*An Environmental, Political, and Social*
*Solutions Handbook with Directories*

# *Macrocosm USA*

*Possibilities for a*
*New Progressive Era...*

First Edition

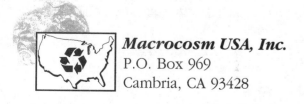

***Macrocosm USA, Inc.***
P.O. Box 969
Cambria, CA 93428

# How to Use this Handbook:

The first part of this book is a reader that contains chapters on many vital issues. Its index can be found near the center of the book, following the last chapter. The second part contains directories broken down as follows and preceeded by its own Subject Index:

❶ Organizations
❷ Periodicals
❸ Media, Computers, & Other Sources
❹ Publishers & Publications Lists
❺ Businesses & Catalogs
❻ References (guides & directories)
❼ People Index

Each entry is preceeded with a dingbat or key letter, for which a glossary appears at the top of every page, providing a flag for quick identification of groups' concern. The center of the book contains the index for the chapters and the directories. Special interest indexing assist in locating entries. A directory of individuals is also included. We suggest, that for easy access of the information, that you purchase inexpensive adhesive index tabs and apply one at the beginning of each section of the directory.

## The Macrocosm Database:

A database of the directory is available for **Works for Windows**, **Works** for PC and Mac, and other ASCII formats. Call for prices (805) 927-8030.

## The Macrocosm Clearinghouse:

**Macrocosm USA, Inc.** will perform specialized searches and reports for you. Macrocosm will also be sending out a newsletter that may be obtained through membership. This membership includes the directory, newsletters, and discounts on the database, services and reports. Call for more details or about our business and nonprofit rates.

Customized mailing labels are also available. Periodic reports and newsletters will focus on specialized areas that will supplement the directory and aid readers in their research.

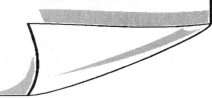

# *Acknowledgments & Disclaimers*

A great deal of what goes into a compilation such as **Macrocosm USA** requires the cooperation and generosity of many people. **Macrocosm USA, Inc.** is now a nonprofit group, and this handbook is the result of three years work and a small volunteer staff.

Special thanks needs to be extended first and foremost to **Macrocosm's** Production Manager, Carl Moodispaugh; Assistant Editor, Henry Tewksbury; and Research Assistants, Lorraine Schulmeister, Eva Uran, Jay Bonestell, Ayme Turnbull, and Ron Landskroner—for their continuous faith and generous contribution of time and materials to this project. Many thanks to cartoons contributed by Belva (Raee) Mattson and Dan Dunivant; to Terri Dunivant, editor of **Earth Journal**, for her editorial assistance and liberal reprint permission; and, J.W. Smith for permission to reprint excerpts of **The World's Wasted Wealth** and his yet unpublished **The World's Wasted Wealth 2**.

Many thanks to: Craig Canan, author of **Progressive Periodicals**, who contributed many of descriptions for periodicals; **Directories in Print** by **Gale Research** whose generous reprint permission provided the descriptions derived for the directories and guides section, "References"; CRISES Press, Inc.'s **APT for Libraries** by Charles Willett; Gregory Wright of **IdeaNet**; **In Context** magazine; **Buzzworm**; John Tibayan, editor of **Creative Resources Guild Directory**; Bill Ellis of **TRANET**; **Invest Yourself Directory** by **The Commission on Voluntary Service & Action**; Charles Leiden, editor of **Compost Patch**; **Co-op America**; **Writer's** magazine; **Holistic Education Review** and **Resource Guide**; **Utne Reader**; **National Wildlife Federation Directory**; and hundreds of others for allowing us to reprint articles.

The following reference guides were indispensable: **Writer's Guide**; **The Interna-**
**tional Directory of Little Magazines and Small Presses** (Dustbooks; Len Fulton, Editor); and **Alternative Press Index**.

**DISCLAIMERS:** Materials printed in **Macrocosm USA** do not imply endorsement by **Macrocosm USA, Inc.** Great care has been taken to insure that no group listed supports violence or hatred. Thousands of entries were written by the groups themselves, who were invited to update entries. If forms were not returned, we were forced to assume that the information that we possessed had not changed. **Macrocosm's** goal is to provide a forum for the disenfranchised and those promoting progressive social change and sustainable development. This guide is entirely assembled by volunteers. **Macrocosm USA, Inc.** cannot make any guarantees as to its accuracy, though every effort has been made maintain the integrity of the material.

Library of Congress Catalog Card Number: 92-080678

ISBN 0-9632315-5-3

*The only thing necessary for the triumph of evil is for good [people] to do nothing.*

Edmund Burke  (1729-1797)

*There are a thousand hacking at the branches of evil to one who is striking at the root.*

Henry David Thoreau (1817-62)

*The whole history of the progress of human liberty shows that all concessions yet made to her august claims have been born of earnest struggle. If there is no struggle, there is no progress. Those who profess to favor freedom, and yet deprecate agitation, are men who want crops without plowing up the ground, they want rain without thunder and lightning. They want the ocean without the awful roar of its many waters.*

Frederick Douglass (c.1817-1895)

*When great changes occur in history, when great principles are involved, as a rule the majority are wrong.*

Eugene V. Debs (1855-1926)

*We have reached a place where it is not a question of "can we live in the same world and cooperate" but "we must live in the same world and learn to cooperate".*

Eleanor Roosevelt (1884-1962)

*Never doubt that a small group of thoughtful committed citizens can change the world; indeed it's the only thing that ever has.*

Margaret Mead (1901-78)

*We must learn to live together as brothers or perish together as fools.*

Martin Luther King (1929-68)

*Growing up in America, we were taught that we inherited a democracy. No one told us that we ourselves had to create one.*

Francis Moore Lappé

*This generation—and perhaps this one alone—carries a historical burden: It may be the last generation that can still avert virtual destruction of humanity and the complex biosphere that has been the gift of evolution over the past three billion years.*

Murray Bookchin

*This book is dedicated to all those who understand that Democracy is not a duty best suited for someone else, but a process and a personal obligation.*

# Editor's Note:

**It is my highest aspiration** that the **Macrocosm** *handbook and database* will revolutionize research, journalism, networking, grassroots activism, politics and, foremost, the way in which we teach the Social Sciences. Access to resources that provide meaningful and creative solutions are not always accessible from mainstream culture. As a result, critical issues are not easily studied. **Macrocosm** attempts to broaden and galvanize a new agenda from seemingly disparate issues into one comprehensible "whole", a macro-cosmic context not readily available from the local newsstand. Hence, the name *macrocosm*.

This handbook is an interdisciplinary text intended to demonstrate how different aspects of human activities are interdependent. Many articles were selected because they presented solutions or succeeded in depicting an integrated world view, even if it might be from a specialized field.

**Macrocosm** offers free directory listings. Over a two-year period 5000+ entities were contacted and invited to map out *possibilities for a new progressive era* and contribute material for reprint. **Macrocosm** tried to focus mainly on grassroots efforts and the alternative press, but well-known liberal concerns are also included.

**Macrocosm** does not pretend to be complete. This is why there is a comprehensive listing of directories and guides. A database is available for those desiring a computerized format. Due to subject and space limitation, reprint difficulties, or simply that material was not forthcoming, many areas remain uncharted.

We invite readers to help us improve future **Macrocosm** editions by sending in relevant material, advice and information on other significant organizations, periodicals and businesses, or simply update their entries by sending in a form. *An entry form is in the back of this book.*

⊕

Within the short period **Macrocosm** has been preparing its directories and chapters, many events have changed the face of the progressive movement. Nelson Mandella was freed. The Cold War turned tepid. Organizations and periodicals that rally around East-West relations are studying a new course. The Strategic Defense Initiative (SDI) continues to hover over our future. MX missile launches and underground testing at the Nevada Test Site are still a fact. President Bush recently announced a reduction in our nuclear arsenal from 21,000 to 6,000; yet, more homeless children than ever shiver every night in cold darkness and hunger.

**The 80's will be remembered** as the *decade of denial* when Americans mortgaged the future of their children: Unprecedented growth in the national debt ($4 trillion) coupled with skyrocketing stock prices and personal credit liabilities. A search for short-term profits and a belief in unlimited growth loosened restrictions, accelerating environmental degradation and human rights violations. Multinationals have moved large chunks of capital out of the U.S. and into developing nations in order to exploit foreign people and resources. A "secret government" bankrolled and tampered with events the public was just beginning to take for granted, beckoning us to re-examine the media's ability for truth.

**If the ecological vision** and economic will of our leaders fails to encourage a philosophy of creative individual power and responsibility, growing cynicism and apathy will see continued voting declines and inertia, where non-participation is a self-fulfilling prophecy contributing to America's decaying democracy.

**Cries for economic conversion** can be heard across the land. The disparity between the rich and the poor has grown wider. The middle class, largely made up of two-income families, has been expected to shoulder an increasing share of taxes; a burden that has financed the military-industrial complex, and the resultant failing institutions and services, and crippled our cities and states. Our tax code has become a complicated, over-politicized pawn for hyperactive corporate lobbies.

**Not only are our tax dollars** squandered on needless government expenditures, but approximately 80% of progressive efforts are expended fighting the establishment and large monied-interests who benefit from huge tax loopholes.

**Oil, due to run out in 30 years,** is the cause of nearly all the Middle East conflicts, the rising cost in living, *and* global warming. To reduce oil demands, the industrial-military complex, including Pentagon and NASA, must begin to develop alternative energy and other appropriate technologies. If the U.S. can put a man on the Moon, it can surely lead the way to safe and sustainable methods by which humans can travel or manufacture.

**Macrocosm's** pages are filled with the unheeded advice and all those fearful *possibilities:* The experts who warned of a recession, the mounting debt, growing poverty, the rise of fascism, environmental calamity, the need for renewable energy, the dangers of over-population, the failure of education, cost prohibitive and unethical health care, the excesses of the military and CIA, and continuing human rights violations.

— *Sandi Brockway*

# Table of Contents

# Foreword

## by Marilyn Ferguson

A friend of mine, a man once famous for his derring-do and now known for his outrageous humanitarianism, remarked, *"I guess I'm a do-gooder now—and do-gooding's more fun than anything!"*

*"Helper's high"* someone has called the feeling, and it is a force to be reckoned with. Recent research shows that we are happiest when we are living up to our ideals.

⊕

*The great unrest in Los Angeles,* where I live, provided plenty of opportunity for *helper's high.* At the peak of the looting a man braved the onslaught to stand guard over his friend's store as if it were his own. *"Please—this is my livelihood,"* he told a crowd of looters. Four or five looters stayed behind to help him protect the store. It was as if they wanted nothing more than to be part of this great event. Helping another person was more edifying than helping themselves.

"Out of the marauding, the looting, and the burning that ruled the night," the *Long Beach Press-Telegram* editorialized, *"a spirit of community and kinship emerged on the city streets Friday morning . . . "*

A multiracial group of neighbors contained the fire in Joe's Liquor Store. Three employees of the *Press-Telegram* helped rescue an elderly woman.

A Long Beach woman, operating from her house, set up a cleanup effort that drew five hundred helpers. A Long Beach organization of two hundred Vietnam veterans set out to see what they could do. Local businesses contributed supplies. Crews of volunteers painted over graffiti, boarded up storefronts, cleaned up debris. Citizens remarked that the streets of Long Beach had never been so spotless.

Then there were the racially diverse members of the Lucky Social Club, a neighborhood-watch group that guarded Lucky's, the only supermarket in the area. Lucky, indeed. One of the members makes his living securing fire-damaged buildings, so he had plenty of yellow "police line" tape. The group sealed off the parking lot, then helped store employees move newspaper racks and other missiles inside. An unarmed group then circled the building, fending off seventy-five or so looters.

One of the participants, a retired bus-driver, had once won a commendation from the police for subduing a mugger. *"If we expect to take back our city, we're going to have to do it in our neighborhoods. There are times when you have to stop the talk and take action."*

A caterer arrived at a Los Angeles shelter for riot victims with two hundred spaghetti dinners, left over from another event, and the cup overflowed. Then the spaghetti was taken to a downtown mission. Dozens of American manufacturers shipped truckloads of food and other goods to the afflicted areas. On Mother's Day a group calling itself **Mothers of All Colors Unite** brought flowers to women staying in shelters with their children. Just as neighbors had cooked for their *adopted* fire crews, now an organization of black firefighters, the Stentorians, barbecued for hundreds of families in need.

In South Central Los Angeles, residents of a small tent city called the **Village of Hope** saved a market whose owners—a Vietnamese woman and her Chinese husband—had shown them kindnesses.

Looters invited the homeless to join them. The homeless declined and urged the looters not to burn the store. At some point during the night, the homeless smelled and saw smoke. They set up a hose brigade, summoned a nearby firefighting crew, and had the fire out within minutes. When the owners returned the next day and despaired over the mess, the homeless set about helping them clean it up.

Help took many forms. Taxi drivers were offering one-dollar fares to the market for people whose neighborhood stores had been burned. At Vermont and Central three men flipped pancakes on a gas grill and offered them to passersby.

*"I was listening for the radio station to announce a phone number for those who wanted to help out,"* a songwriter said, *"but they didn't. So I called up some friends and said, 'Let's make something happen.'"* They set to work cleaning, and their numbers grew as people driving by stopped to help.

*"People came out of nowhere,"* according to a staff member of the Museum of African Art, to save two thousand drums, masks, and other pieces.

Maybe neighbors are the best public servants of all.

⊕

*In analyzing what led to the riots,* the factor that portends unrest throughout the world, someone described the poor as having been *left behind* as others made material gains.

But if the poor have been left behind, so has some vital part of ourselves. Poverty amid plenty, poor schools, and urban decay are a symptom of a deeper lack. What's missing—what we left behind—is the civilizing influence of community.

Community, the sense of belonging, seems elusive in our manic times. Only lightly touched upon by our leaders, community is at the heart of all our visions of Utopia.

Community confers basic dignity. Again and again, the poor have said in many diverse ways, *"Give us some respect. Don't assume that we're less than you, or that we are automatically thieves or gang members."* A landmark study on the root causes of violence in California identified a lack of self-esteem as fundamental. This is now common sense. Or as one person expressed it, *"the emergence of the obvious."* Paradoxically, it was obvious that the explanation was not obvious. Common sense was more than meets the eye.

The thing missing in our society is not an intact nuclear family but a supportive big family. The community. And beyond that, the community of nations, the Family of Man. The larger family that ensures the health and happiness of us all.

⊕

*"Bloom where you are planted,"* someone has said. *Macrocosm U.S.A.* offers us the inspiration and resources to improve the garden wherever we may be.

I am reminded of the words of Olivia Herrera, president of the Civil Service Commission in Long Beach:

*The little things have to be done—then the government will get around to doing the grand things. In the meantime, though, you could starve or freeze. Each one of us must do the tiny thing for unity and dignity. The small gestures of unity and dignity are the fabric of society.*

⊕

Some months ago Sandi Brockway and Carl Moodispaugh invited me to write a forward to this guide and directory. Along the way we both got involved in current politics as well as our writing and publishing chores, and our various projects were delayed. At my end, one crisis (or vital opportunity) after another seemed to interfere with my intention of finishing the forward.

Sandi and Carl were unfailingly compassionate and good-natured about the delays. I vouch for the fact that they live their idealism.

*Macrocosm USA* is a big book compiled by big people who understand complexity and change. Sandi and Carl have pulled together the threads of ten thousand gestures to show us our greatness.

# Preface

by Donella H. Meadows / *In Context*

**It's wonderful,** the recent burst of publications with lists of things we can do to save the planet. It's great to see so much energy behind recycling, energy-efficient light bulbs, and fundraisers for the rain forest.

If we all did 50 simple things to save the planet, that would be a big help. But it wouldn't be enough. The planet—or more accurately our civilization and the natural systems that support it needs more than easy gestures to be saved.

I think everyone knows that. We know that what's needed is an end to our wild population growth and our untrammeled greed. What's needed is real human justice and Earth stewardship. Sometimes I think we get enthusiastic about low-flow faucets and high-mileage cars because they give us the feeling of doing good without seriously challenging our lifestyle.

If we're really interested in saving the environment, and therefore ourselves, there are some not-so-easy things we can and must do.

**About Population:** On the personal level we can stop at two, or one, or none—and learn to love other people's children. On the government level we can give every couple the knowledge and technology to choose the number of their children, and then give them straight, honest reasons why they should choose no more than two. The U.S. government, which used to be foremost in this field, has essentially stopped funding family planning and population education both domestically and internationally. We need to lean hard on our leaders to reverse that policy.

**About Greed:** What we can do individually is define what *enough* means for us and then live it. That doesn't mean living in deprivation or unplugging everything and returning to a previous century. It means: unplugging the nattering sales pitches that tell us we are inadequate unless we buy certain products; achieving security and sufficiency but stopping short of waste and clutter; discovering what life can be about when it isn't about having more stuff, choosing real satisfaction instead of the empty satisfaction of mindless acquisition.

On the government level controlling greed means defining progress by human welfare, not by the growth of the GNP. It means tax, loan, investment, and budget policies that meet real needs rather than promote perpetual swelling. It means ending all the ways the government helps the rich get richer, and all the ways our leaders try to convince us that getting richer is our goal instead of getting better.

**About Justice:** We know that we will never have peace or environmental balance or pride in our collective selves while anyone still lives in poverty. On a personal level what each of us can do is care for just one person in need, to the point where that person can care for himself or herself. And do it not with condescension but with love.

The government can remove obstacles to people's and nations' self-sufficiency. There are many ways to do that—provide truly equal education, forgive crippling debts, ensure that the next set of loans is aimed at sustainable productivity, make trade fair, make technologies available—and that's just the beginning.

**About Stewardship:** Each of us can care for one piece of land. We can beautify a yard or a neighborhood park (and do it without harmful chemicals). We can build up the soil on a farm, or buy produce from a farmer who does. We can manage lovingly a large property and protect it in perpetuity with a conservation easement. We can support a land trust or nature conservancy to do the land caring on our behalf.

As citizens we can insist that governments establish zoning that firmly protects farmland and wildland; create parks that demonstrate nature protection rather than commercialism; manage national lands in a way that does not degrade their resources; provide education and extension services that teach us to treasure land, not to exploit it.

In a mode of genial gesturing, these suggestions sound impossible. In a mode of intent to solve our problems once and for all, they sound obvious. They sound like change, but not sacrifice. And in that mode the simple "planet-saving" steps—recycling, saving energy, stopping the junk mail, refusing the plastic bags at the grocery store—take their proper place as logical, unheroic, helpful parts of a larger whole, a shared, deep commitment to protect and honor the environment that supports us all.

*Donella H. (Dana) Meadows, co-author of* Limits to Growth *and an associate professor at Dartmouth College, writes a self-syndicated newspaper column called "The Global Citizen" that appears in 20 papers and occasionally gets national syndication through the* Los Angeles Times. *Monthly column mailings are available for $20/year from: Dana, P.O. Box 58, Daniels Rd., Plainfield, NH 03781.*

*Excerpted from* In Context, no. 26 *, as it appeared in* Utne Reader, *March/April 1991.*

# Introduction

by Denis Hayes / *Amicus Journal*

For many of my generation, involvement with serious issues—adult issues—began with some form of unconventional politics. Passive disobedience and freedom rides in support of civil rights. The endless town meetings of Vietnam summer. Wearing gas masks down Fifth Avenue on Earth Day. Picketing a state legislature in support of the Equal Rights Amendment. Breaching the exclusion zone around Seabrook or Diablo Canyon. Blocking a train carrying fissionable material to the Rocky Flats bomb factory in Colorado.

We were impatient and idealistic. The first generation with strontium 90 in its bones (from atmospheric nuclear testing), we trusted no one over thirty. Outraged over the state of the world we were inheriting, we vowed that we would pass on to our children a world that was peaceful, just, and ecologically sustainable.

That was twenty years ago. Today, Holden Caulfield is in his early fifties, has a beer belly, and commutes from the suburbs. The angry young women and men of Earth Day—who poured sewage on corporate carpets and pounded polluting automobiles apart with sledgehammers—are now middle-aged. The first generation with strontium 90 in its bones has parented a post-Chernobyl generation with iodine 131 in its thyroids.

Twenty years after Earth Day, those of us who set out to change the world are poised on the threshold of utter failure. Measured on virtually any scale, the world is in worse shape today than it was twenty years ago.

How could we have fought so hard and won so many battles, only to find ourselves now on the verge of losing the war? The answers are complex. But if we can understand the mistakes that led to our current dilemma, we may yet be able to redeem our youthful promises to the next generation.

## Roots of the Modern Environmental Movement

The American *conservation* movement has a long, distinguished tradition, tracing back to such giants as Thoreau, Audubon, Muir, and Leopold. However, the *environmental* movement is of much more recent origin. Individuals such as Rachel Carson and David Brower sounded the environmental alarm in the 1960s, and events such as the Santa Barbara oil spill of 1969 and the Storm King [Hudson River power project] battle in New York gave rise to local waves of concerned activists. But a full-blown national movement emerged only in 1970.

Following the original Earth Day on April 22, 1970, the American conservation move-ment exploded in size and broadened its agenda to encompass modern urban and industrial issues. Old-line organizations saw their memberships double and triple and the new members had broad environmental interests. This new membership—much of it having tested its mettle in the anti-war and civil rights and women's movements—caused many traditional conservation organizations to expand their agendas.

The modern environmental movement has enjoyed a string of spectacular successes on Capitol Hill, in the courts, and in the streets. Earth Day's 25 million participants could not be ignored. Within months, the federal Environmental Protection Agency was created. Congress then swiftly passed the Clean Air Act, the Clean Water Act, RCRA, FIFRA, CERCLA, and a host of other laws that fundamentally changed the rules under which American enterprise operates.

Whenever government agencies or corporations attempted to flout these new laws, environmental groups swiftly hauled them into court. The movement's talented, idealistic lawyers have won hundreds of precedent setting decisions.

When litigation proved to be too slow or ineffective, the environmental movement's guerrillas put their bodies on the line in actions explicitly modeled upon the civil disobedience of the early civil rights movement. Such non-violent, direct action has at least temporarily halted some of the worst whaling abuses and most devastating destruction of old-growth forests.

Yet, despite all these accomplishments, we are in serious trouble, and the problems are compounding with every passing year. There is no evidence that our leaders have the intelligence, the integrity, and the guts to lead us into a new era.

## Lessons From the Last Twenty Years: What Went Wrong?

*Occasionally we were blindsided. Problems snuck up on us before anyone recognized the threat they posed.* We possess only a rudimentary understanding of the complex interactions of life in the biosphere and of the myriad subtle effects of human action upon long-established processes. Comparatively few of the thousands of modern industrial chemicals have been subjected to thorough laboratory or epidemiological tests. We know even less about the cumulative, synergistic effects of long-term exposure to mul-tiple chemicals on human health. We know still less about the effects of these chemicals upon other species and upon the natural cycles—the water cycle, the carbon cycle, the nitrogen cycle, etc.—that shape the living planet.

Even where there is agreement among the experts, the consensus is often later found to have been wrong. If at the time of the first Earth Day, a poll had been taken of industrial chemists asking each to name ten triumphs of modern chemistry, most would probably have listed chlorofluorocarbons. These compounds served a diverse array of beneficial uses, and they appeared to have no undesirable side effects. They are not toxic, carcinogenic, or mutagenic. They do not corrode materials, they are not flammable, and they don't explode.

It was not until 1974—four years after Earth Day—that Professor Sherwood Rowland and his colleagues at the University of California at Irvine discovered that CFCs could pose a theoretical danger to the stratospheric ozone layer which protects the Earth from ultraviolet radiation. And it was not until 1985 that a British team discovered a huge seasonal thinning of the antarctic ozone.

A CFC molecule requires about fifteen years to migrate up to the stratosphere. Therefore, virtually all the damage currently wrought on stratospheric ozone is being caused by CFCs that were released before Professor Rowland conducted his initial studies in 1974. Once in the stratosphere, the chlorine from a single CFC molecule will catalyze the destruction of ozone for about a century on average, during which time it will destroy 100,000 ozone molecules.

CFCs were in use for fifty years before they were found to have any negative side effects. Now it has been determined that the side effects could include the destruction of vital links in the food chain, increases in skin cancer, and harm to human immunological systems.

⊕

*It is always easier to tackle urgent problems than distant threats—even when the distant threats are more important.* In 1978, four years after the oil embargo, the *Washington Post* carried a column heaping thick ridicule upon those energy experts "purporting to describe an unparalleled mis-

**If we can understand the mistakes that led to our current dilemma, we may yet be able to redeem our youthful promises to the next generation.**

fortune that exists, if it exists at all, at an imaginary point where six or seven lines intersect on a graph." Soon thereafter, war erupted between Iran and Iraq; oil production from the two countries fell from 8 million barrels per day to 2 million; and the world price for oil doubled.

This tendency to dismiss "lines intersecting on a graph" remains a staple of American political thought. Among countries, we are what boxers call a counter-puncher. What we do best is respond. Bomb Pearl Harbor and America will pull out all the stops. Launch Sputnik and America will have NASA functioning overnight.

What America does *not* do well is anticipate and avoid problems. Unfortunately, many environmental phenomena involve thresholds that, when passed, cause damage that is essentially irreversible. If we wait until the damage occurs and then respond, it will be too late. The role of governments is to avoid the irreversible. Government has the power to remove redwoods and whales from the financial marketplace before they disappear. Redwoods are protected inside national parks. Rapacious lumber companies cannot harvest a redwood tree that is inside a national park, regardless of what price they are willing to pay. The protected trees are, quite literally, priceless. Whales, likewise, are protected by various laws, treaties, and conventions.

But government has its own limitations. Problems that will be felt only after a politician has retired from office are perceived to be "on someone else's beat." Environmentalists must force the political system to assign high priority to distant but dire threats. We must draw a line in the political sand on *this* side of each irreversible threshold. The public intuitively understands this. Environmental victories are always carried on the shoulders of a mobilized public.

⊕

***The "solutions" we pursue for today's problems can create tomorrow's catastrophes.*** Despite all the environmental literature, both scholarly and poetic, describing how everything is connected to everything else, we have repeatedly ignored this elementary truth. We organized our departments and agencies to solve problems on a piecemeal basis. As a result, we frequently cleaned the air by polluting the water, and cleaned the water by fouling the ground.

We face a serious possibility of making the same error again. For example, some are advocating biodegradable plastics as the

---

## Environmentalists need to reach out to farmers, laborers, the religious community, health care professionals, educators and every other group of prospective supporters.

---

answer to the plastic litter problem. Discarded plastic six-pack holders can strangle birds and other species; plastic "baggies" can wreak untold havoc in marine environments; plastic diapers are clogging our landfills. But the problems posed by biodegradable plastics are themselves serious. For example, when biodegradable plastic is mixed with other plastic, it renders the latter virtually impossible to recycle. Biodegradable (and photodegradable) plastic may have some important uses, such as in medicine and possibly in composting, but it holds no promise as "the" solution to plastic waste.

Nuclear power is another example of a solution being worse than the problem. The nuclear industry is mounting a massive international campaign heralding a new generation of "inherently safe" reactors as the answer to the problem of global warming. But the problems inherent in nuclear fission pose a threat that is at least as intractable as global warming.

⊕

***Time and again, the environmental movement has relied too heavily upon the government.*** The irony in our overreliance on government is not subtle. The punch line of many jokes is, "We are from the government, and we are here to help you."

The government has aggressively promoted unsustainable agricultural practices, an unbalanced transportation system, the nuclear power quagmire, dams with no purpose but pork, and logging policies reminiscent of Paul Bunyan. Government is the nation's largest polluter, and it frequently exempts itself from rules it applies to industry. The toxic brews around nuclear weapons facilities may be the most contaminated sites in the world, and the estimated price tag to clean them up is more than $150 billion.

It would be difficult to find a more compelling example of governmental failure than the responses to the energy crises of the 1970s. The first response was to cook up a pot of Potomac alphabet soup. The AEC and the OCR were folded into ERDA and the FEO (which became the FEA). These were merged with the FPC and redeployed as the DOE, the FERC, and the NRC. The result was congealed chaos.

The second element of Washington's re-

sponse was to study the issue. Thousands of federal studies were undertaken; their data fill large libraries. But to no effect. The government's approach to energy is like the man in the *New Yorker* cartoon who knows all about art but doesn't know what he likes.

Federal studies were supplemented by a raft of private studies, each of which "proved" what its sponsor wanted to hear. The coal industry actually produced studies showing that acid rain is good for the environment. The nuclear industry's reports showed that operating a reactor is safer than operating a health food store. Considered as a whole, they provide great support for an old piece of folk wisdom: Don't ask the barber whether you need a haircut.

The final element of Washington's response was to throw money around. The record here was especially embarrassing. Our excursions into what I call lemon socialism—having the government fund projects that the private sector is too shrewd to finance—produced a notable collection of gold-plated turkeys. The Synfuels Corporation was America's biggest bust before Star Wars. Despite an initial budget of $88 billion—more than the Space Race, the Marshall Plan, and the Interstate Highway program combined—the synfuels program yielded no net energy at all.

On the nuclear side of the house, the Clinch River Breeder Reactor was a classic example of Cheop's Law: Nothing ever gets built on schedule or within budget.

In both cases, failure was fortuitous. A successful synfuels program could have increased America's contribution to global warming threefold, and a successful breeder program would have confronted us with the need to manage thousands of tons of bomb-grade plutonium.

Most of the energy strategies that the government pursued were non-starters, and the situation has deteriorated. U.S. production of oil has been declining since 1971; in July, 1988, for the first time, we imported more than half of all the oil we consumed. Our vulnerability is far greater today than it was in 1973, at the time of the Arab embargo.

If we follow the current course, we can safely predict the international price of oil to begin rising in 1992-93. OPEC presumably has learned its lesson. These next rises will be no more than 20 to 25 percent per year, though sufficient to cause a fiscal hemorrhage.

The obvious solution is to increase the price of oil ourselves—with a carbon dioxide tax and a gasoline tax—so that the revenues will stay at home to be redistribut-

---

## The most dangerous environments are in communities that are least powerful. Poor people and people of color are downwind from most toxic incinerators.

ed and invested. Americans pay between one-half and one-third as much for gasoline as do our industrial allies—all of whom enjoy robust economies and comfortable lifestyles. (The 1990 fuel efficiency standard for France is 39 mpg versus 27.5 for the United States.) A dollar-per gallon gasoline tax would be an important step toward sound energy policy and fiscal integrity. Instead, our leadership resolutely chants its unthinking mantra of "no new taxes," thus guaranteeing that when crude prices soar, the proceeds all will flow to the Middle East.

Not to put too fine a point on it, our national energy program has been a bust. Our leaders have wasted the nation's time, money, and intelligence pursuing a collection of hopeless dead ends.

Continuing to pin environmental hope upon the government is, as Samuel Johnson described a man taking his second wife a triumph of hope over experience.

⊕

***We have not asked enough of our supporters.*** Most environmentalists are willing—even eager—to do more than send money and write letters. We need to appeal to them as consumers, as workers, as investors, and as parents. One of the greatest potential strengths of our movement is the ability to integrate environmental goals into all aspects of a person's life.

All the most successful movements, and all the world's major religions, have succeeded in part because they ask people to improve their behavior. The civil rights movement and the women's movement, for example, ask their supporters for heroic changes in their personal lives.

Environmentalists, on the other hand, have often tried to convince the public that we could all have our cake and eat it too. People were encouraged to believe that, if only we could effect the necessary changes in government and industry, people would not have to change their habits at all.

The answer to air pollution was claimed to be catalytic converters on tail pipes and scrubbers on smokestacks. We have pursued this strategy at enormous cost for twenty years. Yet the sky today in Los Angeles resembles split pea soup. We have been spectacularly successful at cleaning up automobile exhaust. Meanwhile, our cities grew larger. People moved farther away from their jobs, and drove more miles; and their cars idled more at stop lights, drive-through windows, and traffic jams.

It is necessary, but not sufficient, to scrub

## There is not evidence that our leaders have the intelligence, the integrity, and the guts to lead us into a new era. Instead, we must look to ourselves.

pollutants out of exhaust. We must also begin using cleaner fuels and more efficient engines. We also should encourage widespread use of (and improvements in) public transportation. We should promote bicycle riding wherever possible (and bicycle lanes and veloways). We should create incentives for people to live closer to their workplaces to reduce urban commuting and the resulting congestion.

Similarly, we should encourage environmental supporters to be mindful of their values when they go shopping. In Europe, the "green consumer" has become a force to be reckoned with. Environmental labels are commonplace; consumer magazines are devoted to the environmental impacts of products. In the United States, such consciousness is only beginning.

Several of us are exploring criteria for an American environmental label, to be awarded to the best products from the best companies. Such an easy guide would convert environmental consumerism from an esoteric research enterprise into an easy habit. It should have been a mainstay of our efforts for the past two decades.

If everyone used the most efficient light bulbs, the most efficient appliances, the most efficient furnaces, and optimum insulation, average household energy consumption could be cut by more than two-thirds. If everyone ate more organic produce and more local produce, and moved lower on the food chain, energy use in the food system could be cut by two-thirds. If everyone bought the most efficient vehicle having the same internal dimensions as his current car, gasoline use would fall by more than half.

Perhaps no American behavior is more ripe for change than recycling. Sending our natural resources on a one-way trip from the mine to the dump is spherically senseless: it makes no sense no matter how you look at it. We throw away valuable resources, eliminate jobs, waste embedded energy, and destroy the environment—all because people don't put glass in one container and aluminum in another.

Some of our landfills are now richer in resources than some of our mines. But regulatory and tax systems designed to promote exploration and exploitation in a pioneer society have acquired their own inertia and their own vested interests. So we mine virgin ore instead of reducing use, and

repairing, reusing, and recycling substances that have already entered the stream of commerce. To take perhaps the most obscene example, the federal government is currently selling 300-year-old trees in the Tongass for less than the price of a Big Mac.

Comprehensive recycling is essential. At even a 50 percent recycling rate, after just five cycles only 3 percent of the original material is left in the economy. We need to do much better than that.

Comprehensive recycling and composting will require significant government involvement—to end its bias in favor of raw materials, end its bias in favor of landfills and incinerators, provide curbside pick-ups, set standards, and provide near-term markets for recycled goods. But the necessary first step is to ask people to do their part. Environmentalists must comprehensively recycle all their used items, and we must purchase recycled goods whenever possible.

⊕

***The environmental movement has not diversified.*** The most dangerous environments are in communities that are the least powerful. Poor people and people of color are downwind from most toxic incinerators. They are down-gradient from most hazardous waste dumps. They are in the fields when the pesticides are sprayed from planes. They work in factory jobs having the highest exposure to dangerous substances. Yet poor people are not well-represented in the ranks of the environmental movement. In communities racked by the devastation of drugs, plagued with violent crime, suffering school drop-out rates of over 50 percent, experiencing rising problems of homelessness and malnutrition, environmental issues are not considered a "priority." But they should be. The problems are indivisible.

In an important speech in the 1960s at the Riverside Church in New York, the Reverend Martin Luther King came out against the war in Vietnam. The wave of criticism he suffered was intense. To those who challenged him for getting involved in an issue other than civil rights, he replied that African Americans were being drafted in disproportionate numbers and returned home in body bags in disproportionate numbers. There is no more fundamental civil right, he said, than the right to live to be an adult.

Similarly, the right to lead healthy, productive lives means that environmental values should be of great importance to those communities most deeply scarred by environmental degradation.

We environmentalists have to ally our-

## The world is in worse shape today than it was twenty years ago. We have, at most, ten years if we are to avoid cossing some dire environmental thresholds.

selves with others who have good reason to be environmentalists, but who have not traditionally been part of this movement. We need to reach out to farmers, laborers, the religious community, health care professionals, educators, and every other identifiable group of prospective supporters.

Why? Because otherwise we will get rolled. There are not currently enough "card-carrying" environmentalists to win the tough political battles that must be won if the 1990s are to be the Green Decade.

There are probably no more than 10 million dues-paying environmentalists in the country. They are powerful beyond their numbers because they tend to be highly educated, well-paid, and politically active. That is enough to pass some good, narrowly tailored legislation. However, it was not enough to successfully withstand the full frontal assault of the Reagan [Bush] administration.

Our most powerful ally necessarily will be the people. We have no powerful economic institutions on our side. A solar transition will only be achieved if it enjoys enthusiastic backing from a broad cross-section of the entire society. Environmentalists must proselytize much more actively, and much more successfully, than we ever have in the past.

⊕

***We have avoided some hard issues.*** Current population levels are undermining the biological basis for our future. Water tables are plummeting far faster than they are recharged. Topsoil is eroding five times faster than it is replaced; in some parts of Ohio, farms lose two bushels of topsoil for every bushel of corn harvested. Pests display an increasing resistance to pesticides. Deserts are on the march in Africa, Asia, Australia, and America. There is not a single important problem facing the planet that could not be more easily solved with a population of under 5 billion.

The claim sometimes is made that the United States is overpopulated, but India is not. The purported explanation is that the average American consumes twenty times more resources than the average Indian. The core assumption underpinning such an argument is that India will never develop, and that the average Indian's impact on the Earth will remain negligible. While the environmental destruction caused by contemporary Americans is unconscionable and should not be continued or replicated, it is similarly unconscionable to consign the majority of the world's population to perpetual poverty.

Global population growth is an urgent priority, and it must be addressed with substantial family planning assistance and provisions for social mechanisms (e.g., old-age insurance) to undercut the motivations for large families while advancing social

justice. For $4 billion per year, family planning could be provided to all who want it. It might be the single most cost-effective investment available to the world. But right-wing religious zealots have intimidated much of our political leadership, and virtually all national Republican leadership.

Unless human population growth is halted, we will suffer the same ecological collapse that has governed other species that have bred themselves into oblivion. The record of the last two American administrations on population issues—their overt hostility to family planning—has been irresponsible and immoral.

### We Have The Power To Choose Our Future

During the last eight years, the U.S. national debt has tripled. The United States has shifted from being the world's greatest creditor nation to being the world's largest debtor. Hostile takeovers, leveraged buy outs, and greenmail have left our businesses mortgaged to the hilt in unstable junk bonds. The Federal Savings and Loan Insurance Corporation has collapsed under $300 billion of prospective liability. It is not a promising time to look to the federal government for salvation. Instead, we must look to ourselves.

A common feature of all the problems we have been discussing is that none is the result of forces beyond human control. None is caused by sun spots, or the gravitational pull of the moon, or volcanic activity. All are the result of conscious human choices. All can be cured by making other choices.

First, we need to make our own lives congruent with our values. For most of us, there is room for improvement in virtually all spheres. We should conserve energy with easy things, such as replacing incandescent light bulbs with folded fluorescents, which are five times as efficient, insulating our water heater, and doing laundry in cold water. Then we should do the more expensive and difficult things, such as super insulating our dwellings and buying a more efficient furnace and more efficient appliances.

We should pledge not to purchase another new car until we can buy one that meets our needs while getting at least 50 miles per gallon. We should install flow restricters in our faucets and showers and dams in our toilets. We should plant indigenous vegetation. We should search out environmentally sensible soaps and cosmetics, and look for recycled paper and other recycled products. We should eat lower on the food chain, and develop a preference for fresh organic products grown nearby. We should carry our own, reusable string bags to the supermarket, and search out ways to eliminate other unnecessary packaging. We should recycle our metals, glass, paper, and plastics, and

compost all organic waste.

There are many reasons why such lifestyle changes make sense. In the aggregate, they make a huge difference. If everyone used the most efficient refrigerators available, we could save the equivalent of twelve large nuclear power plants. Using the most efficient cars having the same internal dimensions as our current vehicles would cut gasoline consumption in half. Every year, we send more iron and steel to our dumps than we use in the entire automobile industry. The aluminum we throw away every three months could replace the nation's entire fleet of airplanes.

Leading lives that are congruent with your values is a necessary and important first step, but it does not discharge your responsibility. Next you need to explore what you can do as an employee, an investor, a parent, and a member of your church and civic clubs. You should be alert to ways you can lessen the environmental impact of your job, from avoiding Styrofoam coffee cups to suggesting modifications in industrial processes. You should ask your pension fund trustees to adhere to the Valdez Principles in choosing investments. You should set a good example for your children.

Integrating your values into your job and your other activities is another important step, but it still does not discharge your responsibilities. Next, join local and national organizations that share your goals and your philosophy, and proselytize on their behalf. Give gift memberships for Christmas; display their publications on your coffee table; support their campaigns financially and with your volunteer efforts.

Working on behalf of environmental groups that represent your views is vitally important, but this still does not fully discharge your responsibilities. The next step is to become actively involved in politics. Support candidates who share your vision; vigorously oppose those who do not. Invest the time, energy, and financial support needed to win elections. Play the sort of role that causes political friends and foes alike to view you as a person of substance, a person to be reckoned with. Communicate your environmental goals and values to your candidate, and make clear that there are narrow limits on how much compromise is acceptable.

Time is running out. We have, at most, ten years to embark on some undertakings if we are to avoid crossing some dire environmental thresholds.

Individually, each of us can do only a little. Together, we can save the world.

*Excerpted from an article that originally appeared as "The Green Decade," in the* Amicus Journal, *Spring 1990. A similar version appeared in* Natural History, *April 1990, called "Earth Day 1990, Threshold of the Green Decade."*

# Chapter 1

# *War & Peace*

*Ah, love, let us be true*
*To one another! for the world, which seems*
*To lie before us like a land of dreams,*
*So various, so beautiful, so new,*
*Hath really neither joy, nor love, nor light,*
*Nor certitude, nor peace, nor help for pain;*
*And we are here as on a darkling plain*
*Swept with confused alarms of struggle and flight,*
*Where ignorant armies clash by night.*

— "Dover Beach" by Matthew Arnold, 1867

*Every gun that is fired, every warship launched, every rocket fired, signifies, in the final sense, a theft from those who hunger and are not fed, those who are cold and are not clothed. The world in arms is not spending money alone. It is spending the sweat of its laborers, the genius of its scientists, the hopes of its children.*

— Dwight D. Eisenhower (1890-1969)

S. Brockway

*A U.S. Navy transport returning home from the Gulf War as viewed from Alcatraz Island.*

# War on Earth

**by Carl Pope / *Sierra***

*Events in the Persian Gulf remind environmentalists that there's little we can do once the shooting starts. It's in the in-between times that we can help shape tactics and policies that may—indeed, must—someday lead to peace.*

In 1258 the Mongol general Hulagu, commanding his portion of the great nomadic legion forged by his grandfather, Genghis, conquered that part of the world we today call the Middle East. When Baghdad, capital of the Muslim world, fell to his forces, Hulagu burned the city to the ground.

Hulagu's army obliterated not only Baghdad and the other major population centers of the Persian plateau, but also the complex and technically sophisticated irrigation systems between the Tigris and Euphrates rivers, the canals and dams that had made the floodplain of Iraq the Fertile Crescent of ancient civilization.

The underlying cause of the war was the Mongol hunger for a single resource—grass. Nomadic Mongol society depended exclusively on ever-expanding pastures to support its growing herds of horses. By the early part of the 13th century the Mongols had overrun their own grasslands and, rather than change a way and scale of life no longer supportable at home, they poured out of Central Asia. Within two generations they had conquered everyone and everything around them.

The Mongols rejected more complicated

> ***In the future*** *no nation should be free to pollute the common environment and inflict severe ecological and economic damage on other states. In fact, we need a new concept of national security that goes beyond the narrow confines of military security, to embrace economic and ecological interdependence and global environmental hazards. In the field of environment and development there is no such thing as benign neglect. We can no longer live with the pursuit of unilateral advantage at the expense of our common future.*
>
> — Gro Harlem Brundtland, Norwegian Prime Minister and Chairman of the World Commission on Environment and Development.

and diverse ways of life: They despised agriculture, scorned urban society. Only when the world was simplified into a vast pasture could Mongol culture, the civilization of the horse, be truly secure.

Seven and a half centuries later, American and allied forces bombed Baghdad, then invaded and vanquished Iraq. The underlying cause of the war was American hunger for a single resource—oil. In the last several decades, American society has become as dependent on oil as the Mongols were on grass. Likewise, we have exhausted the most productive oil fields of the United States—and, rather than change a way and scale of life we cannot support at home, we use our economic and military power to take the oil we believe we need...indeed, that we believe we are entitled to. Our policies in the Persian Gulf are driven by the desire to make the world safe for the civilization of the internal-combustion engine.

Other values and other concerns were said to be at stake in the war with Iraq. George Bush evoked Munich and Vietnam; the persona of Saddam Hussein gave us reason to tremble. But in our hearts we knew that a similar political crisis in virtually any other Third World country would not have sent half a million American troops into war.

Iraq's share of the Persian Gulf's wealth made it exceedingly important to the industrial nations dependent on the region's oil. So important, in fact, that they had given Saddam Hussein money, sold him weapons, and shared technologies that made it possible for him to invade Kuwait. But his goal—control of the Kuwaiti oil fields—was one they could not tolerate. The annexation of Kuwait would put Saddam at the head of one of the major oil-producing nations in the world, with a capacity to set oil prices equal to that of the Saudis. The possibility that he would take over Saudi Arabia itself was even less tolerable. [There was never any threat to Saudi Arabia, as later revealed by Soviet satellite photos.]

Like many other people around the world, environmentalists were confused and distressed during this time. The causes of the conflict were rooted in a natural resource, its consequences disastrous for the natural world. Yet the maneuvers that led to war seemed impervious to traditional environmental analysis; neither environmental values nor ecology shed light on the increasingly dim situation.

So for months the environmental trumpet, if sounded at all, quavered and faltered. To the extent that the war was a failure of diplomacy and foreign policy, and environ-

mental issues were not central concerns, we were as blind as everyone else, wandering in the bellicose fog where nations stumble from the brink of war into war itself.

Yet the environmental movement *can* help change the habits and policies that draw nations into that fog. In general, the larger environmental organizations, including the Sierra Club, did not adequately meet this challenge. Our failure was not in the aftermath of August 2, 1990. It lay many years earlier.

The oil crisis of the 1970s set in motion a process that could have cured the United States of its dependence on imported oil. Alternative energy technologies and energy efficiency were working faster, and costing less, than anyone had predicted. Then, by deliberate decision of the U.S. government, the process ground to a virtual halt. Some environmentalists continued to work for energy conservation during the dark years of Reagan cutbacks and indifference, of the return of cheap gas and big cars. But neither the Sierra Club nor the environmental movement as a whole gave energy issues the priority they deserved—and that would be required to help the United States kick the oil habit. We could, and should, have done more to resist America's relapse into petroleum addiction in the 1980s.

The tragic events of the past year compel us to recognize that a world economy overly dependent on a single resource, whether it is grass or oil, will inevitably lead us into turmoil. Diversity of energy sources is a mainstay of diplomatic stability, just as biological complexity provides ecological stability.

President Carter never spoke more profoundly than when he said, to much cynical derision, that the struggle to eliminate our dependence on oil was "the moral equivalent of war." Today we see that this struggle is also the ethical and practical alternative to ceaseless conflict among nations.

On January 25, the first in a series of oil spins gushed into the northern Persian Gulf. Within days it appeared that at least three spills, totaling 11 million barrels of oil, had been unleashed. Saudi and American officials charged that the oil had been deliberately released by Iraq from Kuwaiti oil terminals; Iraqi officials countered that allied bombers were responsible for the slicks that were oozing across the fragile, shallow waters of the Gulf. Later reports indicated that about one-third of the oil was, in fact, the result of allied bombing of Iraqi oil tankers anchored off Kuwait, and that the total volume of the spills was far less than initially estimated. U.S. officials who had decried the Iraqi role in the spills as, "environmental terrorism" offered no comment on the conclusion that U.S. bombs had released the equivalent of two *Exxon Valdez* spills.

When Persian Gulf oil became a weapon

of war, the Gulf itself became a victim. This was nothing new: For years the ecosystem of the Gulf had been sacrificed to mine the black gold that lay around and beneath it. The eight years of war between Iran and Iraq had been fought largely in the most delicate part of the Gulf marshes that Saddam Hussein had turned into an electrical and chemical killing zone for young Iranian revolutionary guards—and for any wildlife that had escaped decades of oil production and development.

Now, as the oil slick moved south, the world focused on the Gulf ecosystem for the first time. Here were a rich shrimp fishery, islands where thousands of sea turtles bred, and the home of an awkward, gentle marine mammal called the dugong, related to Florida's manatee. Here millions of birds wintered, and thousands of people made their livelihoods. The oil spill was not the end of the environmental war. In February, as Saddam's army prepared to leave, Iraqi troops exploded the charges they had laid at Kuwait's principal oil-production facilities. Within hours more than 500 oil wells were aflame, and dark clouds began to spread over the region. Photographs taken in the Saudi town of Khafji at noon were surreal midnight portraits, and the rain that fell on the marshes of the Gulf was black with soot.

The Worldwatch Institute concluded that the combination of the spill, the fires, and the direct destruction of the desert ecology by bombs, shells, and tanks made the Gulf war the greatest environmental disaster in modern history.

Once the bombs began to fall, there was little that environmental organizations could do to prevent this tragedy. Tactical suggestions from environmentalists would scarcely have been heeded. Our years of silence on matters of warfare were proven to be a mistake.

We can make up for this now. While we work to build a world that avoids war altogether, we must work to limit those weapons and tactics that are the most destructive. The bombing of hospitals and the use of poison gas are

now viewed with revulsion and prohibited by international convention. We must add to these constraints the targeting of ecosystems and their most sensitive components: wetlands, forests, estuaries, and critical wildlife habitats.

These fragile environments are offered some protection by a multi-lateral treaty ratified by the U.S. Senate in 1979. Nations adhering to this treaty agree not to employ environmental warfare as a tactic against an enemy that also adheres to the treaty. (Though a signatory, Iraq has never ratified the agreement.) However, neither the United States nor Iraq has ratified Protocol 1 to the Geneva Convention, a protocol that contains two provisions prohibiting tactics "intended" or "expected" to cause environmental havoc. Iraq's setting fire to the Kuwaiti oil fields would certainly have been prohibited by Protocol 1, as would, arguably at least, the U.S. bombing of Iraqi oil tankers. Environmentalists must pressure the United States and other nations to ratify and honor this treaty

Nor should we limit ourselves to the concept of environmental warfare that prevailed when the Geneva protocol was developed in 1977. We now understand far better than we did then how devastating such acts of war as the destruction of wetlands or the

> **President Carter never spoke more profoundly than when he said, to much cynical derision, that the struggle to eliminate our dependence on oil was "the moral equivalent of war."**

firing of oil fields can be. Our goal should be to restrict the freedom of military commanders to exploit technology for destructive ends.

The public seems ready for a serious debate on this topic. Though official and media interest in the oil spill turned out to be cynical and short-lived, there was a surprisingly intense public response. As the Saudis rushed to erect booms around wildlife refuges and desalinization plants, the world mourned an environmental tragedy. The shattering of the Gulf's ecology became an emotionally charged issue that brought a distant war closer to home.

When the United States initiated defoliation in Vietnam, there was no spontaneous outcry; environmental scientists had to campaign even to raise the issue. The public response to the Gulf oil spill, although soon eclipsed by the ground war, revealed how far we have come since Vietnam—how ever far we have still to go.

Many Sierra Club leaders were reluctant to comment forcefully on the oil spill in the midst of war. Was it possible to speak out without seeming to value sea cows over children? If the Club had no clearly defined solution to the dilemma posed by the invasion of Kuwait before the spill, did the spill change anything? Probably not. But now that the hostilities have ended, we can and must mobilize to intensify the public revulsion against environmental warfare.

If new forms of arms control make combat a less attractive form of conflict resolution, well and good. We can only hope that ecological awareness will help nations understand

*Highway of Death -- Highway from Al Mutla', Kuwait to Basra, Iraq, after the U.S. and Allied bombing, Feb. 26-27, 1991. It was "like shooting fish in a barrel," said one bomber pilot. The Iraqi's were leaving Kuwait in accordance with the UN resolution and "out of combat." Along with the soldiers killed were Palestinian and Kuwaiti civilians—a clear violation of the Geneva Convention of 1949, common article 3, which outlawed this killing. Photo: International War Crimes Tribunal.*

the folly of war as a solution to their disputes.

Means other than military might do exist, and are in many ways more reliable and certain than war. Sanctions against Iraq were beginning to have an effect; their failure, in the eyes of the world's statesmen, was that they took too long. Because of that rush to judgment, we will never know if sanctions would have forced Saddam to leave Kuwait. An essential value that environmentalists have tried to inculcate in our society is that of patience, of gearing up for the long haul. If the world is to resolve its dilemmas without destroying the biosphere, it must prepare to resolve them more slowly. Quick, simple fixes—such as pesticides and armored divisions—are illusory and dangerous.

The same impatience, hubris, and recklessness that have caused our environmental crises are behind our over reliance on military force. It is up to environmentalists to make explicit these connections, to promote and build on profound changes in public values, and to turn what is still an inchoate desire to protect the environment in time of war into a concrete realization that war's time has passed.

On February 20, 1991, the Sierra Club launched a major, long-term campaign to "detoxify" an economy so dependent on oil. The centerpiece of this campaign is our effort to pass legislation that will increase auto fuel-efficiency 40 percent by the year 2000. Such legislation almost passed the Senate last summer, in the wake of the invasion of Kuwait. It has been reintroduced this session, by Representative Barbara Boxer (D-Calif.) in the House, and by Senator Richard Bryan (D-Nev.). Its passage will reduce American oil consumption by 2.5 million barrels a day by the end of the century, and by 5 million barrels a day in the decade from 2015 to 2025.

By contrast, the Bush administration has offered a plan whose centerpiece is drilling the Arctic National Wildlife Refuge. Experts dispute how productive this would ultimately be. But even if "successful," this approach would yield—at the cost of the nation's last Arctic wilderness—only 300,000 barrels a day, and even that would be exhausted in two decades.

Passage of the Bryan-Boxer bills would mean that the United States could phase out imports from the Persian Gulf altogether by the end of the century. At that point, as we continue to reduce the demands for energy by increasing efficiency, we would also be able to substitute renewable energy resources for an ever-increasing portion of our remaining energy needs. Solar thermal, photovoltaics, and biomass technologies—if supported with research and development funds in the next decade—can easily become more economically and environmentally attractive than conventional fossil-fuel technologies.

The key here is consistency. The Sierra Club must build its campaign to kick the oil habit to the level necessary to pass the Bryan-Boxer bills and to safeguard the Arctic National Wildlife Refuge. We must then continue to mobilize the American people around energy issues until this nation is firmly committed to the most rapid abandonment feasible of our excessive dependence on oil.

The technology to end this dependence is well within our grasp. Long-term economics favors energy efficiency and renewable resources; environmental protection demands them. And finally, as has been proven so painfully this year, our national security requires an end to this dependence; the use of Stealth fighters and M-1A1 tanks as the key tools in our energy strategy has yielded oil-field fires that are consuming millions of barrels of oil a day. The vigorous, sustained pursuit of this campaign over the next decade can be our memorial to the victims—all the victims—of the Gulf war.

Wars have historically been justified not by the benefits they secure for those who fight them, but by appeals to our concern for our children and grandchildren. Yet war impoverishes the ecological systems that our children and grandchildren need to survive. No one today glorifies the prowess of Hulagu's horsemen. Few are even aware of the reasons that supposedly justified his punitive expedition. For centuries he has been remembered for burning Baghdad and destroying the irrigation systems of the Tigris-Euphrates floodplain. Last winter's destruction of the Persian Gulf, the devastation of the desert, the poisoning of the atmosphere, and the relentless bombing of Iraq and Kuwait will be remembered by the great grandchildren of the Iraqi, Kuwait, American, and other allied participants in the Gulf war. They are less likely to remember the war's immediate political origins or its moments of military drama, glorious though these may seem to Americans in the flush of "victory."

Environmentalists should forgive themselves for being caught unprepared by the events of the past months. We cannot be forgiven if we fail to learn their lesson. We have greater capacity to secure the peace of the world than we may have realized. We have a small and inadequate window of time in which to wield that power—but that has always been true of the challenges we have undertaken.

*Excerpted from* Sierra, *May/June 1991.*

*Zapata Oil founder, President George Bush and son, George, Jr., at the opening of Zapata Offshore's first offshore oil drilling rig in Kuwait in 1956. President Bush still owns this company, along with its drilling equipment and oil barge divisions; all of which are now in blind trusts. One month after the Valdez accident Bush put his oil barge company into a "blind trust."*

# CIA out of control

## *With the Cold War over, the intelligence community seeks new bogeymen*

### by Russ W. Baker / *Village Voice*

*I strongly disagree that communism, terrorism, or any other anti-democratic ideology has ever seriously threatened a nation confident in its own democratic values; I just as strongly dispute that it was ever necessary to curtail freedom in order to protect it.*
— Rep. Don Edwards (D-Calif. and ex-FBI agent), *St. John's Law Review.*

Despite new global realities, the American security apparatus keeps on growing and adapting to ensure its long-term survival. As we approach the 21st century, true democracy and open government increasingly move out of our reach. Consider these trends:

• While our cities and transportation systems crumble, the U.S. spy conglomerate thrives healthily. Its budget has quadrupled since 1980, and now consumes more than $35 billion each year. The CIA itself spends more than $5 billion and employs more than 25,000 people, with additional tens of thousands of "unofficial" workers on its payroll worldwide. America's foremost intelligence agency has no comprehensive charter outlining what the CIA may or may not do (the last effort to impose one failed in 1980). And in a time of professed global togetherness, its brutal covert action policies go right on violating international law and the rights of citizens everywhere.

• With the veneer of the Soviet threat torn away, agency actions prove more than ever a thesis shared by numerous former CIA agents—that the national security apparatus is little more than the private army of the *Fortune 500.* Besides the official spy outfits, a vast national security alumni network—positioned everywhere from Wall Street to Bangkok—is setting up private intelligence operations with the cooperation and encouragement of the CIA. In addition, the collaboration with multinational renegades is well-illustrated by the collapsed global empire of the Bank of Credit & Commerce International—already called the largest financial fraud in history. The bank, with which the CIA had maintained close financial ties, engaged in spying, bribery, extortion, kidnapping, and possibly murder. Time magazine, which broke the story, boldly went where few in the media will go: "The discovery of the CIA's dealings with BCCI raises a deeply disturbing question: Did the agency hijack the foreign policy of the United States

and in the process involve itself in one of the most audacious criminal enterprises in history?"

• The vast government intelligence enterprise, which incorporates more than a dozen separate agencies, is funded largely through a secret "black budget," hidden deep within the Pentagon's overall allocation. Having more than quadrupled under Ronald Reagan, the estimated $30 billion black budget is greater than New York City's entire budget, or the total federal outlay for education.

• Most troubling of all, congressional intelligence committees, charged with reining in the madness, are variously asleep at the wheel or helping to steer the ship of state into ever more dangerous waters. Reformist efforts have been virtually laughed out of Congress. One such effort, Sen. Daniel Patrick Moynihan's (D-N.Y.) "End of the Cold War Act of 1991," would transfer all CIA functions to the State Department, and define the agency strictly as an information-gathering unit. Another bill, authored by Rep. Barbara Boxer (D-Calif.), would have eliminated almost all covert action. Moynihan's bill is not expected to pass; Boxer's is even less likely to pass. Meanwhile, President Bush has moved to drastically weaken Congress' recognized responsibility to oversee intelligence activities. He wants to make it clear no one is to stand in the way of his vision of a new world order.

Bush has worked unceasingly to weaken the checks and balances that were instituted following a string of White House-connected scandals in the 1970s. The ad hoc investigative committees, chaired by former Sen. Frank Church and former Rep. Otis Pike, produced reports in 1976 that portrayed the intelligence community as dangerous, often incompetent, and unaccountable to the American people but "utterly responsive to the directions of the president." It is telling that Bush, who was CIA director at the time of the reports, should be the one to immobilize those reforms

Congressmembers' job of oversight is hampered both by a tradition of CIA lying and by their own laziness in pursuing the truth. "We'd go down [to Congress] and lie to them consistently," says ex-CIA officer Ralph McGehee. "In my 25 years, I have never seen the agency tell the truth to a congressional

committee." McGehee, a CIA officer in Vietnam, recounts one particularly juvenile exercise.

That proclivity for untruths continues. In November 1980, CIA analyst John Gentry quit, charging that the agency regularly distorts information to support executive-branch policies. He says it lied for decades about the military strength of the Soviet Union.

Another hot-button phrase in intelligence circles, "crisis management," was a handy excuse for North to draw up a plan that reportedly would have suspended the Constitution in the event of a "national crisis," a situation that might be put into effect by public opposition to a U.S. military invasion abroad. According to the *Miami Herald,* this plan called for rounding up domestic critics and putting them in internment camps.

And while the CIA uses our tax dollars to slavishly serve the interests of megacorporations, these same firms are busy exporting jobs and bilking the government on taxes and Pentagon contracts.

Meanwhile, conservatives around Washington continue to call for intervention against indigenous liberation movements abroad whose only connection with American security is their threat to the cheap labor markets and raw materials prized by the multinational corporations.

Already, 80 percent of the intelligence black budget is controlled by the Pentagon, and is dispensed to a raft of different organizations most Americans have never heard of. The largest, with a budget of $12 billion to $15 billion, is the Air Force's National Reconnaissance Office, which collects satellite data. (The government denies its very existence.) Others include the National Security Agency, which monitors international phone calls, and the Defense Intelligence Agency, which analyzes military information.

With Democrats as well as Republicans refusing to rein in the CIA and other government spooks, only the American people can challenge the national security opiate, just as their mass movements led the fight on civil rights, the environment, and the Vietnam War. Perhaps there's a lesson to be learned from the oppressed peoples of Eastern Europe who broke down the doors of the security agencies in their countries—seizing files and yanking electronics equipment from the walls—and tried to bring the agents to justice.

*Excerpted from* Village Voice, *Sept. 10, 1991.*

In January [1992], this year, 325 FBI agents who used to spy on East Block diplomats were reassigned to investigating [perpetrators of] violent crime and health care fraud.

— *Washington Post National Weekly* April 27-May 3, 1992

# US Role in the New World Order

### by John Stockwell

I worked for George Bush when he was CIA director in 1976 and the agency was trying to prevent a leftist government from ruling in Angola. Like the Iran–Contra team afterward, and many others before us, we had broken various laws and we had perjured ourselves to cover it up—"we" being Secretary of State Henry Kissinger and CIA director William Colby, with people like myself in staff positions supporting them. Bush's policy was *not* to investigate, *not* to dig out the truth, and *not* to punish the perpetrators in order to discipline and clean up the CIA. His policy was to cover up for us. He called it "restoring the CIA's morale."

While at the CIA, Bush was carefully building relationships that would continue when he became vice president and then president. CIA friends would be sprinkled throughout high offices in the Bush presidency, giving the intelligence community, with its dark and cynical ethos about foreign affairs, enormous influence on the U.S. government and national policy.

These contacts were incidental, however, to Bush's broader plan. He used his position as CIA director to bring into the agency a team of right-wing economists who would doctor the intelligence reports in order to publish a bloated assessment of alleged military spending by the Soviet Union. Their report was the foundation for the dramatic arms buildup of the 1980s. During his eight years as vice president, Bush worked quietly with the U.S. government's "secret team," with Oliver North and others involved in Iran-Contra, drug, and terrorist activities, building contacts throughout the national and world security networks.

As president, Bush is more subtle than Reagan, and less noisy, but he is continuing Reagan's policies across the globe. Bush refused the Soviets' offer for both superpowers to abstain from delivering arms to the combatants in Afghanistan; he continued to deliver arms to rebel leader Jonas Savimbi in Angola, who has boasted openly of shooting down passenger planes; he asked for military aid for the contras in Nicaragua so they could continue fighting; and he pressed ahead with vigorous plans to interfere with the elections in Nicaragua. The latter was an eventual success for George Bush and the CIA.

*Excerpted from the book* The Praetorian Guard: The U.S. Role in the New World Order

© Raee Mattson

*by John Stockwell. Copyright © 1991 by John Stockwell; South End Press, 116 St. Botolph St., Boston, MA 02115.*

# Business–as–Usual

### by Sam Day / *Nukewatch Pathfinder*

Every week or two a convoy of unmarked, armored trucks and escort vehicles pulls out of the sprawling Pantex nuclear warhead factory in the Texas panhandle and merges into the stream of traffic headed east on Interstate Highway 40, America's H-bomb alley.

The cargo: several dozen newly minted nuclear warheads, each destined for the nose of an intercontinental ballistic missile capable of reaching and destroying almost any city on Earth. Destination: The U.S. naval base at St. Mary's, Georgia, home of the Atlantic fleet of Trident submarines, which comprise the core of the Pentagon's "nuclear deterrent." Purpose: To maintain business-as-usual in the federal government's nuclear weapons production complex, and to keep it flourishing long after the disappearance of the "enemies" it was erected to deter.

The continued buildup of the Trident fleet, its missiles presumably still targeted on the remnants of the Soviet Union, is only a tiny segment of the post-Cold War U.S. nuclear arms industry. It is the reality behind the peace dividend rhetoric of the Bush Administration and the Congressional Democratic leadership.

A few obsolescent land-based missiles are coming out of the ground in South Dakota; hydrogen bombs once stored at the edge of the runway have been removed at some Air Force installations; Bush has canceled some high-priced weapons orders that never had a prayer of passing Congress and has withdrawn some battlefield nukes that would otherwise have been thrown out in places like Germany and South Korea.

But such steps are mere sops and tokens, designed by the nuclear-military-industrial complex to keep the public off its back while it retrenches and regroups for the future. Unlike its erstwhile superpower rival, which is engaging in unilateral nuclear disarmament with almost unseemly haste and offering to go even faster, the U.S. government is tenaciously resisting change. And so far it is getting away with it.

The withdrawal of the Soviet Union not only from the nuclear arms race, but also from worldwide geopolitical contention, presents this country with an unprecedented opportunity to throw off the same military shackles that brought the Soviet economy to its knees. But the "national security" estab-

> **Recently, President Bush has again said that the United States won the Cold War. My reply to this would be that the long years we spent plunged in the Cold War made losers of us all.**
> — *Mikhail S. Gorbachev*

lishment and its allies have no intention of doing this. For example:

🖎 Impressive at first blush, the Bush Administration's proposed military spending reduction of $50 billion over the next five years actually cuts no more than three percent from the $1.5 trillion previously projected. Cuts of double or even triple that magnitude, proposed by some Democrats, are still puny compared to the need.

🖎 Continued insistence on Star Wars, Trident fleet expansion, the Stealth Bomber and other major weapons is the real measure of the Administration's arms policy, not the *few* cutbacks in isolated systems or the small reductions in numerical inventories.

🖎 Monumental environmental and safety problems in the Department of Energy nucle-

ar weapons production complex are being addressed, not by closure and cleanup of the system but, by reshaping it to continue nuclear weapons production into the 21st century.

🖎 Responding to pressure from the nuclear weapons establishment, the United States continues to be the lone holdout to an international treaty banning the testing of nuclear weapons. Such a treaty is the essential first step to a phasing out of nuclear arms.

Far deeper cuts in military spending, retiring of all major nuclear weapons systems, closing of the nuclear weapons factories, signing of the comprehensive nuclear test ban treaty—are the minimum steps that these times require. A few years ago they would have seemed utopian; today they are the

*realpolitik* of the post-Cold War world.

These are also minimum steps on the path to real national security, toward a nation and world freed of the threat of nuclear oblivion and the dead hand of military spending. We should insist on nothing less from those aspiring to national public office in this election year. And as citizens we should spare no effort to turn today's rekindled dreams of a peaceful and just world order into tomorrow's reality.

*Sam Day received the Martin Luther King Award in 1992 from the Fellowship of Reconciliation.*

*Excerpted from* Nukewatch Pathfinder*, Spring 1992.*

# *Helen Caldicott on* Global Vision and Citizen Action

### by Elizabeth Wolfe / *Matrix*

In ten years the Earth will be in dire straits if we don't take action immediately, said internationally renowned peace activist Dr. Helen Caldicott in Santa Cruz last month. The founder of Physicians for Social Responsibility, author of *Missile Envy*, and a practicing pediatrician in Australia, Caldicott made a sweeping and sober diagnosis of many of the world's environmental and political ills. She called for citizen action on a massive scale to avert disaster.

During her talk, Caldicott returned again and again to one point: the politics of greed and selfishness must be replaced with "the politics of compassion," she said. "Take care of each other. The best way to love everyone is to love yourself, tap into your own soul and there you'll find love, God, creativity."

"We drift toward unparalleled disaster,"

she said. "What are you going to do about it? I know you're all good people, but I'm going to sock it to you. Don't ask me to spoon-feed you: you know what to do."

Her talk covered a wide range of topics, among them:

**The Persian Gulf War**—Making connections between the Gulf War and Hiroshima and the Holocaust, Caldicott said it was the "most obscene thing I've ever seen in my life. It wasn't a war, it was a massacre." The Bush administration, which "works for the corporations, not for you," she said, "orchestrated the war to boost the president's popularity, hold up the military industrial complex, and divert attention from domestic problems."

**The media**—Calling it the "Pentagon's public relations firm," Caldicott blasted the media for its complicity in censoring the Gulf War. She told of a French photographer's pictures of children with charred skin and faces melted away by bombs, "while the American media reported that Baghdad was 'lit up like a Christmas tree'." She further said that the media should not be privately owned and should exist for the sole purpose of educating people.

**Corporations**—"What you have in the U.S. is socialism for the corporations, and capitalism for you guys," she said, recalling how the government bails out companies such as Chrysler.

Calling the U.S. a "weapons-dominated

country," Caldicott said that most corporations are involved in weapons production, among them AT&T, ITT, Amana, General Electric, IBM, Hotpoint, MCI, General Motors, Jeep Eagle, Hewlett Packard and General Foods.

**Nuclear weapons**—"Sixty thousand nuclear weapons still exist in the world. Eighty percent of Americans supported a bilateral nuclear weapons freeze," but Congress nixed it, she said. The U.S. is still preparing for a first strike nuclear capability, she said. In a related point, she reported that one million children are at risk of leukemia due to the Chernobyl disaster.

"If you spent $1 million a day since Jesus was born, you would have spent a trillion dollars," the amount the U.S. spends on weapons in one year, she said. This money must be "transferred from the death industry to saving the planet," she said.

**Women in politics**—"Fifty-three percent of Congress should be made up of women—black women, white women, poor women, rich women," she said. When women comprise less than 30 percent of a political body, "they emulate men, like Thatcher did," Caldicott said. "When we're more than 30 percent, we act like ourselves."

**Consumption**—"The U.S. must lead the effort to avert global disaster because it is the main problem," Caldicott said. With only 5 percent of the Earth's population, the U.S. consumes 40 percent of the world's resources and 25 percent of its energy.

**Overpopulation**—Humans "are like a predatory plague of rabbits," she said. The global population was 1 billion in 1800, it is now 5.2 billion, and by 2040, it could reach 14 billion if measures aren't taken to halt the exponential growth.

**Reproductive rights**—"Contraception and abortion must be freely available to everyone on the globe," she said. Caldicott advocated that RU486, the "abortion pill," be made immediately available in the U.S.

**Global warming**—Unless we act now, the globe could heat up 18 degrees Fahrenheit within 50 years. The major culprits of ozone depletion (which causes global warming) are cars, and refrigerators and air conditioners, which emit chloroflourocarbons. If we stop now, it would take 85 years to achieve 1985 ozone levels, she said.

**Species extinction**—The U.N. and the National Academy of Science predict that if we don't take action now, within 10 years many species will become extinct, Caldicott reported. "There are only 10,000 elephants; there are 5.2 billion humans: that's enough."

**Trees**—"Forests are cathedrals of God," she said. "Trees are the lungs of the Earth." Caldicott said if the destruction of the rain forests in South America, cleared largely for cattle grazing by U.S. fast food chains, does not cease, in ten years they will be gone. "If we continue to chop, half of the Earth's 30 million species that live in the rain forests will become extinct," she said.

**Some of Caldicott's recommendations:**
✔ "Take over Congress," she said. "When are you going to show [your government] the country belongs to you? The whole world is waiting for you." Run independent candidates in every race and "some of you will win. Represent the people, not the transnational nationals." Caldicott pointed out that in Australia, where she recently ran for office, voting is compulsory and the government reimburses candidates 91 cents on the dollar for every vote they receive.

✔ "Educate and mobilize the people."
✔ "Recycling legitimates garbage," Caldicott said. Paper should be made out of bamboo and hemp, not trees.
✔ Have only one child per family. Replace the nuclear family, which is obsolete, she said, with extended families and communities. "Tear down your fences."
✔ Grow your own food; "eat low on the food chain. Don't eat meat."
✔ Have faith. "*But* means *no*," she said. "Stay in the joy, stay out of negativity."

*Excerpted from* Matrix, *April 1991.*

# The Peace Dividend Elimination of World Poverty

### by J.W. Smith /
### *The World's Wasted Wealth*

*Our military economy has created a bulwark of jobs engaged in manufacturing arms and creating a future based on fear, destruction, and waste. Meanwhile, those working to renew respect for Nature have been depicted as destroyers of employment. Yet, if a sane and visionary energy policy and economic conversion were pursued as a "moral equivalent to war," many job insecurities could be avoided. Author and economist, J.W. Smith addresses these issues and proposes solutions. He suggests that with the half of our wealth which is wasted, the world could be capitalized in only 45 years if only 25 percent of that wasted capital was used to produce industry for the world's dispossessed. Upon this premise, he is presently founding The Institute for Economic Democracy. The following is an excerpt from his book,* The World's Wasted Wealth. *[Ed. Note]*

*In military spending and other segments of the economy, we waste over 50 percent of our wealth. Eliminate that waste and we could either be twice as rich, have twice the free time, or provide industrial tools to the Third World and abolish most poverty.*

*— J.W.S.*

Immediately will come warnings from every entrenched mind that it could not be done. But it can. If we can build hundreds of billions of dollars worth of tools of destruction every year when they are not needed, we can build productive tools and loan (or give) them to needy societies. Tools lent for productive purposes can be repaid from the wealth generated; tools for war, when built, subtract from the world's potential wealth

## Military Spending Means Fewer Jobs

Figures based on 1990 fiscal year and 1990 dollars. Source Employment Research Associates, Lansing MI

Number of Jobs created on an equal investment in each area

## Fiscal Year 1992 (numbers in billions)

Source: War Resisters League

and, when used, destroy already produced wealth. The wealth that could have been produced or preserved by that wasted land, labor, and capital is gone forever. It is critical that aid be weighted towards industry for those people to produce their own needs. Products and services such as food and consumer products may not be directly wasted and if there is a crisis it can even be a blessing. But, if it precludes development of local industry and creates dependency in a country that can be self-sufficient and independent, it is a massive waste.

### Measuring the Currently Wasted Capital

Without considering the full social cost to the American community, the combined Pentagon budgets of 1946-1988 represent a mass of resources equivalent to the cost of replacing just about all (94 percent) of everything man-made in the United States (excluding the land) [i.e. every house, railroad, airplane, household appliance, etc.]. But when we take into account both the resources used by the military as well as the economic product forgone, then *we must appreciate the social cost of the military economy, 1946-1988, as amounting to about twice the "reproducible assets" of U.S. national wealth*. What has been forgone for American society is a quantity of material wealth sufficient to refurbish the United States, with an enormous surplus to spare.

Since professor Melman's 1983 calculations, over $1.5 trillion (in 1990 dollars) has been thrown away by the U.S., over $5 trillion by East and West, and over $6 trillion by the world. (Almost one trillion dollars a year are now [1990] spent on arms worldwide.)

The Third World and the First World together spent about $28 trillion on arms since the Second World War (converted to 1990 dollars). That is 5.7 times enough to have industrialized the world over the past 45 years. [The author calculates that only 2.5 percent of an industrialized nation's total wealth are industrial tools caring for civilian needs.] That would have left $24.5 trillion to provide training to run the machines; for training to operate a society (including population control); for initial communications infrastructure to reach the populations with that training; to guarantee food for the elderly so that population control will be accepted (only when a country absolutely could not produce its own); to search for, catalog, and develop resources; and for environmental

---

## The Third World and the First World together spent about $28 trillion on arms since the Second World War.

---

protection. Two-fifths of the world already have relatively stable population levels and that cost could be reduced even further and the world's standard of living raised even faster if the remaining populations were stabilized or reduced.

Over 34 percent of U.S. industry is wasted on arms (1982-91); approximately 10 percent is used to support the infrastructure for the waste distribution territories [unnecessary labor] within the civilian economy; and 20 percent has been idle in the slack economy of the 1980s, of which only half is down time for repairs. This means that fully 54 percent of U.S. industrial capital (not social capital) is wasted, leaving only 46 percent producing for our actual needs and we have calculated that a society can be well cared for at half that consumption rate, or with 23 percent of U.S. per capita industrial capacity.

With approximately 3.5 billion people (70 percent) without modern tools, $4.9 trillion of industrial capital is needed at this time, or 17.5 percent that spent on arms since WWII. Assuming it would require 45 years for the Third World to learn and build social capital as they were being given industrial capital and the world's dispossessed population doubled in that time span, it would require $9.8 trillion. That would be only $217.77 billion annually or 22 percent the $1 trillion currently spent on arms each year worldwide. NATO and Warsaw pact countries accounted for 86 percent of that production, or about $860 billion (1990) and the West spent well over half of that. Thus it would require only 25 percent the money habitually spent on arms by NATO and Warsaw Pact countries to industrialize the world. As the Eastern Bloc has collapsed, this leaves only the West but if we allowed half that spent by the West (over $500 billion), that would still be over twice the $218 billion a year needed to industrialize the world.

Those were the rules under which the Marshall Plan rebuilt Europe. Our policy was "directed not against any country or doctrine but against hunger, poverty, desperation and chaos. Its purpose should be the revival of a working economy in the world so as to permit the emergence of political and social conditions in which free institutions can exist." Any government that was willing to assist in the task of recovery would find full cooperation, but any government that maneuvered to block the recovery of others could not expect help from us. "Furthermore, governments, political parties, or groups which seek to perpetuate human misery in order to profit therefrom politically or otherwise will encounter the opposition of the United States."

The cost of all wars in this century alone could have capitalized the world several times over. It is the battles over world wealth that keeps the world impoverished.

*Excerpted from* The World's Wasted Wealth, *published by New Worlds Press, © 1992 by J.W. Smith.*

# The Clan of One-Breasted Women

### by Terry Tempest Williams / *Ms.*

I belong to a Clan of One-Breasted Women. My mother, my grandmothers, and six aunts have all had mastectomies. Seven are dead. The two who survive have just completed rounds of chemotherapy and radiation.

I've had my own problems: two biopsies for breast cancer and a small tumor removed between my ribs diagnosed as "a borderline malignancy." This is my family history.

Most statistics tell us breast cancer is genetic, hereditary, with rising percentages attached to fatty diets, childlessness, or becoming pregnant after 30. What they don't say is living in Utah may be the greatest hazard of all.

We are a Mormon family with roots in Utah since 1847. *The Word of Wisdom*, a religious doctrine of health, kept the women in my family aligned with good foods: no coffee, tea, tobacco, or alcohol. For the most part, these women were finished having babies by the time they were 30. And only one faced breast cancer prior to 1960. Traditionally, as a group of people, Mormons have a low rate of cancer.

Is our family a cultural anomaly? The truth is, we didn't think about it. Those who did, usually the men, simply said, "bad genes." The women's attitude was stoic. Cancer was a part of life. On February 16, 1971, the eve before my mother's surgery, I accidentally picked up the telephone and overheard her ask my grandmother what she could expect.

"Diane, it is one of the most spiritual experiences you will ever encounter."

I quietly put down the receiver.

Two days later, my father took my three brothers and me to the hospital to visit her. She met us in the lobby in a wheelchair. No bandages were visible. I'll never forget her radiance, the way she held herself in a purple velour robe and how she gathered us around her.

"Children, I am fine. I want you to know I felt the arms of God around me."

We believed her. My father cried. Our mother, his wife, was 38 years old.

15

Two years ago, after my mother's death from cancer, my father and I were having dinner together. He had just returned from St. George, where his construction company was putting in natural gas lines for towns in southern Utah. He spoke of his love for the country: the sandstone landscape, bare-boned and beautiful. He had just finished hiking the Kolob trail in Zion National Park. We got caught up in reminiscing, recalling with fondness our walk up Angels landing on his fiftieth birthday and the years our family had vacationed there. This was a remembered landscape where we had been raised.

> **I watched beautiful women become bald as Cisplatin, Cytoxan and Adriamycin were injected into their veins. I held their foreheads as they vomited green-black bile and I shot them with morphine when the pain became inhuman.**

Over dessert, I shared a recurring dream of mine. I told my father that for years, as long as I could remember, I saw this flash of light in the night in the desert. That this image had so permeated my being, I could not venture south without seeing it again, on the horizon, illuminating buttes and mesas.

"You did see it," he said.

"Saw what?" I asked, a bit tentative.

"The bomb. The cloud. We were driving home from Riverside, California. You were sitting on your mother's lap. She was pregnant. In fact, I remember the date, September 7, 1957. We had just gotten out of the Service. We were driving north, past Las Vegas. It was an hour or so before dawn, when this explosion went off. We not only heard it, but felt it. I thought the oil tanker in front of us had blown up. We pulled over and suddenly, rising from the desert floor, we saw it clearly, this golden-stemmed cloud, the mushroom. The sky seemed to vibrate with an eerie pink glow. Within a few minutes, a light ash was raining on the car."

I stared at my father. This was new information to me.

"I thought you knew that," my father said. "It was a common occurrence in the fifties."

> ### *We don't really test bombs, we do physics experiments.*
> Dr. Robert Kuckuck
> Associate Director for Nuclear Test Experimental Science,
> Lawrence Livermore National Labs

It was at that moment I realized the deceit I had been living under. Children growing up in the American Southwest, drinking contaminated milk from contaminated cows, even from the contaminated breasts of their mothers, my mother—members, years later, of the Clan of One-Breasted Women.

It is a well-known story in the Desert West, "The Day We Bombed Utah," or perhaps, "The Years We Bombed Utah." Above-ground atomic testing in Nevada took place from January 27, 1951, through July 11, 1962. The winds were blowing north, covering "low use segments of the population" in Utah with fallout and leaving sheep dead in their tracks, and the climate was right. The United States of the 1950s was red, white, and blue. The Korean War was raging. McCarthyism was rampant. Ike was it and the Cold War was hot. If you were against nuclear testing, you were for a Communist regime.

Much has been written about this "American nuclear tragedy." Public health was secondary to national security. The Atomic Energy Commissioner, Thomas Murray, was quoted as saying, "Gentlemen, we must not let anything interfere with this series of tests, nothing."

Again, and again, the public was told by its government, in spite of burns, blisters, and nausea, "It has been found that the tests may be conducted with adequate assurance of safety under conditions prevailing at the bombing reservation." Assuaging public fears was simply a matter of public relations. A news release typical of the times stated, "We find no basis for concluding that harm to any individual has resulted from radioactive fallout."

On August 30, 1979, during Jimmy Carter's presidency, a suit was filed entitled *Irene Allen vs. The United States of America*. Allen was the first to be alphabetically listed with 24 test cases, representative of nearly 1,200 plaintiffs seeking compensation from the United States government for cancers caused from nuclear testing in Nevada.

Irene Allen lived in Hurricane, Utah. She was the mother of five children and had been widowed twice. Her first husband, with their two oldest boys, had watched the tests from the roof of the local high school. He died of leukemia in 1956. Her second husband died of pancreatic cancer in 1978.

In a town meeting conducted by Utah Senator Orrin Hatch, shortly before the suit was filed, Allen said, "I am not exactly blaming the government, I want you to know, Senator Hatch. But I thought if my

> **It does not matter whether the United States government was irresponsible, whether it lied to its citizens, or even that citizens died from the fallout of nuclear testing. What matters is that our government is immune.**

testimony could help in any way so this wouldn't happen again to any of the generations coming after us...I am really happy to be here this day to bear testimony to this."

God-fearing people. This is just one story in an anthology of thousands.

On May 10, 1984, Judge Bruce S. Jenkins handed down his opinion. Ten of the plaintiffs were awarded damages. It was the first time a federal court had determined that nuclear tests had been the cause of cancers. For the remaining 14 test cases, the proof of causation was not sufficient. In spite of the split decision, it was considered a landmark ruling. It was not to remain so.

In April 1987, the 10th Circuit Court of Appeals overturned Judge

*Department of Energy photo of the Nevada Desert Test Site. As of July 1992, there has been 941 nuclear tests by the US at this site. The British also do their tests here. Between 1946 and 1958 the US tested in the Bikini Islands. In 1969 the natives were allowed to return to the islands and were re-evacuated in 1978 after residual radiation levels were discovered. Clean-up efforts began in 1988.*

Jenkins' ruling on the basis that the United States was protected from suit by the legal doctrine of sovereign immunity, the centuries-old idea from England in the days of absolute monarchs.

In January 1988, the Supreme Court refused to review the appeals court decision. In our court system, it does not matter whether the United States government was irresponsible, whether it lied to its citizens, or even that citizens died from the fallout of nuclear testing. What matters is that our government is immune: "The King can do no wrong."

In Mormon culture, authority is respected, obedience is revered, and independent thinking is not. I was taught as a young girl no to "make waves" or "rock the boat."

"Just let it go—" my mother would say. "You know how you feel, that's what counts."

For many years, I did just that—listened, observed, and quietly formed my own opinions within a culture that rarely asked questions because it had all the answers. But one by one, I watched the women in my family die common, heroic deaths. We sat in waiting rooms hoping for good news, always receiving the bad. I cared for them, bathed their scarred bodies, and kept their secrets. I watched beautiful women become bald as Cisplatin, Cytoxan and Adriamycin were injected into their veins. I held their foreheads as they vomited green-black bile and I shot them with morphine when the pain became inhuman. In the end, I witnessed their last peaceful breaths, becoming a midwife to the rebirth of their souls. But the price of obedience became too high.

The fear and inability to question authority that ultimately killed rural communities in Utah during atmospheric testing of atomic weapons was the same fear I saw being held in my mother's body. Sheep. Dead sheep. The evidence is buried.

I cannot prove that my mother, Diane Dixon Tempest, or my grandmothers, Lettie Romney Dixon and Kathryn Blackett Tempest, along with my aunts, contracted cancer from nuclear fallout in Utah. But I can't prove they didn't.

My father's memory was correct: the September blast we drove through in 1957 was part of Operation Blumbbob, one of the most intensive series of bombs to be initiated. The flash of light in the night in the desert I had always thought was a dream developed into a family nightmare. It took 14 years, from 1957 to 1971, for cancer to show up in my mother—the same amount of time, Howard L. Andrews, an authority on radioactive fallout at the National Institutes of Health, says radiation cancer requires to become evident. The more I learn about what it means to be a "downwinder," the more questions I drown in.

What I do know, however, is that as Mormon woman of the fifth generation of "Latter-Day Saints," I must question every-

*Non-violence is the answer to the crucial political and moral questions of our time; the need for man to overcome oppression and violence without resorting to oppression and violence. Man must evolve for all human conflict a method which rejects revenge, aggression and retaliation. The foundation of such a method is love.*

— Martin Luther King

*Members of All Saints Episcopal Church, Pasadena, CA, in conjunction with the Nevada Desert Experience, participating in a non-violent civil disobedience action at the Neveda Test Site in February 1990.*

thing, even if it means losing my faith, becoming a member of a border tribe among my own people. Tolerating blind obedience in the name of patriotism or religion ultimately takes our lives.

When the Atomic Energy Commission described the country north of the Nevada Test Site as virtually uninhabited desert terrain, my family members were some of the "virtual uninhabitants."

❋

On March 18, 1988, I crossed the line at the Nevada Test Site and was arrested with nine other Utahns for trespassing on military lands. They are still conducting nuclear tests in the desert. Ours was an act of civil disobedience. But as I walked toward the town of Mercury, it was more than a gesture of peace. It was a gesture on behalf of the Clan of One-Breasted Women.

As one officer cinched the handcuffs around my wrists, another frisked my body. She found a pen and a pad of paper tucked inside my left boot.

"And these?" she asked sternly.

"Weapons," I replied.

Our eyes met. I smiled. She pulled the leg of my trousers back over my boot.

"Step forward, please," she said as she took my arm.

We were booked under an afternoon sun and bussed to Tonopah, Nevada. It was a two-hour ride. This was familiar country to me. The Joshua trees standing their ground had been named by my ancestors who believed they looked like prophets pointing west to the promised land. These were the same trees that bloomed each spring, flowers appearing like white flames in the Mojave. And I recalled a full moon in May when my mother and I had walked among them, flushing out mourning doves and owls.

The bus stopped short of town. We were released. The officials, thought it was a cruel joke to leave us stranded in the desert with no way to get home. What they didn't realize is that we were home, soul-centered and strong, women who recognized the sweet smell of sage as fuel for our spirits.

*Excerpted from* Ms., *September/October 1991.*

# Telephone War Tax Resistance
## *A monthly low-risk action for peace*

The federal excise tax on telephone services has been associated with military spending and intervention throughout most of its history. Originally enacted in 1898 to help finance the US war against Spain, it has been repeatedly renewed and increased to meet the costs of one military intervention after another, including World Wars I and II, and the Korean and Vietnam Wars. In 1990 it was made permanent. The money raised by the tax, like most other taxes, goes into the General Fund. Currently over 50% of these funds are used for military spending.

Thousands of people refuse to pay the 3% federal excise tax each month as a protest against U.S. militarism. The amount you withhold each month may seem small, but this tax generates about $3 billion every year, more am half of which is spent on war and preparations for war. Collectively we send a strong message to the government when we resist this tax. And because the amounts we owe are small, our act of civil disobedience in refusing to pay is relatively risk-free.

### How to Refuse the Telephone Tax

To refuse payment of the telephone tax, deduct the federal (U.S.) excise tax amount itemized on your monthly local and long distance bills, and pay the balance. Enclose a note with the payment including:

① A statement that you are refusing to pay the federal excise tax and why.
② The date of the bill.
③ The amount you are withholding.
④ The signature of the person to whom the bill is addressed.

You can order printed cards from CMTC to enclose with your bill.

Most phone companies will credit you for the withheld taxes. If they do not, contact them and ensure that they understand their responsibilities, otherwise the outstanding balance can accumulate. They are not required to enforce collection of the unpaid taxes, but merely to report the amount to the IRS. Some companies, such as Allnet, have established special billing procedures to accommodate war tax resisters and credit the tax automatically.

### Possible Consequences

In theory the phone company should notify the IRS of your war tax refusal and the amounts of unpaid tax. The IRS usually does nothing with this information, since the cost of collecting the refused taxes would greatly exceed the amounts withheld. You may receive letters from the IRS asking for payment, and in very rare cases they may seize the amount owed plus interest and penalties from bank accounts or garnish wages. A few people have had the tax owed deducted from income tax refunds. The vast majority of telephone tax refusers, however, have never been contacted by the IRS. There is no history of anyone being charged with a criminal offense for withholding telephone taxes. Telephone tax resistance is a low-risk action for peace.

Generally, your phone company cannot legally disconnect your phone service for non-payment of the tax, and could be subject to Federal Communications Commission action if it does, including fines for each day that your service is interrupted. The break-up of AT&T has meant that a lot of new companies are not yet familiar with telephone tax resistance and their responsibilities.

You can reach the Enforcement Division of the FCC at Common Carriers Branch, 2025 M St. NW, Washington, DC 20554; (202) 632-7553. If you need help, contact CMTC.

### What to do With Resisted Telephone Taxes

The other side of withholding the tax money from the militarism of the U.S. government is redirecting it for life-affirming purposes. This makes a positive statement about our priorities and increases our effectiveness.

One way to redirect your telephone taxes is to give them to humanitarian projects in Central America through CMTC's Direct Aid Project for Central America. Ask us for our Direct Aid Project information sheet. This project was set up specifically to redirect telephone taxes. Send us your check marked Direct Aid Project, and you can add solidarity to your tax resistance and help counteract over a century of U.S. intervention in that region.

If you wish your funds to be returnable, you can deposit them in CMTC's Escrow Account. Escrow funds are invested in socially responsible institutions assisting low income communities and minorities. Interest from the Escrow Account helps CMTC to help war tax resisters around the country, and 5% is directly granted to community groups helping to meet human needs. Ask for our Escrow Account brochure to get more information.

*Excerpted from Conscience and Military Tax Campaign flyer (see directories for details).*

> **It is not enough to ban nuclear weapons. If you ban nuclear weapons completely, and even destroy all the existing stock they will be manufactured if war breaks out... We must work toward some system which will prevent war. It requires a different imagination, a different outlook.**
>
> — *Bertrand Russell, 1959*

# Chapter 2

# Developing Nations

**To understand** the perspective of third world people it is first necessary to understand living conditions and economic conditions in these countries.

About one billion people live in extreme poverty in the third world, with only a $20 increase in total income over the last ten years. Sixty-two percent are illiterate; their average life expectancy is fifty years, with an infant mortality rate eight times ours. For one out of every two people in these countries, nutrition is below minimum acceptable standards.

During the next two decades the world will become four times wealthier but the gap between the rich and poor nations is unlikely to change. According to Professor Ann Carter of Brandeis University the "annual per capita incomes in North America will soar by the turn of the century to around $25,000 while indigent citizens of the third world will struggle to survive on $300 a year." Today the poorest 30% of humanity has 3% of the income. The top 20% has 66%.

**Most third world countries** depend on one or two primary commodities like rubber, sisal or jute, tropical crops like tea, coffee or bananas, and minerals like copper, tin, bauxite and aluminum for 50-90% of their earnings. The prices of these commodities are unstable, being controlled by the world's commodities exchanges in Chicago, New York and London.

As a result, the Western countries buy something like $30 billion worth of third world countries' raw materials, process them, and sell them on the world market for $200 billion. The difference is the value added and the jobs created in the so-called rich countries of Europe, Canada, United States, Japan, and Australia.

Obviously, the answer is for the third world countries to process their own raw materials into finished products and retain more of that extra $170 billion.

*Excerpted from a Friends of the Third World brochure.*

# America's Post-Cold War Human Rights Policy

### by Holly J. Burkhalter / *Peace & Democracy News*

Recently I addressed a group of U.S. military officers who had been assigned to our embassies in Latin America to administer American military aid programs and to interact with their Latin American military counterparts. I asked them what the United State's military role in Latin America should be, given the end of the Cold War. Their response was straightforward: to assist governments in combating narcotics production and trafficking, and to aid in defense against subversion.

### The "War on Drugs" in Latin America

The truth of their assessment is vividly demonstrated by the Bush Administration's policy towards Peru. The State Department and White House have been pressuring Peruvian President Alberto Fujimori to accept military assistance since he took office in July, 1990.[1] The key element of the State Department's campaign to pressure Peru was the linking of economic and military aid. If Peru refused military aid, they would get no economic assistance on the grounds that they were not taking effective action against narcotics trafficking. Fujimori and his cabinet resisted the pressure for a year, insisting that theirs would be an alternative strategy based upon economic development and local empowerment. But the country's crippling poverty left Fujimori vulnerable to the State Department's blackmail. Washington won in the end, and in July 1991, the Administration announced its intention to provide Peru with $90 million in anti-narcotics assistance—including a whopping $35 million in military aid.[2]

Washington's eagerness to involve the military in the "war on drugs" in Latin America may also be seen in Argentina, where plans are afoot to involve the Argentine air force, in cooperation with the U.S., in drug interdiction efforts. The Argentine human rights community is outraged, given the role played by the Argentine military in the murder and disappearance of tens of thousands of men, women, and children in the 1970s and 1980s.

Thus the end of the Cold War has not meant an end to the United States' involvement with wholly corrupt and brutal South American armies. The pity of such a strategy is that it invigorates Latin militaries which are either currently engaged in horrific abuses, as in the case of Peru, or which menace civilian governments with coup threats when efforts are made to account for past abuses, as in the case of Argentina. Elsewhere in the hemisphere, Washington continues to pour military aid into El Salvador, notwithstanding the November 16, 1989 murder of the Jesuits in San Salvador and tens of thousands of others—a policy guaranteed to complicate the United Nations' peace efforts in that beleaguered country. The U.S. disengaged from Guatemala's military only reluctantly, following the murder of a U.S. citizen in 1990, but in 1991 the State Department announced that Guatemala will receive $50 million in budgetary support funds, which Congress had frozen on human rights grounds. The anti-narcotics effort in Peru, with its emphasis on the military at the expense of civilian authority, is mirrored in Bolivia and Colombia.

### A Mixed Record in Kenya and Zaire

On the African continent, the Administration's human rights performance is better, if mixed. The democratic revolutions of Eastern Europe have captured the imagination of

---

## The Bush Administration appears not to have noticed that the Cold War is over.

---

Africans, and in country after country, human rights activists, multi-party advocates, and democrats are agitating for change and the United States has been largely sympathetic to the cause. In the case of Ethiopia, the State Department played an enormously significant role in ending decades of civil war by encouraging the Mengitsu regime to leave office and the victorious rebels to enter Addis Ababa with minimal bloodshed. And the State Department's Africa Bureau chief, Ambassador Herman Cohen, has (albeit with strong Congressional urging) ended U.S. military aid to Kenya's Daniel Arap Moi and has persistently and publicly urged him to make significant improvements in human rights.

The United States' important support for democratic change in Kenya has, unfortunately, not been emulated in Zaire. Despite fears by leaders in the U.S. Congress that Mobutu's human rights abuses and extreme corruption in Zaire are setting the stage for a Liberia-like disintegration in the coming year, Washington has pursued a naively optimistic policy of "encouraging" the dictator to engage in democratic discussions to set the stage for future elections. Mobutu, however, is clearly uninterested in relinquishing power and continues to preside over the rapid decay of the entire country. Foreign policy leaders in Congress are of the mind that Mobutu's day is over and the best U.S. policy would be to encourage him to depart the scene. Unfortunately, hard-liners within the Administration (notably the National Security Council) cling to the notion that he can be made to moderate his ways and represents the best hope for Zaire's "transition to democracy."

### China's Outlaw Behavior

Perhaps no example better illustrates the poverty of the U.S. human rights policy than China. Again, the Bush Administration appears not to have noticed that the Cold War is over, and that the long cherished "China card" is now an embarrassing anachronism. How else can one explain a policy in which China, which has engaged in outlaw behavior at every turn (including gross abuses of human rights, international trade depredations, and nuclear and conventional weapons proliferation) continues to be treated as a pampered ally? The Bush Administration has ferociously rejected Congressional limits on China's "most favored nation" trade benefits, and has dodged Congressional demands to bar imports of products made by forced labor. Secretary Baker's recent trip to China yielded absolutely nothing on human rights.

The end of the Cold War has presented an extraordinary opportunity for an end to proxy wars and the bitter human rights abuses that accompany them. The newly significant role of the United Nations in conflict resolution and peacekeeping is another opportunity that has come with the Cold War's demise. But in too many instances, it is business as usual in Washington. It is up to the human rights community and the Congress to insist that the Bush Administration abandon strategies which provoke and prolong human misery at the hands of our repressive friends.

1. The issue of U.S. pressure on Andean governments to accept military aid was thoroughly aired at Congressional hearings on June 20, 1990. Representative Peter Kostmayer of the House Foreign Affairs Committee publicly berated Melvyn Levitsky, the Assistant Secretary of State for International Narcotics Matters, for attempting to force a military solution to the drug problem on reluctant Latin presidents, stating that ambassadors from Peru, Columbia, and Bolivia had complained of the explicit pressure to accept U.S. military aid.

2. Congress blanched at the request, given the appalling human rights record of the Peruvian armed forces. It cut back the Peruvian army's portion considerably, and required that aid be given in three separate branches over the coming year.

*Excerpted from* Peace & Democracy News, *Winter 1992.*

# THIRD WORLD COMPUTERS?

## *It's a tool of imperialist oppression, yes, but also an aid to activists*

### *by Roberto Remo Bissio / third world*

The Third World probably would be better off if there were no computers. Ecologically sound ways of living were firmly established in America when Columbus arrived half a millennium ago. The Quechuas had an advanced computing system *quipus,* where bits and bytes were knots (or the absence of them)that allowed them to control food distribution for 15 million people, roughly equivalent to the number of malnourished people in Peru today. They were also familiar with the wheel-but wise enough to use it only in children's toys.

Still, computers are here. The flow of data across borders allowed banks to spirit $5 billion out of Mexico in two days in 1980. Mainframe computers allowed the military in my country, Uruguay, to classify all of its three million citizens into categories of loyal, neutral (and thus potentially suspect), and enemy. After redemocratization in the 1980s, the files have yet to be found, not to mention eliminated, by the civilian government.

But computers have no ideological bias. Under the threat of a military coup, the Uruguayan parliament granted amnesty to those accused of human rights abuses. Computer technology was thus mobilized for another task-support for a petition campaign to overturn the amnesty law. The fact that over 25 percent of the Uruguayan electorate signed petitions is partially to the credit of a group of committed computer experts and a dozen personal computers.

Such Latin American "hackers" have also stopped electoral frauds in Brazil and saved lives in Colombia, the latter by quick dissemination of alerts released by human rights organizations. In Uruguay we linked 48k Apple-LF computers with mainframe typesetters to publish alternative reference books years before the term "desktop publishing" was coined. Our present access to international electronic mail (known as "e-mail") is shared by several organizations (human rights activists, feminists, members of cooperatives, scholars).

Yes, global electronic data flow is the nervous system of present-day transnational capitalism. But since computers are here, we still might find some use for them.

If we can look at new technologies in new ways, they might speed up our march. But it is up to us to determine where that march will lead.

*Excerpted from* third world, *December 1989, as it appeared in* Utne Reader *July/August 1990.*

> Just as individual riches are not always found to produce a happy life, so the allurements of affluent industrial society fail to provide the kind of shared meanings that make society cohesive and inspire mutual loyalty. Then, too, there is the growing sense in the *lesser developed* societies that modernization does not bring about the development that is best for them in human terms.
>
> *Willis Harman in* New Options
> *April 30, 1990*

---

## AN AMERICAN WOMAN IN GUATEMALA

# Standing Beside the Activists

### *by Barbara Riverwomon / Matrix*

On November 6 [1991], Winnie Romeril, a 24-year-old American woman, spoke in Santa Cruz at the Resource Center for Nonviolence about her 18 months in Guatemala with Peace Brigades International. PBI is a Gandhi-inspired, nonviolent, nonpartisan organization that sends volunteers to areas of conflict as witnesses and peacemakers. In her public talk, Winnie focused on the current political situation in Guatemala, and on the inspiring story of the popular movements that are struggling to resist the extreme state of military and police repression in that country. The next day I encouraged her to talk more about her personal feelings as someone who found herself working in a situation where close friends were killed and tortured for political reasons, where death threats were the order of the day, and where her own life was at some risk. This article draws primarily from that conversation.

In Guatemala, the most common work of PBI volunteers is accompanying popular leaders who have received death threats. "We carry a foreign passport and a camera, and that gives us power the Guatemalans don't have," Winnie said. "And we have the support of the international community. We just walk with activists as they go about their daily business, and that gives them some protection."

How did Winnie make the difficult decision to share the lives of threatened social justice workers in Guatemala? She emphasizes that her mother, who is an Episcopalian priest, has been a strong influence on her life. After leaving her family's home, Winnie majored in Latin American studies at Mount Holyoke College, and studied and lived in Colombia and Costa Rica. Finally, just before leaving for Guatemala, she worked in a battered women's shelter for a year.

"When I was in Guatemala, I had to think a lot about how to deal with fear. And I thought a lot about battered women's syndrome. Battered women and the people of Guatemala both live in an atmosphere of terror," said Winnie. "Only this is not just in your household. The entire society is set up this way.

"Social justice workers use a lot of the tools I learned when I worked in a shelter. They have a plan. They rationalize," she continued. "In Guatemala, activists know their houses may be under surveillance. What can they do? They leave during the daytime and come back in the daytime. They go in and out with someone else, so that if something happens there is a witness, someone to report it. They take a different route to work each day."

Although this makes the work of PBI volunteers sound like high drama, Winnie emphasized that the day-to-day work of PBI volunteers is anything but dramatic. "A lot of the escorting is really boring. You walk around with them, sit outside the room while they are meeting. You get a lot of letters written and a lot of books read!"

Winnie is quite clear about two things. First, as a PBI volunteer, she was very careful to maintain her non-partisan status. At the public lecture, Winnie told the story of a union activist who had been tortured by the police and had escaped. PBI was asked to accompany 24 hours a day, staying with him at a different house each night, until he was able to flee the country. A member of the audience was outraged and asked Winnie why she and her group didn't demand that the U.S. Embassy offer political asylum to the

---

**We carry a foreign passport and a camera, and that gives us power the Guatemalans don't have... We just walk with activists as they go about their daily business, and that gives them some protection.**

---

man. Winnie replied that "it is not our job to demand anything from anybody. That would be crossing over the line of partisanship. If his union wants to demand asylum, we may accompany him to the embassy so that his basic human rights are respected."

The second is that PBI's effectiveness depends on its maintaining a clear profile as an international organization with high-level contacts inside and outside of Guatemala. PBI meets on a regular basis with representatives of the Guatemalan government and carefully cultivates contacts with the country's diplomatic corps. The foreign minister and members of the various embassies in Guatemala have visited the PBI house and have made public statements to the press stating their support for PBI.

Although Winnie made close friends with both men and women in the popular organizations that she worked with, she said she enjoyed working with groups like the Widows Committee (CONAVIGUA) the most.

"...I loved working with the indigenous women in CONAVIGUA. There are villages where all the women who belong to CONAVIGUA are being threatened. Or their sons are kidnapped. Or they are raped. These women are very practical. They are asking for fertilizer, for school supplies for kids. But they are also pushing for investigations into clandestine cemeteries and are pushing for military people to be tried for their crimes. So they are under severe attack."

Winnie not only accompanied the women to their meetings and villages, but joined them in their celebrations. "They have dances, just the women. It's such a trip. They all get together, dance to marimba music, or to salsa or merengue. It's wild. Everybody dances—the children, the teenagers, the old women. An 80-year-old woman pulled me off the bench to dance with her."

Although Winnie hardly commented at all in her public talk about U.S. involvement in Guatemala, she pointed out during the question-and-answer period that it was a matter of public record that the U.S. government was responsible in 1954 for sponsoring a coup that overturned the only popularly elected and reformist government in Guatemalan history, and has continued until this year to help fund a succession of military, or military-controlled, governments.

Winnie concluded by saying that the year and a half in Guatemala was a time of tremendous personal growth for her. "I learned a lot about staying focused, about fighting burnout, about being cautious," she said. "And I learned a lot about my limitations. I also learned how important it is to do what you see needs to be done. If you see something that needs to change, and you see a way to change it, then do it! Don't put things off. You have to use your brain, and your

*PBI Volunteer provides an international, protective presence for the striking textile workers at their occupation of the LUNAFIL factory, Guatemala. Photo from Peace Brigades International.*

common sense, but don't put it off."

*Barbara Riverwomon teaches young children (and worries about what fairy tales to tell them); works with the Santa Cruz Guatemala Committee (and worries about how to transport money, toys and clothes to a sister child-care center in Guatamala City); and tries to practice the art of simple and joyful living—and to stop worrying.*

*Excerpted from* Matrix *(ceased printing), December 1991.*

---

## The Deadly Facts of Life in Central America

- Over 1.6 million Salvadorans (25% of the countries citizens) have abandoned their homes.

- Some 70,000 Salvadorans have been killed in the 10 year civil war.

- 97% of the land in El Salvador has been deforested by the military.

- Over 3,000 tons of U.S. made bombs have been dropped on El Salvador.

- During the civil war in Guatamala in the early 80's, 100,000 lives were lost.

- During the 80's, the U.S. has provided El Salvador with more than 3 billion dollars in aid.

*Source: third world*

# A Helping Hand for War-Torn Nicaragua

After several years of attending Unitarian Universalist Service Committee study courses on Central America, after setting up Sunday morning letter-writing tables, selling Guatemalan crafts, and raising money to send trucks to Nicaragua, Lonna and Richard Harkrader of the Eno River Unitarian Universalist Fellowship in Durham, NC, decided to turn in their activism for good, old-fashioned action. The couple closed up their home, put their construction business on hold, took their two daughters out of school, and headed for Nicaragua.

"We want to show our government how to conduct a relationship with Nicaragua that reflects the Unitarian Universalist value: All the world's people are one family," Lonna said before the trip. "We want our government to change, and of course that change begins with each one of us."

The Harkraders, both of whom served in the Peace Corps in the late '60s, also wanted to expose their children to people coping with very few resources. "As citizens of a country that consumes half the world's resources, we feel it is our responsibility to understand what life is like in less fortunate countries, especially those supplying our raw materials," wrote the Harkraders in a good-bye letter to their fellowship in August of 1990.

The family spent ten months in Central America, helping to build a health clinic in a poor neighborhood of Leon, the second largest city in Nicaragua. They spent the first six weeks of their trip in Guatemala, living with a local family and getting a crash course in Spanish. Then a group called Architects and Planners in Support of Nicaragua matched Richard's construction and architectural skills with the health clinic project, begun six months earlier by a joint USSR-US delegation but never completed. Oxfam America agreed to fund the construction and Richard found laborers willing to work for half wages in exchange for the training their boss would provide. As the cinder block building progressed, the scope of the project changed from a neighborhood clinic to a city-wide health facility that includes a dental clinic and laboratory and serves 50,000 people.

The Harkraders learned firsthand the hardships of life in a country with a 60 percent unemployment rate and a 5 to 10 percent weekly rise in inflation. "I made friends whose parents were struggling to feed their families," recalls Lauren Harkrader, 11. "Every week prices for food went up

because inflation was out of control."

They faced the frustrations of local farmers as they watched ants and iguanas eat up their vegetable garden. They marched with school teachers protesting salaries so low they covered only transportation to and from school. They saw farmers occupy a bank because it would not give them loans to buy seed and fertilizer. Carson Harkrader, 14, walked several miles to a health clinic with a mother seeking medicine for her child, only to discover there was, once again, no medicine to be had. And one morning, after the first deluge of the rainy season, they watched as families dragged away the soggy cardboard that the day before had been the walls to their homes.

The health center was completed in May of 1991, but the Harkraders are disheartened by the continuing lack of foreign investment in this war torn country with its fragile government. Only sister-city relationships with more fortunate communities, established during the Sandinista rule of the '80s, keep Nicaraguan municipalities from economic collapse, they say. They continue to oppose US policy in Nicaragua, and insist that if the country is to remain at peace so that economic activity may begin, the US government must support President Violetta Chamorro's efforts to reconcile with the Sandinistas.

"When our government calls the Sandinista government 'totalitarian' and 'communist', many Americans instantly have a negative reaction," Lonna believes. "What people like us find when they live and work with Nicaraguans who supported the revolution is that they are dedicated, courageous people who want to create a better life for their children."

*Excerpted from* The World, The Journal of the Unitarian Universalist Association, *November/December 1991.*

***Regardless of how you viewed*** the outcome of Nicaragua's recent election, you should know that you helped pay for it. According to William Robinson and David MacMichael's article in *Covert Action* (Winter 1990), U.S. tax dollars provided at least $10 per voter through the National Endowment for Democracy (NED). (An equivalent per-voter expenditure in a U.S. presidential election, by the way, would total $2 billion, but U.S. law specifically prohibits foreign contributions to candidates for federal office.) The NED role in the Nicaraguan election is only the most public in a long and continuing series of little-known interventions sponsored by the organization, which is quietly funding right-wing causes in many places around the globe.

Cloaking itself in the rhetoric of freedom and democracy, NED has instead served as an effective means of U.S. intervention in the political life of other countries. While NED theoretically supports private-sector involvement in promotion of democracy, its actual funding comes from our tax dollars, and many of its grantees exist for the sole purpose of receiving these public funds. In the best Orwellian tradition, NED appears determined to ensure that democracy means right-wing political dominance-wherever in the world it might emerge.

*Excerpted from* Utne Reader, *July-August 1990 from an article by Mary C. Turck.*

# Lawsuit Against U.S. Companies

Hundreds of Costa Rican workers filed a lawsuit in a US court last July 19 against Dow Chemical Corporation, Shell Chemical Corporation and Occidental Petroleum. The workers were left sterile after using the chemical known as DBCP on Standard Fruit Company banana plantations.

The suit charging mass sterility covers 100 employees, although the total number of workers affected ranges from 2,500 to 3,000. Standard Fruit continued to use DBCP in large qualifies on its banana plantations

## The Standard Fruit Company still fails to comply with any of the safety regulations.

until 1984, five years after it was banned in the Unites States.

According to studies carried out in Costa Rica, DBCP causes male sterility and cancer of the skin, liver, kidney, stomach and lungs.

Studies show that the number of new cancers reported per year increased from 1,653 in 1977 to 3,681 in 1983, or from 79.83 per 100,000 inhabitants to 150.86.

The situation is similar in Honduras, Panama and Nicaragua, yet these governments have been insensitive to the health risks run by banana workers. The indiscriminate use of pentachlorophenol, a necessary ingredient in pesticides used to fight pests that attack the banana crop, is prohibited in all industrialized countries because it is a known carcinogen, damages the nervous system, causes, hepatic degeneration and congenital deformation, and also seriously harms the environment.

Despite all this, the Standard Fruit Company still fails to comply with any of the safety regulations established for the application of pesticides, such as the use of masks, overalls and special gloves. In addition it has been shown that this company employs Gramoxone on fruit. According to studies, this pesticide causes serious pulmonary damage as well as male sterility.

*Excerpted from* Barricada Internacional, *October 1991.*

*Banana workers in Central America continue to be exposed to dangerous pesticides.*

F. Escobar

# In Memory of
# Chico Mendes
### by Mev Puleo / *Breakthrough*

By the time he was eleven years old, Chico Mendes was tapping rubber trees alongside his father in the lush Amazon rainforest of Xapuri, Brazil. Like most rubber tappers in the 1950s, his was a poor migrant family exploited by wealthy rubber bosses. In his 44 years of life, Chico chipped away age-old patterns of oppression and domination, protecting not only the rights of rubber tappers, but the very life of the fragile forest.

In his late teens, Chico learned to read and write on weekends while pouring over newspapers with his neighbor, a Bolivian political exile steeped in Marxist analysis. Chico's first project among his people was the formation of literacy circles which also engaged in social analysis. Today, several grassroots schools have educated over a thousand rubber tappers; cooperative health posts have been created in the same spirit.

Chico's main work, however, was union organizing. He long supported worker cooperatives as an alternative to dependency on the rubber bosses. In the seventies he became a leader in the Rural Workers' Union and cofounded the local chapter of the Workers' Party. He also helped plan the First National Encounter of Rubber Tappers in

1985, where the National Council of Rubber Tappers was created.

Chico's life struggle reveals how the defense of rural workers and the defense of the environment are linked. In the 1970s hundreds of landowners and cattle ranchers came to the state of Acre, supported by the government and protected by gunmen. They razed millions of trees and expelled tens of thousands of rubber workers. When legal efforts failed to stop deforestation, rubber workers spontaneously created the tactic of "empate": men, women and children would peacefully approach the work sites and, through conversation or human blockades, stop the advancing bulldozers. In 45 "empates" over the past twelve years, Mendes reported fifteen victories. Defeats were accompanied by arrests and torture; victories brought relief, but added to the ire of the large landowners.

Under the leadership of Chico Mendes, the rubber tappers of Acre also created extractive reserves and the Alliance of Forest Peoples. Extractive reserves are protected areas that preserve the forest while allowing it to be productive through the extraction of rubber, nuts and other natural products. The Alliance of Forest Peoples has made rubber tappers and native peoples—longtime ad-

> **If a messenger from heaven could guarantee that my death would strengthen our struggle, it might be worthwhile. But experience teaches us the opposite. A big funeral and demonstration won't save the Amazon. I want to live.**
> — *Chico Mendes*

versaries—into potent allies facing a common enemy: those who destroy the forest and its peoples. Only such a united effort will save the Amazon.

With his creative local responses to problems with global repercussion, Chico Mendes recently captured world attention. In 1987, this rural, unschooled rubber worker was honored with the Global 500 Award for environmental protection from the United Nations Environment Programme. Unfortunately, the success of his work also attracted the rage of local ranchers. Thus, from 1977 onward, Chico suffered numerous death threats and assassination attempts.

On December 22, 1988, Chico was murdered by several gunmen in the presence of his police "bodyguards." A month earlier, he had written to the Federal Police that certain large landowners, Darli and Alvarino Alves, were trying to harm him and others. Believed to be the assassins, the Alves brothers are still at large. The struggle Chico lived and died for continues as his family and fellow union leaders are still violently threatened, indigenous people are persecuted, and the rainforest is bulldozed for pasture.

When the harassment intensified late last year, Chico affirmed, "If a messenger from heaven could guarantee that my death would strengthen our struggle, it might be worthwhile. But experience teaches us the opposite. A big funeral and demonstration won't save the Amazon. I want to live."

His work is in our hands.

*Excerpted from* Breakthrough, *Summer/Fall 1991.*

24

# EXPORTING IRRESPONSIBILITY

### *Evidence continues to emerge that rich countries dump their toxic wastes in the Southern Hemisphere*

### *by Diane K. Bartz* / third world

*Exported radioactive waste drums*

An Italian waste disposal firm named Jelly Wax deposited more than 2,000 tons of leaky, corroded barrels near Puerto Cabello, Venezuela, in April 1987. Four months later, when area residents began complaining of skin sores, the government's environment ministry took notice. The barrels turned out to contain a witch's brew of chlorinated solvents, pesticide residues and PCBs (poly-chlorinated biphenyls).

An official at the Venezuela Embassy in Washington said, "It was deposited...without proper permission or knowledge, and was not labeled properly." Although Jelly Wax arranged for the waste to be removed, an incensed Venezuelan Congress promptly passed legislation prohibiting the importation of hazardous waste.

In May 1987, the 13-member economic association of English-speaking Caribbean countries, stated its opposition to toxic imports by any Caribbean nation. Thirty-nine Latin American and Caribbean nations—including Belize, Guatemala, Guyana, Haiti, Jamaica, Peru, Saint Lucia and Venezuela—have banned waste imports.

But the shortage of landfill sites and the existence of local environmental regulations which push up the cost of waste disposal in the United States continue to encourage industries and communities to look abroad for places to dump their garbage. Between 1986 and 1988, more than 3.6 million tons of waste were shipped from rich countries to the Third World.

"It costs them from US$250 to US$300 per ton to dispose of wastes in the United States under the new regulations," Environmental Protection Agency's (EPA) Wendy Grieder told the *Chicago Tribune*. Guinea Bissau has accepted "waste for US$40 per ton."

In 1980, 12 companies notified the EPA that they intended to export hazardous waste. By 1987 the number had grown to 465, with officials estimating between 550 and 575 for 1988. This represents only legally exported waste, most of which is sent to Canada and Mexico.

But EPA Inspector General John Martin told the U.S. Congress last July that firms have shipped hundreds of tons of toxic materials abroad without notifying U. S. government officials whose job it is to ensure that the countries which accept the waste will dispose of it safely.

"Our review of the agency's program to control the exports of hazardous waste showed that the program needed major improvements," he said. "It is a program in shambles."

**The case of Guyana—**In one case, two California based firms, Pott Industries and Teixeira Farms International, formed the Guyana Resource Company (GRC) in partnership with the government of Guyana to build an industrial waste incinerator to burn over 60,000 tons annually of industrial oil and paint sludge, waste their companies created.

In September 1988, however, the Guyanese government reversed its decision and rejected its own application to build the plant, causing the firm to pull out of the country after investing some US$250,000 in the waste scheme.

Public opposition to the disposal plan had been fierce. Several environmental activists began hunger strikes and Guyana's Anglican Bishop Randolph George denounced the plan as "a money deal, like drugs."

An angry President Desmond Hoyte described the California firms' owners as "unscrupulous" in an interview last fall. He also said his government had, "No intention of importing any waste into our country, toxic or otherwise."

Belize also reportedly rejected the Pott/Teixeira plan in June 1988. As part of its lobbying efforts, GRC hired American Environmental Audit, another California firm, to prepare a report it could use to sell the program to Congress, which was then considering proposals to curb or ban outright the dumping of waste in Third World countries. The report described the GRC plant as a boon for everyone involved.

But Jonathan Puth, an aide to U.S. Representative John Conyers, was unconvinced. "I am skeptical of any plan which seeks to take advantage of lax environmental regulations," he said. "The basic question is if it's so environmentally sound, why not do it closer to home?"

In the last congressional session, Conyers sponsored legislation banning the export of sludge waste to any country, except Canada or Mexico. That bill is being rewritten to stiffen the proposed regulations and to include Canada and Mexico. The new legislation would establish a permit process, with a public hearing and a permit fee which Puth hopes will be "prohibitively high."

Puth said the new proposal had attracted bipartisan support. Even President George Bush, in a March statement, said he would push for "new legislation that will give the United States government authority to ban all exports of hazardous waste, except where we have an agreement with the receiving country providing for the safe handling and management of those wastes."

Even if regulations are stiffened, experience has shown that greedy corporations will still be able to find counterparts in Third World countries to act as their go betweens.

**Haiti: Philly's bitter garbage—**Haiti's bitter experience with garbage from the U.S. city of Philadelphia is a case in point. Paolino and Sons, a Philadelphia based firm, paid the Liberian flagged ship Khian Sea to haul away 13,476 tons of toxic incinerator ash in August 1986. Samples of the ash showed it contained arsenic, barium, cadmium, lead, mercury and two different types of dioxins between 0.184 and 4.7 parts per billion.

Captain Konstantinos Samos signed a cargo declaration identifying the load as "non-toxic, non-hazardous, nonflammable incinerator ash." In March 1987, the ship's owner, Amalgamated Shipping, tried to cut a deal with Honduras through Honduran promoter Edgardo Pacall.

Pacall told Tegucigalpa the ash was "neither toxic nor dangerous, and was an excellent material for landfills in low-lying zones and swampy areas." Honduras refused Amalgamated's offer to sell the ash for US$22,000.

The Bahamas, Bermuda, the Dominican Republic and Guinea Bissau also rejected the load. In October 1987, after 14 months on the high seas, Felix and Antonio Paul, the brothers of late indicted drug trafficker Colonel Jean Claude Paul, persuaded the Haitian Commerce Department to allow them to import the toxic ash, which they said was fertilizer.

The Khian Sea dumped 3,000 of the 13,000 tons of ash on a peninsula near the city of Gonaives in late January 1988. Port-au-Prince soon caught on and demanded the waste be reloaded onto the ship and threatened to prosecute those responsible for the dumping.

According to Jim Vallete of the environmental organization Greenpeace, the ash is still there. "Some has been repacked in barrels but most is still in a pile," he said. "Some is uncovered, some is covered."

The pile may contain 210,000 pounds of toxic heavy metals, including lead, cadmium, mercury and arsenic. Much of the waste is near the sea and some is being lapped into the ocean. Although the peninsula is lightly populated, there is a small village only a few hundred yards downwind.

Environmental groups in Haiti are persisting in their efforts to get the waste removed. A representative of the Friends of Nature Federation met with Minister of Public Works Franck Paultre in December 1988 to discuss the waste while two grassroots organizations, the Christian Workers Youth and a second church group, organized anti-dumping protests.

The independent Radio Soleil's Gonaive's correspondent, Jean Bouchereau Joseph, visited the dump site in early December. "We saw many dead goats and found many people in the area who had respiratory problems and numerous large lesions," he reported.

**Peru: a giant garbage park?—**In Peru, the U.S. based firm, American Security International (ASI), offered the city of Pisco, some 100 miles south of Lima, $400 million for the rights to build a toxic processing plant near the Paracas National Park. Felipe Benavides, president of the Peruvian National Conservation Federation, denounced the scheme as a plan to turn the park into a "giant garbage dump" and warned it would endanger local plants and wildlife.

ASI, which accepts radioactive and chemical waste from U.S. and European companies, signed a similar agreement with the northern Peruvian city of Paita. But public opposition to the deal forced the city to back out. Benavides said Paraguay had agreed to accept waste from ASI, while Argentina, Colombia, Ecuador, Panama and Venezuela rejected similar deals.

Honduras is considering allowing International Asphalt and Petroleum, a U.S. firm, to build an incinerator near the rainforest at Gracias a Dios. According to Pat Costner, a Greenpeace researcher who has studied the plan, the facility would be used to burn 1.8 million pounds of waste annually, "posing significant risks to the public and the environment."

In December 1988, a subsidiary of Navarette International, NCTB Inc. of New Jersey,

filed an application with the New York Department of Environmental Conservation to build a station to transfer up to 1,000 cubic yards of asbestos daily to Guatemala, saying the asbestos would be used to manufacture brake linings. The subsidiary also produced a letter from the Guatemalan government approving the plan.

Neil Gorfinkel of the White Lung Association, an asbestos watchdog organization, points out that the amount of asbestos slated for shipping so far exceeds the amount Guatemala could use to produce brake linings. He believes the asbestos comes from clean up sites and will be dumped.

### If it's so environmentally–sound, why not do it closer to home?

Such abuses should put Mexico and Canada on edge because their long, porous borders with the United States make detecting illegal waste exports extremely difficult. The Mexican government has banned importing waste for disposal, but allows it for recycling. Greenpeace suspects it may be "sham recycling."

"We know that tens of thousands of tons of steel furnace dust, which has extremely high levels of heavy metals, have been shipped to Mexico," says Vallete. "There may be some reclamation of lead, but you're left with a highly toxic residue which should really be shipped back to the United States. Customs officials don't pay attention."

The EPA's Wendy Grieder disagrees, cautioning, "We have very little evidence of the illegal export of large quantities of waste.

None of that information has made itself public." But, she added, "I'm not saying it's not happening."

**Regulating what should be banned—**Following the Jelly Wax debacle in 1987, Venezuela decided to spearhead the fight for a global treaty banning all international traffic in toxic trash. In March 1989, following 18 months of negotiations, 105 members of the U.N. Environmental Program, based in Nairobi, Kenya, signed an accord that establishes some controls over toxic waste exports.

Early on, Third World countries appeared determined to draft an agreement that would ban all hazardous waste exports. But industrialized countries argued that a ban would stifle free trade. Not only did they successfully limit the document to simple regulation of the waste trade but, as the signing date drew near, the developed countries worked to weaken even those controls.

The final draft was a disappointment to many who argued that regulation implicitly legitimizes a practice that should be ended. Washington endorsed the final agreement but was one of only 11 countries that did not sign it.

The United States sees Latin America and the Caribbean as a cheap dumping ground for its wastes. As tighter environmental regulations and growing volume drive up the price of legal disposal methods, "the export of irresponsibility," as U.S. Representative Conyers puts it, is bound to increase.

*Excerpted from* third world, *December 1989.*

# Double Jeopardy: The Third World

### by Rosalie Bertell / *Ms.*

We must look carefully at the strategies of "First World" governments whose domestic nuclear industry has collapsed. The First World wants to sell its unwanted technology and the Third World is perceived as a good dumping place. Most of the First World is now moving to the Star Wars scenario or to laser beam fusion reactors, so it wants to sell its fission technology (which admittedly was not a good answer to the energy crisis) to the Third World.

When I think of the Third World, I think of indigenous people of the First World as well as those in countries labeled "Third World" or "developing." Two major sources of pollution are uranium mining and milling, often carried out on the land of indigenous peoples—such as Roxby Downs on the land of the aboriginal people in Australia. South Africa has exploited the Namibian people at the Rössing mine. In North America, it is usually the land of Indians that is mined for

uranium. All the radioactive material left at the mine entrance is on their land, so they must live with it.

Nuclear weapons testing was carried out in the Third World at Bikini, Enewetok, and other Pacific-island atolls. The U.S. and Britain set off some 100 nuclear blasts in the Pacific and the French have set off another 167 by now. It is rumored that two nuclear bombs, one atomic and one hydrogen, exploded off the coast of South Africa. Recent reports show that the increase in background radiation in the Southern Hemisphere is greater than the Northern Hemisphere.

Many other Third World countries that don't have uranium mining or are not used for nuclear testing have been affected, too: Brazil, which has thorium reserves, or the Southern Hemisphere as a whole, which has been blanketed with fallout from French nuclear weapons testing in French Polynesia. Peru has already reported finding radio-nuclides in its fish (and fishing is a major industry); the Baja peninsula in Mexico has reported fish contaminated with radionuclides; there has been high fallout of radioactive iodine in Bolivia most likely from the French tests. These are all direct effects.

The *indirect* effects include thermal pollution from released gases. When you set off nuclear bombs, you change air temperature. If you set them off underwater, the hot gas releases change ocean temperature. Possible results include the following: the ocean current, coming up from the South Pole along the South American Pacific coast in 1983, came up warm instead of cold, causing what was called the El Niño effect in Peru, with landslides and rains. It also caused the monsoons to miss Australia and Fiji, which led to drought on the western side of the Pacific and rains and landslides on the eastern side. These effects—like the possible solutions—are all connected.

*Rosalie Bertell has a doctorate in biometry, which is mathematics to understand and predict biological processes. She has been a consultant for the U.S. Nuclear Regulatory Commission and the U.S. Environmental Protection Agency, is president of the International Institute of Concern for Public Health in Toronto, and a founder of the International Commission for Health Professionals in Geneva. Her accessible, demystifying book,* No Immediate Danger, *has been translated into seven languages, and was a best-seller in the U.K. (published by the Woman's Press).*

*Excerpted from* Ms., *September/October 1991.*

# Kerala's Quiet Revolution

## *This Indian state chooses income redistribution over economic growth*

### by Chris Peacock / *Utne Reader*

"If the southern Indian state of Kerala were a separate country, it would place ninth on a list of the world's poorest countries. Yet in terms of quality of life, Kerala is an astonishing success story," writes Alan AtKisson in *In Context* (No. 26). All 29 million people of Kerala have access to health care, while their literacy and life expectancy approaches that of Americans.

Kerala is one of the world's poorest regions. In 1986 Kerala's gross national product averaged $182 per person. Compare that with $290 for India as a whole, and $17,480 in the United States. But by choosing economic redistribution over economic growth and radical political reforms over loans from Western banks, Kerala has brought its citizens vast improvements compared with the rest of India and other low-income countries.

With a history of radicalism dating back to British colonialism and Western-imported Marxism, Kerala's highly organized peasants and workers have struggled for land reform, distribution of wealth, health care, education, and clean water through popular protest and by electing a series of left or left leaning governments.

In 1969 one-and-a-half million tenant farmers and laborers won title to the land they tilled through a combination of protest and government legislation. The massive, thorough, and permanent land reform reduced economic and social inequalities and was key to unlocking further reforms. With a battery of statistics, Richard Franke and Barbara Chasin show in the socialist journal *Monthly Review* (Jan. 1991) that in the 1970s, peasants, unions, and activists agitated for and won clean water and electricity in most villages and the construction of 57,000 new houses. Kerala became number one in India in providing roads, transportation, schools, food distribution, and health centers.

Kerala became India's first literate state in 1991 with 93.66 percent literacy, according to a New Delhi report of the *Inter Press Service* (April 19, 1991), a Third World wire service. "A voluntary people's movement... mobilized volunteers from among the state's educated to teach the illiterate. In most states female literacy is well below the national average of 39 percent. Kerala is the only Indian state where women are as literate as men."

A consistently militant and informed public has kept Kerala's administrations nearly free of the corruption that plagues other states. As Franke and Chasin point out in *Technology Review* (April 1990), "The Kerala model cannot be copied wholesale, but it provides a standard for evaluating and improving the development efforts of other societies." Instead of concentrating on raising per-capita income, poor countries can bring a wide range of benefits to their people by redistributing their meager resources.

*Reprinted from* Utne Reader, *November/December 1991.*

---

Dr. William Alexander of Good Life Study Tours, an affiliate of Food First, conducts educational tours to Kerala and serves as the Principal Investigator for Earthwatch Expeditions. He adds the following:

*In less than 50 years the 30 million Malayalees in the Indian state of Kerala reduced their birthrate from 44 [per 1,000] to 19 [per 1,000] only 3 points above the United States. The answer is too simple for easy belief--genuine democracy, economic control by a poor majority, political sophistication that won't stop.*

---

# Solar Serendipity:

## *Photovoltaic Rural Electrification in Sri Lanka*

### by Neville Williams / *Solar Today*

The Island of Serendib—formerly Ceylon, now Sri Lanka has become a leader in the developing world in the number of rural households powered by solar electricity. Over three thousand Sri Lankan families now derive their electric service directly from the sun, using a single roof mounted PV panel. These solar-home lighting systems are manufactured locally, using indigenous materials, from batteries to lights. The Kyocera solar cells are imported from Japan and the modules are assembled in Sri Lanka.

Thanks to the unique entrepreneurial efforts by the Sri Lankan Firm of Power & Sun, which manufactures Suntec solar modules and electric systems, this country has proved to the world that it doesn't need Western or Northern experts to tell it how to apply solar solutions to rural energy development. With loans from two national development banks, Power & Sun was started 5 years ago by three young Sri Lankans who attended university together in Toronto before returning to their homeland. "The sunshine boys," as they're known around their Colombo Rotary Club, have proved to most non-believers that home solar electric systems can address the needs of the 70 percent of Sri Lankans without access to conventional electricity.

**Charged by the Sun**

A 35-watt Suntec system using a 90 amp car battery can provide approximately 9 ampere hours of power nightly, enough to operate 4 DC, 12v fluorescent lights up to 3 hours each (or 6 lights, 2 hours each), a 12v B&W TV set for 3 hours and a radio for 4 hours. Houses are wired neatly with wall mounted switches and hanging light fixtures in each room, and often boast an exterior or porch light. Inexpensive 12v, 10W fluorescent light fixtures are manufactured locally as a government-sponsored cottage industry and bulbs are imported from China and cost 30 cents. The system price, installed, is close to US$600. There is also a less expensive 20W Suntec model.

Prices will come down with large-volume production. The factory's capacity is 1500 modules per month, but its current production level is much lower while the company concentrates on market building (which, incidentally, the United Nations has identified as the number one barrier to photovoltaics worldwide—not technology or the economics of solar electricity). Sri Lankan-made, rubber-cased car batteries, with their thick plates, work fine in this application, but need to be replaced every 3 years. Imported, long-life, deep-discharge batteries are too expensive for household use. Battery storage provides up to 5 days autonomy during overcast periods without recharging by the sun. Suntec systems include a voltage charge indicator but not a controller. Trial and error field experience has shown that people best manage their own power consumption and battery current by using inexpensive, locally made charge indicators with little red and green lights.

Right now, an estimated 300,000 Sri Lankans are using car batteries in their homes to power lights, radio and TV. These are recharged every ten days by transporting them to a charging station, placing a strain on the national power grid. (At the same time, the national utility is looking at supplementing its hydro generating capacity with a coal-fired power plant.) These 300,000 families (approximately 1.5 million people) are prime candidates for solar power. Recharging their batteries from the sun rather than the grid could, quite possibly, reduce the load enough to avoid having to add conventional generating capacity. PV rural electrification displaces future grid extension, becoming an important pollution abatement.

While Sri Lanka serendipitously enters the solar age on its own, it is also the site of several model international donor programs seeking to make solar rural electrification a reality. BP Solar introduced 1000 home PV lighting systems at a rural village last year as part of an Australian aid project (the 55W BP panels were manufactured by Power & Sun, under license, using BP cells). In 1992, BP plans to begin electrifying 25,000 rural homes, and Dutch aid is reportedly looking at putting in another 6000 solar electric systems in association with the Shell (oil) and Philips (lighting) consortium, and R&S of

Holland. Donor agency subsidization for solar electrification is still required if the solar option is to displace conventional power, which is already subsidized to a larger extent than solar will ever be.

### Where are the Americans?

Notably missing in all this are American companies and U.S. development assistance. The donor-seeded rural PV market is now dominated by the British (BP Solar), the Italians (Helios), the Dutch (R&S), the Germans (Siemens) and the Japanese (Kyocera, Hoxan). This is because these countries tie their aid projects to their export of solar products, which USAID is not permitted to do, (i.e. the Australian-sponsored BP Solar project in Sri Lanka). Also, U.S. solar companies and design firms, despite their substan-

---

## Sri Lanka is poised to become a leading world model for solar rural electrification.

---

tial exports, have so far shown little interest in the rural home PV lighting market in the less developed countries—with the exception of ECD/Sovonics and their solar lantern project and manufacturing line in India, and Photocomm's recent activities in rural Mexico.

However, this admittedly difficult dispersed and decentralized market isn't necessarily closed to U.S. companies. With 2 billion unelectrified people on the planet living in the dark (fully 70 percent of the Third World) it is too vast a market to ignore. Because of worldwide concern over greenhouse gases and global warming, and the environmental problems associated with large hydro projects, there is enormous potential now to divert a portion of the vast energy sector financing currently going to conventional electrical generation into viable solar programs. The World Bank itself is actively looking at lending programs to finance solar rural electrification in Zimbabwe and Sri Lanka; and USAID's Office of Energy noting "new approaches to large-scale power delivery in developing countries, recently stated: "Decentralized renewable energy systems can provide the electric power needs of rural populations, and often can do so at lower costs than either grid extension or diesel power."

### Financing is Critical

Moreover, people in rural areas throughout the world, in the Dominican Republic, Kenya and especially Sri Lanka, have demonstrated a willingness to pay for electricity, and to purchase it from anyone who can provide it. In the Dominican Republic (see *Solar Today,* Mar/Apr 1990), where the first

rural credit scheme for solar was established by Enersol Associates in 1986, a revolving fund managed by a local solar energy development association—a solar co-op—has generated nearly 1500 household PV installations. In Sri Lanka, commercial banks offer 5-year consumer loans to "light up your home with solar power," and Singer Sri Lanka, Ltd., the appliance retailer, also distributes Suntec systems and provides 2-year customer financing.

Price is not the problem; financing is, along with market development. There isn't enough of it at concessional rates, although environmentally unsound conventional power and costly, uneconomic grid extension continue to receive giant subsidies. A residential consumer purchasing solar power is paying for 20 years worth of electricity up front (the life of a PV panel), which is often an unbearable burden.

The Solar Electric Light Fund (SELF) advocates that international donors provide low cost loan funds and interest subsidies to national development banks to be targeted for rural solar development as part of a country's national rural energy plan. SELF also believes in "SELF-help," which means that people pay the actual cost of their own power, which they usually don't do in the case of conventional electric distribution, to the distress of the World Bank. SELF is working with donors to set up technical assistance, technician training and rural credit programs in several countries as an effective way to leverage international aid money.

With an enviable and inexhaustible supply of solar energy—an annual average of 6 peak hours a day—and with 2.3 million homes (over 10 million people) without electricity, including 16,500 unelectrified villages, Sri Lanka is poised to become a leading world model for solar rural electrification. To deliver power to the people by the year 2000, it has no other choice.

*Excerpted from* Solar Today, *November/December 1991.*

---

**In 1989, the U.S. produced 11 billion kilowatt hours from photovoltaic, geothermal, wood, waste, and wind sources out of a total of 2,779 billion kilowatt hours. This was down 1 billion kilowatt hours from the year before.**

# A Peaceful Revolution Whose Time Has Come...
# The Solar Cooker Invasion

## By Barbara Jodry / *PeaceWorks*

When Sacramento biologist Bob Metcalf arrived in Bolivia in 1987, he found the Aymara Indians cooking with sheep dung. Living at 13,000 feet on the shores of Lake Titicaca, the Aymara lacked a dependable supply of firewood to cook potatoes, their staple food. Golf ball size potatoes, thanks to soil stripped of nutrients. In addition, smoky indoor fires in dark huts created health problems for entire families, but especially women and children who spent much time indoors cooking.

Metcalf, invited by the Bolivian government to introduce solar ovens as an alternative cooking method, conducted several workshops in which people in the community built cookers out of cardboard boxes, glass, and other simple materials. The cookers, tested under the cloudless Andean sky, reached temperatures of 250 to 300 degrees. The Aymara soon discovered that solar cooked food is as good or superior to dishes cooked the traditional way.

They learned that the switch from biomass fuel to sun power would reduce pollution inside homes, improve health, and permit them to return natural fertilizer to the soil.

Metcalf's trip, underwritten by the Freedom From Hunger Foundation and the Pillsbury Company, was the first of many he has taken since 1987.

In 1988 he journeyed to El Progreso, Guatemala, to conduct more workshops. Metcalf saw that the daily struggle to collect firewood took up much of the day for women and children. Moreover, local deforestation was directly related to these wood-gathering habits.

His workshops held in 5 villages attracted 145 people. These señoras, like their counterparts in Bolivia, discovered that basic foods such as chicken, corn, rice and potatoes, cooked very nicely. What's more, they could bake bread and cake in the "estufas solares." Metcalf's visit attracted the attention of the wife of then-President Cerezo. She traveled to El Progreso to participate in the community's solar cooked feast shortly before Metcalf returned to Sacramento.

Solar cooking is saving forests and changing lives for thousands of people in countries where diminishing firewood supplies help create food crises. Health improves when

*A woman in Guatemala prepares dinner in a Solar Box Cooker safeguarding her health and the environment.*

people no longer must cook over smoky fires. In some areas firewood for cooking can take a quarter to one third of a family's income. Using a no-cost fuel like the sun enables families to spend more on food and achieve a better diet.

The government of India, independent of U.S. based interests, has supported solar cooking projects for many years, assisting communities with advisors and materials. The subcontinent has by far the largest concentration of solar cookers, an estimated 50,000 to 100,000. Meanwhile, the United Nations Food and Agriculture organization has provided support to Metcalf's activities in Africa and the Middle East.

Since 1978, Metcalf, like a modern Johnny Appleseed, has been sowing a technology gained from Arizona-based Barbara Kerr, who is credited with the development of the low cost, workable, box type cooker which Metcalf uses. A professor in biological sciences at CSUS [California State University at Sacramento], and a bacteriologist, Metcalf is well qualified for his avocation. Throughout the 1980's he led workshops in Sacramento enabling local folks to construct their own solar box cookers. He has encouraged and guided graduate students in environmental studies and the sciences to do research testing safety and reliability factors.

Metcalf practices at home what he preaches abroad. "Why has my family preferred to solar cook since 1978?" he asks.

Five reasons: it saves us time, solar cooked foods have a superior flavor; we avoid heating our house in summer; and we lower our SMUD bill." His fifth reason is more philosophical. "By using a renewable, non-polluting energy source for cooking, we are doing something good for the planet."

Currently Metcalf is president of Solar Box Cookers International (SBCI), a non-profit organization based in Sacramento and dedicated to educating people about the benefits of solar cooking. Since organizing in 1987, SBCI has been disseminating plans, cookers, recipes, and methodology form the Andes to the Sahara, from Central America to Central Africa, and from India to Australia. (A 'Friends of San Juan' delegation to Sacramento's friendship city, San Juan de Oriente in Nicaragua, introduced solar box cookers earlier this year.)

That a U.S. based organization is exporting clean, low cost technology (for a change), available to even the poorest villager in the farthest outpost, should be a source of pride. Like Metcalf and our friends abroad, we can do much to improve the quality of life on our planet by "plugging in the sun."

*Excerpted from* PeaceWorks, *June 1991.*

# RAINFOREST RX

**by Joseph Wallace / *Sierra***

"The Jivaro [of Peru], like most indigenous peoples, use dozens of different plants for medicinal purposes," Walter Lewis says. "These plants have the potential to treat a host of diseases, possibly including cancer and AIDS."

Lewis and his wife, medical microbiologist Memory Elvin-Lewis, are two of a growing number of researchers who search for medicines from plants in the rainforests of Latin America, Asia, and Africa. These plants may accomplish even more: They may provide a means of preserving the dwindling rainforest itself as well as the indigenous tribes struggling to survive there.

"Developing even a few medicines from rainforest plants—and then returning some of the profits to the local people—could help make the forest more valuable to preserve than to destroy," says ethnobotanist Mark Plotkin, vice-president for plant conservation at Washington-based Conservation International. "We shouldn't need an economic reason to save tropical forests, but clearly we do."

He spent years in the forests of Surinam and other tropical countries learning the medicinal lore of local shamans. The knowledge he gained has made him a spokesman for preservation of the tropics' diverse plant life.

Tropical forests contain the vast majority of the world's 250,000 flowering-plant species. Yet only about one percent of them have been thoroughly examined for medicinal properties, says Plotkin; he's concerned that valuable plants may be exterminated before they are ever studied.

Despite their superficial study, scientists have already reaped a valuable harvest—about 120 plant—derived medicinal chemicals from about 100 species. Today, Plotkin points out, nearly a quarter of all prescription drugs contains ingredients derived from plants—including many known to folk wisdom for centuries. Whenever you take an aspirin, for example, you're ingesting a chemical found in the bark of willow trees and sharing an ancient medical tradition with Native Americans. Travel to a tropical country, and it's possible you'll carry an antimalarial medication containing quinine, extracted from the bark of the cinchona tree of South America and first introduced to the developed world by the Jivaro in the early 17th century. And foxglove, a common European plant originally described in the first century, has been touted for centuries for its ability to combat rapid pulse, dropsy, and many other conditions. More recently researchers learned that the same plant also

*Artwork courtesy of* Barricada Internacional

contains digitoxin, the source of digitalis, a potent weapon against heart failure.

In the 1950s and '60s scientists became proficient at synthesizing drugs in the laboratory. They soon developed an attitude that chemist Gordon Cragg of the National Cancer Institute describes as "anything nature can do, we can do better." Most research institutions neglected medicinal plants, yet they couldn't synthesize many of the complex chemicals found in them. Even when

---

**Our best estimates indicate that 50 to 150 plant species will become extinct every day during the next 20 years.**

---

they could recreate natural substances, they often discovered that chemicals made in the lab were far more expensive than those extracted from a plant.

Meanwhile, individual researchers continued to identify, collect, and test plants. Though few in number, these scientists made important contributions to medical knowledge. They found, for example, that a kind of wormwood (Artemisia annua) contains artemisinin, a chemical the Chinese have used to combat malaria for nearly 1,000 years. Scientists who recently confirmed artemisinin's efficacy believe that it can successfully combat the skyrocketing number of malaria strains that have grown resistant to quinine-based medicines.

Native Americans and the early European settlers who learned from them relied on the root of the mayapple (also known as the American mandrake) to treat venereal warts,

parasites, and other conditions. During the past decade etoposide (derived from a chemical found in the root of the mayapple) has become a potent, widely used treatment for testicular and lung cancers.

The most publicized—and by far the most influential—discovery of the past 30 years is the rosy periwinkle, a plant native to Madagascar (and long used medicinally by local people), the leaves of which contain the alkaloids vincristine and vinblastine. Vincristine alone has quadrupled the survival rate for children with leukemia, and both drugs have become important weapons against Hodgkin's disease.

"Each year, sales of vincristine and vinblastine combined exceed $100 million," says Cragg. "The possibility that more such money-makers exist is a powerful incentive to continue the search for medicinal plants."

"We've had tremendous preliminary results from several plants with anti hepatitis B activity," Lewis says.

Elvin-Lewis found she had access to information unavailable to her husband. "The men would tell Walter what plants they thought the women used for contraception," she recalls. "The Jivaro women and I would listen, nod, and remain quiet. Then the men would take Walter off into the forest, and the women would start to smile. They'd say to me, 'Those men don't know anything. We'll show you what we really use.'" The researchers learned that several species in the sedge family, rarely used medicinally by Jivaro men and neglected by most ethnobotanists, are prized by local women. They cultivate the plants, take them along when the tribe moves, and rely on them for a variety of pediatric, gynecological, and contraceptive uses.

Thus far, the temperate-region search has produced several promising leads, as well as one significant success: taxol, a substance in *Taxus brevifolia*, the Pacific yew. Now in final testing stages, taxol has already proven yet to be one of the most effective treatments yet found for ovarian cancer (which claims 12,000 lives a year in the United States alone), and may combat several other types of cancer.

"We had been testing a small number of rainforest plants submitted by Walter Lewis and other scientists all along," explains Gordon Cragg, the branch's director. But once the National Cancer Institute intensified its rainforest efforts in September 1986, it awarded five-year contracts totaling more than $2.5 million to three organizations already skilled at collecting tropical flora: the New York Botanical Garden (for samples from Latin America and the Caribbean), the Missouri Botanical Garden (Africa), and the University of Illinois at Chicago (Southeast Asia). During the life of its contract, each group must identify and deliver 1,500 samples a year to the branch's laboratories.

A few large drug companies—including Glaxo, Eli Lilly, and Merck Sharpe & Dohme—are analyzing plant samples as well, screening them for anti-viral, antibacterial, and anti-cancer activity. Merck's 30-person Natural Products Chemistry department, for example, examines 500 plants a year donated by the New York Botanical Garden. Its staff tests soil organisms and molds as well as plants, and attempts to synthesize promising natural products in the laboratory.

Given the ongoing deforestation of the Amazon and other tropical forests, though, these efforts may not be proceeding quickly enough. "Our best estimates indicate that 50 to 150 plant species will become extinct every day during the next 20 years," says Brian Boom of the New York Botanical Garden. "Most of them are found in the tropics, and most will never have been studied or collected. Who knows what invaluable medicines are contained in plants we'll never even know existed?"

*Joseph Wallace is a freelance writer based in Pleasantville, N.Y. who specializes in natural history and environmental issues.*

*Excerpted from* Sierra, *July/August 1991.*

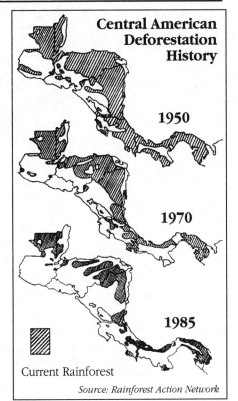

**Central American Deforestation History**

1950

1970

1985

Current Rainforest

*Source: Rainforest Action Network*

# Who Is Really Hungry, and Why?

### by Helen Vukasin / *Manna*

*It is now becoming clear that a factor contributing to Africa's acute food shortages is the way women have been systematically excluded from access to land and from control of modern agriculture.*
— U.N. State of the World's Women, 1985.

In most subsistence societies, women are the prime movers in food production. Yet in those same societies women suffer most from hunger and malnutrition because of poverty and lack of having a voice in the institutions that affect their lives.

Access to food, and especially protein, is the prerogative first of men, second of children and lastly of women. So when there is food, men, considered the bread winners, are fed first, children as the future hope are then fed, and women are fed when there is anything left.

The real causes of hunger are to be found in the social structures that give precedence to men over women, and rich over poor. The move toward sustainable agriculture and food security in developing nations has to include empowerment of women as an integral part of development.

Women constitute one-half and more of the agricultural labor force in many areas of the developing world. In Africa, the division of labor in agriculture places the burden for almost all activities, except cutting the forests and turning the soil and planting, far more on women than on men. Women in Africa account for the following contributions to food production:

- 50% of the planting
- 70% of the weeding and hoeing
- 60% of the harvesting
- 80% of the storage
- 60% of the marketing
- 90% of food processing (husking, grinding, pounding, smoking, drying).

As a group, women are often denied access to food because they:

- are paid less than men
- have a lower status than men
- lack political authority
- operate under social and cultural restrictions on their food intake.

Following are some of the practical ways in which this happens and some of the comments on these conditions made by women in Zimbabwe in a report published by the Zimbabwe Women's Bureau, *"We Carry a Heavy Load."*

**Education.** Girls are often kept at home to help with fuel and water gathering and other domestic tasks. Some schools in developing countries admit only boys. Two times as many women are illiterate as the number of men.

**Technical training.** When technical training is available it is usually offered to males. Often, the nature of such training involves income-generating activities that are identified as male occupations. There is some improvement in Africa where there is an awakening recognition that food security is related to self-sufficiency and that women are the ones who need to learn improved agricultural techniques.

"We need to be taught farming methods to overcome our farming disadvantages."

**Information.** Books and other information that could assist women to improve their lot are more likely to be given to men, if they are even available. Again, the predominance of illiteracy is a constraint on women in making use of such resources.

"The women's [radio] programs are broadcast while we are away working in the fields. We need these types of programs at night so that we can listen to them."

"We have no radios, we don't see newspapers very often and we have never seen a film." Innovations or appropriate technologies offered to or introduced into the community are often offered to men. However, when they are supplied to women, many times the new techniques add chores and increase rather than decrease the burden.

"We want to work with agricultural demonstrators, and learn to improve our farming methods, but our husbands won't allow us to."

**Crops.** As a generalization, women tend to engage in food-producing agriculture. Income-producing crops such as export crops and other cash crops are usually the prerogatives of males. This further deprived women of possible income sources to buy food.

"Just imagine how it hurts. We suffer working on land which doesn't belong to me, and all the money I get from growing things is taken by my husband."

**Land Poverty.** Ownership and control of land are often denied to women. They are allowed to lease or have use of the land without the protection of owning it. Emphasis on cash crops also limits land available to women.

"'The headmen won't give women any land. They say that we don't have any right to use it."

**Income and Wages.** Even when women work for wages, they earn substantially less than men doing the same work. Where men leave the village to work elsewhere, the women back home provide security for unemployed periods, sickness, and retirement.

"Husbands being away mean that they miss all the duties that they are supposed to do at home. So that gives us women extra work to do."

**Finances.** When development assistance brings financial benefits to a village, it is usually not geared to making it easier for women to feed their families.

"I have much difficulty as a woman. I work hard on the farm and yet I get nothing at all. We wives are taken only as laborers."

**Malnutrition.** Women in the child bearing years need more iron and protein than men. Nevertheless, since the man is usually the wage earner he customarily has priority for whatever protein is available to the family.

"The biggest problems facing women is to have many children, year after year, when they can't afford to take care of them. It gives women no free time."

**Decision-making.** Social and cultural norms exclude women from participating in the decision-making processes. They are usually excluded from village councils and elective offices. If they are allowed to have a voice, their reticence to speak out may be a reflection of illiteracy or lack of practice or both.

If we approach hunger and sustainable agriculture only from a technical perspective we may win the battle but lose the war. Women constitute more than half the world's population. If women continue to be deprived of their full share and access to food they will be unable to continue to produce food and to reproduce future generations.

**References:**
*Advocates for African Security, "Lessening the Burden for Women, Women: Key to African Food Security,"* New York, 1988.
Leghorn, Lisa, and Mary Roodkowsky, *Who Really Starves? Women and World Hunger,* Friendship Press, New York, 1977.
United Nations, *"State of the World's Women Report, 1985,"* prepared for the World Conference on the United Nations Decade for Women in Nairobi, Kenya, 1985.
Zimbabwe Women's Bureau, *"We Carry a Heavy Load," Rural Women in Zimbabwe Speak Out,* Compiled by Kate McCalman.

*Helen Vukasin, a IASA Board of Directors member, works with private development assistance groups on relating environmental concerns to small scale development.*

*Excerpted from* Manna, *June 1989.*

# POPULATION PUSHERS

Eleven days after the Supreme Court issued the gag-rule, it quietly made another decision with stronger, more far-reaching consequences, according to the August issue of *Scientific American.* It upheld the legality of the Mexico City policy (so-called because it was announced at a family-planning conference there in 1984). The rule, "...denies US foreign aid to any organization that performs abortions, advises women on abortion or lobbies on behalf of abortion rights—even if these activities are supported by non-US funds."

As a result, many international groups that offer contraception as well as abortion-related services have lost their funding. The Agency for International Development (AID), "the primary dispenser of US foreign aid," used to be a world leader in promoting

birth control, but now, because of the policy, diverts some funds towards groups that are opposed to all forms of artificial contraception. The decision "may actually have led to a rise in the number of unintended pregnancies and abortions in the Third World by reducing the availability of other forms of contraception."

Unsafe abortions are already the leading cause of death of women in their twenties and thirties in six Latin American countries and the second leading killer in another six. An estimated 200,000-plus women die every year due to improper abortions. And now more women will be "turning to unqualified abortion practitioners or trying to abort their pregnancies themselves," thanks to the Mexico City policy.

Afraid that they may lose their funding,

many clinics are now refusing to treat botched abortions as well. "A worker at a clinic in Bangladesh (where botched abortions account for 31% of all recorded maternal deaths) told PCC researchers that even if a woman showed up bleeding and in severe pain, she would be turned away without treatment or even advice."

Although the policy supposedly only affects private groups, many governments dependent on US foreign aid have followed suit with their state-run clinics and hospitals. Said a Kenyan health official, "One does not bite the hand..."

Family-planning groups are lobbying Congress to overturn the decision with legislation. They are hoping that many people, also outraged by the gag rule, will support the rights of Third World women to protect them from the clutches of US patriarchal control.
— *Source:* Wind Chill Factor

*Reprinted from* Earth First!, *Samhain 1991, vol. XII, No. 1.*

# Bartering Helps Farmers Find New Markets

*An interview with Burkinabe grassroots organizer Antoine Sombié*

**by Pierre Pradervand / *African Farmer***

In the face of deteriorating food supplies during the past 15 years, millions of farmers in Africa have started organizing themselves to find their own solutions. One of the most original projects—and one that has huge potential for the entire continent—is the barter operations that farmers' groups in Burkina Faso have set up, first on a national scale, and more recently internationally.

One of the main promoters of these exchanges is Antoine Sombié, a leader of the International Six-S Association (Se servir de la saison sèche en savane et au Sahel, "using the dry season in the savannah and the Sahel"), a non-governmental development organization in Burkina Faso. Formerly a sales representative for a large agro-chemical company, Mr. Sombié left his job to become a grass-roots organizer in the south-west of the country near his home village of Bérégadougou. *African Farmer* interviewed Mr. Sombié [1989] at the Six-S Association's general assembly in Thiès, Senegal.

**How did these exchanges get under way?**

In 1973 the farmers in my region started organizing themselves on a collective self-help basis, called in the local Turka language *wuol*. After a few years, we contacted the Naam organization in northern Burkina Faso to see if we could collaborate. We became partners of the Naam organization.

One of our challenges was excess supply—our farmers produced far more fruit than they could sell at local markets. Initially we worked with private merchants, but we very soon realized that we were being scalped! For instance, merchants would purchase a 130-pound [59 kilogram] box of mangoes for 300 francs CFA [US$1.08] and sell the same box for 5,000 F CFA [US$18]— over 16 times more.

So we decided the only intelligent thing to do was to avoid the middlemen and commercialize our produce directly via barter exchanges with our Naam partners. The farmers in the north would send us sheep in exchange for our fruits—mangoes, pineapples and the like. Thanks to AFDI [Agriculteurs français developpement international]—a French development NGO started and run by French farmers—we were able to acquire a truck for transport, and the Naam organization lent us some others.

**How does the system function?**

We created what are called trade stimulation groups to get the barter operations going. We also suggested to our Naam partners in the north that they set up similar trade groups that would sell the produce acquired from us at their local markets. In our understanding of things, there simply are no poor regions. Every single region has wealth of some kind. They simply have different kinds of production. The north has no fruit, but it has sheep and chickens.

Instead of purchasing the mangoes from our farmers at 300 F CFA a box as the middlemen did, [our farmers' group] would offer [the farmers] 600 to 800 F CFA. Also, instead of retailing the boxes at 4,000 to 6,000 F CFA, we would sell them [to farmers' groups in the north] for 2,500 to 3,000 F CFA or the equivalent in goods, which meant that the consumers in the north could consume fruit at an affordable price. And in addition, we would still make an attractive profit. Our farmers are earning more and the consumers paying less. Everyone wins.

**Do you think that farmers could start marketing their own produce directly in the cities?**

Originally we tried to sell our produce via cooperatives set up by the state. But it didn't work because the civil servants who staffed the cooperatives took the weekends off [and] because it took months and months for the farmers to be paid. So we decided to set up our own marketing network. In the past [year and a half] we have set up our own shops or stalls to sell our produce directly to the consumers in the cities. In BoboDioulasso, we have a major sales outlet that is a cooperative of which our farmers are members.

We purchase the bananas from our farmers at 60 F CFA a kilogram and retail them in the city at 80, 90, maximum 100 F CFA a kilogram. This compares with the retail prices of 150 F CFA for state cooperatives and 150 to 200 F CFA for private merchants. In addition to that, thanks to a special fund we created with the help of the Six-S Association, we pay our farmers cash right away, whereas the merchants may take three to six months to pay, which hardly suits the farmer.

**Do you think these experiences could be duplicated in other African countries?**

Certainly. You see, ultimately the farmer has the same mentality. Farmers are the same from one country to another. In addition to that, ethnic groups straddle the borders. If I go to southern Mali, they are my people, they speak my language.

**What are the main changes you have noticed in recent years?**

A few years ago our only concern was production because of the hunger problem. In recent years there has been considerable improvement in yields [because of better rains], so today we need to have another kind of behavior. In addition to having to be good producers, we also have to be excellent traders and merchants. So we have to teach our farmers' groups not only to produce well, but also to be good tradesmen. We are also encouraging regions to start producing new products. For instance, farmers in the Dissin region in south-west Burkina Faso believed their region could never produce bananas. Today they are practically competing with our region of Bérégadougou, which has been for many years a top banana producer, because the farmers of my region started them in the business.

*Excerpted from* African Farmer, *November 1990.*

## *Sanctions at work*

# The Last Mile

## U.S. Communities and South Africa

In late December, 19 South African political parties including the African National Congress (ANC), the Zulu based Inkatha Freedom Party, and the ruling National Party issued a declaration committing themselves to draft a new constitution and to create a " united, democratic, non-racial and nonsexist" South Africa. Cyril Ramaphosa, the ANC's representative at the talks, struck an optimistic chord, saying, "More than ever, we are convinced that we are walking the last mile."

But the last mile, where all the specifics must be negotiated, remains strewn with land mines and booby traps. Consequently most anti-apartheid organizations, both inside and outside South Africa, have taken the position that sanctions should not be lifted until real democracy is in place. *The question* U.S. communities should now be debating— and few are—is how to ensure that their current sanctions remain effective until the chains of apartheid are completely broken.

## Sanctions Worked

Skeptics of sanctions who insisted that international pressure would not move South Africa toward majority rule were clearly wrong. In just a few short years a concerted international campaign, working alongside the ANC and other major anti-apartheid groups within South Africa, succeeded in isolating the white supremacists of Pretoria and forcing them to undertake major reforms.

All together, local, national, and international sanctions have taken a huge toll on the South African economy. The ACOA believes that over $20 billion in U.S. public funds have been divested from companies doing business in South Africa, including $3.8 billion and $4.2 billion respectively from the retirement funds of California and New Jersey. The Investor Responsibility Research Center (IRRC) calculates that sanctions have cost the South African economy $27 billion—about 20 to 30 percent of the economic growth it would have enjoyed had sanctions not been in place.

Sanctions were also crucial in ending U.S. bank loans to South Africa. When Chase Manhattan, one of the largest U.S. lenders to South Africa, adopted a policy of not making any new loans to Pretoria regime in 1985, the South African government was forced to declare a debt-repayment standstill. Since then, the country has received few new international loans.

According to the IRRC's Alison Cooper, 319 American companies had equity ties to South Africa in 1984; now only 104 do. Roughly a hundred of these companies divested themselves before national sanctions were implemented, which suggests that most of these departures were precipitated not by the Comprehensive Anti-Apartheid Act but by local sanctions.

Perhaps most significantly, sanctions strengthened the forces for reform within South Africa. They pressured President F.W. de Klerk to undertake a number of startling changes. He freed Nelson Mandela and legalized the ANC. He repealed the three "pillars of apartheid": the Population Registration Act, which required every South African to be registered into a racial category at birth; the 1913 and 1936 Land Acts, which restricted blacks from owning 87 percent of the country's land; and the Group Areas Act, which defined where most South Africans could and could not live according to race. De Klerk also opened negotiations for a new national constitution.

These have been bold steps. But do they warrant an end to sanctions?

## The July Coup

Seizing the opportunity to renew business ties with South Africa, President Bush lifted sanctions last July 10th and certified that the five specific conditions of the Comprehensive Anti-Apartheid Act had been met. Under closer scrutiny, however, none of the conditions has been met fully—and some not even remotely.

It's easy to understand why virtually every political, labor, and church representative of black South Africans—except, the conservative Inkatha Party—believes that Bush's decision to lift sanctions was premature. But ironically, Bush's action has turned out to be largely irrelevant.

## States and Cities Stand United

Despite a threat last summer by the U.S. Justice Department that it might sue local jurisdictions that did not follow President Bush's lead and lift sanctions, nearly every state, county, and city has decided to keep the heat on South Africa. In a telephone survey of the 101 cities with sanctions, *Global*

---

# Sanctions should be lifted in phases corresponding to the actual progress being achieved within South Africa.

*—Nelson Mandela*

---

*Communities* found only one, the city of Pittsburgh (PA), seriously considering a move to weaken its law. Moreover, according to both the ACOA and the IRRC, Oregon is the only one of 27 states with anti-apartheid laws that has decided to lift sanctions.

Besides Oregon, states and cities have held firm. "I don't know that anything President Bush would do would cause us to change our policy," said Barry Del Castillo, Town Manager of Amherst (MA). According to Kim Megaro, the First Deputy Purchasing Agent in Chicago: "We're really looking to the United Nations for direction." Grand Rapids (MI) City Treasurer Albert Mooney polled a few city commissioners and found "no interest in repealing."

Gordon Hector, Director of Public Affairs of the New Jersey Turnpike Authority, said that despite the changes in national policy his agency would still be booting Shell Oil franchises off the highway in 1992.

Shortly after Bush lifted sanctions, the mayors of Atlanta, Boston, Chicago, Los Angeles, New York, and Pittsburgh announced that they would not weaken their laws and urged their elected colleagues across the country to do likewise. So did Governor Jim Florio of New Jersey and Governor William Weld of Massachusetts, a conservative Republican.

In his capacity as President of the U.S.

Conference of Mayors, Mayor Raymond Flynn of Boston reiterated that the formal policy of the organization was to retain sanctions and said, "I am ... declaring that the President's decision to lift sanctions was premature. On anti-apartheid action, this government was late to get on board—and the first to jump ship. "

At least three other cities—Fresno (CA), Fairmont (WV), and Erie (PA)—have discussed whether to end sanctions and decided against it. Some jurisdictions went further. Less than two weeks after Bush's announcement, Weschester County (NY) unanimously passed tougher restrictions against banks with ties to South Africa. Richard Gray, Treasurer of Ann Arbor (MI), said that his city was "reviewing its policies and tightening them up."

Some localities may even begin sanctions this year. In 1990 IBM successfully lobbied the city council of Hartford (CT) to table a selective purchasing measure under consideration. But now that several opponents of sanctions were tossed out of office during the most recent election, Hartford anti-apartheid activists are confident that the law will be passed this year.

As a result of continuing local sanctions, U.S. companies are not rushing back to South Africa. Although Lotus and Federal Express recently entered into licensing agreements, and Microsoft is planning to do the same, "no U.S. company to date that has gone back with equity ties," according to the IRRC's William Moses.

## Policies for the Last Mile

Most anti-apartheid organizations within the United States are looking to Nelson Mandela and the ANC for guidance on when to end sanctions. Mandela addressed this question in a speech to the United Nations General Assembly in December. "Sanctions," he said, "should be lifted in phases corresponding to the actual progress being achieved within South Africa." During phase one, which Mandela believes should kick in now, people-to-people activities, including academic exchanges, sports, tourism, and air links, should be resumed. Following this recommendation, the United Nations recently voted to lift the cultural embargo on South Africa and the International Olympic Committee decided to readmit South African athletes to this year's games in Spain.

Mandela suggested that a second phase should begin when the government actually ratifies a new constitution and hands over power to an interim administration; only then can diplomatic relations and most economic ties be resumed. According to the ACOA and TransAfrica, virtually all state and local sanctions fall into this category.

The third and final phase of lifting sanctions, during which countries would be allowed to ship arms and oil to South Africa, would occur only after the election of a new majority government.

If negotiations go well, phase two may be reached by the end of this year. But until that point, most anti-apartheid organizations within the United States and within South Africa are urging U.S. states, counties, and cities to keep up the pressure. This can be done in three ways.

There's a third alternative for states, counties, and cities that goes beyond sanctions. Since 1987, ten U.S. communities have linked up with black townships or so-called "black spots." The earliest links, such as those between St. Paul (MN) and Lawaaikamp, focused international attention on efforts by the South African government to bulldoze black communities. Recently, however, the collaborations have expanded to include pressuring the South African government to provide basic services, upgrading community schools and health care, and supporting local efforts at land reclamation.

Sister-community programs are especially important, because once apartheid is abolished the need for U.S. aid, trade, investment, and technical assistance in the ravaged black communities in South Africa will be enormous. Recognizing this need, Mayor David Dinkens from New York City recently led a delegation to South Africa to prepare the way for greater business ties once democracy is in place.

When Nelson Mandela and the ANC give a green light to renew economic and political relationships with South Africa, U.S. localities must be prepared to act quickly. One recent episode highlights the danger of foot dragging. When Namibia was illegally occupied by South Africa, 58 localities in the United States placed sanctions on companies with trade or investment ties in Namibia. Now, nearly a year after a new constitution was written and free elections were held, only 27 of these laws have been repealed.

When a new government comes to power in South Africa, states, counties, and cities must be prepared to lift sanctions immediately and to assist black communities that will be coping with the deep economic and psychological scars from a century of apartheid. If the outside world fails to support this fragile, young democracy, it could easily slip into another epoch of unjust and authoritarian rule. Even when the last mile is completed, communities worldwide must help South Africa run the next race.

*Excerpted from* Global Communities, *Winter 1991/92.*

# Searching for Justice in the West Bank and Gaza

### by George R. Fouke / *People for a Change*

Journalist Barbara Crossette, in a March 4th article in the *NY Times,* describes [the three-year plan for a Palestinian state] as including "details for setting up an election process, complete with international observers, leading to an interim self-government with legislative functions and power over land, natural resources, water, subsoil, territorial sea, exclusive economic zone and air space." The plan provides for the establishment of "an independent judiciary and police force." It calls for "the cessation of all Israeli settlement activity in the territories, the return of seized property and the release of political prisoners and detainees."

Hana Ashwari, spokeswoman for the Palestinians, summed up the differences between the Palestinian and Israeli approaches toward the future status of the Palestinians: "They [Israelis] start with the assumption that we are inhabitants of the territories with no rights whatsoever." *(SF Chronicle, 2/27/92)*

### PROSPECTS FORM INSIDE ISRAEL

*Jerusalem-based Clergy for Peace is an organization of Jewish and Palestinian clergy. It was founded in 1988, a few months after the intifada began. Members work to help put an end to human rights violations against the Palestinians and to advance the idea of a negotiated settlement. I attended a meeting last February, in Jerusalem, at which Rabbi Jeremy Milgrom, co-director of Clergy for Peace spoke of the obstacles standing in the way of settlement of the Palestinian-Israeli conflict.*

"The press never reports the human side of the Palestinian struggle... As for the broadcast media, it is run in its entirety by the government, which means that it basically serves as a PR agency for government statements..."

"The intifada has made it clear to Israelis that there is virtual unanimity among the Palestinians that their representatives are the [leaders of the] Palestinian Liberation Organization..."

"The polls show that the some Israeli citizens are beginning to recognize that the Palestinian position, the official PLO position, is one of moderation. But the government's claim that the PLO are murderers and

---

**Some Israeli citizens are beginning to recognize that the Palestinian position, the official PLO position, is one of moderation.**

---

that they want everything has won over more and more people..."

"What's gone on in the territories for the last six months for sure, and for longer than that in a semi-milder fashion, has been that the settlers are calling the shots.

There is a tremendous amount of lawlessness that goes on on the part of some to them. ...The settlers went there because they were going to sacrifice their comfort and security in order to make it more difficult for the Israeli government to give back the territories in any possible peace negotiations."

"The settlements [are] obstacles to the peace negotiations, but any time the settlers' security is threatened they think it is perfectly legitimate to shut down normal life of a multitude of people..."

### MILITARY OCCUPATION RULES

Palestinians residing in the Occupied Territories are forbidden to stand on rooftops unless hanging laundry, walk on sidewalks or within 150 meters of a street in non-residential areas after sunset, travel using the airport, move from one town to another without notifying the military governor, be outdoors without identity cards, cover their faces while outdoors, carry the Palestinian flag or anything in the shape of Palestine, drive a car with yellow (non-occupied territories) plates, be outdoors between 9pm and 4am if in Gaza...
—Imad Musa, *Al-Fajr* newspaper

### ON WITH THE TAKEOVER!

"Jewish settlers began a campaign [last week] to increase the Jewish population in the occupied territories by more than 70,000 by the end of the year. Settlement leaders told reporters that their goal is to increase the number of Jewish settlers in the occupied territories from the current 115,000 to 1 million during the next few years."
—SF Chronicle, 4/9/92

### IN FACT...

4,000 Israeli settlers lay claim to 45% of the land in the Gaza Strip, but use 85% of the available potable water, while 850,000 Palestinians live in the remaining territory and must make do with 15% of that water.
—*Middle East Witness Update,* March '92

*Excerpted from* People for a Change *newsletter, May-June 1992.*

*Editor's Note: Shamir (Likud Party) recently lost to the more moderate Labour Party.*

# Taking Aim on the IMF

## by Rainforest Action Network / *Action Alert*

The World Bank and the International Monetary Fund constitute the "lenders of last resort" to the international community. In effect, if the World Bank is a loan shark, the IMF is its muscle. The World Bank loans money; the IMF "restructures" the debtor nation's economy to meet its payments. The IMF is primarily responsible for the crushing austerity programs imposed on indebted Third World countries. More than any other single agency, the IMF pushes those countries to mortgage their environmental futures through the wholesale short-term harvesting of their natural resources.

Like the World Bank, the IMF is one of the most powerful financial institutions on the planet. Like the World Bank, it is funded in part by your tax dollars. Unlike the World Bank, however, the IMF does not study the environmental and social consequences of the projects it promotes. It lacks qualified natural resource ecologists, development economists, poverty experts, and other trained in the very areas its influence on international monetary policy most effects.

And yet the IMF is virtually autonomous. It is accountable, in a real way, to almost no one. There is no external evaluation unit to study whether its goals, such as they are, have been achieved, or whether future projects will have undesirable impacts on the very people they're supposed to help.

Although the US Congress has, in recent years, adopted legislation that in theory mandates reforms within the IMF, little at the institution has changed. By almost every conceivable standard, it continues to have a negative impact on rainforests, health care, education, nutrition, and poverty around the globe. Not surprisingly, those who have suffered most are women and children.

The following sample letter proposed by the Network to the executive director; or they suggest that people lodge their complaints by calling (202) 623-7751.

*Charles Dallara*
*Executive Director from the U.S.*
*International Monetary Fund*
*700 19th Street, NW*
*Washington, DC 20431*

*Dear Mr. Dallara:*
*I do not support the IMF's use of my tax dollars to fund the destruction of the tropical rainforest and the genocide of tribal and other peoples. It is time that you recognize the so-called "Third World debt" for what it really is—bad loans made by incompetent bankers—and take responsibility for relieving, rather than increasing, the inhuman burden those loans have placed on millions of innocent. hard-working people. I urge you to redirect the IMF's priorities away from short-term overdevelopment toward a policy of protecting critical ecosystems and promoting ecologically sound food production.*

*Excerpted from* Action Alert #36, April 1989, *from Rainforest Action Network.*

# Chapter 3

# Demographics
# & Justice Issues

Necessity is the plea for every infringement of human freedom. It is the argument of tyrants; it is the creed of slaves.

*William Pitt*

The law, in its majestic equality, forbids rich and poor alike to sleep under bridges, beg in the streets or steal bread.

*Anatole France*

The notion that man is destined to dominate nature is by no means a universal feature of human culture. If anything, this notion is almost completely alien to the so-called primitive or preliterate communities. I cannot emphasize too strongly that the concept emerged very gradually from a broader social development: the increasing domination of human by human.

*Murray Bookchin,* The Ecology of Freedom

Only very slowly and late have men come to realize that unless freedom is universal it is only extended privilege.

*Christopher Hill*

I have no mercy or compassion in me for a society that will crush people and then penalize them for not being able to stand up under the weight.

*Malcolm X*

America is deeply racist and its democracy is flawed both economically and socially. The black revolution is much more than a struggle for the rights of Negroes. It is forcing America to face all its interrelated flaws—racism, poverty, militarism, and materialism. It is exposing evils that are rooted deeply in the whole structure of society. It reveals systemic rather than superficial flaws, and suggests that radical reconstruction of society itself is the real issue to be faced.

*Martin Luther King*

# Population and Human Needs:
## *A Growing Imbalance*

World population is now at 5.1 billion. Another billion people will be added to our planet over the next ten years, ninety-percent of that growth taking place in the poorer nations of the developing world.

The real issue, however, is how those numbers relate to available resources. It is important to understand the concepts of demographic transition, carrying capacity, and why world population growth has become such a problem.

### Demographic Transition

The term demographic transition refers to the historical shift of birth and death rates from high to low levels. This process tends to happen in three phases:

① Both birth and death rates are high so little growth occurs, if any.

② Death rates fall due to improved living conditions (e.g., better health care, increased food production, expanded social services), but birth rates remain high. In this stage, populations grow rapidly.

③ Economic and social gains combined with lower infant mortality rates reduce the desire for large families and birth rates decline.

When a population is able to maintain a state of zero population growth, then the population is said to have stabilized. Some countries have even advanced to a fourth stage where death rates are higher than birth rates and population has actually declined.

The problem in the developing world is that most of these countries get stuck or "trapped" in the second phase of the demographic transition. Modern medical technology and improved diets reach these populations and decrease death rates before a modern economy has been able to develop and encourage lower birth rates. Populations continue to grow at a rapid pace, outstripping the ability of these countries to meet the needs of such a large number of people. This places undue stress on the land and natural resources as well as negating the modest economic gains of an incipient modern economy. Per capita income declines. If this is accompanied by declines in per capita food production (as in much of sub-Saharan Africa over the last decade), rising food imports will increase external debt putting further stress on the economy. People become unhappy as they lose all hope of attaining a better life for themselves and societies become politically unstable. Population has grown beyond the capacity of the immediate environment to peacefully sustain it.

### Carrying Capacity

Carrying capacity is the amount of life (e.g., plants, animals, humans), which a given amount of land can support. As the world becomes more crowded and overpopulated, disasters such as famine, epidemic diseases and war, due to increasing conflict over scarce resources, would work to bring down the world population count. This is better known as the Malthusian Theory.

In the developing world, population pressures and over-utilization of land resources are turning parts of Africa into desert; drought and famine have increased on that continent. Latin American countries are groaning under the weight of foreign debt as they clear away miles of tropical rainforest and dangerously exploit their natural resources in a mad effort to create the surplus capital they need to industrialize. Urbanization is growing faster than the modern economy necessary to support it. Social unrest and political instability are constant threats; regional and civil wars occur more frequently.

Instead of being "the answer"—technology has only created a new set of problems. It seems that the real answers will be found in the ability to change certain destructive patterns of living. We must learn to understand and respect our environmental limitations, including the carrying capacity of the Earth.

### Growing Imbalances

As the number of people increases, so do the demands for basic human needs like food, safe drinking water, housing, education, health care and employment

As more resources are desired and consumed by the rich countries who have the money to pay for them, fewer resources are available for the economic development of the poor countries who have no way of competing fairly in the world market This creates a growing imbalance between the rich and poor. For example, developed countries make up 21 percent of the world's population yet consume 85 percent of the world's energy.

Developing countries, on the other hand, which lack adequate resources, are hard-pressed to provide basic human needs and services to their citizens. Modest gains in production and economic growth are often diluted or negated by high rates of population growth, discouraging any reasonable hopes for a better life. This swelling in the ranks of the poor beyond the environmental, economic and institutional capacities to meet their needs creates imbalances that seriously threaten the stability of these developing nations. This instability has grave implications for the rest of the world, including the citizens of the United States.

When the rate of per capita food production cannot keep up with the high rates of population growth in countries of sub-Saharan Africa, the resulting food crisis can mean mass malnutrition, famine, and demographic upheavals as refugees migrate to already strained urban areas or across national borders. In instances such as Ethiopia or Sudan, food can become a political weapon in the face of starving populations suffering the effects of civil war.

In fast-growing urban centers of the developing countries such as Mexico City or Sao Paulo, Brazil, large portions of the cities are populated by desperately poor residents living in shanty town squatter homes with no provision for sewage or waste treatment. The nearest source of water for drinking, washing, and cooking also becomes a receptacle for garbage and waste. Without proper sanitation, these areas become the breeding grounds for water-borne diseases and widespread pollution.

The fast-growing poverty of the countryside is causing widespread migration to cities like Manila, which is now home to at least 10 percent of the Philippine population. Urban services are strained beyond capacity and shanty-dwellers are forced to fend for themselves in the urban wasteland that surrounds the city's pockets of affluence. Malnutrition is a way of life for these people, and crime is a constant problem in their city slums.

Since 1983 the overall national income of the Philippines has decreased by nearly 10 percent. Hope of increasing the rural standard of living through agriculture has been thwarted by falling per capita production rates. At the same time, national debt has soared to more than $27 billion. As Filipino citizens loose faith in the abilities of their government to provide a better life, tens of thousands of them are emigrating to the United States each year.

Ironically, the Philippines have also been an important American ally and recipient of large sums of U.S. foreign aid including payments for military base rights. What lessons can be learned from this use of U.S. foreign aid?

### Lessons for Sustainable Population Management

The past decade has been marked by a continuing debate regarding the role of family planning programs—as opposed to the role of economic development—in affecting fertility decline in the developing world.

Emphasis has often been placed on economic growth and development as the cause rather than the effect of declining birth rates. In the developed world, the demographic transition to lower rates of population growth accompanied societal changes related to mandatory education and the rising status of women. As women became educated members of the modern work force, they tended to get married at a later age and have fewer children. As economic incentives shifted, providing more benefits for fewer children became preferred over a greater division of the benefits given to each child in a large family. This put a downward pressure on fertility rates.

In the developing countries, however, economic opportunities and resources are not abundant enough to meet the needs of existing populations or to keep pace with rapid growth rates, especially where the population rate will literally double within a period of 20 to 25 years, less time than it takes to fully regenerate forests or topsoils. These serious limitations in terms of time and available resources entreat the developing countries to consider family planning and population management as critical components of development projects and strategies.

Ronald Leger's address to the International Conference on Strategic Management of Population Programs, "World population growth will not significantly decrease unless we invent new concepts, approaches and methods - and above all a renewed determination to understand poor people's cultures and their ways of thinking and to invent ways to invite their inputs into our decision making process."

*Excerpted from the* NAS Master the Subject, *published by the National Audubon Society.*

# Population Stress:
## *Does it only happen somewhere else?*

If you're like most Americans, "population stress" probably calls to mind places like Ethiopia or India or Mexico. You might think of the more than 5 million babies who die in developing countries each year from the effects of poor sanitation and contaminated food supplies. Or the many millions of hungry, homeless people desperately migrating from one ravaged country to another. But distressing as these problems are, they may seem very remote from the daily bustle of your own life.

Are they really so far away? Clearly, the tragic consequences do not stop at our borders when:

- Political turmoil takes its toll in Haiti and El Salvador, the most densely populated and environmentally degraded countries in this hemisphere.
- Rapidly expanding populations of young people fuel rising discontent in the Middle East
- Explosive growth hampers efforts to provide the most basic human needs in Africa.

This kind of overpopulation "somewhere else" profoundly affects American economic, political, security and environmental interests. And Americans also contribute to the problems. Our impact on global resources, for instance, is staggering. In energy use alone, America's per capita consumption is ten times the world's average.

At home, the United States faces a host of population-linked dilemmas: fouled air and water, unplanned development sprawls, traffic-choked highways, shrinking open space. More and more people are competing for jobs, homes and public services. One million

pregnant teenagers annually, unwanted babies, homeless families, hungry children and jobless workers—all put enormous strain on our government's limited resources.

For many of us, striving for the American dream is becoming a nightmare:

- Suburban towns watch their grassy refuges sacrificed to miles of mammoth commercial complexes.
- Los Angeles residents fight high-rise construction to the cry of "Not yet New York," while Washington and Atlanta commuters worry that traffic will make their cities into "another LA."
- Sun-Belt farmers and city-dwellers struggle in a tug-of-war over scarce water resources.
- Even national parks and wildlife areas suffer from smog and traffic jams.

### *What happened?*

**Too many people.** The U.S. population is growing by more than 2 million each year, yet our government has no national population policy to preserve our quality of life.

**Too many shortsighted leaders.** Bad planning, and plenty of it... or no planning at all. Local and national leaders stubbornly keep their eyes closed to the enormous environmental, financial and social costs of population growth.

**Too much of a good thing.** Progress, growth, bigger, better, more. Great stuff. But then the traffic, long lines, noise, crime and pollution begin to hit us where we live.

*Excerpted from Zero Population Growth brochure.*

### *The Global Dimensions of Hunger*

- Every time the minute hand of the clock sweeps 60 seconds, 28 people die from hunger or related diseases.

- It is estimated that between 500 million and one billion people are hungry. Each year 20 million people, the majority of them children, die from hunger or hunger related diseases.

- One child in every 10 in the world dies before its first birthday. Forty thousand children die each day (15 million each year) from preventable causes.

- In the 83 poorest countries of the world, 3% of the people control 80% of the land.

- In most developing countries, only one person in three has access to clean drinking water. In developed countries such as the United States, more that 90% of the people have clean water readily.

- One person in five worldwide does not have adequate housing 100 million people have no shelter whatsoever.

*Source:* Hunger, Learning for Action; *Church World Service*

39

# Frances Moore Lappé
## Institute for Food and Development Policy

*Frances Moore Lappé was born in 1944 and came to public notice in 1971 with the publication by Ballantine Books of her* Diet for a Small Planet *which has sold three million copies and been translated into French, German, Swedish, Japanese and Spanish.*

In 1975 Lappé and Joseph Collins founded the Institute for Food and Development Policy (IFDP) in San Francisco, a not-for-profit public education and documentation center. Since then IFDP has become internationally recognized for addressing the political and economic roots of world hunger and demonstrating how ordinary citizens can effectively help to end hunger. IFDP now has 20,000 members, a staff of 17 and an annual budget of $1,200,000.

With Collins, Lappé co-authored in 1977 the book *Food First: Beyond the Myth of Scarcity,* which demonstrated that world hunger was a political and economic phenomenon and not due either to food scarcity or over-population. This theme was further developed and updated by her and Collins' *World Hunger: Twelve Myths,* published in 1986 by Food First Books, the imprint of IFDP.

IFDP doesn't suggest "models of devel-opment". Rather its intention is to demon-strate lessons, both positive and negative, to understand and publicize grassroots, non-governmental strategies that work; demo-cratically-controlled initiatives through which the poor are able to transform their lives. To this end IFDP and Lappé have conducted searching, in-depth investiga-tions of food issues in the Philippines, Cuba, Mozambiqué, Tanzania, Bangladesh and Nicaragua. Their books and reports are wide-ly used by grassroots groups in both indus-trial and non-industrial countries. To provide firsthand experience of rural situations, IFDP also organizes Reality Tours in the US and abroad, giving emphasis to such issues as poverty, hunger, and patterns of farming and land ownership.

IFDP is also active in the formal educa-tional sector and has produced both a grade school and a high school curriculum *Explod-ing the Hunger Myths,* filmstrips, slideshows, videos and a comic book for classroom use.

For older students it has published guides to college organizing and to work opportunities for those wishing to promote social change.

Most recently Lappé has been working on a project which explores the underlying ethical values of U.S. society on the one hand and IFDP on the other. It is intended to be a long-term philosophical inquiry into Ameri-can political values, to offer a redefinition of such concepts as "freedom" and "democra-cy". Outside IFDP, Lappé has recently pub-lished *What to Do After You Turn Off the TV,* encouraging families to discover the joys of family life without TV's dominant presence.

*"With a modest budget and a long list of publications, (IFDP) is one of the most estab-lished food "think tanks" and its founder, Frances Moore Lappé, one of the most respect-ed food critics in the country."* (New York Times, October 19th 1980).

*"No society has fulfilled its democratic promise if people go hungry, for by demo-cratic we mean not only particular political structures but whether in the daily lives of its citizens key principles are manifest. The ac-countability of leadership to all those who have to live with their decisions, and the sharing of power so that no-one is left utterly powerless. If some go without food they have surely been deprived of all power. The exist-ence of hunger belies the existence of de-mocracy."*

- Frances Moore Lappé

*Winner of the 1987 Right Livelihood award. Reprinted from the Right Livelihood Awards' Press Release.*

# Welfare: Trickles Down—*NOT!*
## by J.W. Smith / *The World's Wasted Wealth*

In 1984, U.S. social welfare expenditures covering Social Security, Medicaid, Medi-care, came to $592.6 billion (that awesome figure they are supposedly unjustly receiv-ing), of which about $392 billion is consid-ered a right (such as Social Security, earned by a lifetime of work, or education, which prepares a person for work). Social scientist Charles Murray, of the Manhattan Institute for Policy Research, characterizes the remaining $200 billion as welfare or charity. Murray [takes] the negative reaction to the word "welfare" to its maximum. Instead of welfare, most of this $200 billion does not reach those in poverty, it too is considered a right by those above poverty who intercept these funds.

Murray himself admits that only $109 billion of this $200 billion is actually distrib-uted as welfare. This leaves $91 billion wast-ed in distribution. An average wage of just over $18,000 per year would back up Mur-ray's claim that there are five million profes-sionals employed in administering these funds and would account for the $91 billion welfare distribution costs. Most of the re-maining $109 billion distributed as welfare

## For the already affluent, the principle of a negative tax is well established.

still does not reach those in poverty. Much is distributed to people who are above the poverty level for such purposes as student food stamps, school lunch programs, sum-mer youth employment, work incentive pro-grams, vocational rehabilitation, community

health centers, subsidized housing, etc. Most who receive this support do not view it as welfare but as a "right"—just as the oilmen, business people, and farmers view theirs. These middle class citizens protect their self-image by classifying their substantial govern-ment support as due them for being produc-tive citizens. This leaves the poor alone with the shame of welfare, even though they receive only a pittance.

With average per-capita earnings of $2,500, those in poverty would need only an additional $80 billion to double individual income to $5,000, or $20,000 per family of four. This is twice the current poverty level. Thus a modest 40 percent of present welfare expenditures—if it only reached them proportionate to need—would put America's 33.7 million who are officially counted as poor well above poverty.

### A Negative Tax Can Replace the Welfare Bureaucracy

Such a reverse tax would distribute tax money to the poor and make up the difference between low earnings and a predetermined income level above poverty. However, that tax would be far less than now expended to finance the current inefficient welfare system. The five million professionals now processing and investigating welfare claims and distributing payments immediately become redundant.

The thought of using a negative tax to pay someone for doing nothing goes against our cultural training. But consider the support for industry, business, and farmers—that is just a negative tax by a different name. Many billion-dollar corporations have received government subsidies (a negative tax) exceeding the taxes they paid. For example, General Electric earned $2.66 billion in 1981, paid no income tax and received a $90 million rebate (negative tax) from the government Between 1982 and 1985 AT&T received a negative tax of $635.5 million, DuPont $179 million, Boeing $121 million, General Dynamics $90.9 million, Pepsico $89.3 million, General Mills $78.7 million,

Transamerica Corporation $73.2 million, Texaco $68 million, International Paper $59.8 million, Greyhound $53.7 million, and IC Industries $53.7 million. And farmers almost universally receive more money from the government than they pay in taxes. For the already affluent the principle of a negative tax is well established.

### Welfare Disappears

With true insurance, the elimination of legal hocus-pocus, cheap transportation, a public taught responsibility for its own health, and with rights to a productive job, much waste will be eliminated. This will result in a reduction in living costs—which translates into higher living standards. If all have rights to a productive job and the able-bodied share the responsibility to work, negative tax payments should then be an infrequent occurrence in a person's life. There would be no welfare. There need be only those injured, unemployable, or retired who draw negative tax support and this would be their right.

*Excerpted from* The World's Wasted Wealth, © 1992 J.W. Smith, New Worlds Press.

---

## Children in Crisis

**FACT:** Half of all the poor in America are children.

**FACT:** One child in eight under the age of 12 goes to bed hungry every night. 5.5 million children in the richest country in the world.

**FACT:** More than one million children are homeless in the U.S. While their number grows every year, government support for housing programs has dropped 80 percent since 1980.

**FACT:** An African-American infant born in Detroit Indianapolis, or Washington, D.C. is less likely to live to his/her first birthday than a baby born in Jamaica, Chile or Panama.

**FACT:** If present trends continue, by the year 2000, one out of every four children born in the USA will be poor.

These statistics reveal a national failure to meet our children's basic needs.

*Source: Unitarian Universalist Service Committee, Children in Crisis Project.*

---

# THE DISTINCTION BETWEEN "RACISM" AND "PREJUDICE"

### by Michael Novick / *Turning the Tide*

Prejudice is a problem of individuals, animosity based on ignorance, often psychologically rooted in a lack of self-esteem, and a corresponding need to put someone else down to feel "superior". Anyone can be guilty of prejudice.

But racism is much more than this: It is a system, a set of relations between nations and groups of people, based on the denial of a decent life or even life itself to one group so the other group can enjoy privileges.

Racism is rooted in a history of colonialism, conquest and slavery [based] on skin color. Racist thinking and ideas were encouraged to justify and enforce this dehumanizing system.

The powerful groups that have created and benefited from this system have always tried to convince all white people that it's in their advantage to participate. It is similar to the way kids with a weak sense of identity and self-respect get manipulated by the nazis, WAR and the KKK and organized as shock troops or a base.

A process that exploits prejudice and fear, this also depends on the real material differences of most white people compared to most black people. Because racism is designed to put white people on top, we have a special responsibility to oppose and uproot it for the sake of our own humanity and a decent future. No one can be free while continuing to identify with oppressors.

There is only one human race. The way to unite is to recognize and overcome the oppression created by the system of racism. Many nations and cultures, suppressed by the dominant European ones, have a right to

preserve and determine their own destiny.

Not only is racism the problem, men have a special responsibility to oppose male chauvinism, violence against women and homophobia. Jews have a special responsibility to oppose Zionism and brutality against Pales-

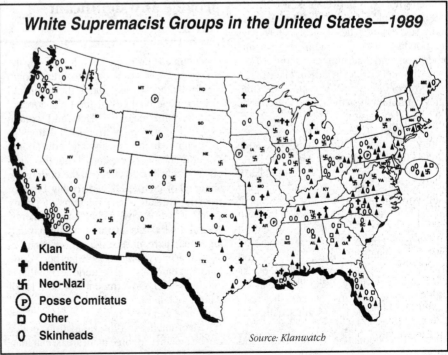

**White Supremacist Groups in the United States—1989**

▲ **Klan**
✝ **Identity**
卐 **Neo-Nazi**
ⓟ **Posse Comitatus**
◻ **Other**
0 **Skinheads**

*Source: Klanwatch*

tinians. Christians have a responsibility to oppose anti-Semitism. This [goes beyond] being "politically-correct". It is trying to face reality and make a better future.

Anti-racists need to participate in the defense of women's clinics, and in an affirmative campaign to extend reproductive freedom; support the self-determination of Black communities, of Native people; to oppose the U.S. war in Central America and the Gulf; and support the efforts of the people of El Salvador, Nicaragua and other countries to build a new, freer life.

Our message needs to be taken into the schools and community groups, to defend artistic and educational freedom from the book burners. Anti-racists need to expose the repressive potential of the "war on drugs" and support the efforts of people to recover from drug abuse without government coercion. Racism has always been one of the biggest obstacles to making any progressive change. People involved in efforts for women's rights, civil liberties, non-intervention, need to get involved in conscious anti-racist action.

Anti-racist action involves not so much fighting with committed racists, as carrying out education and organizing to prevent people from becoming hard-core racists in the first place, [while] challenging the racist [classist] economic and political power structure.

The U.S. is not the only race [class] conscious society. Fighting [occurs] in many countries, involving the Sikhs, the Tamils, the Hindus, the Moslems, loyalists and the Republicans in Ireland, and so on. Based on the slogan, *Think globally, act locally*, P.A.R.T. is composed of white people trying to do what we can about the problem right here.

*Excerpted from* Turning the Tide, *a newsletter from the People Against Racist Terror (PART) located in Los Angeles.*

# The Limits of Gay Rights

### by Gordon O. Parrish / *Fourth Estate (Grey City Journal)*

Aha, you may think, at last the Fourth Estate shows its true colors as another "fag-bashing" reactionary student journal. Wrong! At least as far as this article is concerned. The title does not refer to any moral or philosophical limits on the principles of equality. Rather, it refers to strictly practical considerations. The crux of the gay rights strategy is to appeal to the government to attack institutional discrimination. The glaring defect in this strategy is that anti-gay discrimination is not institutional in nature, but personal.

The gay rights movement, as presently constituted, is rapidly reaching the limits of what it can accomplish. Like other recent civil rights crusaders, gays are relying almost entirely on government action to solve their problems. Since many gays and lesbians are veterans of earlier black civil rights and women's liberation movements, it is natural that they would want to emulate those generally successful tactics. Unfortunately, gays are not like blacks, women, Jews, or any other conventional minority group. They have different characteristics and face different forms of discrimination. Traditional strategies cannot address their needs or provide the relief they desire.

The special circumstance of the gay community are obvious. First, there is no such thing as the gay community. Gays and lesbians come from all races, classes, and walks of life. Racism, sexism, ageism, and any other "ism" you can think of are just as prevalent among homosexuals as they are in the general population. Second, discrimination against gays comes from every corner—all races, nationalities, classes, cultures, and political ideologies. Finally, while blacks were merely seeking the same rights as whites and women just wanted the same opportunities as men, gays are seeking entirely new kinds of "rights." They want acceptance and condonation of behaviors and lifestyles that are unique to them.

Some hard-line conservatives have argued that arts funding, hate crimes data collection, and other legislation are being used to promote "immoral" homosexual behavior. The truth is just the opposite: even if it wanted to, the government can do nothing to promote homosexuality and very little to protect gays from discrimination.

True equality requires that the majority fully accept the minority, a tall order in most cases. In practice, most minority groups have

> ## The problems of the gay community are not rooted in government, and legislative actions cannot provide any significant relief.

concentrated almost exclusively on using the coercive power of the state to break down legal and other barriers against the group and to encourage changes in the behavior and attitude of the majority. Blacks and women benefited handsomely from such actions as their employment, housing and educational opportunities were expanded. But this strategy has only limited effect on the underlying attitudes of people, as can readily be seen from the sad state of race relations after thirty years of active civil rights improvements. Liberals look at this situation with dismay and argue that more must be done. Conservatives argue that everything possible has been done (and that much should be undone, but that is another issue). Government can do a lot of things, but it cannot change men's souls. Only time can do that.

Government anti-discrimination policy can be effective in three main areas: eliminating legal barriers against a minority group, forcing the private sector to drop its own economic barriers, and educating the public to counter irrational prejudices. Unfortunately, none of the three works for the gay community.

Unlike blacks, women, or even immigrants earlier in this century ("No Irish Need Apply"), homosexuals do not suffer from any systematic official discrimination. There have never been any significant legal barriers or Jim Crow laws directed against homosexuals. Yes, there are laws against sodomy in many states, but the vast majority of prosecutions/legal harassment of gays were based on public obscenity or disorderly conduct charges related to the fact that subway restrooms and dark forest preserves used to be the only available places for gays to meet. Sex in public places is simply not acceptable in most communities regardless of the gender of the participants.

Similarly, there are no specific private sector barriers facing gays. There is no such thing as a restrictive covenant in a deed forbidding sale of a property to homosexuals. No country clubs have bylaws barring membership to homosexuals. No corporations have specific policies or quotas against hiring homosexuals.

The proof of this can be seen in the economic health of the gay community. While some homosexuals are poor, there is no such thing as a "gay underclass." On average, gays are no worse off and possibly even better off than most Americans. Certainly the lack of children gives them more disposable income. Since government does not actively oppress gays, there is little that government can do for them. Few would argue, for example, that there should be affirmative action for gays.

There are, of course, a few exceptions, notably the refusal of the military and the intelligence agencies to hire gays. While it is a sore point with gays and many leftist groups are trying to capitalize on it to continue their own long campaign against the national security establishment, the military represents an insignificant fraction of total employment and is at best a minor point.

With few specific barriers to target, gay activists have increasingly been working to pass laws, usually on the local level, to protect their "rights." While such laws may have value as symbols, in terms of concrete accomplishments, they are not worth the paper they are printed on.

In the final analysis, the quest for gay rights is very different from other civil rights struggles. While blacks had to face both a hostile government and enmity from the majority, gays are faced almost exclusively with a public relations problem. Unlike racism, sexism, or anti-Semitism, "homophobic" rules have always been unwritten. And they stem from one source: many "straight" people simply do not like gays.

Moreover, gays are hated for what they do as much as for what they are. Most discrimination stems from ignorance. For example, some whites believe incorrectly that blacks are intellectually inferior or more prone to crime. The government can help dispel misconceptions about homosexuality, but that will not help the gays. Even if the more pernicious myths about gays—that they are hopelessly promiscuous, that they engage in disgusting and unsanitary sexual practices—were removed, many people would still object. It is the reality of homosexuality that disturbs many heterosexuals.

Changing that will require a fundamental transformation in the attitudes of very determined people. The state has never been very good at that sort of thing, and not all the proddings and protests of gay activists is likely to make it any better. Moreover, most gays feel that the real discrimination comes from the rejection by family and friends, as opposed to any official slight. Obviously, the government can do little about that. Gay leaders should abandon attempts to further clutter the law books with useless measures, and concentrate on the long hard struggle to win the hearts and minds of the people.

*Excerpted from* The Fourth Estate, Grey City Journal, *April 20, 1990.*

# Violence at the California-Mexico Border

### by Roberto Martinez / American Friends Service Committee

Human rights violations at the U.S.-Mexico Border continue to increase at an alarming rate. Sixty percent of the border crossings occur and almost 700 U.S. Border Patrol agents are based in the San Diego-Tiajuna border area. This is also where the most violent confrontations take place between the U.S. Border Patrol and undocumented immigrants from Mexico and Central America.

In the last four years, 20 persons have been shot and killed and another 29 wounded by the Border Crime Prevention Unit (BCPU). Of these, at least ten were shot from the back. This unit is now suspended due to protests, numerous lawsuits, publicity and the perception that they are responsible for more violence than they are preventing. The BCPU was made up of six border patrol agents and six San Diego police officers. In the same four years, AFSC documented seven cases of undocumented men, women and children being run over and killed by Border Patrol vehicles and another four injured. One such case took place last August when a 14 year-old boy was run over and killed while runing back across the border. One week later, a 15-year-old boy was shot and wounded in the same area by another border patrol agent who claimed the boy "looked" like he was going to throw a rock.

These cases are among the more spectacular and publicized incidents. But they represent only a very small percentage of a much more widespread problem that occurs not only throughout the border region, but in Latino communities throughout the United States, such as in agricultural areas of north San Diego county.

Last October, several white residents from Encinitas filed complaints with the INS that two border patrol agents chasing two migrant workers shot at the workers because they would not stop. Realizing they were being watched, the agents put away their guns. But, when they caught up to the migrants, one agent held the workers from behind while the other punched them. When the workers fell to the ground, they were kicked and punched some more. The witnesses filed complaints with the Office of Inspector General and the INS Internal Affairs Office. However, it is almost certain that these migrant workers were returned to Mexico the same day to avoid an investigation. We have no way of calculating how many cases of abuse go unreported.

One important factor contributing to the escalation of violence is the lack of a federal statute that punishes federal agents for unjustifiable injuries. Prosecution is left to the local district attorney. No federal agent has ever been charged with criminal negligence in any of the above cases. In March, 1989 Francisco Ruiz Chávez was shot twice in the abdomen by a border patrol agent while trying to protect his wife, who was nine months pregnant. Chavéz was charged with assault of a federal officer, who claimed Chavéz had thrown a rock at him. Since the agent had no visble injuries, and witnesses supported Chavéz' testimony that he never threw a rock, the federal judge acquitted Chavéz. However, the DA refused to prosecute the agent for unjustifiable use of deadly force against Chavéz. Under federal law the worst charge that can be brought against a federal officer is a misdemeanor, punishable by a $10,000 fine and/or one year in jail. Clearly, when a DA refuses to prosecute agents in cases of unjustifiable killings and injuries, this sends a message to these agents that they are virtually immune from prosecution.

The United States and Mexico must not only agree that drug trafficking and immigration are two separate issues, but that whatever agreement or solution they reach must include the respect for human rights and dignity of immigrants from Mexico, Central America and other countries.

Bilateral discussions must be held at every level to address common issues and problems. We must build bridges of communication, not ditches and barriers that can only serve to drive our two countries further apart.

*Excerpted from a newsletter by the American Friends Service Committee, Pacific-Southwest Region, Spring 1990.*

> ## A 15-year-old boy was shot and wounded...by another border patrol agent who claimed the boy *looked* like he was going to throw a rock.

> ## We must build bridges of communication, not ditches and barriers.

# Militarism and Tourism Keep Hawaii a Colony

### by Winona LaDuke & Mililani B. Trask / *Open Road*

Although US maps put Hawaii in a small box off California's coast, Hawaii is really in the Pacific, a separate and struggling geopolitical entity. It also sits in the middle of a very strategic region, and represents the last frontier of U.S. expansionism. Today, on all eight of the Hawaiian Islands, the people and the *aina* (land) are simply trying to survive in what has become someone else's paradise.

Hawaii is the darkest state in the union: Less than 18 percent of the population is Caucasian. Hawaii is also the most militarized state economically, politically and simply in terms of land controlled by the Department of Defense.

Hawaii is the "brain" of the Pentagon's Pacific Command and the headquarters for military activities that control more than half the Earth's surface—from the west coast of North America to the east coast of Africa, from Antarctica to the Arctic.

There are more than 100 military installations in the Hawaiian islands, with fully 10 percent of the state and 25 percent of Oahu under direct control. The land was confiscated by the Pentagon in 1941, and it has become increasingly important to the United States. Hawaii is the loading and reloading base for all of the Pacific. It is in Pearl Harbor Naval Shipyard—Hawaii's largest industrial enterprise—that fuel rods are replaced in the Navy's nuclear-powered submarines. Military spending represents the second-largest income for the state.

The island of Kaho'olawe is the story of Hawaii in a microcosm. Sometimes it doesn't even appear on airlines' maps of the Hawaiian islands, and if it does, it appears as a fetus-shaped island, "totally uninhabited." For centuries, Kaho'olawe had been a monastery for the traditional Hawaiian religion, and the sacred departing place for traditional voyages to Tahiti. In 1941, it was taken by the Department of Defense, and its inhabitants, farmers and ranchers, were moved out. For more than a half-century, the island has been a bombing target for an expanding variety of imaginative military exercises.

In 1990, President Bush ordered a halt to the bombing of Kaho'olawe, and a commission was established to recommend to Congress the "terms and conditions" of returning the island to the state. During public hearings, many Native people demanded that the island be turned over to Ka Lahui Hawaii, a Native Nation created in 1987 at a constitutional convention of native leaders held in Hilo, Hawaii. Kaho'olawe is the only Hawaiian island that is totally Ceded Lands (land to be set aside for Natives), and Natives claim the land should be controlled and managed by the Native Nation. The U. S. military continues to lobby for use of the island for military purposes and for bombing. The Protect Kaho'olawe Ohana (PKO), a multiracial group that has lobbied to stop the bombing for many years, has called for land-banking the island, placing it under the control of the state or the federal government until the United States recognizes the Native Nation. In the meantime, the PKO wants exclusive right to oversee all activities on the island.

Many Native sovereign nations disagree. Ka Lahui and others believe that Native people have an inherent right to be self-governing whether or not the U. S. recognizes this fact. The sovereignty movement in Hawaii is growing stronger and more strident. Returning Kaho'olawe to the state for commercial, tourist, and park uses doesn't address sovereign Native assertions.

The other big industry in Hawaii is, of course, tourism. Haunani Kay Trask, director of the Center for Hawaiian Studies at the University of Hawaii at Manoa, sees the tourist industry as a form of prostitution: "Tourism is not made to sell *haole* (white) culture... It's here because we are the native people of this *aina*. It is our culture that tourists come to see. It is our land that tourists come to pollute... "Tourism, she says, "deforms the culture, so Hawaiians think that to dance the hula is to dance for tourists. Hawaiians grow up thinking our culture is a *haole* interpretation of culture... and if you smile real nice, some *haole* is going to take

> **Tourism, deforms the culture, so Hawaiians think that to dance the hula is to dance for tourists. Hawaiians grow up thinking our culture is a *haole* interpretation of culture... and if you smile real nice, some *haole* is going to take you out.**

you out."

In the end, all this takes a heavy toll on the Hawaiian people and land. As Trask says, "This is not America, this is a colony." The sugar and pineapple plantations were the first wave of colonialism; the military, and finally tourism, are the next waves of colonialism.

*Updated from the Canadian anarchist publication* Open Road *(Winter 1984). Open Road has suspended publication. Winona LaDuke, an Ojibwe, writes and works on behalf of Native causes across North America. Mililani B. Trask is Kia'aina (governor) of Ka Lahui, Hawaii, a Native Hawaiian nation.*

*Excerpted from* Utne Reader, *May/June 1992.*

# Hazardous Waste Disposal
## *A Non-Equal Opportunity Venture*

### by Dr. Michael Zimmerman / *Earth Journal*

A report entitled "Toxic Wastes and Race in the United States" published recently by the United Church of Christ's Commission for Racial Justice, presents some chilling findings. Simply, the racial composition of a community is the single variable best able to explain the existence or nonexistence of commercial hazardous waste facilities in that area. Minorities, mostly blacks and Hispanics, are strikingly over-represented in communities with hazardous waste facilities. Communities with two or more facilities have more than three times the minority representation than do communities without any such installations.

The study has conclusively show that blacks in particular are heavily over-represented within the populations of metropolitan areas with the largest number of uncontrolled toxic waste sites. Although blacks comprise about 11.7 percent of the general population, the percentage of blacks is markedly higher In those cities that top the hazardous waste site list. Three out of every five black and Hispanic Americans live near an uncontrolled toxic waste site, and three of the five largest commercial hazardous waste landfills in America, accounting for 40 percent of the total commercial landfill space in the nation, are in predominantly black of Hispanic neighborhoods.

The US Department of Health and Human Services has documented that African-Americans experience the highest rates of cancer of any US population group. Since there is no reason to believe that the increased incidence of cancer is due to genetic differences between the races, it is not unreasonable to suggest that proximity to hazardous waste sites might be part of the cause.

*Michael Zimmerman is Dean of the College of Letters and Science and a Professor of Biology at the University of Wisconsin at Oshkosh.*

*Excerpted from* Earth Journal, *November 1991.*

# *A Native American Perspective*
# 500 Years after Columbus

### by Carol Heart Looking Horse / Seva

As October 1992 looms ever closer, we "Indians," as we were inappropriately named by Christopher Columbus, find this event to be a positive opportunity to educate the dominant society about our indigenous cultures.

Our ancestors, at the time Columbus landed on San Salvador Island, lived in permanent villages throughout the North American continent that we called Turtle Island. We had sophisticated and advanced knowledge about the seasons and the ability to predict weather variations. Some of our ancestors lived in high rise condominiums, went shopping in malls in Central America, developed the concept of zero, performed brain surgery successfully, and invented medicines which are still in use today, such as aspirin, novocaine, and morphine.

Our ancestors discovered and cultivated many of the foods which we enjoy so much, such as chocolate, gum, cocoa-cola, spices and hot peppers. They also grew about 109 different varieties of potatoes in their fields, as well as the many strains of corn which we have today. Other foods which were unheard of in the Old World were a daily part of their diet. Such foods as tomatoes, watermelons, pineapples, squash and beans were nutritious products of the agricultural societies of Native Americans long before the contact.

It has been estimated by anthropologists that approximately 50 million aboriginal people resided on Turtle Island at that time. The history of this country does not begin

> **A council of elders** from the Lakota (Sioux) Indian tribe declared independence from the United States at a surprise press conference held at Bear Butte, South Dakota, on July 14, 1991. The declaration capped four days of meetings in which elders from South Dakota's reservations agreed that the time for Lakota Sovereignty had come. The new government, proclaimed at Bear Butte, would be traditional in nature and deal with the U.S. government on a nation-to-nation basis only.
>
> The Lakota Declaration of Independence will eliminate all jurisdictional claims currently enforced by state, federal and Bureau of Indian Affairs authorities.
>
> For more information contact the Lakota Sovereign Organization Committee, Box 5686, Rapid City, SD 57709. Phone (605) 348-9463.
>
> *Excerpted from "Lakota (Sioux) Council of Elders Declares Independence", an article by Richard Simonelli,* Men's Council Journal, *Issue 10, August 1991.*

©1992 by Jack Artusio, San Luis Obispo, CA (805) 543-4809

**Let us in the name of the Holy Trinity, go on sending all the slaves that can be sold.**
— Columbus

45

with Christopher Columbus five hundred years ago, but goes back to a time shrouded in mystery when only aboriginal people lived on Turtle Island. We had our own names for the mountains, lakes and rivers, and many of these names are still attached to these places. The Mississippi River, the Black Hills of South Dakota, the states of Iowa, Kansas, and Illinois, to name but a few, are reminders of proud tribes who once inhabited and revered those places.

It is said that we cannot plan our future without knowing our past. Our past in America must include the indigenous people who were such good caretakers of Mother Earth, who lived in balance with her, and whose daily life reflected that balance and harmony.

Many of the tribes do have prophecies, we Lakota among them. Our prophecy tells us that in 1992 there will be a change for the positive for aboriginal people. We are not asking for the return of our original lands, but we are asking for greater understanding about our society, about aboriginal people who still exist today, despite all the events which seemed designed to eliminate us from Turtle Island. We see that the prophecy is coming to pass that in 1992 there will be a change for the better and we hope that the Quincentennial will give us the opportunity to educate the dominant society about who we are.

*Excerpted from* Seva, Spirt of Service, *Spring/Summer 1992.*

# Leonard Peltier:
# A Brief History

*It is not a new development for white society to steal from nonwhite peoples. When white society succeeds it's called colonialism. When white society's effort to colonize people are met with resistance it is called war. But when the colonized Indians of North America meet to stand and resist we are called criminals.*

— Leonard Peltier

In June 1975, a fatal gun battle erupted between FBI agents and members of the American Indian Movement. When the dust settled a Native American and two federal agents lay dead. The courts eventually indicted four members of AIM. Only one was convicted, Leonard Peltier. He was sentenced to two consecutive life sentences in a federal prison. Leonard Peltier has never denied his part in the gun battle, but contends that it was in self-defense.

For over 15 years supporters worldwide have considered Peltier a political prisoner. His support ranges from political and religous leaders to Amnesty International.

New evidence has come forth that helps substantiate Mr. Peltier's claims. Congress is now willing to hold congressional hearings.

Source: *Left Curve*

Norma Jean Croy, a Shasta indigenous woman, was arrested along with her brother, Hooty, in July 1978, after a shoot out involving her friends and the Yreka police in California which began when they got into a scuffle with a store clerk. A police car came onto the scene and gave chase to a car load of "Indians" leaving the scene. The terrified young Shastas fled to the hills where police called for reinforcements. Though the Croys and their friends only had a .22 hunting rifle, and the police were heavily armed, one cop was killed after he shot Hooty Croy in the back as Hooty was checking on his grandmother, where the fire-fight was taking place. Norma Jean was also shot in the back and another man was wounded in the groin as he was trying to surrender.

The cops fired over 200 semi-automatic rounds, the would-be victims only fired six shots. It was clearly self-defense, and racially motivated as well. Yet Hooty was sentenced to death and Norma Jean got life in prison. In 1985, the California Supreme Court finally granted Hooty a new trial. In 1990, he was found not guilty, for reasons of self-defense. Norma Jean, however, remains in prison after 12 years without any release date.

The campaign on behalf of Norma Jean is focusing on getting the California parole board to recognize Hooty's acquittal on the grounds of self-defense as the basis for parole for Norma Jean who was unarmed during the entire incident

***For information contact:***
*Norma Jean Croy Defense Committee
473 Jackson St. 3rd Flr.
San Francisco, CA 94111 (415) 986-5591*
***Write to:***
*Norma Jean Croy CCWF B080701
POB 1508
Chowchilla, CA 93610*

*Editor's Note: With the above information in the parole boards hand, Norma Jean has been denied parole for two years. Her defense attorneys are preparing a federal appeal.*

*Excerpted from* Prison News Service, *September/October 1991. Artwork courtesy of* Left Curve

# Shoshone Sisters Square off Against the Feds over Their Land and Their Rights

On the eve of the Quincentenary of Columbus coming to America, the Western Shoshone Nation is facing further invasion of its homeland in the Great Basin region of the Western US. The Bureau of Land Management has served the Dann sisters, members of the Western Shoshone Nation, with a trespass notice charging them with grazing cattle on land which was recognized as Western Shoshone land by the 1863 Treaty of Ruby Valley but is now claimed by the federal government.

In 1985, the U.S. Supreme Court ruled that the Western Shoshone had been paid for its lands because the Indian Claims Commission awarded the tribe $26 million dollars (about $1.15 per acre) in damages for the "taking" of the land. The Western Shoshone never accepted the money. "Our Mother Earth is not for sale—not now, not tomorrow, or not ever," said Carrie Dann. She recalls that they have been "grazing cattle on

> **Our land is being environmentally destroyed by the U.S. for nuclear testing, strip-mining, water exploration, and military land grants.**

these lands since we were girls just as our grandmother did before us. We have always used our treaty lands without paying fees or getting federal permits. I am grazing livestock on land which the federal government claims, but which we own."

The Western Shoshone National Council is asking supporters to join a nonviolent resistance to the threatened impounding and auctioning of the Dann's livestock and has issued "an urgent call for action and support to defend our homelands from unlawful U.S. government actions...Our land is being environmentally destroyed by the U.S. for nuclear testing, strip-mining, water exploration, and military land grants. These activities affect the health, well-being and culture of our people while giving very little, if anything, in return."

*Excerpted from* Desert Voices, *Fall 1991.*

# The Drug Crisis:
# It Touches All of Our Lives

Nearly everyone in the country can tell of a personal tragedy resulting from drug abuse, drug dealing or drug-related crime. Addicts in our families, crack houses on our streets, increasing violence in our neighborhoods, and drug sales in our schools. And the problem touches every race and every social class. Between 10-12% of all whites, African-Americans, and Latinos abuse drugs. Contrary to images projected by media, 78% of all illegal drug users are white and in New York city alone, 70% are affluent. The worst consequences may be suffered by the next generation: 1 out of every 10 newborns—nearly 375,000—has been exposed to illicit drugs.

### The War on Drugs...
· **It's ineffective.** Despite the Bush Administration's expenditure of over $20 billion in its war on drugs and its proclamation of victory, the crisis has worsened. In fact the number of addicts has increased since 1989, according to the Senate Judiciary Committee. The amount of violent crime has also escalated 11% since last year, the largest leap since 1986, primarily due to drug-related incidents. Since less than 1/3 of the drug war budget is allocated for treatment and prevention, 90% of those

who seek treatment are turned away due to underfunding.

· **It's unfair**. While those who abuse drugs come from every walk of life, people of color suffer disproportionately from the crisis. An FBI study states that while blacks represent 12% of all illegal drug users, blacks are 48% of *all* those arrested on cocaine and heroin charges.

· **It's counterproductive.** Although hundreds of millions of dollars have been poured into crop eradication campaigns, cocaine production has increased 28%, according to the Drug Enforcement Administration. These efforts have actually led to an increase of coca-producing areas.

· **It's dangerously hypocritical**. Small-time street dealers are imprisoned while drug kingpins go free, simply because they have done favors for the federal government. Senate and independent reports prove that our own government—through the CIA and other agencies—has cooperated with drug traffickers in exchange for their support for covert activities and unpopular wars. It was this alliance between government officials and drug running

supporters of the Nicaraguan contras that opened the floodgates of cocaine into our country in the 1980s. Senator Alphonse D'Amato (R-NY) has stated "I am absolutely convinced that we have...had various branches of our government-CIA, etc.—who have worked with drug traffickers for various geopolitical reasons. This is absolutely intolerable."

*Excerpted from a Christic Institute brochure titled "Causes & Cures: A National Teleconference on the Narcotics Epidemic," 11/9/91.*

> **While the Reagan Administration talked tough about fighting drugs, it never followed through on that rhetoric with meaningful actions. In fact...the Contra policy contributed to helping narcotics traffickers move illegal drugs into this country. The Administration failed to realize that the greatest national security threat to the United States in this hemisphere is posed by the flow of drugs—particularly of cocaine—onto our streets.**
> — *Senator John Kerry*
> *Massachussetts*

# Rehabilitating Rehabilitation
## *From the Mean Streets to Delancy Street*
### by Ayme Turnbull / *Macrocosm USA*

With nothing to lose, former heroin addict John Maher knew, there was everything to gain. He knew by experience that men and women who have lived the lives of addicts and criminals can best understand those trying to start life over again. An idea whose time had come is now a reality: A rehabilitation program "run by ex-cons for ex-cons," according to Maher.

In 1972, Maher had approached criminologist Mimi Silbert with hopes of creating this place.

"People are correctly outraged about our drug and crime problem. But we have led them to believe that if we only send enough people to prison the problem will stop. It won't. The years in which we've incarcerated the most people are the years in which our crime rate has been the highest. At some point, we're going to have to teach these people to live a different kind of life," Silbert explained.

She and Maher developed the Delancy Street center for criminal rehabilitation, vocational training, and drug and alcohol treatment for men and women, out of a common desire to create an environment in which "people who would be considered patients elsewhere are in charge." The goal of the program is to help ex-cons and addicts help each other.

Residents live together and teach one another, setting goals for themselves—to attain a high-school degree, a college diploma, to become skilled in a particular field of employment—and achieving them. Participants in the program earn what they receive and meanwhile become productive citizens no longer reliant upon government handouts. Delancy Street residents involve themselves in all types of community service, donate their time and efforts to various charitable organizations and follow a regular work program. Businesses managed and

staffed by Delancy Street residents net $1.9 million per year.

Residents stay for an average of four years, attending rap sessions three times each week and daily meetings and seminars. They are out in the job market during their final year at Delancy Street after receiving training in the areas of sales, manual labor, and office work in enterprises owned by the Delancy Street Foundation. This allows them to develop valuable skills in addition to the vocational, social, and cultural training they already receive through the program.

"I consider Delancy Street unquestionably the best program available to stop drug abuse and teach our young people how to lead successful lives," said former San Francisco mayor Diane Feinstein.

Today there are more than 800 Delancy Street residents in five locations in Los Angeles, San Francisco, Greensboro, N.C., Brewster, N.Y., and San Juan Pueblo, N.M.

"When I started working in prisons, it struck me how trapped, hopeless, and cynical these people were.

"In jail you're responsible for nothing—at Delancy Street, you're responsible for everything you do.

"Most therapy works from the inside out—if you understand your problems, then you'll change your behavior. We work the exact opposite way. We ask our residents, if at first it doesn't come naturally, to 'act as if.'

"Rather than have a 'program' with a paid staff—'experts' treating 'patients'—our philosophy is 'each one teach one.' When you're worrying about somebody else being decent and not lying and not giving up—when you're teaching them how to fight eventually, because you're saying it so much, you come to believe it yourself."

Silbert's philosophy of "each one teach one" has been an obvious success. More than 5000 former addicts and felons have emerged from Delancy Street as changed men and women with new perspectives on life. Many of them had never held a skilled job; over 85 percent had used heroin for more than ten years. One-quarter of the residents are women and half are minorities.

According to Silbert, "It doesn't matter why you were an addict or a burglar. What matters is that you believe in your ability to change."

*Sources:* Reader's Digest *and* California Magazine.

## The Failure of Prisons

### by D'shalom Starr Nation / *Prison News Service*

The conception of the prison ideology began to take form as far back in history as the reign of Louis XIV of France (1643-1715) when the Benedictine monk Mabillon wrote that, "...penitents might be secluded in cells like those of Cathesian monks, and there being employed in various sorts of labor." In 1790, on April 5th, the Quakers in America actualized this concept by erecting the first penitent(iary) house/jail on Walnut street in Philadelphia. Since the American birth of the penitentiary it has grown into a vicious, abominable and fruitless system which now traverses the country. The human misery and wholesale corruption of value systems has been so dramatic in proportion that even the Quakers themselves have joined in mass to oppose and impede its malicious expansion and socially destructive work.

There is voluminous evidence that prisons do not work for the social good. It is irrefutable that prison populations are nearly 50% Afro-American, yet Afro-Americans constitute only 6% of the U.S. population. (Latinos come second on this ill-proportioned scale.) "Black men," wrote George Jackson in 1970, "born in the U.S. and fortunate enough to live past the age of 18 are conditioned to accept the inevitability of prison. For most of us, it simply looms as the next phase in a sequence of humiliations."

In the mid 80s, 47% of the prisoners were unemployed before incarceration.

*Excerpted from* Prison News Service, *November/December 1991.*

> • 804,000 inmates now populate US prisons, up from 330,000 in 1980.
>
> • Nearly 50% of federal inmates are drug offenders, compared with 25% in 1980. The 1991 murder rate in the US was 9.9 per 100,000 people.
>
> — *USA Today, 4/27/92*

## More People are Imprisoned in the U.S. than Anywhere Else in the World

With more than 1 million people behind bars, the United States imprisons a bigger share of its population than any other nation, reports John Flesher of Associated Press. 426 of every 100,000 U.S. residents are incarcerated, at an annual cost of $16 billion. South Africa has the second highest imprisonment rate, with 333 per 100,000 residents. The Soviet Union is third, with 268 per 100,000.

Incarceration in Europe is generally around 35 to 120 per 100,000 residents, and in the Asian countries, from 21 to 140 per 100,000.

Marc Mauer, assistant director of The Sentencing Project, a non-profit research organization which promotes sentencing reforms and alternatives, states that "the same policies which have helped make us a world leader in incarceration have clearly failed to make us a safer nation. We need a fundamental change of direction, toward given programs and policies that work to reduce both imprisonment and crime."

Commenting on the report, Rep. John Conyers of Michigan and chairman of the House Government Operations Committee said "We've got to stop jailing and start rehabilitating. We can build all the jails we think we need and slam the doors on thousands of people, but it won't make a bit of difference until we address the fundamental causes of crime."

The U.S. Sentencing Commission says new sentencing guidelines and tougher penalties for drug law violations may result in a 119% increase in the federal prison population from 1987 to 1997. The proportion of criminals in prison jumped 54% from 1980 to 1987.

According to The Sentencing Project Report, drug-related crime is the biggest cause of the prison population explosion. With the war on drugs waged primarily through the criminal justice system and disproportionately targeting inner-city drug users, the end result is an increasing number of prisoners and an even larger share of black inmates.

A 1989 Delaware study found that the annual cost of imprisoning a criminal was $17,761, while putting the person on probation cost $569 a year. The study said that for every drug offender sentenced to prison,

*Reprinted from* Artpolice, *Summer 1989, vol. 1G, no. 2*

three could be treated in an impatient program and sixteen could be treated as out patients.

*Excerpted from* The Cultivator, *vol. 15, no. 4, 1991.*

# Life in the Big House

### *by Bonnie Urfer* / **the Insider**

FCI Lexington is a maximum security federal prison for women in Lexington, Kentucky. What follows is about the terror, the oppression and incredible mental torture inflicted on each prisoner in the name of justice. It's about the violence we all must learn to live with inside those walls as we desperately try to maintain our sanity and hope, and our tempers.

From the moment I entered the compound and passed the public reception and visiting area, everything grew dingy and closed in. Every door was locked, every window barred. The prison is built in a series of rectangles. Life is compacted into a few of the buildings and the open courtyard of one quadrangle. At most hours of the day, this central area—landscaped with bushes, grass, and decorative benches—is off limits for strolling. We are restricted to the sidewalk that borders the interior perimeters of our prison walls and always in view of a lot of guards.

The Bureau of Prison's guards are sometimes called cops. It's very unfortunate that almost all of them are men. Most of the women incarcerated in Lexington have lived with terrible violence from men who have abused them in numerous ways. I can't quite figure out how a woman can possibly begin to gain an ounce of self-respect and internal strength with an army of men maintaining total and absolute control over her life.

At Lexington, there are 1,250 women. The unit (building) I live in holds 300. Within each unit are long wings of hallways, given the derogatory term "alleys." Fifty women live on my alley. We all share two toilets and two showers. Needless to say, waiting in line to clean oneself or engage in normal bodily functions can be long and painful. The room I reside in holds six women in cramped quarters. Movement is difficult when we're all in the room together. The room itself contains three sets of bunk beds and a locker for each woman, similar to those most of us had in high school. There is no personal space, no place to sit but on one's upper or lower bunk, no privacy whatsoever, and little quiet.

Of the half dozen cops who work the shifts where I live, only one is a woman. As a result, men have the right to walk into any woman's room or the bathrooms or showers anytime they wish, and they do. Most often, they patrol randomly hoping to catch prisoners engaged in any illegal activity, although I often wonder what else they hope to see.

In addition to long lines and daily routines made deliberately difficult and frustrating, there are pages of rules and regulations that

No Picnic

need to be obeyed. Disobeying any one could result in extra duties, lost parole or good time, or additional charges depending on the infraction.

The rule I find most contemptible is the restriction on human contact. There is a lot of pain in prison, a lot of loneliness, a lot of depression. When a person is absolutely forbidden to console another person with a hug of compassion, I consider it inhumane. If two women are caught in an embrace of love, it's almost guaranteed they will be sent to segregation and risk losing all of their earned good time. This rule in no way allows endearment of one to another. It disallows an inherent need for nurturing. It reverses the human urge to love and trust. It's a violence of the worse kind similar to tearing babies from the arms of mothers and then telling them they can look, but never touch. It's damaging to each woman and based on an old fossilized fear of homosexuality, totally disregarding basic imperative needs. This law is in no way diminishes the sexual activities of women in Lexington, but it does build barriers between wise women of any sexual persuasion to engage in simple acts of tenderness not akin to sexuality.

The most difficult thing for me to deal with is the absolute lack of private, quiet space. It's impossible to find a place to go to be alone to think, to meditate, to sort out

## This insanity is everyone's problem. Building more of these hell holes is not the solution.

feelings. It's close to impossible to even find a table and chair to sit at and write, and if you do find one, it's not a silent space. No place is. The atmosphere is one of continuous chaos and tension, busyness and activity, complaints and loud conversation. It keeps a person in a constant state of mental duress, longing for calm and rest. But the Bureau of Prisons is not interested in the mental or physical health of its prisoners. The main purpose of imprisonment has always been, and continues to be, punishment. Lexington does boast periodic programs for drug addicts, but they are flimsy, short-lived, bogus attempts to educate dependent persons on the virtues of independence as each individual is completely dependent on an institution that adheres to nothing but violence and dependence.

We must develop alternatives to this appalling practice of shutting people into boxes, of ignoring the source of crime, of stealing a person's life for a mistake, of punishing children for the errors of their parents, of forcing such intense violence on so many people without regard to the future. This insanity is everyone's problem. Building more of these hell holes is not the solution.

*Bonnie Urfer wrote this article while serving two years for civil disobedience. She is a Nukewatch staff member and co-director of the Progressive Foundation.*

*Excerpted from* the Insider, *a newsletter of the Women's Jail Project, Spring 1991.*

- **Number of Americans sentenced to death since 1900 who were later found to be innocent: 139**

- **Number of Americans who were executed, who were later found to be innocent: 26**

- **2,457 people were on U.S. Death Rows as of 1991**

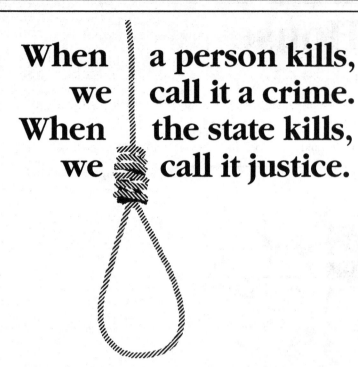

# When a person kills, we call it a crime. When the state kills, we call it justice.

## But is it justice?

- When only the poor are executed.
- When the races of the victim and the accused predict the sentence.
- When innocent people are still sentenced to death.
- When the mentally retarded are executed.

The death penalty does not protect us—instead, it promotes violent crime. An execution costs six times more than a life sentence. The death penalty does nothing to address those most in need—victims' families.

*When the state kills it makes each of us a killer. Killing is no way to show that killing is wrong.*

*Source: Amnesty International, Orange County Newsletter, November 1989*

**In 1988, handguns killed 7 people in Great Britain, 19 in Switzerland, 25 in Israel, 13 in Australia 8 in Canada, and 8,915 in the United States.**

*Source: Handgun Control, Inc.*

# Letters have been saving lives for decades...

*When the first two hundred letters came, the guards gave me back my clothes. Then the next two hundred letters came, and the prison director came to see me. When the next pile of letters arrived, the director got in touch with his superior. The letters kept coming and coming: three thousand of them. The President was informed. The letters still kept arriving, and the President called the prison and told them to let me go.*

— A released prisoner of conscience from the Dominican Republic

*Protests were taking place... the food rations increased and the beatings were fewer. Letters from abroad were translated and passed around from cell to cell, but when the letters stopped, the dirty food and repression started again.*

A released prisoner of conscience from Vietnam.

Thousands of people are in prison because of their beliefs. Many are held without charge or trial. Torture and the death penalty are widespread. In many countries men, women, and children have 'disappeared' after being taken into official custody. Still others have been killed without any pretense of legality. These human rights abuses occur in countries of widely differing ideologies.

Amnesty International is a worldwide movement of people acting on the conviction that governments must not deny individuals their basic human rights. The organization was awarded the 1977 Nobel Peace Prize for its efforts to promote global observance of the United Nations Universal Declaration of Human Rights.

Amnesty International works specifically for:
- ✍ the release of prisoners of conscience -- men, women, and children imprisoned for their beliefs, color, sex, ethnic origin, language, or religion, provided they have neither used nor advocated violence;
- ✍ fair and prompt trials for all political prisoners;
- ✍ an end to torture and executions in all cases.

*Excerpted from Amnesty International brochure.*

**BIG Pictures** ©1991 By Dan Dunivant

*Reprinted from Earth Journal, February 1991.*

# A Day In November

## by James L. Beathard / *Endeavor*

Anytime the death penalty is made a reality in a nation or state problems immediately arise. Naturally, there are the usual and valid criticisms, such as the financial burden such extreme measures impose on a court system. Or the risk run in the unavoidable "questionable" causes and "margin of error" mistakes resulting in an innocent person being executed. And no one can deny the statistical evidence proving that the death penalty at best provides no deterrence and, in fact, appears to exacerbate the frequency of violent crimes. As incontrovertible as these problems are they are still not as damning as the inevitable debasement of society the death penalty causes. So often the words "dehumanizing" and "immoral" are used without any tangible proof so that the claims are easily dismissed by proponents of Capital Punishment as subjective terms, as relative value judgments. But these are not always intangible, apparently mystic or philosophical pronouncements. I have witnessed this debasement occurring in very real, very concrete ways.

The world was unfortunate enough to have witnessed the spectacle that surrounded the Bundy execution. A sizeable proportion of people participated with pleasure in circus atmosphere antics and activities amounting to a nationwide celebration of death. Concerts were staged, commemorative items sold, parties were held and speeches were made all in celebration of the taking of a human life. It was as if the State sanctioned killing had released some malicious facet of human nature in otherwise good people. One might suggest that all the activ-

ity was merely a perception based on selective media coverage. I know different. I've seen it happen when there were no cameras or reporters.

In the very early morning hours one day this last November I had to stop at the Walls Unit (that's the main unit where the administration sections are housed as well as the Death Chamber) on my way to the state's prison medical unit at Galveston. While at the Walls I was left in the transport van wearing

"NEVER GET A PASS JOE THE CRIME RATE IS TERRIBLE OUT THERE!"

©1992 by Raee Mattson

the customary ten-plus pounds of chains and shackles, parked only yards from the Death Chamber, yards from where a friend, Donald Franklin, had been put to death only hours before. The two guards driving the van went to get something to eat, leaving another pair of guards watching the van from outside. These two guards had been on duty during Franklin's execution and while not permitted to watch the execution itself they were, apparent from their conversation, permitted to see the body afterwards. They spoke of this as a privilege and compared the total of bodies from past executions they had each viewed. They spoke of the state of the corpse in disgusting ways, even laughing about

watching one of the other guards placing the victim's hands in degrading positions. A third guard, a younger one, came and joined the conversation, lamenting that he'd not been one of the "lucky ones" who'd seen the body or any of the past ones. The older of the three assured the lad that there were plenty of executions coming up and that he'd see to it the boy got to see at least one of them. At that the other guard pointed out that "the guy in the van" (me) was from Death Row. The young guy seemed excited and asked if that meant, "there was going to be another party tonight". He was visibly disappointed when told that I was only passing through on my way to the medical unit and not there to die. There is no way to describe how watching and listening to those ghouls made me feel, no way to characterize the nausea and disgust that any person with the slightest bit of human compassion would feel.

Such is the effect, even with no cameras or reporters to witness, that State sanctioned killing has on people, what kinds of behaviour and thoughts are elicited. Never have I seen anything of that caliber occur among my fellow inmates on Death Row—never have I seen a "Celebration of Death". What I have seen here are the regrets and the remorse. And that makes we wonder—will society ever learn about compassion, regret, or remorse?

*Originally appeared in* Endeavor, *a prison newsletter.*

*Excerpted from* Prison News Service, *September/October 1991.*

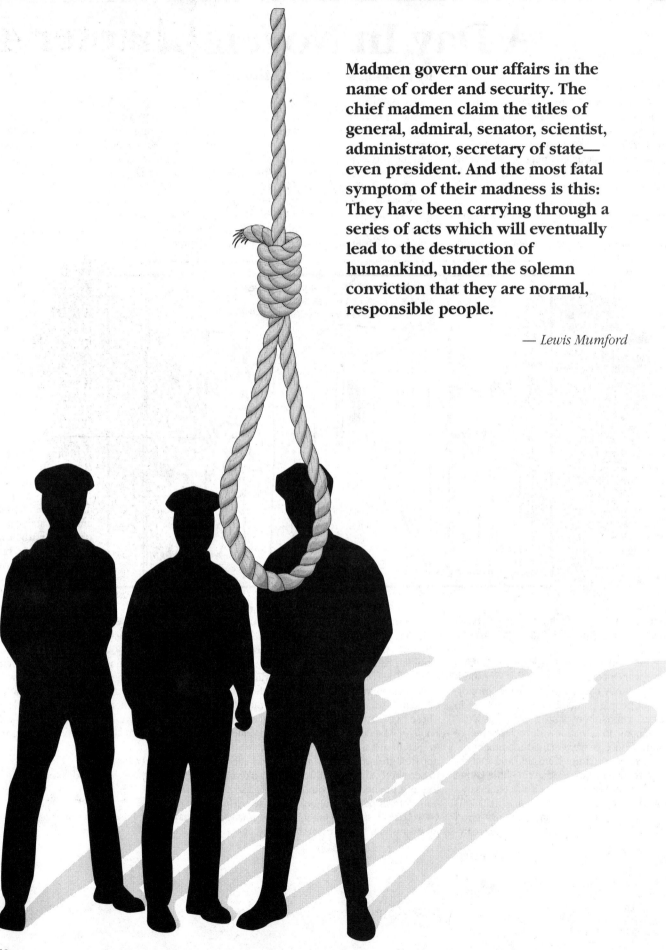

Madmen govern our affairs in the name of order and security. The chief madmen claim the titles of general, admiral, senator, scientist, administrator, secretary of state—even president. And the most fatal symptom of their madness is this: They have been carrying through a series of acts which will eventually lead to the destruction of humankind, under the solemn conviction that they are normal, responsible people.

— *Lewis Mumford*

# Chapter 4

# *Ecology*

The Earth's biosphere is in crisis: a growing hole in the Earth's protective ozone, a dramatic increase in greenhouse gases, a declining biodiversity, and a world population inexorably overtaking its food supply. In our bioregions the crisis comes to us in themes tailored to where we live. The specific events may be polluted and dwindling water supplies, lack of breathable air, loss of forests, wetlands or other natural treasures; but the assault seems ever more pervasive, extending from poisons in our foods to our climate and even into our wilderness retreats.

*Excerpted from "Hands of the Earth" by Karl Ostrom an article that appeared in* The Egg: An Eco-Justice Quarterly, *Winter 1990-1991.*

*We face the question whether a still higher "standard of living" is worth its cost in things natural, wild, and free. For us of the minority, the opportunity to see geese is more important than television, and the chance to find a pasqueflower is a right as inalienable as free speech.*

Aldo Leopold (1886-1948)

# Bioregions and Transnational Zones

### by Rene Wadlow / *Transnational Perspectives*

*A bioregion is an area of land defined, not by political boundaries—cities, states, countries—but by the natural, biological and geological features that cast the real identity of a place. A bioregion can be identified by its mountain ranges and rivers, its vegetation, weather patterns or soil types, or its patterns of animal habitats, whether birds, ground mammals or humans. Bioregionalists further subdivide large regions into individual local watersheds and mountain ranges.*

— Brian Tokar

Bioregionalism can be described as the vision of human society interwoven with the warp and weft of the land, a part of the intricate fabric of life; understanding and working within the natural rhythm and cycles of a particular region. Such a society would be fueled by benign energy sources, such as the sun, wind, water, and biomass. Food and basic commodities can be produced locally, using regenerative, ecological agriculture, intensive gardening, selective forestry, and wholistic resource management. Clean air, clean water, green belts and natural areas are considered inalienable rights of all inhabitants of a region. This definition of inhabitant includes all lifeforms. All species are seen as indispensible parts of the interplay of matter and energy we call life.

Bioregionalism weds the study of ecology and anthropology with an optimistic outlook of a human race backing away from the brink of annihilation by lovingly embracing the Mother Earth.

When we apply an ecological perspective it becomes clear that poor resource management and environmentally destructive practices are socially, economically and spiritually irresponsible. The ethic of exploitation should be replaced with that of stewardship, of maintaining and preserving, respecting and loving the Earth for all time.

A new ethic, embracing plants and animals as well as people, is required for human societies to live in harmony with the natural world on which we depend for survival and well being. Such a new ethic—really a new consciousness—would stress a concern for community and satisfying human relationships. There would be an emphasis on the quality of face-to-face relations, based on mutual aid and reverence for all beings and their environment. Popular participation in decision-making would be an important part of the political and economic structures.

Development would be seen as a means of liberation and fulfillment of the person both as an individual and as a social being. Development would arise from the inner core of the cultural heritage, from the creativity of individuals, through creative exchanges with other groups. Social consciousness would bind people together in a cultural identity with a collective memory but with the organizational ability to respond to new problems with technological adaptability.

Development would take cognizance of the ecological, economic, social and cultural realities with a holistic, not a fragmented, view to ensure that socially, economically, and ecologically-sound development for all the people takes place and that the benefits from development reach the people as a whole.

Although there is a growing realization that such a new ethic is necessary, an analysis of the world society indicates clearly that such an ethic is not operational. The combined destructive impacts of a poor majority of humanity struggling to stay alive and an affluent minority consuming most of the world's resources are undermining the means by which all people can survive and flourish. The poor caught in a daily struggle for enough food and fuel to stay alive strip the land bare of trees and bushes for firewood. They clear steep hillsides for farming only to have the slopes washed out by rains. They overgraze grassy drylands and overfish and overhunt local wildlife. Many migrate to crowded cities where they find shelter in slums and shanty towns, often falling victim to hunger and disease.

At the same time the rich and powerful, both in relative and in absolute terms, continue to exploit resources as if there were no future generations, as if there were no long-range consequences to current actions.

The Earth and its ecological conditions are being increasingly studied, in part through the use of mapping satellites. We have an increasingly accurate picture of the destruction of forests, the desertification of fruitful areas, the loss of topsoil, the salinization of irrigated areas. The "state of the Earth" is increasingly clear. There is even widespread agreement on how to combat these ecological ills through renewable resource development, forest husbandry and replanting, through the use of organic agriculture and other techniques of regeneration.

There are an increasing number of organizations: government programs, non-governmental societies, ecological political parties working to improve the environment and develop a sustainable world society.

Yet the results of all these efforts still fall far short of the needs, and destruction keeps well ahead of regeneration.

One of the paradoxes of the efforts for a sustainable society is that while individuals must see the Earth as a whole, they must also care about units small enough so as to be able to carry out effective action to preserve and restore. The effort to call attention to life in a specific area—large enough to be socially diverse but small enough to be the subject of organized human action—is the contribution of bioregionalism. Bioregionalism has inspired a new sense of place, of attunement with natural cycles, of appreciation of the common whole of which the human and the non-human residents of a region are closely interrelated parts.

> ## The poor caught in a daily struggle for enough food and fuel to stay alive strip the land bare of trees and bushes for firewood.

Awareness of the processes of life in the bioregion encourages local self-reliance while recognizing interregional dependency as well as the connection to the system as a whole. As David Haenke has written: "These bioregions are geographical areas which are defined by natural boundaries, such as rivers, or particular land forms which set them off as distinct from adjacent regions. Each bioregion is further defined by the kinds of flora and fauna that grow within it, which may be unique to it, or just exist in greater numbers of density than in adjoining areas. Unique human cultures which are shaped by the rigors, abundances, and general nature of the bioregion also contribute to its definition. Bioregional boundaries, being created by nature, often cross the arbitrary political lines drawn by humans in their creation of nations, states, and other subunits.

"Bioregionalism deals with the bioregion as a whole system comprised of a set of diverse, integrated natural subsystems (atmospheric, hydrologic, biologic, geologic) run by ecological laws with which humans (as one species among many) must work in cooperation if there is to be a sustainable future. These laws form the basis for the design of all long-term human systems, economic, technological, agricultural, and political. Political ecology is the politics of bioregionalism."

Thus bioregionalism is a useful focus for action, a space large enough to be ecologically meaningful, small enough to correspond to the sense of space of the inhabitants. Bioregions may be (though too often are not) the current political-administrative regions of states.

Bioregionalism as an ideology and as a focus of planning is closely linked to two other concepts: popular participation in meaningful decision-making and trans-frontier cooperation. Disappointment over the slow rate of progress in improving the lives of the poor has led to a reexamination of approaches to development. From a primary focus on economic growth via capital intensive technology and governmental centralized planning, we have seen a shift in emphasis to equity of distribution, the integration of all sectors of society into the modern economic sector, and community self reliance. One result of the emphasis on community is a renewed interest in popular participation in meaningful decision-making.

One answer to why the rural poor stay poor in many countries is that they are rarely well organized, and if they do organize so as to be able to participate meaningfully, they are often repressed.

In some countries, such as Sri Lanka, there is a rich history of rural organizations: village councils, rural development societies, cultivation committees, agricultural productivity committees, women's societies, cooperatives and welfare associations. But in the case of each such association one must ask "who holds the power, and who is left out?" Rural communities in the Third World, as elsewhere, are not homogeneous entities. In most villages there exist sharp contradictions among different groups with conflicts of interest. There are dominance/dependence relations which need to be understood. These relations often give power in rural associations to the already dominant—the larger landlord, the trader, the money lender. These local elite often control institutions of local administration, law enforcement and adjudication.

Nevertheless, a bioregional focus provides a meaningful framework for the empowerment of people. Progress in development needs an area large enough to provide economic and cultural diversity. Such an area must be larger than a single community. Given the importance of ecological factors: land use, water sharing, forests etc, a bioregion provides a framework for the empowerment of people with the idea of power as independent strength, ability, control over one's own life, competence to deal with one's environment out of one's own energy and resources rather than on the basis of dependence.

*Excerpted from* Transnational Perspectives, *vol. 14, no. 2, 1988.*

# What is Global Warming?

Over the past century, the human species has turned the Earth into one huge unplanned experiment. By releasing unprecedented amounts of greenhouse gases (carbon dioxide, methane, chlorofluorocarbons, nitrous oxide and gases that create tropospheric ozone) into the atmosphere, we have in effect, turned up the global thermostat. Greenhouse gases act in a fashion similar to the windshield of a car parked in the sun, allowing light-energy to pass through, but then trapping the re-emitted heat. The greenhouse effect occurs naturally and without it the Earth would be ice-covered and uninhabitable. However, over the past century, human practices have led to an increased buildup of greenhouse gases.

> **"Scientific evidence of global warming is not conclusive in any case."**
>
> President George Bush
> Houston, Texas, July 1991

Scientists already have detected a 1°F temperature rise, which may be due to the greenhouse effect. They predict a further increase of between 4° and 9°F by the middle of the next century if greenhouse gas emissions grow at expected rates. The six warmest years of the century have been in the 1980s, with 1987 and 1988 being the hottest on record. As world population and fossil fuel use grow, greater quantities of greenhouse gases will be released into the atmosphere.

Carbon dioxide (which accounts for approximately half of the global warming trend), nitrous oxide and tropospheric ozone are by-products of burning fossil fuels (coal, oil and gas) and wood. It is important to note that burning natural gas releases 70 percent as much carbon dioxide per unit of energy as oil, and half that of coal. Forests and oceans are natural sinks for carbon dioxide, but are unable to absorb the quantities currently being emitted. Deforestation releases large quantities of carbon dioxide as well as methane, carbon monoxide, ozone and nitrous oxide. Methane, which accounts for 18 percent of the greenhouse effects, also is produced by swamps, cattle, rice paddies, landfills, termites, and fossil fuels. Chlorofluorocarbons (CFCs), used in refrigerators and air conditioners, as foam blowers, as circuit board cleaners and as aerosol propellants, account for 17 percent of the greenhouse effect.

Scientists predict that as global temperatures rise, life on Earth will face a series of potentially disastrous threats. Precipitation will decline in some areas, leading to crop failure and expanding deserts. Elsewhere, rainfall will increase, causing flooding and erosion. Changes in habitat could lead to mass extinctions of plants and animals that are unable to migrate to more compatible climates. And sea levels will rise, flooding coastal areas and causing salt water intrusion into coastal aquifers.

*Excerpted from* Earthline Newsletter, *Earthday 1990.*

# What Consumers can do to Protect the Ozone Layer

There are several things that individual consumers can do to protect the ozone layer. Back in the 1970s, long before the government banned most CFC aerosol sprays, consumers simply stopped buying them once they learned about the damage those aerosols caused to the ozone layer. Here are things that consumers can do today:

**Leaky auto air conditioners are now the single largest source of CFC emissions to the atmosphere in the United States.**

· When your car air conditioning breaks, don't just refill it—get it fixed properly. CFCs are sold in 14-ounce cans at auto supply stores. But if you don't fix the air conditioner's leak, the CFCs you

©1991 Dan Dunivant.
Reprinted from Earth Journal, April 1991

put in it today will head toward the stratosphere next week.

- Find a repair shop that recycles CFCs. A broken auto air conditioner still holds most of its CFC charge. Most repair shops let it loose into the air and refill the unit with new CFCs. But inexpensive machines are now available to capture, clean, and recycle the used CFCs.

- Don't have unnecessary service done to your car's air conditioner. The CFCs inside will only be released into the air. Wait until the air conditioning breaks—and then have it fixed at a repair shop that will recycle the CFCs.

**Some foam plastic packaging materials are made with CFCs.**

- Avoid foam packaging—not only does some of it contain ozone depleting chemicals, but it's also a monumental solid waste problem, since only a tiny fraction of it is recycled.

**Foam plastic building insulation is made with CFCs that eventually leak into the air. Energy-efficient foams made with other blowing agents are still several years away.**

- Consider using fiberglass, cellulose [some cellulose has been determined to contain toxic materials], or other materials. These other materials must be thicker to get the same insulation value. But if you have the space, you can use them without losing energy efficiency.

**Halon fire extinguishers are being marketed for home use. Their ozone-depleting contents eventually leak into the air even if you never have a fire.**

- Don't buy halon fire extinguishers for ordinary home use. Traditional types of fire extinguishers will do the job.

**The ozone depleting chemical methyl chloroform is contained in a surprising number of consumer products, including bug killers and foggers, fabric protectors, waterproofings, spray-on cleaners and spot removers, shoe polish sprays, and other aerosols.**

- Read the contents of these products, and don't buy the ones that contain 1,1,1-trichloroethane, which is how methyl chloroform is listed on product labels. All these items can be made without ozone-depleting chemicals; if you need to use these products, look for ones without methyl chloroform.

**Some CFC aerosols are still on the market, even though EPA banned nonessential uses of CFCs as an aerosol propellant in 1978.**

- Check the contents of aerosols such as photographers' dust removers; boat horns;

and clean sprays for sewing machines, VCRs, and electronic equipment. Although many have stopped using the most harmful kind of CFC, the CFC or HCFC used in these aerosols still destroys the ozone layer. Look for alternative products that don't contain any CFCs. Better still, avoid aerosols whenever possible; even the aerosols that don't contain ozone-depleting chemicals have chemicals that contribute to smog.

Unfortunately, with many products consumers don't have much choice right now. You can't buy a refrigerator without CFCs in it, or a computer that was not made with CFC solvents. But more products made with safe alternatives will be coming on the market over the next few years.

*Excerpted from* NRDC Newsline, *March/April 1990.*

# Biodiversity:
## *The Key to Saving Life on Earth*
### by Donella H. Meadows / *Land Stewardship Letter*

The ozone hole and the greenhouse effect have entered our public vocabulary, but we have no catchy label for the third great environmental problem of the late 20th century. The experts call it "the loss of biodiversity."

Biodiversity obviously has something to do with pandas, tigers and tropical forests. But preserving biodiversity is a much bigger job than protecting rain forests or charismatic megafauna. It's the job of protecting all life—microscopic creepy-crawlies as well as elephants and condors and all life's habitats—tundra, prairie and swamp as well as forests.

Why care about tundra, swamp, blue beetles or little bluestem grasses? Ecologists give three reasons, which boil down to simple self-interest on three levels of escalating importance.

Biodiversity has both immediate and potential economic value. This is the argument most commonly put forward to defend biodiversity, because it's the one our culture is most ready to hear. It cites the importance of the industries most directly dependent upon nature-fisheries, forestry, tourism, recreation and the harvesting of wild foods, medicines, dyes, rubber and chemicals.

Some ecologists are so tired of this line of reasoning that they refer wearily to the "Madagascar periwinkle argument." That obscure plant yields the drugs vincristine and

vinblastine, which have revolutionized the treatment of leukemia. About a third of all modern medicines have derived from molds and plants.

The potential for future discoveries is astounding. The total number of species of life is somewhere between 10 million and 30 million, only 1.7 million of which we have named, only a fraction of which we have tested for usefulness.

The economic value of biodiversity is very

real, but ecologists hate the argument because it is both arrogant and trivial. It assumes that the Earth's millions of species are here to serve the economic purposes of just one species. And even if you buy that idea, it misses the larger and more valuable ways that nature serves us.

Biodiversity performs environmental services beyond price. How would you like the job of pollinating trillions of apple blossoms some sunny afternoon in May? It's conceivable, maybe, that you could invent a machine to do it, but inconceivable that the machine could work as elegantly and cheaply as the honeybee, much less make honey on the side.

Suppose you were assigned to turn every bit of dead organic matter, from fallen leaves to urban garbage, into nutrients that feed new life. Even if you knew how, what would it cost? A host of bacteria, molds, mites and worms do it for free. If they ever stopped, all life would stop. We would not last long if green plants stopped turning our exhaled carbon dioxide back into oxygen. Plants would not last long if a few genera of soil bacteria stopped turning nitrogen from the air into nitrate fertilizer.

Human reckoning cannot put a value on the services performed by the ecosystems of Earth. These services include the cleansing of air and water, flood control, drought prevention, pest control, temperature regulation and maintenance of the world's most valuable library—the genes of all living organisms.

Biodiversity contains the accumulated wisdom of nature and the key to its future. If you ever wanted to destroy a society, you would burn its libraries and kill its intellectuals. You would destroy its knowledge. Nature's knowledge is contained in the DNA within living cells. The variety of that genetic information is the driving engine of evolution, the immune system for life, the source of adaptability—not just the variety of species but also the variety of individuals within each species.

Individuals are never quite alike. Each is genetically unique mostly in subterranean ways that will only appear in future generations. We recognize that is true of human beings. Plant and animal breeders recognize it in dogs, cattle, wheat, roses, apples. The only reason they can bring forth bigger fruits or sweeter smells or disease resistance is that those traits are already present in the genes carried by some individuals.

The amount of information in a single cell is hard to comprehend. A simple one-celled bacterium can carry genes for 1,000 traits, a flowering plant for 400,000. Biologist E.O.

Wilson says the information in the genes of an ordinary house mouse, if translated into printed letters, would fill all the 15 editions of the Encyclopedia Britannica that have been published since 1768.

The wealth of genetic information has been selected over billions of years to fit the ever-changing necessities of the planet. As Earth's atmosphere filled with oxygen, as land masses drifted apart, as humans invented agriculture and altered the land, there were lurking within individuals pieces of genetic code that allowed them to defend against or take advantage of the changes. These individuals were more fit for the new environment. They bred more successfully. The population began to take on their characteristics. New species came into being.

Biodiversity is the accumulation of all life's past adaptations, and it is the basis for all further adaptations (even those mediated by human gene-splicers).

That's why ecologists value biodiversity as one of Earth's great resources. It's why they take seriously the loss of even the most insignificant species; why they defend not only the preservation of species but the preservation of populations within species, and why they regard the rate of human-induced extinctions as an unparalleled catastrophe.

> **"If the United States has to be the only one standing against the Biodiversity Treaty as it now stands, then so be it."**
>
> — President George Bush

We don't know how many species we are eliminating, because we don't know how many species there are. It's a fair guess that, at the rate we're destroying habitat, we're pushing to extinction about one species every hour. That doesn't count the species whose populations are being reduced so greatly that diversity within the population is essentially gone. Earth has not seen a spasm of extinctions like this for 65 million years.

Biodiversity cannot be maintained by protecting a few species in a zoo, nor by preserving greenbelts or even national parks. To function properly nature needs more room than that. It can maintain itself, however, without human expense, without zookeepers, park rangers, foresters or gene banks. All it needs is to be left alone.

To provide their priceless pollination service, the honeybees ask only that we stop saturating the landscape with poisons, stop paving the meadows where bee-food grows and leave them enough honey to get through the winter.

To maintain our planet, our lives and our future potential, the other species have similar requests, all of which add up to: Control yourselves. Control your numbers. Control your greed. See yourselves as what you are, part of an interdependent biological community—the most intelligent part, though you don't often act that way.

So act that way, either out of a moral respect for something magnificent that you didn't create and do not understand, or out of a practical interest in your own survival.

*Excerpted from the* Land Sewardship Letter, *Summer 1990.*

*Greenpeace activists attempting to prevent the rape of the oceans by driftnets, a campaign that often succeeds in saving dolphins. Photo courtesy of Greenpeace.*

# WAR OF THE WORLDS: PEOPLE VS. NATURE

### by Kevin McGuire / *Aqua Terra*

*The following is a report written by an eighteen year old from Eureka Springs [Arkansas]. His alarming and graphic overview of the water crisis merits publication because of its comprehensive perspective.*

In the last few decades, billions upon billions of tons of pollution have been dumped into our world's oceans, lakes, rivers and streams with its effects hard to see. For example, Boston Harbor, or even San Francisco Bay, are still delightful to look at from the shore. What is happening underwater is quite another matter. Scuba divers talk of swimming through clouds of toilet paper and half-dissolved feces, of bay bottoms covered by a foul and toxic combination of sediment, sewage and petrochemical waste appropriately known as "black mayon-

our coastal regions. In Chesapeake Bay, pollution and salinity have decimated fish and oyster harvests. PCBs and heavy metals have been detected in sediments and fish. In New York and New Jersey, hypodermic needles, swabs, IV tubing and other medical wastes have fouled the shores. These incidents are not only occurring in the U.S., but they are also happening all over the world. With help from our government and a little careful planning, we may be able to stop an irreversible effect upon our waters.

The first trouble area that must be dealt with is industrial pollution. From industries come many hazardous wastes such as PCBs polychlorinated-biphenyls, phosphates, nitrates, (heavy) metals such as cadmium, lead, zinc, copper and arsenic. Also, petroleum hydrocarbons that stem from the industrial

inlets. Once the oxygen level in the water has been depleted, both marine plant and animal life are literally choked off. Known as "dead zones" because they leave nothing behind but dead fish and plants, they are also the cause of the red and brown tides that are becoming more common in coastal areas.

There are many frightening incidents where these so-called "dead zones" have quietly destroyed thousands of miles of our once fertile oceans and fresh waters. For example, the nitrate and phosphate pollution from agricultural runoff and industrial discharge have been contributing to a growth of a 3,000 square mile dead zone near the mouth of the Mississippi River in the Gulf of Mexico. In the Great Lakes, the phosphorous pollution, along with other hazardous contaminants, are literally choking off much of

naise." Fishermen haul in lobsters and crabs covered with mysterious "burn holes" and fish whose fins are rotting off. Marine biologists track massive tides of algae blooms fed by nitrate and phosphate pollution.

Across the nation, millions of gallons of murky, raw sewage are leaking through pipes, gushing out of manholes, backing up into basements and washing onto our shores. These waters are alive with pathogens capable of killing us. Because seventy percent of our population lives on or near the coast, our oceans are becoming strained from the intense amount of pollution that is dumped daily into its waters. There are many prime examples of the death and decay of

discharge, radioactive wastes from nuclear reactors and dump sites pollutes our oceans, lakes, rivers, and streams. Many other pollutants, such as acid rain, which is the result of the pollution in the air, wreak havoc on our waters.

Two of the most deadly types of industrial pollution are nitrates and phosphates. These chemicals come from non-point pollution, a grab bag term that refers to all forms of unregulated run-off from the land. Nitrogen and phosphorous compounds that are used mainly in industries as fertilizers. These nutrients which are not in themselves toxic, feed algae blooms, which can gradually suck the dissolved-oxygen content from bays and

the marine life in most of the lakes. When carcasses of more than a dozen whales washed up on Cape Cod in the autumn of 1988, their deaths were attributed to paralytic shellfish poisoning that was passed along the food chain from the toxic chemicals within algae blooms. In that same time period, a red tide off the coast of the Carolinas killed several thousand mullet and all but wiped out the scallop population. The cause was once again the algae blooms. Studies conducted in 1986 showed that large regions of bottom in the North and Baltic Seas were anoxic and lifeless, killed by the deadly algae blooms.

Probably one of the most harmful industrial pollutants is radioactive waste because of its long life span, one year up to three million years; and incredible impact on humans and other animals. These effects range from a quick death due to exposure to large amounts of radiation to a slow and agonizing death from cancer caused by exposure to radioactive substances in small but frequent amounts.

In the United States, there are approximately 15,000 metric tons of spent uranium fuel, still highly radioactive. In the past couple of years, a project to build a repository for radioactive wastes has been thrown back and forth between many prominent U.S. scientists in many fields. According to these scientists, the radioactive substances will remain harmful for approximately 10,000 years within the repository. The wastes will be stored in the best corrosion proof containers known, but they will only last from 300 to 1,000 years.

Ironically, it is the atmosphere's own self-cleaning mechanism that produces the pollution know as acid rain. Across Canada and the northern U.S., it has long been known that entire tracts of wilderness contain lakes and streams that are essentially devoid of aquatic life. Most scientists believe that this is caused by airborne pollutants that return to earth as some type of acid in precipitation.

Acid rain is formed in a very complex set of chemical reactions. Sulfur dioxide and nitrogen oxides are released into the atmosphere by a variety of natural processes including volcanic eruptions and lightning strikes, and by the burning of coal and other fossil fuels. Once in the atmosphere, sunlight causes a series of chemical reactions that transform these gases into sulfuric and nitric acids. Most of the acid molecules end up in cloud droplets. They may remain suspended for a short time in cloud form, but eventually, the molecules are washed out of the air in rain or snow and fall back to earth, where they slowly destroy trees, limestone statues and buildings, and worst of all, they kill rivers, lakes and streams.

After hundreds of studies, scientists now know that 90% of the toxic contaminants in Lake Superior come from the air. It is estimated that 20-25% of all toxic loading in all the Great Lakes comes from the air. These contaminants kill thousands of fish and other marine life, and they also expose the 24 million people who drink from the Great Lakes to whatever is contained in the polluted water droplets.

The final type of industrial pollution is one that is very wide spread because it is out of sight and out of mind. Toxins that mostly rest on the bottom of oceans and fresh waters have a large impact on marine animals. Once contaminated, these animals travel up the food chain, thus contaminating human be-

ings in the end. These events are caused mainly by the large amounts of PCB's, DDT, arsenic, cadmium, copper, lead, zinc, and chlorinated hydrocarbons that many industries discharge directly into the oceans, lakes, rivers, and streams.

Seattle's Elliot Bay, for example, is contaminated with a mixture of copper, lead, arsenic, zinc, cadmium, and polychlorinated-biphenyls (PCBs), all of which were chemicals once widely used by the electrical equipment industry in that area. San Francisco Bay is also contaminated with copper, nickel, cadmium, mercury, and other heavy metals.

*Offshore oil activities endanger oceans and wildlife.*

In the Great Lakes, approximately 400 hazardous chemicals including PCBs, lead, and cadmium have been found. Boston Harbor, whose bottom has been permanently contaminated with chemical waste and toxic metals. Other examples include New York Harbor, parts of the Mississippi estuary in southern Louisiana, and parts of Galveston Bay. Three areas in Puget Sound have been designated toxic-hazard sites due to the intense pollution. Commencement Bay, an inlet surrounded by many different industries, is loaded with petrochemicals, copper, lead, zinc, and arsenic, most of which come from industrial discharge. Due to this pollution, nearby harbors have fish populations that are diminishing rapidly thus causing many fishermen, who rely on their catch, to haul in their nets and find some other type of job.

Bay bottom contamination by heavy metals and organic chemicals pose an environmental double whammy. Many such pollut-

ants become more concentrated as they move up the food chain. Plants and animal bio-accumulate the substances, increasing their concentrations with every step up the aquatic food chain.

The second major problem area in water pollution is the disposal of product refuse such as plastic and medical wastes. In the last couple of years, beaches have been closed due to the tons of filth that have been washing up on the shores in New York, New Jersey, and other beaches all over the U.S. From these pollutants come diseases such as Hepatitis-B, Hepatitis-A, and AIDS. The people driven from the surf by the floating waste have lost their beach and worst of all, their ocean.

Approximately ten pounds or more of solid waste per day per patient are generated in an acute-care medical facility; two to four percent can be defined as potentially hazardous. Such wastes include pathological and surgical waste, clinical and biological laboratory waste, animal carcasses, needles, syringes, patient care items (such as linen, and personal and food service items), drugs, chemicals, and radioactive wastes. Many of these and other medical wastes can be found fouling our beaches and degrading our coastal waters.

In 1988, medical waste began washing up on the sands from Long Island to northern New Jersey. The debris was made up mostly of bloody bandages, syringes, prescription bottles, catheter bags, swabs, and hundreds of vials of blood, some of which tested positive for hepatitis-B and AIDS. Recently found with the medical waste are two inch thick grease balls. These grotesque floating menaces are composed of solid sewage and other organic chemicals.

Another type of product refuse that is growing worse every day is plastic. In recent cleanup programs along 3500 miles of beach front in 25 U.S. coastal states and territories, plastics such as cups, bags, soda bottles, six pack beverage connectors and eating utensils made up 8 of the 12 most prevalent types of flotsam that washed ashore.

Although not inherently dangerous to humans, the plastic desecrates beaches and can be fatal to marine wildlife. Thousands of sea birds, turtles, seals, porpoises and even whales die annually after ingesting or becoming entangled in plastic debris. Plastic is lightweight and strong—its virtues on land. Plastic floats and is nearly immortal—its sins in water. Plastic can take upwards of 500 years to degrade, and much of it is destined to drift about on the surface where much sea life goes on.

Annually, two million sea birds and 100,000 marine mammals die after eating or becoming entangled in plastic debris. Sea turtles choke on plastic bags they mistake for jellyfish. Sea lions are ensnared when they playfully poke their noses into plastic nets and rings. Brown pelicans become so enmeshed in fishing line, that they can literally hang themselves. An estimated 50,000 northern fur seals have died in the Pribilof Islands in Alaska by entanglements in fragments of plastic nets. Baleen whales, finbacks, blues, minkes and humpback whales regularly snag themselves in plastic fish nets which results in their suffocation and death. The nets of Japan's salmon fleet kill up to 750,000 sea birds and 5,000 Dall porpoises each year. The list goes on and on.

Last September [1990], volunteers collected 307 tons of litter from the sands of the Texas Gulf Coast. Two-thirds of this was plastic, including 31,733 bags, 30,295 bottles, and 15,361 sixpack yokes. This year, the Padre Island National Seashore accumulated 673 tons of debris, most of it lightweight plastic

The third major problem area of water pollution is human sewage. Human waste pollution comes mainly from sludge dumping, farm runoff, sewage treatment plant leakage, and general garbage dumping. Human sewage is responsible for a large part of the water pollution facing us today. There are two main reasons for this. First, we have polluted our waters with human wastes since human culture began. Second, most pollution is the result of human wastes (trash, medical waste, unused chemicals, etc.), and therefore, these pollutants are sometimes grouped under the title of human sewage.

Sludge is the name given to treated sewage that comes from treatment plants. Sludge varies considerably in its chemical, physical, and biological characteristics, but most sludge contains toxic metals such as zinc, copper, cadmium, and lead which can be hazardous to marine plants and animals and even humans.

In the last decade, tons of sludge have been dumped into our oceans by the approval of governmental agencies such as the Environmental Protection Agency. For instance, in the past three years, ten million tons of sludge have been dumped 106 miles out from the entrance to New York Harbor. In Boston, fecal and other organic matter has accumulated to levels of several feet at the bottom of the Inner Harbor, due to the excessive spills and dumping that has taken place.

Many clam and oyster beds, that used to be rich and plentiful, closed because they were laced with high concentrations of PCBs.

Today, each person generates approximately 60 gallons of waste water daily. With this amount multiplied by the ever rising population, problems are bound to occur. Our government must help in the disposal of the wastes, but we should also help through conservation and education. If we don't begin to stop now, when our population reaches the level that our waters cannot assimilate it, we will quickly become victims of our own waste.

We are a nation and a world whose incredible amount of garbage and wastes are overwhelming our waters' ability to deal with its disposal. The "toilet" of the oceans and fresh waters is finally backing up. We are slowly killing the life line of the world.

Jacques Cousteau said it best when he said, "The very survival of the human species depends upon the maintenance of an ocean clean and alive, spreading all around the world. The ocean is our planet's life belt."

*Kevin graduated valedictorian from high school and entered an university to study environmental engineering. We are fortunate to have young people like Kevin willing to focus and work on ecological restoration. This report has been edited. The full-length version with bibliography is available for $5.*

*Excerpted from* Aqua Terra, *vol. 1, Issue 1, Spring 1991.*

# How Will the Water Crisis Be Stopped?

## by Pat Costner / *We All Live Down Stream*

This planet is one enormous recycling system. If we produce and release poisons, we end up eating and drinking poisons.

Depending on the current piecemeal approach of federal and state agencies to stop the water crisis is much like expecting seat belt laws to prevent automobile accidents. Driving habits and water use habits are ultimately matters of personal choice.

Historically, U.S. environmental laws have been reactionary remedial responses to already existing problems, not preventative. But, by the primal, unchangeable roles and properties of water, protecting water resources requires prevention—forethought instead of hindsight.

In some countries, the groundwork for effective water resource protection is already being laid. In Holland, a national law allows the government to prohibit the production of chemicals that

©1990 Raee Mattson

OUR DISTRICT is OUT OF **WATER** TODAY! COULD WE HAVE SOME IN A dogie BAG?

cannot be detoxified. In West Germany, over 30 percent of the households are active in a voluntary program to separate garbage into recyclable components.

If the water crisis were mapped—a black dot for each contaminated water supply, every polluter, all the landfills, injection wells and incinerators—North America would be dark. But a pinhole for every individual, community, industry and farm that is working to keep their own wastes out of the water resources would bring a scattering of light.

*Excerpted from* We All Live Downstream *by Pat Costner,* ©1990 The National Water Center, Eureka Springs, Arkansas. Contact the Water Center for water filtration systems recommended for your drinking water needs.

# Chemical and Nuclear Waste: The Cost is too Great

## by J.W. Smith / *The World's Wasted Wealth*

Every exposé on these segments of the economy tells the same story. Corporations are dedicated to finding cheap chemical replacements for food or production—chemicals considered cheap only because the corporate balance sheet conveniently leaves out the cost to society of a destroyed environment and damaged health. Other corporations are then formed to clean up this pollution. In the future, these same corporations could end up owning the remaining pure water and living space. People would then be employed polluting the countryside, others cleaning it up, and still others vending the luxuries of what clean air and water remains to those who can afford to pay.

The one-hundred-billion-dollar nuclear weapons program is a good example. They polluted so much of the countryside and groundwater that it is expected to require much more to clean it up than to build those bombs. Many areas are so polluted (with both chemical and nuclear waste) that they

can never be reclaimed and will become "national sacrifice zones." Some experts have calculated that, at the current level of radiation pollution, nine thousand Americans per year are dying from cancer induced by radiation poisoning. Due to the long-lasting nature of some radiation, that cost will be borne for hundreds or even hundreds of thousands of years.

In studying the pollution problem, *Newsweek* reporter Gregg Easterbrook noted that, "More than 80 percent of [the $100 billion] Superfund spending [legislated for cleaning

up air, land, and water] has gone to consultants and their kinsmen, who have a pecuniary interest in dragging the process out: to keep the meter running."

This unnecessary industry has no connection to our needs for food, fiber, shelter, or recreation. Instead it reduces our quality of life. Industrial pollution could be reduced 50 percent by eliminating this unnecessary production. Some could be turned towards cleaning up the pollution of a waste distribution [unnecessary labor] society, but this industry was never needed. The easiest and cheapest method of clean-up is to not produce those chemical and nuclear wastes in the first place.

*Excerpted from* The World's Wasted Wealth, *published by New Worlds Press,* ©1992 J.W. Smith.

## Toxic Shock:

### *The military is our nation's largest polluter*

The U.S. military is responsible for more than 14,400 pollution sites at 1,579 Army, Navy and Air Force bases nationwide, including Maine's Brunswick Naval Air Station and Loring Air Force Base. Cleanup of the sites, which threaten residents and delays re-use of the closed bases, could cost as much as $200 billion. The military is currently exempt from compliance with state and federal environmental laws and insufficient funding presently available from that budget to clean up their mess. The Pentagon is the nation's largest polluter, but spends just. 4% of its annual budget on environmental restoration.

*Excerpted from* The Quarterly of the Maine Peace Campaign *as it appeared in the* Cultivator. *A more detailed article appeared in* Base Conversion News, *Fall 1990.*

©1990 Raee Mattson

# TRASH: *What Choices Do We Have?*

The landfills that once provided a deceptively simple solution are closing either because they are full or because they do not meet new federal or state standards. One-third of the landfills in the country will be full within five years. Siting of new landfills is difficult because of public opposition. As landfills close and costs of landfilling escalate, the pressure to incinerate mounts. Incinerators, costly to build and operate, are often inefficient and can contribute to serious environmental degradation and threaten public health. Those who resist incineration do so because of legitimate concerns about air pollution and land use, but many also realize that burning waste squanders potentially valuable resources.

People in communities all over the country are beginning to realize that the solution

lies in using garbage as a resource rather than as refuse to be destroyed. Increasingly, localities now choose to recycle rather than to burn thereby greatly decreasing detrimental effects on the environment.

A change in the way we think about waste will also require that we find ways to generate less—and less hazardous—waste in the first place. In industry this means altering manufacturing processes or substituting non-toxic materials for hazardous ones. When dealing with household and commercial waste, "source reduction," as this concept is called, means the elimination of unnecessary packaging, the substitution of biodegradable materials for non-biodegradable ones, and the use of non-toxic products.

Many communities that handle waste successfully have developed an "integrated waste management" system which treats garbage as a resource for the economic and environmental improvement of the community. Articulated in the 1970s, this system is completely local in its analysis of needs and in its decisions about management. Source reduction and recycling are the technologies of choice; incineration and landfilling are used only when necessary.

States can provide technical and financial assistance, promote regional planning, and provide information on markets even though the options chosen for waste

> **People in communities all over the country are beginning to realize that the solution lies in using garbage as a resource rather than as refuse to be destroyed.**

management will depend ultimately on local conditions and needs. The federal government should give solid waste management the priority it requires through funding and technological guidance and by setting national goals for recycling and standards for packaging. A key factor is the educated involvement of each citizen, whether by participation in decision-making or by the improvement of consumer purchasing and disposal practices.

*Excerpted from* Household Waste, *1989; and* Waste, *1988 © Concern, Inc.*

# Guidelines for *Great* Compost

### by Terri Dunivant / *Earth Journal*

❀ Use a variety of materials, and alternate them with enough soil to cover each layer. A good example is 3" of dry leaves and grass clippings 1" of kitchen scraps, and enough soil to cover everything.

❀ Chop or shred large, bulky items like branches or cornstalks. These materials will decompose faster if they are reduced to 1/2" - 3/4" pieces.

❀ Sprinkle water on each layer as you build the pile. You want it to be moist but not soggy. Too much water will cause the pile to compress, blocking air flow and delaying decomposition. Cover your pile if winter rains go on more than a day.

❀ Build the pile to dimensions between 3'x3'x3' and 6'x6'x6'. There is no minimum size, but if it's much smaller or larger, the rate of decomposition will slow down considerably.

❀ Keep the pile aerated. Whether you turn it regularly or build a well–ventilated pile, air is the key to fast composting. The advantage to turning is that it exposes more material to decomposition by beneficial organisms. If you turn the pile every day, your compost could be ready-to-use in just two weeks!

❀ Do not compost meat, bones, dairy products, or grease—they may attract animals

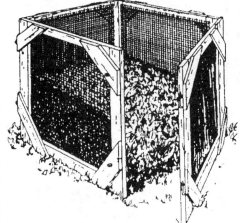

and will cause the pile to stink. (A proper compost pile smells like rich, moist earth.) Also, do not compost cat litter or dog manure, since they may carry diseases that are harmful to humans.

❀ Besides lawn/garden clippings and leaves, you can also compost sawdust, wood ash, straw, rice hulls, seaweed, bird and livestock manure's, tea bags and coffee grounds, vegetable and fruit scraps, nut shells, and blood or bone meal from garden stores.

*Source: Ecology Action of Santa Cruz, California,* The Simple Act of Home Composting.

*Excerpted from* Earth Journal, *August 1991.*

# TRASH STATISTICS

✴ The U.S. discards:
  • over 16 million disposable diapers each year.
  • 16 billion pens
  • 220 million tires
  • enough aluminum to rebuild the entire U.S. commercial airline fleet every 3 months

✴ Americans produce 150 million tons of solid waste annually, or 3.5 pounds per person per day.

✴ Currently, 80% of our generated solid waste is dumped into 6,000 landfills across the U.S.

✴ It is expected that 2,000 landfills will close by 1993. 27 states will completely lose their landfills and will have to truck waste to nearby states.

✴ Japan recycles 50% of their solid waste, Western Europe 30%, America only 10%!

✴ Landfill waste can be used to generate electricity. Currently the U.S only uses 6% of its rubbish to do so. Germany uses 30% of its unrecycled waste.

✴ 80% of our trash is dumped in landfills, 10% incinerated and 10% recycled.

✴ The average American household throws out 15% of all solid food purchased.

✴ Americans toss 1 billion pounds of each year.

✴ Americans only recycle 2% of its plastic products.

This information was derived from, *The Wastoid Handbook,* August 1989 compiled by Leadership America.

# Destruction of America's Ancient Forests

### by Dorene Garvin / *Earth Journal*

California's ancient forests are richly complex ecosystems; the essential home of hundreds of mammals and birds and thousands of invertebrate species. Giant sequoias and coastal redwoods that took root before Caesar reigned are so immense that the base and the crown of one tree live in separate climatic conditions.

California's ancient forests are awesome and beautiful, unique and irreplaceable. They are also nearly extinct.

Timber cutting operations in the redwoods began in the 1820's. The trees were cut with axes and whipsaws, and the logs made into boards on the spot. By 1834, the first water-powered sawmill was built in Sonoma County. As demand for wood increased, more efficient methods were developed, allowing the clear cutting of extensive areas of redwood forest. Cut-over lands were converted for grazing by repeated burning and seeding with grass.

The rate of cutting steadily increased. In 1905, 500 million board feet of lumber was cut; in 1985, more than 3.5 billion board feet was taken. This gross over-harvesting forced hundreds of mills to close because the resource had been so severely depleted.

Today, less than 5% of these ancient forests remain standing. In ten years, if the cutting is not brought under control, this too will be gone.

According to a recent report prepared by the California Department of Forestry, 226% more timber was cut on public lands than was planted during the first half of the 1980's. Each day, as many as 150 ancient giants fall to chain saws.

The largest private owner of old-growth redwoods, Pacific Lumber Company, was taken over by the Maxxam Corporation in 1985. The purchase was financed with high-interest junk bonds, and the cut has since been tripled to make the inflated payments.

### Ancient Forests Can't Be Rebuilt

People are told not to worry about the cutting because "trees are a renewable resource" and are being replanted. However, it takes 200 years of uninterrupted growth for a forest to acquire the characteristics of "old growth." Often, downed Sequoias or Coastal redwoods are replaced with Douglas fir or ponderosa pine because of their rapid growth rates and economic value. These replacement forests are "managed" by clearing competing vegetation and then recut in 40 to 70 years, starting the replanting cycle again. No forest is currently being replanted with the diversity of the original forest. No forests are being left alone for 200 years, and no replanted forests contain spotted owls, Pacific fishers, marbled murelets, red tree voles, Del Norte salamanders or tailed frogs—all animals dependent on old growth forests.

Areas where forests once stood are void of life, the rivers filled with silt, the salmon choked. Deer and elk no longer have protection from the cold in the winter and heat in summer.

So much is lost, and what remains must be protected. The Headwater Forest southeast of Eureka is 3,000 acres of old-growth forest untouched by chainsaws. This is the most intact, pristine watershed in California. But the Headwater is owned by Maxxam-Pacific Lumber, and if all goes their way, this forest will also be felled, systematically, until no trees, no animals, no unique ecosystem remain.

*Excerpted from* Earth Journal, *November 1990.*

## Save a tree...
# STOP THE JUNK MAIL

**DID YOU KNOW...**

♠ Americans receive almost 2 million tons of junk mail every year.
♠ About 44 percent of the junk mail is never even opened.
♠ If only 100,000 people stopped their junk mail, we could save about 150,000 trees every year.

**SIMPLE THINGS TO DO...**

♠ Write to: **Mail Preference Service, Direct Marketing Association,** 11 West 42nd St. PO Box 3861, New York, NY 10163-3861. They'll stop your name from being sold to most large mailing list companies. This will reduce your junk mail up to 75 percent.
♠ **Recycle the junk mail you already get:** If it's printed on newsprint, toss it in with the newspapers. If it's quality paper, make a separate pile for it—many recycling centers accept both white and colored paper.

*Source:* 50 Simple Things You Can Do to Save the Earth, *from The Earthworks Press.*

*Photograph of Oregon Clearcut ©1984 Michael Williams, courtesy of Native Forest Council. The amount of timber taken from the Northwest forests each year is equal to a line of log trucks 20,000 miles long!*

# Rainforest Facts

⚑ The U.S. used to have 1,000 acres of public land for every person. Now there are only three acres for every American.

⚑ Old-growth covered 15 million acres in the Pacific Northwest at one time. During the last century 12 million acres of this forest has been cleared.

*Source: Zero Population Growth Facr Sheet, August, 1989.*

⚑ Tropical rainforest are home to at least 50% of all types of living things—as many as 5 million species of plants and animals. Panama, for example, sustains as many plant species as the entire European continent.

⚑ Today, Earth's tropical rainforest cover approximately 2% of the Earth's surface. Each year, more than 60 million acres of tropical rainforest are degraded or destroyed—nearly 117 acres every minute!

⚑ Rainforests play a critical role in maintaining world climatic stability by generating a significant amount of the world's rainfall and serving as a carbon dioxide "sink" in the fight against global warming.

⚑ Destruction of rainforest results in extinction of at least one species of plant or animal every day.

⚑ 90% of the world's non-human primates are found only in these forests... along with two-thirds of all known plants, 40% of birds of prey and 80% of the world's insects.

⚑ The rainforests are home to 140 million people, many members of indigenous tribes.

⚑ These forests are the source of hundreds of renewable oils, resins, rubber latexes, nuts, fruits, vegetable and medicinal plants. 70% of the more than 3,000 plant species known to be valuable in the treatment of cancer, are found in tropical forest.

⚑ Erosion and siltation of rivers and oceans from rainforests destruction ruins drinking water and irrigation supplies, destroys fish breeding areas and kills marine habitats.

*Source: Greenpeace Rainforest Campaign*

⚑ 87 indigenous tribes have been extinguished by Brazil in this century.

⚑ The U.S. imports 300 million pounds of beef from Central America every year for hamburgers, luncheon meats, baby and pet foods. Calculations reveal that for each pound of beef produced 55 square feet of rainforest, along with its associated animals, must be sacrificed.

⚑ Nearly half the world's rainforests have been destroyed in the last 40 years. In the next 30 years the rest are slated for destruction.

*Source: Rainforest Action Network*

# HEMP

## *A Miracle Plant*

### by Southern Willamette Alliance / *Ahbleza*

Imagine being paid $37,000 by the federal government to plant 270 acres of marijuana (hemp) for two seasons; On today's market that much land in hemp would yield millions of dollars or, more likely, a long jail sentence. But that was a decent income in 1943 and 1944, when the Internal Revenue Service issued Fred E. Coulter of Conrad, Iowa, a special tax stamp as a producer of marijuana. This marijuana was not grown to smoke, but to make rope, landing nets, helmet covers, and linen thread to help the war effort. The U.S. government distributed 400,000 pounds of seeds to farmers and asked them to cultivate hemp because the supply of Manila hemp (abaca) from the Philippines had been cut off by the Japanese. (Synthetic rope had not yet been invented.)

With today's anti-drug hysteria in full swing, our government casts a blind eye toward any item declared illegal, no matter how beneficial that item might be.

Hemp is the strongest, most rot-resistant natural fiber known. With existing technology, dynamite, paper, and particle board can be made from its pulp; rope, twine, linen, canvas, cellophane, and burlap can be made from its fiber. As late as 1938 more than half the linen fabric imported by the United States was made from hemp fiber.

Hemp was hailed as a new billion-dollar cash crop in the February 1938 issue of *Popular Mechanics,* in an article stating that the fiber was used in 5,000 textile products and the hurds (pulp) could be used to make more than 25,000 items.

Hemp could replace petroleum as a fuel for cars and industry. No more worry over imported oil or carbon pollutants. Methanol fuel can be produced by heating hemp hurds (77 percent cellulose), which are the woody particles remaining after the fiber has been removed. Brazil runs 1.2 million cars on methanol produced from sugarcane, a plant with less cellulose than hemp.

Hemp hurds can also be made into paper, and building materials can be formed from hemp fiber, a process that would allow us to save more forests. According to Jason Merrill and Lyster Dewey, authors of a 1916 U.S. Department of Agriculture bulletin on hemp hurds as paper making material, a pulp mill producing 7,500 tons of fiber annually would require 40,500 acres of pulpwood land, compared to 10,000 acres of cultivated hemp.

Until the 1880s, 75 to 90 percent of all paper was made from hemp fiber. (The initial draft of the Declaration of Independence was written on hemp paper.) The promising hemp industry was effectively destroyed when marijuana was made illegal in 1937, and polluting petrochemicals came to be used in many plastic products where hemp might have been employed. The drug qualities of marijuana is now a moot point, however, since French scientists have developed a type of hemp that contains virtually no THC, the psychoactive constituent of cannabis.

*Reprinted from* Ahbleza *(March 1990), as it appeared in* Utne Reader *July/August 1990.*

**MEDICINAL USES**

Relieves pain, nausea, stress and depression associated with AIDS and cancer.

Also effective in treatment of:
Multiple Sclerosis
Epilepsy
Glaucoma
Migraine headaches
Arthritis and rheumatism
Asthma attacks
Anorexia
Menstrual Cramps
Stress

# Take a Stand: Plant a Tree

### by Mary C. Turck / *Earthlight*

What with news about aldicarb and potatoes, burning Brazilian rainforests and the greenhouse effect, hazardous waste and nitrate-polluted goundwater, it's easy to get depressed about environmental issues.

A person who reads all the bad news may feel the problems are too big to be overcome, that the Earth is on an irreversible course toward ecological disaster. Even if one feels there may still be time to change that course, the problems often seem too large for one person to make a difference.

Sinking into depression about the environment is dangerous. People who are depressed lose the energy needed to act. The Earth needs our action more than our tears. So, instead of focusing on the bad news about the environment, let's take time to cheer on the good folks making good news.

Johnny Appleseed is one of the heroes of United States folklore. Johnny, you may remember, walked across the country with his stash of apple seeds. Everywhere he went, he planted apple seeds. He meant his work as a gift to the land and to future inhabitants of the land. Today many people are repeating John-

ny Appleseed's generous gift-giving, planting trees for the future as well as for their own enjoyment.

You or I can't turn around the greenhouse

---

## Whether you live on a farm or in a city or small town, you can plant trees, too.

---

effect or soil erosion single-handedly. But each of us can follow Johnny Appleseed's example by planting trees.

Apple trees, of course, give a tangible reward in a few years. Windbreaks and shelterbelts go one step further, helping control and stop wind erosion of fertile soil while they provide habitat for wildlife. All trees help to preserve and regenerate the air we breathe, fighting against the greenhouse effect.

In 1987 the U.S. Forest Service announced that 2.3 billion trees had been planted for the

fifth consecutive record-breaking year. The Soil Conservation Service in Minnesota's northwest corner proudly reports farmer contracts for the planting of 270 miles of trees for shelterbelts during 1989.

Whether you live on a farm or in a city or small town, you can plant trees, too. The Minnesota Department of Natural Resources has a nationally-recognized guide to backyard plantings, called *Landscaping for Wildlife*, available for $6.95 from Minnesota Documents, 117 University Avenue, St. Paul MN 55155. Seed catalogs and nurseries offer enticing varieties of apple and other fruit trees. Local Soil Conservation Service and Agricultural Extension offices can also help.

Better yet, you can make tree-planting a community-building project. Right now is the right time to start planning a tree-planting project with your church, community group or school. Let's bring Johnny Appleseed back in 1990!

*Copyright ©1989 by Mary C. Turck. Excerpted from the* Earthlight, *Spring 1990.*

---

# HANDLE WITH CARE...

### by Scott Graham & Terri Dunivant / *Earth Journal*

Responsible travel--whether undertaken individually or by joining tours dedicated to traveling responsibly--goes beyond the typical "did that, done that" tourism experience. Responsible travel is more meaningful for visitors and, ultimately, more beneficial and less demeaning to local citizens and their countries.

Resort developments are underway throughout the developing world, where travel is booming. The international tourism industry has more than doubled since 1979, to $200+ billion a year. Destination countries realize less than a quarter of that revenue, but suffer numerous tourist-caused problems that threaten cultures, wildlife, and the environment:

- Indigenous cultures little changed for centuries are threatened by the powerful influences of Western culture that often accompany the arrival of mass tourism in the developing world.
- In popular African game parks, minivans packed with tourists are so numerous and bothersome to wildlife that populations are declining. More than 60 minivans surrounded a mother Cheetah recently, who

tried to carry her cubs to safety outside the circle of overeager tourists. She could only carry one cub at a time in her mouth, and one of them was killed by a predator—also trapped within the circling minivans—before she could return for him.

- In choice trekking areas of the Himalayas and Andes, locals are razing forests and stripping brush from hillsides to supply trekking groups with firewood for cooking and regular hot showers.

Fortunately, as problems such as these have become increasingly apparent, corrective and preventive efforts have been started. International cultural and environmental groups—as well as some travel agencies and tour organizations profiting from the rush of tourists to the developing world—are working to assure that travelers headed to developing countries don't wreak havoc on the places they visit. In addition, these organizations are working to promote tourism that actually benefits the developing world:

- In Africa, local officials—aware of the tourist dollars wildlife represents—are working with international wildlife groups to

strengthen curbs on tourist-caused wildlife abuse in game parks.
- In Brazil, the increasing revenues generated by visitors to the Amazon basin and the lobbying efforts of organizations bringing tourists to the region are convincing the government to save its vast rainforests because of their tremendous long-term value.
- Throughout the developing world, tour operators are helping strengthen local economies and preserve indigenous cultures by limiting the size of tour groups and assuring that their participants stay and eat in locally-owned hotels and restaurants; hire local services; and buy locally-produced arts, crafts, and other goods.

*Scott Graham is author of* Handle With Care: A Guide to Responsible Travel in Developing Countries. *The Noble Press $8.95 167 pp. Excerpted from* Earth Journal, *June 1992.*

*Another useful book for the traveller,* Nature Tourism: Managing for the Environment, *edited by Tensie Whelan and published by Island Press.*

# Suffer the Animals

### by Rose Marie L. Audette / *Environmental Action*

During the 1980s, the animal protection movement stomped and surged onto the national scene.

Members of this growing animal-protection movement share many concerns with environmentalists.

### Animal rights vs. Animal welfare

Like the environmental movement, the animal-protection movement is not a monolith. Through thousands of competing groups, two strains of animal activism can be noted. On the one hand, dating back to the 1800s, there is the "anti-cruelty" or "animal welfare" drive. Traditionally, this camp has appealed to human compassion, kindness, morality--we the powerful humans should not make poor animals suffer.

The second strain—"animal rights"—was launched in 1975 when philosopher Peter Singer published *Animal Liberation.* Singer rejects the Western and JudeoChristian view that humans are superior to their fellow animals by virtue of a god-given soul. "All animals are equal," he proclaims, to believe and to act otherwise is "speciest" just as treating women as inferior to men is sexist. Singer argues that animals can suffer, and therefore their suffering must be given equal weight with human interests.

Singer writes: "I believe that our present attitudes to these beings are based on a long history of prejudice and arbitrary discrimination. I argue that there can be no reason— except the selfish desire to preserve the privileges of the exploiting group—for refusing to extend the basic principle of equality of consideration to members of other species."

Applying this creed (which is to live morally in Singer's view) requires opposing meat-eating, fur-wearing, animal experimentation and more. It means a revolution in human habits.

### The movement's approach:
#### All-out Activism

Building on the ideas in Singer's book, a few activists in the late 1970s and early 1980s launched an animal-rights drive in the United States. The leading animal-rights group today, People for the Ethical Treatment of Animals (PETA), was founded in 1980 with 100 individuals; now it has almost 300,000 members. The Humane Society of the United States swelled from 65,000 members and supporters in 1980 to over a million in 1990. Overall membership in animal-protection groups has been estimated at 10 million. (For convenience, we'll use "animal-protection"

to cover the entire gamut of animal-concern groups.)

The environmental movement has been criticized for its reluctance to call for lifestyle change—we didn't want to be seen as the ones who told Americans they would have to do with less. Animal supporters have no such qualms. They're out to change minds and habits. "Total activism" is the modus operandi. T-shirts intone: Fur coats are worn by

> **Peter Singer says that the pain and suffering caused by human tyranny over nonhuman animals "can only be compared with that which resulted from the centuries of tyranny by white humans over black humans."**

beautiful animals and ugly people. One recent issue of *PETA News* contained a page of slogans ("MEAT IS MURDER" and "EAT BEANS NOT BEINGS" ) that could be xeroxed onto sticky labels for easy posting, as well as a "Barf Bag" to be mailed to L'Oreal objecting to that company's animal testing.

The activism on behalf of animal rights can be extreme. The FBI has labeled the Animal Liberation Front (ALF) a domestic terrorist group. Founded in England in 1976, ALF has conducted about 100 "actions" against research laboratories. In November 1988, a woman was arrested for trying to plant a bomb at the Connecticut headquarters of U.S. Surgical Corp, which animal activists had been picketing for seven years.

PETA is ALF's "media liaison," releasing videotapes and photos to the press within hours of ALF raids. PETA also defends ALF's actions in its press packet. But many in the movement condemn such actions and try to distance themselves from "the crazies," as one animal-rights supporter called them.

Different starting points and priorities also create conflicts. Ben & Jerry's ice cream has forged a pro-environment corpo-

rate image; but animal groups oppose such dairy industry practices as mechanized milking and sending newborn male calves to veal production. A legislator who is a hero to environmentalists may be a villain from the animal-advocate's viewpoint.

Laboratory use of animals poses a similar difficulty. Animal-protection people either want to abolish it completely, or phase it out quickly. Environmentalists, on the other hand, have depended on animal test data to prove that substances are dangerous to human, animal and ecological health.

### Parting of Ways?

"There's a Berlin Wall built between the two movements, animal-rights and environmental safety," says Alex Hershaft of the Farm Animal Reform Movement (FARM). "The issue is homocentricity." Hershaft divides environmentalists in two groups:

People who feel the environment must be preserved "for its own sake" and those who want it protected "because it is useful to humans." Animal supporters don't have any quarrels with the first group, he says, but the second is another story. "Just because we are more crafty doesn't mean we have the right to subjugate everything else."

In the very first paragraph of his seminal book, Peter Singer says that the pain and suffering caused by human tyranny over nonhuman animals "can only be compared with that which resulted from the centuries of tyranny by white humans over black humans." Many people feel that equating animal abuse with slavery is a step too far, while animal abuse should be stopped, that goal can't have equal weight with reducing human suffering. To this objection, PETA suggests the following response: "We should try to alleviate suffering wherever we can. Helping animals is not more or less important than helping human beings—it is all important. Animal suffering and human suffering are noticeably interlinked."

*Excerpted from* Environmental Action, *May/ June 1990.*

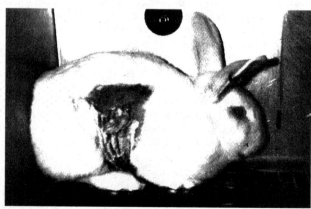

*This rabbit was the victim of one of Gillette's dermal "Death Tests".*
*Source: People for the Ethical Treatment of Animals.*

# Chapter 5

# *Agriculture*

**People have to recognize that peaches don't come out of a can, and milk doesn't come out of a carton. All those products come from agricultural land that is being lost.**

*— Marc Del Piero*
*Chairman, Board of Supervisors,*
*Monterey County, California*

# Agriculture and the Environment

Few people consider agriculture to be an environmental problem. However, mismanaged agricultural lands lead to topsoil loss, water depletion and pollution. With the world's population growing by 95 million people per year (roughly equivalent to Mexico's total population), the pressure on agricultural lands to increase food and fiber production builds. Clearing land for agriculture, especially in tropical regions, leads to large scale deforestation and loss of species diversity.

Soil erosion is a critical problem because tilling the land exposes it to the forces of wind and water. The U.S. has lost more than a third of its topsoil since the first European settlers arrived, and currently loses about three billion tons per year. Last year alone, wind erosion damaged 14 million acre of cropland on the Great Plains. Most soil erosion is caused by rainfall on sloping ground that has been tilled for planting.

Soil erodes much faster when the same crop is planted year after year rather than in an annual crop rotation. The use of chemical fertilizer adds to the problem because, unlike animal manure or cover crops that are plowed under, chemical fertilizer does not add organic material to the soil to rebuild it. In some agricultural areas, an inch of topsoil can be lost in a single year, yet it takes hundreds of years for an inch to be naturally created.

Another problem with modern agriculture is pesticide use. Insecticides are intended to kill insects that destroy crops, but they often harm beneficial predatory insects, birds, fish and mammals, including people. Every year up to two million people suffer from pesticide poisoning worldwide, resulting in about 40,000 deaths. As insects become resistant to pesticides, higher doses must be applied, increasing the risks involved. Over the last 40 years, pesticide use has increased 10-fold, yet crop loss due to pests has almost doubled from 7 to 13 percent.

Dependence on irrigation for crops has severe environmental costs. In the U.S., more than 40 percent of all the freshwater withdrawn from surface and underground sources is used for agriculture. In addition to depleting water in some places, irrigation often causes salt to accumulate in soils where

it damages fertility. Salinization has reduced yields on one quarter of the world's irrigated croplands.

Waste water runoff carrying pesticides, herbicides and fertilizers often contaminates rivers and lakes. The Environmental Protection Agency has determined that agricultural chemicals are the greatest source of surface

*Courtesy of Bill Schaefer,* Land Stewardship Letter, *Spring 1991.*

water pollution in the U.S. Agricultural chemicals have also contaminated groundwater—the source of drinking water for about 40 percent of all Americans. The U.S. Department of Agriculture calculates that 46 percent of all U.S. counties have groundwater susceptible to contamination from agricultural pesticides or fertilizers.

Federal subsidy programs are at the root of many unsustainable farming practices. For example, farmers are currently subsidized according to total bushels harvested—a system that rewards farmers who intensively apply chemicals to produce high yields and penalizes those who rotate crops to increase soil fertility. The price of irrigation water also is subsidized, making it possible for farmers

to continue practices that waste water rather than to adopt water efficient irrigation methods.

## Solutions

Early evidence from the U.S. Department of Agriculture's Low-Input Sustainable Agriculture (LISA) research program indicates that while some farmers who apply fewer chemical pesticides and fertilizers may experience a small initial decline in crop yields, their net profits usually increase due to minimized costs. Low-input practices give small farmers a greater chance to succeed financially, and the land is better off.

In 1989, the National Research Council of the National Academy of Sciences found that many farms using natural techniques of pest control and fertilization could get the same or better crop yields as farms heavily dependent upon chemicals. The report recommends that the U.S. revise its farm programs to encourage sustainable agricultural methods that conserve soil and reduce chemical use.

Integrated Pest Management (IPM) is a well tested system of pest control that minimizes the use of potentially hazardous pesticides by relying more heavily on biological controls (natural predators), genetic modifications (pest-resistant crops), and changes in agricultural practices (crop rotation and diversity in plantings).

Drip irrigation systems reduce water use significantly and decrease the buildup of salt in soils. Computerized watering systems have the potential to reduce water use even further. Some arid areas are not suitable for agriculture at all.

## What You Can Do

· Urge federal officials to ensure that the policies of the U.S. Agency for International Development and the World Bank promote adoption of sustainable agricultural methods.
· Eat lower on the food chain more often.
· If you have a pet, think about replacing part or all of the canned meat in its diet with vegetable protein.

More advice on what you can do, is found in the following articles.

*Excerpted from an Earth Day 1990 Fact Sheet.*

# The Disappearance of Our Soil

*There is far more biological complexity in a handful of soil in Virginia than on the entire surface of Jupiter.*

-Edward O. Wilson
Harvard Professor

- Annually, the amount of topsoil blowing and washing in the world's oceans, lakes, and rivers would fill a train of freight cars long enough to encircle the planet 150 times.
- Each day, in the U.S., enough topsoil erodes away to fill a line of dump trucks 5,600 km (3,500 miles) long.
- Europe loses 1 billion tons annually
- Asia loses 25 billion tons annually
- U.S. loses 7 billion tons annually
- 5.9 billion tons of U.S., annual topsoil erosion is associated with crops destined for livestock and overgrazing of range-land.
- It takes Nature 100-500 years to create one inch of topsoil.
- Currently, we lose an inch of topsoil every sixteen years.
- In the space of a few years, off road vehicles have scoured more soil off parts of California than nature can replace in 1,000 years
- U.S. Department of Agriculture reports that:
  - (a) 200 years ago U.S. croplands had 21 inches of topsoil
  - (b) Today, much of U.S. cropland has 6 inches of topsoil
  - (c) Productivity of U.S. cropland is down 70%

## WHY ARE WE LOSING OUR SOIL?

Wind and flowing water are the two main forces that cause vulnerable soil to erode. Soil is made vulnerable when it is stripped of its natural vegetative cover. The relationship between the plants and the soil is symbiotic: the soil provides the plants with necessary nutrients and; the plants provide the soil with a protective covering. Robbed of that covering through agriculture, logging, construction, cattle grazing, and other human activities, the rate at which the soil erodes is greatly accelerated.

## REASONS BEHIND SOIL EROSION

*Past U.S. farm programs have provided incentives for farming highly erodible soils by encouraging maximum yields and failing to discourage 'sodbusting' (conversion of reserve land to intensive use).*

*Overgrazing of rangelands leads to soil erosion as well. In the 11 western states 48% of the land is owned collectively by the taxpayers and is supposedly "preserved" in national wildlife areas, wilderness areas and national parks. Currently, 80% of this land is being grazed!*

*On our 'public rangelands' (as these areas have come to be called) soil erosion due to overgrazing is severe: 10% of it is in a state of severe or very severe desertification.*

*Those who live amid concrete, plastic, and computers can easily forget how fundamentally our well being is linked to the land.*

—Eric Eckholm
U.S. Environmental Expert

## RESOURCES

*GAIA: An Atlas of Planet Management* General Editor, Dr. Norma Myers, Doubleday, New York, 1984

*Diet For A Small Planet* Frances Moore Lappé, Ballantine Books, New York, 1982

*Environmental Science: An Introduction* G. Tyler Miller, Wadsworth Publishing Company, Belmont, California, 1988

*National Wildlife* February/March 1985 pp, 17-22.

*Excerpted from a 1990 Earth Day Fact Sheet entitled "The Silent Threat: The Disappearance of Our Soil."*

# Regenerating America's Agriculture

### by Cindy Mitlo / *Co-op America Quarterly*

### Sustainable Agriculture on the American Agenda

Today, only twenty percent of our food comes from small farms, and sustainable farms supply an even tinier percentage. The numbers are growing, but it is going to take a new, forceful and creative alliance of farmers and consumers to bring about a truly sustainable relationship between farmers, society and the land.

In order for this new agriculture to come about, three fundamental changes must occur. First, as consumers, we must realize that we have not been paying for many of the environmental, social and medical costs attributed to today's agriculture. These costs are not turning up at the supermarket but in other sectors of the economy.

For example, agriculture uses at least 81% of our nation's water. Not only are supplies being depleted, but groundwater contamination has required the drilling of new municipal and household wells. In 1988, the EPA reported that at least 74 pesticides, some highly carcinogenic, were found in the groundwater of 38 states.

At least one-third of our topsoil has been lost to erosion, and approximately 8 tons per acre continue to erode annually. Cleaning the eroded soil from ditches, lakes and streams costs taxpayers $6 billion per year.

What if food bills reflected these costs? Or the costs of providing medical care to the thousands of farmworkers injured each year from pesticides? Who pays for the costs of unemployment when farms fail? How much do we spend on national security to protect our supply of imported petroleum? Over the coming years we can choose to continue to pay for these costs, or we can work for a healthier system of agriculture.

Secondly, consumers must begin to pay farmers for the direct costs of raising healthy food. Presently, according to The Rocky Mountain Institute, between 3 and 25 cents of each food dollar goes to the farmer, with the rest of it covering processing, packaging, advertising and distribution. Farmers, caught in a financial squeeze between escalating petrochemical costs and declining economic productivity, are becoming an impoverished sector of our society.

At the National Conference on Organic and Sustainable Farming held this March in Washington, D.C., Barry Commoner, (presently the Director of the Center for the Biology of Natural Systems at Queens College, New York) reported that since 1950 agricultural output as a percentage of the GNP had dropped 55%, and the net income of the farmer had decreased by 32% (in uninflated dollars). During the same period, chemical inputs on farms had increased by 484%, yet the yield per unit of chemical used was down by 69%.

Farmers are rediscovering that they can cut costs by replacing chemicals with labor and innovation based on an understanding and respect for nature. Research in organic and sustainable farming—some of it sponsored by the USDA's Low Input Sustainable Agriculture program—has shown that farmers can make a living after the transition. Raising crops free of chemicals often makes them less susceptible to drought and other natural disasters, and the improved soil structure that results from using organic materials like manure is also more drought-resistant. If a greater diversity of crops is grown, the farm as a whole is not vulnerable to the same pests or seasonal weather events. (Cacek and Langner, 1986).

Diversified farms are also protected to a certain extent from price changes in a single commodity. And, since less inputs are needed, the costs are lowered—and so is the need for credit. However, more of the food dollar must go to the farmer so they can receive the economic support they need to farm on the smaller environmentally appropriate scale so critical to long-term sustainability.

Third, farmers and consumers must jointly press for a major change in the structure of government farm programs. These programs have been one of the greatest obstacles for farmers wanting to make their operations more sustainable. New policies are needed to encourage, reward and assist more Farmers in making the transition to sustainable agricultural practices.

It is almost surprising that any farmers are making the transition at all, given U.S. government farm commodity programs. These programs emphasize the monoculture (raising a single crop year after year) of certain erosion-prone crops, penalize farmers for rotating crops, encourage the removal of windbreaks, erosion control crops, and other ecological practices in order to increase production, and necessitate the use of chemicals. The public must realize that farmers have adapted their life-styles, equipment and farming operations to the current resource-depleting, government farm-program system as a way of making ends meet. Most farmers cannot afford to make a change to more sustainable practices unless they are provided with the necessary information, cultural support and economic incentive. Groups like The Land Stewardship Project in Minnesota have been very active in organizing citizen action efforts to improve governmental policies. Through public meetings and farm tours, as well as books, plays and

**It is almost surprising that any farmers are making the transition at all, given U.S. government farm commodity programs.**

videos, they are spreading the message of sustainable agriculture. More importantly, by organizing farmers to experiment with and demonstate sustainable practices on working farms, LSP provides a framework for them to share knowledge and learn from each other.

**Sustainable Agriculture as Reality**

Is it possible for a system of agriculture to resemble this idealistic vision? As many as 30,000 of the nation's 2.1 million farmers are proving that sustainable farming techniques are available, and that they work.

As most of us know, low-input, organic farmers avoid synthetic fertilizers and pesticides, growth regulators and livestock feed additives. Instead, farmers are finding they can replace expensive and non-renewable chemical fertilizers while increasing soil productivity with animal manures, green manures (crops like rye and clover that are grown only to be plowed under), off-farm organic wastes, and rocks with a naturally high mineral content. They employ methods that prevent soil erosion by using cover crops, crop rotation and contour plowing (following the natural contours of the land). Biological pest control and mechanical cultivation can virtually eliminate the use of herbicides or insecticides.

Some of the new farming techniques such as ridge till (a form of conservation tillage) and the use of alternative crops have been developed and introduced in recent years by pioneering farmers. Many practices such as contour plowing, crop rotation and the use of animal manure as fertilizer are not new. They were only abandoned when the "bigger is better" fever took over American agriculture.

**What can we, as consumers, do?**

· Support sustainable farmers by buying foods that have been properly grown, and if need be, paying more for them.
· Tell your supermarket or co-op produce manager that you want organically grown foods.
· Buy locally grown produce in season.
· Look for roadside stands, farmers' mar-

kets, and "You-Pick-'Em" operations.
· Pester your local and state cultural Extension Office—ask for sources of organic livestock and produce, or other food items you want. The more questions they get about healthy food and sustainable farming practices, the more likely they will be to pass the information along to local farmers.
· Support organizations and political leaders who have made a clear commitment to an agricultural system that sustains the land and the people who farm it responsibly.
· Ask your favorite restaurants to use locally and organically produced food.
· Try to convince your local schools and hospitals to switch.
· Get your community and your family involved in planting trees.
· And as much as possible, try to garden! Even if you don't have a yard, try window boxes, patio planters or rooftop gardens. Consider a community plot, where the work and the land can be shared by several families or a church or community group.

In the end, so much comes down to the power we hold in our wallets. It is time for farmers and consumers to band together and create a new food production system in this country. We can insist that our food be grown in a sustainable manner just as we seek ethical financial investments and responsible practices by urban factories. We can no longer wait for Washington to lead American agriculture toward an environmental ethic. We must vote with our dollars, every time we eat!

*Reference:*

*Terry Cacek and Linda Langer, "The Economic Implications of Organic Farming,"* American Journal of Alternative Agriculture, *1986.*

*Excerpted from* Building Economic Alternatives (*now* Co-op America Quarterly*), Summer 1989.*

# Bill Mollison:
## *A Profile*

Bill Mollison was born in 1928 and has been called the "father of permaculture," an integrated system of design encompassing not only agriculture, horticulture, architecture and ecology, but also money management, land access strategies and legal systems for businesses and communities. The aim is to create systems that provide for their own needs, do not pollute and are sustainable. Conservation of soil, water and energy are central issues to permaculture, as are stability and diversity.

Mollison's two early books *Permaculture One: A Perennial Agriculture for Human Settlements* (with David Holmgren, Transworld Publishers, 1978) and *Permaculture Two: Practical Design for Town and Country in Permanent Agriculture* (Tagari Publications, 1979) have sold over 100,000 copies and been translated into four languages. His new book, *Permaculture: a Designer's Handbook* has recently become available from the Permaculture Institute. In addition, Mollison has written various articles and reports on permaculture for governments, educational and voluntary organizations and the general public.

The main focus of the Permaculture Institute is education. Since its inception in 1978,

*All my life we've been at war with nature. I just pray that we lose that war. There are no winners.*

its certificated design courses have attracted more than 2,000 people, most of whom are now active in the practice or education of permaculture around the world. Independent permaculture institutes have been established in several countries and the movement is linked by biannual international conferences and the International Permaculture Journal.

In addition to his work at the Institute, Mollison consults and educates extensively elsewhere in Australia and abroad. He has worked for example on village housing and planting design in Brazil; tropical polyculture systems in Hawaii, Fiji and the Seychelles, and design strategies for city farms in the UK. He has developed a teaching manual in arid land techniques for the Australian Department of Education's Technical and Further Education Colleges and has advised on this topic in Bahrain, Brazil and the USA. The Permaculture Institute endeavors to spread its practical work internationally by training a core of local people in different countries and then assisting them with back-up resources through a Trust in Aid Fund until they are self-sustaining.

Other initiatives of the Institute include the formation of an Earthbank Society, which holds seminars on ethical investment and publishes on alternative economic and financial strategies; and the initiation of a Tree Tithe Programme which voluntarily taxes the proceeds of all permaculture publications to invest in permanent tree-planting. So far the Programme has funded tree-planting groups in South and Central Australia, New South Wales, India, Nepal, Chile and Spain.

*Bill Mollison was the winner of the 1981 Right Livelihood award. Reprinted from the Right Livelihood Awards' press release.*

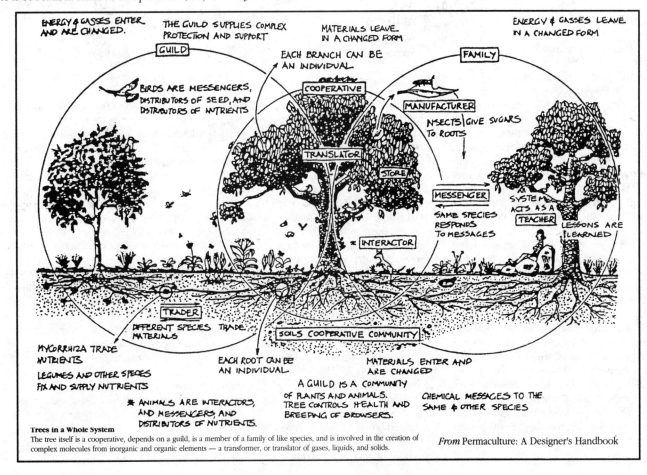

**Trees in a Whole System**

The tree itself is a cooperative, depends on a guild, is a member of a family of like species, and is involved in the creation of complex molecules from inorganic and organic elements — a transformer, or translator of gases, liquids, and solids.

*From* Permaculture: A Designer's Handbook

# Two Vegetarians in Heifer Country

## by Ianto Evans / News from Aprovecho

A year ago Heifer Project International, a prestigious senior development organization, asked Aprovecho to put on a special permaculture course at their headquarters in Arkansas. Their interest was in offering a 2-week interchange between their own international fieldworkers and local people from the Ozarks. They wanted to emphasize what we (farmers in the U.S.) can learn from the Third World, and after extensive inquiries, had concluded that our teaching team would be most suitable. So, in April 1990, Eric Resener and Ianto Evans flew in from the West Coast. What resulted was, I feel, the culmination of six years' effort to provide the best courses on international sustainable systems. We were part of an event that should be exemplary of people-to-people international relations.

Founded in Germany in the 1930's, HPI is funded by churches, and politically extremely reserved. Much of their funding comes from Iowa ranchers. HPI's function is to promote and provide improved breeding stock—heifers, sheep, horses and a broad range of domesticated animals, and to upgrade local breeds in Third World countries. In exchange for donating a bred heifer (sow, ewe, etc.) to a community the first female offspring will in turn be donated to another group. Heifer's whole focus has been, for 50 years, the Rich Countries giving things, specifically domestic animals, to the Poor Countries.

With this in mind, both Eric and I felt somewhat intimidated. Promoting the international meat industry is clearly not part of permaculture. Here are two committed vegetarians, seriously concerned with animal rights, climbing into the jaws of the dragon. Could we conduct ourselves to earn enough respect that the course would be a success? To add to the dilemma, the course was to be held at Heifer's 1200 acre cattle ranch, specifically to coincide with a conference on Women in Livestock Development (WILD women!), many of whose registrants would attend our course. Surely this was the perfect recipe for distrust, disrespect, confrontation and anger.

> Here are two committed vegetarians, seriously concerned with animal rights, climbing into the jaws of the dragon.

Heifer Ranch Director Ed Martsolff and his staff, specifically Jennifer Shumaker, made miracles happen. In some ways Eric and I were observers, the group and setting challenged our honesty and professional skill to the utmost.

At one point Jennifer tentatively asked, "D'you think we'll need to cater for any vegetarians?" I said, "Well, I know of two for certain." The Heifer staff was so cooperative we were able to (as we always do) cater the whole course vegetarian, despite 80% of the participants being enthusiastic carnivores. Jennifer found, in the backwoods of the Ozarks, a remarkable organic farm, whose owner, Mark Cain, moved in with his staff of gourmet cooks and fed us vegan meals so varied, delicious and well presented that the entire group was convinced of the validity of vegetarian food. They were so successful that, given the option of a heavy meat-and-2-vegetable lunch at the ranch cafeteria, almost universally everybody elected to eat at the course kitchen. Hard-bitten cowhands would drift in from their giant tractors to eat with us, in preference to their accustomed meat based diet. The cooks were among the best teachers; consistency of food with theme is essential to good learning.

The previous winter, Jennifer had asked what proportions of Third World people we should plan for. "Ideally," we said, "we'd go for a 3-part balance between Latin Americans, Africans and Gringos."

So often we are dealing mainly with men in what is essentially a woman's preserve, and the difficulty of involving women from traditional cultures: Consistently we stressed the importance of involving women.

By magic, it seemed, Heifer came up with a group comprising almost equal numbers of Latinos, Africans, North Americans and some Asians, about half-a-dozen of each. The course was 60% women, the highest proportion we've ever managed. Dynamite conditions for good interaction! We had a woman ox-driver from Cameroun, a village headwoman from the Philippines, an Indian woman who runs a huge orphanage, and women from Tanzania, Zambia, Honduras and Mexico, all involved in social development at the village level. Men included; two Guatemalans running an ecological grade school in a small isolated town, a Camerounian villager and the son of the Prime Minister of Uganda.

As on ranch land all over the U.S., the soil has been dreadfully abused. By contrast with

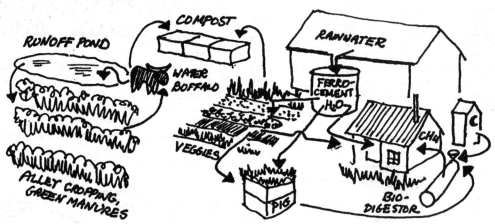

Illustration: Ianto Evans

surrounding woodland, and through noting old soil levels it was clear that huge tracts of Arkansas have lost 2-6 feet of soil since the whites came. Somehow, fate picked the few days before the course to dump 15 inches of rain over the region. We spent our first week perched on the only island of green for miles, the tops of ranch buildings and trees poking up out of the cocoa-colored floods. Talking about the problems of large grazing livestock was almost unnecessary. Nobody disagreed with the course's final conclusions: "The age of large grazing livestock has gone." There are working models of pigpen/biodigester/compost/vegetable plot cycles, a replica Guatemalan country house, carefully integrated contour terrace systems, and nitrogen fixing hedges. We spent much of our time there. The contrast with 1200 acres of overgrazed, overcapitalized, over mechanized chemical ranching was so blatant. Equally, the waste and ostentation of the U.S. are not something most of the participants wanted.

*Excerpted from* News from Aprovecho, *March 1991.*

# MEAT FACTS

Human population of U.S.A.:
**242,000,000**

Number of human beings who could be fed by the grain and soybeans eaten by U.S. livestock:
**1,300,000,000**

Percentage of protein wasted by cycling grain through livestock:
**90**

Pounds of grain and soybeans needed to produce 1 pound of feedlot beef:
**16**

Number of children who will starve to death every day:
**40,000**

Number of pure vegetarians who can be fed by the grain needed to feed 1 meat-eating person:
**20**

Number of people who will starve to death this year:
**60,000,000**

Number of people who could be fed by the grain saved if Americans reduced their intake of meat by 10%:
**60,000,000**

Pesticide residues in the U.S. diet supplied by meat:
**55%**

Pesticide residues in the U.S. diet supplied by dairy products:
**23%**

Pesticide residues in the U.S. diet supplied
by vegetables, fruits, and grains:
**11%**

Percentage of tropical rainforest deforestation directly linked with livestock raising:
**More than 50%**

Amount of forest lost for every hamburger produced from livestock raised on what was Central America forest:
**55 sq. ft. (Size of a small kitchen)**

For every pound of steak the amount of carbon released into the environment has the same greenhouse warming effect as:
**Driving 25 miles in a typical car**

*Sources:* Vegetarian Times, *April 1990;* Diet for a New America, *1987;* World Watch, *May/June 1991*

*Excerpt that appeared in Co-op America Quarterly/Spring 1992.*

## The Pesticide Problem

A 1982 U.S. Congressional staff report indicates that: (i) between 79 and 84 percent of pesticides on the market have not been adequately tested for their capacity to cause cancer; (ii) between 90 and 93 percent of pesticides have not been adequately tested for their ability to cause genetic damage, and (iii) between 60 and 70 percent have not been fully tested for their ability to cause birth defects.

*Excerpted from a National Coalition Against the Misuse of Pesticides guide titled* Pesticide Safety: Myths & Safety.

***According to***
U.S. Geographical Survey scientists, agricultural chemicals, including atrazine and alachlor, attach themselves to water molecules that evaporate from farm fields and return to earth in raindrops, sometimes hundreds of miles away.

Land Stewardship Letter, *Summer 1991, "Herbicides detected in rainfall".*

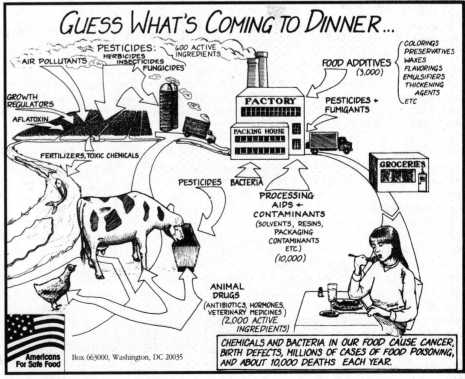

GUESS WHAT'S COMING TO DINNER...

CHEMICALS AND BACTERIA IN OUR FOOD CAUSE CANCER, BIRTH DEFECTS, MILLIONS OF CASES OF FOOD POISONING, AND ABOUT 10,000 DEATHS EACH YEAR.

Americans For Safe Food

Box 663000, Washington, DC 20035

# Food Irradiation
## Could Threaten Our Health

Food irradiation is a preservation process which exposes food to gamma radiation either from the radioactive isotopes cobalt-60 or cesium-137, or from an electron beam. Because radiation penetrates food and *is indiscriminate in its effects,* harmful organisms may be destroyed but *the wholesomeness of the food is affected* as well. While the food itself does not become radioactive, it undergoes many harmful changes. Fruits and vegetables will be irradiated at doses up to 100,000 rads while poultry can be exposed to 300,000 rads (or the equivalent of 30 million chest x-rays.)

Since the 1950's, proponents of food irradiation, including the U.S. Army, the Atomic Energy Commission (AEC), its successor, the Department of Energy (DOE), and the radiation industry, have been pushing for the FDA's approval of food irradiation with little success. It was only in the past decade, in the climate of deregulation, that the FDA approved irradiation for a wide variety of foods. In doing so, the FDA waived its customary approval standards for animal testing, saying that adequate toxicological testing could not be done. At the same time, the FDA admitted, "Studies of sufficiently high quality to support the safety of irradiated foods... are also *not* available." (emphasis added) In fact, the FDA based its approval on *theoretical calculations* from radiation chemistry and physics, not on direct biological testing.

Cobalt-60 and cesium-137, the two radioactive isotopes used in the irradiation process, both have long half lives and are dangerous for many years after their use. Cobalt-60 is hazardous for 50-100 years; cesium-137 for 300-600 years. In addition, cesium-137 is water soluble. When it leaches into ground water supplies, it spreads and is virtually impossible to contain. Although cobalt-60 is currently used in most existing irradiation facilities, cesium-137 is the only isotope available in sufficient quantity to support a thriving food irradiation industry. It is the most abundant radioactive isotope in waste from nuclear weapons manufacture and from nuclear power plants.

Government plans call for the construction of up to 1000 food irradiation facilities across the country — some in the midst of urban neighborhoods; others in rural and farming communities. Irradiation facilities will utilize between one million and ten million curies of radioactive material. In the case of cesium-137, ten million curies is more than 1000 times the cesium released by a 20 kiloton nuclear bomb.

*For more information, please call:* 1-800-EAT-SAFE, *Food & Water, Inc.*

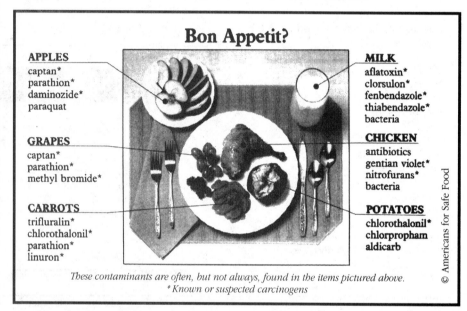

**Bon Appetit?**

**APPLES**
captan*
parathion*
daminozide*
paraquat

**GRAPES**
captan*
parathion*
methyl bromide*

**CARROTS**
trifluralin*
chlorothalonil*
parathion*
linuron*

**MILK**
aflatoxin*
clorsulon*
fenbendazole*
thiabendazole*
bacteria

**CHICKEN**
antibiotics
gentian violet*
nitrofurans*
bacteria

**POTATOES**
chlorothalonil*
chlorpropham
aldicarb

© Americans for Safe Food

*These contaminants are often, but not always, found in the items pictured above.*
*\* Known or suspected carcinogens*

# TAX-EXEMPT BONDS FINANCE FARMER LOAN PROGRAM

Minnesota has a new loan program designed to help young people get started in farming. The program passed by the Legislature this spring introduces so called "aggie bonds" to the state.

A total of $15 million in tax-exempt bonds will be available as a financing tool for beginning farmers and small ag-related businesses to acquire land, livestock, equipment, buildings or install conservation practices at lower interest rates.

The program allows private lenders and sellers to purchase bonds issued by the Minnesota Rural Finance Authority on which the interest is exempt from both federal and state income tax. The lender must "pass on" the interest savings to beginning farmers and ag-related small businesses by making them loans at interest rates up to 2.5 percent lower than market rate.

In past years, federal tax-exempt bonds have been mainly used to fund metropolitan housing redevelopment projects.

The new program focuses on people who have done little or no farming and have few assets. In addition to meeting specific federal eligibility requirements, applicants cannot own or have owned a farm larger than 15 percent of the average farm size in the county of application and cannot have assets in excess of $200,000.

Among the other eligibility requirements for a beginning farmer loan, a prospective borrower must:

- certify that farming will be his/her principal occupation,
- participate in a farm management program for the first five years of the loan,
- file an approved soil and water conservation plan with the county Soil Conservation Service.

Census figures show that nationwide the number of farmers under age 35 has dropped a drastic 70 percent since 1940. Nearly half the nation's food is produced by farmers who will retire in the next 10 years.

Although the new program cannot by itself remedy the problems faced by beginning farmers, Mike Anderson of the Rural Finance Authority, believes it could make a difference in getting new blood into farming.

"One of its purposes is to broaden the resources available to help beginning farmers," Anderson said.

Iowa, Nebraska and Illinois have created similar aggie bond programs.

The program will not be ready to receive applications until September. For more information contact Mike Anderson, Rural Finance Authority, Minnesota Department of Agriculture (612) 296-5943.

*Reprinted from* Land Stewardship Letter, *Summer 1991.*

# Food Coops: The Consumer Link to Sustainable Farming

**by Steve Clark /** *The Land Stewardship Letter*

For Barbara Anderson, of Frederic, Wisconsin, a food coop is a source of nutritious, wholesome food at a low cost. She's a member of the Natural Alternative Coop and especially appreciates being able to obtain bulk organic grains and beans at low prices. "It's the only store in the area where I can buy non-chemical food for my family," she says.

Tim Crampton of Minneapolis says he shops at coops because the people who manage them "care about the consumer and are knowledgeable about food and food production." Crampton credits the coops for increasing his awareness of the importance of sustainable agriculture. "Before I started shopping at coops I never really thought about where my food comes from or how it is raised. Now that I'm conscious of it, I eat healthier, and better from an environmental aspect."

For Linda Miller of Maplewood, a food coop is a place where she can avoid supporting the "food giants" whose ethics she finds questionable. She believes coops are a vital link between small farmers and consumers. "I like the fact that they are not organized to make a profit and they make an effort to buy from local producers. It keeps the money within the community."

Food cooperatives in the Twin Cities area are flourishing. According to coop movement pioneer Kris Olsen, the popularity of coops will continue to grow, as more and more people become concerned about food issues. Twenty years ago, Olsen and several others started The People's Pantry, a "pay-what-you-can experiment" on the West Bank in Minneapolis. After complaints from health inspectors, the Pantry was reorganized as the North Country Coop, becoming the first member–owned food coop in the Twin Cities. Today, North Country is one of 18 storefront coops in the Twin Cities area. Another 30 can be found scattered throughout rural Minnesota, Iowa and Wisconsin. And over three times that many buying clubs are in operation.

"Some people were afraid that once the huge supermarkets started carrying organic products and bulk items the local coops would start to fade," notes Olsen. "But that isn't what's happening. The big stores have a tough time marketing organics and so they end up being far more expensive than the coops."

The secret to the coops' success, says Olsen, is the trust relationship between the buyer and seller. "The big stores have to over-package their organic products in order to differentiate them from the conventional. At coops, the organics are usually sold in bulk just like the other food, and the customer is trusted to tell the cashier the right price."

Pat Kerrigan, produce buyer for Linden Hills Coop agrees. "There's a strong honor system at work here which probably couldn't work in a large supermarket. For one thing, people seem to have an allegiance to coops. It's a whole different relationship from simply being a customer."

Most coops allow both members and non-members to shop. Members elect a board of directors to oversee the operation and hire staff to manage the store. A large percentage of the work is carried out by volunteers or "working members" who then receive a discount on food purchased at the store.

According to P.J. Hoffman of Blooming Prairie Natural Foods (a wholesale distributor), the Twin Cities network of coops is the largest in the country. Hoffman believes that one reason for the growth of coops and buying clubs is that people want to have more control over the food system. With the current trend of foreign and large scale ownership of the food industry, people are realizing there's a place for member and community supported stores, says Hoffman.

"Six to seven years ago it was a nice idea, but most people didn't care one way or the other. Today it is marketable " says Hoffman. "Coops remain as an example of how communities can organize to serve their own needs."

Sometimes what people want is not always available from local producers, especially when it comes to fruit. Like the larger stores, coops are able to obtain from distributors items from California and Mexico—and usually at competitive prices. Kerrigan thinks, however, that the real beauty of coops is their ability to support small food companies—sometimes household enterprises that otherwise would not have an outlet for their products.

"There are over a dozen companies I can think of which have sprung up in the last five years that sell directly and exclusively to coops. It really has become a way for people to become independent of the giant food industry—which brings with it a special sense of security, a sense that a community can achieve at least a degree of self-sufficiency," says Kerrigan.

Melody Nelson, a buyer for Roots and Fruits Cooperative (a wholesale outfit) calls coops the consumer link to sustainable agriculture. "Coops take the time to educate consumers, and to label the food as clearly as possible. That helps the farmer who is making a transition from conventional to organic. We try to buy certified organic first, but that means three years without any chemicals. So we also buy products in transition, and label them accordingly. This info is passed on to the consumer."

Nelson adds that it is very important to support farmers during their transitional phase, because if they can't find a market they're likely to go back to the use of chemicals.

*Excerpted from* The Land Stewardship Letter, *Summer 1990.*

## Community-supported Agriculture: New Hope

*For every one person who entered the profession of farming in 1986, three people left farming to pursue other careers.*

— U.S. Census

Farmland preservation advocates are experimenting with a new tool to keep farms growing crops rather than sprouting houses. Community-supported agriculture is a European practice in which local households pay a portion of a farm's operating costs in exchange for a share of the harvest. Membership fees range from $350 a year for a vegetable farm to $1,000 for a farm that also supplies milk, eggs and meat. Right now, there are about 40 community-supported farms in the United States, accorking to the American Farmland Trust. All are organic.

*Excerpted from* Land Letter, *January 1990.*

## GLEANERS FIGHT HUNGER

*When you reap the harvest in your land, you shall not reap right into the edges of your field, neither shall you glean the fallen ears. You shall leave them for the poor and for the alien.*

- Leviticus 23:22

Food Share is a volunteer group that collects food throughout Ventura County, California. Rather than allow farmers to plow under fruits and vegetables after a harvest, members scavenge the fields, collecting the leftovers to stock their 12,000 square-foot warehouse operation. The produce is then distributed to 160 neighborhood agencies that assist 24,000 families, some as far away as Fresno and Los Angeles. Approximately 4 million pounds of fresh fruits and vegetables are gleaned annually and much more is left behind in the fields. Food Share began in a two-car garage in 1978. Today it boasts of 200 volunteers, mostly retirees, who work one to two days a week, and 26 willing growers.

*Contact: Food Share, Box 4596, Ventura, CA 93004, (805) 647-3944.*

*Source:* Los Angeles Times, *Sept. 14, 1989.*

# Giving Animals a Voice

## by Cathe Compton / *Earth Journal*

*We are used to drinking milk from containers showing 'contented' cows, whose real lives we want to hear nothing about, eating eggs and drumsticks from 'happy' hens, and munching hamburgers from bulls of integrity who seem to command their fate... There are those who never once have considered animal rights.*

— Alice Walker

Why animals' rights when there are so many starving people? Because there *are* so many starving people. Meat consumption causes intense animal suffering and magnifies the world hunger crisis.

Some have estimated the total number of deaths due to lack of food as being 60,000,000 each year. While these people face starvation, we continue feeding to animals the grains and legumes that could be fed directly to people, and could ultimately save these lives. Production of foodstuffs used to feed animals uses up 90% of our agriculture resources and dramatically depletes our vital topsoil and groundwater. Our ability to grow sufficient food for our future needs is in jeopardy.

The family farm of green pastures and open barnyards has been replaced by giant "factory farms." Each year in the United States, nearly six billion cattle, pigs, chickens and other animals are force fed, genetically manipulated, artificially inseminated, and fed huge amounts of antibiotics. Factory farmed animals are treated more like machine parts on an assembly line than beings who feel pain. Most of the "red meat" and poultry that we eat comes from production-oriented factory farms. Slaughter must bring relief from the crowding, deprivation, and mutilation that is routine.

We know that we do not need animals' flesh to survive. Yet we have come to like the taste and smell of these pieces of animals. We don't want to give them up even though doing so means a healthier life for us all.

Each of us must make a decision whether to condone animal exploitation, environmental devastation and world hunger or actively to oppose it. What can be done? We have million opportunities to make our lives count. First, we can become more informed. Some good reading materials include *Diet for a New America* by John Robbins, *Animal Factories* by Jim Mason and Peter Singer, and *Vegetarian Times Magazine.*

We can all personally and directly reduce animal and human suffering by choosing to not eat meat. If we do this, our grocery money will not be used to support the mechanized factory farm system. If Americans reduced their meat consumption by only 10% there would be 12 million more tons of grain to feed the humans that starve to death each year. Our daily food choices will make an important difference. Our consumer buying power is potent. That power counts! Together we can stop the suffering.

*Reprinted from* Earth Journal, *December 1990.*

# Chapter 6

# *Energy & Technological Development*

*Concern for man himself and his fate must always form
the chief interest of all technical endeavors, concern for
the great unsolved problems of the organization of labor
and the distributions of goods—in order that the
creations of our mind shall be a blessing and not a curse
to mankind. Never forget this in the midst of your
diagrams and equations.*

Albert Einstein (1879-1955)
Address, California Institute of Technology [1931]

*Photo from Diablo Project Office*

*1981 protest march at Diablo Canyon nuclear power plant sponsored by Abalone Alliance and Mothers for Peace where over 2000 arrests were made during a two week period. Mothers for Peace has been responsible for monitoring this facility for over two decades. After Diablo Canyon, there has been no new constructions scheduled of nuclear power facilities.*

# Alternative Energy:
## *A Brighter Proposal*

*The United States must do more than stumble toward safer, cleaner, and more economical energy. Here's a way for everyone, even George Bush, to make the leap, before our dependence on fossil fuels and nuclear power weakens us further.*

Since the 1970s environmentalists have been incubating ideas for a national energy policy. To assemble a list of the most timely, important, and practical suggestions for the 1990s, *Sierra* tapped the National Energy Efficiency Platform drafted by the Energy Conservation Coalition (to which the Sierra Club belongs), the Natural Resources Defense Council, the American Council for an Energy-Efficient Economy, and the Alliance to Save Energy.

### Going Farther on a Gallon

Congress should raise the fuel-economy standard for new cars to 45 miles per gallon and for new light trucks to 35 mpg—a technically and economically achievable goal that is 60 percent higher than today's standards. To push average auto efficiencies even higher, Congress should offer rebates to consumers who buy vehicles that exceed the standard and increase the existing "gas-guzzler tax" on those who choose vehicles that fail to meet it. It should also require "truth in testing": Cars currently get about 15 percent lower mileage on the road than in EPA tests.

In an effort to move toward this goal, senators Richard Bryan (D-Nev.) and Slade Gorton (R-Wash.) have introduced a bill that would require 40 mpg for new cars and 30 mpg for light trucks. In the House, a fuel-efficiency bill introduced by Barbara Boxer (D-Calif) would set 45 mpg and 35 mpg standards-and require truth in testing.

The energy and economic savings achieved by such measures would be enormous. A decade after passage, the Bryan-Gorton bill would save us 2.8 million barrels of oil a day. That's ten times as much as the Arctic National Wildlife Refuge would yield under the most optimistic projections, ten times as much as we'd likely to get from more offshore leasing in California, and a million barrels more than we import each day from the Persian Gulf. In addition, consumers would enjoy an annual savings of more than $50 billion in gasoline not purchased, and the atmosphere would be spared more than a million tons of Earth-warming carbon emissions daily.

### A Utility Revolution

From society's standpoint, it makes perfect economic sense to meet increasing demand for electric power with energy efficiency programs wherever possible. By adopting just the cheapest efficiency improvements, those that save a kilowatt-hour at a cost of 0.6 cents or less, we could reduce electrical use in this country by 75 percent, according to the Rocky Mountain Institute. That price tag is several times less than the cost of fuel for a coal-fired or nuclear-power plant-never mind other operating expenses. The Electric Power Research Institute, the utility industry's research arm, posits higher costs, with savings in the 30-percent range, but affirms that efficiency improvements are an extraordinarily good buy.

Some utilities have benefited from this knowledge. By promoting efficiency in 1983 and '84, Southern California Edison reduced the peak demand of its 10 million customers by more than 8 percent. The program cost the utility only about one percent as much as building and running a new power plant.

But for utilities not planning to build a new plant soon, the economics don't work out as well. If they help consumers save energy, sales go down, costs sometimes go up, and they may be on the road to financial disaster.

A few states have taken the lead in making efficiency profitable for the institutions that have traditionally met our power needs. In California, for instance, regulators have divorced utility profits from sales, so utilities can benefit from successful conservation programs. In New York and Massachusetts, regulators have given efficiency a boost by requiring utilities to consider environmental costs when they compare various energy sources.

Congress should encourage state utility commissions to make efficiency more financially attractive. It should also consider amendments to the Public Utility Regulatory Policies Act (PURPA) that would allow efficiency to compete more effectively with other power sources.

### Tougher Appliance Standards

Most of the machines that fill our homes—from furnaces to freezers—were designed in an era of cheap, abundant energy. In many cases more efficient models are now available (or soon will be). Federal appliance-efficiency standards, which set minimums

that all manufacturers must meet, should be upgraded to reflect advances in technology. Congress should adopt state-of-the-art requirements for lighting, windows, and plumbing fixtures as well.

The savings could be enormous. Raising refrigerator and freezer standards by one third, for instance, would reduce electricity use a decade hence by some 18 billion kilowatt-hours per year. That's equal to the yearly output of four large nuclear plants.

### Better Buildings

Energy use in residential and commercial buildings, which swallows up more than a third of the nation's supply, could be cut in half by 2010, according to *Scientific American,* saving $100 billion a year in energy costs.

How could we reap these benefits? The Department of Energy could start by encouraging states to adopt federal energy-efficient building standards. Meeting these rules should also be required of federal-home-loan applicants.

Federal loan programs that promote efficiency should be more widely publicized. Fannie Mae (the Federal National Mortgage Association), Freddie Mac (the Federal Home Loan Mortgage Association), and the Veterans Administration offer larger loans and lower interest rates for energy efficient houses, but only one U.S. homebuyer in 10,000 takes advantage of these programs.

### Redefining Costs

If an energy-guzzling air conditioner costs less than an efficient one, but will run up a bigger bill over time, federal agencies are supposed to purchase the more efficient model because it has a lower "life-cycle cost." In practice, however, the feds rarely do purchase efficiency, because it often entails a bigger initial outlay. Adherence to the life-cycle-cost rule would cut energy use in federal buildings by 20 percent, energy costs by $1 billion a year, and annual carbon-dioxide emissions by 15 megatons.

"Cost" also needs to be redefined when comparing energy sources. If coal's effects on the biosphere were included as part of its overall cost, it would be so expensive that utilities would use it only as a last resort. Some solar-power options, judged by the same standard, would be relatively cheap. And most efficiency improvements would consistently come out at the top of the least-cost list.

Some states have already expanded their notion of costs. In New York, for instance, utility planners add "an environmental cost" of 1.4 cents per kilowatt-hour to the price of fossil-fuel options. It's no coincidence that efficiency programs are expected to reduce peak demand for electricity in the state by 900 megawatts by 1992.

### Federal Research and Development

Many of the energy-efficient technologies touted in this issue originated in federal R&D programs begun in the 1970s. Yet funding for all forms of energy research has dropped since 1980—for energy efficiency by a factor of three; for renewable energy sources by a factor of ten.

We should consider energy R&D a kind of insurance, says University of California energy and resources professor John P. Holdren: "The funding required to develop these alternatives to the point that we can choose intelligently among them is modest compared with the potential costs of having too few choices. "

### Higher Fuel Taxes

In the United States we pay around $1.50 for a gallon of gas. In France the price is more than $3; in Italy, about $4. Most of the variance is due to higher fuel taxes.

Budget legislation passed last year hiked the U.S. gas tax by five cents. This tax should be increased over the next five years by a total of 50 cents, with most of the additional revenues earmarked for mass transit and energy-efficiency programs. To offset the regressive impact of this measure, the government should compensate low-income people through an income-tax credit.

Economists say that such a tax would discourage driving somewhat, reducing gasoline consumption by at least 8 percent. Emissions of carbon dioxide and other damaging substances would shrink proportionally. Meanwhile, back on the highway, we'd be cruising along relatively cheaply.

Another way to raise money for mass transit, efficiency programs, and renewable-energy research would be a carbon tax. Based on the carbon content of fuels (a good indicator of their pollution potential), this levy would boost gasoline prices modestly, but coal prices substantially.

### Foreign Policy

In granting loans or aid to energy projects around the world, the U.S. government should support the alternatives that are least costly, as measured by both environmental and economic impacts. When participating in projects through the World Bank, the United States should oppose schemes that don't meet this "least-cost" test.

Wherever possible, our international aid should encourage energy efficiency. Giving developing countries the money to buy home insulation, compact fluorescent lights, and energy-efficient refrigerators, for instance, could improve living conditions without harming the local-or global-environment.

### Can Science Cure Our Energy Ills?

To some environmentalists, hoping for a grand technological fix for the world's energy dilemma is like waiting for Godot. We can't wait around for whiz-bang solutions, they say: If we simply use less energy, we'll create fewer energy-related problems.

But many technological solutions with real promise get a bad rap. Yes, technology has brought us nuclear power plants (and nuclear waste with nowhere to go) as well as the gasoline engine (and greenhouse gases with nowhere to go). But most of us like being able to heat a kettle of water without first having to build a fire from cow dung. A civilization that rents out seats on space flights to television reporters need not make its citizens shiver to save energy.

Fortunately, energy efficiency and well-designed technology go hand in hand. While we can reduce consumption (by throwing away our car keys, for example), less austere solutions include putting advances in electronics and materials to work in designing more efficient vehicles and cities. Perhaps someday we can even make good on the "space age" promises of fully automated offices and homes, or guided roadways that propel vehicles using benign energy sources. What follows is a look at a few of the technologies—some proven and merely waiting for political and economic support to succeed, and some existing only on paper—that might help ease us away from our dependence on fossil fuels.

### Wind

Energy from the best wind technology is already nearly as cheap as that from conventional energy sources—an all important benchmark of about six to eight cents per kilowatt-hour. (A California residence that relies on electricity for all its energy needs can be expected to use about 800 kilowatt-hours per month.) Already, 1.5 million kilowatts of electricity are generated by California wind farms, and increasingly sophisticated blade materials and designs are being developed to produce even more power with greater efficiency. The disadvantages: So far, wind farms earn their keep only in areas with consistently strong winds (averaging more than 12 miles per hour); they require considerable amounts of land (although the land can be used for other purposes at the same time); and they have been known to kill unsuspecting birds.

### Solar Thermal

The fastest-growing large-scale method of harnessing solar energy, solar-thermal technology, produces about 350 megawatts of power at several plants in California's Mojave Desert. The cost of electricity from these plants is competitive with Southern California's "peak power" rates (what's charged when electrical demand is greatest—for example, in the late afternoon).

Using a variety of techniques, solar-thermal systems collect the sun's energy and use it to heat a fluid to as much as 3,600 degrees Fahrenheit. The heat can be used to generate steam, which can then be used by boiler plants to produce heat or electricity. Like wind and most other solar technologies, solar thermal's effect on the environment is relatively slight: Once in operation these facilities release essentially no pollution and generate no waste. Solar-thermal systems take up large amounts of land, however, and they're built primarily from high-tech components, the manufacture of which (at least for now) is often polluting.

*Some of the 3,500 wind turbines at Altamont Pass, California, operated by U.S. Windpower, the world's largest manufacturer of wind turbines. Photo courtesy of Renew America.*

## Photovoltaics

While solar-thermal technology converts the sun's energy into electricity indirectly, photovoltaic technology does it directly: Light is converted into electricity when it hits a special type of solid-state cell composed of thin layers of semiconductor material. Solar cells have become increasingly economical; within two decades, perhaps, declining production costs and increasing cell efficiency will make them cost-effective for utility-scale uses. These nearly maintenance-free systems already earn their keep in virtually any location not hooked up to an electric-utility system, and in consumer goods such as calculators, watches, and walkway lights. As with solar-thermal technology, photovoltaic systems are benign once in operation, but their production relies on a potentially messy combination of high-tech materials.

*ARCO Solar's 6.5 megawatt solar central station (dismantled) Carrisa Plains, CA. Photo courtesy Renew America.*

## Geothermal Energy

These systems tap heat generated by natural processes underground. They are already in use in New Zealand, Iceland, Italy, the Philippines, and California (where geothermal steam generates about 2 million kilowatts), and under development in Central America, the Soviet Union, and elsewhere. Unfortunately, geothermal resources are commonly found in volcanic areas—often some of the most pristine sites on Earth. With more advanced technology, geothermal energy could be extracted from underground masses of hot rock, a nearly limitless resource.

## Biomass Energy

Biomass is any plant matter that stores the sun's energy through photosynthesis. It can be converted into practical energy simply (by burning wood for heat, for example) or by using complex systems that gasify plant matter and run it through turbine generators to make electricity. In its most primitive forms, biomass is the main source of energy for nearly half the world. It's available anywhere that plants can grow, and (if produced sustainably) adds no carbon dioxide to the environment. Though plentiful, biomass has its limitations: It's a relatively inefficient storehouse of energy, and in many parts of the world it would consume acreage probably best used to grow food crops or left in a wild state.

Biomass is the only renewable energy source capable of producing premium liquid and gas fuels (primarily ethanol) that are already workable alternatives to oil, coal, and natural gas. (Methanol, a much-vaunted alternative fuel, is only a partial solution to our energy problems, since it is very toxic and most often made from natural gas or coal.) In the United States, corn-ethanol production survives only with significant subsidies. Production of ethanol from cane sugar in the tropics is much more attractive, however, because the conversion process is more efficient, land and labor are cheaper, and biomass growth rates are higher. (About half of Brazil's cars run on ethanol made from sugar cane.) The operation can be made even more efficient if the waste can be burned to make electricity at the same time. It's more difficult and expensive to extract ethanol from woody crops, but the technologies do exist.

A process called enzyme hydrolysis could make biomass based alcohol fuels more competitive in the United States.

## Efficient Design

This is a huge area with great conservation potential anywhere energy is used, such as in motors (for everything from home appliances to factory-floor machinery), automobile engines, lighting, space conditioning, and refrigeration.

About half of all energy used in the United States is wasted, and improved efficiency is the cheapest source of "new" energy—although it's not necessarily the easiest to implement. Advances in electronics, manufacturing processes, and complex materials continually conspire to make designed—in energy efficiency less expensive.

On a larger scale, the development of super-efficient electric transmission techniques and storage methods can further increase energy savings. (Unlike liquid and gas fuels, electricity is difficult to store.) "Superconductive" materials being developed reduce electrical resistance nearly to zero; they could maximize the efficiency of electrical wires and provide an effective medium for storing power.

## Solar Hydrogen

Sometime after the year 2000, perhaps, hydrogen fuel produced with solar energy could become the antidote to our fossil-fuel addiction. Hydrogen combustion emits no carbon monoxide, volatile organic compounds, particulates, sulfur dioxide, or carbon dioxide. The only by-products are water vapor and controllable levels of nitrogen oxide. One way to produce hydrogen fuel is by electrolysis-splitting water molecules into hydrogen and oxygen. The key question is where the power for this process will come from. Depending on whom you talk to, the answer could be electricity from nuclear as well as solar sources. Once photovoltaic systems become cost-effective, they could provide the energy for electrolysis.

## Nuclear Fusion

You have to be a true optimist to count on fusion, especially after 1989s "fusion-in-a-jar" fiasco. But it's a tempting idea: Whereas fission creates energy by splitting atoms, fusion joins them together. Enormous amounts of energy are released when the nuclei of two hydrogen isotopes, deuterium and tritium, are fused. Deuterium is a component of water; tritium can be made from naturally occurring lithium and, while radioactive, has only a 12-year half-life. In theory, fusion's only waste product is the inert gas helium. To no one's surprise, however, the technology has serious problems: Using current methods, radioactive waste will be produced, and neutrons that escape during the process make the reactor radioactive. The biggest stumbling block is getting the positively charged nuclei of the hydrogen isotopes to attract each other, which normally occurs only at extremely high temperatures. Fusion occurs naturally in the sun, but it has proved elusive to reproduce under controlled conditions. The hydrogen bomb is the most dramatic example of uncontrolled fusion.

## Solar Energy in Space

On paper, it's appealing: A huge structure containing 10 billion solar cells floating about in high orbit would collect solar energy, convert it into electricity, and beam it to Earth as microwaves. The atmosphere wouldn't block the sun's rays, and collection could take place 24 hours a day. The best estimate of when the right mix of cheap photovoltaics will coincide with regular cargo shuttles into space puts application of this idea deep into the 21st century, however.

## Tapping the Tides

There are endless schemes for exploiting the enormous (but erratic) power of tides, waves, and currents. Tidal power can be harnessed with much of the technology already in use for hydroelectric projects, but it's still very expensive, and effects on local environments can be just as great. In Norway, the world's first commercial wave-energy plant generates 850 kilowatts of electricity. There wave pressure acts like a piston, pushing air in a shaft through an electricity-generating turbine. Another idea that's been successful on a small scale is ocean-thermal-energy conversion, a technology that taps the temperature differences between deep sea-water and the sun-warmed surface in tropical oceans to generate electricity.

## Cogeneration

Only a third of the energy from a boiler in a conventional power plant is converted to electricity. The wasted heat can be tapped by "cogenerators" to produce both heat and electricity. Because cogenerators are usually fired by oil or natural gas, the process isn't really a "fix" for fossil-fuel dependency, but it uses conventional resources more efficiently.

Common-sense strategies and cunning new technologies can be combined for a more comfortable, less costly home.

## High-Tech Lighting

Introduced in the early 1980s, the compact fluorescent lamp is one of the most promising new energy-efficiency tools around. These lamps don't flicker or make faces look ghoulish as the old tube fluorescents did; they emit light as pleasant as an incandescent bulb's. Yet the lamps are so efficient that an 18-watt compact fluorescent provides as much light as a standard 75-watt incandescent bulb.

Each of these new lamps costs at least ten times as much as an incandescent, but it will last up to ten times longer and use only one-fourth as much electricity. If you can afford the up-front cost, you'll save both money and energy over the life of the lamp.

The lamps come in many designs and sizes, so it may take some shopping around to find the ones that best meet your needs. If local merchants don't stock this important energy conserving tool, ask them to consider it. In the meantime, you can shop by mail through: The Energy Federation, 354 B Waverly St., Framingham, MA 01701; Rising Sun Enterprises, P.O. Box 1728, Basalt, CO 81621; or Real Goods, 966 S. Mazzoni St., Ukiah, CA 95482.

The amount of energy that flows out of U.S. windows annually is equal to that delivered each year by the Alaska pipeline. That figure may decline little by little, however, thanks to recent rapid advances in window design.

The first step forward, early in the last decade, was commercial production of "low-emissivity" glass coated with a substance that blocks the flow of heat but not light. Now almost all U.S. glass manufacturers offer this product.

Some windows now on the market have a layer of nontoxic argon gas—an even better insulator than air—sandwiched between two panes of coated glass. This configuration is four times as effective at keeping the heat (or cold) inside your house as a single pane; it is twice as good as most double-pane windows.

Even greater efficiencies are possible. A vacuum between two coated panes can make a window 15 times as efficient as a single pane. Though they are crystal-clear, these vacuum-packed windows perform as well as most insulated walls at night. During the day, by providing heat from sunlight, they act as a solar furnace.

Unfortunately, you can't buy vacuum windows yet; researchers are still working to find a cost-effective manufacturing process. But you can consider a variety of energy-efficient models that take advantage of improvements in energy-saving window technology over the past decade.

## Frugal Refrigerators

Six million refrigerators are sold in the United States every year. If only the most efficient in each size category were purchased, the energy saved annually could replace one large power plant—at one-sixth the cost of building it.

An excellent guide to frugal refrigerators—and other appliances—is *A Consumer Guide to Home Energy Savings*. At the top of the efficiency list are the refrigerators manufactured by Sun Frost (P.O. Box 1101, Arcata, CA 95521). The firm's 16-cubic-foot model, for instance, uses only about a third to a fourth as much energy as its competitors. (It is also more expensive—around $2,400.)

Those who won't be buying refrigerators this year can tend to the ones they already have. Dust the coils at least once a year. Test the door seals; if they can't firmly hold a dollar bill when the door is shut, they should be replaced.

## Savvy Controls

If you're the type who forgets to turn down the heat at night, take heart—you can buy an automatic thermostat ($40-$90) that will do it for you, without fail. The device can also be set to take the chill off your home in the morning before you get out of bed.

Do you have trouble remembering to turn out the lights? Consider purchasing switches that turn lights on when a door is opened and off when it is closed. Or try "people sensors, " which automatically turn off lights when a room is unoccupied for five to seven minutes. Outdoors, try a motion sensing light. Used to illuminate a front porch when someone approaches, for instance, such a light makes it easier to find your keys—and it can discourage intruders.

If you have an electric water heater, a simple $30 timing device will shut it off while you sleep and turn it back on at a given time in the morning. The payback period is less than a year. For more complicated on-off settings, you may need to invest about $100.

(Similar devices for gas water heaters are much more complicated, and therefore not as cost-effective.)

## Shower Power

By decreasing water use, low-flow showerheads and faucet aerators reduce hot-water costs by as much as 50 percent. A top-quality low-flow showerhead costs between $10 and $20 and will pay for itself in as little as four months. Aerators are just a few dollars each. If they aren't available at local stores, try mail-order outlets.

While considering hardware, don't neglect the most basic step in hot-water conservation: Insulate your storage tank. Kits that do the job well are widely available for $10 to $20 and pay for themselves in less than a year.

## Tried and True Ways to Save

- Keep your car well–tuned and maintained. Leave it home or combine trips whenever you can. When buying a car, shop around for the most efficient model. There are wide variations in efficiency within all automobile size and safety classes.

- Fill in the cracks. By putting insulation in your walls and roof and by caulking and weather-stripping doorways and windows, you cut energy consumption and make your house more comfortable. Ask your utility company if it has loan or rebate programs for weatherization.

- Recycle. Making new paper, glass, and metal products from recycled materials saves 40 to 60 percent of the energy required to produce them from virgin materials; it also reduces pollution by an equivalent amount. A move that is equally important in these days when recycling bins are glutted: Expand the market for recycled products by buying them.

- Tap the power of the sun. Purchase useful solar-powered products such as flashlights and outdoor lighting. Consider installing a solar water heater on the roof of your home.

- If you buy an automatic clothes dryer, choose one heated by natural gas. It will produce less carbon dioxide and other pollutants than one fired by electricity that is generated by burning coal or oil.

- If you have a forced-air furnace, check its filter at least once a month during the heating season to see if it needs to be cleaned or replaced. Dust blocks the flow of heat and forces the blower to work harder.

- Oil-fired systems should be tuned up and cleaned by a professional every year. Gas-fired systems need the same treatment every two years. Adhering to this schedule will not only cut your energy costs, it will reduce the air pollution from your system.

*Excerpted from* Sierra, *March/April 1991.*

# BUMPER TO BUMPER, COAST TO COAST

## *Transportation System and Solution Going Nowhere Fast*

Motor vehicles are major contributors to air pollution, ozone depletion, the greenhouse effect, acid rain, and a loss of scenic beauty as roads and parking lots pave over the American landscape.

Are we a nation hooked on the automobile, or can efficient and reasonably priced public transit help us kick the habit? Will technological advances remedy the damaging environmental impacts, or will population growth-and thus vehicle ownership and travel demand-offset any gains made?

### GRRRRidlock

According to the Federal Highway Administration, if no significant improvements are made, congestion will increase more than 400 percent over the next 20 years on the nation's freeways and over 200 percent on non-freeways. Areas with populations under one million, as they experience the push for growth and development, can expect increases of more than 1000 percent.

Population growth clearly plays a role in traffic congestion: more people, more cars. And since the 1970s, as millions of baby boomers and an unprecedented number of women began entering the work force, an added burden has been placed on transportation.

Rapid and uncontrolled suburbanization, which has resulted from the explosive growth in our cities, has pressured our transportation system even further. Between 1980 to 1986, 86 percent of the nation's population increase occurred in metro areas, with about three-quarters of that growth absorbed by the suburbs. In addition, about two-thirds of job growth has been in the suburbs. Mass transit systems built in the 1970s to assist suburban to center city commuters are now insufficient to meet the demands of suburban to suburban travel. This has resulted in an almost total dependence on the automobile.

Call it an insatiable appetite for the car or a lack of alternatives to it, our growing dependence on the car is a large chunk of the gridlock problem. Between 1960 and 1980, while the population grew by 26 percent and the labor force by 38 percent, the number of cars on the road *almost doubled*. There are more cars per person in the United States than in any other country, about one car for every two persons.

We also use the car more often to get around. In cities like Denver, Houston and Los Angeles, about 90 percent of workers commute by car. In European cities, about 40 percent get to work by car, 37 percent use public transit, and the rest walk or bicycle. Only 15 percent of the population in westernized Asian cities, such as Tokyo, drive to work by car.

### Paving the Way

While the American solution to the traffic problem continues to favor building and widening roads, many argue that this is self defeating. In Southern California, for instance, where there are probably more freeways than anywhere else in the world, the average travel speed is 33 mph. It is expected to drop to 15 mph by the year 2000 as population and car ownership continue to grow.

The loss of scenic beauty and valuable land is also at issue as roads and parking lots rob communities of their distinctiveness and this nation of its natural landscape. In U.S. cities, close to half of all urban space goes to accommodate the automobile. In Los Angeles, the figure reaches two-thirds. Over 60,000 square miles of this nation's land (roughly equal to the size of Georgia) has been paved over, including 10 percent of all arable land.

The price of gasoline in this country, which remains well below world levels, not only encourages driving over using public transit, it also promotes consumption over conservation. In 1987, the average U.S. price per gallon of gasoline was 82 cents, as compared to $3.71 in Italy, $2.95 in France, and $2.89 in Japan. The key difference is tax. The average U.S. is 24 cents per gallon; in all other non-communist countries, the tax is over $1.

As America's own oil supplies give in to our gas-guzzling ways, imports have risen to 35 percent of total supply and may go up as high as 60 percent by the year 2000. The U.S. Department of Energy sees this mounting dependence on foreign sources of oil as a major threat to our national security.

> **"We're coming up against the physical limits...the goal has got to be shifted away from moving vehicles to moving people."**

### Environmental Hazard

An estimated 100 million Americans—two out of every five citizens—live in areas with health threatening pollution levels. Dozens of cities, including virtually every major urban area, continue to fail to meet EPA's acceptable levels for carbon monoxide and ozone.

Motor vehicle emissions are a major source of these pollutants. They are responsible for 45 percent of nitrogen oxides and 33 percent of the hydrocarbons that produce smog, acid rain and the ozone problem. They also contribute 75 percent of carbon dioxide, the pollutant that promotes global warming via the greenhouse effect.

According to the American Lung Association, air pollution costs the nation's taxpayers about $40 billion annually in health care. In addition, estimated damage from ozone results in crop losses of between $1.9 billion to $4.5 billion a year.

Less-polluting cars are in the works. But the EPA maintains that the individual auto cannot be improved sufficiently to meet future air quality needs in some metro areas, and that strict limitations on VMT (vehicle miles of travel)—which is largely influenced by population trends—will be required to significantly reduce emissions.

### Getting Out of a (Traffic) Jam

As the social, economic and environmental costs of our dependence on cars become increasingly evident, the search for alternatives is going full speed ahead. Many, like New York City Transportation Commissioner Ross Chandler, feel that public transportation needs to play a larger role: "We're coming up against the physical limits...the goal has got to be shifted away from moving vehicles to moving people."

As many as 30 cities-including San Diego, Buffalo, Sacramento, Dallas, St. Louis, Minneapolis and Miami-have either built or are in the process of building rail transit systems. Other cities like Boston and San Francisco are extending their existing trolley lines.

Urban planners are looking at ways to design suburban centers that are more self-contained and more urban in character, thus leading to a more energy-efficient land use that cuts down on commute distance and that is more effectively served by public transportation.

*Additional copies are available from Zero Population Growth. Single copy free with SASE; write ZPG for information on bulk prices. Publications list available upon request.*

*Excerpted from a ZPG Fact Sheet, prepared June 1989.*

# ENERGY ON THE ROAD
## Transportation and the Environment

Unmistakable sign of crisis is our increasing dependence on foreign oil, a problem that has come to the forefront with the Iraqi invasion of Kuwait. The United States now imports half its oil. We could cut this habit substantially by increasing fuel efficiency and holding the volume of travel constant. For example, by raising the current average fuel economy for all cars from roughly 18 miles per gallon to 21, we could eliminate the need for all US imports of Iraqi and Kuwaiti oil.

There is no single policy that can eliminate congestion, reduce the environmental impact of transportation, and end dependence on foreign oil. Government officials must instead make a wide range of changes on the federal, state, and local levels. As a nation, we should set a goal of reducing the amount of energy used by transportation by at least 20 percent by the year 2005 and aim to end the transportation sector's over reliance on oil. To accomplish this, UCS advocates the following coordinated plan of action:

***Increase motor-vehicle fuel efficiency.*** The federal government should increase the CAFE standard for new cars to at least 40 mpg (30 mpg for light trucks), by the year 2000, and continue to raise the standard in succeeding years. By 2005, this would save up to three million barrels of oil a day, more than we now import from all Arab OPEC nations.

Finally, serious consideration should be given to stricter enforcement of speed limits. This would improve fuel efficiency, since cars burn more gas when driven at high speeds (efficiency can drop 30 percent between 55 and 70 miles per hour).

***Stabilize the number of vehicle miles traveled.*** To reduce energy use, congestion, and pollution, the number of vehicle miles traveled must be stabilized. A variety of policies can accomplish this. If set high enough, taxes on fuel (already mentioned as a way to promote fuel-efficient vehicles) will

prompt people to drive less. In addition, communities can work together to develop regional bicycle and pedestrian plans that will reduce driving. Regional planning can also promote development in those areas with existing mass-transit services and can encourage housing construction in job-rich areas.

If each vehicle carried more people, the number of cars on the road would decrease. Tax relief for employees who share rides would help reduce the number of workers who travel alone to work, as would other carpooling and vanpooling incentives such as preferential parking spaces and flexible work hours. Special high-occupancy vehicle lanes on major commuting roads reward ride

> **An estimated 100 million Americans—two out of every five citizens—live in areas with health–threatening pollution levels.**

sharers with a faster trip. And certainly policies that encourage the use of public transportation rather than private vehicles are desirable.

***Expand the use of clean-burning alternative fuels.*** Motor vehicles could be powered by many fuels other than gasoline. Natural gas, ethanol, methanol, hydrogen, electricity, solar power, and fuel cells could all help reduce oil dependence, and each has its advocates. However, the nation needs a strategy for testing and evaluating these alternative fuels and for determining which should be used where. The federal government should consequently establish regional

demonstration programs with each region focusing on the fuel that best fits its resources and requirements. The results would help determine which fuel(s) should receive the widest national use.

***Alternative fuels will need government intervention to compete with oil.*** A pollutant tax based on vehicle tailpipe emissions would make it more attractive to use cleaner fuels. But even then, it will not be easy to get individual consumers to purchase alternative-fueled vehicles as long as there is no distribution system comparable to the corner gas station. Fleets of vehicles that are fueled at a central location therefore offer the best initial prospects for alternative fuels. Buses, city-owned vehicles, and business fleets could switch over during the next several years.

***Increase mass-transit ridership.*** Mass transit is a fuel-efficient, environmentally sound alternative to private vehicles, but it is not easy to get Americans to forsake their automobiles. Between 1940 and 1989 automobile miles quintupled while mass-transit ridership fell threefold. Urban areas should aggressively market their mass transit services and should subsidize mass-transit passes. Because the maximum tax-free mass-transit allowance employers can give their employees is only $15 monthly, this limit should be increased. Better yet, employers should be given tax incentives for instituting ride share and mass-transit programs for their employees.

***Promote intercity rail travel.*** Trains could be the best way to travel between cities within several hundred miles of each other, but the rail system must be upgraded. Besides doing this, the federal government should work with the states to fund high-speed rail projects. New rail technologies such as high-speed steel-wheel trains and magnetic levitation could make rail travel faster and more attractive. The federal government should cooperate with private businesses to provide high-speed trains along the most highly traveled routes.

*This article is adapted from a UCS report,* Steering a New Course: Transportation, Energy and the Environment. *It is available from the UCS publications department for $9.50 plus 95¢ for shipping.*

*Excerpted from a Union of Concerned Scientists pamphlet.*

# Sustaining What Development?

## *An Alternative Energy Conference Blazes a New Path to "Develop Sustainability"*

### by Geraldo Franco / *third world*

The term "sustainable development" had two distinct meanings during September in Montreal, Canada. It all depended on which conference you were attending—the 14th World Energy Conference or the alternative Green Energy Conference.

**Nuclear power is part of WWII's fallout, and it must be returned to the Pandora's box from which it emerged.**

"Both conferences are talking about sustainable development," explained H'I'ne Lajambe, speaking for the Greens. "But we don't mean the same thing. The World Energy Conference is apparently dedicated to merely sustaining development, while we are committed to a far more challenging task developing sustainability."

To symbolize their differences with the "power conference," while demonstrating that they harbored no ill will, the 250 Greens presented a gift to the official group—a Hiroshima survivor, a full-grown young Oinki tree. As expected, the "powers that be" rejected the offering.

**Saving energy is cheaper than producing more.**

The alternative conference, organized by a coalition of Canadian groups, included several innovative thinkers and activists from around the world. Among them were Bolivian inventor Francisco Pacheco, a man in his late 60s who displayed his patented hydrogen-producing equipment; Amory Lovins of the Rocky Mountain Institute, a physicist and 1983 winner of the Right to Livelihood Award (the alternative Nobel Prize); A.K.N. Reddy, professor at the Bangalore Institute in India and co-author of *Energy for a Sustainable World,* a landmark study of the future of energy; and Jim Bohlen, an environmental activist from British Columbia, Canada, an engineer by trade who works with solar power and is a cofounder of the Canadian Greenpeace.

Lovins' brainchild is the NEGAWATT Revolution. In his paradigm, energy is not a staple good but a service. In part, he plans to make power-guzzling motors, lamps, appliances and other equipment more efficient through correct lubrication and mechanical adjustments.

Saving energy, says Lovins and his staff of scientists, is cheaper than producing more. That simply, is the NEGAWATT Revolution.

A.K.N. Reddy spoke of his experience in India's Karnataka state. But Reddy and others are proposing a solution to the quandary of development toward degradation—a new paradigm for environmental soundness using new mathematical and statistical curves of need satisfaction.

In Karnataka, his new approach eliminated the need for costly imported nuclear power plants or ineffective megaprojects.

Canadian Jim Bohlen argues that we cannot leave a legacy of problems for our children. Nuclear power, for example, is part of World War II's fallout, and it must be returned to the Pandora's box from which it emerged. A developed society must exert a large degree of self-restraint—in contrast to the current consumerist mode. He proposes a change in thinking that would respect the ecosystem, including all animals. He calls for a non-violent revolution, one that is philosophically green and politically mean.

*Excerpted from* third world, *no. 23, December 1989.*

# What's the Crisis?

The 100 nuclear plants in the U.S. have aged rapidly. New defects are found every week. Fines by the NRC for utility violations are mounting. There are no realistic plans for Emergency Evacuation under FEMA. By contrast, Canada has just put a factual booklet in the hands of everyone living in the high danger zone around the CANDU nukes. No help can be expected from Washington so it is up to the people, their county and state governments to put an end to this mounting danger. As new information comes to light about how widely spread the radiation effects from Chernobyl were, it's criminal not to begin a rapid close down of nuclear plants. UK has joined Denmark, Austria, Ireland, Italy and Sweden in moving out of nuclear power, but with twice as many decrepit plants as any other nation, [the] US keeps making the deadly wastes which no one knows how to handle or safely store.

*Source: Women's International Coalition to Stop Making Radioactive Waste, December 1989.*

*Pacific Gas and Electric's Diablo Canyon Nuclear Power Plant, San Luis Obispo, California. This power plant was the last nuclear power plant to be built in the U.S. Photo: Abalone Alliance*

A JUNKIE WILL DO ANYTHING FOR A FIX —

— EVEN KILL.

©1991 Dan Dunivant

*Reprinted from* Earth Journal, *February 1991.*

## Disasters at Nuclear Utilities

*In the past 10 years, nuclear utilities have reported almost 30,000 mishaps at their plants. Even the U.S. Nuclear Regulatory Commission has estimated that the chance of a core-melt accident at a U.S. reactor may be as high as 45 percent over the next 20 years.*

— Ken Bossong, *Business & Society Review* (Summer 1988).

## The Nuclear Push

The nuclear industry is exploiting global warming trends to revive support for nuclear reactors.

It has launched an effort to resell nuclear power as an environmentally and economically sound alternative to the sources of emissions contributing to the greenhouse effect.

The industry's campaign is already having an impact. Three major global warming bills recently introduced in the U.S. Senate would provide major federal support for the re-creation of a "new generation" of nuclear power plants in the United States. A fourth bill has been introduced in the House.

*An alert in* Utne Reader *from Ken Bossong of Public Citizen's Critical Mass Energy Project.*

# No Blood for Oil [or Nukes, Too!]

## by Nancy Culver / Mothers For Peace

The new energy policy introduced by the Bush administration almost guarantees another war over access to oil. It focuses almost exclusively on energy supplies at any cost, and does nothing to reduce dependence on foreign oil. It virtually ignores the fastest, cheapest, and safest "source" of energy: efficiency and conservation. And it all but rejects the available safe alternative energy sources that need only a level playing field to succeed if we remove the decades-old subsidies to the oil, gas and nuclear industries, then solar, wind, and biomass become highly competitive. They have the added benefits of being renewable and not producing acid rain, greenhouse gases, or damage to the ozone layer. Neither do they produce deadly wastes that must be safeguarded for thousands of years. America uses twice as much energy per capita as Germany and three times as much as Japan. Yet those countries are working hard to become even more energy-efficient, thus improving their competitive positions economically.

*Excerpted from SLO [San Luis Obispo, CA] Mothers for Peace Position Paper on the Persian Gulf War.*

# Fueling the Fantasy
## HOW THE RUSH TO GEOTHERMAL ENERGY MAY DESTROY OUR NATION'S LAST RAINFOREST

### by Daphne Wysham / *Greenpeace Magazine*

At first glance, the fierce opposition to the geothermal development of Wao Kele O Puna's 27,785 acres seems misplaced. Yet it is here and in other rapidly dwindling Hawaiian forests that hundreds of species of birds, insects and plants have evolved in tiny niches isolated from the rest of the world.

To tap the heat below the Wao Kele O Puna rainforest, developers plan to build 150 to 200 geothermal wellheads on Kilauea volcano's east rift zone. These would funnel steam to 10 to 20 power plants producing 600 megawatts of electricity phased in between 1995 and 2007. The electricity is then to be transmitted to Oahu over land and along the seabed by way of three 200-mile submarine cables. The cables would pass through nature preserves as well as seismically active areas of ocean floor at depths four to seven times greater than any other cables in the world. The development would require a vast web of concrete and steel steam wells,

*This is an example of a geothermal power plant. It is located at China Lake, California. Photo courtesy of Renew America.*

power plants, pipelines, silica dropout ponds, cooling towers, roads, electrical transmission lines and cables. It is the largest construction project ever undertaken in Hawaii's history.

Since its inception in the late 1970s, the geothermal development has been the target of strong opposition by the Pele Defense Fund and an assortment of other national and international groups. But, for reasons that go far beyond the shores of Hawaii the development is moving forward as planned.

Davianna McGregor, an assistant professor of Ethnic Studies at the University of Hawaii and a member of the Pele Defense Fund, is among those who believe that, in addition to an EIS, an Integrated Resource Planning (IRP) process, already underway, should be completed before any more geothermal wells are drilled. Carried out effectively in California, Nevada, Massachusetts and elsewhere, an IRP requires utilities to project their energy needs over two decades, paying attention to such factors as population growth, future land use and energy efficiency. "We want them to look critically at the way electricity is used, not just how much can be supplied," said McGregor.

Professional engineer and energy consult ant Robert J. Mowris explains it this way: "Supplying electricity to Hawaii is like filling a leaky bucket. Every new, energy-wasting building is another leak. For a utility, the answer is to fill the bucket faster. Instead, why not plug the millions of leaks with energy efficient technologies and establish strong building standards to prevent more leaks from developing?"

If Hawaii's politicians simply heeded the cautious advice of McGregor, Mowris and others, the integrity of the Wao Kele O Puna rainforest could be preserved. However, without public pressure to do so, they may perpetuate the fantasy—of greater profit margins fueled by an endless supply of energy—a fantasy which, like the Hyatt Regency Waikoloa, contributes to the destruction of the real Hawaii it pretends to celebrate.

*Excerpted from* Greenpeace Magazine, *May/ June 1991.*

# Clean Energy Future

Simply choosing the cheapest energy options can guarantee a non-nuclear future. This is already starting to happen. Since 1979 the US has got more than 100 times as much energy from savings as from all expansions of energy supply; more new supply from renewable sources than from non-renewables, and more new electric generating capacity ordered from small hydro-plants and windpower than from coal or nuclear plants or both.

Assured affordable supply of energy is, however, just one of the ingredients of a really secure society. Security also requires other necessities: water, food, shelter. It embraces health, a healthy environment, a flexible and sustainable system of production, a legitimate system of self-government, a durable system of shared values... We build real security above all when we strive to make our neighbors more secure, not less, whether on the scale of the village or the globe.

— *Hunter and Amory Lovins*

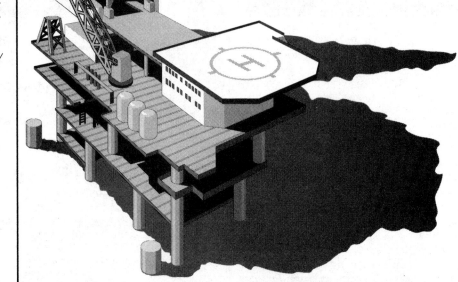

# Chapter 7

# Economics & Labor

Although awareness that the world is on a collision course has been spreading rapidly in recent years, conventional economic strategies offer no solution to the problem. Quite the reverse. Modern communications, especially television, are hooking the rising population of the world more and more firmly on the consumerist values propagated by rich-country businesses and governments. This is evident throughout the non-socialist Third World. Even in the socialist economies, most notably the Soviet Union and China, the reforms now taking place convey that decisions follow more closely the consumerist example of the industrialized West. Meanwhile, as the richest countries gear themselves up to drive still further along the conventional path of economic growth—this being, for example, the stated purpose in the single European market in 1992 and the recent Free Trade Treaty between Canada and the USA—the wealth gap grows wider between rich countries and poor, and between rich people and poor people within each country.

## Rejecting Today's Assumptions

A new economics for people and the Earth must be enabling (for people) and conserving (for the Earth). But those two principles—enabling and conserving—are directly opposed to two basic tendencies of conventional economic practice and thought today:

- The tendency to create and reinforce economic dependency for people, localities, and nations, and to widen the gap between the rich and the poor, the powerful and the weak;
- The tendency to be wasteful of natural resources and damaging to the natural environment.

We also have to reject other basic tendencies and assumptions of today's economic

---

> **Modern economic thinking has its roots in the perception of the English philosophers Bacon and Hobbes—of nature as a limitless resource to be exploited for "the relief of the inconvenience of man's estate," of wealth as power over other people, and of human life as an incessant competitive struggle for power.**

---

order. These include:

- The assumption that the wealth of nations is still what matters and that the paramount unit for economic policy-making must be the nation state;
- A model of human beings as amoral maximizers of their own self-interest who, as economic agents, should not be expected to exercise moral or social choice;
- The notion that economics can be a science that is objective and value-free.

## An Historical Watershed

These features of today's economic practice and thought originated in the 17th and 18th centuries with the deliberate creation of dependency. The common people were pushed off the land, excluded from their subsistence way of life, and made dependent on paid labor. Modern economic thinking had its roots in the perception of the English philosophers Bacon and Hobbes—of nature as a limitless resource to be exploited for "the relief of the inconvenience of man's estate," of wealth as power over other people, and of human life as an incessant competitive struggle for power.

When Adam Smith came to articulate the workings of the modern economy—in place of the vanished medieval economic order that had been based on the rights and obligations of a divinely sanctioned, hierarchal, static society—he followed Bacon's and Hobbes' perceptions of "man" and nature

and society, and Newton's value-free system-building in the sciences. That Smith emphasized the wealth of nations, rather than the wealth of the people or cities or the world, and took material production and consumption as his model of his economic life, reflected the most notable economic phenomena of his own time: the struggles between European nations to dominate overseas trade, and the unprecedented growth of industrial production and its accompanying division of labor.

The new economic order must reflect the very different realities and needs of the 21st-century world—a world perhaps even further removed from Adam Smith's than his [world] was from the Middle Ages. The practices, policies, assumptions, and imperatives of conventional economics place formidable obstacles in the way of active supporters of many specific causes.

## A Task For The 1990's

Those of us who founded The Other Economic Summit (TOES) in 1984 hoped [that] increasing numbers of organizations, movements and groups would come together in a sustained campaign to make sure that enough thinking people worldwide recognize that the 21st century needs a new economic order, and know what they must do to bring it into existence. This initiative has taken root.

*James Robertson of England is the author of* The Sane Alternative and Future Work. *He was one of the founders of The Other Economic Summit (TOES), and is an active member of The New Economic Foundation.*

*Excerpted from* The Egg, An Eco-Justice Quarterly Newsletter, *Spring 1989, "A New Economics For the 21st Century."*

# Re-Defining the Wealth of Nations

## Interview by Elissa Wolfson / *E Magazine*

*Hazel Henderson acquired the title of "economist" the old-fashioned way—she earned it. Henderson began her career in the 1960s, taking on the character building role of New York City housewife shortly after moving here from Britain. Parenthood, with its direct connection to the future, made her worry about the "incredibly polluted" New York City environment. "We'd sit in the park watching the children play, with a Con Ed smoke stack two blocks away. So I began right where I was—with the other mothers in the park."*

*Henderson credits women—who were out in the trenches doing volunteer work, baking cookies, and spearheading radical campaigns—with starting the modern-day environmental movement. "I was part of that first wave," she recalls.*

*Henderson's first major environmental effort, with a large grassroots group called Citizens for Clean Air, found her debating corporate economists on talk shows. In lieu of obtaining a traditional degree, "and then unlearning everything," she began to teach herself economics. By the early 70s, she had mastered her subject well enough to land a six-year stint with the Office of Technology Assessment advisory council, where she found it "a delight" to be in a position to develop better policy tools. "Technology assessment specifically looks at the same phenomenon with different spectacles—those of anthropologists, sociologists, engineers, ecologists and political scientists—not just economists."*

*Henderson has since added the intriguing title of "futurist" to her job description. She is author of two books* Creating Alternative Futures *(Putnam, 1978) and* The Politics of the Solar Age *(Knowledge Systems, 1988)—and has published articles in over 200 journals, including* Harvard Business Review *and* The New York Times. *She also holds executive seminars at Fortune 500 companies, serves on numerous advisory and editorial boards and is a much sought-after speaker. E Magazine caught up with Henderson at New York's Sarah Lawrence College last spring, prior to that evening's lecture and reception. Impeccably dressed and radiating class, Henderson possesses a formidable combination of traits which have served the environmental movement well. With her razor-sharp intelligence, refreshingly direct manner and striking blue eyes, Hazel Henderson is the proverbial iron fist in the velvet glove.*

**E: What sparked your interest in economics?**

**Henderson:** When I began to study economics I realized it was based largely on assumptions that were unreal: that air and water were free, that natural resources would *always* be available at the right price. Nowhere in the teaching of economics was an absolute scarcity of anything ever mentioned.

Conventional economics also uses an unrealistic model of human nature as competitive and selfish—a model which does not fit people raising children or doing volunteer work.

Quite simply, if you ignore the unpaid work that happens in every society, fewer people will do it. People say "I'm not respected here so I'll get a real job." So you end up with nobody home watching the kids or doing volunteer work. Once this occurred to me, I was no longer intimidated by all the fancy math.

**Are you saying that, with all the abundance and cooperation going on in nature, our economic models aren't based on the way the world really works?**

That's right. They're based on the Darwinian theory that competition is everything. Whereas in nature there is just as much symbiosis and cooperation as competition.

Current economic theory is far too one dimensional. When you have a multi-dimensional world, the quality of life needs to be measured in a multi-dimensional way. This one discipline called economics, with one measure called the GNP, can't be in the catbird seat while all other disciplines with very useful insights are taking minor roles.

**What is the Gross National Product (GNP) and how did it became the only measure of our country's economic well-being?**

The GNP is a crude measure of development based upon a country's per-capita production. It was developed during World War II, the idea being to develop an indicator that would value war production more highly than civilian production so as to mobilize society's resources. But nobody at the end of the war said, "Hey, now we need to rethink this." By that time it had been picked up by many other countries and it began to be an arbiter of progress.

The problem is that GNP only measures production; it places a value on bullets, cars and missiles, and none on the environment or on children—our most precious resource. It's like evaluating the health of a patient with only a blood pressure gauge. This is why decision-making is so skewed when education and the environment are seen as worthless, it doesn't make any sense to spend money on them.

The United Nations, then the World Bank, picked up this thinking when all the nations were being created after the war. They stated, in effect, "You don't get a loan unless you set up a system of national accounts based on the GNP."

Then the Employment Act of 1946 mandated that the economy be managed both for growth and full employment. Economists claimed to have the formula, and politicians believed them. We began with targets like two percent unemployment. When we couldn't meet these targets, we changed the numbers. By the late 70s, we had a roaring case of this disease called stagflation"—which is unemployment accompanied by inflation—and finally people began losing faith in economists. In testifying before the Joint Economic Committee (JEC) in the 70s, I'd simply say that inflation consisted of all the variables that economists left out of the original model by sweeping all the social and environmental costs under the rug.

In the 70s when all the bills were coming due, we had to pay to clean up our water. But instead of subtracting these costs, the work of pollution control companies was added in as more useful production. So we had more and more of this double counting where a company would pollute with one division, then set up another division to clean up the pollution, and it would all be counted as pluses in the GNP. Since pristine ecosystems have no value, events like the Exxon Valdez, for example, perversely increase the GNP!

And education is treated as a cost rather than as an investment, because building schools and paying teachers is measured by the GNP, but literacy is not.

## You have proposed an alternative to the GNP called the Country Futures Indicators (CFI).

Basically, these are all very commonplace and sensible indicators of the quality of life. All countries collect data on education, literacy, health care, life expectancy and political participation. Not all countries have information on the real cost of pollution, but it's not impossible to get.

The CFI is simply a group of categories necessary for providing us with a well-rounded view of a country's quality of life. Each country is going to construct it a little bit differently, to reflect its own priorities and culture. I'm not trying to invent something new. I'm simply saying that we need to construct a scorecard which takes all of these elements into account.

## How does the U.S. stack up on the CFI?

Not very well on voter participation, health care or literacy—in fact, Iraq's literacy rate is higher than ours. The Scandinavian countries rank high overall, along with Switzerland. In one province in India [Kerala], they have a very high quality of life, but one of the lowest per capita incomes in the world—$200 a year. And countries like Costa Rica also rank quite high, the main reason being that they do not have military spending eating up everything.

What clouds the view of traditional indicators is the emphasis on per capita income rather than on the quality of life, what I'd call "true wealth." Jacksonville, Florida has compiled many "quality of life" indicators of which only one is per capita income.

## Would your plan need to be mandated by a centralized government in order for it to work?

I don't think so. One of the problems with macroeconomic theory is this top-down idea. That is definitely why the Soviet economy fell apart. If we can't manage countries from the top down, what makes us think we can manage the world that way?

There is also a lot of top-down management in the West, and in large corporations. The big debate today is not about whether the economy should be regulated, but simply

what rules of interaction do we need? We need to level the global playing field upward and put an ethical floor beneath it. Then we'd begin to reward the most responsible countries and companies instead of the least.

## How can we begin to build this green global economy?

On five different levels. As individuals we can shop and invest in a socially responsible manner, and—as citizen activists demand that prices include social and environmental costs. Once that occurs, many products will leave the marketplace—their wastefulness will become apparent and they will be absolutely unaffordable. Then there is the local government level. Here people must demand recycling centers and renewable energy.

Next there is the corporate level. It doesn't matter how many citizens recycle if industries are still producing tons of crap and are not redesigning their products to be more environmentally-friendly. It's hard to imagine companies getting into the business of de-emphasizing consumption, but utilities are now finding it quite profitable—and imperative—to do so.

The fourth level is the national government—changing the scorecards, as we discussed, and then "greening" the tax code in order to discourage unhealthy behavior. "Sin" taxes, like those on tobacco and alcohol, would still count—but so would pollution sins like depletion, waste, obsolescence and pollution. German models indicate this would generate so much revenue that you would actually have to reduce income taxes in order to keep the economy revenue neutral

The fifth level is the global level, installing that ethical floor, and forging treaties between nations. These five levels provide different roles for different souls. Some people love working at the local level, others at the national; some love to crusade against irresponsible corporations, some love being planetary citizens. And they are all needed.

## How do you address the popular perception that living in a less materialistic way would diminish our quality of life?

That's why I want to change the economic indicators—so people can confirm their sense that, "Well, my salary didn't go up, but now we can swim in that river that was polluted last year."

## You sound optimistic.

Being pessimistic is a waste of time. Having a child and grandchild automatically makes you an excellent futurist!

*Excerpted from* E Magazine, *September/October 1991.*

# Clearing the Water

## Excerpted from a speech by Jim Hightower, Chairman of the Financial Democracy Campaign, Amherst, MA—April 28, 1991

What's the Financial Democracy Campaign about? It's about what kind of values we're going to try to embrace and implement as a society. We're suggesting that we implement those values on which this country supposedly was founded, and I am talking radical stuff here now. I'm talking about economic fairness, social justice, equal opportunity, and stewardship of our resources.

Of course, we've been going quite the opposite direction over the last couple of decades...We've been trying to implement a pernicious philosophy of greed. It's pernicious because its based on a philosophy of trickle-down. Even if trickle-down worked, it says a very ugly thing about people, doesn't it? It says that only a handful of people really matter. The rest of you don't count. If you're good folks and sit down there with your bowls open then maybe a little of this stuff will trickle down to you. But really it's a philosophy that says, "I got mine, you get yours;" "never give a sucker an even break;" "caveat emptor," "I'm rich and you're not;" adios chump." It has been a policy of course

of enriching the rich.

Eighty percent of American families lost income during the 1980's. The wealthiest one percent had a 74% increase in their income, and they started off better than most of us. They started at $314,000 average income, ended with $540,000. The wealthiest one half of one percent of the American people—that's 400,000 families—now own more than all the bottom 90% of the people own. That's what we're really contending with. And nowhere do you see this government relationship with wealth any clearer than in this S & L rip-off that we've just had.

My Aunt Eula used to say, "The water won't ever clear up until you get the hogs out of the creek." It's just that simple. The hogs are in the creek. They're fouling the economic and environmental waters of our country. Now I don't know how much you folks know about hogs, but you don't get a hog out of the creek by saying, "Here hog, here hog." You put your shoulders to it, and you shove the hog out of the creek. That's what it takes, and that's the kind of politics we have to have—

a politics that's going to go out and rally folks. And the folks are ready.

Now I know people say, "Well if that's the case then why'd they vote for Bush?" Well they didn't, did they? Half of the people didn't vote in the 1988 Presidential election, and half of those who did said they were not voting for the person they marked on the ballot, they were voting against the other person. That's three quarters of the American people who either don't vote or vote no. Because we don't have the politics that offers a clear alternative and a vision that people will respond to. We've got to have a politics that talks to those people so that they hear it and are willing to respond to it. And we've got to get a hold of the process for the long haul. And that's what the Financial Democracy Campaign hopes to be a part of.

*Excerpted from* Community Economics, *no. 23, Summer 1991.*

## The $250 Billion Political Cover-up

### *The administration hid the S&L scandal from the public for far too long*

#### by Chris Norris & Peter Tira / *San Francisco Bay Guardian*

While most Americans recognize the savings and loan scandal as one of the most costly governmental blunders ever, few know how much the administration's attempts to cover it up added to the price tag. Had the problem been honestly addressed before the 1988 presidential elections, Federal Home Loan Bank Board officials estimate, the government could have saved the country $250 billion. Instead, staff members were told to play down the problem so it wouldn't hurt Bush's candidacy. (Remember "Read my lips; no new taxes"?)

*Sources: "The Great American Bailout, " a 58-minute documentary co-produced by The Center for Investigative Reporting and* Frontline, *aired October 22, 1991.*

*Excerpted from the* San Francisco Bay Guardian *as it appeared in the* Utne Reader, *May/June 1992. This article was selected as "The Top Ten Censored Stories of 91."*

# FDIC In$urance Lo$$e$

## by J.W. Smith / *World's Wasted Wealth*

The Federal Deposit Insurance Corporation (FDIC) is a congressionally chartered private insurance agency for bank deposits. This $16-billion (1987) private insurance fund is about 3 percent of total insured deposits. One large bank failure can deplete it. Yet the name "federal" is so convincing as a government agency that even sophisticated financial writers refer to it as a government guarantee.

Added to those burdens, the U.S. Federal Reserve is being counted on (though it has not accepted) to be "lender of last resort" for Eurodollar deposits.

In April 1987, the Federal Savings and Loan Insurance Corporation (FSLIC) reported $2 billion in reserve against an estimated $8 billion in expected losses. Just three months later, they reported the latter might be as high as $26 billion. A year later the official estimated cost had climbed to $36 billion and six months later to $100 billion, while analysts are saying the economy is going strong. If there is a severe recession, the cost could be much more. "Taxpayers have to realize: They're going to pay." Eight months later (June 1989) Congress is voting to bail out six hundred savings and loans; analysts predict the eventual cost could be anywhere from $125 billion to $325 billion depending on the interest rates and time spans used in calculations. The higher figure is fourteen hundred dollars for every man, woman, and child in America. It was bidding for finance capital that created this debt trap.

Though the proper function of banks is to finance essential commerce while paying reasonable interest on savings, their present purpose is to maximize earnings for their shareholders. To do this, they must have money to lend and they must bid for it. Each participant is forced into the game, as there are no other sources—it is monopolized by bidding power.

This process can make money market instruments risky speculations. This became apparent during the bankruptcy of the Penn Central Railroad, which had borrowed heavily through commercial paper. The railroad's collapse created a $6-billion sell off of commercial paper. This was absorbed by the Fed's lending of funds to any bank to cover loans normally serviced by the money markets.

The need for the Fed to be lender of last resort was again demonstrated during the collapse of the Continental Illinois National Bank in 1984. The total rescue costs came to $7.5 billion. And Federal Reserve Board officials admitted that there were now ten a year of these "breathless moments."

Much is ending up in risky speculation when it could be providing homes and employment for family, neighbors, and friends. Most money market funds have four things in common which create high risk when the economy enters one of its periodic severe recessions: they are unsecured IOUs; they evade the regulatory requirements of the Federal Reserve; when included as part of the banking system, these exterior bank loans cause the parent banks to exceed the normal reserve requirements; and they are financed by "hot" money that zips back and forth across the financial landscape but will disappear if the market appears risky.

All central banks are trying to protect themselves from the consequence of this speculation by inserting money into their economy each time a part of this pyramid starts to collapse. In this effort, "the FDIC went from a corner drug store to being Sears and Roebuck in three years." During these breathless moments, although it can later be redeemed through taxes, the Fed must print any money not covered by insurance reserves.*

"Interest on the national debt is transferred from the ordinary taxpayer to the rich, who hold a disproportionate amount of the treasury notes." The $2-trillion national debt in 1986 equaled $10,048 [today it is more than $4 trillion] for every man, woman, and child in the U.S. The pyramid of government-guaranteed loans just described raises this another $3.6 trillion. If we conservatively assume 50 percent of that debt would be uncollectable in a severe depression, each American citizen, from cradle to nursing home, will owe the money monopolists almost $20,000, or $60,000 per average *family. As* values will have collapsed, they will have received nothing in trade for this debt. They would be in the same predicament as most Third World countries—they would be in a debt trap.

* It is interesting to note that those who loan money almost always have first mortgage; when borrowers default, the lender will promptly repossess the mortgaged property. When these money monopolists get in trouble, Uncle Sam (the public) is asked to bail them out. But repossession is never contemplated.

*Excerpted from* The World's Wasted Wealth, *published by New World Press, © J.W. Smith.*

# Monopoly Money Gains

## by William Greider / *Secrets of the Temple*

While Continental borrowed more from the Fed and from its "safety net" of private banks, Volcker, Isaac and Conover worked out the terms for the federal rescue. The FDIC would guarantee an infusion of at least $1.5 billion and were asked to put up $500 million as an expression of confidence. Present were executives from seven banks—Morgan, Chase, Citibank, Chemical, Manufacturers Hanover, Bankers Trust and Bank of America—who were to sell the package to twenty-five or thirty other major banks.

It was the federal government that would save the banks from possible calamity, including the seven banks assembled at the table. All of them, in varying degrees, were vulnerable to the same sort of panic that had brought down Continental. They all depended heavily on the daily money-market borrowing required by "managed liabilities" banking. They were all overexposed on foreign lending.

Eight days after the "run" began [May 17, 1984], the federal regulators announced the largest bailout in the history of banking. The FDIC would pump $4.5 billion in immediate new capital into the bank, assuming liability for the bulk of Continental's bad loans while it searched for a new owner to take over the institution. The Federal Reserve promised that, in the meantime, it would lend whatever was necessary in short-term funds to keep Continental afloat. In the course of fulfilling that promise, the Fed made emergency loans to Continental Illinois that rose to a breathtaking $8 billion.

The Continental bailout posed an awkward precedent that federal regulators could not explain away. If there was any doubt before, Continental starkly established that the largest banks would never be allowed to fail, whatever the cost to the government. Badgered on the question in House hearings,

the Comptroller conceded that, yes, the eleven largest multinational banks would not be allowed to fail.

The most striking political fact of the Continental rescue, however, was the absence of controversy. Aside from small bankers, there was almost no reaction from the general public and very little criticism from politicians. The dimensions of the crisis were so awesome and complex that perhaps ordinary people felt they could not question the decisions. Another possibility was that most Americans regarded the government intervention as unexceptional. When the largest, most influential enterprises were imperiled, the government would come to their rescue. That was how people expected the American system to work.

[By] midsummer, [Continental] was the largest bank, not seventh. Meanwhile, federal regulators could find no willing buyers. Chemical, Citibank and First Chicago all took a look at Continental's books and shared their pessimistic assessments with the government agencies: the bank had $4 billion in bad loans, not $2.7 billion, as the federal regulators had believed. No one offered a good explanation as to why the private bankers found problems that the government regulators did not see. In any case, no one wanted to buy the carcass.

Therefore, in late July, the federal government bought the bank. The idea was, of course, offensive to the freemarket ethic that still dominated American politics, yet this *was* done without controversy—and under Ronald Reagan, the most conservative President to govern in many decades. Conservative commentators were silent as the govern-

ment executed its massive intrusion in the free marketplace.

The nationalization of Continental was, in fact, quintessential act of modern liberalism—the state intervening in behalf of private interests and a broad public purpose. The rescue of Continental also amounted to a vast bailout for the creditor classes. Perhaps that was why the conservative commentators did not complain. In the past, conservative scholars and pundits had objected loudly at any federal intervention in the private economy, particularly emergency assistance for failing companies. Now, they hardly seemed to notice. Perhaps they would have been more vocal if the deed had been done by someone other than the conservative champion, Ronald Reagan.

The assumption was that the government would own Continental until it was back on its feet and operating profitably again, then it would sell the bank back to private investors. By early 1986, the FDIC reported a loss to date of $1.24 billion on the bad loans it has assumed from Continental, but it would be many years before anyone knew the full cost to the public. It might also be many years before the federal government could get out of the banking business.

The banking crisis did not end with the rescue of Continental Illinois, however. Fear and nervousness continued to stalk some of the largest banks in the country. The financial markets buzzed with rumors of another impending crisis, perhaps on the same scale. Before the summer was over, the tremors in American banking would have a direct, distorting impact on the Federal Reserve's monetary policy—and, therefore, damaging consequences for the American economy.

*Excerpted from* Secrets of the Temple *by William Greider; 1987 © Simon & Schuster.*

# Why Economic Conversion?

## by Michael Closson / *Positive Alternatives*

For a few short months after the Berlin Wall came tumbling down, economic conversion was—in a word—fashionable. Public officials and ordinary citizens recognized that, as the need for Pentagon spending diminished, vulnerable workers, communities and companies required assistance to adjust to a non-military future.

Then Iraq invaded Kuwait. Suddenly, the Pentagon budget was once again a sacred cow. The rationale for military spending shifted. Third world chaos and access to foreign oil supplanted the "Red Menace." But, the result was the same—a renewed focus on military solutions to the world's problems.

Yet, if the crisis in the Gulf tells us any-

thing, it demonstrates that security comes neither from nuclear weaponry nor from playing policeman for the world with conventional forces.

Real security will only be attained when we seriously turn our money and talents to the critical human and environmental problems confronting our society and the globe. Otherwise, we may soon follow on the heels of the Soviet Empire, staggered not by a lack of talent or resources, but by a stubborn refusal to acknowledge the problems or act on them.

Our best hope for the future is to educate our children, rebuild our crumbling cities and infrastructure, restore our precious environment, care for our sick and disabled and,

> **In 1980, corporate chief executives earned roughly 40 times the income of average factory workers; by 1989 CEO's made 93 times blue collar workers.**
>
> Source: *The Politics of Rich and Poor: Wealth and the American Electorate in the Reagan Aftermath* by Kevin Phillips.

91

as is pointed out below, develop a comprehensive energy policy for the next century.

Economic conversion is a key component of this dramatic shift. The development of conversion plans will lessen political resistance to military cuts and their implementation will ease the transition of workers and communities to peaceful pursuits.

Equally as important, conversion can stimulate visionary thinking and action. At the national level, conversion planning is intimately related to the development of new technologies and a sound energy policy. For example, it is difficult to imagine a serious commitment to alternative energy development without a redirection of the nuclear weapons work at national laboratories such as Lawrence Livermore. At the local level, the conversion of a military base or defense plant not only insures continuing prosperity but can also empower citizens to begin positively shaping other aspects of their lives.

Saddam Hussein has provided the Pentagon and its minions with a temporary reprieve. But the end of the Cold War and the enormous problems confronting American society will mean a substantial transfer of resources from the DoD—the only signifi-cant source of money available to deal with the problems confronting the nation—to other areas of government during the 1990s. As a result, military bases will continue to be closed, weapons systems like the Stealth bomber will be cancelled and thousands of troops will be pulled out of Europe. In this context, conversion planning, which is underway in cities and states across the country, will continue to be an idea whose time has come.

*Excerpted from* Positive Alternatives, *Fall 1990.*

# Setting the Trend

## *Maine outshines every other state in its campaign to adjust to changes in federal military spending*

### by Michael Closson / *Bulletin of Municipal Foreign Policy*

Although few in numbers, the people of Maine think big when it comes to addressing the problem of military dependency. In fact, spurred on by the energetic efforts of the non-profit Peace Economy Project (PEP), no other state in the union can match Maine's variety of conversion-related activities.

Maine's most military-dependent region is the Bath-Brunswick area. Military-related employment accounts for 46 percent of all jobs in that area and for 54 percent of its total wages. Concerned citizens there have moved to confront likely Pentagon cuts by establishing the Bath-Brunswick Conversion Task Force. Its members represent a diverse group of stakeholders. They will concentrate upon identifying creative economic development strategies for the region. As part of that effort, the Task Force is preparing a grant proposal to the Pentagon's Office of Economic Adjustment for funds made available by economic adjustment legislation included in the 1991 Defense Authorization Act.

Not to be outdone, activists have developed an initiative to be considered by town meetings across the state this spring. The initiative, "Reinvest in Hometown America," asks municipalities to pass resolutions calling for: (1) reduced military spending, (2) the reinvestment of federal resources to meet environmental, economic and social needs, and (3) federal assistance to design and implement local economic adjustment, conversion and diversification processes. Re-cently, four towns decided not to wait and immediately adopted the resolution. The state legislature and Maine's Conference of Mayors are also considering signing on in support of the initiative.

A successful outcome from this flurry of activity is by no means certain, but the energy and diverse talents applied to the problem give cause for optimism. The state has already developed a model for others to emulate. Conversion adherents are hopeful that the old political adage rings true in this case as well: "As goes Maine, so goes the nation."

*Excerpted from* Bulletin of Municipal Foreign Policy, *Spring 1991. Ed. Note: publication has been absorbed by* Global Communities.

## Alternative Investments
### Community Development Loan Funds

Community development loan funds are non-profit organizations that "recycle" capital into communities, targeting the people that need it most. They make loans—at low-cost rates—to community organizations, both nonprofit and for-profit, that develop affordable housing, employment opportunities, and other resources and services for low-income, unemployed and otherwise economically disadvantaged people.

Community development loan funds make excellent investment options for people interested in building and rebuilding communities at the grassroots level. Although these are usually low-yield investments, investors know that their money is going directly to people who will use it to build homes and start responsible businesses. They are also low-risk: The National Association of Community Development Loan Funds (NAC-DLF) reports that of the over $88 million loaned by their member funds, only $1.1 million, or 1.3 per-cent, has been lost. Of that, all but $15,000 was absorbed by the funds, so losses to investors were only .02 percent.

NACDLF, a member of Co-op America and the Social Investment Forum, is a group of 40 member funds working across the country for healthy communities. Contact them to find a loan fund in a region of your concern: *NACDLF, 924 Cherry St., 3rd Floor, Philadelphia, PA 19107-5085, 215-923-4754.*

*Excerpted from* Co-op America Quarterly, *Spring 1992.*

# Renewing Our Communities

### by Anne Zorc / *Co-op America Quarterly*

"Smoke-stack chasing." That's the game most small towns play when the traditional basic industry—agriculture, mining, or manufacturing—no longer sustains the job market or local economy. Small towns end up competing against cities for new industries when old ones fail. Even if a small town "wins," they often lose because of costly incentive packages, environmental clean-up costs, uncontrolled growth, fluctuating economies, and other long term repercussions.

What if towns looked at Main Street, not Wall Street, for economic solutions? In the late 80s the Rocky Mountain Institute (RMI) designed a step-by-step Economic Renewal Program encouraging towns to utilize local resources and skills to control their own economies and improve the job market while maintaining a healthy environment and community. Community volunteers, leaders and economic development professionals learn to stop frantically recruiting industry and start mobilizing the economic potential existing in the town.

The Economic Renewal Program begins with a town meeting where the community agrees upon goals for a "preferred future." Town leaders attend seven community workshops, study a casebook of success stories, and analyze their town's economic infrastructure and business needs using a workbook. Four principles guide RMI's Program. Their *Business Opportunities Casebook* explains the four principles using examples of small town models:

### Principle One

*"Plugging the leaks"* means stopping dollar drains from the local economy. Money kept in the community has a "multiplier effect" that generates higher wages, buying, investment and, ultimately, jobs. One method is "Buy Local" programs that encourage people and businesses to buy local goods. A successful example, the Oregon Marketplace, matches producers and suppliers. One such match was between a local bicycle carriage manufacturer with a local wheel maker. The local supplier was more reliable and cheaper than the wheel factory in Taiwan where the manufacturer originally bought wheels. More importantly, the money remained in the local economy.

### Principle Two

Often ignored by town leaders, small businesses are the lifeblood of local economies. *Principle number two, "support existing businesses"* can mean downtown revitalization programs, such as one in a Colorado town en route to Rocky Mountain National Park that resulted in a 58% increase in sales tax revenue. Or it can mean business assistance centers, such as the Briarpatch Network in the San Francisco area that reported a failure rate of only one-fifth of the national average for small businesses in an identical three year period.

### Principle Three

*Encouraging new local enterprises should be on every town's agenda.* For example, the first sparks of Digital Equipment Corporation flew in an abandoned wool mill.

### Principle Four

*"Appropriate"* is the keyword in RMI's *fourth principle:* "Recruit appropriate new businesses." Towns should target businesses that meet unfulfilled needs and won't compete with existing local enterprises. Leaders should weigh the social and environmental effects of new businesses as well as the economic ones. The Program suggests marketing unique characteristics of the town instead of costly incentive packages to attract businesses. For example, a brochure advertising a large number of machine trade workers lured new business to Franklin County, MA.

*Excerpted from* Co-op America Quarterly, *Spring 1991.*

# Bartering for a Better Community

### by Anne Zorc / *Co-op America Quarterly*

Modern economic theory dictates that the wealth of a community depends upon its cash supply. Here are two non-profit economic models that build a community's wealth with the skills, goods and labor of its citizens.

### LETS

The Local Economic Trading System (LETS) maintains community trade regardless of the fluctuations of money and employment in local economies.

LETS, a nonprofit venture, makes its own currency. The currency, approximate in value to the federal dollar, allows members to barter goods and services. Accounts work like bank accounts; members are charged a small transaction fee (in the local currency), and they receive monthly statements. The "bank" is a computer system that records transactions. It's like an interest-free line of credit from the community.

Here is an example: John has book-shelves that need to be painted, but he doesn't have the time. In our conventional monetary system, John hires a painter—unless he is constrained by not having enough cash. In a traditional barter system, John would have to offer a service to the painter in exchange for the service he needs. Instead, John looks in the LETS monthly newsletter that lists members' goods and services and finds a listing for Susan, a professional painter. Susan paints John's bookcases and John calls up the LETS twenty-four hour answering service and credits Susan's account with 75 units of the local currency from his account. Later, his account will be replenished when someone else uses John's landscaping service.

Initially, communities worry that some members will run up a large "commitment" without repaying in kind. Although this is possible, it has not been a problem. The availability of member balances to all members is one practical deterrent. In the current economic system, people incur debt because they lack money. With LETS, as long as members have skills—from baby-sitting to word processing—and goods to trade, they can easily and affordably get the services and goods they need. People can offer one or more things. Neither is there a reason to hoard local currency because, unlike federal money, it is always available to be re-earned, and it generates no interest in the "bank."

How does the community benefit? On an economic level, citizens can continue to trade goods and services despite a cash shortage. The local currency strengthens community self-reliance because it circulates in the local economy, can always be re-earned, and is unaffected by the fluctuations of the federal dollar market. LETS creates buying power and employment opportunities for the unemployed and cash-poor.

Invented as an innovative solution for an economically depressed community in Vancouver, Canada, with a limited cash supply,

LETS is in use in anywhere from 50 to 200 communities in Australia, New Zealand, Canada and England, and the number is growing in the United States.

In Los Angeles the Coop Resources and Service Project runs a LETSystem with 200 accounts. Lois Aarkin, director, describes LETS as a "community-building device" that combats "the alienation of big-city life that is the root of many of LA's social problems."

### Service Credits

Service credit systems equate one hour of service to one unit of currency. Primarily designed for the elderly, these non-taxable systems provide services such as meal preparation, shopping, adult and child day care, home maintenance, and tutoring in ten states across America. The most successful program is in Miami where about 4,000 service hours are generated each month.

The service credit systems work on different models. In the "blood bank model' volunteers provide services to each other and earn credits that they later can "draw down" when they need similar services. Participants trade services directly, one-to-one, in the "barter model." For example, an elderly person may baby-sit in return for a drive to the store from the parents. In the "insurance model" membership organizations pool credits as insurance for members that lack sufficient credits to pay for services they need. Younger members, for example, in a church program may donate credits to the service pool.

Although anyone can earn credits, many of the service credit systems in place limit the spending of credits to persons over sixty. Younger people, however, are encouraged to donate credits to grandparents or elderly members. The service credit program benefits all age groups because it utilizes everyone's skills and encourages interaction.

Even a bed-ridden elderly woman can earn credits in a telephone reassurance program. The system guarantees a work force that cannot become unemployed. The encouragement of unskilled labor removes the stigma normally attached to low-end service jobs. Furthermore, the employment of the elderly, infirm and young frees them from the limited roles of consumers of the traditional economic system. Most importantly, the non-transferability of service credits outside the community encourages both an investment and stake in the community.

*Excerpted from* Co-op America Quarterly, *Spring 1991.*

*Citizens in the Berkshires, encouraged by the Schumacher Society, sell regional currency like the ones depicted in the above illustration, good for products and services. These trade dollars allow the farms and businesses, in lean times, to get cash advances from their patrons. Jane Jacob's recent book,* Cities and the Wealth of Nations, *illustrates "how national currencies stifle the economies of regions."*

# Mutual Aid

## *Microenterprise loan programs demand that small businesses rely on their peers*

### by Aaron Jaffe / *City Limits*

A Russian immigrant who worked as a civil engineer in his homeland can't get that kind of job in the United States. He wants to start his own cleaning business. A man from El Salvador wants to buy an auto body repair shop, so he can take advantage of the years of experience he had back home. Another woman, also from El Salvador, makes dresses with an old sewing machine in her apartment.

These are the people John Waite wants to help.

Waite, director of the microenterprise program at the Church Avenue Merchants' Business Association (CAMBA) in North Flatbush, Brooklyn, says microenterprises may be an important part of helping these and other small entrepreneurs to escape poverty.

Microenterprise loans are a new phenomenon in the sea of economic programs for lower-income New York businesses. They're meant for people who wouldn't normally be able to get a bank loan, would-be entrepreneurs putting together small, labor-intensive businesses with virtually no credit history, little bookkeeping experience and very little collateral. All they have to put up for the money is their word—and the word of three or four other would-be entrepreneurs from the same community.

That's the trick to microenterprise loans—support groups made up of four or five peers, each of them receiving a loan for their business and each of them responsible for one another. Instead of material collateral, the system is based on honor and mutual dependence. its a way to help people take care of themselves.

## The Bangladesh Model

The best known model for the method of peer-group loans is the Grameen Bank in Bangladesh, which started giving microenterprise loans in 1977. A 98 percent repayment rate on an average loan of just $67 opened eyes in the United States, where poverty in some neighborhoods is nearly as bad as in some third-world nations.

The organization that has the most international success with the model is ACCION International, a 31-yearold program based in Cambridge, Massachusetts. Working mostly in Latin America, ACCION has about 100,000 clients and more than $55 million in outstanding loans, with payment rates of the same caliber as Grameen's.

CAMBA's loan program is still being hammered together, and won't start handing out money until later this month. But Waite says he is already meeting with prospective clients. Not all of them are happy with the peer group idea.

But Jeff Stern of the Local Development Corporation of East New York sees it differently. He's working with the East Williamsburg Valley Industrial Development Corporation to start a microenterprise program with part of a $200,000 grant the groups received from the state Urban Development Corporation. The peer groups "provide stronger ties so people don't take the money and run," says Stern. "It minimizes risk."

Minimizing risk is definitely important to CAMBA's Waite, who works primarily with immigrants from Southeast Asia, Russia and Eastern Europe, along with immigrants from the Caribbean Islands and Latin America. Many of his clients don't have a good credit history. Another problem, he says, is that many of them are recognized by the government as political refugees from their homelands, meaning they automatically qualify for public assistance a month after arriving. "Some of them get used to it," he says.

News of the international success of microenterprise programs has attracted attention at the federal level, where two bills supporting the model are winding their way through the house. Rep. Tony Hall (Democrat, Ohio), the chairman of the House Select Committee on Hunger, introduced the "Freedom From Want Act" last May. Part of the bill seeks to expand current employment and training projects to include microenterprises, making it easier for people on welfare to start businesses without having their benefits curtailed.

*Aaron Jaffe is a reporter for the* Asian Wall Street Journal Weekly.

*Excerpted from* City Limits, *May 1992.*

# Community Housing and Land Trusts

## by Gregg Ramm / Institute for Community Economics

One fundamental cause of poverty is an inequitable pattern of ownership—too many absentee owners draining money out of poor neighborhoods. ICE [Institute for Community Economics] has helped organize over 100 community land trusts in 23 states over the past decade. These groups are helping low-income people regain control over their land, their housing and their communities.They offer a glimpse of the seemingly insurmountable challenges confronting low-income communities.

The economic and social health of a community, rural or urban, depends a great deal on who owns and controls the land and how that land is used.

Pedro Rodriguez a homeowner, leaseholder and board member with the United Hands/Manos Unidas Community Land Trust. In North Philadelphia, the several hundred members of United Hands are taking back their neighborhood from absentee landlords and drug dealers, and creating permanently affordable housing on community-owned land. It has already created homeownership opportunities for 29 families and plans to develop 100 more housing units in the coming year! Pedro reminds us:

*"United Hands is one of the most vibrant community organizing projects in the entire city. We want to revitalize our community by bringing in and developing a new type of homeowner—people who are not just looking out for themselves but are also looking out for the entire community. We have learned that you can put out new concepts of property in a way that people will accept and will adapt as a viable way of living within the community."*

> ***Farms,*** and indeed our entire agricultural economy, are dangerously threatened today by the conversion of farmland to other uses, as well as by the disappearance of family farms and the growth of agribusiness. The demand for land to build houses, highways and shopping centers keeps growing, but the amount of land always remains constant. As a result, land prices are skyrocketing. This has made it virtually impossible for would-be-farmers to buy land to farm.
>
> There are hundreds of Community Land Trusts today in the United States. Over 50 of them deal with rural land. The widespread growth of community land trusts represent a broad-based property ownership reform movement.
>
> *Excerpted from "Community Farm of Ann Arbor" promotional material.*

Three thousand miles from Philadelphia, off the coast of Washington state, the residents of Lopez Island are also battling for community control in a vastly different setting. They are confronting the devastating impact of a wealthy tourist economy on land values. As Sandy Bishop, director of the Lopez Community Land Trust, describes it:

*From June of 1989 through June of 1990, the average price of a home went from $69,000 to $204,000—a rise of 196 percent! Basically, it wiped out a whole strata of people that could not afford housing."*

In the San Juan Islands, the members of Lopez CLT are fighting to maintain their land, their homes and their way of life. The CLT has $500,000 committed for its first project and will break ground in April.

Today, the struggle for ownership and control of the land takes many forms. In rural areas these struggles often place land directly in the forefront:

- In northern Minnesota, Native Americans have organized the **White Earth Land Recovery Project** to regain control of lost reservation lands.

- The **Wisconsin Farmland Conservancy** was organized by farmers from Wisconsin to help put families back on the land and to foster sustainable agriculture.

- The **Addison County Community Trust**, in Middlebury, Vermont, acquires mobile home park land to preserve its use by mobile home park residents and purchases development rights to land in the county to preserve open space and farmland.

In cities, the struggle often takes a different form, not easily recognized as a fight over land.

This call to action comes from the **Dudley Street Neighborhood Initiative** (DSNI), based in inner-city Boston. DSNI has undertaken the enormous task of taking back ownership of, then developing, the vast stretches of vacant land in this disinvested neighborhood that is home to 14,000 people. The land that DSNI acquires—through eminent domain powers granted by the City as well as through more conventional means—will be placed into a community land trust. The community land trust will assure that the people in the community will always have a say as to how the land is used. And the land trust will assure that housing developed on that land will be permanently affordable for future generations.

In cities, "neighborhood" is often the word we use to describe the land we occupy as a community, and the creation of decent affordable housing is often the most important goal for its use. Yet land is much more than the ground that supports the buildings on it—land is the foundation of our community. Any struggle over land—any effort to rebuild a neighborhood—inevitably leads beyond the development of affordable housing. This is certainly true in Cabbagetown, a neighborhood in Atlanta which faces substantial gentrification pressures because of its proximity to downtown.

**Cabbagetown Revitalization and Future Trust** (CRAFT) is a community land trust, a member of ICE's CLT Affiliate Program and a borrower from ICE's Revolving Loan Fund, which works to provide affordable home ownership opportunities to residents of the historic Cabbagetown neighborhood.

CRAFT has already completed 18 units of housing and is working on more. Yet CRAFT is an important example of why a community land trust must be a community advocate as well as a competent developer of affordable housing.

Like many neighborhoods, Cabbagetown is experiencing increased drug dealing and violence. Yet, unlike most housing developers, who build and leave, CRAFT has a real stake in the future of the neighborhood and confronts these problems. Recently, CRAFT organized several meetings of residents to discuss an appropriate response to increased drug dealing in the neighborhood. Through intimidation, the drug dealers tried to nip this organizing effort in the bud.

Representatives of CRAFT demanded that the City respond to the violence in the neighborhood. The residents got a response—the police have become visible and active in the neighborhood and perpetrators have been arrested.

ICE is working with dozens of groups around the country like CRAFT. Many of these groups operate on shoestring budgets. They often barely have funds to pay staff.

But the struggle for the land, for control and ownership of our neighborhoods and communities, will continue. Land trusts respond to today's needs and preserve opportunities for future generations.

*Excerpted from Institute for Community Economics, Inc. letters dated Nov. 11, 1991 & May 4, 1992.*

# Environmental Investing

## by Cindy Mitlo / *Co-op America Quarterly*

Interest in "environmental investing" has been markedly increasing, in step with public outcry at the state of our biosphere. Many investors use an environmental screen as one of several for choosing investments. However, as citizens demand action—to protect our water supplies, recycle our garbage and clean up toxic waste—and governments attempt to comply, new industries are being born and others are growing fast. So, other investors as well as those managing investment vehicles are designing portfolios solely around this criterion. Financial analysts see environmental industries as good investments, and expect them to continue growing into the nineties, faster than industry as a whole.

First Affirmative Financial Network of Colorado Springs explains what makes them good prospects for investing: "Most pro-environment companies are relatively new, small capitalization companies, beginning to show high revenue growth. They are held by few institutions and trade primarily on the secondary exchanges. Companies providing these services are relatively immune to economic downturns due to their essential nature and to government regulation and/or funding."

Strategies for environmental investing parallel those for social investing. Individuals and organizations can screen their portfolios to eliminate environmental offenders—heavy polluters, makers of throwaway products, wasters of natural resources. They can also invest pro-actively by directing their money toward firms working to clean the environment or keep it clean.

This is an important distinction to make. Environmental industries fall roughly into two groups—those trying to clean up the mess we've made and those making stewardship of the planet a priority by developing new, clean methods of getting what we need; industries involved in cleaning include everything from hazardous and solid waste disposal to groundwater consulting and recycling services. These are the kinds of companies investment analysts recommend—the magnitude of the clean-up problem guarantees a market for their essential services well into the future. Riskier from an investment standpoint are those entrepreneurial companies working on environmentally sound technology: alternative energy, solar power, biological pest control for farming, advanced composting systems, and solar aquatic waste-water systems, for example. Much less risky are companies working with known technologies on cleaner systems such as natural gas utilities.

There is a third group that environmental and social investors might want to consider for their portfolios: manufacturers of products and services that are necessary and important and who have made a significant commitment to environmentally sound manufacturing. H.B. Fuller, the maker of specialty adhesives and related products, is one such company. CEO Anthony Anderson has put in place a set of environmental standards for the company that are the highest in the chemical industry. They employ everything from state-of-the-art scrubbers and water cleansing systems to dramatically reduce the air, ground, and water pollutants they release—and their stated vision is "zero pollution."

Social investment mutual funds, which

**ENVIRONMENTAL SHOPPING TIPS**

· **AVOID THROW-AWAY PACKAGING** by choosing products with little packaging and ones that are packaged in recycled or recyclable materials.

· **REUSE** grocery bags, jars and other containers to reduce the need for new bags and storage containers.

· **BUY DURABLE GOODS** whenever possible. Try to avoid such one-time use items as:. styrofoam cups, paper plates, and

· **SPEAK OUT** and tell store managers that you prefer products with less packaging and recycled/recyclable packaging.

routinely screen their portfolios for issues like nuclear weapons, South African connections and employee relations, are often just as stringent when it comes to environmental issues.

For example, the New Alternatives Fund focuses entirely on companies involved in alternative energy and environmental protection, and looks for strong evidence of environmental responsibility. They have purchased stock in companies like Zurn Industries, which builds alternative energy plants, and have divested themselves of shares of PPG, which makes energy efficient windows but is also involved in toxic waste sites.

Parnassus Fund believes that protecting the environment makes good economic sense, and has invested in CRS Sirrine, a construction company addressing acid rain. Pax World Fund evaluates the environmental intent of a company by the amount of capital they have historically devoted to pollution control, and also stresses the importance of natural gas.

The Valdez Principles, developed by CERES, a group of environmental and consumer organizations, will prove (as did the Sullivan Principles on apartheid) investing strategy can make a difference in corporate behavior.

*Excerpted from* Co-Op America Quarterly, *Summer 1991*

# Valdez Principles

**A company which signs the Valdez Principles pledges to:**

1. Protect the biosphere from pollutants.
2. Use natural resources in a sustainable manner.
3. Minimize the production of waste and dispose waste using safe methods.
4. Use environmentally safe energy sources and conserve energy as much as possible.
5. Minimize health, safety, and environmental risks to employees and communities.
6. Market only products and services that minimize adverse environmental impacts.
7. Take responsibility for any harm done to the environment by fully restoring it and compensating those people adversely affected.
8. Disclose to employees and to the public incidents that cause environmental harm or pose health and safety hazards.
9. Have at least one member of the board of directors be qualified to represent environmental interests.
10. Conduct and make public annual environmental audits of progress towards implementing these principles.

# The Voluntary Green Tax

**by Dave Albert /** *Green Business: Hope or Hoax?*

New Society Publishers, for which I work, produces and distributes books that promote fundamental social change through nonviolent action.

However, the production and distribution of our books contribute to the environmental depletion that many of our books decry. While our books are printed on at least partially recycled paper, trees are cut down to manufacture them. Our advertising broadsheets are printed with recycled ink, but liquid industrial wastes are still produced in the process. The trucks that haul the newspapers to the recycling plants, the paper to the presses, and the finished books to customers burn petroleum products and pollute the air.

These costs or, more correctly, the cost of restoring the environment to the state in which it existed before such economic activity took place, are external to the exchange that happens in the marketplace and nowhere figured into the price of the product or service exchanged.

## The Green Tax

After taking account of all these considerations, we came up with the idea of a voluntary "Green Tax," a convenient way for consumers to share in offsetting the environmental costs of products. In 1989 we started to give our customers an opportunity to participate in the tax by adding a line on our catalog order form, with a note of explanation as to what the "tax" is for. We suggested 9 percent though we must note that the actual environmental costs of all "externalities" accumulated over time—building and maintenance of roads, air and water pollution, environmental costs of power generation, etc. might occasionally approach 100 percent of the purchase price of many commodities!

We dispense the accumulated "Green Fund," using 50 percent of the funds generated for actual environmental restoration (tree planting, river and ocean cleanup, re-inhabitation projects) and 50 percent for environmental education and direct action. We decided to use most of the restoration funds in our own bioregion, especially in the neighborhoods of our businesses, so that we can monitor their effectiveness, and take part in the projects themselves. We've' used the other half of the funds nationally and even internationally. Since instituting our Green Tax, we have given away some $10,000 to more than fifty groups and organizations.

> **Only eighteen months after we started, some one hundred plus businesses have instituted some version of the *Green Tax*.**

## Growth in Campaign

With no advertising, solicitation, or coordination except a note in our catalog, the Green Tax idea seems to have caught on very quickly. Only eighteen months after we started, some one hundred plus businesses have instituted some version of the Green Tax. One business, TOPS Learning Systems in Canby, Oregon, which produces innovative science materials for classrooms, has gone so far as to add the Green Tax to invoices sent to school districts and has experienced a very high compliance rate.

Probably the most advanced manifestation of the Green Tax thus far has been the creation of the Finger Lakes Bioregional Green Fund in upstate New York. Started by Steve Siergirk of Acorn Designs, a producer of stationery and other products featuring environmental designs on recycled paper, the Fund has expanded to include dozens of businesses. Among the members thus far are seven restaurants, several gift shops, two print shops, a tire store, a general store, a video store, and a pet shop.

Each business displays a "Green Fund" logo on their windows or doors, and keeps a rack with display material at the checkout register. Clerks ask customers whether they would like to add a "Green Tax" to the amount of their purchase, and refer them to the printed materials (provided by the Fund) if they have any questions about its operation. A Green Tax director has been hired to collect the funds monthly, to recruit new businesses, and to ensure that each business is properly equipped. A volunteer board made up of business members and representatives of the environmental community makes decisions about the disbursement of funds. And, every month, the local newspaper has agreed to run a Green Fund column, talking about one of the member businesses and reporting on disbursement.

While we are proud of the contributions our customers are making to restoring the environment, we would be naive to think that this could ever approach the level truly needed to make a long-term difference. What we do hope the Green Tax will do, if it spreads widely enough, is provide a simple way to begin dialogue among larger segments of the population at the grassroots level so that more lasting answers can be found. And by acknowledging our "environmental debt" as a business, we expect the maintenance of the Green Fund to be not only a consciousness raiser for customers, but for ourselves as well.

*Excerpted from* Green Business: Hope or Hoax?, © *1991, New Society Publishers.*

# Green Business and Labor

### by David Morris / *Co-op America Quarterly*

In Europe, the environmental movement builds on the struggles and successes of the labor movement. In the United States, the links between the two are still undeveloped. The greening of the American economy should include a respect for labor as well as a respect for nature.

Union members in the U.S. today are an endangered species. The proportion of the U.S. private work force that belongs to unions has plummeted, from 30 percent in the mid 1950s to 12 percent in 1990. At this rate, by the end of this decade, unions outside the public sector will be little more than a memory.

Much of the business community and the White House tell us this is a positive development. No unions means higher productivity, more innovation, greater competitiveness. Right?

Wrong. "The most competitive national economies," a recent *Harvard Business Review* article concludes, have "far higher levels of unionization than the United States."

Our competitors know a good thing when they experience it. Among 17 major competitors the workforce is becoming more, not less, unionized, rising on average from 48 percent in 1970 to 53 percent in 1987.

In these countries, labor is at the table when fundamental decisions affecting labor are made. It should come as no surprise that one result is that workers are treated with a dignity that is lacking in the U.S. In Sweden, union stewards can close a plant they believe is unsafe. In the U.S. in 1989 alone more than 3600 workers filed appeals with the federal government for being fired for protesting unsafe working conditions. Swedish managers can't lay off anyone without one month's notice, 6 months for employees over 45. The average blue collar worker in this country in the late 1980s received only 7 days notice before losing his or her job; 2 days when not backed by a union.

German corporations with over 1,000 employees must have an equal number of labor and management representatives on the board of directors. But suggest to American managers that even one worker representative be on their boards and they go balk. Employees of Pacific Enterprises, a utility holding company, own about 21 percent of the company's stock; board and officers own only 1.5 percent. Yet when the Utility Workers Union of America recently put up a candidate for one of 15 seats on the board, management spent $260,000 in a successful effort to defeat him. CEO Richard Farman insists, "I do not believe that a union leader can serve on the board without placing himself in the position of creating a conflict of interest."

Most American managers treat labor not as a partner but as the enemy. The Congressional Office of Technology Assessment informs us that computers now monitor 10 million workers, often without their knowledge or permission. Employers are now firing workers who are overweight, who smoke off duty, or have high cholesterol levels. Two thirds of all firms recently surveyed by the America Management Association test for drugs, "even when there is no suspicion of drug use and no obvious case for testing," says Eric Greenberg, the Association's research editor.

In countries where labor has power, it also has respect. And since more than 90 percent of us are workers, that respect spills over from the workplace to the entire society. It is no accident that the U.S., where labor has the least power, also is the only industrialized country lacking universal health insurance.

When labor has power, everyone has more leisure time. The average American worker spends 1,900 hours a year on the job. A German, Dutch or Danish employee works the equivalent of 4 weeks less each year than their American counterpart, yet boasts a standard of living at least as high as ours.

Today the environmental movement is trying to educate us that nature has a cost. In Europe the analogy with the history of the labor movement comes easily to mind even to business people. The head of AB Flakt, a Swedish engineering firm recently observed, "We treat nature like we treated workers a hundred years ago. We included then no cost for the health and social security of workers in our calculations, and today we include no cost for the health and security of nature."

*Excerpted from* Co-op America Quarterly, *Fall 1991.*

# Building Bridges

### *Coalitions with Social-movement Activists Offer New Hope for Labor Unions*

### by Jeremy Brecher & Tim Costello / *Z Magazine*

The usual media images of working peoples' political views over the past quarter century have focused on reactionary "hard hats" beating up on peace demonstrators and narrow-minded "Reagan Democrats," disgusted with kooks and troublemakers from radical social movements, abandoning traditional blue-collar political loyalties. A closer look at the political sympathies of America's working class reveals a different reality: widespread cooperation between grassroots union activists and activists from other movements: Women's, environmental, minority, peace, and others.

This cooperation is proving to be an important means of renewing the labor movement and overcoming some of its widely recognized ills, such as its isolation from the growing female and minority segments of the work force, its lack of rank and file participation, and the public perception of organized labor as a special interest group rather than as an advocate for the needs of all working people.

The separation of labor from other social movements has been a crucial obstacle to social change in the United States, making it easy for those who benefit from the status quo to divide and conquer any potential opposition. An alliance of labor and community movements would have considerable political clout because it would speak for the overwhelming majority of the population—a majority that is today largely excluded from political and economic decision making, but if mobilized would represent an enormous social force.

Throughout the 1980s there was little effective national opposition to the right-wing corporate offensive spearheaded by the Reagan and Bush administrations. But facing up to the failure of their individual political strategies, activists from diverse movements began reaching out to one another.

The result is a new era of political bridge building: Once isolated movements are now beginning to redefine themselves as part of an emerging alliance. Community labor coalitions, such as the Naugatuck Valley Project in Connecticut and the Tri-State Conference on Steel in the Pittsburgh area, forced corporations to bargain with them over the closing or sale of plants and developed worker buyout plans as a way of preserving and developing the local economy.

At the same time, as the Democratic Party became less and less responsive to labor and other social movements, activists from a wide range of movements began running candidates from their own ranks, often challenging conservative Democrats as well as

Republicans. Institutions such as the Legislative Electoral Action Project in Connecticut, Pro-Pac in New Mexico, the Minnesota Alliance for Progressive Action, and local Rainbow coalitions (spawned by Jesse Jackson's 1988 campaign) recruit and support candidates and keep them accountable after they're elected.

Community labor coalitions differ from traditional ideological politics in that they do

> **The separation of labor from other social movements has been a crucial obstacle to social change in the U.S., making it easy for those who benefit from the status quo to divide and conquer.**

not demand agreement on a single party line. They depend instead on a political culture that recognizes how concerns will vary for different groups in the coalition and accepts that at times it is necessary to agree to disagree. Catholic activists and feminists, for instance, may agree completely on dozens of issues yet find an irresolvable conflict on abortion rights. The experience of these coalitions shows that such conflicts can be bridged creatively in many but not all instances.

Suspicion and hostility rooted in past

conflicts and long-standing prejudices also impede political bridge building. Baiting of groups within a community labor alliance for their association with alien forces is not uncommon; at a recent coalition meeting that included gay rights activists, for example, a labor delegate demanded to know, "Why is our union making a coalition with 'lifestyle' groups?"

Some groups have been able to design specific political programs to help unify different groups. The New Haven Community Labor Alliance in Connecticut, for example, developed and won a plan for cafeterias in local schools that united parents whose children would be fed and low-income communities for which the cafeterias would provide jobs. Activists in the peace movement and workers in military industries jointly supported the Minnesota Jobs with Peace campaign, which drafted a plan for converting the state's industries from military to peacetime production—demonstrating that even longtime antagonists can work together.

*This article was adapted from the book* Building Bridges: The Emerging Grassroots Coalition of Labor and Community *by Jeremy Brecher and Tim Costello. Copyright ©1990 by Jeremy Brecher and Tim Costello. Published by Monthly Review Press, New York. Reprinted by permission of the authors.*

*Excerpted from* Z Magazine, *April 1990.*

# A New Alliance

### by Brian Ahlberg / *Utne Reader*

Almost all the large environmental organizations still pursue a determinedly upper middle-class, conservationist agenda. And organized labor still often joins its employers in opposing environmental regulation that threatens jobs. Nonetheless, recent labor struggles linking environmental degradation to dangerous working conditions and a diminished quality of life for workers have raised ecological awareness among union members.

Environmental and labor groups have found themselves suddenly thrust together as common opponents to proposed "free-trade" agreements, especially with Mexico, advocated by big business and the Bush administration. Free trade means that corporations can move production to where both labor and the environment can be most

> **Environmental and labor groups have found themselves suddenly thrust together as common opponents to proposed *free-trade* agreements.**

harshly exploited. Or they can merely threaten to move and use the pressure of competition to lower labor and environmental standards at home.

A *Public Citizen* report called "Runaway Deregulation: The Consumer and Environmental Case Against Fast Track" argues that, under fast track, the administration could achieve through trade agreements what it has been unable to accomplish in other ways—rolling back protections in areas such as pesticides, asbestos, clean air, clean water, worker safety, meat inspection, and species conservation. If Congress or states tried to enforce stricter regulations on these matters, they could be overruled as violations of international free trade agreements.

Writing in the *Northeast Midwest Econom-*

*From: Industrial Workers of the World*

ic Review (April 22, 1991), the biweekly report of the non-partisan think tank Northeast Midwest Institute, AFL-CIO secretary treasurer Thomas Donahue argues that NAFTA [North American Free Trade Agreement] would "pave the way for hundreds of thousands of jobs to be exported to Mexico." Donahue predicts that such a freetrade arrangement not only would harm U.S. workers, but would turn the whole of Mexico into a replica of the U.S.-Mexico border area

where nearly 2,000 *maquiladora* factories now operate. The *maquilas,* set up by U.S. companies to take advantage of cheap Mexican labor and lax regulation, have turned "much of the border region into a sinkhole of abysmal living conditions and environmental degradation," according to the *Wall Street Journal,* cited by Donahue.

In this fight against the fast track on free trade, environmental and labor organizations have established the tentative beginnings of

a political partnership. Ideally, they will continue as allies to combat some of the negative effects of the increasing corporate control of all the world's resources. Because neither movement can win on its own, the shaky combination represents one of the few hopeful developments for American politics in the '90s.

*Excerpted from* Utne Reader *July/August 1991.*

# Protecting Jobs *and* Owls

> Even if we run out of [spotted] owls, which is more important, a damned bird or the economic well-being of an entire class of people?
> — Collin King, Loggers Solidarity

**by Tom Knepher / *Earth Journal***

There is a massive flaw in the bottom-line mentality that forces us to choose between the environment and economic well-being. Philosopher Ivan Illich writes, "Money devalues what it cannot measure," and the value of an ecosystem, whether it is a lake in New York or a forest in Washington, cannot be measured in dollars. Its destruction hurts everyone, but is especially hard on those who earn their livelihood from it.

Unfortunately, the workers affected by this destruction have been set by their employers against environmental groups that would do the most to preserve their way of life. A look at the "owls vs. jobs" controversy in the Pacific Northwest provides insight into the challenges facing both workers and environmentalists across the nation.

Timber companies tell us that protecting the spotted owl or restricting the "harvest" of old-growth trees will destroy the thriving economy of the Pacific Northwest, but independent studies paint a very different picture. The number of timber-related jobs in Washington and Oregon dropped from over 130,000 in 1979 to barely 100,000 in 1986 while timber production increased from 11.2 billion to 12.3 billion board feet. Even if no spotted owl habitat is set aside, another 20,800 more timber industry jobs may be lost over the next decade.

These jobs, like so many others, have been lost to automation and exports. New equipment has cut the number of employees needed to turn out 1 million board feet of timber by 35 percent, and a mill that produced 2,000 board feet of plywood veneer per employee in 1978 now has each worker turning out 10,000 board feet.

Jobs that remain are endangered by massive exports of raw logs. In 1988, 25 percent of Oregon and Washington's harvest—3.7 billion board feet—was shipped to Japan.

Weyerhaeuser and ITT Rayonier exported more logs through one Washington port that year than were cut on the Olympic and Mount Baker-Snoqualmie National Forests combined. In May 1988, Weyerhaeuser, which had $1.5 billion worth of exports in 1987, announced that it was closing its seventy-year-old-growth sawmill in Snoqualmie, Washington, for lack of trees.

Logs aren't the only thing being exported. In 1989, Louisiana Pacific (LP), one of the largest timber companies, bussed workers to Redding, California, to protest against the spotted owl just one week before company plans were revealed in local papers to open a huge mill in Mexico—where laborers are paid less than $2.00 an hour.

What kind of jobs are being lost? Professor David E. Krumm, in his study *Limitations on the Role of Forestry in Regional Economic Development*, found that throughout the region, "Wages are below the national average, skills are limited...and there are very few technical and managerial positions with high salaries. Limited opportunities exist for women, and many woods workers are self-employed with inadequate protection."

At the same time the timber industry is losing jobs, the area is gaining them. Jobs in the Pacific Northwest increased by 320,000 in 1987-89, many in tourism and recreation-based industries that will suffer if the ancient forests are lost. It would seem to make economic sense to save the old growth and retrain the loggers. But the timber companies are loath to give up their profits—LOP reported over $2 billion in sales in 1989—and the loggers are equally reluctant to give up their ways of life. These are the real conflicts—jobs vs. corporate profits and the end of a way of life.

At the same time, environmentalists have often neglected the legitimate concerns of workers and rural communities, allowing themselves to be depicted as "elitists" and "preservationists" who would lock resources

away forever. George Marston, editor of *High Country News*, says, "A vision that sees only land and wildlife has the same weakness as a vision that sees only ore bodies and old-growth forests. A vision that does not recognize the small communities and rural human activities that accompany the land and wildlife has an enormous blindspot."

The recent elections showed that when economic issues compete with the environment, economics win. Environmentalists have been slow to make this connection, but as economist Hazel Henderson has noted, business has long shifted the blame for declining productivity "onto workers and other scapegoats such as environmentalists and 'welfare chiselers.'"

It is time to forge effective alliances between the "scapegoats" and put responsibility for both economic and environmental decline back where it belongs. These alliances will depend on an increased appreciation by both sides of the concerns of the other. They will also depend on compromise and political savvy and a willingness to set aside old stereotypes.

The coalition of commercial fishermen and environmental groups opposing offshore oil drilling on the West Coast is an excellent example of the way these partnerships can work.

As workers and environmentalists— which are not mutually exclusive groups— begin to understand and respect each other, more coalitions will arise. As PCFFA President Nat Bingham wrote during Redwood Summer, environmentalists and loggers "have to sit down and figure out the answer to the forestry problem. Each group has something vital to contribute to the solution. United as we are on the oil issue, we can solve this problem for ourselves." Indeed, we can.

*Excerpted from* Earth Journal, *February, 1992.*

# Labor and Grassroots Activists
# Seek Common Ground for the 90's

### by Lois Gibbs / *Everyone's Backyard*

I went to an exciting conference in Niagara Falls, NY last November sponsored by the NY AFL-CIO, Toxics In Your Community Coalition, NY Environmental Institute, NY Council on Occupational Safety and Health, Ecumenical Task Force, Love Canal Homeowners Association, UAW 686, IBEW 2213, NY Council of Churches, Statewide Occupational Health Center, Public Employees Federation, and the Environmental Planning Lobby.

This conference may mark a special place in history where barriers between workers and community activists are finally removed. I finally saw the jobs versus environment issue honestly discussed. Concrete ideas were put on the table. The most promising idea was OCAW leader Tony Mazzochi's *Superfund for Workers*.

This conference reinforced my belief that workers and community people not only have a lot in common, but are usually the same people, only bearing different labels, often by their own choice. I come from Love Canal, where this was our daily reality.

Workers used to be cowed into silence, but this is changing. They're beginning to realize we're fighting the same enemy.

Workers and the community are also victimized in the same way by government agencies that work to protect corporate interests. In the same way that they use the "hearing" (without listening) process to snow the community over pollution issues, they try to snow workers on workplace safety. Whether you're a community pollution victim or a worker exposed to an unsafe workplace, you get 10 minutes to pour your heart out, with support from the few experts who will work for our side. Then on come the experts from industry and government to tell us "There's no cause for alarm" and that, besides, we don't want regulations that will stand in the way of progress and cause companies to lose money.

Labor and grassroots activists have been kept divided for a long time by industry and government who frame the issues as a choice between jobs or the environment. It's part of public policy, for example, in "cost-benefit analysis," where government weighs the expected benefit to public health against the expected economic loss, which everyone is supposed to translate into jobs.

OCAW's Tony Mazzochi may have an answer to protecting workers and their communities. Establish a "Superfund for Workers." Tony wants to see a fund to help workers cope with losing work when plants shut down or run away. The fund would support their families and allow workers to go to school or get retraining. It expands on the toxic waste Superfund idea. A company that abandons a community leaves damage to be "cleaned up." Obligation for clean-up falls on companies that caused it and government that let it happen. As Tony puts it, it's only fair to treat workers as well as the dirt left behind when a company dumps on and then dumps a community.

The idea was a big hit with both grassroots activists and workers at the Niagara Falls conference. They saw ways this idea can bridge our self-interests and wanted to discuss ways not only to get it, but how to make it work as a tool for community-labor solidarity. With this "insurance" for financial security, we could form even closer alliances to work on other issues like reducing pollution, toxic exposure and mutual health and safety concerns.

In these hard times, the only way to win such a plan is to unite. If we recognize that workers and the community are one and the same in most of the places where we live, we can focus on the issues that will bring us together to take on the common foe. Since 1978, when Love Canal started the Grassroots Movement for Environmental Justice, we've seen a lot of successes and more than a few failures in building relationships between workers and grassroots activists. We've learned a lot.

*Excerpted from* Everyone's Backyard, *January/February 1990.*

# Union and Environmentalists
# Working Together

### by Laura McClure / *EcoSocialist Review*

If a company is spewing toxic substances into the air and water, it's a reasonable guess that workers' bodies are being poisoned. Take Lordstown, Ohio, a small town built around a complex of General Motors auto and truck plants. These plants spew an estimated three million tons of toxic emissions into the air every year. The facilities received 750 citations for health violations from the state of Ohio late last year, and 438 of the violations were deemed deliberate.

Inside the plants, workers are being poisoned by "fugitive emissions"—evaporation from storage tanks, leaky valves, and what workers charge is a faulty ventilation system. Charles Reighard, forty-three, used to spray primer in the car assembly plant at Lordstown. "I had absolutely no protection—no mask, no ventilation—the company didn't want to provide it," says Reighard. Now Reighard is out on disability. "What its done to me is its damaged my immune system, and I'm now sensitized not just to hydrocarbon fumes, but to almost everything—hair spray, perfume. I get headaches and vomit. Sometimes I black out."

Reighard is an organizer for Workers Against Chemical Hazards (WATCH), which is trying to force GM to clean up its plants, inside and out. They've organized public hearings, initiated studies, and joined with local environmentalists fighting an incinerator GM operates in the area. "We don't think all this damage has to happen to produce autos," says Reighard.

GM is using a potent weapon against WATCH: job blackmail. It's threatening to shut down production if workers and the community force a cleanup. "They've already announced they're going to move the truck plant, and they're saying that their workmen's compensation cases are too high. We're saying, if you'd clean up the plant, you'd automatically save money on your medical bill," says Reighard.

Job blackmail like GM's is the main obstacle to the building of environmental-labor coalitions. Even when the demand is for cleanup, not for shutdown, workers often have to fear for their jobs. And in areas like Lordstown, where the economy is dominated by a single employer, workers stand to lose not just a job, but the chance for any job in the area. Workers who try to sell their houses to get the money to move away find that their houses are unmarketable in a community with no jobs and streets lined with for-sale signs.

Sometimes labor-environmental coalitions are born during strikes or lock-outs, when workers have less to lose and more to gain by challenging corporate practices.

Paperworkers in Jay, Maine, had been working and living with toxins from International Paper's Androscogin Mill for years. But when they went on strike in 1987, they were on the lookout for weapons to use against the company, and what they found was pollution. The plant emits dioxin into nearby streams, poisoning fish and endangering the water supply. The union joined with local community and environmental groups, eventually resulting in stricter state laws on emissions.

In theory, unions will back proposals to provide laid off people with income security or money for retraining. But in practice, unions find it politically difficult to push this agenda, which is like a tacit concession that certain jobs will be lost, that certain members will be cut loose.

At the Rocky Flats nuclear weapons facility in Colorado even the Department of Energy acknowledged that the aging plant should be phased out. The nation's only producer of plutonium triggers for warheads, it has been shut since November [1990], after a scarifying series of safety hazards was revealed.

Adrienne Anderson, the Denver-based Western director of the National Toxics Campaign, says that some Rocky Flats workers are beginning to think about what will happen if the plant shuts down for good.

The National Toxics Campaign through the local Jobs with Justice coalition in Denver, has begun a discussion with union workers about both clean up of the plant and

alternatives for those who may be laid off. There's also been discussion about reducing the health risks to workers. Anderson says a lot of Rocky Flats workers fear that if they lose their job at the plant, they'll never find another one: "They're such high health insurance risks, employers might be loathe to take them on." Says Anderson, "This just underscores the need for a federal program to protect these people."

*Laura McClure is a freelance writer living in New York City.*

*Excerpted from the* EcoSocialist Review, *Spring 1991. This article originally appeared in DSA's national magazine* Democratic Left.

# Worshipping Work

## by Walter Johnson / The New Internationalist

*"You can't eat for eight hours a day nor make love for eight hours a day—all you can do for eight hours is work. Which is the reason why man makes himself and everybody else so miserable and unhappy."*

—William Faulkner

Faulkner's feelings about work are in no way unique. Throughout history work has usually been viewed either as a curse or, at best, as a necessary evil. Most people in the pre-industrial era showed no strong inclination to work more than was necessary to maintain a fairly low standard of living. Even today, in the few remaining hunter-gatherer societies, there is no such thing as a "work ethic" which relentlessly drives people to their tasks. Some tribes will not hunt for food unless compelled by agonizing hunger. When this point is reached they will do whatever is necessary, for however long it takes, to satisfy their hunger, after which they will return to their hammocks until such hunger arises again.

It was just such an intermittent commitment to work that frustrated the early colonizers of Africa—they resorted to the imposition of cash taxes to force reluctant tribes, who had no need for money, to accept the discipline of the labor market. Many of these tribes had previously consumed only what was available and not tried to produce surpluses. In spite of this, or perhaps because of it, they were still able to support themselves, including a large proportion of the tribe that did not work at all. This belies our present belief that only an affluent, industrialized

society can afford a large, "non-productive" population.

Modern notions have it that people should be willing to work day after day, well beyond the point at which their basic needs are satisfied. Work is seen as the measure of a person's moral worth and character. Today it is not work but the lack of it which stigmatizes the individual and relegates him or her to the margins of "the good life." Sociological studies from the 1930s to the present show that individuals who need or want work, and are unable to find it, experience higher levels of alcoholism, drug abuse, divorce and other forms of unhappiness.

All this would have been incomprehensible to the ancients. So why is the loss of work or the inability to find it so traumatic for those affected? What accounts for our strange addiction to work?

According to the renowned German sociologist Max Weber, the roots of this "work

> **Increasingly there were few alternatives to wage employment. It was work in the factories or starve. Under these circumstances it is easy to see how the value of a job, any job, became so important.**

ethic" can be traced back to the Protestant Reformation some 400 years ago. One of the more prominent of the reformers, John Calvin, believed that our salvation or eternal damnation was predestined from the beginning of time. No one could know whether they were one of the few predestined to life eternal or one of the many damned to everlasting death. According to Calvin, salvation could never be certain but there might be clues that indicated who was elected by God. People who succeeded in work and lived exemplary lives were seen as the most likely candidates for salvation.

It wasn't long before the predestinarian views of salvation were supplanted by a simple belief that one could actually earn one's way into heaven through diligent effort. What became firmly implanted was a general cultural belief that hard work, of any kind, was good and idleness was wicked. This "Protestant Work Ethic" was ideally suited to the then-emerging system of industrial capitalism, which required both a disciplined work force and entrepreneurs who would limit their consumption and re-invest savings to produce even greater wealth.

It is highly unlikely, however, that most people ever believed that all work was moral and meaningful. This was essentially an ideology for self-satisfied entrepreneurs who were soon to be the dominant class within industrial societies. For the factory hands who labored in the 'dark satanic mills' the reality of daily life was a constant rebuke to the fanciful notions of ideologues.

The necessity of earning a living in the new capitalist cash economy uprooted people from their traditional communal patterns and threw them into a dog-eat-dog competition for available jobs. Many who were unaccustomed to factory work at first resisted the changes. Manufacturers often resorted to using children as laborers since they had known no other form of work and were therefore less resistant to entering the factory. Increasingly there were few alternatives to wage employment. It was work in the factories or starve. Under these circumstances it is easy to see how the value of a job, any job, became so important. To be without work in the cash economy was to be without value as a human being. Hence the special misery of the unemployed right to the present day.

Work became the central function for atomized individuals cut off from their communal roots. It determined what time they got up, what they did all day, whom they did it with and how much time they had left at the end of the day for 'leisure'. This form of work became an enforced activity, rather than a creative and satisfying one. The factory system limited the extent to which workers could exercise their capacities as human beings. The workers did not own their tools, did not own the product of their labor and did not have the right to make any decisions as to the nature of their labor. Rather than finding fulfillment and happiness at their jobs, workers instead exhausted their mental and physical energies, experiencing what Karl Marx called 'alienation'.

The source of the work ethic, then, was the insecurity and material scarcity which people experienced as a consequence of the nature of early capitalism. However, the unprecedented productivity of this new system soon made it possible to produce a large surplus with relatively little labor input, bringing about an increase in wages and a decrease in the hours of work. Union organization and the growth of the welfare state also helped mitigate the insecurity of the earlier period.

How did the work ethic persist in the face of such changes? The resilience and longevity of capitalism stems from its ability to create new forms of psychological insecurity and material scarcity at the same time as it eliminates the old forms. Thus it engineered consumerism, and the continued maldistribution of income and wealth served to create a host of artificial needs and wants that could only be satisfied through a renewed commitment to work.

There must be a better way to satisfy human needs than this. If we accepted the notion of work as something meaningful rather than simply the source of money, there would be no need to engage in the production of waste, as in the case today. We need to redefine work. Our best teachers are people who now enjoy their work. In general they do work that allows them to express their personalities. It offers them a sense of fulfillment and balance which transcends the usual quest for money and status. Work is an integral part of their lives, not simply a chore to be endured for eight hours a day and forgotten.

We have to develop a co-operative ethic which attaches value to a broader range of human activities. There would be no problem finding jobs if learning, or caring for children, or community action were considered to be work. The work ethic doesn't work any more because the type of jobs that sustained it are rapidly disappearing. The challenge is to find new ways for people to keep occupied while remaining securely attached to the larger human community. If we are successful we may finally discover the cure for what De Tocqueville called 'the disease of work'.

> **If we accepted the notion of work as something meaningful rather than simply the source of money, there would be no need to engage in the production of waste.**

*Walter Johnson is a former car worker and the author of two books on work. He lives in Quebec.*

*Excerpted from* The New Internationalist, *December 1986.*

# Volunteerism, Work & Service

## by Carrol Joy / *The Cultivator*

I have a pile of clippings in front of me from magazines and newspapers around the USA that claim to detect a new era of volunteerism among "yuppies" and other well-paid professionals. Pragmatic as well as inspired, these new volunteers are putting their skills to work in the service of society in some very interesting ways.

For example:
- Employees at Apple Computer help children in hospital wards play computer games;
- The president of Dillon Read has formed an organization to decrease the drop-out rate of inner-city students;
- Five young Wall Street analysts and consultants created a clearinghouse for those from the financial sector who want to volunteer help to the homeless and other good causes.

My favorite example from this collection comes from the *New York Times*. It is the story of the "Mad Housers," a group of architects, industrial designers and bank employees who on weekend nights secretly—and illegally—erect simple but livable huts for the homeless in Atlanta, Georgia. The group uses salvaged materials to construct tiny dwellings (about six feet by eight feet) complete with bed and shelves.

> **As a society we are less than enthusiastic about paying a living wage to people who seek first and foremost to serve from the heart.**

Like the smart business people they are, the Mad Housers field-tested their product: they left the prototype in place to see whether anyone would inhabit it. Within a few days, it had not only been inhabited, but moved to a less conspicuous spot and reassembled in a more functional manner.

### Tremendous Addition

There's no question but that competent professionals willing and able to give freely of their education, skills and contacts are a tremendous addition to the cadre of volunteers in this country. I commend them and applaud the work that they, and all of their coworkers in the vineyard, contribute to a needy world.

Having said all that, however, I must confess this happy news has only reinforced my uneasiness about the state of the nation. Why, I found myself wondering, should all of these good and essential deeds be left to the vagaries of volunteerism? Why is not such work, crucial as it is to individuals and to society, considered "real" work for which people are hired and paid decently? And why is nobody in high places—at least here in the United States—asking these questions?

If you think about it, the way we distinguish "real" jobs from volunteer jobs implies a distinction between work (what you do to earn a living) and service (action called forth in response to genuine need). Nowhere is this distinction clearer than when corporations publicly defend their "charitable" acts to stockholders as just plain good business. Clearly altruism and compassion are not marketable commodities, nor are they, in and of themselves, of much material value. Translating this in terms of jobs and wages, it means that as a society we are less than enthusiastic about paying a living wage to people who seek first and foremost to serve from the heart.

It would seem the work we most approve of and value—if payment and position in society are any measure—lies in the province of finance, business, and professional expertise of the kind we get from lawyers and medical specialists. That they can command the extraordinary salaries and fees we pay them is surely an indication we think their contribution is indeed important. More important, certainly, than teachers, social workers and other non-profit employees whose services we only grudgingly purchase. Far more important, certainly, than the advocate for the teenage mother, the relief worker struggling in a Third World refugee camp, or the nurse in a charity hospital.

And how much more valuable, then, must the financiers, business people, and profes-

sional experts be to us than the teacher's helper, the neighbor delivering "meals on wheels" to elderly shut-ins, or the full-time employee working nights and on weekends to prepare meals for the homeless—all volunteers who are unpaid, unappreciated, and unrewarded by society.

I think somewhere in the depths of our national psyche we feel that if one is really dedicated to human welfare and truly altruistic, he or she will be willing to work for very little or for free: Virtue is to be its own reward.

### Scandalous Proportions

What makes this situation troubling, as well as irrational, is that it perpetuates unnecessary human misery. If we place so little value on supporting those who *help* people live decent and dignified lives, how much less we must value the *recipients* of their help. And indeed, our social and legislative system's neglect of the public served by volunteers and underpaid workers—poor women and children, the displaced, and those outside the mainstream of society has reached scandalous proportions.

> **The answer may turn out to be some form of a guaranteed minimum wage for any activity that makes such a contribution and the opportunity to earn more through free enterprise.**

Equally disturbing, this model of work, jobs and pay stifles compassion, creative social problem-solving, and the desire to serve. How many have been driven out of teaching, advocacy for the underclass, community services, because they could not earn a liveable wage—and because they received so little recognition or appreciation by society? How many close their ears to calls for help, or deny their own urge to give because there is so little social validation for these impulses? And what must be the effect on our youth, as they discover there is no room for their altruism and their idealism in the job market?

Well, it's easier to describe problems than to solve them, and I have no magic answers to offer. Ultimately, both the public and private sectors will have to be brought around to the view that *anything* one does that makes a contribution to the physical, social, mental and spiritual well-being of people and planet—in the community, nation, and world—is real work, and should be supported. The answer may turn out to be some form of a guaranteed minimum wage for any activity that makes such a contribution and the opportunity to earn more through free enterprise. A new fusion of capitalism and socialism, combining the best of both worlds.

*Excerpted from* The Cultivator, *vol. 14, no. 4; vol. 15, no. 1, 1989.*

---

> *In the usual (though certainly not in every) public decision on economic policy, the choice is between courses that are almost equally good or equally bad. It is the narrowest decisions that are most ardently debated. If the world is lucky enough to enjoy peace, it may even one day make the discovery, to the horror of doctrinaire free-enterprisers and doctrinaire planners alike, that what is called capitalism and what is called socialism are both capable of working quite well.*
>
> John Kenneth Galbraith (b. 1908)

# Chapter 8

# *Urban Crisis*

*If we strip away the rhetoric of the right and the left, a surprising consensus emerges. There is broad agreement that America has developed an underclass, although some would prefer another term. There is sharp disagreement about the causes of this underclass, but rarely about its effects.*

*Those on the right tend to use words like "pathology," "passivity," and "hostility"; those on the left tend to speak of "despair," "hopelessness," and "alienation"—different words that often mean the same thing. As Jacob Riis warned more than a century ago, a "few generations" of slum life might produce monsters. For the first time in America's relatively young history, the ghetto has become a permanent home for too many broken families.*

*For some, upward mobility is a lie, and organized society is the enemy; for others, the temporary crutch of welfare has turned into a straitjacket of permanent dependency.*

*Whether you are compassionate or scared, the underclass should command your attention.*

— *Ken Auletta*
*from his book*
The Underclass, 1984

***Over the past few years,*** many policy makers have focused their attention on the emerging *underclass* of persons trapped at the bottom of the socioeconomic ladder. Definitions of the underclass vary, but the concept usually refers to persons who are persistently poor and living in deteriorating urban neighborhoods. In addition to these criteria, some analysts also define the underclass to be persons who engage in dysfunctional or antisocial behaviors, such as teenage pregnancy, dropping out of school, criminal activity, substance abuse, welfare dependency, or chronic unemployment.

Most researchers agree that the size of the urban underclass is relatively small—perhaps only 7 percent of the entire poverty population, according to one estimate. But as a group, the underclass seems to be growing more rapidly than the poverty population as a whole. Blacks comprise 70 percent of the underclass population. However, black people who live in urban underclass neighborhoods represent only a small share (perhaps 15 percent) of all black people in poverty.

What these data suggest is that most of the poverty population, including blacks who are poor, do not live in urban ghettos. Indeed, the poverty rates of Stewart County, Georgia, Tallahatchie County, Mississippi, and Hidalgo County, Texas are considerably higher than the rates of poverty in Newark, New Jersey or Detroit, Michigan. Poverty in America reaches beyond the central cities to medium—and small-sized communities, as well as to rural areas.

In many ways the most troublesome aspect of poverty, both now and in the future, is that socioeconomic mobility seems to be increasingly difficult for those on the edge of society. Obtaining a good education or marketable skills, finding transportation to the areas where jobs exist, or even developing relationships with successful role models have all become more problematic for people living in poverty areas. Furthermore, in a political climate of budget deficits and fiscal constraints, it may be difficult to direct public resources to areas of greatest need.

Attacking the problems of poverty and fostering the means for achieving upward mobility will encompass a broad range of policy options, among them:

✓ Programs that help young children get a better start on life—quality day care and school enrichment programs are essential components of such assistance.

✓ Programs that help pregnant teens prepare for their role as parents and assist them in completing school.

✓ Job training and job counseling programs that help unemployed or welfare-dependent people become self supporting.

✓ Programs that help make housing more affordable, not only for first-time home buyers but also for those who rent.

✓ A reappraisal of tax policies and income generating plans that will enable government at the federal, state, and local levels to finance programs to assist persons in need.

*Excerpted from* America in the 21st Century, *a booklet from Population Reference Bureau, Inc.*

# Main Street U.S.A.
## *Lobby or Lose It*

Cities are now experiencing the worst fiscal crisis since the Great Depression. According to the National League of Cities (NLC) almost two-thirds of all local governments cannot meet expenses this year, and their fiscal outlook for the coming years does not look much better.

### The Plight of U.S. Cities

Every day seems to bring more bad news to U.S. cities. For example, despite worsening problems of trash, crime, crack, homelessness, and AIDS, New York City has just fired 6,000 employees. Among the programs cut were those aimed at reducing infant deaths, preventing lead poisoning in children, and delivering meals to the homes of a thousand elderly citizens.

Across the country, no area of municipal services has been spared the budget cutter's axe. Houston cut 358 jobs from its fire department. Sacramento has delayed the opening of a new library. Minneapolis and St. Paul are reducing public transportation for the disabled. The District of Columbia has scaled back its drug rehabilitation programs.

According to Cook County Clerk David D. Orr, over the course of this year 49,000 people living in the city, of Chicago will find themselves homeless, half a million will live in inadequate dwellings, and half the city's children will go to school hungry. Forty percent of those living in Chicago are paying more than 30 percent of their income for rent and the city's murder rate is at an all time high. What has been the national response? Between 1985 and 1991, federal support was throttled back 14 percent for health and human services, 25 percent for job training and placement, 47 percent for community economic development, 55 percent for transportation, and a whopping 92 percent for housing. Overall, the city lost half of its federal assistance.

Chicago is hardly alone. A survey of 50 cities by the U.S. Conference of Mayors found that the percentage of city budgets covered by federal funds had decreased 64 percent over the past decade.

Mayor Mary Moran of Bridgeport (CT) recently petitioned for protection under chapter 9 of the U.S. bankruptcy code, and other cities may soon follow suit. In July the Boston-based law firm of Burns & Levinson sponsored a panel discussion on alternatives to bankruptcy, including receivership, and representatives from 39 cities attended.

Nor are these problems restricted to the country's largest metropolitan areas. "It's misleading," says Paul Thornton, chair of the NLC small cities council.

In Gorham (ME), a community of 11,000 people, general spending has been slashed by 16 percent—or a million dollars. Potholes are being ignored, capital expenditures delayed, and police laid off. Gorham's school budget also has been cut by $733,000, which has meant teacher layoffs, fewer classes, and cutbacks in extracurricular programs like sports.

Local governments once counted on states to make up for budgetary shortfalls. Over the past decade state aid to municipalities has grown from under $17 billion to $29.5 billion. But with most states now experiencing unprecedented deficits—and thirteen of them, according to the National Conference of State Legislators, projecting deficits greater than $500 million or 5 percent—local aid programs are being eliminated. According to Stephen Moore of the Cato Institute, it's " the easiest area for [states] to cut back on. This is passing down the financial pinch to the city governments."

What's responsible for these budget crunches? One big factor is the recession, which has reduced tax revenues and also put more people on public assistance. Another item state administrators say is "out of control" is Medicaid, which increased 25 percent this past year. Prison expenses are also rising; last year the states spent $18 billion for corrections, nearly 30 percent more than they paid in 1988.

Many cities complain that the federal government's vision of "new federalism" is to put more responsibilities onto cities with-

> **Many cities complain that the federal government's vision of *new federalism* is to put more responsibilities onto cities without providing the money to pay for them.**

out providing the money to pay for them. Two-thirds of fifty cities recently surveyed by the U.S. Conference of Mayors cited new federal environmental mandates as particularly costly. Cities now must clean up their water supplies, cut lead pollution, construct sewage treatment plants, and meet federal clean air standards all with no additional federal money.

### The Hidden Role of the Pentagon

Where has all the federal money gone? Look no further than the Pentagon. Military spending increased from $232 billion in 1980 to $300 billion in 1990 (all figures are in 1990 dollars). Throughout the decade, the Reagan and Bush Administrations pumped $579 billion *additional dollars* into national defense, that is, above 1980 spending levels.

Using data from the Advisory Commission on Intergovernmental Relations, we have calculated that over the same period states and cities lost $78 billion in federal aid. Not only did every dollar cut from cities go to the military budget—so did most of the dollars borrowed from overseas.

The Reagan/Bush rearmament program hurt the financial well-being of state and local government in at least two other ways. First, in the early 1980s Reagan threw cities a double whammy by increasing defense spending while simultaneously cutting taxes, which saddled the country with an unprecedented national debt.

Under the Bush Administration, as was true for the previous eight years, the deficit remains a perfect excuse to avoid revamping the nation's social and economic health.

> **If we phased out our commitments to NATO, which consume roughly $150 billion of the military budget (roughly half), we could shrink the Pentagon's budget still further.**

There is still another way the arms race has hurt cities. A growing body of evidence suggests that high levels of military spending are associated with unemployment and lower productivity. Germany and Japan have been allocating roughly four and 1 percent of their national R&D budgets, respectively, to military innovation. The United States, in contrast, has been spending nearly two-thirds of its R&D on better weapons. More than a quarter of our scientists and engineers are working on defense projects, while the best German and

Japanese minds are building better cars, computers, and fax machines.

Far from comprising a small part of cities' financial woes, military spending is perhaps the single biggest cause.

Fortunately, there are many ways to shrink the Pentagon's budget with no loss in national security. According to *New York Times* Pentagon correspondent Richard Halloran, at least $100 billion per year could be saved by eliminating waste, fraud, and inefficiency. Given the virtual disappearance of the Soviet threat around which most of our defense strategies have been built Brookings Institution analyst William W. Kaufman estimates that defense spending could be cut to $160 billion by the end of the l990s. If we phased out our commitments to NATO, which consume roughly $150 billion of the military budget (roughly half), we could shrink the Pentagon's budget still further.

**What Can Cities Do?**

If the peace movement, existing city lobbyists, the NLC, and the U.S. Conference of Mayors all lack the resources to match the enormous lobbying forces of defense contractors, to whom can cities turn for help? The answer is simple—themselves.

A decade ago, nearly a thousand local jurisdictions passed resolutions to "freeze" the nuclear arms race. It was an effective tool for mobilizing public opinion against the arms race, but it wound up delivering very little. Congressional members who supported the freeze turned around and voted for MX missiles and B-1 bombers—and paid no political price. In retrospect, the freeze movement made a major tactical error. It should have also asked local governments to hire a lobbyist whose mission would have been to

## Table 1

### Levels of Federal Assistance to State and Local Governments

#### (millions of 1990 dollars)

| | Outlay in 1980 | Outlay in 1990 | Net Loss |
|---|---|---|---|
| Action | 211 | 189 | 22 |
| Community Development Block Grants | 6188 | 3239 | 2949 |
| Economic Development Assistance | 1666 | 0 | 1666 |
| Education Research and Improvement | 546 | 270 | 276 |
| Elderly & Handicapped | 1193 | 680 | 513 |
| Employment Training and Placement | 11207 | 4107 | 7099 |
| Energy Conservation | 910 | 414 | 496 |
| General Revenue Sharing | 10872 | 0 | 10872 |
| Legal Services | 516 | 337 | 178 |
| Mass Transit | 5085 | 2449 | 2636 |
| National Endowment of the Arts | 241 | 174 | 67 |
| National Endowment of the Humanities | 249 | 171 | 78 |
| Small Business Administration | 3011 | 548 | 2463 |
| Social Service Block Grants | 4383 | 2952 | 1430 |
| Vocational and Adult Education | 1369 | 955 | 414 |
| Urban Development Action Grants | 355 | 221 | 134 |
| Waste Water Treatment | 6889 | 2413 | 4476 |

**Source: Greg Specter, National Priorities Project, (413) 584-9556**

reverse the arms race and cut military spending. Had a thousand city lobbyists descended on the nation's capital, the political clout of defense contractors over the past decade might have been seriously eroded.

Now, half a trillion dollars of defense increases later, cities must recognize that they cannot afford not to have their own lobbyists.

Yes, a lobbyist costs money perhaps one or two hundred thousand dollars a year. But for a large city not to invest this amount of money so as to save millions or tens of millions of dollars annually is fiscally irresponsible. Even a medium-sized city could

> **More than a quarter of our scientists and engineers are working on defense projects, while the best German and Japanese minds build better cars, computers, and fax machines.**

rationalize setting up such an office. The city of Palo Alto, California, for example, received over $300,000 per year in General Revenue Sharing; now it receives nothing. Certainly it makes sense for Palo Alto to spend $100,000 per year to retrieve $300,000 per year.

Small cities or cities experiencing especially harsh financial difficulties might consider investing in part of a lobbying office. Twenty neighboring towns, each contributing $5,000, could support one or two lobbyists in Washington. Alternatively, a city might agree to open up its phones, photocopy machines, and mailing privileges to local peace groups before big defense-spending votes.

A related commitment must come from each city's local elected officials. Frank Shafroth notes that mayors and council members have an impact when they personally "buttonhole" their representatives in Washington. "As long as there are just eight people here and our little budget," says Shafroth, "we're never going to take on the Pentagon or half the other people in this town. But we do have bodies, and they're bodies that are elected by the same people that elect members to the House and Senate."

The bottom line is that every city should do *something*. New national priorities must begin with new local priorities. Unless we make it absolutely clear, in dollars and cents, that we are committed to saving our cities, how can we expect members of Congress to do otherwise?

As long as cities approach the defense budget in a business-as-usual way, we can be sure that a $300 billion per year defense budget will continue to destroy our cities. Everyone knows that cutting the defense budget is the only real route to saving our cities. "We say it in private," one lobbyist told us, "but we don't say it in public." It's high time for cities to end their silence—and their complicity.

*Excerpted from* Global Communities, *Autumn 1991.*

# OPERATION URBAN STORM

## A New Generation of Activists is Fighting to Bring Back the Cities

### by Vicki Kemper / *Common Cause Magazine*

Many people associate the War on Poverty with liberal spending policies that do little to motivate individuals or cure entrenched dependency, and they usually point to the inner cities as evidence. In fact, most of the Johnson administration's Great Society initiatives were successful in the 1960s, when the economy was strong and growing. Studies by Congress' General Accounting Office, congressional committees and private groups indicate that specific programs—WIC, the nutrition program for pregnant women and young children; prenatal care; Head Start for poor preschoolers; childhood immunization; specialized education programs; job training; and Medicaid—have been highly cost-effective.

While such programs may have eased the plight of the poor, the War on Poverty "vision" did nothing to address unemployment, underemployment and other basic economic realities that make and keep people poor, says University of Chicago sociologist and author William Julius Wilson. As industries, much of the middle class and many social institutions deserted the cities, poverty became concentrated there, making it more visible and seemingly intractable. The nation's changed and weakened economy, the devaluation of welfare benefits and the Reagan administration's regressive tax policies have sabotaged anti-poverty efforts, leaving the poor poorer and millions of others scrambling to stay above the poverty line.

In 1989 the nations' poverty rate of 12.8 percent, representing more than 31 million Americans, was higher than it was in 1970. Today one out of every five American children is poor; one out of every eight children suffers from hunger; and 40,000 U.S. children, or 9.1 of every 1,000 born, die each year before their first birthday—a rate surpassed by only 19 countries in the world.

Virtually everyone agrees that throwing money at the problem isn't enough—particularly when there is less money to throw around. Activists and policy experts are calling for new strategies, more comprehensive and confrontational than '60s-style solutions, which would reorder national priorities and redistribute dwindling resources. They say the antipoverty policies of the '90s must challenge America's increasing economic segregation, a separation of class and race so severe that it evokes comparisons with South African apartheid. If Americans want their cities and the people in them to survive, they can no longer stand by as

middle and upper-class taxpayers abandon the cities, taking the tax base with them, says Hartford city manager, Gene Simpson. Regional governments, or some other means of spreading the wealth—and the responsibility—must become part of the debate over where to go from here.

It is not the War on Poverty but "society [that] has failed," says Hyman Bookbinder, who was executive officer of President Johnson's Task Force on Poverty. "It tired of the war too soon, gave it inadequate resources and did not open up new fronts as required." Testifying before the House Committee on Government Operations last March, Manhattan Borough President Ruth Messinger called on the government to launch "Operation

---

**They say the anti-poverty policies of the '90s must challenge America's increasing economic segregation, a separation of class and race so severe that it evokes comparisons with South African apartheid.**

---

Urban Storm." "Now that the liberation of Kuwait has been accomplished," she said, "the federal government [should] immediately undertake the liberation of the millions of Americans in our cities [who are] trapped by the tyranny of poverty, illiteracy, hunger, unemployment, crime and hopelessness."

### Dividing Lines

Hartford [CT] is a crowded, decaying city where property taxes are the main source of revenue but only half the property is taxable and three-fourths of city residents live in rental units. One out of four residents lives below the poverty line, and one out of five receives some sort of welfare. The city's unemployment is way above state and national rates. Some core businesses have moved their operations out of town or out of the country, and downtown landmarks have been razed to make room for new buildings that haven't come, leaving vacant lots and eyesores.

"Hartford is an island of poverty in the midst of a vast ocean of affluence," says the Rev. James Kidd, pastor of the city's Asylum Hill Congregational Church. The *Hartford Courant* recently completed a special series

on the city's problems and concluded that of all "metropolitan cities explored as comparisons, none is so fragmented and stratified as Greater Hartford."

Yet Hartford's problems are not unique among Connecticut's cities. Located a few suburbs south of Hartford is New Haven, the nation's seventh poorest city. In June the city of Bridgeport, located in the states wealthiest county, became the nations first major city to file for bankruptcy.

"Cities are in a death spiral," says Frank Shafroth, chief Washington lobbyist for the National League of Cities.

### Surrendered Cities

In a May 8, 1991 television address, New York City Mayor David Dinkins explained his city's fiscal crisis this way: "Our city, like every urban center, has been abandoned in the past decade by the federal government." For its part the Bush administration shows no intention of changing course—and few in Congress are pressing the issue. "There's almost a conspiracy of silence between the Democrats and Republicans in Congress and between the White House and Congress not to talk about urban problems," says Rep. Christopher Shays (R-Conn.), whose district includes Bridgeport.

Faced with the inevitable dilemma of cutting services or raising taxes, many cities have had to do both, driving out industries, jobs and middle-class residents in the process. Philadelphia has lost some 200,000 private sector jobs in the past 15 years, and Hartford has suffered a net loss of 40,000 residents since 1950 and more than 10,000 jobs in the current economic downturn.

With New York facing a budget deficit of $3.5 billion, Dinkins announced in May he would be forced to slash essential services by $1.5 billion unless the state government, which has a $6 billion budget gap of its own, came to the rescue. "Mayor Dinkins is in a no win situation," says Shafroth of the National League of Cities. "If he cuts services, people will leave. If he raises taxes, people will leave. Both will cause people to leave the city—the very people the city needs most."

This cycle has been repeated so often, and in so many American cities, that suburbanization has become "the dominant demographic trend in the nation," writes Thomas Byrne Edsall in the May issue of the *Atlantic*. From 1986 to 1987 more than two million Americans moved to the suburbs; between 1980 and 1990, 19 major cities lost population, all but seven of them in growing metropolitan regions.

Increased suburbanization is restoring the racial and economic segregation that the civil rights movement and Great Society programs sought to eliminate. It "is working to intensify the geographic separation of the races, particularly of whites from poor blacks," writes Edsall. It has also resulted in "a geographic separation of the haves and have-nots," observes Michael Wald, a professor at Stanford University Law School.

A Bush administration plan could make matters worse. It would convert $15 billion in federal grants—for housing, drug enforcement assistance, education, and social services—into single block grants to states. The nation's mayors, horrified that the plan would allow state governments to spend the money as they see fit, fear that governors, faced with their states fiscal crises, would leave mere crumbs for the cities.

### Battle Plan

Hartford City Manager Gene Shipman has a plan to make city poverty a direct interest of suburbanites: He wants to move poor people right into their protected backyards. "The doughnut syndrome," where cities are in the hole and suburbs get the dough.

He has come up with the following plan to reverse the city's long decline:

- Require the suburbs to join a regional government that would involve the joint provision of some services and a transfer of resources from suburban coffers to the city of Hartford.
- Tear down three public housing projects and relocate the 1,000 families who live there to the suburbs.
- Levy a one percent earnings tax on suburban residents who work in Hartford, which he believes would raise $50 million for the city and make possible a 25 percent cut in property taxes.
- Lay off some city employees to bring a bloated bureaucracy under control.
- "Privatize" the direct delivery of services to the poor, reducing city outlays and increasing efficiency.
- Redirect the city's resources away from social services and toward "core municipal functions": economic development and the provision of street maintenance, water and sewer services, police and fire protection and the like.
- Emphasize programs that move poor people into jobs and self-sufficiency.

Shipman says that once he stops Hartfords' decay, he'll move on to his second goal: keeping the middle class in the city. He would use both a carrot and a stick. The carrot: federal and state investment in urban schools, infrastructure and industry, which would provide opportunities for poor people to work themselves into the middle class. The stick: Penalize those who leave with commuter taxes. "You need to pay a premium for the luxury of living in suburbia if that's what you choose to do," he says.

Finally, Shipman would also relocate some housing and services for the poor to the suburbs. Moving poor people into the suburbs would free them from "inhuman conditions" in the city and expose them to a different, motivating life-style, he says.

### Front-line Victories

With the prospects for outside help so dim, local officials, community organizers and anti-poverty groups are doing what they

*Reprinted from ArtPolice, Summer 1989, vol. 1G, no.2*

can to rescue cities and their residents from the slide into greater decay. While Hartfords' problems are pervasive, the city also has its success stories. Some of the most effective organizations are using a combination of public and private funds to help poor people break the cycle of dependency and become self-sufficient. To cite a few:

**Jobs.** America Works of Connecticut has adopted an "all-win" strategy to get poor women off welfare, says chief officer Lee Bowes. The women win because the program teaches them job skills, shows them how to get along in the workplace, finds them jobs, pays them to intern for two to three months, and then provides them with the support they need to make it as regular employees—whether it's helping them get to work on time or making sure their kids are picked up from school.

Private employers and the state government also win. The state pays America Works $4,000—about one-third the annual cost of keeping a family of three on welfare—for each welfare recipient placed in a job. The state also continues to provide day care and medical benefits to the working woman for a year after she gets off the welfare rolls. Companies that hire America Works clients get a federal tax benefit of up to $4,500 if the employee stays on the job for more than a year—and 75 percent do.

Since 1985 America Works have placed some 1,000 former welfare recipients in jobs, Bowes says.

**Intervention.** While America Works tries to place poor women in jobs, the 1,400 members of Asylum Hill Congregational Church—some 80 percent of them suburbanites, and almost all of them white—are working to break the poverty cycle at an earlier stage. Three years ago the church raised $400,000 to guarantee college educations for a middle-school class of 79 kids. About 100 church members and three staff members work with the children in the "Dreamer Project," says pastor James Kidd.

Church members also run Saturday morning and weekday tutoring programs for kids, and they pay the salary of a community social worker at the nearby middle school. Church members have begun a new project to sponsor families in homeless shelters, providing financial assistance, helping them "work the system" and eventually helping them find housing in the suburbs. It's "a way of rescuing families," Kidd says.

The church also helps run a soup kitchen, offers courses on urban problems, supports housing-renovation projects, and even ran a full-page newspaper ad that declared, "We Love Hartford" and encouraged others to become involved in efforts to help the city.

"It's a justice issue," Kidd says of his church's activism. "The key thing is personal involvement and support. "People [in privately run programs] care about the neighborhood and about the kids," he says. "The city doesn't."

**Change.** For the Rev. Mark Welch, director of the Christian Activities Council's Metropolitan Training Institute, "boosterism" and efforts to, "serve the poor with programs" are important but ultimately insufficient responses to "the moral imperative of the '90s." "We believe in justice before charity," he says. "Just tinkering with the system won't do it; we need systematic and structural change."

Welch emphasizes the importance of community activism in the style of the late Saul Alinsky: helping poor people figure out what they need most from the system and organizing them to fight for it. The Asylum Hill Organizing Project, Project Mash and other community groups mobilize low-income residents to work for tenants' rights, better schools and increased neighborhood safety. They also promote housing rehabilitation and job training and placement.

Community investment is also key, Welch says. The Christian Activities Council (CAC), a mission of the United Churches of Christ, sponsors a minority-owned and operated corporation that manages some 180 apartments in the city for low-income people.

**Vision.** One key to solving the city's problems is making people believe that it's possible, activists say. With a $25,000 seed grant from the private Knox Foundation, organizers are forming a task force of 45 community leaders—from business, government, community, education, labor, religious and other groups—to implement a new "vision process" for Hartford.

"There is a mood of pessimism and hopelessness in this town, and it's important to attack that," says Knox Foundation President Ivan Backer.

More than a dozen studies and plans have been conducted since 1980; they produced hundreds of recommendations but little has been done. Backer hopes community involvement will make the process different.

### Children First

Because poverty is having an increasing impact on the nations children, advocates for the poor are finding allies in unexpected places. Suburbanites, business executives, pro-family groups and crime fighters are beginning to acknowledge the long-term impacts of neglecting the nation's children. In March the CEOs of AT&T, BellSouth, Prudential, Honeywell and Skychefs appeared before the House Budget Committee to call for a doubling of funding for the WIC program. The executives warned that as many as 40 percent of the nation's children are headed for educational failure unless more is done to meet their health, social and developmental needs before they reach school age.

Right now, more people are moving into poverty than escaping from it. Between February and March the number of families receiving Aid to Families with Dependent Children (AFDC), or "welfare," increased by 68,000—the 20th consecutive monthly increase and the largest single monthly increase since 1975, according to Rick Ferreira, policy associate at the American Public Welfare Association.

That increased the total number of AFDC recipients to an all-time high of 4.4 million families, or 12.6 million people, two-thirds of them children. Yet welfare is hardly a ticket out of poverty; the purchasing power of welfare benefits has decreased by 42 percent since 1970, according to the Center on Budget and Policy Priorities. Monthly welfare payments currently average $135.36 per individual and $390.86 per family, Ferreira says.

Taken together, the declining effectiveness of government income programs, increased unemployment and lower earnings are responsible for two-thirds of the dramatic increase in child poverty, according to the Childrens Defense Fund. About one-fourth of the increase is due to the greater proportion of children living in single-parent families, the report says.

Marian Wright Edelman, president of the Childrens Defense Fund, has called for nearly $6 billion in new federal spending on children, much of it to expand current immunization, daycare and Head Start programs.

One-stop assistance centers are being launched in several school districts across the country. They include social workers, daycare centers, health care clinics, job training and counseling. In Maryland, parents can go to Family Support Centers for assistance in childrearing, health and nutrition counseling, education and job training.

On the economic policy level, the Childrens Defense Fund, the Progressive Policy Institute and others have called for an increase in the personal income-tax exemption for low and middle-income families with children; further expansion of the Earned Income Tax Credit to decrease the penalties and increase incentives for poor people to work; an increase in the minimum wage; passage of some version of the Family and

Medical Leave Act, which was vetoed by President Bush last year; more money to alleviate hunger and homelessness; and the reform of divorce laws to protect children and ensure the payment of child support.

"To be born in a ghetto is to be consigned a fate no American should have to suffer," writes Nicholas Lemann, author of *The Promised Land: The Great Black Migration and How it Changed America.*

Robert Reich, political economist at Harvard University and author of *The Work of Nations: Preparing Ourselves for 21st-Century Capitalism,* warns that the gap between rich and poor communities is "widening into a chasm." This trend toward greater economic segregation "raises fundamental questions about the future of American society," he says. "The stark political challenge in the decades ahead will be to reaffirm that, even though America is no longer a separate and distinct economy, it is still a society whose members have abiding obligations to one another."

Gene Shipman couldn't agree more. "We have a moral imperative to act," he says. "We can't afford to throw away our cities or the people in them."

*Excerpted from* Common Cause Magazine, *July/August 1991.*

# Danaan Parry, Stewardship & Urban Youth

## by Carolyn Moran / *Talking Leaves*

**CM:** What's going on with your work at the high school level?

**DP:** Last summer the whole month of July we were in Bedford/Stuyvesant in Brooklyn, New York, where we did an urban Peace Trees project. This involved high school students from all over the world, including a large contingent of black inner-city high schools. We brought 5 incarcerated kids from New Jersey who had been thrown out of high school and locked up for various charges. We convinced the New Jersey Department of Corrections to do a pilot program where 5 of those kids and 2 of their counselors, the guards, would be a part of this program. We all lived together for a month at Pratt University. Every day we would go out and tear up the concrete in the streets and plant trees. We don't plant trees in nice green parks. We got permission from the city to tear up abandoned parking lots, to tear up center dividers in streets. In fact in Fulton Boulevard in Brooklyn there wasn't even a center divider; we took the turn lane and dug it up by hand. We don't use power tools. This way we really get into working and having a great time. These high school kids are at a wonderful age because they have an incredible amount of energy which in that environment is

usually directed toward self-destruction. If you redirect it a little bit, you have this power plant of incredible energy where they can do 10 times as much work as you could do with a soil erosion. Kids come from the Middle East and they see the world in a totally different way than the high school kids do here.

There are different trainings every night. We separate the groups into men and women—the men will go off with men counselors and the women with women counselors and we will spend an hour talking about what it is like to be a man or a woman in Jordan, in Seattle, etc. Then we come back together and share that information. There will be a Catholic girl and a Protestant girl and they will be so into communicating with the high school boys what it is like to be a woman that the barriers between them disappear. They wind up hugging each other and crying together about what it's like in Northern Ireland to be a woman and what they have to put up with.

*Excerpted from* Talking Leaves, *April 1992, "Warrior of the Heart, An Interview with Danaan Parry," a former Atomic Energy Commission physicist and Clinical Psychologist, and founder of Earthstewards Network.*

# Cities on Drugs

## by Michael Shuman / *Bulletin of Municipal Foreign Policy*

> *We can begin to make real headway against drugs if we're ready to harness our local governments to reshape national policy-makers, assist desperate Third World farmers, and put real controls on multinational chemical companies.*

January [1990] was business as usual in the nation's capital. More than one person was gunned down in the city's drug wars every day—only a slight increase over the previous year's rate of carnage.

Local leaders were proclaiming victory in the "war on drugs," while Mayor Marion Barry was being hauled off to a rehabilitation facility in Florida for allegedly smoking crack in front of FBI cameras. And President George Bush was proposing a budget with trivial increases for fighting drugs while continuing to earmark $150 billion for war preparations in Central Europe that everyone agrees are absurd.

Faced with hypocrisy at every turn, it is hard to know what local officials and citizens can do about drugs. Clearly they can no longer do nothing. Economists now estimate that the total cost of drug abuse in America, including the cost of crime, law enforcement, and health problems, exceeds $60 billion per year, damages that are falling primarily on poor, urban blacks who can least afford them. If cities begin wisely using the tools of municipal foreign policy, they have a chance of making a dent in the drug mess.

### WHAT WON'T WORK

Following the lead of [former] Drug Czar William Bennett, too many local officials have taken to the stump demanding more stringent law enforcement: If only we could incarcerate more crack dealers, give them longer sentences (including the death penalty), capture more contraband at our borders, wipe out more coca fields, and extradite more drug lords, all of our problems would be solved.

But statistics tell another story. Between 1980 and 1988, according to author Tina Rosenberg, the United States spent $10 billion to fight illicit cocaine imports, sales and use. During the same period, the supply of cocaine in the United States increased by a factor of ten, its street price dropped by four-fifths, and its purity rose from 12 to 80 percent.

Rooting out the coca fields and makeshift labs in Latin America has been similarly difficult. Drug trafficking earns Colombia between $2-4 billion each year; coffee, in contrast, Colombia's largest legal export, earned $1.7 billion in 1988 and only a billion in 1989. Fewer and fewer Colombians are willing to destroy their most successful multinational business just because Uncle Sam doesn't like it. According to Rosenberg, drug trafficking "is an accepted, even an admired activity. There is no segment of Colombian society that has not made its pact with cocaine: the military, the guerrillas, the banks, the Catholic Church, industry, the courts, the police." It is for this reason that U.S. gunboats cannot help.

### PROMISING NEW STRATEGIES

What other options, then, are there? While there are no easy or cheap ways out of the drug epidemic, there are at least three approaches with more promise than direct interdiction, each of which requires creative municipal action.

### 1. REGULATE U.S. CHEMICAL COMPANIES

We must begin by regulating more vigorously one of the parts of the cocaine business from which American companies profit—selling processing chemicals that transform Latin America's coca paste into cocaine. According to the U.S. Drug Enforcement Agency, nearly half of the ether, acetone, and methyl ethyl ketone (MEK) exported in 1987 to Colombia, Bolivia, Peru, and Ecuador was used for processing coca. Exxon and Shell, for example, have shipped Colombia enormous quantities of MEK, well beyond any legitimate industrial uses by that country.

State and local government should pass disclosure regulations that supplement loose federal regulations. Look carefully at the chemical companies in your own backyards, ask for records of their foreign transactions, and make sure that they are not part of the problem. If you or other cities discover companies that seem to be involved in the chemical-cocaine chain, your city should refuse to enter contracts with or invest in them.

### 2. PROMOTE LATIN AMERICAN DEVELOPMENT

Another approach to stopping drug traffic is to give Latin American farmers a profitable alternative to growing coca. The United States must stop sabotaging Latin America's legal industries. Last year, we scuttled an international coffee agreement that caused the price of Colombia's largest legal export to tumble by 40 percent. At the same time, the Department of Commerce decided to protect our domestic flower growers at the expense of Colombia's flower farmers, the nation's fourth largest group of legal exporters.

More importantly, we should provide grants, loans, technology, and other assistance that could give farmers direct incentives to stop growing coca. So long as the average coca farmer can earn an income six times higher than other farmers—for a crop that is resistant to most pests and enjoys a relatively stable price—the incentives for illicit agriculture will remain irresistible. Yet, in our misguided quest for interdiction, we now give Colombians twenty times more for crop eradication and law enforcement than for all forms of development assistance.

Every American city should adopt one town or village in Peru, Bolivia or Colombia, and work side-by-side with Latin Americans to promote economic alternatives to growing coca. Like our counterparts in Europe who now have nearly one thousand Third World links dedicated to sustainable development, we should send our sister communities farming equipment, provide small-scale loans, and help build roads, bridges, water systems and schools.

For $25 billion—between one-half and one-eighth the total cost of the bailout for the savings and loan industry we could pay *every* rural family in Latin America $1,000 not to grow coca (that's the typical annual income for a coca farmer). That would be half the cost cities are now paying in crime, sickness and other drug damages. Third World development is no longer just charity; it is an essential, cost-effective means of protecting our cities.

### 3. CUT THE PENTAGON'S BUDGET

Ultimately, our efforts to end drug abuse must reduce demand at home. The war on drugs will never be won without a revived war on poverty.

Any new commitment to eradicating hunger, homelessness, illiteracy, unemployment, and addiction will require tens of billions of dollars. And unless we are willing to increase taxes, which President Bush has sworn never to do, we must slash the military budget.

It is essential for cities to send lobbyists to Washington to push for deeper cuts in military spending and renewed social services. Moreover, cities must educate their citizens to understand the need for new national budget priorities—now.

We can begin to make real headway against drugs if we're ready to harness our local governments to reshape national policy-makers, assist desperate Third World farmers, and put real controls on multinational chemical companies. The time has come to break loose of our dependency on Washington and begin the local initiatives that can win the war on drugs. If we fail, we will have no one to blame but ourselves.

*Excerpted from* Bulletin of Municipal Foreign Policy (ceased printing), *Spring 1990.*

# Hyper-Cities Indicate Larger Ills

## by Pete Brady / *New Times*

According to the United Nations Population Fund, population growth can be directly tied to economic and social health; no longer can we truthfully say "The more the merrier."

"The fastest-ever growth in human numbers is compounded by widespread poverty and deprivation," says Fund spokesperson Dr. Nafis Sadik. "The fastest-ever growth in human consumption of resources is compounded by political and economic systems unaware of any limits to growth."

According to Sadik's research, population growth and increased poverty are directly correlated in developing countries and in the United States. Where fertility and immigration rates are high, societal conditions are substandard, poverty is rampant, illiteracy rates are high, and women's lives are charac- terized by exploitation, lack of political and social freedom and early death.

Population growth also fuels the trend toward megacities which dehumanize and victimize their inhabitants.

"In 1950, only 29 people in every 100 lived in cities. All the world's urban areas contained 734 million people, and only two cities—London and New York—housed more than 8 million people," Sadik said. "But by 1990 the world's urban population had tripled, and 45 people of every 100 lived in cities or towns. There are now 20 hyper-cities with more than 8 million people each."

Sadik's researchers note that American cities like Los Angeles and Third World cities like Calcutta often have strikingly similar features— sprawling areas of abject poverty comprised of recent immigrants and other powerless people living in squalid conditions.

Unprecedented population growth in Africa, Latin America and Asia has spurred international migration to record levels. The United States took in an average of 610,000 permanent immigrants annually during the 1980s, the highest number in history except for the 1900-1920 period. This number is compound by an estimated half a million illegal immigrants each year.

*Pete Brady lives in Sacramento, California.*

*Excerpted from "L.A.: A Sympton of Larger Ills" which appeared in the* New Times *(San Luis Obispo, CA), May, 28, 1992.*

# Days of the Dragon, Flight L.A. of the Phoenix

## by Marilyn Ferguson • *Brain/Mind & Common Sense Bulletin*

So the Big One finally happened and it wasn't at all what we expected. It wasn't the 8.0 tremor on the Richter Scale, ripping through the network of faults underlying Los Angeles, the most international of cities. The great, seismic shock issued from a courtroom: *Not guilty,* the jury said. And three aftershocks. *Not guilty, not guilty, not guilty.*

Within hours the great Dragon of indignation, breathing fire, began moving, inch by inch, then slashing here, there and everywhere with its talons. In Los Angeles it was embodied in an army of the possessed and the dispossessed, acting out the communal rage, torching friends and enemies alike, plundering neighbors and neighborhoods, much as people crazed by pain bang their heads against the wall.

Warring gangs made peace to avenge themselves on "the pigs." "Crips and Bloods Together," read one graffito, and another said, "Mexicans and Crips and Bloods together TONITE." The Dragon's army swelled with arsonists and other mercenaries, with pyromaniacs, adolescents, urban flotsam and jetsam of every kind, children, thrill-seekers. The Dragon's counterparts flared their nostrils in San Francisco, Las Vegas. Seattle, Atlanta, New York, even in Eugene, Oregon.

Just in time, the Phoenix shook off its torpor. Through the eyes of helicopter cameras, it saw the Dragon wreaking havoc.

Armies of angels banded against the destruction, linking in front of neighborhood stores, warning-off looters; toting coffee to firemen, even to "pigs"; grabbing hoses and buckets; rescuing innocent people from the Dragon's random ire.

Prayer strengthened the Phoenix, and it rode on warm currents of common sense. A Korean store-owner calmly invited the crowds to enter his store, admitting five at a time, offering-up his merchandise and asking only that they break nothing. They took, they left.

A strange hypnotic calm was gathering above and around the array of infernos. Among those watching the spectacle, civic outrage at the vandalism slowly gave way to despair, then a kind of understanding. In the quick turn of events and the smoke of war, viewers could not clearly detect a villain.

The Phoenix spread its wings more fully on the Day After. The army of broom-wielding helpers swelled, filling the streets, sweeping up the debris in parking lots around the burned shells. They came from the affected neighborhoods and throughout the city; from Beverly Hills, even from Simi Valley. With so many hands, so many brooms flying, Phase One of the cleanup took little more than a single day.

The events in Los Angeles can be seen as mere history or as a watershed; they will have the meaning we give them. One possible story: The world as we know it—the world of black and white, of easy, righteous answers—ended in fire. Our common spirit, the "rough beast slouching toward Bethlehem," was born in the ashes of Los Angeles. If we imagine well, perhaps it will stretch its wings and bear us up, as it did those dark hours.

*Excerpted from* Brain/Mind & Common Sense Bulletin, *May 1992.*

# Greening Our Cities

## by Alex Levine

There needs to be a profound shift in the fundamental premises and activities of city living. Urban people have to adopt conserveration values and carry out more responsible practices in wide areas of daily life. Municipal governments need to restructure their priorities so that long-term sustainability can become a feasible goal. With such a large portion of the population removed from the land and from access to resources, ways to secure some share of the basic requirements of food, water, energy, and materials will have to be found within the confines of cities.

Cities need to become "green." They must be transformed into places that are life-enhancing and regenerative. [Ed. note: What follows are recommendations on how city residents can begin "greening" their city. These recommendations were written for the San Francisco Bay area but almost all of them are applicable to other cities and towns.]

*Adapted from* **A Green City Program for San Francisco Bay Area And Beyond** *by Peter Berg, Beryl Magilavy and Seth Zuckerman*

## URBAN PLANTING
### What benefits can cities reap from urban planting?

- More livable cities. Cities typically devote almost all of their land area to buildings and streets. That's an impoverishing choice—aesthetically, physically and spiritually. Trees, bushes and grasslands are beautiful, and complement the beauty of human artifacts. They provide shade when its hot and shelter from winter storms and wind.
- Closer-knit communities. Sidewalk planting projects present an opportunity for residents to work together on bettering their neighborhoods. Unified neighborhoods are less vulnerable to crime, litter and other problems of urban blight.

### Here are few practical ideas for municipal policies that can be undertaken immediately to promote urban planting.

- Repeal ordinances and procedures that stand in the way of the literal greening of the cities (e.g. those that impede the planting of street trees and sidewalk strips).
- Offer, sponsor or subsidize classes in urban gardening.
- Make available some city park land for citizen planting and gardening; plant fruit trees in parks and maintain them as public orchards.

### Longer-term visions for municipal action include:

- Assist in the establishment of local composting centers for parks and gardens in the city.
- Require developers to set aside a certain percentage of the area of their developments as plantable space, in rooftop and window planter boxes and in sidewalk strips.
- Make city money available to neighborhood associations, homeowners or renters for urban revegetation and tree planting, in the form of either tax incentives or a district levy.
- Encourage the growth of local commons, either by offering incentives to landowners to donate or grant long-term leases on plantable vacant lots, or by acquiring land and making it available to local residents.

## SMART TRANSPORTATION

Smart transportation means seeking appropriate, ecologically sound solutions to people's transportation needs, instead of trying to solve them all with more asphalt and single occupancy vehicles. It means using a combination of techniques—such as self-propelled transit (foot and bicycle), buses, ride-sharing and proximity (working and playing near home)—to complement the role of the automobile, and giving preference to cycling and walking.

### What benefits can cities gain from smart transportation?

- More workable cities. Decreased use of automobiles will mean less noise, cleaner air and unclogged roads.
- Decreased dependence on imported energy. Motor vehicles consume a large fraction of the fossil fuels used in cities and leave us vulnerable to price hikes and gas shortages.
- Reduced municipal expenditures. Decreased traffic cuts highway maintenance costs, damage from accidents and fuel charges. New developments that incorporate smart transportation principles can slash infrastructure costs by narrowing roads and using more land for people, less for streets and related services.

### What can cities do to promote smart transportation?

- Levy a local gasoline tax, higher parking taxes and an auto tax to help fund public transit, compensating for subsidies to auto transit (e.g. freeway construction and maintenance).
- Create auto-free pedestrian malls in dense sections of town to encourage foot traffic and to prevent congestion and parking problems.
- Install bike racks on some buses and allow bikes on trains to facilitate the bike-to-mass-transit connection and reduce the need for parking and shuttles at transit stations.
- Require developers to shoulder some of the transportation costs generated by their development (for instance, by coordinating vanpools or providing shuttles to commuter rail).
- Adopt mixed-use zoning policies to enable dwellings, workplaces and places of entertainment to be near each other for access by proximity instead of transportation; discourage housing-only subdivisions,

commuter suburbs and urban sprawl.

- Promote services such as car and vanpooling, which require low capital investment and offer high flexibility. For example, provide tax incentives to employers to organize vanpools for their workers or offer cash bonuses to employees who use ride sharing.
- Greatly expand facilities for cyclists, such as racks, lanes and off-street paths.

***Longer-term visions for municipal action include:***

- Reduce the width of all but arterial streets and their maximum speed limits to make streets more hospitable to pedestrians and cyclists.
- Design some streets to include culdesacs connected by bike paths, thus making the bicycle a swifter vehicle than the automobile in many instances (as was done in the Village Homes development in Davis, California).

## SUSTAINABLE PLANNING

Sustainable planning refers both to the process of planning and its focus. Good planning examines the overall, cumulative effects of proposed changes in land use, and judges them in the context of the region's natural features such as climate, watercourses, seismic history and animal and plant lifecycles. It is developed at the grassroots level with active citizen participation in setting the agenda and proposing policies.

***What benefits can cities reap from sustainable planning?***

- Livability over the long term. The prosperity of a region is rooted in the health of the ecosystems that support it— the land, the air and the water. Sustainable planning considers proposed development with a view to preserving and improving these systems.
- Sustainable planning involves people in the choices that determine the ecological functioning of their regions and thus brings home the effect of people's actions on their environment.

***What can cities do to promote sustainable planning?***

- Establish a staff to serve as sustainable planning advocates. They would counter balance powerful monied interests that exert pressure on the planning process. A model could be the Public Staff Division of the Public Utilities Commission, which acts as a rate payer advocate before the commission in rate cases.
- Actively solicit neighborhoods' visions of their futures through methods such as attitude and preference polls and well-publicized, ongoing town-hall-style meetings.
- Emphasize a long-term, regional perspective in city planning.
- Discourage or prohibit the conversion of valuable agricultural land into low-density

suburbs that require a high investment in roads and city services and increase dependency on the automobile. Promote instead "proximity policies" that encourage people to live near their workplaces.
- Identify "sacred places" (ranging from parks to landmark buildings to cafes and teen hangouts) that may not be removed or disturbed.

***Longer-term visions for municipal action include:***

- Adopt "statutes of responsibility" that delineate the obligations of officials and agencies to preserve the health of the city and its inhabitants, and that require developers to internalize costs generated by their development and currently imposed on the public. These range from water and sewer use to air pollution and encroachment on open space.
- Wherever possible, reverse cars' domination of the landscape, recapture land devoted to the automobile (sometimes approaching 60 percent of urban land area) for other uses, and restrict the allocation of more land to car-related use.
- As a way to reduce urban sprawl, use city money to buy, move or demolish buildings that are located in ecologically sensitive or valuable areas (e.g. along waterfront, creeks or hilltops) and are near the end of their useful lives.

## RENEWABLE ENERGY

Fossil fuels such as oil and gas come from finite reserves created by the decay of plants over millions of years, which cannot be regenerated on a human time-scale. In contrast, renewable energy sources come from natural flows in the environment, such as sunlight and falling water. If designers take into account fluctuations in weather and climate, these flows are consistent and dependable enough to serve as reliable energy sources. Coupled with improvements in the efficiency of all energy use, renewable sources can supply all of a city's energy needs.

***What benefits can cities gain from renewable energy?***

- Reduced pollution.
- Lower energy costs. The first prerequisite for smart use is improving the efficiency with which we use energy. The next cheapest energy strategy is conversion to renewable sources: These sometimes cost more to build than other technologies, but they cost much less to run because the fuel is free.
- Improved base of local jobs. Money spent on oil leaves the city and enriches people in far away places. With renewables and energy efficiency, much of the work takes place in the communities or regions where the energy is to be used, so money spent on energy keeps circulating in the area, creating more jobs through a "multiplier effect." (For example, the people who

build your solar greenhouse spend their wages at local restaurants, barbershops and grocery stores.)

***What can cities do to promote renewable energy?***

- Set an example of smart energy use by demonstrating applications of energy efficiency and renewable energy in municipal buildings, such as libraries, schools and firehouses.
- Sponsor energy education programs, displays on renewable energy and the distribution of information.
- Make a more vigorous effort to reach low-income households eligible for free weatherizations.
- Pass ordinances requiring that homes and apartments be weatherized when sold (as has been done in San Francisco, Berkeley and elsewhere) or by a certain deadline (as has been done in Portland).

## RECYCLING AND REUSE

Recycling and reuse mean salvaging discarded materials rather than burying or burning them. They may be used again in their original form (such as returnable bottles or old chairs or doors), reused for a different purpose (such as paper pressed into artificial logs), decomposed organically (such as the composting of kitchen scraps), or reprocessed (such as the recovery of the glass or metal content from bottles, aluminum cans or auto engines).

***What benefits can cities reap from recycling and reuse?***

- Lower city costs. Recycling and reuse programs offer an economical way for cities to dispose of their discards while paying lower disposal fees. Because they salvage value from the supply of discards, recycling and reuse programs can reduce the necessity and cut the costs of dumping garbage in landfills, while generating income from products people want to dispose of.
- More job opportunities. Recycling programs generate a large part of their own revenues, supporting their own employees.
- Reduced pressure on wilderness resources. Recycling cuts the demand for raw materials such as wood and metals. Composting also makes it possible to return the nutrients from kitchen scraps and yard trimmings to the soil.
- Elimination of the need for incineration.

***Here are a few municipal policies that could be undertaken to promote recycling and reuse:***

- Institute curbside pickup of separated recyclables, provide or sell special containers for materials to be recycled.
- Buy recycled materials for municipal use as a way of creating markets for recyclables.
- Raise tonnage fees for landfill disposal. Offer an alternative to the flat monthly

home garbage fee that charges according to the volume actually thrown away.

### GETTING STARTED

Single proposals in the Green City Program are modest in impact, but it will be the cumulative effect that counts. Each step will lead in the direction of realignment toward a society that sees its long-term interest in the well-being of the whole planet.

While the Green City Program can serve as a blueprint for a more ecologically sound future, it will just remain a set of good ideas until individuals turn their energies toward implementing its goals—until people take it as their own agenda and set to work on personal, community and governmental levels to see that it gets done.

*Adapted from* A Green City Program for San Francisco Bay Area And Beyond *by Peter Berg, Beryl Magilavy and Seth Zuckerman ©1990 Wingbow Press/Planet Drum Foundation.*

*Excerpted from* Co-op America Quarterly.

# COHOUSING COMMUNITIES:
## *A Way to a Sustainable Future*

### by Ken Norwood & Kathleen Smith / *Open Exchange*

At Shared Living Resource Center (SLRC), we receive many calls from people wanting to move to the country. People dream of the community and belonging that existed in most small towns and villages of yore. Yet in an attempt to escape the problems of the cities, new ones are created— freeways, shopping malls, single family lots and houses, congestion, air pollution, and noise spread, destroying farmland and the remaining open space. The social isolation and loneliness follow as well.

The problems are in the institutions we create and support, caused by our individualistic and separatist world view which exploits people and land for profit. Individual, separated houses mean more cars, appliances, heaters, more trips to the store, and more "stuff" in general, which means big money for business. It also means more resource depletion and pollution, and more isolation.

> **Many people are seeking alternatives not provided by the traditional housing industry, and some are ready to do something about it.**
>
> — *Kathryn McCamant and Charles Durrett*

Since the 1970's Ken Norwood has educated about and designed Shared Living Communities based on the premise that "Without a sense of community our society will deteriorate." These communities are simply a modern day adaptation of the extended family compound and village which humankind has lived in for thousands of years—an instinctual human way of living.

The cohousing model, well advanced in Denmark, is becoming increasingly popular in the United States through the work of Charles Durrett and Kathryn McCamant, au-

thors of the book *Cohousing.* Several village cluster type communities have opened. Doyle Street in Emeryville, Muir Commons in Davis, and the Winslow Cohousing near Seattle. These communities are organized around everyday activities, like villages, and have the potential for strengthening relationships beyond our small nuclear families. With the emphasis on sharing meals as a common bonding experience, people eat more healthily and affordably, and gain emotional support by sharing stories, ideas, and concerns.

*Excerpt adapted from an article which appeared in* Open Exchange, *July/August/September 1992. Ken Norwood, Executive Director, and Kathleen Smith, Associate Director, of Shared Living Resource Center, a community education and design nonprofit, are currently writing a book,* Shared Living Communities: Designs for Ecological Living. *For more information see the directories for the Center. Ken Norwood is the Planner and Architect for the Center. The following designs reflect two of the many such possibilites in cohousing.*

Cohousing *by Kathryn McCamant and Charles Durrett is available from Ten Speed Press (800) 841-2665.*

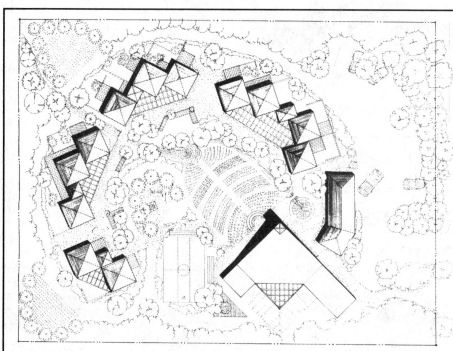

A *Village Cluster Community* is composed of newly constructed or remodeled private units of various sizes, grouped around extensive common facilities in a central house. Examples are found in some American intentional communities and Scandanavian cohousing communities. These are advanced, state-of-the-art intentional/cooperative communities which may have 30 or more units clustered around village-like streets, self-sufficient gardens, a central kitchen, dining and social halls, work studios, and number of shared amenities. These communities can be organized, designed, financed and built by a group acting as their own developer, or sponsored by for-profit or nonprofit housing developers.

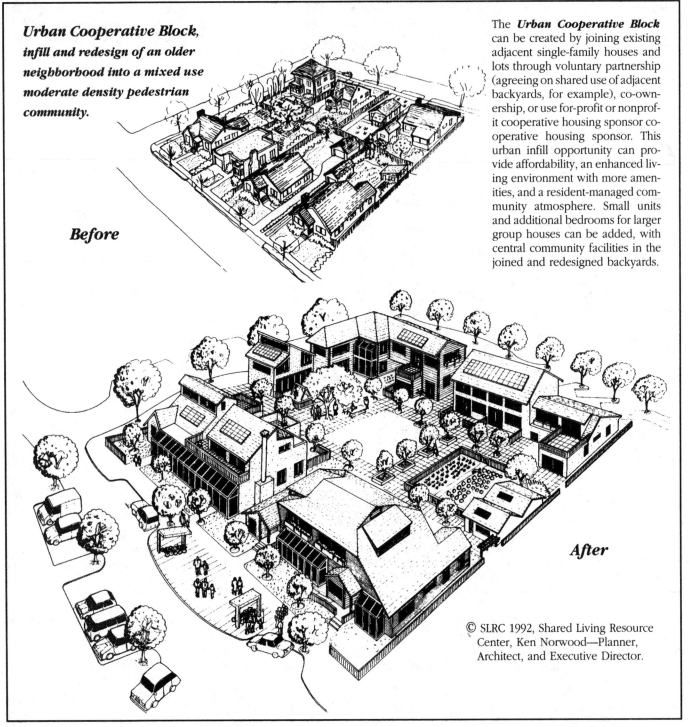

***Urban Cooperative Block,*** *infill and redesign of an older neighborhood into a mixed use moderate density pedestrian community.*

**Before**

The ***Urban Cooperative Block*** can be created by joining existing adjacent single-family houses and lots through voluntary partnership (agreeing on shared use of adjacent backyards, for example), co-ownership, or use for-profit or nonprofit cooperative housing sponsor cooperative housing sponsor. This urban infill opportunity can provide affordability, an enhanced living environment with more amenities, and a resident-managed community atmosphere. Small units and additional bedrooms for larger group houses can be added, with central community facilities in the joined and redesigned backyards.

**After**

© SLRC 1992, Shared Living Resource Center, Ken Norwood—Planner, Architect, and Executive Director.

# Vegetable Gardens Atop Skyscrapers

For seven years, poet, novelist, and former Vietnam corpsman Dan Barker has been giving away vegetable gardens—525 of them to date—in the needy neighborhoods of Portland, Oregon. Funded by private foundations and trusts, Barker builds free backyard gardens from frames, trellises, and seeds and gives advice on post control and tips in cooking. Barker's project complements the community garden movement thriving in many cities. With vegetables sprouting everywhere from skyscraper rooftops to former abandoned lots, a community garden fullfils needs for camaraderie as well as for fresh produce.

*From an article that first appeared in* The Sun *and excerpted from its reprint in* Utne Reader. *In the Los Angeles area,* Burwood Journal, *produced by* Survival News Service, *advises urban residents on similar endeavors.*

# Chapter 9

# *Education*

*it will be a great day*
*when*
*our schools*
*get all the money*
*they need*
*and the air force*
*has to hold*
*a bake sale*
*to buy a*
*bomber*

*Recycling and shopping ecologically are almost pointless when one-third of California's high school students drop-out, and most who graduate can't read much. How can these people inherit a world? Even if we give them a greener world, are they equipped to keep it that way?*

*Michael Ventura, from his list of solutions in* LA Weekly, *March 9, 1990.*

Laments about our schools are nothing new. Everyone is an expert, it seems, when it comes to education. While most critics point to the lack of funding or the shortage of teachers, John Gatto insists the problem goes deeper; we've turned our schools, he says, into "torture chambers."

John Gatto teaches seventh grade at Junior High School 54 on Manhattan's Upper West Side.

What follows [on the next page] is the text of the speech he gave on being named *Teacher of the Year.*

— **Sy Safransky**
**Editor,** *The Sun*

# Why Schools Don't Educate

## by John Gatto / *The Sun*

We live in a time of great social crisis. Our children rank at the bottom of nineteen industrial nations in reading, writing, and arithmetic. Our teenage suicide rate is the highest in the world. In Manhattan seventy percent of all new marriages last less than five years.

Our school crisis is a reflection of this greater social crisis. We seem to have lost our identity. Children and old people are penned up and locked away from the business of the world to a degree without precedent; nobody talks to them any more. Without children and old people mixing in daily life, a community has no future and no past, only a continuous present. In fact, the name "community" hardly applies to the way we interact with each other. We live in networks, not communities, and everyone I know is lonely because of that. In some strange way school is a major actor in this tragedy, just as it is a major actor in the widening gulf among social classes. Using school as a sorting mechanism, we appear to be on the way to creating a caste system, complete with untouchables who wander through subway trains begging and sleeping on the streets.

I've noticed a fascinating phenomenon in my twenty-five years of teaching—that schools and schooling are increasingly irrelevant to the great enterprises of the planet. No one believes anymore that scientists are trained in science classes, or politicians in civics classes, or poets in English classes. The truth is that schools don't really teach anything except how to obey orders. This is a great mystery to me because thousands of humane, caring people work in schools as teachers and aides and administrators, but the abstract logic of the institution overwhelms their individual contributions. Although teachers do care and do work very, very hard, the institution is psychopathic, it has no conscience. It rings a bell, and the young man in the middle of writing a poem must close his notebook and move to a different cell, where he learns that man and monkeys derive from a common ancestor.

Our form of compulsory schooling is an invention of the State of Massachusetts around 1850. It was resisted—sometimes with gun—by an estimated eighty percent of the Massachusetts population, the last outpost in Barnstable on Cape Cod not surrendering its children until the 1880s, when the area was seized by militia and children marched to school under guard.

Now here is a curious idea to ponder. Senator Ted Kennedy's office released a paper not too long ago claiming that *prior* to compulsory education the state literacy rate was ninety-eight percent, and after it the figure never again reached above ninety-one percent, where it stands in 1990.

Here is another curiosity to think about. The home-schooling movement has quietly grown to a size where one and a half million young people are being educated entirely by their own parents. Last month the education

STUDY & STRUGGLE

*I have never let my schooling interfere with my education.*

—*Mark Twain (1835-1910)*

press reported the amazing news that children schooled at home seem to be five or even ten years ahead of their formally trained peers in their ability to think.

We need to realize that the school institution "schools" very well, but it does not "educate".

Schools were designed by Horace Mann and Barnas Sears and W.R. Harper of the University of Chicago and Thorndyke of Columbia Teachers College and others to be instruments of the scientific management of a mass population. Schools are intended to produce, through the application of formulae, formulaic human beings whose behavior can be predicted and controlled.

To a very great extent schools succeed in doing this. But our society is disintegrating, and in such a society the only successful people are self-reliant, confident, and individualistic. Well-schooled people are irrelevant. They can sell film and razor blades, push paper and talk on telephones, or sit mindlessly before a flickering computer terminal, but as human beings they are use-

less—useless to others and useless to themselves.

It is absurd and anti-life to be part of a system that compels you to sit in confinement with people of exactly the same age and social class. That system effectively cuts you off from the immense diversity of life and the synergy of variety. It cuts you off from your own past and future, sealing you in a continuous present much the same way television does.

It is absurd and anti-life to be part of a system that compels you to listen to a stranger reading poetry when you want to learn to construct buildings, or to sit with a stranger discussing the construction of buildings when you want to read poetry.

It is absurd and anti-life to move from cell to cell at the sound of a gong for every day of your youth, in an institution that allows you no privacy and even follows you into the sanctuary of your home, demanding that you do its "homework."

"How will they learn to read?" you say, and my answer is, "Remember the lessons of Massachusetts." When children are given whole lives instead of age-graded ones in cellblocks, they learn to read, write, and do arithmetic with ease if those things make sense in the life that unfolds around them.

But keep in mind that in the United States almost nobody who reads, writes, or does arithmetic gets much respect. We are a land of talkers; we pay talkers the most and admire talkers the most and so our children talk constantly, following the public models of television and schoolteachers. It is very difficult to teach the "basics" anymore because they really aren't basic to the society we've made.

In centuries past the time of a child and adolescent would be occupied in real work, real charity, real adventures, and the real search for mentors who might teach what one really wanted to learn. A great deal of time was spent in community pursuits, practicing affection, meeting and studying every level of the community, learning how to make a home, and dozens of other tasks necessary to becoming a whole man or woman.

But here is the calculus of time the children I teach must deal with:

Out of the hundred sixty-eight hours in each week, my children sleep fifty-six. That leaves them one hundred twelve hours a week out of which to fashion a self.

My children watch fifty-five hours of television a week, according to recent reports.

That leaves them fifty-seven hours a week in which to grow up.

My children attend school thirty hours a week, use about eight hours getting ready, going and coming home, and spend an average of seven hours a week in home-work—a total of forty-five hours. During that time they are under constant surveillance, have no private time or private space, and are disciplined if they try to assert individuality in the use of time or space. That leaves twelve hours a week out of which to create a unique consciousness. Of course my kids eat, too, and that takes some time—not much, because we've lost the tradition of family dining. If we allot three hours a week to evening meals, we arrive at a net amount of private time for each child of nine hours.

Think of the things that are killing us as a nation: drugs, brainless competition, recreational sex, the pornography of violence, gambling, alcohol, and the worst pornography of all—lives devoted to buying things, accumulation as a philosophy. All are addictions of dependent personalities and that is what our brand of schooling must inevitably produce.

I want to tell you what the effect is on children of taking all their time—time they need to grow up—and forcing them to spend it on abstractions. No reform that doesn't attack these specific pathologies will be anything more than a facade.

① The children I teach are indifferent to the adult world. This defied the experience of thousands of years. A close study of what big people were up to was always the most exciting occupation of youth, but nobody wants to grow up these days, and who can blame them? Toys are us.

② The children I teach have almost no curiosity, and what little they do have is transitory; they cannot concentrate for very long, even on things they choose to do. Can you see a connection between the bells ringing again and again to change classes and this phenomenon of evanescent attention?

③ The children I teach have a poor sense of the future, of how tomorrow is inextricably linked to today. They live in a continuous present; the exact moment they are in is the boundary of their consciousness.

④ The children I teach are ahistorical; they have no sense of how the past has predestined their own present, limiting their choices, shaping their values and lives.

⑤ The children I teach are cruel to each other; they lack compassion for misfortune, they laugh at weakness, they have contempt for people whose need for help shows too plainly.

⑥ The children I teach are uneasy with intimacy or candor. They cannot deal with genuine intimacy because of a lifelong habit of preserving a secret self inside an outer personality made up of artificial bits and pieces of behavior borrowed from television, or acquired to manipulate teachers.

⑦ The children I teach are materialistic, following the lead of schoolteachers who materialistically "grade" everything—and television mentors who offer everything in the world for sale.

⑧ The children I teach are dependent, passive, and timid in the presence of new challenges. This timidity is frequently masked by surface bravado, or by anger or aggressiveness, but underneath is a vacuum without fortitude.

Between schooling and television, all the time children have is eaten up. That's what has destroyed the American family; it no longer is a factor in the education of its own children.

## What can be done?

First, we need a ferocious national debate. We need to scream and argue about this school thing until it is fixed or broken beyond repair, one or the other. If we can fix it, fine; if we cannot, then the success of home-schooling shows a different road that has great promise. Pouring the money back into family education might kill two birds with one stone, repairing families as it repairs children.

Genuine reform is possible, but it shouldn't cost anything. We need to rethink the fundamental premises of schooling and decide *what* it is we want all children to learn, and *why.* For one hundred forty years this nation has tried to impose objectives from a lofty command center made up of "experts," a central elite of social engineers. It hasn't worked. It won't work. It doesn't work because its fundamental premises are mechanical, anti-human, and hostile to family life. Lives can be controlled by machine education, but they will always fight back with weapons of social pathology—drugs, violence, self-destruction, indifference, and the symptoms I see in the children I teach.

It's high time we looked backward to regain an educational philosophy that works. One I like particularly well has been a favorite of the ruling classes of Europe for thousands of years. I think it works just as well for poor children as for rich ones.

At the core of this elite system of education is the belief that self-knowledge is the only basis of true knowledge. Everywhere in this system, at every age, you will find arrangements that place the child *alone* in an unguided setting with a problem to solve. Sometimes the problem is fraught with great risks, such as the problem of galloping a horse or making it jump. Sometimes the problem is that of mastering solitude, as Thoreau did at Walden pond, or Einstein did in the Swiss customs house.

We need to invent a curriculum where each kid has a chance to develop uniqueness and self-reliance.

We've got to give kids independent time right away because that is the key to self-knowledge, and we must reinvolve them with the real world as fast as possible so that the independent time can be spent on something other than more abstractions. This is an emergency. It requires drastic action to correct. I think we need to make community service a required part of schooling, it is the quickest way to give young children real responsibility.

For five years I ran a guerrilla school program where I had every kid, rich and poor, smart and dipsy, give three hundred twenty hours a year of hard community service. Dozens of those kids came back to me years later, and told me that this one experience changed their lives, taught them to see in new ways, to rethink goals and values.

Independent study, community service, adventures in experience, large doses of privacy and solitude, a thousand different apprenticeships—these are all powerful, cheap, and effective ways to start a real reform of schooling. But no large-scale reform is ever going to repair our damaged children and our damaged society until we force the idea of "school" open—to include *family* as the main engine of education.

If we use schooling to break children away from parents—and make no mistake, that has been the central function of schools since John Cotton announced it as the purpose of the Bay Colony schools in 1650 and Horace Mann announced it as the purpose of Massachusetts schools in 1850—we're going to continue to have the horror show we have right now.

The curriculum of family is at the heart of any good life. The way to sanity in education is for our schools to take the lead in releasing the stranglehold of institutions on family life, to promote during school time confluences of parent and child that will strengthen family bonds.

Our greatest problem, in getting the kind of grassroots thinking going that could reform schooling, is that we have large, vested interests profiting from schooling just exactly as it is, despite rhetoric to the contrary.

We have to demand that new voices and new ideas get a hearing, my ideas and yours. A decade-long, free-for-all debate is called for now, not any more "expert" opinions. Experts in education have never been right; their "solutions" are expensive, self-serving, and always involve further centralization. Enough.

Time for a return to democracy, individuality, and family.

*Excerpted from* The Sun, 1990. *It also appeared in* A Voice of the Children *Fall 1990.*

# Helping Students Confront a World of Change and Crisis

## by Shelley Kessler / *Curriculum Quarterly*

*Without virtue, without the education of the heart, expertise and ambition easily become demonic. How can society survive if education does not attend to those qualities which it requires for its very perpetuation.*
*James Laney*
*"The Education of the Heart",*
Harvard Magazine

As parents and teachers today, we watch our teenagers confront a world of change and crisis that includes rampant use of drugs, AIDS, divorce and family dissolution, threat of nuclear and/or environmental annihilation, and loss of faith in traditional values and in our political leadership. These and other issues often making growing up terrifying and may make life seem meaningless. The symptoms of this often overwhelming challenge to young people have reached epidemic proportions.

- **1 out of 4 teens will become a problem drinker in high school**
- **1 American teen commits suicide almost every 90 minutes**
- **4 of every 10 girls will be pregnant before leaving high school**
- **1 out of 4 teens will drop out of high school**

As a mother of three boys, I share the deep concerns of all parents and teachers who are raising teenagers in these times and know that caring, creativity and commitment are crucial at this time. On the east coast, I had directed an agency specializing in preventive programs for adolescents. Five years ago when I arrived in California I heard about a school called Crossroads that was taking bold steps to create a unique, innovative and comprehensive program to address these needs. I was hired to chair the newly created Department of Human Development. (Human Development includes ethics, community service and Mysteries.)

Initiated six years ago with a course designed as a "rite of passage" for seniors, the Mysteries program has evolved and expanded in response to its success and high demand among satisfied students and their families. As of Fall 1989, we will offer Life Skills for 7th and 8th graders. Transitions for

9th grade and Mysteries for Sophomores and Seniors. Although technique, topic and pace vary according to age, each of these classes is a place where students can raise their life issues and talk; where their own sense of self-esteem is enhanced because they are listened to; where a sense of solidarity is gained by learning that everyone is struggling with the same issues. Students learn that the questions are just as important as answers in education, and that a place is needed to explore the questions that have no obvious "right answer."

In Mysteries, students learn such skills as conflict resolution, stress management, group problem solving and decision-making; they receive information about sexuality, drugs, rape prevention, AIDS, and prejudice. Mysteries gives them tools for enhancing their creativity, imaging new solutions and experiencing their own resilience in the face of challenge and of new conditions.

For me, the most rewarding aspect of Mysteries is that our students learn to tolerate and enjoy diversity, to learn to be themselves and to find deep common threads as human beings. By fostering a sense of deep connection to others and to the Earth in all its manifestations, Mysteries encourages a sense of responsibility to the self, to others

and to the planet. And, most unique of all in the educational setting, students in Mysteries are encouraged to recapture their ability to play, to express joy and love, and to go "home" within themselves and within their school community.

Just as the child develops emotionally, intellectually and physically, he or she develops spiritually as well. In working with teenagers, I see a longing for spiritual experience and development which manifests itself as a longing for connection to one's own self and to those beyond oneself, for a sense of meaning or purpose in life, for the mysterious dimension of non-ordinary experience, for wholeness. Drugs and sex for teens are both a search for connection, mystery and meaning and an escape from the pain of not having a genuine source of spiritual fulfillment. I believe that our program is unique in acknowledging this dimension of adolescent development and in creating non-religious methods which foster spiritual satisfaction and growth for our teenagers.

Through this program, perhaps we can find ways to prepare our students for the times in which they live and provide tools which give them the power to design their own desired futures.

*Please contact: Shelley Kessler at Crossroads School, 1714 21st St., Santa Monica, CA 90404 (213) 829-7391.*

*Excerpted from* Curriculum Quarterly, *Spring, 1989.*

# *Waldorf Schools*

# R$_X$ for U.S. Education Crisis

## by Eric Utne / *Utne Reader*

The U.S. is becoming a nation of badly educated, ill-informed nincompoops. You've heard the litany of alarming statistics already.

Whatever the cause, it's time for fresh thinking and new approaches. My own preference is for *Waldorf education.* My 18-year-old son, Leif, attended a Waldorf school in Lexington, Massachusetts, from nursery school through eighth grade. Waldorf schools emphasize the arts, nature, and spiritual values; keep their students with the same teacher for all of grammar school; teach knitting, geometry, and the recorder to six year olds; do not teach kids how to read or do math until they're at least seven years old; and generally turn out young people who get into the colleges of their choice, but more importantly are well prepared for life.

The Waldorf School movement is rapidly expanding, with more than 500 schools

across the globe. There are public schools in Switzerland that base their curriculums on Waldorf School principles, and this is beginning to happen in Sweden as well. Waldorf schools are opening this fall in Moscow, Romania, and East Germany, and a teacher training school will open soon in Hungary, where the movement is exploding. The board of education in Milwaukee recently passed a resolution to open a Waldorf school within the Milwaukee Public School system by Fall 1991. I hope Milwaukee welcomes Waldorf into the public school system, and I hope this form of education becomes the basis of public school curriculums throughout the United States. And I hope it happens soon.

*Excerpted from* Utne Reader, *November/December 1991.*

# War Toys and Stereotyping in the Home and Classroom

## by Kate Donnelly / *Stop War Toys Campaign*

Children learn in many ways. Toys and television are a major influence on what the world is like outside their own homes.

War toys and war play have been a serious and growing problem in the classroom. Many teachers have expressed mixed feelings of confusion, exasperation and ambivalence about how to handle war play, and where to set limits on war toys. Some teachers believe there is a need for this type of play in the development of the child, but are not very comfortable allowing the play and the toys, in their classrooms.

Recent studies on the effects of war toys and aggressive behavior come to the conclusion that playing with war toys increases anger and aggression in children.

Because war toys have a preset storyline, with characters in roles already spelled out on the packages, there is little room for creative play. No longer do children make up characters and stories—instead they imitate what they see on TV. War toys do not encourage sharing and cooperation, nor do they teach children how to solve conflicts non-violently. They are, as one day care center director put it, "Unfriendly toys."

Many children, caught up in the heat of mock battles, show a total disregard for the needs and rights of other children, and they show this in many ways, from "accidentally" running over a child not involved in the play, to actually pushing, hitting, and hurting each other.

Often teachers are confused as to what

*Center on War and the Child*

actually is or is not a war toy. It is hard to know where to draw the line—what to allow into the classroom, what to ban. A good checklist from the Institute for Peace and Justice in St. Louis, defines war toys:

A toy of violence is a toy that:
- Teaches that war is an acceptable way of settling disputes
- Encourages play at hurting and killing others
- Falsely glamorizes military life, combat and war
- Reinforces sexist stereotypes of male dominance and female passivity
- Depicts ethnic or racial groups in a negative way
- Fosters unnecessary aggressive competition
- Creates the need for an enemy
- Hurts other children or animals

According to Nancy Carlsson-Paige and Diane Levin, in their book *The War Play Dilemma*, we have four options in dealing with war play. First, we can simply ban war play, although this approach does not address the developmental needs that children have for this type of play. Second, we can ignore warplay, as long as there is no actual hurting being done. Third, we can allow the play within specific limits, i.e. no "real" guns, only outside, only by mutual consent, etc. or lastly, as teachers we can actively facilitate the play, and help children learn about conflict resolution through non-violent, as opposed to violent, means. We can still, however, ban the actual war toys from the classroom, perhaps even set up a "demilitarized zone" where the children can leave their toys while at school.

*Resource packets are available from Stop War Toys Campaign for $6 each.*

*This article appeared in* Sharing Space, A Newsletter of Children's Creative Response to Conflict, *February 1990.*

# Upattinas Educational Resource Center

## by Sandra Hurst / *Home Education Magazine*

The Upattinas Educational Resource Center began as an alternative school in 1971, formed by families and teachers who were interested in experimenting with a combination of free school and open classroom ideas. It grew and developed as a school for the next nineteen years, waxing and waning with the times and the need for alternative kinds of schools.

During those years, a growing number of people who liked the philosophy of such schools, but who either lived too far away or did not have the funds to support private schooling for their children, began to school their children at home. It was an unpopular thing to do and many found themselves in need of some sort of umbrella organization that would help them to find their way through the maze of laws and customs that

impeded their progress toward their goals. At the same time, many families who had other philosophical reasons to keep their children at home also began to home school.

Because of our philosophy of empowerment of families to work with their children according to their own beliefs and ideals, Upattinas School became a resource for many of these people. We provided counseling as to working with their school districts, helped with preparation of letters of intent, and loaned textbooks to those who felt that they needed them. We were told clearly by the state officials that we could not permit home schooling—only the District Superintendent could do that. But we could provide a resource and educational consultation for them.

Within the past year the school has undergone a metamorphosis and has become still more of a resource for people who wish to get their education outside of traditional schooling. While still working with people who home school under the confines of their state laws and more structured traditions, Upattinas has become a resource for those who prefer to "unschool"; that is to say, to learn in ways natural to themselves and their environments without restrictions as to hours or credits.

Counselling takes the form of helping people see what they do in their everyday lives that is already educational, encouraging their active involvement in their neighborhoods or environs. We support children of all ages being involved in the work of the family or in jobs outside of their homes—real jobs—not classes about getting jobs. We support and sponsor travel programs which take young people farther away from home and into the natural world. We encourage their use of all the many different kinds of learning places available to them—community colleges, museums, art centers, YM/YWCAS, individual tutors, friends, community members.

When it is important to either the family or the individual student, we also allow involvement in classes which are a part of the ongoing life of the Center. These classes are developed according to the needs of the people involved in any given year. They may be academic or elective types of classes, but all are developed with the involvement of the students. They are taught by people who know and understand the philosophy of participation in decision-making and who are prepared to work with students according to their individual needs.

Students who wish, at the high school level, may work toward a diploma by collecting the credits needed to fulfill the requirements of the Commonwealth of Pennsylvania. They do this in their own time, according to their own needs and interests. They may fashion their own independent study courses with the help of staff at the Center, or they may take classes in any of the above mentioned educational institutions, or at Upattinas. For each credit they wish to receive they must write an essay evaluation of the work done and present some of that work to a staff member. When they have completed all the requisite credits they are graduated with a diploma which is recognized as a diploma from a licensed private academic school. The

Center has a full roster of certificated teachers for facilitating this program.

The Upattinas Educational Resource Center also has two computers available for use by our families and is currently working to get a grant for more computers. These can be made available for individual use by enrolled students, but they are also available for people who want to try out the academic programs to see if they are appropriate for a given student. We have a resident expert who can advise about and teach computer skills.

Because our Center has lovely space for meeting and playing, we also carry on a series of workshops and parent support groups and special programs for children and adults. While the children play, these groups sit over tea and chat on actual specific things like math and science; art and craft workshops; experiential days for exploring musical instruments; and virtually anything suggested by our community. We also anticipate developing several-day retreats for those interested in immersing themselves in special interests. For example, one of our families is developing a performance in drums, dance, and the African American experience. A two-day workshop will involve participants in whatever aspects of the experience they might enjoy—from actually dancing and drumming, to sharing readings and discussions.

People who enjoy working with others or sharing their special gifts and interests have begun to offer their services to the Resource Center, and this promises to be a wonderful new direction for us. A chamber music group which needs to test out its new concert series

will do its dress rehearsal here for our families; people who write poetry will bring their poetry reading group here so that we can listen in; a staff member who loves esoteric movies has organized a movie night at the Center. We are limited only by the imaginations of our community.

Our Center is funded by a variety of sources: tuition, individual class fees, rental of spaces, donations for specific programs and donations to the over-all program, and occasional foundation grants. We are a 50lC3 non-profit corporation which is cooperative in nature. Our board of directors is elected from the constituent group and other interested community members. Our community includes anyone who is interested in becoming involved and who accepts our basic premises: cooperative, non-coercive learning; participant control through democratic process; non-discrimination as to race, religion, sex, or other individual difference.

*Sandra Hurst is an Educational Consultant with twenty-seven years of public and private school experience. She is also a member of the Board of Directors of the National Coalition of Alternative Community Schools, an international support group for organizations which are designed to share education in non-coercive and nondiscriminatory programs. More information can be requested by writing to Upattinas Educational Resource Center, 429 Greenridge Road, Glenmoore, PA 19343; or calling Sandy at (215) 458-5138.*

*Reprinted from* Home Education Magazine, *May/June, 1991.*

# Undergrad Director Sees Role as Educating Activists

### by Debra Lee / *World View*

Jeff Unsicker holds up the toy bicycles and cars made by his sons and their African playmates, admiring the craftsmanship and ingenuity. Constructed from bits of wire and insulation cord, pieces of rubber and crushed coke cans, the vehicles are intricately detailed and functional. Wheels and pedals turn, car windows open, there's even a trailer hitch on one automobile. The vehicles seem to symbolize what Unsicker, School for International Training's director of the World Issues Program, hopes to bring to the undergraduate program: the integration and creative use of resources.

"We need to invent new ways of utilizing resources creatively, to use what's in the environment, to be proactive, efficient, and creative. There's great chemistry here at SIT and I want to be a catalyst for activating it," says the 40-year old Unsicker, who took over

the directorship last summer.

Unsicker emphasizes the importance of teamwork and says he is committed to working with the students and the six-member World Issues Program faculty to find ways to "diversify, expand, and make the program more dynamic." Integrating the human resources—faculty and students—in all SIT programs, including College Semester Abroad, is one way of accomplishing his objectives.

"I believe very strongly that the strength of the school cannot be realized until we integrate programs," Unsicker contends.

The World Issues director brings to SIT a strong academic background in both international studies and education, as well as significant experience in curriculum development, teaching, consulting, student advising, and education administration.

©Nanci Leitch

*SIT Undergrad Director Jeff Unsicker.*

dent advising, and education administration.

A native of San Diego, California, he holds

graduate degrees from Stanford University—an M.A. in International Education Administration and Policy Analysis and a Ph.D. in International Development Education.

Unsicker describes his life's work as the response to a "calling" to social activism. "Long ago, I realized that I'm a social activist. That's what motivated me. I'm an idealist, a romantic, but also a pragmatist. I believe in working to change society, to reduce injustice."

The director believes that the 25-35 students who graduate through the World Issues Program each year are cut from similar cloth. They are committed to social change.

It was Unsicker's passion to have a hand in training these activists, whom he defines as "those who believe their careers must contribute to the betterment of the world," that led him to SIT.

"The people who come here are already committed; this program integrates scholar-ship with activism, theory with practice. That's the exciting thing about SIT," he says. "It's at the nexus."

Confident of his mission in life and challenged by the vision and creativity required to pursue it, Unsicker smiles at how he contradicts the meaning behind the German origin of his name—Unsicker. "I'm told it means 'uncertain'" he grins.

*Excerpted from* World View, *Summer 1991.*

---

*If by now you haven't concluded that the arts are a crucial part of any effort to reinvigorate learning, Eric Oddleifson will convince you. Eric is President of The Center for Arts in the Basic Curriculum, an association whose agenda is clear. Not only do they believe art education will enhance the traditional curriculum; they believe "the arts should be the basis of education" because "the deepest and most lasting learning is participatory and whole-brained. This is precisely what the arts offer." Their publications offer some impressive data to back up their case. Contact the center at 58 Fearing Road, Hingham, MA 02043 for more information on their publications and services.*

# THE CASE FOR THE ARTS

## By cutting back on arts to strengthen their basic core curricula, schools may be taking a giant leap backward

### by Eric Oddleifson / *In Context*

In their efforts to improve the schooling of American children, educators and the communities they serve are striving to develop schools that will teach our youngsters to be more productive and competitive workers in business and industry. From their understanding of the test scores of American children, the reformers infer that our schools must teach more mathematics, more science, more language skills. Prescribed remedies for the problems range from "back to basics," to a more rigorous curriculum, to alternative private school systems, to parental "choice" of schools. In almost every case, budgetary constraints become the "enemy" as greater demands are placed on the schools and they appear to be, like Alice, running faster just to "stay in the same place."

To make time for expanded math, science and language studies, the reformers reduce or eliminate time for the arts—music, visual arts, theater, dance, and creative writing.

But the research of cognitive psychologists and the experience of schools that teach the arts as a part of the basic curriculum—strongly suggest that this prescription will not produce the results the reformers seek. In fact, research into the records of students in several schools indicates that *a curriculum that devotes 25% or more of the school day to the arts produces youngsters with academically superior abilities*. There is compelling evidence to suggest that schools should increase the time devoted to teaching the arts. The supposedly "nonessential" subjects of music, theater, dance, and art promote the kinds of thinking, enthusiasm, self-esteem and discipline that are necessary requisites for learning.

Many people do not associate the arts with "thinking." We are aware of the art "product" the song, the picture, the play—but we are less aware of the *process* which creates that product. Yet the arts are not so much a result of inspiration and innate talent as they are a person's capacities for creative thinking and imagining, problem solving, critical judgment, and a host of other mental processes. The arts represent forms of cognition every bit as potent as the verbal and logical/mathematical forms of cognition that have been the traditional focus of public education.

Still, some educators and educational psychologists remain skeptical about the practical benefits of arts study. The argument runs this way: "If you want to improve science education, improve science, not the visual arts. Math is improved through math education and not through music." When budgets are tight, the arts tend to be the first subjects curtailed—though this attitude may be changing.

### VERTICAL AND HORIZONTAL

There are very good reasons to teach the arts both vertically and horizontally within the traditional core curriculum. An examination of what the study of an art form requires when taught *vertically*—that is, as a stand-alone subject—points to very practical benefits that may accrue. The arts:

- activate mental energy by awakening and educating the imagination, the seat of our thought processes themselves;
- are a model of "learning by doing" and engaging students with the real world (the apprenticeship model of learning, with teacher as coach);
- develop aspiration to achieve, to get better, to excel;
- require hard work to per fect the techniques demanded by the specific art form;
- require discipline, and the continuing need to practice to hone technique;
- require long-term commitment; and
- require cooperation and collective

123

accountability in a group performance—music, theater, and dance.

Others have observed that the arts develop higher order (critical and creative) thinking skills, including (1) the ability to deal with complexity and ambiguity; (2) the capacity for sound judgment, (3) attention to purpose (exploring alternative goals) as much as results; and (4) the ability to consider differing viewpoints and defer judgment.

Interestingly enough, these are precisely the skills the business community now so avidly seeks in its new employees. Not finding them, it is calling for a radical restructuring of the American educational system.

When the arts also taught *horizontally*—that is, used together with traditional academic approaches to articulate and understand a particular subject or theme—learning becomes more integrated. Students employ the style of learning that suits them best, and the arts become a support to the curriculum. Such "integrative learning" changes the way the classroom runs, as well as the content. It uses a problem-based structure, and is similar to a "studio" in this respect. Outstanding artistic work can occur, giving an important aesthetic content to the broad themes being studied. Teachers become excited about their new roles as facilitators, and a culture of high standards and high academic achievement within a school is the result. School becomes an exciting place to be.

In fact, the most important benefit of the arts may be *the education of the imagination*.

*Excerpted from* In Context, *no. 27, Winter 1991.*

# Learning Through Service
## *By caring for others, students learn how to care for themselves and their world*

### by Kate McPherson / *In Context*

*By the time they reach college, many students have learned to refer to the larger society beyond the walls of academe as the "real world". The separation this reflects is perhaps one of the most ironic, and tragic, aspects of traditional educational models—we isolate learners from the very culture we profess to be preparing them for. Yet for many students, a deep encounter with those in need may be the most educational thing that ever happens to them.*

*Kate McPherson is Director of Project Service Leadership, which assists schools and communities in implementing service learning programs. Her project is one of four regional centers funded by the Kellogg Foundation to provide such assistance throughout the country. Contact Kate at 2810 Comanche Dr., Mt. Vernon, WA 98273, 2061428-7614, or the National Youth Leadership Council at 1-800-366-6952, for more information.*

Youth Service America, a national clearinghouse for community service programs, estimates that high school volunteers donate 17 million hours of unpaid service annually at an estimated dollar value of almost 60 million.

Such programs not only meet important local community needs, but teach students about responsible citizenship by giving their studies real-life applications and helping to create a positive transition into adulthood.

Service learning provides a hands-on, collaborative approach to learning. It also engages students in real problem solving and in exercising their own initiative—opportunities that are rare in most school curricula. Here are some examples from Washington State:

🔸 Students in Gig Harbor tutor new immigrants who speak the foreign language that the students are studying. With Spanish, for example, students develop a more thorough understanding of the language and a greater appreciation for Hispanic culture. Developing a lesson plan gives them practice in finding effective ways to explain an idea. And by conversing about the tutorial subject in Spanish, students develop a more integrated understanding of the subject's content.

🔸 Social studies students at Lakeside School and Kennedy High School in Seattle are spending time with homeless families providing meals, gathering supplies, and working in shelters. For these students, homelessness is no longer just a word, but a complex political and economic issue with real names and faces, sounds and sights.

🔸 Industrial arts students at Foss High School in Tacoma apply their skills in design and problem-solving by working on projects such as a chair designed and built for an eighteen-month old child with multiple sclerosis. This project involved determining which materials would provide the needed stability and mobility, and developing an expandable design to grow with the child.

### A Profound Effect

The value of student service to the community is important, but just as important is the effect of service on the students themselves. This is perhaps best reflected in excerpts from their own writing about their experiences. From a student who worked at a homeless shelter:

*For me, this experience was eye-opening, stereotype-breaking, and attitude-changing. I really grew attached to some of the kids at the shelter, and found myself wanting to return to see them again. I am a person who was initially opposed to the whole learning thing... but I have changed my attitude almost completely (which is not something I do very often). You can be told about poverty until you think you have heard all there is to know about it. Until you witness poverty and homelessness first hand, however, it will not have an impact. It does not take much exposure to a human need to get personally involved and begin to care about a situation. I am convinced that just a little time required in community service will yield a lifetime of dedication to help.*

From a student who worked in a teen runaway shelter:

*The way in which I was personally benefited the most was by what I realized by the end of that Saturday night. I was feeling good about myself and was, in fact, on a small ego trip. After all, just look at what I had done—I must have spent thirteen hours collecting clothes and five hours slaving over an oven baking (and eating) peanut butter cookies. I essentially gave up my whole Saturday to feed the hungry. But after watching these teenagers, who had so little material wealth compared to myself and who could be satisfied with what I considered garbage, I began to see the truth. A very uncomfortable notion crept into my mind—the idea that these kids were, if anything, superior to myself. Not in what they had, but in who they were.*

More and more districts across the country are infusing service into their K-12 curriculum, seeing it as central to their educational mission and as a powerful tool for creating partnership between communities and schools. Service fosters an ethic of caring and community within the school. As service becomes an expected component of classroom goals and a part of teacher student discussions, schools develop into more compassionate environments where students care for others—and are themselves cared for.

*Excerpted from* In Context, *no. 27, Fall 1990.*

# Chapter 10

# *Health*

*Look to your health; and if you have it, praise God...*
*for health is... a blessing that money cannot buy.*

So wrote Izaak Walton some 340 years ago. Our modern society pays little heed to that homespun advice. Today, this nation's health care system is driven by the idea that if we spend enough money, we can buy better and better health.

The cost of health care has skyrocketed in recent years and continues to accelerate. In 1989, the U.S. spent $604 billion on health care. We spend more on health care per capita and as a percentage of our economy than any other industrialized nation—12 percent of GNP, a number expected to jump to 15 percent by the year 2000. Health care is a huge burden for government and thus for taxpayers—at all levels. The public sector funds over 40 percent of health care expenses, mostly through Medicare for seniors and Medicaid for the poor. It is estimated that health spending will comprise 20 percent of the Federal budget by 1996.

Government, businesses—many of which purchase health insurance for their employees—and individuals all face a health care crisis.

At a hearing I held in the House Budget Committee, we were told that the biggest factor in rising costs is the proliferation of new technologies—the machines and procedures that are preventing and curing more illnesses and keeping us alive longer than ever. Rising labor costs and the aging of our population are also important factors.

## Millions Lack Insurance

Despite the amount we expend, millions of Americans lack access to quality health care. Some 33 million Americans have no private health insurance and are ineligible for public programs. Most go without care. Nearly one-third are children.

While Medicare cost controls enacted by Congress have produced some savings, the overall impact has been marginal. The situation is virtually out of control. Emergency treatment is in order.

What we need to do is slow the rise in health costs; provide health insurance or coverage for those who do not have access to health care; preserve flexibility so that individuals can still choose the type of health care they want; and prevent increases in, or reduce, red tape and paperwork. And we must do all of these things without bankrupting the nation's taxpayers.

In a nutshell, we need to make difficult choices about how to get the most health care for the most people at a cost that we, as a society, decide we can afford.

How we do that is a decision that must be made during the 1990's. It is one of the most important we will make as a society in preparation for the 21st century.

## Two Approaches

Two basic approaches are being examined in the Congress.

One is to provide a national health insurance plan similar to the Canadian health plan. The Federal government would provide comprehensive health insurance for all Americans. Individuals would continue to choose their physicians, but all fees would be set and paid to the provider by the government.

Such a plan could reduce paperwork and ensure access to care for all. However, it could be very costly and would require a substantial tax increase. Access to certain medical procedures could become more difficult, and some question whether the government could run such a massive program effectively. Many also believe this system is too "radical" to be acceptable to the American people.

The other approach also guarantees basic care for all Americans. It requires employers to either purchase health insurance for their employees or contribute to a public program to cover uninsured workers and the unemployed.

This "play or pay" approach for businesses would also guarantee access to care, and at less additional cost to the average taxpayer. However, it would place a burden on some businesses that currently do not provide insurance for their workers, and it would not change significantly the current paperwork—heavy third party private insurance payor system.

## Cost Controls

Cost controls would have to be part of either approach. But who bears the burden? Should doctors and hospitals be forced to charge less and accept reduced incomes? Should we limit the availability of costly tests and equipment—ration them to reduce unnecessary use?

Should individuals always pay deductibles and co-payments to ensure that they bear some of the cost every time they employ the health care system?

These are difficult questions. How we resolve the health care dilemma will tell much about what kind of society we want to be in the 21st century.

*"The Growing Health Care Crisis: America Seeks a Cure," originally appeared as an article from a newsletter by Congressman Leon Panetta, (D. CA), Reports to the 16th District, Summer 1991.*

# Waste: The Consequence of Medical Extravagance

## by J.W. Smith / *The World's Wasted Wealth*

*It was an ominous sign that [operation] procedures most beneficial for the surgeons themselves seemed to grow at the fastest rate. Through the 1970s, for example, the frequency of heart operations for men tripled; the coronary bypass came into widespread use. Researchers now question whether the bypass is really worth it for many recipients—life is prolonged for just one in ten. But bypass operations are unquestionably worth it for surgeons, whose fees average $5,000 for a few hours' work... Fee-for-service surgeons, for example, are twice as likely to perform a coronary bypass as HMO [Health Maintenance Organizations] surgeons.*

*— Gregg Easterbrook,* "The Revolutions in Medicine," Newsweek, *December '87.*

### Routine Operations

In a 1985 investigation, the Senate's Special Committee on Aging charged that unnecessary operations for hernias, hemorrhoids, gallstones, enlarged prostates, heart disease and other conditions were cutting short the lives of thousands of Americans and wasting billions of dollars. Significantly, these operations increased 130 percent after Medicare was enacted. The American College of Surgeons and the American Surgical Association concluded that 4.5 million operations per year—30 percent of the total—are unnecessary, and an additional 50 percent perhaps beneficial but not essential to save or extend life. Assuming only *half* the expected mortality rate, that would cause about 30,000 needless deaths a year.

That 50 percent of these operations are unnecessary is demonstrated by comparing the U.S. system with British medical practice. Not working under the *cut-for-a-fee* system, surgeons there operate only one-half as often as their American counterparts. I know of no evidence that suggests the British would be better off with twice the number of operations. Instead, the free medical care would suggest that their doctors are only operating when necessary.

### Births

In 1984, over 20 percent of the births in the U.S. were Cesarean, twice the rate of ten years earlier; by 1988 they were almost 25 percent. Cesarean births generate much higher fees and require twice the length of hospitalization. They are also hazardous and

an open invitation to further medical complications. Nor did these operations improve infant mortality rates. In 1971, the U.S. ranked fourteenth from the top while Holland ranked third. Most births in Holland occur at home with the help of midwives, and hospitals are used only if problems are foreseen.

### Defensive Medicine

In 1983, due to the high cost of malpractice insurance, 6 percent of the obstetricians quit and 25 percent had abandoned this practice by 1989. Many of the almost 25 percent of all births that are by Cesarean section are performed by doctors trying to avoid being sued. Other defense strategies

"BUT SIR THIS IS THE THIRD TIME YOU TOOK OUT HER 'APPENDIX'"

© 1992 Rae Mattson

are X rays, exploratory surgery, and blood tests. These defensive practices have been estimated as accounting for 25 percent of America's health bill.

### Drugs

A Senate subcommittee hearing in 1977 concluded that 30,000 people died each year from adverse reactions to prescribed drugs, while other studies suggested 100,000. Expecting to disprove such damning indictments, the Pharmacists Association and the American Medical Association (AMA) conducted their own investigation. They were astonished when their own study showed that "Medications in hospitals alone killed from 60,000 to 140,000 Americans per year, and make 3.5 million others more or less seriously ill."

A study by the National Institutes of Health found that 60 percent of all medication and 80

to 90 percent of all antibiotics used were unnecessary and "the federal government in 1980 estimated that only one Valium prescription in thirty was really medically necessary." A British study showed that "More than half of all adults and almost a third of all children take medication every day. Yet 90% of the time people get well (or can get well) without therapeutic intervention."

The notorious sedative thalidomide caused 16,000 infant deaths and led to another 8,000 children being born without arms or legs. And the anti-arthritic pill Oraflex killed 124 before it was pulled off the market.

Besides the thousands of chemical drugs on the market that cause these unwanted reactions, there are three thousand different antibiotics with thirty thousand derivatives. Yet experienced clinicians judge that from two to four dozen basic drugs would suffice for 98 to 99 percent of drug-treatable illnesses. Indiscriminate use of these antibiotics has produced many drug-resistant bacteria. Significantly, the death rate from one of these resistant diseases—bacteremia—is now up to pre-antibiotic levels. Most such problems are avoided by countries like Czechoslovakia and China, which use only ten to fifteen antibiotics for all their health needs, saving the potent ones for emergencies.

Inside one's body (and outside) there is an ecological balance of microorganisms that is the key to good health. These "normal bacteria provide a natural host defense mechanism against infection, [and] only occasionally, in well-understood diseases when the balance is upset, is medical intervention helpful." Many times it is antibiotics which create this imbalance. Given hygienic living conditions and nutrition, good health is the normal condition of man and animal.

### Medical Technology and Patents

One million older Americans have cataract surgery each year at a cost of four billion dollars, of which two billion is considered overcharge. One-third of these operations are unnecessary, and Medicare is being charged anywhere from $310 to $700 for an intraocular lens valued at $50.

### The Greater the Need, the Higher the Charge

Few have challenged or even recognized the unfair tax upon the unfortunate created by vastly overpriced products and services.

Witness the hearing aid... Each is only a tiny amplifier, yet it costs ten to twenty times as much as a radio, which is hundreds of times larger and much more complicated.

The same overcharges are present with patented drugs which are critical to patient treatment. Witness the prescription drug MPTP. With the first clue that it might be of benefit in treating Parkinson's disease, the price skyrocketed from eleven dollars a gram to ninety-five hundred dollars. This scene was replayed when AZT (azidithymidine) showed promise in controlling the AIDS virus. The cost to these desperate people shot up to ten thousand dollars per year. This high price is not for developing this drug. "The discovery was made at the National Cancer Institute lab in Detroit and all original research was done at U.S. government expense.

These drugs are astoundingly cheap to manufacture and "for 120 years doctors, drug manufacturers, and the pharmacopoeia convention have considered that *to patent an essential medicine is morally indefensible.*" It is the patents that preserve them as private property and entitle the owners (not the discoverers) to charge all the market will bear.

The prices noted for mechanical, electrical, and chemical medical services are above the true value of the labor involved in developing, manufacturing, and distributing these essential products. A mechanical, electrical, or chemical engineer could quickly expose these high-priced items as simple, inexpensive technology. There should be no need to make fortunes on others' misfortunes.

**The High Cost of Dying**

Twenty-eight percent of America's medical bills are incurred during the last year of life. Until our era the vast majority of Americans died at home. Today 80 percent die in hospitals. An estimated 10,000 Americans are being sustained in what doctors call "persistent vegetative state." Maintaining life in an ICU [intensive care unit] costs a minimum of $100,000 dollars annually. That's roughly 1 billion dollars per year to keep heartbeats present in the forever comatose.

In the survival time of terminally ill patients, there is no statistical difference between home care and hospital care Companionship and care of relatives, the comfort of a familiar environment, the security of religion, and narcotics to relieve pain could

equal or exceed hospital care during a patient's last days.

Almost universally these patients have made it clear that they would prefer a quiet, dignified death. Yet to extend life a few more days, terminal patients are kept on life support systems, spending more than a person can normally expect to save in a lifetime. In Holland, where voluntary euthanasia is a practical option for the terminally ill, one out of six chooses it rather than face a tortured, painful death.

Is this not strange? In this country it is not normal to support a terminally ill patient's right to a dignified death and a doctor would be considered negligent if he or she failed to make every effort to keep the person alive a few more days—even if it costs tens or hundreds of thousands of dollars. At the same time, there is no adequately functioning mechanism for calling this same doctor to account when unnecessary exploratory surgery, invasive treatment, or drug prescription causes death in a healthy individual who could otherwise have lived for many more years.

*Excerpted from* The World's Wasted Wealth, © *1992 J.W. Smith, New Worlds Press.*

# The Bu$ine$$ of Medicine

### by Steve Eabry / *Earth Journal*

When is the last time you went to a fancy restaurant and handed over your Diner's Club card before you were seated? Do you bring your credit rating along to the garage when you bring your car in for service? Why is it, then that we accept the way physicians' office and hospital personnel insist on knowing our ability to pay before they unlock the door to the examining room?

We keep hearing of consumers being billed for services not received. There have been numerous studies demonstrating the vast numbers of unnecessary tests and operations, and the often inaccurate results of lab testing. Instead of charging a uniform fee for an office visit, some doctors are breaking down bits and pieces of a visit, "unbundling," in order to charge more.

More people are getting less and paying more. Our medical education system and philosophy may be technically magnificent and clinically solid, but in becoming a business, it has lost its true purpose. As the medical profession grew, a medical industry developed to support the profession. Today, the industry is driving and controlling the profession.

Are you getting fed up with the business and medical practices of doctors, hospitals and other medical entities? What can you do? First, I'd suggest that you become the expert

on the peculiarities and problems of your body and those of family members. Don't give that power over to the medical wizards. Become an expert on the availability of local health care also, and use it appropriately.

Support doctors and facilities where you are treated well and feel comfortable. Let others know of your experience. Also, let others know of bad experiences. Don't help to cover up poor practice, even if it may be embarrassing to have to admit it. Complain to the local medical association, Better Business Bureau and Chamber of Commerce.

There are many services and organizations working to improve medical care which you might want to support and learn from, and support groups for most any disease condition. These can often be found through the 800 information operator and are very helpful in learning what others with similar conditions have tried, what worked and what didn't.

*Steve Eabry is a biologist who, while working for the state of New York, was responsible for evaluating the effects of electric generating plants and transmission lines on humans as well as natural systems. He has monitored development in EMF effects reserach since 1976, and continues to study the therapeutic applications of EMFs. Steve and his wife are*

*California State certified Natural Health Counselors and Massage Therapists offering a variety of body therapy in San Luis Obispo, California.*

*Excerpted from* Earth Journal, *June 1992.*

# Chemical Poisoning: The 20th Century Disease

### by Terri Dunivant / *Earth Journal*

*When Atascadero [CA] resident Lynn Montandon came home from Dunsmuir she was tired and sick, but determined to go back and help the people in that poisoned town. Montandon is a registered nurse and the founder of the Response Team for the Chemically Injured, a statewide network of volunteers—many of whom including Montandon, suffer from life-threatening illnesses related to chemical poisoning. This is her story.*

"There were 20,000 gallons of a biocide, metam sodium, that was spilled into the Sacramento River at Dunsmuir when a Southern Pacific train derailed. The chemical killed everything in its path, contaminating the river for fifty miles down to Lake Shasta, which is the drinking and irrigation supply for Redding.

"It was an unmarked tanker and, according to the residents, the SP denied that it was anything at all. These people called us, knowing that they're being kept in the dark; not being told the truth. They described symptoms of poisoning: rashes, burning eyes, throat and chest pains, coughing with mucus, bloody diarrhea, weakness, dizziness, fatigue, headaches.

"I know that 400 people had been seen either in the hospital or at the emergency center that had been set up at the high school,

> **98 percent of all cancers are related to chemical exposure. A study by the EPA states that 99% of the population has one or more toxic chemicals stored in their fatty tissues, and that many of these chemicals are linked to cancer. 95 percent of mother's milk is toxic.**

but many said they felt the hospital staff weren't aware of what to do. Now the people are developing secondary infections; a lot of the children are also developing pneumonia.

"The Response Team is made up of medical professionals and lay people whose concern is for the victims of chemical poisoning, so we went to Dunsmuir to evaluate the victims and set up a triage, to work with the hospital and the labs.

"When people found out we were there they would come, many crying, and say, "I'm sick, my children are sick, I can't go home, I don't have any money. What am I to do, sleep in the car? It's very sad.

"We held an open forum, along with an epidemiologist from the hospital and others, to discuss chemical poisoning and answer questions. Two hundred people came, many of them sick.

"A reporter asked me afterwards if I thought their symptoms might be caused by mass hysteria. So ignorant; I tried not to laugh. I told him the rashes are the body's natural response to try and get rid of the poison. Some of the people up there will develop multiple chemical sensitivity; some will develop cancer.

"I know what it's like to have to live with this kind of illness. Most of the people

working on the Response Team are also victims of chemical injuries. The chemically injured, who are also called 'environmentally ill,' 'multiple- or hypersensitive,' usually become sick through an accumulation of poisons in their bodies that causes an immune system breakdown. It adds up, all the things you're exposed to.

"'Universal reactors' are people who can't tolerate any kind of chemical around them. Some people can only tolerate one kind of food until they can build their immune systems back up. Some people have to live away from everyone; they live in tents, barns, cars.

"Chemical accumulation in the body can continue until it becomes life-threatening, or a sudden massive exposure like the Dunsmuir spill can trigger serious chemical illness and disease. Multiple-sensitivity is indeed a recognized disorder, although it wasn't for a long time. They call it the 20th Century disease.

"My husband is the city attorney for Santa Maria and Atascadero, [California]. Three years ago, he prosecuted a case against a company that was dumping chemicals in the ground—the owner went to jail.

"We plan to return to Dunsmuir the first week of August to continue our work, but we need help. People who are sick have been displaced from their homes. There is no government assistance or help from SP or the chemical company yet, and Dunsmuir is a depressed community. Everybody has been paying for operations out of their own pockets, putting people up, feeding them.

"Medical professionals who are willing to absorb the costs themselves are needed. We need money as well, and people can deduct donations written to the **Shasta Recovery Fund—3H Foundation, c/o Response Team for the Chemically Injured, Box 608, Atascadero, CA 93423.** People can also call me at (805) 461-3662."

*Excerpted from* Earth Journal, *August 1991.*

# A Bond That Surpasses:
## *Supportive Therapy Groups for Women With Cancer*

*I knew her scarcely a week, and yet I knew her very well. Cancer patients have a bond that surpasses a healthy person's understanding.*

— C. Ryan, *A Private Battle*

*Matrix editor's note: Any discussion of women's health would be incomplete without understanding the epidemic proportions to which cancer among women has grown. The following is an interview with Sabra Larsen and Deborah Abbott, two Santa Cruz women who work with and offer support groups for cancer patients.*

**Matrix**: Tell us about the groups you're offering.

**Sabra Larsen**: A Bond That Surpasses are eight-week supportive therapy groups for women who have cancer. We hold the view that every cancer is unique and every woman with cancer is unique with her particular needs. For example, one woman may have confidence in dealing with her doctors, but have a difficult time talking about her feelings or asking for help. Another may have a good network of friends, but a stressful, inflexible job that may be undermining her recovery.

Our groups will offer women a wide range

of resources and therapeutic tools to help them through their process of living with cancer—everything from day-to-day self care; to tending to feelings; to exploring beliefs, relationships and lifestyle; to education about the physical and social aspects of cancer.

**Matrix**: What has moved you to do these groups?

**Deborah Abbott**: Much of what propels me to do this work, quite honestly, is my anger. One in three women will have some form of cancer in her lifetime. Two out of three women with cancer will die from it. *The*

*American Cancer Society estimates that 242,000 women will die from cancer in the United States this year.*

My anger comes from my growing awareness of how privately most of these women are struggling with their illnesses. Not only do women with cancer receive little support, most must keep on giving it. They come home from chemotherapy treatments and between vomiting episodes, they're making dinner for their kids.

Out of the very real fear of losing their jobs and/or medical benefits, women are continuing to work in the face of the profound exhaustion that comes with radiation therapy. I am angry that this cancer epidemic is of such enormous proportions (*contrast the 120,000 U.S. deaths from AIDS over the past ten years with the 242,000 women dying of cancer this year alone*), and that our community has not adequately responded to or cared for its women with this life-threatening illness. Our groups will be the only ones, to our knowledge, that provide a small, ongoing, in-depth and woman-focused space in which women with cancer can do the work of healing.

**Matrix**: How about you Sabra? What has moved you to offer these groups?

**Sabra**: As a cancer survivor myself, I know how terrifying and overwhelming a cancer diagnosis is, and how vital support is in the treatment and recovery process. Some studies say that support is the most important ingredient for mobilizing the immune system.

Like Deborah, part of my motivation in offering these groups is simply the need for them. I've been a social worker with Santa Cruz County Hospice for the past six years and am struck by the fact that a woman in the terminal stages of cancer has many more resources available to her than a woman in the early stages or one whose cancer is not terminal.

Having cancer is often considered shameful, a personal failure. Cancer is blamed on an individual being too fat, eating too much fat, not eating enough fiber, not exercising enough, repressing feelings, being a cancer personality, etc. Even the American Cancer Society's slogan, "The best prevention is early detection!" may lead women to believe that they got cancer because they didn't do breast self-exams, didn't go their doctors soon enough or get their Pap smears or mammograms often enough.

While early detection is critical in diagnosing cancer in its early stages, and thus improving a woman's chances for survival,

detection does not prevent a woman from getting cancer in the first place.

**Deborah**: As women, it's probably much less threatening to volunteer to help a man with AIDS. I can get an HIV test; you can get an HIV test. If it's negative, there are fairly clear steps we can take to avoid getting the virus.

But cancer is not only one virus, it is many diseases. There are not such clear measures for prevention. I can stop eating meat, swim more often, buy organic produce and meditate. You can stop smoking, start taking vitamins and cut out the alcohol. We can believe that these steps will prevent us from getting cancer and we can privately think that if only women with cancer had taken these steps, they too would be cancer free.

In the meantime, we may avoid getting close to a woman with cancer, because if we do, we may well discover that she too ate organic, exercised daily and went to therapy. Her story will challenge the myth that we are safe. A woman with cancer mirrors our own vulnerability to cancer.

It is possible to reduce our individual exposure to carcinogens somewhat. Quitting smoking is the most significant step we can take, since 30 percent of cancers are caused by cigarettes. We can make a number of dietary changes (such as cutting back on fat and increasing fiber) and we can keep our immune systems healthier (e.g. by reducing physical and emotional stressors). But people with Environmental Illnesses are the "canaries in the mines," warning us that the environment is toxic in more subtle and powerful ways than simply the cigarettes we smoke and the food we eat.

We do not see cancer as an individual failure but as a societal one—an epidemic due to living in a time and place where polluting the world is more profitable than protecting it.

**Sabra**: Our groups do not have a prescribed formula for recovery, but respond to the women and their particular needs, and incorporate many approaches to 'getting well again."

**Matrix**: What are your future plans?

**Deborah**: These groups are just a beginning. We're very excited about the prospect of opening a women's cancer resource center. We'll be following in the footsteps of groups such as the Oakland Women's Cancer Resource Center.

We'd like to offer a wide variety of workshops as well as groups for Spanish-speaking women, children with cancer, caregivers, women in the post-treatment phase, women

> We do not see cancer as an individual failure but as a societal one—an epidemic due to living in a time and place where polluting the world is more profitable than protecting it.

of color and lesbians. We particularly want to make the center available to women whose access to resources is limited.

*For more information, call (408) 464-2168.*

*Excerpted from* Matrix *(ceased printing), November 1991.*

## The 10 Worst Food Additives

1. Acesulfame-K
2. Artificial Colors
3. Aspartame
4. BHA & 5. BHT
6. Caffeine
7. Monosodium Glutamate
8. Nitrite
9. Saccharin
10. Sulfites

*Source:* Center for Science in the Public Interest's book, *Safe Food: Eating Wisely in a Risky World*

## What War on Drugs?

Annual death rates from substance abuse:
Tobacco—346,000
Alcohol—125,000
Alcohol & Drugs—4,000
Heroin/Morphine—4,000
Cocaine—2,000
Marijuana—75

*Source: National Institute on Drug Abuse*

## TOBACCO AND ALCOHOL ADS:

### SOCIAL INSANITY

#### by J.W. Smith / *The World's Wasted Wealth*

What about the insanity of spending billions on advertising cigarettes, whiskey, and beer? Our agriculture is then employed in raising crops for these health-damaging habits and the government pays more hundreds of millions of dollars to these farmers in crop support. Then more millions are employed trying to stem the damage caused by these habits. The cigarette industry alone is a $17.5 billion a year industry (1990) plus the cost of caring for that damaged health which is surely the greater cost. If we allowed that $50 billion of those wasted dollars could be saved by eliminating the promotion of such deadly lifestyles and instead promoting against it, 2.5 million people would be free for honest employment.

*Excerpted from* The World's Wasted Wealth, *published by New Worlds Press,* ©1992 J.W. Smith.

# Has the AIDS Tragedy been Distorted by Media and Partisan Politics?

## by James DeMeo, Ph.D. / *Pulse of the Planet*

By the late 1980s, it was clear that a "heterosexual AIDS epidemic" had not taken place in the USA, or Europe, and that some of the statistics had been cooked. The so-called "epidemic" of AIDS has not entered the heterosexual sphere to any significant extent, mainly because it was not, and still is not, easily transmittable through ordinary means, sexual or otherwise.

Gay males and intravenous drug users were most seriously at risk, particularly in certain cities such as San Francisco or New York, where large numbers of gay men and intravenous drug users were concentrated.

Gonorrhea, syphilis, hepatitis and other infectious diseases were deeply rooted in the gay community long before AIDS appeared, solely because of the highly promiscuous, anonymous, and unsanitary nature of many gay sex practices. These infectious diseases also exist among heterosexual populations, and are often transmitted via heterosexual genital contact. But not AIDS—to any significant degree—which in nearly all cases requires a blood-borne route of infection. For this reason, AIDS is a relatively difficult disease to catch.

In select brothels in Nevada and Amsterdam, Holland, for example, where anal intercourse and intravenous drug use are forbidden, the risk of AIDS through vaginal or oral intercourse is demonstrated to be exceedingly small, even nonexistent. Street prostitutes in New York and elsewhere have tested positive in high percentages mainly due to their use of shared intravenous drugs. This also appears to be a major factor in the current increase of AIDS among inner-city populations of teenagers, where such drug use is more common. Therefore, lesson from the data on AIDS is not "abstinence," or even questionably effective "safe sex" practices. The lesson is, *instead, know your partner!*

"Official science" says that abstinence or condoms are the only rational solutions. Evidence also suggests that "safe sex" practices are relatively ineffective for curbing the very real epidemic among the high-risk gay groups, but you would not know this from the widely publicized propaganda for condoms. The effectiveness of condoms in preventing the spread of AIDS is another question entirely.

Among heterosexual teens in New York City, clean injection needles and effective drug treatment programs to reduce intravenous drug use, not condoms, are needed to stem the problem.

The various Christian moralists have also been disinterested in the facts about AIDS transmission, and have spread false or misleading information about the risks for casual infection, leading to many regrettable incidents. The AIDS mythology conveniently supports the anti-sexual agenda of fundamentalists.

AIDS is also big business, and millions of dollars are now going into various big-time medical research programs, education programs, and social programs, few of which emphasize directly to high risk populations just what their actual risk factors are—these continue to be the blood transmission routes of promiscuous anal intercourse and the sharing of infected drug needles.

* 1992: Since writing this review the author, Dr. DeMeo, has become completely persuaded by the scientific findings of Dr. Peter Duesburg. These findings indicate that HIV has no connection to AIDS. If this is the case, then some of the statistics provided by the Center for Disease Control (contained in adjacent boxes) are not supportable.

*Excerpted from* Pulse of the Planet #3. *It appeared as a review of the book* The Myth of Heterosexual Aids, How A Tragedy has been Distorted by Media and Partisan Politics *by Michael Fumento (Basic Books, NY, 1990, 411 pages, $22.95).*

---

# AIDS: The Equal Opportunity Disease

- At this time, AIDS is the fifth leading cause of death for women in this country.
- Women are the fastest growing group affected by the virus.
- The World Health Organization estimates there are in excess of 100,000 women between the ages of 15-49 who are infected with the virus.
- Women comprise 10 percent of the total cases in the world.
- Women infected with the virus will die faster than men. For every month a man lives, a woman will live a week.
- Of women infected with HIV, 53 percent are African-American and 26 percent Latinas. Most are single mothers and heads of households.

*Excerpted from "Racism, Sexism, Classism & Homophobia, Tales From a Government-Sponsored Conference" by Gloria Nieto, an article which appeared in* Matrix, *November 1991.*

---

## AIDS FACTS - 1991

- 1.2 million people nationwide have tested HIV positive; 168,000 have AIDS:
    - 59% are homosexual/bisexual males;
    - 22% drug abusers;
    - 12% are female;
    - 6% are heterosexual males;
    - 1% transfusers and hemophiliacs.
- Since 1979, 108,000 have died from AIDS in the United States.
- As of 1990, roughly 61% of all the reported cases worldwide occurred in the U.S.
- High risk groups include, in order of risk factors: Homosexual/bisexual males; intravenous drug users; partners of people in high risk areas; people who received blood transfusions before 1985, in particular hemophiliacs; children born to infected mothers; female heterosexuals; male heterosexuals.
- 58% of AIDS cases were white; 26 are black; 15% are Hispanic; 1% Asian.
- 45% of Hispanic and blacks AIDS cases are drug related compared to 14% for whites.
- 79% of women infected with HIV are African American or Latina, most are single mothers.
- 40% of children born to HIV-mothers become positive.
- In the U.S., AIDS is the ninth leading cause of death among children ages 1-4; it is the fifth leading cause of death among women.
- Roughly 46% of all cases reside in New York and California, in particular San Francisco and New York City and surrounds. Higher incidence of drug-related transmission is reported in the East.

# Planting Seeds of Hope for the Mentally Ill

### by Kathy Johnston / *New Times*

"The delusions we have are pretty interesting," says Bob, 38, who's been diagnosed as mentally ill, a manic-depressive.

Bob is talking with other workers at Growing Grounds Farm, a special San Luis Obispo, CA plant nursery where all members of the workforce are also mentally ill. They stand around a table, planting young Lilies-of-the-Nile into gallon containers and sharing their tales.

"It's like being in a 24-hour horror movie," adds Tim, a schizophrenic.

Mental illness is not well understood even by medical professionals. And among the general public it's image is even worse, with widespread misconceptions fueled by sensationalized, erroneous media stereotypes. All of which is why Growing Grounds Farm opened its doors last week for a special open house, inviting the curious—and even the apprehensive—to better understand an all-too-common human affliction.

"People have this ax murderer concept which I find is the furthest thing from the truth," says Charles, 37, who suffers from depression. "All the people out here are real nice and very low key."

Therapist Gerald Clare, who works with mentally ill people through the SLO county Health Services sits on a Community Mental bench outside a greenhouse.

"Schizophrenics are not to be feared," she explains. "They are not violent. A lot of lay people think they are psychotic, but they're much more often the victim of an assault than the perpetrator. They're usually gentle people.

Some mental illnesses are biological and some are sociological, "the nature-nurture issue," he says. Schizophrenia, for example, is strictly biological, a brain chemistry disorder. Other mental problems are related to childhood in a dysfunctional family.

"Mental illness isn't either/or, it's a continuum," says Clare. "The ability to cope with your problems is not a black and white thing." Depression, he says, is the most common form of mental illness, affecting one-third of the population at some time in their lives.

"People who come here benefit, from having some success in their lives and a supportive working environment that's flexible enough to meet their needs. It's a double entendre—Growing Grounds Farm—since

it's not just lettuce growing here, it's people."

Veronica, 40, lays out little lettuce seedlings ready for planting in the fields. Once grown, the organically grown lettuce is harvested daily for use in local restaurants.

Diagnosed with schizophrenia, Veronica doesn't tell people about her disability unless she knows them well. "A lot of people are against people with mental illness.

Barbara Barnard says she's encountered prejudice against her son, who's a schizophrenic. She's now president of a support group, the Alliance for the Mentally Ill.

"My son had his own janitorial business when he was diagnosed with schizophrenia. It's such a stigma. Even people I'd known for years shied away from me when they found out my son was mentally ill. Had he had a brain tumor, they would have been helpful and supportive.

She says her son takes medication regularly to control his symptoms, and now lives independently after having spent some time working at the Growing Grounds Farm.

Charles waters some newly transplanted flower seedlings and talks to a reporter. "Maybe the chemicals in my brain just aren't right. But I know even as a kid I wasn't very happy. It was real strange growing up. My mom had mood swings, and she'd yell and scream about nothing. You never knew where you stood."

He adds, "This place has helped me deal with people. Two years ago I couldn't have talked to you, I was so shy mid withdrawn. But this is like my extended family; everyone's so nice."

Art is a 59 year-old who suffers from mental depression and anxiety with panic, after losing his 30-year job with a local trucking company. "I call this place my home now," he says, as he plants cuttings of a drought-resistant shrub. "These little cuttings will grow to gallon-size plants in about four months. It feels real good to see them go out the gate."

Kay, 45, says she couldn't believe it when a doctor told her she was schizophrenic. "I was devastated. When you break a leg, you can deal with it. But when you find out your brain is crippled, it's so hard to handle."

Gary, 40, credits medication for straightening out the chemical imbalances in his brain. "With the meds, I'm 100 percent A-OK. Without it, I go into astral hell. My eyes don't

> **Depression is the most common form of mental illness, affecting one-third of the population at some time in their lives.**

---

# The [Un]Acceptable Discrimination

Michael Landwehr of the Council for Disability Rights in Chicago, born with spina bifida. He was disabled during surgery when he was 12 and is in a wheelchair.

"I have been denied an apartment based on my disability," says Michael Landwehr. "Last year I was uprooted from home when the commuter train I took to work refused to let me continue riding without an attendant. I was told I could not buy a ticket in the first-class section of an airliner unless I also purchased a ticket for an attendant. I have been denied jobs and promotions on the basis of my disability. Every day I am denied access to public transportation

"Hundreds of thousands of disabled persons remain incarcerated in nursing homes and institutions, isolated from every aspect of community life, denied their right to vote, denied the right to education and employment.

Disabled people remain the most unemployed and underemployed in the country. For every dollar earned by a non disabled white male, a disabled white male earns 52 cents, a disabled minority male earns 25 cents, and a disabled minority woman earns 12 cents."

For more information contact: ADAPT, (303) 7339324; Disability Rights Education and Defense Fund, (202) 986-0375; Project on Women and Disability, (617) 277-5617.

*Excerpted and adapted from "America's Apartheid" by Nat Hentoff, which appeared in* The Village Voice*, March 4, 1986.*

---

close, and I end up on Venus.

Gary is the only one of the group working in the potting shed who says he has relationships with non-mentally ill people: "My normal friends are weirder than me."

*Excerpted from* New Times *(San Luis Obispo), June 4, 1992.*

# What, Meat Worry?

### by Bonnie Liebman / *Nutrition Action Newsletter*

Whether Neal Barnard is right or wrong, he's certainly got people talking.

Last April, everyone from *Newsweek* to *The New York Times* reported on a startling new proposal by Barnard's Physicians Committee for Responsible Medicine. The "New Basic Four Food Groups," said Barnard at a Washington, D.C., press conference, should consist of fruits, vegetables, legumes, and whole grains. That's it.

Everything else from French bread to flounder, cottage cheese to chicken, and skim milk to olive oil would end up in the "optional" category. This isn't just a vegetarian diet. We're talking vegan (no meat, fish, poultry, eggs, or dairy).

One press conference isn't enough to convince a nation to give up red meat, not to mention the foods that fill half our refrigerators. But millions of Americans are eating less beef and pork. And many of them are nervous about nutrients they may be missing. They shouldn't be.

Ever wonder why you see so many ads from the Pork Producers and the Beef Industry Council? It's because people are eating less red meat.

Some are cutting back to avoid fat. Others are motivated by ethics. Whatever the reason, in 1990 we ate less than 120 pounds of red meat per person, 12 percent less than in 1980 and 20 percent less than in 1971, our peak year.

But many people fear that eating less red meat is risky. And while some may maintain their composure if a piece of chicken or fish replaces the hunk of beef or pork on their plate, take away all four and they really start to sweat.

As it turns out, the one nutrient that troubles them most—protein—is the last one to fret over.

**Protein Panic.** "Protein is not a concern at all," says Jeanne Freeland-Graves of the University of Texas at Austin. "That's an old wives' tale."

- The typical adult gets at least 50 percent more protein than the Recommended Dietary Allowance (RDA). Young children average three times the RDA.
- Protein isn't found just in meat and milk. The third largest source of protein in the average American's diet is white bread, rolls, and crackers.
- Lacto-ovo vegetarians (who eat dairy and eggs) needn't worry about mixing complementary proteins. The protein in milk products and eggs has a "complete" array of the amino acids that your body can't make.

- Only vegan [VEE-gun] children (who eat no dairy or eggs) could conceivably be at slight risk, because 35 percent of a child's protein must be complete (it's only 20 percent for adults). But most vegan meals mix complementary foods like beans and rice or bread and peanut butter, so it's rarely a problem—as long as the child is getting enough food.

**Iron Overload.** If there is any nutrient non-red-meat-eaters should worry about, it's iron, not protein.

Beef is loaded with iron, and nutritionists have long worried that eating too little beef will cause anemia, especially in women of childbearing age (who lose iron during menstrual periods).

But the iron story is not as simple as it sounds. While most nutritionists are eager to tell people what to eat to get enough iron, James Cook of the University of Kansas Medical Center isn't.

"Men, post menopausal women, and chil-

---

**The *New Basic Four Food Groups* should consist of fruits, vegetables, legumes, and whole grains.**

---

dren under 18 don't develop iron deficiency," says Cook. "And the women who have anemia shouldn't rely on diet to alleviate it. They should take an iron supplement."

That's because "there are so many competing effects on iron absorption that, with a varied diet, they cancel each other out," he says.

For example, you might have an iron-rich chicken leg for lunch, but you might also have coffee, tea, a calcium supplement, or some egg yolk, bran, or other foods that interfere with your body's ability to absorb the iron.

Cook is also reluctant to give advice on how to get more iron because "a large number of people suffer from too much iron, and the problem may be as bad as for those who suffer from too little." Cook is talking about a disease called hemochromatosis, which is a genetic defect that affects three to five out of every thousand people. Their bodies accumulate excess iron, and the results can be disastrous.

**Iron-Poor Blood.** Of course, no one's saying it's good to be *low* in iron. First there's anemia, which leaves people tired and out of breath. And iron depleted women may feel cold, sleep poorly, and have poorer memo-

ries, according to preliminary studies that need to be confirmed. [1-3]

Are people who eat less red meat at greater risk? Perhaps.

Iron-deficiency anemia is no more common among vegetarians than non vegetarians, in part because the body adapts. The less iron you eat, the more your body absorbs.

But many women have iron levels that are below normal, (though not low enough to cause anemia), and few studies have examined iron levels in vegetarian women. One small study, by Bonnie Worthington-Roberts of the University of Washington, found that pre-menopausal women who were lacto-ovo vegetarians or fish-and-poultry eaters had lower iron levels than women who ate red meat . [4]

"The incidence of true anemia is four to five percent of pre-menopausal women, which is not as high as people think," says Worthington-Roberts. "But we don't have a good handle on the number of women with low iron stores."

In the meantime, says Worthington-Roberts, "all women should at least get their hematocrit and hemoglobin analyzed annually."

**Inscrutable Zinc.** If you're eating less red meat, zinc is another nutrient nutritionists might warn you about. But as far as researchers now know, it isn't much of a problem.

"Adults have an incredible capacity to adapt to marginal intakes of zinc by decreasing excretion and maybe by increasing absorption," says Janet King of the University of California at Berkeley. Exceptions are:

- pregnant women (they have greater needs),
- diabetics whose blood sugar levels are uncontrolled (they lose zinc in their urine), and
- people who have experienced trauma (such as surgery, burns, or gunshot wounds).

Unfortunately, you can't take a test to find out if you're getting enough zinc.

"We don't have a good way to evaluate zinc status," says King. The amount of zinc in your hair or saliva is unreliable, and once the level in your blood drops, you're really deficient.

Only in children is it easy to know who is getting enough zinc. Kids who are deficient don't grow.

So what can you do if your doctor is concerned that your child is growing too slowly? "Give them zinc and see if growth improves," says King. To play it safe, stick with the RDA (10 mg per day for children under 11). Don't go overboard.

Fortunately, you don't need red meat to get zinc. There's plenty in seafood, poultry, milk, and legumes.

**Vegetables in the News.** So, non-or less-red-meat-eaters, cross protein off your worry list. If you're a pre-menopausal woman, keep iron in mind, and if your child isn't growing well, don't forget zinc.

If you're still concerned, why not take a multi-vitamin-and-mineral supplement that provides 100 percent of the USRDA (15mg for zinc and 18 mg for iron)? Just make sure it has copper, and that you're not at risk for hemo-chromatosis.

"I know it's against most others in my profession, but I don't see anything wrong with a supplement with RDA levels as a margin of safety," says nutritionist Freeland-Graves.

One thing is certain. Taking a supplement is healthier than loading up on red meat.

[1] *Am. J. Physiol. 246:* R380,1984.
[2] *Fed. Am. Soc. Exper. Biol. J 2:* A434,1988.
[3] *AM. J. Clin. Nutr. 53:* P- 1 6, 22, 28, 199 1.
[4] *Am. J Clin. Nutr. 47:*275,1988.

*Excerpted from* Nutrition Action Healthletter, *June 1991.*

# Meat-eaters vs. Vegetarians

- Training in nutrition received during 4 years of medical school by average US physician: 2.5 hours
- Most common cause of death in US: Heart disease
- How frequently a heart attack kills in US: Every 45 seconds
- Risk of death from heart attack for average American man: 50%
- Risk of death from heart attack for American man who consumes no meat: 15%
- Risk of death from heart attack for American man who consumes no meat, dairy products or eggs: 4%
- Leading sources of saturated fat and cholesterol in American diets: Meat, dairy products and eggs
- Cholesterol found in all grains, legumes, fruits, vegetables, nuts, seeds: None

- Chance of dying from heart disease if you do not consume cholesterol: 4%
- Increased risk of breast cancer for women who eat butter and cheese 2-4 times a week compared to once a week: 3.2 times higher
- Increased risk of fatal prostate cancer for men who consume meats, dairy products and eggs daily as compared to sparingly: 3.6 times higher
- The average measurable bone loss of female meat-eaters at age 65: 35%
- The average measurable bone loss of female vegetarians at age 65: 18%
- Meat Board advertisements claim; "Today's meats are low in fat"—Their ad campaigns show servings with: 200 calories—Reality: The servings of beef they show us are half the size of an average serving and have been surgically defatted with a scalpel.
- Dairy industry advertising claim: Milk is nature's most perfect food—Reality: Milk is nature's most perfect food for a calf, who has four stomachs, will double its weight in 47 days, and can weigh up to 1000 pounds within a year
- Sperm count of average American male compared to 30 years ago: Down 30%
- Amount of total antibiotics used in US fed routinely to livestock: 55%
- Staphylococci infections resistant to penicillin in 1960: 13%
- Staphylococci infections resistant to penicillin in 1988: 91%—Major contributing cause: Breeding of antibiotic resistant bacteria in factory farms due to routine feeding of antibiotics to livestock

*Source:* Diet for a New America *by John Robbins.*

# No Zinc Without Copper

If you're taking a zinc supplement, don't forget to take copper.

Scientists have long known that too much zinc can impair the body's ability to absorb copper. Because copper is used to make red blood cells, impaired absorption can lead to anemia.

But more people-especially the elderly-may now be at risk, warns Donald Frambach of the University of Southern California School of Medicine.

"A recent study suggested that 100 mg of zinc per day may retard the progression of age-related macular degeneration, the leading cause of blindness among elderly Americans," says Frambach, who adds that "many elderly Americans are now taking zinc supplements."

One popular supplement, Ocuvite, which contains 40 mg of zinc per tablet, has a recommended dose of one to two tablets per day. (The U.S. Recommended Daily Allowance USRDA—for zinc is 15 mg.)

Earlier studies have shown that as little as 50 mg of zinc can impair copper absorption. To play it safe, never take any zinc without also taking the USRDA of copper, which is 2 mg. That should provide enough copper to cover up to 50 mg of zinc, says Peter Fischer of Health and Welfare Canada.

If you take a vitamin-and mineral supplement, make sure it has both.

*J. Am. Med. Assoc. 264:*1441, 1990, and *265:* 869, 1991.

*Excerpted from* Nutrition Action Health-letter, *June 1991.*

## *Potentially toxic daily doses of vitamins:*

Vitamin A ..................... 25,000-50,000 IU
Vitamin D ................................ 50,000 IU
Vitamin E ................................. 1,200 IU
Vitamin C ...................... 1,000-5,000 Mg
Thiamin (B-1) ............................ 300 Mg
Riboflavin (B-2) ....................... 1,000 Mg
Niacin (B-3) ............................. 1,000 Mg
Pyridoxine ............................ 100-200 Mg
Folacin ...................................... 400 Mg
Biotin ......................................... 50 Mg
Pantothenic Acid ..................... 1,000Mg
Calcium ................................. 12,000 Mg
Phosphorus ........................... 12,000 Mg
Magnesium ............................. 6,000 Mg
Iron ......................................... 100 Mg
Zinc ......................................... 500 Mg
Copper ..................................... 100 Mg
Flouride ................................. 4-20 Mg
Iodine ......................................... 2 Mg
Selenium ..................................... 1 Mg

*Source: National Research Council*

| Food | Estimated Absorbable | |
|---|---|---|
| | Zinc (mg) | Iron (mg) |
| Oysters (3 oz) | 155 | 1.5 |
| Wheat germ (1 oz) | 4.7 | 0.2 |
| Bottom rounded steak (3 oz) | 3.9 | 0.4 |
| Clams (3 oz) | 2.3 | 3.1 |
| Tofu, firm (4 oz) | 2.0 | 1.1 |
| Lentils/Chickpeas (¾ cup, cooked) | 1.9 | 0.4 |
| Kidney/Pinto beans (¾ cup, cooked) | 1.4 | 0.3 |
| Shrimp (3 oz) | 1.3 | 0.3 |
| Cheddar cheese (1.5 oz) | 1.3 | 0.3 |
| Chicken breast (4 oz) | 1.1 | 0.2 |
| Green peas (½ cup, cooked) | 1.0 | 0.1 |
| 1% milk (1 cup) | 1.0 | 0.0 |
| Peanut butter (2 Tb) | 0.9 | 0.1 |
| Spinach (½ cup, cooked) | 0.7 | 0.3 |
| Light tuna in water (3 oz) | 0.4 | 0.3 |
| Whole wheat bread (2 sl) | 0.3 | 0.2 |
| Broccoli or Kale (½ cup, cooked) | 0.3 | 0.1 |

*Daily Goals: Iron--1.8 mg for menstruating women, 1.3 mg for other adults. Zinc--2.5 mg.*

# The Calcium Myth

### by Judy B. Schermerhorn / *Earth Journal*

The National Dairy Council spends tens of millions of dollars trying to convince the American population that osteoporosis can be prevented by drinking more milk and consuming more dairy products. However, the *only* research even faintly suggestive of the benevolence of consuming dairy products has been paid for by the National Dairy Council itself.

Nathan Pritikin is considered by many to currently be the foremost expert on nutrition. People flock to his Longevity Centers in huge numbers, sometimes facing major coronary bypass operations or confined to wheelchairs, and often go jogging home within the month. Nearly all improve tremendously.

The heart of Pritikin's program is his *diet*. Pritikin studied the medical research on osteoporosis and found no basis whatsoever for the Diary Council recommendation of 1200 mg of calcium a day.

In our country, according to Pritikin, "those who can afford it are eating 20% of their total calories in protein, which guarantees negative mineral balance—not only of calcium, but of magnesium, zinc, and iron. It's all directly related to the amount of protein you eat."

The body must have calcium in the blood for such vital functions as controlling muscular contractions, including the heart, transmission of nerve impulses, blood clotting, and other essential vital tasks. When the level of calcium in the blood is insufficient, the body undergoes a series of biochemical reactions to draw calcium from the bones to bring it to the blood.

No matter how much calcium is taken in, the correspondence between excess protein intake and bone resorption is direct and

---

**High protein diets in general, and meat-based diets in particular, lead to a gradual but inexorable decrease in bone density, creating the development of osteoporosis.**

---

consistent. The result is that high protein diets in general, and meat-based diets in particular, lead to a gradual but inexorable decrease in bone density, creating the development of osteoporosis.

The reason excessive protein intake depletes the body of calcium is this: the blood must be kept at an essentially neutral pH level. If our blood becomes too acidic, we die. If the diet contains many acid-forming foods, then the body must withdraw calcium from the bones and use this alkaline mineral to balance the pH level of the blood. Meat, poultry, eggs, fish, and dairy products are the most acid-forming of foods and therefore are the foods which cause calcium to be drawn from the bones to restore the pH balance. Most fruits and vegetables, in contrast, become alkaline in the body and so require *no* depletion of calcium stores from the bones to maintain the neutrality of the blood.

The body's ability to absorb and utilize the calcium in foods is directly dependent on the ratio of calcium to phosphorous in these foods. In addition to their neutral pH level, the calcium/phosphorous ratio in vegetables and fruits is high, making the calcium easily utilized by the body. Foods whose calcium is least available, because their calcium/phosphorous ratio is so low, are chicken, liver, beef, pork, and fish. Green leafy vegetables have the highest calcium/phosphorous ratio and therefore contain the most usable calcium. We can improve our health by reducing our protein intake and increasing our intake of fresh fruits and vegetables. Pass the salad, please!

*Judy B. Schermerhorn, a health writer in Templeton, California, actively practices vegetarian health and nutrition with her family.*

*Excerpted from* Earth Journal, *March 1991.*

# Popular Herbal Formulas for Minor Health Conditions

### by L. Carl Robinson, M.H., Ms. T., T.T / Yarrow Institute (*See* Robinson Research Institute)

*Throughout man's history, the beneficial uses of plants have played an important part in health and well-being. The medicinal effects of plants, discovered originally by trial and inspiration in many lands and cultures, are only now being scientifically explored through the science of pharmacology. Today, many companies provide convenient dosage forms of popular herbs and herb formulations.*

• Blood Pressure (high)—garlic and cayenne combinations.
• Blood sugar (low) balancer—licorice root combinations.
• Calcium enricher (muscle cramps, nervousness)—comfrey, oatstraw and shavegrass combinations.
• Herbal expectorant/anti-asthmatic/bronchial expectorant—comfrey, mullein and garlic liquid extracts.
• Relaxant (Gentle)—Lady slipper combinations (Traditional Native American).

© 1991 Raee Mattson

• Respiratory/Chest & Lung Strengthener—Comfrey & Mullein combinations (Traditional European)
• Ulcers/Antiseptic properties—myrrh and golden seal
• Weight & Appetite controller—chickweed & licorice combinations (contemporary/Traditional English).

*L. Carl Robinson holds a Master of Herbology in herbal pharmacology and is a Therapy Technician with extensive research in modern nutrition and herbology.*

*Warning: This information is not intended to be used in the diagnosis, treatment, or mitigation of any disease condition. Seek the advise of a physician for any condition which requires professional care.*

*Excerpted from Robinson Research Institute brochure, "Herbs and Your Health." Hundreds of great herbal recommendations!*

# Chapter 11

# *Feminism & the Family*

It was women's concern with speaking out on issues such as slavery, peace, and religious rights that led them to their concern with women's rights. In 1840, there was an anti-slavery convention in London to which several American female delegates were denied seating. American historians have traced the 1848 Seneca Convention directly back to these women who were denied their ability to speak out on the issue of slavery. These women came back and said, "We are going to have to demand our own rights as women before we have the right to speak on other issues."

There [is] this interplay between women's concern for themselves and others in nonviolent actions [from] the abolition and prohibition movements [to] the peace, environmental and human rights movements. [The] inability to stand up for these issues [have] led them to fight for their own rights.

— *Carolyn Stephenson (University at Hawaii at Manoa). Excerpted from* Nonviolent Sanctions, News from the Albert Einstein Institution.

*"American HERSTORY, Mystory, Ourstory" Collage ©1988 by Sanda Aronson and photo by Stanley Willard. This collage celebrates women in American History, particularly women excluded from the mainstream history: disabled women and other minority group women. It was created by invitation for the national conference, "American Herstory" for the 200th anniversary of the US Constitution at the Atlanta College of Art*

*(1/26-3/5/88), and was one of a few selected for a 2-year touring show sponsored by the Southern Arts Federation. The artist may be contacted by writing: Sanda Aronson, Box 20781, New York City, NY 10025. Ms. Aronson is the founder of Disabled Artists Network.*

*Reprinted with permission from the artist.*

# A Declaration of Interdependence

### by Libby Bassett & Mim Kelber / *Women's Environmental Development Organization*

**W**hen in the Course of Human Events, it becomes necessary to create a new bond among the peoples of the Earth, connecting each to the other, undertaking equal responsibilities under the laws of nature, a decent respect for the welfare of humankind and all life on Earth requires us to Declare our Interdependence.

We recognize that humankind has not woven the web of life; we are but one thread within it. Whatever we do to the web, we do to ourselves. Whatever befalls the Earth befalls also the family of the Earth.

We are concerned about the wounds and bleeding sores on the naked body of the Earth: the famine; the poverty; the children born into hunger and disease; the destruction of forests and fertile lands; the chemical and nuclear accidents; the wars and deaths in so many parts of the world.

It is our belief that man's dominion over nature parallels the subjugation of women in many societies, denying them sovereignty over their lives and bodies. Until all societies truly value women and the environment, their joint degradation will continue.

Women's views on economic justice, human rights, reproduction and the achievement of peace must be heard at local, national, and international forums, wherever policies are made that could affect the future of life on Earth. Partnership among all peoples is essential for the survival of the planet.

If we are to have a common future, we must commit ourselves to preserve the natural wealth of our Earth for future generations.

### **A**s women we accept our responsibility and declare our intention to:

- Link with others—young and old, women and men, people of all races, religions, cultures and political beliefs—in a common concern for global survival;
- Be aware in our private, public and working lives of actions we can take to safeguard our food, fresh water, clean air and quality of life;
- Make women's collective experiences and value judgments equal to the experiences and value judgments of men when policies are made that affect our future and future generations;
- Expose the connections between environmental degradation, greed, uncontrolled militarism and technology devoid of human values. Insist that human and ecological values take absolute precedence when decisions are made in national affairs;
- Change government, economic and social policies to protect the well-being of the most vulnerable among us and to end poverty and inequality;
- Work to dismantle nuclear and conventional weapons, build trust among peoples and nations, and use all available international institutions and networks to achieve common security for the family of Earth.

**W**e also declare that, whenever and wherever people meet to decide the fate of the planet, it is our intention to participate on an equal footing, with full and fair representation, equivalent to our number and kind on Earth.

*Drawn from the words and philosophies of the drafters of the U.S. Declaration of Independence (July 4, 1776); Chief Seattle to President Franklin Pierce (1855); Wangari Maathai, founder, Green Belt Movement, and Chair, National Council of Women of Kenya (1988); The UN Population Fund (1988); Women's Foreign Policy Council, The World Commission on Environment and Development (1987); Spiritual and Parliamentary Leaders Global Survival Conference, Oxford (April 1988).*

*Reprinted with permission from Women's Environmental Development Organization, 1990.*

The experience of being a woman was once centered in transience: evanescent beauty, fading love. As wives and daughters, women lived contingent lives. The future belonged to them only in dreams. Today women are beginning to be in a better position than men to understand—and to teach what it means to invest in the long term, for themselves, for other women, for the human community.

Feminism is a long-term project. We are all aware of its uneven history, of how, for instance, feminism went into eclipse after World War II. The task now is to lengthen its present, to combine today's efforts with a sustained awareness that will not burn out. We need to emulate the double rhythm of successful high-tech companies. They must develop new products constantly; at the same time, they have a long-term pattern of growth as they carry experience from one project to the next.

Feminism has always had at least three different agendas. One concerns the development and fulfillment of women as individuals. The second concerns social justice for all women and involves political goals that depend on solidarity for their achievement. And the third concerns the way society as a whole will change when women are full participants. Today, as contemporary feminism begins to span generations and thus to reflect the aspirations of women of all ages, we face the risk that our agendas will diverge or that one of them will be lost. These agendas have different rhythms of progression: They unfold in different kinds of time, and in order to integrate them into a single vision, we will have to change our ways of thinking about time. The future, therefore, is a feminist issue. Start worrying about the future: your own, far longer than it would once have been; the future of your daughters and daughter surrogates, your nieces and proteges, and all those who follow after; and the future of the world we will leave them.

The sense that women today are moving forward as a group can obscure the fact that women are becoming steadily more diverse. As we discover how different we are, the feminist agenda of individual fulfillment becomes more complex. Being an adult female in the United States today involves a profoundly personal and improvisatory act of creation. Decisions no longer automatically follow from well-understood social roles and relationships. They must be made one by one. Yet the commitments that follow on our decisions now can extend over 50 years of healthy maturity rather than the 25 or 30 years of adult productivity that a woman could anticipate in the past. Perhaps more than men, women are beginning to visualize the composition of life on an extended scale. But this also involves recognizing different high points, rhythms, and surges. We have begun to acknowledge new starts and new

# Claiming the Future

## *A vision of women to span the generations*

### by Mary Catherine Bateson / *Lears*

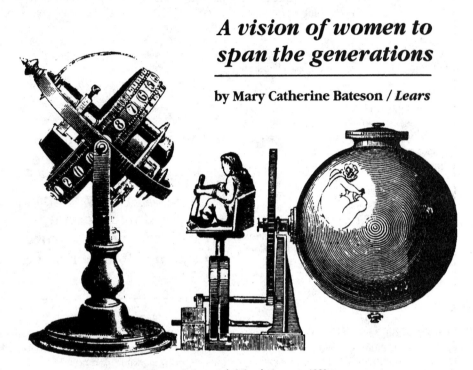

*Woman Empowered* © Sanda Aronson 1989

transitions, rejecting archaic definitions of when alternatives are closed off; of what it means to be "too old."

Social forms have yet to be adjusted to the fact that women on average have more good working and learning years than men, more than enough to balance a few years taken off from a career outside the home and invested in child care. If some women choose, for a while, to advance more slowly at the office than some male colleagues, a realistic assessment of their skills should allow them to move faster later—and keep moving longer. The immediate problem for younger women is short-term thinking on the part of employers; for older women it becomes sexism recycled as ageism. The struggle for equal opportunity recurs at every age; it turns out to entail a struggle for recognition of continued growth and of the capacity to sustain and transfer learning from one context to another, from the home, for example, to the workplace.

Females need to get the maximum benefit from their peak growth periods. In many organizations, if you do not achieve a particular rank by a particular age, you never will,

however much you continue to develop. On the other hand, once a rank is achieved it can be kept through years of declining productivity.

Twenty years ago we realized that we would have to rethink what it means to be a woman. Today we realize that we have to rethink the meaning of being an adult of either sex.

Adulthood now demands new understanding for young and old: for those cutting new pathways through decades that would once have been decades of decline and for adolescents hesitating to make commitments that may bind them far into extended futures. In the past, women were often treated like children. Today we are not only grown-up—we are learning to be a new kind of grown-up. We are not only reevaluating all of our traditional commitments but changing our understanding of what it is to make and sustain commitments freely. Men, too, are moving—not always gracefully— toward a new balance of freedom and commitment.

Adulthood is not just longer; it has room for many changes and choices, as manifested by the number of "housewives" who have gone back to school after 15 or 20 years at home and launched new careers and often new partnerships. Two incarnations in a single lifetime. Two adulthoods. Sometimes three. But those are only the obvious examples. Increasingly we will be learning to layer our potentials, to explore multiple roles at the same time and find new ways to pace ourselves.

How does the growing individual sense of possibility affect the search for justice for all women? Here there is reason for concern.

Reaction has been in the air, and common political goals are receding. It is not that the battle for women's rights is won—it isn't—but that much of our attention has shifted. In some ways our sense of individual possibility conflicts directly with the requirements of political solidarity. We are rightly offended by the idea that women are essentially alike. For example, the attitude that a token woman on a committee or in the cabinet or on the Supreme Court can represent the "women's point of view" is no longer acceptable. We have also learned, on those occasions when several women are present, to resist the male tendency to treat women's individual views as interchangeable. Biology does affect destiny, but it is clearly true that female biology does not determine for us identical destinies.

All this makes us less likely to unite for political action. We have learned to reject stereotypical views of groups of women that suggest that each woman's behavior can be predicted from such labels as housewife or spinster or flirt. And so it is not surprising that increasing numbers of women are uncomfortable with the often caricatured label "feminist," even if they take the goals of feminism for granted. Younger women especially may reject the label as part of claiming the right of independent thought.

It is because we are discovering and nurturing so much individuality that solidarity has to be relearned constantly. The strategy of reaction builds on this, eroding rights piecemeal from groups of women, starting with the least powerful—mothers on welfare, say, or pregnant teenagers. Not you, not me. Not yet. The recent diminishing of abortion rights warns us that our gains are fragile; the current resurgence of pro-choice activism demonstrates that the consensus is there but not the habit of vigilance or the conviction that the rights of individual women will be safest when those of all women are protected.

Stereotypes can also cause confusion with regard to the third agenda, the changes we anticipate in society when women are full participants. Because adult men and women today have grown up under the influence of powerful gender stereotypes and expectations, it may take generations to discover what qualities are genuinely distinctive to each sex and not socially induced. Liberated

men and women often revert to familiar roles when their own children are born, so patterns reecho across generations.

Then, too, the commitment to change may produce its own rigidities and overcompensations. Women carry the marks of exploitation and disparagement, but because sex roles complement each other, neither women nor men have been permitted their full growth. Only pervasive and mutual change can make all of us whole. Furthermore, the movement away from the linkage of gender with "home" (as the woman's sphere) and "work" (as the man's sphere) means that progress on one front often creates imbalance on the other. Our efforts to build new patterns are often out of sync, leaving us limping along in shoes that don't match.

---

**In the past, women in the home cleaned up after men who spent their working hours creating slag heaps and toxic dumps, perhaps because they never learned to clean up after themselves anywhere.**

---

Child care and elder care are like clean air—as long as they were freely available, they were taken for granted, and no one understood their value. We now know that women are not necessarily nurturing and caring and that we cannot count on women for all the necessary tasks of social maintenance. Society can meet these needs either by forcing the work on some group that has no alternative or by dividing it in a more equitable fashion. Looking to the future, feminism must envision a society in which the tasks and values traditionally assigned to women are appealing to both sexes, with appropriate resources allocated and appropriate skills developed. We must not allow class or race to replace gender as the basis of coercion.

The personality traits that women were trained to adopt—and men were trained to reject—are needed as part of the overall social fabric. Rejecting those values is not a good solution. Indeed, stereotypical female traits are badly needed in many settings where women have been excluded. In the past, women in the home cleaned up after men who spent their working hours creating slag heaps and toxic dumps, perhaps because they never learned to clean up after themselves anywhere. We are a lethally messy species. Housekeeping and maintenance are important—to rivers and cities and forests as well as within the home. It's no use

for women to foster growth at home while in factories and offices individuals are stunted and treated as replaceable parts. Caring is not a specialty to be limited to one gender or setting but a human responsibility.

Though we don't know which traits will prove in the long run to be distinctively feminine, there are certain areas where I believe women, for at least the next generation, can begin to compensate for distortions that have developed in our male-oriented society. Women have received, through improvements in contraception and in general medical care, an immensely precious gift of time. As we become aware of that gift, and learn to use it, we may in turn be able to teach the whole society something about living in time, about not foreclosing the future. But long-term thinking is not sufficient unless it is combined with attention to the needs and problems of the present. Traditionally women have had better peripheral vision than men—not literally but in the sense that their lives required simultaneous attention to multiple needs and a high tolerance for interruption. In hunting-and-gathering societies the hunter would go off to hunt an antelope with skill and intense concentration, while the woman would combine the gathering task with caring for children of different ages, constantly adjusting to their development over time as she watched for problems out of the corner of her eye. The hunter had specific, narrow goals; the woman was the one who learned to roll with the punches and respond to multiple needs. Everyone made a great fuss when the hunter brought back meat for a feast, but somewhere along the way the woman probably invented agriculture. Women may yet help us to make the transition from a society addicted to short-term profit to one committed to long-term stability, simply by virtue of their broader and deeper focus of attention.

The ability to bridge short-term demands—those interruptible efforts of every day—with long-term needs encompassing visions that span generations is a faculty that must be cultivated to protect the future. A woman can learn to stir the soup and take a business call from Tokyo at the same time, with a baby balanced on one hip. She automatically saves whatever is on the computer screen when she hears a step in the hall, and gets back to it later with undiminished interest. She has had to learn a flexible pattern of attention that may make her more able to deal with complexity over the long term, to see and care more widely. Women have had to develop the ability to respond to immediate needs without losing track of long-term goals. Is this biological? We don't know, but if it is learned, then surely it is more important to share it than to outgrow it.

The need to embrace flux and discontinuity as opportunities for growth while planning for long-term viability may seem paradoxical. Certainly our society is failing in this respect. It is on a treadmill of short-term goals and yet rigidly unable to choose and plan for real change. The political process staggers from election to election, budget to budget. Our narrow focus has led us to accumulate debt and deplete the Earth. New companies may fail on their first quarterly report and major technologies remain undeveloped because the lead time seems too long. Through the art of child-rearing, women have traditionally been arbiters of the paradoxical claims of immediate need and long-term possibility. No one expects the birth of a child, much less its maturation, to occur in the short time scale that is increasingly important in the male-dominated economic sphere; patience with the slow pace necessary for certain types of development is part of a woman's traditional role. Child-raising requires steady change and adaptation, not unlike the combination of long-term commitment and responsive improvisation needed by a great newspaper. Multiple rhythms, high intensity in the moment and long-term planning.

Awareness of the long term is relevant to all three feminist agendas. Only in a context where the long term is valued can individual women fully prove their potential—for instance, only an institution or a corporation with a long-term vision can recognize the value of a work force, or a worker, developing over time. The same kind of vision can lead a corporation or a community to protect the environment. It is in this area of long-term thinking that women have critical insights to offer. Once men were planners and women were dependent on their decisions. Today we have made our claim on time and gained access to the future. We need to hang on to it, to take and make time.

It is here that we may have our greatest moral impact, for the return to a longer sense of time has built into it a greater ethical sensitivity. A sense of time that spans generations must, in this mobile world, also span space and human diversity and acknowledge global interdependence. It reminds us that the bills for pollution and human exploitation may take a long time coming due, but they will be extremely costly when they come. Women cannot be expected always to be better than men, but theirs is a much needed wisdom, and they have the potential to share it.

*Mary Catherine Bateson is Clarence Robinson Professor of Anthropology and English at George Mason University. Her most recent book is* Composing a Life *(Atlantic Monthly Press).*

*Excerpted from* Lear's, *February 1990.*

# Are men still the breadwinners?

## by Ken Clatterbaugh / *Changing Men*

There is a common complaint among men that many, if not most, of the costs of being a man come from our social role as *providers*. Men who are providers, the argument goes, spend too much time at work and neglect their families, their children, and themselves. Men who are providers are overly competitive with each other, and this rivalry prevents them from forming bonds of trust with other men. Women in male-female families are economically dependent on men who provide for them, while men, overly involved in their work, need women as their emotional and physical caretakers. Both women and men come to resent these dependencies, with divorce and violence as a result.

The conditions of work in the United States, however, are changing rapidly. We may soon have to abandon this idea that the costs of being a man arise from the fact that men are providers. In reality, the male provider role is fading.

Of the new workers entering the job force in the next 10 years, 64 percent will be women. Work opportunities in manufacturing and agriculture, two areas that traditionally have been overwhelmingly male and paid a wage capable of supporting a family, are declining.

Meanwhile, women are gaining in income relative to men. By 1988 women ages 16-24 were earning 90 percent of the median weekly earnings of men in the same group.

(Those with college educations were even closer together.) Meanwhile, women ages 25-35 earned 78 percent of men's earnings. Women ages 40-65 earned 60 percent relative to men's earnings.

Although the poor are largely women and children, the latest figures show a sharp rise in the rate at which men are falling into poverty; the rate of increase for men living in poverty is 50 percent compared to a rate for women of around 10 percent per year.

Black and Hispanic men have suffered the most since the late 1970s. In 1979 Hispanic men, for instance, had median weekly earnings for full-time work 74 percent that of white men; by 1986 that had declined to 69 percent. In some cases minority and working-class women are doing better than the men. More black women than black men have college degrees, and black women have slightly lower unemployment rates. Hispanic women who work full time have a median weekly earning 82 percent that of full-time white workers, compared to 69 percent for Hispanic men.

It is among the richest 20 percent of the

**The dominant fact is that the male role as provider is rapidly disappearing.**

population that women are making the most gains. These are the women who have the education and family support to compete with men successfully. This is the class where men do earn enough to be providers in the traditional sense of the word, but increasingly so do the women.

The traditional male provider role in American life has always been strongest in middle-income families. But now many of those families desperately need two incomes to maintain their buying power against inflation, tax increases, declining real wages, and plant closings. In younger male-female middle income families there is a much greater balance between the earnings of the man and the woman.

The dominant fact is that the male role as provider is rapidly disappearing.

*Excerpted from the men's movement magazine* Changing Men, *Winter/Spring 1991.*

# Halting the Oppression of Children

### by Rachel Burger & Liz Roberts / *Peacework*

In the 14 years of the war in Vietnam, some 58,000 US citizens were killed—an average of more than 4000 per year. Americans may not realize that the violence of abuse and neglect that goes on in our country today causes the deaths of some 5000 children every year.

As workers in the battered women's movement, we are aware too of the frequency of abuse of women by their partners.

Violence against women is not the problem of a few sick families. It is practically the norm. Ending the violence against women and children in our society will require social and political change, not just social services.

In only 11 states is corporal punishment banned in public school systems; about 150,000 children per year are forced to seek medical attention for injuries resulting from physical punishment in school.

Our society systematically denies the reality of the violence in many children's lives, and ignores the way most children are subject to adult control and intimidation. Even within the battered women's movement, violence against children has not received the attention it deserves. Woman abuse is child abuse; observing your mother being beaten is as damaging as being beaten yourself. In addition, a high proportion of children in shelters have themselves been the victims of physical, sexual, and/or emotional abuse. Yet, even though there are two children for every battered woman in a shelter, many programs commit little or no staff time, money or energy to children's programs.

We need to realize that adults have consistently undermined children's self-respect, their sense of well-being, and their ability to approach problems creatively. In fact, children know from their own experience how destructive violence is. But to liberate their tremendous capacity to find creative solutions to conflict, we must name the violence that is at the root of child-beating practices in this country.

The oppression of children is perpetuated by the many ways this society fails to support parents. Mothers are expected to know "by instinct" how to relate to children. Abusive behavior is stigmatized so that parents seeking help often feel blamed and humiliated. There is little genuine relief for parents in the form of quality, affordable daycare, community-based parent education and support groups, or support groups for children. Women who "drop out" to raise their children may be working harder than they ever have before, but are still asked "So what are you doing these days?," as if parenting were not in itself demanding and stimulating work. We need to recognize that any work which challenges this society's treatment of children is critical in the movement for peace and social justice as working for nuclear disarmament, doing anti-racism organizing, or fighting violence against women.

Often, our treatment of children teaches the ground rules for oppression. When we say "Because I said so" to a child, we teach her that "might is right," and that she should not challenge authority. When we spank a child, saying it's "for your own good," we deny the truth that violence is always a misuse of power. When we insist that a child "Go kiss Aunt Mary," we teach her that other people are entitled to make choices about her own body. When we order children around, we forget the principles of negotiation and mutual respect that we try to apply in our relationships with other adults.

Adults have more power than children, greater access to resources, greater knowledge of the world, more freedom to choose the people with whom we will be intimate, and a larger, stronger physical presence. If we examine how we use this power in relationships to children, more children can be freed to use and develop their own power: the power to think, to create, to say what they're feeling, to express their likes and dislikes, to be whole human beings.

Each of us can take responsibility for challenging the oppression of children in our personal lives and in our political and work lives. We can change the way we relate to children by listening carefully, and respecting children's understanding of their lives; by respecting children's feelings; by being honest and direct with children; by respecting children's physical space; by getting in touch with what it was like to be a child and by using this to identify with children,

We do not have to take on children's liberation as another exhausting cause. But if we can open ourselves to questioning values and challenging harmful practices, small and large changes will follow. As parents, teachers, social justice activists, policy-makers and therapists, if we take children more to heart, we will truly be working for peace.

*Rachel Burger is a child advocate at Transition House in Cambridge. Liz Roberts is a child advocate at Harbor Me, in Chelsea, MA.*

*Excerpted from a special issue of* Peacework, Domestic Violence and Nonviolence, *1989.*

## STATISTICS ON DOMESTIC VIOLENCE

- Wife abuse maims and murders more women annually than do automobile accidents, muggings and rapes combined.
- One third of all female homocide victims were murdered by their husbands or boyfriends in 1985.
- Of the violent crimes included in the FBI's Uniform Crime Reports in 1984, homocide was the least likely to be committed by a stranger. 57% of all homocide victims were killed by an acquaintance or a relative, as compared to 18% killed by a stranger.
- National Crime Statistics show that in almost three-fourths of spouse-on-spouse assaults, the victim was divorced or separated at the time of the incident.
- As many as 35% of women who visit treatment facilities have abuse-related symptoms, either physical or stress-related.
- 25% of all victims of domestic violence are beaten when they are pregnant.

### Devastating Impact on Children

- Children who grow up in violent homes are five times more likely to become batterers or victims themselves than are children from nonviolent homes.
- Children in homes where domestic violence occurs are physically abused or seriously neglected at a rate 1500% higher than the national average in the general population.
- One study shows that 79% of violent delinquents reported witnessing extreme violence between their parents (compared to only 20% of nonviolent delinquents).

*Statistics compiled by the California Alliance Against Domestic Violence with the assistance of the San Francisco Family Violence Project.*

# Parents Anonymous:
## *Peace Begins at Home*

If peace and human rights are to become universal, they need to begin within the family. For many people, violence begins when they are children, and despite their best intentions, continues throughout their lives.

I grew up in a violent family. Abuse—physical, emotional and sexual—began when we were very young. When I was small, I was a helpless victim, but as I grew closer in size to my father I became a formidable enemy. I could protect myself with whatever was at hand: butcher knife, hot iron, etc. The violence took on new shapes; one had to "sleep with one eye open" and be ready to fight or run at all times.

In the outside world the peace movement was in full swing. Human rights and nonviolence appealed to me. Wouldn't it be wonderful if people didn't have to fight or be frightened or feel they had no right to exist? When we escaped from my father's grip permanently, I became nonviolent. I worked for peace, and peace became my way of life.

This peace slowly disappeared and the teachings of my family emerged after I became a parent. We learn to parent from our parents. I found myself yelling constantly at my daughters, then name calling, and eventually threatening. After that came the pushing, spanking, and pinching. All this time I was terrified. How many times I had been hit for telling my parents that I would never be like them; daily now, I became more like them.

As if my lack of parenting skills wasn't tough enough, I was a single parent, on welfare, living a life of absolute hopelessness.

The guilt I felt was immense, and the guiltier I felt the worse I behaved. The cycle of child abuse had come full circle against my will. One day all the pain, hurt, and anger of my life exploded. I held a stick, about to hit my daughter. All I could see was my father's hand holding that stick. At the last moment, I turned away, beating the stick against her desk until it shattered. I felt nothing but terror. What if I had hit her? What if next time I can't stop? What if they put me in jail? What kind of person am I? What about my vow of nonviolence?

With the help of an excellent therapist, I put my kids in foster care for a year and a half. I also joined a group that brings peace to families, Parents Anonymous. P.A. is a network of self-help groups for parents who are struggling in their relationships with their children. Each group is facilitated by a volunteer from the human service field and a parent member of the group. Members talk about whatever is causing stress in their lives:

kids, spouses, their own childhoods, school, agencies, etc.

Parents Anonymous groups are free, confidential, and safe. Some provide transportation and child care. Groups are nonjudgmental and open to anyone wishing to develop a better relationship with their children. Parents Anonymous is also starting groups for adults abused as children, who are not parents.

It's easy to say, "I could never hurt a

> **For many people, violence begins when they are children, and despite their best intentions, continues throughout their lives.**

child," but the reality is that each and every parent has slipped, at one time or another, and hurt our kids. Perhaps it was something we said that hurt; a spanking that went too far; maybe the day we didn't listen to something really important that the child had to say.

Nonviolence begins at home. If you wish to help bring peace to families by volunteering your time or joining a group, call Parents Anonymous at 1-800-882-1250.

*Excerpted from a special issue of* Peacework, Domestic Violence and Nonviolence, 1989.

# *Why Can't We Recognize That Child Sexual Abuse Is a Problem That Can Be Prevented?*

### by Cordelia Anderson, M.A / Illusion Theater

Since sexual abuse is seldom talked about or reported, local, state or federal statistics may not accurately illustrate the scope of the problem. Low statistics probably do not mean cases are not there, just that few people talk about them or believe they occur. People do not want to believe sexual abuse could happen to "their children" or in "their community" or by "their friend or relative," but it does. Over 80% of the sexual abuse of children is by someone the child knows, not a stranger.

As a first step toward prevention we must begin to realize that sexual abuse is common. Researchers are finding that approximately one in four girls, and one in ten boys is sexually abused by the age of 18.

However, accepting that sexual abuse is a problem is not enough, and we must be willing to take some type of action to prevent it. Treatment can help sex offenders to acknowledge their responsibility for the abuse, to accept the damage caused by their actions and to change their behavior. Treatment for both victims and offenders is critical to prevention because it begins to break cycles of victimization and abuse.

Children are vulnerable to adults and look to adults for protection. Most children who are victims of sexual abuse are tricked, not forced by the offender. The offender is likely to be someone the child knows and trusts and the child may not believe this person would hurt her/him. Primary prevention efforts such as direct education programs for chil-

dren inform them of their right to trust their feelings, to say "no" and to tell someone about any touch or behavior that confuses, scares or hurts them. Without information and support for disclosing, it is unlikely that a child would talk about a sexual assault.

> **People do not want to believe sexual abuse could happen to *their children* or in *their community* or by *their friend or relative,* but it does.**

The following are some statistics on the problem of child sexual abuse:

- 15-38% of all girls and 3-10% of all boys are victims of sexual abuse before the age of eighteen. (D. Finkelhor, 1982; Diane Russell, 1981; King County Rape Relief, 1979; J.T. Landis, 1956)

- Over 90% of the abusers are men. (National Center of Child Abuse and Neglect, 1981)

- 70-85% of children are sexually abused by someone they know. (King County Rape Relief, Washington; Minnesota Program for Victims of Sexual Assault, Saint Paul, Minnesota; Ann Burgess, 1975; Vincent De Francis, 1969)

- Most incidents (two-thirds) of child sexual abuse are not reported to any adult. (*Newsweek Magazine,* August 9, 1981)

- 33% of sex offenders had some form of sexual trauma as children (in comparison with the finding that only 1/10 of adult male non-offenders report similar victimization in their lives). (A.N. Groth, 1979, *Men Who Rape*). While this does *not* mean that all children who are abused grow up to be offenders, it does illustrate the importance of early intervention.

- In a study conducted by Tory Haden at the University of Minnesota, it was found that 77% of 110 children who are elective mutes were abused.

- 33% of teenage prostitutes were sexually abused in their home by a family member

and 65% were sexually assaulted by non-family members. *(The Enablers Study, The Link, 1979)*

- Child sexual abuse is not restricted to any one social or economic class. (Burgess, Finkelhor, Sandford)

- Pornography is a $7 billion-a-year business and child pornography is estimated to be over $500 million (Women Against Violence Against Women in Media). Note: The impact or role of pornography in the

awareness of sexual abuse is debatable. We believe that violent, exploitive and abusive images of women/children give the idea that sexual abuse is acceptable and grossly confuse healthy sexuality with the abusive use of sex. Therefore, while pornography may not be the sole cause of sexual abuse, it does perpetuate it.

*Excerpted from* Child Sexual Abuse Prevention: How to Take the First Steps *by Cordelia Anderson, M.A. Director of Child Abuse Prevention Program, Illusion Theater.*

# Interrupting the Violence of Rape

## by Janet Meyer / *Peacework*

The hotline rings. I pick it up, as I have probably a thousand times before, hoping that it's not a crisis this time. A voice on the other end of the line begins, "Is this where I call to get a speaker?" Whew. I explain that we do a lot of public education. What is she looking for? "Well, we have a number of young ladies at our church who will be going off to college this fall, and we want someone to come and talk to them about rape prevention. Can you do it?"

The request seems simple enough. Many people have similar questions for those of us who work at the Rape Crisis Center. "Is it best to fight back or not?" "What should women do to protect themselves?" "Do you recommend self-defense courses or carrying Mace?" They want answers; they want someone to help them feel they have some control over the risks they or their loved ones are facing.

The answers I have for them are not easy answers. I tell them that I will not speak to women about rape prevention. Women, by and large, do not rape. They do not want rape. They do not ask for rape. They do not deserve rape. They are, in short, not responsible for rape or its prevention. Men are. I can speak to men about rape prevention. I can speak to women about the choices involved in resisting rape, and some of the possible consequences of those choices. I believe it is everyone's responsibility to understand that there is a war going on against women and children in this country, and not enough of us are paying attention.

One in three women in this country will be raped during her lifetime. Of these women, nearly 70% will know her attacker, whether he be a lover, acquaintance, co-worker or relative. The truth is that people you know are raped by people they know. And the fact affects our choices when we try to either prevent or resist the violence of rape and other sexual assault.

When a woman looks into the eyes of the man raping her, more often than not she is

looking into the eyes of someone who, just a short time ago, she had reason to trust.

When women are raped, they struggle with questions about the appropriate response to violence both in the immediate moment and over the long term. They must consider their relationship with the attacker, their own values, and the particular circumstances of the rape. Only one in ten rape survivors reports her rape to the police.

When we face questions about the right response to rape on a societal level, we must face questions about who gets convicted in our racist and classist legal system and what violence they face in the prisons of this country. What do we believe is the proper punishment for rape? What is the role of the prison system in a feminist's view of a just society? How do we require men to take

responsibility for their violence, when the criminal justice system only perpetuates and teaches greater violence? What justice is there when only three in a thousand rapists ever serve a jail term for their crime?

I believe that we must not confuse nonviolence and passivity, or deny our righteous anger and just rage at this unwarranted violation of one-third of the women in our country. There is no justice in allowing ourselves to be victims. Nonviolence means calling ourselves and our opponents to be our highest selves. We must face the tough questions, challenge men to respect women's right to control their bodies, and interrupt violence of every kind.

*Excerpted from a special issue of* Peacework, Domestic Violence and Nonviolence, *1989.*

# Exposing Glamorized Degradation
## *The Beauty Myth* and *Dreamworlds*

### by Pamela Scott, MFCC / *Women's Press*

There are important contributing cultural factors that subliminally add up to extreme female identity distortion. Naomi Wolfe, author of *The Beauty Myth*, and Sut Jhally, author of *Dreamworlds—Desire, Sex, and Power in Rock Videos*, have quite eloquently pointed them out.

Jhally, a University of Massachusetts Professor, has produced a fifty minute video of assembled clips from MTV that demonstrate how stylish objectification of women can hide an indoctrination in masochism. The women portrayed in the popular music videos are shown as either inhumanly passive mannequins, anonymous interchangeable body parts, or insatiable nymphomaniacs ... all existing on the screen to be used, abused,

> **Violent sexual imagery took its energy from male anger and female guilt at women's access to power.**

and controlled by men (usually the male band members). Pervasive themes of sexual violence and degradation are displayed, and rape myths are consistently reinforced ("The bitch deserved it," "No" means "Yes," etc.).

During the final segment of Jhally's video, the vicious rape scene from the Jody Foster film "The Accused" is juxtaposed with the music videos, and they fit together all too well.

The "dreamworld" Jhally refers to is the land of male sexual fantasy, and he points out that MTV is meant to function as a giant commercial geared to exploit the emerging sexuality of the adolescent male population.

In *The Beauty Myth*, author Naomi Wolfe has compiled a comprehensive body of political, historical, and sociological evidence that women in America are at present caught in a "beauty backlash" that is being used by the male power structure of our society as a sophisticated political weapon against the women's movement. "The more legal and material hindrances women have broken through, the more strictly and heavi-

ly and cruelly images of female beauty have come to weigh upon us."

Wolfe also extensively discusses the rise of sexual violence. "Violent sexual imagery took its energy from male anger and female guilt at women's access to power." She cites a UCLA study of 14 to 18 year-olds where more than 50 percent of the boys and nearly half of the girls thought it was okay for a man to rape a woman if he was sexually aroused by her.

The reality is that males are conditioned to

behave abusively towards women, and women are conditioned to see themselves as objects worthy of abuse. As long as all of us continue to tolerate such negative media images, violence against women will be accepted as commonplace and normal.

Naomi Wolfe's book *The Beauty Myth* is published by William Morrow. Sut Jhally's *Dreamworld* is available at (413) 584-4269.

*Excerpted from* Women's Press, *October 1991.*

# A Potential Landmark for Female Human Rights

## by Gayle Kirshenbaum / *Ms.*

A crucial initiative for female human rights is working its way through the United Nations system; framed around the rights of women in prostitution, the initiative would broaden all women's rights: the first U.N. Convention Against Sexual Exploitation.

The "industrialization of prostitution" has greatly expanded the proprostitution constituency over the last two decades. Sex tourism and mail order bride agencies are proliferating; some countries identify sex tourism as an official, planned source of national income. The development of multinational conglomerates, specializing in "packages of sexual services," have transformed entire villages in Southeast Asia into prostitution-tourism centers for military and business men.

The convention proposal must be taken up by the U.N. Commission on Human Rights for it to be launched into the U.N. system. The elements as submitted are:

• It is a fundamental human right to be free

of sexual exploitation in all its forms.
• Sexual exploitation is a practice by which person(s) achieve sexual gratification or financial gain or advancement through the abuse of a person's sexuality by abrogating that person's human right to dignity, equality, autonomy, and physical and mental well-being.
• Sexual exploitation takes the forms of, but is not limited to, sexual harassment, rape, incest abuse, wife abuse, pornography, and prostitution. Exploitation of prostitution includes casual, brothel, military, pornographic prostitution, and sex tourism, mail order bride markets, and trafficking in women.
• As sexual exploitation violates human rights, in prostitution we must de-penalize the prostitute, penalize the customer and anyone who promotes prostitution for sexual gratification, financial gain, or advancement including pimps and procurers.

• Sexual exploitation violates the human rights of *anyone,* female or male, adult or child, Western or Third World persons, subjected to it. Therefore this definition rejects the use of any of these distinctions to determine exploitation as artificial and serving to legitimize prostitution.
• Sexual exploitation preys on women and children made vulnerable by poverty and underdevelopment, refugee and displaced persons, and states' economic policies which promote immigration for labor.
• The sexual exploitation of women through prostitution victimizes women both within and outside of prostitution.

Letters of support for this new U.N. Convention can be sent to: The Commission on Human Rights, c/o The Centre for Human Rights, U.N. Office, 8-14 Avenue de la Paix, 121 1, Geneva 1 0, Switzerland. For information or to make donations, write to: Coalition Against Trafficking in Women, Calder Square, P.O. Box 10077, State College, Pa. 16805.

*Excerpted from* Ms., *September/October 1991.*

## *Neo-Nazis Attack Women's Rights*

# Abortion Rights & Racist Terror

## by Michael Novick / *Turning the Tide*

The violence committed by Operation Rescue in its attempts to close down women's clinics, and the violations of women's right to choose, are part of a larger strategy by the right wing to turn back the gains of the women's movement and other progressive forces. Within the so-called "right-to-life" movement, racists and other fascist-right forces are seeking to build a mass base and to sharpen the tools of repression and intimidation with which to crush all dissent. For example, in Dallas, Texas recently, five Klansmen marched with Operation Rescue to shut down a clinic. They proclaimed that

the Ku Klux Klan opposes abortion.

This is not an isolated instance. Tom Metzger, a national racist organizer based in southern California, has long proclaimed that "abortion is white genocide." In Florida, John Burt, the leader of the anti-abortion forces, is the former state grand dragon of the KKK.

But the linkage of racism to the anti-abortion movement is not restricted to hardcore neo-Nazis. Pat Buchanan, former presidential adviser and a syndicated columnist, in August proclaimed that Islam would destroy Western civilization because white Europeans and Americans, under the domina-

tion of Planned Parenthood, were not having enough babies.

This racist organizing leads not only to continued attacks against women and women's clinics, but also to violence against gay men and lesbians, Jews, Moslems, Blacks, Hispanics, Native Americans and Asians.

*Call the Anti-Klan Hotline, (213)281-7928, or write People Against Racist Terror (PART).*

*Excerpted from* Turning the Tide.

# Abortion:
## *The Courts, The Church, The Conscience*

### *An Excerpt from a Sermon Preached by Dr. George F. Regas, Rector, July 16, 1989*

As a priest of the Church and as an ethicist, I want to stand up and be counted as pro-choice, keeping abortion legal, safe and available to all—rich and poor alike. But I seek a society in which abortion is less and less necessary. We live in a society where there is one abortion to every three live births, so count me among those who favor public policies that will reduce the number of abortions without coercing women. The only way that is possible is to create a different kind of nation.

- The society we seek must have as its primary agenda the rights of the born, the improved quality of life for those who come into this marvelous world, adequate care and protection from the first stirrings to the final groans. My grievance is severe with so many of the anti-abortion advocates who demand justice for the unborn, but who also advocate the dismantling of social programs that provide a decent life for children once they enter the world.

- Some politicians speak eloquently of their concern for the innocent fetus; but it is the cruelest irony how so many of these anti-abortionists have no interest in the things that make that newborn child healthy and beautiful. It's brutal to force a poor mother to have a child and then deny her healthy prenatal care. For many poor people in America life begins at conception and ends at birth. If we are to reduce abortions, we must reaffirm by work and action the rights of the born.

- The society we seek provides good, affordable child-care so a woman can have children and still work, a society where her wages are just and she is able to climb out of the "feminization of poverty," a society where men accept an equal responsibility for the care and nurture of children.

- The society we seek doesn't flaunt and exploit sex at every turn. Vast numbers of adults today participate in the devaluing of human sexuality by separating sex from love and commitment. Can we embrace sex in all its mystery and loveliness as

*Dr. George F. Regas, Rector of All Saints Episcopal Church, Pasadena, California.*

sacramental? Yes, passionate, ecstatic life but a sexual love where a whole life is shared with the readiness to exercise self discipline and to bear the children of that love.

- The society we seek says life is sacred everywhere, for if it is cheap anywhere, it is cheap everywhere. The right to life pertains to the unborn, but it is also extended to prisoners on death row, the poor and elderly in urban ghettos, and all the children of this planet.

President Nixon was extremely vocal in his support of the anti-abortion movement in the spring of 1971—calling for the sanctity of life and denying legal abortion to women. He did that at the very time he was ordering the most ferocious carnage of the Vietnam War.

Only as we see every human being across this planet as a sacred person to be cherished—only then will we see emerging a society where abortion is less and less a necessary option.

*All Saints Church is dedicated to ministries that feed and shelter the homeless, care for refugees, provide health care to poor children, educate the community about the ravages of drug abuse, reach out to those suffering with AIDS and their caregivers, develop affordable hous-*

*ing, build bridges of understanding with churches in northwest Pasadena and south central Los Angeles. In cooperation with Pastor Joe Hardwick of the Praises of Zion Church in Watts, All Saints is organizing exchange visitations. All Saints has also collected food, clothing and money in order to assist those who suffered as a result of the riots in Los Angeles.*

WOULD HE BE MORE CAREFUL ...

IF IT COULD HAPPEN TO HIM?

*Courtesy of Planned Parenthood*

# PROTECT THE RIGHTS OF THE UNBORN

**PROTECT** their right to clean air and water, to live in a nontoxic environment and to have the use of resources such as minerals, forests, water, air and topsoil.

**PROTECT** their right to see an old growth forest, to experience the diversity of life and to live an uncrowded, meaningful life.

Protect their right to continued life on this planet. Protect their right to a future.

HOW? By using less, wasting less, consuming less and conserving more. A child born in an industrial nation will have 30-100 times the environmental impact of a Third World child.

**PRACTICE** birth control. If birth control

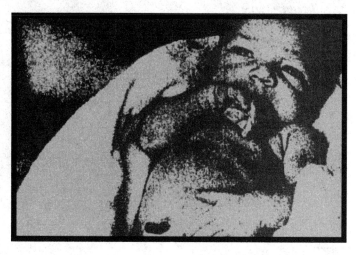

fails, use safe, early term abortion. Overpopulation of humans is depleting Earth's resources and causing mass extinctions of other species. Soon there will be nothing left...

*Reprinted from Population Pressure.*

## *Profile:* Planned Parenthood

### by Sandy Baer / *Earth Journal*

Our children are at risk, and Planned Parenthood is underway with a 10-year initiative to reduce adolescent child-bearing in the United States. Far too many American children are living a deprived childhood that may well prevent them from experiencing a healthy, productive adolescence and adulthood.

Launched in 1989, Planned Parenthood's *First Things First* initiative aims to reduce the number of births to teens 50% by the year 2000. Nearly 500,000 children are born to teens every year. *First Things First* is being joined by such diverse organizations as the American Psychiatric Association, the Girls Clubs of America, the YWCA and Catholics for a Free Choice.

Nationally, thirteen million American children under 18 (five million of whom are under six) live in families whose incomes are below the federal poverty level. Another three million children under six live in families with incomes just above the poverty line.

Almost 80% of the one million teenagers who become pregnant every year do so unintentionally. Close to half of them give birth each year. Furthermore, the US continues to have the highest teenage pregnancy rate of all developed countries—one in ten

teenagers will become pregnant.

With a patient population averaging 18 to 25 years of age, demand for reproductive health care services is high at Planned Parenthood's clinics. The majority of these patients are seeking contraceptive services. More than 1,723,000 women received these services nationally in 1989. Of these, 31% were teen women aged 15 to 19 years.

Planned Parenthood reports that contraception patients prefer the birth control pill (75.6%). Surprisingly, use of intrauterine devices (IUDs) remained constant in 1989, reversing a trend of the last nine years. IUD use has been declining because of several factors: its cost, an extensive list of potential side effects, and the fact that there are only two kinds on the market. Diaphragm use continued to decline in 1989 as well. On the other hand, the percentage of patients choosing vaginal chemical contraceptives and/or condoms rose more than one-half a percentage point. It seems likely that the publicity and patient education surrounding the added value of the condom as a protection against HIV infection has led more patients to choose this method.

The outlook for the development of new birth control methods in the United States

remains bleak. The development and approval processes for new drugs in the US are so costly and cumbersome that pharmaceutical firms are unwilling to commit resources to contraceptive development. The fear of litigation also has a chilling effect on the pharmaceutical research and development. And the US government has steadily reduced federal funding for contraceptive research: it was less than $9 million in 1989, which is about what it takes to support the US Defense for 15 minutes!

After many years of review, the Food and Drug Administration (FDA) recently approved marketing and distribution of Norplant, the long-acting (five-year) contraceptive, consisting of tiny hormone-releasing rods implanted under the skin of the upper arm. Similar contraceptives have been available in Europe, Canada, and parts of Asia for at least ten years.

Children born to teenage parents are more likely to become teen parents themselves, more likely to be welfare recipients, and more likely to earn lower wages if employed.

*Excerpted from* Earth Journal, *February 1991.*

# Poverty Is a Women's Issue

### by Marita O'Neill / *Maine Progressive*

There is a war going on in Maine and in the nation. Its name is poverty and its worst casualties in the 1980s were women and children. As we look to the 1990s, it is time to acknowledge this battle as a women's issue.

Increasingly, health care has become inaccessible to our nation's poorest citizens, most of them women and children.

Today, 80 percent of the poor people in the United States are women and children. More than half of the children in female headed households, one out of every five children, are poor. Poverty is a women's issue and should be the single most pressing issue on the agenda of the women's movement in the 1990s.

Women have a responsibility to themselves and their children to emphasize that poverty, like rape, is not a "choice" but an act of violence. There are many racist stereotypes that portray African-American men and women as choosing welfare over work. This myth hides the fact that African-Americans, women especially, have been excluded from mainstream jobs in this country and forced into the low-paying service sector or into "underground" work that is not only illegal but often life threatening. Often women find themselves unable to maintain their families on a minimum wage with no health or child care benefits. They choose AFDC for one simple reason: it is their only survival option. It is not a way out of poverty.

In 1988 the total number of AFDC recipients was about eight million. Of that number, seven million were children. In 1960, the average monthly AFDC payment per family was $393. In 1986 it dropped to $354. It would be hard to imagine anyone "choosing" to raise a family in the environment of violence such poverty breeds.

We must also start making the connections between poverty and military spending. President Reagan spent $1.5 trillion on military programs between 1981 and 1986, while diseases of malnutrition that are most commonly found in some of the worst famine areas of Africa were cropping up in America's ghettoes.

As we demand "choice" in the 90s, we should remember that many women do not have some of the most basic choices. Theirs is a life of economic terrorism. When we demand choice we should recognize that women must have control of their own lives and of the futures of their children. For many women, a life of poverty denies them those rights, denies them the most basic "choice"— to live without fearing for their survival.

*Excerpted from the* Maine Progressive, *February 1991.*

# People In Progress (PIP)
## *More than Shelter for the Homeless*

In a statewide survey of homeless people conducted in 1989 by the Minnesota Coalition for the Homeless, 65% of homeless people in emergency shelters and transitional housing were women and children. In its eighth year of operation, **People in Progress (PIP),** run by the St. Paul YWCA, is the largest emergency shelter/transitional housing program in the state and noted for a comprehensive program of support services in addition to housing. *76% of the YWCA's approximately $2 million budget is related to these services.*

Clients entering the shelter receive food, clothing, chemical dependency and mental health assessment referrals, health screening for children, a clean furnished private room for each woman with additional beds for her children, *and 24 hour security.* Other supportive services include case management, basic skills and life stabilization classes, child care, financial stabilization, referrals to employment/training programs, literacy classes, and opportunities to enroll in regular health and fitness programs of the YWCA.

### Transitional Housing

In 1989, 192 women and children elected to utilize the Y's case management system and entered the transitional housing program for up to six months in the YWCA building itself. Sixty four women and children moved to off site transitional housing in an 18 unit apartment complex, where they can live up to 2 years with help from the YWCA to achieve stability in their lives. 46 women and children received rent subsidies to rent their own apartments.

Women entering transitional housing are required to set goals, make monthly reports, and take responsibility for progress towards self-sufficiency, full time employment and permanent housing. During the day mothers are at jobs, or job training or in school while children are in school or day care. All residents must attend monthly residents' meetings, maintain the grounds and public space. Graduates of the program are also expected to attend residents' meetings and to mentor a mother in the emergency housing program, in partial payment for the help they received. YWCA staff act as family in providing on going help with the problems of daily living. ("We are their Mom").

When a family is ready to move out to their own apartment, the Y calls a group in suburban Church of the Way for help. The volunteers get to know the family, provide such things as transportation for the move, help with painting, furnishings, and at times money for start up costs.

### After The Transition, What?

Outcomes are measured in terms of housing status and employment status of participants.

"Half of the people who enter PIP, living as they are, crisis by crisis, are completely unmotivated." says Pamela McCrea, the director. "Thirty days of emergency shelter and stabilization is not enough time to get that motivation, but after a month the funding stops." In the transitional housing program, the YWCA has two years before the participant must go out on her own. During that time federal funding guidelines require her to be full time in school, job training or employed. She must also learn parenting and homemaking skills. If she is lucky enough to find an affordable apartment (subsidized or Section 8) in the city, she can continue to use the YWCA support network. Unfortunately, most of the available subsidized apartments are rural or in the suburbs, with no available transportation to the city where the jobs, schools and support services are. Without a community, it is very easy to drop back into the patterns of crisis living and more homelessness.

*Excerpted from* Neighborhood Caretaker, *1990.*

# A Last Resort

## *Adoption should be a solution that suits children, not childless couples*

### by Marsha Riben / *The Dark Side of Adoption*

We must stop glorifying adoption and recognize it for what it is: a second-best solution for all. Adoption is currently being promoted as the solution for infertility and for unplanned pregnancy. Just as divorce should not be offered as a cure-all for every marital problem, new solutions need to be sought for infertile couples and pregnant women and couples who don't have the means to raise a child. Because every adoption begins with a tragedy, it should, like divorce, be a last resort to be used only after attempts to keep the family together have failed.

Here are some reforms:

**Adoption** needs to return to its original goal of serving the needs of the children. We need to find homes for children who need homes, not to find babies for the childless. There are now 36,000 children in this country—in foster homes or institutions—who are free for adoption. Legislation is needed to encourage and subsidize the adoption of "special needs" children, particularly in terms of medical expenses and insurance coverage for children with preexisting medical conditions.

Because it involves the welfare of innocent children, adoption requires many safeguards. All adoptions therefore need to be handled through reputable and licensed state and religious agencies.

The current practice of private, independent adoption often employs the use of gimmicks such as newspaper advertising that lure women to give up their babies by offering financial remuneration under the guise of payment for services. Adoption laws, which now vary greatly from state to state, need to be standardized and regulated.

While maintaining high standards, licensed agencies can and should "borrow" practices, such as openness between adoptive and birth parents, that currently make private adoptions more appealing. Licensed agencies would arrange the placement only after both the adopting and surrendering parents had received family counseling.

**Infertility** needs to be recognized and dealt with as a medical problem similar to a disability, not a social problem. We need more preventive programs such as cleaning up the environment and finding cures for the newer and more resilient strains of venereal diseases that are sometimes responsible for the rising infertility rates.

Psychological counseling and self-help groups for the infertile need to view the loss of fertility as a loss that needs to be addressed and grieved, perhaps forever.

**Prevention** of many "unplanned" pregnancies could be accomplished through sex education programs and by the availability of birth control. Also, pressuring teenage mothers to put their babies up for adoption may be wrong-headed. Teenagers can and do make excellent parents if they are given the proper support. In less-industrialized nations, women generally bear children in their teens and early twenties when they are most fertile and healthy, and they enjoy strong family and community support systems.

**Single parents** need to be recognized as capable parents regardless of age, education, race, or economics. Government programs intended to offer temporary aid to those in need should be expanded, not ended. Fifty-five percent of American children have working mothers, yet America is the only advanced industrialized nation with no national maternity leave.

Single mothers who indicate a need to surrender their children to adoption should be required to see an independent family counselor who considers single mothers and their children as legitimate families and who would help clients to explore all their options.

No final plans should be made prior to the birth and for at least 30, and preferably 90, days afterwards.

When everyone involved in adoption puts the needs of the children foremost, and when all those who care about children join hands to work together toward the mutual goal of humanizing adoption, the adoption triangle can be softened into a circle of love, respect, and mutual understanding.

*Excerpted from the book* The Dark Side of Adoption *by Marsha Riben. Copyright ©1988 by Marsha Riben. Available for $12.95 from 45-06 Hunters Glen Dr., Plainsboro, NJ 08536.*

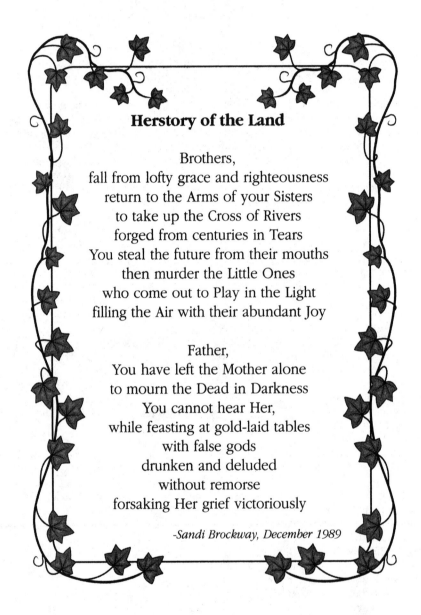

### Herstory of the Land

Brothers,
fall from lofty grace and righteousness
return to the Arms of your Sisters
to take up the Cross of Rivers
forged from centuries in Tears
You steal the future from their mouths
then murder the Little Ones
who come out to Play in the Light
filling the Air with their abundant Joy

Father,
You have left the Mother alone
to mourn the Dead in Darkness
You cannot hear Her,
while feasting at gold-laid tables
with false gods
drunken and deluded
without remorse
forsaking Her grief victoriously

*-Sandi Brockway, December 1989*

# Chapter 12

# *Politics*

*The decayed condition of American democracy is difficult to grasp, not because the facts are secret, but because the facts are visible everywhere. Symptoms of distress are accumulating freely in the political system and citizens are demoralized by the lack of coherent remedies.*

*Given the recurring, disturbing facts, a climate of stagnant doubt has enveloped contemporary politics, a generalized sense of disappointment that is too diffuse and intangible to be easily confronted.*

*The things that Americans were taught and still wish to believe about self-government—the articles of civic faith we loosely call democracy—no longer seem to fit the present reality.*

—William Greider
from *Who Will Tell the People, The Betrayal of American Democracy,* ©1992

BIG Pictures © 1991 by Dan Dunivant

*Reprinted from* Earth Journal, *July 1991*

149

# A Social Disease of Pandemic Proportions

### by Richard Gaines / *Miami New Times*

In retrospect, the greater horror and tragedy resided in the national somnolence.

If we knew—at some level—about the failure of our political system, which allowed determinant power and influence to be concentrated in the hands of an anonymous lobby, we stoically bore that knowledge as if it were an inevitable condition of life in the American democracy.

If we knew of the moral failure of our economic system, which concentrated unaccountable wealth in the hands of a few and doomed countless millions to unconscionable destitution, we stoically bore that knowledge as if it were an unavoidable inefficiency in a capitalism that had proved its mettle in the century's great ideological showdown.

If we knew that Martin Luther King's dream of racial harmony proved to be a mirage, we came to accept the racial fissures as an unfortunate law of imperfect life.

This the American public did with increasing determination. We turned off to the festering social failures that seemed as irradicable as AIDS. We tuned in to *The Cosby Show,* a lying exemplar of black middle-class assimilation (which, ironically and appropriately, ended its own eight-year run on the worst night of the riots in South Central L.A.). And we dropped out of a democratic politics grown pathetically irrelevant. We had become a nation adrift, inured to mediocrity, understandably convinced that our fate was fixed and there was damn little we could do about it.

What we wanted and what we got was distraction. *Lifestyles of the Rich and Famous, E.T., Rescue 911, Unsolved Mysteries* individual, isolated sagas of triumph and tragedy, served our need. The appetite for these distractions was greater, because the realities from which we were seeking refuge were so troubling and seemingly immutable.

The educator John Silber, president of Boston University, diagnosed the national

---

**For its very survival's sake, America must re-examine old presuppositions and release itself from many thing that for centuries have been held sacred. For the evils of racism, poverty and militarism to die, a new set of values must be born. Our economy must become more person-centered than property and profit centered. Our government must depend more on its moral power than its military power.**

*-- Martin Luther King*

---

distemper in his prophetic 1989 book *Straight Shooting.* "Our society is in trouble and we all know it." he wrote. "We know that something is terribly wrong—the way we might know in our own bodies that we are seriously ill. When we have an internal intimation of serious illness, it is hard even to talk about the way we feel. We sense that talking about it might make it worse."

Now, thanks to Rodney King, four cops twelve jurors, and countless anonymous thieves, arsonists, and murderers, we have been given a wake-up call.

The sinful maldistribution of wealth, power, and opportunity, the inequities between white and nonwhite, the failures of the political system have penetrated the American consciousness.

Ills that previously have been treated in isolation and with precarious results, from Boston to Brooklyn to Miami, now, as a result of these events—from the emotionless reading of the jury verdict to the apocalyptic scenes televised around the globe—will demand and possibly receive the nation's full attention.

As if, thanks to Rodney King etal., the fundamental failures of the nation, ignored, overlooked, and rationalized since the other King ignited moral outrage a generation ago, had not become the only *real* political issues before the American people, now suddenly awakened from a restless sleep.

Now. There's plenty to talk about, argue about, debate, and vote on. Plenty to do.

*Writer Richard Gaines lives in Miami.*

*Excerpted from* Miami New Times *with permission from AlterNet.*

---

# Bringing Politics Home

## *Big government creates more problems than it solves*

### by Sam Smith / *The Progressive Review*

A while back, *USA Today*—America's second largest circulation newspaper held a dinner to honor its retiring publisher. It boasted that the dinner would be attended by some of the nation's "best and brightest." Prominently mentioned on the guest list were Vice President Dan Quayle, Lee Atwater, and South Dakota Senator Larry Pressler. America is in trouble.

In the book *Systemantics,* John Gall argues that "systems tend to oppose their proper functions." The ideal proper function of the American system is life, liberty, and the

pursuit of happiness. Yet as it gropes its way into the 21st century, the system in reality increasingly endangers human life, denies personal liberty, and represses individual happiness.

Unfortunately, complex systems that are failing have little capacity to save themselves, in part because the solutions come from the same source as the problem.

Complex systems usually try to save themselves by doing the same thing they have been doing badly all along—only harder. This is because the salvation of the system is

considered far more important than the solution of any problems that might be causing the system to fail. Solutions that bring into question the effectiveness of the system itself are not tolerated.

We have seen some classic examples of this phenomenon in recent times. The Vietnam War quickly became a battle to justify the decision to enter it. In the Alaskan oil spill, we found ourselves relying upon the world's most powerful government and the world's largest corporation to repair the damage caused by *their* policies.

The question we should be asking is not what the system should be doing but whether the existing system can do anything except to make matters worse.

Ironically, the crisis we now face results in no small part from our willingness to turn over individual and community responsibilities to the very system that we now ask to save us.

Functions formerly performed by family, community, and church have now been assumed by government and, to an increasing but unacknowledged degree, by the private corporation. Conservative rhetoric and liberal defensiveness keep our focus on the threats of centralization coming from government, but in many ordinary aspects of human life, corporate centralization is just as intrusive. WalMart stores, for instance, try to discourage employees from fraternizing outside the job.

Even when the question is one of state control, conservatives deserve far more responsibility for the rampant centralization in our society than they get. Both liberals and conservatives have consistently favored state centralization, the difference being that conservatives have tended to want the government to assume controlling functions while liberals and progressives want government to take over caring functions. Thus under conservatives we get more missiles and prisons, while under liberals we get more day-care centers and nursing homes.

To break this cycle, we must change not only our political policies but also the very way we regard politics. Until we bring politics home—devolving its power, abdicating its expertise, and undermining its arrogance—we will remain trapped in a temple to a false god.

*Excerpted from* The Progressive Review, *May 1989.*

## The System is Much Worse Today Than 10 Years Ago

Over the past decade, there has been a remarkable change in the distribution of funds between congressional incumbents and challengers, particularly in the House of Representatives. For practical purposes, House challengers as a group have been *defunded* during this period.

In 1980, House challengers raised $36 million. Ten years later, they raised $37 million. No growth.

House incumbents, meanwhile, went from raising $72 million in 1980 to $181 million in 1990, a 150 percent increase.

The role of PACs in bringing about this extraordinary advantage for incumbents is instructive.

In overall giving, PACs distributed $110 million more in 1990 than in 1980—and $109 million of the $110 million went to incumbents.

In 1990 challengers actually raised **less** from PACs than they did in 1980: $7 million in 1990 versus $7.3 million in 1980. Incumbents, meanwhile, jumped from $25 million to $87 million in PAC money during the same period.

*Excerpted from* Common Cause, *June/August 1991.*

- **Congressional staff has grown from 2,000 to 12,000 since 1947**

- **Number of congressional committees has grown from 38 in 1947 to 301 today**

- **Average length of bills has gone from four pages to 20 pages in the last 20 years**

- **Only 3% of bills introduced are ever enacted; the Senate spends 25% of its time calling the roll**

*Source: Washington Post Weekly, 11/18-24/91*

# Why Americans Hate to Vote

### by Brian Ahlberg / *MPIRG Statewatch*

The United States stands at the bottom of a list of industrialized democracies when it comes to the percentage of people who vote. Just barely a majority (50.1 percent) of eligible voters cast a ballot for president in 1988. Nationwide turnout for the 1990 election was a dismal 36 percent.

Why do so few Americans vote?

First, it's important to note that voting in the United States is skewed according to class and race. In the 1980 general election, for example, an estimated 70 percent of Americans with incomes over $25,000 a year voted, while only 25 percent of those with incomes below $10,000 a year did.

America is also unique in requiring personal, periodic voter registration. Some nations register citizens automatically through government records. Great Britain and Canada pay public servants to register voters door-to-door.

In addition, most states in the United States don't allow registration by postcard, and only a handful of states allow election-day registration. Voter registration is not conducted—in fact is often not allowed—at offices of social service agencies that serve low– and moderate-income citizens.

Finally, American elections are held on a working Tuesday, instead of on a weekend or a declared holiday as in Western Europe.

But Joshua Cohen, professor of political science and philosophy at MIT, and Joel

IT'S BEAUTIFUL. YOU LOOK HIP, HAPPENING - IT'S A LOOK THE VOTERS'LL REALLY RESPOND TO...

DEMOCRATIC LEADERSHIP COUNCIL

©1991 Terry Laben

Rogers, professor of law at University of Miami, argue that low voter participation in the United States has more to do with the substance of American politics than with its mechanical procedures. In a report called "Rules of the Game," they point out that when public policy routinely ignores the

concerns of the poorest parts of the population, those people have little incentive to enter the political system.

America's two-party system further diminishes political involvement, Cohen and Rogers say. The two parties' position on most issues are very close together—a

shrewd strategy for maximizing votes when there are only two parties, but a situation that limits the range of political debate and diminishes the range of choices voters have.

*Excerpted and updated from* MPIRG Statewatch (*Jan./Feb. 1987*).

# *Why Not Here?*
# Prospects for Green Politics in America

### by Kirkpatrick Sale / *Greenpeace Magazine*

There are two large answers to "Why not here," neither of which gives much encouragement to those who, like me, have been trying to make Green politics happen in this country.

The first is more or less technical, a combination of some hard and uncomfortable facts. There is no proportional representation in America, on any level, and minority parties do not get into office or have access to the kind of funding provided by European electoral systems. This makes the task for third parties almost insuperable, one made all the worse by the fact that all such efforts naturally meet the considerable resistance of the two established parties, whose operatives are in charge of the petition, authorization, registration and voting processes. National organizing is made difficult by the vastness of this country and the timid and homogenous national media.

The second is more or less political, or perhaps philosophical. The people attracted to the American Green banner over the last five years did not start from and have not achieved (and may not even want) a coherent political philosophy behind which to organize. The movement has instead taken as its model the amalgam of politics by which the German Greens began, trying to join disparate forces with disparate political interests into a coalition. This has left the Green movement as a loose connection of local organizations, and these no more than gathering places for anyone with vaguely left-liberal politics and a concern for the environment.

That said, I still believe there is a potential role for Green politics in America. I think it is possible to imagine that, as time goes on and the environmental crises multiply, there will arise a need for a specifically ecological politics, grounded in such principles as bioregionalism and biocentrism. The Greens may see themselves as the public, the active, the electoral arm of that politics: the people debating the state fish and game departments, lobbying the legislative committees, pressuring town zoning and planning boards, putting up school board and water district candidates, running for town coun-

cils. Not by fiat but simply by experience will arise the two essential ingredients of such a politics: first, that it is local (statewide at most), ensuring that as many decisions as possible are made at the local, even neighborhood, level; second, that it understands environmental issues, and especially the protection and preservation of natural systems, as its primary political agenda.

While I say it is "possible to imagine such a Green role," I am not convinced by any means that it is a certainty. It will require a sense of modesty that many nationally minded young activists do not possess; an acceptance of small victories that the instant-gratification generation finds difficult; a single-minded focus on ecological questions that the loose umbrella coalitions have not been capable of. And it will take a much more earnest and apocalyptic understanding of the perils we face, of the cultural forces that cause them and the wrenching difficulties of escaping them than I have found in Green circles I have seen in the last decade. Still, I do not know any other way to go.

*Kirkpatrick Sale is author of* Human Scale, Dwellers in the Land, *and most recently,* The Conquest of Paradise, *a book that explores the legacy of Christopher Columbus.*

*Excerpted from* Greenpeace Magazine, *July/August 1991.*

## What GREEN Means

The new Committees of Correspondence stand in the tradition of earlier American democratic, non-violent, and populist movements, and have a kinship to the Green Parties in other countries and to such movements as Polish Solidarity and the base communities of Latin America.

We seek to bring people together from the many thousands of neighborhood and community groups, religious congregations, women's groups, labor unions, farmers' alliances, and environmental and peace groups that have been growing since the early civil rights movement inspired a new broad, popular, and locally based citizen's movement to fulfill the democratic promise of this country.

Common goals are emerging from this grassroots ferment—to rebuild communities and restore a shared sense of democratic values, to democratize political and economic power and establish just distributions of wealth and income and opportunity, to end exploitation of the Third World, to reharmonize our economy and technology with nature and create a future for our children.

*From "Our Roots and Heritage" brochure, Green Committee of Correspondence Clearinghouse.*

# *How to Get Global Issues on the Political Agenda*

### by Fritjof Capra / *Shared Vision*

Strategies for global survival are not part of the agenda of today's political leaders, nor are they the concern of the majority of the world's business leaders, scientists or religious leaders. They are, however, a concern for most people and especially for most women. So, there is a tremendous gap between the so-called leaders of the world and the people they are supposed to lead.

It is up to us to introduce these issues into

the political dialogue. Let me propose six ideas to form the context of our work. The Earth is our common context—regardless of our differing cultural backgrounds—and this realization is the source of our ethical actions.

- There is a distinction between spirituality and religion. The spiritual dimension is common to all humanity. It is the experience of being connected to the cosmos as a whole, of a sense of belonging that gives meaning to life.

- The major problems of our time are systemic; they cannot be understood in isolation. They need a systemic, or holistic, approach to be solved.
- The immediate goal of our strategies is global survival. The long-term goal is building a sustainable future. As the Worldwatch Institute defined it in the *State of the World 1988*, "A sustainable society is one that satisfies its needs without diminishing the prospects of future generations."
- Global survival and creating a sustainable future require a profound change of values. A central aspect of this change is a shift from domination to partnership— partnership between men and women, between nations, and between human beings and nature.
- The goals of global survival and of creating a sustainable future are the basis for real security. The notion of "national security" is outdated; there can only be global security. Ultimately, sustainability equals security.

I have tentatively identified six areas in which challenges could be formulated. The examples given are general; the actual challenges would need to be much more specific:

- *Energy:* Design sustainable energy scenarios, shifting from fossil fuels to improved efficiency and renewable sources of energy.

- *Arms race:* Shift resources from military expenditures to create a secure sustainable future.
- *Population and development:* Recognize the link, and then design strategies for population stabilization and sustainable development.
- *Forestry and food:* Preserve tropical rainforests; reforest; monitor soil losses; establish "food first" policies; reduce pesticide use.
- *Industrial production:* Ban CFCs to protect the ozone layer; cut industrial waste to one-third.
- *Human rights:* Define international standards—including the right to basic needs—and link these rights to economic and resource security.

*Dr. Capra founded The Elmwood Institute dedicated to the convergence of politics, ecology and spirituality. Born in Austria, he received his PhD. from the University of Vienna and has done research in high-energy physics at several European and American universities. He has written and lectured extensively on the philosophical implications of modern science. He is the author of* The Turning Point: Science, Society and the Rising Culture *and the bestselling* The Tao of Physics, *which has been translated into a dozen languages. He now lives in Berkeley, California.*

*Excerpted from* Shared Vision, *Spring 1988.*

# Reaching the Decision Makers

### by Suzanne Iudicello / *The Volunteer Monitor*

The ultimate goal of a legislative campaign is to reach the decision makers—the legislators. How does a group do this?

The Center for Marine Conservation followed the model outlined below in our successful campaign for the introduction and passage of legislation prohibiting plastic dumping in the ocean (the Marine Plastic Pollution Control Act).

#### 1. *Document the issue*
Learn the science; get all the facts and statistics. Make sure you know exactly what you're talking about.

#### 2. *Publicize your cause*
Build support for your cause through a public information campaign. Publish brochures and posters.

Linking your facts and information to issues of public concern is crucial to winning support and getting media coverage.

#### 3. *Build a constituency*
Get your message to other organizations and enlist their support. Attend their meetings and make presentations; write articles for their newsletters.

#### 4. *Reach the decision makers*
At this point, if you've been successful, you are already reaching the decision makers indirectly. You have built such a groundswell that the legislators have heard about your issue from their constituents and through the media.

You can also reach the decision makers directly. Organize a letter-writing campaign. Call or visit legislators to talk about the problem. if you don't mention a specific bill, but just provide educational information, you are not lobbying.

The amount of influence you will have depends on your credibility. If your facts are solid, and you have built a reputation for trustworthiness in prior contacts with legislators, you may be asked to testify at legislative hearings.

*Suzanne Iudicello is program counsel for the Center for Marine Conservation.*

*Excerpted from* The Volunteer Monitor, *Spring 1992.*

## *Beyond* NIMBY
### <u>N</u>ot <u>I</u>n <u>M</u>y <u>B</u>ack<u>Y</u>ard

What does it take to activate people to protect the environment? Very often the catalyst is a direct threat to the health and well-being of their own personal environments. Nothing mobilizes someone faster than a contaminated drinking water supply, a hazardous–waste leak, a nuclear reactor accident, or a potential shopping mall in his or her own backyard.

The issue then becomes personalized, and primal survival energies surface. Some of the most well–oiled and financed corporate machines have regretted tangling with grassroots activists operating from a place of instinct and conviction. Parents protecting their young, people defending their families and neighbors, are powerful and formidable foes.

So powerful, in fact, that reaction to a community threat has been immortalized by the acronym "NIMBY"—or "Not In My BackYard."

There is an emerging distinction, though, between a short–term and locally focused NIMBY attitude, and a perception of environmental responsibility that considers the *entire world as everyone's backyard*. Current global environmental threats demand we foster a grassroots fighting spirit towards dangers that may not yet be so apparent in our own communities. Once we begin to view all places as part of our worldwide backyard, and see that air, water and land pollution know no boundaries, it is much easier to feel a stake in the outcome, take a stand, and join with others to protect our common world.

"Protecting Everyone's BackYard" (PEBY) is the new rallying cry of the globally alert. That means taking it to the streets not only for issues close to home, but for environmental and social injustice problems affecting all of us in the global family.

For instance, PEBYers are just as uncomfortable shipping hazardous waste to another state as disposing of it in the local landfill. Instead, they examine the causes of problems (such as increased waste generation creating a need for more waste disposal facilities) and seek preventive maintenance measures (such as encouraging waste reduction).

*Excerpted from* One Person's Impact, *January/February 1992.*

# You Can Fight

## CITY HALL

*Local politics stirs people's interest, but bureaucratic barriers discourage participation*

**by David Morris / Utne Reader**

While a great number of Americans purport to hate politics and don't want any part of it, a good many of them still get riled up about local issues and become fervently involved in town, municipal, and county government.

The reason is that local politics, unlike national politics, can truly be empowering for everyday citizens. The hostility many Americans harbor toward the abstract process of politics fades as decision making and public debate move closer to home. A recent study from the Kettering Foundation, *Citizens and Politics: A View from Main Street*, says, "We have found that people's perception of having a diminished voice in national politics does not hold as true on the local level."

City governments are the closest and most responsive to the people. The scale of the jurisdiction invites holistic thinking. It's possible to see—and do something about—the connections among, say, traffic patterns, development plans, zoning laws, and public transportation. Cities also have the right to fashion rules that govern much of their residents' commercial and personal conduct.

Local politics means many things. In the late 1950s, for example, an outside investor purchased Toledo's beloved Mud Hens, a Class AAA minor league team, and moved them away. The aroused citizenry persuaded the Lucas County supervisors to guarantee financing to purchase another baseball team

and move them to Toledo. The Mud Hens aren't moving anywhere anymore. No longer can private entrepreneurs trifle with the fans' deep loyalties and emotions. Rooting for the home team in Toledo meant more than buying tickets. It meant getting involved in local politics.

In Los Angeles, local politics has meant taking on Detroit's automakers and, quite possibly, redesigning America's urban transportation system from the ground up. In January, 1989, the city council unveiled its electric car initiative, an automotive design competition to award a contract to deliver 10,000 electric vehicles over five years. For years, electric cars had been hailed as a transportation form of the future all over the world. But no one did anything significant on a national or state level to bring this grand idea closer to reality until Los Angeles' city government stepped in to solve a local problem.

Los Angeles, with four times Hawaii's population of 1.1 million, has 100 times the number of people lacking health insurance. Large cities can learn from small states about the possibilities of exercising authority. Hawaii's 17-year-old health insurance program insures 98 percent of the population compared to the fewer than 80 percent who are insured nationally. The cost of living in Hawaii is 30 percent above the national average, but its health insurance premiums are well below the national average.

When a single city lacks the power to change the rules, an alliance of cities may be the answer. St. Paul, like many cities, worried that the amount of plastic in the garbage stream was steadily increasing, but that little recycling was occurring. The city enacted an ordinance prohibiting the sale of plastic packaging unless the manufacturers created a market for the recycled material. Concerned that if it acted alone the manufacturers would simply remove their products from the city's stores, St. Paul enlisted the support of eight nearby cities, including Minneapolis, which implemented similar laws.

The exercise of power by people in local communities worries some. Communities, the argument goes, are by nature resistant to change. To give communities power, therefore, is to erect roadblocks to progress.

Yet we are learning that one person's roadblock may be another person's shortcut. Consider the much maligned not-in-my-backyard movement. Tufts University political scientist Kent Portney told the *New York Times* that because of it, "We're losing facil-

ities faster than they're being replaced, whether it's prisons, power plants, or hazardous waste treatment facilities." Former Environmental Protection Agency chief William D. Ruckelshaus agrees. "There is no society on Earth that has empowered the citizen the way we have," he says, but adds that in doing so, "We are disadvantaging ourselves versus the other developed countries in the world."

Ruckelshaus and Portney may have a point. But they might miss an even more important point: As more communities say no to prisons and power plants and waste facilities, we will be forced to develop solutions that strike deeper at the causes of social problems by reducing the need for prisons, power plants, and garbage dumps. Emptying the prisons of people convicted of victimless crimes like prostitution, homosexuality, and personal drug use would significantly reduce the need for more prisons. Aggressively pursuing higher levels of energy efficiency limits the need for new power plants. Recycling waste and substituting benign chemicals in the industrial process diminish the need for landfills and incinerators.

However, despite the possibilities offered by local politics, voter turnout at local elections is much lower even than the much-lamented turnouts at national elections.

Local apathy stems, in part, from the fragmentation of duties among many government bodies. A city might control garbage collection, for instance, while the counties regulate landfills and incinerators. The city dispenses welfare. The county deals with public health. A regional agency oversees sewage. Another delivers water. The educational system is run by an entirely separate government, and libraries and parks also have their own commissions. State agencies oversee environmental protection. Still other state agencies regulate electric and gas systems.

Trying to make an impact on this bewildering array of elected and other agencies is often strenuous, unrewarding work that can dampen citizen enthusiasm and encourage apathy and cynicism.

Besides this paralyzing fragmentation of authority, local governments increasingly find their hands tied and authority preempted by higher levels of government. Local governments are free to regulate barking dogs and backfiring motorcycles. But the federal government prohibits them from regulating much noisier jet planes. Even a municipally owned airport cannot impose a mandatory curfew on jet takeoffs. When New York City tried to prohibit the transport of nuclear

> **Economic and social misery increases in direct proportion to the size and power of the central government of a nation or state.**
>
> — *Kirkpatrick Sale,* Human Scale

materials through its congested streets, the federal Department of Transportation successfully sued to overturn the ordinance.

Compounding this lack of authority and the jurisdictional fragmentation is the widespread belief that the world's problems are much too large to be tackled by local communities.

Local politics also suffers from citizens' tendencies to be involved only when a particular issue raises their ire—making local governments spasmodic, reactive, and negative. People are motivated by struggles against a garbage incinerator, or a new shopping mall, or a high-rise, or tax increases. While these movements can be thrilling examples of democracy in action, their political energy largely disappears when they have succeeded, or failed. Despite flashes of

brilliant innovation, especially in the area of environmental protection, local politics has yet to fully realize its potential for making American politics more meaningful.

We need political parties on the municipal level. These municipal parties need not be tied to, or tied down by, our present national parties. Their job would be to offer a political platform that ties the pieces of the territory together, one that can be presented not only to the city council, but also to the sewage authority, to the school board, to the energy regulatory agency. Their goal would be not only to elect people to office, but also to involve and empower the citizenry.

The creation of real municipal political parties depends on our overcoming the lack of a sense of connectedness even among people who live close together. Without a

sense of community, local politics is doomed to be the same empty experience that most people find national politics to be.

Alexis de Tocqueville, the 19th-century observer of American democracy, once described local politics as the "primary school of government." This is where we learn the lessons of democracy that we later apply at the state and national level. So far the report card reads "Needs improvement."

*David Morris, co-director of the Washington, DC based Institute for Local Self-Reliance, is also the author of* The New City States, *available for $10 from the Institute, 2425 18th St. NW, Washington, DC 20009.*

*Excerpted from* Utne Reader, *November/December 1991.*

# Conflict Resolution and Negotiation

## by Katherine Baril / *The Volunteer Monitor*

In my work as a mediator in environmental disputes, I've learned that if you humiliate your adversary you may win today but you will lose tomorrow. A farmer who is forced to fence a stream will manage that fence so that it fails. But if the farmer has worked jointly with other parties to arrive at a solution, he or she will make that solution work.

Different people—farmers, industrialists, community activists—see pollution issues very differently. For example, consider the debate in the Northwest over clear-cutting (cutting down all the trees in an area at 60- to 80-year intervals) versus selective forestry (cutting a percentage of the trees at more frequent intervals). Environmentalists argue that selective forestry causes less disturbance to wildlife habitat and allows continued vegetative cover. But industrial foresters

point out that selective forestry causes soil compaction from the repeated entry of heavy equipment and also requires substantially more road construction.

To address such conflicts of value, we need new negotiation techniques, new processes that promote equity, fairness, and lively debate. We must learn to:

- separate the personality from the problem
- talk about real needs, not positions
- pay attention to nonverbal cues
- generate agreements that focus on long-term interdependent relationships
- anticipate that these agreements will be monitored for their impacts and changed as necessary
- engage all affected parties in the dramatic process of developing solutions that pro-

tect resources and meet everyone's needs.

I have seen such processes lead to strong, long-term, mutually beneficial coalitions between former enemies. We can no longer afford polarization or finger pointing. The issues are too important, and time is too short.

*Katherine Baril is an attorney specializing in community-based public policy and environmental conflict management and a law resources agent with Washington State University Cooperative Extension.*

*Excerpted from* The Volunteer Monitor, *Spring 1992.*

# What is Advocacy?

## by Eleanor Ely / *The Volunteer Monitor*

According to the dictionary, to advocate is "to plead a cause." Environmental advocacy is one of a whole spectrum of activities encompassed in the more general concept of "stewardship." To create a somewhat artificial distinction, cleanups, restorations, and resource management activities can be thought of as ways of taking care of a resource; monitoring as a kind of watching over it; and advocacy as speaking out on behalf of the resource.

This "speaking out" can take many forms. It can be on a scale as big as a nationwide legislative campaign. But "talking to your

neighbor over the back fence is advocacy, too," as Nancy Stafford, a Washington State volunteer monitor, points out.

In between these two extremes are almost limitless possibilities for championing your cause at a local, state, or national level through activities like testifying at public hearings or town meetings, negotiating with developers, reporting violations to enforcement agencies, working to pass local zoning regulations, reviewing permits, taking polluters to court, and educating your community.

Because the word "advocacy" is frequent-

ly associated with confrontation, some in the environmental monitoring movement are cautious about using the term. Esperanza Stancioff, a technical advisor to monitoring programs in the state of Maine, says, "In rural areas, you can have a 'community project to protect a resource,' but don't use the words 'activist' or 'advocate.' Advocacy is seen as adversarial."

Advocacy can be adversarial, but it doesn't have to be. "Be a part of the community—don't attack the community," advises Stancioff. Susan Handley, public involvement coordinator for EPA Region 10, agrees.

"There is advocacy for confrontation and there is advocacy for cooperation. Things get done when people work together."

On the other hand, there are times when you have to roil the waters. John Payne, associate director of San Francisco BayKeeper, observes that advocacy usually involves a combination of cooperation and confrontation. "To be effective," he says, "you have to be able to exhibit both qualities within the same five minutes."

Whatever the level of confrontation, advocacy is without integrity unless it rests on a foundation of truth. If monitoring groups take an honest look at their data, and learn from it, they are likely to promote realistic solutions rather than push preconceived positions.

*Excerpted from* The Volunteer Monitor, *Spring 1992.*

# MONITORS ADD POWER TO GRASSROOTS ADVOCACY

## by Cynthia Poten / *The Volunteer Monitor*

As all good grassroots environmental advocates know, stopping bad projects or changing bad laws is tough work. The cards are stacked against us. Most of us are nonprofit groups, which means we have limited funds and our lobbying activities are restricted by law. Meanwhile, the profit sector has all the money it needs to lobby extensively, buy studies and experts, engage in long-term planning, and advertise its cause.

More often than not we function in a reactive mode, responding to proposals already gathering speed as they journey through the regulatory or lawmaking process. We get our information late and sometimes cannot obtain vital data.

But there's a new force: volunteer monitoring.

People performing scientific observations of their local resources represent a substantial strengthening of the environmental advocacy movement.

Besides collecting data for long-term trend assessment, volunteer monitors can also provide information that can be put to use immediately.

In addition to chemical water quality testing, our volunteers perform comprehensive visual surveillance. Our reporting form calls for (1) mapping of stream characteristics, land uses, discharge pipes, and other human impacts; (2) details on stream conditions (e.g., color, odor, streambed coatings, presence of algae, aquatic vegetation), and habitat characteristics; (3) threatened and endangered species sightings; and (4) pollution incidents and other threats to stream health.

The frequent and regular presence of monitors, not only on the water but on land and in the air, allows for a broad range of observations and for cross-checking. Volunteer pilots, for example, have the best view of mud pollution after storm events and of pollution plumes from pipes and oil spills. Land observers are best able to determine the exact location of an offending pipe.

The information provided by our visual surveillance monitors requires substantial follow-up. We investigate incident reports and report documented problems to agencies. We track agency responses, and if illegal activities continue, we push for enforcement action. We report threatened and endangered species sightings to appropriate agencies and record them in our file of stream inventories, along with habitat characteristics, land uses, and stream conditions.

The explosion of interest in volunteer monitoring translates into a lot more people actively committed to protecting their local environment. People who are investing time and energy in monitoring have a stronger motivation to speak out on behalf of a resource—to attend municipal meetings, comment at public hearings, and write elected officials—especially since they are also armed with reliable information on local conditions.

Many of our volunteer monitors are affiliated with local grassroots organizations. These groups receive our reports, which include volunteer data and discussions of local and regional issues.

We encourage local groups to develop protection strategies for their regions and to call on us for help with advocacy problems. Because we are a four-state regional organization, we can help bring local issues to the regional arena. Thus, the relationship of our volunteer network to other grassroots organizations is based on shared data, mutual concern about issues, and cooperation in getting out the troops.

*Cynthia Poten is the Delaware Riverkeeper.*

*The Delaware Riverkeeper Network is a project of the Watershed Association of the Delaware, an American Littoral Society affiliate. We serve over 200 volunteer monitors in the Delaware estuary and are expanding the project to the Delaware Water Gap in spring of 1992. For more information, call (609) 397-4410 or write to P.O. Box 753, Lambertville, NJ 08530.*

*Excerpted from* The Volunteer Monitor, *Spring 1992.*

# ROUNDTABLES

## by Ken Cooke / *The Volunteer Monitor*

The monitoring group invites as panelists representatives from local government agencies, local university experts, the Chamber of Commerce, environmental control officers for major industries, and leaders of area environmental groups. These officials serve as a panel of experts.

The roundtable is promoted through normal outreach efforts, including news releases, flyers, and invitations to key community groups. A large public turnout, though nice, is not essential for the meeting to be worthwhile. Just having the panelists together at one time is valuable in itself. Often local officials rarely get a chance to talk to one another. The volunteer group can perform a vital community service by getting these people face to face.

The panelists are not asked to give formal presentations. This allows more time for the panelists to interact informally with the facilitator, the audience, and each other concerning the issues. In preparation for the meeting, panelists are given a list of questions the facilitator is likely to ask and an advance copy of the monitoring results so they can digest the findings beforehand.

The monitoring that the group has done gives them legitimacy, and the fact that they are hosting the meeting gives them a measure of control. The monitoring group has some power to ask questions and to be heard, and often they can get commitments from the public officials.

These forums work well in school settings, using student facilitators. Audiences of 100 or more can he generated by inviting science, social studies, and other classes to participate. The roundtables are often videotaped and cable-cast over local community access channels.

*Ken Cooke is program coordinator for Kentucky Water Watch, a statewide public participation program, administered by the Kentucky Division of Water, which includes citizen water quality monitoring, community education, and stream rehabilitation. For more information, contact Kentucky Water Watch Program, Division of Water, 18 Reilly Road, Frankfort, KY 40601 (502)564-3410.*

*Excerpted from* The Volunteer Monitor, *Spring 1992.*

# Chapter 13

*From the poetry quarterly,* **Mr. Cognito.**

# Media, the Arts, and Reflections on the Information Age

*In art the mass of people no longer seeks consolation and exaltation, but those who are refined, rich, unoccupied, who are distillers of quintessences, seek what is new, strange, original, extravagant, scandalous. I myself, since Cubism and before, have satisfied these masters and critics with all the changing oddities which passed through my head, and the less they understand me, the more they admired me. By amusing myself with all these games, with all these absurdities, puzzles, rebuses, arabesques, I became famous; and that very quickly. And fame for a painter means sales, gains, fortunes, riches.*

*And today, as you know, I am celebrated, I am rich. But when I'm alone with myself, I have not the courage to think of myself as an artist in the great and ancient sense of the term. Giotto, Titian, Rembrandt were great painters. I am only a public entertainer who has understood his times and exploited as best he could the imbecility, the vanity, the cupidity of his contemporaries. Mine is a bitter confession, more painful than it may appear, but it has the merit of being sincere.*

—Pablo Picasso
(from an interview with Giovanni Papini in Libro Nero, 1952)

> *What is missing in American life is a sense of context... in our journalism the trivial displaces the momentous because we tend to measure events by how recently they have happened... We've become so obsessed with facts that we've lost touch with the truth.*
>
> —Ted Koppel, ABC News

Activists are painfully aware that mass media all too seldom present the progressive viewpoint. We see that ownership of media outlets by fewer and fewer corporations is coinciding with increased news manipulation and censorship. On top of that, we are seeing the influence of tightly organized and vocal right-wing groups on the media. How can the media claim objectivity when, as frequently happens, the U.S. government is the sole source for a story on a controversial issue?

# Getting Good Press

**by Ann Harbaugh / *L.A. Peace Directory***

## Collective Voice Needed

While most of us are troubled by media handling of its gatekeeper role in news dissemination, how many of us take responsibility for another factor shaping the news— *the relative silence of the progressive voice in the face of media bias and misrepresentation?* Certainly, some progressive groups and individuals do excellent and sustained media work. But most of us need to become more skillful and vocal media activists. Let's take a cue from the success of right-wing groups and develop a louder, clearer, more tenacious collective voice. However, let ours be a voice that, unlike the right wing, seeks *inclusion* of our viewpoints rather than *exclusion* of opposing thought.

## The Press Release

The single most important tool for getting media coverage is the press release. A release may contain an announcement, a calendar listing, information on an event, or a feature story or interview idea, among other things. Write your release concisely and clearly and include all pertinent information, preferably on one page. Answer the five W's: *Who, What, When,* and *Where* in the first paragraph and *Why* in a subsequent paragraph. Releases are cut from the bottom up, depending on available space, so place the most important facts at the beginning and less vital information toward the end.

To compete successfully with the many releases media outlets receive, make yours as professional as possible. Use your organization's letterhead. Type double-spaced with wide margins, on one side of the paper only. One page is preferable. If you need two pages, include all the primary information on the *first* page and type *-MORE-* at the end of the page. If your release is one page, type *-END-* or ### at the bottom.

At the top, left of the page, type *FOR IMMEDIATE RELEASE* with the date underneath, or *FOR RELEASE AFTER:* followed by the desired release date. Opposite this line on the right-hand side, type *CONTACT* followed by the name of your group's contact person and, below that, the phone number.

Below this, center your headline typed in capital letters. Use an active verb. The headline should summarize your release and arouse interest. To call attention to a good opportunity for photos, at the bottom of the page type *PHOTO OPPORTUNITY* and a brief description of what will take place.

## Press Release Distribution

Once you have lovingly crafted your press release, get it to the *appropriate* people. For events, send out two mailings. Check on the deadlines for calendar listings and do your first mailing to meet these deadlines. Plan your second mailing to arrive about 4 days before the event and send it to the Assignment Editor. If there is a reporter who has covered your issue or an editor of a specific section covering your issue, be sure they receive copies too. Send yet another copy to the City Editor.

Media staff titles differ from place to place and a few papers request that all releases be sent to one individual for routing to the appropriate person. Do some research to determine the people who should receive your release.

## Following Up with Phone Calls

Follow up with phone calls to increase your likelihood of receiving coverage. When you call, *never* tell an editor what to print or air. Make a pitch for your story. Talk about the importance of your story and its relevance. Encourage them to cover events.

## Media Contact Lists

For the most effective media work, establish relationships with reporters, editors, and producers. Use a media contact list to keep track of your dealings with these people. This list should include the media person's name, outlet, address, phone number, interests, and how that individual responded to your previous contacts. It's good to include deadlines and day of publication for non-daily papers, or day of airing for radio or TV programs. Any time you interact with that person, note the date and the outcome.

## Media Advisories

Media Advisories resemble press releases but are used differently. Advisories can provide background for ongoing issues in the news. If your organization has a knowledgeable, articulate spokesperson as a news source on an issue, write a media advisory announcing that person's availability. Consider including a press kit with the advisory.

## Press Kits

A press kit supplements information in the press release and is given to the members of the press at events and news conferences. You can also mail one along with your feature story idea. Press kits may contain your group's background, biographies, supporting documentation or background on your issue, press clippings, and/or the text of a statement. Use a folder or report cover with an identifying label on the cover.

## Feature Stories

A feature story about your organization and people can provide tremendous publicity. Features are in-depth articles about issues and people in the news. They frequently describe the background of current news stories and are often written by a beat reporter who interviews one or more people. You can suggest an idea for a feature story to a media outlet. Do some preliminary research to target appropriate outlets.

Once you've determined the best outlets and have practiced presenting your idea clearly, concisely, and with confidence, you're ready to make a "pitch call." The pitch call gives you the opportunity to convince the editor, reporter, or producer that your idea is relevant, timely, and of interest to that publication's audience.

You can also present your feature story idea in a letter. This letter can be longer than a press release (up to two pages) and can contain more than one idea or focus. Whether you call or write, mention a local angle ("hook") for your feature to interest the media contact and, ultimately, the general public. You can also offer to arrange interviews with people in your organization. Anything you do to make the reporter's job easier will increase your chances of turning your feature idea into a published article.

To place a radio or TV feature story, prepare your pitch, then phone for an appointment to discuss the idea with your contact. In some cases a contact will ask for a letter describing the proposed story.

## Letters to the Editor

A letter to the editor is another way to express the views and concerns of your organization. Write yours clearly and succinctly using your organization's letterhead. If possible, cite a recent news story by name and date. In a letter to the editor you can state your organization's views with more compelling passion than in other forms requiring stricter objectivity.

Of course, individuals may write letters to the editor on their own stationery.

### "Op-Ed" Pieces

Many newspapers feature an op-ed (opposite the editorial) page written by the general public. Usually, op-ed pieces range from 750-1,000 words but requirements vary, so check with the newspaper first.

Acceptance of an op-ed piece is more likely if its author (or at least the person signing it) has some name recognition and stature in the community and if the issue is controversial. The piece should present a persuasive counter-argument to an opponent's view, and ask for reader responses in some way such as calling, writing, or attending an event.

### Support from Celebrities

Having celebrities and public figures associated with your issues and events always increases the probability of getting good press. Be on the lookout for the *Creative Resources Guild Directory* containing, among other people, names of media, art, music, entertainment industry figures interested in supporting progressive issues. (Call John Tibayan, the Guild's executive director, at (310) 390-1470 for more information.)

*Excerpted from* L.A. Peace Directory, 1989.

# Activism on the Airwaves

## Grassroots TV? You bet!

by Dwight Oestricher / *City Limits*

In two small rooms, crammed with videotapes from around the country, a three-person operation shoots the New York-based Deep Dish TV network onto America's cable television systems.

The purpose of the network is to link activists from all walks of life through cable television programs on subjects such as environmental racism, censorship and police brutality. It's a far cry from "America's Funniest Home Videos," and a radical alternative to the tabloid sleaze of local news stations and the milk-toast placidity of public television.

Deep Dish is "a replacement more than a supplement to commercial TV," says executive director Steve Pierce. "Their first priority is to sell you something, not to challenge people's thinking or get them to communicate with each other. The mainstream media gives you newspeople reporting the news. We give you the people who are living the news, grassroots organizers telling you the real story."

What's more, at Deep Dish, it's local organizers and independent video producers who make the shows—taking control of the airwaves and making public access channels live up to their name. Here's how it works: the Deep Dish staff chooses a topic for a program, then sends out mailings to cable access channels and independent video producers asking if they can contribute. Those who send in acceptable outlines receive funding (a few hundred dollars) and receive guidance from the Deep Dish staff.

Regional coordinators take the finished product and edit the raw footage into a program that is eventually beamed out via satellite. Each program has a budget of about $2,000, half of which goes into production and purchasing satellite time.

"In their own communities these independent activists get isolated," says Pierce. "As well as actual geographical distances between these people there are also cultural

## Deep Dish is a replacement more than a supplement to commercial TV.

and racial boundaries. We have built a network of activists, producers and programmers who are using TV to organize and work together."

Programs this season included "Teaching TV," a compilation of more than 20 different projects produced by youth around the country; "Sexual Politics and the Revolution," which looked at sex, class and gender attitudes in black and Hispanic communities; and "Idiot Box Savant," a survey of public access programs that included a studio and home audience discussion from Milwaukee on the racism and homophobia present in newspaper coverage of the Jeffrey Dahmer murder case.

### Town Hall on TV

There are also live programs, like "Slow Death in the Cities," a town hall meeting on environmental issues broadcast from the Borough of Manhattan Community College, and "We Interrupt this Schedule to Bring You," a live performance in honor of World AIDS Day.

Last season, shows on the Gulf War looked at discrimination against Arab-Amer-

icans, the history of America's involvement in the region, plus the demonstrations and teach-ins against the war going on across the country.

The shows are fast-paced and throw multitudes of information at the viewer. A series on censorship included a piece on political prisoners in the United States, and coverage of people currently incarcerated was interspersed with archival footage of Malcolm X and Huey Newton. Added to this was a town meeting at which a man recalls how his anger at finding none of his cultural heroes in history books at school in Puerto Rico later turned him into a fighter for Puerto Rican independence.

The Deep Dish approach is perhaps best exemplified in "Vibrant Voices: People of Color Speak Out," where an image of a black woman in dreadlocks is superimposed over the picture of the all-white, all-male board of directors of a commercial television network. She asks: How can these men relate to the masses?

### Collective Creation

Deep Dish was created in 1986 by Paper Tiger, a New York City-based television production collective. The collective wanted to distribute its weekly media criticism and analysis show beyond local public access channels and Deep Dish was born to beam their efforts nation-wide. But once the network was born, it grew into an entity of its own with input from people across the country.

"I guess our greatest contribution is that we are helping people to make TV," says program director Martha Wallner. "A lot of people forget that programs are being made by human beings. Public access is all about people getting involved in the movements, the causes that affect our lives."

*Excerpted from* City Limits, *January 1992.*

# Desert Snow Storm
## *CBS and NBC withheld footage of Gulf War carnage*

### by Chris Norris & Peter Tira / *San Francisco Bay Guardian*

At the height of the air war against Iraq, NBC and CBS executives refused to air some of the most compelling footage of the entire Persian Gulf War. Videotapes by Emmy award-winning Maryanne Deleo and Jon Albert showed images of Iraq's devastated countryside and anguished families, which powerfully contradicted administration claims of minimal damage to civilians.

Yet despite unanimous approval of the piece, NBC president Michael Gartner killed it. At CBS, the night before the videotape was to air on CBS Evening News, executive producer Tom Bettag—who had approved the footage for the news segment—was fired, and the piece was spiked by CBS as well.

*Source: San Francisco Bay Guardian, March 20, 1991, "Sights Unseen" by Dennis Bernstein and Sasha Futran. This story was selected as one of the "Top 10 censored stories of '91" by Carl Jensen of Project Censored. Excerpted from San Francisco Bay Guardian, January 22, 1992.*

# Radio Activist Mbanna Kantako: *In His Own Words*

We're talking about censorship and freedom of speech, and we should talk about why the FCC exists. Why does the FCC tell us what to say and what not to say?

It's a fact that none of you in this room, or none of you know anyone who controls the life in America. It's controlled by the major corporations that basically control the world. How do they do it? Does this country tell you the facts, the truth, and then allow you to make a rational decision based on the facts and the truth? Has it ever done that? It controls you by fear and misinformation. This is why our station is under attack. The very reason that the government has to control what you hear is so that you go along with what they're doing.

How hot is this issue in Springfield? When we first came on the air, we were a community-based organization known as the Tenants Rights Association. We basically were using the radio because the local media had distorted or left out our intents on different demonstrations or different positions that we had stated clearly. They would change it around, or just lie, or just ignore it. So we basically came on the air so that the views of the Association would be heard.

At first, out of not knowing our rights, we went off the air for a couple of weeks. Then we came back on, and we've been on ever since. Now we've joined the Zoom Black Magic family. We call the FCC the *thought patrol*, and recommend to everyone when you leave here tonight: go find a catalog, borrow yourself a transmitter, find yourself a blank space on the dial, and go to work.

What is going on is, you have a few—what is it, one half of one percent—who control the majority of all this country's wealth. If you give the same message of individualism, then they will not only leave you on the air, they'll give you a bigger transmitter! But if you start talking about people coming together to fight against the system that's oppressing all of humanity, all across the planet, then they will find you.

Just look at events around the world. The Solidarity movement in Poland. Much of that was brought about by what they called clandestine radio broadcasts. Look at Romania. When the people decided to overthrow the government, what did they go after and fight for the hardest—the TV and the radio stations.

If a law is killing you—and we can go back to the Declaration of Independence here—it is not only your right, it is your duty to throw off those chains and provide a new guard for yourself. This is what we're saying. The FCC has no right to urinate on your head and tell you it's raining. You know better than that. That's why I say get you a transmitter. So when they turn that dial, they hear 15 commercial stations, and they hear 15 liberation stations.

> ## Why does the FCC tell us what to say and what not to say?

> ## We use radio because, the local media distorted our positions.

# MEDIA COVERAGE & CENSORSHIP

Worldwide, both big-business and alternate media recognized the International War Crimes Tribunal as an historic event. Why, then, did big-business media in the U.S. completely blank out Tribunal coverage, not even allowing the critical or condescending stories usually reserved for progressive events? They all knew of the Tribunal. They made up *half* of the 93 journalists who signed in on Feb. 29, 1991. A letter from Ramsey Clark reminded heads of media corporations of their responsibility to report the news. Yet individual journalists told the Tribunal media staff that an attempt to cover the Tribunal could lead to their being fired. All evidence points to systematic, co-ordinated censorship within the U.S. of the Tribunal's work. Only continued effort can bring the Tribunal's truth to the people of the United States.

*Excerpted from a International War Crimes Tribunal brochure.*

*Mbanna Kantako Cresis (formerly Dewayne Readus) is a radio activist with Zoom Black Magic Liberation Radio (now Black Liberation Radio and formerly WTRA) of Springfield, Illinois. These remarks are excerpted from a forum entitled "Censorship On The Radio: What Next?" which was held at the Guild Complex in Chicago on Friday, January 19, 1990. Cresis' talk was part of a panel discussion which included such other radio activists as Black Rose and Mr. Ebony of Zoom Black Magic, Fresno, CA; Tony Fitzpatrick of Chicago's WLUP, and Lee Ballinger, Associate Editor of Rock and Roll Confidential who put the panel together and is presently doing cultural organizing throughout the United States around the issue of music censorship.*

*Excerpted from Cultural Democracy, Spring 1990.*

# The Pen is Still Mighty

## by Pete Brady / *New Times*

In an era when opinion polls show that the public ranks journalists and the media just slightly above attorneys, used car salesmen, and Supreme Court nominees on standards of reliability, professionalism and honesty, it is heartening to note that sometimes journalists do get it right.

*Sacramento Bee* reporter Tom Knudson spent eight months, 200 interviews and traveled 10,000 miles researching a recently published series on the decline and fall of our fabled Sierra Nevada mountain range.

He found the Sierras in deep trouble due to timber practices, mining, population growth, air pollution, water projects, livestock grazing and the drought.

Running Knudson's series was a courageous decision for the *Bee*, a newspaper which is to the North State what the *L.A Times* is to the South State.

Environmental activist Karen Pickett commented that "newspapers have a hard time criticizing the timber industry. After all, paper products are their lifeblood, and many of them have sweetheart deals with the industry which honest reporting about industry practices could well jeopardize. We find that they're quite willing to go after industries with which they have no direct advertising or production links, but in timber country, for example, the media is going to tow the party line regardless of what the truth is."

The Knudson series pulled no punches, however, containing candid statements from Forest Service officials who said the government's management of Sierra national forests and parks is almost completely dominated by economic rather than environmental concerns.

---

**Forest Service environmental impact documents were written to support timber cutting rather than to scientifically and completely evaluate the impacts of logging operations.**

---

One Forest Service biologist said Forest Service environmental impact documents were written to support timber cutting rather than to scientifically and completely evaluate the impacts of logging operations.

Knudson also found that soil erosion which muddies Sierra streams and rivers is taking its toll on hydroelectric facilities which officials describe as "drowning in mud." Inestimable tons of mud piling up behind dams threatens to severely affect hydroelec-tric generating capacity in the near future, according to PG&E spokespersons, and much of the silt is coming from clear-cut or overgrazed mountain slopes which can no longer hold soil.

Kevin Eckery, vice-president of industry affairs for the California Forestry Association, didn't like Knudson's articles. He said the series was a "two-dimensional analysis of a three-dimensional issue."

Eckery said the articles were biased against the timber industry, but when contacted by phone Eckery did not dispute the articles' contention that logging operations had severely harmed the Sierra.

California's Resources Secretary Douglas Wheeler recently announced that Knudson's articles prompted plans for an "environmental summit" this month which will discuss proposals to create a new national park in the Sierras, and explore other ways to save the Sierra ecosystem.

Just another case of the pen being mightier than the sword, or the chainsaw.

*Excerpted from the* New Times *(San Luis Obispo), December 7, 1991.*

# Enough Already

## *How Much Is Too Much When It Comes to Freedom of Expression?*

### by Richard Neville / *New Times*

*The man is naked and in pain, pummeled by a gang of thugs. Snarling abuse, the ringleader of the thugs bastes the victim with excrement and globs it into his gob. Dogs bark, onlookers mock and a bejeweled moll surveys the high jinx. The man is then urinated upon and the toughs strut off to a fancy restaurant.*

Welcome to the opening of "one of the finest movies to come out of Britain in the last decade," according to Derek Malcolm of *The Guardian*, who described it as "Magnificent."

Soon the woman is being punched in the stomach by her husband, the ringleader. Another diner is kneed in the groin. A child is molested and abducted. A kitchen helper is tortured.

More guests are set upon; one of them is soaked in soup and forcibly fed. The wife reappears, embroidered with bruises, and another woman is stabbed in the cheek with a fork. By the time the child is savaged for the second time, I flee the cinema, sensing that worse is in store.

A glossy promotional flier is full of critics' praise for the film I just walked out on. "A masterpiece of movie invention," headlines a review reprinted in full from Britain's *Financial Times*. The British entertainment weekly Blitz was more succinct: "Sex, murder, cannibalism," it raved. "It's all there and more ...quality erotica." Other critics agreed: "breathtaking" ... "dazzling" ... "brilliant" ... "In essence, this new film by Peter Greenaway—*The Cook, The Thief, His Wife and Her Lover*—is considered a cornucopia of multiplying subtle resonances, biblical allusions, frozen painterly gestures, and mobile revelations ..."

As I slunk homeward, I wondered who was the craziest: the filmmaker, his critics, our culture, or me? At the core of my confusion is a paradox. I am part of a generation that spent its formative years fighting for the freedom of expression. We had trials, street demonstrations, an alternative press, pirate radio stations, sit-ins on the David Frost show, the burning of bras and the unbanning of books. An era that began with the liberation of *Lady Chatterley's Lover* ended with canonization of the *Sex Pistols*.

Perhaps it's because we put so much energy into this defense of freedom that it goes against the grain to pass judgment on anything that is obviously obnoxious, especially if it is deft, daring or unusual. With a tolerant shrug, we move from a Robert Mapplethorpe "masterpiece" of a bum-encased bullwhip to a pop video of Alice Cooper on

# BIG Pictures ©1992 Dan Dunivant

*Reprinted from Earth Journal*

a bed of nails wielding his whip on a steamy nymph. And who dares deride an artistic work for its immorality, with the censorship lobby still alive and twitching in the wings?

The generation that came of age in the '60s and '70s lives in a post-modernist Valhalla, where negative judgment is considered passé. And the matter is complicated by the panache and technical wizardry of many of today's dark artists. The top prize at this year's Cannes festival went to *Wild at Heart*, a film "laced with torrid sex scenes and stomach-churning violence," according to Reuters News Service. The director, David Lynch, earlier made headlines with *Blue Velvet* (currently saturating the video outlets), a movie that shocks audiences with its mixture of violence and sexual terror and perhaps redeems itself by exposing small-town complacency and corruption. In other words, like so much of today's cultural fare, it is powerful, erotic, and nasty. But, in this era of mounting cataclysm, who needs it? Just as the Cannes audience greeted this latest award with a mixture of cheers and boos, I believe it is time for those concerned about the rising tide of degradation and violence to come out of the closet.

*London Fields*, the new novel by Martin Amis, is breathtaking in its intelligence. It has verve, imagination, wit and cold, cold heart. All the major characters are vile, including a baby. The book is un-put-downable, until you put it down. Then you wonder why you've been spending so much time with such murderous creeps. The book's meanness of spirit remains in the brain like a drug, a Largactil of the soul. In a way, we, the cultural consumers, are often lured back as unwitting guests to a macabre, Greenaway-ish feast in the company of demented gangsters, witnessing acts of sadistic brutality. Why do we stay, when our very presence is an act of collusion?

"But the music," a friend said, when I quizzed her about the ending of *The Cook*, etc. "Wasn't it wonderful?" I suppose so. Notable too, were the costumes, the "painterly" colors, the direction, the acting, the

mood. But I wanted to know what finally happened to Alan Howard, the bookish adulterer in the film. His death was so gruesome, she explained, that she would rather not discuss it; anyway, the lover was finally cooked and served for dinner. Yum, yum.

Okay, so we appreciate that the director is gifted, but what is he saying? What is the film's insight into the human condition? When the end credits roll, what is the audience left with? What we are left with is this: a load of the same substance that was smeared on the nude man in the beginning,

---

**In art, as in life, this is not the time for nihilism, sadism or spiritual defilement. Most of us are aware that barbarity is commonplace. But, with environmental disruption facing us all, the time is urgent for cleansing the atmosphere and ridding the soil and the sea of pollutants.**

---

with a difference. Unlike the victim in the film, the audience does not have the benefit of a hosing down.

In art, as in life, this is not the time for nihilism, sadism or spiritual defilement. Most of us are aware that barbarity is commonplace. But, with environmental disruption facing us all, the time is urgent for cleansing the atmosphere and ridding the soil and the sea of pollutants and poisons.

This also applies to our culture. For as surely as toxic residues kill the fish and the fowl, so the sludge of mean-spirited filmmakers and writers kill our spirit. It is renewal that is needed now, honor and optimism, not the sordid excesses of artists talented in merely shocking us.

The Jungian psychologist James Hillman, in a wonderful Schumacher Lecture, explained the problem of "psychic numbing." Hillman suggests the "shocking possibility" that the more we shrink away from the world and into our private lives, focusing on the interior psyche, the more we contribute to the decay of civilization. "Reawakening the

sense of soul in the world," he believes, "goes hand-in-hand with an aesthetic response—the sense of beauty and ugliness—to each and everything, and this in turn requires trusting the emotions of desire, outrage, fear and shame... Outrage, in particular, has a social function, responding to moral and aesthetic atrocities, and leading us into the fray."

According to a report in the *Sydney Morning Herald* (May 15, 1990), a dozen children aged between four and eight were recently treated in Cairns hospital for sexually transmitted diseases. They came from the Kowanyama community on Cape York peninsula. In another remote aboriginal community, men forced children as young as 7 to engage in acts depicted in pornographic videos. Elsewhere, a 5-year-old boy suffered internal injuries after older boys tried to emulate a scene from a video.

The source of this nightmarish report was attributed to a consultant to the Australian Prime Minister's Department, Judy Atkinson, who said that these acts of brutality were increasing with the wider availability of videos. "Because it's on film," she explained, "it must be somehow normal, so it's all right to get out and do it." Exactly. This is an extreme and tragic case of what so many of us are suffering in one degree or another: a loss of our sense of normality. If the VCR at Kowanyama is ever loaded with the tape of *The Cook, The Thief, His Wife and her Lover*, then it's only a matter of time before the first victims are admitted to Cairns hospital.

Coprophilia and cannibalism finally will have arrived, courtesy of one of the finest films to come out of Britain in the last decade.

*Richard Neville is a freelance journalist currently living in Australia. During the '60s, he was an editor for London's famed underground magazine Oz.*

*Excerpted from New Times (San Luis Obispo, CA), September 20-27, 1990.*

# In Praise of Censorship
## *There's too much art anyway*

### by Quentin Crisp / *The Hungry Mind Review*

I am unsympathetic to the fuss caused by the National Endowment for the Arts' withdrawal of financial support for Mr. Mapplethorpe's photographic exhibition. The aesthetes behaved like precocious children who, as soon as anything is forbidden, want it. It stands to reason that any group of people gathered under a heading that includes the word *national* must act in accordance with the general public's wishes, and we all know from long experience that most people are deeply disturbed by representation of sexual activity of any kind—let alone anything kinky.

In any case, no art should be subsidized by a nation that is heavily in debt. Art we do not need; artmaking should be made so difficult an occupation that only the most dedicated practitioners would persist. As things stand at the moment, every flat surface in New York is a stage, and every incompetent waitress is a closet actress. If censorship were more strict, artists in whatever medium might work more carefully and, with luck, produce less.

Of course, I hold these views because I am by nature a philistine. I only took up writing, drawing, and other occupations loosely connected with the arts because my bizarre appearance automatically disqualified me for real work. If I had been compelled to rely on my talent, I should have died very young. I learned to evoke the indulgence of my employers. That is the only art for which I ever had any aptitude.

*Quentin Crisp is the author of the autobiography* The Naked Civil Servant.

*Excerpted from* Hungry Mind Review, *Summer 1991.*

## Big Battle, Bigger Wars

### by Steven Marks
### *The Original Art Report*

As a playwright, I'm in the war against censorship *and* for free speech but the sight of artists running to the wrong ramparts in opposing Senator Jesse Helms and his ilk depresses me.

A more pernicious suppression of art (I call it "Big Censorship") is practiced by bloated government bureaucracies like the National Endowment for the Arts and any big art museum.

Big Art embraces radical chic (such as Andres Serrano's "Piss Christ") into its ethos without batting an eye. At the same time, it smugly blasts the reactionary, bourgeois attitudes of the artistically illiterate masses while falsely championing itself as the defender of free speech.

I say free speech is denied when a subsidiary of Big Art, any local art gallery, allows its choice of art shows or members to be dictated by corporate buying decisions.

Neither is it free speech when funding decisions are made by people seeking to refill the coffers of their organizations, public or private, by supporting artistic works that will reflect well upon their choices.

That artists have allowed this to happen to them is evidence of a lack of chutzpah on their part. It seems, at times, they are unwitting dupes or willing partners in the censorship of their own work because they want to be recognized by Big Art's artistic authority so badly.

*Excerpted from* The Original Art Report (TOAR).

# STRIKING OUT WITH THE ART STRIKE 1990–93

*We call on all cultural workers to put down their tools and cease to make, distribute, sell, exhibit, or discuss their work from 1 January 1990 to 1 January 1993. We call for all museums, agencies, 'alternative' spaces, periodicals, theaters, art schools, etc., to cease all operations for the same period.*
— Art Strike call, 1989

The Art Strike 1990-1993 must rank as one of the most memorable and successful failures of the decade, memorable because so many people reacted so strongly to it, and successful because it failed so completely.

The Art Strike was designed to question a series of assumptions about art and the artist, the role of the artist, the role of art within culture, the institutions of art, and particularly the identity of the artist herself. Modeling itself upon traditional ideas of the strike and the withdrawal of labor, it was hoped that it would create new situations for intensifying the class war and shattering commodity culture.

The idea quickly circulated through the international network of underground magazines, Xerox posterists, and others involved in the overlapping milieu of marginal and underground cultures. Art Strike Action Committees (ASAC) were established in the USA, England, Ireland and Uruguay as points of contact and to disseminate propaganda. At the beginning of 1989 the ASAC in San Francisco hosted a well-attended, week-long series of public discussions, propaganda workshops, and performances exploring the issues raised by Art Strike, culminating at the end of the year with a final 24 hour orgy of art making and creativity after which all the works were interred in a time capsule buried deep in the basement of Artists Television Access, (the alternative space hosting the event). All that remains today of this action is a bronze plaque set into the concrete floor that reads "ARTSTRIKE 1990-1993."

Artists' reactions to the Art Strike have varied between two extremes. Some find the idea hilariously funny, while others convulse in undisguised anger at an idea that threatens their whole way of life.

Many have felt that the Art Strike is one big conceptual art piece and that try as they may, they all unwittingly become part of the piece. Some have felt that it was all a conspiracy on the part of the Art Strikers to wipe out their competitors and claim their share of the market place. Many who have participated in the Art Strike have found that since giving up making art, and the subsequent boycotting of the gallery/museum establishment with all its boozy opening receptions, that they've had more time to engage in a range of other, more worthwhile pursuits like gardening, correspondence, getting engaged with political activities, earning some decent money for once, going back to school, spending more time nurturing their personal relationships, and reading, to name just a few.

For people in other countries the idea of the Art Strike may sound appealing, but different cultural contexts bring their own unique perspectives, as this Art Striker from Yugoslavia makes clear.

*Now that I have learned the reasons for the international Art Strike 1990-1993 I declare that I will support it, but in Yugoslavia, country where I am living and making art, an Art Strike would have no sense because:*

*1. There is no art market here yet.*

*2. Prices of artworks are so low that you don't sell at all. You make art for pleasure, philosophical and creative reasons.*

*3. We have only few art critics and curators, and they have no power or influence upon artists.*

*4. You don't have to pay the galleries for having your own exhibition, but galleries pay you for that. Shows are not commercial at all, so alternative artists can exhibit in official gallery spaces.*

*5. The serious culture hardly exists here. It is repressed by the primitive, peasant culture, so our aim is to develop and support culture here.*

*So I am suggesting all art strikers come and settle in Yugoslavia during the period 1990-1993 and continue making art and exhibitions.*

It's no coincidence that the three years framed by the Art Strike have generated such profound changes in political and social structures across the globe. Whole countries have struck back at the outmoded and repressive ideologies imposed upon them for so long. So, with the remaining months left of the Art Strike, let's finish the job off and rid ourselves of 'art' and 'culture' once and for all!

Anti-©opyright 1992.

*Excerpted from Art Strike Action Committee (Iowa City).* Give Up Art *handbook available for $2 from: 221 West Benton St. Iowa City, IA 52246. The editor, Sandi Brockway, is observing the Art Strike and has worked on this book,* Macrocosm, *instead of doing "Art."*

# *Where Do We Go From Here?*
## A Message From an Activist Artist

### by Guillermo Gómez-Peña / *High Performance*

My generation was born and raised in a world of multiple crises and continuous fragmentation. Our current lives are framed by the sinister Bermuda triangle of war, AIDS, and recession. We seem to be closer than ever to the end, and precisely because of this, our actions have twice as much meaning and moral weight, though perhaps less repercussion.

Our fragile contemporaries are starving, migrating, and dying at a very young age and the art we are making already reflects this sense of emergency. But it is not enough to just make art. We must step outside the safe arena of art.

As the '90s unfold, U.S. artists, cultural organizers, and intellectuals must perform central roles in the making of our society. We must fine tune our multiple roles as intercultural diplomats, border philosophers, alternative chroniclers, and activists for world glasnost and local gringostroika. More than ever, we must practice, promote, and demand access, tolerance, dialogue, and reform.

We must defend the survival of the art world as a demilitarized zone. We must continue to support the community centers and the alternative spaces, the last bastions of political and cultural freedom, which are facing potential extinction. The large institutions must try to keep the smaller ones from sinking, for without them the large institutions would lose their roots and their seeds.

Successful painters might contemplate donating the proceeds of the sale of an artwork to a community center or an alternative space.

We must listen carefully to other cultures that have a long history of facing repression, censorship, and exclusion. Native Americans, Latinos, African-Americans, and Asian-Americans have been fighting these battles for centuries.

We must rebuild community through our art, for our communities have been dismembered.

We must dialogue and collaborate with artists from other disciplines and ethnic communities, as well as with political activists, educators, lawyers, journalists, cultural critics, academics, and social scientists. Together, we can develop a national consensus of priorities and strategies for the new decade.

*Excerpted from* High Performance, *Fall 1991.*

# Art for All People
## *Community-oriented art inspires*

### by Linda Frye Burnham / *High Performance*

I'm finding it harder than ever to sit through art events, especially gallery art by white yuppies. It's lost its resonance for me. I guess I just don't make that good an audience any more. There's too much going on outside. Real life is calling. I can no longer ignore the clamor of disaster—economic, spiritual, environmental, political disaster—in the world in which I move. In that context, most art just has no "oomph," as an artist friend puts it.

Fortunately, I'm not the only one who feels that way. All around me I see artists creating dynamic experimental projects in the communities where they live. The most interesting art I see now happens in the interaction between non-artists and artworld refugees. In prisons, in hospitals, in schools, in community centers, on Skid Row, in shelters for the homeless, in soup kitchens, in AIDS hospices, in refugee asylums, in protest groups, in environmental study coalitions, in free law and healthcare facilities, in childcare centers, in retirement communities. One of the most stimulating art projects I know about is happening, not in a major museum or theater, but on the streets of Skid Row, where John Malpede is directing the Los Angeles Poverty Department, an award-winning performance art group made up of homeless people that is currently touring Europe.

Others are making art projects with gang kids, pregnant Central American refugees, prisoners on death row. And I mean they are making art, not therapy (though the results are undeniably therapeutic). In contrast to institutionally trained art teachers, these artists are taking wildly non-traditional approaches to their subjects, expanding the definition of community art the way they expanded the definition of fine art in the '70s. They are exercising the ideas that formed the postmodern agenda: that art is not made in a vacuum, that it is part and parcel of everyday life and politics, that creative exchange is essential to human development and brings it to flower, that cross-cultural interface is a matter of survival and vice versa, that no man is an island.

I'm tired of the gallery as hideout, the

museum as bastion of culture. I'm tired of art sitting in the driveway of the real world like a stalled car. It's the same with all the other institutions of this era: We need some really good mechanics who aren't afraid to get their hands dirty.

Artists are the most amazing thinkers I have ever known, and bullheaded enough to take on insurmountable tasks, believing their crazy ideas can change things. Many times over the last few years I have listened to some mad daydream of Malpede's and shaken my head, knowing his plans won't work. And they do. And everybody lives through it and comes out smiling.

How many of you would try to produce a play written by and starring a schizophrenic who, only months ago, was stalking the streets screaming angrily at the sky, and who, even now that he is an award-winning writer, won't sleep indoors?

As Americans, we declare that we own the right to pursue happiness, and most of us think we won't be happy till we're rich. But Albert Schweitzer once said, *"You will never be happy until you have found a way to serve."*

*Excerpted from* High Performance *(No. 38/ 1987).*

# Strange Biology

## *What's wrong with nature films?*

### by Jim Nollman / *Whole Earth Review*

Why is it that so few nature films bother to present nature in the traditional sense, as a place of the spirit? Why do so few describe the cusp between humans and nature in the deep ecological sense of being a primary source of communion? Instead, year after year we watch a continuing parade of field biologists promoting the classic scientific schism between observer and observed, with nature as a vast wildlife laboratory presided over by stewarding scientists.

We need to invent a new kind of nature film, a form of documentary that tinkers with the edges of allegory and myth.

Three prototypes come to mind—*Roger and Me, Koyaanisqatsi,* and *My Dinner with Andre.* Each one paves an unconventional path toward the re-enchantment of the nature film. Each bucks the form upon which it has been based.

*Roger and Me* did more to connect to an audience with its curious blend of humor, staging, and actual documentary footage than any number of pious rust-bowl documentaries. Why not take the same kind of sardonic chance with a nature film, utilizing that same brilliantly dogged interview style in the African veldt? Find some articulate Namibian whistleblower to act as host. Let him go interview rhino poachers, rhino scientists, starving native people, South African militia, insurgent guerrillas, officials of the World Bank, Hong Kong pharmacists, and the emir of Kuwait showing off his collection of rhino-horn daggers.

Imagine an entire series of nature travelogues based on the speeded-up wizardry of *Koyaanisqatsi.* I would love to see that style employed to shoot a film about the year 1991, set entirely in the Arctic National Wildlife Refuge.

Following the lead of *My Dinner with Andre,* how about an entire genre of nature films that show creative people—artists, children, musicians, poets, native people, and seekers—interacting and communing with animals as if they were peers and teachers instead of merely subjects and specimens?

How about a whale film entitled *Talking to Beluga?* Instead of the usual gang of whale scientists, why not ask a few creative artists up to the Arctic and film them attempting to communicate with one of these fascinating, beautiful, most intelligent, and least known creatures on the planet? Invite a guitarist, a rap musician, a ceremonialist, a synchronized swimmer, an ice sculptor, a psychic, a chanting Tibetan lama. A tap dancer on a metal raft. Or a neon artist. Be sure to let the whales themselves initiate the interaction.

Someone once said that war is too important to leave to the generals. I believe that nature is too important to leave to the scientists. Creative filmmakers of the world, unite. Go forth and reinvent the nature film. We need a new vision of nature and we need it now.

*Jim Nollman is author of* Spiritual Ecology *and founder of Interspecies Communication, Inc. which produces* Interspecies *Newsletter.*

*Excerpted from* Whole Earth Review *Fall 1991.*

# *Is Folk Art Real Art?*

### by Seitu Ken Jones / *Utne Reader*

After 27 years as a railroad worker, Maurice Carlton became a folk artist. Of course, no one in our neighborhood used the term "folk artist," and while some people called Maurice an artist, others called him crazy. He called himself a toy inventor: Gathering material from garbage cans and dumpsters, he transformed broken dolls, toy trucks, hair dryers, old TVs, and tennis rackets into marvelous works of art. Maurice made telescopes that could see into the future and back into the past at the same time. He created weather vanes, crowns, and public shrines throughout the neighborhood.

His work dealt with the collective condition of the African-American community in St. Paul, in sometimes obvious and sometimes subtle ways. Maurice, who recently died, made art and created sculptures from a deep well of passion for serving African-American youth and protecting the earth. He worked within an aesthetic he developed from the communal experience of African-American life.

Maurice's work aptly illustrates the debate about an art form that seems to be gathering chic these days. Celebrities from Barbara Streisand to Bill Cosby are collecting folk art, and premier collections put together by Abby Aldrich Rockefeller and Herbert W. Hemphill, Jr., recently toured the country. But what and whose work qualifies as folk art? Are museums and exhibits truly representing the work of "common people"? Are arts administrators playing up "innocuous" folk art to avoid controversial art?

Would Maurice's work be considered folk art by the art world? He never referred to himself as a folk artist. I come from a family of quilters, trained and untrained painters, and seamstresses, but we didn't look on such artistic output as folk art. We called it what it was: a quilt, a painting, a dress, a chair. But the work was both decorative and functional, had its own aesthetic standard, and often made a statement on crucial political, social, and cultural issues. Maurice's work has inspired and informed my own work as an artist, and surely the work of many others. Aren't these solid criteria for art? Doesn't his work belong in a museum?

Yet, as Margaret Rog notes—in the Minneapolis/St. Paul alternative weekly *The Twin Cities Reader (May 22, 1991)*—in her review of the "Treasures of American Folk Art From the Abby Aldrich Rockefeller Folk Art Center" exhibit, most of the quilts, trade signs, portraits, decoys, toys, townscapes, and other items were made by "white middle-income people, many of whom also worked as dentists, teachers, shop owners, and the like." Curator Ann Kohl told Rog that "ethnicity is not really a question in this show."

Folk art needs not only to be represented in museum collections, but also to be recognized for its diversity, vitality, and source of inspiration.

In some parts of the art world, folk art isn't taken seriously. Check out museum catalogs from across the country, and see what gets reviewed in *Art in America, Artforum,* or *Artpaper*—not much happening with folk art. From my perspective, the old, narrow, largely white interests of the museum and art world remain protected from the vibrant, sometimes rough, fresh, and equally valid art

that goes on outside it. Fortunately, the Maurice Carltons of the world will create with or without the museums and other gatekeepers of the art world. We need them more than they need us.

*Excerpted from the* Utne Reader *November/ December 1991.*

# Computer Networks for Activists
## *PeaceNet: powerful tool connects progressives in 80 countries*
### by Andrew Lang / *Convergence*

*Commercial computer networks like CompuServe and Prodigy link the home or office personal computer with a growing array of information services. With a few simple commands, your computer can reach electronic newspapers, wire services, stock quotations and weather reports. But one of the best-kept secrets of the information age is that the peace and environmental movements now have their own computer networks. Activists throughout the world are using these networks to discuss strategy, share information and debate issues.*

*One of these progressive networks is PeaceNet. This article will introduce you to PeaceNet and explain how you can connect your computer to electronic networks at very little cost.*

The Christic Institute uses PeaceNet and other telecommunication networks to send electronic mail, contact supporters and organize on-line "conferences" linking together field offices and local chapters with the national staff.

PeaceNet is the largest computer network serving the peace movement in the United States. More than 8,000 activists, local peace centers and national organizations use PeaceNet's growing library of news and information.

Anyone who uses a personal computer at home or the office can get involved. You will need:

• **A modem.** This inexpensive device allows computers to exchange data over ordinary phone lines. A new modem can cost less than $80.

• **A communications program.** Modems usually come equipped with a program that enables you to dial other computers, transfer files and send electronic mail.

• **A PeaceNet account.** PeaceNet charges an initial fee of $15, plus a $10 monthly fee billed either directly to your address or your credit card. An additional fee is charged for the number of minutes you spend on the system. Access to PeaceNet is less expensive during *"offpeak"* hours in the evening and on weekends.

Hundreds of "conferences" available on PeaceNet will keep you informed on developments censored by the mass media. A "conference" can either be an alternative news service or an electronic discussion in which anyone can participate. A conference title usually consists of two or three words separated by periods. When you type *christic.news,* for example, the system will connect you to the Christic Institute's news service.

As you continue to explore PeaceNet, you will find serious news and background articles on disarmament, ethnic strife in the USSR, threats to the environment, the Federal budget, social policy, economics and human rights, plus organizing alerts and information needed for action campaigns.

A subscription to PeaceNet provides the following advantages:

• **PeaceNet is immediate.** A bulletin or news story posted on PeaceNet is available within seconds. You don't have to wait two or three days to read the information.

• **PeaceNet is an active medium.** On many conferences you are not simply a passive reader of information: You can respond simply by typing a comment on your computer screen. Many conferences are not only electronic "news services" but provide for reader reaction and response. Other conferences are designed to help users to discuss strategy and plan demonstrations.

• **PeaceNet connects you with hundreds of organizations and thousands of activists.** You can browse through PeaceNet's catalogue of more than 800 conferences and visit the organizations or news service that interest you the most.

• **PeaceNet allows you to send and receive "electronic mail."** PeaceNet's electronic mailroom may also be used to post messages to fellow PeaceNet subscribers and to electronic addresses on other computer networks around the world. You can also use PeaceNet for telexes, faxes and telegrams. PeaceNet provides a special service to send faxes to Senators and Members of Congress.

• **PeaceNet is international**. PeaceNet will let you discuss issues and plan strategies with activists in more than 90 countries. PeaceNet is part of a wider family of progressive networks in Nicaragua, Brazil, Australia, the United Kingdom, Canada, Sweden, the Soviet Union and Germany.

Supporters of the Christic Institute can also read news from our investigations and participate in electronic discussions on "Christic DataBank," a computer "bulletin board system" (BBS) in Washington, D.C. The BBS is available from 9 a.m. to 9 p.m. Eastern time at (202) 529-0140 and accepts calls from 1200 to 9600 bits per second.

Initial access to Christic DataBank is free. All you need is a computer and a modem. For a modest charge you can spend more time on the system and transfer files directly from our computer to yours.

*Excerpted from* Convergence, *Summer, 1991.*

# AlterNet
### *An Alternative Press Wire Service*

AlterNet was launched in November 1987 by the Institute for Alternative Journalism, a nonprofit organization devoted to research on public policy issues and journalism.

AlterNet is linked to its subscribers via a computer network, which ties together more than fifty papers in the U.S. and in Canada. This on-line network is maintained by PeaceNet, a nonprofit global computer network based in San Francisco. AlterNet has syndicated more than 4,000 stories. Its users have ready access to an evergreen story bank of over 1,800 articles, plus a current story database of over 200 articles.

AlterNet's mission is to serve non-daily, alternative, community media and tailors those offerings to the individual editors' wants and needs. Its editorial offerings come from a wide variety of sources, and cover a broad range of topics. Many articles first appeared in local papers or are originals written exclusively for AlterNet member papers. AlterNet works with public interest and advocacy groups in Washington and around the country.

Although its primary mission is to provide a syndication service, the AlterNet weekly index offers story ideas, news for and about its member papers, resource guides and information. In keeping with its goal of maintaining an interactive service, AlterNet also offers its members the opportunity to post queries, job listings and the like free of charge on its weekly index. AlterNet's weekly index of stories is mailed on Friday; editors wishing to see a story contact us and it is mailed immediately. If you are interested in a regular feature—a column, for example-- we send it to you automatically.

AlterNet's electronic delivery system is designed to let editors retrieve stories from a computer bulletin board at their convenience. Downloading from AlterNet saves the trouble of re-keying copy. In addition, the system is designed to let papers send copy to AlterNet's electronic mailbox for redistribution, and it permits editors to communicate directly with one another.

We maintain a comprehensive index of all our stories, and we are able to generate for editors on demand a list of our inventory that may be of use.

*Source: AlterNet press release.*

# *Can We Talk?*
## *The impact of global communications*
### by Howard Frederick

For thousands of years, people had little need for long-distance communication because they lived very close to one another. The medieval peasant's entire life was spent within a radius of no more than 25 miles from his or her place of birth. In the 1830's, it took as long as two years to send a letter and receive a reply. Even at the beginning of our century, the average person still lived in the countryside and knew the world only through travelers' tales.

This painfully slow communication had a dramatic effect on war and peace. Two of America's most devastating wars were due in part to communications breakdowns. In 1941, the US had just installed a new device to detect planes and ships—radar. The surprise attack on Pearl Harbor was no surprise at all. Inexperienced technicians had noticed a large blip on the screens 200 miles out. They tried and failed to raise their command by radio. They eventually got through by

phone and explained the situation to the duty officer. He told the technicians that they were seeing a group of bombers due in from the United States and told them "not to worry about it."

The Gulf of Tonkin incident was due partially to a communications breakdown. The US warship Maddox was hit by violent thunderstorms while on maneuvers in the Gulf. The captain received false signals afterwards from erratically functioning electronic equipment. He incorrectly identified these signals as an attack by the North Vietnamese. This was used as justification by Johnson to commit forces to Vietnam without Congressional approval—thanks to a breakdown in communications technology.

All the channels mentioned to this point— from radar to military communications—are highly centralized and rest in the hands of the military, government, and transnational corporations. But today, a worldwide meta-

network of highly decentralized technology has arisen—computer networks, fax machines, amateur radio, VCR, video cameras, and the like. For the first time in history, the forces of peace have the communication tools previously reserved for the governing elite.

Advocacy groups from all over the globe have started to link and successfully effect the course of peace and war:

ſ During the 1989 Tiananmen Square protest, Chinese students transmitted detailed, vivid reports by fax, telephone and computer network to activists throughout the world, making a protest that might once have been suppressed globally visible. Telephone circuits also circumvented official controls during the attempted coup in the Soviet Union in August 1991.

ſ Computer networks became a major outlet for uncensored news of the Persian Gulf War and its effects on the Third World,

## Electronic Global Suggestion Box

The winner of the 1992 Social Invention Award sponsored by the Body Shop, is Gregory Wright of California for his "IdeaNet" Electronic Global Suggestions Box. Accessible by computer and modem from around the world, it will act as a repository for any ideas and projects people send in—so that "people's creativity can be continuously and effectively harnessed." IdeaNet should be up and running in 18 months.

Users will be able to mark schemes out of 100, and an average mark and a top 20 will develop, so that users avoid drowning in a sea of electronic material, as tends to happen on some present computer networks. IdeaNet will link other Idea Gathering Organizations (IGOs) around the world, including social invention centers in Stockholm, Moscow, Giessen (Germany) and the Institute for Social Inventions in London.

More information can be obtained from IdeaNet. See listing in the Media section of the directory.

*Source: Institute for Social Inventions, 20 Heber Rd., London NW2 6AA, United Kingdom.*

Israel and the Arab countries, as well as the worldwide anti-war movement. Competing action groups used computers to agree on common platforms, plot strategies and plain events across vast distances.

✠ The APC networks played a major role in resourcing the 1992 United Nations Conference on Environment and Development (UNCED) in Brazil, including an information-sharing service that made U.N. documents available worldwide.

Other worldwide APC environmental and social justice projects range from helping U.S. students monitor river water quality to getting out the news of a neo-Nazi skinhead attack on foreigners in a Dresden, Germany neighborhood. Tens of thousands of messages a day pass back and forth within the "APC village," and the number grows everyday.

Our challenge is to guarantee that today's

silenced majorities, which include all of civil society, can engage in the political dialogue so vital to true democracy.

*Howard H. Frederick, Ph.D, teaches Politics and Society at the University of California at Irvine. He can be reached on-line at "hfrederick@igc.org".*

*This article was adapted from various material written by Howard Frederick.*

# Too Much Information:
## *Toxic Waste of the Mind*
### by Diana Prizio / *The Cultivator*

*The mind that tends towards discrimination increases illumination.*
— Patanjali, Indian Mystic

To describe ours as a fast-paced society is a dated understatement. No one denies that we exist in such a style. We attempt, as individuals, all sorts of ways to slow down, to get away from the input, the screen, the telephone. But then we go to the movies, or read another book, or visit a friend, and take in more information. The concept of *Information Sickness* doesn't get front page coverage. Sounds too much like something George Orwell created. Besides, there are too many other facts considered (by whom?) to be more pertinent to our lives. Our increasing stress level does get some airplay and gives us brief pause, and doctors still do recommend that we need to "get away from it all," but where, indeed, is a body to go?

The point being that it seems desirable to exercise discretion about the quality of information we allow into our brains. A certain amount comes in uninvited, for sure (it's known that we receive radio transmissions through the fillings in our teeth: the volume is so low that we don't often *consciously* hear them)—but we can learn to shut the door on a great deal of it.

If I started talking about meditation now, I would lose some readers. And there are plenty of books and people who describe those benefits better than I. Fact is, most feel there's simply not enough time to meditate. Who can afford to do nothing? We can. It could be called diminishing our impact. *It is better to do nothing than to waste time.*

Speaking of time, Jeremy Rifkin states that:

*The computer introduces an entirely new time frame and with it a new vision of the future. The clock measures time in relationship to human perceptibility. It is possible to experience an hour, a minute, a second, even a tenth of a second. With computers, however, the nanosecond (a billionth of a second) is the primary measurement of time. The snap of a finger, for instance, is equivalent to the passage of 500 million nanoseconds. This marks a radical turning point in the way human beings relate to time. Never before has time been organized at a speed beyond the realm of consciousness.*

*As we move into fifth and sixth-generation computers, this new concept of time will pose a variety of problems. Computers of the 21st century are likely to be able to make decisions*

*on a wide range of activities in nanosecond time. Events being processed in the computer world will exist in a time realm that we will never be able to experience. This new 'compu-time' represents the complete separation of time from human experience and the rhythms of nature.*

*Psychologists and sociologists have begun to study the impact of this time on both individuals and society at large. Their findings suggest that the effects of this changing time orientation may become a central social problem over the next century. According to Craig Brod, one of the growing number of psychologists specializing in computer-related distress, "those who live with computer workers invariably complain that disputes over time are a major source of friction.*

*"Long-term computer users often suffer from the constant jolt back and forth between two time worlds. As they become more enmeshed in the new time world of the computer, they become less and less able to readjust to the norms and standards of the traditional clock.[1]*

...such as walking down the road, preparing a meal, growing a garden, listening to a symphony, noticing the birds. Studies done with computer operators had them stand in line to wait their respective turns for periods of four to seven minutes. Once they'd reached the head of the line, each was asked how long they'd had to wait. Responses varied from 15 minutes to 35 minutes, and all expressed impatience at the wait.

My espousing methods and advice on conquering the sickness called Information would only be adding to the problem. We all have discovered ways in which we can experience mental quiet, even for a few moments at a time.

Experiment with this: make a concerted effort not to listen to or read the "news" for a longer-than-personally-normal period of time. See how, without asking, we are presented with various pieces of information as they become relevant to us. Filtering the news in this way can enable us to have more discretion about where to concentrate our efforts. Like the squeaky wheel, the most urgent needs will persist: they won't allow us to ignore them.

By this process of elimination, the true elements of life become more clear—our friends, our children, the ways in which we personally interact with the rest of the world.

We begin to actually *see* the faces of the people we pass as we ride to work, the configurations of the clouds in the sky, the graffiti on the wall of the building.

Unless we learn to discriminate, the history of the last quarter of the 20th century may be seen as a superabundance of unfascinating facts representing a generation of vacuous, non-questioning minds. Excessive information leads us to mental saturation. Minimal

messages can arouse healthy inquiry and invite the curiosity so vital to maintaining an interest in life.

1. Jeremy Rifkin, *Time wars: The Primary Conflict in Human History,* Henry Holt and Company, NY 1987.

*Excerpted from* The Cultivator, *volume 14, no. 4; volume 15, no. 1, 1989.*

# Information & Evolution

**by Theodore Roszak / *Macrocosm USA***

In classical metaphysics, the term "being" once functioned as a cosmic catch-all, the murky essence of everything. These days there are those who believe information is the *Be-all* and *End-all* of existence. In a recent book, two renowned cosmologists, examining "Life and the Final State of the Universe," conclude that "*everything* human beings do, not just their thinking, is purely and simply a form of information processing." They predict a time when we may have to recruit fundamental matter itself (in the form of positronium atoms) to pack away all the information we have collected. Finally, when some super-intelligent species has "stored an infinite amount of information, including *all* bits of knowledge which it is possible to know," we will have reached the Omega Point.[1]

Look behind this glorification of information, and you find a fascinating bit of cultural history. In the years just before World War II, Claude Shannon of Bell Labs had developed a radically new approach to communication called "Information Theory." Challenged to justify the odd meaning his theory ascribed to "information," Shannon agreed that his definition might be "more trouble than it is worth." But before he could find a substitute, Alan Turing, John Von Neumann, Norbert Wiener had launched information a triumphant new career. Wiener, due largely to the rapid development of computers during the war, believed that his new science of cybernetics had mastered one of the fundamental properties of life and mind: the transfer and feedback of information.

Meanwhile, in the early fifties, Watson and Crick had deciphered the double helix, and with it (so they thought) the basic chemistry of genetics. As we have learned from Thomas Kuhn, scientists work from paradigms, which they explore, exhaust, and discard. The history of science can very nearly be written as

There are those who see machine intelligence as a species in the making, well on its way to becoming fitter to survive than its human inventor.

**The computer liberates the brain from "the weakness of the mortal flesh" and turns us into "a race of immortals."**

a succession of models each carrying the theoretical imagination a little farther into the unknown. The New Biology was no exception. It, too, needed a paradigm. It was waiting in the new field of Cybernetics. Almost spontaneously, geneticists began speaking the language of information theory. DNA was a "code"; the double helix was a "bit-string" stored in the "memory" of the cell. The gene was a "biocomputer" that was "programmed" to process "data" stored in the amino acids.

Although the New Biology may have borrowed its basic paradigm from cybernetics, it eventually lent information a glamour

it might never have acquired in any other way. Information, became the secret of life. From a data-processing mechanism as tiny as the DNA helix, all the ordered complexity of life on Earth has supposedly evolved. Here was an astonishing demonstration of how much could be pieced together out of mere particles of data. The mechanistic model of the universe had always needed something cleverer and more subtle than steam engines and dynamos on which to model the supple intricacies of life. Even the clock, that oldest of smart machines, had never quite filled the bill as a convincing replica for the mysteries of the brain or cellular chemistry. The computer, especially as it got smaller and faster, was just the machine to save the mechanistic paradigm from extinction—though, of course, that paradigm was now left suspended precariously above the physicist's invisible domain of fields and energies and baffling probabilities. This was hardly the solid foundation of absolute matter on which mechanistic science had always hoped to be based.

The computer model also brings with it a troubling gap. Hardware must have its software; and software does not create itself. It derives from intelligence. In the case of the universe at large, *whose* intelligence? At a certain point, the computer paradigm of nature betrays embarrassingly Deistic connotations—as if God, formerly the great

---

## Properly handled, the computer model might return us to that perception of mindlikeness in nature that was common to both Aristotle and our animistic forebears.

---

watchmaker in the sky, had been updated into the cosmic computer programmer. The anthropomorphic element in such a line of speculation runs the risk of becoming plain silly. But on the other hand, if there is mentality *of some kind* at work beneath the surface of nature, it would most likely manifest itself as just the sort of buzz and sizzle we find in the strange vibrations and resonances that underlie so-called physical reality. Properly handled, the computer model might return us to that perception of mindlikeness in nature that was common to both Aristotle and our animistic forebears.

How far can the computer paradigm can be extended in biology. If the living cell is any sort of information processor, its subtlety is vastly beyond anything the most sanguine cognitive scientist might imagine. There is an evolutionary memory involved in genetic chemistry that goes well beyond decoding a bit-string. Whatever "master genes" or "jumping genes" may be, they represent hierarchical levels of control that no computer program can even approximate.

But if biology has a less and less easy fit with the computer model, computer science is far from finished with biological imagery. What other machine besides the computer was ever spoken of as going through "generations?" Even more dramatic is the use that information technicians frequently make of the evolutionary paradigm. Genes may or may not process information; but the notion that computers "evolve" is commonplace. Nor is the term always used metaphorically. There are those who see machine intelligence as, quite literally, a species in the making, well on its way to becoming fitter to survive than its human inventor. Information technology reaches a stage at which individual human brains can be fully simulated and then downloaded into microchips. The body becomes dispensable; personal identity becomes obsolete. "In the final step your old

body is disconnected. The computer is installed in a shiny new one, in the style, color, and material of your choice." This is what Hans Moravec of Carnegie-Mellon University sees in our future, and he looks forward to the day. Marvin Minsky likes the idea too. "It's hard to see anything against it," he comments. "People will get fed up with bodies after a while." Minsky has worked his way to the conclusion that "life" has become a disposable concept; the future of biology lies with energetics and information processing—in short, with thinking machines.[2]

In 1978 when *Time* magazine ashed Robert Jastrow of NASA to provide the big picture for its first major issue on computers, he predicted human obsolescence. The future of life on Earth, he was certain, lies with "the child of man's brain rather than his loins."

*Human evolution is a nearly finished chapter in the history of life. ... We can expect that a new species will arise out of man surpassing his achievements as he has surpassed those of his predecessor, Homo erectus. ... The new kind of intelligent life is more likely to be made of silicon.*

Like Moravec, Jastrow looks forward to the time when the brain will make its home in a cozy box. Any day now "a bold scientist will be able to tap the contents of his mind and transfer them into the metallic lattices of a computer." This he views as "the mature form of intelligent life in the Universe," the point at which the computer liberates the brain from "the weakness of the mortal flesh" and turns us into "a race of immortals."[3]

What we have here is a body-denying asceticism that has haunted the history of mathematics since the days of Pythagoras; freely mixed with the Frankensteinian arrogance that Mary Shelley long ago warned us was the guaranteed best way of making monsters.

1. John D. Barrow and Frank Tipler, *The Anthropic Cosmological Principle*, Oxford University Press, pp. 660, 677.
2. Moravec and Minsky as quoted in Max Dublin's excellent new book *Futurehype*, Dutton, 1991.
3. Jastrow, *The Enchanted Loom: Mind in the Universe*, Simon & Schuster, 1984, p. 166

*Theodore Roszak is Professor of History at California State University, Hayward. He is the author of* The Making of a Counterculture, The Cult of Information: The Folklore of Computers *and the* True Art of Thinking, *and the science fiction novel* Bugs. *His latest works include the novel* Flicker *("a secret history of the movies") and* The Voice of the Earth, *(a reconnaissance of "ecopsychology") both published by Simon & Schuster.*

We want to be famous as a writer, as a poet, as a painter, as a politician, as a singer, or what you will. Why? Because we really don't love what we are doing. If you loved to sing, or to paint, or to write poems—if you really loved it—you would not be concerned with whether you are famous or not... Our present education is rotten because it teaches us to love success and not what we are doing. The result has become more important than the action. ...it is good to hide your brilliance under a bushel, to be anonymous, to love what you are doing and not to show off. It is good to be kind without a name. That does not make you famous, it does not cause your photograph to appear in the newspapers. Politicians do not come to your door. You are just a creative human being living anonymously, and in that is richness and great beauty.

*—Krishnamurti*

# Chapter 14

# *Ethics & Spirituality*

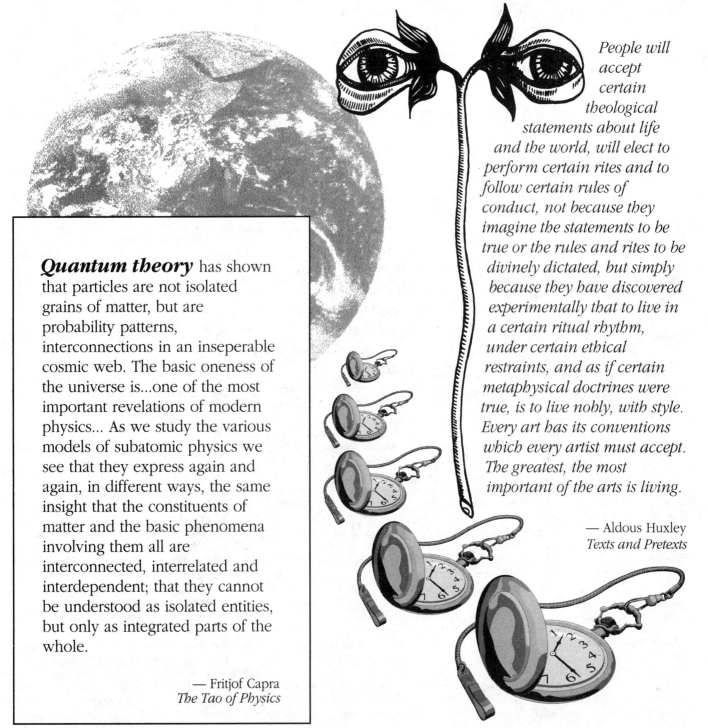

**Quantum theory** has shown that particles are not isolated grains of matter, but are probability patterns, interconnections in an inseperable cosmic web. The basic oneness of the universe is...one of the most important revelations of modern physics... As we study the various models of subatomic physics we see that they express again and again, in different ways, the same insight that the constituents of matter and the basic phenomena involving them all are interconnected, interrelated and interdependent; that they cannot be understood as isolated entities, but only as integrated parts of the whole.

— Fritjof Capra
*The Tao of Physics*

*People will accept certain theological statements about life and the world, will elect to perform certain rites and to follow certain rules of conduct, not because they imagine the statements to be true or the rules and rites to be divinely dictated, but simply because they have discovered experimentally that to live in a certain ritual rhythm, under certain ethical restraints, and as if certain metaphysical doctrines were true, is to live nobly, with style. Every art has its conventions which every artist must accept. The greatest, the most important of the arts is living.*

— Aldous Huxley
*Texts and Pretexts*

# Thomas Berry:
# *Dreaming of a New Earth*

### An Interview by Bernard Connaughton & Jo Roberts / *The Catholic Worker*

*Thomas Berry is presently the director of the Riverdale Center for Religious Research in New York City. On a cloudy January day, we visited with Tom Berry in his home situated beneath the branches of a great 500-year-old oak tree on a hillside overlooking the Hudson River. We listened as he spoke of the desecration of the natural world by the human species, and read from his recent book,* The Dream of the Earth. *The following is taken from our day together.*

[Here in the West,] we have lost sight of our integral relationship with the natural world. And we have developed a technology that enables us to transcend the basic biological law, that every species has opposing species or environmental conditions so that no one species can overwhelm another—a law of limits. But through our technology, we pride ourselves on not being subject to these limitations, on outwitting nature.

We see this transcendence as our destiny. We are not satisfied with the human condition. Our millenial expectations become disastrous as we look to live beyond the limits that are normal and natural to us as human beings; and so we get this ideal of limitless progress.

The dynamics of science, of technology, of our whole industrial setup, are not scientific, but visionary. We keep inventing, inventing, inventing, trying to get beyond the human condition into some kind of wonderworld. But the more we try to get wonderworld, the more we go into wasteworld.

Other societies are limited because of their lack of technological development, their lack of dedication to a state transcending the human condition. But, in the West, we have this lack of reconciliation with the normal conditions of life, and so we go about burning up the energies of the planet in trying to get beyond the planet—a sort of pulling ourselves up by our own bootstraps. We can invent things that have immediate advantages, but we don't see the long term disadvantages.

Take the greenhouse effect. We can't trust our scientists, because they are telling us [about it] at this late date—why weren't they telling us about it a century ago? Well, they say, we couldn't know. That's just the point! The scientists didn't know. And that's why scientists have to learn a decent amount of humility, of caution—so that they don't make

up all these fertilizers and these genetic engineering processes, when they don't know the consequences of what they're doing.

A person says: "There's energy in the coal, there's energy in the oil, why shouldn't we use it to heat our houses, to give us transportation? Why not dig it up and use it?" Well, it's very simple: There's a purpose in the petroleum, there's a purpose in the coal. That purpose is to store the basic carbon so that the balance of carbon, oxygen, and so forth on the surface of the Earth can be worked out in such a way that the plant life can absorb the carbon dioxide and, under the energy of the sun, can convert it into living matter. Then the living matter can go through its processes. It's what you might call the carbon cycle—everything is balanced out and you have the ozone layer and so forth.

> **We have developed a technology that enables us to transcend the basic biological law; we pride ourselves on not being subject to these limitations, on outwitting nature.**

That took a long time to be worked out. The oil and the coal began to be stored about two hundred million years ago. Now, if you take the oil and the coal out of the ground, break it up and put the residues back into the atmosphere, the chemistry of the planet is changed, and the ozone layer is destroyed.

The scientists should have known about this a long time ago, and should have been very careful about disturbing the chemical balance of things. But they weren't concerned. They said: "Oh, well, we'll manage that when we get to it," not realizing that there are certain disadvantages that they can't rectify. The ocean and the atmosphere will never again be as pure as they were before this. The balance that existed before will never return. The rainforests, once they've gone, will never come back, not as they have been.

When we disturb the outer world, we are destroying living forms, the animals and the trees. Presently, we are losing probably ten

thousand species a year. We only know of 1,600,000 species.

We should be clear about what happens when we destroy the living forms of this planet: The first consequence is that we destroy modes of Divine presence. If we have a wonderful sense of the Divine, it is because we live amid such awesome magnificence. If we have refinement of emotion and sensitivity, it is because of the delicacy, the fragrance, and indescribable beauty of soul and music and rhythmic movement in the world about us. If we grow in our life vigor, it is because the earthly community challenges us, forces us to struggle to survive, but, in the end, reveals itself as a benign providence. But, however benign, it must provide that absorptive drama of existence whereby we can experience the thrill of being alive in a fascinating and unending sequence of adventures.

If we have powers of imagination, these are activated by the magic display of color and sound, of form and movement, such as we observe in the clouds of the sky, the trees and bushes and flowers, the waters and the wind, the singing birds, and the movement of the great blue whale through the sea. If we have words with which to speak and think and commune, words for the inner experience of the Divine, words for the intimacies of life, if we have words for telling stories to our children, words with which we can sing, it is again because of the impressions we have received from the variety of beings around us.

If we lived on the moon, our minds and emotions, our speech, our imagination, our sense of the Divine would all reflect the desolation of the lunar landscape.

The change that is taking place on the Earth and in our minds is one of the greatest changes ever to take place in human affairs, perhaps the greatest, since what we are talking about is not simply another historical change or cultural modification, but a change of geological and biological as well as psychological order of magnitude.

What is happening is psychic devastation and an imaginative emptiness. It is not simply the physical loss of resources in an economic sense. It is even more devastating to us inwardly than it is to the planet outwardly.

It is not easy to be aware of just what is happening. Take the drug scene, for instance, take the dullness in people's lives at present. This is all related to this radical isolation from the spontaneities and the invigorating and ever renewing qualities of the natural world. The natural world renews itself; bridges and concrete roads and machines don't. That's why it is already determined that our children, and our children's children, are going to live amid the ruined infrastructure of the industrial world and amid the ruins of the natural world itself. And they are going to have to face a restructuring process with diminished psychic and spiritual resources that is the real terror of what we are doing.

While such an order of magnitude can produce a paralysis of thought and action, it can, we hope, also awaken in us a sense of what is happening, and move us to a program of reinhabiting the Earth in a truly human manner. It could awaken in us an awareness of our need for all the living companions we have here on our homeland planet. To lose any of these splendid companions is to diminish our own lives.

It is in this context that we have to do some thinking and some restructuring of the existing order. One of the temptations is to avoid the basic issue and to seek to ameliorate the existing circumstance. The real transformation requires a rejection of one pattern for another, and that is where wisdom comes in—how to survive an existing circumstance while putting a new order of things into functioning, without crippling the new process.

We need confrontational tactics, transformational tactics, and creative vision, so as to confront the existing order in its full level of destructiveness.

So the question is, as Chesterton once said, how to be sufficiently dissatisfied with the situation in order to change it, and how to be sufficiently satisfied to think that it *can* be changed, to be motivated to change that is, how to reject something and create something at the same time.

The same role does not belong to everybody. Some people may have the role of enabling us to survive in the present, some may have the role of challenging the present very directly, some may have the role of inventing the new. Some may have the role of transforming the system from within, in a way that would be radically transformative, and not merely enabling it to survive. You have to survive the present while creating a viable future.

This is where we are at the present time, and my own work is to identify the complex of forces that are at work, with the general idea of establishing a context and a direction in which to move that will be adequate for the tough work that needs to be done.

*Excerpted from* The Catholic Worker, *March-April, 1989.*

# Compassion in Action:
## *First Steps on the Path of Service*

*A new book by Seva's board members Ram Dass and Mirabai Bush is a part of Seva's work to spread awareness about compassionate action.*

### An Excerpt from the Preface
In 1985, Ram Dass and Paul Gorman published *How Can I Help?* which explored "the nature of conscious service." The incredible response it evoked led to another question-how do we *begin* to act compassionately for change? What are the first steps toward the conscious relief of suffering? Especially, how do we begin those actions that may not happen naturally and spontaneously, the kind that stretch the arm's reach.

As we explored the issues that arose, we thought that an autobiographical reflection by Ram Dass might provide an entrance into what is for many of us a new arena. We felt that one person's journey could remind others that the development of compassionate action is a continual process, one of discovering ever new questions, rather than answers. This narrative is followed by a reflection on the nature of service as a spiritual practice, or "the path of action." To help that process begin, we have added some "first steps": thoughts and encouragement for entering the world of service, stories and quotes from many people already there, and resources and suggestions on where to begin.

### An Excerpt from
### "An Autobigraphical Exploration"
As I look back on my earlier attitudes about service, I see how rooted in fear they were. I was afraid of the massive unawakened suffering of the world. I was afraid that if I opened myself to it, I would drown in it. To protect myself, I needed the boundary definition that "I only work with people who want to awaken." I felt pity for others, and I was willing to help from a distance with a donation of money or even time, but basically I had no direct business with the suffering mass of humanity.

The fear I was experiencing was strikingly exemplified in a class I was teaching in New

---

**We were afraid that if we truly opened our hearts to the suffering of the people around us, we would be unable to set limits, to define boundaries.**

---

York City. It was the second or third meeting of the class on compassionate action that we had convened in a basement room at St. John the Divine Cathedral in New York City. The class was jointly sponsored by the Cathedral, the Seva Foundation, the Open Center, and radio station WBAI. There were, perhaps, two hundred of us who had come together to become involved around the issue of homelessness. We all had agreed that during the course we would each in one way or another become involved with the plight of homeless folks in the city.

Some of us volunteered to cook and serve in soup kitchens; some to monitor overnight shelters in church basements; some to lobby against unfair housing practices such as warehousing empty apartments, or legislation that unfairly benefitted real estate developers; some to work on the streets with mental patients who were lost between the bureaucratic cracks; some to help the men and women who were living on the streets to unify and organize and stage demonstrations to bring attention to their plight.

We were to keep diaries of our experiences and share these entries at an open microphone at each class, so that we could increase our collective awareness of the ways in which we were both the problem and the solution in the ever-worsening homelessness situation.

One woman wanted to share an experience she had had right outside her apartment building. She explained that during the past many months, when she left her apartment to go either to the bus or to the store, she would pass the same man begging at the corner of her street. He had a paper coffee cup with a few coins in it which he would jiggle as each person went by.

The woman reported that sometimes she would put a quarter in the cup and sometimes she wouldn't. After telling us this, she smiled somewhat embarrassedly and admitted that she had evolved a sort of budget for giving him $2.50 per week. She said that she regularly spread the giving of the money over the week.

"As a result of this course," she said, "I

realized that though I gave him money, I had never really acknowledged his existence as a fellow human being. When I examined why that was, I saw that I was afraid. But what was I afraid of? I wasn't afraid that he was going to rape me or anything like that. I wasn't even afraid he might take my purse. After all we had been passing each other regularly all this time. No," she said,

"What I was afraid of was that if I opened up to him, he'd end up living in my apartment."

In the discussion that followed the reflective and empathetic silence that her remark elicited in the group, we saw the abstract issue involved. We were afraid of our own hearts' caring. We were afraid that if we truly opened our hearts to the suffering of the

people around us, we would be unable to set limits, to define boundaries...

*Excerpted from* Compassion in Action, First Steps in the Path of Service, *copyright ©1992 by Ram Dass and Mirabai Bush. Published by Harmony Books, a division of Crown Publishing Group.*

# Creative Advocacy

## *South Bronx People for Change combines feisty activism and religious faith*

### by Karen R. Brown / *City Limits*

The South Bronx is internationally renowned as an urban wasteland, but for the people who live in the area it is simply home, a place to sleep, work, raise a family and build a better future. At the heart of this struggle is South Bronx People for Change, a feisty church based community group that aims to ensure dignity and respect for the South Bronx and its citizens.

The organization's most recent success was the reopening of Fire Engine Co. 41, a turn of the century firehouse on 330 East 150th Street. As well as letter-writing and lawsuit-filing, People for Change conducted nightly prayer vigils in front of the firehouse for 600 consecutive days. They also demonstrated at the fire commissioner's house, held a 115th birthday party for the firehouse and constructed a mock graveyard with tombstones memorializing South Bronx residents killed in fires since the firehouse's closing.

Mary Meade, a People for Change member who helped lead the protests, recalls, "We spoke to everyone, and had 50 people at all the parades and functions—the Firemen's Ball, the Polaski Day parade, the Columbus Day parade. You name it, we were there. We were right behind them and we drove them crazy!"

Over the years South Bronx People for Change members have organized a wide array of creative campaigns to improve their eight local neighborhoods. There have been sit-ins to save buildings from demolition; protests to demand improved postal service; tenant organizing in city-owned buildings; as well as petitions and committees demanding more police on foot patrol to fight drugs and better street lighting on a main street in Hunts Point, to name just a few efforts.

The core of People for Change's work takes place within eight church based social action groups. Church members within these groups determine which issues to organize around, and how the organizing should be done. People for Change staff members oversee up to three campaigns each, but

their primary function is nurturing local leaders who can eventually work on their own.

### Belief in God

The starting point for this organizing method is a straightforward belief in God. "Faith has always been the foundation upon which we build our political skills," states Ramirez. People for Change is an ecumenical organization that includes Catholics, Methodists, Episcopalians and Baptists. As Ramirez puts it, "All are religious people ... who believe God is on our side to change the South Bronx, and without God, we can go nowhere."

### Out of the Ashes

One of their greatest challenges is ensuring community involvement in the rehabilitation of 722 units of low income housing in the Highbridge section. The apartments are located in 23 city-owned buildings that were slated for demolition by the housing department in the late 1970s. Back then, People for Change fought the city and saved the buildings from the wrecker's ball.

"We stand for having the community meaningfully participate in all decisions affecting their future," says Ramirez.

*Excerpted from* City Limits, *February 1991.*

# Safeguard Earth for the Seventh Generation

### Libby Bassett / *Shared Vision*

What is the most important thing leaders must have? The answer, according to Oren Lyons' Native American tradition, is vision—"to see way into the future."

"The decisions that make us leaders must reflect on the welfare of the seventh generation to come. That," he believes, "is a profound instruction."

As a leader of the Haudenosaunee, he said he was taught "not to think of our families or of our generation, but to look at the future. We are told to plant our feet carefully on Mother Earth because of the faces of all future generations looking up from it."

"What I saw at the Moscow meetings (of the Global Forum) was an effort that is truly global, a serious commitment by international

> **In every deliberation, we must consider the impact of our decision on the next seven generations.**
>
> *Iroquois Tribe*

al leaders to clarify issues and to somehow organize to meet these problems. I saw the commitment—it is very important—and I was impressed with its sincerity."

He said the disasters occurring in the natural world eventually will come to every single person—if not in this generation, then in the next or the next. We all will become victims of processes occurring today unless we respect life and exert our leadership to safeguard Mother Earth for the seventh generation.

"We see humans as a special being, powerful but no more than equal with the rest of life." Chief Lyons said Native Americans "think it is presumptuous to say animals do not have souls. Man has been given the

*Chief Oren Lyons*

animals, although today humans do not operate under the natural laws.

"We have options with our intellect, which makes us dangerous,' he said. "The human gift of intellect makes us capable of great invention, but with this gift comes responsibilities."

One responsibility overlies all others, Chief Lyons said: 'The Great Spirit, being our creator, said people have a duty, and it seems to be the only one he gave us. He said people must give thanks for what they have.

From this simple dictum, all Native American thanksgiving ceremonies have developed. Chief Lyons said his people celebrate the time of planting; the maple tree, leader of all trees; the first fruit (the strawberry is the spiritual leader of all plants). They give thanks for beans, the staff of life; for squash; for the American corn that now foods 75% of the world; and for the general harvest, which Native Americans taught white settlers to celebrate.

Thanksgiving ceremonies take place all around the world, Chief Lyons noted—from

intellect to understand the concept of death early on. This makes him different from the other animals. But he is under the law of

aborigines in Australia to Africans on the land. All native peoples understand the need to be respectful and work with the elements, he said.

The Circle of Elders to which he belongs has operated since 1974. Before that, the same group of traditional elders had traveled the United States in a Unity Caravan of Hopis, Lakota, Creeks, Navajos, Iroquois and others, carrying the message of Indian ways, trying to make the continuum more visible to those who had been forcefully dislocated from the land and their culture.

Any elder can join the Circle of Elders, Chief Lyons said, as it travels in North America. Although it is a spiritual group, it also serves as a forum for information, for support, for the guidance of children and the welfare of the people and their lands.

*Oren Lyons, Chief Joagquisho of the Haudenosaunee or Iroquois Confederation, is a Native American elder and spiritual leader, and a member of the Global Forum Steering Committee and Planning Group for the 1990 Global Forum on Environment and Development for Survival.*

*Excerpted from* Shared Vision, *Spring, 1989.*

# Grassroots Religious Ecology Works

### by Leigh Eason / *Everyone's Backyard*

In October, 1987, I had control of my life. I stayed home with my infant son and did cross-stitch to earn extra money. We were the "perfect family," a throw-back to the 50s. We'd worked hard to be the "perfect family." Not that we had earned lots of money from my husband's job. We didn't. Like most American families, we weren't even middle income. But we struggled through the loss of 3 children. We wept together, mourned together, and at the birth of our healthy son, rejoiced together. We worked hard.

But one evening as I looked in the precious face of our son, I wondered how many other women did the same sort of "work," how many families would have to give up and remain childless.

I worried about Alabama's rank as second highest in infant mortality. AL's statistics crossed all lines. The miscarriage rate in some AL counties is twice the national average. I felt the environment played some role in this and asking pastors on both sides of the abortion issue what was the difference between babies dying from environmental poisoning and abortion.

In November, 1987, our *"Perfect family"* went off to Emelle, AL, the world's largest hazardous waste dump. It was such a long way to Emelle that I hadn't even thought about how the dump would impact on the

state's environment. But mainly, I hadn't thought about the complacency it bred in most Alabamians. At the dump, we joined in a prayer vigil. The minister asked us to hold hands and recite the Lord's Prayer. Seven words stuck in my mind: *"On Earth, as it is in Heaven.'"* There's no way Alabama could believe the Lord's Prayer and turn its head on 7 of the words. All those losses and sickness, greed and complacency wasn't like Heaven.

## What was the difference between babies dying from environmental poisoning and abortion?

As I gazed at the dump, I saw my waste being buried and I had done nothing to stop it.

After Christmas, we planned to start a Christian Stewardship to the Environment group.

We began programs to educate people to take responsibility for the environment. We held a workshop to teach alternatives to bad environmental practices. The transformation in the area was not overnight but it was dramatic.

I'm no longer in control of my life. My phone rings day and night. The vision of a

community working through its churches for environmental justice is working. Like an infant, it gets lots of attention. It gets on its feet at times and begins to run, and falls, but grows more independent. In March, 1988, we formed Vision. Vision's slogan was adapted from Psalm 24:1: "The *Earth is the Lord's... Please help preserve it."*

Since March, 1988, Vision took on a project a month. Even though some projects aren't finished, we've won everything we've set out for.

Membership grew from 7 faithful to over 200. We have members in 3 states and helped organize church groups as far away as California.

Each year we have a Christian Stewardship Conference. Our long range goal is a world where activism is respected because it's Christian (Christ-like) and each person knows how s/he can and should be responsible for the Earth's well-being. Vision's long-range goal is more than church organizing. It's to make those words in the Lord's Prayer make a difference, for if His will be done, it will be done *"on Earth as it is in Heaven."*

*Excerpted from* Everyone's Backyard, *a newsletter of Citizens' Clearinghouse for Hazardous Wastes, Inc., June 1990.*

# Christianity and the New Age:
## *Finding Common Ground*
### by Judith Meynell with Father Dirumuid O'Murchu / Findhorn Foundation

Many people see the Christian Church and the "New Age" as apparently contradictory, or at least hugely different and irreconcilable. To encourage a dialogue between the two streams of thought, I recently brought together a group of fifteen people at the Findhorn Community in Scotland for a weekend. The main presenter was Father Dirumuid O'Murchu, a Catholic priest and social psychologist, whose comments I outline further below.

My own experience of Christianity and the deeply spiritual new movement is that both are fundamentally seeking to live out the same values but through a different expression. I perceive them as complementary paths and, without question, ones that could learn from each other.

Taking just the simple message that Jesus Christ preached 2000 years ago—the message of love, peace and justice—we could then leave behind the structure that has built up around this message in the form of our churches, their patriarchal domination, and the rigidity of some of the forms of worship.

In this way the Christian faith could be regarded not as a guardian of the old but as a catalyst of the new.

I also see that this process of integrating two seemingly conflicting streams could be applied to many other polarities of life—capitalism and communism, the individual and the collective, business and spirituality, orthodox and alternative medicine—to name only a few. But what better area to start creating this third way than in the fundamental belief systems and religions of our society. The following selections [are] from Father O'Murchu's presentations.

### The Church In Crisis

Christianity is faced with a very serious identity crisis, which theologians have been noting for centuries. Namely that in the life and teaching of Jesus himself, there is very little allusion to the notion of the Church.

The Church has a frightening capacity for denial and rationalization. In the past twenty years formal Church membership in Europe and the United States has declined to a meager 10-15%, while in most of our churches business goes on as usual. Even when churches had to close down, few asked serious questions; in fact attention tended to focus on a scapegoat to blame for the crisis, rather than on its cause.

Without openly acknowledging and seriously addressing the priority of the reign of

**In the life and teaching of Jesus himself, there is very little allusion to the notion of the Church.**

God as the core vision of the Christian faith, the Church cannot hope to engage meaningfully with our rapidly changing world. Conversely, by adopting the vision and challenge of the reign of God, the Church can assume a whole new cultural relevance.

### The Church of the Future

The Church has a greater chance of being true to its founder when it gives priority not to the foundations of the past, but to the adaptations that need to be made for the Church to be relevant to each new set of cultural circumstances. A Church in tune with the vision of God's new reign must be fluid, flexible, creative, and above all, future-oriented.

It can never justify itself in being denominational, racist, sexist, sectarian or closely aligned with any one national identity. A truly Christian Church must be global, broad and

inclusive: not in the traditional sense of converting everybody to its point of view, but by being a catalyst and model for the inclusiveness and unity that cherishes all the diversity and richness of universal life.

Justice, love and peace must be adopted with a whole new approach to the dominantly patriarchal values of power and control. Power is something to be given away, even to the extent of turning the other cheek. The one that threatens you is the one you must cherish in a new way, even to the extent of loving the enemy who hates you. Just for a moment, consider how perversely the Church has disregarded this challenge by its collusion in warfare and brutality, to the point of concocting the notion of a "just war."

It is not enough to condemn the injustice all around us; we must be just, fair and equitable in all our dealings, putting love, reconciliation and forgiveness above all other considerations.

### The Evolutionary Context

We are in a new evolutionary phase which many people feel they are being drawn towards at this time, characterized by a new sense of the unity of all life and the disintegration of traditional dualities and polarities.

Transitions from one major culture to the next remain largely unexplored, but what seems clear is that all these transitions are marked by upheavel, chaos, and disintegration and death of a declining cultural system. Yet there is continuity, perhaps at the level of what Jung called the "collective unconscious."

Nothing, no matter how sacred or supernatural, escapes the impact of global change and its consequent "death experience." Therefore, in humility and openess to truth, we have to acknowledge that something as sacred and mysterious as religions and Churches will also disintegrate and die. This is not pessimism and travesty, because central to the Christian belief system is the profoundly archetypal truth that all death has a density, namely rebirth or "resurrection."

Churches and religions alike must face the paradoxical truth that new life is only possible through the letting go and death of the old. In the rebirth that follows will be the joyous rediscovery of the fundamental truths that underpin all religions.

*Excerpted with permission from* One Earth, The Findhorn Foundation & Community Magazine.

# The Goddess Revived
## *The Rise of Ecofeminism*

### by Kitty Mattes / *Amicus Journal*

"Arachnophobia," a movie in which a community battles evil spiders with heroic tides of pesticides, was a major hit at theaters this summer; in the end, chemical-wielding man wins out over web-weaving insect. While reinforcing people's fears of the natural world, the movie glorifies the technological fix, and crudely illustrates the mentality environmentalists are up against. Humans increasingly control and stand apart from other forms of life. Among environmentalists, the deepening global crisis is leading to new modes of thought. Recent movements such as Green philosophy, bioregionalism, and deep ecology all seek to rearrange and reharmonize humankind's relationship to nature.

Eco-feminism, an intriguing manifestation of this quest, is rooted equally in environmentalism and women's liberation—two powerful movements that flowered in the 1970s. Combining the feminist and ecological perspectives, ecofeminism makes the woman/nature connection.

"Nature-hating and woman-hating are particularly related and associated," says Ynestra King, "and are mutually reinforcing." King has become the major spokesperson for ecofeminism through her activism, writing, and teaching over the last fifteen years. Currently, she teaches at the New School for Social Research in New York; her forthcoming book is titled *Women and the Reenchantment of the World*. Ecofeminism links human liberation and respect for nonhuman nature, explains King. Ecology is incomplete without feminism, she says, because it does not recognize the necessity of ending the oppression of women; and feminism is disembodied without the ecological perspective, which "asserts the interdependence of living things."

Everything on the feminist agenda—equal rights, quality of work, child care, reproductive choice, and domestic violence—is interconnected, just as the feminist agenda is connected to the environmental agenda.

Charlene Spretnak, whose books include *The Lost Goddesses of Early Greece* and *The Politics of Spirituality,* sees ecofeminism as one of the "new ecologies" that include Green politics, deep ecology, bioregionalism, "creation oriented spirituality," and animal rights. While mid-1970s feminist studies of domination are seminal to ecofeminism, Spretnak particularly emphasizes the impetus and inspiration of recent work on ancient goddess cultures.

Archeologists studying graves and temples in Eastern Europe and the Middle East

("Old Europe"), have uncovered flourishing, unstratified farming societies where females and males had equal power, according to Marija Gimbutas, professor of archeology at the University of California. Religion centered on goddess figures; the female principle was conceived as creative and eternal, the male as spontaneous and ephemeral. This culture reigned until about 3500 BC, Gimbutas claims, when incursions by nomads gradually succeeded in destroying it.

Nomad society was based on the grazing of large herds and on small patrilinear units, with the hero as horseman and warrior. "In contrast to the sacred myths of pre-Indo-

---

**Ecology is incomplete without feminism because it does not recognize the necessity of ending the oppression of women; and feminism is disembodied without the ecological perspective, which "asserts the interdependence of living things."**

---

European peoples, which centered around the moon, water, and the female," Gimbutas has written, the religion of Indo European peoples was "oriented toward the rotating sky, the sun, stars, planets, and other sky phenomena, such as thunder and lightening!' Eventually, the holistic, Earth-oriented goddess cultures were displaced by the hierarchy and domination of patriarchy. Some ecofeminists even date the beginning of our cultural history from 8000 BC, the midpoint of the period when agriculture was first developed.

The ecofeminist view also claims some notable male voices. In his book, *The Dream of the Earth*, environmental philosopher Thomas Berry shows how the values and attitudes that emerged after the historical shift to patriarchy underpin our four, central modern institutions: empire, church, nation, and corporation, all of which are hierarchical and male-dominated. Kirkpatrick Sale, a prominent spokesperson for Green values, whose latest book is *The Conquest of Paradise,* hails ecofeminism, especially as he sees it establishing a direct political link between men and women that is lacking in the traditional feminist movement.

But among ecofeminism's most obvious

allies, there is also serious criticism of the movement. The ecofeminist stance on international population control programs that they are tainted by racist and coercive overtones—puts them at odds with those environmentalists who consider curbing world population an urgent priority. Greens claim that ecofeminism does not exist as a separate philosophy at all, because their own philosophy incorporates the goals of ecofeminism. The "Ten Key Values" that form the basis of Green politics include "postpatriarchal values," which some see as an accurate description of the ecofeminist view. Traditional feminists decry the woman/nature connection at the very core of ecofeminism, calling it a throwback to biological determinism. The identification of women with nature reinforces the Earth Mother stereotype, say feminists, and revives the "essentialism" and romanticization of women they have fought so hard to discredit. From nurturer on a pedestal to tramp in the gutter, the patriarchal woman is defined by her relationship with males, and feminists have always condemned such stereotypes. In this light, ecofeminists risk perpetuating women's marginality and "otherness!'

Women are now looking beyond the goal of integrating themselves into the work force, for example, and questioning the nature of work and the structure of the workplace itself. Day-care is no longer the more appealing alternative to mothering, as women and men are revaluing child care, and questioning the role the state plays in it.

Ecofeminism simultaneously celebrates interconnectedness and diversity. Life is a web, not a hierarchy; within it diversity is essential for both healthy ecosystems and healthy societies. We are all different, but no one's difference is more important than another's. Since our very differences are valuable, all forms of domination are unhealthy. On a political level this stand can be linked to the recognition of the intrinsic worth of nonhuman life (hence animal rights), of indigenous peoples (cultural survival), and of the integrity of minority cultures (as opposed to assimilation).

The celebration of differences may explain why more women of color are to be found in the ranks of the ecofeminists than among the traditional feminists.

Third World women, most of whom find themselves without status in their cultures, also gain empowerment in ecofeminism. Their health and livelihoods are directly linked with environmental quality. Vandana

Shiva, a physicist and ecofeminist in Delhi, India, maintains that "maldevelopment"—a model of progress based on the colonizing, modern West—means destruction for women, nature, and subjugated cultures. She calls for reinstatement of precolonial standards of productivity as the basis for a development based on conservation and ecology.

In Brazil, ecofeminism began to take shape in 1984 as people protested against the testing of experimental contraceptive drugs on poor women. An ecofeminist group has emerged in Brazil, called the Network in Defense of the Human Species; the group plans an international conference next year in Salvador, Brazil.

[The] concern—that the costs of a deteriorating environment fall hardest on those who can least afford it—is shared by all ecofeminists. The population issue must be looked at in the context of other issues, she believes. The United States, with 5 percent of the world's population, produces 25 percent of global warming gases, for example. "Let's face it," says King, "it's the rich, white people who pollute!' Studies have repeatedly documented the relationship between rising economic and social opportunities for women and declining birthrates.

The ecofeminist celebration of diversity and sense of place is shared by Greens and is basic to bioregionalism.

Right now, it is a bit too soon to speak of true environmental politics in the United States. A tiny fraction of the American people has made meaningful life-style changes, but the national agenda consists mainly of approaching environmental problems through the legal system. The gap between philosophy and action keeps American environmentalism tenuous and peripheral. Western European countries are taking far more significant steps-in farm policy, recycling, pollution reduction, and family planning—due to cohesive political pressure. The danger in all "isms" is that they can be reduced to academic bombast or pop-press prattle. Ecofeminism may well inform a future solution to the planetary crisis—and may even play a significant role. But at this time and in this place, it is still only a good idea.

*Excerpted from the* Amicus Journal, *Fall 1990.*

# *Where are the Ethics in Men's Spirituality?*

### by Jack Straton / *Changing Men*

What is "male spirituality?" Substantially missing, that's what. Men are spiritual as members of institutionalized religions or non-traditional spiritual paths, and are the dominant force within most religious organizations. But seldom are men engaged spiritually as men. There are two possible exceptions that I will consider, the Mythopoetic and Ending Men's Violence movements. I will contrast them in order to reveal what each is missing and propose a unifying focus. I begin by defining some terms I will be using.

## Mythopoetic Movement as Ritual

I believe the Mythopoetic movement to be a ritual enterprise rather than a spiritual one, and the complete lack of discussion of ethics within it is what keeps it from being more than the crust of a spiritual endeavor. In what follows, I will focus on the work of Robert Bly, since he is universally recognized as the Crown Poet of the Mythopoetic movement.

The "Gathering for Men" that I attended in Washington, DC in 1987 was a masterpiece of ritual. Robert Bly told us tales, piping us from the land of the Fairies into the land of the Hairies, as Michael Meade, another leader of the Mythopoetic movement, wormed his way into our guts with his drums. Five hundred sons felt pain over five hundred absent fathers—and resentment over five hundred mothers who tried to snatch their balls. "And women today complain that men are too aggressive," said Bly, "but if we hadn't been aggressive 30,000 years ago, the tigers would have devoured all the women." "RrrrRRRAAWWWRRRRr," roared the men.

A day of intense ritual for men, and worse than scant attention paid to ethics. Men were taught in a group-heightened, drum-deepened state how to blame women for their ills. Meade guided us through a story in which we were to casually "kill the slave girls."[1] And then instead of quizzing us on the ethics of bondage and murder, he got 499 men to invisibilize their crimes by focusing their attention on an overt task, choosing loyalty to our father or to the King. Intentional or otherwise, the lesson in erasing women was given. Scared the holy shit out of me, at best this ceremony had the same relationship to a coherent spirituality as a basketball buddyship (a "doing" connection) has to intimate friendship (a "feeling" connection). It was "spear-ritual," not "spiritual."

## Dualism Hides Reality

Bly claims that men cast away the '50s cowboy role in response to the Feminist movement, and in the '70s the world filled up with "soft, sensitive males" who wandered purposelessly through life.

I would like to know exactly where these "soft males" of the '70s were and are. Diana Russell's 1981 survey[2] has shown that rape (not just the reporting of rape) has been on the rise since the 1950s. The 1985 survey by Mary Koss of 6,159 college students on 32 college campuses revealed that one in 13 men had committed rape or attempted rape, and that 1 in 4 admitted to having committed some form of sexual aggression.[3] They show that the "soft male" is a myth of the Mythopoetics.

## Sensitivity or Control?

If men are feeling lost today, it is not because we are too sensitive. In fact we are seldom sensitive enough. How many men do you know who sense their sisters' pain enough to actually do something to stop it? Men who are feeling lost today are responding to feeling out of control. The solution is to examine our need to control.

If we are to control anything, let us learn to control ourselves. We may find ourselves reexpressing power over...our lives. We may learn a new form, the power...to embrace personal integrity, courage and wholeness. Finally, we may join with those heralds of men's spirituality, the radical profeminist activists, to embrace power in the interests...of our gay friends, our women friends and our friends of varied hues.

## Ending Men's Violence—Spirituality in Action

I believe that the best example of men's spirituality in action as men lies in the group of men working to end men's violence. Here is a clearly defined ethical system based on a supreme commitment to service on behalf of others. For the most part, there is a real sense of connection between individuals within this movement and the women and men they are working for. And it is not just an empathy for the victims of men's violence, through friendship, respect or self identification as such. Men who challenge other men to stop being violent are acting toward them in the most loving way possible. To do otherwise is to damn abusers to a hell of their own making.

## Beyond Self

The Ending Men's Violence movement is profoundly ethical—it wants to change the world—yet it scares men away. Robert Bly clearly has a type of magnetic attraction, but he misdirects the men he influences.

Since both movements have fallen short of their potential, it is useful to present a path toward that goal.

What is it that men need to concentrate on in order to develop an ethical male spirituality? Central is our need to understand the difference between the world in which we live and the world we construct within our heads. The trademark of the Fundamentalist is a need to bind oneself securely to a bedrock of belief about reality. But the world is wider and more unknowable than our puny concepts of "world" can contain. Our attempts to manipulate the world to our own ends are bound to leave us in pain and frustration if we are attached to our narrow idea of what the world should be.

The world is not magically identical with our "idea of the world," yet, paradoxically, the only world available to our experience is the internally constructed one. For example, we all know that those men who swagger the most are likely those who are feeling smallest inside.

### Beyond Control

My world view and self view are based upon a life that has learned to acknowledge change, and even chaos, as fundamental parts of existence. Meditation, yoga, art, music and heartfelt rap sessions have helped me cope with a world made up of change, showing me the interconnectedness of the spinning "leaves" and swirling "waters."

Most simply put, my personal story and that of many others suggests that men need to find some process, be it drumming, hiking, meditation or eros that reminds us not to get too attached to our bloated or limited idea of ourselves. Whatever the self is, our idea of our "self" is not the whole story. And from this understanding comes Great Mystery and rightful humility. A world beyond our control is a world beautiful beyond belief.

*Jack Straton is a Spokesperson for the National Organization for Men Against Sexism He is also a quantum theorist at California State University, Fresno.*

**References:**
1. "The slave girls within us" we were later told when I challenged him on this.
2. *Sexual Exploitation: Rape, Child Sexual Abuse, and Workplace Harassment,* by Diana Russell (Sage: Beverly Hills, 1984) pp. 53-56.
3. M.P. Koss, C. A. Gidycz and N. Wisniewski, *J. Consulting and Clinical Psychology,* 55,162 (1987).

*Excerpted from* Changing Men, *Issue 23, Fall/Winter 1991.*

# From Dominance to Partnership

### by John Rowan / *Changing Men*

Patriarchy is perhaps the biggest problem of today. In a patriarchal system women are put down and oppressed and most things female are devalued. The consciousness of man is distorted and limited.

Among spiritually-minded people, patriarchy is just as much of a problem. John Southgate once did a survey of 200 intentional communities and found that 80% of them had one charismatic male leader. The women usually took service roles, just as in the outside world.

Even humanistic psychology, which places so much emphasis on equality and genuine encounter, perpetuates patriarchial systems. It was once found that in the biggest and most important growth center (Esalen), 80% of the leaders were men but 80% of the participants were women.

So this thing called patriarchy is all pervasive.

In her book, *The Chalice and the Blade,* Riane Eisler suggests that rather than use the word "patriarchy," which arouses so many quibbles, we talk about *dominance* cultures and *partnership* cultures.[1] She explores 30,000 years of history and prehistory to show that there have been partnership cultures at intervals all through that time, where men and women have worked together without having to set up structures of dominance and oppression.

It is important to realize that she is not talking about matriarchy; her terminology is specifically chosen to avoid any suggestion that women simply want to take over, in exactly the same way that men have taken over historically. She is talking about genuine partnership.

### Approaches to Partnership

So the question now is, how do we move from a dominance culture to a partnership culture? What do we do about it? I want to suggest that we can choose to work on this from at least three different positions.

The first approach has to do with *taking practical action.* This is very important. On a personal level, men have started to take more interest in child care, to admit that they are emotional beings and to question the all-importance of their careers. On a political level, laws have been passed in many countries now to make the treatment of women more equal. Rules and instructions and advertisements have been reworded.

But all work is limited because there is something else which has to be dealt with at the same time. Many women and men find that in attempting to change their personal behavior, they meet with mysterious blocks. They fully intend to live in a different way, but find that the old ways persist or come back. This is because there are unconscious forces at work here, which have been described by psychoanalysts and others. So it seems that there is another position we can work from, and this second position has to do *with the personal unconscious.* Both women and men have to explore their relations with their mothers, with their fathers and with their own inner conflicts. One of the most important areas here is the way in which the masculine excludes and dominates the feminine in our culture. We have to question this deeply.

The third approach to partnership is the least understood and the most necessary. This is the work from a *spiritual or transpersonal* position. By that I mean the position at which we leave the intellect and operate in terms of symbols, images, metaphors, fairy stories, legends and myths.

## Paganism and Partnership

There are of course many spiritual and religious traditions, and many say something about the relationship between the female and the male, and how it could or should be. One tradition which seems to deal successfully with this relationship is the pagan tradition—what we sometimes call the Old Religion, or Wicca.

In paganism, pre-Christian tradition which has been revived in the past 40 years in many different countries, the main deity is the Great Goddess. She is often described as a threefold Goddess the Maiden, the Mother and the Crone corresponding to the three phases of the moon: waxing, full and waning. But she is not just a moon goddess, she is the Great Cosmic Mother of All. She is to be found everywhere and in all things. Her consort and partner is the Horned God, who relates to her with love and respect, but he never tries to be independent of her.

In trying to understand the relationship between the Great Goddess and the Horned God, I have found the Tantric doctrine of the Shakti very helpful. Shakti is the female power, and all the power there is. If the god wants to move, he has to draw on the Shakti energy—without it, he is powerless.

## Kali Ma

Here is a little of what Barbara Walker says about Kali Ma, the Great Goddess:[3]

Kali was the basic archetypal image of the birth-and-death Mother, simultaneously womb and tomb, giver of life and devourer of her children: the same image portrayed in a thousand ancient religions. Brahmans assigned Kali's three functions to three male gods, calling them Brahma the creator, Vishnu the preserver and Kali's archaic consort Shiva the destroyer; but the Nirvana Tantra treated the claims of male gods with contempt: *...so long as the living man does not know the supreme truth in regard to Her ... his desire for liberation can only give rise to ridicule...O fair-eyed Devi, just as rivers and lakes are unable to traverse a vast sea, so Brahma and other gods lose their separate existence on entering the uncrossable and infinite being of Great Kali. Compared with the vast sea of the being of Kali, the existence of Brahma and the other gods is nothing but such a little water as is contained in the hollow made by the cow's hoof. Just as it is impossible for a hollow made by a cow's hoof to form a notion of the unfathomable depths of a sea, so it is impossible for Brahma and other gods to have a knowledge of the nature of Kali.*

The Yogini Tantra said of Kali, "Whatever power anything possesses, that is the Goddess." Shakti, "Power," was one of her important names. Without her, neither man nor god could act at all. Contrary to the Western idea of her as a purely destructive Goddess, she was the fount of every kind of love, which flowed into the world only through her agents on Earth, women. Thus it was said a male worshipper of Kali "bows down at the feet of women," regarding them as his rightful teachers.

## Connectedness

So that is the Goddess.

Alan Bleakley suggests the image of the string of a musical instrument such as a violin or guitar.[4] If the string is too loose, no music. If the string is too tight it snaps and again no music. But if the tension is just right, music can come out and something new can be created; so it is between men and women.

In my workshops, I explore this spiritual material, because it is the least well-known of the three approaches to partnership that we have mentioned. I approach it through myth and ritual because that is its language.

But throughout, the emphasis remains on the *relationship between the male and the female, both within the person and between people.* Only if this relationship is right, taking on the feminist critique of dominance cultures, and taking power issues seriously, will we break out of the confines of our cultural conditioning.

## References

1. Riane Eisler, *The Chalice and the Blade* (Harper & Row: San Francisco, 1990). A modern classic, with an important contribution to make. The basis of this article.
2. Bob Cornell, *Gender and Power* (Polity Press: Cambridge 1987). Essential reading on the central issue of power in society.
3. Barbara G. Walker, *The Women's Encyclopedia of Myths and Secrets* (Harper & Row: San Francisco, 1983). Reworking of the who field from a feminist standpoint.
4. Alan Bleakley, *Fruits of the Moon Tree* (Gateway Books: London. 1984) A rhapsodic and original account of some important themes by a poet.

*Excerpted from* Changing Men, *Issue 23, Fall/ Winter 1991.*

IF THE CIRCLE SYMBOLIZES WHOLENESS, AND THE SPIRAL REPRESENTS CHANGE, THEN THE BALANCE WITHIN THESE TWO SHAPES IS THAT ONLY CHANGE CAN ARRIVE AT WHOLENESS

©1992 Cielle Tewksbury

*Coming full circle...endings and beginnings; in how many cultures would I discover that ancient, repeated theme. Whether walking the medicine wheel, the labyrinth, the sacred hoop, the mandala or the maze in the cathedral at Chartres, I felt it again and again and again.*

*Cielle Tewksbury, the artist, lives on a farm in Marlboro, Vermont. She teaches Tai Chi and presents seminars, in New England and on the West Coast, on exploring comparative symbols in movement.*

# Inspiration and Intolerance: The Double Truth

### by John Bowker / *Shared Vision*

Religions offer, to many people in all countries of the world, life, meaning and hope. In some circumstances they are (exactly as Marx observed) the heart of a heartless situation, the sigh of the oppressed creature. But they are equally the inspiration of art, music, dance, drama, architecture. They give substance to the dreams of the human spirit. They give guidance on how to live wisely and appropriately in ways which lead beyond this world into life beyond death.

How, then, does it come about that religions are involved in virtually all the bloody, intransigent and apparently insoluble conflicts in the world? Northern Ireland, the Middle East, Sri Lanka, Sikhs in Amritsar, people in the Philippines, South Africa, Afghanistan—while in other areas, such as Cyprus and the border between India and Pakistan, where there is an uneasy peace, but with a comparable background of warfare and violence—in all these, religion is not the sole cause, but it is deeply involved. How, also, does it happen that all religions in their past, and some still in the present, exhibit the spiritual equivalent of political totalitarianism, with all the consequences of oppression, intolerance and terrorization? How is it that the poet, John Clare, could, in 1824, finish reading Fox's *Book of Martyrs* and conclude, "The sum of my opinion is that Tyranny and Cruelty appear to be the inseparable companions of Religious Power, and the Aphorism is not far from the truth that says, 'All priests are the same'."?

The answer lies in recognizing that *both* realities about religions (both inspiration and intolerance) are true at one and the same time: Religions are so important to their adherents that they would rather die than abandon them; for them there are more important things in life than living: "I will never give up my faith...Whatever happens, if the worst comes to the worst, my faith cannot be snatched from me. That's a part of my body, that's something attached to my heart that only dies when I die." But the beliefs and practices which sustain that kind of commitment do not float about in a random way. They have to be organized if they are to be transmitted from one life, or from one generation, to another. So it comes about that religions are highly systematized. They are organized into *systems* for the processing of information. Indeed, they are historically the earliest human cultural achievement for protecting and transmitting precisely that religious information which has proved true and successful in guiding human lives from the cradle to the grave and beyond the grave.

But systems have boundaries, sometimes literally so (in terms of geography), but always metaphorically so. And where you have boundaries, there you have border incidents: where a religious system comes under pressure, either literally by invasion, or metaphorically by (for example) conceptual and practical erosion, as in the process of secularization, it is predictable that there will be a defensive (or sometimes offensive) conservation of the system and what it stands for. This can be seen at the present time from Teheran to the Vatican, from Belfast to Amritsar.

Hence the extreme importance of the Oxford Conference. At the moment, we are all too polite about religion. We emphasize the good and inspiring truths, and look for agreement between religions on the great themes of hope and peace, justice and generosity; and all that is indeed part of the picture. All religions have inclusive voices of friendship and reconciliation, and these need to be encouraged and reinforced. But it is essential also to recognize that religious involvement in conflict and warfare is neither exceptional nor aberrant. All religions, including those which advocate ahimsa (nonviolence) and peace, justify warfare in some circumstances. Therefore politicians and statesmen must take seriously the involvement of religions in the political and economic process of the world, and stop regarding religions as inoffensive options which lie at the edges of life, rather than (for the majority of people alive today) at the center.

The time is extremely short. It is now certainly conceivable that we are in the last decades of human life as we know it on this planet. Religions won't be the only cause of that catastrophe if it happens. But if we want them to become a part of the resistance to it, then we must bring them into a more formal and deliberate connection with each other Only then can we really begin to pray—and to act for the peace of Jerusalem; and of Belfast, land of Soweto, of Warsaw, of Amritsar, of El Salvador, of Cyprus, of Teheran and Baghdad. There have been all too many evils and disasters in the past, and in the history, of religions. But the point of departure for all religions is not only to recognize those disasters, but to repent of them, and to turn back in *the power which religion also offers* to the renewal and the redemption of the Earth.

*Professor John Bowker is Dean of Chapel, Trinity College, Cambridge University, and Adjunct Professor in the Universities of Pennsylvania and North Carolina State. Author of* The Religious Imagination, Worlds of Faith, Licensed Insanities, *and* The Sense of God, *he is someone who, as the Bishop of Salisbury said of him, "takes religion out of the ghetto and indicates the ways in which it is of burning concern to every one of us ."*

*Excerpted from* Shared Vision, *Spring 1988.*

> **Hitherto, man had to live with the idea of death as an individual; from now onward [hu]mankind will have to live with the idea of its death as a species.**
>
> — *Arthur Koestler (1905-1983)*

# Reader's Index

# Directory Subject Index

## Subject Headings

Abortion Rights
Acid Rain
Adoption
Africa
Agriculture
AIDS
Air Pollution
Alliances
Alternative Consumer—
    Cruelty-Free
Alternative Consumer—Ecological
Alternative Consumer—Health
Alternative Consumer—
    Socially-Responsible Investing
Alternative Consumer—
    Third World
Alternative Political Parties &
    Issues
Animal Rights
Antartica
Anti-authoritarian
Anti-draft
Anti-Nuclear Issues
Apprenticeships
Appropriate Technology
Architecture
Arctic
Arms Control
Arts
Asia

Battered Women
BBS/Computer Networking
Beautification
Bioregionalism
Biotechnology
Birth
Boycotts
Broadcasting
Budget Priorities

Caribbean
Censorship
Central America
Chesapeake Bay
Child Abuse
Child Support
Children's Rights
Civil Disobedience
Civil Liberties, Censorship, &
    Freedom of Expression
Co-housing
Coalitions
Community Economics
Computer Networking
Conflict Education
Conflict Resolution
Conservation
Consumer Protection
Consumer Rights
Cooperatives
Corporate Responsibility

Counseling
Criminal Justice System

Day Care
Death & Dying
Death Penalty
Democratic Socialism
Demographics
Developing Nations
Disabled's Issues
Disarmament
Diversity
Divestment
Draft Evasion
Drylands

East-West Relations
Economic Conversion
Economics
Education
Electronic Democracy
Energy
Energy Efficiency
Environment
Equal Rights

Faith
Family
Family Farms
Family Issues
Family Planning
Farm Workers
Farmland
Feminism
Film
Fine Arts
Food Distribution
Foreign Policy
Forests/Third World
Forests/U.S.
Freedom of Expression
Fundraising
Future

Gay
Global Understanding
Global Warming
Government Accountability
Graphics
Great Lakes
Green Consumer
Green Politics
Gun Control

Hazardous Toxic Waste
Health
Herbal Remedies
Holistic Education
Homelessness
Homeschooling
Homeworkers
Housing
Hunger

Ideation
Immigration/Refugees

Indigenous Peoples—
    Developing Nations
Intentional Communities
Cohousing
Interfaith
International Law
Internships
Intervention—Developing Nations
Invention/Ideation
Investing

Jobs
Justice
Juvenile Law

Labor
Land Trusts
Latin America
Lesbian
Letter Writing
Literacy
Literature
Lobbying—Animal Rights
Lobbying—Developing Nations
Lobbying—Environmental
Lobbying—Feminism
Lobbying—Minority Rights
Lobbying—Other Justice Issues
Lobbying—Peace

Media
Media Watch/Responsibility
Medicare
Men's Liberation
Mentoring
Mid-East
Minority Rights
Monopolies
Multilogues
Municipal Issues
Music

National Health
National Security
Native Americans
Networks/Networking
Nonviolence
Nonviolent Civil Disobedience
Nuclear Test Ban
Nutrition

Occupational Safety
Organic
Over-population

Pacific/Pacific Rim
Passive Resistance
Peace
Peace Dividend
Permaculture
Pesticide Issues
Philanthropy
Physically-Challenged
Poetry
Polar
Political Prisoners
Politics

Population Issues
Poverty
Preventative Medicine
Prisons
Pro-Choice
Psychology
Public Health

Racism
Rainforests
Rape/Sexual Abuse
Recreation
Recycling  (See Waste Mgmt.)
Renewable Energy
Repatriation
Rural Communities
Rural Relocation

Science
Self-Help—Health
Self-determination
Seniors
Sexual Abuse
Socially Responsible Investing
Soil
Solar
South Africa
South America
Soviet Relations
Space
Spiritual
Substance Abuse

Taxation
Telecommunications
Terminal Illness
Theater
Third World
Third World Alternative Markets
Toxic Waste
Trade
Transformation
Transportation
Travel

Unions
United Nations
Urban

Vegetarianism
Veterans
Victims' Rights
Vitamins
Volunteering
Voting

War Tax Resistance
Waste Management
Water
Welfare Rights
Wetlands
Whistle-blowing
Wildlife
Wind
Women's Rights
Worker Ownership
Workplace Democracy

tary Tax Campaign; Draft Notices; Militarism Resource Project News; Objector; On Watch; Reporter for Conscience' Sake;

## Anti-Nuclear Issues

❶ Abalone Alliance; Architects, Designers, and Planners for Social Responsibility; Center for Defense Information; Citizens Against Chemical Contamination; Citizens Against Rocky Flats Contamination; Citizens Energy Project; Coalition for Nuclear Disarmament; Coalition For Safe Power; Committee for Nuclear Responsibility; Concerned Citizens for Nuclear Safety; Critical Mass Energy Project; Don't Waste California; Federation of American Scientists; Friends of the Earth; Fund for Peace; Greenpeace USA; Ground Zero Center for Nonviolent Action; Hanford Education and Action League; Health and Energy Institute; Human Ecology Party; INFACT; INFACT(GE Boycott); Interfaith Center for Corporate Responsibility; Interfaith Center to Reverse the Arms Race; International Alliance of Atomic Veterans; International Physicians for the Prevention of Nuclear War; Jewish Action for Nuclear Responsibility; Lawyers' Committee on Nuclear Policy; Librarians for Nuclear Arms Control; Mobilization for Survival; Mothers Embracing Nuclear Disarmament (MEND); Mothers For Peace; Nevada Desert Experience; Northwest Nuclear Safety Campaign; Nuclear Control Institute; Nuclear Free America; Nuclear Free America; Nuclear Information and Resource Service; Nuclear Information Center; Nukewatch; Peace Pac; Physicians For Social Responsibility (PSR); Recreators For Social Responsibility; Red River Peace Network (RRPN); Resource Center For Nonviolence; Riverside Church Disarmament Program; Rocky Mountain Peace Center; Safe Energy Communication Council; Sane/Freeze; Section on Social Responsibility, Canadian Psychological Association; Seeds of Peace; Sojourners Fellowship; Student/Teacher Organization to Prevent Nuclear War; Tellus Research Program; Terra; Union of Concerned Scientists; Unitarian Universalist Peace Network; Wilmington College Peace Resource Center; Women Strike For Peace; Women's International League for Peace and Freedom;

❷ Advocate; Beyond War; Bulletin of the Atomic Scientists; Catalyst; Convergence; CPSR Newsletter; Desert Voices; FAS Public Interest Report; Greenpeace Magazine; Ground Zero; Groundswell; In Brief; INFACT News; Lawyers' Committee on Nuclear Policy Newsletter; LNAC Almanac; MYTHbusters; New Abolitionist; Northern Sun News; Nuclear Chronicle; Nuclear Power in Crisis; Nuclear Resister; Nucleus; Nukewatch Pathfinder; Pacific Bulletin; Peace Planter; Progress; PSR Reports; RWC Waste Paper; Stone & Sling; Test Banner;

❸ Disarmament; NIRSNET; Peace Education Resources Catalog: Audio-Visuals;

❹ Peace Education Resources Catalog: BOOKS;

❺ EcoWorks, Inc.;

❻ All Things Nuclear; Citizen Diplomats: Americans Ending the Cold War; Concerned Citizen's Guide to National Security; Conscientious Investor's Guide to Socially-Responsible Mutual and Money Market Funds; Investment Services & Directory of Alternative Investments; Language of Nuclear War: An Intelligent Citizen's Dictionary; Nuclear Free America; Nuclear Waste Digest & Nuclear Waste Primer; Nuclear Weapons Chart; Nuclear Weapons Databook; Swords into Plowshares: Nonviolent Direct Action for Disarmament; Teacher's Resource Guide; Towards a Nuclear Free Future: A Guide to Organizing a Local Nuclear Free Zone Campaign; Uncovering the Nuclear Industry: A Research Guide; Understanding Nuclear Weapons and Arms Control: A Guide to the Issues; Waging Peace: A Handbook for the Struggle to Abolish Nuclear Weapons;

## Apprenticeships

See Jobs; Mentoring; Volunteering;

## Appropriate Technology

See also Solar; Wind;

❶ Alliance to Save Energy; Alternative Energy Resources Organization (AERO); Appalachia Science in the Public Interest; Appropriate Technology International; Appropriate Technology Transfer for Rural Areas; Council on International and Public Affairs; Critical Mass Energy Project; Forum on Renewable Energy & Climate Change; Foundation on Economic Trends; Greater Yellowstone Coalition; Health and Energy Institute; Mothers For Peace; National Center For Appropriate Technology (NATAS); National Consumer Law Center; Rocky Mountain Institute; Science for Peace; University Research Expeditions Program (UREP);

❷ Alternator; Both Sides Now; Burwood Journal; Nuclear Power in Crisis; Rain; TRANET;

❹ Lorien House; Survival News Service;

❺ Environmental Concerns; Lehman's Non-Electric Catalog; Orrin International Trade Co.; SaveEnergy Co.; Signal;

❻ Alternative America; Business Environmental Lending Library; Business Opportunities Workbook, Implementing Economic Renewal Projects; Communities for Conservation and Action: A Manual for Building Community; Healthy Harvest IV: A Directory; Human Factors Society - Directory; Power of the States: a Fifty-State Survey of Renewable Energy; RAINBOOK: Resources for Appropriate Technology; State of the States;

## Architecture

❶ American Institute of Architects Environmental Resources Committee, LA Chapter; Center for Human Environments; Eco-Home Network; Mega-Cities Project; Shared Living Resource Center; Virginia Polytechnic Institute and State University;

❷ Design Spirit; ECO; Ecolution; Livability; Shared Living Community;

❺ Native Self-Sufficiency Center;

## Arctic

See Polar;

## Arms Control

Too numerous; see related topics or contact Macrocosm for specialized searches or database.

## Arts

See related topics or all entries flagged ✎;

## Asia

❶ Human Rights Watch; Indochina Project;

❷ Action Alert; Asia & Pacific Update; Asian Affairs: An American Review; Asian Rights Advocate; Bulletin of Concerned Asian Scholars; Indochina Issues; Indochina Newsletter; Korea Biweekly Report; Philippine Resource Center Monitor; South Asia Bulletin; Southeast Asia Chronicle; third world; Veteran Affairs News; Vietnam Today;

❸ Asian American Media Reference Guide;

❺ Exotic Gifts; From The Rainforest; Marketplace: Handwork of India; Rainbow World Imports; SRI Advisors;

❻ Alternative Directory of South Asian Non-Governmental Organizations; Asia and Pacific: A Directory of Resources; Asian Studies Newsletter; Human Rights Directory: Asia & the Pacific;

## Battered Women

❶ Batterers' Group; Boulder County Safehouse; Center for Women's Global Leadership; National Coalition Against Domestic Violence; World Conference on Religion and Peace;

❷ No Longer Silent; Victimology: An International Journal;

❸ Clearinghouse on Child Abuse and Neglect Information;

❹ Volcano Press;

❻ Battered Women's Directory; Safe, Strong, and Streetwise; Talking It Out: A Guide to Groups For Abused Women;

## BBS/Computer Networking

❶ Action Linkage; Aquarian Research Foundation; Networking Institute Inc.; Pennsylvania Resources Council; SeniorNet;

❷ Conflict Resolution Notes; PICA News;

❸ Agenda Project; Alternatives: The Computer Bulletin Board Dedicated to Progressive Social Change; BBS Bible USA; Cleveland Free-Net; Communications & Computer Multilogues; Community Memory Project; ConflictNet; Connected Education, Inc.; Connecting with Nature (WORLDPEACEU); DataNet; EcoLinking, Everyone's Guide to Online Information; EcoNet; Ed-Line; Electronic Information Exchange System (EIES); ElfNet; Fulcrum: The R & D Network for the Development of Human Systems; Fund Raising Management - Non-Profit Software Package Directory Issue; GEMNET; Global Action Network; Global Business Network; Global Electronic University; Global Suggestion Box for Ideas to Promote Global Harmony; Global Systems Analysis and Simulation (GLOSAS) Project; HandsNet; Holistic Education Community Network; HomeoNet; IdeaNet; Institute for Global Communications; Meta Network; New Computerized World Information Service; NIRSNET; Pacific Telecommunications Council; PeaceNet; Public Electronic Network (PEN); Public-Access Xanadu(TM) or PAX(TM); R.A.C.H.E.L. (Remote Access Chemical Hazards Electronic Library); RecycleLine; Some Things Special; WELL (Whole Earth 'Lectronic Link);

❺ Signal;

❻ Networking: People Connecting with People;

## Beautification

❶ America the Beautiful Fund; American Pedestrian Association; Keep America Beautiful, Inc.; League to Save Lake Tahoe; National Wildflower Research Center; Scenic America;

❷ Hortideas; Sign Control News; Vision;

❸ KAB: It's More Than a Slogan;

❻ Clean Team Manual; Multi-Material Recycling Manual; Shading Our Cities, A Resource Guide For Urban Community Forests Communities; Signs For Main Street: Guidelines;

## Bioregionalism

See also Permaculture;

❶ Alaska Bioregional Network; Alliance for the Wild Rockies; Bioregional Women's Collective; Center for Rare Tropical Bird Conservation; Community Economic and Ecological Development Institute (CEED); Cumberland Green Bioregional Council; Driftless Bioregional Network; Fourth World Movement; Institute for Social Ecology; New England Wild Flower Society, Inc.; North American Bioregional Council; Northcoast Environmental Center; Planet Drum Foundation; San Antonio Bioregional Research Group;

❷ Boundary Waters Journal; California; Center for Rural Affairs Newsletter; Cultivator; Decentralize!; Green Synthesis; Katuah; Mesechabe; Networker; New Catalyst; New Wealth; Northwest Conservation: News and Priorities; Pollen: Journal of Bioregional Education; Raise the Stakes; Small Farm Advocate; Vermont Life; Washington Post Magazine;

❹ Yankee Books;

❻ Bioregional Bibliography; Bioregional Directory; Going Off the Beaten Path; Green City Program for the Bay Area and Beyond;

## Biotechnology

❶ Center For Science Information; Foundation for Biointensive Agriculture; Foundation on Economic Trends; Friends of the Earth; National Association of Biology Teachers;

❷ geneWATCH; NGO Networker;

## Birth

❻ Ambulatory Maternal Health Care and Family Planning Services; Directory of Nurse-Midwifery Practices; Directory of Women's Health Care Center; Encyclopedia of Public Affairs Information Sources; Healthy Mothers, Healthy Babies - Directory of Educational Materials; NAPSAC Directory of Alternative Birth Services & Consumer Guide; Reaching Out: A Directory of National Organizations Related to Maternal and Child Health; Starting Early: A Guide to Federal Resources in Maternal and Child Health; Total Nutrition for Breast-Feeding Mothers; Whole Again Birth Catalog: A Sourcebook for Choices in Childbirth; Wise Woman Herbal for the Childbearing Year;

## Boycotts

See also Investing;

❶ Action for Corporate Accountability (ACA); Austin United Support Group; Boycott Committee; Boycott of Conscience; Boycott Shell Campaign; Casa Chile; Chile Committee; Coalition to Boycott Domino's Pizza; Coke Divestment Campaign; Colorado Earth First!; Companies Which Cut Rainforests Boycott; Conference of Consumer Organizations; Council on Economic Priorities; Educators Against Racism and Apartheid; Fresh Fruit/Vegetable Workers Union, UFCW Local 78B; Friends of Animals; Georgians Against Smoking Pollution; In Defense of Animals (IDA); INFACT; INFACT(GE Boycott); Institute for Consumer Responsibility; Institute for Gaean Economics; Interfaith Center for Corporate Responsibility; Irish National Caucus; Jemez Action Group; Labor Letter; National Coalition on Television Violence; National Family Farm Coalition; National War Tax Resistance Coordinating Committee; Neighbor to Neighbor; Neighbor to Neighbor; Nuclear Free America; Nukewatch; Operation PUSH; People for the Ethical Treatment of Animals (PETA); Rainforest Action Network; Snake River Alliance; Stop War Toys Campaign; War Resisters League; Waste Oil Action;

❷ Boycott Shell Bulletin; Council on Economic Priorities Research Report; Food and Justice; INFACT News; National Boycott News; NCTV News; Nukewatch Pathfinder; Peace Planter; Progressive Student News; Rainforest Action Network Alert; Tobacco and Youth Reporter;

❸ Bringing Bad Things to Light;

❻ Better World Investment Guide; Conscientious Investor's Guide to Socially-Responsible Mutual and Money Market Funds; General Electric Shaping Nuclear Weapons Policies for Profits; Investment Services & Directory of Alternative Investments;

## Broadcasting

❶ Edge of Life Center; Educational Communications; National Citizens Committee For Broadcasting; Oasis Group; Recording for the Blind; Union for Democratic Communications; World Peace University;

❷ Columbia Journalism Review; GBH/The Members' Magazine; Independent; Journal of Popular Film and Television; Telemedium; Threepenny Review;

❸ Affiliated Media Foundation Movement - AMFM; Alternative Radio; Americans Dialogue; Children's Television Workshop; CNN (Cable News Network); Connecting with Nature (WORLDPEACEU); Creative Resources Guild; CRG Resource Directory; Deep Dish TV, The First National Satellite Access Network; Directory of Information and Referral Services in the United States and Canada; Econews; Environment Today; Environmental Media Association; Environmental News Service; Environmental Viewpoints; Gaia Institute; Global Vision TV & Radio; KPFA-FM94; Mushalko's Radiophonic

Lab; Nationwide Black Radio Directory; Nature NewsBreak; New Dimensions Radio and Tapes; New Era Media; Other America's Radio; Pacifica Cassette Tapes Catalogue; Pacifica Radio; Pacifica Radio Archive Catalog; Peace Through The Airwaves; Peaceful Warrior Productions; Peacemakers Television; Peaceworks; Radio For Peace International; RadioWest; Skylink Satellite Communications, Inc.; There is a Solution; Turner Broadcasting System; University of the Air; Whole Life Radio Network KFOX-93.5; Xchange Television;

**Budget Priorities**

See also Government Accountabilty; Taxation;
❶ Campaign to Cut Military Spending In Half; Center on Budget and Policy Priorities; Citizens Against Government Waste; Common Cause; Comprehensive Security Project; Employment Research Associates; Federal Incentive Awards Program; Full Employment Action Council; INFACT; National Governors' Association;
❷ Campaign Report; Common Cause Magazine; INFACT News;
❻ Access: A Security Information Service;

**Caribbean**

See also Latin America;
❶ Data Center; Transafrica;
❷ Callaloo; Caribbean Newsletter; Cuba Update; Unidad Borinquena;
❻ Directory of Puerto Rican Organizations; Human Rights Directory: Latin America & the Caribbean;

**Censorship**

See Civil Liberties;

**Central America**

See also Latin America;
❶ Central America Working Group; Central American Resource Center; Committee In Solidarity with the People of El Salvador (CISPES); Committee In Solidarity With The People Of Guatemala; Data Center; Ecumenical Program On Central America & the Caribbean (EPICA); Independent Commission of Inquiry on the US Invasion of Panama; Institute of Maya Studies; MADRE; Mayan Crafts; Medical Aid for El Salvador; Methodist Federation for Social Action; National Labor Committee in Support of Human Rights in El Salvador; National Sanctuary Defense Fund; Neighbor to Neighbor; Network in Solidarity With the People of Guatemala; Network of Educators Committees on Central America; Nicaragua Interfaith Committee For Action; Nicaragua Network; Nicaragua Solidarity Network; Wisconsin Coordinating Council on Nicaragua; Witness for Peace;
❷ Alert!: Focus on Central America; Barricada Internacional; CARECEN Speaks; CENSA's Strategic Report; Central America Bulletin; Central America Monitor; Central America NewsPak; Challenge: A Journal of Faith and Action in Central America; El Estiliano and N.I.C.A.; Focus; Labor Report on Central America; Links; MADRE Speaks/MADRE Informa; News Notes; Nicaragua Information Center Bulletin; Nicaragua Network News; Periodic Reports from CARECEN; Report on Guatemala; Students United for Peace Newsletter; Telegraph News; Tidewater Nicaragua Project Foundation Newsletter; Update; Veteran; Witness for Peace; Witness for Peace Newsbrief;
❸ Central America; El Salvador Media Project; Video Project 1992 Catalog: Films and Videos for a Safe and Sustainable World;
❺ Alternative Trading News; One World Trading Co.; Paraclete Society International; Pueblo to People; Rainbow World Imports; Thread of Hope; World Peace by Nina Grand;
❻ Directory of Central America Organizations; Directory of National Organizations Dealing With Central America; Human Rights Directory: Latin America & the Caribbean; List of Declared Public Sanctuaries; Rainforest: A Guide to Research & Tourist Facilities at Selected Tropical Sites in Central & South America; What's Wrong, Who's Right in Central America? A Citizen's Guide;

**Chesapeake Bay**

❶ Alliance for the Chesapeake Bay; Chesapeake Bay Foundation; Clean Water Action Project;
❷ Chesapeake Bay Magazine;
❻ Chesapeake Citizen Directory;

**Child Abuse**

See also Children's Rights;
❶ Action for Children; American Humane Association; Boulder County Safehouse; Feminists Against Pornography; Free Arts for Abused Children; Illusion Theater Prevention Program; National Center For Missing & Exploited Children; National Coalition Against Domestic Violence;
❷ In Touch; Protecting Children; Victimology: An International Journal;
❸ Advocate's Guide to the Media; Child Abuse and Neglect and Family Violence Audiovisual Catalog; Clearinghouse on Child Abuse and Neglect Information;
❻ Child Find Photo Directory of Missing Children; Child Sexual Abuse Prevention: How To Take The First Steps; Courage to Heal: A Guide for Women Survivors of Child Sexual Abuse; Directory for Exceptional Children; Directory of Child Abuse; Guide to Resources in Holistic Education; Missing Children; National Directory of Child Abuse Prosecutors; National Directory of Children & Youth Services; National Directory of Runaway Programs; North American Directory of Programs for Runaways, Homeless Youth and Missing Children; Parental Kidnapping: An International Resource Directory; Programs to Strengthen Families: A Resource Guide; Safe, Strong, and Streetwise; Sexual Abuse Prevention Education: An Annotated Bibliography; Sexual Assault and Child Abuse: A National Directory of Victim Services and Prevention Programs;

**Child Support**

❶ Welfare Warriors;
❷ American Family; CDF Reports; Welfare Mothers Voice; National Congress for Men - Directory;

**Children's Rights**

See also Child Abuse;
❶ Action for Children; Action for Corporate Accountability (ACA); Boulder County Safehouse; CARE International; Children International; Children's Defense Fund; Children, Inc.; Free Arts for Abused Children; Interfaith Impact for Justice and Peace; National Center For Missing & Exploited Children; National Child Nutrition Project; Promise the Children; Save the Children; Welfare Warriors; World Conference on Religion and Peace;
❷ Black Child Advocate; CDF Reports; Ford Foundation Letter; INFACT News; Victimology: An International Journal; Welfare Mothers Voice; Youth Law News;
❸ Adoption; Advocate's Guide to the Media; Child Abuse and Neglect and Family Violence Audiovisual Catalog; Living Stage Theater Company;
❹ Children's Book Press;
❻ Adoption Directory; Child Find Photo Directory of Missing Children; Children and Adolescents with Mental Illness: A Parents' Guide; Council for Health & Human Service Ministries - Directory Services; Directory for Exceptional Children; Directory of Child Abuse; Guide to Resources in Holistic Education; Missing Children; National Directory of Child Abuse Prosecutors; National Directory of Children & Youth Services; National Directory of Runaway Programs; North American Directory of Programs for Runaways, Homeless Youth and Missing Children; Parental Kidnapping: An International Resource Directory; Parental Kidnapping: How to Prevent an Abduction and What to Do If Your Child is Abducted; Society for Research in Child Development; State Youth Employment Initiatives: A Resource Guide and Framework for Action;

**Civil Disobedience**

See Nonviolence; Nonviolent Civil Disobedience; War Tax Resistance;

**Civil Liberties, Censorship, & Freedom of Expression**

❶ American Civil Liberties Union (ACLU); Americans for Religious Liberty; Center for National Security Studies; Meikeljohn Peace Institute; National Committee Against Repressive Legislation; Project Censored; Women's Institute For Free Press;
❷ A.C.L.U. News; AIM Magazine; American Atheist; American Right to Read Newsletter; Censorship News; Civil Liberties; Civil Liberties Alert; Civil Liberties Review; Crisis; First Principles; Forum; Free Inquiry; Freedom of Information Report; Freedom to Read Foundation News; Freedom Writer; Gauntlet; Index on Censorship; Liberty; Mother Jones; Newsletter on Intellectual Freedom; Progressive; Public Eye Magazine; Rights; SPLC Report; Voice of Reason Newsletter; Workers World; Youth Law News;
❸ Artist Equity Association; Human Rights Film Guide;
❻ Books on Trial: A Survey of Recent Cases; Equal Rights Amendment: An Annotated Bibliography of the Issues; Using the Freedom of Information Act, A Step by Step Guide;

**Co-housing**

See Cooperatives; Intentional Communities;

**Coalitions**

Too numerous; see related topics or contact Macrocosm for specialized searches or database.

**Community Economics**

See Rural Communites; Intentional Communities; Cooperatives;
❶ Accion International; ACORN; Appalachia Science in the Public Interest; Association for Enterprise Opportunities; Atlantic Center for the Environment; California Community Foundation; Center for Community Change; Center for Community Self-Help; Center for Democratic Renewal; Center for Economic Revitalization; Center for Holistic Resource Management; Center for Neighborhood Technology; Center for Urban Affairs; Community Educational Service Council, Inc. (CESCI); Community Information Exchange; Community Information Resource Center; Community Regeneration; Community Service Inc.; Cooperative Resources and Service Project; Ecologia (Ecologists Linked for Organizing Grassroots Initiatives); Fair Trade Campaign; Farallones Institute; Fellowship for Intentional Community; Foundation for International Community Assistance; Fourth World Movement; Freedom From Hunger Foundation; Good Life Study Tours; Institute for Community Economics, Inc.; Institute for Local Self-Reliance; Intermediate Technology Development Group of North America; International Society for the Preservation of Rain Forests; Land Trust Alliance; Livingston Economic Alternatives in Progress; National Association of Housing Cooperatives; National Association of Neighborhoods; National Association of Service and Conservation Corps; National Congress for Community Economic Development; National Self-Help Resource Center; Organize Training Center; Partners For Livable Places; Plenty USA; Progressive Community Associates (PCA); School of Living (SOL); Schumacher Society; Shared Living Resource Center; The Other Economic Summit (TOES); US Conference of Mayors;
❷ Accion International Bulletin; Backwoods Home Magazine; Business Ethics; Communities: Journal of Cooperation; Community Change; Community Economics; Community Service Newsletter; Cooperative Housing Bulletin; Fourth World Review; Green Revolution; Jubilee Partners Report; NAN Bulletin; NAN Displacement Reporter; Neighborhood Works; Network News; Rain; Shared Living Community; Vermont Vanguard Press, Statewide Weekly;
❹ Accion International Publications List; C. Olson & Company; Community Bookshelf; Seven Locks Press;
❺ Co-op Resources & Service Project (CRSP); Community Capital Bank; Cooperative Fund of New England; Eco Solar; Environmental Federation of California; Financing Ozark Rural Growth & Economy (FORGE); First Nations Financial Project; Forest Trust; InDios Co-op; N.B.A. Credit Union; National Federation of Community Development Credit Unions; Native Self-Sufficiency Center; Pendle Hill; Project Now Inc.; Self-Help Credit Union; South Shore Bank; Women's World Banking (WWB);
❻ Beyond 25 Percent: Material Recovery Comes of Age; Business Opportunities Workbook, Implementing Economic Renewal Projects; Communities for Conservation and Action: A Manual for Building Community; Council for Urban Economic Development (CUED) - Directory; Farms of Tomorrow; Guide to Community Education Resources; Intermediate Technology Development; National Priorities Action Packet; SourceBook: Guide to Clubs, Groups, Associations, and Organizations;

**Computer Networking**

See BBS/Comuputer Networking;

**Conflict Education**

See also Global Understanding;
❶ American Youth Work Center; Center on War and the Child; Children's Creative Response To Conflict Program; Circle Pines Center; Educators for Social Responsibility; New World Action; Samantha Smith Center;
❷ Forum; Rethinking Schools; WarChild Monitor;
❻ Annotated Bibliography for Teaching Conflict Resolution in Schools; Friendly Classroom for a Small Planet; Young Peacemakers Project Book;

**Conflict Resolution**

Too numerous; see Conflict Education or Global Understanding or contact Macrocosm for specialized searches or database.

**Conservation**

Too numerous; see related topics or contact Macrocosm for specialized searches or database.

**Consumer Protection**

❶ ACORN; Alliance to Save Energy; American Council on Consumer Interests; Americans for Safe Food; Center for Auto Safety; Center for Science in the Public Interest; Center for the Study of Services; Citizen Action; Citizens Energy Project; Citizens for Tax Justice; Community Nutrition Institute; Conference of Consumer Organizations; Congress Watch; Consumer Education & Protection Association (CEPA); Consumer Education Resource Center; Consumer Federation of America; Consumer Pesticide Protection Project; Consumers Union; Council on Economic Priorities; Friends of the Earth; Government Accountability Project (GAP); HALT - an Organization for Americans for Legal Reform; Health Research Group; National Citizen's Coalition for Nursing Home Reform; National Consumer Law Center; National Consumers League; National Institute for Science, Law and Public Policy; National Insurance Consumer Organization; National Pesticide Telecommunication Network; National Rural Electric Coopera-

Appendix Guide to Subject Index: ❶ Organizations; ❷ Periodicals; ❸ Media; ❹ Publishing; ❺ Business; ❻ Reference

tive Association; National Women's Health Network; Public Citizen; Society For Nutrition Education; Southwest Research & Information Center; Tobacco Products Liability Project; US Public Interest Research Group (USPIRG);
❷ Archives of Environmental Health; Checkbook; Citizen Action News; Citizen Agenda; Collation; Congress Watcher; Consumer Action News; Consumer Reports; Consumer's Voice; Consumers Digest; Council on Economic Priorities Research Report; Directions; Environ; Health and Development; Health Facts; Health Letter Newsletter; IMPACT; Journal of Environmental Health; Lemon Times; Nation; NCLC Reports (National Consumer Law Center); Network News; Public Citizen; Quality Care Advocate; Safe-Food Gazette; Science for the People; Seattle's Child; Wary Canary; Zillions;
❹ Center for Auto Safety Publications Brochure;
❺ Gift Shopping For A Better World;
❻ Better World Investment Guide; Choices: Realistic Alternatives in Cancer Treatment; Consumer Sourcebook; Consumer's Dictionary of Food Additives; Consumer's Resource Handbook; Consumers' Guide to Hospitals; Directory of State and Local Consumer Organizations; Food Pharmacy; Free Range Meat Directory; Lemon Book; National Clearinghouse for Legal Services; Product Safety Book: The Ultimate Consumer Guide; Truth in Produce;

**Consumer Rights**
See Consumer Protection;

**Cooperatives**
See also Intentional Communities;
❶ 21st Century Society; American Institute of Cooperation; Aprovecho Institute; Artists' Housing; CEED Institute; Center for Community Self-Help; Co-op Resource Center; Community Catalyst Project; Cooperative Alumni Association, Inc.; Cooperative Education Project; Cooperative League of the USA; Cooperative Resources and Service Project; Cultural Survival; Federation of Egalitarian Communities; Fellowship for Intentional Community; Mayan Crafts; Michigan Alliance for Cooperatives; National Association of Housing Cooperatives; National Cooperative Business Association; National Native American Co-op; National Rural Electric Cooperative Association; Oberlin Student Co-operative Association; Puget Sound Co-op Federation/Foundation; School of Living (SOL);
❷ Burwood Journal; Co-op America Quarterly; Communities: Journal of Cooperation; Cooperative Action; Cooperative Grocer; Grassroots Economic Organizing (GEO) Newsletter; Ideas and Action; Jubilee Partners Report; Shelterforce;
❹ Community Bookshelf; Survival News Service;
❺ Artesanias Indigenas; Avon Hills Consumer Housing Coop, Inc.; Catalyst Group; Cherry Hill Cannery, Inc.; Co-Aqua; Co-op Alumni Association; Co-op America Alternative Catalog; Co-op Resources & Service Project (CRSP); Cooperative Fund of New England; Deva Lifewear; Diarchy Development; Exotic Gifts; Far Reaches Catalog; Happy Home; High Cotton Co.; ICA Revolving Loan Fund; Indianapolis Arts Cooperative; InDios Co-op; Industrial Cooperative Association; LYDIA - A Women's Cooperative Interchange; Marketplace: Handwork of India; Mission Traders; National Cooperative Bank; Paraclete Society International; Pueblo to People; Puget Sound Co-op Federation/Foundation; R.E.I. (Recreational Equipment International); Self-Help Credit Union; Thread of Hope; Twin Oaks Hammocks; UGAN (Union des Artisans du Nord); World Peace by Nina Grand;
❻ California Co-op Directory; Co-op America Organizational Member Directory; Colorado Directory; Cooperative Communicators Association - Membership Roster; Directory of Agencies Assisting Cooperatives in Developing Countries; Directory of Collectives (West Coast Directory of Collectives); Finding Co-ops; North American Students of Cooperation - Campus Co-Op Directory; Whole Arts Directory;

**Corporate Responsibility**
See also Boycotts; Socially-Responsible Investing;
❶ ACORN; Act Now: Business for a Change; Action for Corporate Accountability (ACA); Austin United Support Group; Boycott Committee; Boycott of Conscience; Boycott Shell Campaign; Citizen-Labor Energy Coalition; Coalition to Boycott Domino's Pizza; Coke Divestment Campaign; Colorado Earth First!; Common Cause; Common Ground USA; Corporate Crime Reporter; Data Center; Employment Research Associates; Environmental Defense Fund (EDF); Fairness & Accuracy in Reporting; Financial Democracy Campaign; Fresh Fruit/Vegetable Workers Union, UFCW Local 78B; Georgians Against Smoking Pollution; Government Accountability Project (GAP); Greenpeace USA; HALT - an Organization for Americans for Legal Reform; Henry George Foundation of America; In Defense of Animals (IDA); Industrial Crisis Institute; INFACT; INFACT(GE Boycott); Interfaith Center for Corporate Responsibility; Intermediate Technology Development Group of North America; Investor Responsibility Research Center; Irish National Caucus; Jemez Action Group; Labor Letter; Neighbor to Neighbor; Nuclear Free America; Operation PUSH; People for the Ethical Treatment of Animals (PETA); Public Citizen; Student Environmental Action Coalition (SEAC); War Resisters League; Waste Oil Action;
❷ Bridging the Gap; Business Ethics; Common Cause Magazine; Corporate Examiner; Dossier; Freedom of Information Report; Greenpeace Magazine; Groundswell; Health Facts; Health Letter Newsletter; INFACT News; Multinational Monitor; Nation; Nuclear Power in Crisis; Public Citizen; Wall Street Green Review;
❸ FAIR Resource Lists;
❹ Prevailing Winds Research;
❺ Co-op America Alternative Catalog; Enviro-Media, Inc.; Wysong Corporation;
❻ Business Recycling Manual; Co-op America Organizational Member Directory; Conscientious Investor's Guide to Socially-Responsible Mutual and Money Market Funds; Consumer Sourcebook; Consumer's Resource Handbook; Corporate Environmental Data Clearinghouse; Corporation Responsibility Monitor; Guide to the Management of Hazardous Waste; Investment Services & Directory of Alternative Investments; Transnational Corporations and Labor: A Directory of Resources;

**Counseling**
❶ Al-Anon/Alateen Family Group Headquarters; Alcoholics Anonymous; Institute for Individual and World Peace; Jubilee House Community Inc.; Planned Parenthood Federation of America; Spiritual Emergency Network;
❷ Journal of Group Psychotherapy, Psychodrama and Sociometry; Self-Help Reporter;
❸ There is a Solution;
❻ 100 Best Treatment Centers for Alcoholism and Drug Abuse; Children and Adolescents with Mental Illness: A Parents' Guide; Courage to Heal: A Guide for Women Survivors of Child Sexual Abuse; Directory of Counseling Services; Directory of Hotlines and Crisis Intervention Centers; Directory of Organizations Serving People with Disabilities; Directory of Organizations, Associations, Self Help Groups & Hotlines for Mental Health & Human Services Professionals; Directory of Services for the Widowed in the United States and Canada; Displaced Homemaker Program Directory; Family Resources Database; Help for Children from Infancy to Adulthood: A National Directory of Hotlines, Helplines, Organizations, Agencies & Other Resources; National Congress for Men - Directory; National Directory of Children & Youth Services; National Register; Parental Kidnapping: How to Prevent an Abduction and What to Do If Your Child is Abducted; Parents & Friends of Gays - International Directory; Post-Traumatic Stress Disorder, Rape Trauma, Delayed Stress and Related Conditions; Programs to Strengthen Families: A Resource Guide; Recovery Resource Guide; Register of Marriage and Family Therapy Providers; SER Network Directory; Who's Who in Addiction Treatment and Recovery;

**Criminal Justice System**
See also Death Penalty; Drug Issues; Juvenile Law; Political Prisoners;
❶ Amnesty International; Causes and Cures; Christic Institute; Handgun Control Inc.; HEMP (Help Eliminate Marijuana Prohibition); Institute on Black Chemical Abuse; National Black Organizations Against Alcohol & Drug Use; National Center for Innovations in Corrections; National Coalition Against the Death Penalty; National Parents Resource Institute For Drug Education; Prisoner Legal Services; Women's Jail Project;
❷ California Prisoner; Crime and Social Justice; Neighborhood Caretaker; Prison News Service; Workers World; Zenger;
❻ Crime in America: Historical Patterns and Contemporary Realities; Pre-trial Detainee Manual; Recovery Resource Guide;

**Day Care**
❶ Welfare Warriors;
❷ American Family; CDF Reports; Child Care ActioNews; City Limits; Family Day Care Bulletin; Welfare Mothers Voice;
❻ Current Issues in Day Care; Directory of Child Day Care Centers; Healthy Mothers, Healthy Babies - Directory of Educational Materials; Programs to Strengthen Families: A Resource Guide; Reaching Out: A Directory of National Organizations Related to Maternal and Child Health; School's Out—Revised;

**Death & Dying**
❶ Californians Against Human Suffering; Hemlock Society; National Coalition Against the Death Penalty; National Council on Death and Dying; Natural Death Centre; Neptune Society;
❷ Hemlock Quarterly;
❹ Aurora Press; Celo Books; IBS Press, Inc.;
❻ Dealing Creatively with Death: A Manual of Death Education and Simple Burial; Directory of Services for the Widowed in the United States and Canada; Guide to the Nation's Hospices; Hospice Alternative: A New Context for Death and Dying;

**Death Penalty**
See also Criminal Justice System; Political Prisoners;
❶ American Civil Liberties Union (ACLU); Amnesty International; National Coalition Against the Death Penalty;
❷ Amnesty International Orange County Newsletter; Brethren Peace Fellowship Newsletter; California Prisoner; Civil Liberties Alert; Crime and Social Justice; Lifelines;
❸ Human Rights Film Guide;

**Democratic Socialism**
❶ Center for Social Research and Education; Democratic Socialists of America; Socialist Party USA;
❷ Activist Journal; Commonwealth Report; Democratic Left; Democratic Socialist REPORT & REVIEW; DSA Green News; In These Times; May Day!; Our Struggle/Nuestra Lucha; People's World; Radical America; Socialism and Democracy; Socialist;

**Demographics**
See related topics or all entries flagged **D**;

**Developing Nations**
See related topics or entries flagged with **T**;

**Disabled's Issues**
See Physically-Challenged;

**Disarmament**
Too numerous; see related topics or contact Macrocosm for specialized searches or database. See Disabled's Rights Gay/Lesbian; Minority Rights; Native Americans; Racism; Sexism;

**Diversity**
See Minority Rights; Wildlife/Endangered Species;

**Divestment**
See also South Africa;
❶ Africa Fund; American Committee on Africa; Boycott Shell Campaign; Coke Divestment Campaign; Interfaith Center for Corporate Responsibility; Methodist Federation for Social Action;
❷ Progressive Student News;
❻ Conscientious Investor's Guide to Socially-Responsible Mutual and Money Market Funds; In Whose Interest: A Guide to US-South Africa Relations; Investment Services & Directory of Alternative Investments;

**Draft Evasion**
See Anti-draft;

**Drylands**
❶ Desert Fishes Council; Native Seeds/SEARCH; Running Rain Society; Southwest Regional Permaculture Institute;

**East-West Relations**
❶ Citizen Exchange Council; Cooperation Project; Institute for Soviet-American Relations; Jewish Labor Committee; Topsfield Foundation; US-USSR Reconciliation Projects;
❷ International Security News Clipping Service; International Workcamper Newsletter;
❻ Organizations Involved in Soviet-American Relations;

**Economic Conversion**
❶ 1% For Peace; Alternative Revenue Service; Campaign to Cut Military Spending In Half; Center for Economic Conversion; Center on Budget and Policy Priorities; Church of the Brethren; Common Agenda Coalition; Comprehensive Security Project; Defense Budget Project; Fund for Peace; Human Ecology Party; Institute for Space and Security Studies; Interfaith Center for Corporate Responsibility; Interfaith Center to Reverse the Arms Race; National Campaign for a Peace Tax Fund; National Commission for Economic Conversion & Disarmament; National Governors' Association; National Jobs With Peace Campaign; National Rainbow Coalition; People For A Change; US Conference of Mayors;
❷ Advocate; Base Conversion News; Breakthrough; Campaign Report; New Economy; Nuclear Times; Peace Conversion Times; Peace Newsletter; Peace Tax Fund Newsletter; People For A Change, Building Ourselves A Base; Positive Alternatives; Veterans For Peace Journal;
❺ Tax Resistor's Penalty Fund;
❻ Conscientious Investor's Guide to Socially-Responsible Mutual and Money Market Funds; From Star Wars to the Alternative; Investment Services & Directory of Alternative Investments; National Priorities Action Packet; Suggestions for Organizers;

**Economics**
See related topics or all entries flagged **$**;

**Education**
See related topics or all entries flagged ✍;

**Electronic Democracy**
See Broadcasting; BBS/Computer Networking; Telecommunications;

**Energy**
See related topics or all entries flagged ✪;

**Energy Efficiency**
❶ Act Now: Business for a Change; Alliance to Save Energy; American Council for an Energy-Efficient Economy; American Petroleum Institute; American Public Transit Association; American Solar Energy Society; Conservation & Renewable Energy Inquiry & Referral Service (CAREIRS); Conservation Law Foundation of New England; Consumer Energy Council of America; Earth Day Resources; Electricity Consumers Resource Council; Energy Conservation Coalition; Environmental Action Foundation; Health and Energy Institute; Northwest Power Planning Council; Rocky Mountain Institute; Solar Box Cookers International;
❷ Earth Day 2000; Home Resource Magazine; Journal of Hydrogen; Mother Earth News; Real Goods News; Solar Today;
❹ American Council for an Energy-Efficient Economy Publication List; Cheshire Books;
❺ Eco Solar; EcoAlternatives; EcoWorks, Inc.; Energy Auditor & Retrofitter; Heart Interface; International Environment Consultants; New Millennium Technologies; Planetary Solutions; Resources Conservation; SaveEnergy Co.; Westgate Enterprises;
❻ Practical Home Energy Savings; Resource-Efficient Housing Guide;

**Environment**
See related topics or entries flagged **E**;

**Equal Rights**
❶ Coalition to Boycott Domino's Pizza; Federation of Organizations for Professional Women; Leadership Conference on Civil Rights; National Council of Women of USA; National Organization for Women; Women's Legal Defense Fund;
❷ Human Ecology Forum; Tradeswoman; Women Library Workers Journal; Women's Agenda; Women's Rights Law Reporter;
❸ Pacifica Cassette Tapes Catalogue;
❻ Equal Rights Handbook; Sex Law: A Legal Sourcebook on Critical Sexual Issues for the Non-Lawyer; Working Woman's Guide to Her Job Rights;

**Faith**
Too numerous; see entries flagged with S; or contact Macrocosm for specialized searches or database.

**Family**
See related topics or entries flagged ♥;

**Family Farms**
❶ American Agricultural Movement; Center for Rural Affairs; Farm Aid; Institute for Alternative Agriculture; Land Trust Alliance; National Farmers Organization; National Land for People; National Save the Family Farm Coalition; Rural American Women, Inc.;
❷ American Journal of Alternative Agriculture; Center for Rural Affairs Newsletter; Family Farm Networker; North American Farmer; Prairie Journal; Rain; Rural Advance; Small Farm Advocate;
❺ F.U.T.U.R.E. Organics, Inc.; Nichols Garden Nursery Inc.; Vermont Land Trust; Worm's Way;
❻ Farms of Tomorrow;

**Family Issues**
❶ Action for Children; Alliance for Parental Involvement in Education (AlIPIE); Aware Parenting Institute; Boulder County Safehouse; Center of the American Experiment; Family Resource Coalition; Feminists Against Pornography; Human Lactation Center Ltd.; Mothers and Others for a Livable Planet; National Center For Missing & Exploited Children; National Coalition Against Domestic Violence; National PTA; Parenting in the Nuclear Age; Pathfinder Fund; Planned Parenthood Federation of America; Population Council; Population Environment Balance, Inc.; Population Services International; Presbyterian Peacemaking Program; Welfare Warriors;
❷ American Family; Child Care ActioNews; Family Day Care Bulletin; Feminist Studies; Hopscotch; Indigenous Women; Loving More Journal; MADRE Speaks/MADRE Informa; Mothering; Parents; Thinking Families; Welfare Mothers Voice;
❸ Adoption; Child Abuse and Neglect and Family Violence Audiovisual Catalog; Clearinghouse on Child Abuse and Neglect Information;
❹ Alliance for Parental Involvement in Education (AlIPIE) Book & Resources Catalog; Compcare Publishers; Meadowbrook Press; Mountain Meadows Press; Parenting Press, Inc.; Resource Publications, Inc.;
❺ Baby Works; Babykins International, Inc.;
❻ 100 Best Treatment Centers for Alcoholism and Drug Abuse; Adoption Directory; Ambulatory Maternal Health Care and Family Planning Services; Child Find Photo Directory of Missing Children; Child Sexual Abuse Prevention: How To Take The First Steps; Current Issues in Day Care; Custody Handbook; Directory of Child Abuse; Directory of Family Planning Grantees, Delegates, and Clinics; Directory of US-Based Agencies Involved in International Health Assistance; Displaced Homemaker Program Directory; Family Resources Database; Healthy Mothers, Healthy Babies - Directory of Educational Materials; Missing Children; National Congress for Men - Directory; National Directory of Child Abuse Prosecutors; National Directory of Runaway Programs; Parental Kidnapping: An International Resource Directory; Parental Kidnapping: How to Prevent an Abduction and What to Do If Your Child is Abducted; Planned Parenthood Affiliates, Chapter & State Public Affairs Offices Directory; Polyfidelity Primer; Programs to Strengthen Families: A Resource Guide; Reaching Out: A Directory of National Organizations Related to Maternal and Child Health; Register of Marriage and Family Therapy Providers; Self-Help Sourcebooks; Sexual Abuse Prevention Education: An Annotated Bibliography; Sexual Assault and Child Abuse: A National Directory of Victim Services and Prevention Programs; Society for Research in Child Development; Solo Parenting: Your Essential Guide; Starting Early: A Guide to Federal Resources in Maternal and Child Health; Total Nutrition for Breast-Feeding Mothers; Whole Again Birth Catalog: A Sourcebook for Choices in Childbirth; Wise Woman Herbal for the Childbearing Year;

**Family Planning**
❶ Association for Voluntary Surgical Contraception; Basic Foundation, Inc.; Catholics For Free Choice; International Women's Rights Action Watch; National Audubon Society Population Program; National Family Planning and Reproductive Health Association; Pathfinder Fund; Planned Parenthood Federation of America; Population Communications Services; Population Council; Population Environment Balance, Inc.; Population Services International; World Population Society;
❷ Conscience; International Family Planning Perspectives; No Longer Silent; Population Newsletter; Studies in Family Planning; Voice;
❸ Reproductive Rights;
❻ Ambulatory Maternal Health Care and Family Planning Services; Dictionary of Demography: Biographies; Directory of Family Planning Grantees, Delegates, and Clinics; Directory of US-Based Agencies Involved in International Health Assistance; Directory of Women's Health Care Center; Family Planning Information Centers; Nongovernmental Organizations in International Population Crisis Committee; Planned Parenthood Affiliates, Chapter & State Public Affairs Offices Directory; T.A.P.P. Sources: A National Directory of Teenage Pregnancy Prevention; Wise Woman Herbal for the Childbearing Year;

**Farm Workers**
❶ National Farm Worker Ministry; National Farmers Organization; United Farm Workers Union;
❷ Franciscan Worker; Rural Advance;
❻ Migrant Health Services Directory;

**Farmland**
See also Family Farms; Soil; Organic; Rural Communities;
❶ Agricultural Council of America; American Farmland Trust; American Institute of Cooperation; California Certified Organic Farmers (CCOF); Codel, Inc.; Concern, Inc; Food First; Institute for Agriculture and Trade Policy; Institute For Food and Development Policy; International Alliance for Sustainable Agriculture; International Council for Local Environmental Initiatives; Land Stewardship Project; Mothers and Others for a Livable Planet; National Farm Worker Ministry; Native Seeds/SEARCH; North American Wildlife Foundation; Public Voice for Food and Health Policy; United Farm Workers Union; World Food Institute;
❷ Action Alert; American Farmland; Exchange; Food First News; Land Letter; Land Stewardship Newsletter; Maine Organic Farmer & Gardner; NGO Networker;
❻ Chesapeake Citizen Directory; Education and Training Opportunities; Healthy Harvest IV: A Directory; Migrant Health Services Directory;

**Feminism**
See related topics or entries flagged **F**;

**Film**
Too numerous; see Media Section or contact Macrocosm for specialized searches or database;

**Fine Arts**
❶ Pacific University of Hawaii;
❷ Art Works; Community Murals Magazine; Earth's Daughters; Kaleidoscope; Yellow Silk: Journal of Erotic Arts;
❸ Performing and Fine Artists for World Peace;
❻ Whole Arts Directory;

**Food Distribution**
❶ Bread for the World; Food Industry Crusade Against Hunger; Food Marketing Institute; Food Research and Action Center; Institute for Agriculture and Trade Policy; International Fund for Agricultural Development; National Food and Energy Council; Second Harvest National Food Bank Network; Trees For Life; US National Committee For World Food Day;
❷ ECHO Development Notes; Food First News; Hunger Notes;
❹ C. Olson & Company;
❺ Tucson Cooperative Warehouse;
❻ Healthy Harvest IV: A Directory;

**Foreign Policy**
See Intervention—Third World;

**Forests/Third World**
❶ Ancient Forests International; Arctic to Amazonia Alliance; CARE; Georgians Against Smoking Pollution; International Society for the Preservation of Rain Forests; Rainforest Action Network; Rainforest Foundation;
❷ Life Lines; Rainforest Action Network Alert;
❺ Community Products, Inc.; Ecotour Expeditions; From The Rainforest;
❻ International Tree Project Clearinghouse; Rainforest: A Guide to Research & Tourist Facilities at Selected Tropical Sites in Central & South America;

**Forests/U.S.**
❶ Acid Rain Foundation, Inc.; America the Beautiful Fund; American Forest Council; American Forestry Association; American Wilderness Adventures; Association of Forest Service Employees For Environmental Ethics; Boulder Rainforest Action Group; Children of the Green Earth; Colorado Earth First!; Companies Which Cut Rainforests Boycott; Conservation International; Creating Our Future; Earth First! Tropical Timber Campaign; Earth Island Institute; Earth Plan, Inc.; Earthwatch; Environmental Protection Information Center (EPIC); Forest Ecosystem Rescue Network (FERN); Forest History Society; Forests Forever; Friends of the Ancient Forest; Friends of the Earth; Friends of the Trees Society; Friends of UNEP; Greater Ecosystem Alliance; Greater Yellowstone Coalition; Hug-a-Tree; Industrial Workers of the World; Jewish National Fund; League to Save Lake Tahoe; Lighthawk; LM Research Institute; National Arbor Day Foundation; National Forest Action Center; National Woodland Owners Association; Native Forest Council; New Forests Fund; PCI Tours; Planetary Survival Alliance; Planning and Conservation League; Rainforest Alliance; Rainforest Information Center; Save America's Forests; Save the Rainforest, Inc.; Save-The-Redwoods; Siskiyou Action Project; Siskiyou Regional Education Project; Texas Committee on Natural Resources; TreePeople; Wilderness Expeditions;
❷ American Forests; Earth First!; Forest & Conservation History; Forest Watch; Global Releaf Report; Industrial Worker; Inner Voice; International Environmental Affairs: Journal for Research & Policy; Land Letter; National Woodlands Magazine; Networker; Olympic Ancient Forest Report; Robin Newsletter; Save-The-Redwoods Bulletin; Tree Song; Tropicus; World Rainforest Report;
❸ Environmental Media Association;
❹ Feline Press; Idea House Publishing Co.;
❺ Conservatree Paper Co.; Earth Care Catalog; Eco Solar; Forest Trust; John Rossi Company; Nichols Garden Nursery Inc.; Treekeepers;
❻ Acid Rain Foundation - Directories; Global Ecology Handbook; Global Releaf Citizen's Action Guide; Green Front Report; International Green Front Report; National Resources for the 21st Century; Shading Our Cities, A Resource Guide For Urban Community Forests Communities; United Nations List of National Parks and Protected Areas;

**Freedom of Expression**
See Civil Liberties;

**Fundraising**
See also Philanthropy;
❷ Grassroots Fundraising Journal; Peace Developments;
❸ Fund Raising Management - Non-Profit Software Package Directory Issue;
❺ Action Resource Guide; Enlightened Living; Last Word; Linda Q. Perrin & Associates; Progressive Resources For Grassroots Organizing & Fundraising; Resource Catalog; Rural Praxis, Inc.; Whale Gifts Collection; Working Assets Long Distance Program;
❻ Church Funding Resource Guide; Environmental Grantmakers Directory; Fund Raising Counselors & Organizations; Funding - Social Responsibility; Fundraiser's Guide to Human Service Funding; Grantseekers Guide: A Funding Source Book; Guide to Gifts and Bequests: A Directory of Philanthropically Supported Institutions; National Data Book; National Foundations; National Fund Raising Directory; National Guide to Corporate Giving; National Guide to Funding in Aging; Organize!; Peace and World Order Studies: A Curriculum Guide; Public Media Center's Index of Progressive Funders; Resources Mailing Lists; Search for Security: The ACCESS Guide to Foundations in Peace, Security, and International Relations; Where to Go to Find Information on Grant Funds and Fundraising; Whole Nonprofit Catalog; Wise Giving Guide;

**Future**
See Ideation and other related topics; or entries flagged **?**;

**❷** CARECEN Speaks; Central American Refugee Defense Newsletter; El Rescate; Lucha/Struggle; Refugees; Spotlight; Telegraph News; Unitarian-Universalists in Support of Sanctuary Newsletter;
**❸** Human Rights Film Guide;
**❹** Denali Press;
**❻** Dictionary of Demography: Biographies; Directory of Central America Organizations; List of Declared Public Sanctuaries; Refugee and Immigrant Resource Directory 1990-1991; United States Committee for Refugees - Directory;

## Indigenous Peoples— Developing Nations

**❶** American Committee on Africa; Arctic to Amazonia Alliance; Clergy and Laity Concerned; Committee In Solidarity with the People of El Salvador (CISPES); Committee In Solidarity With The People Of Guatemala; Cultural Survival; Institute for Development Anthropology; Institute for World Understanding of Peoples, Cultures and Languages; International Society for the Preservation of Rain Forests; North American Coordinating Committee of Non-Governmental Organizations on the Question of Palestine; Pan-American Indian Association and Adopted Tribal Peoples; Plenty USA; Rainforest Foundation; Seva Foundation;
**❷** Action Alert; Asia & Pacific Update; Asian Rights Advocate; Catalyst: Economics for a Living Earth; Cultural Survival Quarterly; Development Update; Focus; Indigenous World; Native Peoples Magazine, The Arts and Lifeways; Other Side; Pacific Bulletin; Transition;
**❸** Third World Organizing;
**❹** Denali Press; Path Press;
**❺** RainForest Essentials, Ltd.; World Peace by Nina Grand;
**❻** Guide to Liberation Theology for Middle-Class Congregations;

## Intentional Communities/Cohousing
See also Cooperatives;
**❶** Appalachian Community Services; Aprovecho Institute; Center for Communal Studies; Communal Studies Association; Community Catalyst Project; Community Economic and Ecological Development Institute (CEED); Community Educational Service Council, Inc. (CESCI); Community Service Inc.; Federation of Egalitarian Communities; Fellowship for Intentional Community; Progressive Community Associates (PCA); Shared Living Resource Center; Turtle Island Earth Stewards;
**❷** Communities: Journal of Cooperation; Free Spirit; New Wealth; Seedling; Shared Living Community; Social Anarchism: A Journal of Practice & Theory;
**❹** Community Bookshelf;
**❺** One Source; Twin Oaks Hammocks;
**❻** Alternative America; Builders of the Dawn; Communities - Directory of Intentional Communities Issue; Directory of Intentional Communities;

## Interfaith
Too numerous; see entries flagged with S; or contact Macrocosm for specialized searches or database.

## International Law
See also National Security;
**❶** Alliance for Justice; American Society of International Law; Center for International Policy; Coalition to Stop US Intervention in the Mid-East; Fourth Freedom Forum Inc.; Independent Commission of Inquiry on the US Invasion of Panama; International Human Rights Law Group; International War Crimes Tribunal; Pace Peace Center; Union for Democratic Communications;
**❷** American Journal of International Law; Convergence; CovertAction Information Bulletin;

**❻** An International Directory of Information on War, Peace, and Security; Search for Security: The ACCESS Guide to Foundations in Peace, Security, and International Relations; Strategy Workbook;

## Internships
See Jobs; Mentoring; Volunteering;

## Intervention—Developing Nations
See also Divestment;
**❶** Africa Faith and Justice Network; Alternative Revenue Service; American Committee on Africa; Association for the Advancement of Policy Research & Development in the Third World; Carnegie Endowment for International Peace; CATO Institute; Center for Defense Information; Center for Strategic & International Studies; Center of Concern; Center on Budget and Policy Priorities; Citizens Network for Foreign Affairs; Coalition for Peace in the Horn of Africa; Coalition to Stop US Intervention in the Mid-East; Committee In Solidarity with the People of El Salvador (CISPES); Committee In Solidarity With The People Of Guatemala; Council on Foreign Relations; Council on International and Public Affairs; Educators Against Racism and Apartheid; Fellowship of Reconciliation Task Force on Latin America; Foreign Assistance Action Project; Foreign Policy Association; Independent Commission of Inquiry on the US Invasion of Panama; Indochina Project; Institute for Defense and Disarmament Studies; Institute for Foreign Policy Analysis; Inter-Hemispheric Education Resource Center; International Center for Development Policy; International War Crimes Tribunal; Mobilization for Survival; NARMIC; National Security Archive; Neighbor to Neighbor; Network in Solidarity With the People of Guatemala; Roosevelt Center for American Policy Studies; Sane/Freeze; Southwest Research & Information Center; United Methodist Church; US Catholic Conference; Witness for Peace; Women's Foreign Policy Council; World Affairs Council; World Policy Institute;
**❷** Asian Affairs: An American Review; Barricada Internacional; Center Focus; Central America Report; Focus; Foreign Policy; Foreign Policy Magazine; Headline Series; Indochina Issues; Indochina Newsletter; Lucha/Struggle; Nation; News & Views; NGO Networker; Peace Review; Resource Center Bulletin; Veteran; Veteran Affairs News; Washington Newsletter; World Policy Journal; World Press Review;
**❸** Public Interest Video Network;
**❹** Indonesia Publications;
**❻** Great Decisions; Guide to Liberation Theology for Middle-Class Congregations; Handbook on Military Taxes and Conscience; In Whose Interest: A Guide to US-South Africa Relations; World Peace and World Order Studies: A Curriculum Guide;

## Invention/Ideation
**❶** ABC's for the 21st Century Project; Action Linkage; Aquarian Research Foundation; Brahma Kumaris; Brain Exchange; British Consortium for Innovation; Celebration of Innovation: An Exposition Showcase of Creativity, Innovation and Invention; Center for Peace Through Culture; CIVITEX (Civic Information and Techniques Exchange); Community Regeneration; Council for Prosperity; Eastern Europe Constitution Design Forum; Federal Incentive Awards Program; Forum 2000; Global Cooperation for a Better World; Ideas Banks for Unconventional Ideas in Science, Medicine and Sociology; Innovative Design Fund; Institute for 21st Century Studies; Institute for Social Inventions; International Network for a UN Second Assembly; Invent America; Inventors Workshop International Education Foundation; Mega-Cities Project; Mississippi 2020 Network; National Association of Suggestion Systems; National Center for Innovations in

Corrections; National Learning Foundation; Networking Institute Inc.; New Civilization; One World; Parliament of Innovators; Pate Institute For Human Survival; Planetary Society; Planners Network; Post-Industrial Future Project; Quality Team Tracking Program; Right Livelihood Awards Foundation; Roundtable Discussions; SeniorNet; Third Millenium Project; Together Foundation for Global Unity; Tomorrow Today: A Pavilion of Possibilities; Transformation 2000; Union for Democratic Communications; World Future Society; World Information Systems;
**❷** 2000 / The Millennium Magazine; 21st Century Society Newsletter; Brain/Mind Bulletin; Current; Free Spirit; Futurific Magazine; Futurist; Green Living Magazine; Invent!; Liberty; Master Switch Weekly; Nuclear Times; Omni; Rain; Trajectories; Working Papers for a New Society; Z Magazine;
**❸** Agenda Project; Alternatives: The Computer Bulletin Board Dedicated to Progressive Social Change; Community Memory Project; DataNet; Ed-Line; ElfNet; Fulcrum: The R & D Network for the Development of Human Systems; Global Electronic University; Global Suggestion Box for Ideas to Promote Global Harmony; Global Systems Analysis and Simulation (GLOSAS) Project; Holistic Education Community Network; IdeaNet; Kids' Internationally Distributed Superstation (KIDS); New Computerized World Information Service; Visions;
**❻** Business Environmental Lending Library; Educator's Guide: An Agenda for the 21st Century; Encyclopedia of Social Inventions; Encyclopedia of World Problems and Human Potential; Fringes of Reason; Ideas Index: Fresh Ideas for Democratic Ideals; Networking: People Connecting with People; Peace Pact Guide; Planetwork; World Future Studies Newsletter - Membership Directory Issue;

## Investing
See also Boycotts;
**❶** Action for Corporate Accountability (ACA); Africa Faith and Justice Network; Austin United Support Group; Boycott Committee; Boycott of Conscience; Boycott Shell Campaign; California Community Foundation; Center for Business Ethics; Center for Economic Revitalization; Co-op America; Coalition for Environmentally Responsible Economics; Coalition to Boycott Domino's Pizza; Coke Divestment Campaign; Colorado Earth First!; Earth Share; Environmental Federation of America; Fresh Fruit/Vegetable Workers Union, UFCW Local 78B; Georgians Against Smoking Pollution; In Defense of Animals (IDA); INFACT (GE Boycott); Institute for Gaean Economics; Interfaith Center for Corporate Responsibility; Investor Responsibility Research Center; Irish National Caucus; Jemez Action Group; Labor Letter; Neighbor to Neighbor; New Consumer, Ltd.; Nippon Ecology Network; Nuclear Free America; Operation PUSH; People for the Ethical Treatment of Animals (PETA); Tele-Effective Securities, Inc.; War Resisters League; Waste Oil Action;
**❷** Business Ethics; Catalyst: Economics for a Living Earth; Clean Yield; Community Economics; Good Money; International Living; Investing from the Heart; Wall Street Green Review;
**❺** Albion Financial Associates; Amy Domini - Loring, Wolcott, & Coolidge; Bank Credit Card OBSERVER; Calvert Group; Chrysalis Money Consultants; Clean Yield Group; Co-op America Alternative Catalog; Co-op Resources & Service Project (CRSP); Common Good Loan Fund; Community Economic and Ecological Development Institute (CEED); Community Products, Inc.; Consumers United Insurance Company; Cooperative Fund of New England; Creative Financial Concepts; Diarchy Development; Ethical Investments, Inc.; Financial Alternatives; Fi-

nancial Network Investment; First Affirmative Financial Network; Franklin Insight; Franklin Research and Development Corporation; Freedom Environmental Fund; Global Resource Bank; Good Money Publications, Inc.; New Alternatives Fund; Paraclete Society International; Pax World Fund; Peter D. Kinder & Co.; Progressive Asset Management; Progressive Securities; Project Now Inc.; Sand County Venture Fund; Social Banking Programs; Social Responsibility Investment Group; South Shore Bank; SRI Advisors; Vermont National Bank; Worker Owned Network; Working Assets; Working Assets Funding Service; Working Assets Money Fund;
**❻** Better World Investment Guide; Co-op America Organizational Member Directory; Conscientious Investor's Guide to Socially-Responsible Mutual and Money Market Funds; Directory of Environmental Investing; Economics As If The Earth Really Mattered: A Catalyst Guide to Socially Conscious Investing; Guide to Socially Responsible Investing; How to Make the World a Better Place, a Beginner's Guide; Investing in America's Corporate Conscience; Peace Catalog; Socially Responsible Buyer's Guide; Socially Responsible Financial Planning Guide;

## Jobs
See also Volunteering;
**❶** Access: Networking in the Public Interest; Accion International; Appalachian Trail Conference; Association for Enterprise Opportunities; California Conservation Corps; CEIP Fund; Full Employment Action Council; Goodwill Industries of Southern California; Human Environment Center; Labor Research Association; National Committee for Full Employment; National Jobs With Peace Campaign; National Youth Work Alliance; Student Pugwash, USA; Travellers Earth Repair Network (TERN); Zoovival;
**❷** AALC Reporter; Agriculture Employment Bulletin; Earth Work; Economic Notes; Environmental Opportunities; International Employment Hotline; International Living; Job Seeker; Jobs Impact Bulletin; Monday Developments; Peace Chronicle; RNA Advisor; Struggle; Women's Research Network News;
**❹** Garret Park Press; Ten Speed Press;
**❺** Paraclete Society International; Project Now Inc.; Worker Owned Network; World Peace by Nina Grand;
**❻** Affirmative Action Register; Church Funding Resource Guide; Complete Guide to Environmental Careers; Corporation Responsibility Monitor; Directory of Peace Studies Programs; Directory of Public Interest Legal Internships/The NAPIL Fellowships Guide; Directory of Public Service Internships: Opportunities for the Graduate, Post-Graduate & Mid-Career Professional; Directory of Undergraduate Internships; Directory of Washington Internships; Good Works: A Guide to Careers in Social Change; Great Careers: The Fourth of July Guide to Careers, Internships, and Volunteer Opportunities in the Nonprofit Sector; Guide to Careers and Graduate Education in Peace Studies; Guide to Careers in World Affairs; Helping Out in the Outdoors; National Center for Resources in Vocational Education; New Careers, A Directory of Jobs and Internships in Technology & Society; Overseas List - Opportunities For Living and Working in Developing Countries; SER Network Directory; State Youth Employment Initiatives: A Resource Guide and Framework for Action;

## Justice
See related topics or entries flagged **J**;

## Juvenile Law
**❷** Youth Law News;
**❻** Crime in America: Historical Patterns and Contemporary Realities; National Directory of Children & Youth Services; National Directory of Runaway Programs; North American Directory

of Programs for Runaways, Homeless Youth and Missing Children;

**Labor**

See related topics or entries flagged **L**;

**Land Trusts**

❶ Community Economic and Ecological Development Institute (CEED); Cooperative Resources and Service Project; Federation of Egalitarian Communities; Highwind Association; Institute for Community Economics, Inc.; Land Trust Alliance; School of Living (SOL); Trust for Public Land; Trust For the Future; Turtle Island Earth Stewards; WOMLAND (Women of Matriarchal Beliefs on Sacred Land);

❷ Business Ethics; Community Economics; Exchange; New Wealth;

❺ First Nations Financial Project; Forest Trust; New Land Trust; Vermont Land Trust;

❻ Conscientious Investor's Guide to Socially-Responsible Mutual and Money Market Funds; National Directory of Conservation Land Trusts;

**Latin America**

See also Caribbean; Central America; South America;

❶ Fellowship of Reconciliation Task Force on Latin America; Georgians Against Smoking Pollution; Human Rights Watch; Pueblo to People; Questers Tours and Travels; Washington Office on Latin America;

❷ Latin America Update; Lucha/Struggle; Solidarity/Solidaridad; third world; Washington Report on the Hemisphere;

❸ Radio For Peace International;

❹ University of Arizona Press;

❺ Artesanias Indigenas; Stephanie Schuster, Inc.;

❻ Directory of Inter-American and Other Associations in the Americas.; Human Rights Directory: Latin America & the Caribbean;

**Lesbian**

See entries that are flagged **G**;

**Letter Writing**

See Multilogues;

**Literacy**

❶ Cartoonists Across America; Children's Defense Fund; Lauback Literacy; Women's Computer Literacy Center;

❷ Struggle;

❹ Dawn Horse Press;

❻ National Directory of Community Based Adult Literacy Programs;

**Literature**

See also Journalism;

❶ Mark Trail/Ed Dodd Foundation; Omega Institute;

❷ American Voice; Atlantic; Bloomsbury Review; Callaloo; Catalyst; Comics Journal; Contact II Magazine; Contemporary Literature; Cream City Review; Critique: Studies in Contemporary Fiction; Earth's Daughters; Five Fingers Review; Gauntlet; Granta; Harper's Magazine; Hopscotch; Index on Censorship; Mississippi Mud; New England Review; North American Review; Out West; Outdoors Unlimited; Parabola; Publisher's Weekly; Sage: A Scholarly Journal on Black Women; SAMISDAT; Shoe Tree; Signs: Journal of Women in Culture & Society; Sulfur; Turnstile; Utne Reader; Women: a cultural view; Working Classics; Writer; Wyoming, The Hub of the Wheel; Yellow Silk: Journal of Erotic Arts;

❸ KPFA-FM94; Pacifica Radio;

❹ AMOK; Big Books from Small Presses; Borgo; Children's Book Press; City Lights Review; Dawn Horse Press; Four Walls Eight Windows; Gaia Catalog Co. & Bookstore; Oxford University Press; Telos;

❻ Alternative Publications: A Guide to Directories, Indexes, Bibliographies and Other Sources; International Directory of Little Magazines and Small Presses; Seeds of Peace: A Catalog of Quotations; Writer's Handbook;

**Lobbying—Animal Rights**

❶ American Anti-Vivisection Society; Friends of Animals;

❷ PETA News;

**Lobbying—Developing Nations**

❶ Central America Working Group; Lawyers Committee For International Human Rights; Results; Transafrica;

❷ Multinational Monitor; News & Views;

**Lobbying—Environmental**

❶ 20/20 Vision National Project (East); Air and Waste Management Association; American Forest Council; American Forestry Association; American Littoral Society; American Oceans Campaign; Americans for the Environment; Clean Water Action Project; Common Agenda Coalition; Don't Waste California; Energy Conservation Coalition; Environmental Defense Fund (EDF); Environmental Policy Institute; Environmental Protection Information Center (EPIC); Friends of the Earth; Institute for Alternative Agriculture; Interfaith Impact for Justice and Peace; Land and Water Fund of the Rockies; Massachusetts Campaign to Clean Up Hazardous Waste; National Campaign Against Toxic Hazards; Native Forest Council; Natural Resources Defense Council; Northcoast Environmental Center; Northern Alaska Environmental Center; Sierra Club; Sierra Club Population Committee;

❷ EDF Letter; Environmental Update; Sierra;

❺ Earth Cards;

❻ Corporate Environmental Data Clearinghouse; Environmental Disputes; Making Polluters Pay: A Citizens' Guide to Legal Action and Organizing; Understanding Environmental Administration and Law;

**Lobbying—Feminism**

❶ American Civil Liberties Union (ACLU); Center for Women's Policy Studies; National Abortion Rights Action League; National Council of Women of USA; National Women's Political Caucus;

❷ Woman Activist;

**Lobbying—Minority Rights**

❶ Congressional Black Caucus Foundation; National Congress of American Indians; National Council of La Raza;

❷ Point of View;

**Lobbying—Other Justice Issues**

❶ American Association of Retired Persons; American Civil Liberties Union (ACLU); Americans for Religious Liberty; Children's Defense Fund; Common Cause; Jericho; National Coalition to Ban Hand Guns; National Lawyers Guild; NORML (National Organization to Reform Marijuana Laws); Unitarian Universalist Association;

❷ Common Cause Magazine; Network; Report to Presbyterians from Washington;

❻ National Coalition For the Homeless;

**Lobbying—Peace**

❶ Arms Control Association; Business Executives for National Security; Center for Defense Information; Council for a Livable World; Friends Committee on National Legislation; Gray Panther Network; Jewish Peace Lobby; Legislative Strategies and Lobbying Network; National Campaign for a Peace Tax Fund; National Conference of Catholic Bishops; National Mission For Church and Society; National Peace Institute Foundation; National Rainbow Coalition; Network, National Catholic Social Justice Lobby; Pax Christi USA; Peace Pac; Peace With Justice Week; Professionals' Coalition for Nuclear Arms Control; Southern Christian Leadership Conference; Union of American Hebrew Congregations; Unitarian Universalist Association of Congregations; US-USSR Bridges for Peace; Women's International League for Peace and Freedom;

❷ FAS Public Interest Report; Peace and Freedom; Peace Institute Reporter; Professional; Women's Agenda;

**Media**

See related topics or entries flagged **M**;

**Media Watch/Responsibility**

❶ Center for Environmental Information; Center for War, Peace, and the News Media; Fairness & Accuracy in Reporting; Institute for Media Analysis; Media Access Project; Media Alliance; National Coalition on Television Violence; National Forum Foundation; Political Research Associates; Project Censored; Scientists' Institute for Public Information; Union for Democratic Communications; Viewers for Quality Television;

❷ 10 Best Censored Stories; Deadline; Documents to the People; Extra!; Lies of Our Times; Media & Values; NCTV News; Perpetual Notions Newsletter; Propaganda Review; SIPIscope; St. Louis Journalism Review; World Press Review;

❸ Action For Children's TV; Association for Responsible Communication - ARC; FAIR Resource Lists; Media Watch; This Way Out;

❹ Institute for Media Analysis - Publications List;

**Medicare**

❷ Foodlines; A Chronicle of Hunger and Poverty in America; Senior Citizens News;

❺ Consumers United Insurance Company;

❻ Age Care Sourcebook: A Resource Guide for the Aging and Their Families;

**Men's Liberation**

❶ Austin Men's Center; Center for Partnership Studies; Green Committees of Correspondence; Los Angeles Men's Center; Men's Center of Los Angeles; National Organization for Men Against Sexism;

❷ Changing Men, Issues in Gender, Sex & Politics; Green Letter; Icarus Review; Journeymen; Man!; Men's Council Journal; Sacred Path; Wingspan;

❻ Changing Men, Issues in Gender, Sex, and Politics - Resource Directory; Equal Rights Handbook; National Congress for Men - Directory;

**Mentoring**

❷ Mentor;

**Mid-East**

❶ Coalition to Stop US Intervention in the Mid-East; Forum Travel; Institute for Palestine Studies; International War Crimes Tribunal; Interns for Peace; Jewish Labor Committee; Jewish Peace Lobby; North American Coordinating Committee of Non-Governmental Organizations on the Question of Palestine; Palestine Solidarity Committee;

❷ Al Fajr Palestinian Weekly; Brethren Peace Fellowship Newsletter; Dossier; Israel Horizons; Jewish Affairs; Jewish Currents; Journal of Palestine Studies; Middle East Report; Other Israel; Voices for Peace;

❹ Prevailing Winds Research;

❻ Middle East Human Rights Directory; Middle East: A Directory of Resources;

**Minority Rights**

See also Racism; Native Americans;

❶ American Arab Anti-Discrimination Committee; Black Student Alliance; Center for Third World Organizing; Coalition of Hispanic Health & Human Services Organization; Congress of National Black Churches; Congressional Black Caucus Foundation; Dakota Indian Foundation; Ground Zero Center for Nonviolent Action; Highlander Research & Education Center; Institute on Black Chemical Abuse; John Brown Anti-Klan Committee; Leadership Conference on Civil Rights; League of United Latin American Citizens; National Black Caucus of Locally Elected Officials; National Council of La Raza; National Institute Against Prejudice and Violence; National Minority AIDS Council; National Puerto Rican Coalition; National Urban League; Partisan Defense Committee; People For A Change; Running Strong for American Indian Youth; Southern Christian Leadership Conference; Southern Poverty Law Center; United Church of Christ Commission for Racial Justice;

❷ AALC Reporter; Bill of Rights in Action; Bill of Rights Journal; Black Child Advocate; Black Collegian; Black Enterprise; Black Film Review; Black Scholar; Class-Struggle Defense Notes; Fighting Back; Freedomways; Highlander Reports; International Review of Third World Culture and Issues; Jubilee Partners Report; Law Report; MALDEF Newsletter; Minority Engineer; Minority Rights Group; Minority Trendsletter; Monitor; National Black Law Journal; Our Struggle/Nuestra Lucha; Point of View; Prison News Service; Southern Exposure; Transition; Washington Post Magazine; Workers World;

❸ Living Stage Theater Company; Third World Organizing;

❹ Denali Press; University of Minnesota Press;

❻ Affirmative Action Register; Alliance For Cultural Democracy Membership Directory; Alternative Press Index; Black Americans Information Directory; Black Resource Guide; Directory of African American Religious Bodies; Directory of Financial Aids for Minorities; Directory of Hispanic Organizations; Directory of Private Fair Housing Organizations; Directory of Special Programs for Minority Group Members: Career Information Services, Employment Skills Banks, Financial Aid Sources; Ethnic Information Sources of the United States; Financial Aid for Minorities in...; Guide to Multicultural Resources; Hispanic American Voluntary Organizations; Hispanic Americans Information Directory; Hispanic Resource Directory; Migrant Health Services Directory; Minority Business Development Agency - Directory of Regional & District Offices and Funded Organizations; Minority Organizations: A National Directory; Negro Almanac: A Reference Work on the African American; SER Network Directory; Whole Arts Directory; World Directory of Minorities;

**Monopolies**

See Corporate Responsibility;

**Multilogues**

❶ Action Linkage; Communication Task Group; Designing New Civilization; Economics; GPE Network; Green Party Multilogue; Illich Network; Mondragon Type Communities; Planetary Consciousness; Politics and Government Multilogue; Process Education; Roundtable Discussions; TNI Multilogue;

❷ Letter Exchange;

❸ Communications & Computer Multilogues;

**Municipal Issues**

❶ Alliance for Justice; Common Cause; Conference on Alternative State and Local Policies; Employment Research Associates; International Council for Local Environmental Initiatives; National Association of Neighborhoods; National Association of Towns and Townships; National League of Cities;

❷ Common Cause Magazine; Global Communities;

❸ Public Electronic Network (PEN);

❻ Building Municipal Foreign Policies: An Action Handbook for Citizens and Local Elected Officials; National Priorities Action Packet; Organizations Master Index;

**Music**

❶ Free Arts for Abused Children; Omega Institute;

❷ Art Works; Critical Inquiry; Dynamic; F.U.T.U.R.E. Newsletter; High Performance; Mini-Mag; Option; Sassafras; Sing Out! Magazine; Sound Choice; Talkin' Union; The Original Art Report (TOAR); Threepenny Review; Voices;

❸ Creative Resources Guild; KPFA-FM94; Ladyslipper Inc.; New Era Media; Pacifica Radio;

Peacemakers Television; Redwood Records; Steven Bergman Enterprises;
❹ Gaia Catalog Co. & Bookstore; Indiana University Press; Pyramid Books New-Age Collection;
❺ Earth Sounds; Gentle Wind;
❻ American Association for Music Therapy - Membership Directory; Association of Hispanic Arts News - Directory of Hispanic Arts Organizations Section; Common Ground: Resources for Personal Transformation;

**National Health**
❶ Coalition for A National Health System; Medical Reform Group; National Assembly of National Voluntary Health and Social Welfare Organization; National Health Federation;
❷ Foodlines; A Chronicle of Hunger and Poverty in America; Journal of Health Politics, Policy & Law; Senior Citizens News;
❺ Consumers United Insurance Company;

**National Security**
See also International Law;
❶ Business Executives for National Security; Center for National Security Studies; Committee for National Security; Five College Program in Peace and World Security Studies; Forgotten Families; Fourth Freedom Forum Inc.; Institute for Security and Cooperation in Outer Space; Institute for Space and Security Studies; Rocky Mountain Institute; Topsfield Foundation;
❷ Convergence; Dossier; Inforum; International Security News Clipping Service; Veteran Affairs News;
❹ Prevailing Winds Research;
❻ Access: A Security Information Service; Alternative Defense Project; An International Directory of Information on War, Peace, and Security; Building Municipal Foreign Policies: An Action Handbook for Citizens and Local Elected Officials; Concerned Citizen's Guide to National Security; Lower Midwest Grassroots Peace Directory; Mid Atlantic Grassroots Peace Directory; New England Grassroots Peace Directory; Northwest & Pacific Rim Grassroots Peace Directory; Search for Security: The ACCESS Guide to Foundations in Peace, Security, and International Relations; South Grassroots Peace Directory; Southwest Grassroots Peace Directory; Strategy Workbook; United States in Search of Enemies; Upper Midwest Grassroots Peace Directory; Western States Grassroots Peace Directory;

**Native Americans**
❶ Arctic to Amazonia Alliance; Bear Tribe Medicine Society; Big Mountain Support Committee; Conservatory for Nature Culture; Cultural Survival; Dakota Indian Foundation; Hopi Epicenter for International Outreach; Huichol Center; Indian Law Resource Center; Institute for the Study of Natural Systems; Learning Alliance; Mayan Crafts; National Congress of American Indians; National Native American Co-op; Native American Prisoners Rehabilitation Research Project; Native Seeds/SEARCH; Pan-American Indian Association and Adopted Tribal Peoples; Running Rain Society; Running Strong for American Indian Youth; Section on Social Responsibility, Canadian Psychological Association; Seva Foundation; South & Meso American Indian Information Center (SAIIC); Western Shoshone National Council;
❷ Akwesasne Notes; American Indian Law Newsletter; Bayou La Rose; Circle; Cultural Democracy; Cultural Survival Quarterly; Eagle; huracan; Indian Report; Indigenous Women; Indigenous World; NARF Legal Review/NCBL Notes; National Self-Sufficiency; Native Nations; Native Peoples Magazine, The Arts and Lifeways; Native Self-Sufficiency; New World Times; Northeast Indian Quarterly; Other Side; Prison News Service; Rethinking Schools; SAIIC Newsletter (South & Meso American Indian Information Center Newsletter); Veteran Affairs News; Western Shoshone Nation Newsletter; Whispering Wind Magazine;
❸ Third World Organizing; White Buffalo Multi-Media;
❹ Bear & Company, Inc.; Book Publishing Company; Denali Press; Naturegraph Publishers; University of Arizona Press;
❺ Ikwe Marketing Collective;
❻ American Indian Index - A Directory of Indian Country, USA; American Indian Index: A Directory of Indian Country USA; American Indian Reference Book; Bureau of Indian Affairs Higher Education Grant People; Federal Programs of Assistance to American Indians; Guide to Multicultural Resources; Indian Reservations: A State and Federal Handbook; Native American Archives: An Introduction; Native American Directory: Alaska, Canada, United States; Native American Policy Network - Directory; North American Human Rights Directory; Red Pages: Businesses Across Indian America; Sources of Financial Aid Available to American Indian Students;

**Networks/Networking**
Too numerous; see related topics or contact Macrocosm for specialized searches or database.

**Nonviolence**
❶ 20/20 Vision National Project (East); After the Fall; Batterers' Group; Center on War and the Child; Coalition to Stop US Intervention in the Mid-East; Crossing; Episcopal Peace Fellowship; Fellowship of Reconciliation (FOR); Friends World Committee for Consultation; Green Committees of Correspondence; Ground Zero Center for Nonviolent Action; Independent Commission of Inquiry on the US Invasion of Panama; Institute for Peace and Justice; Institute for the Practice of Nonviolence; International War Crimes Tribunal; Lutheran Peace Fellowship; NARMIC; New World Action; Pax Christi USA; Peace Brigades International; Resource Center For Nonviolence; Southern Christian Leadership Conference; Unitarian Universalist Service Committee; US Institute of Peace; Witness for Peace; Women's International League for Peace and Freedom;
❷ American Friends Service Committee Newsletter; Both Sides Now; Brethren Peace Fellowship Newsletter; Center Update; Changing Men, Issues in Gender, Sex & Politics; Decentralize!; Fellowship Magazine; Green Letter; Nonviolent Sanctions; Pax Christi USA; Peace-Work; Point; Sojourners; Spotlight; USIP Journal; WarChild Monitor;
❹ Albert Einstein Institution Publications List; New Society Publishers;
❻ Citizen Diplomats: Americans Ending the Cold War; Guide to War Tax Resistance; Handbook of Nonviolence; Handbook on Military Taxes and Conscience; People Power: Applying Nonviolence Theory; Resources on Gandhi; Seeds of Peace: A Catalog of Quotations; Swords into Plowshares: Nonviolent Direct Action for Disarmament;

**Nonviolent Civil Disobedience**
See also Nonviolence; War Tax Resistance;
❶ American Peace Test; Civilian-Based Defense Association; Earth Action Network; Greenpeace USA; Nukewatch; Social Movement Empowerment Project;
❷ Advocate; Civilian-Based Defense: News & Opinions; Greenpeace Magazine; Ground Zero; Nukewatch Pathfinder; Practical Strategist; Test Banner;
❸ Empowerment Project;
❻ Handbook for Nonviolent Action; MAP Training Manual; Power of the People, Active Nonviolence in the United States; Waging Peace: A Handbook for the Struggle to Abolish Nuclear Weapons;

**Nuclear Test Ban**
❶ American Peace Test; Campaign Against Proliferation; Committee for Nuclear Responsibility; Human Ecology Party; Librarians for Nuclear Arms Control; Nevada Desert Experience; Rocky Mountain Peace Center; Sane/Freeze; Seeds of Peace; Women Strike For Peace;
❷ Desert Voices; LNAC Almanac;

**Nutrition**
See also Vegetarianism;
❶ Action for Corporate Accountability (ACA); Americans for Safe Food; Bastyr College of Natural Health Sciences; Blue Star; Center for Science in the Public Interest; Center for the Biology of Natural Systems; Citizens for Alternatives in Nutrition and Health Care; Community Nutrition Institute; Cooking for Survival Consciousness; Eden Acres, Inc.; Farm Verified Organic; Food and Water, Inc.; Foster Parents Plan, Inc.; Health Plus; Human Ecology Action League; National Child Nutrition Project; National Coalition Against the Misuse of Pesticides; National Coalition to Stop Food Irradiation; National Food and Energy Council; National Institute of Nutritional Education; National Women's Health Network; Natural Food Associates; Natural Food Institute; Organic Growers and Buyers Association; People for the Ethical Treatment of Animals (PETA); Physicians Committee For Responsible Medicine; Project Concern International; Public Voice for Food and Health Policy; Robinson Research Institute; Rodale Foundation, Press and Research Center; Rodale Institute; Society For Nutrition Education; US National Committee For World Food Day; Vegetarian Society Inc.; Women and Food Information Network; World Food Institute;
❷ Action Alert; American Council for the UN University Newsletter; Body & Soul; Children's Digest; Connecting the Dots; Conscious Choice; Cultivator; Delicious!; Eagle; Environ; Food First Development Report; Food Irridiation Alert!; Foodlines; A Chronicle of Hunger and Poverty in America; Health Foods Business; Herb Quarterly; Human Ecologist; Mother Earth News; Natural Food and Farming; Natural Health World; Network News; New Farm; Nutrition Action Healthletter; Prevention; Safe-Food Gazette; True Food; World Hunger Action Newsletter;
❸ Advocate's Guide to the Media;
❹ Crossing Press; IBS Press, Inc.;
❺ Advanced Medical Nutrition; Arrowhead Mills, Inc.; Cherry Hill Cannery, Inc.; F.U.T.U.R.E. Organics, Inc.; L & H Vitamins; Natural Lifestyle Supplies; Organic Farms, Inc.; Outpost Natural Foods; Preventic's, Inc.; Shaklee Corp.; Tucson Cooperative Warehouse; Walnut Acres Organic Farms; WSA Community Pharmacy;
❻ Common Ground: Resources for Personal Transformation; Consumer's Dictionary of Food Additives; Directory of US-Based Agencies Involved in International Health Assistance; Food Pharmacy; Free Range Meat Directory; Healing Wise: The Second Wise Woman Herbal; Healthy Harvest IV: A Directory; Healthy Healing; National Association of Meal Programs - Directory; New Consciousness Source Book: Spiritual Community Guide; Nutrient Data Bank Directory; Organic Network; PETA Guide to Compassionate Living; Prescription for Nutritional Healing; Quick Guide to Food Additives; Tech and Tools Book: A Guide to Technologies Women Are Using Worldwide; Total Nutrition for Breast-Feeding Mothers;

**Occupational Safety**
See also Consumer Protection;
❶ Amalgamated Clothing & Textile Workers Union; Center for Occupational Hazards; Commission on Voluntary Service and Action; Industrial Crisis Institute; National Farm Worker Ministry; Occupational Safety and Health Law Center; Public Citizen;
❷ Art Hazards News; Health Letter Newsletter; Health Science; Labor Center Reporter; Labor Occupational Health Program Monitor; Occupational & Health Magazine; RNA Advisor; Science for the People; Voluntary Service in Action;
❺ Applied Ergonomics;
❻ Whole Arts Directory;

**Organic**
See also Pesticides;
❶ Agrecology Program; Bio-Dynamic Farming and Gardening Association; California Action Network; California Certified Organic Farmers (CCOF); Committee for Sustainable Agriculture; Cooking for Survival Consciousness; Ecology Action; Eden Acres, Inc.; Elfin Permaculture; Farm Verified Organic; Gaia Services; Institute for Alternative Agriculture; Land Stewardship Project; Native Seeds/SEARCH; Natural Food Associates; Natural Food Institute; Natural Organic Farmers Association; Ocean View Farms; Organic Food Network; Organic Growers and Buyers Association;
❷ Acres USA, A Voice For Eco-Agriculture; Bio-Dynamics; Both Sides Now; Cultivar; F.U.T.U.R.E. Newsletter; Food Irridiation Alert!; Fresh Connections; International Permaculture Solutions Journal; Land Stewardship Newsletter; Maine Organic Farmer & Gardner; Natural Food and Farming; Natural Health; New Farm; NOFA-Notes; Nutrition Action Healthletter; Organic Farmer, The Digest of Sustainable Agriculture; Organic Gardening with Bountiful Gardens; Organic Times;
❺ Arrowhead Mills, Inc.; Beneficial Insectary; Bountiful Gardens; Cherry Hill Cannery, Inc.; Dubose Natural Farm; Earthsong; F.U.T.U.R.E. Organics, Inc.; Financing Ozark Rural Growth & Economy (FORGE); Gardener's Supply; Ikwe Marketing Collective; Necessary Trading Company; New American Food Company; Organic Farms, Inc.; Outpost Natural Foods; Pure Products for Personal Care and Natural Healing; Redwood City Seed Co.; Tucson Cooperative Warehouse; Walnut Acres Organic Farms; Worm's Way;
❻ Education and Training Opportunities; Farms of Tomorrow; Fertile Soil; Healthy Harvest IV: A Directory; International Permaculture Species Yearbook (TIPSY); Organic Network; Organic Wholesalers Directory; Resources of International Permaculture (TRIP); Truth in Produce;

**Over-population**
See Population Issues;

**Pacific/Pacific Rim**
❶ Gaia Pacific: The Art of Activism;
❷ Asia & Pacific Update;
❹ Indonesia Publications;
❻ Asia and Pacific: A Directory of Resources; Human Rights Directory: Asia & the Pacific;

**Passive Resistance**
See Anti-draft; Civil Disobedience; Nonviolence;

**Peace**
See related topics or entries flagged ☮;

**Peace Dividend**
See Economic Conversion;

**Permaculture**
See also Bioregionalism;
❶ Alter Project; Aprovecho Institute; Central Rocky Mountain Permaculture; Elfin Permaculture; Forest Ecosystem Rescue Network (FERN); Friends of the Trees Society; North American Permaculture; Permaculture Institute of North America; Running Rain Society; School of Living (SOL); Southwest Regional Permaculture Institute;
❷ Alternator; ECO; Fresh Connections; International Permaculture Solutions Journal; Katuah;

Appendix Guide to Subject Index: ❶ Organizations; ❷ Periodicals; ❸ Media; ❹ Publishing; ❺ Business; ❻ Reference

Permaculture Activist; Robin Newsletter; Sustainable Living in Drylands;
❻ Education and Training Opportunities; Green Front Report; International Permaculture Species Yearbook (TIPSY); Permaculture: A Practical Guide for a Sustainable Future; TRIP (The Resources of International Permaculture);

**Pesticide Issues**
See also Organic;
❶ Concern, Inc; Consumer Pesticide Protection Project; Fresh Fruit/Vegetable Workers Union, UFCW Local 78B; Louisiana Toxics Project; Mothers and Others for a Livable Planet; National Pesticide Telecommunication Network; Northwest Coalition for Alternatives to Pesticides; Pesticide Watch; Rodale Institute; Terra; United Farm Workers Union;
❷ Alternator; Common Sense Pest Control Quarterly; Dirty Dozen Campaigner; Global Pesticide Monitor; IPM Practitioner; Journal of Environmental Quality; Journal of Pesticide Reform;
❺ Chem-Free Exterminating Alternatives; Chemfree Environment;
❻ Chesapeake Citizen Directory; Network Guide of Organizations; Pesticide Handbook: Profiles for Action; Pesticides: A Community Action Guide;

**Philanthropy**
See also Volunteering;
❶ California Community Foundation; Council on Foundations; Dakota Indian Foundation; Environmental Data Research Institute; Foundation for a Compassionate Society; Foundation for International Community Assistance; Independent Sector; National Committee for Responsive Philanthropy; Permanent Charities Committee; Richard and Rhoda Goldman Fund; Right Livelihood Awards Foundation; Running Strong for American Indian Youth; Southern California Association for Philanthropy (SCAP); Women and Foundations/Corporate Philanthropy;
❷ Artpaper; Resist;
❸ Fund Raising Management - Non-Profit Software Package Directory Issue;
❹ Jossey-Bass Inc.;
❻ Activist Guide to Religious Funders; America's Newest Foundations: The Sourcebook on Recently Created Philanthropies; Annual Register of Grant Support: A Directory of Funding Sources; ARIS Funding Reports; Charitable Organizations of the US; Church Funding Resource Guide; Dictionary of Demography: Biographies; Directory of Building and Equipment Grants; Directory of Foundation Funding Sources; Directory of Women's Funds; Encyclopedia of Associations: National Organizations of the US; Encyclopedia of Associations: Regional, State, and Local Organizations; Environmental Grantmakers Directory; Facts on Grants: A Report on Grantmaking of the Charles Stewart Mott Foundation; Foundation Directory; Foundation Grants Index Annual; Foundation Grants to Individuals; Fund Raising Counselors & Organizations; Fundraiser's Guide to Human Service Funding; Grantseekers Guide: A Funding Source Book; Guide to Gifts and Bequests: A Directory of Philanthropically Supported Institutions; Handicapped Funding Directory; Health Funds Grants Resources Yearbook; International Organizations; Inventory of Private Agency Population Research; Invest Yourself, The Catalog of Volunteer Opportunities; Major Private Organizations; National Data Book; National Foundations; National Fund Raising Directory; National Guide to Corporate Giving; Organizations Master Index; Peace and World Order Studies: A Curriculum Guide; Philanthropy and Volunteerism; Public Media Center's Index of Progressive Funders; Resource Directory for Volunteer Programs; Search for Security: The ACCESS Guide to Foundations in Peace, Security, and International Relations; Taft Foundation Reporter; Third Sector Directory; Where to Go to Find Information on Grant Funds and Fundraising; Whole Nonprofit Catalog; Wise Giving Guide;

**Physically-Challenged**
❶ Achievement House; Appalachian Community Services; Center on Human Policy; Disabled Artists' Network; Goodwill Industries of Southern California; Housing for Independent People; Medical Aid for El Salvador; Mental Health Law Project; National Assault Prevention Center; Paralyzed Veterans of America; Recording for the Blind; Seva Foundation;
❷ Berkeley Women's Law Journal; Directions; Disability Rag; Health-Care Revue; Independent Living; Kaleidoscope; RE:view; Young and Alive;
❸ Direct Link/REACH;
❹ Human Policy Press Catalogue;
❺ High Cotton Co.; Jacaranda Imports; Marketplace: Handwork of India; Treekeepers;
❻ Academy of Dentistry for the Handicapped-Referral/Membership Roster; Accent on Living - Buyers Guide; AFB Directory of Services for Blind and Visually Impaired Persons in the United States; Affirmative Action Register; Aging Myths: Reversible Causes of Mind and Memory Loss; Alzheimer's Disease Treatment Facilities and Home Health Care Programs; American Annals of the Deaf; Annotated Registry of Independent Living Programs; Assistive Technology Sourcebook; Caring for Alzheimer's Patients: A Guide for Family & Health Care Providers; Caring for the Mentally Impaired Elderly: A Family Guide; Caring for the Sick; College and Career Programs for Deaf Students; Directory for Exceptional Children; Directory of Agencies and Organizations Serving Deaf-Blind Individuals; Directory of Independent Living Programs; Directory of National Information Sources on Handicapping Conditions and Related Services; Directory of Organizations Interested in People with Disabilities; Directory of Organizations Serving People with Disabilities; Directory of Residential Centers for Adults with Developmental Disabilities; Directory of Resources for Adults with Disabilities; Directory of Selected Early Childhood Programs; Financial Aid for the Disabled and Their Families; Handicapped Driver's Mobility Guide; Handicapped Funding Directory; HEATH Resource Directory; Human Factors Society - Directory; International Directory of Adult-Oriented Assistive Device Sources; International Directory of Periodicals Related to Deafness; International Telephone Directory of TDD Users; Library Manager's Guide to Hiring and Serving Disabled Persons; Library Resources for the Blind and Physically Handicapped; Mental Health Directory; National Accreditation Council for Agencies Serving the Blind and Visually Handicapped - List of Member Organization; Programs Demonstrating Model Practices for Integrating People with Severe Disabilities into the Community; Self-Help Sourcebooks; Special Child: A Source Book for Parents of Children with Developmental Disabilities; Special Recreation Compendium of 1,500 Resources for People with Disabilities; Spinal Network: The Total Resource for the Wheelchair Community; Understanding the Law; Unrestrictive Environment;

**Poetry**
❶ Omega Institute;
❷ Contact II Magazine; Eagle; Five Fingers Review; Green Politics; Heresies: A Feminist Publication on Art and Politics; Hopscotch; Index on Censorship; Kaleidoscope; Minnesota Review; Mr. Cogito; New England Review; North American Review; On the Line; Pig Iron; Poetry: San Francisco Quarterly; Red Bass; SAMISDAT; San Fernando Poetry Journal; Shoe Tree; Sing Heavenly Muse! Women's Poetry & Prose; Story Friends; tricycle; Turnstile; Wide Open Magazine; Wyoming, The Hub of the Wheel; Yellow Silk: Journal of Erotic Arts;
❸ Peacemakers Television;

**Polar**
❶ Alaska Bioregional Network; Alaska Conservation Foundation; Arctic to Amazonia Alliance; Cousteau Society; Green Party of Alaska; Greenpeace USA; National Audubon Society; Northern Alaska Environmental Center; Oceanic Society Expeditions; Zoetic Research/Sea Quest Expeditions;
❷ Greenpeace Magazine; Northern Line;
❹ Alaska Northwest Books;
❻ Alaska Conservation Directory; Public Interest Group Directory;

**Political Prisoners**
See Criminal Justice System; Civil Liberties; Civil Disobedience;
❶ American Committee on Africa; Amnesty International; Center for Constitutional Rights; Center for Victims Of Torture; Defenders Project; Family Reunification Project; Forgotten Families; International League For Human Rights; Partisan Defense Committee; Women's Jail Project;
❷ Amnesty International Orange County Newsletter; Bayou La Rose; California Prisoner; Class-Struggle Defense Notes; Into the Night; Issues and Concerns; Law Report; Movement Support Network News; Nommo; Open Road; Organizer; Prison News Service; Turning the Tide;
❻ Crime in America: Historical Patterns and Contemporary Realities; Human Rights Directory: The Commonwealth; Human Rights Directory: Western Europe; North American Human Rights Directory;

**Politics**
See related topics or entries flagged **P**;

**Population Issues**
See also Family Planning;
❶ Africare; Alan Guttmacher Institute; Association for Voluntary Surgical Contraception; Basic Foundation, Inc.; Californians for Population Stabilization; CARE; Carrying Capacity Network; Catholics For Free Choice; Center for Immigration Studies; Center for Population Options; Dean and Virginia Institute for Population and Resource Studies; Environmental Fund; Environmental Policy Institute; Foreign Assistance Action Project; Global Environment Project Institute; Global Tomorrow Coalition; International Planned Parenthood Federation; National Audubon Society Population Program; National Family Planning and Reproductive Health Association; Negative Population Growth; Pathfinder Fund; Planned Parenthood Federation of America; Population and Environmental Psychology; Population Communication; Population Communications Services; Population Council; Population Crisis Committee; Population Environment Balance, Inc.; Population Institute; Population Reference Bureau; Population Resource Center; Population Services International; Save Our Earth; Sierra Club Population Committee; United Nations Population Fund; US Committee For Refugees; Women's Foreign Policy Council; World Population Society; Zero Population Growth;
❷ Balance Report; Carrying Capacity News/FOCUS; Clearinghouse Bulletin; Conscience; Family Planning Perspectives; Have You Heard?; Human Survival; International Family Planning Perspectives; No Longer Silent; NRDC Newsline; Popline; Population and Development Review; Population Bulletin; Population Newsletter; Population Reports; Population Today; Studies in Family Planning; Washington Memo; World Eagle;
❸ Fax Alert Service;
❻ Activist's Handbook; Community Researcher's Guide To Rural Data; Dictionary of Demography: Biographies; Directory of US-Based Agencies Involved in International Health Assistance; Global Ecology Handbook; Inventory of Population Projects in Developing Countries Around the World; Inventory of Private Agency Population Research; Major Private Organizations; Nongovernmental Organizations in International Population Crisis Committee; Population Handbook; Population Programmers and Projects: Guide to Sources of International Population Assistance; Scarcity and Growth Reconsidered; State of the Earth Atlas; World Population Data Sheet; World Population Fundamentals of Growth, Student Chartbook;

**Poverty**
See Homelessness; Hunger;

**Preventative Medicine**
❶ American Council For Drug Education; American Lung Association; Association of Occupational and Environmental Clinics; Gesundheit Institute; Health Plus; Hesperian Foundation; Holistic Alliance International; Human Ecology Action League; National Black Organizations Against Alcohol & Drug Use; National Parents Resource Institute For Drug Education; National Prevention Network; Robinson Research Institute; US Conference of Mayors AIDS Program;
❷ Arizona Networking News; Body & Soul; Eagle; Environ; Health Foods Business; Health Science; HerbalGram; Human Ecologist; Medical Self-Care; Natural Food and Farming; Smoking and Health Review; Wary Canary;
❺ L & H Vitamins; Shaklee Corp.; WSA Community Pharmacy; Wysong Corporation;
❻ American Cancer Society Cancer Book; Ask Your Doctor, Ask Yourself; Common Ground: Resources for Personal Transformation; Food Pharmacy; Healthy Healing; Prescription for Nutritional Healing;

**Prisons**
See Drug Issues; Criminal Justice System; Political Prisoners;

**Pro-Choice**
❶ Alan Guttmacher Institute; American Civil Liberties Union (ACLU); Catholics For Free Choice; International Planned Parenthood Federation; National Abortion Rights Action League; National Family Planning and Reproductive Health Association; National Organization for Women; People for the American Way; Pro-Choice Task Force; Religious Coalition For Abortion Rights; Reproductive Rights National Network; Women's Foreign Policy Council;
❷ Conscience; Family Planning Perspectives; International Family Planning Perspectives; No Longer Silent; Turning the Tide; Voice; Washington Memo;
❸ Reproductive Rights;
❻ Dictionary of Demography: Biographies; National Abortion Federation - Membership Directory; Sex Law: A Legal Sourcebook on Critical Sexual Issues for the Non-Lawyer;

**Psychology**
Too numerous; see Counseling and related topics or contact Macrocosm for specialized searches or database.

**Public Health**
See also AIDS;
❶ American Groundwater Trust; American Public Health Association; Association of Occupational and Environmental Clinics; Birmingham Environmental; Coalition of Hispanic Health & Human Services Organization; Conservation Law Foundation of New England; Freshwater Foundation; Global Warming Watch; Government Accountability Project (GAP); Holistic Alliance International; INFORM; International Institute Of Concern For Public Health; Learning Alliance; Medical Reform Group; National As-

sembly of National Voluntary Health and Social Welfare Organization; National Association of Community Health Centers, Inc.; National Coalition Against the Misuse of Pesticides; National Environmental Health Association; National Toxics Campaign Fund; Project Concern International;

❷ American Journal of Public Health; Archives of Environmental Health; Behavioral Medicine; Doctor-Patient Studies; Health and Environment Digest; Human Ecology Forum; INFORM Reports; International Health & Development; Nation's Health; Smoking and Health Review; WHO Chronicle; World Health;

❹ World Health Organization Publications Catalogue;

❻ California Toxics Directory; Citizen's Toxics Protection Manual; Directory of Facilities Obligated to Provide Uncompensated Services; Directory of Family Planning Grantees, Delegates, and Clinics; Groundwater: A Community Action Guide; Inventory of Private Agency Population Research; Migrant Health Services Directory; Social Services Organization;

## Racism

See also Minority Rights; Native Americans;

❶ Africa Fund; American Committee on Africa; Anti-Defamation League; Center for Democratic Renewal; Conflict Resolution Center International, Inc.; Episcopal Church Public Policy Network; Global Options; Jews For Racial and Economic Justice; Louisiana Coalition Against Racism and Nazism; Political Research Associates; Upstate Coalition Builders;

❷ Black Vet; Breakthrough; Collective Voice; Crisis; Dimensions: A Journal of Holocaust Studies; Human Ecology Forum; Human Rights Quarterly; Interracial Books for Children Bulletin; Klanwatch Intelligence; Links; Organizer; People For A Change, Building Ourselves A Base; Social Justice: A Journal of Crime, Conflict & World Order; Southern Fight-Back; Witness;

❸ Community Issues;

❹ New Seed Press;

❻ Human Rights Directory: The Commonwealth; Human Rights Directory: Western Europe; Toxic Wastes and Race in the US;

## Rainforests

See Forests;

## Rape/Sexual Abuse

❶ Center for Women's Global Leadership; Feminists Against Pornography; Illusion Theater Prevention Program; National Center For Missing & Exploited Children; National Clearinghouse on Marital and Date Rape; Women Against Pornography;

❷ In Touch; Victimology: An International Journal;

❻ Campus Gang Rape: Party Games?; Child Sexual Abuse Prevention: How To Take The First Steps; Courage to Heal: A Guide for Women Survivors of Child Sexual Abuse; National Clearinghouse on Marital and Date Rape; Post-Traumatic Stress Disorder, Rape Trauma, Delayed Stress and Related Conditions; Recovering from Rape; Recovery: How to Survive Sexual Assault; Safe, Strong, and Streetwise; Sexual Abuse Prevention Education: An Annotated Bibliography; Sexual Assault and Child Abuse: A National Directory of Victim Services and Prevention Programs;

## Recreation

See also entries flagged ➜ for Travel;

❶ American Hiking Society; American Recreation Coalition; Appalachian Mountain Club; Circle Pines Center; Eastern Co-op Recreation School; Imagine Tours; International Bicycle Fund; National Audubon Society Expedition Institute; National Celebration of the Outdoors; National Organization for River Sports; National

Speleological Society; National Wildlife Federation's Conservation Summits; Outdoor Industry Conservation Alliance; Outdoor Writers Association of America; R.E.I. Adventures; Rails-To-Trails Conservancy; Recreators For Social Responsibility; Sea Quest Expeditions; Wildlife Camp; Windsurfers for Clean Water; Woman's Circle; Woodswomen;

❷ American Hiker; Appalachia; Backpacker Magazine; Bicycle Guide; Boundary Waters Journal; IBF News; Out West; Outdoor America; Outdoors Unlimited; Outside; Portable Dwelling Newsletter; Ranger Rick; Signpost Magazine; Silent Sports; South Carolina Wildlife; Walking Magazine; Wilderness;

❹ Backcountry Publications; Falcon Press Publishing Co. Inc.; Johnson Books, Inc.; Mountaineers Books; Outdoor Books; Sierra Club Books; Stackpole Books; Ten Speed Press;

❺ Backroads Bicycle Touring; Biological Journeys; Budget Europe; Easy Going Travel; High Country Adventures; International Expeditions; Laughing Heart Adventures; Nature Quest; R.E.I. (Recreational Equipment International);

❻ Helping Out in the Outdoors; Soft Paths;

## Renewable Energy

See also Solar; Wind; Appropriate Technology;

❶ American Hydrogen Association; American Solar Energy Society; Bio-Energy Council; Center for Renewable Resources; Citizens for Clean Energy; Conservation & Renewable Energy Inquiry & Referral Service (CAREIRS); Critical Mass Energy Project; Earth Day Resources; Forum on Renewable Energy & Climate Change; Fund for Renewable Energy and the Environment; Geothermal Education Office; National Audubon Society; Renewable Fuels Association; Safe Energy Communication Council; US Biomass Industries Council; US Export Council for Renewable Energy;

❷ Connecting the Dots; Earth Day 2000; Garbage; Home Resource Magazine; Independent Energy; Peace Conversion Times; Real Goods News; Renewable Resources Journal;

❸ Safe Planet;

❺ Heart Interface; Leslie Manufacturing; Solar Car Corporation;

❻ Business Opportunities Workbook, Implementing Economic Renewal Projects; Communities at Risk; Communities for Conservation and Action: A Manual for Building Community; Going Off the Beaten Path; Power of the States: a Fifty-State Survey of Renewable Energy; SYNERJY - A Directory of Renewable Energy;

## Repatriation

❶ Going Home Campaign;

## Rural Communities

See also Family Farms; Farmland; Rural Relocation;

❶ Center for Rural Affairs; Center for Rural Studies; Community Information Exchange; Congressional Black Caucus Foundation; Greener Pastures Institute; Land Stewardship Project; League of Rural Voters; National Association of Towns and Townships; National Catholic Rural Life Conference; National Land for People; National Rural Electric Cooperative Association; National Save the Family Farm Coalition; North American Farm Alliance; Planners Network; Plenty USA; Rural American Women, Inc.; Rural Coalition;

❷ Catholic Rural Life; Center for Rural Affairs Newsletter; Community Transportation Reporter; Country Journal; Greener Pastures Gazette; North American Farmer; Permaculture Activist; Post Amerikan; Prairie Journal; Prairie Naturalist; Prairie Paper; Ruralite; Small Farm Advocate;

❹ Community Bookshelf;

❺ Financing Ozark Rural Growth & Economy (FORGE); Forest Trust; Paraclete Society International;

❻ Community Researcher's Guide To Rural Data; Creating Successful Communities, A Guidebook to Management Strategies; International Rural Sociology Association - Membership Directory; Resource Guide for Creating Successful Communities; Rural Sociological Society; Saving America's Countryside: A Guide to Rural Conservation;

## Rural Relocation

❶ Greener Pastures Institute; Rural Network;

❷ Advocate; Country Journal; Greener Pastures Gazette;

❻ Rural Sociological Society;

## Science

❶ American Association for the Advancement of Science; American Institute of Biological Sciences; American Museum of Natural History; Appalachia Science in the Public Interest; Association for Women in Science; Center for Science in the Public Interest; Computer Professionals for Social Responsibility; Earth-Base Projex; Einstein Experience; Federation of American Scientists; Florida Solar Energy Center (FSEC); Foundation for Advancements in Science and Education; Institute of Noetic Sciences; National Center For Appropriate Technology (NATAS); Orgone Biophysical Research Lab; Planetary Society; Progressive Science Institute; Science for Peace; Scientists' Institute for Public Information; Smithsonian Institution; Speak Truth to Power Project; Student Pugwash, USA; Volunteers in Technical Assistance (VITA); Water Pollution Control Federation;

❷ 3-2-1: Contact; American Biology Teacher; American Scholar; Bear Essential News for Kids; Black Enterprise; Brain/Mind Bulletin; Bucknell Review; Bulletin of Science Technology & Society; Centennial Review; geneWATCH; Global Electronics; Green Teacher; Minority Engineer; Omni; Owl; Perspectives on Science and Christian Faith; Pulse of the Planet; Rain; ReVision: The Journal of Consciousness and Change; Science and Society; Science for the People; Scientific Worldview; Scientist; SIPIscope; Skeptical Inquirer; Smithsonian Magazine; US Kids; Wildlife Conservation;

❸ Media Resource Service; Videotape Referral Service;

❹ Enslow Publishers; Facts On File Publications; New Science Library; Oxford University Press; Plenum Publishing Corp.; University of Arizona Press;

❺ Real Goods Alternative Energy Sourcebook;

❻ Directory of Research Grants; Institute for Theological Encounter with Science and Technology - Membership Directory; Mudpies to Magnet; New Careers, A Directory of Jobs and Internships in Technology & Society; Science & Religion; Tech and Tools Book: A Guide to Technologies Women Are Using Worldwide; Women and Technology Project;

## Self-Help — Health

❶ Jubilee House Community Inc.; Wellness Community;

❷ Eagle; Environ; Self-Help Reporter; Wary Canary; Wide Open Magazine;

❸ Sageline;

❹ Health Communications, Inc.; Humanics Publications; IBS Press, Inc.; Impact Publishers; Ten Speed Press;

❻ Ask Your Doctor, Ask Yourself; Directory of Organizations, Associations, Self Help Groups & Hotlines for Mental Health & Human Services Professionals; Parents & Friends of Gays - International Directory; Programs to Strengthen Families: A Resource Guide; Reaching Out: A Directory of National Organizations Related to Maternal and Child Health; Recovery, Incorporated - Directory of Group Meeting Information; Self-Care and Self-Help Groups for the Elderly:

A Directory; Self-Help Organizations and Professional Practice; Self-Help Sourcebooks;

## Self-determination

See Disabled's Rights Gay/Lesbian; Minority Rights; Native Americans;

## Seniors

❶ American Association for International Aging; American Association of Retired Persons; Gray Panther Network; Gray Panthers National Office; Interfaith Impact for Justice and Peace; National Caucus & Center on Black Aged; National Citizen's Coalition for Nursing Home Reform; National Council of Senior Citizens; National Council on the Aging; National Senior Citizens Law Center; SeniorNet; World Conference on Religion and Peace;

❷ Collation; Health-Care Revue; Mature Years; Modern Maturity; Neighborhood Caretaker; Prime Times; Senior Citizens News; Senior Magazine;

❸ Sageline;

❹ Celo Books;

❺ Project Now Inc.;

❻ Age Care Sourcebook: A Resource Guide for the Aging and Their Families; Aging Myths: Reversible Causes of Mind and Memory Loss; Alzheimer's Disease Treatment Facilities and Home Health Care Programs; Caring for Alzheimer's Patients: A Guide for Family & Health Care Providers; Caring for the Mentally Impaired Elderly: A Family Guide; Caring for the Sick; Directory of Adult Day Care in America; Directory of Episcopal Facilities for the Elderly; Directory of Resources for Aging, Gerontology, and Retirement; Encyclopedia of Senior Citizens Information Sources; Gray Panther Network - Listing of Local Groups Issue; Home Health Care: A Complete Guide for Patients and Their Families; Human Factors Society - Directory; National Guide to Funding in Aging; Self-Care and Self-Help Groups for the Elderly: A Directory; Senior Citizens Service Organizations Directory; Spices of Life: The Well-Being Handbook For Older Americans; Where Can Mom Live? A Family Guide to Living Arrangements for Elderly Parents; Young and Old Together;

## Sexual Abuse

See Rape;

## Socially Responsible Investing

See Boycotts; Investing; See Alternative Consumer—Socially-Responsible Investing;

## Soil

❶ American Farmland Trust; Land Stewardship Project; Native Seeds/SEARCH; Soil and Water Conservation Society; Soil Remineralization; World Association of Soil and Water Conservation;

❷ Journal of Soil and Water Conservation; Land Stewardship Newsletter;

❺ Natursoil Company;

❻ Fertile Soil;

## Solar

See also Renewable Energy; Wind; Appropriate Technology;

❶ American Hydrogen Association; American Solar Energy Society; Citizens for Clean Energy; Conservation & Renewable Energy Inquiry & Referral Service (CAREIRS); Florida Solar Energy Center (FSEC); Interstate Solar Coordinating Council; Passive Solar Industries Council; Solar Box Cookers International; Solar Electric Light Fund; Solar Energy Industries Association (SEIA); Solar Energy Research Institute; Solar Retrofit Consortium;

❷ Home Magazine; Home Power Magazine; Home Resource Magazine; Hydrogen Today; Independent Energy; International Solar Energy Intelligence Report; Journal of Hydrogen; Photovoltaic Insider's Report; PV Network News; PV News; re news digest; Solar Industry Journal; Solar Today;

❺ Eco Solar; Fafco Solar Heating Systems; Integral Energy Systems; Jade Mountain Import-Export Co.; New Alternatives Fund; Real Goods Alternative Energy Sourcebook; Sandia National Laboratories (SNLA); Solar Car Corporation; Solar Power Wagon; Sun Watt/Skyheat Association;
❻ Solar Electricity Today; Solar Energy Applications; Solar Energy Education Directory;

**South Africa**
See also Divestment;
❶ Boycott Shell Campaign; Coke Divestment Campaign; Educators Against Racism and Apartheid; Interfaith Center for Corporate Responsibility; Methodist Federation for Social Action; Project South Africa; Transafrica;
❷ ANC Weekly News Briefing; Boycott Shell Bulletin; IDAF News Notes/Focus in Southern Africa; International Review of Third World Culture and Issues; Kagenna; Nommo; Progressive Student News; Southern Africa Perspectives; Student Anti-Apartheid Movement Newsletter; Students United for Peace Newsletter; Toward Freedom;
❸ California Newsreel;
❺ SRI Advisors; Conscientious Investor's Guide to Socially-Responsible Mutual and Money Market Funds; In Whose Interest: A Guide to US-South Africa Relations; Strangers in Their Own Country: A Curriculum Guide on South Africa;

**South America**
See also Latin America;
❶ Ancient Forests International; Data Center;
❷ Chile Newsletter; Report on Science and Human Rights;
❺ From The Rainforest;
❻ Rainforest: A Guide to Research & Tourist Facilities at Selected Tropical Sites in Central & South America;

**Soviet Relations**
See East-West Relations;

**Space**
❶ Arms Race in Space Project; Institute for Security and Cooperation in Outer Space; Institute for Space and Security Studies; Planetary Society; Speak Truth to Power Project;
❷ Space and Security News;
❸ DataNet;

**Spiritual**
See related topics or entries flagged **S**;

**Substance Abuse**
See also Drug Issues;
❶ Action on Smoking and Health; Al-Anon/Alateen Family Group Headquarters; Alcoholics Anonymous; American Council For Drug Education; American Lung Association; Birmingham Environmental; Causes and Cures; Group to Alleviate Smoking Pollution (GASP); Institute on Black Chemical Abuse; M.A.D.D. (Mothers Against Drunk Driving); National Black Organizations Against Alcohol & Drug Use; National Prevention Network; Remove Intoxicated Drivers (RID-USA); Tobacco Products Liability Project; World Conference on Religion and Peace;
❷ Eagle; Neighborhood Caretaker; Parabola; Tobacco and Youth Reporter;
❸ There is a Solution;
❹ Compcare Publishers; Health Communications, Inc.; New Idea Press, Inc.;
❻ 100 Best Treatment Centers for Alcoholism and Drug Abuse; Alcoholism Information & Treatment Directory; American Academy of Psychiatrists in Alcoholism & Addiction - Membership Directory; Association of Halfway House Alcoholism Programs of North America (AHHAP) - Membership Directory; Drug, Alcohol, and Other Addictions: A Directory of Treatment Centers and Prevention Programs Nationwide; Encyclopedia of Drug Abuse; Mental Health Directory; National Association of Substance Abuse Trainers; National Directory of Alcoholism and Drug Abuse Treatment and Prevention Programs; National Directory of Drug Abuse and Alcoholism Treatment and Prevention Programs; National Prevention Network - Directory; National Treatment Directory Alcohol and Addiction; Rehab: A Comprehensive Guide to the Best Drug-Alcohol Treatment Centers in the US; Self-Help Sourcebooks; Substance Abuse Training Program; Who's Who in Addiction Treatment and Recovery;

**Taxation**
See also Budget Priorities; Government Accountabilty;
❶ Alternative Revenue Service; Citizens Against Government Waste; Citizens for Tax Justice; Conscience Canada, Inc.; Employment Research Associates; Financial Democracy Campaign; Finger Lakes Green Fund; Henry George Foundation of America; Institute for Economic Democracy; Living Economy Network; National Taxpayers Union;
❷ Nolo News; Peace Tax Fund Newsletter; Pragmatist, A Utilitarian Approach;

**Telecommunications**
See also BBS;
❶ British Consortium for Innovation; Telecommunications Co-op Network; Telecommunications Research and Action Center; Unison Institute;
❸ Environmental News Service; Fax Alert Service; Green Newsline; Kids' Network; Pacific Telecommunications Council; Presbytell; Sageline;

**Terminal Illness**
See Death & Dying;

**Theater**
❶ A.C.T.S. - Artists Contributing to the Solution; PeaceWorks;
❷ Alternate Roots; Artpaper; Heresies: A Feminist Publication on Art and Politics; High Performance; In Touch; Plays, The Drama Magazine for Young People; The Original Art Report (TOAR); Threepenny Review;
❸ Alternate Roots; Creative Resources Guild; CRG Resource Directory; Living Stage Theater Company;
❻ American Dance Therapy Association - Membership Directory; Association of Hispanic Arts News - Directory of Hispanic Arts Organizations Section; Child Sexual Abuse Prevention: How To Take The First Steps; Sexual Abuse Prevention Education: An Annotated Bibliography;

**Third World**
See related topics or entries flagged **T**;

**Third World Alternative Markets**
❶ Friends of the Third World, Inc.; Mayan Crafts; Pueblo to People; Trade-Aid, Inc.;
❷ Catalyst: Economics for a Living Earth; Investing from the Heart;
❺ Abundant Life; Alternative Gift Markets; Alternative Trading News; Daily Planet; Earth Sounds; Easy Going Travel; Exotic Gifts; Fallen Empire; From The Rainforest; Jubilee Crafts; Mission Traders; One World Trading Co.; Orrin International Trade Co.; Paraclete Society International; Plowsharing Crafts; Pueblo to People; Rainbow World Imports; RainForest Essentials, Ltd.; Seva Catalog; Stephanie Schuster, Inc.; Thread of Hope; UGAN (Union des Artisans du Nord); World Peace by Nina Grand;
❻ Co-op America Organizational Member Directory; Conscientious Investor's Guide to Socially-Responsible Mutual and Money Market Funds;

**Toxic Waste**
Too numerous; see related topics or contact Macrocosm for specialized searches or database;

**Trade**
❶ CATO Institute; Coalition for Fair Trade and Social Justice; Fair Trade Campaign; Institute for Agriculture and Trade Policy; International Trade & Development Policy Education Foundation;
❺ Paraclete Society International; World Bank;

**Transformation**
Too numerous; see entries flagged with S; or contact Macrocosm for specialized searches or database.

**Transportation**
See also Renewables;
❶ Act Now: Business for a Change; American Pedestrian Association; American Public Transit Association; Californians For Transportation Solutions; Commuter Transportation Services, Inc.; Henry George Foundation of America; Institute for Transportation and Development Policy; International Bicycle Fund; International Conference on Appropriate Transportation; Mega-Cities Project; Texas Committee on Natural Resources; US Conference of Mayors; Aerovironment; Alternative Transportation News; Community Transportation Reporter; IBF News; re news digest; Adamson Design; Backroads Bicycle Touring; Budget Europe; Green Tortoise Adventure Travel; International Environment Consultants; White Industries; Association for Commuter Transportation - Membership Directory; Bicycling in Africa; Wildlife Reserves and Corridors in the Urban Environment;

**Travel**
See entries that are flagged ✈;

**Unions**
AFL-CIO; Amalgamated Clothing & Textile Workers Union; American Federation of Government Employees; American Federation of State, County & Municipal Employees (AFSCME); American Federation of Teachers; Association for Union Democracy; Bakery, Confectionery, & Tobacco Workers International Union; Boycott Committee; Citizen-Labor Energy Coalition; Coalition to Boycott Domino's Pizza; Communications Workers of America; Data Center; Food & Allied Service Trades (AFL-CIO); Front Lash, Inc.; Full Employment Action Council; Industrial Workers of the World; International Association of Machinists & Aerospace Workers; International Brotherhood of Electrical Workers; International Brotherhood of Teamsters, Chauffeurs, Warehousemen & Helpers of America; International Chemical Workers Union; International Ladies' Garment Workers Union; Jewish Labor Committee; Labor Education and Research Project; Labor Heritage Foundation; Labor Letter; National Association of Letter Carriers; National Association of Social Workers; National Forum Foundation; National Labor Committee in Support of Human Rights in El Salvador; National Writers Union; Oil, Chemical and Atomic Workers International Union; Sheet Metal Workers International Association; Teamsters For a Democratic Union;
❷ AALC Reporter; Art Works; BC&T Report & News; CLUW News; Convoy Dispatch; Food and Justice; Ideas and Action; Industrial Worker; Information Bulletin; International Labor Reports; Jobs Impact Bulletin; Labor History; Labor Notes; Labor Occupational Health Program Monitor; Labor Research Review; Labor Today; Machinist; People's Daily World; Struggle; Union; Union Democracy Review; Workers World;
❺ Co-op Alumni Association;
❻ Directory of National Unions & Employee Associations;

**United Nations**
❶ Campaign for UN Reform; Center for UN Reform Education; Defenders Project; Earth Protection Group; Family Reunification Project; Friends of the United Nations; Friends of UNEP; Global Cooperation for a Better World; Global Forum of Spiritual and Parliamentary Leaders on Human Survival; Inter-American Foundation; International League For Human Rights; International Network for a UN Second Assembly; International War Crimes Tribunal; Our Planet in Every Classroom; Peace Studies Unit; People's Assembly for the UN; United Nations; United Nations Association of the USA; United Nations Association of USA; United Nations Environment Programme; World Association for World Federation;
❷ Global Report; Human Rights Quarterly; Inter-Dependent; Toward Freedom; UN Chronicle; WHO Chronicle; Window on the World; World Federalist News; World Peace News;
❸ United Nations Films & Videos;
❻ Environmental Guidelines for World Industry; International Development Resource Books;

**Urban**
See related topics or entries flagged **U**;

**Vegetarianism**
See also Nutrition;
❶ Beyond Beef Campaign; EarthSave Foundation; Farm Animal Reform Movement (FARM); Jewish Vegetarians of North America; Web of Life Foundation;
❷ Alive and Well on Planet Earth; Farm Report; Hygienic Community Network News (HCN); Jewish Vegetarians Newsletter; Land Stewardship Newsletter; Sproutletter; Vegetarian Journal; Vegetarian Living; Vegetarian Times; Vegetarian Voice;
❹ Book Publishing Company;
❺ Amberwood;
❻ SproutChart/SproutGuide; Vegetarian Health Directory; Vegetarian Voice - Local Vegetarian Organizations Section;

**Veterans**
❶ Amvets; Citizen Soldier; Forgotten Families; International Alliance of Atomic Veterans;
❷ Black Vet; Point; Veteran; Veteran Affairs News;
❻ Mental Health Directory; Post-Traumatic Stress Disorder, Rape Trauma, Delayed Stress and Related Conditions;

**Victims' Rights**
❶ Commission on Voluntary Service and Action; National Senior Citizens Law Center; Tobacco Products Liability Project;
❷ Victimology: An International Journal; Voluntary Service in Action;
❺ AIKI Works;
❻ Parental Kidnapping: How to Prevent an Abduction and What to Do If Your Child is Abducted; Sexual Assault and Child Abuse: A National Directory of Victim Services and Prevention Programs; Sunny Von Bulow National Victim Advocacy Center;

**Vitamins**
See Preventative Medicine;

**Volunteering**
See also Jobs;
❶ Access: Networking in the Public Interest; Acid Rain Foundation, Inc.; American Cetacean Society; American Forestry Association; American Lung Association; American Red Cross; American Youth Work Center; Appalachian Trail Conference; Aprovecho Institute; California Earth Corps; Caribbean Conservation Corporation; Center for Marine Conservation; Clean Water Action Project; Coalition for National Service; Colorado Environmental Coalition; Commission on Voluntary Service and Action; Congressional Institute for the Future; Coolidge Center for Environmental Leadership; Defenders of Wildlife; Ducks Unlimited; Earth Island Institute; Earthwatch; Environmental Data Research Institute; Environmental Law Institute; Environmental Protection Information Center (EPIC); Foundation for Field Research; Free Arts for Abused

Children; Freshwater Foundation; Friends of Animals; Friends of Peace Pilgrim; Friends of Vista; Fund for Animals; Greenpeace USA; Habitat for Humanity International; Hawk Migration Association of North America; Hawk Mountain Sanctuary; Hawkwatch International, Inc.; Hudsonia Limited; Humane Society of the US; Hunger Project; Independent Sector; INFORM; Interaction; International Council for Bird Preservation; International Ecological Society; International Oceanographic Foundation; International Voluntary Services (IVS); Involvement Corps; Lake Michigan Federation; Land and Water Fund of the Rockies; Legacy International; Lighthawk; Mennonite Central Committee; Mission: Wolf; National Assembly of National Voluntary Health and Social Welfare Organization; National Association of Service and Conservation Corps; National Parents Resource Institute For Drug Education; National Parks and Conservation Association; National Youth Work Alliance; Nature Conservancy; North American Association for Environmental Education; North American Loon Fund; North American Wildlife Park Foundation, Inc.; Northern Alaska Environmental Center; Northshield; On Beyond War; Peregrine Fund, Inc.; Permanent Charities Committee; Rails-To-Trails Conservancy; Recording for the Blind; Resource Center For Nonviolence; Results; Save Our Streams Program; Sea Shepherd; Seeds: Christians Concerned About Hunger; Southern Christian Leadership Conference; Student Conservation Association, Inc.; Student Pugwash, USA; Texas Committee on Natural Resources; Travellers Earth Repair Network (TERN); Unitarian Universalist Service Committee; University Research Expeditions Program (UREP); Volunteers for Peace Workcamps; Volunteers in Technical Assistance (VITA); Wildlife Conservation International; Windhorse Touring and Trading; Witness for Peace; WorldTeach; Youths for Environment and Society;

❷ Challenge: A Journal of Faith and Action in Central America; Developments; Earth Work; Friends of Peace Pilgrim Newsletter; International Workcamper Newsletter; Monday Developments; Northern Sun News; Peace Chronicle; Spotlight; Victimology: An International Journal; Voluntary Service in Action;

❹ Jossey-Bass Inc.;

❻ AFB Directory of Services for Blind and Visually Impaired Persons in the United States; All-in-One Guide to European-Atlantic Organizations; Alternative Directory of South Asian Non-Governmental Organizations; Alternatives to the Peace Corps: Gaining Third World Experience; Bay Area Green Pages, The Local Handbook for Planet Maintenance; Complete Guide to Environmental Careers; Directory of Peace Studies Programs; Directory of Public Interest Legal Internships/The NAPIL Fellowships Guide; Directory of Public Service Internships: Opportunities for the Graduate, Post-Graduate & Mid-Career Professional; Directory of Undergraduate Internships; Directory of US-Based Agencies Involved in International Health Assistance; Directory of Volunteer Centers; Directory of Washington Internships; Encyclopedia of Associations: National Organizations of the US; Encyclopedia of Associations: Regional, State, and Local Organizations; Fish and Wildlife Reference Service; Gale GlobalAccess: Associations; Good Works: A Guide to Careers in Social Change; Great Careers: The Fourth of July Guide to Careers, Internships, and Volunteer Opportunities in the Nonprofit Sector; Green City Program for the Bay Area and Beyond; Helping Out in the Outdoors; Hispanic American Voluntary Organizations; International Organizations; International Workcamp Directory; Invest Your-self, The Catalog of Volunteer Opportunities; Jewish American Voluntary Organizations; Lend a Hand: The How, Where, and Why of Volunteering; Making Things Happen; National Center for Resources in Vocational Education; National Volunteer Clearinghouse for the Homeless; New Careers, A Directory of Jobs and Internships in Technology & Society; Organizations Master Index; Organize!; Overseas List - Opportunities For Living and Working in Developing Countries; Philanthropy and Volunteerism; Public Interest Group Directory; Reaching Out: A Directory of National Organizations Related to Maternal and Child Health; Resource Directory for Volunteer Programs; SourceBook: Guide to Clubs, Groups, Associations, and Organizations; Student Conservation Association Catalog; Voluntary Agencies Directory; Volunteer Vacations; Volunteer! The Comprehensive Guide to Voluntary Service in the US and Abroad.;

## Voting

❶ Americans for the Environment; Coalition for Free and Open Elections; Eastern Europe Constitution Design Forum; Interfaith Impact for Justice and Peace; League of Rural Voters; League of Women Voters; Project Vote Smart;

❻ Civilian Congress; It's a Free Country! A Young Person's Guide to Politics & Elections; Nuclear Waste Digest & Nuclear Waste Primer; Thinking Globally...Acting Locally: A Citizen's Guide to Community Education on Global Issues;

## War Tax Resistance

❶ Alternative Revenue Service; Conscience and Military Tax Campaign; Conscience Canada, Inc.; Friends World Committee for Consultation; National Campaign for a Peace Tax Fund; War Resisters League;

❷ Conscience and Military Tax Campaign; God and Caesar; Network News; Peace Tax Fund Newsletter;

❺ Tax Resistor's Penalty Fund;

❻ Guide to War Tax Resistance; Handbook on Military Taxes and Conscience; War Tax Manual for Counselors and Lawyers;

## Waste Management

Recycling is too numerous; see related topics or contact Macrocosm for specialized searches or database.

❶ Aluminum Association; Dean and Virginia Institute for Population and Resource Studies; Don't Waste California; Environmental Research Foundation; INFORM; Military Toxics Network; National Recycling Coalition; StopStyro;

❷ Clean Water Action News; Garbage; R.A.C.H.E.L'S Hazardous Waste News;

❸ W.O.W. Series of Video Tapes on the Solid Waste Crisis;

❺ Community Recycling and Resource Recovery;

❻ Business Recycling Manual; Citizens' Guide to Plastics in the Ocean: More Than A Litter Problem; Guide to the Management of Hazardous Waste; Solid Waste Education Recycling Directory; We All Live Downstream - a Guide to Waste Treatment That Stops Water Pollution;

## Water

❶ American Cave Conservation Association; American Farmland Trust; American Groundwater Trust; American Water Resources Association; Association of State and Interstate Water Pollution Control Administration; Association of State Drinking Water Administrators; Chesapeake Bay Foundation; Clean Water Action Project; Colorado Environmental Coalition; Concern, Inc; Environmental Hazards Management Institute; Food and Water, Inc.; Freshwater Foundation; Global Water; INFORM; Jemez Action Group; Kansas Area Watershed Council; Lake Michigan Federation; League to Save Lake Tahoe; National Association of Conservation Districts, Inc.; National Audubon Society; National Clean Water Coalition; National Water Center; National Water Resources Association; New Alchemy Institute; North American Lake Management Society; North American Native Fishes Association; North American Water Office; Northshield; Ocean Arks International; Ocean View Farms; Quebec-Labrador Foundation Canada (QLF); Sierra Club Legal Defense Fund; Soil and Water Conservation Society; Texas Committee on Natural Resources; Water Pollution Control Federation; Williams Watershed Protection Agency; Windsurfers for Clean Water; World Association of Soil and Water Conservation;

❷ Aqua Terra - Water Concepts for an Ecological Society; Clean Water Action News; Health and Environment Digest; Hydata-News & Views; Journal of Environmental Quality; Journal of Hydrogen; Journal of Soil and Water Conservation; Keep Tahoe Blue; Mono Lake Newsletter; US Water News; Water Resources Bulletin;

❺ Co-Aqua; Conservation Concepts; EcoAlternatives; Resources Conservation; Seventh Generation Catalog; Waste Not;

❻ Chesapeake Citizen Directory; Citizen's Directory For Water Quality Abuses; Citizen's Handbook on Groundwater Protection; Controlling Nonpoint-Source Water Pollution, A Citizen's Handbook; Drinking Water: A Community Action Guide; Groundwater: A Community Action Guide; Mono Lake Guidebook; Practical Home Energy Savings; Repair Manual For Planet Earth: Steps You Can Take To Heal the Land, Water, Wildlife, and Cities of America; We All Live Downstream - a Guide to Waste Treatment That Stops Water Pollution;

## Welfare Rights

❶ Coalition of Hispanic Health & Human Services Organization; Congressional Black Caucus Foundation; National Assembly of National Voluntary Health and Social Welfare Organization; Welfare Warriors;

❷ Campaign Report; CDF Reports; Disability Rag; Foodlines; A Chronicle of Hunger and Poverty in America; Indian Report; NLADA Cornerstone; Welfare Mothers Voice;

❻ Council for Health & Human Service Ministries - Directory Services; Guide to Resources in Holistic Education; National Directory of Children & Youth Services; National Directory of Private Social Agencies;

## Wetlands

❶ Association of State Wetland Managers, Inc.; Ducks Unlimited; International Ecological Society; National Audubon Society; Nisqually Delta Association; North American Lake Management Society; Williams Watershed Protection Agency;

❷ Ducks Unlimited; National Wetlands Newsletter; Networker;

❻ Chesapeake Citizen Directory; Creating Successful Communities, A Guidebook to Management Strategies; United Nations List of National Parks and Protected Areas; We All Live Downstream - a Guide to Waste Treatment That Stops Water Pollution;

## Whistle-blowing

❶ Government Accountability Project (GAP);
❷ Bridging the Gap;

## Wildlife

Too numerous; see entries flagged with "E" or contact Macrocosm for specialized searches or database.

## Wind

See also Renewable Energy Solar; Appropriate Technology;

❶ American Wind Energy Association;

❷ Home Power Magazine; International Solar Energy Intelligence Report; re news digest; Wind Energy Weekly; WindLetter;

❹ American Wind Energy Association Publication List; Cheshire Books;

❺ Integral Energy Systems; Jade Mountain Import-Export Co.;

❻ Wind Energy for a Growing World;

## Women's Rights

See Battered Women; Empowerment; Equal Rights; Family Planning; Men's Liberation; Rape/Sexual Abuse; and all entries flagged with "F";

## Worker Ownership

See Workplace Democracy;

## Workplace Democracy

❶ Arthur Morgan School; Association For A Democratic Workplace; Association for Enterprise Opportunities; Association for Union Democracy; Backcountry Homeworker's Exchange; Center for Community Self-Help; National Center for Employee Ownership; National Farm Worker Ministry; National Farmers Organization; United Farm Workers Union; Women's Project of the Association for Union Democracy;

❷ Bayou La Rose; Franciscan Worker; Grassroots Economic Organizing (GEO) Newsletter; Ideas and Action; Mother Jones; Neighborhood Works; Networking Newsletter; Rural Advance; This Time;

❹ New Society Publishers;

❺ American Capital Strategies; Consumers United Insurance Company; Democratic Workplaces; Deva Lifewear; Employee Partnership Fund; Great Alaska Catalog; ICA Revolving Loan Fund; InDios Co-op; Industrial Cooperative Association; Worker Owned Network; WSA Community Pharmacy;

❻ Migrant Health Services Directory;

# ① Organizations

| A | = Agriculture | D | = Demographics | ✪ | = Energy | ? | = Future | L | = Labor | S | = Spiritual |

A = Agriculture    D = Demographics    ✪ = Energy    ? = Future    L = Labor    S = Spiritual
➤ = Animal Rights    ♿ = Disabled    E = Environment    G = Gay/Lesbian    M = Media    T = Third World
✎ = Arts    $ = Economics    ♥ = Family    H = Health    ✵ = Peace    ✈ = Travel
⊄ = Computers    ✍ = Education    F = Feminism    J = Justice    P = Politics    U = Urban

---

✎ ♦ **A.C.T.S. - Artists Contributing to the Solution**
c/o SCWCA
1727 N. Spring St.
Los Angeles, CA 90012  (714)532-5519
**Concern(s):** arts; environment; activism; sustainability; preservation; theater. A group of artists dealing with global environmental issues. Under the auspices of the Southern California Women's Caucus for Art, A.C.T.S. will present a year-long series of events, exhibits, panels and performances dealing with the environment. **Contact(s):** Suvan Geer (Coordinator).

✪ ♦ **Abalone Alliance**
2940 16th St., #310
San Francisco, CA 94103  (415)861-0592
**Concern(s):** energy; environment; anti-nuclear. A coalition of environmental and anti-nuclear groups that organized demonstrations at Diablo Nuclear Power Plant with the assistance of Mothers for Peace and others. Presently working on Don't Waste California to stop radioactive waste disposal.

✍ ♦ **ABC's for the 21st Century Project**
c/o Countdown 2001
110 North Payne St.
Alexandria, VA 22314
**Affiliation:** Countdown 2001. **Concern(s):** education; economics; future; politics; ideation; trade. Offers workshops for business education and government leaders on how to lead organizations into the 21st century. **Other Resources:** See EDUCATOR'S GUIDE: AN AGENDA FOR THE 21ST CENTURY. Nonprofit. **Est.:** 1985.

♿ ♦ **Academy of Dentistry for the Handicapped**
See ACADEMY OF DENTISTRY FOR THE HANDICAPPED-REFERRAL/MEMBERSHIP ROSTER.

P ♦ **Academy of Political Science**
475 Riverside Dr.
New York, NY 10115-0122  (212)870-2500
**Concern(s):** politics; education; students. Innovative insights into the political sciences. offering an excellent curriculum for the politically-minded person.

✍ ♦ **Academy of World Studies**
2820 Van Ness Ave.
San Francisco, CA 94109
**Concern(s):** education; peace; global understanding; world order. Courses in various languages with a global perspective. **Contact(s):** Bennet Skewes-Cox (President).

L ♦ **Access: Networking in the Public Interest**
50 Beacon St.
Boston, MA 02108  (617)720-5627
**Concern(s):** labor; jobs; volunteers. Job listings in nonprofits, public interest law, and state government. Personal computerized job search services and information on volunteer opportunities. **Member:** Co-op America.

T ♦ **Accion International**
130 Prospect St.
Cambridge, MA 02139  (617)492-4930
**Concern(s):** Third World; economics; education; community self-reliance; development; jobs. Founded to reduce poverty in the Americas. Since 1973, it has focused on creating jobs and income opportunities among the poor by providing loans and basic business training to the self-employed poor. It has become an internationally recognized leader in micro-enterprise development and has worked in virtually every Latin American country and several US areas. In 1990, it provided loans to 67,000 small businesses, creating 42,000 jobs and benefiting 300,000 family members. **Other Resources:** Books about micro-enterprise assistance, ACTION INTERNATIONAL BULLETIN, annual report, and other general information about its programs. ACTION INTERNATIONAL PUBLICATIONS LIST available. Nonprofit. **Est.:** 1961. **Fax:** (617)876-9509. **Contact(s):** Gabriela Romanow (Director of Communications), Libbie Shufro (Resource Development).

♿ ♦ **Achievement House**
Box 3060
San Luis Obispo, CA 93406  (805)543-9383
**Affiliation:** United Way. **Concern(s):** health; disabled. A unique environment where handicapped adults are trained to be employable. A thrift shop, nursery, woodshop, and mailing center, all located in a wooded setting. **Other Resources:** Newsletter, THE ACHIEVER.

E ♦ **The Acid Rain Foundation, Inc.**
1410 Varsity Dr.
Raleigh, NC 27606  (919)828-9443
**Concern(s):** environment; recycling; acid rain; forests; volunteers. Purpose: To foster greater understanding of global atmospheric issues by raising the level of public awareness, supplying educational resources and supporting research. Current Emphasis: Acid rain, global atmosphere, recycling and forest ecosystems. **Other Resources:** Volunteer Programs: Education, development, library and marketing. See directories under same name. **Dues:** $35/yr. **Contact(s):** Harriett S. Stubbs, Ph.D (Executive Director), Joane Harer (Administrative Assistant).

$ ♦ **ACORN**
300 Flatbush Ave.
Brooklyn, NY 11217  (718)789-5600
**Concern(s):** economics; demographics; politics; justice; grassroots organizing; community self-reliance; consumer rights; rape/sexual abuse; housing; corporate responsibility. The Association of Community Organizations for Reform Now (ACORN) is the nation's largest movement organization of low and moderate-income people. It has grown to a membership of over 75,000 member families since the early 60's. Made up of neighborhood organizations who work on direct action campaigns to fight to preserve affordable and decent housing, prevent rape, force banks and corporations to be accountable to local communities and more. **Est.:** 1960.

✪ ♦ **Act Now: Business for a Change**
c/o Aurora Press
Box 573
Santa Fe, NM 87504
**Concern(s):** energy; politics; economics; environment; global warming; air pollution; efficiency; resource management; transportation; conservation; corporate responsibility; trade. A partnership of companies and customers working to pressure Congress to fight global warming and air pollution by requiring greater gas economy requirements for car manufacturers. Goal: By the year 2000 standards should be 40mpg. "We are Aurora Press, Real Goods, Seventh Generation, Ben & Jerry's, The Body Shop, Rhino Records, Earth Care Paper, Smith & Hawkin, Utne Reader, Working Assets, and more."

G ♦ **Act Up (AIDS Coalition to Unleash Power)**
135 W. 29th St., 10th Fl.
New York, NY 10001  (212)564-AIDS
**Concern(s):** health; justice; public health; AIDS; gay/lesbian. A diverse nonpartisan group of individuals, united in anger, and committed to direct action to end the AIDS crisis. **Est.:** 1987. **Fax:** (212)989-1797.

♥ ♦ **Action for Children**
ONGA A-4A, 866 UN Plaza
New York, NY 10017
**Affiliation:** NGO Committee on UNICEF. **Concern(s):** family; justice; child abuse; children.

$ ♦ **Action for Corporate Accountability (ACA)**
3255 Hennepin Ave. S, #255
Minneapolis, MN 55408-9986  (612)823-1571
**Concern(s):** economics; Third World; justice; health; boycott; corporate responsibility; socially-responsible investing; children; nutrition. BOYCOTT NESTLE/AMERICAN HOME PRODUCTS — They are the largest marketers of infant formula in the Third World. Products: All Nestle including Beech-Nut items, Carnation, Coffeemate non-dairy creamer, Hills Brothers Coffees, Libby's MJB Coffees, Nescafe, Nestea, Nestle's chocolate, Stouffer's, and Taster's Choice. All AHP products including Advil, Anacin, Chef Boyardee, Easy Off items, Gulf Light, Kwik Light, and Wizard Charcoal lighters, Jiffy popcorn, Gulden's Mustard, Dristan, Easy-Off... **Other Resources:** To protest, write to: Alan MacDonald, Nestle Co, 100 Manhattanville Rd., Purchase, NY 10577; John Stafford, American Home Products, 685 Third Ave., New York, NY 10017. Write ACA for more information. **Contact(s):** Janice Mantell, Carol-Linnea Salmon (Associate Director).

⊄ ♦ **Action Linkage**
Box 684
Bangor, ME 04401
**Concern(s):** media; peace; future; multilogues; ideation; computer networking. Primary purpose is to link people together in ways that are not normally available to them. Currently assisting in a project called IdeaNet, a scheme to develop a Global Suggestion Box through computer networking presently in the multilogue stage. **Other Resources:** Publishes GENERAL COMMUNICATION MULTILOGUE. See also, IdeaNet and ACTION LINKAGE NETWORKER newsletter. **Contact(s):** Cat Eldridge (General Coordinator).

H ♦ **Action on Smoking and Health**
2013 H St. NW
Washington, DC 20006  (202)659-4310
**Concern(s):** health; substance abuse; hazardous/toxic. This organization provides legal action for non-smokers. **Other Resources:** See SMOKING AND HEALTH REVIEW.

A ♦ **Adaptations**
See FRESH CONNECTIONS Newsletter.

J ♦ **Affiliate Network Project**
432 Park Ave. S
New York, NY 10022  (212)684-1221
**Affiliation:** International League for Human Rights. **Concern(s):** justice; Third World; networking. Working to strengthen domestically based human rights groups worldwide and present their concerns in international human rights forum.

J ♦ **Affirmative Action, Inc.**
See AFFIRMATIVE ACTION REGISTER under Directories.

T ♦ **Africa Faith and Justice Network**
3700 Oak View Terrace NE
Washington, DC 20017  (202)832-3412
**Concern(s):** Third World; justice; economics; Africa; faith; socially-responsible investing; foreign policy. An international advocacy group trying to challenge African policies and influence legislation. They oppose military support for countries in Africa that do not support human rights. Focus is mainly on North Africa, but they still support issues concerning the rest of the continent. **Other Resources:** Publishes COUNTRY REPORT, a newsletter on individual countries of North Africa; and, ISSUES that deals with debt and war. **Contact(s):** Sister Maria Browne.

T ♦ **Africa Fund**
198 Broadway
New York, NY 10021  (212)962-1210
**Concern(s):** Third World; justice; environment; wildlife/endangered species; Africa; divestment; discrimination; racism. This organization covers many aspects of Africa from endangered species to apartheid. **Other Resources:** See STUDENT ANTI-APARTHEID MOVEMENT NEWSLETTER and SOUTHERN AFRICA PERSPECTIVES. **Contact(s):** Jim Fowler.

T ♦ **Africa News Service**
See AFRICA NEWS.

T ♦ **Africa Watch**
See Human Rights Watch. **Contact(s):** Rakiya Omaar (Director), Janet Fleischman (Research Associate).

T ♦ **African National Congress of South Africa**
See ANC WEEKLY NEWS BRIEFING.

T ♦ **African Studies Association**
See DIRECTORY OF AFRICAN AND AFRO-AMERICAN STUDIES IN THE UNITED STATES.

E ▶ **African Wildlife Foundation**
1717 Massachusetts Ave. NW
Washington, DC 20036 (202)265-8394
**Concern(s):** environment; Third World; wildlife/endangered species; Africa. AWF has worked in 25 countries with the belief that Africa's wildlife could be protected only by the Africans themselves. Projects include ivory boycotts and protecting the Mountain Gorilla. **Other Resources:** See WILDLIFE NEWS. Projects include ivory boycotts and protecting the Mountain Gorilla. **Est.:** 1961. **Member:** Global Tomorrow Coalition; Environmental Federation of America. **Contact(s):** Paul T. Schindler (President).

L ▶ **African-American Labor Center/AFL-CIO**
See AALC REPORTER.

T ▶ **Africare**
440 R St. NW
Washington, DC 20001 (202)462-3614
**Concern(s):** Third World; demographics; feminism; development; Africa; hunger; population growth. This organization is concerned with issues of overpopulation, hunger and development throughout Africa.

L ▶ **AFL-CIO**
815 16th St. NW
Washington, DC 20006 (202)637-5000
**Concern(s):** labor; unions. The largest labor union in the US encompassing many types of professions. Unfortunately some key members have demonstrated strong anti-communist sentiments and involvement with CIA and Third World intervention. The Institute recruits people for employment with AFL-CIO to conduct union representation camps. **Other Resources:** See LABOR LETTER and Communications Workers of America. **Contact(s):** Lane Kirkland (President). **Other:** AFL-CIO Organizing Institute, 1444 I St. NW, #216, Washington, DC 20005 (202)408-0700.

✌ ▶ **After the Fall**
2161 Massachusetts Ave.
Cambridge, MA 02140
**Affiliation:** American Friends Service Committee. **Concern(s):** peace; nonviolence; grassroots/ community organizing. This New England group serves as an example of how local grassroots and community efforts can successfully work for world peace. **Other Resources:** Publishes PEACEWORK.

T ▶ **Agency for International Development**
State Building, 320 21st St. NW
Washington, DC 20523 (202)663-1451
**Concern(s):** Third World; development; hunger. This organization deals with Third World development. Its strives to increase the productivity and increase the standard of living of less fortunate nations.

A ▶ **Agricultural Council of America**
1250 I St. NW, #601
Washington, DC 20005 (202)682-9200
**Concern(s):** agriculture; politics; reform; farm policy; lobbying. This council deals with the agricultural issues in the US today. It tries to bring about reform to the problems facing agriculture by successfully lobbying in Congress.

A ▶ **Agriculture Department**
14th & Independence SW
Washington, DC 20250 (202)447-8732
**Concern(s):** agriculture; health; environment; hazardous/toxic waste. This department ensures the quality and safety of the food we eat (yeah, sure).

A ▶ **Agroecology Program/UCSC**
University of Calif., Santa Cruz
Santa Cruz, CA 95064 (408)459-4140
**Concern(s):** agriculture; environment; organic; sustainability; social ecology. A research and education group working toward the development of ecological, socially, and economically sustainable agricultural systems. On the UCSC campus, the Program manages the 25-acre Farm and 4-acre Garden, which are open to the public. **Other Resources:** Publishes CULTIVAR, excellent, expensively printed rundown on organic methods everywhere.

T ▶ **Agutu School Fund**
1369 Brenner Ave.
St. Paul, MN 55113 (612)636-5645
**Concern(s):** Third World; education; Africa; children. Sells African cookbooks and cards to raise money to build a school in a Ugandan village, where there is presently no school. Seeking funding for the school. **Member:** Co-op America.

H ▶ **AIDS Action Council**
2033 M St. NW
Washington, DC 20036 (202)293-2886
**Concern(s):** health; AIDS; public health. An umbrella organization for 380 AIDS service providers, it advocates for sound public policies on AIDS and health issues relating to AIDS. **Contact(s):** Jean Flately McGuire.

E ▶ **Air and Waste Management Association**
Box 2861
Pittsburgh, PA 15230
**Concern(s):** environment; politics; global warming; recycling; lobbying; reform; leadership. Goals: A clean environment, proper leadership, and promoting a sense of responsibility for air quality and waste management. **Dues:** $75/yr.

H ▶ **Al-Anon/Alateen Family Group Headquarters**
200 Park Ave. S
New York, NY 10003 (212)254-7230
**Affiliation:** Alcoholics Anonymous. **Concern(s):** health; substance abuse; counseling. This is the bay group to AA. These are specials groups that support the children, spouses and possible "co-dependents" of recovering alcoholics. It is believed that the entire family is in need of guidance and support through the process towards wellness.

F ▶ **Alan Guttmacher Institute**
2010 Massachusetts Ave. NW 5th Fl.
Washington, DC 20036 (202)296-4012
**Concern(s):** feminism; demographics; pro-choice; population growth; analysis. Independent organization for research, policy analysis in Washington and public education activities in NY. Supported by nearly 60 foundations and organizations. For more than 20 years anticipated critical reproductive health issues throughout the world. Work is geared to enhance and defend reproductive rights with special focus on disadvantaged classes. Publications target government officials, clinicians and personnel, gynecologists, sex-ed teachers, other social scientist in related areas. **Other Resources:** Publications list available. Publishes journals, FAMILY PLANNING PERSPECTIVES, and INTERNATIONAL FAMILY PLANNING PERSPECTIVES. Also, a newsletter, WASHINGTON MEMO. Reports, ISSUES IN BRIEF, covers public policy in many topic areas. Nonprofit. 111 Fifth Ave., New York, NY 10003-1089 (212)254-5656.

E ▶ **The Alaska Bioregional Network**
HCRO 3, Box 8496
Palmer, AK 99645
**Affiliation:** Planet Drum Foundation. **Concern(s):** environment; bioregionalism; polar.

E ▶ **Alaska Conservation Foundation**
430 W. 7th Ave., #215
Anchorage, AK 99501 (907)276-1917
**Concern(s):** environment; conservation; polar. This movement has organized a statewide Assembly, has a collective lobbying presence in Juneau and participates in the electoral process through a Political Action Committee, An increasing number of national environmental organizations either have offices and /or representatives here. **Other Resources:** Publishes ALASKA CONSERVATION DIRECTORY.

✌ ▶ **The Albert Einstein Institution**
1430 Massachusetts Ave., 6th Fl.
Cambridge, MA 02138 (617)876-0311
**Concern(s):** peace; education; research; analysis; conflict resolution. The Albert Einstein Institution supports and conducts research, policy studies, and education concerning the nature and potential of nonviolent sanctions in comparison to violent ones, for solving the problems of aggression, dictatorship, genocides, and oppression. **Other Resources:** Books, monographs, conference reports, and a quarterly newsletter, NONVIOLENT SANCTIONS and a publications list. **Est.:** 1983. **Fax:** (617)876-0837. **Contact(s):** Roger Powers (Special Projects Coordinator), Jane Gharibian (Administrative Coordinator). (617)876-0311.

H ▶ **Alcoholics Anonymous**
468 Park Ave. S
New York, NY 10016 (212)686-1100
**Concern(s):** health; counseling; substance abuse. Their famous 12 step program is now being used for just about every addiction known to man from over-eating, obsessive relationships to the cocaine habit. Still considered the most effective form of treatment for alcoholics and their families, AA has rivaled most psychological treatments of the disorder. Their famous prayer is used by believers and non-believers as well. **Other Resources:** A famous prayer, "God grant me the serenity to accept the things I cannot change, the courage to change the things I can, and the wisdom to know the difference."

F ▶ **All Saints Episcopal Church**
See Pro-Choice Task Force and VOICE newsletter.

E ▶ **All Species Project**
804 Apdaca Hill
Santa Fe, NM 87501
**Affiliation:** Institute for Gaean Economics. **Concern(s):** environment.

P ▶ **All-Peoples Congress**
Box 1819, Madison Square Station
New York, NY 10159 (212)741-0633
**Concern(s):** politics; grassroots organizing; lobbying. This is an organization that believes in representation of all the people not just a select few, and a world government that will represent the will of the people and not of the wealthy nations. **Other Resources:** Newspaper, FIGHTING BACK. **Office:** 146 W. 25th St. New York, NY 10001. **Contact(s):** Gavrielle Gemma.

E ▶ **Alliance for Environmental Education**
10751 Ambassador Dr., #201
Manassas, VA 22110 (703)335-1025
**Concern(s):** environment; education. Alliance merges the economic sense of business, manpower of organized labor, experience of environmentalists, grassroots organization of citizens' groups, the commitment and skill of educators and the technical talents of government, focusing them on the common need for more effective environmental education. The Alliance is comprised of more than 35 business, labor, educational and environmental organizations. Collectively, these organizations represent more than 15 million people. **Other Resources:** Works as a partner with the US Environmental Protection Agency in order to establish centers in universities, colleges, and institutions throughout the US. **Dues:** $100-250/yr.

P ▶ **Alliance for Justice**
1601 Connecticut Ave. NW
Washington, DC 20009 (202)332-3224
**Concern(s):** politics; peace; justice; foreign policy; international law; municipal; constitutional rights. Its purpose is to focus the resources and talents of members on key generic issues which vitally affect the effectiveness and survival of the public international law movement. Devotes most of its efforts to ensuring access to the courts and administrative process for persons who historically have not been represented in the legal and administrative process and on securing a reliable financial base for public international law. **Est.:** 1981.

✌ ▶ **Alliance for Our Common Future**
1835 K St. NW
Washington, DC 20006 (202)223-1770
**Affiliation:** National Peace Institute Foundation. **Concern(s):** peace; justice; world order; disarmament; reform. Coalition of about 70 organizations concerned with world order, arms control, disarmament, peace, and justice. Objectives include: reducing nuclear & conventional armaments and military spending worldwide, using freed-up resources to meet human needs, developing and strengthening structures (i.e. UN & World Court) for the peaceful settlement of international disputes and to promote economic and social justice; enforcing international standards of human rights and environmental protection. **Other Resources:** See WORLD DEMOCRACY NEWS.

✍ ▶ **The Alliance for Parental Involvement in Education (AllPIE)**
Box 59
East Chatham, NY 12060-0059 (518)392-6900
**Concern(s):** education; family; childhood. Encourages and assists parents who wish to be involved in their children's education, through two newsletters, consultation, workshops, book catalog, referrals service, conference. **Other Resources:** Publishes a newsletter, book and resources catalog, pamphlets, conducts workshops, seminars, and conferences, and provides referrals and other resources. See OPTIONS IN LEARNING newsletter. Nonprofit. **Est.:** 1989. **Dues:** $20-$60/memberships.

✌ ▶ **Alliance for Survival**
200 N. Main St., #M-2
Santa Ana, CA 92701 (714)547-6282
**Concern(s):** peace; energy; politics; arms race; conflict resolution; leadership; grassroots organizing. A grassroots organization dedicated to ending the arms race, non-violent conflict resolution, and promoting a clean environment and a sustainable culture. "We work to involve individuals in the democratic process and stress everyone's personal responsibility to make a difference." **Other Resources:** PEACE CONVERSION TIMES. Support, networking & coalition building with and for the entire progressive community in Orange County, CA. Nonprofit. **Est.:** 1980. **Circ.:** 7M. **Fax:** (714)547-6322. **Contact(s):** Marion Pack (Executive Director), Jeannie Bernstein (President of Board).

E ▶ **Alliance for the Chesapeake Bay**
600 York Rd.
Baltimore, MD 21212 (301)377-6270
**Concern(s):** environment; water; ocean/rivers; Chesapeake Bay. **Other Resources:** CHESAPEAKE CITIZEN DIRECTORY.

E ▶ **Alliance for the Wild Rockies**
Box 8731
Missoula, MT 59807 (406)721-5420

**Concern(s):** environment; economics; wilderness; wildlife/endangered species; bioregionalism; social resistibility. A bioregional alliance of conservation organizations and businesses working to protect wildlands, wildlife habitat and water quality in Montana, Idaho, Wyoming, Oregon, Washington, Alberta, and British Columbia. "We have a petition supporting our bioregional federal lands proposal, The Wild Rockies National Lands Act." **Other Resources:** Newsletter, THE NETWORKER. "We work with 110 member groups and businesses and conduct 'Forest Watch' programs. We've developed computer maps of the bioregion." **Est.:** 1988. **Fax:** (406)721-5912. **Contact(s):** Mike Bader (Executive Director), Cass Chinske (President, Board of Directors).

### ✑ ◗ The Alliance For Cultural Democracy
Box 7591
Minneapolis, MN 55407 (415)346-8031
**Concern(s):** arts; justice; diversity; discrimination; Native peoples; culture; grassroots organizing. Supports community cultural participation; believes in cultural pluralism; understands the necessity to integrate the struggles for cultural and political, and economic democracy in the US. The initiatives for cultural democracy take place on a grassroots level in communities, neighborhoods, and among activist artists and other progressive cultural workers. Preserving local cultures is the task of architects, planners, activists, artists and all progressives. **Other Resources:** Publishes a membership directory and quarterly magazine, CULTURAL DEMOCRACY. **Dues:** $25; $50 organization. **Other:** Fools Paradise, Pawnee, IL 62558. Ron Sakolski.

### M ◗ Alliance of Information & Referral Systems
See DIRECTORY OF INFORMATION AND REFERRAL SERVICES IN THE UNITED STATES AND CANADA.

### ☯ ◗ Alliance to Save Energy
1725 K St. NW, #914
Washington, DC 20006-1401 (202)857-0666
**Concern(s):** energy; environment; economics; demographics; efficiency; air pollution; conservation; consumer rights; appropriate technology; housing. Coalition of government, business, consumer and labor leaders dedicated to increasing the efficiency of energy use. Conducts research and pilot projects to stimulate investment in energy efficiency and use experience in these activities to formulate policy initiatives and conduct educational programs. Focus includes the environment, affordable housing, competitiveness, national security and economic development. **Other Resources:** Booklets, articles, reports, manuals, computer software and other material. Nonprofit. **Contact(s):** James L. Wolf (Executive Director).

### A ◗ The Alter Project
Slippery Rock University
Slippery Rock, PA 16057
**Concern(s):** agriculture; environment; permaculture. **Other Resources:** See THE ALTERNATOR (periodicals).

### ☯ ◗ Alternative Energy Resources Organization (AERO)
44 North Last Chance Gulch, #9
Helena, MT 59601
**Concern(s):** energy; agriculture; environment; appropriate technology; air pollution; conservation.

### A ◗ Alternative Farming Systems Information Center
National Agricultural Library
Beltsville, MD 20705 (301)344-3755
**Affiliation:** National Agricultural Library. **Concern(s):** agriculture. **Other Resources:** See EDUCATION AND TRAINING OPPORTUNITIES, a directory.

### M ◗ Alternative Press Center
See ALTERNATIVE PRESS INDEX under directories.

### ♟ ◗ Alternative Revenue Service
War Resisters League
339 Lafayette St.
New York, NY 10012 (212)228-0450
Affiliation War Resistors League, National War Tax Resistance Coordinating Committee, Conscience and Military Tax Campaign. **Concern(s):** peace; Third World; economics; war tax revolt; militarism; economic conversion; peace dividend; peace tax; intervention; foreign policy; taxation. A project of the War Resisters League, National War Tax Resistance Coordinating Committee, Conscience and Military Tax Campaign, that is designed to respond to the social crisis in the US and the related need for change in US foreign policy. Copies of the ARS EZ Peace Form available.

### ☯ ◗ Alternative Sources of Energy, Inc.
See INDEPENDENT ENERGY newsletter.

### ✝ ◗ Alternatives to Animal Research
175 W. 12th St., #16G
New York, NY 10011
**Concern(s):** environment; animal rights.

### E ◗ The Aluminum Association
900 19th St., NW
Washington, DC 20006 (202)862-5100
**Concern(s):** environment; recycling; waste management.

### L ◗ Amalgamated Clothing & Textile Workers Union
15 Union Square
New York, NY 10003 (212)242-0700
**Concern(s):** labor; health; justice; unions; discrimination; occupational safety. This union is trying to make working conditions for textile workers better. It attempts to bring fair employment, occupational safety, and improved health benefits into the textile and clothing industry. **Other Resources:** National Labor Committee in Support of Human Rights in El Salvador and CLUW NEWS. **Contact(s):** Jack Sheinkman (President), Dave Dyson.

### E ◗ America the Beautiful Fund
1501 H St. NW
Washington, DC 20005 (202)638-1649
**Concern(s):** environment; agriculture; conservation; beautification; preservation; forests; food production. Charitable organization dedicated to the preservation of the best of our American values, self-sufficiency, good citizenship and freedom while preserving the man-made and natural beauty of America. Operates Operation Green Plant, the shipping of seeds to the 15,000 community projects that grow food for the elderly, the handicapped and the confined, to improve decaying neighborhoods and to show that growing plants can give people and communities new hope as they beautify and nourish America. **Contact(s):** Paul Bruce Dowling (Executive Director).

### T ◗ America-Israel Council for Israeli-Palestinian Peace
See VOICES FOR PEACE under periodicals.

### H ◗ American Academy of Psychiatrists in Alcoholism & Addiction
See membership directory under same name.

### A ◗ American Agri-Women
1342 West San Jose
Fresno, CA 93711 (209)439-7277
**Concern(s):** agriculture; feminism. **Contact(s):** Ruth E. Johnston.

### A ◗ American Agricultural Movement
100 Maryland Ave. NE
#500A, Box 69
Washington, DC 20002 (202)544-5750
**Concern(s):** agriculture; politics; economics; farmland; family farms. Brought together by common concerns and strengthened by diversity, AAM works to make sure that the rest of the country knows not only who they are, but the problems that the American agriculture community faces. Through AAM's PAC, governed by producing farmers, we can get our hard-earned money into the hands of influential candidates whose interests parallel our own. **Other Resources:** The REPORTER newspaper. **Est.:** 1977. Updates: (202)544-6024. **Contact(s):** Larry Mitchell.

### ✍ ◗ American Anthropological Association
See ANTHROPOLOGY AND HUMANISM QUARTERLY.

### ✝ ◗ American Anti-Vivisection Society
801 Old York Rd.
Noble Plaza, #204
Jenkintown, PA 19046 (215)887-0816
**Concern(s):** environment; politics; animal rights; lobbying. Believes that it is morally wrong to conduct testing on live animals. It fights for stronger legislation controlling this. **Est.:** 1883.

### ♟ ◗ American Arab Anti-Discrimination Committee
4201 Connecticut Ave. NW, #500
Washington, DC 20008 (202)244-2990
**Concern(s):** peace; justice; conflict resolution; minority rights; racism. The largest Arab-American organization in the country. It is an organization dedicated to the promotion of the civil and legal rights of people of Arab descent, including resistance to racism, discrimination, and stereotyping of Arab-Americans. ADC has over 25,000 members organized into 70 chapters throughout North America. **Other Resources:** Publishes ADC TIMES, a monthly membership newsletter; sends action alerts; makes available speakers, films, publications and other resources; sponsors two-month summer internships in DC for college students in other ADC offices. **Dues:** $25, $20/students, $35/family.

### P ◗ The American Assembly
Columbia University
412 Altschul Hall
New York, NY 10027-6598 (212)854-3456
**Concern(s):** politics; analysis; reform; grassroots organizing. Holds nonpartisan meetings and public discussions to illuminate issues of US policy. **Fax:** (212)662-3655.

### H ◗ American Association for International Aging
1133 20th St. NW
Washington, DC 20036 (202)833-8893
**Concern(s):** health; seniors. This association is an advocate for seniors rights in our societies. **Contact(s):** Dr. Helen K. Kerschner.

### H ◗ American Association for Marriage and Family Therapy
See REGISTER OF MARRIAGE AND FAMILY THERAPY PROVIDERS under directories.

### H ◗ American Association for Music Therapy
See Membership Directory under same name.

### ✍ ◗ American Association for the Advancement of Science
1333 H St. NW
Washington, DC 20005 (202)326-6400
**Concern(s):** education; justice; science. Founded to respond to concerns about violations of basic human rights of scientists, engineers, and science students, and restrictions on international scientific communications. Prepares recommendations in response to cases involving important scientific principles. In the past, it has focused on human right violations of scientists in Eastern Bloc countries. **Other Resources:** See REPORT ON SCIENCE AND HUMAN RIGHTS and SCIENTIST under periodicals. **Est.:** 1977. **Contact(s):** Richard C. Atkinson (President), Walter E. Massey (Chairman).

### H ◗ American Association for World Health
2021 L St. NW
Washington, DC 20036 (202)265-0286
**Concern(s):** health; Third World. **Contact(s):** Rod Leonard.

### H ◗ American Association of Retired Persons
601 E St. NW
Washington, DC 20004 (202)434-2277
**Concern(s):** health; justice; politics; lobbying; seniors. **Contact(s):** Horace B. Deets (Executive Director).

### H ◗ American Association of Retired Persons (AARP)
See DIRECTORY OF SERVICES FOR THE WIDOWED IN THE UNITED STATES AND CANADA.

### H ◗ American Association of Sex Educators, Counselors & Therapists
See NATIONAL REGISTER under Directories.

### H ◗ American Association of Suicide
See DIRECTORY OF SUICIDE PREVENTION/CRISIS INTERVENTION AGENCIES IN THE UNITED STATES.

### F ◗ American Association of University Women Education Fund
2401 Virginia Ave. NW, Public Policy Office
Washington, DC 20037 (202)872-1430
**Concern(s):** feminism; education. **Contact(s):** Sarah Harder (President), Anne Bryant. (202)785-7700.

### E ◗ American Association of Zoological Parks and Aquariums
Oglebay Park
Wheeling, WV 26003 (304)242-2160
**Concern(s):** environment; oceans; conservation; wildlife/endangered species. 146 accredited zoos and aquariums are represented by this professional organization. This establishment promotes wildlife conservation and education and is currently focussing on captive propagation. **Dues:** $30/yr. for Associates.

### ♟ ◗ American Baptist Church Peace Concerns Program
Box 851
Valley Forge, PA 19482-2451 (215)768-2451
**Affiliation:** American Baptist Church USA. **Concern(s):** peace; spiritual; politics; faith; militarism; foreign policy. A group that develops and disseminates information and resources on the nuclear arms race, military spending, United Nations, and religious foundation for peacemaking. **Other Resources:** Publishes a newsletter, SWORDS INTO PLOWSHARES; also, THE ECONOMY OF PEACE. **Est.:** 1980., Charles W. Sydnor (215)768-2202. **Other:** Office of Government Relations, 110 Maryland Ave. NE, Washington, DC 20002 Robert Tiller , Director. (202)544-3400.

**H ♦ American Board of Examiners in Psychodrama, Sociometry, and Group Psychotherapy**
See Directory under same name.

**H ♦ American Botanical Council and Herb Research Foundation**
See HerbalGram under periodicals.

**F ♦ American Business Women's Association**
See WOMEN IN BUSINESS under periodicals.

**✈ ♦ American Camping Association**
See SOFT PATHS under Directories.

**E ♦ American Cartridge Recycling Organization**
3870 La Sierra, #266
Riverside, CA 92505    (714)359-8570
**Concern(s):** environment; recycling. An association dedicated to improving the cartridge recycling industry. One goal is to increase public awareness and educate consumers on the environmental impact of recycling. Nonprofit.

**E ♦ American Cave Conservation Association**
Box 409
Horse Cave, KY 42749    (502)786-1466
**Concern(s):** environment; wildlife/endangered species; water; conservation. Its goal is to preserve groundwater, endangered species, mineral formations, and archeological finds through protection of caves and karstlands. Sponsors clean-ups, restoration and cave gating projects. **Other Resources:** Museum/educational museum, technical services and consulting, training seminars, project support and a clearinghouse. **Dues:** $25/yr.

**E ♦ American Cetacean Society**
Box 2639
San Pedro, CA 90731-0943 (310)548-6279
**Concern(s):** environment; education; wildlife/endangered species; oceans; research; conservation; volunteers. The oldest whale conservation group in the world. ACS is a volunteer, membership organization with nine chapters located across the country. Works to protect whales, dolphins, porpoises and the oceans they live in through education, research and conservation projects. **Other Resources:** See WHALEWATCHER journal and WHALENEWS newsletter. **Dues:** $25/yr. **Member:** Global Tomorrow Coalition. **Contact(s):** Donald R. Patten (President).

**J ♦ American Civil Liberties Union (ACLU)**
132 W. 43rd St.
New York, NY 10036    (212)944-9800
**Concern(s):** justice; politics; feminism; civil liberties; freedom of expression; pro-choice; constitutional rights; reform; law; lobbying; capital punishment; criminal system. Founded with the purpose to define specific guarantees in the Bill of Rights: freedom of speech, the press, religion, association and assembly, due process of law, and equal treatment under the law. This is its national office. In recent years it has become rather controversial for defending murderers, Nazis and Klansmen, expressing a sometimes strong anti-religious bias. They are supporters of pro-choice and other related issues. **Other Resources:** General information, public policy reports; See newsletters CIVIL LIBERTIES and A.C.L.U. NEWS, and FIRST PRINCIPALS, co-sponsored with Center for National Security Studies. See guide, USING THE FREEDOM OF INFORMATION ACT. Committee for Public Justice **Est.:** 1920. **Dues:** $20+/yr. (212)944-5736(Committee). **Contact(s):** Ramona Ripston (Executive Director (S.Calif.)), Norman Siegel (Director). (202)544-1681. **Other:** American Civil Liberties Union Legislative Office, 122 Maryland Ave. NE, Washington, DC 20002 Morton Halperin, Executive Director.

**H ♦ American College of Nurse-Midwives**
See DIRECTORY OF NURSE-MIDWIFERY PRACTICES.

**E ♦ American Committee for International Conservation**
c/o Center for Marine Conservation
1725 DeSales St. NW, #500
Washington, DC 20036 (202)429-5609
**Affiliation:** Center for Marine Conservation. **Concern(s):** environment; conservation. An association of NGO's concerned with international conservation activities; stimulates coordination of members' overseas activities; and assists activities of IUCN. **Contact(s):** Roger McManus (Secretary), J. Michael McCloskey (Vice Chairman).

**T ♦ American Committee on Africa**
198 Broadway
New York, NY 10038    (212)962-1210
**Concern(s):** Third World; justice; peace; foreign policy; Africa; divestment; indigenous peoples; political prisoners; racism. This committee maintains research, education and divestment plans on South Africa. Distributes literature and maintains a speakers bureau. **Other**

**Resources:** See ACOA ACTION NEWS. **Contact(s):** Richard Knight, Jennifer Davis (Executive Director).

**☙ ♦ American Committee on US-Soviet Relations**
109 11th St., SE
Washington, DC 20003    (202)546-1700
**Concern(s):** peace; disarmament; conflict resolution. Committee determined during the 80's to achieve a detente between the Soviet Union and the US. **Other Resources:** See EAST-WEST OUTLOOK. **Contact(s):** Jeanne Mattison.

**A ♦ American Community Gardening Association**
325 Walnut St.
Philadelphia, PA 19106
**Concern(s):** agriculture. Promotes the growth of community gardening and can help individuals contact ones in their areas. Nonprofit. **Est.:** 1979. **Dues:** $25/yr. and up.

**E ♦ American Conservation Association**
30 Rockefeller Plaza, #5402
New York, NY 10112    (212)649-5600
**Concern(s):** environment; conservation. A non-membership, educational and scientific organization formed to advance knowledge and understanding of conservation and to preserve and develop natural resources for public use. [The list of trustees tells the editor that its members rank among those who make up the 10% who own most of the country's wealth.] Nonprofit. **Est.:** 1958. **Contact(s):** George R. Lamb (Executive Vice President), Lawrence Rockefeller (Chairman of the Board).

**☼ ♦ American Council for an Energy-Efficient Economy**
1001 Connecticut Ave. NW, #535
Washington, DC 20036    (202)429-8873
**Concern(s):** energy; environment; economics; efficiency; air pollution; conservation; research. An organization dedicated to advancing energy-conserving technologies and policies. Conducts research, analysis, advocacy and information dissemination. Projects include: energy efficiency and the environment; utilities; transportation; buildings; appliances, light and equipment; conservation research and development; energy efficiency in developing countries. **Other Resources:** Publications catalogue available. Publishes and distributes books, reports and conference proceedings. CONSUMER GUIDE TO HOME ENERGY SAVINGS. Nonprofit. **Contact(s):** Liz Burke (Chairman), Glee Murray.

**✍ ♦ American Council for the UN University**
See AMERICAN COUNCIL FOR THE UN UNIVERSITY NEWSLETTER, WORK IN PROGRESS newsletter, and FUTURE MIND, a guide.

**H ♦ American Council for Voluntary International Action**
See CONSUMER HEALTH PERSPECTIVES under periodicals.

**H ♦ American Council For Drug Education**
204 Monroe St.
Rockville, MD 20850    (301)294-0600
**Concern(s):** health; education; substance abuse; preventative medicine.

**$ ♦ American Council on Consumer Interests**
238 Stanley Hall, University of Missouri
Columbia, MO 65211    (314)882-3817
**Concern(s):** economics; health; consumer rights; consumer protection. **Contact(s):** Dr. Barbara Slusher.

**✍ ♦ American Council on Education**
1 Dupont Circle NW, #800
Washington, DC 20036    (202)939-9300
**Concern(s):** education. See GUIDE TO EDUCATIONAL PROGRAMS IN NON-COLLEGIATE ORGANIZATIONS. **Contact(s):** Barbara Turlington.

**E ♦ American Council on the Environment**
1301 20th St. NW
Washington, DC 20036    (202)659-1900
**Concern(s):** environment.

**H ♦ American Dance Therapy Association**
See Membership Directory under same name.

**D ♦ American Demographics**
See periodical under the same name.

**J ♦ American Ethical Union**
See periodicals for YOUR WASHINGTON ETHICAL ACTION OFFICE REPORTS, WASHINGTON REPORTS, and CENSORSHIP NEWS.

**A ♦ American Farmland Trust**
1920 N St. NW, #400
Washington, DC 20036    (202)659-5170
**Concern(s):** agriculture; environment; conservation; natural re-

sources; sustainability; soil; water; farmlands; farm policy. The nation's only nonprofit organization solely dedicated to protecting America's farmland. Through field offices across the country, it works with farmers, business people, legislators and conservationists to preserve our most productive resource for future generations. Seeks to promote a productive, sustainable agriculture by preventing farmland conversion, conserving soil and water, and lessening the environmental impact of agricultural land use. **Other Resources:** A magazine, AMERICAN FARMLAND. Nonprofit. **Dues:** $15/yr. **Member:** Global Tomorrow Coalition; Environmental Federation of America. **Contact(s):** Ralph E. Grossi (President).

**L ♦ American Federation of Government Employees**
1325 Massachusetts Ave. NW
Washington, DC 20005    (202)737-8700
**Concern(s):** labor; unions. **Contact(s):** John N. Sturdivant (President), Kenneth T. Blaylock.

**L ♦ American Federation of State, County & Municipal Employees (AFSCME)**
1625 L St. NW
Washington, DC 20036    (202)452-4800
**Concern(s):** labor; unions. See PUBLIC EMPLOYEE magazine. **Contact(s):** Gerald W. McEntee (President).

**L ♦ American Federation of Teachers**
555 New Jersey Ave., NW
Washington, DC 20001    (202)879-4400
**Concern(s):** labor; education; politics; unions. **Contact(s):** Barbara Van Blake, Duane Kelly (816)483-0753. **Other:** 10311 East 42 St., Kansas City, MO 64133.

**E ♦ American Fisheries Society**
5410 Grosvenor Lane
Bethesda, MD 20814-2199 (301)897-8616
**Concern(s):** environment; wildlife/endangered species; conservation. The world's oldest and largest organization dedicated to strengthening the fisheries profession, advancing fisheries science, and conserving fisheries resources. Publishes four major journals and is also a major publisher of reference works including textbooks and manuals. **Other Resources:** See the DIRECTORY OF NORTH AMERICAN FISHERIES AND AQUATIC SCIENTISTS. **Dues:** $43.50/yr. **Contact(s):** Carl R. Sullivan (Executive Director).

**E ♦ American Forest Council**
1250 Connecticut Ave. NW
Washington, DC 20036 (202)463-2455
**Concern(s):** environment; politics; forests; lobbying. Industry lobbying outfit that claims, according to its advertisement in Natural History Magazine, to be planting 6 million tress per day. This group supports many fringe beliefs of the progressive movement, i.e. tree farming.

**E ♦ American Forestry Association**
Box 2000
Washington, DC 20013 (202)667-3300
**Concern(s):** environment; politics; forests; conservation; global warming; lobbying; volunteers. The nation's oldest citizen conservation group. Operates TreeNet and Global Releaf, a campaign to plant 100 million healthy trees by 1992 in order to assist in reversing global warming trends. Through action-oriented programs, it attempts to enlist the interest and support of citizens, industry and government in order to improve and maintain the health and value of trees and forests. **Other Resources:** See THE GLOBAL RELEAF REPORT newsletter and GLOBAL RELEAF CITIZEN'S ACTION GUIDE. Volunteer & internship positions available. See AMERICAN FOREST Magazine and guide NATIONAL RESOURCES FOR THE 21ST CENTURY and SHADING OUR CITIES. **Dues:** $24/yr. **Member:** Environmental Federation of America. **Office:** 1516 P St., NW Washington, DC 20036. **Contact(s):** R. Neil Sampson (Executive Director). DC 20036.

**✍ ♦ American Forum for Global Education**
45 John St., #1200
New York, NY 10038    (212)732-8606
**Concern(s):** education; global understanding. Works with institutions and organizations to build global perspectives into basic school curriculum; provides programming, consulting services; designs conferences and workshops to increase understanding and improve communications among businesses, schools, communities, and government. Has developed teaching strategies for K-12 classes. Many resource materials available. **Other Resources:** See ACCESS newsletter and NEW GLOBAL RESOURCE BOOK. **Contact(s):** Willard M. Kniep.

**H ♦ American Foundation for AIDS Research**
1515 Broadway
New York, NY 10019    (212)719-0033
**Concern(s):** health; AIDS; public health; research. Mission is to find

biomedical and psychosexual research on AIDS. It raises money for scientific research and education projects relating to methods of prevention and a cure for AIDS. **Other Resources:** Publishes AMFAR EXPERIMENTAL TREATMENT DIRECTORY. See AIDS INFORMATION RESOURCES DIRECTORY. **Contact(s):** Donald Moschberger.

**D ◆ American Friends Service Committee**
1501 Cherry St.
Philadelphia, PA 19102   (215)241-7000
**Concern(s):** demographics; peace; spiritual; justice; faith; conflict resolution; refugees; immigration; hunger; militarism. Provides education about the connections between world hunger and militarism, the role of multi-national corporations, and many other issues relevant to hunger. As a Quaker organization, they believe that everyone, whatever age, race, faith or nationality, can be guided by an "inner light" of love and peace—and that eliminating the evils that oppress people will help them to discover that light on their own. A textbook, a meeting place, a shovel or a packet of seeds makes profound changes. **Other Resources:** Various publications, slide shows, videos, films, and speakers are available. Scores of programs and projects. Literature and audio/video material available. See NARMIC. A multitude of projects and publications. **Contact(s):** Dan Seeger, Stephen G. Cary. (215)241-7163. **Other:** Mexico-US Border Program, Primitivo Rodriguez.

**A ◆ American Fruitarian Society**
See Organic Food Network.

**✪ ◆ American Gas Association**
1515 Wilson Blvd.
Arlington, VA 22209   (703)841-8400
**Concern(s):** energy; resource management.

**✍ ◆ The American Geographical Society**
156 5th Ave., #600
New York, NY 10010-7002   (212)242-0214
**Concern(s):** education; environment; global understanding. While stressing ecological issues abroad and in the US this organization seeks, through publications, awards, travel programs, lectures and consulting, to disseminate geographical knowledge. **Other Resources:** Publishes THE GEOGRAPHICAL REVIEW and FOCUS magazine, educational travel program.

**E ◆ The American Groundwater Trust**
6375 Riverside Dr.
Dublin, OH 43017   (614)761-2215
**Concern(s):** environment; health; education; water; public health. Its goal is to increase public awareness and emphasize the importance of the drinking water supply for nearly 50% of the American population.

**E ◆ The American Hiking Society**
1015 31st St. NW
Washington, DC 20007-4490   (703)385-3252
**Concern(s):** environment; recreation. The nation's only nonprofit organization dedicated to protecting the interests of hikers and preserving America's footpaths, with over 70 club affiliates. These clubs maintain a public information service to provide hikers and other users with facts regarding facilities, organization, and ecological guidance in trail usage. **Other Resources:** Publishes directory, HELPING OUT IN THE OUTDOORS; also publishes a newsletter 8X/year. Magazine, AMERICAN HIKER; also periodic legislative alerts on trail issues in DC. "Volunteer Vacations" train individuals in trail development. Nonprofit. **Dues:** $25/yr. **Contact(s):** Louise Marshall (President). (202)833-8229.

**H ◆ American Holistic Medical Association**
See Directory of Members under same name.

**☛ ◆ American Horse Protection Association**
1000 29th St. NW, #T-100
Washington, DC 20007   (202)965-0500
**Concern(s):** environment; animal rights; wildlife/endangered species. Fights for the humane treatment of horses, wild or domestic, through litigation, investigation and public awareness about the care and treatment of horses. It works to protect their burros, to prevent abuse in competitions and transportation, and solve the problems of neglect and mistreatment. **Dues:** $15/yr.

**☛ ◆ American Humane Association**
Box 1266
Denver, CO 80201   (303)695-0811
**Concern(s):** environment; feminism; justice; animal rights; child abuse. Its goal is to prevent the neglect, abuse, cruelty and exploitation of animals and children and to insure that their rights, welfare and interests are effectively and humanely guaranteed by our society. **Other Resources:** See THE ADVOCATE magazine, SHOPTALK newsletter and Legislative Alerts, and PROTECTING CHILDREN newsletter. **Dues:** $15-$50/yr. **Office:** 9725 East Hampden Ave. Denver, CO 80231. Washington, DC 20041-0352 Adele Douglass , Director. (202)543-7780.

**S ◆ American Humanist Association**
See HUMANIST magazine.

**✪ ◆ American Hydrogen Association**
219 S. Siesta Lane, #101
Tempe, AZ 85281   (602)921-0433
**Concern(s):** energy; environment; renewables; solar; appropriate technology. AHA supports a transition from fossil fuels to solar hydrogen technologies including fuel cells. It is dedicated to education, research and science and believes an information gap exists within the scientific and educational community, industry, the political establishment, the media, and the public. A grassroots organization that wants to help make a lasting transition from the fossil depletion economy, to a renewable solar-hydrogen economy. **Other Resources:** See newsletter, HYDROGEN TODAY! and JOURNAL OF HYDROGEN magazine. Publications list available. **Est.:** 1990. **Fax:** (602)967-6601. **Contact(s):** Roy McAlister (President), Herb Hayden (Vice President, Engineering).

**J ◆ American Indian Law Center**
See AMERICAN INDIAN LAW NEWSLETTER.

**J ◆ American Indian Program/Cornell University**
See NORTHEAST INDIAN QUARTERLY.

**U ◆ American Institute of Architects Environmental Resources Committee, LA Chapter**
3780 Wilshire Blvd., #900
Los Angeles, CA 90010   (213)380-6692
**Concern(s):** urban; economics; environment; architecture; land use. The Committee works to encourage sustainable architecture & development in the region... "Serving the needs of the present without limiting the ability of future generations to meet their own needs." It has endeavored to demonstrate the process by creating a prototype: design of the "Eco-Expo Environmental House of Tomorrow... Today.". (213)815-1345.

**E ◆ American Institute of Biological Sciences**
730 11th St. NW
Washington, DC 20001   (202)628-1500
**Concern(s):** environment; agriculture; health; education; research; science. The institute strives to coordinate the efforts of persons engaged in biological research, education and other applications of the biological sciences including agriculture, the environment and medicine. **Other Resources:** Produces a monthly journal and bi-monthly newsletter.

**$ ◆ American Institute of Cooperation**
50 F St. NW, #900
Washington, DC 20001   (202)626-8740
**Concern(s):** economics; agriculture; cooperatives; alternative markets; research; trade; farms; farm policy. This institute provides research and networking for and about cooperatives. They deal with the principles of business, attitude, and philosophy of cooperatives and ways that these can be improved. Primarily deals with farm cooperatives. **Other Resources:** Publishes AIC Newsletter. **Contact(s):** David C. Thomas.

**✪ ◆ American Institute of Mining, Metallurgical, and Petroleum Engineers**
345 E. 47th St., 14th Fl.
New York, NY 10017   (212)705-7695
**Concern(s):** energy; resource management; trade.

**S ◆ American Jewish Committee**
165 E. 56th St.
New York, NY 10022   (212)751-4000
**Concern(s):** spiritual; peace; politics; faith. See COMMENTARY under periodicals. **Contact(s):** Rabbi Marc Tannenbaum (Director, International Relations). (212)687-6200. **Other:** 711 Third Ave., New York, NY 10017.

**☸ ◆ American Jewish Congress Task Force on Nuclear Disarmament**
See IN BRIEF under periodicals.

**L ◆ American Labor Education Center**
See AMERICAN LABOR newsletter.

**✍ ◆ American Library Association**
See WOMEN'S LEGAL RIGHTS IN THE US: Bibliography and FREEDOM TO READ FOUNDATION NEWS.

**M ◆ American Library Association Government Documents Roundtable**
See DOCUMENTS TO THE PEOPLE under periodicals.

**E ◆ American Littoral Society**
Sandy Hook
Highlands, NJ 07732   (201)291-0055
**Concern(s):** environment; politics; ocean/rivers; conservation; lob-

bying. A national public interest organization of professional and amateur naturalists founded by a small group of divers, naturalists, and fishermen to encourage better understanding of aquatic environments and provide a unified voice advocating protection of the delicate fabric of life along the shore. Sponsors field trips and general store. The shore and adjacent wetlands, bays and rivers - the littoral zone - is the special area of interest and concern for members. Chapters throughout the US. **Other Resources:** See UNDERWATER NATURALIST, COASTAL REPORTER under periodicals. Chapter newsletter and incidental bulletins covering such coastal subjects. Nonprofit. **Est.:** 1961. **Dues:** $20/yr.

**E ◆ American Lung Association**
1740 Broadway
New York, NY 10019-4374   (212)315-8700
**Concern(s):** environment; health; global warming; substance abuse; preventative medicine; volunteers. A voluntary agency concerned with the conquest of lung disease and the promotion of lung health which includes preventing and controlling air pollution. **Other Resources:** AMERICAN REVIEW OF RESPIRATORY DISEASE, and THE AMERICAN REVIEW OF RESPIRATORY CELL AND MOLECULAR BIOLOGY. **Est.:** 1904. **Member:** Global Tomorrow Coalition. **Contact(s):** John R. Garrison (Managing Director), Ronald White (Air Conservation Manager). (202)785-3355.

**H ◆ American Lung Association**
See Clean Air Council.

**✍ ◆ American Montesorri Society**
See MONTESORRI LIFE under periodicals.

**☸ ◆ American Movement for World Government**
1F Adrian Court
Peekskill, NY 10566
**Concern(s):** peace; world order. American campaign to establish a world government. **Other Resources:** Public relations projects, including newspaper and magazine advertising, publishes WORLD PEACE NEWS, a quarterly. **Contact(s):** R. W. Harrington (President).

**E ◆ American Museum of Natural History**
79 Central Park W
New York, NY 10023   (212)769-5100
**Concern(s):** environment; education; wildlife/endangered species; global understanding; science; research. The museum covers the history of the world from the natural view, i.e. geological, environmental, and wildlife changes. **Other Resources:** See NATURAL HISTORY MAGAZINE.

**E ◆ American Oceans Campaign**
725 Arizona Ave.
Santa Monica, CA 90401   (310)576-6162
**Concern(s):** environment; energy; politics; ocean/rivers; wildlife/endangered species; lobbying. This organization is primarily concerned with coastal pollution, offshore oil drilling, and net fishing. It works with many conservation and environmental organizations around the country to lobby the government into passing responsible legislation on the oceans, drilling, and fishing. Has a legislative office in Washington, DC. **Other Resources:** Publishes, AOC quarterly newsletter; HOUSEHOLD HAZARDOUS WASTE WHEEL; and a video, HELP SAVE PLANET EARTH. Nonprofit. **Fax:** (310)576-6170. **Contact(s):** Ted Danson (President), Casey Coates-Danson (Vice President). **Other:** 235 Pennsylvania Ave., SE, Washington, DC 20003(202)544-3526.

**E ◆ American Paper Institute**
260 Madison Ave.
New York, NY 10016   (212)340-0600
**Concern(s):** environment; recycling. Offers information on how individuals or community groups can initiate newspaper, cardboard, or office-paper recycling programs. Write for a list of companies that use recycled cardboard in their packaging. (202)463-2588. **Other:** 1250 Connecticut Ave. NW, #210, Washington, DC 20036.

**☸ ◆ American Peace Network**
610 Ethan Allen Ave
Takoma Park, MD 20712-5425   (301)891-2997
**Concern(s):** peace; disarmament; conflict resolution. The organization's purpose is to abolish war to insure human survival. **Other Resources:** Publishes periodical, THE PEACEBUILDER. **Est.:** 1985. **E-Network:** PeaceNet. **Fax:** (301)891-2997. **Contact(s):** Peter Zuckerman (President).

**☸ ◆ American Peace Test**
Box 26725
Las Vegas, NV 89126   (702)386-9834
**Affiliation:** Greenpeace. **Concern(s):** peace; nonviolence; civil disobedience; militarism; test ban; disarmament. A grassroots organization begun by a few dedicated people working to stop nuclear weapons testing at the Nevada Test Site and now based on a national network of active local groups. It is a nonviolent campaign to end the

nuclear arms race and testing through direct action and enabling committed citizens to take a stand at DOE facilities. Only by changing the way we react to the violence around us will we bring about change in the world. **Other Resources:** Publishes TEST BANNER, a newsletter. Testing Alert Network membership ($25/year) puts you on a phone tree. Testing alert hotline: (702) 386-9831. **Est.:** 1986. Hotline: (702)731-9646.

E ◆ **American Pedestrian Association**
   Box 624
   Forest Hills, NY 11375
**Concern(s):** environment; urban; beautification; conservation; transportation; planning. The pedestrian's right to safety, mobility, space, and wilderness, without congestion is fought through unilateral planning to prevent vehicular encroachment. It promotes and environmental trust fund designed to guarantee pedestrians better parks and pathways. **Dues:** $5/yr.

☺ ◆ **American Petroleum Institute**
   1220 L St. NW, #900
   Washington, DC 20005  (202)682-8000
**Concern(s):** energy; resource management; conservation; efficiency. An institute dedicated to the use of petroleum and other natural resources in a responsible and manageable way. They also believe in conservation of energy in order to extend the resources that we already have.

✍ ◆ **American Planning Association**
See guide, EDUCATIONAL MATERIALS IN PLANNING and PLANNING newsletter.

H ◆ **American Psychological Association**
   1200 17th St. NW
   Washington, DC 20036  (202)955-7600
**Affiliation:** American Psychological Association. **Concern(s):** health; peace; Third World; psychology. International Affairs Office publishes a newsletter, PSYCHOLOGY INTERNATIONAL. See PSYCHOLOGY OF WOMEN QUARTERLY. Organizations include Population and Environmental Psychology and Society for the Psychological Study of Social Issues.

H ◆ **American Public Health Association**
   1015 15th St. NW
   Washington, DC 20005  (202)789-5600
**Concern(s):** health; environment; public health; hazardous/toxic waste. The largest organization of public health professionals in the world, representing more than 32,000 members from 77 occupations of public health. APHA brings together all health professionals and related fields in a multi disciplinary environment concerned with a broad set of issues affecting personal and environmental health. Establishes coalitions with related associations and groups to encourage health practices consistent with APHA goals. **Other Resources:** See THE AMERICAN JOURNAL OF PUBLIC HEALTH and THE NATION'S HEALTH. **Contact(s):** Seiko Baba Brodbeck.

U ◆ **American Public Transit Association**
   1201 New York Ave., NW, #400
   Washington, DC 20005  (202)898-4000
**Concern(s):** urban; energy; transportation; conservation; efficiency. This is an association of public transit organizations. Their combined efforts have resulted in a better transportation policy in many cities.

E ◆ **American Recreation Coalition**
   1331 Pennsylvania Ave. NW, #726
   Washington, DC 20004  (202)662-7420
**Concern(s):** environment; recreation. The national voice for recreation interests. A federation of more than 100 organizations representing enthusiasts, private sector providers of recreation opportunities and producers of recreation goods. Acts as a national advocate for activities which are a part of nearly every American's lifestyle--from fishing to camping, from boating to bicycling, from skiing to snowmobiling and more. Nonprofit. **Est.:** 1978. **Contact(s):** Derrick A. Crandall (President), Mary Beth Keller

H ◆ **American Red Cross**
   17th & D St. NW
   Washington, DC 20006  (202)737-8300
**Concern(s):** health; demographics; hunger; preventive health; public health; volunteers; AIDS; homelessness. This organization is founded on the belief of volunteerism in order to help your fellow human. They provide relief in natural and man made disasters. Also, they help maintain the nations blood supply and feed and clothe the homeless. **Other Resources:** Blood donor information—(800)272-0024.

E ◆ **American Rivers**
   801 Pennsylvania Ave. SE, #400
   Washington, DC 20003  (202)547-6900
**Concern(s):** environment; politics; ocean/rivers; preservation; law. Founded to protect America's rivers by assisting with state and local river preservation efforts. This group's major focus is on the preserva-

tion of rivers and corridors in the National Wild and Scenic River Systems and works to inventory and develop strong laws for rivers warranting protection. Members write officials, attend hearings, and work locally and nationally. Internships for college students and recent graduates available in conservation, communication and other areas. **Est.:** 1973. **Dues:** $20+/yr. **Member:** Environmental Federation of America.

✍ ◆ **American Scientific Association**
See PERSPECTIVES ON SCIENCE AND CHRISTIAN FAITH under periodicals.

E ◆ **American Society for Agronomy**
See JOURNAL OF ENVIRONMENTAL QUALITY.

☂ ◆ **American Society for the Prevention of Cruelty to Animals (ASPCA)**
   441 E. 92th St.
   New York, NY 10128  (212)876-7700
**Concern(s):** environment; animal rights. Protects every kind of animal —the abandoned, the sick and the hurt, the abused and the hungry. No animals should suffer because of human selfishness, indifference or carelessness. Works to pass and enforce humane laws nationwide. **Other Resources:** See ASPCA REPORT. Operates full-service shelters and ambulance rescue services, veterinarian hospitals and spay-neuter clinics; provides adequate care and shelter for animals needing such help. **Est.:** 1866. **Contact(s):** John F. Kullberg (President).

J ◆ **American Society of Criminology**
   1314 Kinnear Rd.
   Columbus, OH 43212
**Concern(s):** justice; urban; education; criminal system.

⚖ ◆ **American Society of International Law**
   2223 Massachusetts Ave. NW
   Washington, DC 20008  (202)265-4313
**Concern(s):** peace; world order; conflict resolution; international law. An organization that stresses conflict resolution through the legal process and not force. **Other Resources:** Publishes AMERICAN JOURNAL OF INTERNATIONAL LAW. **Contact(s):** Marilou M. Righini.

E ◆ **American Society of Mammalogists**
   Department of Zoology
   Brigham Young University
   Provo, UT 84602  (801)378-2492
**Concern(s):** environment; wildlife/endangered species; research. Through publications, aiding research and other activities, this society seeks to promote the interests of mammalogy worldwide. **Dues:** $23/yr.

☺ ◆ **American Solar Energy Society**
   2400 Central Ave., #B-1
   Boulder, CO 80301  (303)443-3130
**Concern(s):** energy; environment; solar; efficiency; conservation; air pollution; renewables. Provides technical and scientific information on renewable energy as well as support and direction on the use and benefits of alternative energy sources. ASES is a membership organization which publishes a number of publications as well as organizing conferences and roundtable discussions. **Other Resources:** Publishes a magazine, SOLAR TODAY and a Publications Catalog. **Other:** 850 W. Morgan St., Raleigh, NC 27603 (919)832-6303.

E ◆ **American Water Resources Association**
   5410 Grosvenor Ln, #220
   Bethesda, MD 20814-2192  (301)493-8600
**Concern(s):** environment; water; resources; research. An organization dedicated to the advancement of interdisciplinary water resources research, planning, management, development, and education. With over 3,000 members worldwide, AWRA provides a forum for the collection, organization, and dissemination of ideas and information in the physical, biological, economic, social, political, legal, and engineering aspects of water related problems. **Other Resources:** Publications catalog available. Publishes the WATER RESOURCES BULLETIN and HYDATA-NEWS AND VIEWS, a newsletter.

E ◆ **American Wilderness Adventures**
   7500 E. Arapahoe Rd., #355
   Englewood, CO 80112  (303)771-0380
**Concern(s):** environment; education; wilderness; wildlife/endangered species; forests; preservation; natural resources; social ecology. This organization seeks to provide the public with rewarding outdoor adventures while promoting the preservation and wise use of wilderness, wetlands, wildlife, free-flowing rivers, watersheds and fisheries. Nonprofit. **Est.:** 1977. **Dues:** $25/yr. (800)322-WILD. **Contact(s):** Sally A. Ranney (President), Clifton R. Merritt.

☺ ◆ **American Wind Energy Association**
   777 N. Capitol St. NE., #805
   Washington, DC 20002  (202)408-8988

**Concern(s):** energy; environment; wind; renewables. An association of companies and organizations involved in alternative energy choices, specifically wind. **Other Resources:** Videos and slide presentations available. Solar Energy Industries Association; US Biomass Industries Council; See WIND ENERGY WEEKLY, WIND LETTER, and WIND ENERGY FOR A GROWING WORLD DIRECTORY. Publications list available. **Est.:** 1974. **E-Network:** Econet. **ID:** 'awea'. **Fax:** (202)408-8536. MCI Mail: AWEA.. **Contact(s):** Randy Swisher (Executive Director), Dianne Eppler (Director of Operations).

✈ ◆ **American Youth Work Center**
   1751 N St. NW, #302
   Washington, DC 20036  (202)785-0764
**Concern(s):** education; peace; travel; conflict resolution; youth; volunteers. American and German youth workers will exchange positions under a grant. Other USIA funded programs conducted by AYWC have been with the U.K., France, Israel and Africa. **Other Resources:** COVERING THE GLOBAL VILLAGE: A HANDBOOK FOR THE STUDENT PRESS; NATIONAL DIRECTORY OF RUNAWAY PROGRAMS; NORTH AMERICAN DIRECTORY OF PROGRAMS FOR RUNAWAYS, HOMELESS YOUTH AND MISSING CHILDREN.

H ◆ **Americans Against Human Suffering, Inc.**
See Californians Against Human Suffering.

E ◆ **Americans for a Safe Future**
   16830 Ventura Blvd. #Y
   Encino, CA 91436  (818)784-4411
**Concern(s):** environment; politics; grassroots organizing; activism. Organizes petition drives, lobbying and activism concerning critical environmental issues. Most recent is the "Ward Valley Urgent Alert II" in California. **Other Resources:** Volunteers needed. **Fax:** (818)784-4596.

P ◆ **Americans for Democratic Action**
See ADA Today under periodicals.

J ◆ **Americans for Religious Liberty**
   Box 6656
   Silver Springs, MD 20916  (301)598-2447
**Concern(s):** justice; spiritual; politics; faith; civil liberties; conflict resolution; lobbying; freedom of expression. A public educational organization dedicated to preserving the America tradition of religious, intellectual and personal freedom in a secular democratic state. Annual dues are $20 for individuals, $25 for families, $10 for students and limited income. Through its publications, speakers bureau, coast-to-coast media appearances, research, testimony before Congress, litigation activity, and coalition building, it strives to make a difference. **Other Resources:** Publishes newsletter, THE VOICE OF REASON. Nonprofit. **Contact(s):** John M. Swomley, Jr. (President), Ed Doerr (Executive Director).

A ◆ **Americans for Safe Food**
   1875 Connecticut Ave. NW, #300
   Washington, DC 20009  (202)332-9110
**Affiliation:** Center For Science in the Public Interest. **Concern(s):** agriculture; environment; health; hazardous/toxic waste; nutrition; consumer protection. Making consumer demand known to supermarkets, grocers, and government officials will stimulate the production and availability of contaminant-free food. That is the goal of ASF. It is supported by a coalition of over 80 consumer, environmental, farm and rural advocacy groups. **Other Resources:** See SAFE FOOD ACTION and THE SAFE-FOOD GAZETTE newsletters; FREE RANGE MEAT DIRECTORY. **Contact(s):** Roger Blobaum (ASF Director), Michael F. Jacobson (Executive Director).

E ◆ **Americans for the Environment**
   1400 16th St. NW, Box 64
   Washington, DC 20036  (202)797-6665
**Concern(s):** environment; education; politics; activism; lobbying; petition; voting. A national, nonpartisan educational institute which serves as the political skills training arm of the environmental community. Provides political skills training, educational materials, and organizational assistance for hundreds of environmental activists in more than 30 states. Our workshop leaders and training materials are available to help citizens understand how political campaigns work and how to effectively get involved in campaigns. Nonprofit. **Est.:** 1982. **Contact(s):** Johanna Barry (Executive Director).

E ◆ **Americans for Wilderness Coalition**
   Box 4784
   Missoula, MT 59806
**Concern(s):** environment; wilderness.

P ◆ **Americans United for the Separation of Church and State**
   8120 Fenton St.
   Silver Springs, MD 20910  (301)589-3707
**Concern(s):** politics; spiritual; analysis; constitutional rights; civil liberties; reform. This organization strives to achieve what the consti-

tution required. Separation of church and state. Believes this important in order to maintain a country for the people by the people. **Other Resources:** See CHURCH AND STATE under periodicals.

**T ▸ Americas Watch**
See Human Rights Watch. **Contact(s):** Mary Jane Camejo (Research Associate).

**J ▸ Amnesty International**
322 8th Ave.
New York, NY 10001 (212)807-8400
**Concern(s):** justice; Third World; political prisoners; death penalty; prisons; criminal system. A mass membership, grassroots organization with 3,600 chapters acting within the confines of a strictly defined mandate limiting it to work on behalf of political prisoners' human rights and specific issues affecting them such as torture, executions, and disappearances practicing "case adoption" to boost prisoners' morale through letters, supplies, release requests, freedom from pre-trial torture or intimidation, access to family, right to a fair trial or appeals, adequate medical care. **Other Resources:** Publishes AMNESTY ACTION and AMNESTY INTERNATIONAL ORANGE COUNTY NEWSLETTER. Nonprofit. **Contact(s):** John G. Healey (Executive Director). **Other:** 777 UN Plaza, New York, NY 10017(212)867-8878.

**D ▸ Amvets**
4647 Forbes St.
Lanham, MD 20706-6175 (301)459-9600
**Concern(s):** demographics; justice; health; veterans. An organization that raises money to help support a wide variety of veterans' causes. Their most visible way of doing this is through their nationwide thrift stores.

**E ▸ Ancient Forests International**
Box 1850
Redway, CA 95560 (707)923-3015
**Concern(s):** environment; Third World; forests; research; preservation; South America. An alliance of conservationists dedicated to helping preserve, study and increase awareness of the Earth's few still-intact temperate forest ecosystems. Our current emphasis is on the old-growth rainforests of Southern Chile, currently threatened by the multi-national timber industry. We raise funds for the preservation of park-quality tracts.

**♈ ▸ Animal Legal Defense Fund**
See Legal Action For Animals.

**♈ ▸ Animal Protection Institute of America**
Box 22505
Sacramento, CA 95822-9986 (916)731-5521
**Concern(s):** environment; animal rights; wildlife/endangered species; law. Through publications, animal rights and legislative issues and education, this organization seeks to eliminate the pain, fear and suffering inflicted on animals and to preserve species threatened with extinction. **Other Resources:** Curriculum available, "Know a Teacher" literature. **Contact(s):** Duf Fischer (Executive Director). **Other:** 2831 Fruitridge Rd., Sacramento, CA 95820.

**♈ ▸ Animal Rights Mobilization (ARM!)**
Box 1553
Williamsport, PA 17703 (717)322-3252
**Concern(s):** environment; politics; animal rights; grassroots organizing. A national grassroots organization, it serves as a coordinating body, information clearinghouse and research center. ARM! believes that animal exploitation can be ended only through a mass movement for animals, and the success of this movement depends on the strength of local grassroots groups. Evolving out of Trans-Species Unlimited, a direct-action organization, ARM! continues the Fur-Free Campaign and Cornell University Cat Campaign. **Other Resources:** See MOVEMENT Magazine. Trans-Species Unlimited. Hotline: (800)CALL-ARM.

**♈ ▸ Animal Rights Network**
456 Monroe Turnpike
Monroe, CT 06468 (203)452-0446
**Concern(s):** environment; animal rights. This network strives for the preservation of animals rights in this country and abroad. This network believes that all creatures not just humans have a right for a pain free life. **Other Resources:** See ANIMAL'S AGENDA magazine. **Contact(s):** Dana Stutchell, Kay Sievers (Co-directors).

**♈ ▸ Animal Welfare Institute**
Box 3650
Washington, DC 20007 (202)337-2332
**Concern(s):** environment; animal rights; wildlife/endangered species. Stopping cruelty in animal testing; protecting whales and dolphins; curbing and stopping the pet trade, and promoting humane treatment and transportation of wildlife. **Other Resources:** Publishes a newsletter. **Est.:** 1951. **Contact(s):** Christine Stevens (President).

**J ▸ Anti-Defamation League**
823 UN Plaza
New York, NY 10017 (212)490-2525
**Concern(s):** justice; discrimination; racism. A clearinghouse for virtually every aspect of the far right. **Other Resources:** See handbook, EXTREMISM ON THE RIGHT and DIMENSIONS: A JOURNAL OF HOLOCAUST STUDIES.

**J ▸ Anti-Racist Action**
Box 7471
Minneapolis, MN 55407
**Concern(s):** justice; racism; discrimination; minority rights; sexism Anti-racist skinheads and others join together to fight discrimination of all forms.

**♈ ▸ The Anti-Vivisection Society**
801 Old York Rd., #204
Jenkintown, PA 19046-1685 (215)887-0816
**Concern(s):** environment; animal rights. This society wishes to end the exploitation of animals for research, testing and education. Believes that animal testing is scientifically unsound and ethically wrong. **Other Resources:** See periodical, ANIMAL EXPERIMENTS ARE A DYING TRADITION.

**✍ ▸ Antioch University West**
2607 2nd Ave.
Seattle, WA 98121 (206)441-5352
**Concern(s):** education; curriculum. "...offers individualized Master of Arts program with maximum student freedom in designing a curriculum in a field of the student's choice. This non-residential program is for a self-directed proactive learner who wants to study in his/her community and be totally involved in determining the learning process. Accredited. Financial aid available." **Price:** $1/ea. **Contact(s):** Linda McRae-Campbell.

**✪ ▸ Appalachia Science in the Public Interest**
Box 298
Livingston, KY 40445 (606)453-2105
**Concern(s):** energy; economics; education; environment; agriculture; science; community self-reliance; appropriate technology. Makes science and technology responsive to the needs of the poor in central Appalachia through demonstration of low-cost housing, organic gardening and renewable energy projects, publication of A.T. materials and environmental education literature and reports. **Other Resources:** Free publications list. Nonprofit. **Est.:** 1977. **Frequency:** 4/yr. **Subscription:** $5/yr. **Circ.:** 3.4M. **Contact(s):** Al Fritsch.

**$ ▸ Appalachian Community Services**
Box 428, 80 E. Benjamin Dr.
New Martinsville, WV 26155 (304)455-5666
**Concern(s):** economics; justice; intentional communities; disabled's rights. An alternative community for socially marginal adults unable to live by themselves. No age restriction. **Other Resources:** Free brochure. **Member:** Co-op America. **Contact(s):** Wess Harris.

**E ▸ Appalachian Mountain Club**
5 Joy St.
Boston, MA 02108 (617)523-0636
**Concern(s):** environment; recreation. Sponsors programs of recreational service and conservation in the northeastern states including trail and shelter maintenance, preservation, research, outdoor education, publication of guide books and maps, operation of 9 unit public hut systems, self service and full service camps, varied activities and educational programs for members and non-members. **Other Resources:** See APPALACHIA JOURNAL. Also publishes APPALACHIA BULLETIN and AMC guide books. **Est.:** 1876. **Contact(s):** Earle Perkins (President), Andrew J. Falander (Executive Director).

**E ▸ Appalachian Trail Conference**
Box 807
Harpers Ferry, WV 25425 (304)535-6331
**Concern(s):** environment; conservation; preservation; jobs; volunteers. A private organization dedicated to the preservation and wise management of the Appalachian Trail and its surrounding lands. ATC conducts a variety of programs designed to protect, manage, and promote the Appalachian Trail and its associated lands through public acquisition. Projects involving protection, stewardship, and suppling information, provides year round work. **Other Resources:** Publishes the APPALACHIAN TRAILWAY NEWS magazine, guidebooks, and maps for the Trail, and other books for the different categories of Trail visitors. Nonprofit. **Dues:** $18+/yr. **Contact(s):** David N. Startzell (Executive Director), Margaret C. Drummond (Chairperson). (404)78-9557.

**$ ▸ Applied Ergonomics**
13734 39th Ave. NE
Seattle, WA 98125 (206)361-1890
**Concern(s):** economics. **Contact(s):** Jack Litewka.

**✪ ▸ Appropriate Technology International**
1331 H St. NW
Washington, DC 20005 (202)879-2900
**Concern(s):** energy; appropriate technology.

**A ▸ Appropriate Technology Transfer for Rural Areas**
Box 3657
Fayetteville, AR 72702 (501)575-7570
**Concern(s):** agriculture; energy; development; appropriate technology; research. A USDA Extension Service program designed to collect and disseminate information on low-input/sustainable agriculture and diversification. Technical specialists respond by sending tailored information, providing referrals, or discussing appropriate alternatives. (800)346-9140. **Other:** 7777 Walnut Grove Rd., Memphis, TN 39119.

**E ▸ The Aprovecho Institute**
80574 Hazeltine Rd.
Cottage Grove, OR 97424 (503)942-9434
**Concern(s):** environment; energy; Third World; education; demographics; agriculture; labor; conservation; land use; development; intentional communities; sustainability; permaculture; cooperatives; volunteers. "This worldwide Oregon based institute is a tiny group of volunteers. We help individuals and groups make the best use of the inevitable changes that come with diminishing resources. We research and promote sustainable alternatives to the wastefulness of industrial consumerism. Our focus is a sustainable development, permaculture, and deconsumerization of the US. We teach the lessons of Nature, wise land use, local self-reliance and cooperative family employment. Funded by donations." **Other Resources:** Courses, training, workshops, consultancies and publications. Also, a international phone and mail service of information on our fields of concern. See NEWS FROM APROVECHO newsletter. Nonprofit. **Est.:** 1976. **Dues:** $15, supporting; $100, full member.

**✈ ▸ APT Tours**
1150 Janes Rd.
Medford, OR 97501 (503)773-2435
**Concern(s):** education; Third World; travel; development. Conducts tours developed in cooperation with host country advisors and guides. Designs "mini-projects" to allow interaction between host and tour participants. **Contact(s):** Grove Adee.

**☮ ▸ Aquarian Research Foundation**
5620 Morton St.
Philadelphia, PA 19144 (215)849-1259
**Concern(s):** peace; demographics; justice; environment; politics; future; media; militarism; hunger; homelessness; computer networking; ideation. Research into future & World Transformation. Present projects: "Where's Utopia?" - Hour video with Soviet scientist on various cooperative and communal solutions; abolishing military systems; low cost and free computer networks for communities, world changers. **Other Resources:** AQUARIAN ALTERNATIVES newsletter, Community Guides, Natural Birth Control Book, friendship, relationship. Seeking helpers, community to join. Call anytime. (215)849-3237.

**E ▸ Archaeological Conservancy**
415 Orchard Dr.
Santa Fe, NM 87501 (505)982-3278
**Concern(s):** environment; conservation. Organization dedicated to the permanent preservation of the most significant prehistoric sites in the US, usually through acquisition. Cooperates with government, universities, museums, and private conservation organizations to acquire lands for permanant archaeological preserves. **Other Resources:** A newsletter, THE ARCHAEOLOGICAL CONSERVANCY. Nonprofit. **Est.:** 1979. **Contact(s):** Mark Michel (President), Ric Windmiller (Director/California Office). (916)685-2342. **Other:** 7402 Charrington Ct., Indianapolis, IN 46254 Sylvia Ball , Director. (317)291-9857.

**☮ ▸ Architects, Designers, and Planners for Social Responsibility**
225 Lafayette St., #205
New York, NY 10012 (212)431-3756
**Concern(s):** peace; disarmament; anti-nuclear; analysis; research. A national organization of design professionals and students. ADPSR assists the public in understanding the catastrophic consequences of nuclear and conventional war. "We believe that the continuous preparation for war seriously impairs humanity's potential for economic and social justice." This NY-based group joined similar groups around the country in 1984 to establish the national organization ADPSR, which now has 10 chapters. **Other Resources:** See ADPSR NEWS. Nonprofit. **Est.:** 1982. **Contact(s):** Jim Morgan, Anne Herscher (Executive Director).

**E ⬧ Arctic to Amazonia Alliance**
Box 73
Strattford, VT 05072    (802)765-4337
**Concern(s):** environment; Third World; justice; Native Americans; indigenous peoples; forests; polar. An alliance of indigenous and non-indigenous peoples organizations to promote education and activism around cultural and biological diversity. **Other Resources:** Newsletter.

**⬧ Ark Communications Institute**
1640 School St., #104
Moraga, CA 94556    (510)631-0112
**Concern(s):** peace. **Contact(s):** Linda Lazare.

**⬧ Arms Control and Disarmament Agency**
US State Department
2201 C St. NW
Washington, DC 20451    (202)647-9610
**Concern(s):** peace; disarmament. An agency of the US State Department. They are not our best hope, and certainly not our only hope, but many a redress can be submitted or demonstrated here, with or without a guarantee of success.

**⬧ Arms Control Association**
11 Dupont Circle NW, #900
Washington, DC 20036    (202)797-4604
**Concern(s):** peace; politics; disarmament; lobbying. This association promotes public support of arms control through the press, programs, publications and conferences. **Other Resources:** Publishes a newsletter, ARMS CONTROL TODAY and FOREIGN POLICY MAGAZINE. **Est.:** 1971. **Contact(s):** Pete Scoville (President), Spurgeon M. Keeny, Jr. (Director). **Other:** 2400 N St. NW, Washington, DC 20037 (202)797-6450.

**⬧ Arms Race in Space Project**
5115 S. A1A Highway
Melbourne Beach, FL 32951 (407)952-0600
**Affiliation:** Institute for Space and Security Studies. **Concern(s):** peace; energy; politics; arms race; space; government accountability. Research/educational project exposing dangers of weapons in space. Dr. Bowman directed "Star Wars" under Ford and Carter, then became most outspoken critic when Reagan turned it into program to develop new offensive weapons disguised as defense. Project gets the truth to members of Congress and American people. Nonprofit. **Est.:** 1982. **Contact(s):** Dr. Robert M. Bowman (President).

**⬧ Arthur Morgan School**
1901 Hannah Branch Rd.
Burnsville, NC 28714    (704)675-4262
**Concern(s):** education; economics; labor; alternative; workplace democracy; worker ownership. This school teaches individuals economic principles which defy the old school, such as employee ownership, reinvestment, workplace democracy. **Contact(s):** Margot Preston.

**⬧ Artists for Social Responsibility**
Johnson State College
Building 52
Johnson, VT 05656
**Concern(s):** arts; peace; economics; activism. An organization that shows the ways artists are being socially responsible in our society. Also, reports on ways that other artists are not being socially responsible. **Other Resources:** Publishes a newsletter. **Contact(s):** Sophie Sollberger.

**⬧ Artists' Housing**
1442 E. Baltimore St.
Baltimore, MD 21231    (301)675-9087
**Concern(s):** arts; demographics; economics; housing; cooperatives. Cooperative housing with studios and living spaces for artists. **Other Resources:** Free brochure. **Member:** Co-op America.

**T ⬧ Asia Resource Center**
See SOUTHEAST ASIA CHRONICLE magazine and INDOCHINA NEWSLETTER.

**T ⬧ Asia Watch**
See Human Rights Watch.

**D ⬧ The Aspen Institute**
See COMMUNITY RESEARCHER'S GUIDE TO RURAL DATA (directories).

**L ⬧ Association For A Democratic Workplace**
Box 2092
Jasper, OR 97438-0299 (503)683-8184
**Concern(s):** labor; economics; health; workplace democracy. A national membership organization providing progressive health care and financial plans, training, resources, and contacts necessary to achieve a truly democratic workplace. Individual and business members. **Contact(s):** Cynthia Wooten.

**T ⬧ Association for Asian Studies, Inc. (AAS)**
See ASIAN STUDIES NEWSLETTER.

**⬧ Association for Childhood Education**
11141 Georgia Ave., #200
Wheaton, MD 20902    (301)942-2443
**Concern(s):** education; childhood. **Contact(s):** Gil Brown.

**⬧ Association for Community Based Education**
See NATIONAL DIRECTORY OF COMMUNITY BASED ADULT LITERACY PROGRAMS, DIRECTORY OF FOUNDATION FUNDING SOURCES, and CENTSITIVITY, a directory.

**⬧ Association for Commuter Transportation**
See Membership Directory under same name.

**E ⬧ Association for Conservation Information**
408 S. Polk St.
Albany, MO 64402    (816)726-3677
**Concern(s):** environment; conservation; wildlife/endangered species; resources; networking; research. A league of information and education agencies, organizations, and professionals whose major role is providing natural resource, environmental, wildlife or related information and education to the public through diverse means. ACI does not itself prepare information for the public, but helps train the staffs of member organizations and provides means to exchange skills and ideas. Government forestries, private organizations and individuals are among the type of members. **Other Resources:** Publishes BALANCE WHEEL, a quarterly newsletter; and, a ACI membership directory. Nonprofit. **Contact(s):** Rod Green (President).

**S ⬧ Association for Creative Change**
See ASSOCIATION FOR CREATIVE CHANGE WITHIN RELIGIOUS AND SOCIAL SYSTEMS—DIRECTORY.

**$ ⬧ The Association for Enterprise Opportunities**
Center for Enterprise Development West
353 Folsom St.
San Francisco, CA 94105    (415)321-7663
**Affiliation:** Center for Enterprise Development. **Concern(s):** economics; labor; education; worker ownership; homeworkers; workplace democracy; jobs; community self-reliance. A new coalition of more than 150 advocates of microenterprise, self-employment, and entrepreneurial training, especially for low income persons. A number of its members provide loans to help start small businesses.

**⬧ Association for Experiential Education**
See JOURNAL OF EXPERIENTIAL EDUCATION.

**T ⬧ Association for the Advancement of Policy Research & Development in the Third World**
Box 70257
Washington, DC 20024    (202)723-7010
**Concern(s):** Third World; development; foreign policy.

**⬧ Association for Transarmament Studies**
3636 Lafayette Ave.
Omaha, NE 68131
**Concern(s):** peace; education.

**L ⬧ Association for Union Democracy**
500 State St.
Brooklyn, NY 11217    (718)855-6650
**Concern(s):** labor; feminism; unions; workplace democracy; empowerment. The only national nonprofit organization dedicated solely to the issues surrounding democracy in the US and Canadian labor unions. **Other Resources:** Newsletter, UNION DEMOCRACY REVIEW; advice, legal support, advocacy; Women's Project. Nonprofit. **Est.:** 1969. **Dues:** $25/yr. **Fax:** (718)855-6799. **Contact(s):** Susan Jennik (Executive Director), Brett Nair (Office Manager).

**D ⬧ Association for Voluntary Surgical Contraception**
122 E. 42nd St.
New York, NY 10168    (212)351-2500
**Concern(s):** demographics; health; feminism; education; population growth; family planning; research. To insure through education, research and service, that women and men everywhere have access to safe and effective voluntary contraceptive sterilization. **Other Resources:** Publishes AVSC NEWS, and BIOMEDICAL BULLETIN. **Est.:** 1943. **Contact(s):** Joseph E. Davis, MD (Chair), Hugo Hoogenboom (Executive Director).

**S ⬧ Association for Wholistic Living**
See WHOLISTIC LIVING NEWS.

**F ⬧ Association for Women in Science**
1522 K St. NW
Washington, DC 20005    (202)408-0742
**Concern(s):** feminism; education; science.

**H ⬧ Association For Humanistic Psychology**
1772 Vallejo
San Francisco, CA 94103    (415)346-7929
**Concern(s):** health; psychology; reform. This organization stresses a new approach to psychology. It has to be done from a humanist point of view!

**M ⬧ Association of Alternative Newsweeklies**
c/o Jane Sullivan
Bay Guardian, 2700 19th St.
San Francisco, CA 94110    (415)824-7660
**Concern(s):** media; press. Contact this group to find out about local newsweeklies in your area.

**⬧ Association of American Colleges**
See Project on the Status and Education of Women and guide, CAMPUS GANG RAPE: PARTY GAMES?

**E ⬧ Association of Botanical Gardens & Arboreta**
Box 206
Swathmore, PA 19081    (215)328-9145
**Concern(s):** environment; preservation.

**E ⬧ Association of Forest Service Employees For Environmental Ethics**
Box 11615
Eugene, OR 97440    (503)484-2692
**Concern(s):** environment; politics; forests; preservation; wildlife/endangered species; government accountability. Promotes ecologically sustainable management practices in public agencies, especially the forest service. Encourages even anonymous membership if you are a government employee, as it acknowledges the "pressure that can be brought to bear on individual employees for sticking their necks out." **Other Resources:** Publishes INNER VOICE newspaper. Local chapters on national forests; education; speaking; support of free speech rights of federal employees. Nonprofit. **Est.:** 1989. **Dues:** $20/yr. includes newspaper. **Contact(s):** Jeff DeBonis (Executive Director), Erin Bonner (Assistant Director).

**H ⬧ Association of Halfway House Alcoholism Programs of North America (AHHAP)**
See Membership Directory under same name.

**⬧ Association of Hispanic Arts (AHA)**
See ASSOCIATION OF HISPANIC ARTS NEWS - DIRECTORY OF HISPANIC ORGANIZATIONS SECTION.

**⬧ Association of International Colleges and Universities**
See Directory under same name.

**E ⬧ Association of Interpretive Naturalists**
Box 1892
Ft. Collins, CO 80522    (303)498-8844
**Affiliation:** National Association of Interpretation. **Concern(s):** environment; conservation; wildlife/endangered species; wilderness.

**H ⬧ Association of Occupational and Environmental Clinics**
1010 Vermont Ave., NW
Washington, DC 20005    (202)347-4976
**Concern(s):** health; preventative medicine; public health. National membership organization of individuals and clinics committed to the prevention of occupation/environmental diseases and health hazards through the provision and development of high quality access health services. **Contact(s):** Laura Welch.

**E ⬧ Association of State and Interstate Water Pollution Control Administration**
444 N. Capitol St., NW
Washington, DC 20001    (202)624-7782
**Concern(s):** environment; health; water; hazardous/toxic waste.

**E ⬧ Association of State Drinking Water Administrators**
1911 N. Fort Myer Dr.
Arlington, VA 22209    (703)524-2428
**Concern(s):** environment; health; water; hazardous/toxic.

**E ⬧ Association of State Wetland Managers, Inc.**
Box 2463
Berne, NY 12023
**Concern(s):** environment; wetlands. Created to promote and enhance protection and management of wetland resources and to better apply science to such management efforts. Seeks to strengthen state, federal, and local wetlands programs by facilitating and improving effective federal, state, and local cooperation, and by integrating public, private, and academic efforts to achieve wetland protection and management goals. **Other Resources:** Publishes a quarterly newsletter. Nonprofit.

**H ▸ Association of Transpersonal Psychology**
Box 3049
Stanford, CA 94305
**Concern(s):** health; psychology.

**E ▸ Association of Vermont Recyclers**
See AVR TEACHER'S RESOURCE GUIDE FOR SOLID WASTE AND RECYCLING.

**✻ ▸ Association of Veterinarians for Animal Rights**
530 E. Putnam Ave.
Greenwich, CT 06830    (203)869-7755
**Concern(s):** environment; animal rights. Group of veterinarians who are opposed to the unethical treatment of animals including testing. They lobby for laws to be enacted for the protection of animals. **Contact(s):** Dr. Neil C. Wolff, Dr. Ned Buyukmichi.

**P ▸ Association to Unite the Democracies**
Box 75920
Washington, DC 20013   (202)544-5150
**Concern(s):** politics; peace; world order. Formerly, Federal Union, advocates federation of established democracies first, others becoming eligible as they become democratic internally; see also Center for the Study of Federalism. **Office:** 1506 Pennsylvania Ave. SE Washington, DC 20003. **Contact(s):** Ira Strauss (Executive Director).

**⚔ ▸ Athletes United for Peace**
See AUFP NEWSLETTER.

**E ▸ Atlantic Center for the Environment**
39 S. Main St.
Ipswich, MA 01938    (508)356-0038
**Affiliation:** Quebec-Labrador Foundation, Inc. **Concern(s):** environment; economics; conservation; natural resources; oceans/rivers; wildlife/endangered species; community investment. The Quebec-Labrador Foundation (QLF) is a nonprofit organization incorporated in the US and Canada. The Atlantic Center is an umbrella term for QLF programs. Through a variety of projects, QLF works to build support for conservation of natural resources within cultural contexts. Broadly defined, the primary program areas of QLF are rivers and watersheds; wildlife and habitats; rural landscapes and community development. **Other Resources:** See NEXUS under periodicals. Nonprofit. **Est.:** 1963. **Dues:** $25-$500/yr. **E-Network:** Econet. **ID:** 'qtautictr'. **Fax:** (508)356-7322. **Contact(s):** Brent Mitchell (Director/Conservation & Communications), Kathleen Blanchard **Other:** New England Field Office, Box 217, Montpelier, VT 05602 Tom Horn , Vice President Programs. (802)229-0707.

**E ▸ Atmospheric Impact Research Center**
See ACID RAIN FOUNDATION - DIRECTORIES.

**⚔ ▸ Atomic Scientist Association**
See BULLETIN OF THE ATOMIC SCIENTISTS.

**L ▸ Atran Center for Jewish Culture**
See Jewish Labor Committee.

**E ▸ Audubon Naturalists Society**
8490 Jones Mill Rd.
Chevy Chase, MD 20815(301)652-9188
**Concern(s):** environment; education; wildlife/endangered species; conservation; children. Woodend, a 40-acre nature sanctuary in suburban Maryland, is the society's home. They teach the importance of preservation, conservation and renewing natural resources, especially in the DC area. **Other Resources:** ATLANTIC NATURALIST, a newspaper, and NATURALIST NEWS. Children's classes, family programs, teacher training, school programs, conservation forums, field studies classes for adults, forays and field trips, bookshop, informational brochures. Nonprofit. **Est.:** 1897. **Dues:** $20/yr. **Member:** Audubon Alliance; Global Tomorrow Coalition. **Fax:** (301)951-7179. **Contact(s):** Ken Nicholls (Executive Director), Kathy Rushing (PR Director).

**F ▸ Austin Men's Center**
1611 W. 6th St.
Austin, TX 78703    (512)477-9595
**Concern(s):** feminism; men's liberation. A center that promotes the idea that men do not have to be "macho" to be men. Shows alternative lifestyles of families including the man performing the traditional role of the house wife. **Other Resources:** Publishes MAN! Magazine. **Contact(s):** John Lee.

**S ▸ Austin Seth Center**
See REALITY CHANGE under periodicals.

**L ▸ Austin United Support Group**
711 4th Ave., NE
Austin, MN 55912    (507)437-4110

**Concern(s):** labor; economics; justice; boycott; corporate responsibility; socially-responsible investing; discrimination. BOYCOTT HORMEL — They are accused of unfair labor practices. Products: Black Label bacon and hams, Broiled and Browned sausage, Cure 81 hams, Cure Master hams, KiLusso Genoa salami, Dinty Moore stews, Dubuque products, Fast 'N Easy bacon, Frank 'N Stuff franks, Fresh Farm catfish, Great Beginnings products, Jennie-O turkeys, Light and Lean Canadian bacon and ham, Little Sizzlers sausage, Mary Kitchen roast beef and corned beef hash, Old Smokehouse barbecue sauce... Burger King & Pizza Hut. **Other Resources:** To protest, write to: Hormel, 501 16th Ave., NE, PO Box 800, Austin, MN 55912.

**✍ ▸ The Aware Parenting Institute**
Box 206
Goleta, CA 93116    (805)968-1868
**Concern(s):** education; family; childhood. Founder is author of the revolutionary books "The Aware Baby" and "Helping Young Children Flourish." The Institute sponsors lectures, workshops, classes, and consultations with Dr. Solter. Goals are to promote gentle and effective parenting for a peaceful world. **Est.:** 1990. **Contact(s):** Aletha Solter (Founder).

**L ▸ Backcountry Homeworker's Exchange**
Provident Press
RR2 Box 233A
Monson, ME 04464
**Concern(s):** labor; feminism; economics; homeworkers. This network provides information and common ground for homeworkers. The Networking Newsletter has free ads for members and brief news clips of interest to women who work at home. **Other Resources:** See NETWORKING Newsletter.

**S ▸ Bahai National Office of External Affairs**
1606 New Hampshire Ave. NW
Washington, DC 20009   (202)265-8830
**Concern(s):** spiritual; peace; faith. A national network of individuals and local institutions which promote the oneness of humankind and religion through educational programs; children's, youth and women's activities; social committees; and affiliation with the United Nations. **Other Resources:** Publishes WORLD ORDER Magazine; and a newsletter, US BAHAI REPORT. **Est.:** 1927. **Contact(s):** Anita Chapman.

**✈ ▸ Baikal Foundation**
See Cooperation Project.

**L ▸ Bakery, Confectionery, & Tobacco Workers International Union**
10401 Connecticut Ave.
Kensington, MD 20895   (301)933-8600
**Concern(s):** labor; politics; unions; lobbying. Represents approximately 145,000 workers in the US and Canada. Publishes BC&T NEWS, a membership tabloid, ten times a year and BC&T Report, a monthly leadership newsletter. It also handles public relations, legislative and political activities. **Contact(s):** Carolyn J. Jacobson (Director of Public Relations).

**T ▸ The Bank Information Center**
2025 I St. NW
Washington, DC 20006   (202)466-8191
**Affiliation:** International Center for Development Policy. **Concern(s):** Third World; economics; environment; development; sustainability. A clearinghouse for environmental information on multilateral development bank (MDB) funded projects which monitors the activities of the MDBs and provides information and documents to overseas non-governmental organizations that are assessing or verifying the environmental public health and economic impact of bank projects in specific countries. Also promotes reform of MDB information and environmental policies. **Other Resources:** Library and databases on environmental policy, multilateral development banks, and development. **Contact(s):** Chad Dobson.

**J ▸ Baptist Joint Committee on Public Affairs**
200 Maryland Ave. NE
Washington, DC 20002   (202)544-4226
**Concern(s):** justice; spiritual; peace; faith. **Other Resources:** Magazine, REPORT FROM THE CAPITOL. **Contact(s):** Jeannette Holt.

**✈ ▸ Baptist Peace Fellowship of North America**
499 Patterson St.
Memphis, TN 38111    (901)324-7675
**Concern(s):** education; peace; spiritual; faith; travel. A network of 3,000 Baptists organized in regional groups throughout Canada, the US, Puerto Rico, and sponsors Friendship Tours.

**⚔ ▸ Baseball Diplomacy**
See Bats Not Bombs.

**D ▸ The Basic Foundation, Inc.**
Box 47012
St. Petersburg, FL 33743    (813)526-9562
**Concern(s):** demographics; environment; feminism; population growth; natural resources; family planning. Advocates the preservation of natural resources through limitation of population growth. Nonprofit. **Member:** Co-op America. **Contact(s):** Paul Goldberg.

**H ▸ Bastyr College of Natural Health Sciences**
144 NE 54th
Seattle, WA 98105    (206)523-9585
**Concern(s):** health; holism; nutrition. Bastyr College is the nation's only accredited college offering courses and degree programs in scientifically based medicine and whole foods nutrition. Graduate and undergraduate degrees in Naturopathy, Acupuncture, Oriental medicine and Nutrition. **Other Resources:** ENCYCLOPEDIA OF NATURAL MEDICINE co-authored by Joseph Pivrorro, Jr., College President.

**E ▸ Bat Conservation International**
Box 162603
Austin, TX 78716    (512)327-9721
**Concern(s):** environment; wildlife/endangered species; sustainability. Sponsors projects in North America, Latin America and the Pacific Islands as well as worldwide education efforts to protect the bats and the health of the ecosystems that rely on them. Encourages better management and research initiatives. **Dues:** $25/yr.

**⚔ ▸ Bats Not Bombs**
Box 34166
Los Angeles, CA 90034   (310)458-8124
**Affiliation:** Baseball Diplomacy. **Concern(s):** peace; conflict resolution. Peace Through Sports. "Since 1986, we've been arranging sports events with countries to improve US relations with Central American countries. We hosted Nicaragua in California in 1986, took our team to Mexico to play Cuba in 1987. In 1989 took the USA all stars to play Cuba, Nicaragua, Dominican Republic, Panama, and Mexico in Nicaragua." **Est.:** 1986. **Contact(s):** Andrew Liberman (Executive Director). (213)413-3191.

**F ▸ The Batterers' Group**
412 Dayton St.
Yellow Springs, OH 45387-1706   (513)225-3197
**Concern(s):** feminism; peace; battered women; nonviolence. Clinical social workers who treat people who batter. "We work towards nonviolence individually, and ultimately globally." **Member:** Co-op America.

**✎ ▸ Bay Area Center for Art & Technology**
See magazine, PROCESSED WORLD.

**J ▸ Bear Tribe Medicine Society**
c/o Sun Bear
Box 9167
Spokane, WA 99209
**Concern(s):** justice; spiritual; health; Native Americans; holism; diversity. **Contact(s):** Sun Bear.

**E ▸ Berkeley Ecology Center**
See Ecology Center.

**S ▸ Bethaheva's Concern**
Box 276
Clifton, NJ 07011-0276
**Concern(s):** spiritual; politics; environment; faith; reform; transformation. Christians meet New Agers easily sums up this group. Interesting combination of New Age thoughts to Old Age ideas. **Other Resources:** See CHRISTIAN *NEW AGE QUARTERLY. **Est.:** 1983.

**P ▸ Better Government Association**
230 N. Michigan Ave.
Chicago, IL 60601    (312)641-1181
**Concern(s):** politics; media; government accountability. Founded to combat waste, inefficiency, and corruption in government. Frequently works with the national news media on a variety of investigation projects. **Est.:** 1923. **Contact(s):** Peter M. Manikas. (202)223-6164. (312)641-1181.

**M ▸ Better World Society (dissolved)**
(202)659-1833
**Concern(s):** media; peace; environment; demographics; film; world order. All calls are being diverted to the Population Crisis phone number above. **Member:** Global Tomorrow Coalition. **Contact(s):** Ted Turner (Chairman), Dr. Glenn A. Olds (Public Relations). **Other:** 1 CNN Center, Box 105366, Atlanta, GA 30348-5366 Elaine Jones , Director, Program Development.

**A ▸ Beyond Beef Campaign**
1130 17th St., #630
Washington, DC 20036

**Concern(s):** agriculture; environment; health vegetarian; animal rights. 100,000 activist nationwide educating the public about the benefits of reduced beef consumption in terms of social justice, sustainable agriculture, and environmental preservation. **Other Resources:** Newsletter. **Dues:** $25/yr.

**E ♦ Big Bend Natural History Association**
Box 68
Big Bend National Park, TX 79834 (915)477-2236
**Concern(s):** environment; natural resources. Goals: To facilitate the growth of appreciation for the scenic, scientific and historical value of Big Bend through research, books, maps, and illustrative material, and sponsoring seminars. **Dues:** $25/yr.

**J ♦ Big Mountain Support Committee**
Box 33686
San Diego, CA 92103 (619)277-0991
**Concern(s):** justice; Native Americans. **Member:** Alliance for Survival. **Other:** Big Mountain Legal Office, Box 1509, Flagstaff, AZ 86002.

**A ♦ Bio-Dynamic Farming and Gardening Association**
Box 550
Kimberton, PA 19442 (215)423-2263
**Concern(s):** agriculture; organic certification. An organization that promotes using natural fertilizers and pesticides in growing crops and gardens. **Other Resources:** See periodicals for BIODYNAMICS. See directories for FARMS FOR TOMORROW. Free brochure on community supported farms (CSA's) plus a national list of operating CSAs, to find one near you. Publishes many helpful books.

**✪ ♦ Bio-Energy Council**
11403 Waples Mill Rd.
Oakton, VA 22124 (703)715-6644
**Concern(s):** energy; environment; renewables; conservation. **Other Resources:** See Nature Conservancy and Izaak Walton League of America. 715-6644.

**A ♦ Bio-Integral Resource Center**
Box 7414
Berkeley, CA 94707 (510)524-2567
**Concern(s):** agriculture; environment; health; hazardous/toxic waste. Provides information on least-toxic methods for managing any pests found in homes or gardens. **Other Resources:** See periodicals for IPM PRACTITIONER and THE COMMON SENSE PEST CONTROL QUARTERLY; 50 publications on individual pests are available. **Est.:** 1978.

**E ♦ Bioregional Women's Collective**
c/o Constance Maytum
4114 Interlake Ave. N
Seattle, WA 98109
**Concern(s):** environment; feminism; bioregionalism.

**E ♦ Birmingham Environmental**
230 Lee Valley, #40
Pelham, AL 35124
**Concern(s):** environment; health; air pollution; public health; substance abuse. Discover how much secondhand cigarette smoke you inhale. Our passive smoking badge shows you exactly how many cigarettes you knowingly smoke. **Other Resources:** Passive Smoke Badge.

**J ♦ Black Student Alliance**
Student Center, Rm. SC06
Graduate Ctr., 33 W. 42nd St.
New York, NY 10036 (212)642-2545
**Concern(s):** justice; racism; discrimination; minority rights. Seeks to find ways to minimize the effects of racism in New York and provide a foundation for challenging racism in an ongoing, thoughtful way. Nonprofit.

**J ♦ Black Veterans for Social Justice**
See periodicals for BLACK VET.7

**H ♦ Blue Star**
Box 800
El Prado, NM 87529
**Concern(s):** health; nutrition; holism. This organization believes in natural organic health practices.

**⚼ ♦ Boise Peace Quilt Project**
See periodicals for PEACEFUL PIECES.

**E ♦ Bolton Institute For A Sustainable Future**
4 Linden Square
Wellesley, MA 02181-4709 (617)235-5320
**Concern(s):** environment. An independent organization for research and public education about the values which lie back of our choices about limits-to-growth issues. **Other Resources:** Publications list

available upon request. **Est.:** 1972. **Contact(s):** Elizabeth Dodson Gray, David Dodson Gray (Co-directors).

**⚐ ♦ Boston Women's Teachers' Group**
See RADICAL TEACHER under periodicals.

**♥♥ ♦ Boulder County Safehouse**
Box 4157
Boulder, CO 80306
**Concern(s):** family; justice; children; battered women; child abuse.

**E ♦ Boulder Rainforest Action Group**
Environmental Center
Box 2, University of Colorado
Boulder, CO 80309 (303)492-8300
**Concern(s):** environment; forests.

**⚐ ♦ Boy Scouts of America**
1325 Walnut Hill Lane
Irving, TX 75015-2079 (214)580-2000
**Concern(s):** education; environment; youth; activism. Outdoor programs for boys and young men which aim to build moral strength and character, citizenship, and mental, physical and emotional fitness. **Dues:** $7/yr.

**L ♦ Boycott Committee**
Teamster Local 391, Box 929
Kernersville, NC 27825
**Concern(s):** labor; economics; justice; boycott; corporate responsibility; socially-responsible investing; unions; discrimination. BOYCOTT HOLLY FARMS/TYSON FOODS — Unfair labor practices. Products: All Holly Farm and Tyson Foods products. **Other Resources:** Holly Farms Corp., P.O. Box 17236, Memphis, TN 38187-0236; Tyson Foods, 2219 West Oaklawn Dr., Springdale, AR 72764.

**L ♦ Boycott of Conscience**
630 3rd Ave., 5th Fl.
New York, NY 10017 (212)818-1130
**Concern(s):** labor; economics; justice; boycott; corporate responsibility; socially-responsible investing; discrimination. BOYCOTT TWA — They are accused of unfair labor practices. **Other Resources:** To protest, write to: Carl Icahn, TWA, 605 Third Ave., New York, NY 10158.

**T ♦ Boycott Shell Campaign**
c/o United Mine Workers America
900 15th St. NW
Washington, DC 20005 (202)842-7350
**Concern(s):** Third World; economics; justice; environment; boycott; corporate responsibility; socially-responsible investing; South Africa; divestment. BOYCOTT SHELL — They have not divested from South Africa. Products: Shell Gasoline; Motor Oils- Aeroshell, Fire and Ice, Rimula, Rotella, Shell Super X, Shell X-100; Auto products - Comfort Ride, Meridyne radios, Sentinel batteries, Shell Radial Ride + Radial II + Shellride + Superlife, Superlife, Super Shell Aramid, Super Shell Snowshoe; Home Products - Child Protector Tops, Citrus Blossom air freshener, Heritage furniture polish, Home Freshener, Open Air air freshener, Shell Flea Collar... **Other Resources:** To protest, write to: Shell Oil, Frank H. Richardson, 1 Shell Plaza, Houston, TX 77001 (800) 331-3703; and Royal Dutch/Shell Petroleum, L.C. Van Wachem, 30 Carel Van Bylandtlaan, The Hague, Netherlands. Publishes a newsletter, BOYCOTT SHELL BULLETIN.

**? ♦ Brahma Kumaris**
401 Baker St.
San Francisco, CA 94117
**Concern(s):** future; ideation. Invites people to submit their vision of a better world to a Global Cooperation Bank, and to participate in "creative groups" (4-8 people), a thousand of which are functioning in 50 countries.

**⚐ ♦ Brain Based Education Network**
See Institute for Learning and Teaching.

**? ♦ The Brain Exchange**
116 Coleridge St.
San Francisco, CA 94110
**Concern(s):** future; ideation. Intermittently offers monthly "brainstorming salons."

**D ♦ Bread for the World**
802 Rhode Island Ave. NW
Washington, DC 20018 (202)269-0200
**Concern(s):** demographics; spiritual; agriculture; politics; hunger; faith; food production; food distribution; leadership; reform. A Christian citizens' movement which approaches hunger as a public policy issue. Its 48,000 members are organized by congressional district into local groups nationwide. They work with their member of Congress in support of US policies and practices that give hungry people a chance to overcome hunger and in seeking changes in policies that

don't. Provides voting records of members of the US Congress on hunger. Educates public about hunger by monthly newsletters & training events. **Other Resources:** Monthly newsletter, BREAD FOR THE WORLD; educational materials about the causes of hunger, hunger education and training events. Produces 12 minute video solving infant mortality and child hunger...worldwide. **Contact(s):** Arthur Simon (Executive Director). (800)82-BREAD.

**S ♦ Brethren in Christ Church**
Board Brotherhood Concerns
Box 2
Mount Joy, PA 17552
**Concern(s):** spiritual; peace; faith. See Mennonite Central Committee.

**⚼ ♦ Brethren Peace Fellowship**
Box 455
New Windsor, MD 21776 (301)775-2254
**Concern(s):** peace; education; spiritual; faith; activism. This organization is concerned with Christian peace education. It is very active in the peace movement with its peace vigils and support groups for peacemakers. **Est.:** 1967. **Contact(s):** Dale Aukerman (Coordinating Secretary).

**? ♦ British Consortium for Innovation**
37 Bedford Square
London, WC1 3HW England
**Concern(s):** future; economics; media; agriculture; health; justice; labor; ideation; trade; invention; telecommunications. Facilitates idea-sharing among a large number of companies and organizations involved in international banking, law, agriculture, telecommunications and health management, and seeks to design business structures that will not inhibit creativity.

**⚐ ♦ The Buckminster Fuller Institute**
1743 S. La Cienega Blvd.
Los Angeles, CA 90035 (310)837-7710
**Concern(s):** education; environment; planning.

**J ♦ Bulldozer Collective**
See PRISON NEWS SERVICE under periodicals.

**J ♦ Bureau of Indian Affairs**
See BUREAU OF INDIAN AFFAIRS HIGHER EDUCATION GRANT PEOPLE under directories.

**⚐ ♦ Bureau of Public Affairs**
See Department of State Publications under publishers.

**F ♦ Business and Professional Women-USA**
2012 Massachusetts Ave. NW
Washington, DC 20036 (202)293-1100
**Concern(s):** feminism; politics; economics; discrimination; analysis; empowerment; sexism. This organization is a watchdog on hiring and firing practices of the business world. They take the side of the female professional and give counseling and legal advice. Hotline (202)833-5524. **Contact(s):** Irma Brosseau.

**⚼ ♦ Business Executives for National Security**
601 Pennsylvania Ave. NW
Washington, DC 20004 (202)737-1090
**Concern(s):** peace; economics; education; politics; trade; national security; lobbying. Works towards reducing the threat of nuclear war through lobbying and public education. They also strive for better national security by encouraging sensible military spending. **Other Resources:** Publishes a newsletter, TRENDLINE. **Est.:** 1982. **Contact(s):** Marcia Johnston (Executive Director), Stanley Weiss (President).

**A ♦ California Action Network**
Box 464
Davis, CA 95617 (916)756-8518
**Concern(s):** agriculture; environment; organic; organic certification; pesticides. Publishes the 1990 ORGANIC WHOLESALERS DIRECTORY & YEARBOOK, a listing of over 200 wholesalers, distributors, and manufacturers of organic food and farm supplies in the US and Canada. **Other Resources:** A quarterly newsletter. Produces a comprehensive handbook on certification, and an annual list of California Organic growers, CALIFORNIA WHOLESALER'S DIRECTORY.

**A ♦ California Certified Organic Farmers (CCOF)**
Box 8136
Santa Cruz, CA 95061-8136 (408)423-2263
**Concern(s):** agriculture; organic farming. An organization of farmers who have been certified not to use non-organic pesticides on their crops. **Other Resources:** Publishes a good statewide newsletter.

**S ♦ California Community Foundation**
3580 Wilshire Blvd., #1660
Los Angeles, CA 90010

**Concern(s):** spiritual; economics; philanthropy; community investment; socially-responsible investing. The concept of a community foundation has been called the wave of the future in private philanthropy. CCF is a tax exempt philanthropic pool where hundreds of individual funds are placed together so that even modest charitable contributions enjoy all the professional administration of a multi-million-dollar fund. Since inception, the foundation has granted more than $60 million to projects dedicated to improving the quality of life in Southern California. Nonprofit. **Est.:** 1915.

**E ▸ California Conservation Corps**
1530 Capitol Ave.
Sacramento, CA 95814 (916)445-8183
**Affiliation:** State of California. **Concern(s):** environment; education; labor; urban; conservation; youth; jobs. An environmental youth work program started by Gov. Jerry Brown that trains youths 18-23 in fire fighting, flood fighting, oil spill control, disaster relief, conservation and environmental awareness. A model program for other states and counties youth conservation programs, it also teaches English as a second language, G.E.D., Conservation Awareness, Career Counseling and offers college classes. Program builds a good work ethic in youth and opens up many career paths. Suffering severe cutbacks. **Other Resources:** Helitack Firefighting program, C.D.F.; Backcountry Trails programs; Internships at State Parks and Zoo's. **Est.:** 1976.

**E ▸ California Department of Conservation**
Division of Recycling
1025 P St., #401
Sacramento, CA 95814 (916)323-3743
**Concern(s):** environment; recycling. It is responsible for administering the California Beverage Container Recycling and Litter Reduction Act, with the goals of reaching an 80% beverage container recycling rate and ensuring convenient consumer recycling opportunities in an effort to save energy, conserve natural resources and extend the life of the state's landfills. **Other Resources:** See CALIFORNIA CO-OP DIRECTORY.

**✍ ▸ California Department of Education**
See YOUND AND OLD TOGETHER under directories.

**E ▸ California Earth Corps**
2420 28th St. #11
Signal Hill, CA 90806
**Affiliation:** Earth Island Institute. **Concern(s):** environment; education; activism; youth; volunteers. Fighting to restore marshes, bays, and to stop radioactive waste. Dedicated to conserving, protecting and restoring the biosystems. **Other Resources:** Monthly newsletter AT THE CORPS. Nonprofit. **Dues:** $15-$100/yr. includes newsletter.

**E ▸ California Institute of Public Affairs**
See WORLD DIRECTORY OF ENVIRONMENTAL ORGANIZATIONS; INTERNATIONAL PEACE DIRECTORY; CALIFORNIA ENVIRONMENTAL DIRECTORY; CALIFORNIA TOXICS DIRECTORY; and, CIPA: COMPLETE LIST OF BOOKS AND REPORTS IN PRINT under publishers.

**E ▸ California Integrated Waste Management Board**
1020 9th St., #300
Sacramento, CA 95814 (916)322-3330
**Concern(s):** environment; recycling. Newly created state agency, implementing policies to reduce waste, increase recycling and minimize environmental risk from waste management operations. It assists local governments, business and industry in identifying waste reduction and recycling options and developing markets for recycled materials. Free information on recycling and household toxics. (800)553-2962.

**✏ ▸ California Lawyers for the Arts**
315 W. 9th St., #1101
Los Angeles, CA 90015-4210 (213)623-8311
**Concern(s):** arts; justice; activism; reform. An organization providing legal services and information for the arts community. "We provide alternative dispute resolution, educational programs, and legal referrals for artists of all disciplines. We offer Copyright Clinics, Arts Arbitration and Mediation Services, small workshops and other seminars on various business and legal self-help topics for artists." Nonprofit. **Est.:** 1974.

**H ▸ Californians Against Human Suffering**
5750 Wilshire Blvd., #561
Los Angeles, CA 90036 (213)937-6295
**Affiliation:** Americans Against Human Suffering, Inc.. **Concern(s):** health; death/dying. A campaign to pass the California Death With Dignity Act. **Contact(s):** Robert L. Risley (Founder/Chairman), Michael White (President). **Other:** 3200 Cutter Way, Sacramento, CA 95818 (916)454-3686

**E ▸ Californians Against Waste**
909 12th St., #201
Sacramento, CA 95814 (916)443-5422
**Concern(s):** environment; recycling. A grass-roots organization that lobbies in support of a waste reduction and recycling. Its Foundation works closely with CAW in public education, research and advocacy programs for recycling and resource renewal in California. "Buy Recycled Campaign." **Est.:** 1977. **Fax:** (916)443-3912. **Contact(s):** Sandra Jerabek (Executive Director), Jeni Haas.

**D ▸ Californians for Population Stabilization**
916 J St. , #915
Sacramento, CA 95814 (916)446-1033
**Concern(s):** demographics; environment; population growth. An organization dedicated to stabilizing population growth in California in order to protect and preserve the State's environment, ecology and resources. It believes that overpopulation is the ultimate environmental threat. **Other Resources:** Public education, media campaigns, public policy and advocacy, and grassroots organizing. Publishes quarterly newsletter, CAPS. **Est.:** 1986. **Contact(s):** Barbara Alexander (Executive Director), Benny Chien, MD (President).

**U ▸ Californians For Transportation Solutions**
The Planning and Conservation League
909 12th St. #203
Sacramento, CA 95814
**Affiliation:** Planning and Conservation League. **Concern(s):** urban; energy; environment; transportation; conservation; global warming. A coaliton of environmental, transportation, labor and business organizations dedicated to providing a sensible transportation system for California's future. **Other Resources:** California Clean Air and Rail Transit Initiative. **Contact(s):** James K. Knox (Campaign Director).

**✍ ▸ Calvert School**
105 Tuscany Rd.
Baltimore, MD 21210 (301)243-6030
**Concern(s):** education; alternates; childhood. Elementary school curriculum which extends from Kindergarten to 8th Grade. Our courses have been used to educate hundreds of thousands of children since 1906 and is fully accredited by the Maryland State Department of Education. Parents who plan homeschooling should check with state statutes. No approval necessary if used as a supplement to regular schooling. A planned, structured curriculum for the basic subjects. Teaching manuals to assist the inexperienced parent. **Subscription:** $230-425/yr.

**✌ ▸ Campaign Against Proliferation**
c/o SANE-Freeze
1819 H St. NW. #640
Washington, DC 20006 (202)862-9740
**Concern(s):** peace; disarmament; test ban. Sends out regular updates and action suggestions from the International Comprehensive Test Ban Campaign, a coalition of over 61 countries working together in support of a CTB Treaty. Presently, due to funding, the Campaign Against Proliferation is operating out of the Sane/Freeze offices. The group was previously known as the Comprehensive Test Ban Coalition. Nonprofit. **Fax:** (202)862-9740. **Contact(s):** Adrian Jemott (Coordinator:).

**✌ ▸ Campaign for Peace and Democracy**
Box 1640, Cathedral Station
New York, NY 10025 (212)666-5924
**Concern(s):** peace; Third World; politics; justice; labor; feminism; grassroots organizing; disarmament. Founded in 1982 to organize Western peace activists to defend the rights of independent movements in the East and to enlist East bloc activists to oppose US policy in Latin America and elsewhere. Maintains network of contacts in East European environmental, labor, women's, minority, and peace movements; expanding to include contacts in Central America, Africa, Asia, and Middle East. **Other Resources:** Publishes PEACE AND DEMOCRACY NEWS provides information and contacts to US journalists, activists, academics for citizen-based democratic social change movements in Eastern Europe and the USSR and vice versa, organizes seminars and forums. **Est.:** 1982. **Contact(s):** Joanne Landy (Executive Director), Thomas Harrison (Associate Director).

**✌ ▸ Campaign for UN Reform**
418 7th St. SE
Washington, DC 20003 (202)546-3956
**Affiliation:** World Federalist Association. **Concern(s):** peace; United Nations; world order. Rates Congressmen and Senators on global issues alone, particularly roll call votes on funding UN agencies. Also maintains an active legislative program. They believe that the UN provides the most practical framework for the creation of a dependable global structure capable of assuring world peace. Campaign includes: Global Statesmanship ratings; voting guides; assistance to politicians who support a strengthened UN; and, maintains active lobby. **Other Resources:** Publishes newsletter, UN REFORM CAMPAIGNER. **Contact(s):** Eric Cox (Executive Director).

**✌ ▸ Campaign for World Government**
552 Lincoln Ave.
Winettka, IL 60093 (312)446-7177
**Concern(s):** peace; world order. Working toward the goal of a world federation all-inclusive, democratic in its own structure, with enforcement of world federal laws directly on individual citizens wherever they live. The world federation would have only those powers granted to it under some kind of constitution. The aim is to include all nations, but to be members, each nation would have to adopt the constitution. This would expand government under popular control and replace the anarchy among nations. **Contact(s):** Georgia Lloyd (Executive Director). (312)835-1377.

**$ ▸ Campaign to Cut Military Spending In Half**
Council for a Livable World Education Fund
110 Maryland Ave. NE
Washington, DC 20002 (202)543-4100
**Affiliation:** Council for a Livable World. **Concern(s):** economics; peace; peace dividend; budget; economic conversion. The US spends $300 billion annually on the military. This campaign suggests we can cut that in half by the year 2000 or sooner. This could result in nearly a $700 billion savings. Hotline: (202)543-0006.

**T ▸ Campaign To End Hunger**
936 N. 34th St., #200
Seattle, WA 98103-8869 (206)448-2445
**Affiliation:** Planet Earth Foundation. **Concern(s):** Third World; education; hunger; development; global understanding. Designed to promote action to change the conditions that allow hunger to persist. These conditions threaten the world all people share. Global security, the planetary environment, and the world environment all will gain when we have ended hunger. **Other Resources:** Publishes GUIDE TO ACTION. **Contact(s):** Keith Blume (Executive Director), Carla Cole (Director). (800)888-8750.

**✍ ▸ The Campus Outreach Opportunity League (COOL)**
386 McNeal Hall, University of Minnesota
St. Paul, MN 55108-1011 (612)579-2011
**Concern(s):** education; politics; students; grassroots organizing. Nationally youth-led organization that produces publications, organizes conferences, and makes campus visits to help get things going on campus and in community. From campus ideals to community involvement. Something's happening on campus. Students are building a new movement based on communication service. **Other Resources:** Hosts national and local conferences. **Contact(s):** Julia Scatliff (Executive Director), Bill Hoogterp. (612)624-3018.

**✍ ▸ Campus Services**
See Council on International Educational Exchange.

**✏ ▸ Canadian Institute of Cultural Affairs**
See EDGES MAGAZINE.

**H ▸ Cancer Control Society**
2043 N. Berendo St.
Los Angeles, CA 90027 (213)663-7801
**Concern(s):** health; prevention; research; analysis. This organization focuses on analyzing experimental treatments and therapies for cancer. **Other Resources:** Publishes, CANCER CONTROL JOURNAL.

**T ▸ CARE**
8354 Beverly Blvd.
Los Angeles, CA 90048 (213)653-7772
**Concern(s):** Third World; demographics; health; environment; development; hunger; forests; population growth; conservation. A worldwide network dedicated to helping poor people improve their lives. "We reach 30 million people in 40 nations in Africa, Asia, and Latin America. In 1990 CARE planted 30 million trees worldwide."

**D ▸ CARE International**
660 1st Ave.
New York, NY 10016 (212)686-3110
**Concern(s):** demographics; agriculture; Third World; justice; hunger; children. Dedicated to famine relief throughout the world. It primarily deals with children. Some of their programs supply seeds and tools to aid communities with self reliance. Nonprofit. **Contact(s):** Elizabeth Waldstein, Nancy Blum (Public Relations). (212)979-6265. **Other:** CARE, Inc./Washington Liaison Office, 2025 I St. NW, #1001, Washington, DC 20006. Marianne Leach (202)223-2277.

**F ▸ Career Women's Network**
Communication Creativity
Box 213, County Rd. FF 38
Saguache, CO 81149
**Affiliation:** Communication Creativity. **Concern(s):** feminism; economics; trade.

**E ♦ Caribbean Conservation Corporation**
Box 2866
Gainesville, FL 32602 (904)373-6441
**Concern(s):** environment; wildlife/endangered species; conservation; oceans/rivers; volunteers. An international, public foundation with the purpose of sponsoring long-term scientific studies, preservation and conservation of the Atlantic Green Turtle. CCC continues to support and collaborate on projects in the US and other parts of the world, and is active in environmental education and natural resources management. Currently, volunteers are tagging turtles, collecting data and monitoring the sites of the largest green turtle nesting colony in the Atlantic at Tortuguero, Costa Rica. **Dues:** $35/yr. **Fax:** (904)375-2449. **Contact(s):** Colin Phipps (President), Dr. Archie Carr (Technical Director). **Other:** Box 3048, Tallahassee, FL 32315.

**T ♦ Caribbean Workers Council**
See CARIBBEAN LABOR under periodicals.

**☙ ♦ Carl Rogers Peace Project**
1125 Torrey Pines Rd.
La Jolla, CA 92037
**Concern(s):** peace; education; activism. For all of those brought up on sweet Carl, who died in 1987, this seems appropriate. **Other Resources:** Publishes an organizational directory.

**☙ ♦ Carnegie Endowment for International Peace**
1737 Cambridge St.
Cambridge, MA 02138-7299(202)797-6400
**Concern(s):** peace; education; Third World; research; foreign policy; analysis. School related activities. An operating foundation that does not make grants but conducts research in a broad range of issues in international affairs. Promotes research, education, and discussion on foreign policy issues, including arms control. **Other Resources:** See FOREIGN POLICY (journal). **Contact(s):** Thomas L. Hughes (President), Michael V. O'Hare (Director, Finance/Education). (212)572-8200.

**D ♦ Carrying Capacity Network**
1325 G St. NW, #1003
Washington, DC 20005 (202)879-3044
**Concern(s):** demographics; environment; population. A network and clearinghouse designed to address the relationships between environmental protection, resource use, population, economic growth, achieving a sustainable society and related issues. It facilitates cooperation and information dissemination among a diverse set of activists through its publications, Fax Alert Service, and other clearinghouse services. **Other Resources:** Publishes a quarterly newsletter, CARRYING CAPACITY NEWS/FOCUS; CLEARINGHOUSE BULLETIN; FAX ALERT SERVICE. See also, Population Environment Balance. Nonprofit. **Est.:** 1989. **Dues:** $35, organization $50-80. **E-Network:** Econet. **ID:** 'Smabley'. **Fax:** (202)879-3019. **Contact(s):** Stephen M. Mabley (Network Coordinator).

**✐ ♦ Cartoonists Across America**
Box 670
Lompoc, CA 93438 (805)735-5134
**Concern(s):** arts; media; education; trade; graphics; literacy. Environmental cartoonists that promote literacy among children and adults through cartoons.

**T ♦ Casa Chile**
Box 3620
Berkeley, CA 94703 (510)845-9398
**Concern(s):** Third World; economics; boycott. An organization which disagrees with supporting the fascist state of Chile. **Other Resources:** See CHILE NEWSLETTER.

**E ♦ Cascade Holistic Economic Consultants**
See FOREST WATCH magazine.

**$ ♦ Catalyst (Institute for Gaean Economics)**
See newsletter, INVESTING FROM THE HEART.

**☙ ♦ Catholic Peace Fellowship**
See CATHOLIC PEACE FELLOWSHIP BULLETIN.

**J ♦ Catholic Worker Movement**
See newspaper, CATHOLIC WORKER.

**F ♦ Catholics For Free Choice**
1436 U St. NW, #301
Washington, DC 20009-3916 (202)638-1706
**Concern(s):** feminism; spiritual; demographics; population growth; pro-choice; faith; family planning; reform. A national education organization that supports the right to legal reproductive health care, especially to family planning and abortion. CFFC also works to reduce the incidence of abortion and to increase women's choices in childbearing and through advocacy of social and economic programs for women, families, and children. **Other Resources:** Publishes journal, CONSCIENCE. **Contact(s):** Denise Shannon (Director of Communications), Frances Kissling (President).

**P ♦ CATO Institute**
224 2nd St. SE
Washington, DC 20003 (202)546-0200
**Concern(s):** politics; economics; Third World; justice; foreign policy; civil liberties; trade; third party. This institute focuses on issues dealing with foreign policy, civil liberties, and socio-economic issues with a strong libertarian slant. **Other Resources:** Publishes a magazine, INQUIRY. **Contact(s):** Ed Crane (President).

**P ♦ Caucus for a New Political Science**
See NEW POLITICAL SCIENCE under periodicals.

**✍ ♦ Caucus on Social Theory and Art Education**
See BULLETIN OF THE CAUCUS ON SOCIAL THEORY AND ART EDUCATION.

**U ♦ Causes and Cures**
Christic Institute
1324 N. Capitol St. NW
Washington, DC 20002 (202)797-8106
**Affiliation:** Christic Institute. **Concern(s):** urban; health; justice; politics; grassroots organizing; public policy; interfaith; constitutional rights; substance abuse; CIA; drugs; criminal justice. A project that is an effort to involve communities in the discussion and solutions involving drugs in America and covert operations. **Other Resources:** Educational and organizing material available including video of their first teleconference.

**E ♦ CEED Institute**
1807 2nd St., Studio 2
Santa Fe, NM 87501 (505)986-1401
**Concern(s):** environment; economics; urban; sustainability; cooperatives; planning. An organization that is planting the seeds of sustainable community by demonstrating practical models for new ecological neighborhoods and environmentally responsible community enterprises. CEED established the "Seed Ecological Living Center" which combines a "Community Green Store" specializing in ecological products with artisans. **Est.:** 1988.

**E ♦ The CEIP Fund**
68 Harrison Ave.
Boston, MA 02111-1907(617)426-4375
**Concern(s):** environment; labor; jobs; Great Lakes. Currently offering jobs in Florida, California, the Northeast, Pacific Northwest and Great Lakes regions. CEIP averages about 300 job openings a year and offers counseling, conferences and workshops on environmental vocations for private and public organizations for college students, career changers and other job seekers. **Other Resources:** See COMPLETE GUIDE TO ENVIRONMENTAL CAREERS under directories. **Est.:** 1972.

**? ♦ Celebration of Innovation: An Exposition Showcase of Creativity, Innovation and Invention**
Box 637
Mill Valley, CA 94942 (415)383-5064
**Affiliation:** Institute for the Study of Natural Systems. **Concern(s):** future; ideation. An exposition tribute to the creative genius in us all" held in San Francisco in Fall 1987, planned as a prototype for future events, included a Regenerating America Contest held in cooperation with Rodale Press's Regeneration Project; an Inventions Contest "looking for bold new ideas in communications, transportation and energy conservation"; international participation in new idea sharing via satellite communications. **Est.:** 1987.

**✍ ♦ Center for a Common Security**
Williams College
Williamstowm, MA 01267
**Concern(s):** education; students. Growing out of the efforts of a handful of concerned Williams College undergraduates, CCS continues to engage college students across the country through their dynamic educational and outreach programs.

**☙ ♦ Center for a New Creation**
845 N. Lincoln
Arlington, VA 22201
**Concern(s):** peace. **Contact(s):** Joan Urbanzcyk.

**✍ ♦ The Center for Applied Human Ecology**
Huxley College
Western Washington University
Bellingham, WA 98225
**Concern(s):** education; Third World; global understanding; development. Promotes a semester abroad offering Third World experience, understanding of the process of technological development, and practical hands-on experience meeting human needs through understanding the process of technological development. Students will live with urban and rural families and work on village development projects. **Other:** Promotes a semester abroad offering Third World experience,

understanding of the process of technological development, and practical hands-on experience meeting human needs.

**$ ♦ Center for Auto Safety**
2001 S St. NW, #410
Washington, DC 20009 (202)328-7700
**Concern(s):** economics; health; consumer rights; consumer protection. Established to reduce deaths from defective automobiles, badly constructed highways and defective mobile homes. Also, educates and advises consumers and attorneys on warranty rights and other legal rights. See IMPACT and LEMON TIMES under periodicals; and, CENTER FOR AUTO SAFETY PUBLICATIONS LIST. See, also, under directories, THE LEMON BOOK. **Other Resources:** See THE LEMON BOOK. Publications brochure lists Books, Periodicals, Reports & Information, Auto Defect Packets, Fuel Economy Publications, Consumer Action Guides and Arbitration Manuals available from CAS Publications Dept. Over 100 items available. **Est.:** 1970. **Contact(s):** Debra Barclay (Communications Director).

**$ ♦ Center for Business Ethics**
Bentley College
450 Beaver St.
Waltham, MA 02154-6270
**Concern(s):** economics; socially-responsible investing; alternative consumer; trade. **Contact(s):** Robert E. Frederick.

**P ♦ Center for Changes**
See Against the Current (periodicals).

**E ♦ Center for Clean Air Policy**
444 N. Capitol St. NW, #526
Washington, DC 20001 (202)624-7709
**Concern(s):** environment; air pollution.

**E ♦ Center for Coastal Studies**
Box 826
Provincetown, MA 02657 (617)487-3622
**Concern(s):** environment; wildlife/endangered species; oceans/rivers. An organization dedicated to the preservation of the coastal environment and to saving whales through research and education. **Other Resources:** COASTWATCH newsletter. **Office:** 59 Commercial St. Provincetown, MA 02657.

**✍ ♦ Center for Collaborative Education**
1573 Madison Ave., #412
New York, NY 10029 (212)348-7821
**Concern(s):** education. **Contact(s):** Heather Lewis (Director).

**✍ ♦ Center for Communal Studies**
8600 University Blvd.
Evansville, IN 47712 (812)464-1727
**Concern(s):** education; economics; research; intentional communities. A research and international center with archival materials on 90 historic and 350 current communal groups. CCS headquarters Fellowship for Intentional Communities and Communal Studies Association, and is a support facility for the International Communal Studies Association. **Other Resources:** Conferences, classes and publications. See, also, Communal Studies Association and Fellowship for Intentional Community. **Est.:** 1976. **Member:** Fellowship for Intentional Community.

**$ ♦ Center for Community Change**
1000 Wisconsin Ave. NW
Washington, DC 20007 (202)342-0519
**Concern(s):** economics; demographics; politics; community self-reliance; self-determination; poverty; community investment. For two decades with support of individuals and institutions who believe that poor people can help themselves, the Center has been helping people build strong communities. While organizing poor communities is an essential step toward changing those communities, the impact of national policies cannot be ignored. As a result, the center has always worked both to increase or protect the resources available to poor communities and to ensure that those resources are used effectively. **Other Resources:** See COMMUNITY CHANGE newsletter under periodicals. **Contact(s):** Ann Roberts, Tim Saasta, Allen Fishbein.

**$ ♦ Center for Community Self-Help**
Box 3259
Durham, NC 27705 (919)683-3016
**Concern(s):** economics; labor; community investment; cooperatives; worker ownership; community self-reliance. Provides technical support for worker-owned businesses and helps low-income people create ar save jobs through worker-ownership. Established The Self-Help Credit Union in 1983 to provide credit to members of democratically managed establishments. Nonprofit. **Dues:** $25; $12 limited.

**( ♦ Center for Computer Assistance**
See Direct Link/REACH.

**✌ ▸ Center for Conflict Resolution**
4400 University Dr.
Fairfax, VA 22030
**Concern(s):** peace; conflict resolution. **Other Resources:** DIRECTORY OF PEACE STUDIES PROGRAMS. See also, Consortium on Peace, Research, Education and Development (COPRED).

**E ▸ Center for Conservation Biology**
Dept. of Biological Sciences
Stanford University
Stanford, CA 94305 (415)723-5924
**Concern(s):** environment; education; conservation.

**J ▸ Center for Constitutional Rights**
666 Broadway
New York, NY 10012 (212)614-6464
**Concern(s):** justice; politics; political prisoners; constitutional rights; reform; criminal system. A national institution dedicated to preserving the Constitution as a living document belonging to all the people. CCR is both a defender of constitutional rights and a catalyst for extending those rights. Is a relentless foe of those who ignore the Constitution's mandate and twist its meanings to deny freedom and equality to those less privileged and powerful than themselves. Founded by lawyers Arthur Kinoy, William Kunstler, and the late Ben Smith, Peter Weiss dedicated to creative use of law. **Other Resources:** See MOVEMENT SUPPORT NETWORK NEWS. Freedom Now!: National Campaign for Amnesty and Human Rights for Political Prisoners (project). Periodic list of US political prisoners. See, also, Riptide Communications (media) and Fund for Human Dignity. **Contact(s):** Morton Stavis (President), Patricia Maher (Executive Director).

**T ▸ Center for Cuban Studies**
See CUBA UPDATE under periodicals.

**✌ ▸ Center for Defense Information**
1500 Massachusetts Ave. NW
Washington, DC 20005 (202)862-0700
**Concern(s):** peace; Third World; politics; disarmament; anti-nuclear; foreign policy; research; analysis; lobbying. The foremost independent research organization in the country analyzing military spending, policies, and weapons systems. The staff consists of retired admirals, generals, and other former officers, as well as civilians with extensive military training analysis. This expertise backs up the Center's commitment to end nuclear weapons build-ups and prevent nuclear war, yet advocates a strong national defense. **Other Resources:** Started the Women's Agenda in 1985; produced TV series, AMERICA'S DEFENSE MONITOR. See THE DEFENSE MONITOR and WOMEN'S AGENDA newsletters. **Contact(s):** Rear Admiral Gene R. LaRocque (Director), Rear Admiral Eugene J. Carroll, Jr. (Deputy Director).

**J ▸ Center for Democratic Renewal**
Box 50469
Atlanta, GA 30302 (404)221-0025
**Concern(s):** justice; politics; racism; discrimination; grassroots/community organizing. Formerly the National Anti-Klan Network, it gathers news from the front lines, providing training, information and help to stop the destructive trends of the Klan nationwide. **Other Resources:** See THE MONITOR newsletter.

**✌ ▸ Center for Dispute Resolution**
1337 Ocean Ave.
Santa Monica, CA 90401 (310)451-1615
**Concern(s):** peace; labor; conflict resolution. A mediation and training organization with extensive experience in resolving organizational disputes, workplace disputes and helping peace groups and others work better as a team. CRD works with corporations, schools, unions, nonprofit organizations, divorcing couples, and parties in litigation to settle their disputes amicably. **Other Resources:** Publishes newsletter. Nonprofit. **Est.:** 1983. **Fax:** (310)394-3453. **Contact(s):** Kenneth Cloke (Director).

**✌ ▸ Center for Economic Conversion**
222-C View St.
Mountain View, CA 94041-1344 (415)968-8798
**Concern(s):** peace; economic conversion; disarmament. Provides public education about the economic impact of the arms race and helps communities who are economically dependent on the military to convert their economic base to a more peaceful, conventional one. Resource list is available. Is dedicated to creating a sustainable future and building a society of peace, jobs, and justice. Founded to educate the public about the need for positive alternatives to excessive military spending and largely supported by members and donors nationwide. **Other Resources:** See BASE CONVERSION NEWS and POSITIVE ALTERNATIVES under periodicals. Also, SUGGESTIONS FOR ORGANIZERS under directories. **Est.:** 1975. **E-Network:** PeaceNet. **ID:** 'jwoke@igc.org'. **Fax:** (415)968-1126. **Contact(s):** Michael Closson (Director).

**$ ▸ Center for Economic Revitalization**
64 Main St.
Montpelier, VT 05602 (802)223-7943
**Affiliation:** Institute for Gaean Economics. **Concern(s):** economics; socially-responsible investing; community investment. This center focuses on ways that cities, companies, and various other entities can revitalize themselves.

**$ ▸ Center for Enterprise Development**
See Association for Enterprise Opportunities.

**E ▸ Center for Environment and Development**
1709 New York Ave. NW, #700
Washington, DC 20006 (202)638-6300
**Affiliation:** World Resources Institute. **Concern(s):** environment; Third World; conservation; sustainability; development. This group tries to find the balance between development and conservation by proposing socially responsible development. **Contact(s):** Thomas Fox.

**E ▸ Center for Environmental Information**
46 Prince St.
Rochester, NY 14607-1016 (716)546-3796
**Concern(s):** environment; education; media; global understanding; media watch. Attempts to resolve the growing dilemma on where to find nonpartisan, timely, accurate, and comprehensive information on environmental issues. It is funded by membership dues, fees, contracts, grants, and contributions. CEI seeks to remove barriers and find construction solutions for individuals, public officials, businesses, and organizations through publications, education programs and information services while stressing ethics, laws, communication and global environmental change. **Other Resources:** Publications, library services, conference and program coordination. Nonprofit. **Est.:** 1974. **Dues:** $25/yr.

**✈ ▸ Center for Global Education**
Augsburg College
731 21 Ave. South
Minneapolis, MN 55454 (612)330-1159
**Concern(s):** education; Third World; travel. It coordinates travel seminars to Latin America, Southern Africa, the Philippines, and the Middle East, with the purpose of introducing participants to the reality of poverty and injustice, examining the root causes of those conditions, and reflecting on the role and responsibility of North American citizens to enter into public debate on foreign policy concerns. **Other Resources:** Publishes GLOBAL PERSPECTIVES newsletter. **Est.:** 1982. **Contact(s):** Mavis Anderson, Joan Moline (Coordinators).

**H ▸ Center for Health Administration Studies**
See DOCTOR-PATIENT STUDIES newsletter.

**H ▸ Center for Holistic Resource Management**
5820 4th St. NW, #12
Albuquerque, NM 87107 (505)344-3445
**Concern(s):** health; environment; economics; urban; holism; natural resources; community self-reliance. Promotes a holistic approach to managing natural and human resources; dedicated to restoring the vitality of communities and the resources on which they depend. **Other Resources:** Provides regular courses in Holistic Resource management and specialized training for community development needs. Publishes quarterly newsletter. Nonprofit. **Est.:** 1984. **Circ.:** 2M. **Other Formats:** Private BBS for members, planned to go public. **Fax:** (505)344-9079. **Contact(s):** Shannon A. Horst (Director of Public Awareness), Mike Ziomko (Director of Development).

**E ▸ Center for Human Environments**
25 W. 43rd St.
New York, NY 10036 (212)944-1751
**Concern(s):** environment; urban; economics; planning; architecture.

**D ▸ Center for Immigrant Rights**
48 St. Marks Place
New York, NY 10003 (212)353-9690
**Concern(s):** demographics; justice; immigration; refugees. **Contact(s):** Ruben Quiroz. (212)505-6890.

**D ▸ The Center for Immigration Studies**
1815 H St. NW
Washington, DC 20006 (202)466-8185
**Concern(s):** demographics; Third World; environment; immigration; population growth; research; analysis. A tax-exempt institute dedicated to research and policy analysis on the broad social, economic, environmental and demographic effects of immigration on American society. The Center uses research, policy analysis, publications, and dialogue to meet the nation's need for sound and balanced information to aid the search for effective immigration laws and practices geared to America's changing interests and conditions. **Other Resources:** Publishes periodical, SCOPE. Nonprofit. **Fax:** (202)466-8076. **Contact(s):** David Simcox (Executive Director).

**✌ ▸ Center for Innovative Diplomacy (retired)**
See BUILDING MUNICIPAL FOREIGN POLICIES: AN ACTION HANDBOOK FOR CITIZENS AND LOCAL ELECTED OFFICIALS under directories.

**✌ ▸ Center for International Policy**
1755 Massachusetts Ave. NW
Washington, DC 20036 (202)232-3317
**Concern(s):** peace; Third World; justice; international law. Analyzes and studies US policy towards the Third World and its impact on human rights and needs. **Other Resources:** Publishes newsletter, INDOCHINA ISSUES; and INTERNATIONAL POLICY REPORTS. **Est.:** 1975. **Contact(s):** William Goodfellow (Director).

**M ▸ Center for Investigative Reporting**
309 Pennsylvania Ave. SE
Washington, DC 20003 (202)546-1880
**Concern(s):** media; press; journalism; responsibility. A nonpartisan organization which sells stories related to environmental and other issues to news agencies. Nonprofit.

**E ▸ Center for Marine Conservation**
1725 DeSales St. NW, #500
Washington, DC 20036 (202)429-5609
**Concern(s):** environment; wildlife/endangered species; rivers/oceans; volunteers. Through the preservation and conservation of marine habitats, preventing marine pollution, managing fisheries for conservation, the center seeks to preserve and protect endangered marine species. **Other Resources:** Sea Turtle Rescue Fund and CITIZENS' GUIDE TO PLASTICS. Catalog, WHALE GIFTS COLLECTION. See, also, American Committee for International Conservation. Volunteer positions available. **Dues:** $20/yr. **Member:** Environmental Federation of America. **Contact(s):** Roger E. McManus (President).

**H ▸ Center for Medical Consumers**
See HEALTH FACTS under periodicals.

**P ▸ Center for National Policy**
317 Massachusetts Ave. NE
Washington, DC 20002 (202)546-9300
**Concern(s):** politics; peace; Third World; law; government accountability. **Other Resources:** CHEMICAL WEAPONS CONVENTION BULLETIN.

**✌ ▸ Center for National Policy**
See CHEMICAL WEAPONS CONVENTION BULLETIN.

**J ▸ Center for National Security Studies**
122 Maryland Ave. NE
Washington, DC 20002 (202)544-1681
**Affiliation:** Fund for Peace. **Concern(s):** justice; politics; peace; civil liberties; foreign policy; national security. Resists incursions against civil liberties justified on national security grounds, pursuing that goal through a carefully designed program of research, litigation, public education, and government relations. Has substantive expertise on national security matters; experience in negotiating with the intelligence community, executive agencies, and the Congress; and the research and litigation skills necessary to influence policy on national security issues when civil liberties are at stake. **Other Resources:** Publications list available. Publishes FIRST PRINCIPLES: NATIONAL SECURITY and CIVIL LIBERTIES (co-sponsored by the ACLU Foundation and the Fund for Peace). **Est.:** 1974.

**$ ▸ Center for Neighborhood Technology**
2125 W. North Ave.
Chicago, IL 60647 (312)278-4800
**Concern(s):** economics; urban; politics; community investment; development; community self-reliance; planning; grassroots organizing. Publishes TAKING CHARGE OF YOUR LOCAL ECONOMY and other materials on neighborhood approaches to community needs. Presently helping church-based credit unions become community lenders. **Other Resources:** NEIGHBORHOOD WORKS newsletter. **Member:** Co-op America.

**✍ ▸ Center for Non-Traditional Education**
See directory, CENTSITIVITY.

**H ▸ Center for Occupational Hazards**
5 Beekman St.
New York, NY 10038 (212)227-6220
**Concern(s):** health; labor; arts; environment; hazardous/toxic waste; occupational safety. A center which studies risks in a variety of different occupations and notifies the workers of these risks. **Other Resources:** See newsletter, ART HAZARDS NEWS.

**F ▸ The Center for Partnership Studies**
Box 51936
Pacific Grove, CA 93950

**Affiliation:** Earth Trust Foundation. **Concern(s):** feminism; peace; future; men's liberation. Established to apply the partnership concepts that were introduced in Riane Eisler's The Chalice and the Blade: Our History, Our Future, and is dedicated to building the cultural and structural foundations for a world of partnership between women and men, social, ethnic, political, economic and religious groups, among families, nations and with nature. We are developing integrated approaches to education and communication to maximize opportunities for interactions based on mutual respect. **Other Resources:** The PARTNERSHIP NEWS newsletter is available for $25. See EQUAL RIGHTS HANDBOOK under directories. Nonprofit. **Est.:** 1987. **Contact(s):** Riane Eisler (Co-director/founder). **Other:** 25700 Shafter Way, Carmel, CA 93923

⚥ **Center for Peace and Conflict Studies**
See CENTER FOR PEACE AND CONFLICT STUDIES NEWSLETTER.

? **Center for Peace Through Culture**
c/o Janice Vann
325 W. 86 Ave. Apt. 6A
New York, NY 10024-8304  (212)645-1653
**Concern(s):** future; arts; peace; culture; ideation. Holds conferences at which it utilizes "an interdisciplinary process we have designed called Creative Synthesis" organized around annual themes, and publishes reports on the results. Goals: To uplift people through the arts and develop a cultural and learning center in the form of an international city.

⚥ **Center for Peaceful Change**
See PEACE & CHANGE under periodicals.

E **Center for Plant Conservation**
125 Arborway
Jamaica Plain, MA 02130  (617)524-6988
**Concern(s):** environment; endangered species; conservation. Focussing most of its attention on Hawaii, Florida, California, Texas and Puerto Rica, the center seeks to conserve and protect indigenous plants through research, education, cultivation at 19 affiliated garden and arboreta in the US, and offsite germplasm collections in the National Collection of Endangered Plants.

P **Center for Policy Alternatives**
1875 Connecticut Ave. NW
Washington, DC 20009  (202)387-6030
**Concern(s):** politics; reform. A nonpartisan public policy center focusing on innovation at the state and local level. NCPA links policy ideas, constituencies, and forward thinking political leaders together. **Other Resources:** Newsletter, WAYS AND MEANS; Conference on Alternative State and Local Policies. **Contact(s):** Jeffrey Tyrens (President), Linda Tarr-Whelan (Executive Director).

$ **Center for Popular Economics**
Box 785
Amherst, MA 01004  (413)545-0743
**Concern(s):** economics; environment; alternative ; social ecology. Teaches workshops on "economics for people, not for profits." Goal is to make economics accessible to people working for social change. **Other Resources:** Free brochure and book list. Nonprofit. **Contact(s):** Natasha Harmon.

D **Center for Population Options**
1025 Vermont Ave. NW
Washington, DC 20005  (202)347-5700
**Concern(s):** demographics; environment; Third World; population growth. Seeks to educate the masses on how to control an explosive population crisis. There is only so much resources for the world and at todays growth rates those will be exhausted. Believes in providing contraceptives to underdeveloped countries and other means of birth control.

H **Center for Psychology in the Public Interest**
21 W. Euclid Ave.
Haddonfield, NJ 08033  (609)429-2012
**Concern(s):** health; psychology. Psychological consulting and psychotherapy practice. "The understanding of problems always starts with a consideration of the impact of social factors" such as class, employer-employee relations, etc. **Member:** Co-op America.

P **Center for Public Dialogue**
10615 Brunswick Ave.
Kensington, MD 20895
**Concern(s):** politics; economics. **Contact(s):** Walter Rybeck (President).

E **Center for Rare Tropical Bird Conservation**
19th & Parkway
Philadelphia, PA 19103  (215)299-1182
**Concern(s):** environment; education; wildlife/endangered species; bioregionalism. Center that preserves the tropical biodiversity and bird conservation through conservation education programs, research and

training of biologists in the New World Tropics.

E **Center For Reflection on the Second Law**
8420 Camellia Dr.
Raleigh-Durham, NC 27613
**Concern(s):** environment; conservation; wilderness. Released a "Declaration" in which the conference-goers who attended recently held conference on "The Land," set forth their deeply ecological beliefs about the land and some political proposals.

S **Center for Religion, Ethics, and Social Policy**
c/o Eco-Justice Project
Anabel Taylor Hall, Cornell University
Ithaca, NY 14853  (607)255-4225
**Affiliation:** Eco-Justice Project. **Concern(s):** spiritual; justice; interfaith.

☺ **Center for Renewable Resources**
1400 16th St. NW, #710
Washington, DC 20036  (202)232-2252
**Affiliation:** Renew America. **Concern(s):** energy; environment; resources; natural resources; conservation; renewables. **Other Resources:** Fund For Renewable Energy & the Environment **Contact(s):** Tina C. Hobson (Executive Director), Denis Hayes (Chairman). (202)232-2252.

F **Center for Research on Women**
See WOMEN'S RESEARCH NETWORK NEWS (periodicals).

E **Center for Resource Economics**
Island Press
1718 Connecticut Ave. NW
Washington, DC 20009  (202)667-6982
**Affiliation:** Island Press. **Concern(s):** environment; agriculture; economics; energy; resource management. **Other Resources:** See ANNUAL ENVIRONMENTAL SOURCEBOOK and Island Press. **Office:** 1718 Connecticut Ave. NW Washington, DC 20009. (202)232-7933. **Other:** Star Route L, Box 38, Covelo, CA 95428-9800 Kenneth A. Cook , Legislative Hotline. (202)667-6982.

✈ **Center for Responsible Tourism**
2 Kensington Rd.
San Anselmo, CA 94960 (415)258-6594
**Concern(s):** education; economics; Third World; alternative consumer; travel; development. Exists to change the attitudes and practices of North American travelers and to persuade them to be part of the struggle for justice in tourism in the Third World. **Other Resources:** List of resources available. See RESPONSIBLE TRAVELING newsletter.

A **Center for Rural Affairs**
Box 405
Walthill, NE 68067  (402)846-5428
**Concern(s):** agriculture; family farms; rural communities. Was formed by rural Nebraskans concerned about the role of public policy in the decline of family farms and rural communities. The Center's purpose is to provoke public thought about social, economic and environmental issues affecting rural America, especially the Midwest and Plains regions. **Other Resources:** See CENTER FOR RURAL AFFAIRS NEWSLETTER and SMALL FARM ADVOCATE newsletter. **Contact(s):** Marty Strange (Director).

A **Center for Rural Studies**
2305 Irving South
Minneapolis, MN 55405 (612)377-5656
**Concern(s):** agriculture; environment; politics; food; land; rural communities. Established for political action and education on food, land and agriculture issues. **Est.:** 1971.

P **Center for Science in the Public Interest**
1875 Connecticut Ave. NW
Washington, DC 20009  (202)332-9110
**Concern(s):** politics; health; education; economics; environment; hazardous/toxic waste; nutrition; consumer rights; preventative; science; government accountability. Provides the public with reliable, up-to-date information about the effects of science/technology on society, chief focus on food/health; developing a national health policy which features health promotion and disease prevention; investigates, monitors and exposes industry and government's failure to implement a sound nutrition/health policy for US. The nation's leading consumer group, best known for work on food labeling, additives, deceptive advertising, organic agriculture and watchdogging. **Other Resources:** NUTRITION ACTION NEWSLETTER, books, posters, computer software, videos, and slide charts. See, also, Americans for Safe Food. **Est.:** 1971. **Fax:** (202)265-4954. **Contact(s):** Richard Layman (Marketing Division).

A **Center For Science Information**
4252 20th St.
San Francisco, CA 94114  (415)553-8772

**Concern(s):** agriculture; environment; biotechnology. Purpose: To educate decision makers and journalists about the environmental applications of biotechnology. **Fax:** (415)566-1048. **Contact(s):** Elizabeth Atcheson (Vice President).

P **Center for Social Research and Education**
2940 16th St.
San Francisco, CA 94103  (415)255-2296
**Concern(s):** politics; peace; education; Democratic Socialism; reform. An educational organization aiming to promote democratic socialization. **Other Resources:** See magazine, SOCIALIST REVIEW. **Est.:** 1970. **E-Network:** PeaceNet. **ID:** 'csre'.

P **Center for Socialist History**
See CENTER FOR SOCIALIST HISTORY INTERBULLETIN.

⚥ **Center for Strategic & International Studies**
Georgetown University
1800 K St. NW
Washington, DC 20006  (202)887-0200
**Concern(s):** peace; Third World; education; foreign policy.

T **Center for Study of Americas**
See CENSA's STRATEGIC REPORT under periodicals.

A **Center for the Analysis of World Food Issues**
261 Roberts Hall
Cornell University
Ithaca, NY 14853  (607)256-3035
**Affiliation:** Cornell University. **Concern(s):** agriculture; Third World; demographics; food production; hunger.

A **Center for the Biology of Natural Systems**
163-03 Horace Harding Boulevard
Flushing, NY 11365  (718)670-4180
**Concern(s):** agriculture; health; nutrition. **Contact(s):** Barry Commoner.

E **Center for the Great Lakes**
See GREAT LAKES DIRECTORY.

⚥ **Center for the Study of Armament & Disarmament**
California State University
5151 University Dr.
Los Angeles, CA 90032
**Concern(s):** peace; disarmament.

$ **Center for the Study of Commercialism**
1501 16th St. NW
Washington, DC 20036-1499  (202)332-9110
**Concern(s):** economics; health; media; environment; analysis; psychology.. National organization that opposes the increasing commercialism of American life. Will document and publicize the infusion of commercial interests into all corners of American life, including education, broadcasting and sports. Will seek to help immunize citizens against the compulsive-impulsive fostered by the purveyors of "more." Will promote a lifestyle of moderate consumption, civic involvement and environmentalism. Will achieve its goals through publicity, conferences and education. **Contact(s):** Michael Jacobson.

$ **Center for the Study of Services**
806 15th St. NW
Washington, DC 20005  (202)347-7823
**Concern(s):** economics; consumer rights. Established to provide consumers with good to reasonably priced, high quality services. By studying and rating service firms and publishing the findings, they hope to improve the local service market and to foster similar organizations in other cities. **Other Resources:** See CHECKBOOK magazine.

J **Center for Theology and Public Policy**
4500 Massachusetts Ave. NW
Washington, DC 20016  (202)885-9100
**Concern(s):** justice; urban; spiritual; politics; peace; Third World; disarmament; hunger; development; interfaith. Research center for theology and public policy in five areas: disarmament, health care, urban issues, minority rights, world political economy; emphasis on North/South relations and world hunger. **Contact(s):** James Nash (Executive Director).

T **Center for Third World Organizing**
3861 Martin Luther King Jr. Way
Oakland, CA 94609  (510)654-9601
**Concern(s):** Third World; justice; labor; minority rights. Research and training organization which trains and places labor and community organizers and researches issues which disproportionately affect people of color in the US. **Other Resources:** See ACTIVIST GUIDE TO RELIGIOUS FUNDERS (directory) and MINORITY TRENDSLETTER (periodical).

## Center for UN Reform Education
139 E. McLellan Ave.
Livingston, NJ 07039

**Concern(s):** peace; education; world order; United Nations. Conducts UN reform seminars, workshops for members and staff of "mainstream" organizations; develops, distributes educational materials on reform and restructure of the UN system. **Contact(s):** Myron Kronisch (Executive Director).

## U ▶ Center for Urban Affairs
Community Studies, Northwestern University
2040 Sheridan Rd.
Evanston, IL 60201

**Concern(s):** urban; education; community. **Contact(s):** John McKnight (Director).

## Center for US-USSR Initiatives
3268 Sacramento St.
San Francisco, CA 94115    (415)346-1875

**Concern(s):** peace; politics; Soviet Union; grassroots organizing; conflict resolution. "Our philosophy, 'When the people lead, the leaders will follow,' undergirds all our programs. We go directly to citizens to assess issues, stimulate ideas and work toward solutions. While we feel that a cooperative relationship with governments is necessary, we believe that ultimately ordinary citizens have the intelligence to address their own problems and the wisdom to implement solutions and that one citizen or citizens can start an avalanche of social awareness." **Other Resources:** See WHEN PEOPLE LEAD...(newsletter). **Contact(s):** Sharon Tennison (President).

## J ▶ Center for Values and Social Policy
University of Colorado
Boulder, CO 80309-0232

**Concern(s):** justice; politics; environment.

## J ▶ Center for Victims Of Torture
722 Fulton St. SE
Minneapolis, MN 55414

**Concern(s):** justice; health; political prisoners; psychology. Provides support, treatment, and therapy for survivors.

## Center for War, Peace, and the News Media
10 Washington Pl.
New York University
New York, NY 10003    (212)998-7960

**Concern(s):** peace; media; disarmament; media watch. Addresses issues related to press coverage of the arms race. Identifies how the press can misinform the public on peace and war issues. **Other Resources:** See DEADLINE (bulletin).

## Center for War/Peace Studies
218 E. 18th St.
New York, NY 10003    (212)475-1077

**Concern(s):** peace; world order. Publisher of major periodicals on peace issues; does in-depth research; develops, advocates specific proposals, e.g., the Binding Triad method of voting in the UN General Assembly. purpose is to transform the United Nations into an organization that can cope with global problems of international conflict, economics, human rights, and the environment, through the development of the Binding Triad proposal for global decision-making in the UN. **Other Resources:** Newsletter, GLOBAL REPORT. **Est.:** 1977. **Fax:** (212)260-6384. **Contact(s):** Richard Hudson (Executive Director).

## F ▶ Center for Women's Global Leadership
Rutgers University
27 Clifton
New Brunswick, NJ 08903    (908)932-8782

**Affiliation:** Douglas College. **Concern(s):** feminism; education; justice; peace; politics; battered women; rape/sexual abuse; militarism; sexism; activism; leadership. In Progress: An annotated directory of groups and bibliography of theoretical and practical works about women, violence and human rights, ranging from sexuality to militarism. Essays, editorials, and thinkpieces will outline ways in which women, from varying cultures, perceive these issues. For the time being, the Center plans to house the Women's Leadership Institute (5/91), facilitate visiting scholars, gather resources for policy makers, activists and educators in these areas. **Other Resources:** GENDER VIOLENCE: A DEVELOPMENT AND HUMAN RIGHTS ISSUE booklet; others to follow.. **Date Publ.:** 7/91. **E-Network:** Reilly@Zodiac - Rutgers. **ID:** Reilly. **Fax:** (908)932-8011. **Contact(s):** Charlotte Bunch (Director), Niamh Reilly (Program Associate).

## F ▶ Center for Women's Policy Studies
2000 P St. NW
Washington, DC 20036    (202)872-1770

**Concern(s):** feminism; politics; analysis; lobbying. An organization that analyzes the policies being passed into legislation on their effects on the female population. **Contact(s):** Carol Foreman (Executive Director).

## Center for World Order Alternatives
475 Riverside Dr., #570
New York, NY 10115    (212)870-3290

**Affiliation:** Global Education Associates. **Concern(s):** peace; Third World; world order. A New York- and Third World-based "global forum...to redefine the concepts of sovereignty and security, formulate world security alternatives and develop transitional strategies for achieving those alternatives." (212)870-3291.

## Center of Concern
3700 13th St. NE
Washington, DC 20017    (202)635-2757

**Concern(s):** peace; justice; Third World; spiritual; world order; foreign policy; hunger; development; intervention; faith. An independent, interdisciplinary team engaged in social analysis, theological reflection, policy advocacy and public education on issues of peace and justice. rooted in a faith commitment and guided by a global vision, current programs focus on international development, peace initiatives, economic alternatives, women in society and church, the cultural crisis, and social theology. Engages in an extensive program of workshops and writing to help North Americans understand the global scene. **Other Resources:** Publishes RESOURCE CATALOG; Newsletter, CENTER FOCUS; and Books, TORCH IN THE NIGHT and CATHOLIC SOCIAL TEACHING: OUR BEST KEPT SECRET (Orbis Books). See, also, Coalition for Peace in the Horn of Africa. **Contact(s):** Peter J. Henriot (Executive Director), James Hug.

## ♥ ▶ The Center of the American Experiment
45 S. 7th St.
Minneapolis, MN 55402

**Concern(s):** family. A new emphasis on 'social capital' is needed to put children and the family in proper perspective in the American dream. This organization is promoting a new concern for the family. Only children who grow up in a loving two-parent family will become sensitive citizens able to lead America out of its deteriorating condition. No government programs alone will change the behavior to one that is required.

## Center on Budget and Policy Priorities
777 N. Capitol St. NE, #710
Washington, DC 20003    (202)408-1080

**Concern(s):** peace; Third World; economics; foreign policy; budget; economic conversion. This center studies and reports on how our government spends money on different aspects of the budget. This includes foreign policy and defense. They also focus on how the "peace dividend" will be spent. **Other Resources:** Defense Budget Project. **Contact(s):** Robert Greenstein.

## Center on Conscience and War
610 Rutherford Ave.
Charlestown, MA 02129    (617)242-9606

**Affiliation:** Pax Christi. **Concern(s):** peace; spiritual; faith. **Contact(s):** Michael W. Hovey (Executive Director).

## ⚿ ▶ Center on Human Policy
200 Huntington Hall
University Station
Syracuse, NY 13244-2340    (315)443-3851

**Affiliation:** Syracuse University. **Concern(s):** health; justice; education; disability rights; disabled. A policy, research, and advocacy organization involved in the national movement to insure the rights of people with disabilities. Since its founding, the Center has been involved in the study and promotion of open, integrated settings for people with disabilities. **Other Resources:** Publishes the following guides, THE NON RESTRICTIVE ENVIRONMENT and UNDERSTANDING THE LAW. Slides, videos and media Packages available. HUMAN POLICY PRESS CATALOG (publishers); PROGRAMS DEMONSTRATING MODEL PRACTICES (directories). Nonprofit. **Est.:** 1971. **E-Network:** SpecialNet. **ID:** 'nyctr.human.policy'. **Fax:** (315)443-4338. **Contact(s):** Steve Taylor (Director), Rachael Zubal (Publications coordinator).

## Center on War and the Child
Box 487
Eureka Springs, AR 72632    (501)253-8900

**Concern(s):** peace; education; conflict resolution; nonviolence; youth. Focuses on militarization of children and children as civil and international conflict victims. Challenges society's institutions and practices glorifying and enhancing war in the mind of the child; informs and educates members and public; mobilizes public response; advocates for children. Conducts research regarding the effects of war on children and processes by which the institution of war is culturally transmitted to children. **Other Resources:** See WARCHILD MONITOR. **Est.:** 1987. **Dues:** $18/yr, $23/organization. **Fax:** (501)253-7149. **Contact(s):** Richard Parker, Ph. D. (Director), Samuel Hilburn (Associate Director).

## T ▶ Central America Health Rights Network
See LINKS under periodicals.

## T ▶ Central America Research Institute
See CENTRAL AMERICAN BULLETIN.

## T ▶ Central America Resource Center
See DIRECTORY OF CENTRAL AMERICA ORGANIZATIONS.

## T ▶ Central America Working Group
712 G St. SE
Washington, DC 20001    (202)546-7010

**Concern(s):** Third World; justice; politics; lobbying; Central America. Hotline: (202)667-0990. **Other:** (202)797-7010.

## T ▶ Central American Historical Institute
See UPDATE under periodicals.

## T ▶ Central American Refugee Center
See PERIODIC REPORTS FROM CARECEN and CARECEN SPEAKS under periodicals.

## T ▶ Central American Refugee Defense Fund
See CENTRAL AMERICAN REFUGEE DEFENSE NEWSLETTER.

## T ▶ Central American Resource Center
Box 2327
Austin, TX 78768

**Concern(s):** Third World; Central America. **Other Resources:** See CENTRAL AMERICAN NEWSPAK under periodicals. Provides a directory.

## Central Committee for Conscientious Objectors
Western Regional Office
Box 42249
San Francisco, CA 94101    (415)474-3002

**Affiliation:** Central Committee for Conscientious Objectors. **Concern(s):** peace; politics; justice; education; anti-draft. Provides military and draft counseling, legal help, and guidance in nonviolence. Produces written and audiovisual materials geared especially for high school and college groups. **Other Resources:** See CCCO NEWS NOTES and OBJECTOR under periodicals. **Office:** 1251 Second St. San Francisco, CA (415)695-7755; 552-6433. **Contact(s):** Robert A. Seeley (Editor). (415)566-0500. **Other:** Eastern Regional Office, 2208 South St., Philadelphia, PA 19146 Lou Ann Merkle (215)545-4626.

## A ▶ Central Rocky Mountain Permaculture
Box 631
Basalt, CO 81621-0631    (303)927-4158

**Concern(s):** agriculture; environment; economics; permaculture; social ecology. Offers design courses that give the student the opportunity to recognize and learn about natural ecosystems and their design and implementation to create balance environments along with the social and economic benefits inherent in a sustainable ecology. This is an eight acres of remote Colorado mountain terrain, one which supports the house, intensive garden, greenhouses, and small animals. Send for a schedule of their regular conferences.

## ✍ ▶ Central States Resource Center
809 S. Fifth
Champaign, IL 61820    (217)344-2371

**Concern(s):** education. A regional conservation organization primarily concerned with water policy, solid, hazardous, radio-active waste issues. Organizational and research assistance is provided to persons and organizations involved in related activities. **Other Resources:** Publishes periodicals, RIVERS; ROADS; and TOXIC WASTE. **Est.:** 1972. **Contact(s):** John W. Thompson (Executive Director), Bruce M. Hannon (President). (217)352-3646.

## ☉ ▶ Centre for Alternative Technology (England)
See GREEN TEACHER under periodicals.

## ? ▶ The Centre For Our Common Future
Palais Wilson
52 Rue des Paquis
Geneva, CH-1201 Switzerland

**Concern(s):** future. **Contact(s):** Warren H. Lindner (Executive Director).

**S ◆ Charles Stewart Mott Foundation**
See FACTS ON GRANTS: A REPORT ON GRANTMAKING OF THE CHARLES STEWART MOTT FOUNDATION and GUIDE TO COMMUNITY EDUCATION RESOURCES (directories).

**E ◆ Chesapeake Bay Foundation**
162 Prince George St.
Annapolis, MD 21401    (301)268-8816
**Concern(s):** environment; education; water; ocean/rivers; Chesapeake Bay; preservation. A membership organization established to promote the environmental welfare and proper management of Chesapeake Bay including its tidal tributaries. **Other Resources:** Publishes CBF newsletter and the BAYWATCHER BULLETIN. Nonprofit. **Contact(s):** William C. Baker (President), Betty Caldwell (Vice President). **Other:** 214 State St., Harrisburg, PA 17113 Thomas P. Sexton III (717)234-5550.

**T ◆ Chicago Religious Task Force on Central America**
See LIST OF DECLARED PUBLIC SANCTUARY under directories.

**♥ ◆ Child Care Action Campaign**
See CHILD CARE ActioNews under periodicals.

**♥ ◆ Child Find of America, Inc.**
See CHILD FIND PHOTO DIRECTORY OF MISSING CHILDREN under directories.

**J ◆ Child Keyppers International**
See MISSING CHILDREN under directories.

**✍ ◆ Children and Community Network**
14556 Little Greenhorn Rd.
Grass Valley, CA 95945
**Concern(s):** education; homeschooling. a nationwide network for home schoolers, unschoolers, alternative schoolers and those looking for child-oriented community, neighbors and friends. **Contact(s):** Lynne Knowles.

**✇ ◆ Children as Peacemakers Foundation**
950 Battery St.
San Francisco, CA 94111
**Concern(s):** peace; education; childhood.

**T ◆ Children International**
Box 419055
Kansas City, MO 64141
**Concern(s):** Third World; justice; hunger; children. **Contact(s):** Joseph Gripkey.

**E ◆ Children of the Green Earth**
Box 31087
Seattle, WA 98103    (206)781-0852
**Concern(s):** environment; education; forests. A worldwide association of individuals committed to re-greening the Earth by helping the youth plant and care for trees and forests. **Other Resources:** Newsletter, TREE SONG. **Est.:** 1980. **Contact(s):** Michael Soule, Dorothy Craig (206)754-7842.

**E ◆ Children's Alliance For Protection of the Environment**
8117 Greenwich Meridian
Austin, TX 78759
**Concern(s):** environment; education. By learning through action, children around the world will initiate local actions and global networking to not only raise the consciousness of adults but also to participate in recycling, reforestation, beach cleanup or other projects which will beautify.

**✇ ◆ Children's Campaign for Nuclear Disarmament**
See CHILDREN'S CAMPAIGN FOR NUCLEAR DISARMAMENT NEWSLETTER.

**✍ ◆ Children's Creative Response To Conflict Program**
Box 271
Nyack, NY 10960    (914)358-4601
**Affiliation:** Fellowship of Reconciliation (CCRC). **Concern(s):** education; peace; conflict resolution; childhood. Established by the New York Quaker Project on Community Conflict. Years of nonviolence training taught the staff that the seeds of violence are ingrained in children at a very early age. The program is specially designed so participants experience ways to examine conflicts and develop solutions. We present four themes: Cooperation, Communication, Affirmation, and Conflict Resolution. Advanced training available on mediation, bias awareness, and problem-solving. **Other Resources:** Publishes handbook, THE FRIENDLY CLASSROOM FOR A SMALL PLANET, and newsletter, SHARING SPACE, as well as many other publications and materials for the classroom. **Est.:** 1972. **Contact(s):** Paula Cuth Conner.

**J ◆ Children's Defense Fund**
122 C St. NW
Washington, DC 20001    (202)628-8787
**Concern(s):** justice; demographics; education; politics; children; hunger; poverty; lobbying; literacy; youth; childhood. Through carefully planned, long-term large-scale programs and policies educates and encourages prevention investment in children before they get sick, drop out of school, or get into trouble. Preference given to disadvantaged. Gathers data, publishes reports, provides information. Specialists in health, education, child development, adolescent pregnancy prevention, youth employment. Monitors government policies, lobbies in Congress and provides assistance to concerned entities. **Other Resources:** See AN ADVOCATE'S GUIDE TO THE MEDIA; newsletter, CDF REPORTS; THE HEALTH OF AMERICA'S CHILDREN (annual book); STATE YOUTH EMPLOYMENT INITIATIVES (directories). Publications guide. **Contact(s):** Marian Wright-Edelman (Executive Director).

**✍ ◆ Children's Environments Research Group**
NYU Graduate School & Univ. Ctr
33 W. 42nd St.
New York, NY 10036    (212)944-2335
**Concern(s):** education; childhood. Provides a link between University scholarship and the development of designs, policies, and programs that both improve the quality of environments for children and enhance children's interactions with them. **Other Resources:** Publishes CHILDREN'S ENVIRONMENTS quarterly.

**♥ ◆ Children's Foundation**
See FAMILY DAY CARE BULLETIN under periodicals.

**T ◆ Children, Inc.**
Box 5381
Richmond, VA 23220    (800)538-5381
**Concern(s):** Third World; justice; hunger; children. **Contact(s):** Mrs. Jeanne Clark Wood.

**T ◆ Chile Committee**
Box 12313
Philadelphia, PA 19119
**Concern(s):** Third World; justice; economics; boycott. Chilean products boycott.

**✍ ◆ Chinook Learning Center**
Box 57
Clinton, WA 98236
**Concern(s):** education; environment; spiritual; transformation. This center attempts to educate people in the need to be one with nature again.

**T ◆ Chol-Chol Foundation**
1307 N. Ode St.
Arlington, VA 22209    (703)525-8844
**Concern(s):** Third World; agriculture; education; development; hunger. A grassroots organization working to end world hunger by teaching peasant farmers the basic notions of modern agriculture, animal husbandry, and forestry. **Other:** A grassroots organization working to end world hunger by teaching peasant farmers the basic notions of modern agriculture, animal husbandry, and forestry.

**T ◆ Christian Children's Fund**
Box 26511, 203 E. Carey
Richmond, VA 23261    (804)644-4654
**Concern(s):** Third World; justice; hunger; faith.

**S ◆ Christian Church (Disciples of Christ)**
Department of Church in Society
Box 1986
Indianapolis, IN 46206    (317)353-1491
**Concern(s):** spiritual; peace; faith. **Other Resources:** See ISSUES AND CONCERNS newsletter. **Contact(s):** Rolland G. Pfile. **Other:** 222 Downey Ave., Indianapolis, IN 46206.

**J ◆ Christian Relief Services**
See Running Strong for American Indian Youth.

**P ◆ The Christic Institute**
8773 Venice Blvd.
Los Angeles, CA  90034 (310)287-1556
**Concern(s):** politics; justice; education; spiritual; grassroots organizing; public policy; interfaith; constitutional rights; intervention; CIA; drugs; criminal system. Organized Democracy Watch: A campaign for lawful and open government, a citizens' action campaign destined to build a national consensus against covert activity. An interfaith, law and public policy center specializing in investigations, legal work, and public education. A team of lawyers and related professionals best known for winning the Silkwood settlement and cracking open the Iran-Contra Scandal. Membership has grown to 40,000. The government has been trying to destroy the Institute. **Other Resources:** See CONTRAGATE ALERT newsletter and CONVERGENCE newsletter.

Produced COVER-UP, an award-winning film on the Iran-Contra scandal. Video and audio tapes available. Causes and Cures, a project designed to stop drugs. **Other Formats:** Internet, user name - 'christic@igc.org'. **E-Network:** PeaceNet. **ID:** 'christic'. **Fax:** (310)287-1559. **Contact(s):** Sara Nelson (Executive Director), Daniel Sheehan (General Counsel).

**✇ ◆ Christophers**
See CHRISTOPHERS NEWS NOTES under periodicals.

**T ◆ Church Committee on Human Rights in Asia**
See ASIAN RIGHTS ADVOCATE (periodicals).

**S ◆ Church of All Worlds**
See GREEN EGG (periodicals).

**✇ ◆ Church of God Peace Fellowship**
Box 2337
Anderson, IN 46018-3337    (317)643-0049
**Concern(s):** peace; spiritual; faith.

**J ◆ Church of the Brethren**
110 Maryland Ave. NE
Washington, DC 20002    (202)546-3202
**Concern(s):** justice; peace; spiritual; politics; faith; disarmament; foreign policy; peace dividend. Provides a witness to government on peace and justice issues, and assists church members in making their citizenship reflective of their faith. **Other Resources:** Brethren Press (publisher); SERRV SLEF-HELP HANDCRAFTS (catalog). **Est.:** 1962. **Contact(s):** Leland Wilson, Mr. Shantilal Bhagat (312)742-5100. **Other:** 1451 Dundee Ave., Elgin, IL 60120.

**F ◆ Church Women United**
475 Riverside Dr.
New York, NY 10115    (212)870-2347
**Concern(s):** feminism; demographics; justice; peace; spiritual; faith; empowerment; poverty. Engages in advocacy by seeking to influence public policy on justice issues, especially those that affect the pauperization of women and children. Promotes women's concerns in the international forum and keeps informed about world issues. Forming coalitions with the ecumenical movement to strengthen their effectiveness in working on justice and peace issues in the US and internationally. Functions through 1,800 local and 52 state units that are committed to the empowerment of women. **Other Resources:** See CHURCHWOMAN, a quarterly magazine with accompanying newsletter, CHURCH WOMEN ACT. **Contact(s):** Doris Anne Younger (General Director), Claire Randall.

**T ◆ Church World Service**
475 Riverside Dr.
New York, NY 10115-0050 (212)870-2257
**Affiliation:** National Council of Churches. **Concern(s):** Third World; justice; global understanding; hunger; development; faith. A shared ministry of 32 Protestant & Orthodox communions worldwide serving as the service arm of the Council. Since its founding, it has responded to requests for relief and assistance in more than 70 countries. In partnership with private, church & ecumenical organizations it works with those directly affected by famine, drought, natural or human-caused disasters - and assists in developing long-term solutions. **Other Resources:** The Film Library, Box 969, Elkhart, IN 46515. At the same address is the Education and Fundraising Program. See, also, CROP Office on Global Education. **Est.:** 1946. (800)456-1310/Global disaster hotline. **Contact(s):** J. Richard Butler (Executive Director).

**✍ ◆ Circle Pines Center**
8650 Mullen Rd.
Delton, MI 49046    (616)623-5555
**Concern(s):** education; peace; environment; conflict resolution; youth; recreation. A cooperative recreation and education center founded to teach co-operation. An accredited children's summer camp located on 284 acres of woods and meadows in Southwest Michigan, adjoining state lands and spring-fed Stewart Lake. Education for cooperative democracy. Open year-round. **Est.:** 1938. **Contact(s):** Mary Olson, Tom Van Hamman (Co-Directors).

**P ◆ Citizen Action**
Box 33304
Washington, DC 20033-3304    (202)857-5153
**Affiliation:** Citizen Action. **Concern(s):** politics; health; environment; energy; grassroots organizing; consumer protection; air pollution. A national citizens organization with statewide affiliates in 24 states and 2 million individual members nationwide. Works to increase citizen participation in economic and political decision-making at all levels; to provide clear and workable policy alternatives on the environment, health care, insurance rates, the family and other areas of crisis, and to win meaningful, concrete improvements in the quality of peoples' lives. **Other Resources:** CITIZEN ACTION NEWS. See Citizen-Labor Energy Coalition; and National Campaign Against Toxic Hazards. **Office:** 1300 Connecticut Ave. NW Washington, DC

20036. **Contact(s):** Heather Booth. (202)857-5168.

### ✈ ◆ Citizen Exchange Council
12 W. 31st St.
New York, NY 10001   (212)643-1985

**Concern(s):** education; peace; travel; East-West. Works for improved US-Soviet understanding by arranging cultural, professional and educational exchanges. **Other Resources:** Publishes a newsletter, COMMUNIQUE. **Est.:** 1962.

### J ◆ Citizen Soldier
175 5th Ave., #1010
New York, NY 10010   (212)777-3470

**Concern(s):** justice; veterans. GI/veteran rights organization that is dedicated to the principle that our military should respect, to the fullest possible extent, the civil and human rights of its members. Accepts no funds from any government agency and is not connected to any business, law, firm, or political party. Believes that service members should participate fully in civilian society and that any attempt to isolate GIs or treat them as "second class" citizens should be opposed. **Other Resources:** Newspaper, ON GUARD. Nonprofit. **Est.:** 1975. **Contact(s):** Tod Ensign.

### ☢ ◆ Citizen-Labor Energy Coalition
1300 Connecticut Ave. NW
Washington, DC 20036 (202)857-5153

**Affiliation:** Citizen Action. **Concern(s):** energy; politics; economics; labor; consumer; policy; monopolies; grassroots organizing; unions. Established to win a national energy policy for the development of jobs and safe, renewable energy sources; to build a grassroots citizens movement that can challenge the power of the energy corporations of unions, senior citizens, public interest groups, and community organizations throughout the US. **Est.:** 1978. **Contact(s):** Edwin Rothchild. **Other:** 600 W. Fullerton Ave., Chicago, IL 60614(312)929-9125.

### H ◆ Citizens Against Chemical Contamination
9496 School St.
Lake, MI 48632-9503   (517)588-9845

**Concern(s):** health; environment; politics; hazardous/toxic waste; anti-nuclear. Citizens group founded in response to an aerial spray program against the gypsy moth in central Michigan. "We are also active against nuclear power, toxic waste disposal, wood fired power plants and serve an educational role by informing the public about chemicals in the environment. National coverage and constituency." **Est.:** 1978.

### $ ◆ Citizens Against Government Waste
1301 Connecticut Ave. NW
Washington, DC 20036   (800)USA-DEBT

**Concern(s):** economics; politics; education; government accountability; reform; taxation; budget. This organization is fighting government mismanagement and waste at all levels. It was established to inform the American public about the findings of the Grace Commission. Nonprofit. **Est.:** 1984. **Contact(s):** George S. Goldenberger (President). (202)467-5300.

### ☷ ◆ Citizens Against Rocky Flats Contamination
1660 Lafayette St.
Denver, CO 80218   (303)832-4508

**Affiliation:** American Friends Service Committee. **Concern(s):** peace; environment; anti-nuclear. Trying to get the Rocky Flats Nuclear Weapons Plant cleaned up and to get it to stop emitting plutonium. A great group - it needs donations, grants, and fundraising help. **Contact(s):** Jan Pilcher.

### E ◆ Citizens Clearinghouse for Hazardous Wastes
Box 6806
Falls Church, VA 22040   (703)237-2249

**Concern(s):** environment; health; hazardous/toxic waste. Started by Lois Gibbs of Love Canal, they offer technical and practical assistance (in areas such as recycling legislation) to those working to change environmental policy at the local level; provides networking information and sponsors leadership training conferences. Helps local groups fight toxics, incinerators, and toxic landfills. This organization wins high marks for bringing low- and middle-income people into environmental activism. **Other Resources:** See EVERYONE'S BACKYARD newsletter, ACTION BULLETIN, ENVIRONMENTAL HEALTH MONTHLY; and under directories MAKING POLLUTERS PAY; SOLID WASTE ACTION GUIDE BOOK; and FIGHT TO WIN ON HAZARDOUS WASTE. Many other resources available. **Contact(s):** Lois Gibbs (Executive Director).

### ☢ ◆ Citizens Energy Project
215 Pennsylvania Ave. SE
Washington, DC 20003-1180   (202)546-9707

**Affiliation:** US Public Interest Research Group. **Concern(s):** energy; economics; anti-nuclear; policy; consumer rights. A research and advocacy organization working on a range of energy policy issues with

an emphasis on solar energy development and opposition to nuclear power. Over the years it has issued over 200 books and shorter reports. Nonprofit. **Est.:** 1973.

### H ◆ Citizens for Alternatives in Nutrition and Health Care
Box B-12
Richlandtown, PA 18955

**Concern(s):** health; nutrition; alternative consumer. **Contact(s):** Catherine Frompovich.

### ☢ ◆ Citizens for Clean Energy
515 Lee Hill Rd.
Boulder, CO 80302   (303)443-8591

**Concern(s):** energy; solar; renewables. Promotes solar and other renewable energy sources in combination with hydrogen as an alternative to fossil fuels. First project: promotional video. **Member:** Co-op America.

### $ ◆ Citizens for Tax Justice
1311 L Street NW
Washington, DC 20005   (202)626-3780

**Concern(s):** economics; politics; labor; justice; consumer rights; taxation. A national coalition of unions, national public interest groups, and state and local citizen organizations involved in tax issues that seeks tax justice for working people, the elderly, and those on fixed incomes; and opposes measures to shift the tax burden onto these groups. **Other Resources:** Provides research, technical assistance, lobbies Congress and works with national and state press to get tax reform for low and middle income people. **Est.:** 1979. **Contact(s):** Kathy Ceronsky.

### E ◆ Citizens For A Better Environment
501 2nd St., #305
San Francisco, CA 94107-1431   (415)243-8373

**Concern(s):** environment; health; urban; hazardous/toxic waste. The mission of CBE is to prevent and reduce toxic hazards to human health and the environment, specifically from pollution of air, water, and land in major urban areas.

### P ◆ Citizens Global Action
Box 19742
Portland, OR 97219   (503)228-6736

**Concern(s):** politics; peace; law; foreign policy. Builds a visible and measurable constituency for legislators already working at both the national and international level to shape global policy in the common public interest. The Registry is a vital service which links citizens and their elected representatives. Legislators will receive regular reports on their growing constituency. Citizens will receive news on the activities of the legislators they support. Works closely with Parliamentarians Global Action. **Office:** 1837 SW Elm Portland, OR 97201. **Contact(s):** Gary Pagenstecher, Anne Pagenstecher.

### T ◆ Citizens Network for Foreign Affairs
1634 I St. NW
Washington, DC 20006   (202)639-8889

**Concern(s):** Third World; foreign policy. **Contact(s):** John H. Costello.

### M ◆ Civil Liberties Committee
See PUBLIC EYE MAGAZINE.

### ☷ ◆ Civilian-Based Defense Association
Box 31616
Omaha, NE 68131   (402)558-2085

**Concern(s):** peace; politics; nonviolence; civil disobedience; grassroots organizing. A grassroots national membership organization encouraging citizens to be interested in nonviolent civilian-based defense—a possible future way for nations to deter and resist aggression. The association keeps members informed of worldwide discussion and developments relating to this defense policy. **Other Resources:** Newsletter, CIVILIAN-BASED DEFENSE; News and Opinion Publications and Resources available. **Office:** 3636 Lafayette **Contact(s):** Melvin G. Beckman, Philip D. Bogdonoff.

### U ◆ CIVITEX (Civic Information and Techniques Exchange)
National Civic League
1445 Market St., #300
Denver, CO 80203   (800)223-6004

**Affiliation:** National Civic League. **Concern(s):** urban; future; media; ideation. "The computer home of hundreds of case studies of successful community programs." Sell profiles of various solutions to civic problems. **Contact(s):** Eric Duran, Chris Gates. (303)571-4343.

### E ◆ Clean Air Council
Juniper & Locust Sts.
Philadelphia, PA 19107   (215)545-1832

**Affiliation:** American Lung Association. **Concern(s):** environment;

energy; air pollution. Citizens' organization devoted to cleaner, healthier air. Formed to solve serious regional problems with air pollution; to serve as an advocate for changes and improvements in the way pollution is controlled; to oversee government and industry efforts to clean the environment.

### E ◆ Clean Ocean Action
Box 505
Sandy Hook, NJ 07732   (201)872-0111

**Concern(s):** environment; ocean/rivers. A broad-based coalition of over 115 conservation, fishing, boating, diving, women's business, service, and community groups. Collectively, we represent hundreds of thousands of concerned citizens with a wide range of experience and expertise on ocean pollution issues. "United, we can command the attention of public officials who have the power to once and for all, stop ocean pollution." The only regional coalition that provides a full time office, research, education and action for clean oceans. **Other Resources:** Publishes ACTION newsletter. **Est.:** 1984. **Contact(s):** Dery Bennett (President), Cindy Zipf (Executive Director). (212)535-7204. **Other:** Box 268, Gracie Station, New York Regional Office, New York, NY 10028

### E ◆ Clean Water Action Project
1320 18th St. NW, #300
Washington, DC 20036 (202)457-1286

**Affiliation:** Clean Water Fund. **Concern(s):** environment; politics; health; water; Chesapeake Bay; rivers; hazardous/toxic waste; lobbying; volunteers; Great Lakes. Through various volunteer programs in 27 locations, this project works for clean and safe water at an affordable price, to curb the use of chemicals, and promote safe solid waste management systems and protection of our natural resources. Utilizes environmental law enforcement, pesticides safety and groundwater protection, solving the garbage crisis as a means to this end. Chesapeake Bay, the Great Lakes, the Atlantic Coast and other endangered natural resources are its primary interests. **Other Resources:** CLEAN WATER ACTION NEWS; see GUIDE TO HOUSEHOLD ALTERNATIVES and HOME SAFE HOME (directories). Nonprofit. **Dues:** $24, $40/organization. **Contact(s):** David Zwick (Executive Director).

### ☷ ◆ Clergy and Laity Concerned
198 Broadway, #305
New York, NY 10038   (212)964-6730

**Concern(s):** peace; justice; Third World; spiritual; militarism; interfaith; indigenous peoples; grassroots organizing; discrimination. An interfaith and multiracial network of 57 chapters and action groups in 31 states, working primarily in and through the religious community for justice and peace. Founded to mobilize the religious community to oppose US intervention in Vietnam. In 1982 CLC created the Third World Caucus composed of people of color within the CALC network who are committed to the goal of making CALC and the larger community more responsive to the concerns of people of color in the US and abroad. **Other Resources:** Publishes CALC REPORT; educational pamphlets, speakers, slide shows, and packets on special issues. See, also, Columbus In Context **Est.:** 1965. **Contact(s):** Lawrence Wofford, George W. Webber.

### E ◆ Climate Institute
324 4th St. NE
Washington, DC 20002 (202)547-0104

**Concern(s):** environment; global warming; networking. Creates an interchange among climate researchers and analysts, policymakers and planners, opinion makers and the public, through conferences and symposia, video and audio tapes, books and papers. A worldwide bridge between scientists, government, and private decision makers on greenhouse warming and stratospheric ozone depletion. **Other Resources:** CLIMATE ALERT newsletter. **Contact(s):** Stephen Leatherman (Chairman), John C. Topping, Jr. (President).

### E ◆ Climate Protection Institute
5833 Balmoral Dr.
Oakland, CA 94619   (510)331-8618

**Concern(s):** environment; global warming. **Contact(s):** Bill Prescott.

### $ ◆ Co-op America
2100 M St. NW, #310
Washington, DC 20063 (202)872-5307

**Concern(s):** economics; environment; alternative consumer; socially-responsible investing; green consumer. Association linking socially responsible businesses and consumers in a national network, a new alternative marketplace; to build more cooperation, justice, accountability and environmental responsibility into the economy. Allows consumers to align their buying habits with their values. Also enables businesses, co-ops and nonprofits which put people ahead of profits to expand their markets. Boasts a membership of 52,000 individuals and 590 organizations. **Other Resources:** See CO-OP AMERICA QUARTERLY and ALTERNATIVE CATALOG. Each Fall the quarterly feature a directory of members, many who were listed in Macrocosm. Publishes SOCIALLY RESPONSIBLE FINANCIAL PLANNING GUIDE. CIRCLE OF POISON KIT available for $1. **Est.:** 1982. **Contact(s):** Paul Freundlich (Executive Director), Alisa Gravitz (Director). (800)424-COOP.

**$ ▸ Co-op Resource Center**
1442 A. Walnut St., #415
Berkeley, CA 94709
**Concern(s):** economics; cooperatives.

**F ▸ Coalition Against Trafficking in Women**
Calder Square, Box 10077
State College, PA 16805
**Concern(s):** feminism; justice; sexism. A United Nations non-governmental organization involved with protecting the rights of women in prostitution. It believes that prostitution is a form of slavery and a violation of human rights and seeks to establish an international instrument capable of curtailing its proliferation. Seeks prosecution for the perpetrators, not the women.

**H ▸ Coalition for A National Health System**
49 Corwin Ave.
Rochester, NY 14609 (716)266-6136
**Concern(s):** health; national health. Association of individuals and organizations for a national health care program which provides high quality, comprehensive personal health care; is universal in coverage, locally controlled, rationally organized, equitably finances, with no out-of- pocket charges, is sensitive to the particular health needs of all, and is efficient in containing cost. **Other Resources:** Reprint/research service. Bibliography of related articles on national health care and related issues (enclosed). **Est.:** 1977. **Dues:** $5-50; National groups $500-1000; State $100-500. **Contact(s):** Anthony DiMarco (Coordinator).

**E ▸ Coalition for Clean Air**
122 Lincoln Blvd., #201
Venice, CA 90291-2826 (310)450-3190
**Concern(s):** environment; global warming. Newsletters, flyers and information on air quality control issues.

**$ ▸ Coalition for Environmentally Responsible Economics**
711 Atlantic Ave.
Boston, MA 02111 (617)451-3252
**Affiliation:** Social Investment Forum. **Concern(s):** economics; environment; socially-responsible investing. A project of the Social Investment Forum. Responsible for writing up the Valdez Principles. **Contact(s):** Gordon Davidson (Executive Director), Joan Bavaria/ Denis Hayes (Co-chairs).

**$ ▸ Coalition for Fair Trade and Social Justice**
518 17th St. #200
Oakland, CA 94612 (510)763-6584
**Concern(s):** economics; labor; Third World; trade. To link Northern California and North America, to educate each other about the past and pending effects of free trade initiatives, and develop strategies and actions to address the problems that arise from initiatives such as the North American Free Trade Agreement and General Agreement on Trades and Tariffs. Promotes the creation of equitable and ecological alternatives to current economic policies. Consists of labor, Latin-concerned, ecological and educational organizations and individuals.

**P ▸ Coalition for Free and Open Elections**
Box 355
Old Chelsea Station, NY 10011
**Concern(s):** politics; voting. See BALLOT ACCESS NEWS (periodicals).

**✍ ▸ The Coalition for National Service**
5140 Sherier Place, NW
Washington, DC 20016 (202)363-6850
**Concern(s):** education; urban; economics; volunteers.

**☮ ▸ Coalition for Nuclear Disarmament**
40 Witherspoon
Princeton, NJ 08542
**Concern(s):** peace; anti-nuclear; disarmament. **Contact(s):** John Field (Director).

**T ▸ The Coalition for Peace in the Horn of Africa**
3700 13th St. NE
Washington, DC 20017 (202)635-2757
**Affiliation:** Center of Concern. **Concern(s):** Third World; peace; justice; foreign policy. An association of more than 60 US NGO's which have pledged to work on US policy issues in Sudan, Somalia, and Ethiopia. The formation of the Coalition is a reflection of the growing concern on the part of many that the root cause of the crisis facing the peoples of the Horn must begin to be addressed by US policy, and that band-aids are no longer sufficient to salve the conscience of the US public. **Contact(s):** John Pendergast (Co-Chair).

**E ▸ Coalition for Recyclable Waste**
See TIPS ON HOW TO REDUCE YOUR WASTE (directories).

**☢ ▸ Coalition For Safe Power**
408 SW 2nd St., #406
Portland, OR 97204 (503)295-0490
**Concern(s):** energy; environment; anti-nuclear.

**D ▸ Coalition for the Homeless**
500 8th Ave.
New York, NY 10018 (212)695-8700
**Concern(s):** demographics; justice; politics; homelessness; poverty; hunger. An advocacy and direct service organization dedicated to the principles that decent shelter, sufficient food, and affordable housing are fundamental rights in a civilized society. The coalition has been working through litigation, public education, and direct services to see that goals are met to eliminate the irrationalities, inefficiencies and contradictions of a system which, rather than allowing people to be self-sufficiency, perpetuate the cycle of dependency. **Other Resources:** Operates Legislative Alert System, a telephone tree and letter chain that places swift, effective pressure on representatives. Their Direct Action Network is a group that organizes demonstrations, rallies and other direct actions. **Est.:** 1981. **Contact(s):** Kristen Morse.

**E ▸ Coalition of Coastal Communities**
1 State St.
Providence, RI 02920 (401)272-3434
**Concern(s):** environment; ocean/rivers. A coalition of coastal communities that helps protect the ocean and river environments of their communities.

**J ▸ Coalition of Hispanic Health & Human Services Organization**
1501 16th St. NW
Washington, DC 20036 (202)387-5000
**Concern(s):** justice; health; minority rights; public health; welfare rights.

**F ▸ Coalition to Boycott Domino's Pizza**
c/o LASC
4120 Michigan Union
Ann Arbor, MI 48109
**Concern(s):** feminism; justice; labor; environment; Third World; economics; boycott; corporate responsibility; socially-responsible investing; sexism; discrimination; equal rights; unions. BOYCOTT DOMINO'S PIZZA — The Michigan Coalition suggests that owner Tom Managhan's practices span the gamut of possible violations, from women's rights, to anti-union and discriminatory employee practices, to socially irresponsible and environmentally unsound development, to support of right-wing activities at home and abroad. Products: Domino's Pizza, Domino Farms. **Other Resources:** To protest, write to: Tom Monaghan, CEO, 30 Frank Lloyd Wright, Ann Arbor, MI 48105. **Other:** NOW, 2307 Mershon, Saginaw, MI 48602.

**T ▸ Coalition to Stop US Intervention in the Mid-East**
36 E. 12th St.
New York, NY 10003 (212)254-2295
**Concern(s):** Third World; peace; Mid-East; intervention; foreign policy; international law; militarism; nonviolence. This coalition attempts to bring about a stop to all US intervention in the Middle East. This organization did intensive research into the US-Iraq War. **Other Resources:** See, also, International War Crimes Tribunal. **E-Network:** PeaceNet. **ID:** 'afreeman'. **Contact(s):** Ramsey Clark. **Other:** 2489 Mission St. #28, San Francisco, CA 94110(415)821-6545.

**E ▸ Coast Alliance**
235 Pennsylvania Ave. SE
Washington, DC 20003-1107 (202)546-9554
**Concern(s):** environment; ocean/rivers. A corporation formed by a number of groups and individuals concerned about the effects on the US coasts of unprecedented development pressure. Was founded for the purpose of increasing public awareness of the coast's immense value, bringing new, important scientific facts about coastal ecology to public attention, encouraging groups nationwide to work for protection of valuable coastal resources and urging federal, state, and local governments to protect coastal ecosystems. **Other Resources:** Publishes — AND TWO IF BY SEA, FIGHTING THE ATTACK ON AMERICA'S COASTS — a citizen's guide. Nonprofit. **Est.:** 1979. **Contact(s):** Beth Millemann (Director).

**E ▸ The Coastal Society**
Box 2081
Gloucester, MA 01930-2081 (508)281-9209
**Affiliation:** Renewable Natural Resources Foundation. **Concern(s):** environment; ocean/rivers. An international multi-disciplinary organization dedicated to promoting the understanding and wise use of coastal environments including the shoreline, coastal waters, and adjacent land areas. The society's coastal orientation is unique and inspires membership from many professions and nations. **Other Resources:** Publishes a quarterly, BULLETIN, with information on coastal management, current policy developments, research, and education. Also offers several publications. List available. Nonprofit. **Est.:** 1975. **Dues:** $25/yr. includes BULLETIN. **Circ.:** 500. **Fax:** (508)281-9371. (508)281-9333. **Contact(s):** Thomas E. Bigford (Executive Director). **Other:** Renewable Natural Resources Foundation, 5410 Grosvenor Lane, Bethesda, MD 20814.

**T ▸ Codel, Inc.**
475 Riverside Dr.
New York, NY 10115 (212)870-3000
**Concern(s):** Third World; environment; agriculture; spiritual; development; hunger; faith; farm policy. An ecumenical Christian consortium that supports community based projects in developing countries. They provide technical and financial support for the developing countries through an environmental and development program. They stress the relationship between the environment and development in third world countries. They try to identify printed material that is for the common man to use in the field not the research lab. **Other Resources:** Publishes a free bimonthly newsletter, CODEL NEWS. Provides Educational and Training programs, overseas workshops and workshop reports. **Fax:** (212)870-3345. **Contact(s):** Rev. Nate Vanderwerf, Mary Ann Smith (Environmental Director).

**T ▸ Coke Divestment Campaign**
92 Piedmont Ave., NE
Atlanta, GA 30303 (404)586-0460
**Concern(s):** Third World; justice; environment; economics; boycott; corporate responsibility; socially-responsible investing; animal rights; divestment; South Africa. BOYCOTT COCA-COLA — They have not divested from South Africa and they also sponsored a rodeo. Products: Belmont Springs distilled water, Bright and Early drinks, Butter-Nut coffee, Coca-Cola (classic, diet, cherry, etc.), Fanta, Five-Alive, Fresca, Hi-C soft drinks, Maryland Club coffee, MAX energy drinks, Mello Yello, Minute Maid juices, Mr. PIBB, Nemasket Spring water, Ramblin' Root Beer, Saniba, Sprite, TAB, Columbia Pictures, Embassy Television, RCA/Columbia Pictures Home Video... **Other Resources:** To protest, write to: Carl Ware, V.P. of Urban Affairs, PO Drawer 1734, Atlanta, GA 30301. Write CDC for more information. **Contact(s):** Malkia M'Buzi, Tandi Gabashe. **Other:** International Society for Animal Rights, Inc., 421 South State St., Clarks Summit, PA 18411.

**E ▸ Colorado Earth First!**
Box 1166
Boulder, CO 80303
**Concern(s):** environment; economics; boycott; corporate responsibility; socially-responsible investing; forests. BOYCOTT AMERICAN EXPRESS CO. — Partner in venture to build ski resort in San Juan Mountains, Colorado. Products: credit cards and services. **Other Resources:** To protest write to: James D. Robinson, Chairman, AMEX, World Finance Center, New York, NY 10258 (800) 528-4800. **Other:** Earth First! Grizzley Task Force, Box 6151, Bozeman, MO 59715 (406)587-3356.

**E ▸ Colorado Environmental Coalition**
777 Grant St., #606
Denver, CO 80203-3518(303)837-8701
**Concern(s):** environment; air pollution; land; water; wilderness' natural resources; volunteers. Citizens' coordinating council, employing paid staff and volunteers, engaged in education, study, and legislative action in such areas as pollution, wilderness, land use planning, energy, water resources, mining, timber cutting and urban problems. **Other Resources:** Publishes the COLORADO ENVIRONMENTAL REPORT Newsletter. **Est.:** 1965. **Contact(s):** Dorothy Cohen (Office Manager), Donald Thompson (President). (303)320-4895.

**✍ ▸ Columbus in Context**
c/o Clergy and Laity Concerned
198 Broadway, #305
New York, NY 10038 (212)964-6730
**Affiliation:** Clergy and Laity Concerned. **Concern(s):** education; justice; spiritual; politics; militarism; interfaith; indigenous peoples; grassroots organizing; discrimination. A clearinghouse for alternative, progressive approaches to marking the Quincentenary of the 1492 voyage of Columbus. Rather than celebrating his discovery, educators need to recognize his violence to Native Americans and the role of the Columbus myth in supporting later generations of racism and colonialism. **Est.:** 1965. **Contact(s):** Lawrence Wofford, George W. Webber.

**P ▸ Commission for the Advancement of Public Interest Organizations**
1875 Connecticut Ave. NW
Washington, DC 20009 (202)462-0505
**Concern(s):** politics; economics; health; analysis; research; grassroots organizing; lobbying. Established to investigate ways of expanding and promoting the public interest movement, its organizations, and its constituency. **Other Resources:** See PERIODICALS OF PUBLIC INTEREST ORGANIZATIONS: A CITIZEN'S GUIDE (directories). **Est.:** 1974.

**♿ ▸ Commission on Accreditation of Rehabilitation Facilities**
See DIRECTORY OF ORGANIZATIONS SERVING PEOPLE WITH DISABILITIES.

**J ▸ Commission on Social Action of Reform Judaism**
Union of American Hebrew Congregations
838 5th Ave.
New York, NY 10021 (212)249-0100
**Affiliation:** Union of American Hebrew Congregations. **Concern(s):** justice; Third World; feminism; spiritual; faith; reform; civil liberties. Synagogue social action is the process of translating the principles of Judaism into action in our communities, the nation, and the world. It cooperates with other groups in American life, Jewish and non-Jewish, in seeking to implement the positions on social issues taken by the Union at its biennial convention. Issues: race relations, civil liberties, Soviet Jewry, separation of church/State, Israel, poverty, abortion reform, women's rights, Jews in Arab lands, etc. **Contact(s):** Albert Vorspan (Director), Rabbi David Saperstein 2027 Massachusetts Ave NW, Washington, DC 20036.

**H ▸ Commission on Voluntary Service and Action**
Box 117
New York, NY 10009 (212)974-2405
**Concern(s):** health; justice; environment; volunteers; occupational safety; victims' rights; conservation. The coordinating and consultive body representing non-government voluntary service in North America. 200 member organizations address concerns including workers' rights, environment, health, justice. **Other Resources:** A directory, INVEST YOURSELF ($6 and $1.50 for postage- US). A quarterly journal, VOLUNTARY SERVICE IN ACTION ($4/each, $14/4 issues). Volunteer and member inquiries welcome. **Est.:** 1946. **Other Formats:** 3.5' disc, word. **Labels:** 200. **Fax:** (212)974-2849. **Contact(s):** Susan Angus (Editorial Coordinator), Jim Rosenberg (Circulation). (212)768-8624.

**☮ ▸ Committee Against Registration and the Draft**
731 State St.
Madison, WI 53703 (608)257-7562
**Concern(s):** peace; anti-draft. Coalition of local and national groups opposing registration and the draft from an anti-racist, anti-interventionist perspective. Also works on related military personnel issues (GI & veterans rights). **Other Resources:** Publishes periodicalS, ANTI-DRAFT and CARD NEWS SERVICE. **Est.:** 1979. **Contact(s):** Gilliam Kerley (Executive Director), Kim Amelor (Associate Director).

**P ▸ Committee for National Security**
1601 Connecticut Ave. NW, #3011
Washington, DC 20009 (202)745-2450
**Affiliation:** Council on Economic Priorities. **Concern(s):** politics; environment; foreign policy; national security; foreign policy. The Committee is made up of many former government officials and other affluent people. It directs and offers ideas to the director, who publishes briefing papers, sets up lecture tours, and other public information ideas along with the CNS staff. **Other Resources:** "We publish briefing papers on subjects relevant to national security at the time (like: chemical weapons, ballistic missiles, US Defense Budget, etc.)." **Est.:** 1980. **Fax:** (201)381-6298. **Contact(s):** Jonathan Brown (Research Assistant), John Parachini (Director). **Other:** Council on Economic Priorities, 30 Irving Plaza, New York, NY 10003

**✪ ▸ Committee for Nuclear Responsibility**
Box 11207
San Francisco, CA 94101
**Concern(s):** energy; peace; environment; health; anti-nuclear; hazardous/toxic waste; test ban. **Contact(s):** Dr. John W. Gofman. **Other:** Box 546, Yachats, OR 97498.

**P ▸ Committee for Responsive Politics**
See Project Vote Smart.

**A ▸ Committee for Sustainable Agriculture**
Box 1300
Colfax, CA 95713 (916)346-2777
**Concern(s):** agriculture; environment; organic; sustainability.

**T ▸ Committee in Solidarity with Latin American Nonviolent Movements**
See periodical SOLIDARITY/SOLIDARIDAD.

**T ▸ Committee In Solidarity with the People of El Salvador (CISPES)**
Box 12056
Washington, DC 20005 (202)265-0890
**Concern(s):** Third World; justice; Central America; intervention; indigenous people. Committee focuses on the problems with the people of El Salvador. Focuses on bringing a mutual solidarity and understanding between the two peoples of the US and El Salvador. **Other Resources:** Alert!: Focus on Central America. **Office:** 1314 14th St., NW Washington, DC **Contact(s):** Angela Sanbranno.

**T ▸ Committee In Solidarity With The People Of Guatemala**
494 Broadway
New York, NY 10012 (212)219-2704
**Concern(s):** Third World; justice; Central America; indigenous peoples; intervention; development. Committee focuses on the problems caused by interventions in the internal affairs of this beautiful Central American country. Attempts to bring about a mutual solidarity and understanding between the peoples of the US and Guatemala. **Other Resources:** Publishes UPDATE ON GUATEMALA, a bimonthly newsletter. **Other:** 225 Lafayette St., Room 212, New York, NY 10012 (212)219-2704.

**☮ ▸ Committee Oppose to Militarism and the Draft**
See periodicals for DRAFT NOTICES.

**P ▸ Common Agenda Coalition**
870 Market St., #1228
San Francisco, CA 94102 (415)788-7961
**Affiliation:** Tides Foundation. **Concern(s):** politics; economics; justice; environment; economic conversion; social justice; lobbying; grassroots organizing. "Reordering federal priorities from military to human and environmental needs." Coordinates the activities of a wide spectrum of groups working towards this goal. **Est.:** 1990. **Contact(s):** Steve Gibson, Elizabeth Stevenson.

**P ▸ Common Cause**
2030 M St. NW
Washington, DC 20036 (202)833-1200
**Concern(s):** politics; economics; justice; energy; government accountability; lobbying; reform; municipal; foreign policy; budget; constitutional rights; conservation; corporate responsibility. A leading force in the battle for honest and accountable government at the national, state, and local level. Does not accept government grants or money from foundations, labor unions, or corporations for its financial support. Its purpose was to join individuals from across the nation in an effort to lobby officials on national issues of mutual concern. Also reports special interest campaign contributions in congressional races, standards of ethics, military spending, lobby disclosure, etc. **Other Resources:** Publishes COMMON CAUSE MAGAZINE. Nonprofit. **Est.:** 1970. **Circ.:** 270M. **Contact(s):** Fred Wertheimer (President).

**$ ▸ Common Ground USA**
2000 Century Plaza, #238
Columbia, MD 21044 (301)740-1177
**Concern(s):** economics; politics; justice; urban; demographics; reform; policy; housing; monopolies; planning; sustainability. A membership organization dedicated to influencing public policy. "We advocate solving problems by attacking their causes, not superficial symptoms. Issues of concern include property tax reform, cutting government subsidies and monopolies, affordable housing, and urban sprawl." **Other Resources:** GROUNDSWELL newsletter. **Est.:** 1985. **Contact(s):** Hanno Beck (Executive Director), Steven Cord (Chief Operating Officer).

**☮ ▸ Common Heritage Institute**
620 Yale Ave.
Swathmore, PA 19081
**Affiliation:** Villanova University. **Concern(s):** peace; energy; world order; resource management. Formerly, World Order Research Institute; major research on Law of the Sea issues, implications for management and use of other resources, etc. See also World Association for World Federation. **Contact(s):** John Logue (Director).

**✍ ▸ Communal Studies Association**
c/o Center for Communal Studies
8600 University Blvd.
Evansville, IN 47712 (812)464-1727
**Affiliation:** Center for Communal Studies. **Concern(s):** education; economics; research; intentional communities. Encourages the preservation of historic communal sites, and the study of past and present communal societies with quarterly newsletters, annual journals and conferences. **Est.:** 1975. **Dues:** $20/yr. **Member:** Fellowship for Intentional Community.

**F ▸ Communication Creativity**
See Career Women's Network.

**T ▸ Communication for Development**
265 Rock Run Rd.
Falmouth, VA 22405 (703)752-2710
**Concern(s):** Third World; feminism; development. **Contact(s):** Russell B. Sunshine.

**M ▸ Communication Task Group**
537 Jones St.
San Francisco, CA 94102
**Concern(s):** media; multilogues. **Contact(s):** Ann Weiser.

**L ▸ Communications Workers of America**
501 3rd St. NW
Washington, DC 20001 (202)434-1100
**Affiliation:** AFL-CIO. **Concern(s):** labor; media; unions. **Contact(s):** Morton Bahr (President).

**P ▸ Communist Party USA**
See POLITICAL AFFAIRS and DYNAMICS under periodicals.

**✍ ▸ Community Catalyst Project**
1531 Fulton St.
San Francisco, CA 94117
**Concern(s):** education; economics; research; cooperatives; intentional communities. Provides research, networking, and technical support for intentional communities and co-ops. It's travelling networker has visited nearly 300 communities over the past 3 years. Research about the history, philosophy, and realities of shared living and shared work is reviewed with each group visited (and with the public) though slide shows and informal discussions. **Other Resources:** Periodic newsletter. **Est.:** 1988. **Dues:** Donations. **Member:** Fellowship for Intentional Community.

**$ ▸ Community Economic and Ecological Development Institute (CEED)**
Box 9844
Santa Fe, NM 87504 (505)986-1401
**Concern(s):** economics; environment; education; health; agriculture; intentional communities; social ecology; bioregionalism; land trusts; holism; sustainability. Ecological villages are having a new burst of growth and need a clearinghouse to keep each informed of the other. Residential learning communities which are ecologically sound, economically successful and socially desirable can become models which link lifestyles of industrial and third world countries. CEED is establishing such a community in New Mexico and already links with similar communities in Tunisia, Scotland, Spain and England. **Other Resources:** See SEEDLING newsletter and NEW WEALTH journal. Explores issues for a sustainable future such as: ecological living options; cohousing & community building; land trusts and affordable housing; sustainable agriculture; whole person education, etc. **Office:** 1807 2nd Stee 87501. **Contact(s):** David Mulligan.

**$ ▸ Community Educational Service Council, Inc. (CESCI)**
c/o Shannon Farm
Route 2, Box 343
Afton, VA 22930
**Concern(s):** economics; education; community self-reliance; intentional communities. Provides short-term, low-interest loans to businesses owned by intentional communities from coast to coast. Those interested in investment opportunities or loan applications are encouraged to contact CESCI. **Est.:** 1954.

**D ▸ Community for Creative Nonviolence**
425 2nd St. NW
Washington, DC 20001 (202)393-4409
**Concern(s):** demographics; urban; politics; poverty; homelessness; grassroots organizing; hunger; housing. Provides shelter for the homeless and abused. **Contact(s):** Mitch Snyder (deceased) (Founder;).

**D ▸ Community Housing Improvement Program**
429 Normal Ave.
Chico, CA 95928
**Concern(s):** demographics; urban; housing; planning.

**U ▸ The Community Information Exchange**
1029 Vermont Ave. NW, #717
Washington, DC 20005 (202)628-2981
**Concern(s):** urban; agriculture; economics; demographics; networking; development; community investment; trade; rural communities; housing. An information service for people working on housing and investing in urban neighborhoods and rural communities. **Other Resources:** A database of 300 community-based cases. Nonprofit. **Member:** Co-op America.

**$ ▸ Community Information Resource Center**
Box 42663
Tucson, AZ 85733-2663 (602)326-7397
**Affiliation:** NEST, Inc.. **Concern(s):** economics; community self-reliance. The CIRC is an information utility, communications hub, consulting resource and organizing service agency. Its mission is to facilitate the emergence of structures which empower the community through information, collection, sharing, and utilization. **Other Resources:** See GREEN REVOLUTION (periodicals). **Est.:** 1990. **E-Network:** Econet. **ID:** 'sol'. **Contact(s):** Thomas H. Greco, Jr. (Director). **Other:** NEST, Inc., Box 41144, Tucson, AZ 85717.

**H ▸ Community Nutrition Institute**
2001 S St. NW, #530
Washington, DC 20009 (202)462-4700
**Concern(s):** health; economics; consumer rights; nutrition. Dedicated to providing a safe, nutritious, affordable and accessible food supply for all Americans. **Est.:** 1970. **Contact(s):** Rodney Leonard. Rodney Leonard.

**$ ▸ Community Regeneration**
Rodale Institute
222 Main St.
Emmaus, PA 18049 (215)967-5171
**Affiliation:** Rodale Institute. **Concern(s):** economics; urban; future; community investment; community self-reliance; planning; ideation. A network sponsored by the Institute which provides information and new ideas to help people enhance their capacities, build healthy communities, strengthen their local economies and improve their living environment." **Dues:** $25/yr. **Subscription:** Membership. **Contact(s):** Jeff Bercuvitz (Executive Editor).

**$ ▸ Community Service Inc.**
Box 243
Yellow Springs, OH 45387
**Concern(s):** economics; community self-reliance; intentional communities. Dedicated to promoting the small community (intentional and otherwise) as a basic institution for economic, social, and spiritual development. **Other Resources:** Books, workshops, consultation. Free booklist. Publishes bimonthly newsletter, holds annual conference, and maintains a catalog of mail-order literature. Nonprofit. **Est.:** 1940. **Dues:** $20/yr. **Member:** Co-op America.

**✪ ▸ Community Transportation Association of America**
See COMMUNITY TRANSPORTATION REPORTER (periodicals).

**E ▸ Commuter Transportation Services, Inc.**
3550 Wilshire Blvd., #300
Los Angeles, CA 91352 (213)365-6828
**Concern(s):** environment; energy; urban; trade; recycling; transportation. Formed more than 16 years ago in response to the gas crisis, the nation's largest private nonprofit corporation dedicated to helping commuters - on their own or as employees - find alternatives to driving alone each day. It offers most services at no charge. Nonprofit. **Est.:** 1974. (213)380-RIDE.

**E ▸ Companies Which Cut Rainforests Boycott**
Institute for Gaean Economics
64 Main St.
Montpelier, VT 05602 (802)223-7943
**Affiliation:** Institute for Gaean Economics. **Concern(s):** environment; economics; boycott; green consumer; forests. BOYCOTT the following companies: SCOTT PAPER CO., 277 Pleasant St., #104, Dartmouth, Nova Scotia B27 4BJ, Canada; KIMBERLY CLARK CORP., P.O. Box 61900, DFW Airport Station, Dallas, TX 75261; COCA-COLA CO., Drawer 1734, Atlanta, GA 30301; GEORGIA-PACIFIC CORP. 133 Peachtree St., NE, Atlanta, GA 30303; RJR NABISCO, Inc., 300 Galleria Parkway, Atlanta, GA 30339; and CASTLE & COOKE, INC., 10900 Wilshire Boulevard, Los Angeles, CA 90024. **Other Resources:** Call or write for more details. **Contact(s):** Susan Meeker-Lowery.

**▸ Compassion For Animals Foundation**
See ANIMAL'S VOICE magazine.

**$ ▸ Comprehensive Security Project**
5115 S. A1A Highway
Melbourne Beach, FL 32951 (407)952-0600
**Affiliation:** Institute for Space and Security Studies. **Concern(s):** economics; peace; education; budget; peace dividend. Reshape national priorities and federal budget to provide military, economic, environmental, health-care, and legal/political security to American people. Investigate proposals for converting weapons industry to provide non-polluting energy. Would cut defense budget 75%, double teacher pay, establish National Health system, revitalize cities, strengthen UN & World Court. **Est.:** 1982. **Contact(s):** Dr. Robert M. Bowman (President).

**✌ ▸ Computer Professionals for Social Responsibility**
Box 717
Palo Alto, CA 94302-0717
**Concern(s):** peace; education; energy; labor; science. A national organization working on issues concerning technology, peace, privacy, workplace, and education. **Other Resources:** CPSR NEWSLETTER.

**D ▸ Concern America**
Box 1790
Santa Ana, CA 92702 (714)953-8575
**Concern(s):** demographics; urban; hunger; homelessness.

**E ▸ Concern, Inc**
1794 Columbia Rd. NW
Washington, DC 20009 (202)328-8160
**Concern(s):** environment; agriculture; health; hazardous/toxic waste; natural resources; water; farmland; pesticides. A tax-exempt organization that provides environmental information and guidelines for community action. **Other Resources:** Publishes, WASTE: CHOICES FOR COMMUNITIES; FARMLAND: A COMMUNITY ACTION GUIDE; DRINKING WATER: A COMMUNITY ACTION GUIDE; GROUNDWATER: A COMMUNITY ACTION GUIDE; PESTICIDES: A COMMUNITY ACTION GUIDE; GLOBAL WARMING & ENERGY CHOICES; HOUSEHOLD WASTE. Nonprofit.

**E ▸ Concerned Citizens for Nuclear Safety**
712 Calle Grillo
Santa Fe, NM 87501 (505)983-1111
**Concern(s):** environment; peace; anti-nuclear. Our vision is rejoin the sacred hoop. The circle that unites us all, the planet Earth. Our focus is solving the problem of radioactive waste. The governments of the world insist that nuclear technology is safe but they never speak publicly on the problem of nuclear waste. It is this angle we are pursuing in hopes of closing down nuclear bomb and power plants. We are also working with the Pueblo Indians of New Mexico in hopes of bringing together a united voice. **Contact(s):** Wayne Wilcox (Outreach Coordinator). (505)986-1973.

**✍ ▸ Concerned Educators Allied for a Safe Environment**
17 Gerry St.
Cambridge, MA 02138 (617)864-0999
**Concern(s):** education; environment; peace.

**✪ ▸ Concerned Neighbors in Action**
Box 3847
Riverside, CA 92509 (714)681-9913
**Concern(s):** energy; politics; health; hazardous/toxic waste: grassroots organizing. These concerned neighbors are fighting to get the EPA to stop procrastinating and do something about a hazardous waste dump known as the Stringfellow Acid Pits. This small but effective organization is a great example of community organization; through their efforts they have gotten bottled water trucked in, state funding for a new clean, safe water supply, and new technologies for cleanup of waste introduced. **Other Resources:** Publishes a quarterly newsletter, STRINGFELLOW NEWS. Nonprofit. **Est.:** 1979.

**J ▸ Confederation of American Indians**
See INDIAN RESERVATIONS: A STATE AND FEDERAL HANDBOOK.

**$ ▸ Conference of Consumer Organizations**
Box 158
Newton Center, MA 02159 (617)552-3674
**Concern(s):** economics; health; consumer protection; alternative consumer; boycott. **Contact(s):** Fr. Robert McEwen.

**P ▸ Conference on Alternative State and Local Policies**
Center for Policy Alternatives
1875 Connecticut Ave. NW
Washington, DC 20009 (202)387-6030
**Affiliation:** Center for Policy Alternatives. **Concern(s):** politics; municipal; public policy. Established to provide a major meeting place and forum for ideas of progressive elected officials, community organizers, political activists, and technically trained experts interested in alternative policies and programs at the state and local levels. Holds an annual national meeting and frequent regional, statewide and issue conferences focussing on their complex problems. Economic strategies aimed at issues of energy, tax referendum, agriculture, and fact closings. **Other Resources:** Newsletter, WAYS AND MEANS. **Est.:** 1975. **Contact(s):** Linda Tarr-Whelan (Executive Director).

**✌ ▸ Conflict Resolution Center International, Inc.**
7514 Kensington St.
Pittsburgh, PA 15221 (412)371-1000
**Concern(s):** peace; justice; conflict resolution; racism; discrimination; diversity. CRCI seeks to be a clearinghouse or resource center assisting everyday people who are working on resolving conflict in their own communities. Specifically, they are concerned with neighborhood disputes and racial, ethnic and religious conflict. **Other Resources:** Publishes a journal, CONFLICT RESOLUTION NOTES. Extensive library on conflict resolution, annotated index for sale. Book: THE MOVE CRISIS IN PHILADELPHIA: EXTREMIST GROUPS AND CONFLICT RESOLUTION ($9.95 + $1.50 postage). **Dues:** $20/yr. **Subscription:** Membership. **E-Network:** ConflictNet (PeaceNet). **ID:** 'crcii'. **Fax:** (412)371-1000. **Contact(s):** Paul Wahrhaftig.

**J ▸ Congress of National Black Churches**
1225 I St. NW
Washington, DC 20005 (202)371-1091
**Concern(s):** justice; spiritual; politics; economics; discrimination; faith; minority rights. An organization dealing with the role of blacks in todays social, economic, and political environment. **Contact(s):** Dr. Elisha Byrd.

**P ▸ Congress Watch**
215 Pennsylvania Ave. SE
Washington, DC 20003-0757 (202)546-4996
**Affiliation:** Public Citizen. **Concern(s):** politics; economics; lobbying; consumer rights. The legislative advocacy arm of Public Citizen, a consumer organization founded by Ralph Nader. Attorneys, organizers, and staffers go before the US Congress on behalf of the average consumer. **Other Resources:** Newsletter, CONGRESS WATCHER. **Est.:** 1971. **Contact(s):** Michael Waldman.

**U ▸ Congressional Black Caucus Foundation**
1004 Pennsylvania Ave. SE
H2-344 House Annex II
Washington, DC 20515 (202)675-6730
**Concern(s):** urban; agriculture; justice; diversity; racism; discrimination; law; lobbying; welfare rights; rural communities; ethnic concerns; minority rights. Seeks to preserve our national commitment to fair treatment for urban and rural America, the elderly, students, small businessmen and women, middle and low income wage earners and the economically disadvantaged. Engaged in public policy analysis, legislative education and research. Started by 13 Black members of the House to strengthen their effort to address legislative concerns of minorities. Full employment to welfare reform, South Africa to human rights, minority business to education. **Other Resources:** Publishes magazine, POINT OF VIEW. Nonprofit. **Est.:** 1970. **Contact(s):** Julian C. Dixon (President), Ron V. Dellums (Chairman). (202)226-7790.

**$ ▸ Congressional Institute for the Future**
409 3rd St. SW
Washington, DC 20024 (202)863-1700
**Concern(s):** economics; politics; future; volunteers. Bank your service credits as you volunteer service to the elderly, poor or neighbors. The idea and demonstrations of computer banks in which service credits can be saved until needed or exchanged for services you need has reached Congress. Reports on possible legislation which would provide Federal support for the establishment of Service Credit Banks.

**✌ ▸ Connexions Information Sharing Services**
427 Bloor St. West
Toronto, ON M5S1X7 Canada (416)960-3903
**Concern(s):** peace; environment; justice; feminism. Provides information and services for activists, voluntary, and self-help organizations and for all seeking reliable and up-to-date information on social concern issues. Works to build links between people who are striving to create positive solutions to social, environmental, economic and international problems. **Other Resources:** Publishes the CONNEXIONS ANNUAL and DIGEST. Mailing lists of organizations, libraries, and individuals interested in environmental, peace and women's and social justice materials are available. Provides consulting and publishing services **Est.:** 1975. **Other Formats:** DBase III+ database. **Labels:** 11000. **Contact(s):** Ulli Diemer (Coordinator), Karl Andur (Computer Systems).

**✌ ▸ Conscience and Military Tax Campaign**
4534 1/2 University Way NE
Seattle, WA 98105 (206)547-0952
**Concern(s):** peace; anti-draft; militarism; war tax revolt. Advises resisters and encourages war tax resistance. Seeks signatures on resolutions that state that when 100,000 is reached all will resist military taxes together. Recognizes the importance of withholding on a large scale in order to assert US citizen's rights of conscience. In support of the Peace Tax Fund Bill which, if passed would permit the full payment of taxes for nonviolent, non-military programs. **Other Resources:** Literature list available; CMTC Information Packet (incl. Wm. Durland's "People Pay For Peace" on war tax refusal); see CONSCIENCE AND MILITARY TAX CAMPAIGN, with information, ideas, and strategies about the War Tax Resistance Movement. **Est.:** 1979.

⚔ ◗ **Conscience Canada, Inc.**
Box 601, Station E
Victoria, BC V8W 2P3 Canada
**Concern(s):** peace; economics; war tax revolt; anti-draft; taxation. Deals with issues on conscientious objection to military taxation.

✪ ◗ **Conservation & Renewable Energy Inquiry & Referral Service (CAREIRS)**
Box 8900
Silver Springs, MD 20907    (800)523-2929
**Concern(s):** energy; environment; efficiency; appropriate technology; renewables; solar; conservation. Provides information on full spectrum of renewable energy technologies and energy conservation. In addition, the Service maintains contact with a nationwide network of public and private organizations specializing in technical or regionally-specific information. An information service directed to the general public, educators, consumers, etc. Provides factsheets about what solar technology is and how it can be utilized and makes referrals on specific and general inquiries about renewable energy.

E ◗ **Conservation Education Association**
Northland College
Ashland, WI 54806    (615)632-8103
**Concern(s):** environment; education; conservation. It encourages local, state and national conservation programs by disseminating news, ideas and suggestions on conservation and environmental education through annual conferences and reports, a newsletter, other publications, special projects and cooperation organizations and agencies active in this field. **Contact(s):** John R. Paulk. **Other:** TVA, 1B35 Old City Hall, Knoxville, TN 37902.

E ◗ **The Conservation Foundation**
1250 24th St. NW, #500
Washington, DC 20037  (202)293-4800
**Affiliation:** World Wildlife Fund (US). **Concern(s):** environment; Third World; health; conservation; land use; hazardous/toxic waste; research; development. A research and public education organization promoting wise use of the Earth's resources. Conducts research and/or provides technical assistance in land use, toxic substances, risk assessment, water resources, environmental dispute resolution, environmental issues in developing countries, and reports periodically on environmental conditions and trends. **Other Resources:** Publishes CONSERVATION FOUNDATION LETTER; RESOLVE; Successful Communities (a field program); Books, Films, Reports, and Conferences. Publications Catalog available. CONTROLLING NONPOINT-SOURCE WATER POLLUTION (directories). See World Wildlife Fund. Nonprofit. **Est.:** 1948. **Contact(s):** Kathryn S. Fuller (President), Douglas Wheeler (Executive Vice President).

E ◗ **Conservation International**
1015 18th St. NW, #1000
Washington, DC 20036  (202)429-5660
**Concern(s):** environment; conservation; wildlife/endangered species; forests. A membership organization whose mission is to help develop the capacity to sustain biological diversity and the ecosystems and ecological processes that support life on Earth. Works with private organizations, government agencies, and universities in many tropical countries to develop the capacity to preserve critical habitats through effective eco-projects. Provides assistance in science, fundraising, management training, conservation planning, legal and policy analysis and public education. **Other Resources:** See TROPICUS newsletter. **Dues:** $15/yr. **Contact(s):** Charles J. Hedlund (Chairman), Peter Seligman (President).

E ◗ **Conservation Law Foundation of New England**
3 Joy St.
Boston, MA 02108-1497(617)742-2540
**Affiliation:** Conservation Law Foundation. **Concern(s):** environment; energy; health; conservation; law; efficiency; pollution; natural resources; resource management; public health. Energy efficiency, resource management, public health, and pollution control are the primary goals of CLF's attorneys, scientist and policy makers. **Dues:** $30/yr, $15/students.

E ◗ **Conservatory for Nature Culture**
RFD 2 Box 330
Brooks, ME 04921    (207)722-3112
**Affiliation:** Goodbye Columbus Day! (A movement to de-mythify Columbus). **Concern(s):** environment; education; justice; Native American; students. A small (12-student) private facility organized by Native American women to provide a comfortable, low-key environment for the exploration and understanding of native culture and skills. Residence takes place as two-week sessions during summer months. Also is called "School That is Not," located in the Penobscot Nation. **Other Resources:** Some of the grandmother-founders will travel to do lectures and workshops. See CULTIVATOR under periodicals. Nonprofit. **Est.:** 1990. **Member:** Womland Trust (Women Owning Maine Land in Trust). **Contact(s):** Georgia Mitchell (Grand-

mother/Director).

✍ ◗ **Consortium on Peace Research Education and Development (COPRED)**
George Mason University
4400 University Dr.
Fairfax, VA 22030    (703)323-2806
**Affiliation:** Center for Conflict Resolution. **Concern(s):** education; peace; conflict resolution; research; networking. An educational organization founded to foster research and education in the areas of peace and conflict resolution. Purpose is to advance peace studies at all levels. It encourages interchange and support among peace educators, researchers, professionals, and practitioners. At present, special emphasis on developing services for the growing number of peace studies programs at colleges and universities. Network of cross-fertilization among 220 groups and individuals. **Other Resources:** Activities and services: Networking and information exchange; consultation; conferences, seminars and workshops, research projects and resource development; publications. See newsletter, PEACE CHRONICLE and DIRECTORY OF PEACE STUDIES PROGRAMS. Nonprofit. **Est.:** 1970. **Dues:** $20, $125 institution; includes Chronicle. **Labels:** 220. **Fax:** (703)764-6515. **Contact(s):** Maire A. Dugan, Ph. D. (Executive Director).

J ◗ **Constitutional Rights Foundation**
See BILL OF RIGHTS IN ACTION newsletter.

$ ◗ **Consumer Action**
See CONSUMER ACTION NEWS.

$ ◗ **Consumer Education & Protection Association (CEPA)**
6048 Ogantz
Philadelphia, PA 19140  (215)424-1441
**Concern(s):** economics; health; consumer rights; consumer protection. Membership organization of consumers in Philadelphia area which handles consumer complaints, mortgage foreclosures, utilities and insurance rate increases, etc. **Other Resources:** Newsletter. **Dues:** $15/yr, membership and newsletter. **Member:** Co-op America.

$ ◗ **Consumer Education Resource Center**
350 Scotland Dr.
Orange, NJ 07050    (201)676-6663
**Concern(s):** economics; education; consumer rights. Serves as a clearinghouse, training and technical assistance center for consumer educators planning and implementing educational and information programs. **Est.:** 1978. (800)872-0121. **Contact(s):** Robert Berko.

✪ ◗ **Consumer Energy Council of America**
2000 L St., NW, #802
Washington, DC 20036  (202)659-0404
**Concern(s):** energy; politics; policy; efficiency; lobbying; law. The nation's oldest public interest energy policy organization committed to shaping a national energy policy that will provide consumers with an adequate supply of energy at fair and reasonable prices. CECA is a broad-based coalition. representing consumer's interests in energy issues before Congress, the Administration, the courts and other public forums. **Est.:** 1973. **Contact(s):** Ellen Berman (Executive Director). (202)662-9744.

$ ◗ **Consumer Federation of America**
1424 16th St. NW
Washington, DC 20036  (202)387-6121
**Concern(s):** economics; health; agriculture; politics; consumer rights. Advocates the consumer point of view on Capitol Hill and before agencies and the courts. An organization comprised of other organizations. Assists its members through a state and local resource center, which provides them with ideas on issue, fundraising and organizing. In turn, its members assist in national lobbying efforts. **Other Resources:** See DIRECTORY OF STATE AND LOCAL CONSUMER ORGANIZATIONS. **Est.:** 1968. **Contact(s):** Steve Brobeck (Executive Director).

$ ◗ **Consumer Handbook Information Center**
See CONSUMER'S RESOURCE HANDBOOK.

A ◗ **Consumer Pesticide Protection Project**
425 Mississippi St.
San Francisco, CA 94107    (415)826-6314
**Concern(s):** agriculture; environment; economics; health; hazardous/toxic waste; consumer rights; pesticides. A network of environmentalists, consumers, and labor groups working to promote practical pesticide reduction, and in the process, promote excellence in American agriculture. **Other Resources:** See also National Toxics Campaign. **Contact(s):** Craig Merilees.

$ ◗ **Consumers Education & Protection Association (CEPA)**
See CONSUMER'S VOICE (periodicals).

$ ◗ **Consumers Union**
2001 S St. NW
Washington, DC 20009  (202)462-6262
**Concern(s):** economics; consumer rights. Established to provide consumers with information and counsel on consumer goods and services; to give information on all matters relating to the expense of the family income and to initiate and cooperate with individual and group efforts seeking to create and maintain decent living standards. **Other Resources:** See CONSUMER'S REPORT magazine and ZILLIONS (periodicals). **Est.:** 1936. **Other:** 256 Washington St., Mt. Vernon, NY 10553(915)667-9400.

E ◗ **Context Institute**
Box 11470
Bainbridge, WA 98110  (206)842-0216
**Concern(s):** environment; economics; education; sustainability. Mission: To facilitate widespread, effective, direct participation in the development of a humane and sustainable world. Principles: Recognition of the capacity of individuals to effect change; awareness of existing ways to implement humane and sustainable systems; priorities clarity—over which actions are both important and effective; how-to knowledge and skills for taking priority actions; the spread and accumulation of decentralized learning; and higher visibility of such movements. **Other Resources:** Publishes IN CONTEXT, a quarterly magazine. Offers consulting services and computer mediated seminars, Nonprofit. **Est.:** 1983. **E-Network:** Econet. **ID:** 'incontext'. **Fax:** (206)842-5208. **Contact(s):** Robert Gilman (Executive Director), Diane Gilman (Associate Director).

⚭ ◗ **Convention of American Instructors of the Deaf**
See AMERICAN ANNALS OF THE DEAF (directories).

E ◗ **Convention on International Trade in Endangered Species of Wild Fauna and Flora (CITES)**
3705 Cardiff Rd.
Chevy Chase, MD 20815(301)654-3150
**Concern(s):** environment; wildlife/endangered species. A treaty, ratified by nearly 100 nations committed to the wise use of endangered and threatened plant and animal species, working to prevent their extinction due to uncontrolled exploitation. Programs include: study of endangered species; assistance to countries seeking to enforce treaty provisions; monitoring legal trade and illicit trafficking; advising Third World country participants on preserving living resources; and educating the public. **Other Resources:** See CITES ARK newsletter. **Fax:** (301)652-6390. **Contact(s):** George A. Furness, Jr. (Senior Advisor to the CITES Secretariat).

H ◗ **Cooking for Survival Consciousness**
Box 26762
Elkins Park, PA 19117    (215)635-1022
**Concern(s):** health; agriculture; environment; nutrition; organic; pesticides. **Contact(s):** Beatrice Wittels.

✍ ◗ **The Coolidge Center for Environmental Leadership**
1675 Massachusetts Ave., #4
Cambridge, MA 02138-1836(617)864-5085
**Concern(s):** education; Third World; environment; development; sustainability; development; global understanding; volunteers. Students and mid-career professionals from developing nations in US graduate programs are helped to become effective and informed decision-makers and leaders so that they find creative and long-term solutions to critical environmental problems at home and worldwide. Encourages mutual support and information exchange through collaboration with alumni and nongovernmental organizations, and supplies materials on sustainable development to university faculty. **Other Resources:** Many resource, reference and research materials available. Volunteer positions available. Provides a newsletter. **Dues:** $15-100/yr. **Contact(s):** Bruce J. Stedman (Executive Director).

✈ ◗ **The Cooperation Project**
c/o Mir Initiative
Box 28183
Washington, DC 20038-8183    (202)857-8037
**Affiliation:** Mir Initiative & Baikal Foundation. **Concern(s):** education; peace; environment; East-West; travel. "The joint work of an American nonprofit and a Soviet non-governmental organization. Our purpose is to promote multicultural perspectives of environmental and social issues. The drop of the Iron Curtain has allowed greater cooperation between people of the East and West than was possible before..." This Project brings people from many different cultures and continents together to share their skills and collaborate in effecting

positive solutions to problems. **Other Resources:** International voluntary workcamps, citizen diplomacy programs, internships. Presently doing an ecology video of Lake Baikal, Siberia, building an ecologically-clean hotel, and offering work experience in that area. Nonprofit. **Contact(s):** Alexandra van der Sleefen. (202)232-1930.

$ ◗ **Cooperative Alumni Association, Inc.**
250 Rainbow Lane
Richmond, KY 40475    (606)623-0695
**Concern(s):** economics; cooperatives. **Contact(s):** Jack McLanahan.

✍ ◗ **Cooperative Children's Books Center**
See ALTERNATIVE PRESS PUBLISHERS OF CHILDREN'S BOOKS: A DIRECTORY.

$ ◗ **Cooperative Communicators Association**
See Membership Roster under same name (directories).

✍ ◗ **Cooperative Education Project**
Box 8032
Ann Arbor, MI 48107    (313)663-3624
**Affiliation:** Michigan Alliance of Cooperatives. **Concern(s):** education; economics; labor; cooperatives. Program for public and private K-12, adult, and higher education to foster the attitudes, shifts, and economics of cooperation - sponsored by the Alliance, providing professional development and curriculum resources. **Other Resources:** Publishes newsletter, COOPERATIVE ACTION. **Office:** 273 E. Liberty Plaza Ann Arbor, MI 48104. **Contact(s):** Ebba Hierta (Executive Director).

D ◗ **Cooperative Housing Foundation**
1010 Wayne Ave., #240
Silver Springs, MD 20901    (301)587-4700
**Concern(s):** demographics; Third World; hunger; poverty; homelessness; development. A private foundation concerned with helping families throughout the world building better housing and better communications. currently CHF directs the great bulk of its efforts toward helping low income persons in developing countries to meet their housing needs. Nonprofit. **Contact(s):** Jim Trousdale.

$ ◗ **Cooperative League of the USA**
1401 New York Ave. NW., #1100
Washington, DC 20005-2102    (202)638-6222
**Concern(s):** economics; cooperatives. The only national confederation of co-ops of all kinds in the US today, it promotes co-op development domestically and internationally. Also educates and provides technical assistance. **Other Resources:** See, also, Society for International Development. Nonprofit. **Est.:** 1945.

H ◗ **Cooperative Power**
See ISSUES IN RADICAL THERAPY (periodicals).

$ ◗ **Cooperative Resources and Service Project**
3551 White House Pl.
Los Angeles, CA 90004  (213)738-1254
**Concern(s):** economics; environment; urban; cooperatives; conservation; research; trade; land trusts; community self-reliance. A training, education, and development center for all kinds of cooperatives. "We sponsor the Ecological Urban Village, the Ecological Revolving Loan Fund, the Local Exchange Trading System, the Shared Housing Network, the Jerry Voorhis Co-op Library, the Co-op Housing Roundtable and much more."

T ◗ **Cooperative Trading Project**
See Friends of the Third World, Inc.

✍ ◗ **Copen Foundation**
357 Hunterbrook Rd.
Yorktown Heights, NY 10598
**Concern(s):** education. **Contact(s):** Peter Copen.

$ ◗ **Corporate Crime Reporter**
Box 18384
Washington, DC 20036  (202)429-6928
**Concern(s):** economics; politics; corporate responsibility; government accountability; criminal system. **Office:** 1322 18th St. Washington, DC 20036.

⚹ ◗ **Council for a Livable World**
110 Maryland Ave. NE
Washington, DC 20002  (202)543-4100
**Concern(s):** peace; politics; disarmament; law; lobbying. Founded by nuclear physicist Leo Szilard and other scientists working in the early days of atomic weapons. The goal of these men and women was to warn the public and Congress of the threat of nuclear war and lead the way to rational arms control and nuclear disarmament. The DC program provides senators with technical and scientific information that helps to make intelligent decisions about nuclear arms control and strategic weapons. Contributes to peace politicians selected by contributors. **Other Resources:** Contributes to peace politicians;

phone hotline with alerts on nuclear war and issues before Congress. Publishes a newsletter, PEACE PAC project. See also, Campaign to Cut Military Spending in Half. **Est.:** 1962. Hotline: (202)543-0006. **Contact(s):** Jerome Grossman (Chairman), John Isaacs (President). **Other:** 20 Park Plaza, Boston, MA 02116. Wayne Jaquith, Boston Director. (617)542-2282.

J ◗ **Council for Democratic & Secular Humanism**
See FREE INQUIRY magazine.

? ◗ **The Council for Prosperity**
20 Heber Rd.
London, NW2 6AA England  (4481208 2853
**Concern(s):** future; ideation; invention. Acts as advocate for the interests of future generations. It publishes a Declaration of the Rights of Prosperity, and has a youth wing "Adopt a Planet" with 1000 pounds in prize money for children adopting and improving parts of their local environment. **Other Resources:** Legal assistants and lawyers who can represent the interests of future generations at planning enquiries and similar forums. **Est.:** 1990. **Fax:** (4481 452 6434. **Contact(s):** Nicholas Albery (General Secretary).

U ◗ **Council for Urban Economic Development**
See directory under same name.

⚹ ◗ **Council of Cooperation & Goodwill**
419 Main St.
Huntington Beach, CA 92648-5199
**Concern(s):** peace; spiritual. **Other Resources:** Newsletter.

$ ◗ **Council on Economic Priorities**
30 Irving Place, 9th Fl.
New York, NY 10003    (212)420-1133
**Concern(s):** economics; environment; peace; consumer rights; alternative consumer; boycott; green consumer; boycott. A research organization which publishes newsletter and studies on corporate social responsibility, the environment and defense spending. Ms. Marlin recently won the Right Livelihood Award. **Other Resources:** See SHOPPING FOR A BETTER WORLD, THE BETTER WORLD INVESTMENT GUIDE, INVESTING IN AMERICA'S CORPORATE CONSCIENCE, and COUNCIL ON ECONOMIC PRIORITIES RESEARCH REPORT. See Committee for National Security, and Corporate Environmental Data Clearinghouse. Nonprofit. **Est.:** 1969. (800)822-6435. **Contact(s):** Alice Tepper Marlin (President), Myra Alperson (Director for Social Responsibility).

T ◗ **Council on Foreign Relations**
56 E. 68th St.
New York, NY 10021    (212)734-0400
**Concern(s):** Third World; foreign policy. This organization promotes discussion of international issues among influential elites. **Other Resources:** Publishes a journal, FOREIGN AFFAIRS; and Annual Report. **Est.:** 1921.

$ ◗ **The Council on Foundations**
1828 L St. NW , #300
Washington, DC 20036  (202)466-6512
**Concern(s):** economics; politics; spiritual; philanthropy. A membership organization. Nonprofit. **Contact(s):** Debbie Vinson.

T ◗ **Council on Hemispheric Affairs**
See WASHINGTON REPORT ON THE HEMISPHERE (periodicals).

✍ ◗ **The Council on International and Public Affairs**
777 UN Plaza
New York, NY 10017    (212)972-9877
**Concern(s):** education; peace; energy; Third World; research; appropriate technology; global understanding; foreign policy. A research and educational publishing group founded to promote the study and understanding of national and international problems and affairs. **Other Resources:** Publishes a book, HOW TO END THE NUCLEAR NIGHTMARE. **Est.:** 1954. **Other:** 6 Valley Trail, Center on the Hudson, New York, NY (212)953-6920.

✈ ◗ **Council on International Educational Exchange**
205 E. 42nd St.
New York, NY 10017    (212)661-1414
**Affiliation:** Campus Services. **Concern(s):** education; travel. See DIRECTORIES OF HOTLINES AND CRISIS INTERVENTION CENTERS and VOLUNTEER! THE COMPREHENSIVE GUIDE TO VOLUNTARY SERVICE IN THE US AND ABROAD (directories). (212)695-0291.

✍ ◗ **Council on Interracial Books for Children**
See INTERRACIAL BOOKS FOR CHILDREN BULLETIN (periodicals).

E ◗ **Council on Ocean Law**
1709 New York Ave. NW
Washington, DC 20006  (202)347-3766
**Concern(s):** environment; ocean/rivers. Founded to support and promote the establishment of a stable and balanced regime of law for the world's oceans, and to educate about the importance of widely

accepted international agreement on rules to govern the rapid expansion of ocean uses. In carrying out these purposes, COL supports and monitors the observance of international agreements and other developments in ocean law that serve the interests of all states - both industrialized and developing. **Other Resources:** Publishes OCEANS POLICY NEWS newsletter. **Est.:** 1980. **Contact(s):** Lee A. Kimball (Executive Director).

✍ ◗ **Council on Social Work Education**
See DIRECTORY OF COLLEGES AND UNIVERSITIES WITH ACCREDITED SOCIAL WORK DEGREE PROGRAMS.

✍ ◗ **Countdown 2001**
110 N. Payne St.
Alexandria, VA 22314    (703)684-4735
**Concern(s):** education; future; global understanding. An organization of educators who are committed to helping young people develop essential learning for future-like critical thinking and a global perspective. Founded by Dr. Sherry Schiller, a long-time futures educator, it offers educators: partnership in a dynamic network of leading practitioners who are preparing students for effective citizenship in the 21st century; instructional packages (including lessons, classroom activities, and resource guides. **Other Resources:** Partners receive newsletters and participate in special events and workshops. See ABC's for 21st Century project and EDUCATOR'S GUIDE: AN AGENDA FOR THE 21ST CENTURY. Nonprofit. **Est.:** 1985. **Fax:** (703)684-4737. **Contact(s):** Sherry L. Schiller, PhD (Founder/President).

E ◗ **Cousteau Society**
930 W. 21st St.
Norfolk, VA 23517    (804)627-1144
**Concern(s):** environment; ocean/rivers; polar. "Environmental problems stem from widespread ignorance about how the living systems of Earth work...and how they do not." The Society emphasizes education through research, lectures, videos, books and other publications. Currently working on an Antartican international natural reserve. **Other Resources:** Publishes THE DOLPHIN LOG and THE CALYPSO LOG magazines, bimonthly and monthly newsletter, CALYPSO DISPATCH. **Dues:** $20, $28 family. **Fax:** (804)627-7547. **Contact(s):** Jean-Michel Cousteau, C.L.S. Merriam (Research/Communications).

E ◗ **Creating Our Future**
2669 Le Conte Ave
Berkeley, CA 94709-1024
**Concern(s):** environment; education; peace; students; forests; homelessness; global warming. Social change and environmental issues are brought to and from young people. High school and college-level activists have joined in projects and demonstrations to create awareness of apartheid, rainforest destruction, homelessness, ozone depletion, recycling, the Israeli/Palestinian affair, and other issues. As well as a newsletter, COF has a summer program to train youths to organize and lead their own local campaigns. **Other Resources:** See listing under manuals. Speakers available.

J ◗ **Crime and Social Justice Association**
See CRIME AND SOCIAL JUSTICE newsletter.

✍ ◗ **CRISES Press, Inc.**
1716 SW Williston Rd.
Gainesville, FL 32608    (904)335-2200
**Concern(s):** education; media; justice; environment; press. Critical Research Institute for Social and Environmental Sciences displays books and journals to librarians at ALA conferences with their Alternative Book Exhibit. "Marketing alternative publications that don't paper over the problems", it is entirely supported by publisher fees. **Other Resources:** Publishes a descriptive catalog. (Planned, 1992) It will be publishing a library book-selection tool reviewing titles overlooked or misrepresented by CHOICE, LIBRARY JOURNAL, etc. To be supported by subscriptions. Nonprofit. **Est.:** 1991. **Contact(s):** Charles Willett (President), Lisa Barr (Secretary).

☺ ◗ **Critical Mass Energy Project**
215 Pennsylvania Ave. SE
Washington, DC 20003  (202)546-4996
**Affiliation:** Public Citizen. **Concern(s):** energy; environment; antinuclear; appropriate technology; renewables. A powerful voice in the movement to end reliance on nuclear power and to promote safe, economical, and environmentally sound energy alternatives. **Est.:** 1974.

D ◗ **CROP Office on Global Education**
2115 N. Charles St.
Baltimore, MD 21218    (301)727-6106
**Affiliation:** Church World Service. **Concern(s):** demographics; education; Third World; peace; global understanding; hunger; development. Mandated to inform and sensitize the US public about the root causes of hunger, the limitations of global resources, and the interdependence of all people. The Office works in a collaborative and cooperative style, animating and supporting existing initiatives in global

education in the US as well as providing educational programming. **Contact(s):** Tom Hampson. **Other:** Box 968, Elkhart, IN 46515. Joan Wuischpard. (219)264-3102.

### ☸ ◆ The Crossing
906 S. 49th St.
Philadelphia, PA 19143
**Concern(s):** peace; spiritual; nonviolence; transformation. A place to have conferences dedicated to nonviolent social change.

### ✈ ◆ Crossroads Africa
475 Riverside Dr.
New York, NY 10115     (212)870-2210
**Concern(s):** education; Third World; travel; Africa; development.

### ✍ ◆ Crossroads School
See Mysteries Program.

### ☸ ◆ Crusade to Abolish War and Armaments by World Law
174 Majestic Ave.
San Francisco, CA 94112
**Concern(s):** peace; world order; disarmament. Promotes various actions for world government. **Contact(s):** Mia Lord (Director).

### J ◆ Cultural Survival
53-A Church St.
Cambridge, MA 02138   (617)495-2562
**Concern(s):** justice; Third World; labor; diversity; Native Americans; indigenous peoples; cooperatives. Founded by social scientists from Harvard University who were concerned with the fate of tribal peoples and ethnic minorities worldwide. "Small traditional societies are extinguished not by abstract historical processes but by greed and incomprehension. It designs, sponsors and implements culturally sensitive development programs that will include tribal people and ethnic minorities as participants and beneficiaries. Forms cooperatives and sells native products. Famous for Rainforest Crunch. **Other Resources:** Publishes CULTURAL SURVIVAL QUARTERLY. **Est.:** 1972. **Contact(s):** Jason Clay.

### E ◆ Cumberland Green Bioregional Council
4014-C Utah Ave.
Nashville, TN 37209
**Concern(s):** environment; bioregionalism.

### ✍ ◆ D.E.E.R. (Developing Educational and Environmental Resources)
Box 422
Sturgeon Bay, WI 54235 (414)743-6777
**Affiliation:** Whitetails Unlimited, Inc. **Concern(s):** education; environment. Project that stresses educational programs to help curtail the wreckless destruction of the environment.

### J ◆ Dakota Indian Foundation
201 S. Main St.
Box 340
Chamberlain, SD 57325
**Concern(s):** justice; spiritual; education; Native American; diversity; minority rights; philanthropy. **Contact(s):** Joseph E. Morrison (Executive Director).

### P ◆ Daniel Deleon Election Committee
Box 362
Newaygo, MI 49337
**Concern(s):** politics; alternative party. "Our work amounts to an advertising campaign promoting the writings and speeches of Daniel DeLeon. We pass out leaflets that reads in part 'Vote for Daniel DeLeon' and a message that capitalism must be replaced with socialism before there can be substantial environmental improvement. Dedicated to political action for socialism. **Other Resources:** Brochure and leaflets. **Est.:** 1986. **Contact(s):** Thomas E. Girard (Founder).

### L ◆ Data Center
464 19th St.
Oakland, CA 94612     (510)835-4692
**Concern(s):** labor; justice; economics; Third World; media; development; Central America; South America; Caribbean; unions; corporate responsibility; press. A user-supported library and resource center dedicated to collecting, organizing, and providing access to information concerning the political economy of the US and the world. **Other Resources:** Fees for walk-in use and "search service" mail requests. See CENTRAL AMERICA MONITOR, PLANT SHUTDOWNS MONITOR; CORPORATION RESPONSIBILITY MONITOR, a monthly clipping service. Nonprofit. **Subscription:** $420/yr. **Pages:** 100. **Member:** Co-op America. **Contact(s):** Mary Welter (Librarian), Fred Goff (Director).

### D ◆ The Dean and Virginia Institute for Population and Resource Studies
Stanford University
Stanford, CA 94305
**Concern(s):** demographics; environment; energy; population growth; natural resources; waste management. Its objective is to become a national and international leader in the interdisciplinary study of population growth and its effects on social structures, national economies, resource availability, and the environment throughout the world. The ultimate goal is to produce understanding of, and improvement in, the conditions that now exist for many of the world's plant, animal, and human populations. There are to be three facets to this endeavor: research, education and formulation of policy. **Contact(s):** Marcus W. Feldman (Director), Fred O. Pinkham (Associate Director).

### E ◆ Dearborn Naturalists Association
4901 Evergreen Rd.
Dearborn, MI 48128     (313)425-7715
**Concern(s):** environment.

### E ◆ Defenders of Wildlife
1244 19th St. NW
Washington, DC 20036   (202)659-9510
**Concern(s):** environment; wildlife/endangered species; conservation; volunteers. A national membership organization dedicated to the protection and restoration of all native wild animals and plants in their natural habitats through education and appreciation, reducing environmental hazards, and reasoned advocacy. Projects: Restoration of the grey wolf to Yellowstone; protecting marine mammals from plastic debris and discarded fish nets; strengthening the National Wildlife Refuge System. **Other Resources:** See DEFENDERS magazine. Also conducts an activist network that includes nearly 6,000 individuals. Volunteer positions available at any of the four regional offices. **Dues:** $20, $15/students-seniors/yr. **Member:** Global Tomorrow Coalition; Environmental Federation of America. **Contact(s):** Rupert M. Cutler (President).

### J ◆ Defenders Project
432 Park Ave. S, #1103
New York, NY 10016    (212)684-1221
**Affiliation:** International League for Human Rights. **Concern(s):** justice; peace; United Nations; political prisoners. Concerned with protecting rights of human rights advocates and organizations through promotion of new international standards.

### ☸ ◆ Defense Budget Project
777 N. Capitol St. NE, #710
Washington, DC 20002-4239     (202)408-1517
**Affiliation:** Center on Budget and Policy Priorities. **Concern(s):** peace; economics; politics; analysis; peace dividend; economic conversion; government accountability. An independent research organization which analyzes defense budget and spending issues and national security policy. It is funded by grants from major foundations. Established to provide timely commentary on and analysis of defense budget, defense spending and national security issues for policymakers, the media and the public. Nonprofit. **Est.:** 1983. **Contact(s):** Natalie Goldring, Stephen Alexis Cain.

### E ◆ Delphys Foundation
Box 4009
Santa Barbara, CA 93140     (805)684-1356
**Concern(s):** environment; wildlife/endangered species. Goal: to establish a worldwide clearinghouse, library and archive to facilitate open ocean, free ranging (vs. captive) dolphin and whale research. Nonprofit.

### P ◆ Delta Greens
7725 Cohn St.
New Orleans, LA 70118
**Concern(s):** politics; environment; Green.

### P ◆ The Democracy Project
c/o Globalvision
215 Park Ave. S, #1814
New York, NY 10003    (212)260-2022
**Concern(s):** politics; economics; health; urban; grassroots organizing; crime. Action institute focusing on four areas: economic democracy, political democracy, health, safety regulation and crime. **Other Resources:** Publishes books, reports, studies and articles. See IDEA INDEX: FRESH IDEAS FOR DEMOCRATIC IDEALS (directories). **Contact(s):** Mark Green, David Corn.

### P ◆ Democratic Socialists of America
15 Dutch St., #500
New York, NY 10038-3705   (212)962-0390
**Concern(s):** politics; Democratic Socialism. A national political organization committed to building a broad progressive alliance of unions, minorities, feminists, peace activists, gays/lesbians, and community organizations. DSA is committed to implementing an agenda of social justice, economic democracy, a democratic foreign policy and racial and sexual equality. A 5000+ member organization with 40 local chapters. DSA works for immediate reforms of America's social, economic, and political systems, as well as to promote socialist ideals. **Other Resources:** DSA-YS is the largest multi-issue radical student and youth organization in the country. See THE ACTIVIST; ECOSOCIALIST REVIEW. DEMOCRATIC LEFT; RELIGIOUS SOCIALISM; COMMONWEALTH REPORT; and DEMOCRATIC SOCIALIST REPORT & REVIEW (periodicals). **Contact(s):** Patrick Lacefield.

### ♿ ◆ Department of Education
See DIRECTORY OF RESOURCES FOR ADULTS WITH DISABILITIES.

### H ◆ Department of Health and Human Services
See DIRECTORY OF FACILITIES OBLIGATED TO PROVIDE UNCOMPENSATED SERVICES.

### U ◆ Department of Housing & Urban Development
See DIRECTORY OF INFORMATION RESOURCES IN HOUSING AND URBAN DEVELOPMENT.

### H ◆ Department of Human Nutrition & Food Systems
See NUTRIENT DATA BANK DIRECTORY.

### F ◆ Department of Labor
See WORKING WOMAN'S GUIDE TO HER JOB RIGHTS (directories).

### E ◆ Department of Natural Resources
See RECYCLING STUDY GUIDE (directories).

### ✍ ◆ Department of Special Education Programs
See DIRECTORY OF SELECTED EARLY CHILDHOOD PROGRAMS.

### U ◆ Department of Urban Development
See DIRECTORY OF PRIVATE FAIR HOUSING ORGANIZATIONS.

### E ◆ Desert Bighorn Council
Box 5431
Riverside, CA 92517
**Concern(s):** environment; endangered species; wildlife/endangered species. Attempting to establish viable populations of bighorn sheep to its historic range though translocation and habitat improvement. Encourages research, conservation, and scientific study. **Est.:** 1957. **Dues:** $15/yr. **Contact(s):** Donald J. Armentrout.

### E ◆ Desert Fishes Council
407 W. Line St.
Bishop, CA 93514
**Concern(s):** environment; drylands; wildlife/endangered species. Desert flora and fauna.

### E ◆ The Desert Protective Council
Box 4294
Palm Springs, CA 92263
**Concern(s):** environment; wilderness. Works to place serving areas in protective categories by having them designated as wilderness, wild and scenic rivers, areas of Critical Environmental Concern (ACECs) or parks, refuges, preserves, and sanctuaries. Efforts are being made to strengthen agency budgets for naturalist and interpretive services, as well as for enforcement of existing laws. Develops educational materials on desert resources and issues. **Other Resources:** Publishes EL PAISANO, quarterly newsletter and unscheduled publications and alerts from DPC and cooperating organizations. **Contact(s):** Bill Neill.

### E ◆ Desert Tortoise Council
Box 1738
Palm Desert, CA 92261  (619)431-8449
**Concern(s):** environment; endangered species; wildlife/endangered species. Attempting to establish viable populations of tortoise-to its historic range though translocation and habitat improvement. Encourages research, conservation, and scientific study. Serves as an advisory council for tortoise preservation, fish and wildlife, and other appropriate agencies on matters pertinent to the desert tortoise. **Est.:** 1975. **Dues:** $12/yr. $300/yr. for lifetime. **Contact(s):** Dana Pearson, Mike Guisti (Co-chairmans). (310)422-6172.

### M ◆ Designing New Civilization
16255 Ventura Boulevard, #605
Encino, CA 91436-2354
**Concern(s):** media; multilogues.

### U ◆ Development Alternatives, Inc.
4811 Chippendale Dr., #208
Sacramento, CA 95841  (916)344-5345
**Concern(s):** urban; planning. **Contact(s):** Don Humpal.

### ? ◆ Development Group for Alternative Policies (GAP)
1400 I St. NW, #520
Washington, DC 20005  (202)898-1566

**Concern(s):** future; environment; energy; economics; policy.

**T ❖ Development International, Inc.**
Box 28097
Atlanta, GA 30328    (404)257-1977
**Concern(s):** Third World; development. **Contact(s):** George R. O'Day.

**F ❖ Development Law and Policy Program**
Center for Population & Family Health
Columbia University, 60 Haven Ave.
New York, NY 10032
**Affiliation:** International Women's Rights Action Watch. **Concern(s):** feminism; justice; Third World; sexism. International consortium of scholars and activists monitoring implementation of the UN Convention on the Elimination of All Forms of Discrimination Against Women. Reports on law and policy changes in connection with Convention's principles. Seeks ongoing information from women's groups and other nongovernmental sources on the situation of women worldwide to aid CEDAW in its periodic review of conditions in nations ratifying the Convention. **Other Resources:** Publishes WOMEN'S WATCH.

**T ❖ Development Resources**
7201 Wisconsin Ave.
Bethesda, MD 20814    (301)951-5546
**Concern(s):** Third World; feminism; development. **Contact(s):** Jayne Millar Wood.

**✍ ❖ Dialectics Workshop**
See SCIENCE AND NATURE (periodicals).

**E ❖ Digit Fund**
See DIGIT NEWS or Morris Animal Foundation.

**♿ ❖ Disabled Artists' Network**
Box 20781
New York, NY 10025
**Concern(s):** health; arts; justice; disabled; disabled's rights. An information exchange and living bulletin board of disabled artists in the visual and sculptural arts. Services: introducing artists to one another, exchanging information about opportunities, shows, competitions, galleries, working on public education and services for professional disabled artists. **Price:** S.A.S.E. **Contact(s):** Sanda Aronson (Executive Director).

**☣ ❖ Disarm Bazaar Coalition**
1006 M St. NW
Washington, DC 20001    (202)682-9056
**Concern(s):** peace; disarmament. Organization trying to end the annual Air Force Association exhibition of weapons at Sheraton Hotel. Educates the public and puts pressure on Sheraton. **Member:** Co-op America. **Contact(s):** Paul Magno.

**☣ ❖ Disarmament Resource Center**
942 Market St., #708
San Francisco, CA 94102
**Concern(s):** peace; disarmament.

**S ❖ Disciples of Christ**

**Other Resources:** See Christian Church and ISSUES AND CONCERNS newsletter. **Contact(s):** Rev. John Humbert (President).

**L ❖ Displaced Homeworkers Network**
See DISPLACED HOMEMAKERS PROGRAM DIRECTORY.

**H ❖ Do It Now Foundation**
See NEWSERVICE (periodicals).

**E ❖ Dolphin Network**
3220 Sacramento St.
San Francisco, CA 94115    (415)931-0948
**Affiliation:** Washington Research Institute. **Concern(s):** environment; wildlife/endangered species. Abroad network of people and organizations concerned with protecting the dolphins, the threat of drift nets, animal assisted therapy, and the Heinz and StarKist policies to can tuna caught by only dolphin safe methods. A project of the Washington Research Institute. **Other Resources:** Publishes DOLPHIN NET newsletter. Nonprofit.

**E ❖ Dolphin Research Center**
Box 2875
Marathon Shores, FL 33052 (305)289-0002
**Concern(s):** environment; education; wildlife/endangered species; research. This a research and education center that manages the largest non-commercial dolphin facility in North America. "Our research projects have included language studies, oil detection and avoidance with dolphins, and improved husbandry practices." **Other Resources:** Dolphin critical care facility. **Est.:** 1961.

**D ❖ Domestic Human Needs Network**
110 Maryland Ave. NE, #509
Washington, DC 20002  (202)543-2800
**Affiliation:** Interfaith Impact for Justice and Peace. **Concern(s):** demographics; justice; economics; spiritual; interfaith. **Other Resources:** NETWORKER newsletter. (800)424-7290.

**E ❖ Don't Waste California**
2940 16th. St., #310
San Francisco, CA 94103    (415)861-0532
**Concern(s):** environment; energy; politics; health; anti-nuclear; lobbying; waste management; hazardous toxic waste. A growing coalition of concerned California citizens and organizations committed to responsible radioactive waste policies and practices that is working in conjunction with Nuclear Information and Research Service and Greenpeace to change federal policies and priorities responsible for this nightmare. They are concerned that California will become a national dumpsite, while citizens bear the tax burden and lose their rights to the democratic processes. Against short-sighted energy policies. **Other Resources:** Their present concern is the proposed dump site in Ward Valley, 15 miles from the Colorado River. (310)426-1021. **Other:** Box 8781, Orange, CA 92664. (714)491-0657.

**E ❖ Driftless Bioregional Network**
Route 3, Box 163
Winona, MN 55987
**Concern(s):** environment; bioregionalism.

**E ❖ Ducks Unlimited**
1 Waterfowl Way
Long Grove, IL 60047    (312)438-4300
**Concern(s):** environment; wildlife/endangered species; conservation; wetlands; volunteers. Membership organization founded to help restore and enhance critically needed waterfowl breeding habitat in Canada. Major activities include: an international wetlands conservation effort, working in Canada, the US and Mexico; active wetlands restoration and management projects, designed to provide the best waterfowl habitat possible; and organization of wildlife professionals fighting to secure the future of wetlands and waterfowl across North America. Supportive of hunters. **Other Resources:** See DUCKS UNLIMITED magazine. Over 5,000 volunteer fund-raising chapters throughout the US. **Contact(s):** Matthew B. Connolly, Jr. (Executive Vice President).

**P ❖ Dynamic Balance Party**
Box 909
Lompoc, CA 93438
**Concern(s):** politics; economics; alternative party. Provides list of "Seven Key Issues." **Contact(s):** Robert Theobald.

**J ❖ The Eagle Connection**
457 Scenic Rd.
Fairfax, CA 94930    (415)457-4513
**Concern(s):** justice; health; spiritual; environment; economics; social justice; transformation. 100 transformative organizations: retreat and growth centers, social action groups, journals, holistic health practitioners, alternative schools, and natural food stores. These groups tend to be shifting from self-growth to activist concerns: a yearning for community; and a growing acknowledgment of the need to reach out to other classes and ethnic groups. Goals: Development non-hierarchical yet effective leadership; give up "us-versus-them" mentality; turn despair into empowerment. **Contact(s):** John Broomfield, Jo Imlay (Co-founders).

**E ❖ Earth Action Network**
1711 Martin Luther King Way, #D
Berkeley, CA 94709    (510)649-1895
**Concern(s):** environment; politics; peace; civil disobedience; nonviolence. Seeks to build a diverse coalition of environmental, labor, cultural, peace and social justice, anti-intervention, community and minority organizations and groups, and develop an ecological sustainable future dedicated to nonviolence and an alternative community based on nonhierarchical authority that is neither capitalist nor state socialism. Famous for their Wall St. actions. **Other Resources:** A monthly Network paper and the Community Action Network Bulletin Board (BBS). **Other Formats:** BBS: (510) 843-8788. **Contact(s):** Stephen.

**E ❖ Earth Birthday Celebration Project**
183 Pinehurst Ave., #34
New York, NY 10033    (212)928-1463
**Concern(s):** environment; education. Encourages children to learn about the environment and contribute toward its health. **Contact(s):** Clifford Ross (Executive Director).

**E ❖ Earth Day International**
800 Yates St.
Victoria, BC V8W 1L9 **Canada**
**Concern(s):** environment. The International Environmental Network

Headquarters that coordinates 3000 environmental groups in 141 countries. **Other Resources:** See Business Environmental Library (directories). **Contact(s):** Jim Crabtree (International Coordinator).

**E ❖ Earth Day Resources**
116 New Montgomery, #530
San Francisco, CA 94105    (800)727-8619
**Concern(s):** environment; energy; sustainability; activism; efficiency; renewables; recycling. This is the organization that took over for the original 1990 Earth Day people. **Other Resources:** Newsletter, EARTHDAY 2000. Nonprofit. **Dues:** $20/yr. **Contact(s):** Christina L. Desser (Chairman), Eric Ridenour (Coordinator).

**☣ ❖ Earth Democrathon**
Box 359
Welches, OR 97067
**Concern(s):** peace; world order. Promotes statewide referendums, hopes to expand to national issues and ultimately go global on geofederation.

**E ❖ Earth First!**
Box 5871
Tucson, AZ 85703    (602)622-1371
**Concern(s):** environment; conservation; wilderness; wildlife/endangered species. Whereas, many environmental groups are members of the American political establishment and essentially adopt the anthropocentric (human-centered) view, EF! sets forth the pure, hardline "no-compromise" position of those who believe that Earth comes first. **Other Resources:** See Earth First! Tropical Timber Campaign and EARTH FIRST! newspaper.

**E ❖ Earth First! Tropical Timber Campaign**
Box 83
Canyon, CA 94716    (415)376-7329
**Affiliation:** Earth First!. **Concern(s):** environment; forests; conservation; preservation. The branch of EF! that is concerned with the tropical Rainforests. **Contact(s):** Karen Picket.

**E ❖ Earth Island Institute**
300 Broadway, #28
San Francisco, CA 94133    (415)788-3666
**Concern(s):** environment; economics; green consumer; animal rights; rainforests; ocean; wildlife/endangered species; conservation; preservation; sustainability; volunteers. Purpose is to initiate and support internationally-oriented projects for the protection and restoration of the environment. Identifies crucial and emerging environmental issues; motivates rapid and effective public action; builds networks among international constituencies. Agenda focuses on rain forests and marine life preservation with support for Central America's environmental struggles. Successful in showing how environmental issues tie in with international politics. **Other Resources:** EARTH ISLAND JOURNAL; Tuna/Dolphin Boycott; Environmental Project on Central America; international Save the Dolphin Project; Rainforest Action Network; Sea Turtle Restoration Project, Urban Habitat Program; California Earth Corps. Volunteers needed. Nonprofit. **Est.:** 1982. **Dues:** $25, $15/student. **Fax:** (415)788-7324. **Contact(s):** David R. Brower (Chairman/Founder), David Phillips (Co-director).

**E ❖ Earth Plan, Inc.**
14755 Ventura Blvd., #687
Sherman Oaks, CA 91423    (818)789-1570
**Concern(s):** environment; economics; forests; trade. The "A Gift of a Tree"(TM) gift certificate will cause a tree to be planted in the Lacondan Maya Rain Forest in your name. Or, if you choose, you may select another option which is described on the back of the certificate: a plant-it-yourself Tree Starter kit.

**E ❖ Earth Protection Group**
Box 2833
Malibu, CA 90265    (213)658-4273
**Concern(s):** environment; politics; peace; activism; grassroots organizing; United Nations. "We feel if a coalition to fight a war can come together, why can't an environmental coalition be established to fight global environmental disasters? We are working to bring an awareness to the United Nations of this intention."

**E ❖ Earth Regeneration Society, Inc.**
1442A Walnut St.
Berkeley, CA 94709    (510)525-4877
**Concern(s):** environment; conservation; resources; global warming. They argue that funds for CO-2 control and climate stabilization must be diverted from military uses. By creating jobs in soil and forest restoration the development of alternative energy sources could be actualized by: 1) Stopping the use of fossil fuels, 2) halting deforestation and starting reforestation programs, and 30 remineralize the soils to provide healthy, rich soils for proper plant and tree growth. **Contact(s):** Alden Bryant.

**E ▸ Earth Share**
3007 Tilden St. NW, #4L
Washington, DC 20008 (202)537-7100
**Affiliation:** Environmental Federation of America. **Concern(s):** environment; economics; health; alternative consumer; socially-responsible investing. A program in association with the Sprint Donation Program that permits you to designate a percentage of your monthly long distance usage to the Federation. "One gift supports all of the member agencies, protecting America and the world's health and natural resources now and forever." Nonprofit. **Est.:** 1990. **Fax:** (202)537-7101. (800)875-3863. **Contact(s):** Kalman Stein (Executive Director).

**E ▸ Earth Trust Foundation**
20110 Rockport Way
Malibu, CA 90265 (310)456-8300
**Concern(s):** environment; peace; politics; social ecology; sustainability. Provides a forum for seminars, symposia, workshops that increase personal awareness and social responsibility from a global perspective. **Other Resources:** See Center for Partnership Studies.

**✍ ▸ Earth-Base Projex**
Box 1328
Bloomington, IN 47402
**Concern(s):** education; energy; science. Open to entries of all ages and judged in age categories the contest urges school classes to enter. Projects are expected to be simple, efficient, and complete with design papers and a working model. The Alternative Energy Science Fair and Contest is being held in July 1991.

**H ▸ Earth-Spirit, Inc.**
See Flower Essence Society.

**✍ ▸ Earthmind**
720 Brooks Ave.
Venice, CA 90291 (310)396-1527
**Concern(s):** education; environment; research. A research and education organization. **Other Resources:** See ALTERNATIVE TRANSPORTATION NEWS. **Est.:** 1972.

**E ▸ Earthnet**
Box 330072
Kahului, Maui, HI 96733 (808)262-5452
**Concern(s):** environment; networking. Its concern is that the saving of the Earth from environmental destruction must be the one overriding commitment of all people. Interactive support must be rapid and global. A computer campaign for the Earth, it is now in the design phase and currently is under testing.

**E ▸ Earthright Institute**
Gates-Briggs Bldg., #322
White River Junction, VT 05001 (802)295-7734
**Concern(s):** environment; efficiency; recycling. Environmental information, education, and referral. Also, energy-efficient light bulbs, canvas shopping bags, stickers to re-use envelopes. **Member:** Co-op America.

**H ▸ Earthsong Foundation**
617 E. Alameda
Santa Fe, NM 87501 (505)986-0323
**Concern(s):** health; spiritual; transformation; holism. A Taoist & Hawaiian, healing, teaching & meditation foundation located in Santa Fe, New Mexico. Individual services offered include Hawaiian Shamanic healing, individual High Self readings, belief system healing and clearing, pas lives work, Hypnotherapy and meditation instruction. **Contact(s):** H. Elizabeth Burke, Christopher M. Burke.

**✌ ▸ The Earthstewards Network**
Box 10697
Bainbridge Island, WA 98110 (206)842-7986
**Affiliation:** Holyearth Foundation. **Concern(s):** peace; spiritual; environment; conflict resolution; global networking. "Agents of conscious, loving change who individually commit themselves to a program of service which they themselves have conceived. In small ways and in large ways, within themselves and within their sphere of influence, they facilitate the shift from a system based on competition, aggression, suspicion and intolerance to a new consciousness based on cooperation, sharing, openness, and acceptance. **Other Resources:** Newsletter. Parry, formerly a psychologist then nuclear physicist with the Atomic Energy Commission before working with Mother Teresa, is author of ESSENE BOOK OF DAYS; THE EARTHSTEWARDS HANDBOOK; WARRIORS OF THE HEART, LEADERSHIP FOR THE 21ST CENTURY. Nonprofit. **Est.:** 1980. **Dues:** $25/yr. includes newsletter. **Frequency:** 6/yr. **Subscription:** $18/yr. **Pages:** 8. **Circ.:** 4M. **E-Network:** PeaceNet. **Contact(s):** Danaan Parry (Director), Diana Glasgow (Project Director).

**H ▸ EarthSave Foundation**
Box 949
Felton, CA 95018 (408)423-4069
**Concern(s):** health; environment; spiritual; energy; nutrition; conservation; transformation; vegetarian; animal rights. Provides education and leadership for transition to more healthful and environmentally sound food choices, non-polluting energy supplies and a wiser use of natural resources. It points the way to an ecologically sustainable future, in harmony and vital partnership with the web of life. Educates people about the cumulative impact of America's food choices and how it affects our health, happiness and the future of life on Earth. **Other Resources:** See CONNECTING THE DOTS newsletter. Founder, John Robbins authored DIET FOR A NEW AMERICA. A fact booklet, REALITIES, is available for $1.50. Nonprofit. **Office:** 706 Frederick St. Santa Cruz, CA 95062-2205. Hotline: (213)964-4455. **Contact(s):** John Robbins. **Other:** Los Angeles, Box 6567, Malibu, CA 90265

**✈ ▸ Earthwatch**
680 Mt. Auburn St.
Box 403-CA
Watertown, MA 02272 (617)926-8200
**Concern(s):** education; environment; forests; conservation; volunteers; travel. "To preserve our environment, we must understand it." Members support over 120 field scientists in their efforts to uncover the mysteries of our world. Members spend one to three weeks working at research sites, contributing time, money, and enthusiasm. Over 100 scientific research expeditions all over the world that volunteers can participate in - anthropological digs, observing dolphins, monitoring sea turtles. Nonprofit. **Dues:** $25/yr. **Member:** Co-op America. **Contact(s):** Brian Rosborough (President).

**E ▸ Earthworm, Inc.**
186 South St.
Boston, MA 02111 (617)426-7344
**Concern(s):** environment; recycling; conservation. Offers hotline/referral service to individuals interested in establishing recycling programs in their offices or in finding a program near their homes. Organizes school and community group presentations and provides advice and start-up funds for new recycling ventures and grassroots efforts. Publishes list of companies that sell recycled paper products.

**✍ ▸ Eastern Co-op Recreation School**
49 West 96th St., #4C
New York, NY 10025 (212)866-5362
**Concern(s):** education; recreation; youth. Workshops in recreational leadership training: how to lead people of all ages in singing, dancing, performing skits, and playing cooperative games. **Member:** Co-op America.

**P ▸ The Eastern Europe Constitution Design Forum**
20 Heber Rd.
London, NW2 6AA England (4481208 2853
**Concern(s):** politics; future; peace; ideation; invention; voting; grassroots organizing; research; East-West. A network for action, research, support and consultancy for Eastern Europe's emerging democracies wanting help with constitution design or electoral systems. **Other Resources:** International meetings for constitution designers, helpline for expert advice. Publishes forum newsletter. **Est.:** 1990. **Frequency:** Irregular. **Subscription:** Donation. **Pages:** 2. **Circ.:** 250. **Fax:** (4481 452 6434. **Contact(s):** Nicholas Albery (Secretary).

**E ▸ Eco-Home Network**
4344 Russell Ave.
Los Angeles, CA 90027 (213)662-5207
**Affiliation:** Resources & Services Project. **Concern(s):** environment; urban; sustainability; architecture; planning. Recent scientific findings show that the way we humans inhabit our planet is causing problems which threaten our very survival. This Network is a community of people creating an ecological future for our cities. The demonstration home is open for tours on Sundays and Tuesdays. **Other Resources:** See ECOLUTION newsletter. **Dues:** $20, $25 household, $50 institutions/businesses. **Contact(s):** Julia Russell (Founder/Executive Director), Bob Walter (President). (213)388-5338.

**E ▸ The Eco-Justice Project and Network**
Anabel Taylor Hall
Cornell University
Ithaca, NY 14853 (607)255-9240
**Affiliation:** Center for Religion, Ethics and Social Policy/Genesee Area Campus Ministries. **Concern(s):** environment; agriculture; spiritual; interfaith. A healthy environment and a good society depend upon the values of stewardship, justice, and community. Programs include: Sufficient and Sustainable Agriculture; Untangling the Waste Knot; Energy Conservation and Efficiency; Good Work; Economics as Stewardship; Eco-Just Living; Environment and Social Justice as Peace and Security Issues; Eco-Justice as an Ethical Perspective. Many programs are geared for campus groups, community organizations and churches, and include slides, visuals and videos. **Other Resources:** Sponsors conferences and workshops, produces audio-visuals, provides consultation services and leadership training. See EGG, A JOURNAL OF ECO-JUSTICE and Center for Religion. **Est.:** 1974. **Dues:** $25/yr. **Contact(s):** Mary Jeanette Ebenhack (Eco-Justice Project Executive Director), William E. Gibson (Editor). (607)255-4225.

**E ▸ Ecologia (Ecologists Linked for Organizing Grassroots Initiatives)**
Box 199
Harford, PA 18823 (717)434-2873
**Concern(s):** environment; peace; politics; community organization; activism; East-West. An NGO created to provide direct linkages between grassroots environmental groups in the US, Soviet Union, and Eastern Europe. Initiates cooperative projects with a concrete local focus designed to respond to these concerns. It also promotes the development of democratic decision-making skills. Environmental activism provides an important pathway to political participation for citizens who have never before participated in grassroots democratic movements. **Other Resources:** ECOLOGIA newsletter, a monthly publication mailed at no charge to Soviet Union and Eastern Europe. **Est.:** 1989. **Subscription:** $18/ yr. **Fax:** (717)945-7572. **Contact(s):** Randy Kritkausky (Ecologia President), Carolyn Schmidt (Ecologia Newsletter Editor).

**A ▸ Ecology Action**
5798 Ridgewood Rd.
Willits, CA 95490
**Concern(s):** agriculture; organic. An organization that emphasizes organic gardening along with other important agricultural aspects of the environment. **Other Resources:** Publishes ORGANIC GARDENING WITH BOUNTIFUL GARDENS. **Contact(s):** John Jevons.

**E ▸ Ecology Center**
2530 San Pablo Ave.
Berkeley, CA 94702 (510)548-2220
**Affiliation:** Berkeley Ecology Center. **Concern(s):** environment; agriculture. This organization operates the oldest recycling program in California and serves as a comprehensive environmental information center. It strives to develop and demonstrate sound alternatives to environmentally destructive practices. It can also supply you with the names and addresses for sources for untreated, non-hybrid, open pollinated, heirloom, or native seeds. **Other Resources:** Monthly newsletter, recycling hotline, bookstore, library and clipping files. Nonprofit. **Est.:** 1969. **Contact(s):** Dave Kershner.

**E ▸ Ecology Center of Southern California**
Box 35473
Los Angeles, CA 90035 (310)559-9160
**Affiliation:** Educational Communications, Inc.. **Concern(s):** environment; education; media; activism; research; networking; conservation; press. A regional conservation group serving an area of over 15 million people. Its many functions include being a clearinghouse, referral service, speakers bureau, and activist arm of the environmental movement. **Other Resources:** See Educational Communications. **Est.:** 1958.

**E ▸ Ecology For Knowledge Network**
Box 57
Orangeburg, NY 10962
**Concern(s):** environment; health; conservation; hazardous/toxic waste; networking. "Orthic man measures his actions in terms of their value in preserving life on planet earth. Economic man measures his actions in terms of the use and exchange of scarce natural resources. Orthic man would quickly end pollutants which produce the problems caused by economic man."

**$ ▸ Economic Policy Institute**
1730 Rhode Island Ave. NW, #812
Washington, DC 20036 (202)775-8810
**Concern(s):** economics.

**$ ▸ Economic Renewal Program**
See BUSINESS OPPORTUNITIES WORKBOOK, IMPLEMENTING ECONOMIC RENEWAL PROJECTS and Rocky Mountain Institute.

**M ▸ Economics**
Box 365
Adamsville, RI 02801
**Concern(s):** media; economics; multilogues. **Contact(s):** Richard T. Borden.

**E ▸ Ecoropa**
See ECOCURRENTS (periodicals).

**U ▸ EcoVillage**
3551 White House Place
Los Angeles, CA 90004 (213)738-1254
**Affiliation:** Los Angeles Mutual Housing Association. **Concern(s):** urban; environment; demographics; conservation; preservation; inner city; planning; sustainability; housing. EcoVillage has been in the planning stages for eight years. Currently planned from an 11 acre Department of Water and Power owned land fill five miles northeast of downtown L.A. Nonprofit.

**T ▸ Ecumenical Program On Central America & the Caribbean (EPICA)**
1470 Irving St.NW
Washington, DC 20010 (202)332-0292
**Concern(s):** Third World; politics; Central America. Educates the American public about social and political struggles in Central America and the Caribbean and about US impact on development of these societies. EPICA is a small press and solidarity organization which publishes educational materials on Central America and the Caribbean and offers faith-based forums such as delegations and workshops using a popular education model on El Salvador, Guatemala and Nicaragua. **Other Resources:** See CHALLENGE: A JOURNAL OF FAITH AND ACTION IN CENTRAL AMERICA (periodical). **Est.:** 1968. **E-Network:** Peacenet. **ID:** 'epica'. **Fax:** (202)332-1184. **Contact(s):** Minor Sinclair.

**A ▸ Eden Acres, Inc.**
12100 Lima Center Rd.
Clinton, MI 49236 (517)456-4288
**Concern(s):** agriculture; economics; health; organic; alternative consumer; nutrition. **Other Resources:** See Organic Network (directories).

**✌ ▸ The Edge of Life Center**
1800 S. Robertson Blvd., #161
Los Angeles, CA 90035 (310)398-2843
**Concern(s):** peace; environment; media; education; activism; broadcasting; press; networking. The foundation fosters world peace and environmental consciousness through our newsletter, radio broadcasts, grassroots networking, publishing books and articles, and producing consciousness-raising events. "We are members of all the major environmental and peace organizations, and teach workshops on how each person counts." **Contact(s):** Barry Klein (Director), Jill Gwin (310)398-5732.

**D ▸ The Edna McConnel Clark Foundation**
250 Park Ave.
New York, NY 10177-0026 (212)986-7050
**Concern(s):** demographics; homelessness. This foundation has taken on the task of finding who is really homeless, taking action to solve the problem. Their study, Families on the Move, chronicles the stories of nine formerly homeless families and their struggles to make a positive and permanent adjustment. The recommendations based on their experiences could help break the cycle of homelessness.

**✍ ▸ Educational Communications**
Box 35473
Los Angeles, CA 90035 (310)559-9160
**Affiliation:** Ecology Center of Southern California. **Concern(s):** education; media; environment; broadcasting; activism. Produces EcoNews, radio and TV programming on the environment. See, also, COMPENDIUM NEWSLETTER; DIRECTORY OF ENVIRONMENTAL ORGANIZATIONS; and ENVIRONMENTAL DIRECTIONS and ENVIRONMENTAL VIEWPOINTS, radio interview shows. **Est.:** 1958. **Contact(s):** Nancy Pearlman (Executive Producer).

**T ▸ Educational Concerns for Hunger Organization (ECHO)**
See ECHO DEVELOPMENT NOTES (periodicals).

**$ ▸ Educators Against Racism and Apartheid**
164-04 Goethals Ave.
Jamaica, NY 11432 (201)836-6644
**Concern(s):** economics; Third World; education; peace; boycott; South Africa; foreign policy. Promotes materials, teacher education, and a new curriculum for schools in the NY area and beyond. Specifically, they plan to demonstrate "20 Ways" to bring the issues of racism and apartheid into subject areas where they are not usually addressed, such as math, art, or English. Education and action projects to help end apartheid. Developed curriculum and newsletter for use in schools. APARTHEID IS WRONG: Curriculum for Young People, grades 1-12. **Est.:** 1982. **Contact(s):** Paula Bower (Co-chairperson).

**✌ ▸ Educators for Social Responsibility**
23 Garden St.
Cambridge, MA 02138 (617)492-1764
**Concern(s):** peace; education; conflict resolution; militarism; disarmament; students. A teachers' organization that offers curricula and professional development addressing the socially significant controversies of the nuclear age. Publications reflect pedagogical emphasis on dialogue, questioning, cooperative problem-solving, nonviolent conflict resolution, an informed decision making. Curricula designed to encourage participation, assist in development of conscience, and empower students and teach contemplation. **Other Resources:** Offers publications and professional development; trains teachers in nuclear education and develops teaching guides. Produces a newsletter. A growing network of local chapters and professional development programs. See FORUM magazine. **Contact(s):** Susan Alexander (Executive Director), Sheldon Berman (President).

**✌ ▸ Einstein Experience**
1839 Edgeland Ave.
Louisville, KY 40204
**Concern(s):** peace; energy; education; world order; science. An education project which provides an introduction to this century's information explosion. Examines widely held assumptions in light of current technological capacities and provides information supporting the contention that humanity now possesses the technical capacity to eliminate hunger, overpopulation, environmental destruction, and nuclear war. Supports people in taking individual responsibility to act on this opportunity by working toward a unified world. **Contact(s):** Michael Kessler.

**✪ ▸ Electric Power Research Institute**
3412 Hillview Ave.
Palo Alto, CA 94303 (415)855-2000
**Concern(s):** energy.

**✪ ▸ Electricity Consumers Resource Council**
1333 H St. NW
Washington, DC 20005-3905 (202)682-1390
**Concern(s):** energy; environment; conservation; efficiency; resource management.

**S ▸ The Eleventh Commandment Fellowship**
Box 14667
San Francisco, CA 94114
**Concern(s):** spiritual; peace; faith. "Thou shall not kill."

**A ▸ Elfin Permaculture**
7781 Lenox St.
Jacksonville, FL 32221
**Concern(s):** agriculture; environment; organic; permaculture. "Permaculture is the design process of bringing our lives back into participation with the process of Earth. Permaculture proponent Bill Mollison warns of global destruction unless we learn to live with Earth rather than continuing to prey upon her. It is based on the conviction that the Earth shows us solutions to halt the destruction of the biosphere." **Other Resources:** See THE INTERNATIONAL PERMACULTURE SPECIES YEARBOOK (TIPSY) (directories) and ROBIN, the newsletter of the Solutions Network. Also Forest Ecosystem Rescue Network (FERN) and RESOURCES OF INTERNATIONAL PERMACULTURE (TRIP) (directories). **Contact(s):** Dan Hemenway, Cynthia Baxter.

**E ▸ Elmwood Institute**
Box 5765
Berkeley, CA 94705 (510)845-4595
**Concern(s):** environment; spiritual; social ecology; transformation. A think tank for ecological and philosophical ideas with a strong bent toward the political, to "nurture new ecological visions by promoting a cultural transformation from the mechanistic Western, patriarchal worldview to a more holistic one. Proponents of the "New Physics" and economics working towards a "paradigm shift." Projects include series of reports on ecological practices in business and government, special publications, symposia and dialogues. **Other Resources:** See ELMWOOD NEWSLETTER, features noted writers such as Hazel Henderson Ernest Callenbach, Charlene Spretnak, Chellis Glendinning, and others. **Est.:** 1984. **Fax:** (510)845-1439. **Contact(s):** Fritjof Capra (Founder).

**$ ▸ Employment Research Associates**
115 W. Allegan St., #810
Lansing, MI 48933 (517)485-7655
**Concern(s):** economics; labor; politics; peace; budget; monopolies; government accountability; municipal; taxation. An independent economic consulting firm which specializes in analyzing the impact of government policies on the US economy. Has established a national reputation for producing carefully researched, clearly written reports which show the impact of changes in government expenditures on the economies of cities, states, and the nation. **Other Resources:** Reports and publications available. Nonprofit. **Contact(s):** Marion Anderson (Director). **Other:** 474 Hollister Bldg., Lansing, MI 48933.

**D ▸ The End Hunger Network**
222 N. Beverly Dr.
Beverly Hills, CA 90210 (310)273-3179
**Concern(s):** demographics; hunger. A corporation dedicated to focusing the power of the communications media and the entertainment community on helping to create the popular and political will to end the deaths due to hunger. By creating coalitions of nonprofit agencies, business, government, media, and entertainment personalities, the Network creates media events, programs, and educational materials. The Network's goal is to stimulate the increased awareness and involvement needed to enact solutions. Nonprofit. **Contact(s):** Jerry Michaud.

**✪ ▸ The Energy Conservation Coalition**
235 Pennsylvania Ave. SE
Washington, DC 20003 (202)546-9554
**Affiliation:** Environmental Action Foundation. **Concern(s):** energy; environment; politics; efficiency; acid rain; global warming; lobbying. Representing 20 national public interest organizations, promoting energy efficiency as part of an environmentally sound and cost-effective solution to the problems of acid rain, global warming, smog and loss of wilderness. A political lobbying organization. **Other Resources:** See Environmental Action, Inc. and ENVIRONMENTAL ACTION magazine. (202)745-4870. **Contact(s):** Nancy Hirsch, Nicholas A. Fedoruk (Director).

**✪ ▸ Energy Research Foundation**
537 Harden St.
Columbia, SC 29205-2230 (803)256-7298
**Concern(s):** energy; nuclear. Trying to clean up its regional nuclear weapons plant.

**✪ ▸ Environmental and Energy Studies Institute**
122 C St. NW, #700
Washington, DC 20001 (202)628-1400
**Concern(s):** energy; environment; air pollution. Independent nonpartisan organization mobilizes congressional leadership for a healthy environment and economy. Seeks incentives for energy efficiency, water conservation, pollution prevention and international cooperation. **Member:** Environmental Federation of America. (202)546-3200.

**E ▸ Environmental Action Coalition**
625 Broadway
New York, NY 10012 (212)677-1601
**Concern(s):** environment; activism; conservation; preservation. This coalition is striving for better care of our environment through activism, lobbying, and education. **Other Resources:** See Radioactive Waste Campaign.

**E ▸ Environmental Action Foundation**
6930 Carroll Ave., #600
Tacoma Park, MD 20912 (301)891-1100
**Concern(s):** environment; energy; education; politics; health; efficiency; hazardous/toxic waste. A brainchild of Nadar's, this organization concentrates on education, research, training, and political action in relation to electric utilities, nuclear power, hazardous waste, and toxins. See Energy Conservation Coalition; Solid Waste Alternatives Project (SWAP); and a yearly publication, DIRTY DOZEN, that discusses the 12 top polluters in the country. **Other Resources:** See POWERLINE, a journal of their Energy Project; and WASTELINE, newsletter of their Solid Waste Project; ENVIRONMENTAL ACTION magazine; MAKING POLLUTERS PAY: A CITIZEN'S GUIDE TO LEGAL ACTION AND ORGANIZING; WRAPPED IN PLASTICS; and "Fact Packets." **Member:** Environmental Federation of America. **Contact(s):** Phillip J. Perkins (Director), Ruth Caplan (Executive Director). (202)466-5045.

**P ▸ Environmental Community of Democratic Socialists of America**
See EcoSocialist REVIEW (periodicals).

**$ ▸ Environmental Construction Network**
RR 1
Caledon East, ON LON 1E0 **Canada** (519)941-6499
**Concern(s):** economics; environment; health; urban; trade; sustainability; alternative consumer; hazardous/toxic. Information exchange for environmentally responsible design, construction, and operation of built space. Emphasis on nonallergic and toxic components. **Contact(s):** Ed Lowans.

**E ▸ Environmental Data Research Institute**
797 Elmwood Ave.
Rochester, NY 14620 (716)473-3090
**Concern(s):** environment; economics; philanthropy; volunteers. Purpose: Established to provide the environmental community with information on organizations, publications, and funding. "EDRI has developed a comprehensive database of environmental grants, which we use to provide detailed custom reports on who's giving money, who's getting it, where it goes, and for what purpose." Current Emphasis: Analysis of funding by topic (biodiversity, energy, toxics,

etc.), activity (research, advocacy, etc.), geographic region and scope. **Other Resources:** Volunteer Programs, some internships are available. **Est.:** 1989. **Fax:** (716)473-0968.

### E ♦ Environmental Defense Fund (EDF)
1616 P St. NW, #150
Washington, DC 20036 (202)387-3500
**Concern(s):** environment; law; corporate responsibility; lobbying. Staff of lawyers, scientists and economists conducts research, public education, litigation, and administration and legislative advocacy on environmental issues; international interests focus on role of multinational development banks in encouraging exploitation of resources for export. Lawsuits for wildlife, clean air, environment and public health. Currently focussing on solid waste management, global climate change, tropical rainforest deforestation and toxin control. **Other Resources:** See EDF LETTER. Publications list available and brochure describing everything you ever wanted to know about recycling, COMING FULL CIRCLE: SUCCESSFUL RECYCLING TODAY. Summer internships. See Questers Tours and Travels. **Dues:** $20/yr. **Member:** Global Tomorrow Coalition; Environmental Federation of America. (800)CALL EDF. **Contact(s):** Frederic D. Krupp (Executive Director), Michael J. Bean (Wildlife Program Director). **Other:** 257 Park Ave. South, New York, NY 10010(212)505-2100.

### E ♦ Environmental Education Association of Oregon
Box 40047
Portland, OR 97240 (800)322-3326
**Concern(s):** environment; education.

### E ♦ Environmental Education Group
3201 Corte Malpaso, #304
Camarillo, CA 93012 (805)484-8738
**Concern(s):** environment; demographics; energy; education; conservation; housing. An educational center and demonstration community for the study and promotion of Ecosystems management and resource-conserving design.

### E ♦ Environmental Federation of America
3007 Tilden St. NW, #4L
Washington, DC 20008 (202)537-7100
**Concern(s):** environment; health; education; economics; alternative consumer; socially-responsible investing; conservation; preservation; hazardous/toxic waste; wilderness; natural resources. A federation of 24 environmental and conservation agencies that help prevent human health problems from air, water and toxic pollution; protect and conserve fresh water, marine and land based resources, preserve biological diversity and wildlife habitat; and develop educational programs which promote a sound and balanced use of natural resources. **Other Resources:** See, Earth Share, a program that allows you to invest through long distance dialing. Nonprofit. **Est.:** 1990. **Fax:** (202)537-7101. (800)875-3863. **Contact(s):** Kalman Stein (Executive Director).

### D ♦ The Environmental Fund
1325 G St. NW, #1003
Washington, DC 20005 (202)879-3000
**Affiliation:** Carrying Capacity Network. **Concern(s):** demographics; environment; population growth. **Other Resources:** Publishes THE OTHER SIDE and TEF data; SAVING THE DREAM, QUALITY OF LIFE IN AMERICA.

### E ♦ Environmental Grantmakers Association
See ENVIRONMENTAL GRANTMAKERS DIRECTORY.

### E ♦ Environmental Hazards Management Institute
Box 932, 10 Newmarket Rd.
Durham, NH 03824 (603)868-1496
**Concern(s):** environment; health; hazardous/toxic waste; recycling; water; pollution. An Institute that provides useful and timely information on hazardous and toxic wastes. Also provides information on water conservation and pollution and useful ways to recycle. **Other Resources:** Sells the HOUSEHOLD HAZARDOUS WASTE WHEEL, WATER SENSE WHEEL, and RECYCLING WHEEL.

### H ♦ Environmental Health Center
8345 Walnut Hills, #205
Dallas, TX 75231 (214)368-4132
**Concern(s):** health; hazardous/toxic waste. **Contact(s):** Dr. Gerry Ross.

### E ♦ Environmental Health Watch
4115 Bridge Ave., #104
Cleveland, OH 44113 (216)961-4646
**Concern(s):** environment; health; hazardous/toxic waste; communities; preventive health. Information and assistance on environmental health issues for local individuals and community groups. **Other Resources:** HEALTHY HOUSE CATALOG. **Member:** Co-op America.

### E ♦ Environmental Law Institute
1616 P St. NW, #200
Washington, DC 20036 (202)939-3800
**Concern(s):** environment; law; volunteers. Nationally recognized nonpartisan research and education center on environmental law and policy providing information and analysis services to a growing international constituency of professionals in law, government, finance, industry, and advocacy organizations. Staff includes lawyers, journalists, economists and scientist who do not litigate or lobby. Special interest include: Transboundary pollution, global warming, medical, solid and hazardous clean-up and wetlands protection. **Other Resources:** See ENVIRONMENTAL LAW REPORTER; THE ENVIRONMENTAL FORUM; NATIONAL WETLANDS NEWSLETTER; DIRECTORY OF STATE ENVIRONMENTAL AGENCIES. Reference, LAW OF ENVIRONMENTAL PROTECTION, and many others. Internships available, and volunteers needed for publications. Nonprofit. **Est.:** 1969. **Member:** Environmental Federation of America. **Contact(s):** J. William Futrell (President).

### E ♦ Environmental Leadership Training Institute
Lincoln Filene Center
Tufts University
Medford, MA 02155 (617)381-3451
**Concern(s):** environment; politics; education; leadership; grassroots organizing; students. Promotes active citizenship. The center serves as a bridge between Tufts University and community, acting as catalyst, convener, and sponsor of programs to develop community leadership and effective democratic institutions. The Center is based on the premise that active citizenship is a major component of healthy community life. Concern with justice and equal opportunity, communication, inter-cooperation, and promotion of individual rights and public responsibilities are themes. **Contact(s):** Nancy Anderson, Tara Mitchell (617)381-3291.

### $ ♦ Environmental Management Committee
See Inter-American Development Bank (business).

### E ♦ The Environmental Network (TEN)
Box 5490
Fullerton, CA 92635 (714)870-8822
**Concern(s):** environment; economics; alternative markets; green consumer. "The network, through its distributors, attempts to promote environmental awareness while making available to the consumer what we believe to be the finest environmentally-safe, cruelty-free, continually expanding line of products for home and garden, personal care, health care, baby care and pet care." Nonprofit.

### E ♦ Environmental Policy Institute
218 D St. SE
Washington, DC 20003 (202)544-2600
**Affiliation:** Friends of the Earth. **Concern(s):** environment; demographics; politics; population growth; lobbying. An environmental organization which takes steps around the world to influence public policy to protect our future. **Other Resources:** Publishes monthly newsletter, ENVIRONMENTAL UPDATE. Friends of the Earth and Oceanic Society are members of the Institute. **Member:** Global Tomorrow Coalition. **Contact(s):** Michael Clark (President), Brent Blackwelder; Jack Doyle.

### E ♦ Environmental Protection Agency
See ENVIRONMENTAL ORGANIZATION DIRECTORY; PUBLIC INTEREST GROUP DIRECTORY; HOUSEHOLD HAZARDOUS WASTE (directories). See also, Public Information Center; and Alliance for Environmental Education.

### E ♦ Environmental Protection Information Center (EPIC)
Box 397
Garberville, CA 95440 (707)923-2931
**Concern(s):** environment; education; forests; conservation; wildlife/endangered species; lobbying; volunteers. EPIC is a resource center for volunteer activists, encouraging educational activity and participation in the democratic process. Despite its small budget, EPIC is waging on-going court battles to defend the forests form destructive, illegal logging practices. Donations to EPIC are tax-deductible. **Est.:** 1977. **Contact(s):** Jama Chaplin, John Angus.

### E ♦ Environmental Research Foundation
Box 73700
Washington, DC 20056-3700 (202)328-1119
**Concern(s):** environment; health; hazardous/toxic waste; waste management. "Provides technical assistance to environmental groups to strengthen democracy at the local level. We gather technical information, translate it into laymen's terms, then disseminate it using our weekly newsletter, our database, and direct personal assistance." **Other Resources:** Weekly newsletter, RACHELS HAZARDOUS WASTE NEWS; BBS, R.A.C.H.E.L.; and a publications list. **Est.:** 1981. **Office:** 1432 U St. NW Washington, DC 20009.

**Contact(s):** Robin Zeff (Associate Director), Maria Pellerano (Director of Finance).

### E ♦ Environmental Sabbath Project
UNEP
United Nations
New York, NY 10017 (212)963-8139
**Affiliation:** United Nations Environmental Programme. **Concern(s):** environment; spiritual; transformation; reform; interfaith. **Contact(s):** Noel J. Brown.

### E ♦ Environmental Studies Institute
See ENVIRONMENTAL PERIODICALS BIBLIOGRAPHY (directories).

### E ♦ Environmental Support Center
1905 Queen Ave. N, #126
Seattle, WA 98109
**Concern(s):** environment; grassroots organizing. A new organization designed to increase the effect of state and local environmental organizations through help with fundraising, especially in the workplace, giving camps, media, and organizational development.

### E ♦ Environmental Task Force
See Re: Sources (periodicals).

### E ♦ EOS Institute
26662 Calle Ultima
Capistrano Beach, CA 92624 (714)493-3568
**Concern(s):** environment; education; research; resource management; sustainability. A proposed education center and demonstration community for the study and promotion of Ecosystems management and resource-conserving design.

### P ♦ Episcopal Church Public Policy Network
815 2nd Ave.
New York, NY 10017 (212)867-8400
**Affiliation:** Episcopal Church Center, Office of Peace and Justice. **Concern(s):** politics; education; peace; demographics; environment; justice; energy; health; spiritual; faith; poverty; hunger; racism; discrimination. A network of Episcopalians who have affirmed their ministry of advocacy by joining together to receive information on national legislative issues, specifically those on which the Church has a state policy. The areas are: Food, Policy/Hunger, Peace/Disarmament, Economic and Social Justice, Racism/Discrimination, Health and Welfare, Energy and Ecology. Interacts with other ecumenical organizations committed to advocacy efforts. **Other Resources:** Numerous brochures and leaflets available. Ask! Publishes quarterly publication, JUBILEE JOURNAL, devoted to issues of the poor. (800)334-7626.

### 🕊 ♦ The Episcopal Peace Fellowship
Box 28156
Washington, DC 20038 (202)783-3380
**Affiliation:** Fellowship of Reconciliation. **Concern(s):** peace; spiritual; faith; nonviolence. A body of Episcopalians dedicated to discovering and practicing the Biblical concept of peace: shalom. This includes a commitment to renounce, so far as is possible, participation in war and other forms of violence. EPF assists Episcopalians and others to follow Christ's call to be peacemakers, through prayer, study, education, and action. Thus, the Fellowship endeavors to develop within the Church a community of Christians pledged to peace, justice, reconciliation, and nonviolence. **Other Resources:** Publishes quarterly newsletter, newsletter for local chapters, pamphlets on peace and justice issues, and bulletin inserts for parishes. Draft counseling assistance & materials, peace education resource materials, videos, speakers. Nonprofit. **Est.:** 1939. **Dues:** $25, $35/couple; $5/limited income. **E-Network:** PeaceNet: ID: 'epf'. **Office:** 1317 G St. NW Washington, DC 20005. **Fax:** (202)393-3695. (408)252-3181. **Contact(s):** Mary Miller (Executive Secretary), Ann P. McElroy (Chair). (408)252-1998. **Other:** Fellowship of Reconciliation, Box 271, Nyack, NY 10960.

### H ♦ Episcopal Society for Ministry on Aging
See DIRECTORY OF EPISCOPAL FACILITIES FOR THE ELDERLY.

### 🖉 ♦ Esalen Institute
Big Sur, CA 93920
**Concern(s):** education; health; spiritual; holism; transformation; conflict resolution. This retreat provides workshops and seminars for you to discover the inner self and realize inner peace. Great place to get away from it all and soak in its sulpher hot springs.

### $ ♦ Essential Information
See MULTINATIONAL MONITOR (periodicals).

### P ♦ Ethics & Public Policy Center
1015 15th St. NW
Washington, DC 20005 (202)682-1200
**Concern(s):** politics; justice.

**D ♦ Evangelical Lutheran Church Hunger Program**
Office of Church in Society
8765 W. Higgins Rd.
Chicago, IL 60631     (312)380-2709
**Concern(s):** demographics; hunger. **Contact(s):** Reverend John L. Halvorson, Barbara Lundblad (312)380-2700.

**P ♦ Evangelicals for Social Action**
Lancaster Ave. & City Line Ave.
Ardmore, PA 19151     (215)645-9390
**Concern(s):** politics; education; justice; spiritual; faith; grassroots organizing; research. Multi-issue organization with programs in education and public policy research. They are very strong in the field of grassroots community organizing. **Contact(s):** Ronald J. Sider, Van Temple (215)645-9390.

**✈ ♦ Experiment in International Living**
Kippling Rd.,Box 676
Brattleboro, VT 05301     (802)257-7751
**Affiliation:** School for International Studies. **Concern(s):** education; Third World; travel. Private organization that has been a leader in international education and exchange. Invented the homestead concept of learning the culture of another country by living as a member of one of its families. Has grown into a broadly diversified worldwide organization which promotes international understanding through citizen exchange, career-oriented higher education, language instruction and projects in international development and training. **Other Resources:** See School for International Training. Nonprofit. **Contact(s):** John G. Sommer.

**$ ♦ Fair Trade Campaign**
Box 80066
Minneapolis, MN 55408 (612)339-0586
**Concern(s):** economics; Third World; environment; spiritual; health; hazardous/toxic waste; development; community self-reliance; trade. FTC is a coalition of farm, church, consumer, and environmental groups urging Congress to protect American sovereignty, phase out export dumping and assist Third World self-reliance.

**M ♦ Fairness & Accuracy in Reporting**
130 W. 25th St., 8th Fl.
New York, NY 10001     (212)633-6700
**Concern(s):** media; politics; economics; media watch; press; responsibility; corporate responsibility; government accountability. Media watch group. Monitors and challenges bias in the daily press, networks, PBS. The national media watch group offers well-documented criticism in an effort to correct bias and imbalance. FAIR focuses public awareness on the narrow corporate ownership of the press, the media's persistent Cold War assumptions and their insensitivity to women, labor, minorities, and other public interest constituencies. Advocates greater media pluralism. **Other Resources:** EXTR🖉 newsletter and FAIR RESOURCE LISTS, a mini-directory of resources, general factoids, and alternative press. **Fax:** (212)727-7668. **Contact(s):** Jeff Cohen (Executive Director). (202)332-FAIR.

**♥ ♦ Family Life Information Exchange**
See DIRECTORY OF FAMILY PLANNING GRANTEES, DELEGATES, AND CLINICS.

**♥ ♦ Family Resource Coalition**
230 N. Michigan, #1625
Chicago, IL 60601
**Concern(s):** family. See PROGRAMS TO STRENGTHEN FAMILIES: A RESOURCE GUIDE. .

**J ♦ Family Reunification Project**
432 Park Ave. S, #1103
New York, NY 10016     (212)684-1221
**Affiliation:** International League for Human Rights. **Concern(s):** justice; peace; United Nations; political prisoners. Helps those detained by their governments and unable to rejoin with their families. .

**T ♦ Famine Foods for Africa**
695 Cragmont Ave.
Berkeley, CA 94708-1329     (510)528-3213
**Concern(s):** Third World; demographics; education; agriculture; Africa; hunger. The goals are: to identify all edible plants in Africa, provide information on their nutritional value, and illustrate in text and picture the growing plants so that they can be identified in the field. The food encyclopedia, once completed, will not only provide valuable information in times of ecological disaster but will identify indigenous plants which might be developed commercially. **Contact(s):** Robert L. Freedman.

**♨ ♦ Farallones Institute**
15290 Coleman Valley Rd
Occidental, CA 95465     (707)874-3060
**Concern(s):** education; economics; community self-reliance. Established to develop social and physical tools to live equitable and

autonomous lives. Seeking to be free from the commodity dependence that pervades contemporary society. **Est.:** 1969.

**A ♦ Farm Aid**
21 Erie Street, #20
Cambridge, MA 02139     (617)354-2922
**Concern(s):** agriculture; family farms; farmland.

**🌱 ♦ Farm Animal Reform Movement (FARM)**
Box 30654
Bethesda, MD 20824     (301)530-1737
**Concern(s):** environment; agriculture; health; animal rights; vegetarian. A public interest organization formed by animal, consumer, and environmental protection advocates to expose and stop animal abuse and other destructive impacts of factory farming. Each year, FARM conducts four major national campaigns through a network of hundreds of local groups and individual activists. **Other Resources:** See newsletter, THE FARM REPORT. Nonprofit. **Est.:** 1981. **Dues:** $20-$1000/yr. **Price:** Free. **Contact(s):** Alex Hershaft (President), Michael Winikoff (Legislative Coordinator).

**A ♦ Farm Verified Organic**
Box 45
Redding, CT 06875     (203)544-9896
**Concern(s):** agriculture; environment; health; organic certification; nutrition; green consumer.

**A ♦ Farming Alternatives Project**
443 Warren Hall
Cornell University
Ithaca, NY 14853     (607)255-9832
**Concern(s):** agriculture. **Contact(s):** Judy Green.

**? ♦ Federal Incentive Awards Program**
Office of Personnel Management
US Government, 1900 E St. NW
Washington, DC 20415 (202)376-3800
**Concern(s):** future; economics; ideation; budget. Under this program, 37 individuals or groups have won awards for money-saving suggestions since its inception. In 1987, 169,000 people (about 7% of all federal employees) submitted suggestions; about 43,000 of the ideas were implemented, saving the government some $386 million! **Est.:** 1954.

**⚭ ♦ Federalist Caucus**
Box 19482
Portland, OR 97219
**Concern(s):** peace; politics; disarmament; law. Transnational registry of voters who are philosophically and politically supportive of national legislators in Parliamentarians Global Action and/or Arms Control & Foreign Policy Caucus of US Congress; sends annual reports. **Contact(s):** Neal Potter (President), Elizabeth R. Dana

**D ♦ Federation for American Immigration Reform**
1666 Connecticut Ave. NW, #701
Washington, DC 20009 (202)328-7004
**Concern(s):** demographics; justice; Third World; immigration; refugees.

**⚭ ♦ Federation of American Scientists**
307 Massachusetts Ave. NE
Washington, DC 20002 (202)546-3300
**Concern(s):** peace; environment; energy; education; health; hazardous/toxic waste; science; anti-nuclear. Conducts research and lobbying on problems that affect science and society, including arms control and disarmament. This organization promotes the development of teaching materials, resources and curricula concerning nuclear war. **Other Resources:** Publishes a bulletin, CHEMICAL WEAPONS CONVENTION BULLETIN; PUBLIC INTEREST REPORT; and FAS PUBLIC INTEREST REPORTS. Sponsors Nuclear War Education Project.

**$ ♦ Federation of Egalitarian Communities**
Box FB4
Tecumseh, MO 65760     (417)679-4682
**Concern(s):** economics; justice; intentional communities; cooperatives; land trusts. A network of several communities, each of which shares income and resources, and practices nonviolent and nondiscriminatory behavior. Each FEC community holds its land, labor, and other resources in common, and is committed to equality, ecology, and participatory democracy. Group size ranges from small homesteads to small villages. Assembles twice a year. **Other Resources:** A directory of 200 communities is available from Sandhill Farm. **Subscription:** $20/yr. **Member:** Co-op America.

**E ♦ Federation of Organizations for Conservation of Urban Space**
Box 1711
Santa Monica, CA 90406     (310)459-6398
**Concern(s):** environment; politics; urban; preservation; government

accountability. Since 1970, FOCUS' major activities include: circulating a "City Hall Watchers Guide," monitoring unnecessary street and private tree removals by local governments, alerting residents citywide to pending local government actions that will harmfully impact their neighborhoods. **Est.:** 1970.

**F ♦ Federation of Organizations for Professional Women**
2001 S St. NW
Washington, DC 20006 (202)328-1415
**Concern(s):** feminism; labor; politics; equal rights. Established to attain equal opportunity for women in education and employment. **Other Resources:** See WOMEN'S YELLOW BOOK (directories). **Est.:** 1972.

**⚭ ♦ Federation of Scientists**
See guides, FROM STAR WARS TO THE ALTERNATIVE and ALL THINGS NUCLEAR (directories).

**$ ♦ Fellowship for Intentional Community**
Center for Communal Studies
8600 University Blvd
Evansville, IN 47712     (816)464-1727
**Affiliation:** Center for Communal Studies. **Concern(s):** economics; community self-reliance; intentional communities; cooperatives. A North American network of groups and individuals interested in supporting and promoting intentional community, based on common values of cooperation and peaceful transformation. The FIC helps to gather and make available information for people looking for a home in a community or otherwise seeking valuable insights into the dynamics of their lives. Provides a forum for sharing among a wide range of intentional communities, networks and support organizations, and people seeking a community. **Other Resources:** Co-published the 1990/91 DIRECTORY OF INTENTIONAL COMMUNITIES. Nonprofit. **Est.:** 1987. **Dues:** $15, $25, $40/yr. **Contact(s):** Laird Schaub (Secretary), Caroline Estes (President). (503)964-5102.

**⚭ ♦ Fellowship of Reconciliation (FOR)**
Box 271
Nyack, NY 10960     (914)358-4601
**Concern(s):** peace; education; justice; spiritual; conflict resolution; militarism; interfaith; nonviolence; disarmament. FOR sponsors programs and educational projects concerned with racial justice, disarmament, US/USSR reconciliation, and conflict resolution in schools, in addition to providing literature and resources on nonviolence and peacemaking. An interfaith pacifist organization first inspired by the Quakers, FOR members are from many religious and ethnic traditions with chapter in over 28 countries. Provides literature, audiovisuals and other resources on nonviolence and peacemaking. **Other Resources:** Children's Creative Response to Conflict; FELLOWSHIP MAGAZINE & SHARING SPACE newsletter. Racial & Economic Justice; US-USSR Reconciliation; Disarmament; Mid-East; Nonviolence; Latin America; Young Peacemakers Projects Luthern/Episcopal Peace Fellowships. **Est.:** 1914. **Contact(s):** Al Hassier, Fran Levin.

**T ♦ Fellowship of Reconciliation Task Force on Latin America**
515 Broadway
Santa Cruz, CA 95063     (408)423-1626
**Concern(s):** Third World; justice; peace; Latin America; intervention; foreign policy. A program which helps heal the wounds created by the American government and their intervening foreign policy.

**S ♦ Fellowship of Religious Humanists**
See RELIGIOUS HUMANISM (periodicals).

**F ♦ Feminist Business and Professional Network (FBPN)**
See directory under same name.

**F ♦ The Feminist Institute**
Box 30563
Bethesda, MD 20824     (301)951-9040
**Concern(s):** feminism; politics. Policies for social change concerning women's issues. **Est.:** 1985. **Contact(s):** Caroline Sparks (President).

**F ♦ Feminists Against Pornography**
Box 6731, Yorkville Station
New York, NY 10128
**Concern(s):** feminism; family; sexism; rape/sexual abuse; child abuse.

**🌱 ♦ Feminists for Animal Rights**
Box 10017, N. Berkeley Station
Berkeley, CA 94709     (415)547-7251
**Concern(s):** feminism; environment; sexism; animal rights. This organization wishes to expose the connection between animal abuse and abuse of women. **Other Resources:** Publishes a magazine.

**F ▸ Feminists for Reason**
See APPEAL magazine.

**$ ▸ Financial Democracy Campaign**
2009 Chapel Hill
Durham, NC 27707 (919)419-1841
**Concern(s):** economics; agriculture; politics; environment; government accountability; reform; corporate responsibility; grassroots organizing; taxation. Mr. Hightower was formerly with the Commissioner of the Texas Department of Agriculture. Presently the focus is the S & L bailout. **Other Resources:** Starting a radio program. **Contact(s):** Tom Schlesinger, Steve Kest (Coordinators). **Other:** 739 8th St. SE, Washington, DC 20003 Jim Hightower, Chairman/Founder.

**$ ▸ Finger Lakes Green Fund**
Box 6578
Ithaca, NY 14851 (607)387-3424
**Concern(s):** economics; environment; taxation; green consumer. A collective of businesspeople who have agreed to collect a Green Tax that pays into a fund for environmental nonprofits.

**E ▸ Fish and Wildlife Reference Service**
See FISH AND WILDLIFE REFERENCE SERVICE NEWSLETTER and listing under same name in directories section.

**✍ ▸ The Five College Program in Peace and World Security Studies**
Hampshire College
Amherst, MA 01002 (413)549-4600
**Concern(s):** education; peace; national security; students. See directories section for GUIDE TO CAREERS AND GRADUATE EDUCATION IN PEACE STUDIES. **Contact(s):** Dr. Michael Clare (Director).

**✌ ▸ Florida Coalition for Peace and Justice**
Box 2486
Orlando, FL 32802 (407)422-3479
**Concern(s):** peace; justice; politics. **Contact(s):** Bruce Gagnon.

**✪ ▸ Florida Solar Energy Center (FSEC)**
300 State Rd., #401
Cape Canaveral, FL 32920
**Affiliation:** University of Central Florida. **Concern(s):** energy; education; solar; alternative; science. FSEC is the energy institute of the State University System of Florida, under the administration of the University of Central Florida, Orlando. The State Legislature established FSEC in 1974 to conduct research on alternative energy technologies, to ensure the quality of solar energy equipment sold in Florida, and to educate people about their energy options. The Center conducts state, federal and privately supported research in solar water heating, photovoltaics, energy use in buildings, etc. **Est.:** 1974.

**H ▸ Flower Essence Society**
Box 459
Nevada City, CA 95959 (916)265-9163
**Affiliation:** Earth-Spirit, Inc. **Concern(s):** health; environment; education; holism. Currently the largest and most active branch of Earth-Spirit. Members are health practitioners throughout the world who support research and educational programs that deepen the understanding of flower essences as a therapeutic modality. Donations support vital field and clinical research work concerning many North American plant species and help sustain educational efforts. **Other Resources:** Their Flower Essence Services offers a catalog which is devoted exclusively to the preparation of flower essences and related goods and services. Publications list available. Order: (800)548-0075. **Contact(s):** Richard Katz, Patricia Kaminski (Co-directors).

**✈ ▸ Folkways Travel**
14600 SE Aldrigd Rd.
Portland, OR 97236 (800)225-4666
**Concern(s):** education; travel. Study, research, and development tours all over the world, including Vietnam and Burma. **Member:** Co-op America.

**L ▸ Food & Allied Service Trades (AFL-CIO)**
815 16th St. NW, #406
Washington, DC 20006 (202)737-7200
**Concern(s):** labor; agriculture; unions. **Contact(s):** Keith Mestrich.

**A ▸ Food and Water, Inc.**
225 Lafayette St., #612
New York, NY 10012 (212)941-9340
**Concern(s):** agriculture; environment; health; natural resources; water; nutrition; hazardous/toxic waste. See Food Irradiation Alert! under periodicals. (800)EAT-SAFE. **Contact(s):** Michael Colby, Christina Roessler **Other:** 3 Whitman Drive, Denville, NJ 07834(201)625-3111.

**A ▸ Food for Survival**
See Second Harvest National Food Bank Network.

**D ▸ Food for the Hungry**
Box E
Scottsdale, AZ 85252 (602)955-8438
**Concern(s):** demographics; hunger. **Contact(s):** Ted Noble, Bruce Bell, Ted Yamamori.

**D ▸ Food First**
145 9th St.
San Francisco, CA 94103 (415)864-8555
**Affiliation:** Institute for Food and Development Policy. **Concern(s):** demographics; agriculture; Third World; hunger; development; food production and distribution; policy; poverty. This is the action arm for the Institute for Food and Development Policy. **Other Resources:** See Good Life Study Tours. **Contact(s):** Frances Moore Lappe, Marilyn Borchadt

**D ▸ Food Industry Crusade Against Hunger**
1750 K St. NW
Washington, DC 20006 (202)429-4555
**Concern(s):** demographics; agriculture; hunger; food distribution; food production. **Contact(s):** George Scharffenberger.

**A ▸ Food Marketing Institute**
1750 K St. NW
Washington, DC 20006 (202)452-8444
**Concern(s):** agriculture; demographics; hunger; food distribution; food production. **Contact(s):** Barbara McBridge, Dagmar Farr

**D ▸ Food Research and Action Center**
1875 Connecticut Ave. NW
Washington, DC 20009 (202)986-2200
**Concern(s):** demographics; agriculture; Third World; food production; food distribution; hunger; poverty; homelessness. Through field organizing, litigation, research, public information, and advocacy FAC seeks to alleviate hunger, malnutrition, and poverty in America by playing a role in the development and formulation of government policies concerning these issues. Nonpartisan advocacy group that works primarily on federally-funded assistance programs; monitors federal policy developments; prepares publications; conducts trainings; and answers questions about funding anti-hunger programs. **Other Resources:** See newsletter, FOODLINES and National Anti-Hunger Coalition. Nonprofit. **Est.:** 1970.

**T ▸ Foreign Assistance Action Project**
801 Pennsylvania Ave. SE
Washington, DC 20003 (202)547-9009
**Affiliation:** National Audubon Society Population Program. **Concern(s):** Third World; demographics; politics; foreign policy; government accountability; population growth. Seeks to make ecologically sustainable development the centerpiece of all Foreign Assistance decision-making. Particularly concerned with over-population and its impact on the world's natural resources. **Other Resources:** See AUDUBON ACTIVIST and AUDUBON ACTION ALERTS. Many other informational and organizing materials and resources. (202)547-9017.

**T ▸ Foreign Policy Association**
729 7th Ave.
New York, NY 10019 (212)764-4050
**Concern(s):** Third World; foreign policy; intervention. Objective is to stimulate an informed, thoughtful and articulate public opinion on foreign policy issues facing the US. By bringing the facts and a broad range of views and perspectives before the American people, FPA strives to encourage greater public understanding and involvement in international issues. Annual catalogue of publications available. **Other Resources:** See guides, GREAT DECISIONS; GUIDE TO CAREERS IN WORLD AFFAIRS; TEACHER'S RESOURCE GUIDE; periodicals, HEADLINE SERIES and FOREIGN POLICY PREVIEW newsletter. Annual catalogue of publications available. Nonprofit. **Est.:** 1918. **Contact(s):** John W. Kiermaier (President), Mia T. Kissil (Executive Secretary). **Other:** 1800 K St., NW, Washington, DC 20006

**E ▸ The Foresight Institute**
10108 Hemlock Dr., Box 13267
Overland Park, KS 66212 (913)383-3359
**Concern(s):** environment; education. Dedicated to healing Mother Earth through publications, training and awards. Officially founded in August 1989 after one year of research, travel and planning. Founder, Twyla Dell, is a professional speaker and writer and former employee of the EPA. She wrote The Call of the Rainbow Warrior which is about a businessman who becomes an environmental convert when he is visited in dreams by the Rainbow Warrior. Also published 101 Ways to Save the Earth. They offer a variety of leadership programs. **Other Resources:** Ms. Dell is a speaker, her husband consults businesses. The Environmental Bookshelf; The Environmental Leadership Program; Rainbow Warriors International, a membership program for responsible student environmental action; Foresight Press. **Est.:** 1989. **Fax:** (913)383-2454. **Contact(s):** Twyla Dell (Founder/President), Kelly Butts (Director of Marketing).

**A ▸ Forest Ecosystem Rescue Network (FERN)**
7781 Lenox St.
Jacksonville, FL 32221
**Affiliation:** Elfin Permaculture. **Concern(s):** agriculture; environment; permaculture; forests. It administers these programs: Tree Bank, Fate of Our Forests Conferences, ROBIN newsletter, Fate of Our Forests slide lectures and organizing weekends for local FERN Chapters. The latter two are only at request and organizing of local groups. **Est.:** 1984. **Contact(s):** Dan Hemenway, Cynthia Baxter (Coordinators).

**E ▸ Forest History Society**
701 Vickers Ave.
Durham, NC 27701 (919)682-9319
**Concern(s):** environment; forests; conservation. Its educational emphasis is dedicated to advancing the historical and ecological understanding of human interconnectedness with forested environments. **Other Resources:** Publishes a journal, FOREST & CONSERVATION HISTORY. **Dues:** $25+/yr.

**E ▸ Forests Forever**
Box 410041
San Francisco, CA 94141 (415)647-9160
**Concern(s):** environment; forests. A California group presently petitioning in California to have a forest reform initiative put on the California ballot. This initiative bans clearcutting, protects California's old-growth (ancient) forests, defines and mandates sustained yield. **Other:** Box 3240, San Rafael, CA 94912. Cecilia Lanman.

**J ▸ Forgotten Families**
Box 2745
Bangor, ME 04402 (207)947-9819
**Concern(s):** justice; peace; politics; foreign policy; national security; CIA; government accountability; veterans; political prisoners. Dedicated to assisting families affected by the Cold War or covert operations, with special attention given to those families whose loved one has died or disappeared as a result of involvement in CIA/covert operations. Assists in Freedom of Information Act and investigations. A nonpolitical organization that attempts to be more of a support group than to advocate foreign policy. **Other Resources:** See VETERANS AFFAIRS NEWS. Nonprofit. **Est.:** 1989. **Other Formats:** ION. **E-Network:** Prodigy. **ID:** 'bbmc57a'. **Fax:** (207)945-6499. **Contact(s):** Sherry Sullivan (President/Investigator). (207)469-6883.

**? ▸ Forum 2000**
P.B. 5140
Majorstua 0301
Oslo, 3 Norway (02)13 85 85
**Concern(s):** future; ideation; networking. "Through networking and by serving as a catalyst, organizer and channel for new ideas, Forum aims at contributing to increased communication and enhanced consciousness by promoting new ideas within a wide spectrum, and stimulating new activities, new initiatives and by creating nontraditional networks in Scandinavia and transnationally." **Contact(s):** Sven Bjork (Coordinator). (02) 53 40 14.

**✈ ▸ Forum International**
91 Gregory Lane, #21
Pleasant Hill, CA 94523 (510)671-2900
**Concern(s):** education; environment; travel. Educational organization involved with ecosystems field studies and ecotourism. **Other Resources:** Publishes ECOSPHERE magazine. **Member:** Co-op America.

**✪ ▸ Forum on Renewable Energy & Climate Change**
I.C.R.C.
801 N. Fairfax St. #304
Alexandria, VA 22314-1757
**Affiliation:** I.C.R.C.. **Concern(s):** energy; environment; conservation; renewables; appropriate technology. Sponsored by The Climate Institute, EPA, US Export Council for Renewable Energy and World Resources Institute.

**✈ ▸ Forum Travel**
4606 Winthrop St.
Pittsburgh, PA 15213 (412)681-4099
**Concern(s):** education; Third World; travel; Mid-East. Full-service travel agency specializing in study tours of the Middle East. Nonprofit. **Member:** Co-op America.

**T ▸ Foster Parents Plan, Inc.**
157 Plan Way
Warwick, RI 02886 (800)225-1234
**Concern(s):** Third World; demographics; health; hunger; poverty; homelessness; nutrition. Non-sectarian/non-political agency for inter-

national development based on one-to-one sponsorship of children overseas, assisting 450,000 children and their families in over 26 nations in Africa, Latin America, the Caribbean and Asia. Combines personal correspondence with grassroots assistance individually tailored to the needs of each situation emphasizing participation, self-help, nutrition and health, education, water and sanitation, income-generation, agricultural and community development. **Contact(s):** Kenneth H. Phillips (President). (401)738-5600 ext. 316.

S ◆ **Foundation Center**
See FOUNDATION GRANTS INDEX ANNUAL; FOUNDATION DIRECTORY; FOUNDATION GRANTS FOR INDIVIDUALS; NATIONAL DATA BOOK; NATIONAL FOUNDATIONS; NATIONAL GUIDE TO CORPORATE GIVING; NATIONAL GUIDE TO FUNDING IN AGING; PHILANTHROPY AND VOLUNTEERISM (directories).

F ◆ **Foundation for a Compassionate Society**
227 Congress Ave
Austin, TX 78701-4021
**Concern(s):** feminism; spiritual; health; empowerment; psychology; transformation; philanthropy. Promotes the hypothesis that women's nurturing, including its unpaid labor, forms a hidden economic system of free gift-giving different from the Western exchange economic system. Women can build upon what they do best so that all people can develop a different kind of ego structure directed towards others. By validating the gift-giver and raising nurturing to the highest level of respect, a new paradigm will create a new system of human well-being.

✍ ◆ **Foundation for Advancements in Science and Education**
Park Mile Plaza
4801 Wilshire Blvd.
Los Angeles, CA 90010     (213)937-9911
**Concern(s):** education; energy; environment; science.

A ◆ **Foundation for Biointensive Agriculture**
390 Leland Ave., #3B
Palo Alto, CA 94306
**Concern(s):** agriculture; environment; food production; biotechnology.

$ ◆ **Foundation for Economic Education**
See FREEMAN (periodicals).

E ◆ **Foundation for Field Research**
Box 2010
Alpine, CA 92001     (916)445-9264
**Concern(s):** environment; education; global understanding; research; volunteers. Volunteers pay a tax-deductible donation to join projects with archeologists, marine biologists, botanists, paleontologists and zoologist on worldwide scientific expeditions.

$ ◆ **Foundation for International Community Assistance**
2504 E. Elm St.
Tucson, AZ 85716
**Concern(s):** economics; Third World; philanthropy; development; community self-reliance.

$ ◆ **Foundation for National Progress**
See MOTHER JONES magazine.

$ ◆ **Foundation for Personal and Community Development**
See COMMUNITIES: JOURNAL OF COOPERATION.

☪ ◆ **Foundation for PEACE**
See PEACE IN ACTION (periodicals).

P ◆ **Foundation for Study of Independent Social Ideas**
See DISSENT magazine.

$ ◆ **The Foundation on Economic Trends**
1130 17th St. NW, #630
Washington, DC 20036   (202)466-2823
**Affiliation:** Greenhouse Crisis Foundation. **Concern(s):** economics; environment; energy; agriculture; politics; health; hazardous/toxic waste; global warming; biotechnology; appropriate technology. Activities are centered around the environmental, economic, and ethical concerns raised by the development and commercialization of emerging technologies. By education, litigation, and grassroots organization, the Foundation is focusing public attention and scrutiny on the present revolutions in technology. It hopes to encourage examination of emerging technologies in their full social and economic context, taking both benefits and potential adverse impacts into consideration. **Other Resources:** The only national organization for more than 10 years that has consistently and actively monitored biotechnology research and regulation warning that unless properly regulated and used, biotechnology will cause far-reaching environmental damage. **Mem-**

**ber:** Global Greenhouse Network. **Contact(s):** Jeremy Rifkin (President).

☪ ◆ **Fourth Freedom Forum Inc.**
803 N. Main St.
Goshen, IN 46526     (800)233-6786
**Concern(s):** peace; international law; national security. A private operating foundation established to provide a medium for discussion of alternative methods of international security. **Other Resources:** See INFORUM (periodical) and video, CIVILIZED DEFENSE PLAN. Nonprofit. **Contact(s):** Marc Hardy (Executive Director). (219)534-3402.

$ ◆ **Fourth World Movement**
3030 Sleep Hollow Rd
Falls Church, VA 22042
**Concern(s):** economics; politics; environment; justice; world order; bioregionalism; community self-reliance; grassroots organizing; diversity. Affirms self-rule by urban neighborhoods, rural villages and distinct ethnic groupings, and seeks to break down all big powers into ethnic or bioregional units.

S ◆ **Franciscans**
See FRANCISCAN WORKER and HAVERSACK newsletters .

J ◆ **Free Arts for Abused Children**
6955 Fernhill Dr.
Malibu, CA 90265     (310)457-5531
**Concern(s):** justice; feminism; education; arts; child abuse; children; childhood; music, dance, graphics; volunteers. FAAC introduces creative arts activities to victims of child abuse as outlets through which they can grow. Volunteers in dance, drama, writing, music, painting, sculpting and film increases the child's self-worth and build character by unlocking the child's imagination. Children participating in this ongoing process learn new ways to channel emotion, release anger and come to know the meaning of success. Nonprofit.

D ◆ **Freedom From Hunger Foundation**
Box 2000, 1644 Da Vinci Court
Davis, CA 95617     (916)758-6200
**Concern(s):** demographics; agriculture; economics; politics; hunger; food production; community self-reliance; grassroots organizing. "Backs self-help credit programs (1) all are based on finding and implementing new ways to make people self-sufficient, (2) we concentrate on the individual, (3) we never seek to run the projects ourselves; our job is to get proven programs launched. Our local staff goes to the field, does whatever is necessary, and then moves on." **Contact(s):** David Crowley (President/CEO).

M ◆ **Freedom to Read Foundation**
See FREEDOM TO READ FOUNDATION NEWS.

J ◆ **Freedomways Association**
See FREEDOMWAYS (periodicals).

L ◆ **Fresh Fruit/Vegetable Workers Union, UFCW Local 78B**
600 S. Main St., #5
Salinas, CA 93901     (209)784-8058
**Concern(s):** labor; environment; health; feminism; justice; economics; boycott; corporate responsibility; socially-responsible investing; pesticides; hazardous/toxic waste; sexism; discrimination. BOYCOTT CASTLE & COOK — They have a record of harmful pesticide use and discrimination against women. Product: Dole bananas and pineapples. **Other Resources:** To protest, write to: George Horn, VP, 10900 Wilshire Blvd., Los Angeles, CA 90024.

E ◆ **Freshwater Foundation**
2500 Shadywood Rd.
Orono, MN 55331     (612)471-8407
**Concern(s):** environment; health; water; public health; volunteers. This foundation has three goals: To insure freshwater for human consumption, industry and recreation; to sponsor public education, increase awareness, and find solutions; and, to support scientific research confronting our freshwater supply problems. **Other Resources:** Volunteers needed. Internship available in computer mapping and research projects. See HEALTH AND ENVIRONMENT DIGEST. **Dues:** $25+/yr.

☪ ◆ **Friends Committee for Consultation, Section of the Americas**
See HANDBOOK ON MILITARY TAXES AND CONSCIENCE.

☪ ◆ **Friends Committee on National Legislation**
245 2nd St. NE
Washington, DC 20002   (202)547-6000
**Concern(s):** peace; justice; politics; spiritual; disarmament; interfaith; militarism; lobbying. Works towards a non-military world order based so firmly on justice, spiritual unity, and voluntary cooperation that there would be no place for war. Today, through congressional

testimony, direct lobbying, and publications, FCNL's legislative staff and constituency informs members of Congress, their staffs, and colleague organizations about peace and social justice issues. Just as importantly, it works with grassroots activists nationwide to educate and organize for peace & social justice. **Other Resources:** See WASHINGTON NEWSLETTER and INDIAN REPORT (periodicals); Action Alerts, providing timely and informative calls for action to improve lobbying efforts at home; HOW-TO Series; ISSUES IN BRIEF Series. **Est.:** 1943. Hotline: (202)547-4343. **Contact(s):** Nancy Alexander, Alison D. Oldham (Legal Action Coordinator).

E ◆ **Friends Committee on Unity with Nature**
7700 Clarks Lake Rd.
Chelsea, MI 48118     (313)475-9976
**Concern(s):** environment; spiritual; interfaith; sustainability. "To the Testimony of conscientious objection to war, let us add conscientious protection of our planet." This organization has two primary goals: the development of a clear witness on environmental issue among Friends and like-minded people, and the support of informed, spirit-led action. This organization has a commitment to a sustainable future. **Other Resources:** See newsletter BEFRIENDING CREATION and guide, GENTLY WALKING ON THE EARTH. Nonprofit. **Est.:** 1987. **Dues:** $10/yr. donation. **E-Network:** Econet. **ID:** 'pymcun'. **Contact(s):** Isabel Bliss (Clerk), Ted Bernard (Assistant Clerk). (614)594-2893.

T ◆ **Friends for Jamaica**
See CARIBBEAN NEWSLETTER.

🐾 ◆ **Friends of Animals**
Box 1244
Norwalk, CT 06856-1244   (203)866-5223
**Concern(s):** environment; politics; animal rights; wildlife/endangered species; oceans; lobbying; boycotts; law; volunteers. An international animal protection organization dedicated to eliminating human brutality to animals. Programs are as follows: A breeding control service; wildlife and marine mammal protection including the fur trade, national refuge, public lands; a wild animal orphanage and rehabilitation center in Liberia; protection of animal used in experiments and testing; protection of farm animals. **Other Resources:** Committee for Humane Legislation in DC. Volunteers needed in each branch for low cost breeding programs, as well as grassroots activities and other services. **Est.:** 1957. **Dues:** $20/yr. (203)866-5223.

E ◆ **Friends of Opal Creek**
Box 318
Mill City, OR 97360
**Concern(s):** environment; conservation. .

☪ ◆ **Friends of Peace Pilgrim**
43480 Cedar Ave.
Hemet, CA 92344     (714)927-7678
**Concern(s):** peace; spiritual; activism; interfaith; volunteers. An group of volunteers dedicated to carrying on the message of Peace Pilgrim, a woman who dedicated her life to simplicity and carrying the message of peace by foot from 1953-81. "Overcome evil with good, falsehood with truth, hatred with love." Without money or organizational backing she reached thousands on dusty roads, in great churches, on TV and radio, and colleges. She spoke and wrote mainly about inner peace. **Other Resources:** Offers books, FRIENDS OF PEACE PILGRIM newsletter, posters, cassette tapes, and much more. Ocean Tree Books, a publisher. Nonprofit. **Contact(s):** Ann Rush (President), John Rush (Secretary Treasurer).

E ◆ **Friends of the Ancient Forest**
Box 3499
Eugene, OR 97403
**Concern(s):** environment; forests; conservation.

E ◆ **Friends of the Earth**
218 D St. SE
Washington, DC 20003   (202)544-2600
**Affiliation:** Environmental Policy Institute. **Concern(s):** environment; peace; energy; agriculture; health; politics; lobbying; antinuclear; air pollution; hazardous/toxic waste; biotechnology; global warming; consumer protection; forests. Citizen-based international networks for action on environmental, consumer protection and peace issues; promotes conservation, restoration and rational resource use through public education and campaigning at local, national and international levels. Activist members in over 30 nations works to stop rainforest destruction, nuclear proliferation, and pesticide abuse. "Using scientific, economic, and political information, we are fighting programs and legislation that threaten our Earth." **Other Resources:** See ENVIRONMENTAL UPDATE, a monthly newsletter, OCEAN MAGAZINE, and award-winning magazine, NOT MAN APART. Lobbies in DC and other state capitals. See, also, Environmental Policy Institute. **Dues:** $25, $15-student/low-income/senior. **Member:** Global Tomorrow Coalition; Environmental Federation of America. **Contact(s):** Alan Gussow (President), Geoff Webb (202)543-4312.

**E ♦ Friends of the River**
Fort Mason Center
Building C, 3rd Fl.
San Francisco, CA 94123    (415)771-0400
**Concern(s):** environment; ocean/rivers. Founded to protect and preserve free-flowing streams and rivers and implement wise energy resource and water management policies worldwide. Currently focusing on securing federal wild and scenic protection for over 100 rivers and streams in national forests in California and a comprehensive protection of the Colorado River Basin. **Est.:** 1974. **Dues:** $25, $40/family: $50/business. **Other:** Ft. Mason Center, San Francisco, CA 94123(415)771-0400.

**E ♦ Friends of the Sea Otter**
Box 221220, Dept. D
Carmel, CA 93922    (408)625-3290
**Concern(s):** environment; wildlife/endangered species; oceans; preservation. Anything having to do with protecting the California sea otter and protecting its nearshore habitat along the central coast, such has oil spill prevention and response, water quality, reduced mortalities and public education. **Other Resources:** Publishes a newsletter, THE OTTER RAFT. Also provides educational presentations and operates a center. **Dues:** $15/yr: $100/life. (408)373-2747.

**T ♦ Friends of the Third World, Inc.**
611 W. Wayne St.
Fort Wayne, IN 46802-2125 (219)422-6821
**Affiliation:** Cooperative Trading Project. **Concern(s):** Third World; economics; development; trade; alternative markets; alternative consumer. Networking and technical assistance to alternative trading organizations. Sponsors annual national conference on alternative trading. Also imports and sells a variety of Third World Products, such as Nicaraguan coffee. Printing cooperative offers discounts to community groups and nonprofits. **Other Resources:** See ALTERNATIVE TRADING NEWS, a catalog. **Contact(s):** Jim Goetsch. (219)422-1650. **Other:** Networking and technical assistance to alternative trading organizations. Sponsors annual national conference on alternative trading. Also imports and sells a variety of Third World Products, such as Nicaraguan coffee. Printing cooperative offers, discounts to community groups and nonprofits.,

**E ♦ Friends of the Trees Society**
Box 1064
Tonasket, WA 98855    (509)486-4726
**Concern(s):** environment; agriculture; forests; trees; permaculture. This Society is a network of individuals, local groups, and international organizations working to preserve forests and plant trees. Friends of the Trees has published a wide range of material; organized dozens of conferences, courses, workshops, and an annual spring tree sale. **Other Resources:** See newsletters, GREEN FRONT REPORT and INTERNATIONAL GREEN FRONT REPORT. Conducts permaculture design courses; and Forestry conference. See, also, Travellers Earth Repair Network (TERN). Nonprofit. **Est.:** 1978. **Dues:** $10/yr.; $250/life. **E-Network:** Econet. **ID:** 'fott'. **Fax:** (509)486-4726. **Contact(s):** Michael Pilarski (Director), Carol Lanigan (Office Manager).

**☸ ♦ Friends of the United Nations**
730 Arizona Ave., #329
Santa Monica, CA 90401    (310)451-1810
**Concern(s):** peace; United Nations; networking. An independent public relations consulting group dedicated to promoting the UN in the US. It is committed to publicize, inform and educate others about the goals and activities of the UN so that a more knowledgeable public opinion can develop. Through serving as a networking and consulting resource, it helps facilitate the distribution of UN materials with NGO's and governmental organizations, educational institutions, corporations, and entertainment and media industry. **Other Resources:** See Transmissions Project. **Contact(s):** Irving Sarnoff (Executive Director).

**E ♦ Friends of the Wolf**
5 Country Lane
Scotts Valley, CA 95006-3305    (916)753-8625
**Concern(s):** environment; wildlife/endangered species; conservation. .

**E ♦ Friends of UNEP**
2013 Q St. NW
Washington, DC 20009  (202)234-3600
**Concern(s):** environment; peace; United Nations; forests; wildlife/endangered species; air pollution. Established to help the UN Environmental Programme in two main ways: First, by building public support for UNEP and its cooperating organizations which safeguard and enhance the global environment, and second, by tracking and reporting to UNEP key trends in US public. **Est.:** 1984. **Contact(s):** Richard Hellman (President).

**D ♦ Friends of Vista**
1000 Wisconsin Ave. NW
Washington, DC 20007  (202)342-0717
**Concern(s):** demographics; justice; development; hunger; poverty; volunteers. **Contact(s):** Lisa Woll.

**☸ ♦ Friends Peace Committee**
See NVC Newsletter.

**☸ ♦ Friends World Committee for Consultation**
Section of the Americas
1506 Race St.
Philadelphia, PA 19102  (215)241-7250
**Affiliation:** American Friend Service Committee. **Concern(s):** peace; justice; politics; Third World; spiritual; war tax revolt; interfaith; militarism; nonviolence; grassroots organizing. **Other Resources:** Publishes HANDBOOK ON MILITARY TAXES AND CONSCIENCE, and FEAR GOD AND HONOR THAT EMPEROR, a manual on military tax withholding for religious employers.

**✈ ♦ The Friendship Force**
675 S. Omni International
Atlanta, GA 30303
**Concern(s):** education; travel.

**L ♦ Front Lash, Inc.**
815 16th St., NW
Washington, DC 20006  (202)783-3993
**Affiliation:** AFL-CIO. **Concern(s):** labor; unions. Organizes and implements labor movement projects involving the minimum wage, child labor, boycott & strike support.

**L ♦ Full Employment Action Council**
c/o Industrial Union
815 16th St. NW.
Washington, DC 20006-4104        (202)842-7800
**Affiliation:** Industrial Union/AFL-CIO. **Concern(s):** labor; economics; politics; jobs; budget; unions. Established to educate the public on policies to achieve a full employment economy. **Other Resources:** See JOBS IMPACT BULLETIN; and National Committee for Full Employment. **Est.:** 1974.

**☛ ♦ Fund for Animals**
200 West 57th St.
New York, NY 10019    (212)246-2096
**Concern(s):** environment; animal rights; wildlife/endangered species; volunteers. Focuses on animal protection and the belief that all animals, wild or domestic, deserve the right to be free from fear, pain and suffering, especially sport hunting. **Other Resources:** Volunteers works in 26 field offices across the US. Operates a wildlife sanctuary and rabbit reserve. **Dues:** $10, $25/family. **Contact(s):** Cleveland Amory (President). (212)246-2632.

**T ♦ Fund for Free Expression**
See Human Rights Watch and INDEX ON CENSORSHIP (periodicals).

**P ♦ Fund for New Priorities**
171 Madison Ave.
New York, NY 10016    (212)685-8848
**Concern(s):** politics; government accountability; leadership; law; reform; lobbying. Since their first conference on the military budget this group of business executives and professionals have organized 60 Congressional conferences at the Capitol to encourage debate on vital public policies between Congress, public institutions, informed citizens and the media, strives to influence government policies, and strengthen citizens voice in the political process at every level. **Other Resources:** Working with groups of political leaders nationwide to create the Foundation for Democracy. Purpose: To articulate the liberal agenda and focus on new and imaginative ways of using the media and related technologies to inspire future generations. **Est.:** 1969. **Contact(s):** Maurice S. Paprin (President), Joseph Krevisky (Executive Director).

**☸ ♦ Fund for Peace**
345 E. 46th St.
New York, NY 10017    (212)661-5900
**Concern(s):** peace; justice; economics; media; anti-nuclear; economic conversion; peace dividend. Committed to the elimination of unacceptable levels of military spending, the preservation of human rights, social and economic justice; and to an open, informed society at home and abroad. Projects: Center for Defense Information; Center for International Policy; Institute for the Study of World Politics; Citizens' Dialogue Program; Entertainment Summit, co-sponsor, Mediators Productions. See Alternative Defense Project and Center for National Security Studies. **Other Resources:** Often works with other organizations to expand international cooperation, justice and human rights in the quest of an enduring peace. Sponsors autonomous programs, e.g., IN THE PUBLIC INTEREST, a radio broadcast. **Contact(s):** Nina K. Solarz (Executive Director).

**☉ ♦ Fund for Renewable Energy and the Environment**
1400 16th St. NW, #710
Washington, DC 20036 (202)232-2252
**Affiliation:** Center for Renewable Resources. **Concern(s):** energy; environment; resource management; renewables. An educational forum and network dedicated to the development of a safe and sustainable environment. Supported by a membership of concerned individuals as well as by charitable foundations. **Other Resources:** See Renew America, one of its projects. Nonprofit. **Contact(s):** Tina C. Hobson (Executive Director), Denis Hayes (Chairman).

**P ♦ Fund For Constitutional Government**
122 Maryland Ave. NE
Washington, DC 20002 (202)546-3732
**Concern(s):** politics; justice; media; government accountability; constitutional rights; law; journalism. Established to actively promote an accountable, honest performance from government, including relations with corporations and labor unions, through journalistic and litigation activities. **Est.:** 1974. **Contact(s):** Anne Zill.

**G ♦ Fund For Human Dignity**
666 Broadway
New York, NY 10012    (212)614-6464
**Affiliation:** Center for Constitutional Rights. **Concern(s):** health; justice; education; AIDS; gay/lesbian. A national gay and lesbian education foundation. It operates a hotline and the National AIDS Education Program, a clearinghouse which collects, produces, and distributes educational materials nationwide. **Contact(s):** Sherrie Cohen, Jin Soo Kim.

**☛ ♦ Fur-Bearer Defenders**
Box 188950
Sacramento, CA 95818  (916)391-4617
**Concern(s):** environment; animal rights. Joins forces with caring people, determined to open the public's eyes to what REALLY goes on in the backwoods, wildlife preserves—and yes, even the urban areas of our land. Conducts the leghold trap campaign. **Contact(s):** George V. Clements (Executive Director).

**E ♦ Gaia Pacific: The Art of Activism**
Box 53
Del Mar, CA 92014        (619)481-6784
**Concern(s):** environment; arts; peace; Third World; education; activism; culture; conflict resolution; Pacific/Pacific Rim. This project strives to promote both environmental awareness and change through multi-disciplinary forms of art, aimed at communities throughout the Pacific Rim. Based in San Diego, it presents events throughout the year. It unites international artists and environmentalists to strengthen and diversity the network of activists who are working for the common goal of preserving the ecosystems of the Pacific. "Art is not a mirror which reflects culture, it is a hammer with which to shape it." **Contact(s):** Mary Hsi (Director).

**A ♦ Gaia Services**
RFD 3, Box 84
St. Johnsbury, VT 05819(802)633-4152
**Affiliation:** Information & Communications for Ecological Agriculture. **Concern(s):** agriculture; environment; organic. **Contact(s):** Grace Gershuny.

**♿ ♦ Gallaudet Research Institute**
See directories section for COLLEGE AND CAREER PROGRAMS FOR DEAF STUDENTS.

**✍ ♦ Garden Club of America**
598 Madison Ave.
New York, NY 10022    (212)753-8287
**Concern(s):** education; environment; conservation. A national organization with member clubs from coast to coast and in Hawaii. Dedicated conservation of natural resources, protection of the environment, control of pollution, wise land use, and historic preservation. Active support of billboard and sign control. **Other Resources:** Educational packet, THE WORLD AROUND YOU. Nonprofit. **Est.:** 1913. **Contact(s):** Mrs. J. Wrinkle (Corresponding Secretary), Mrs. D. MacGraw (Conservation Chairman).

**A ♦ Garden Society**
See GARDEN under periodicals.

**G ♦ Gay Lesbian Alliance Against Discrimination/ SFBA**
5140 Castro St., #B
San Francisco, CA 94114    (415)861-4588
**Concern(s):** justice; health; gay/lesbian; AIDS.

**S ♦ General Conference Mennonite Church**
Commission on Home Ministries
Box 347
Newton, KS 67114    (316)283-5100

**Concern(s):** spiritual; peace; justice; politics; faith. **Other Resources:** See newsletter, GOD AND CAESAR.

**F ♦ General Federation of Women's Clubs**
1734 N St. NW
Washington, DC 20036-2290    (202)347-3168
**Concern(s):** feminism; politics. **Fax:** (202)835-0246.
**Contact(s):** Phyllis J. Dudenhoffer (International President).

**E ♦ Georgia Environmental Project**
429 Moreland Ave.
Atlanta, GA 30307    (404)521-3731
**Concern(s):** environment; activism. Works to protect Georgia's environment through organizing, lobbying, research, and litigation. Also, store of environmentally-sound products. **Member:** Co-op America.

**T ♦ Georgians Against Smoking Pollution**
Box 450981
Atlanta, GA 30345    (404)296-9526
**Concern(s):** Third World; environment; economics; boycott; corporate responsibility; socially-responsible investing; forest; Latin America. BOYCOTT TOBACCO COMPANY SUBSIDIARIES — GASP maintains that the tobacco industry adversely affects the Third World, Latin American rainforests, and individual human lives. **Other Resources:** Send $.50 and an SASE to GASP in order to receive a complete list of tobacco subsidiaries and their products.

**E ♦ Geothermal Education Office**
664 Hilary Dr.
Tiburon, CA 94920    (800)866-4436
**Concern(s):** environment; energy; renewables.

**✍ ♦ Gerber Educational Resources**
Box 2997
Kirkland, WA 98083
**Concern(s):** education. Offers courses, consulting, workshops, and publications on "education for world transformation". Promotes holistic approaches to learning, involving self-empowerment; authentic emotional connections among co-learners, and synergistic methods.

**H ♦ Gesundheit Institute**
2630 Robert Walker Place
Arlington, VA 22207
**Concern(s):** health; alternative consumer; preventative medicine; holistic. One man's answer to modern corporate medicine through a completely selfless holistic and human approach. One doesn't need malpractice insurance to cure through humor, pleasure, and caring.

**✍ ♦ Girl Scouts of the USA**
830 3rd Ave.
New York, NY 10022    (212)940-7500
**Concern(s):** education; feminism; empowerment; childhood. The national organization offers informal education and recreation program designed to help each girl develop her own values and sense of worth as an individual. It provides opportunities for girls to experience, to discover, and to share planned activities that meet their interest. **Other Resources:** Publication, GIRL SCOUT LEADER. **Contact(s):** Betty Pillsbury (President), Mary Rose Main (Nat'l Executive Director). (212)940-7700.

**✈ ♦ Girls Clubs of America**
30 E. 33rd St.
New York, NY 10016    (212)689-3700
**Concern(s):** education; demographics; health; travel; hunger; youth; childhood; empowerment; juvenile. A national service and advocacy organization for the rights and needs of all girls. Traditional and non-traditional activities including career development, juvenile justice, alcohol and drug abuse, sexuality education and rights for youth programs. **Contact(s):** Mary Jo Gallo.

**E ♦ Glass Packaging Institute**
1801 K St. NW, #1105-L
Washington, DC 20006  (202)887-4850
**Concern(s):** environment; recycling. **Other Resources:** Publishes list of glass collection and recycling centers in 27 states and a guide for anyone interested in planning, building, and operating a multi-material recycling center.

**E ♦ Global Action Plan for the Earth (GAP)**
449A Route 28A
West Hurley, NY 12491  (914)331-1312
**Concern(s):** environment; activism; networking. Started on Earth Day 1990, GAP already has country coordinators in Australia, Canada, the Netherlands, Norway, Sweden, US, and USSR. **Est.:** 1990.

**✍ ♦ Global Alliance for Transforming Education**
4202 Ashwoody Trail
Atlanta, GA 30319    (404)458-5678
**Concern(s):** education; spiritual; global understanding; transforma-

tion. A global network of educators dedicated to proclaiming and promoting a vision of education that fosters personal greatness, social justice, peace, and a sustainable environment. GATE recognizes that a paradigm shift is needed to affect mainstream education and seeks to accomplish this through programs and activities supported by membership. It further recognizes that there are individuals and other educational, social and political organizations prepared to commit to educational transformation. **Other Resources:** Conferences, reports and newsletter. Holistic Education Community Network. **Est.:** 1990. **Dues:** $15/yr. **Other Formats:** 'GANG' via Connect. **E-Network:** Internet or Peacenet. **ID:** 'gange dcjon.das.net'. **Fax:** (404)454-9749. (708)393-2177. **Contact(s):** Dr. Phil Gang, Dr. Nina Lynn (Executive Leaders). (802)365-7616.

**✡ ♦ Global Christian Peace Conference**
See North American Christian Peace Conference.

**✡ ♦ Global Concerns Center**
2131 W. Berwyn Ave.
Chicago, IL 60625    (312)728-6336
**Concern(s):** peace.

**? ♦ Global Cooperation for a Better World**
28 Baker St.
London, W1M 4DF England 01-487-4634
**Concern(s):** future; peace; politics; grassroots organizing; ideation; networking. An initiative to collect ideas and actions now underway in 80 countries. The organizers suggest people form "creative groups" in their family, school or organization to manifest ideas in the three headings of inner life, relationships with other people, and the man-made and natural environment.

**✍ ♦ Global Cooperation for a Better World**
Regional Coordinating Office
866 UN Plaza
New York, NY 10017    (212)688-1335
**Concern(s):** education; peace; world order; United Nations; conflict resolution. An international project dedicated to the UN that looks beyond the world's problems and aims to encourage people towards a positive vision for the future. Developed the Creative Workshop, used worldwide; 1) Creating the vision together, 2) Defining essential methods and values within the vision, 3) Deciding on recommended plans of action, both personal and collective. The goal is to teach people how to better cooperate and visualize a better world. All topics covered.

**✈ ♦ Global Education Associates**
475 Riverside Dr., #456
New York, NY 10115    (212)870-3290
**Concern(s):** education; peace; spiritual; justice; environment; Third World; world order; networking; research; interfaith; travel. An educational organization which facilitates the efforts of concerned people of diverse cultures, talents, and experience, in contributing to a more humane and just world order. Has a network of associates in some 70 countries who collaborate in research, writing, and education programs related to this goal. Our goal is to catalyze a transnational, multi-issue movement for world order based on values of peace, social justice, ecological balance, and participation in decision making. **Other Resources:** See THE WHOLE EARTH PAPERS; and BREAKTHROUGH magazine. Filmstrips, audio and video tapes, consulting, speakers, educational programs, monograph and books. See Center for World Order Alternatives and GLOBAL EDUCATION RESOURCE GUIDE and BOOK CATALOG. Nonprofit. **Contact(s):** Gerald & Patricia Mische (Co-Directors).

**✈ ♦ Global Educational Experiences**
430 Belmont Ave.
Doylestown, PA 18901
**Concern(s):** education; travel. Offers intercultural travel for teachers.

**E ♦ Global Environment Project Institute**
Box 1111
Ketchum, ID 83340    (208)726-4030
**Affiliation:** Global Environment Foundation. **Concern(s):** environment; education; economics; demographics; resources; conservation; preservation; global understanding; population growth. A tax-exempt organization generating projects concerned with educating the public about global environmental issues, the goal of a sustainable world economic development, including overpopulation, resource depletion, and environmental degradation. GEPI emphasizes the connection between global issues and local problems suggesting ways that individuals can work responsibly towards solutions. **Other Resources:** Teacher training workshops, film festivals, programs for students, teachers and the public; environmental public resource library including directories, teaching tools, films and videos. See also Global Action Network. Nonprofit. **Est.:** 1986. **Contact(s):** Cindy Thiede (Deputy Director), Tom Hormel (Founder).

**✈ ♦ Global Exchange**
2141 Mission St., #202
San Francisco, CA 94103    (415)255-7296
**Concern(s):** education; travel. "Reality tours" - see and learn about environmental destruction in Brazil, grassroots organizing in the Philippines, the environmental movement in India, and so forth. **Other Resources:** Quarterly newsletter. **Member:** Co-op America.

**✡ ♦ Global Family**
112 Jordan Ave.
San Anselmo, CA 94960 (415)453-7600
**Concern(s):** peace; environment; world order. Supports and celebrates the shift in consciousness from separation and fear to unity and love. It is an international peace networking organization committed to creating a healthy, sustainable world. **Contact(s):** Marian Culhane.

**✡ ♦ Global Forum of Spiritual and Parliamentary Leaders on Human Survival**
304 E. 45th St.
New York, NY 10017    (212)953-7947
**Affiliation:** UNICEF. **Concern(s):** peace; spiritual; environment; justice; politics; world order; interfaith; reform; leadership; United Nations. "To change the harmful ways we deal with each other and our environment, we must learn to use our skills and knowledge to replenish the Earth and safeguard it for future generations. This requires a profound change in values-change that can lead to positive action. It helps to create this change by involving spiritual and parliamentary leaders in an intensive dialogue on critical survival issues. Political and religious leaders are central to the process of positive change." **Other Resources:** Newsletter, SHARED VISION. **Contact(s):** The Very Rev. James Parks Morton (Co-chairman), Akio Matsumura (Executive Coordinator).

**E ♦ Global Greenhouse Network**
1130 17th St. NW, #630
Washington, DC 20036  (202)466-2823
**Affiliation:** Foundation on Economic Trends. **Concern(s):** environment; energy; global warming. Comprised of key public interest organizations and legislators from 35 countries. Its primary mission is to raise awareness and mobilize public opinion regarding the greenhouse effect and global warming trends. **Contact(s):** Jeremy Rifkin.

**✍ ♦ Global Learning**
See GLEANINGS newsletter.

**✈ ♦ Global Learning Center**
2020-A E. Central St.
Wichita, KS 67214
**Concern(s):** education; travel. An independent international dialogue and learning organization which looks forward to working with libraries, schools, businesses, religious congregations, civic, labor and fraternal groups. Planned services include seminars and workshops on global issues; helping teachers set up international exchanges; international protocol for business people; providing information to foreign visitors. Nonprofit. **Contact(s):** Pam Ann Hatcher.

**✈ ♦ Global Learning Inc.**
1018 Stuyvesant Ave.
Union, NJ 07083    (201)964-1114
**Concern(s):** education; demographics; travel; hunger. Promotes global education. Consults on curriculum development and with hunger groups. **Contact(s):** Jeffrey Brown.

**J ♦ Global Options**
Box 40601
San Francisco, CA 94140
**Concern(s):** justice; peace; economics; feminism; racism; conflict resolution; sexism. Research and educational work on behalf of progressive causes; regular, lively seminars on controversial issues; publication of our well-respected journal, SOCIAL JUSTICE; delegations to Eastern Europe and other socialist countries; research on contemporary political issues such as the Nicaraguan elections, US media coverage of Cuba, varieties of democracy in Eastern Europe, and the politics of race and gender at home. **Other Resources:** As a Global Options Associate, you will receive four issues of SOCIAL JUSTICE, our newsletter DATALINE, and occasional papers issued by GO researchers, as well as an open invitation to GO's seminar series and special events. Tax-exempt. **Dues:** $100/associate.

**E ♦ Global Tomorrow Coalition**
1325 G St. NW, #915
Washington, DC 20005-3104    (202)628-4016
**Concern(s):** environment; demographics; future; resources; sustainability; population growth. A national alliance of 120 organizations and individuals concerned with global trends in environmental degradation, population growth, and natural resource management, committed to creating a more sustainable future. Active in both non-formal public education work through a series of national conferences called Global Scope and a formal education through the publication of a

series of teacher packets on the CITIZEN'S GUIDE TO SUSTAINABLE DEVELOPMENT and CITIZEN'S GUIDE TO GLOBAL ISSUES. **Other Resources:** See INTERACTION newsletter. Internships available in legislative research, global issues forums and office management. See GLOBAL ECOLOGY HANDBOOK and CONTACT DIRECTORY: LOCAL ACTION ON GLOBAL ISSUES (directories). **Contact(s):** Don Lesh (President), Walter Corson

**E ▶ Global Warming Watch**
Public Health Institute
853 Broadway, Rm. 2014
New York, NY 10003
**Affiliation:** Public Health Institute. **Concern(s):** environment; global warming; public health.

**E ▶ Global Water**
602 S. King St., #402
Leesburg, VA 22075    (703)478-8652
**Concern(s):** environment; Third World; agriculture; education; water; development; hunger. Founded to educate the public as to the severity of the world's water problems, at home and abroad and to begin the process of solving some of these problems by funding demonstration projects. Some of these projects are now underway in the Third World, bringing water where there was none and making unsafe water safe. **Est.:** 1982. **Other:** 2119 Leroy Pl, Washington, DC 20008

**T ▶ Going Home Campaign**
SHARE Foundation
401 Michigan Ave. NE
Washington, DC 20017   (202)319-5540
**Affiliation:** SHARE Foundation. **Concern(s):** Third World; demographics; repatriation; refugees; immigration. **Other:** Box 24, Cardinal Station, Washington, DC 20064

**✾ ▶ Going to the Source**
5445 Varnum
Baldensburg, MD 20710
**Concern(s):** peace. **Contact(s):** Diane Stanton-Rich.

**E ▶ Goldman Environmental Foundation**
1090 Sansome St., 3rd Fl.
San Francisco, CA 94111    (415)788-1090
**Concern(s):** environment.

**✈ ▶ Good Life Study Tours**
30 El Mirador Court
San Luis Obispo, CA 93401   (805)541-3101
**Affiliation:** Food First Institute. **Concern(s):** economics; education; environment; community self-reliance; travel. "Human exploitation of Earth's resources must be reduced. Lifestyles of excessive consumption must be modified while maintaining high life quality. We provided direct participatory lifestyle learning within families and communities of a low consumption culture - low birth rates and high standards for health, education, and longevity." Specializes in Kerala, India. Nonprofit. **Est.:** 1989. **Dues:** $25/yr. **Contact(s):** William M. Alexander (Director). **Other:** Food First Institute, 145 Ninth St., San Francisco, CA 94103

**J ▶ Goodbye Columbus Day!**
See Conservatory for Nature Culture.

**♿ ▶ Goodwill Industries of Southern California**
342 San Fernando Rd.
Los Angeles, CA 90031   (213)223-1211
**Concern(s):** justice; environment; health; recycling; disabled's rights; jobs. Helps disabled people become independent, tax-paying citizens through vocational training, job placement and employment. By collecting, refurbishing and marketing household and industrial discards, the Southland's premier recycler is 95% self-supporting. During 1990, It served 1,565 individuals and placed 158 in private industry. Nonprofit. (213)222-5131.

**E ▶ Gopher Tortoise Council**
Florida Museum of Natural History
Gainesville, FL 32611
**Concern(s):** environment; wildlife/endangered species; preservation. Through educational efforts, research programs, management and legislative protection, members serve in advisory positions in order to protect the tortoise and its upland habitat. **Dues:** $5/yr; $100/life.

**P ▶ Government Accountability Project (GAP)**
810 1st St. NE
Washington, DC 20002   (202)408-0034
**Concern(s):** politics; economics; labor; health; energy; consumer rights; public health; whistle-blowing; government accountability; corporate responsibility. Public interest organization supporting public employees and corporate workers who seek to prevent waste, corruption and threats to public health/safety. Has developed a unique

program that offers desperately needed legal counsel and representation to government and corporate whistle-blowers and local citizen groups; investigative services to state and local government bodies; legal education to law students pursing public interest careers; and information to the general public on above issues. **Other Resources:** Publishes quarterly newsletter, BRIDGING THE GAP. Nonprofit. **Est.:** 1977. **Contact(s):** Louis Clark (Executive Director).

**M ▶ GPE Network**
950 Martinsburg Rd.
Mount Vernon, OH 43050
**Concern(s):** media; multilogues. **Contact(s):** Mark Kinney.

**✍ ▶ Grace Contrino Abrams Peace Education Foundation, Inc.**
3550 Biscayne Blvd., #400
Miami, FL 33137    (305)576-5075
**Concern(s):** education; peace; conflict resolution. Develops programs to offer young people nonviolent alternatives to youth crime and gang violence. Programs emphasize conflict resolution and professional training. **Other Resources:** Publishes PEACE WORKS newsletter and other materials. **Member:** Co-op America.

**E ▶ Grand Canyon Trust**
1400 16th St. NW, #300
Washington, DC 20036    (202)797-5429
**Concern(s):** environment; preservation; natural resources; wilderness. Advocates the preservation and wise management of the Grand Canyon and Colorado Plateau, with special focus on air pollution, Utah Wilderness designation and the Glen Canyon Dam operations. **Dues:** $15/yr.

**✾ ▶ Grandmothers for Peace**
909 12th St.
Sacramento, CA 95814   (916)444-5080
**Concern(s):** peace; activism. Similar to the group Mothers for Peace this one is an activist group for the senior. Peace must be the responsibility of all. **Contact(s):** Barbara Wiedner.

**S ▶ Grantsmanship Center**
See WHOLE NONPROFIT CATALOG (directories).  .

**E ▶ Grassroots Coalition for Environmental and Economic Justice**
Box 1319
Clarksville, MD 21029    (301)964-3574
**Concern(s):** environment; spiritual; politics; education; interfaith; activism; social justice; conservation; grassroots organizing. Several hundred churches and synagogues in Maryland, N.Y., N.J., and Pennsylvanian which are working together for environmental justice. "Our program is designed to appeal to average people because we are convinced that by involving very large numbers of church and synagogue members, we can truly achieve environmental justice." **Other Resources:** A newsletter, VOICE OF THE EARTH; and an action manual $10. **Est.:** 1988. **Frequency:** 10/yr. **Subscription:** $10/yr. **Price:** $1/ea. **Bulk:** 15% off/24. **Pages:** 4. **Circ.:** 300. **Contact(s):** John Conner (Director), Iona (Co-director).

**T ▶ Grassroots International**
Box 312
Cambridge, MA 02139   (617)497-9180
**Concern(s):** Third World; demographics; justice; development; hunger. Activist development and information agency providing material aid to democratic Third World social change movements. "The partnerships we build at the grassroots level provide us with a unique basis to inform the US public about Third World conflicts" and the US role in them. "We focus on strategically important areas where national movements are challenging economic and social inequalities and repressive political systems." **Other Resources:** Projects range from emergency relief, public health programs, and literacy training to publications and worker-managed cooperatives. Current priorities are Africa, the Philippines, and the Middle East, primarily funding relief and development projects. **Contact(s):** Dan Connell (Executive Director), Sarah McCarthy (Information Coordinator).

**P ▶ Grassroots Leadership**
See newsletter, GRASSROOTS.

**H ▶ Gray Panther Network**
311 S. Juniper St., #601
Philadelphia, PA 19107
**Concern(s):** health; peace; justice; politics; seniors; discrimination; lobbying. Radical seniors working for peace and social justice. **Contact(s):** Maggie Kuhn (Founder).

**H ▶ Gray Panthers National Office**
1424 16th St. NW
Washington, DC 20036    (202)387-3111
**Concern(s):** health; politics; seniors; lobbying. Works on issues of social justice of concern to older Americans in particular: forced

retirement, nursing home abuse, good housing, basic health care for all. All ages welcome to participate. Directory available. **Member:** Co-op America. **Contact(s):** Frances Humphreys.

**E ▶ Great Bear Foundation**
See BEAR NEWS (periodicals).

**E ▶ Greater Ecosystem Alliance**
Box 2813
Bellingham, WA 98227   (206)671-9950
**Concern(s):** environment; forests. **Other Resources:** Newsletter, NORTHWEST CONSERVATION: NEWS AND PRIORITIES. **E-Network:** Econet. **ID:** 'gea'. **Fax:** (206)271-8429.

**E ▶ Greater Yellowstone Coalition**
Box 1874
Bozeman, MT 59717    (406)586-1593
**Concern(s):** environment; energy; appropriate technology; preservation; conservation; forests. This coalition is comprised of 75 organizations and 3500 individuals who don't want to see Yellowstone, one of the largest essentially intact ecosystems in the temperate zones, ruined by inappropriate oil and gas development, logging, grazing and other excessive development. **Other Resources:** Internship available. **Dues:** $20-500/yr.

**E ▶ Green & Rainbow Activists for a Democratic Society**
Box 5194
New York, NY 10185
**Concern(s):** environment; politics; activism; Green; alternative party; grassroots organizing. New York Greens link with Rainbow activists in order to bring the green movement into today's politics. It recognizes that there are more greens in the world than just those who claim membership in a Green Party. All who espouse ideas of democracy social justice, peace, and ecology are invited to join the GRADS debate on unity of the broader movement.

**E ▶ Green Committees of Correspondence**
Box 30208
Kansas City, MO 64112   (816)931-9366
**Concern(s):** environment; politics; justice; economics; feminism; peace; nonviolence; men's liberation; sustainability; Green. Rooted in the 10 key values: Ecological Wisdom, Grassroots Democracy, Social Responsibility, Nonviolence, Decentralization, Community-based Economics, Post-patriarchal Values, Respect for Diversity, Global Responsibility and Sustainability. Greens comprise over 200 local groups and a dozen budding Green parties. We practice a value-based politics and believe that neither social nor environmental problems can be solved in isolation from each other. **Other Resources:** GREEN LETTER newsletter; GREEN LETTER, IN SEARCH OF GREENER TIMES magazine; and GREEN SYNTHESIS QUARTERLY which is sent to all members. **Est.:** 1984. **Contact(s):** Jim Richmond (Coordinator).

**E ▶ Green Earth Foundation**
Box 327
El Verano, CA 95433    (707)935-7257
**Concern(s):** environment; spiritual; education; transformation. An educational organization dedicated to the healing and harmonizing of the relationships between humanity and the Earth. Through its publications and other projects, the foundation aims to help bring about changes in attitudes perceptions, and world views that are based on ecological balance and respect for the integrity of all life-forms on Earth. **Other Resources:** Publishes newsletter, GREEN EARTH OBSERVER. Nonprofit. **Est.:** 1988. **Dues:** $25/yr.; $15 low income. **E-Network:** Peacenet/Econet. **ID:** 'rmetzner'. **Contact(s):** Ralph Metzner (President). (707)935-0906.

**S ▶ Green Fire Foundation**
See EARTH ETHICS/EVOLVING VALUES FOR AN EARTH COMMUNITY.

**E ▶ Green Media Group**
See BAY AREA GREEN PAGES, THE LOCAL HANDBOOK FOR PLANET MAINTENANCE (directory).

**M ▶ Green Party Multilogue**
1115 Tennessee
Lawrence, KS 66044
**Concern(s):** media; politics; multilogues; Green. By-mail-community which discusses to present and future of the Green Party. This multilogue is for those who want to exchange ideas on Green Politics and build a Green Community. **Contact(s):** Paul Justus.

**P ▶ Green Party of Alaska**
GPA Coordinating Office
106 W. Bunnell Ave.
Homer, AK 99603
**Concern(s):** politics; environment; Green; alternative party; polar. **Other Resources:** Publishes GREEN PARTY OF ALASKA newsletter.

241

**P ▸ Green Program Project**
Box 111
Burlington, VT 05402
**Concern(s):** politics; environment; Green; social ecology. Extensive left green/social ecology literature list, GREEN PERSPECTIVES.

**D ▸ Greener Pastures Institute**
Box 1122
Sierra Madre, CA 91025 (818)355-1670
**Concern(s):** demographics; urban; agriculture; rural relocation; rural communities. Formerly Relocation Research in Bend, Oregon, the founder started this "pre-move counselling service" as a clearinghouse for prospective ex-urbanites. By offering unbiased information about various US locations, it helps people avoid needless financial and emotional stresses related to the moving process. A future goal includes doing research on how voluntary population dispersal and decentralization can impact the seriously declining quality of life of our major urban areas. **Other Resources:** See GREENER PASTURES GAZETTE. Brochure with recommended reading material available on request. Classes, consulting, books and publications for sale. **Fax:** (818)440-9471. **Contact(s):** William L. Seavey (Director).

**E ▸ Greenhouse Crisis Foundation**
1130 17th St. NW, #630
Washington, DC 20036 (202)466-2823
**Affiliation:** Foundation on Economic Trends. **Concern(s):** environment; energy; global warming. Established to reverse the potential catastrophic results of the Greenhouse Effect, by educating the public as to what alternative solutions can be researched, explored, and implemented. **Other Resources:** Guides, 101 WAYS TO HELP SAVE THE PLANET and GREENHOUSE CRISIS, A CITIZEN'S GUIDE. **Fax:** (202)429-9602. Telex: 904059-WSH. **Contact(s):** Jeremy Rifkin (President).

**E ▸ Greenline Membership Program**
Conservatree Information Services
10 Lombard St., #250
San Francisco, CA 94111 (415)433-1000
**Affiliation:** Conservatree Paper Co.. **Concern(s):** environment; peace; recycling. Greenline members receive bi-monthly mailings, including ESP News, Conservatree's newsletter on recycled paper issues. Designed to keep policy makers, businesses and consumers up to date on recycled paper issues, ESP News covers important new initiatives, legislation, and new developments. Members also receive an extensive introductory kit. **Est.:** 1976. **Frequency:** 6/yr. **Subscription:** $29/yr.; $49 business. **Pages:** 12. **Circ.:** 25M. **Fax:** (415)391-7890. **Contact(s):** David Assmann (Vice-President).

**E ▸ Greenpeace USA**
1436 U St. NW
Washington, DC 20009 (202)462-1177
**Concern(s):** environment; energy; peace; politics; health; animal rights; ocean/rivers; wildlife/endangered species; nonviolence; civil disobedience; anti-nuclear; polar; corporate responsibility; government accountability; hazardous/toxic waste; volunteers. An international organization that advocates grassroots nonviolent direct action to save whales, seals, wolves, stop nuclear tests and stop toxics. Fathered the "Rainbow Warrior" which was blown-up by French agents in Australia. Advocates nuclear disarmament, public education, nonviolent direct action, research, and worldwide organizing, anything that might grab the attention of the media and bring these injustices to public attention. **Other Resources:** See GREENPEACE ACTION Magazine; EVERYONE'S GUIDE TO TOXICS IN THE HOME; STEPPING LIGHTLY ON THE EARTH. Volunteers accepted at 23 locations around the world. Pundit Watch on PeaceNet/EcoNet. See, also, American Peace Test and Planetary Survival Alliance. **Dues:** $15/yr. Info: (202)319-2444. **Contact(s):** Peter Bahouth (Executive Director), Peter Dexter (Media Director). (202)232-1590. **Other:** Box 3720, Washington, DC 20007

**A ▸ Gross National Waste Product Forum**
4201 S. 31 St., #616
Arlington, VA 22206 (703)578-4627
**Concern(s):** agriculture; economics; sustainability; food production. Conducts research on the effects of wasteful practices in the agricultural/food sectors on the economy.

**☮ ▸ Ground Zero Center for Nonviolent Action**
16159 Clear Creek Rd NW
Poulsbo, WA 98370 (206)779-6673
**Concern(s):** peace; economics; politics; anti-nuclear; discrimination; minority rights; nonviolence. The railroad tracks that carry Trident missile components across the country pass through many urban Black communities which have been devastated by our budgetary focus on developing weapons like the Trident. Our group applies a long-term campaign of nonviolence as a way of life trying to learn from and apply insights of Gandhi, M.L. King and Jesus. **Other Resources:** Quarterly newspaper of reflection; weekly leafleting campaign at 2 local naval installations; nonviolence training and some civil disobedience. **Est.:** 1978. **Frequency:** 4/yr. **Subscription:** $10/donation. **Pages:** 12. **Circ.:** 9M. **Contact(s):** Karol Schulkin, Renee Krisko (Core Members). (206)697-1470.

**H ▸ Group to Alleviate Smoking Pollution (GASP)**
Box 12103
Boulder, CO 80303
**Concern(s):** health; environment; substance abuse; air pollution.

**T ▸ Guatemala News and Info Bureau**
See REPORT ON GUATEMALA (periodicals).

**L ▸ H.O.M.E., Inc. (Homeworkers Organized for More Employment)**
See newsletter, THIS TIME.

**J ▸ Habitat for Humanity International**
Habitat & Church Sts.
Americus, GA 31709-3498 (912)924-6935
**Concern(s):** justice; demographics; Third World; economics; housing; poverty; hunger; homelessness; development; volunteers. Hundreds of thousands of families in America live in deplorable living conditions: bug invested ghetto flats; dilapidated rural shacks; decaying, crumbling apartments. Habitat has set up 445 revolving loan funds to build housing for the poor and a network of 100,000+ committed volunteers globally has been developed to build and remodel modest homes. Interest-free, nonprofit home loans are offered the poor who then pay back into the revolving loan fund to help someone else in need. **Other Resources:** See newsletter, HABITAT WORLD. Nonprofit. **Dues:** $25/yr. **Contact(s):** Geoff Van Loucks, David Eastis.

**D ▸ Hadassah**
50 W. 58th St.
New York, NY 10019 (212)355-7900
**Concern(s):** demographics; justice; spiritual; faith; refugees. A nation-wide Jewish women's charity/relief organization named after the Biblical character, Hadassah (who later became Queen Esther that saved her people from destruction). Actually, Hadassah was the Hebrew name of Henrietta Sold, a modern-day Hadassah. She was responsible for organizing youth immigration to Israel (then Palestine) in the 30's that enabled thousands of children to flee from Nazi persecution (Youth Alia). **Contact(s):** Thelma Wolf.

**J ▸ HALT - an Organization for Americans for Legal Reform**
1319 F St. NW, #300
Washington, DC 20004 (202)347-9600
**Concern(s):** justice; economics; politics; consumer rights; reform; monopolies; self-determination. National consumer organization that works to reform the civil legal system and educate people so they can handle their legal affairs simply, affordably and fairly. Its legislative agenda includes ending lawyers' monopoly over legal services, simplifying legal processes, reducing costs, providing alternatives to lawsuits and bringing public accountability to the regulation of the legal profession. **Est.:** 1978. **Contact(s):** Richard Hebert.

**D ▸ Hand To Hand**
Box 881
Camden, ME 04843 (207)326-9643
**Concern(s):** demographics; hunger. **Contact(s):** Charlie Frair.

**J ▸ Handgun Control Inc.**
Box 96627
Washington, DC 20077-7307 (202)898-0792
**Concern(s):** justice; urban; politics; gun control; criminal system; drugs; inner city. A citizen's organization formed by handgun victims that persuaded Congress to continue a ban on the interstate sale of handguns; won major victories to outlaw armor-peircing "cop killer" bullets, new machine guns and undetectable plastic guns; victories in Maryland keeping Saturday Night Special ban in place. Promoted Brady Bill and Assault Weapon Bill. **Est.:** 1983. **Office:** 1225 Eye St. NW, #1100 Washington, DC 20005. **Contact(s):** Charles J. Orasin (President), Sarah Brady (Chair). N.T. Pete Shields , Chairman Emeritus.

**☮ ▸ Hanford Education and Action League**
S. 325 Oak St.
Spokane, WA 99204 (509)624-7264
**Concern(s):** peace; environment; politics; anti-nuclear; activism. Works to clean up the Hanford Nuclear Weapons Plant.

**E ▸ Harbinger Communications**
50 Rustic Lane
Santa Cruz, CA 95060 (408)427-2510
**Affiliation:** Peninsula Conservation Foundation. **Concern(s):** environment; conservation; preservation. Dedicated to promoting comprehensive, far-sighted environmental planning and education. "We try to increase the amount of public participation in all aspects of the planning process and to educate them through information sharing." **Other Resources:** See HARBINGER FILE (directories). Nonprofit. **Est.:** 1970. **Contact(s):** Bill Leland.

**E ▸ Hawk Migration Association of North America**
Box 3482, Rivermont Station
Lynchmont, VA 24503 (804)847-7811
**Concern(s):** environment; wildlife/endangered species; conservation; volunteers. Conducts research on the wintering habits of raptors in Central and South America and North American nesting habitats. Dedicated to the conservation of birds of prey throughout education and research. **Other Resources:** Slide show available to the public on eastern and western birds of prey and some research awards available. Volunteer hawkwatchers welcome. **Dues:** $10/yr.

**E ▸ Hawk Mountain Sanctuary**
RD 2
Kempton, PA 19529 (215)756-6961
**Concern(s):** environment; wildlife/endangered species; conservation; preservation; volunteers. Environmental education, ecological and avian research and conservation policy are utilized to create a better understanding of birds of prey and their natural environment. **Other Resources:** Various volunteer opportunities. Internships in research, education and raptor care. **Dues:** $20/yr.

**E ▸ Hawkwatch International, Inc.**
Box 35706
Albuquerque, NM 87176-5706 (505)255-7622
**Concern(s):** environment; education; wildlife/endangered species; preservation; volunteers. Purpose: The conservation of birds of prey and their habitats in western US through research and public education. Supports six field projects to monitor trends and migration patterns of migratory raptors in the Rocky Mountain West. Current Emphasis: Standardized counts of migrating raptors at strategic observation points and large-scale capture and banding. **Other Resources:** Volunteer Programs, Spring and Fall research and education internships. Volunteer banders also needed. **Dues:** $15, $25 Family. **Office:** 1420 Carlisle NE, #100 Albuquerque, NM 87110. (505)265-5393.

**E ▸ Hazardous Waste Control Research Institute**
9300 Columbia Rd.
Silver Springs, MD 20910-1702 (301)587-9390
**Concern(s):** environment; health; hazardous/toxic waste.

**E ▸ Heal The Bay**
1640 5th St., #112
Santa Monica, CA 90401 (310)394-4552
**Concern(s):** environment; oceans/rivers. A coalition of people and organizations who are working to achieve swimmable and fishable coastal waters that meet the goals of the Federal Clean Water Act "to restore and maintain the chemical, physical, and biological integrity of the nation's waters." It informs the public, elected officials and the media about the bay, the causes and effects of pollution and ways to deal with existing problems so that the Bay can begin the process of healing itself. Nonprofit.

**H ▸ Health and Energy Institute**
Box 5357
Takoma Park, MD 20912 (301)585-5541
**Concern(s):** health; energy; politics; efficiency; conservation; appropriate technology; lobbying; anti-nuclear. Goals are to preserve a healthy environment and promote human health and life. This organization conducts research, seminars, and testifies before Congress and other agencies. Tracks radiation litigation, and assists radiation victims. **Est.:** 1978. **Contact(s):** Kathleen Tucker (Director).

**H ▸ Health Plus**
Box 22001
Phoenix, AZ 85028
**Concern(s):** health; nutrition; preventative medicine. Dr. Ariola's nutritional advice.

**H ▸ Health Policy Advisory Center**
See HEALTH/PAC BULLETIN and Reproductive Rights National Network.

**H ▸ The Health Research Group**
2000 P St. NW., #605
Washington, DC 20036-0757 (202)833-3000
**Affiliation:** Public Citizen. **Concern(s):** health; consumer protection. Fights for protections against unsafe foods, drugs, and workplaces, and for greater consumer control over health decisions. Publishes the monthly HEALTH LETTER newsletter. **Other Resources:** See HEALTH LETTER newsletter.

**♿ ▸ HEATH Resource Center**
See HEATH RESOURCE DIRECTORY.

**A ▶ Heifer Project International**
1015 S. Louisiana St.
Little Rock, AR 72202    (501)376-6836
**Concern(s):** agriculture; Third World; hunger; interfaith. An ecumenical entity dedicated to alleviating world hunger through long-term livestock development projects by providing a continual source of nourishment, and means for achieving self-sufficiency by giving needy families an animal and training to care for it. In return, each family agrees to "pass on the gift" by giving offspring of the animal and training to another neighbor in need. During the last four decades HPI has sent animals to people in over 110 countries and over 30 states. Nonprofit. **Contact(s):** Jerry Bedford, Sherry Campbell.

**E ▶ Helen Dwight Reid Educational Foundation**
See ENVIRONMENT magazine.

**♿ ▶ Helen Keller National Center**
See DIRECTORY OF AGENCIES AND ORGANIZATIONS SERVING DEAF-BLIND INDIVIDUALS.

**T ▶ Helsinki Watch**
See Human Rights Watch.

**H ▶ Hemlock Society**
Box 11830
Eugene, OR 97440
**Concern(s):** health; death/dying. The Society seeks to raise public, medical, and legal consciousness about euthanasia. There has recently been some murky personal business in connection with the founder, his ex-wife, and her parents. Controversy surrounds his books. Many feel that his reading material should not be so easily accessible without proper guidance. Some AIDS victims and others, though, might find the information useful during those final moments. **Other Resources:** Publishes HEMLOCK QUARTERLY, a guidebook, LET ME DIE BEFORE I WAKE; and, ASSISTED SUICIDE: THE COMPASSIONATE CRIME. Nonprofit. **Est.:** 1980. **Frequency:** 4/yr. **Subscription:** $20/yr. **Price:** Free sample. **Contact(s):** Derek Humphry.

**P ▶ HEMP (Help Eliminate Marijuana Prohibition)**
5632 Van Nuys, #210
Van Nuys, CA 91401
**Concern(s):** politics; justice; drugs; reform; criminal system. Not only do they extoll the medical benefits (helps cataracts), but Hemp can grow fast and effectively as a replacement for trees in the making of paper, chipboard and other building products. It has been demonstrated that much of the deforestation going on today could be avoided by growing Hemp crops. Commercial Hemp has insignificant amounts of THC, the psychogenic substance that has made it necessary for its criminalization. Of course, this group also believes this should be legalized. **Contact(s):** Jack Herer (Director).

**J ▶ Henry George Foundation of America**
2000 Century Plaza, #238
Columbia, MD 21044    (301)740-1177
**Concern(s):** justice; urban; economics; environment; demogrpahics; housing; transportation; monopolies; social justice; planning; land use; taxation. Devoted to long-term solutions to problems of affordable housing, urban sprawl, natural resource depletion, transportation, land use, and unfair taxation. "We believe justice is the world's best medicine and apply it with wonderful results." **Other Resources:** Consulting services to municipal governments facing fiscal challenges. See COMMON GROUND USA and GROUNDSWELL newsletter. **Est.:** 1926. **Fax:** (301)997-1608. **Contact(s):** Hanno Beck (Asst. Director), Steven Cord (Director).

**H ▶ Hesperian Foundation**
Box 1692
Palo Alto, CA 94302
**Concern(s):** health; politics; justice; preventative medicine. Publishes WHERE THERE IS NO DOCTOR (David Werner & Daniel Perlman, eds.) and newsletter on the political and social aspects of health.

**E ▶ High Country Foundation**
See HIGH COUNTRY NEWS.

**P ▶ Highlander Research & Education Center**
Route 3, Box 370
New Market, TN 38720    (615)933-3443
**Concern(s):** politics; justice; demographics; peace; education; grassroots organizing; minority rights; racism; self-determination; poverty. Grassroots community organizing is taught for empowerment of working and poor people. Rosa Parks and Dr. Martin Luther King, Jr., were inspired here, and the center continues to inspire common people to organize more effectively for themselves, their neighbors, and their environment. **Other Resources:** Publishes HIGHLANDER REPORTS.

**$ ▶ Highwind Association**
Route 2
Plymouth, WI 53073
**Concern(s):** economics; environment; intentional community; land trusts. An intentional community created to help restore the balance between people and the Earth. Using informal shared discovery, education and research, it is seeking to interrelate, in the spirit of wholeness, new concepts in ecology, sustainable agriculture, relationships and community. We're currently engaged in "living-learning" educational programs, on-site cottage industries, creation of a national think tank to influence the values of Federal policymakers. **Other Resources:** Studying the concept of placing our 128 acres into a land trust so that our land cannot be privately owned or bought and sold in the future.

**H ▶ Holistic Alliance International**
Box 3000
Flanders, NJ 07836
**Concern(s):** health; environment; preventative medicine; public health; alternative consumer; holism. A fundraiser for environmental issues, an umbrella for networking organizations and, in conjunction with the Public Health Office of Morristown, New Jersey, is forming a coalition for Preventative Medicine Model. As a member you will receive discounts for holistic services and products, have a voice in solutions for health issues and share in contributing to the well-being of ourselves and others. Nonprofit. **Est.:** 1988.

**☮ ▶ Holyearth Foundation**
See Earthstewards Network.

**D ▶ Homelessness Information Exchange**
1830 Connecticut Ave. NW
Washington, DC 20009    (202)462-7551
**Concern(s):** demographics; hunger; homelessness; poverty; networking. From their database come a number of newsletters addressing different aspects of the problem of homelessness. **Other Resources:** Newsletter, HOMEWORDS.

**H ▶ Homeopathic Educational Services**
See HOMEOPATHY: MEDICINE FOR THE 21ST CENTURY (directories).

**J ▶ Hopi Epicenter for International Outreach**
22 S. San Francisco St., #406
Flagstaff, AZ 86001
**Concern(s):** justice; spiritual; Native Americans; transformation.

**E ▶ Household Hazardous Waste Project**
901 S. National Ave.
Box 87
Springfield, MO 65804    (417)836-5777
**Concern(s):** environment; health; hazardous/toxic waste. **Other Resources:** Publishes GUIDE TO HAZARDOUS PRODUCTS AROUND THE HOME.

**♿ ▶ Housing for Independent People**
25 E. Hedding St.
San Jose, CA 95112    (408)294-9756
**Concern(s):** demographics; health; justice; housing; disabled; disabled's rights. Housing developer for low to moderate income people. Specializing in housing for the disabled. Nonprofit. **Member:** Co-op America.

**E ▶ Hudson Bioregional Council**
See BIOREGIONAL BIBLIOGRAPHY (directories).

**E ▶ Hudsonia Limited**
Bard College Field Station
Annandale, NY 12504
**Concern(s):** environment; education; conservation; volunteers. While stressing scientific research, education and conservation, this organization provides technical consulting for landowners, nonprofit organizations, citizen's groups and government agencies. **Other Resources:** Volunteer positions available.

**E ▶ Hug-a-Tree**
6465 Lance Way
San Diego, CA 92120    (619)286-7536
**Concern(s):** environment; forests. **Contact(s):** Jacqueline Heet.

**J ▶ Huichol Center**
Box 1430
Cottonwood, AZ 86326    (602)634-3946
**Concern(s):** justice; Native Americans. A community, medical and art center founded to help Huichol Indians in Mexico. Provides an alternative to working in pesticide-covered tobacco fields. Jewelry, arts, and crafts. **Member:** Co-op America.

**H ▶ Human Ecology Action League**
Box 66637
Chicago, IL 60666    (312)665-6575

**Concern(s):** health; environment; social ecology; nutrition; hazardous/toxic waste; preventative medicine. Provides information and current news on food allergies, chemical sensitivities, ecological illness, and related subjects. **Other Resources:** See THE HUMAN ECOLOGIST newsletter.

**P ▶ The Human Ecology Party**
20 Sunnyside Ave., #A-156
Mill Valley, CA 94941    (800)733-2357
**Affiliation:** San Francisco Medical Research Foundation.
**Concern(s):** politics; health; environment; peace; energy; economics; alternative party; social ecology; anti-nuclear; test ban; economic conversion; decentralization. This party is "a synthesis of the Republican, Democratic, and Green parties... an educational process designed to activate higher consciousness and align humanity with a comprehensive program which creates Health and Freedom for All. Through the law of synergy and direct political action, we are confident we will realize this majestic and inspired vision." Advocates a decentralized energy policy, supports Comprehensive Nuclear Test Ban Treaty, economic conversion, tax reform and improved health care. **Other Resources:** Offers a program, books, video, and catalog. Plans to convert Alcatraz into The Global Peace Center, and create a Global Family Television Network. **Contact(s):** Raphael Ornstein, M.D. (SFMRF Director), James Marti (Project Director).

**$ ▶ The Human Economy Center**
Box 14, Department of Economics
Mankato State University
Mankato, MN 56001    (507)389-5325
**Concern(s):** economics; analysis. Created to provide encouragement, exchange of information, and new developments for those who see the necessity for a new kind of economics. Membership includes a subscription to newsletter. **Other Resources:** Newsletter, THE HUMAN ECONOMY NEWSLETTER. **Member:** Co-op America.

**E ▶ The Human Environment Center**
1001 Connecticut Ave. NW, #82
Washington, DC 20036    (202)331-8387
**Concern(s):** environment; justice; urban; education; conservation; natural resources; jobs; discrimination. Serves and cultivates common aims of the environmental and social equity movements. The Center promotes racial integration in the environmental and natural resource professions, improvement of urban environments and—the major focus of current work— expansion of youth conservation and service corps programs. **Other Resources:** See HEC NEWS newsletter. See, also, National Association of Service and Conservation Corps. **Est.:** 1976. **Contact(s):** Margaret Fosenberry.

**♿ ▶ Human Factors Society**
See HUMAN FACTORS SOCIETY—DIRECTORY.

**♥ ▶ The Human Lactation Center Ltd.**
666 Sturges Highway
Westport, CT 06880    (203)259-5995
**Concern(s):** family; birth.

**P ▶ The Human Party**
c/o Dr. Larry Holden
Box 1026
Loveland, CO 80539    (717)647-9933
**Concern(s):** politics; alternative party. Dr. Holden has for the last six years been engaged full-time in bringing to birth the Human Party, neither Democratic nor Republican, neither "left" nor "right", his candidacy is not merely symbolic or an egghead's "visionary dream." He "hopes to build unity along with support and bring together groups that espouse different humanitarian, spiritual, and conservationist causes" into one powerful constituency. - Chapin, S.F. Examiner. **Other Resources:** See THE FLIGHT OF THE EAGLE newsletter. **Contact(s):** Dr. Larry Holden (Founder).

**J ▶ Human Rights Documentation Project**
Box 460597
San Francisco, CA 94146
**Concern(s):** justice; peace; East-West. Founded by Association of Humanitarian Lawyers. Collects reports on human rights violations for persons engaged in US/Soviet dialogue on human rights. Current goal is to bring together US & Soviet legislators in public forum on human rights. **Est.:** 1988.

**J ▶ Human Rights Internet**
c/o Human Rights Centre, University
of Ottawa, 57 Louis Pasteur
Ottawa, ON K1N 6N5 Canada    (613)564-3492
**Concern(s):** justice; peace. International communications network and clearinghouse on human rights, focusing on activities of nongovernmental organizations. Serves human rights advocacy organizations worldwide, promotes teaching and research. Directories include: AFRICA: HUMAN RIGHTS DIRECTORY & Bibliography; HUMAN RIGHTS DIRECTORY: Eastern Europe & the USSR; HUMAN RIGHTS

243

DIRECTORY: Latin America & the Caribbean; NORTH AMERICAN HUMAN RIGHTS; HUMAN RIGHTS DIRECTORY: Western Europe: and more... **Other Resources:** Publishes the HUMAN RIGHTS INTERNET REPORTER. Other directories: MIDDLE EAST HUMAN RIGHTS DIRECTORY; HUMAN RIGHTS DIRECTORY: ASIA & THE PACIFIC; HUMAN RIGHTS DIRECTORY: THE COMMONWEALTH. **Est.:** 1976. **Dues:** $75/institution: $50/individual: with Reporter and 50% privileges. **Fax:** (613)564-4054.

**T ♦ Human Rights Watch**
1522 K St. NW
Washington, DC 20005   (202)371-6592
**Affiliation:** Fund for Free Expression. **Concern(s):** Third World; justice; politics; Africa; Asia; Latin America; government accountability. An organization that links the five Watch communities—Africa Watch, Americas Watch, Asia Watch, Helsinki Watch and Middle East Watch—and coordinates and supports their efforts to monitor the human rights practices of governments. In situations of sustained armed conflict, including armed conflicts within a country, HRW monitors violations of the laws of war by both sides. Publicizes violations of human rights and launches international protests against governments that commit abuses. **Other Resources:** Publishes HUMAN RIGHTS WATCH newsletter. **Contact(s):** Holly Burkhalter (Director). **Other:** 485 5th Ave., New York, NY 10017 Aryeh Neier, Executive Director. (212)972-8400.

**☂ ♦ Humane Farming Association**
1550 California St., #2
San Francisco, CA 94109
**Concern(s):** agriculture; environment; health; animal rights. **Contact(s):** Bradley Miller (Director).

**☂ ♦ The Humane Society of the US**
2100 L St. NW
Washington, DC 20037   (202)452-1100
**Concern(s):** environment; animal rights; volunteers. National animal-welfare organization. In addition to extensive informational, legislative, investigative, and legal work, the HSUS also operates a separate education division, The National Association for the Advancement of Humane Education (NAAHE), and a bioethics division, the Center for Respect of Life and Environment (CRLE). Focus on marine mammal protection, domesticated and wild animals, laboratory animal welfare and more. Volunteers welcome. **Other Resources:** See HSUS NEWS magazine, ANIMAL ACTIVIST ALERT newsletter, SHELTER SENSE, CHILDREN AND ANIMALS magazine and KIND NEWS newspaper. "The Shame of Fur" Campaign; "Be a P.A.L.—Prevent a Litter" Campaign. Also, CAREERS WORKING WITH ANIMALS, a guide. **Dues:** $10/yr. **Member:** Global Tomorrow Coalition. **Contact(s):** John A. Hoyt (President).

**T ♦ Humanitas International Human Rights Committee**
Box 818
Menlo Park, CA 94026   (415)324-9077
**Concern(s):** Third World; justice; peace. See HUMANITAS INTERNATIONAL NEWSLETTER.

**D ♦ Hunger and Development Coalition of Central Ohio**
299 King Ave.
Columbus, OH 43201   (614)424-6203
**Concern(s):** demographics; environment; Third World; hunger; development. "A coalition of organizations and individuals in Central Ohio who are working collectively on issues related to the survival of our planet and all of its inhabitants. Understanding that all issues are interconnected, we seek solutions where today's needs can be met for all without sacrificing future generations of life on Earth." **Other Resources:** Global Learning Center - resources for Central Ohio reflecting our members' issues; Global Store - products from self-help cooperatives around the world to promote our wholeness and oneness; Environmental roundtable. See OUR COMMON FUTURE newsletter. Nonprofit. **Est.:** 1986. **Dues:** $25, $100 organization. **Contact(s):** Marilyn Welker (Program Coordinator).

**D ♦ The Hunger Project**
1388 Sutter St.
San Francisco, CA 94109-5452   (415)928-8700
**Concern(s):** demographics; Third World; education; hunger; volunteers. An organization committed to prioritizing the issue of world hunger through far-reaching educational campaigns and strategic global initiatives. More than 6 million individuals in 152 countries have committed themselves to this objective. Volunteers mobilize all sectors of society through presentations in schools, fund-raising events, newspaper articles and local agencies. See THE BUSINESS OF ENDING HUNGER, a quarterly newsletter, and resource guide, ENDING HUNGER. **Other Resources:** See newspaper, A SHIFT IN THE WIND; a twice monthly report, WORLD DEVELOPMENT FORUM; AFRICAN FARMER magazine; HUNGER PROJECT PAPERS; video,

FAMINE AND CHRONIC, PERSISTENT HUNGER: A LIFE AND DEATH DISTINCTION and curriculum aids. Nonprofit. **Other:** 1 Madison Ave., New York, NY 10010 Jean Holmes , Executive Director. (212)532-4255.

**E ♦ Idaho Conservation League**
Box 844
Boise, ID 83701   (208)345-6933
**Concern(s):** environment; conservation.

**? ♦ Ideas Banks for Unconventional Ideas in Science, Medicine and Sociology**
Bureau of Applied Sciences Ltd.
42A High St., Newport
Isle of Wight, PO30 1SE England   (0983)521067
**Concern(s):** future; economics; trade; ideation; invention; networking. "Converting unconventional ideas into action and products" is the primary aim of this effort. **Fax:** (0983) 821573. **Contact(s):** Bruce Denness.

**M ♦ Illich Network**
6 Hemlock Terrace
Waltham, MA 02154
**Concern(s):** media; economics; multilogues. **Contact(s):** Gene Burkart.

**✍ ♦ Illusion Theater Prevention Program**
528 Hennepin Ave. , #702
Minneapolis, MN 55403 (612)339-4944
**Concern(s):** education; health; feminism; childhood; AIDS; rape/sexual abuse; child abuse. "Through our pioneering collaboration of prevention specialists and professional artists, we create and present prevention plays, workshops, and educational resources. Topics: Rape, child abuse, AIDS and related areas." **Other Resources:** Publishes newsletter, IN TOUCH, and guide, CHILD SEXUAL ABUSE PREVENTION: HOW TO TAKE THE FIRST STEPS and SEXUAL ABUSE PREVENTION EDUCATION: AN ANNOTATED BIBLIOGRAPHY. **Publisher:** ETR Associates. **Member:** National Family Life Network. **Contact(s):** Cordelia Anderson, MA (Director). **Other:** ETR Associates, Box 1830, Santa Cruz, CA 95061.

**H ♦ Imagine Tours**
American Lung Association
917 Third St.
Davis, CA 95616   (800)228-7041
**Concern(s):** health; environment; recreation. Bicycle tours, alternative transportation plans, corporate wellness programs.

**☂ ♦ In Defense of Animals (IDA)**
816 W. Francisco
San Rafael, CA 94901   (415)453-9984
**Concern(s):** environment; economics; boycott; corporate responsibility; socially-responsible investing; animal rights. BOYCOTT PROCTER & GAMBLE — They continue to use animal testing. For a complete list of products, contact IDA. **Other Resources:** To protest, write to: J.G. Smole, CEO, Procter & Gamble, Fifth & Sycamore Sts., Cincy, OH 45202.

**T ♦ Independent Commission of Inquiry on the US Invasion of Panama**
36 E. 12th St.
New York, NY 10003   (212)254-2295
**Concern(s):** Third World; peace; Central America; intervention; foreign policy; international law; militarism; nonviolence. This commission attempts to find out the truth behind the invasion of Panama and the atrocities that took place during and after the invasion. **Contact(s):** Gavrielle Gemma (Project Director), Teresa Gutierrez (Assistant Director).

**♿ ♦ Independent Living Research Utilization**

**Other Resources:** See ANNOTATED REGISTRY OF INDEPENDENT LIVING PROGRAMS; DIRECTORY OF INDEPENDENT LIVING PROGRAMS; and INDEPENDENT LIVING (periodicals).

**S ♦ Independent Sector**
1828 L St. NW
Washington, DC 20036   (202)223-8100
**Concern(s):** spiritual; justice; demographics; volunteers; philanthropy; research. Designed to preserve and enhance the traditions of giving, volunteering and not-for-profit sectors through public education to improve the public's understanding of the volunteer sectors; communicates within the sectors to identify shared problems and oppositions; does research on the nonprofit sector; coordinates interconnections between these sectors and government; encourages effective operation and management; and attempts to maximize benefit and service to individuals and society. **Est.:** 1980.

**✍ ♦ Independent Study**
University of Minnesota
Minneapolis, MN 55455 (800)234-6564
**Concern(s):** education; alternative. "With correspondence, audio, or video courses from the University of Minnesota Department of Independent Study, you can choose from 400 credit courses that will fit in your busy schedule and location. Enrollments are open, take up to a year to complete a course, and register by mail." Other: (612)624-0000.

**J ♦ Indian Law Resource Center**
601 E St. SE
Washington, DC 20003   (202)547-2800
**Concern(s):** justice; politics; Native Americans; law.

**E ♦ Indian Peaks Working Group**
337 Spruce St.
Boulder, CO 80302   (303)442-7337
**Concern(s):** environment.

**J ♦ Indian Resource Development (IRD)**
See SOURCES OF FINANCIAL AID AVAILABLE TO AMERICAN INDIAN STUDENTS (directories).

**T ♦ Indochina Project**
318 4th St. NE
Washington, DC 20002   (202)547-5075
**Concern(s):** Third World; justice; peace; Asia; foreign policy; development. An organization concerned with US foreign policy towards the peoples and governments of Vietnam, Laos, and Cambodia. The projects seeks ways to develop better understanding of the countries of Indochina and their relations with the US. It undertakes other activities designed to stimulate dialogue and enhance public awareness of Laos, Vietnam, and Cambodia. **Other Resources:** See INDOCHINA ISSUES, a journal. Nonprofit.

**$ ♦ Industrial Crisis Institute**
649 E. 19 St.
Brooklyn, NY 11230   (718)859-3435
**Concern(s):** economics; environment; labor; corporate responsibility; monopolies; occupational safety; social ecology. Individuals and organizations from all over the world, concerned about economic, social and cultural problems associated with industrial activities. Industrial activities bring jobs, products, taxes and economic prosperity to communities and nations. However, they are also the source of environmental degradation, large scale industrial accidents, product injuries and occupational hazards. Preventing such crises and coping with them requires an understanding of their causes and consequences. **Contact(s):** Paul Shrivastava. (717)524-1821.

**L ♦ Industrial Union/AFL-CIO**
See Full Employment Action Council.

**L ♦ Industrial Workers of the World**
1476 W. Irving Park Rd.
Chicago, IL 60613-1921 (312)549-5045
**Concern(s):** labor; environment; unions; forests. The Wobblies are still agitating for one big industrial union, but are not taken as seriously as they were in the early 1900's, when they were shot and jailed for their actions, but through their paper they are still the voice of the underdog, attempting to link labor with environmental issues. This is the International Committee. **Other Resources:** See newspaper, INDUSTRIAL WORKER. **Office:** 1095 Market #204 San Francisco, CA 94103. (415)863-WOBS.

**☙ ♦ INFACT**
Box 3223
South Pasadena, CA 91031 (818)799-9133
**Concern(s):** economics; peace; politics; socially-responsible investing; boycotts; corporate responsibility; government accountability; anti-nuclear; militarism; budget. Grassroots organization, of 6 regional offices and nearly 4 million consumers form every region and 40+ countries, that runs campaigns for corporate responsibility currently targeting GE's leading role in producing and promoting nuclear weapons. Only by a massive, international public opposition to large nuclear weapons industries and their powerful lobbies can there be change. **Other Resources:** See INFACT NEWS and SOCIALLY RESPONSIBLE BUYER'S GUIDE. Booklets, INFACT BRINGS GE TO LIGHT; GENERAL ELECTRIC SHAPING NUCLEAR WEAPONS POLICIES FOR PROFITS; video BRINGING BAD THINGS TO LIGHT and NUCLEAR WEAPONMAKING CAMPAIGN UPDATE newsletter. **Contact(s):** Ruth Shy, Lynn Martin, Eve Martin (213)255-0287. **Other:** INFACT International, Box 80016, Minneapolis, MN 55408; 256 Hanover St. , Boston, MA 02113. Kathy Pillsbury/Catherine Brady.(617)742-4583. GENERAL ELECTRIC produces critical components for more nuclear weapons systems than any other company. Products: GE lightbulbs, lighting accessories, GE Medical Systems equipment, GE & RCA consumer electronics, GE-Finances credit cards, Roper lawn equipment, GE & Hotpoint appliances, GE con-

struction materials, GE Capital, Kidder, Peabody & Co., GEnie on-line computer service. To protest, write to: John Welch, CEO, GE, 3135 Easton Turnpike, Fairfield, CT06431 (800)626-2000.

### E ▶ INFORM
381 Park Ave. S, #1301
New York, NY 10016    (212)689-4040

**Concern(s):** environment; energy; health; natural resources; public health; hazardous/toxic waste; waste management; air pollution; water; volunteers. A research organization that identifies and reports on practical actions for the preservation and conservation of natural resources and public health. It's current research focuses on some of this country's most critical environmental problems: industrial toxic waste generation, municipal solid waste management, alternative vehicle fuels and threats to land and water resources. **Other Resources:** See INFORM REPORTS and BUSINESS RECYCLING MANUAL; BOOK NEWSLETTER. Volunteer positions available in research assistance and communications. Nonprofit. **Est.:** 1974. **Dues:** $35/yr. **Contact(s):** Joanna D. Underwood.

### A ▶ Information & Communications for Ecological Agriculture
See Gaia Services.

### ? ▶ Innovative Design Fund
860 UN Plaza
New York, NY 10017    (212)759-8544

**Concern(s):** future; ideation. Gives grants for fabricating prototypes of innovative designs of products for the "immediate designed environment."

### $ ▶ Institute for 21st Century Studies
1611 N. Kent St., #610
Arlington, VA 22209-2111    (703)841-0048

**Concern(s):** economics; peace; justice; environment; Third World; spirtual; faith; ideation. An independent, charitable, and educational organization assisting both industrialized and developing nations to explore alternative strategies for achieving sustainable economic development and security. Such strategies are essential for countries facing the complexities of international competition, population growth, resource management, environmental protection, and national security. **Other Resources:** See Third Millenium Project. Nonprofit. **Contact(s):** Gerald O. Barney (Executive Director).

### A ▶ Institute for Agriculture and Trade Policy
212 Third Ave. North, #301
Minneapolis, MN 55401 (612)338-3382

**Concern(s):** agriculture; economics; Third World; policy; development; trade; hunger; food production; food distribution. **Contact(s):** Mark Ritchie.

### A ▶ Institute for Alternative Agriculture
9200 Edmonston Rd., #117
Greenbelt, MD 20770    (301)441-8777

**Concern(s):** agriculture; environment; politics; sustainability; lobbying; research; family farms; farmland; organic. A research and education organization that encourages and facilitates the adoption of low-cost, resource-conserving, and environmentally-sound farming methods. The Institute serves as: a sponsor of research and education outreach programs; a voice for alternative agriculture in Washington; and a contact for farmers and others who seek information on diversified, sustainable farming systems. **Other Resources:** See ALTERNATIVE AGRICULTURE NEWS newsletter and AMERICAN JOURNAL OF ALTERNATIVE AGRICULTURE. Nonprofit. **Est.:** 1983. **Member:** Global Tomorrow Coalition. **Contact(s):** Garth Youngberg (Executive Director).

### ? ▶ Institute For Alternative Futures
108 N. Alfred St.
Alexandria, VA 22314    (703)684-5880

**Concern(s):** future; health; media; research; analysis; planning; networking. A research and consulting firm that specializes in trends analysis in health care, the pharmaceutical industry, and information technology. Also works out long-range planning projects with local and state governments. **Other Resources:** Publications list available. **Member:** Global Tomorrow Coalition. **Contact(s):** Clement Bezold (Executive Director). (800)552-5461.

### $ ▶ Institute for Community Economics, Inc.
57 School St.
Springfield, MA 01105    (413)746-8660

**Concern(s):** economics; demographics; justice; environment; community self-reliance; social ecology; housing; land trusts; community investment; poverty. A national organization which provides technical assistance, low-cost financing, and educational resources to community groups working to produce and preserve affordable housing, jobs and social services in low-income areas. Coordinates a network of over 100 community land trusts in 26 states. Offers socially responsible investment opportunities through its $10 million nationwide Re-

volving Loan Fund. **Other Resources:** Some staff live in community housing, receive a modest monthly stipend, health care and paid vacations. Extra stipends given to family members. See COMMUNITY ECONOMICS newsletter. Free resource list available. Also, COMMUNITY LAND TRUST HANDBOOK. Nonprofit. **Est.:** 1967. **Dues:** $15/yr, includes newsletter. **Labels:** 7000. **Member:** Co-op America. **Contact(s):** Greg Ramm (Director), Andrew Baker (Media Coordinator).

### E ▶ Institute for Conservation Leadership
2000 P St. NW
Washington, DC 20036-2266    (202)466-3330

**Affiliation:** National Wildlife Federation. **Concern(s):** environment; politics; education; conservation; leadership. America's only leadership training program developed exclusively for conservation and environmental leaders. The Institute is a joint effort of the conservation and environmental community. Provides training, consulting services and follow-up so that local leaders can answer these questions: What is leadership? What keeps a conservation organization healthy, growing and effective: and; How do I plan my group's future and build a stronger organization for the long haul? **Contact(s):** Diane Russell.

### $ ▶ Institute for Consumer Responsibility
Box 95770
Seattle, WA 98115-2770    (206)523-0421

**Concern(s):** economics; boycott. This institute keeps an eye on companies and helps organize consumer boycotts of organizations that are guilty of bad practices. **Other Resources:** See NATIONAL BOYCOTT NEWS. Nonprofit. **Est.:** 1985. **Contact(s):** Todd Putnam (President), Timothy Muck (Secretary-Treasurer). (206)524-7726.

### ☙ ▶ Institute for Defense and Disarmament Studies
2001 Beacon
Brookline, MA 02146

**Concern(s):** peace; Third World; disarmament; intervention. Conducts research and fosters public education on long-term trends in worldwide military forces and on alternative policies for arms control and disarmament. Encourages non-intervention and growth of democratic institutions. Their alternatives would gradually limit the role of armed forces to national defense and ultimately a stable peace, the abolition of nuclear weapons, and reduction of conventional forces and military spending to levels commensurate with genuinely defensive defense. **Other Resources:** See THE ARMS CONTROL REPORTER, a monthly research service; THE PEACE RESOURCE BOOK (annual); DEFENSE AND DISARMAMENT ALTERNATIVES, a bulletin; Alternative Defense Network project; and, audiovisual and other materials. Nonprofit. **Est.:** 1979. **Contact(s):** Randall Forsberg (Executive Director).

### $ ▶ Institute for Development Anthropology
State University of New York
at Binghamton
Binghamton, NY 13902

**Concern(s):** economics; Third World; environment; development; social ecology; indigenous peoples.

### ⚏ ▶ Institute For Earth Education
Box 288
Warrenville, IL 60555    (708)393-3096

**Concern(s):** education; environment; alternative; conservation; preservation; activism. The Institute hosts international and regional conferences, supports local branches, publishes books and program materials, conducts workshops and provides a seasonal members' journal, in order to develop and disseminate focused educational programs that will help build an understanding of, appreciation for and harmony with Earth and its life. **Other Resources:** Printed materials available. **Dues:** $20-100/yr. (509)395-2299.

### ✪ ▶ Institute For Ecological Policies
9208 Christopher St.
Fairfax, VA 22031    (703)691-1271

**Concern(s):** energy; environment; politics; grassroots organizing; legislature. Established to represent, propose, and advocate positive, constructive, environmentally sound alternatives in a variety of issue areas, especially energy. "Our primary goal is to encourage citizens to become actively involved in local and state governments." **Est.:** 1978.

### $ ▶ The Institute for Economic Democracy
Box 56
Terre Haute, IN 47808    (812)232-6323

**Concern(s):** economics; politics; peace; justice; taxation; government accountability; reform. Author øf THE WORLD'S WASTED WEALTH: THE POLITICAL ECONOMY OF WASTE, J.W. Smith, invites others to join this Institute. He will promote economic reform in all sectors of society and call for economic reform that would truly cut out waste of all kinds. **Other Resources:** See New Worlds Press under publishers. **Contact(s):** J.W. Smith (Founder).

### ⚏ ▶ Institute for Educational Studies
See Holistic Education Community Network in media section.

### ✪ ▶ Institute for Energy & Environmental Research
6935 Laurel Ave.
Takoma Park, MD 20912    (301)270-5500

**Concern(s):** energy; environment.

### D ▶ Institute For Food and Development Policy
145 9th St.
San Francisco, CA 94103    (415)864-8555

**Concern(s):** demographics; agriculture; environment; Third World; hunger; development; food production and distribution; policy; poverty. Its three goals: (1) Free people from the myths that deny hope and block action against hunger, poverty, and other social problems. (2) Educate people about positive democratic developments in US and elsewhere. (3) Help people define core public values necessary to guide public change. Conducts research, analysis, education, provides leadership on international problems of hunger, and creates positive social development. **Other Resources:** FOOD FIRST BOOKS CATALOGUE OF RESOURCES (educational materials). See ALTERNATIVES TO THE PEACE CORPS (directories); Good Life Tours; Project Public Life; Food First and FOOD FIRST NEWS & FOOD FIRST DEVELOPMENT REPORTS; and FARMING ACTION ALERTS. **Contact(s):** Frances Moore Lappe, Marilyn Borchadt.

### T ▶ Institute for Foreign Policy Analysis
c/o Central Plaza Bldg. 10th Fl.
675 Massachusetts Ave
Cambridge, MA 02139-3309(617)492-2116

**Concern(s):** Third World; education; politics; foreign policy; government accountability. This institute publishes a wide variety of educational material on the foreign policies of the US government.

### $ ▶ Institute for Gaean Economics
64 Main St.
Montpelier, VT 05602    (802)223-7943

**Affiliation:** Center for Economic Revitalization. **Concern(s):** economics; environment; boycott; socially-responsible investing; green consumer; social ecology; alternative consumer. This organization believes that the emphasis should not be on the purse, but that economics should be conscious of the Earth, morality, peace and justice. A great institute! **Other Resources:** See newsletters CATALYST and INVESTING FROM THE HEART. All Species Project; Center for Economic Revitalization; Companies Which Cut Rainforest Boycott. **Contact(s):** Susan Meeker-Lowrey. **Other:** Box 364, Worchester, VT 05682.

### S ▶ Institute for Global Issues
Wainwright House
Rye, NY 10580

**Concern(s):** spiritual; education; global understanding; interfaith. An interfaith learning center. **Contact(s):** Daniel Martin.

### S ▶ Institute for Individual and World Peace
2101 Wilshire Blvd.
Santa Monica, CA 90403    (310)828-0535

**Concern(s):** spiritual; health; peace; education; counseling; psychology; transformation. An organization that promotes the idea that as individuals find inner peace, we will experience greater peace in the world. Nonprofit.

### ✈ ▶ Institute For International Cooperation and Development
Box 103
Williamstown, MA 01267    (413)458-9828

**Concern(s):** education; Third World; travel. Dedicated to promoting global understanding. Offers travel and study courses to Central America and Asia, as well as solidarity work programs in Angola, Mozambique, and Nicaragua. Anyone 18 years or older can participate. Nonprofit. **Est.:** 1986. **Fax:** (413)458-9466. **Contact(s):** Esther Neltrup (Administrative Director).

### $ ▶ Institute for International Economics
11 Dupont Circle, NW
Washington, DC 20036  (202)328-9000

**Concern(s):** economics; Third World; development. **Fax:** (202)328-5432.

### S ▶ Institute for Labor and Mental Health
See TIKKUN magazine.

### ⚏ ▶ The Institute for Learning and Teaching
449 Desnoyer
St. Paul, MN 55104    (612)644-2805

**Affiliation:** Brain Based Education Network. **Concern(s):** education; childhood. An organization dedicated to increased learning by all students, assisting schools and districts with decentralized decision making and staff development. **Other Resources:** Sponsors The Brain Based Education Network and its NETWORKER newsletter.

Nonprofit. **Dues:** $25/yr. **Contact(s):** Wayne B. Jennings (Editor), Jonelle Ringnalda (Assistant Editor).

### $ ◆ Institute for Local Self-Reliance
2425 18th St. NW
Washington, DC 20009  (202)232-4108

**Concern(s):** economics; community self-reliance. Assists grassroots groups, local government, and small business by providing relevant technical data and policy analysis to achieve sustainable economic development. The Institute focuses on materials policy, reduction in consumption of raw materials, market development for recycled materials, closed loop manufacturing, the shift to renewable resources, and energy efficiency. **Other Resources:** Publishes a series of facts sheets, FACTS TO ACT ON. See BEYOND 25 PERCENT: MATERIAL RECOVERY COMES OF AGE (directories). Nonprofit. **Est.:** 1974. **Fax:** (202)332-0463. **Contact(s):** Neil Seldman (President), Ingrid Komar (Media Coordinator).

### M ◆ Institute for Media Analysis
145 W. 4th St.
New York, NY 10012   (212)254-1061

**Concern(s):** media; media watch. Analyzes and counters myths, propaganda, biases, and disinformation in print and broadcast media. **Other Resources:** See also COVERTACTION INFORMATION BULLETIN and LIES OF OUR TIMES. Other, OUR RIGHT TO KNOW. Produces a publication list of books, monographs, journals, tapes, and more. **Est.:** 1986. **Contact(s):** William H. Schaap (Director).

### T ◆ Institute for Palestine Studies
Box 25697, Georgetown Station
Washington, DC 20007  (202)342-3990

**Concern(s):** Third World; Mid-East. An independent Arab research and publication center specializing in the history and development of the Palestinian problem, the Arab-Israeli conflict, and their peaceful resolution. IPS is not affiliated with any political organization or government. **Other Resources:** IPS publishes the JOURNAL OF PALESTINE STUDIES, various books, publications, and media list available. Nonprofit. **Est.:** 1963. **Dues:** $24; $36/institution includes JOURNAL. **Office:** 3501 M St. NW Washington, DC 20007. **Fax:** (202)342-3927. **Contact(s):** Dr. Hisham Sharabi.

### ◈ ◆ Institute for Peace and International Security
91 Harvey St.
Cambridge, MA 02140-1718 (617)547-3338

**Concern(s):** peace; education; politics; research; analysis; grassroots organizing; activism. IPIS works to develop and popularize political alternatives to the Cold War and Peace through Strength. To this end the IPIS (1) strengthens analysis and collaborative research efforts, (2) actively share this work through education, (3) accelerate public involvement in foreign policy and decision making. Stresses Common Security. **Other Resources:** See STRATEGY WORKBOOK (directories). **Contact(s):** Pam Solo, Paul F. Walker (Co-directors).

### ◈ ◆ The Institute for Peace and Justice
4144 Lindell Blvd.
St. Louis, MO 63108   (314)533-4445

**Concern(s):** peace; demographics; justice; education; spiritual; interfaith; hunger; family; nonviolence; conflict resolution; diversity. An independent center engaged in creating resources and providing learning experience in peace education and social justice for schools, religious institutions, families and counsellors. Focus is on hunger and global ecomomic injustice, parenting for peace and justice, multiculturalizing education, nonviolent conflict resolution and cooperation in the schools, and integrating spirituality/ministry with social justice. **Other Resources:** Resource catalog. Programs: Parenting for Peace & Justice (newsletter); Faith and Parenting; Educating for Peace & Justice; Youth Workers Network Resources & Services: workshops and consulting for families, schools, religious groups; extensive library. Not-for-profit. **Contact(s):** Kathy McGinnis, James McGinnis

### P ◆ Institute for Policy Studies
1601 Connecticut Ave. NW
Washington, DC 20009  (202)234-9382

**Concern(s):** politics; peace; foreign policy. A center of progressive thought and action on Capitol Hill. Independent of government, it serves as a crucible, think-tank, conscience. Accepts no corporate funds or government contracts. Three working groups: Post-Cold War Planning for a New Foreign Policy, The Social and Political Effects of Global Economic Integration, and the State of Democracy. European sister organization, The Transnational Institute, was founded in 1975 to address the disparities between the rich and poor. **Other Resources:** See magazine, GLOBAL COMMUNITIES, which was formerly THE BULLETIN OF MUNICIPAL FOREIGN POLICY produced by the Center for Innovative Diplomacy. Guides, DIRT RICH, DIRT POOR and IN WHOSE INTEREST. See, also, Planners Network. **Contact(s):** Robert L. Borosage (Director), Frances T. Farenthold (Chairman).

### P ◆ Institute for Public Affairs
See IN THESE TIMES newspaper.

### ☯ ◆ Institute for Security and Cooperation in Outer Space
3400 International Dr. NW
Washington, DC 20008  (202)537-0831

**Concern(s):** energy; peace; space; disarmament; national security. See DataNet under media. **Contact(s):** Connie Van Praet (Director, Research/Operation).

### J ◆ Institute for Social & Cultural Change
116 Saint Botolph St.
Boston, MA 02115      (617)266-0629

**Concern(s):** justice; media; arts.

### P ◆ Institute for Social & Cultural Communications
See Z Magazine.

### E ◆ Institute for Social Ecology
Box 89
Plainfield, VT 05667      (802)454-8493

**Concern(s):** environment; agriculture; economics; health; social ecology; holism; bioregionalism. Integrates the study of human and natural ecosystems through understanding interrelationships of culture and nature. It advances a critical, holistic world view suggesting that creative human enterprise can construct an alternative future, harmonizing people's relationships with each other. Draws on studies in the natural sciences, feminism, anthropology, and philosophy, to provide a critique of current trends and offer reparative measures. Examines ways to create sustainable communities. **Other Resources:** Using Central Vermont as a laboratory, the Institute explores bioregional solutions to global problems. **Contact(s):** Paula Emery (Assistant Director).

### ? ◆ The Institute for Social Inventions
20 Heber Rd.
London, NW2 6AA England   081 208 2853

**Concern(s):** future; ideation; invention. The institute encourages new and imaginative non-technical ideas and projects which improve the quality of life or help create more human-scale societies. $2,500 awarded each year to the best ideas from around the world. Promotes social inventions and social inventiveness in Great Britain and around the world. Publishes the ideas of its members in periodical journals and networks with other idea-soliciting organizations worldwide. **Other Resources:** Publishes ENCYCLOPEDIA OF SOCIAL INVENTIONS ($40), SOCIAL INVENTIONS JOURNAL ($40/year), ALTERNATIVE MOSCOW GUIDE ($10), and much more. Annual Social Inventions Competition. Nonprofit. **Est.:** 1985. **Dues:** $40/includes journal. **Frequency:** Annual. **Subscription:** $40/yr. **Price:** $10/ea. **Pages:** 48. **Circ.:** 600. **Fax:** (4481 452 6434. **Contact(s):** Nicholas Albery (Chairman).

### P ◆ Institute for Social Justice
739 8th St. SE
Washington, DC 20003  (202)547-9292

**Concern(s):** politics. A national resource and training center of principles and skills of community organizing. **Other Resources:** Publishes a journal, THE ORGANIZER. **Est.:** 1972.

### ✐ ◆ Institute for Southern Studies
See SOUTHERN EXPOSURE (periodicals).

### ◈ ◆ Institute for Soviet-American Relations
1601 Connecticut Ave. NW, #301
Washington, DC 20009  (202)387-3034

**Concern(s):** peace; education; foreign policy; East-West; travel; conflict resolution; research. This Institute tries to improve relations between the superpowers by opening channels of communication and exchange in order to bring about a nonviolent conflict resolution. It is trying to develop a broad network of responsible interchanges in the fields of culture, trade, science and education, and tourism. **Other Resources:** See journal, SURVIVING TOGETHER and, guides ORGANIZATIONS INVOLVED SOVIET-AMERICAN RELATIONS and HOSTING SOVIET VISITORS. **Est.:** 1983. **E-Network:** Peacenet. **ID:** 'isar'. **Fax:** (202)667-3291. **Contact(s):** John Sturino (Systems Coordinator).

### ◈ ◆ Institute for Space and Security Studies
5115 S. A1A Hwy.
Melbourne Beach, FL 32951-3210      (407)952-0600

**Concern(s):** peace; energy; politics; space; national security; peace dividend; government accountability; CIA. Created to expose the danger of "Star Wars" weapons in space, ISSS has become a powerful independent voice for the security of the American people (military security, economic security, environmental security, health-care security, legal/political security). We expose government lies (KAL-007, Challenger, Contragate, nuclear testing, MIA, JFK's murder, etc.). **Other Resources:** SPACE & SECURITY NEWS; lectures on above issues by Dr. Robert M. Bowman; videotapes; book: STAR WARS: DEFENSE OR DEATH STAR? See, also, Arms Race in Space Project; Speak Truth to Power; and Comprehensive Security Project. Nonprofit. **Est.:** 1982. **Member:** Alliance for Our Common Future. **Contact(s):** Dr. Robert M. Bowman (President).

### E ◆ Institute for the Future
2740 Sand Will Rd.
Menlo Park, CA 94025-7095 (415)854-6322

**Concern(s):** environment; future; global warming; research. Is distributing a documentary film, "Stopping the Coming Ice Age," and a book, The End: The Imminent Ice Age & How We Can Stop It (Celestial Arts).

### ◈ ◆ Institute for the Practice of Nonviolence
Box 170670
San Francisco, CA 94117

**Concern(s):** peace; nonviolence.

### E ◆ Institute for the Study of Natural Systems
Box 637
Mill Valley, CA 94942   (415)383-5064

**Concern(s):** environment; spiritual; justice; Native Americans; transformation. A series of video and audio tapes which recreate the Hopi Indian creation myth, with twelve different Indian tribes participating and a blend of modern and ancient instruments and music. **Other Resources:** See CELEBRATION OF INNOVATION: AN EXPOSITION SHOWCASE OF CREATIVITY, INNOVATION AND INVENTION (directories).

### P ◆ Institute for the Study of World Politics
1755 Massachusetts Ave. NW
Washington, DC 20036  (202)797-0882

**Concern(s):** politics; peace; world order.

### S ◆ Institute for Theological Encounter with Science and Technology
See Membership Directory under same name.

### ☯ ◆ Institute for Transportation and Development Policy
1787 Columbia Rd. NW, 3rd Fl.
Washington, DC 20009  (202)387-1434

**Concern(s):** energy; Third World; peace; development; transportation. Provides bicycles to those who need them most, working in some of the toughest places to empower people with the mobility, freedom, and efficiency of the bicycle. ITDP demonstrates that transportation development can be equitable, economical, and environmentally sustainable, and that ordinary people across America can contribute skills and resources to make such development happen. **Other Resources:** Operates Bikes Not Bombs Campaign Project and newsletter Update; project and newsletter, AEROVIRONMENT; and, Transportation Alternatives Project. **Contact(s):** Michael Replogle (President), Ken Hughes (Executive Director).

### ✈ ◆ Institute for World Understanding of Peoples, Cultures and Languages
939 Coast Blvd., #19DE
La Jolla, CA 92037      (619)454-0705

**Concern(s):** education; Third World; justice; energy; travel; indigenous peoples.

### ✈ ◆ Institute of Cultural Affairs
1301 Longfellow St. NW
Washington, DC 20011  (202)882-6284

**Concern(s):** education; Third World; development; travel. A private organization concerned with empowering the human factor in development in communities and the workplace. It is networked with other national ICAs through ICA International, located in Brussels. Conducts annual summer Alternative Workcamps, a project of the Perspectives in Development Series. Works domestically and abroad. Nonprofit. (212)475-5020.

### L ◆ Institute of Industrial Relations
See LABOR CENTER REPORTER (periodicals).

### ✈ ◆ Institute of International Education
1400 K St. NW
Washington, DC 20005  (202)898-0600

**Concern(s):** education; travel. Boasts a 550+ membership of universities. It administers overseas educational exchanges and provides information on foreign study. **Other Resources:** A membership only newsletter called EDUCATION ASSOCIATE, and a learning traveler series. **Est.:** 1919. **Contact(s):** Alex Patico. **Other:** 809 UN Plaza, New York City, NY 10017. (212)883-8200.

### T ◆ Institute of International Health and Development
See magazine, INTERNATIONAL HEALTH AND DEVELOPMENT.

**T ▸ Institute of Maya Studies**
3280 S. Miama Ave.
Miami, FL 33129
**Concern(s):** Third World; Central America.

**H ▸ Institute of Noetic Sciences**
475 Gate Five Rd., #300
Sausalito, CA 94965-0909
**Concern(s):** health; education; spiritual; psychology; science; transformation. "Founded to expand the knowledge of the nature and potentials of the mind and spirit, and apply that knowledge to advance health and well-being for humankind and our planet. We are explorers, and the most compelling frontier of our time is human consciousness. Our quest is the discovery of the "new story" for humanity—one which so integrates science and spirituality that reminds us of our wholeness and connectedness, not only to each other and to the Earth, but to the inner self." **Other Resources:** NOETIC SCIENCES REVIEW; NOETIC SCIENCES BULLETIN; AN INTELLIGENT GUIDE — a resource for the latest books, audiotapes, and videotapes on health and healing, exceptional abilities, and emerging ideas about our changing values. **Est.:** 1973. **Dues:** $35/yr. includes periodical. **Contact(s):** Willis Harmon (President), Edgar Mitchell (Founder).

**✍ ▸ Institute of Psychohistory**
See JOURNAL OF PSYCHOHISTORY (periodicals).

**E ▸ Institute of Scrap Recycling Industries**
1325 G St. NW
Washington, DC 20005 (202)466-4050
**Concern(s):** environment; recycling.

**J ▸ Institute of Social Service Alternatives**
See CATALYST: A SOCIALIST JOURNAL OF SOCIAL SERVICES (periodicals).

**S ▸ Institute of Transpersonal Psychology**
See Spiritual Emergency Network.

**U ▸ Institute of Urban Life**
See DIRECTORY OF COMMUNITY ORGANIZATIONS — CHICAGO.

**H ▸ Institute on Black Chemical Abuse**
2614 Nicollet Ave.
Minneapolis, MN 55408 (612)871-7878
**Concern(s):** health; justice; urban; substance abuse; drugs; ethnic concerns; minority rights.

**S ▸ Institute on Religion & Democracy**
1331 H St. NW
Washington, DC 20005 (202)393-3200
**Concern(s):** spiritual; politics; economics; transformation; interfaith.

**U ▸ Institute on the Church in Urban Society**
See METRO MINISTRY NEWSLETTER.

**D ▸ Insurgent Sociologist**
See CRITICAL SOCIOLOGY (periodicals).

**✌ ▸ Integrated Strategies**
806 Descano Way
San Rafael, CA 94903
**Concern(s):** peace; world order. **Contact(s):** Gordon Feller.

**M ▸ Intellectual Freedom Commission of the American Library Association**
See NEWSLETTER ON INTELLECTUAL FREEDOM.

**✍ ▸ Inter-American Foundation**
1515 Wilson Blvd.
Rosslyn, VA 22209 (703)841-3800
**Concern(s):** education; Third World; politics; United Nations; research; networking. Publishes Guide to NGO (non-governmental organizations) Directories.

**T ▸ The Inter-Hemispheric Education Resource Center**
Box 4506
Albuquerque, NM 87196 (505)842-8288
**Concern(s):** Third World; education; development; hunger; foreign policy; global understanding. A private organization which produces books, reports, and audiovisuals for use in colleges, churches, and activist organizations about US foreign relations with Third World countries, particularly Central America and the Caribbean. The goal of the Resource Center is to use information as a catalyst for social change. This is done through the publication of books and reports, participation in seminars, and educational sessions. **Other Resources:** Publishes quarterly newsletter, RESOURCE CENTER BULLETIN. Free list of educational services. Seminars and educational briefing sessions, books, reports. Nonprofit. **Est.:** 1979. **Labels:** 3500. **Fax:** (505)256-0071. **Contact(s):** Deb Preusch (Director), Jodi Gibson (Administration Aide).

**T ▸ Interaction**
1717 Massachusetts Ave. NW
Washington, DC 20036 (202)667-8227
**Concern(s):** Third World; justice; demographics; development; hunger; refugees; immigration; volunteers; policy. Is an inclusive coalition of more than 100 American private and voluntary organizations engaged in international humanitarian efforts, including disaster relief, refugee protection, assistance, and resettlement, long-term development, public policy, and educating the American public on international development issues. **Other Resources:** See publications brochures, TOUCH THE FUTURE: AN AGENDA FOR GLOBAL EDUCATION IN AMERICA and periodical, MONDAY DEVELOPMENTS. **Contact(s):** Dr. Peter J. Davies. (212)777-8210. 200 Park Ave. South, New York, NY 10003

**$ ▸ Interfaith Center for Corporate Responsibility**
475 Riverside Dr., #566
New York, NY 10115 (212)870-2295
**Concern(s):** economics; peace; Third World; spiritual; interfaith; corporate responsibility; alternative consumer; divestment; socially-responsible investing; boycott; anti-nuclear; corporate responsibility; economic conversion; peace dividend; South Africa. A coalition of Protestant and Roman Catholic agencies which hold corporations accountable by sponsoring shareholder resolutions, divesting stock, conducting public hearings and investigations, publishing special reports. It challenges nuclear weapons production, investment in South Africa, and Star Wars, and other issues concerning peace, economic justice, and stewardship of the Earth. Coordinates corporate shareholder's resolutions on South Africa for churches. **Other Resources:** See newspaper, CORPORATE EXAMINER; guides, THE CONSCIENTIOUS INVESTOR'S GUIDE TO SOCIALLY-RESPONSIBLE MUTUAL MONEY MARKET FUNDS and INVESTMENT SERVICES & DIRECTORY OF ALTERNATIVE INVESTMENTS; GUIDE TO CHURCH ALTERNATIVE INVESTMENT FUNDS—1991. **Dues:** $35/yr. **Contact(s):** Tim Smith. (212)870-2936.

**✌ ▸ Interfaith Center to Reverse the Arms Race**
132 N. Euclid Ave.
Pasadena, CA 91011 (818)449-9430
**Concern(s):** peace; education; justice; spiritual; anti-nuclear; disarmament; peace dividend; interfaith. Primary mission is to educate the religious community about the threat of nuclear destruction, and to stimulate action, on moral ethical, and religious grounds. Encourages interfaith cooperation in its effort to educate and empower citizens of all faiths to overcome militarism and violence as a solution to political problems. It also promotes a redefinition of federal budget priorities. **Other Resources:** RAR led in the formation of the Religious Leaders Network which is the model for a national consortium on religious leaders. **Contact(s):** Pierce O'Donnel (President), Dr. Judith Glass (Executive Director). (213)681-4292.

**✪ ▸ Interfaith Coalition on Energy**
Box 26577
Philadelphia, PA 19141 (215)635-1122
**Affiliation:** Philadelphia's Religious Community. **Concern(s):** energy; spiritual; interfaith; conservation. Mission is to inspire congregations to use less energy and to practice environmental stewardship. **Other Resources:** Videotapes, workshop, various booklets and workbooks, product evaluation, on-site energy surveys, research and telephone consultation. Publishes the ICE MELTER NEWSLETTER. **Est.:** 1980. **Frequency:** 4/yr. **Subscription:** $20/yr. **Price:** $5/ea. **Pages:** 12. **Circ.:** 10M. **Fax:** (215)635-1903. **Contact(s):** Andrew Rudin (Project Coordinator).

**♈ ▸ The Interfaith Council for the Protection of Animals and Nature**
4290 Raintree Lane NW
Atlanta, GA 30327
**Affiliation:** Humane Society of the US. **Concern(s):** environment; spiritual; interfaith; animal rights; wildlife/endangered species. A national conservation and animal protection group, composed of people of various faiths from all parts of the country who are working to save "God's Creation." "We believe that human welfare is inextricably linked with the health of the Earth's ecology and its diverse life forms." **Contact(s):** Lewis G. Regenstein (Executive Director). **Other:** 2841 Colony Rd., Ann Arbor, MI.

**T ▸ Interfaith Hunger Appeal**
475 Riverside Dr., #635
New York, NY 10115 (212)870-2035
**Concern(s):** Third World; demographics; justice; spiritual; hunger; development; global understanding; interfaith. Main thrust is in the area of development education. A domestic educational and awareness agency sponsored by Catholic Relief Services, Lutheran World Relief, Church World Services and the American Jewish Joint Distribution Committee. While continuing work overseas, it promotes awareness of global hunger and poverty throughout our communities on issues related to hunger: global indifference, underdeveloped economies, aggravated debt, insulted environment, bad public policy & political unrest. **Other Resources:** Publishes newsletter. Projects: PSA Campaign; "Hunger Causes a World of Problems"; Collegiate Curriculum Development Program; guide books; publishes EDUCATION FOR DEVELOPMENT, a report. **Contact(s):** Robert J. Coll (Executive Director).

**✌ ▸ Interfaith Impact for Justice and Peace**
110 Maryland Ave. NE, #509
Washington, DC 20002 (202)543-2800
**Concern(s):** peace; demographics; justice; feminism; politics; environment; agriculture; energy; economics; spiritual; interfaith; poverty; lobbying; voting; family; sustainability; discrimination; children; seniors; grassroots organizing. Protestant, Jewish, Muslim and Catholic national organizations join to brings grassroots groups and individual and congregational members to DC to convert their values into votes for justice and peace. Issues: Domestic Poverty & Human Needs; International Peace; Civil, Human, & Voting Rights; Economic Policy & Sustainable Development; Energy, Environment & Agriculture; Justice for Women & Families. Formerly Interfaith Action for Economic Justice & National Impact. **Other Resources:** Magazine, INTERFAITH IMPACT, legislative hotline, 6 Issue Networks, action alerts, and Congressional memberships. $10 for additional Issue Networks/NETWORKER newsletters. Publications list. **Dues:** $30/yr.; includes magazine & 1 issue Network. **E-Network:** HandsNet. **ID:** HN00146. **Fax:** (202)547-8107. Hotline: (800)424-7292. **Contact(s):** Christie Goodman (Communications). (202)547-8107.

**H ▸ Intergovernmental Health Policy Project**
2021 K St. NW 800
Washington, DC 20006 (202)872-1445
**Concern(s):** health; politics; justice; AIDS; research; law. IHPP's State AIDS Policy Center tracks state AIDS legislation, regulations, and appropriations. It publishes newsletters, books, and other materials for state health officials and decision-makers. It tracks state spending on a number of AIDS issues, including testing, treatment, and prevention education. **Contact(s):** Caitlin Ryan.

**H ▸ Interhelp**
Box 86
Cambridge, MA 02141 (408)262-0792
**Concern(s):** health; peace; justice; environment; feminism; psychology; activism; empowerment. A global network of activists bringing spiritual and psychological insight to the work for peace, justice, and healing. Give community workshops to help individuals share their pain for the world, reconnect, and direct their energies towards social action. Provide psychological and spiritual support for activists through consultation and organizing support groups. **Other Resources:** Publish quarterly newsletter/journal AWAKENING. Hold regional and national gatherings. **Contact(s):** Amy Mar. **Other:** 3640 Ocean View Ave., Los Angeles, CA 90066. Bernard Somers , Contact Person. (310)398-3595.

**$ ▸ Intermediate Technology Development Group of North America**
777 UN Plaza, #9A
New York, NY 10521 (212)972-9877
**Concern(s):** economics; demographics; environment; community self-reliance; sustainability; monopolies. Disseminates information about community revitalization and economic decentralization, and works with many other groups to launch a campaign for a just and sustainable society through TOES (The Other Economic Summit). **Other Resources:** See INTERMEDIATE TECHNOLOGY DEVELOPMENT under Directories. **Contact(s):** Cynthia Morehouse.

**A ▸ International Alliance for Sustainable Agriculture**
1701 University Ave. SE, #202
Minneapolis, MN 55414 (612)331-1099
**Concern(s):** agriculture; environment; Third World; economics; politics; sustainability; networking; farmland. Promotes sustainable agriculture worldwide through research documentation, network building, education and public outreach by linking members in sixty countries. It has brought together consumers, farmers, researchers, business leaders, government officials and a spectrum of agriculture, environment, health, church and consumer groups. Endorsed '90 farm bill, Valdez Principles, humane animal care, no-pesticide usage through education, collaboration, networking and policy developments. **Other Resources:** See MANNA newsletter and RESOURCE GUIDE TO SUSTAINABLE AGRICULTURE IN THE THIRD WORLD. Slide shows available. Speakers bureau and internships. **Dues:** $5-$1000/yr. **Contact(s):** Terry Gips (President).

**E ▸ International Alliance of Atomic Veterans**
Box 32
Topock, AZ 86436 (602)768-7515
**Concern(s):** environment; peace; health; hazardous/toxic waste; veterans; anti-nuclear.

**H ▶ International Association of Counseling Services**

See DIRECTORY OF COUNSELING SERVICES.

**✻ ▶ International Association of Educators for World Peace**

See PEACE PROGRESS (periodicals).

**L ▶ International Association of Machinists & Aerospace Workers**
1300 Connecticut Ave. NW
Washington, DC 20036  (202)857-5200

**Concern(s):** labor; unions. **Other Resources:** See the MACHINIST magazine. **Contact(s):** George J. Kourpias (President).

**U ▶ International Bicycle Fund**
4887 Columbia Dr. S
Seattle, WA 98108       (206)767-3927

**Concern(s):** urban; energy; economics; environment; education; health; transportation; development; planning; global understanding; recreation. A nongovernmental organization promoting bicycle transportation. The four main areas of activities are: Transportation Planning, Economic Development, Safety Education, and International Understanding. **Other Resources:** BICYCLING IN AFRICA, a handbook, and IBF newsletter. Nonprofit. **Est.:** 1982. **Contact(s):** David Mozer (Director).

**L ▶ International Brotherhood of Electrical Workers**
1125 15th St. NW
Washington, DC 20005  (202)833-7000

**Concern(s):** labor; unions. **Contact(s):** John J. Barry.

**L ▶ International Brotherhood of Teamsters, Chauffeurs, Warehousemen & Helpers of America**
25 Louisiana Ave. NW
Washington, DC 20005  (202)624-6800

**Concern(s):** labor; unions. **Contact(s):** William J. McCarthy (President).

**D ▶ International Catholic Migration Committee**
1319 F St. NW
Washington, DC 20001  (202)393-2904

**Concern(s):** demographics; Third World; justice; spiritual; faith; hunger; development; refugees; immigration.

**T ▶ International Center for Development Policy**
731 8th St. SE
Washington, DC 20004  (202)547-3800

**Concern(s):** Third World; peace; development; foreign policy; research; conflict resolution. Brings together influential private citizens and leading members of Congress to promote peace and democracy around the world. A foreign policy organization focused on relations with Asia, Africa, Latin America and the Soviet Union, the center conducts programs of research, publication, overseas travel and hosts foreign visitors to inform the press, Congress, US government officials, and the public of the impact of American policies abroad. **Other Resources:** See Bank Information Center. **Contact(s):** Robert E. White (President), Lindsay Mattison (Executive Director).

**F ▶ International Center for Research on Women**
1CRW/MNHC Project/1CRW
1717 Massachusetts Ave. NW
Washington, DC 20003  (202)797-0007

**Concern(s):** feminism; education; justice; research.

**T ▶ International Center for the Dynamics of Development**
4201 S. 31st St.
Arlington, VA 22206

**Concern(s):** Third World; agriculture; urban; development.

**L ▶ International Chemical Workers Union**
1655 W. Market St.
Akron, OH 44313

**Concern(s):** labor; unions. **Contact(s):** Frank D. Martino (President).

**✈ ▶ International Christian Youth Exchange**
134 W. 26th St., 4th Fl.
New York, NY 10001      (212)206-7307

**Concern(s):** education; spiritual; faith; travel.

**E ▶ International Conference on Appropriate Transportation**
49 E. Houston St.
New York, NY 10012      (212)431-0600

**Concern(s):** environment; energy; transportation. This network helps newcomers and one another to show off their ideas and coordinates "Lightwheels" a traveling festival which "raced" the inventions from Washington to New York last summer. **Contact(s):** Steven Stollman.

**E ▶ International Council for Bird Preservation**
1250 24th St. NW
Washington, DC 20037  (202)778-9563

**Affiliation:** National Audubon Society. **Concern(s):** environment; wildlife/endangered species; preservation; volunteers. This council monitors the status of susceptible bird populations worldwide; fosters international cooperation to induce the provision of financial and technical assistance to countries where local expertise and funds are scarce; maintains a volunteer network in over 110 countries. Its goal is to preserve the diversity, distribution, abundance and natural habitats of bird species throughout the world and to prevent the extinction of any species or subspecies. **Dues:** $35+/yr. **Contact(s):** Kimberly Young.

**E ▶ International Council for Local Environmental Initiatives**
Toronto City Hall
100 Queen St. W, 8th Fl., E. Tower
Toronto, ON M5H 2N2 Canada

**Concern(s):** environment; agriculture; decentralization; municipal; foreign policy; grassroots organizing. This organization is taking over the environmental work of the Center for Innovative Diplomacy.

**E ▶ International Crane Foundation**
Rt 1, Box 230c, Shady Lane Rd.
Baraboo, WI 53913

**Concern(s):** environment; wildlife/endangered species. Crane preservation.

**T ▶ International Defense and Aid Fund for Southern Africa**
See newspaper, IDAF NEWS NOTES/FOCUS IN SOUTHERN AFRICA.

**T ▶ International Development Conference**
1401 New York Ave. NW, #1100
Washington, DC 20005  (202)638-3111

**Concern(s):** Third World; education; development; global understanding. A coalition of individuals associated with leading national organizations; it is a meeting ground for a variety of sectors and interests concerned about US-Third World issues and about educating Americans about these issues. IDC chairs and manages the affairs of a new national effort, Worldwise 2000, which is devising a national agenda for the 1990s as the Decade for International Understanding. It plans to link the formal and informal education sectors around international education. **Other Resources:** See newsletter IDEAS AND INFORMATION ABOUT DEVELOPMENT EDUCATION which has recently expanded to include news about media. **Est.:** 1951. **Contact(s):** Robert J. Berg.

**T ▶ International Development Exchange (IDEX)**
777 Valencia St.
San Francisco, CA 94110     (415)621-1494

**Concern(s):** Third World; development. IDEX supports small-scale community development projects in Asia, Africa, and Latin America while involving US citizens directly and actively in development issues. The Third World community receives financial support to get their project off the ground, while the American sponsor has a chance to learn about the challenges and realities of communities working for positive change. **Other Resources:** Publishes IDEX UPDATE. **Est.:** 1985. **E-Network:** Appletops. **ID:** Jessica Pitt. **Contact(s):** Rebecca Buell (Executive Director), Jessica Pitt (Outreach Director).

**T ▶ International Development Institute**
3114 Circle Hill Rd
Alexandria, VA 22301

**Concern(s):** Third World; development. **Contact(s):** Dr. Peter Nelson.

**T ▶ International Development Network**
110 Maryland Ave. NE, #509
Washington, DC 20002  (202)543-2800

**Affiliation:** Interfaith Impact for Justice and Peace. **Concern(s):** Third World; development. **Other Resources:** INTERNATIONAL DEVELOPMENT NETWORKER newsletter. (800)424-7290.

**E ▶ International Ecological Society**
1471 Barclay
St. Paul, MN 55106-1405     (612)774-4971

**Concern(s):** environment; education; social ecology; wetlands; wildlife/endangered species; research; preservation; conservation; animal rights; volunteers. Volunteer staffed international organization dedicated to environmental protection and the encouragement of better understanding of all life forms. Efforts include Save the Whales, prohibition of leghold trap, wetland protection, urban natural areas protection, campaigns against primate research, prohibitions on rodeo cruelties, alternatives to animal testing, and many more. **Other**

**Resources:** ECO-HUMANE LETTER; SUNRISE; brochures and posters. Nonprofit. **Contact(s):** R. J. F. Kramer (President), Richard J. Ebensteiner (Educational Director).

**✍ ▶ International Educational Development, Inc.**
Box 7066
Silver Springs, MD 20910

**Concern(s):** education; Third World; global understanding.

**T ▶ International Food Policy Research Institute**
1776 Massachusetts Ave. NW
Washington, DC 20036  (202)862-5600

**Concern(s):** Third World; demographics; economics; hunger. Established to identify and analyze alternative national and international strategies for improving the food situation of the low-income countries and peoples of the world. Their research program is broad and designed to stimulate worldwide interaction among researchers, policymakers, and administrators. **Contact(s):** John W. Mellor (Director Ex Officio), Barbara Rose.

**T ▶ International Fund for Agricultural Development**
1889 F St. NW
Washington, DC 20006  (202)289-3812

**Concern(s):** Third World; demographics; agriculture; hunger; poverty; homelessness; food production; food distribution. A fund set up that assists farmers worldwide in developing environmentally correct forms of agriculture. **Other Resources:** HUNGER NOTES.

**🐾 ▶ International Fund for Animal Welfare**
411 Main St.
Box 193
Yarmouth Port, MA 02675     (617)362-4944

**Concern(s):** environment; animal rights; wildlife/endangered species. An international animal welfare organization dedicated to protecting wild and domestic animals from cruelty. Projects include: harp and hood seal preservation in Canada, dog and cat abuse in the Philippines and South Korea, elephants in Africa, the use of animal in laboratory testing, and whales and other marine mammals worldwide. **Other Resources:** Sponsors Pilot whale stranding network on Cape Cod for Massachusetts residents. **Contact(s):** Richard Moore (Executive Director), Brian Davies (Founder/President).

**J ▶ International Human Rights Law Group**
1601 Connecticut Ave. NW.
Washington, DC 20009  (202)232-8500

**Concern(s):** justice; Third World; peace; social justice; international law. Provides legal services and educational programs in international human rights law; assists non-governmental agencies in preparing complaints on human rights violations to be filed before international, regional, and domestic courts. Devotes substantial resources to protecting due process rights and rights necessary for meaningful political participation; observes elections in various countries; trains lawyers in the practice of international rights law. **Est.:** 1978.

**E ▶ International Institute for Environment and Development**
1709 New York Ave. NW
Washington, DC 20006  (202)638-6300

**Concern(s):** environment; Third World; development. **Contact(s):** David Runnals (Vice President/Dir. North American Office).

**☯ ▶ International Institute For Energy Conservation**
420 C St. NE
Washington, DC 20002  (202)546-3388

**Concern(s):** energy; environment; economics; Third World; conservation.

**H ▶ International Institute Of Concern For Public Health**
830 Bathurst St.
Toronto, ON M5R 3G1 Canada

**Concern(s):** health; public health. **Contact(s):** Rosalie Bertell.

**L ▶ International Ladies' Garment Workers Union**
126 Baxter St.
New York, NY 10013      (212)274-0023

**Concern(s):** labor; unions. **Contact(s):** Jay Mazur (President).

**J ▶ International League For Human Rights**
432 Park Ave. S, #1103
New York, NY 10016      (212)684-1221

**Concern(s):** justice; peace; United Nations; political prisoners. Currently has four major projects: 1) Strengthening review of human rights in UN system though critical evaluation of reports submitted by governments to UN human rights bodies. Emphasis on areas with serious abuses "that do not regularly come under scrutiny elsewhere in the UN system." **Other Resources:** See, 2) Defenders Project 3) Family Reunification Project 4) Affiliate Network Project. **Est.:** 1942.

✍ ▸ **International Learning Institute**
Box 60-C
Petaluma, CA 94953
**Concern(s):** education; Third World.

E ▸ **International Marinelife Alliance**
94 Station, #645
Higham, MA 02043 (617)749-5387
**Concern(s):** environment; wildlife/endangered species; oceans/rivers. Supports practical and positive measures to restore the health and diversity of marine environments in developing countries. IMA seeks sustainable solutions through village-level education and training, research, economic and technical cooperation to bring harmony between woman/man, marine life and the environment. It encourages wise use of resources and harvesting methods that ensure long-term yields and widespread benefits with emphasis on community level cooperation. **Other Resources:** Publishes SEA WIND bulletin. **Fax:** (617)749-6544. **Contact(s):** Dr. Vaughn R. Pratt.

✌ ▸ **International Network for a UN Second Assembly**
301 E. 45th St.
The Delegate - 20B
New York, NY 10017 (212)983-3353
**Affiliation:** People's Assembly for the UN. **Concern(s):** peace; future; United Nations; networking; ideation. The Medical Association for the Prevention of War, Physicians For Social Responsibility and part of International Physicians for the Prevention of Nuclear War, have teamed up to propose a Second Assembly. To encourage a more democratic, UN appointees should be "guided only by their humankind identity, and therefore global and regional—not national—considerations." Various methods under discussion. Open to many organizations and might work with members of European Parliament. **Other Resources:** FOURTH APPEAL, a 10-page document widely circulated among the UN Secretariat during the General Assembly, is available for those interested in UN policy making and reform. At this time there are over 100 member organizations throughout the world. Nonprofit. **Est.:** 1975. **Contact(s):** Dr. Harry Lerner (US Convenor).

E ▸ **The International Oceanographic Foundation**
4600 Rickenbacker Causeway
Key Bisqane
Miami, FL 33149-9900 (305)361-4888
**Concern(s):** environment; education; ocean/rivers; volunteers. An organization devoted to the ocean, our last great frontier on Earth. It has members in nearly 90 different countries of the world. The objectives of the Foundation are to provide the general public with authoritative unbiased information about the world oceans and their importance to the human race, and to encourage their scientific investigation. **Other Resources:** Publishes SEA FRONTIER/SEA SECRETS, a bimonthly magazine. IOF Sea Safaris. Sponsors expeditions and maintains a museum, Planet Ocean. Volunteers inquire. Nonprofit. **Est.:** 1953. **Dues:** $18/yr. **Contact(s):** Edward T. Foote II (President). (305)361-4888.

H ▸ **International Organization of Consumers Union**
See PESTICIDE HANDBOOK: PROFILES FOR ACTION (directories).

✌ ▸ **International Peace Academy**
777 UN Plaza
New York, NY 10017-3521 (212)949-8480
**Concern(s):** peace; education; conflict resolution. An NGO which provides courses in Conflict Resolution designed for diplomats, military officers, academicians, and policy planners. **Contact(s):** Thomas G. Weiss (Executive Director).

✌ ▸ **International Peace Research Association**
Antioch College
795 Livermore
Yellow Springs, OH 45387 (513)767-6444
**Concern(s):** peace; education; environment; feminism; Third World; media; conflict resolution; militarism; research; development. Promotes national studies and teaching related to the pursuit of world peace; Facilitates contacts and cooperation between scholars and educators globally; Encourages worldwide dissemination of results of peace research. Members in 70+ countries working around issues of Communications, Ecological Security, Nonviolence, Peace Movements, Weapons Technology and Disarmament, Militarism and Women and many more. **Other Resources:** Publishes the IPSA NEWSLETTER, quarterly, and a membership directory. Nonprofit. **Est.:** 1965. **Dues:** $30, $15 low income. **E-Network:** PeaceNet. **ID:** 'antiochcol'. **Fax:** (513)767-1891. **Contact(s):** Paul Smoker (Secretary General).

✌ ▸ **International Peace Science Society**
See periodicals for CONFLICT MANAGEMENT AND PEACE SCIENCE.

✌ ▸ **International Peace Walk**
32 Rustic Way
San Rafael, CA 94901 (415)453-0792
**Concern(s):** peace; East-West; conflict resolution. Conducts walking tours of the Soviet Union with American and Soviet walkers. Participants meet local residents and experience local culture. **Member:** Co-op America.

✌ ▸ **International Physicians for the Prevention of Nuclear War**
126 Rogers
Cambridge, MA 02142 (617)868-5050
**Concern(s):** peace; anti-nuclear; disarmament. Physicians working to lessen the threat of nuclear war. by holding international forums, supporting international research and promoting multi-hemispheric exchanges. **Other Resources:** See IPPNW REPORT, and Update. **Est.:** 1980. **Contact(s):** William L. Monning (Executive Director).

F ▸ **International Planned Parenthood Federation**
Western Hemisphere Division
902 Broadway
New York, NY 10010 (212)995-8800
**Affiliation:** Planned Parenthood Federation of America. **Concern(s):** feminism; demographics; population growth; planned parenthood; pro-choice. Is one of the six regions of the worldwide IPPF, global headquarters are in London where they exchange information, experience and new ideas with family planning associations in Asia, Africa, and Europe. There are 23 national associations and a subregional organization, the Caribbean Family Planning Affiliation, with 21 members covering French, Dutch and English-speaking countries of that area. Provides services to 7 million+ with one million new a year. Goal: accessibility to everyone. **Est.:** 1952.

🐾 ▸ **International Primate Protection League**
Box 766
Summerville, SC 29484 (803)871-7988
**Concern(s):** environment; wildlife/endangered species; endangered species; preservation; animal rights. The League works to protect all primates in the wild and in captivity. Maintains a gibbon sanctuary; supports overseas sanctuary projects; uncovers illegal trafficking. **Dues:** $20/yr. **Contact(s):** Shirley McGreal.

E ▸ **International Rivers Network**
301 Broadway, #B
San Francisco, CA 94133 (415)986-4694
**Concern(s):** environment; ocean/rivers. Against costly dams finances by the US that destroy wildlife, natives, and enrich corrupt politicians and industries while introducing diseases and doing reverse land reform; Pro-river; Pro-rainforest; anti-dams. **Other Resources:** Publishes THE WORLD RIVERS REVIEW (periodicals). **Contact(s):** Phil Williams (Executive Director).

A ▸ **International Rural Sociology Association**
Michigan State University, Sociology Department
c/o Dr. Harry K. Schwarzweller
East Lansing, MI 48824
See directory by same name.

H ▸ **International Service Association For Health**
1712 Clifton Rd NE
Atlanta, GA 30329 (404)634-5748
**Concern(s):** health. **Contact(s):** Ellen Hayes Wright.

🐾 ▸ **International Society for Animal Rights, Inc.**
421 S. State St.
Clarks Summit, PA 18411
**Concern(s):** environment; animal rights.

E ▸ **International Society for the Preservation of Rain Forests**
3302 N. Burton Ave.
Rosemead, CA 91770 (818)572-7273
**Concern(s):** environment; economics; health; Third World; forests; ocean/rivers; indigenous peoples; community self-reliance. An organization that works at government and village levels to help people develop positive, sustainable usage of rainforest; develop species survival sanctuaries, river dolphin preserves, and community reserves for preservation of pristine forest; collect and distribute clothing, medicine, etc. among Indians and river people. **Contact(s):** Roxanne Kremer.

A ▸ **International Sprout Growers' Association (ISGA)**
7300 Lincolnshire , #200
Sacramento, CA 95823 (916)399-9846
**Concern(s):** agriculture; food production. **Contact(s):** Craig Johnson.

T ▸ **International Trade & Development Policy Education Foundation**
1911 N. Fort Myer Dr., #702
Arlington, VA 22209 (703)243-1456
**Concern(s):** Third World; education; economics; agriculture; hunger; development; trade; research. Formed in a response to the continuing need for greater awareness of the importance of national trade and development activities. The Foundation believes that the US, its economy, its social structures and its security, derive significant benefits from our involvement in international development activities, foreign trade, and other forms of international involvement. It recognizes that there is a serous need to inform Americans about the importance of international activities. **Other Resources:** Publications and video on foreign assistance. **Est.:** 1983. **Contact(s):** Daniel E. Shaughnessy (President), Raymond A. Hoehle (Executive Director).

T ▸ **International Voluntary Services (IVS)**
1424 16th St. NW, #204
Washington, DC 20036 (202)387-5533
**Concern(s):** Third World; development; volunteers. A corporation which has placed over 1,200 skilled technicians in 30 countries world wide in the fields of agriculture, health care, small business, cooperatives, and appropriate technology. **Other Resources:** Newsletter, DEVELOPMENTS. Nonprofit. **Est.:** 1953. **Fax:** (202)387-4234. **Contact(s):** Suzanne Beane Stafford (Interim Executive Director), Andrea Brock (Director, Communications).

T ▸ **International War Crimes Tribunal**
36 E. 12th St., 6th Fl.
New York, NY 10003 (212)254-5385
**Affiliation:** Coalition to Stop US Intervention in the Mid-East. **Concern(s):** Third World; peace; Mid-East; intervention; foreign policy; international law; militarism; nonviolence; research; United Nations. This Commission, through the UN, is attempting to bring to international justice the people responsible for war crimes during Operation Desert Storm. They are currently bringing 19 charges against Bush, Quayle, Cheney, Powell, Shwarzkopt and others involved in the war that has resulted in 250,000 Iraqi deaths. **Other Resources:** Free brochure, Special requests for information. WAR CRIMES, by Ramsey Clark is available for $12.95 + $2 S&H. Video, NOWHERE TO HIDE with Ramsey Clark for $25 + $3 S&H. Also, Commission of Inquiry for the International War Crimes Tribunal. **E-Network:** PeaceNet. **ID:** 'afreeman'. **Fax:** (212)979-1583. **Contact(s):** Ramsey Clark (Co-founder), Jelayne Miles (Co-coordinator). **Other:** 2489 Mission St. #28, San Francisco, CA 94110. Vic Becker, (415)821-6545.

E ▸ **International Wildlife Coalition**
Box 388
North Falmouth, MA 02556-0388
**Concern(s):** environment; wildlife/endangered species; oceans. This international coalition works for the preservation of wildlife not only on land but the ocean wildlife. It accomplishes this by not only working to preserve wildlife but the wilderness too. They publish educational brochures and pamphlets. **Other Resources:** See WHALEWATCH newsletter and Whale Adoption Project. **Office:** 634 North Falmouth Highway North Falmouth, MA 02556. **Contact(s):** Dan Morast (Executive Director).

F ▸ **International Women's Rights Action Watch**
Center for Population & Family Health
Columbia University, 60 Haven Ave.
New York, NY 10032 (212)854-1754
**Concern(s):** feminism; justice; demographics; family planning. **Other Resources:** See Women, Public Policy and Development Project; Development Law and Policy Program: WOMEN'S WATCH newsletter.

F ▸ **International Women's Tribune Center**
777 UN Plaza
New York, NY 10017 (212)687-8633
**Concern(s):** feminism; economics; Third World; demographics. **Other Resources:** Publishes newsletter, TRIBUNE and TECH AND TOOLS BOOK: A GUIDE TO TECHNOLOGIES WOMEN ARE USING WORLDWIDE (directories).

T ▸ **Interns for Peace**
150 5th Ave., #911
New York, NY 10011 (212)255-8760
**Concern(s):** Third World; peace; Mid-East. This organization has two main goals: development of positive relations between Israel's Jewish and Arab citizens through cooperative, mutually beneficial activities. **Other Resources:** Publishes ISRAEL HORIZONS. **Est.:** 1978. **Fax:** (212)627-1287. **Contact(s):** Arieh Lebowitz (Editor).

**J ▶ Interreligious Foundation for Community Organization**
See IFCO NEWS (periodicals).

**E ▶ Interspecies Communication, Inc.**
See INTERSPECIES NEWSLETTER.

**☺ ▶ Interstate Solar Coordinating Council**
900 American Center Bldg
St. Paul, MN 55101    (612)296-4737
**Concern(s):** energy; solar. A membership organization formed to help coordinate renewable energy programs between state governments. It provides recommendations for policy planning, certification of solar energy equipment, and a directory of contacts and programs in state government.

**? ▶ Invent America**
510 King St., #420
Alexandria, VA 22314
**Concern(s):** future; ideation; invention. An inventions contest for inventive young Americans.

**? ▶ Inventors Workshop International Education Foundation**
3201 Corte Madeira, #304
Camarillo, CA 93012    (805)484-9786
**Concern(s):** future; ideation; invention. The largest of the ethical inventor organizations in the USA," one of whose goals is "to improve the national climate for inventors and inventions." Alternative energy and environmental innovations. Annual tradeshow: "Inventech", monthly publications. Seminars. National radio show monthly **Other Resources:** INVENT! magazine; LIGHTBULB newsletter. "Inventors Bookshop" publications and A.V.'s. Membership for children, adults, and students. Nonprofit. **Est.:** 1971. **Frequency:** 6/yr. **Subscription:** $35/yr. **Price:** $5/ea. **Circ.:** 20M. **E-Network:** Inventnet. **Fax:** (805)388-3097. **Contact(s):** Alan Arthur Tratner (President).

**P ▶ Invert**
See MAINE PROGRESSIVE.

**$ ▶ Investor Responsibility Research Center**
1755 Massachusetts Ave. NW
Washington, DC 20036    (202)234-7500
**Concern(s):** economics; peace; politics; socially-responsible investing; research; corporate responsibility. This center provides information and conducts research on business issues that relate to corporate impact on society, focusing on socially responsible investing. An independent corporation that provides timely reporting and analysis to institutional investors and others. **Other Resources:** Publishes a newsletter, NEWS FOR INVESTORS, a monthly newsletter; and annual survey of voting results on shareholders resolutions; in-depth reports on social responsibility issues. Nonprofit. **Est.:** 1972. **Contact(s):** Margaret Carroll (Executive Director).

**$ ▶ Involvement Corps**
15515 Sunset Blvd., #108
Pacific Palisades, CA 90272    (310)459-1022
**Concern(s):** economics; trade; volunteers. This program helps businesses and organizations establish volunteer work programs and involvement. Nonprofit. **Est.:** 1968.

**✈ ▶ IOF Sea Safaris**
Box 499900
Miami, FL 33149    (305)361-4888
**Affiliation:** International Oceanographic Foundation. **Concern(s):** education; travel. Travel program for members of I.O.F. Travelers learn about natural history and ocean life while on a cruise ship. **Member:** Co-op America.

**J ▶ The Irish National Caucus**
413 E. Capitol St. SE
Washington, DC 20003    (202)544-0568
**Concern(s):** justice; labor; economics; boycott; corporate responsibility; socially-responsible investing; discrimination; faith. BOYCOTT FORD MOTOR COMPANY — The Fair Employment Agency has found Ford guilty of discrimination against Catholics. Products: all Ford automobiles. **Other Resources:** To protest, write to: Mr. D.E. Peterson, CEO, Ford Motor Company, Dearborn, MI 48121. (313) 322-3000.

**T ▶ Israeli Council for Israeli-Palestinian Peace**
See THE OTHER ISRAEL (periodical).

**✍ ▶ It's Our World Too**
Box 326
Winterport, ME 04496
**Concern(s):** education; peace; global understanding; youth; students; childhood. A youth organization founded by kids for kids.

Purpose of newsletter is to provide any student, anywhere, rich or poor, with an opportunity to share ideas and concerns on the subject of the arms race/peacemaking and related issues. **Est.:** 1982.

**E ▶ The Izaak Walton League**
RR 1, Box 769
Ottumwa, IA 52501-9801    (515)682-8610
**Concern(s):** environment; education; wilderness; conservation; acid rain; resources; wildlife/endangered species. Is one of America's oldest and most respect conservation organizations. Today, the League boasts a membership of 50,000 all working together to defend the nation's soil, air, woods, water, and wildlife. It promotes citizen involvement in local environmental protection efforts; educated the public about emerging resource threats, presses for strong laws to protect natural resources and enforces these laws. Pursues clean water, acid rain reduction, improved wildlife habitat, outdoor ethics. **Other Resources:** See OUTDOOR AMERICA magazine. Maintains an Action Network, sending out insider reports on Washington development and special "alerts." Publishes CITIZEN'S DIRECTORY FOR WATER QUALITY ABUSES, and SPLASH, a newsletter for Save Our Streams Program. **Est.:** 1922. **Member:** Environmental Federation of America. **Contact(s):** Jack Lorenz (Executive Director). **Other:** Legislative Offices, 1401 Wilson Blvd., Arlington, VA 22209. (703)528-1818.

**E ▶ The Jane Goodall Institute**
Box 26846
Tucson, AZ 85726    (602)792-2075
**Concern(s):** environment; wildlife/endangered species; Africa. The Institute is dedicated to ongoing support and expansion of field research on wild and captive chimpanzees and to publicizing their unique status and needs to insure their preservation in the wild and their psychological well-being in captivity. **Other Resources:** Projects include: Field research at Gombe Stream Research Centre in Tanzania; ChimpaZoo study of active chimpanzees in zoos of other captive colonies in the US; and conservation activities targeting wild and captive chimps, including those in labs. **Dues:** $25+/yr.

**E ▶ Jemez Action Group**
Box 8659
Santa Fe, NM 87504    (505)984-1428
**Concern(s):** environment; health; economics; boycott; corporate responsibility; socially-responsible investing; hazardous/toxic waste; water. BOYCOTT STONE-WASHED JEANS — Mining pumice for the stonewashing process has a deleterious effect on New Mexico's environment. Products: Stone-, acid- indigo-, snow-, & white-washed denim jeans. **Other Resources:** To protest, write to: Richard Cook, General Manager, Copar Pumice Co., P.O. Box 38, Espanola, NM 87532.

**D ▶ Jericho**
926 J St., #410
Sacramento, CA 95814    (916)441-0387
**Concern(s):** demographics; politics; justice; spiritual; interfaith; poverty; homelessness; hunger; lobbying. Follows a Judeo-Christian scriptural bias towards the poor and oppressed summoning us to free those most in need. Issues that have the potential for opening up structures to the poor and powerless in decisions which effect their lives. Social analysis and a comprehensive view of the interrelationship of multifaceted issues and interlocking structures is required for a systemic change, that recognizes local, national, and international linkages. **Other Resources:** JERICHO TRUMPET newsletter, legislative alerts, and workshop invitations are included with membership. Two programs: A Voice for Justice & Education for Justice, one works in the legislature, the other to promote a greater public understanding. **Dues:** $30-500/yr. **Contact(s):** Sister Shiela Walsh (Executive Director), John M. McCoy (President).

**☪ ▶ Jewish Action for Nuclear Responsibility**
87 Hillary Lane
Penfield, NY 14526
**Concern(s):** peace; spiritual; faith; anti-nuclear. **Contact(s):** Joyce S. Herman (Secretary).

**L ▶ Jewish Labor Committee**
25 E. 21st St.
New York, NY 10010-6297    (212)477-0707
**Affiliation:** Atran Center for Jewish Culture. **Concern(s):** labor; spiritual; education; Third World; justice; economics; peace; faith; unions; discrimination; Mid-East; East-West. Founded by the International Ladies' Garment Workers' Union, Amalgamated Clothing Workers' of America, Worksmans' Circle, and Jewish Daily Forward Association, in response to the rise of Nazism in Europe. It works to enhance Jewish security by mobilizing the support of the American labor movement for Israel, Soviet Jewry, and other related issues. During post WWII, it was involved with relief/rehabilitation for survivors. Seeks

to strengthen ties between labor and the Jewish community. **Other Resources:** Publishes the JEWISH LABOR COMMITTEE REVIEW, and an annual survey, CRITIQUE OF TRADE UNION RIGHTS IN COUNTRIES AFFILIATED WITH THE LEAGUE OF ARAB STATES. **Est.:** 1934.

**S ▶ Jewish National Fund**
42 E. 69th St.
New York, NY 10021    (212)879-9300
**Concern(s):** spiritual; environment; forestry; conservation; faith. **Contact(s):** Dr. Joseph P. Sternstein (President).

**☪ ▶ Jewish Peace Fellowship**
See SHALOM - THE JEWISH PEACE LETTER.

**☪ ▶ The Jewish Peace Lobby**
4431 Lehigh Rd., #141
College Park, MD 20740 (301)589-8764
**Concern(s):** peace; Third World; politics; Mid-East; conflict resolution; lobbying; self-determination; faith. The only American Jewish peace organization working full-time to directly affect American foreign policy in the Middle East. They believe that the US has a crucial role to play in promoting a peaceful resolution of the Israeli-Palestinian conflict based on Israel's right to secure borders and the Palestinian right to self-determination and statehood. JPL maintains a Washington office which lobbies Congress and the Administration and organizes local lobbying committees throughout the US. **Other Resources:** Sends out WASHINGTON ACTION ALERTS with legislative updates and suggestions for action.

**S ▶ Jewish Vegetarians of North America**
Box 1463
Baltimore, MD 21203    (301)366-VEGE
**Concern(s):** spiritual; health; vegetarian; animal rights; faith. An educational group that promotes vegetarianism within the Jewish tradition and explores the relationship between Judaism, dietary laws, and vegetarianism. Sponsors annual weekend conference in New York state. Topics also include health, ethics, food, economics, animal rights, ecology, and world hunger. **Other Resources:** JEWISH VEGETARIANS Newsletter. Nonprofit. **Est.:** 1983. **Dues:** $24/yr. includes newsletter. **Frequency:** 4/yr. **Subscription:** $12/yr. **Pages:** 16. **Circ.:** 800. **Other Formats:** Cheshire/self-adhesive/mag tape. **Contact(s):** Charles Stahler, Debra Wasserman.

**U ▶ Jews For Racial and Economic Justice**
200 W. 72nd St., #49
New York, NY 10023    (212)721-3585
**Concern(s):** urban; justice; spiritual; faith; discrimination; racism; ethnic concerns; racial tensions. Founded by a coalition of Jewish writers, professional, religious and labor leaders, educators and community activists. Seeks to be a clear, outspoken Jewish presence in the struggle for racial and economic justice in New York City, to bring issues of racism and social justice to the forefront in the Jewish community, and to cooperate with African-American, Latino, Asian-American and others. Has been in the forefront in addressing such historical issues as Jewish participation in the slave trade. **Est.:** 1990. **Contact(s):** Marilyn Neimark, Donna Nevel

**J ▶ Jobs for Progress, Inc.**
See SER NETWORK DIRECTORY.

**☪ ▶ Joel Brooke Memorial Committee**
See WORKING FOR PEACE: AN ANNOTATED RESOURCE GUIDE.

**J ▶ John Brown Anti-Klan Committee**
220 9th St. #443
San Francisco, CA 94103    (415)330-5363
**Concern(s):** justice; racism; discrimination; minority rights. **Other Resources:** Occasional newspaper, NO KKK, NO FASCIST USA, that is very useful in following skinhead activity.

**P ▶ Joint Center for Political &Economic Studies**
See National Black Caucus of Locally Elected Officials.

**H ▶ Jubilee House Community Inc.**
902 Boulevard
Statesville, NC 28677    (704)872-9230
**Concern(s):** health; peace; counseling; self-help. Retreat for burned-out peace and justice workers. **Other Resources:** Free newsletter. **Member:** Co-op America.

**$ ▶ Jubilee Partners**
See JUBILEE PARTNERS REPORT (periodicals).

**🐾 ▶ Justice for Animals**
148 S. Lehigh St.
Trucksville, PA 18708    (717)696-4956
**Concern(s):** environment; animal rights; wildlife/endangered species.

**E ▸ Kansas Area Watershed Council**
Box 1512
Lawrence, KS 66044
**Concern(s):** environment; agriculture; water; conservation.

**E ▸ Keep America Beautiful, Inc.**
Mill River Plaza
9 West Broad St.
Stamford, CT 06902 (203)323-8987
**Concern(s):** environment; recycling; conservation; beautification. National public education organization dedicated to improving waste handling practices in American communities. Informs and educates citizens on litter control and alternatives for handling solid waste. Through its principal program, the KAB SYSTEM, it is influencing more responsible attitudes and behavior toward the environment. **Other Resources:** See MULTI-MATERIAL RECYCLING MANUAL; VISION Newsletter; KAB: IT'S MORE THAN A SLOGAN Video; WASTE IN PLACE and WASTE: A HIDDEN RESOURCE Curriculums; CLEAN TEAM MANUAL. **Contact(s):** Roger W. Powers (President).

**A ▸ The Kerr Center for Sustainable Agriculture**
Box 588, Hwy 271S
Proteau, OK 74953-0588 (918)647-9123
**Concern(s):** agriculture; environment; sustainability; social ecology. "We strive to provide leadership, education, and technical assistance to the agricultural community seeking ecologically sound methods of producing food and sustaining farm livelihood. Also, we acknowledge the interdependence of biological, social and spiritual relationships in promoting stewardship and health of the land and people it supports." Suports the meat and organic agriculture. **Other Resources:** KCSA NEWSLETTER, information dissemination, host/cohost conferences, sponsor field days, tours, speakers list, and on-farm research.Directory, RESOURCES FOR SUSTAINABLE AGRICULTURE AND ALTERNATIVE ENTERPRISES. **Est.:** 1986. **Fax:** (918)647-8712. **Contact(s):** Heidi C. Carter (Education Coordinator), Teresa A. Maurer (Associate Program Director).

**✌ ▸ Kids for Peace**
Beacon Hill School
170 Alton Dr.
Beaconsfield, QC H9W 2Z3 Canada
**Concern(s):** peace; education; childhood. Developing programs to bring peace consciousness to the whole community.

**P ▸ Kindred Spirits**
See KINDRED SPIRITS JOURNAL (periodicals).

**A ▸ Koinonia Partners**
See KOINONIA NEWSLETTER.

**✍ ▸ L-CIPSSI Curriculum Services**
26801 Pine Ave.
Bonita Springs, FL 33923 (813)992-6381
**Concern(s):** education; homeschooling. Customized home schooling curriculum programs. "Our kindergarten-12th grade programs with convenient write-in text books start at only $200 and contain: math, science, social studies, language arts, reading, grammar, spelling, and more." Your teacher's supplies will include: teacher's editions and/or answer keys, schedule, report card, certificate of promotion, crate & files for organizing programs, and more. **Other Resources:** Call or write for your free custom curriculum questionnaire and please specify grade level. Nonprofit. **Fax:** (813)992-6473.

**D ▸ L.I.F.E. - Love is Feeding Everyone - Hunger Action Group**
310 N. Fairfax Ave., 2nd Fl.
Los Angeles, CA 90036 (213)936-0895
**Concern(s):** demographics; justice; hunger. Founded by actors Dennis Weaver and Valerie Harper and other concerned individuals from the entertainment and business communities, it is a hunger action group which helps feed over 50,000 needy people in the Los Angeles area each week. We reclaim salvageable food from grocery stores and other sources and distribute it to other organizations or agencies who then distribute directly to needy families. Nonprofit. **Est.:** 1984.

**L ▸ Labor Center**
See LABOR CENTER REPORTER (periodicals).

**L ▸ Labor Education and Research Project**
7435 Michigan Ave.
Detroit, MI 48210 (313)883-5580
**Concern(s):** labor; education; unions. Established to educate and aid in communications between union activists who want to "put the movement back in the labor movement." **Other Resources:** Publishes LABOR NOTES. **Est.:** 1978.

**✐ ▸ Labor Heritage Foundation**
815 16th St. NW, #301
Washington, DC 20006 (202)842-7880
**Concern(s):** arts; labor; activism; unions. Seeks to revive the tradition of labor, music, and art and increase its use in union activities, including rallies, boycotts and strike, in order to educate and organize the labor movement and the public. Focuses on artistic and cultural works which addresses the current concerns of working people. **Other Resources:** A referral service and information clearinghouse for labor artists and cultural activities. Assistance to unions in planning and coordinating activities. Co-sponsors regional arts/song exchanges, concerts, and festivals. See ART WORKS newsletter. Nonprofit. **Est.:** 1984. **Dues:** $30/yr.; $50 sponsor includes newsletter. **Fax:** (202)842-7838. **Contact(s):** Joanne Delaplaine (Executive Director).

**L ▸ Labor Letter**
Union Labor & Services Trade Dept./AFL-CIO
815 16th St. NW
Washington, DC 20006 (202)637-5000
**Affiliation:** AFL-CIO. **Concern(s):** labor; justice; economics; boycott; corporate responsibility; socially-responsible investing; unions. LABOR BOYCOTTS — To get a complete list of official labor boycotts contact Labor Letters.

**T ▸ Labor Network on Central America**
See LABOR REPORT ON CENTRAL AMERICA (periodicals).

**L ▸ Labor Occupational Health Program**
See LABOR OCCUPATIONAL HEALTH PROGRAM MONITOR (periodicals).

**L ▸ Labor Research Association**
145 W. 28th St.
New York, NY 10001 (212)714-1677
**Concern(s):** labor; economics; jobs; analysis; research. This organization does research and analysis of economic trends concerning labor. **Other Resources:** See ECONOMIC NOTES (periodicals).

**E ▸ Lake Michigan Federation**
59 E. Van Buren
Chicago, IL 60605 (312)939-0838
**Concern(s):** environment; energy; water; rivers; pollution; volunteers. The Federation promotes clean-up programs and wise planning in order to insure, protect and preserve Lake Michigan, its tributaries and shorelines. **Other Resources:** Volunteers inquire.

**E ▸ The Land and Water Fund of the Rockies**
1405 Arapahoe, #200
Boulder, CO 80302
**Concern(s):** environment; lobbying; volunteers. "to provide free legal aid to grassroots environmental groups in Arizona, Colorado, Idaho, Montana, New Mexico, Utah, and Wyoming. LAW Fund staff attorneys and a regional network of local volunteer attorneys supply advice and counsel, and will litigate for client groups." **Other Resources:** Volunteer Programs: Pro Bono Attorney Program, "Adopt-A-Forest," opportunity for technical experts. **Est.:** 1990. **Dues:** $25, $15/ student, low income/senior: $50/special.

**E ▸ Land Educational Association Foundation**
See LAND/LEAF (periodicals).

**A ▸ The Land Institute**
2440 E. Water Well Rd.
Salina, KS 67401 (913)823-5376
**Concern(s):** agriculture; environment; education; sustainability. Educational-research organization which examines technology and ideas which could sustain the long-term ability of the Earth to support a variety of life and culture. **Other Resources:** Publishes the LAND REPORT. Publications list is available. Offers on-site interdisciplinary classes in sustainable agriculture to ten interns each year. **Contact(s):** Wes Jackson, Dana Jackson.

**A ▸ The Land Stewardship Project**
14758 Ostlund Trail North
Marine-on-St. Croix, MN 55047 (612)433-2770
**Concern(s):** agriculture; environment; education; farm policy; sustainability; soil; organic; conservation; resources; land; rural communities. The Project seeks to foster a stewardship ethic towards our precious farmlands, an ethic that will lead to more careful use of the land by individuals and to needed changes in public policies affecting our soil and water. The ideal to which they are striving is that one day Americans, as a nation, will hold our country's farmlands in the same high ethical regard we now reserve for our national parks and wilderness areas. Focuses on urban and rural Upper Midwest US. **Other Resources:** Publishes LAND STEWARDSHIP NEWSLETTER and LAND NOTES, a column on land ethics for local newspapers. Nonprofit. **Contact(s):** Ron Kroese (Executive Director), Lee Ronning. **Other:** 512 W. Elm St., Stillwater, MN 55082.

**A ▸ Land Trust Alliance**
1017 Duke St.
Alexandria, VA 22314 (703)820-4940
**Concern(s):** agriculture; environment; economics; family farms; conservation; land; wilderness; land trusts; community investment. A national network of nonprofit local and regional land conservation organizations that provides programs and services to help land trusts reach their full potential, foster public policies supportive of land conservation and build public awareness of land trust and their goals. **Other Resources:** See NATIONAL DIRECTORY OF CONSERVATION LAND TRUSTS; journal, EXCHANGE. Provides educational materials and technical assistance for land trusts and other land conservation professionals. Internships available; volunteers needed countrywide. Nonprofit. **Dues:** $30+/yr. **Contact(s):** R. Dean Tice (Executive Director). (703)683-7778.

**T ▸ Lasting Links**
6165 Leesburg Pike, #109
Falls Church, VA 22044 (703)241-3700
**Concern(s):** Third World; development; hunger. **Contact(s):** Raymond W. Konan.

**J ▸ Latino Commission, DSA**
See OUR STRUGGLE/NUESTRA LUCHA (periodicals).

**✍ ▸ Lauback Literacy**
Box 131
Syracuse, NY 13210 (315)422-9121
**Concern(s):** education; literacy. An educational corporation whose purpose is to enable illiterate adults and older youth to acquire the listening, speaking, reading, writing and mathematical skills they need to solve the problems they encounter in daily life; to take full advantage of opportunities in their environment; and to participate fully in the transformation of their society. Nonprofit. **Office:** 1320 Janesville Ave., Syracuse, NY 13210.

**✌ ▸ Lawyers Against Nuclear Arms Control**
See LANAC NEWSLETTER.

**J ▸ Lawyers Committee For International Human Rights**
330 7th Ave, #10N
New York, NY 10001
**Concern(s):** justice; politics; Third World; refugees; immigration; law; lobbying. Public interest law center working to promote compliance with internationally recognized principles regarding human rights and refugee law. Provides legal support to other human rights organizations; participates in selected court cases where human rights law is relevant; monitors laws limiting US foreign assistance to countries with a consistent pattern of human rights violations; provides legal representation to applicants for political asylum in the US. **Other Resources:** Publishes NEWSBRIEFS. **Est.:** 1978.

**✌ ▸ Lawyers' Committee on Nuclear Policy**
666 Broadway
New York, NY 10012 (212)674-7790
**Concern(s):** peace; politics; anti-nuclear; conflict resolution; law. A national educational association of lawyers and legal scholars concerned with legal aspects of the nuclear weapons debate. Supports global security and the abolition of nuclear weapons through the promotion and strengthening of nonviolent legal mechanisms for resolving international disputes. "Our Statement on the Illegality of Nuclear Warfare" has become a classic in its field. **Other Resources:** Publishes newsletter under same title, and provides a literature list. Nonprofit. **Est.:** 1981. **Frequency:** 5/yr. **Contact(s):** David Birman (Executive Director).

**F ▸ Leadership Conference of Women Religious L-I-F-E**
8808 Cameron St.
Silver Springs, MD 20910 (301)588-4955
**Concern(s):** feminism; spiritual; peace; interfaith. **Contact(s):** Sr. Margaret Nulty.

**J ▸ Leadership Conference on Civil Rights**
2027 Massachusetts Ave. NW
Washington, DC 20036 (202)667-1780
**Affiliation:** Religious Action. **Concern(s):** justice; feminism; politics; spiritual; discrimination; racism; minority rights; law; equal rights; interfaith. Coordinates civil rights advocacy. A major coalition of concerned organizations. It seeks to advance civil rights for all Americans through investigation and enforcement of federal legislation. "Our goal is to achieve equal rights in a free, plural, democratic society." A national organization represents blacks, Hispanics, Asian Americans, women, labor, the aged, the handicapped, major religious groups, minority businesses and professions across the country. **Est.:** 1950. **Contact(s):** Arnold Aronson (Co-founder).

**E ▸ League of Conservation Voters**
1707 L St. NW
Washington, DC 20036 (202)785-8683
**Concern(s):** environment; politics; leadership; conservation. A national, nonpartisan political action committee formed to help elect conservation-minded candidates to office. "We support candidates

with outstanding environmental records running in close elections and endorse others who deserve recognition." The League makes cash campaign contributions and does extensive field organizing in key races. The League Board includes leaders from major national and state environmental organizations. Board members serve as individuals, not as representatives. **Other Resources:** Publishes the NATIONAL ENVIRONMENTAL SCORECARD (directories), a record of representatives' votes on planet-saving issues. **Est.:** 1970. **Contact(s):** Roger Stephenson (Director), Jim Maddy (Executive Director).

**A ▸ League of Rural Voters**
212 3 Ave. North, #301
Minneapolis, MN 55408 (612)827-6055
**Concern(s):** agriculture; politics; rural communities; voting. An organization dedicated to increasing the informed and effective participation of rural voters in the political and policy-making process. The League is also involved in a variety of educational, training and support work on critical local, state, national and international issues with farm and rural groups across the nation. **Contact(s):** Julie Ristau. (612)338-3382.

**J ▸ League of United Latin American Citizens**
2716 Fredericksburg St.
San Antonio, TX 78201 (512)376-6131
**Concern(s):** justice; Third World; diversity; minority rights. This organization analyzes and researches issues effecting Hispanics from immigration to education. **Other Resources:** Publishes a newsletter, AVISO; and a magazine, LATINO. **Est.:** 1929. **Contact(s):** Jose Garcia De Lara (President), Elva Perez.

**P ▸ The League of Women Voters**
1730 M St. NW
Washington, DC 20036 (202)429-1965
**Concern(s):** politics; feminism; law; voting. League Action Service (LAS) provides up to the minute accounts on congressional action on a wide variety of national issues. Through the periodic newsletter Report from the Hill and strategically timed Action Alerts, LAS subscribers know when their letters or phone calls will have the greatest impact on their members of Congress. **Other Resources:** Newsletter, REPORT FROM THE HILL; strategically timed Action Alerts; Membership magazine, THE NATIONAL VOTER, catalog of League publications and materials. Guides, NUCLEAR WASTE DIGEST and THINKING GLOBALLY...ACTING LOCALLY. **Contact(s):** Nancy M. Newman (President), Grant P. Thompson (Executive Director).

**E ▸ League to Save Lake Tahoe**
Box 10110
S. Lake Tahoe, CA 95731 (916)541-5388
**Concern(s):** environment; rivers; water; conservation; forests; preservation; air pollution; beautification. This League seeks to reverse the water and air quality decline at Lake Tahoe. They are dedicated to preserving the environmental balance, scenic beauty and recreational opportunities of the Basin. **Other Resources:** KEEP TAHOE BLUE newsletter. **Dues:** $35/yr.

**✍ ▸ Learning Alliance**
494 Broadway
New York, NY 10012 (212)226-7171
**Concern(s):** education; environment; feminism; health; justice; public health; Native Americans. An independent organization offers workshops, conference, training, and ongoing projects on a wide range of community and social issues including ecology, social justice, women's issues, personal and community health, combatting racism, arts, culture, and Native American issues. Nonprofit. **Est.:** 1985. **Contact(s):** David Levine (Executive Director).

**P ▸ Left Green Network**
Box 372
West Lebanon, NH 03784 (802)295-1544
**Concern(s):** politics; alternative party; Green. Hopes to enhance the vitality, diversity, and political coherence of the North American Green movement, while advancing a united but pluralistic Left Green agenda with the broader movement. Principles: Ecological Humanism; Social Ecology; Racial Equality; Ecofeminism; Gay/Lesbian Liberation; Grassroots Democracy; Cooperative Commonwealth; Human Rights; Non-Aligned Internationalism; Independent Politics; Direct Action; Radical Municipalism; Strategic Nonviolence; Democratic Decentralism. **Other Resources:** Publishes monthly, LEFT GREEN NOTES; and, quarterly, GREEN POLITICS.

**✈ ▸ Legacy International**
346 Commerce St.
Alexandria, VA 22314 (703)297-5982
**Affiliation:** United Nations. **Concern(s):** education; environment; Third World; politics; travel; volunteers; grassroots organizing. An organization affiliated with UN that offers a unique summer leadership instruction for international youths. On 126 rural Blue Ridge Mountains, young people from various ages, races, relations, and national origins participate in training programs dedicated to community organizing, environmental responsibility; leadership; global issues; and cross-cultural relations. **Other Resources:** See Youth For Environment and Society (YES). **Contact(s):** Jean Philipson.

**♈ ▸ Legal Action for Animals**
205 E. 42nd St.
New York, NY 10017 (212)818-0130
**Affiliation:** Animal Legal Defense Fund. **Concern(s):** environment; animal rights; wildlife/endangered species. Provides legal services on behalf of animals in trouble. The only public interest law firm in the country devoted to animal problems. Assists with cruelty complaints, companion animal eviction proceedings, veterinarian malpractice, and defense of civil disobedience on behalf of animals. Also tackles broader issues, including the plight of lab animals, wildlife, fur and food animals, animals used for entertainment and in zoos as well as providing legal support for other animal advocacy groups.

**✌ ▸ Legislative Strategies and Lobbying Network**
1616 P St. NW, #320
Washington, DC 20036 (202)332-4823
**Affiliation:** Professionals' Coalition for Nuclear Arms Control. **Concern(s):** peace; politics; disarmament; lobbying; law. A special service designed for local, regional and statewide coalitions that provides up-to-date legislative information, telephone and written consultation and recommendations for specific lobbying actions upon request. **Est.:** 1984. **Contact(s):** David Cohen (President/Lobbyist), Robert K. Musil, Becky Weaver (Executive Director).

**✍ ▸ LERN (Living Education Resources Network)**
Box 1448
Manhattan, KS 66502 (913)539-LERN
**Concern(s):** education. Publishes an alternative almanac for educators. Quotes, dates, historical events from the great thinkers in adult and continuing education adorn this calendar, well designed for planning and keeping notes of yearly meetings, deadlines and events. All royalties go to continuing the work of John Ohlinger and his Basic Choices which links educators worldwide with ideas which challenge the standard educator's notions. **Other Resources:** See AN ALTERNATIVE ALMANAC FOR EDUCATORS. **Office:** 1554 Hayes Drive Manhattan, KS 66502.

**P ▸ Libertarian Socialists**
Box 171, Station D
Toronto, ON M6P 3J8 Canada
**Concern(s):** politics; alternative party. A political party that advocates the idea that socialism is about freedom, the transformation of daily life, critical thought, and collective and individual liberation. **Other Resources:** Publishes THE RED MENACE. A set of articles and discussion papers on liberation is available for $5. **Est.:** 1973.

**✌ ▸ Librarians for Nuclear Arms Control**
Box 60552
Pasadena, CA 91106 (818)799-6193
**Concern(s):** peace; education; disarmament; anti-nuclear; test ban. **Other Resources:** See LNAC ALMANAC (periodicals). **Contact(s):** Janet Jenks.

**☢ ▸ Life Guard Idaho**
Box 4090
Ketchum, ID 83340 (208)726-7728
**Concern(s):** energy; environment; health; nuclear; hazardous/toxic waste. Works to clean up nuclear weapons plant pollution.

**E ▸ Lighthawk**
Box 8163
Santa Fe, NM 87504 (505)982-9656
**Concern(s):** environment; forests; sustainability; volunteers. Their goal is to enhance our species capacity to sustain biological diversity, intact ecosystems and processes that support life on this planet. Emphasis is on the American national forest system with a stronger focus on the Pacific Northwest rain forests. They encourage the use of aircraft in order to shed light on and correct the mismanagement and empower others to do the same. Always looking for volunteer pilots with at least 1000 hours. **Dues:** $35/yr.

**P ▸ Lincoln Filene Center for Citizenship**
See CITIZEN PARTICIPATION newspaper.

**T ▸ Links, Inc.**
1200 Massachusetts Ave. NW
Washington, DC 20005 (202)842-8686
**Concern(s):** Third World; demographics; development; hunger. **Contact(s):** Dr. Regina Jollivette Frazier.

**$ ▸ Living Economy Network**
School of Peace Studies
University of Bradford
Bradford, BD7 1DP England
**Concern(s):** economics; politics; decentralization; alternative party; taxation. Paul Elkins, former director of The Other Economic Summit (TOES), is launching this Network: of social scientists from around the world who share the decentralist/globally responsible political philosophy. Immediate goal is to produce an annual book and build relationships with other groups. Ultimate goal is to forge a new "school of economic thought" like Keynesianism or Marxism. Concept paper available. **Contact(s):** Paul Elkins.

**✍ ▸ Living Education Resource Network**
See ALTERNATIVE ALMANAC FOR EDUCATORS (directories).

**E ▸ Living From the Heart**
11186 N. Thrush
Parker, CO 80134 (303)841-2437
**Concern(s):** environment; wildlife/endangered species. LFH, The Dolphin Experience takes you to the Florida Keys to swim with and "be" with dolphins. Being with dolphins in their natural habitat facilitates an expansive level of awareness. Our niche in the global ecosystems of life is brought into clear, sharp focus. We strive for the attainment and understanding of the alpha state through programs of spiritual enlightenment, personal and planetary growth. We are very concerned about conservation issues that affect our oceans, land, and air. (303)841-5016.

**$ ▸ Livingston Economic Alternatives in Progress**
Box 156, Old City Hall
Livingston, KY 40445 (606)453-9800
**Concern(s):** economics; community self-reliance. An organization working toward greater economic self-sufficiency for local people. Sponsors Golden Kentucky Products, which sells sorghum, honey, and locally-made candy. **Other Resources:** Brochure available. Nonprofit. **Member:** Co-op America.

**E ▸ LM Research Institute**
Main St.
Harrisville, NH 03450 (603)827-3048
**Concern(s):** environment; forests; preservation. Through the Johnny Elmseed Community Service Project, sponsored by the Boy Scouts, they distribute the new disease-resistant American Liberty elm to cities and colleges. Solicits support from the private sector in order to provide funds for university research on elm disease prevention. (800)FOR-ELMS.

**U ▸ London Research Center**
See Mega-Cities Project.

**E ▸ Long Branch Environmental Educational Center, Inc.**
Route 2, Box 132
Leicester, NC 28748
**Concern(s):** environment.

**F ▸ Los Angeles Men's Center**
9012 Burton Way
Beverly Hills, CA 93759 (818)701-9898
**Concern(s):** feminism; health; men's liberation; empowerment. "Over 20 years as a therapist and teacher tells me that we are fast approaching the time when men en masse will take up the banner of the spiritual warrior. Men are giving up the hard-line masculine model to feel a new energized passion for life. To facilitate this global process I have created the Los Angeles Men's Center." **Other Resources:** The Sacred Path Workshops, monthly speaker breakfasts, a newsletter, seminars, individual counseling, ongoing weekly support groups.

**U ▸ Los Angeles Mutual Housing Association**
See EcoVillage.

**J ▸ Louisiana Coalition Against Racism and Nazism**
806 Perdido St., #205
New Orleans, LA 70112 (504)523-2811
**Concern(s):** justice; urban; racism; discrimination; ethnic concerns.

**E ▸ Louisiana Toxics Project**
616 Adams St.
New Orleans, LA 70118 (504)865-8708
**Concern(s):** environment; agriculture; hazardous/toxics wastes; pesticides. **Contact(s):** Darryl Malek-Wiley.

**J ▸ Low Income Housing Information Services**
See National Low Income Housing Coalition.

**S ▸ Lucis Trust**
See World Goodwill and Lucis Producations (media).

**S ▸ Lutheran Office for Governmental Affairs**
122 C St. NW, #300
Washington, DC 20001 (202)783-7507
**Affiliation:** Evangelical Lutheran Church in America. **Concern(s):** spiritual; peace; politics; faith; government accountability; militarism; law. (202)783-7508.

## ✿ ♦ Lutheran Peace Fellowship

2481 Como Ave. West
St. Paul, MN 55108     (612)644-1140
**Affiliation:** Fellowship of Reconciliation. **Concern(s):** peace; spiritual; nonviolence; militarism; faith. Lutherans who share a vision of peace as shalom - the presence of justice. As individuals, Fellowship members seek to practice peace in ways that build alternatives to war and the militarism that feeds it. It works within the church to nurture a community of Christians who renounce participation in war and who espouse nonviolence as the means of reconciliation in parish, nation, and the world community. Has widened its dialogue to discuss the immorality of war preparation. **Contact(s):** Tom Witt.

## ✆ ♦ Lynx Educational Fund for Animal Welfare

10573 W. Pico Blvd., #155
Los Angeles, CA 90064     (310)838-7178
**Concern(s):** environment; animal rights. An organization devoted solely to the preservation of fur-bearing animals. Its goal is to create a climate of opinion which ensures that wearing fur garments is no longer glamorous or acceptable. Nonprofit. **Est.:** 1985.

## H ♦ M.A.D.D. (Mothers Against Drunk Driving)

669 Airport Freeway
Hurst, TX 76054     (817)268-6233
**Concern(s):** health; education; substance abuse. Central office.

## T ♦ MADRE

121 W. 27th St.
New York, NY 10001     (212)627-0444
**Concern(s):** Third World; justice; feminism; development; Central America. **Contact(s):** Sarah Santana (Executive Director). See MADRE Speaks/MADRE Informa magazine.

## A ♦ Maine Organic Farmer & Gardner Association

See MAINE ORGANIC FARMER & GARDNER magazine and guide, TRUTH IN PRODUCE.

## E ♦ Manomet Bird Observatory

Box 936
Manomet, MA 02345     (508)224-6521
**Concern(s):** environment; wildlife/endangered species. The Center applies long-term environmental research and scientific education. Their studies improve understanding of wildlife populations and natural systems and foster conservation action throughout the Americas. Training in field biology is offered to college students and program support for science educators in schools. Focus remains on the ecology and conservation of neotropical migrant land birds, migration ecology and conservation of shorebirds and management of N. American fisheries. **Other Resources:** Field biology training program and international shorebird survey. Field techniques workshops for Latin American biologists. **Dues:** $25/yr.

## E ♦ Marine Mammal Stranding Center

Box 733
Brigantine, NJ 08203     (609)266-0538
**Concern(s):** environment; wildlife/endangered species. Tries to help beached whales and learn what causes the beaching.

## E ♦ Mark Trail/Ed Dodd Foundation

Box 2807
Gainesville, GA 30503     (404)532-4274
**Concern(s):** environment; education; arts; activism; conservation; childhood; graphics; literature. Dedicated to the conservation ideals and teachings of the comic strip character Mark Trail and his creator, the late Ed Dodd. It teaches today's children/tomorrow's leaders to make sound environmental decisions, and to voice these decisions skillfully. **Other Resources:** Internships available. Environmental writing workshops. Nonprofit. **Est.:** 1986. **Contact(s):** Rosemary Dodd (Executive Director), Frank Norton, Jr. (Chairman).

## ✿ ♦ Maryknoll Justice and Peace Office

Box 534
Maryknoll, NY 10545     (914)941-7590
**Concern(s):** peace; justice; spiritual; politics; faith. **Other Resources:** See NEWS NOTES (periodicals). **Contact(s):** Sister Helene O'Sullivan, Michael Gable **Other:** Maryknoll Fathers & Brothers Justice & Peace Office, 3700 Oakview Terrace NE, Washington, DC 20017. (202)832-1780.

## E ♦ Massachusetts Campaign to Clean Up Hazardous Waste

29 Temple Place
Boston, MA 02111     (617)292-4810
**Concern(s):** environment; politics; health; education; hazardous/toxic waste; lobbying. Attempting to clean up the hazardous wastes in the state by action, lobbying for stricter laws on hazardous wastes, and education of the public on the dangers of hazardous wastes.

## J ♦ Massachusetts National Lawyers Guild

See PUBLIC EYE MAGAZINE.

## ✆ ♦ Massachusetts Society for the Prevention of Cruelty to Animals

See ANIMAL (periodicals).

## E ♦ Mattole Restoration Council

4062 Wilder Ridge Rd
Garberville, CA 95440-4613
**Concern(s):** environment; conservation; preservation. This council focuses on restoring the environment in this region. Everything from the watershed areas to the wilderness areas. **Other Resources:** Newsletter.

## $ ♦ Mayan Crafts

1101 N. Highland St., #506
Arlington, VA 22201
**Concern(s):** economics; Third World; trade; Central America; Native American; cooperatives. Markets traditional handmade weavings produced by Guatemalan Maya Indian refugees, displaced people, widows, and co-ops. Nonprofit. **Member:** Co-op America.

## D ♦ Mazon - Jewish Response to Hunger

2940 Westwood Blvd., #7
Los Angeles, CA 90064     (310)470-7769
**Concern(s):** demographics; spiritual; faith; hunger. **Contact(s):** Irving Creamer.

## M ♦ Media Access Project

2000 M St. NW
Washington, DC 20036     (202)232-4300
**Concern(s):** media; politics; justice; electronic democracy; press; media watch; responsibility. A public interest law firm working to assure that the print and broadcast media inform the public fully and fairly on important issues involving the environment, consumerism, civil rights, the economic and the political process. Advises local and national organizations seeking to make broadcast stations more responsive in the areas of programming and employment. Represents these groups in their efforts to obtain access to the broadcast and print media. **Est.:** 1971. **Contact(s):** Andy Schwartzman (Executive Director).

## M ♦ Media Alliance

Fort Mason Center
Building D
San Francisco, CA 94123     (415)441-2557
**Concern(s):** media; media watch; responsibility. This organization strives for better journalism in the US. It wants to expose the cover ups that take place by the government in the media. This alliance also wishes to increase the ethical standards of journalism in the US. **Other Resources:** See MEDIA & VALUES and PROPAGANDA REVIEW (periodicals). **Contact(s):** Micha X. Peled (Executive Director).

## T ♦ Medical Aid for El Salvador

6030 Wilshire Blvd, #200
Los Angeles, CA 90036     (213)937-3596
**Concern(s):** Third World; health; Central America; disabled. Dedicated to providing medical care for the victims of the war in El Salvador. Prosthetics Project provides artificial limbs to war-wounded amputees. Children's Project brings ill and wounded children to US for surgery. Provides medical supplies, equipment, and training to Salvadoran health care providers. Nonprofit. **Est.:** 1980. **E-Network:** PeaceNet. **ID:** 'maes'. **Fax:** (213)935-7404. **Contact(s):** Mario Velsquez (Executive Director), Kim Groves (Assistant to the Director).

## H ♦ Medical Reform Group

Box 366, Station J
Toronto, ON M4J4Y8 Canada     (416)588-9167
**Concern(s):** health; national health; public health. An organization of physicians, medical students, and others concerned with health care, believes health care is a right, and that social, economic and political changes are needed to produce better health. **Other Resources:** Publishes a newsletter, MEDICAL REFORM. **Est.:** 1979. **Frequency:** 6/yr. **Subscription:** $25/yr, includes newsletter. **Pages:** 16. **Contact(s):** Dr. Haresh Kirpalani (Editor).

## U ♦ Mega-Cities Project

c/o London Research Center
81 Black Prince Rd.
London, SE 1 7SZ England     735 4250
**Affiliation:** London Research Center. **Concern(s):** urban; future; environment; networking; sustainability; ideation; invention; sustainability; architecture; planning; transportation. Identifies innovations which are helping to make cities better places to live and work in, and disseminates information about these innovations so that they can be adopted in other places.

## J ♦ Meikeljohn Peace Institute

Box 673
Berkeley, CA 94701     (510)848-0599
**Concern(s):** justice; politics; peace; civil liberties; social justice. An archival library to house case files from human rights cases for use by other attorneys, et al, as models; and to house historic materials—National Lawyers Guild papers and files on McCarthyism, etc. Purpose and goals are to defend, strengthen, and extend civil rights and liberties, economic rights, and the right to peace. Publishes and distributes books and pamphlets and answers requests. Formerly Meikeljohn Civil Liberties Institute. See periodical, GUILD PRACTITIONER. **Est.:** 1984. **E-Network:** PeaceNet. **ID:** 'peacelaw'. **Office:** 1715 Francisco St. **Contact(s):** Ann Fagan Ginger.

## F ♦ Men's Center of Los Angeles

9012 Burton Way
Beverly Hills, CA 90211
**Concern(s):** feminism; men's liberation. **Other Resources:** See THE SACRED PATH newsletter.

## E ♦ Mendocino Environmental Center

106 W. Stanley
Ukiah, CA 95482     (707)468-1660
**Concern(s):** environment. **See** The MENDOCINO COUNTRY ENVIRONMENTALIST and MENDOCINO COMMENTARY newspapers. **E-Network:** Econet. **ID:** 'bball'. **Fax:** (707)462-2370.

## ✿ ♦ Mennonite Central Committee

21 S. 12th St.
Akron, PA 17501     (717)859-1151
**Concern(s):** peace; spiritual; justice; faith; volunteers. A relief, development, and service organization of North American Mennonite and Brethren in Christ churches. Currently about 1,000 MCC workers - about 650 of them volunteers - serve in more than 50 countries, including the US and Canada, in areas of health, development, education, social services, agriculture, appropriate technology and disaster relief. **Other Resources:** GUIDE TO PEACE RESOURCES available. See FOOD AND HUNGER NOTES (periodicals). **Est.:** 1920. **E-Network:** Mennolink. **ID:** UCC. **Fax:** (717)859-2171. Telex: 90-2210. **Contact(s):** Hershey Leamon. (202)544-6564. **Other:** 21 S. 12th St., Akron, PA 17501.

## ♿ ♦ Mental Health Law Project

1101 15th St. NW
Washington, DC 20015     (202)467-5730
**Concern(s):** justice; health; politics; disabled rights; psychology. A public interest organization, using a comprehensive program of test-case litigations, educational outreach, and federal policy advocates to clarify and protect the legal rights of people who are labeled "mentally" or "developmentally" disabled. Our attorneys focus on key social-policy problems confronting these clients, identifying specific objectives and advocating changes in these areas. **Est.:** 1972.

## ✐ ♦ Mesechabe Foundation & Center for Gulf South History & Culture

See MESECHABE magazine.

## T ♦ Methodist Federation for Social Action

76 Clinton Ave.
Staten Island, NY 10301     (718)273-4941
**Concern(s):** Third World; justice; peace; spiritual; faith; divestment; South Africa; Central America. This organization was formed to promote democracy and justice in foreign countries and to apply pressure on corporations to divest, and stop intervention in Central America. **Other Resources:** See SOCIAL QUESTIONS BULLETIN.

## J ♦ Mexican American Legal Defense and Education Fund (MALDEF)

See MALDEF NEWSLETTER.

## $ ♦ Michigan Alliance for Cooperatives

Box 8032
Ann Arbor, MI 48107     (313)663-3624
**Concern(s):** economics; cooperatives. A localized version of Co-op America. This alliance is comprised of over 2000 local businesses and organizations. **Other Resources:** See Cooperative Education Project and newsletter, COOPERATIVE ACTION.

## ✍ ♦ Mid-Atlantic Radical Historians' Organization (MARHO)

See RADICAL HISTORY REVIEW (periodicals).

## T ♦ Middle East Research & Information Project

See magazine, MIDDLE EAST REPORT.

## T ♦ Middle East Watch

See Human Rights Watch.

## L ♦ Midwest Center for Labor Research

See LABOR RESEARCH REVIEW (periodicals).

## H ♦ Midwest Migrant Health Information Office

See MIGRANT HEALTH SERVICES DIRECTORY.

## ✿ ♦ Militarism Resource Project

See MILITARISM RESOURCE PROJECT NEWS (periodicals).

**E ▶ Military Toxics Network**
c/o Dyan Oldenburg
2802 East Madison #177
Seattle, WA 98112     (206)328-5257
**Affiliation:** National Toxics Campaign Fund. **Concern(s):** environment; anti-nuclear; politics; hazardous/toxic waste; waste management; grassroots organizing; government accountability. A national network of grassroots activists from around the country concerned about military pollution in their communities whose purpose is to organize people locally to monitor and influence the clean-up, waste management and pollution prevention practice of military installations and contractors. The Pentagon produces about 1.5 billion pounds of hazardous waste per year. **Other Resources:** A starter kit is available. **Fax:** (206)328-5267. **Contact(s):** Dyan Oldenburg.

**❀ ▶ Milwaukee Peace Center**
See Peace Education Resource Center.

**✪ ▶ Mineral Information Institute, Inc.**
1125 17th St., #2070
Denver, CO 80202     (303)297-3226
**Concern(s):** energy; environment; natural resources.

**❀ ▶ Minnesota Library Association Social Responsibilities Roundtable**
See MSRRT NEWSLETTER.

**J ▶ Minority Business Development Agency**
See Directory under same name.

**J ▶ Minority Rights Group**
See periodical under same name.

**✈ ▶ Mir Initiative**
See Cooperation Project.

**E ▶ Mission: Wolf**
Box 211
Silver Cliff, CO 81249     (303)425-3320
**Concern(s):** environment; education; wildlife/endangered species; preservation; volunteers. An educational group offering traveling programs, when animals agree. "Mostly we house 26 wolves and wolf dogs, and offer anyone interested to visit, volunteer, to come learn about wolves and their place in nature and how we all can take part in environmental issues to improve the natural world." **Est.:** 1988. **Contact(s):** Kent Weber, Dana Weber.

**? ▶ Mississippi 2020 Network**
Box 31292
Jackson, MS 39206-1292
**Concern(s):** future; ideation. A membership association of Mississippians and others "who believe ordinary people can transform the future by introducing images of new social possibilities." **Contact(s):** Bob Kochtitsky (Director).

**E ▶ Missouri Botanical Garden**
Box 299
St. Louis, MO 63166-0299
**Concern(s):** environment; preservation.

**♿ ▶ Mobility International USA**
See WORLD OF OPTIONS: A Guide to International Educational Exchange, Community Service and Travel for Persons with Disabilities.

**❀ ▶ Mobilization for Survival**
45 John St., #811
New York, NY 10038     (212)385-2222
**Concern(s):** peace; energy; Third World; environment; justice; disarmament; intervention; social justice; anti-nuclear. Nationwide organization working for disarmament, non-intervention, safe energy, human needs. Quarterly publication. Works to highlight connections among nuclear arms race, military intervention, nuclear power, and lack of commitment to social and economic justice. Provides a variety of action-oriented resources. **Other Resources:** See MOBILIZER magazine; NORTHERN SUN NEWS; and guides, TOWARDS A NUCLEAR FREE FUTURE and UNCOVERING THE NUCLEAR INDUSTRY. **Contact(s):** Michael G. Burns. **Other:** 135 W. 4th St., New York, NY 10012. (212)673-1808.

**J ▶ Mohawk Nation**
See AKWESASNE NOTES newspaper.

**M ▶ Mondragon Type Communities**
4131 Larwin Ave.
Cypress, CA 90630
**Concern(s):** media; multilogues. **Contact(s):** Bill Holden.

**E ▶ Monitor Consortium**
1506 19th St. NW
Washington, DC 20036 (202)234-6576
**Concern(s):** environment; analysis. Clippings of environmental articles from many environmental sources.

**E ▶ Mono Lake Committee**
See MONO LAKE NEWSLETTER and MONO LAKE GUIDEBOOK.

**✎ ▶ Montessori World Educational Institute**
Box 3808
San Luis Obispo, CA 93403  (805)541-3100
**Concern(s):** education; alternative. Founded by a group of educators for the purpose of making information, training, and materials related to the Montessori Method of Education more easily accessible to parents and educators. It provides training for persons wishing to work with pre-primary, primary, and elementary age children. Course work is offered that enables a teacher to earn a degree while continuing regular work. Nonprofit. **Est.:** 1979. **Contact(s):** Bob Blodget, Marilyn Blodget: (Co-founders).

**E ▶ Morris Animal Foundation**
45 Inverness Dr. East
Englewood, CO 80112-5480 (303)790-2345
**Affiliation:** Digit Fund. **Concern(s):** environment; wildlife/endangered species. Trying to protect endangered mountain gorillas.

**A ▶ Mothers and Others for a Livable Planet**
40 W. 20th St.
New York, NY 10011     (212)727-2700
**Affiliation:** Natural Resources Defense Council. **Concern(s):** agriculture; family; environment; activism; pesticides; policy. A project of the NRDC that works to ensure a safe, pesticide free food supply. But, also works for solutions to other environmental problems facing families. **Other Resources:** Publishes a newsletter, TLC. Nonprofit. **Fax:** (212)727-1773. **Contact(s):** Wendy Gordon Rockefeller (Chairperson).

**❀ ▶ Mothers Embracing Nuclear Disarmament (MEND)**
Box 2309
La Jolla, CA 92038     (619)454-3343
**Concern(s):** peace; feminism; anti-nuclear; disarmament. A national education organization inspired by mothers and other nurturers with the hope, the means, and the belief in their own ability to take actions that reduce the risk of nuclear war. Supports multi-lateral, verifiable reductions and other efforts to promote understanding between nations and encourages a new approach to national security. MEND has set up a network of chapters and community contacts throughout the country and one in India. **Other Resources:** Quarterly newsletter, PROGRESS; regular Communiques; and, A CONCERNED CITIZEN'S GUIDE TO NATIONAL SECURITY. Nonprofit. **Contact(s):** Maureen Pecht King (Executive Director).

**❀ ▶ Mothers For Peace**
6465 Corral de Piedra
San Luis Obispo, CA 93401  (805)773-3881
**Concern(s):** peace; environment; energy; militarism; anti-nuclear; appropriate technology. Founded "by our sadness and frustration at the needless loss of life in Vietnam. Our shared values have kept us together as we have opposed that which would destroy, and worked for that which would promote life, the environment, and peace." The Gulf War has furthered their resolve to demand a serious energy plan and condemn military solutions to conflict. This is the group that has put up a fight against Diablo Canyon Nuclear facility for nearly 20 years. **Other Resources:** Position paper available. Also offers a yearly scholarship of $1500 to someone committed to working for a saner, safer world on the Central Coast. **Est.:** 1969. **E-Network:** Peaceline-(805) 541-1394. **Contact(s):** Nancy Culver, Jane Swanson (805)595-2605.

**E ▶ Mountain Lion Foundation**
Box 1896
Sacramento, CA 95812  (916)442-2666
**Concern(s):** environment; economics; wildlife/endangered species. An educational organization whose programs focus on today's critical wildlife problems. "Our gift line is designed to show the power and natural grace of the American lion and is produced with the highest regard for environmental integrity." Nonprofit.

**F ▶ Ms. Foundation For Women**
141 5th Ave. #6S
New York, NY 10011
**Concern(s):** feminism. **Other Resources:** See also MS. MAGAZINE. **Contact(s):** Gloria Steinem.

**E ▶ Myrin Institute**
See ORION magazine.

**✎ ▶ Mysteries Program**
Crossroads School
1714 21st St.
Santa Monica, CA 90404     (310)829-7391
**Affiliation:** Crossroads School. **Concern(s):** education; spiritual; holism; transformation; childhood. An innovative new program that helps children adapt to the ambivalence of our times, grow strong and creative, and develop life sustaining values; gives students the tools and the experience to combat the root causes of self-destructive behavior—low self-esteem, stress, isolation, and poor decision-making skills; teaches students to tolerate and enjoy diversity, develop compassion and a sense of responsibility and empowerment, joy, play, love and connectedness. Junior and high school level. **Contact(s):** Shelley Kessler.

**❀ ▶ NARMIC**
1501 Cherry St.
Philadelphia, PA 19102  (215)741-7277
**Affiliation:** American Friends Service Committee. **Concern(s):** peace; education; Third World; spiritual; global understanding; interfaith; conflict resolution; nonviolence; disarmament; foreign policy. A research and resource group of the Peace Education Division of the AFSC. It was established to provide action-orientated research on the US Military establishment and the use of US weapons in Vietnam. Today, drawing on its extensive database, NARMIC is working to provide social change groups with educational resources on the impact of US military and economic policy on foreign policies. **Est.:** 1969.

**✎ ▶ The Naropa Institute**
2130 Arapahoe Ave.
Boulder, CO 80302     (303)444-0202
**Concern(s):** education. A private, Buddhist-inspired, nonsectarian liberal arts college offering undergraduate and graduate degrees in the arts, social sciences, and humanities. It is dedicated to fostering the study and interplay of Western disciplines and Eastern contemplative practices. A highly cross-cultural approach that draws from the spiritual traditions of Montesorri, Waldorf, and Krishnamurti.

**P ▶ The Nation Institute**
72 Fifth Ave.
New York, NY 10011     (212)463-9270
**Concern(s):** politics; justice; law. **Other Resources:** Project, Supreme Court Watch.

**F ▶ National Abortion Federation**
See Membership Directory under same name.

**F ▶ National Abortion Rights Action League**
1101 14th St. NW
Washington, DC 20005  (202)408-4600
**Concern(s):** feminism; politics; pro-choice; lobbying. Learn how you can support the Freedom of Choice Act. Keep abreast of proposed legislation and become an effective lobbyist for Pro-Choice. Participate in the clinic defense campaign to keep clinics open despite zealous attempts by "Operation Rescue." Hundreds of proposals to impose mandatory waiting periods, husband consent requirements, and outright bans on all or most abortions will be hitting tens of state legislatures. Restrictions have already been enacted in many states and territories. **Other Resources:** Presently campaigning for a Freedom of Choice Act. Goal is to bring the issue to the voting booth for women. **Est.:** 1970. **Dues:** $20+/yr. **Contact(s):** Kate Michelman (Executive Director). **Other:** 1337 Third St. Promenade, #306, Santa Monica, CA 90401.

**♿ ▶ National Accreditation Council for Agencies Serving the Blind and Visually Handicapped**
See List of Member Organizations under same name.

**A ▶ National Agricultural Library**
See Alternative Farming Systems Information Center.

**H ▶ National AIDS Network**
1012 14th St. NW
Washington, DC 20005  (202)347-0390
**Concern(s):** health; education; public health; community education; AIDS. National resource and information center for over 750 community based organizations providing AIDS education, support services, and technical assistance to local organizations focusing on AIDS. **Other Resources:** Publishes quarterly and monthly magazines, a video directory, and technical pamphlets. **Contact(s):** Christopher Hall, Anne Lewis.

**J ▶ National Alliance Against Racist & Political Repression**
See ORGANIZER (periodicals).

**T ▶ National Alliance of Third World Journalists**
See ALLIANCE REPORT (periodicals).

**D ▶ National Alliance To End Homelessness**
1518 K St. NW, #206
Washington, DC 20005  (202)638-1526
**Concern(s):** demographics; urban; hunger; poverty; homelessness. **Contact(s):** Nan Roman, Susan G. Baker (Chairman).

**D ▸ National Anti-Hunger Coalition**
1875 Connecticut Ave. NW
Washington, DC 20009 (202)986-2200
**Affiliation:** Food Research and Action Center. **Concern(s):** demographics; hunger; poverty. A grassroots organization of low-income people, their allies, and interested groups to multiply the impact of low-income people on the policy decisions that affect our lives; to increase the amount of national resources devoted to the prevention of hunger and its causes; to expand public awareness of hunger and its relationship to government fiscal policies and priorities; and to nurture leadership potential within low-income communities; works with Food Research and Action Center. **Est.:** 1979. **Contact(s):** Michele Tingling-Clemmons.

**♈ ▸ National Anti-Vivisection Society**
53 West Jackson Boulevard
Chicago, IL 60604 (312)427-6065
**Concern(s):** environment; animal rights.

**E ▸ National Arbor Day Foundation**
100 Arbor Ave
Nebraska City, NE 68410 (402)474-5655
**Concern(s):** environment; education; forests; conservation. An educational organization dedicated to tree planting and conservation. **Other Resources:** Programs include, Trees for America, Tree City USA, Conservation Trees, Celebrate Arbor Day, and the National Arbor Day Center. Publishes TREE CITY USA BULLETIN and ARBOR DAY. **Dues:** $10/yr.

**✍ ▸ National Assault Prevention Center**
Box 02005
Columbus, OH 43202 (614)291-2540
**Concern(s):** education; health; youth; disabled. Programs in local schools to help children and the handicapped understand abuse and how to prevent it. Helps other organizations set up similar programs. **Member:** Co-op America.

**H ▸ The National Assembly of National Voluntary Health and Social Welfare Organization**
1319 F St. NW, #601
Washington, DC 20004 (202)347-2080
**Concern(s):** health; politics; public health; national health; lobbying; welfare rights; volunteers.

**✍ ▸ National Association for Legal Support of Alternative Schools (NALSAS)**
See National Coalition of Alternative Community Schools and NATIONAL DIRECTORY OF ALTERNATIVE COMMUNITY SCHOOLS.

**✌ ▸ National Association for Mediation in Education (NAME)**
525 Amity St.
Amherst, MA 01002 (413)545-2462
**Concern(s):** peace; education; conflict resolution. Promotes the development, implementation, and institutionalization of school and university-based conflict resolution programs and curricula. NAME is the primary national and international clearinghouse for information resources, technical assistance, and training in the field of conflict resolution in education. **Other Resources:** Publishes FOURTH R newsletter and ANNOTATED BIBLIOGRAPHY FOR TEACHING CONFLICT RESOLUTION IN THE SCHOOLS (directories). Nonprofit. **Est.:** 1984. **Dues:** $30, $50/organization. **Contact(s):** Annette Townley (Executive Director), Rachel Goldberg (Project Assistant).

**E ▸ National Association for Plastic Container Recovery**
5024 Parkway Plaza Bl., #200
Charlotte, NC 28217 (704)357-3250
**Concern(s):** environment; recycling.

**P ▸ National Association for Public Interest Law (NAPIL)**
1118 22nd St. NW
Washington, DC 20036 (202)466-3686
**Concern(s):** politics; justice; education; reform. A small public interest organization founded by law students to remove the barriers confronting law students and lawyers interested in pursuing public interest careers. **Other Resources:** Publishes DIRECTORY OF PUBLIC INTEREST LEGAL INTERNSHIPS and the NAPIL FELLOWSHIPS GUIDE. Legal services. **Contact(s):** Michael Caudell-Feagan, Sue Schreiber.

**J ▸ National Association for the Advancement of Colored People**
588 Vance Ave
Memphis, TN 38126-2202 (901)521-1343
**Concern(s):** justice; politics; demographics; diversity; poverty. Established to insure the political, educational, social, and economic equality of black citizens; to achieve equality of rights and eliminate race prejudice among people of the US; to eliminate racial discrimination. **Other Resources:** See CRISIS magazine. **Est.:** 1909. **Contact(s):** J. LeVonne Chambers (Director, Legal Defense /Education Fund), Benjamin Hooks (Executive Director). (212)245-2100.

**✐ ▸ National Association for Young Writers**
See SHOE TREE (periodicals).

**E ▸ National Association of Biology Teachers**
11250 Roger Bacon Dr., #19
Reston, VA 22090 (703)471-1134
**Concern(s):** environment; education; conservation; animal rights; preservation; biotechnology. Focuses on the concerns of biology teachers. Projects include: Middle school teacher training, biotechnology labs and equipment loan programs, alternative use of animals in the classroom and elementary education environmental curriculum. **Other Resources:** Publishes periodical, The AMERICAN BIOLOGY TEACHER.

**H ▸ National Association of Community Health Centers, Inc.**
1330 New Hampshire Ave. NW, #122
Washington, DC 20036 (202)659-8008
**Concern(s):** health; public health. **Contact(s):** Joanne Orijel.

**E ▸ National Association of Conservation Districts, Inc.**
Box 855
League City, TX 77574-0855 (713)332-3402
**Concern(s):** environment; agriculture; conservation; natural resources; water. This organizations strives to preserve natural resources through conservation and alternative energy means. It maintains relations with organizations and government agencies and publishes information about the districts. Conservation, development, self-government is the theme of the district movement. **Est.:** 1946. **Office:** 408 East Main St. League City, TX 77574-0855. **Contact(s):** Ernest C. Shea (Executive Vice President), Ronald G. Francis (Director, Communications).

**✌ ▸ National Association of Evangelicals**
1023 15th St. NW, #500
Washington, DC 20005 (202)789-1011
**Concern(s):** peace; justice; spiritual; faith. This organization addresses the issues of peace, human rights, and national security simultaneously, believing they are interdependent. **Other Resources:** Publishes newsletter, WASHINGTON INSIGHT.

**$ ▸ National Association of Housing Cooperatives**
1614 King St.
Alexandria, VA 22314 (703)549-5201
**Concern(s):** economics; community self-reliance; cooperatives. A national federation of housing cooperatives, professionals, organizations, and individuals promoting the interests of cooperative housing communities. The only national housing cooperative organization. **Other Resources:** Newsletter, COOPERATIVE HOUSING BULLETIN; journal, workshops. Nonprofit. **Est.:** 1950. **Dues:** Sliding scale based on type of membership. **Fax:** (703)549-5204. **Contact(s):** Pamela M. St. Clair (Deputy Director), Herbert J. Levy (Director).

**E ▸ National Association of Interpretation**
Box 1892
Fort Collins, CO 80522 (303)498-8844
**Concern(s):** environment; justice; cultural integrity. A professional organization that represents all those whose job it is to convey the meanings and relationships between people and their natural, cultural and recreational world. It serves the needs and interest of interpreters employed by agency organizations concerned with natural and cultural resources, conservation and management. **Other Resources:** Association of Interpretive Naturalists. **Dues:** $40, $25/student.

**L ▸ National Association of Letter Carriers**
100 Indiana Ave. NW
Washington, DC 20001 (202)393-4695
**Concern(s):** labor; unions. **Contact(s):** Vincent R. Sombrotto (President).

**H ▸ National Association of Meal Programs**
See Directory under same name.

**P ▸ National Association of Neighborhoods**
1651 Fuller St. NW
Washington, DC 20009 (202)332-7766
**Concern(s):** politics; economics; grassroots organizing; community self-reliance; municipal. A unique, multi-issue member organization of blocks, clubs, community councils, umbrella groups, city-wide neighborhood coalitions and individual citizens. They have come together to: speak with a unified voice on issues of local and national importance; educate and be educated on programs, advocate issues and techniques and to promote neighborhood movement. **Other Resources:** NAN BULLETIN and NAN DISPLACEMENT REPORTER, both monthlies. Referrals to neighborhood associations, citywide coalitions, and community development corps. **Est.:** 1975. **Contact(s):** Stephen Glaude (Executive Director).

**H ▸ National Association of People With AIDS**
Box 34056
Washington, DC 20043 (202)898-0414
**Concern(s):** health; education; public health; AIDS. An advocacy and service organization for people with AIDS. It has 84 affiliates in 41 states and DC. It sponsors a speakers bureau with nearly 500 presenters, over 100 of whom are people of color and 50 of whom are women. In addition, many NAPWA affiliates sponsor their own speakers, bureaus and public education programs. **Other Resources:** AIDS on-line database for area codes 703, 301, or 202 use (703)998-3144, all others call (800)926-2792. Modem settings should be: 8 bits, No parity, 1 stop bit. **Office:** 1413 K St. NW, 10th Flr. Washington, DC 20005. **Fax:** (202)898-0435. **Contact(s):** Stephen Beck.

**E ▸ National Association of Service and Conservation Corps**
1001 Connecticut Ave. NW, #827
Washington, DC 20036 (202)331-9647
**Affiliation:** Human Environment Center. **Concern(s):** environment; education; economics; urban; conservation; volunteers; community development; youth. Promotes youth corps at the federal, state, regional, county and municipal levels and serves as a forum for identifying policy issues affecting members. It seeks to broaden a national consensus for youth service and provide information and technical assistance to existing and developing conservation and service corps programs. Sponsors national and regional conferences, monitors and reports on corps programs, is developing a national data collection system and staff training program. (202)331-8387.

**L ▸ National Association of Social Workers**
7981 Eastern Ave., Legislative Affairs
Silver Springs, MD 20910 (301)565-0333
**Concern(s):** labor; health; politics; unions. See directory, SELF-HELP ORGANIZATIONS AND PROFESSIONAL PRACTICE. **Contact(s):** Eileen McGowan Kelly, Susan Hoechstetter.

**A ▸ National Association of State Departments of Agriculture**
1616 H St. NW
Washington, DC 20006 (202)628-1566
**Concern(s):** agriculture; environment. Composed of Department of Agriculture executive heads from 50 states and trust territories for the betterment of American agriculture and general welfare of the people; promotes unity and efficiency in the administration of all agricultural statutes and regulations; develops, through teamwork, cooperation between the departments and person interested or engaged in agriculture. **Contact(s):** S. Mason Carbaugh (President), Robert Amato (Asst. Executive Secretary).

**H ▸ National Association of Substance Abuse Trainers & Educators**
See directory by same name.

**? ▸ National Association of Suggestion Systems**
230 N. Michigan Ave., #1200
Chicago, IL 60601 (312)372-1770
**Concern(s):** future; ideation. The NASS helps companies and government agencies operating or contemplating employee suggestion systems, and sponsors the "Suggester of the Year" competition. **Est.:** 1942.

**P ▸ National Association of Towns and Townships**
1522 K St. NW, #730
Washington, DC 20005 (202)737-5200
**Concern(s):** politics; agriculture; environment; recycling; rural communities; municipal. Produces a training package on recycling for community leaders, Why Waste a Second Chance?, which includes a guidebook, a video focusing on small community case studies and a user's guide to assist in conducting training sessions.

**E ▸ National Audubon Society**
950 3rd Ave.
New York, NY 10022 (212)832-3200
**Concern(s):** environment; energy; wildlife/endangered species; acid rain; land; water; natural resources; conservation; wetlands; air pollution; renewables; polar. Dedicated to: long-term protection and the wise use of wildlife, land, water, and other natural resources; the promotion of rational strategies, and other natural resources; the promotion of rational strategies for energy development and use, and to the protection of life from pollution, radiation, and toxic substances. Focuses on the interaction of population, resources and the environment and stresses renewable energy sources, wetlands, old-growth forests conservation, and clean air. **Other Resources:** See AUDUBON ACTIVIST newsletter and AUDUBON magazine. Projects, Saving

the Platte River; protecting the Arctic National Wildlife Refuge; Audubon Activist Network; Citizen's Acid Rain Monitoring Network; Expedition Institute; Population Program. **Est.:** 1905. **Dues:** $20/introductory offer. **Member:** Global Tomorrow Coalition. Hotline: (202)547-9017. **Contact(s):** Peter A. A. Berle (President). (212)546-9100. **Other:** 801 Pennsylvania Ave., SE, #301, Washington, DC 20003 Elizabeth Raisbeck , Vice President, Governmental Affairs. (202)547-9009.

✈ ◆ **National Audubon Society Expedition Institute**
Box 170
Readfield, ME 04355    (207)685-4333
**Affiliation:** National Audubon Society. **Concern(s):** education; environment; recreation; wildlife/endangered species; travel. A traveling education program stressing environmental education which offers year-long and semester expeditions proving undergraduate and high school students and alternative to traditional education. Students learn hiking, backpacking, cooking, outdoor living and group consensus decision making. Tuition ranges from $6,100 to $10,400. Exciting list of courses offered. **Fax:** (207)685-4333.

E ◆ **National Audubon Society Population Program**
666 Pennsylvania Ave. SE, 2nd floor
Washington, DC 20003  (202)547-9009
**Affiliation:** National Audubon Society. **Concern(s):** environment; demographics; feminism; family planning; population growth. Supports family planning assistance here and abroad; works' for adoption of a national population policy; testifies at congressional hearings on federal legislation to establish a mechanism for continuous monitoring of international trends in population, resources, and environment, and for providing our leaders with greater foresight capability; cooperates with private and public organizations. **Other Resources:** Publishes POPULATION PROGRAM ACTIVITY REPORT (monthly/bimonthly) and POPULATION Newsletter. Audiovisual and Print Resources list available. See Foreign Assistance Action Project. **Contact(s):** Patricia Baldi (Director).

P ◆ **National Black Caucus of Locally Elected Officials**
1301 Pennsylvania Ave. NW
Washington, DC 20004  (202)626-3120
**Affiliation:** Joint Center for Political and Economic Studies. **Concern(s):** politics; justice; law; minority rights. This organization is comprised of black elected officials. Their goal is to see that the minorities have more of an equal representation in government, both local and federal.

J ◆ **National Black Child Development Institute**
See BLACK CHILD ADVOCATE magazine.

H ◆ **National Black Organizations Against Alcohol & Drug Use**
22 Chapel St.
Brooklyn, NY 11201
**Concern(s):** health; urban; preventative medicine; substance abuse; ethnic concerns; drugs.

E ◆ **National Campaign Against Toxic Hazards**
1300 Connecticut Ave. NW
Washington, DC 20036  (202)857-5153
**Affiliation:** Citizen Action Fund. **Concern(s):** environment; hazardous/toxic waste; lobbying.

⚯ ◆ **National Campaign for a Peace Tax Fund**
2121 Decatur Pl. NW
Washington, DC 20008  (202)483-3751
**Concern(s):** peace; politics; economics; peace dividend; lobbying; war tax revolt. An organization working towards the passage of the Peace Tax Fund bill - which would mean that anyone morally opposed to war could have the current military percentage of his or her federal income tax redirected to a new Peace Tax Fund, spendable only for peacemaking policies. **Other Resources:** PEACE TAX FUND NEWSLETTER, free to members. **Fax:** (202)265-1297. **Contact(s):** Marian Franz (Executive Director).

A ◆ **National Catholic Rural Life Conference**
4625 NW Beaver Dr.
Des Moines, IA 50310    (515)270-2634
**Concern(s):** agriculture; spiritual; rural communities; faith. **Contact(s):** Joseph K. Fitzgerald.

H ◆ **National Caucus & Center on Black Aged**
1424 K St. NW, #500
Washington, DC 20005  (202)637-8400
**Concern(s):** health; justice; urban; ethnic concerns; seniors. **Contact(s):** Samuel J. Simmons.

E ◆ **The National Celebration of the Outdoors**
1250 24th St. NW, #500
Washington, DC 20037  (202)293-4800

**Affiliation:** World Wildlife Fund. **Concern(s):** environment; wilderness; recreation.

E ◆ **National Center for Atmospheric Research**
Box 3000
Boulder, CO 80307    (303)497-1000
**Concern(s):** environment; global warming.

♥ ◆ **National Center for Education in Maternal and Child Health**
See directories section for REACHING OUT and STARTING EARLY.

$ ◆ **National Center for Employee Ownership**
2201 Broadway, #807
Oakland, CA 94612-3024    (510)272-9461
**Concern(s):** economics; labor; demographics; worker ownership; workplace democracy. A private membership, information and research corporation established to provide reliable, objective and comprehensive information about employee ownership and participation. Nonprofit. **Contact(s):** Corey Rosen.

A ◆ **National Center for Food and Agricultural Policy**
See Resources for the Future.

H ◆ **National Center for Homeopathy**
See DIRECTORY OF UNITED STATES HOMEOPATHIC PRACTITIONERS.

J ◆ **National Center for Innovations in Corrections**
George Washington University
Washington, DC 20052  (202)994-1522
**Concern(s):** justice; future; ideation; prisons; reform; criminal system. A clearinghouse for creative thinking in an area of society in great need of creative thinking. **Contact(s):** Judith Schloegel (Director).

♥ ◆ **National Center for Prosecution of Child Abuse**
See NATIONAL DIRECTORY OF CHILD ABUSE PROSECUTORS.

J ◆ **National Center for the Protection of Children**
See DIRECTORY OF CHILD ABUSE.

J ◆ **National Center for Youth Law**
See YOUTH LAW NEWS (periodicals).

☯ ◆ **National Center For Appropriate Technology (NATAS)**
Box 2525
Butte, MT 59702    (800)428-2525
**Concern(s):** energy; education; agriculture; appropriate technology; conservation; science. NATAS is an information service which provides technical information and assistance on energy conservation and renewable energy technologies. It works with individuals and business, helping them implement specific projects as well as referring them to local assistance and contractors. Provides various resources, training and grants for low-cost, self-built, decent technology in energy, housing, agriculture and transportation for, but not exclusively, low-income persons. Nonprofit. **Est.:** 1976. **Contact(s):** George Everts. (406)494-4572. **Other:** 1212 New York Ave., Washington, DC 20335 Joseph F. Sedlak. (202)289-6657.

♥ ◆ **National Center For Missing & Exploited Children**
(703)235-3900
**Concern(s):** family; justice; child abuse; rape/sexual abuse; children. See PARENTAL KIDNAPPING: HOW TO PREVENT AN ABDUCTION AND WHAT TO DO IF YOUR CHILD IS ABDUCTED. Hotline: (800)843-5678.

S ◆ **National Charities Information Bureau**
See WISE GIVING GUIDE (periodicals).

J ◆ **National Child Nutrition Project**
1501 Cherry St.
Philadelphia, PA 19102  (215)496-9003
**Affiliation:** American Friends Service Committee. **Concern(s):** justice; health; demographics; spiritual; nutrition; hunger; poverty; children; interfaith. **Contact(s):** Sandra Sherman.

H ◆ **National Citizen's Coalition for Nursing Home Reform**
1224 M St. NW
Washington, DC 20005  (202)393-2018
**Concern(s):** health; justice; economics; seniors; constitutional rights; consumer protection. A coalition of 300 groups that seeks to improve the long-term health care system and quality of life for nursing home residents, educate and make heard the citizens and consumers affected by nursing home legislation, it also strives for improvement in work conditions for nurses aides and other workers. NCCNHR operates an information Clearinghouse referring callers to local groups. **Other Resources:** Publishes two periodicals, QUALITY CARE ADVOCATE and COLLATION. **Est.:** 1975.

M ◆ **National Citizens Committee For Broadcasting**
Box 12038
Washington, DC 20005  (202)462-2520
**Concern(s):** media; electronic democracy; broadcasting; film. This organization seeks to foster a more democratic and responsible communications system in America, based on the premise that the best means to achieve this goal is to increase direct citizen access to the means of communications. Programs are designed to promote increasing diversity, choices, and participation in all forms of media, with a growing emphasis on electronic warfare and emergency communications technology. **Est.:** 1967.

U ◆ **National Civic League**
See CIVITEX (Civic Information and Techniques Exchange).

E ◆ **National Clean Water Coalition**
1400 16th St. NW
Washington, DC 20036  (202)797-6886
**Concern(s):** environment; water; ocean/rivers. **Contact(s):** Deon Ferris.

F ◆ **National Clearinghouse on Marital and Date Rape**
2325 Oak St.
Berkeley, CA 94708    (510)548-1770
**Concern(s):** feminism; health; justice; rape/sexual abuse; sexism. A project of the former Women's Historic Resource Center, is an organization of consultants, residents, speakers, and resources for legislative and medical advocates, writers, the media, students, and campus and community people. **Contact(s):** Laura X.

M ◆ **National Coalition Against Censorship**
See BOOKS ON TRIAL: A SURVEY OF RECENT CASES.

♥ ◆ **National Coalition Against Domestic Violence**
Box 15127
Washington, DC 20003-0127    (202)638-6388
**Concern(s):** family; feminism; battered women; child abuse.

J ◆ **National Coalition Against the Death Penalty**
1501 Cherry St.
Philadelphia, PA 19102  (215)241-7118
**Affiliation:** American Friends Service Committee. **Concern(s):** justice; politics; death penalty; capital punishment; reform; criminal system; prisons. A coalition that is dedicated to ending capital punishment in the US.

A ◆ **National Coalition Against the Misuse of Pesticides**
701 E St. SE
Washington, DC 20003  (202)543-5450
**Concern(s):** agriculture; environment; health; public health; food production; hazardous/toxic waste; nutrition. A membership organization providing useful information on pesticides and alternatives to their use. The staff supports local action to promote independent scientific review of the dangers of pesticide exposure and carry out community organizing projects to promote alternative pest management. Focuses public attention on the serious public health, environmental and economic problems associated with the use and misuse of pesticides. **Other Resources:** See PESTICIDES AND YOU newsletter and NETWORK GUIDE OF ORGANIZATIONS. Nonprofit. **Dues:** $20/yr. **Member:** Environmental Federation of America. **Contact(s):** Jay Feldman (Executive Director).

⚯ ◆ **National Coalition Building Institutes**
See Upstate Coalition Builders.

E ◆ **The National Coalition for Marine Conservation**
Box 23298
Savannah, GA 31403    (912)234-8062
**Concern(s):** environment; ocean/rivers; conservation. The only national organization devoted exclusively to conserving ocean, fish, and protecting the marine environment for the benefit of all Americans. Four basic principles are: the long-term productivity of the ocean, for the benefit of all, should be the primary objective of marine conservation and management; conservation of all forms of marine life requires that we also protect the natural environments they need for survival; sound resource management based on scientific principle. **Other Resources:** Publishes the MARINE BULLETIN. **Est.:** 1973. **Contact(s):** Ken Hinman (Executive Director).

📖 ◆ **National Coalition of Alternative Community Schools**
58 Schoolhouse Rd.
Summertown, TN 38483(615)964-3670
**Affiliation:** National Association for Legal Support of Alternative Schools (NALSAS). **Concern(s):** education. The largest and most comprehensive network of innovative schools and educators in this country. NCACS members have been on the cutting edge of educa-

tional change since the organization's funding. Members include homeschoolers, independent schools, public school alternatives, colleges, educational resource centers and individuals throughout the US and in several foreign countries. **Other Resources:** Membership networks, regional and national conferences. See NATIONAL DIRECTORY, and NATIONAL COALITION NEWS. Nonprofit. **Est.:** 1975. **Dues:** $20/yr. includes News. **Contact(s):** Michael Traugot (National Office Coordinator), Mary Ellen Bowen (News Editor). **Other:** National Association for Legal Support of Alternative Schools (NALSAS), Box 2823, Santa Fe, NM 87504.

**M ▸ National Coalition on Television Violence**
Box 2157
Champaign, IL 61825 (310)278-5433
**Concern(s):** media; economics; media watch; responsibility; boycott. This coalition is against violence on television. Lists of advertisers and networks being targeted. Successfully boycotted FRIDAY THE 13TH/FREDDY'S NIGHTMARE — The coalition is concerned about the extreme brutality of these programs. Write for a list of advertisers and network being targeted. **Other Resources:** Publishes NCTV NEWS. **Contact(s):** Dr. Carole Lieberman (Chairperson/Research Director).

**J ▸ National Coalition to Abolish the Death Penalty**
See LIFELINES (periodicals).

**J ▸ National Coalition to Ban Hand Guns**
100 Maryland Ave. NE
Washington, DC 20002 (202)544-7190
**Concern(s):** justice; politics; gun control; lobbying; legislative; criminal system. A coalition of people and groups who want to see a ban or, at least, better control on handguns. (Press Contact). (202)547-1690.

**H ▸ National Coalition to Stop Food Irradiation**
(800)EAT-SAFE
**Concern(s):** health; environment; agriculture; nutrition; hazardous/toxic waste; food production. A national organization founded in response to the increasing threat of food irradiation, a technology designed to use radioactive waste products to extend the shelf life of meats, grains, produce, herbs and spices. As a result of this exposure, nutrients are depleted and new chemicals are formed in the food (many toxic and carcinogenic). The risk of nuclear accidents is also greatly increased. It works on both political and grassroots levels to educate and legislate on these issues. **Other Resources:** See FOOD IRRADIATION ALERT! newsletter. There are over 90 chapters, affiliated groups, and supporting organizations worldwide. Nonprofit. **Est.:** 1984. **Contact(s):** Mary Carroll Randall.

**$ ▸ National Commission for Economic Conversion & Disarmament**
Box 15025
Washington, DC 20003 (202)462-0091
**Concern(s):** economics; peace; economic conversion; disarmament; peace dividend. **Other Resources:** Publishes THE NEW ECONOMY newsletter. **Office:** 1801 18th St. NW Washington, DC 20009. **Contact(s):** Seymour Melman (Program Director), Jonathan Feldman (National Coordinator).

**J ▸ National Committee Against Repressive Legislation**
236 Massachusetts Ave. NE, #406
Washington, DC 20002 (202)543-7659
**Concern(s):** justice; politics; constitutional rights; law; freedom of expression. Established to educate the public and Congress about pending federal legislation which infringes upon First Amendment rights of free speech, press, assembly, and association, and to mobilize citizens' actions to oppose such legislation or to support legislation which expands and protects the right to freedom of political thought. **Est.:** 1960. **Contact(s):** Kit Gage.

**✍ ▸ National Committee for Citizens**
See Network, For Public School.

**U ▸ National Committee for Full Employment**
306 E. 12th St., #819
Kansas City, MO 64106-2418 (816)842-5177
**Affiliation:** Full Employment Action Council. **Concern(s):** urban; politics; labor; inner city; jobs; unemployment. Works with inner city programs to help end unemployment in the US. **Other:** Full Employment Council, 1710 Paseo, Kansas City, MO 64108.

**$ ▸ National Committee for Responsive Philanthropy**
2001 S St. NW, #620
Washington, DC 20009 (202)387-9177
**Concern(s):** economics; demographics; politics; alternative consumer; lobbying; philanthropy. Formed to improve the accountability and accessibility of philanthropic institutions and to increase their responsiveness to groups which are working to achieve social justice, equal opportunity and fair representation for disenfranchised people in our economic and governmental systems (organizations advocating for minorities, women, poor people and the elderly and for consumer, environmental and other public interest causes). **Other Resources:** See RESPONSIVE PHILANTHROPY newsletter. **Contact(s):** Robert O. Bothwell (Executive Director), Steve Paprocki (Director, Field Operations).

**S ▸ National Conference of Catholic Bishops**
3211 4th St. NE
Washington, DC 20017-1194 (202)541-3000
**Concern(s):** spiritual; peace; justice; politics; faith; activism; lobbying. One of three departments of the USCC, the national public policy agency of the US Catholic Bishops. The department reflects the bishops' concern for justice by applying the principle of Catholic social teaching to issues in the public forum and developing policy positions for adoption by the bishop body. The department has two offices: Domestic Social Development and International Justice and Peace. The first delves in economy, labor, federal budget, voting rights, energy, health, housing. **Other Resources:** Bimonthly newsletter. **Contact(s):** Rev. Robert N. Lynch (General Secretary), Fr. J. Bryan Hehir. (202)659-6797.

**P ▸ National Conference of State Legislatures**
444 N. Capitol St. NW, #500
Washington, DC 20001 (202)624-5400
**Concern(s):** politics; law. **Contact(s):** Irv Stolberg.

**$ ▸ National Congress for Community Economic Development**
1875 Connecticut Ave. NW
Washington, DC 20009 (202)234-5009
**Concern(s):** economics; demographics; justice; energy; community self-reliance; homelessness; hunger; poverty; social ecology; self-determination. The only national association of community-based organizations active in economic development. Major purposes are to increase resources available to community development corporations and help them utilize these resources effectively. The activities NCCED undertakes to meet these goals includes: policy development, communications, information sharing, network development, conferences and applied research contracts. NCCED is controlled entirely by membership organizations. **Est.:** 1970. **Contact(s):** Robert Zdeneck (President).

**F ▸ National Congress for Men**
See Directory by same name.

**T ▸ National Congress for Puerto Rican Rights**
See UNIDAD BORINQUENA (periodicals).

**J ▸ National Congress of American Indians**
900 Pennsylvania Ave. SE
Washington, DC 20004 (202)546-9404
**Concern(s):** justice; politics; Native Americans; lobbying. **Contact(s):** Suzan Harjo.

**F ▸ National Congress of Neighborhood Women**
1129 Catherine St.
Brooklyn, NY 11211 (718)388-6666
**Concern(s):** feminism; politics; empowerment; grassroots organizing. Established to provide a voice for poor and working class neighborhood women's concerns. To strengthen women's leadership role in their neighborhoods by giving support, information, training, and recognition for their work. To encourage an emerging women's consciousness with the multi-racial character of the communities in which they live. (Contact Institute for Social Ecology, Plainfield, VT). **Other Resources:** Publishes monthly newsletter and NEIGHBORHOOD WOMEN QUARTERLY. **Est.:** 1975. **Contact(s):** Sandy Love.

**$ ▸ National Consumer Law Center**
236 Massachusetts Ave. NE
Washington, DC 20002 (202)543-6060
**Concern(s):** economics; energy; politics; consumer rights; appropriate technology. A corporation working in the consumer and energy fields and seeking to further the interests of low-income consumers. Specifically, the Center provides technical assistance, publications and training related to low-income energy and consumer issues. Some publications are distributed by the National Clearinghouse for Legal Services. Publications list available. **Other Resources:** See ENERGY UPDATE and NCLC REPORTS newsletters. Nonprofit. **Est.:** 1969. **Contact(s):** Charles E. Hill. **Other:** 11 Beacon St., Boston, MA 02108. (617)523-8010.

**$ ▸ National Consumers League**
815 15th St. NW, #516
Washington, DC 20005 (202)639-8140
**Concern(s):** economics; consumer rights. Established to ensure consumer representation for citizens before government and industry decision-makers. **Other Resources:** NCL BULLETIN. **Est.:** 1899. **Contact(s):** Linda Colodner.

**$ ▸ National Cooperative Business Association**
1401 New York Ave. NW, #1100
Washington, DC 20001 (202)638-6222
**Concern(s):** economics; labor; trade; cooperatives. A national membership and trade association representing America's cooperative business community, from small buying clubs to Fortune 500 companies. **Other Resources:** See directory, FINDING CO-OPS. **Member:** Co-op America. **Fax:** (202)638-1374. **Contact(s):** Robert O. Bothwell (Executive Director), Peggy Sheehan.

**T ▸ National Council For International Health**
1701 K St. NW
Washington, DC 20006 (202)833-0070
**Concern(s):** Third World; health; hunger; poverty; development. "Our goal is to improve health worldwide by actively focusing scarce resources on life and death issues, increasing US awareness and response to international health needs, and by providing vigorous leadership to achieve this goal. We exist to serve the underdeveloped world, but we also help to apply what is learned abroad to serve the underprivileged in urban and rural areas of the US." NCIH is funded through grants from private individuals, foundations, corporations, and government. **Other Resources:** See DIRECTORY OF US-BASED AGENCIES INVOLVED IN INTERNATIONAL HEALTH ASSISTANCE with more than 500 member organizations listed. Nonprofit. **Est.:** 1971. **Dues:** $60, $40 student. **Circ.:** 2M. **Fax:** (202)833-0075. **Contact(s):** Richard McHale (Media Manager), Julian Kilker (Assistant Comm. Manager). (202)833-5900.

**F ▸ National Council For Research on Women**
Sara Delano Roosevelt Memorial House
47-49 E. 65th St.
New York, NY 10021 (212)570-5001
**Concern(s):** feminism; research. A coalition of 60+ centers/organizations that support/conduct feminist research, policy analysis, and educational programs, formed to bridge traditional distinctions among scholarship, policy, and action programs, it works to strengthen ties with other national and international organizations and coalitions. Member centers, affiliates, and sponsored projects link 10,000+ women and men scholars and practitioners worldwide, serving the academic community, public policy makers and the public. **Other Resources:** Newsletter, WOMEN'S RESEARCH NETWORK NEWS. See DIRECTORY OF NATIONAL WOMEN'S ORGANIZATIONS; DIRECTORY OF WOMEN'S MEDIA; OPPORTUNITIES FOR RESEARCH & STUDY; WOMEN'S MAILING LIST DIRECTORY; INTERNATIONAL CENTERS FOR RESEARCH ON WOMEN. **Est.:** 1981. **Fax:** (212)570-5380.

**J ▸ National Council of Churches Human Rights Office**
475 Riverside Dr.
New York, NY 10115 (212)870-2916
**Concern(s):** justice; education; spiritual; faith; global understanding. Four priorities: human rights defense and advocacy; network (building); constituency education; and public outreach. **Other Resources:** Periodicals, MARK-UP, ACTION ALERT!, and ASIA & PACIFIC UPDATE. Also, Church World Service and Friendship Press. **Other:** National Council of Churches (National Office), 110 Maryland Ave. NE, Washington, DC 20002. William Fore , Director. (202)544-2350.

**J ▸ National Council of La Raza**
810 1st St. NE
Washington, DC 20006 (202)289-1380
**Concern(s):** justice; health; politics; minority rights; lobbying; grassroots organizing; public health; AIDS. A resource and information clearinghouse, coordinating body, and funding source for Hispanic organizations. It has 120 affiliations in 21 states. Does research and advocacy in support of all Hispanic minorities, and provides technical assistance and programmatic support to Hispanic communities-based organizations. **Other Resources:** Seeks to expand and improve AIDS education and services for the Hispanic community. It works with 80 La Raza affiliates nationwide to disseminate AIDS educational materials. Publishes AGENDA bimonthly. **Contact(s):** Charles Kamaski. (202)293-4680. **Other:** AIDS Project, 20 F St. NW, Washington, DC 20001. Norma Lopez. (202)628-9600.

**J ▸ National Council of Negro Women**
1211 Connecticut Ave. NW
Washington, DC 20036 (202)659-0006
**Concern(s):** justice; feminism; discrimination; minority rights; racism; sexism. **Contact(s):** Dorothy Height (President), Gayla Cook.

**H ▸ National Council of Senior Citizens**
925 15th St. NW
Washington, DC 20005 (202)347-8800

**Concern(s):** health; politics; seniors; lobbying. This council fights for the rights of seniors in our society today. **Other Resources:** See SENIOR CITIZEN NEWS (periodicals). **Contact(s):** Lawrence Smedley. (202)624-9500.

**F ♦ National Council of Women of USA**
777 UN Plaza
New York, NY 10017     (212)697-1278
**Concern(s):** feminism; politics; sexism; lobbying; equal rights.
**Contact(s):** Mira Berman.

**H ♦ The National Council on Death and Dying**
250 West 57th St.
New York, NY 10107     (212)246-6973
**Concern(s):** health; death/dying. Encourages everyone to right-up a Living Will in order to avoid the pain of being kept alive with tubes. This Council was the result of the Society for the Right to Die and Concern for Dying merging in order to form the largest patients' rights agency of this kind in the US. **Other Resources:** Membership includes up to four copies of Living Will Declarations, each designed for your particular state. Nonprofit. **Dues:** $20-100/yr. **Contact(s):** Evan R. Collins (President).

**♥ ♦ National Council on Family Relations**
See FAMILY RESOURCES DATABASE (directories).

**H ♦ National Council on the Aging**
409 3rd St. SW
Washington, DC 20024  (202)479-1200
**Concern(s):** health; seniors. **Contact(s):** Dr. Daniel Thursz, Betty R. Ransom.

**✍ ♦ National Education Association**
1201 16th St. NW
Washington, DC 20036  (202)833-4000
**Concern(s):** education; politics. Works to elevate the character and advance the interest of the teaching profession and to promote the cause of education in the US. **Est.:** 1857. **Contact(s):** Keith Geiger (President), Don Cameron (Executive Director).

**J ♦ National Emergency Civil Liberties Committee**
See RIGHTS and BILL OF RIGHTS JOURNAL (periodicals).

**☉ ♦ National Energy Specialist Association**
518 NW Gordon
Topeka, KS 66608     (913)232-1702
**Concern(s):** energy; conservation. A technical assistance association of companies producing energy conservation equipment. NESA mainly answers questions about energy conservation technology, its construction and availability. **Other Resources:** Also publishes a quarterly journal and a monthly newsletter on energy conservation.

**E ♦ National Environmental Health Association**
720 S. Colorado Blvd.
South Tower, #970
Denver, CO 80222
**Concern(s):** environment; health; research; analysis; public health. A professional society of persons who promote educational and professional curriculum for colleges and universities, holds conferences, conducts national professional registration and continuing education programs. Works also with governmental public health agencies, public health agencies and environmental health education, and industry. **Other Resources:** Publishes JOURNAL OF ENVIRONMENTAL HEALTH. **Dues:** $15-$350, inquire.

**A ♦ National Family Farm Coalition**
80 F St. NW , #714
Washington, DC 20001  (202)737-2215
**Concern(s):** agriculture; economics; demographics; boycott; family farm. A clearinghouse for information on small and moderate sized family farm issues; advocacy and lobbying for the organizations that represent small and moderate sized family farmers. Send SASE for a list of producers and stores that support a Bovine Growth Hormone boycott. **Contact(s):** Susan Denzer. **Other:** Box 414, Circle, MT 59215. (406)485-3324.

**F ♦ National Family Planning and Reproductive**
   **Health Association**
122 C St. NW, #380
Washington, DC 20001-2109     (202)628-3535
**Concern(s):** feminism; demographics; population growth; family planning; pro-choice. A coalition of over 1,000 family planning providers, state-county-local health departments, hospital-based clinics, affiliates of PPF of America, family planning councils, independent free-standing clinics, individual health care professionals and consumers. This network provides reproductive health care services to over five million people, and is dedicated to improving and expanding the delivery of family planning and reproductive health services and programs. **Other Resources:** NFPRHA NEWS and NEPHRA ALERT. **Est.:** 1971. **Contact(s):** Scott R. Swirling (Executive Director), Ellan

Lapidas. (202)-7742.

**A ♦ National Farm Worker Ministry**
Box 302
Delano, CA 93216     (805)725-7445
**Concern(s):** agriculture; labor; demographics; health; farm workers; hazardous/toxic waste; food production; occupational safety. An experienced ecumenical organization with seventy years of service to farm workers. It is recognized as the church's foremost advocate for farm worker justice, especially among those affected by toxic pesticides. **Contact(s):** Pat Drydyk, OSF (Executive Director).

**A ♦ National Farmers Organization**
777 N. Capitol St. NE
Washington, DC 20002  (202)371-0711
**Concern(s):** agriculture; labor; politics; farm workers; farm policy; lobbying; family farms. **Other:** 720 Davis Ave, Corning, IA 50841. (515)322-3131.

**A ♦ National Farmers Union**
10065 Harvard, 7th Fl.
Denver, CO 80251     (303)337-5500
**Concern(s):** agriculture; politics. Believes that the soil, water, forest and other natural resources of the nation should be used and conserved in a manner to pass these resources on undiminished to future generations and that publicly and privately owned land and resources should be administered in the interest of all the public. **Other Resources:** Publishes the NATIONAL FARMERS UNION WASHINGTON newsletter. **Est.:** 1902. **Contact(s):** Leland H. Swenson (President), William Owen (Treasurer). **Other:** Legislative Office, 600 Maryland Ave. # 202 W, Washington, DC 20024 Michael V. Dunn , Vice-President/Legislative. (202)554-1600.

**G ♦ National Federation of Parents & Friends of**
   **Gays**
See PARENTS & FRIENDS OF GAYS - INTERNATIONAL DIRECTORY.

**E ♦ National Fish and Wildlife Foundation**
18 & C St. NW, #2556
Washington, DC 20024  (202)208-3040
**Concern(s):** environment; wildlife/endangered species; oceans/ rivers. Goal is to protect wetlands and restore leadership training for wildlife professionals while striving to develop partnerships between conservation organizations, public agencies and industry to benefit the nation's fish, wildlife and plant resources. **Other Resources:** Limited internships in DC. **Contact(s):** Charles H. Collins (Executive Director).

**A ♦ National Food and Energy Council**
409 Vandiver West, #202
Columbia, MO 65202     (314)875-7155
**Concern(s):** agriculture; energy; health; food production; food distribution; nutrition. **Contact(s):** Richard Hiatt.

**E ♦ National Forest Action Center**
900 17th St. NW
Washington, DC 20006  (202)833-2300
**Affiliation:** Wilderness Society. **Concern(s):** environment; forestry. **Other Resources:** Publishes bimonthly FOREST ISSUES BULLETIN. **Contact(s):** Jay Watson.

**P ♦ National Forum Foundation**
107 2nd St. NE
Washington, DC 20002  (202)543-3515
**Concern(s):** politics; labor; media; analysis; unions; media watch; press. Provides the nation's press with the views of national experts on timely public issues. It is funded as a public service by AFSCME, the public employee union. **Contact(s):** Mary O'Driscoll.

**G ♦ National Gay & Lesbian Task Force**
1734 14th St. NW
Washington, DC 20009  (202)332-6483
**Concern(s):** justice; gay/lesbian. A variety of publications concerning hate crimes against gays and lesbians.

**✍ ♦ National Geographic Society**
17 & M St. NW
Washington, DC 20036  (202)857-7000
**Concern(s):** education; environment; environment; wildlife/endangered species; global understanding. Supports important worldwide research and exploration, such as Cousteau, Goodall, Leakey and Ballard; new programs to improve geographic literacy among youngsters; develops films, filmstrips, and software, and other materials throughout the US and Canada. **Other Resources:** Publishes National Geographic WORLD and National Geographic TRAVELER. Also award-winning PBS TV Specials and EXPLORER, a weekly program. NATIONAL GEOGRAPHIC MAGAZINE for free with membership. See Kid's Network (media). **Dues:** $21/yr. **Contact(s):** Gilbert M. Grosvenor (President), Melvin M. Payne (Chairman). (800)638-4077.

**✍ ♦ National Geographic Society Educational**
   **Services**
Dept. 88
Washington, DC 20036  (800)368-2728
**Concern(s):** education; youth; global understanding. National Geographic Society's new program for improving the geographic literacy of America's youngsters. (201)628-9111.

**P ♦ National Governors' Association**
444 N. Capitol St. NW
Washington, DC 20001  (202)624-5300
**Concern(s):** politics; economics; law; budget; planning; economic conversion. These elected officials have presented plans to the federal government that offer solutions to our decaying infrastructures. They call for prioritizing funds and taking some of the tax burdens off the states or the citizens in order to do so. As long as no one is listening in the Whitehouse, these plans are useless. **Contact(s):** John DeWitt.

**H ♦ National Health Federation**
21 West Foothill Blvd.
Monrovia, CA 91016-2147  (818)357-2181
**Concern(s):** health; justice; national health. This organization works in the defense of human or civil rights throughout this country in the health profession.

**H ♦ National Health Law Program**
See HEALTH ADVOCATE newsletter.

**✍ ♦ National Home Education Research Institute**
25 West Cremona St.
Seattle, WA 98119
**Concern(s):** education; alternative; research. Engages in educational research with a focus on home education. Aims to educate the public about home education and to assist home educators in their efforts. Supports scholarly research and publishes various materials in the field of home education.

**H ♦ National Hospice Organization**
See GUIDE TO THE NATION'S HOSPICES (directories).

**J ♦ National Housing Institute**
See SHELTERFORCE (periodicals).

**J ♦ National Institute Against Prejudice and**
   **Violence**
31 South Green St.
Baltimore, MD 21201     (301)328-5170
**Concern(s):** justice; racism; discrimination; minority rights. A research and policy organization focusing on the study of violence and intimidation motivated by prejudice. It has published many useful studies about racist programming on cable TV. An excellent source of information on current policy issues such as hate-crimes legislation.

**⚖ ♦ The National Institute for Dispute Resolution**
1901 L St. NW, #600
Washington, DC 20036  (202)466-4764
**Concern(s):** peace; conflict resolution; analysis. Acts as a clearinghouse for conflict resolution and management programs.

**P ♦ National Institute for Science, Law and Public**
   **Policy**
1424 16th St. NW, #105
Washington, DC 20036  (202)462-8800
**Concern(s):** politics; health; agriculture; consumer protection; law. **Other Resources:** See HEALTHY HARVEST directory. **Contact(s):** Deborah Preston.

**E ♦ National Institute for Urban Wildlife**
10921 Trotting Ridge Way
Columbia, MD 21044-2831  (301)596-3311
**Concern(s):** environment; urban; wildlife/endangered species; sustainability. A scientific and educational organization dedicated to wildlife research, management and conservation education · programs and activities that will encourage the discovery of practical procedures for maintaining or enhancing the wildlife species in urban, suburban and developing areas. **Other Resources:** See WILDLIFE RESERVES AND CORRIDORS IN THE URBAN ENVRIONMENT (directories). **Dues:** $25/yr.

**✈ ♦ National Institute for Work & Learning**
1255 23rd St. NW
Washington, DC 20037  (202)862-8845
**Concern(s):** education; Third World; travel; development.

**H ♦ National Institute of Adult Daycare**
See DIRECTORY OF ADULT DAY CARE IN AMERICA.

**♿ ♦ National Institute of Disability & Rehabilitative**
   **Services**
See DIRECTORY OF NATIONAL INFORMATION SOURCES ON HANDICAPPING CONDITIONS AND RELATED SERVICES.

**H ▸ National Institute of Mental Health**
See MENTAL HEALTH DIRECTORY.

**H ▸ National Institute of Nutritional Education**
5600 S. Syracuse Circle, #205
Greenwood Village, CO 80111
**Concern(s):** health; education; nutrition.

**H ▸ National Institute on Aging Information Center**
See SELF-CARE AND SELF-HELP GROUPS FOR THE ELDERLY: A DIRECTORY.

**H ▸ National Institute on Drug Abuse**
See NATIONAL DIRECTORY OF DIRECTORY OF DRUG ABUSE AND ALCOHOLISM TREATMENT AND PREVETION PROGRAMS.

**$ ▸ National Insurance Consumer Organization**
344 Commerce St.
Alexandria, VA 22314 (703)549-8050
**Concern(s):** economics; consumer rights. Established to educate insurance consumers. Seeks to reform insurance institutions and provide expert advise to consumers and testimony before regulators and courts. **Est.:** 1980. **Contact(s):** Robert Hunter (President).

**☮ ▸ National Interreligious Service Board for Conscientious Objectors**
1601 Connecticut Ave. NW, #750
Washington, DC 20009 (202)483-4510
**Concern(s):** peace; spiritual; interfaith; anti-draft. Sponsored by a broad coalition of religious groups to aid conscientious objectors. Provides attorneys for those needing legal counsel. **Other Resources:** Publishes a newsletter, THE REPORTER FOR CONSCIENCE' SAKE?

**☮ ▸ The National Jobs With Peace Campaign**
76 Summer St.
Boston, MA 02110 (617)338-5783
**Concern(s):** peace; politics; labor; peace dividend; economic conversion; jobs. Campaign designed to convert the huge military job structure to one of peace. **Other Resources:** See CAMPAIGN REPORT, a newsletter. **Contact(s):** Ann Wilson (National Co-chair), Jill Nelson (Executive Director).

**T ▸ National Labor Committee in Support of Human Rights in El Salvador**
15 Union Square W
New York, NY 10003 (212)242-0700
**Affiliation:** Amalgamated Clothing & Textile Workers Union. **Concern(s):** Third World; justice; labor; Central America; unions. This labor committee attempts to show support of the establishment of human rights in El Salvador. **Contact(s):** Dave Dyson, Charles Kernaghan 732-5411.

**A ▸ National Land for People**
People, Food and Land Foundation
35751 Oak Spring Drive
Tollhouse, CA 93667 (209)855-3710
**Affiliation:** People, Food and Land Foundation. **Concern(s):** agriculture; environment; health; family farms; food production; rural communities. Established to preserve and expand family farm opportunities and to develop a more democratic, nutritious and ecologically sound food system. The elements of NLP's spiral strategy are: 1) public policies favoring a small farm economy, 2) economic organization of small farmers through distribution and marketing, 3) non-chemical, arid land growing practices for small farmers, 4) low-tech energy structures and adaptations, 5) organization of and assistance to food co-ops and 6) rural land trusts. **Contact(s):** George Ballis.

**P ▸ National Lawyers Guild**
55 Avenue of the Americas
New York, NY 10013 (212)966-5000
**Concern(s):** politics; justice; lobbying; social justice. A national membership organization of over 7000 legal practitioners. The guild provides legal support for virtually every struggle in this country for economic, social and environmental justice. The guild is considered the conscience of the US bar. **Other Resources:** Publishes periodicals GUILD NOTES and ON WATCH by their Military Law Task Force. **Est.:** 1937. **Contact(s):** Michael Cowan. **Other:** 853 Broadway #1705, New York, NY 10003. Nicholas G. Sileo. (212)260-1360.

**P ▸ National League of Cities**
1301 Pennsylvania Ave. NW
Washington, DC 20004 (202)626-3000
**Concern(s):** politics; peace; grassroots organizing; municipal. This is a coalition of cities working for the interests of the local area over the national. It believes in more autonomy from the federal system yet, maintaining federal assistance. **Contact(s):** Alan Beals (Executive Director), Douglas Peterson.

**✍ ▸ National Learning Foundation**
Box 405
Vienna, VA 22183
**Concern(s):** education; future; ideation.

**J ▸ National Legal Aid and Defender Association**
1625 K St. NW
Washington, DC 20006 (202)452-0620
**Concern(s):** justice; reform; constitutional rights; social justice; criminal system. Established to promote, advocate, and assure high quality legal services to poor persons in civil and criminal cases. **Other Resources:** See NLADA CORNERSTONE (periodicals). **Est.:** 1911.

**J ▸ National Low Income Housing Coalition**
1012 14th St. NW, #1006
Washington, DC 20005-3406 (202)544-2544
**Affiliation:** Low Income Housing Information Services. **Concern(s):** justice; demographics; homelessness; housing; hunger; poverty; housing. Established to provide decent housing, suitable environments, adequate neighborhoods and freedom of housing choice for low income people. The coalition works toward these goals through lobbying Congress and the Administration for better, sufficiently funded housing programs and through production publications to inform people of housing legalities. It is the foremost advocacy group for low income housing. **Est.:** 1974. **Contact(s):** Kate Crawford (Associate Director). (202)662-1530.

**H ▸ National Minority AIDS Council**
300 I St. NE, #400
Washington, DC 20003 (202)544-1076
**Concern(s):** health; justice; public health; AIDS; minority rights. A coalition of local organizations dealing with AIDS in minority communities. Focuses on empowerment issues and assists community organizations in locating educational and training resources. It publishes monthly reports for its members and others. **Contact(s):** Lynelle Johnson.

**S ▸ National Mission For Church and Society**
Episcopal Church
815 2nd Ave.
New York, NY 10017 (212)867-8400
**Affiliation:** Episcopal Church. **Concern(s):** spiritual; peace; justice; demographics; politics; faith; lobbying; hunger; homelessness; social justice. Public Ministries is a part of the National Mission for Church and Society of the Episcopal Church. Public Ministries develop action alerts and programs in response to social policy decisions of the Church's General Convention and Executive Council. Offices include: Jubilee Ministries; Peace and Justice; Hunger; Ministry on Aging; Social and Specialized Ministries, Housing; Coalition for Human Needs; and, the Washington Office of the Episcopal Church. **Other Resources:** See THE WITNESS; THE EPISCOPALIAN; THE EPISCOPAL PEACE FELLOWSHIP NEWSLETTER (periodicals). See, also, Episcopal Church Public Policy Network and Episcopal Peace Fellowship. (800)228-0515. (800)334-7626. **Other:** Episcopal Church Center, 110 Maryland Ave. NE, Washington, DC 20002. (202)547-7300.

**J ▸ National Native American Co-op**
Box 5000
San Carlos, AZ 85550
**Concern(s):** justice; economics; cooperatives; Native Americans. Events, trading posts, pow-wows, media, tribes, brochures, etc. Forward SASE for American Indian information packets. **Other Resources:** See NATIVE AMERICAN DIRECTORY.

**S ▸ National Network of Grantmakers**
See GRANTMAKERS GUIDE; A FUNDING SOURCE BOOK.

**F ▸ National Organization for Men Against Sexism**
c/o Our Town Family Center
Box 26665
Tucson, AZ 85726 (602)881-0991
**Concern(s):** feminism; men's liberation. Formerly National Organization for Men (1981) and National Organization of Changing Men (1984). Yearly conferences explore men's options in solidarity with the women's, gay, civil rights, and other progressive liberation movements. **Other Resources:** See CHANGING MEN magazine. **Est.:** 1990.

**E ▸ National Organization for River Sports**
314 N. 20th St.
Box 6847
Colorado Springs, CO 80904 (719)473-2466
**Concern(s):** environment; recreation; rivers; preservation. Goals: To fight for access rights for river runners that are being placed in jeopardy by governmental regulations and preservation of the few remaining whitewater rivers from dams and other development. **Dues:** $15/yr.

**F ▸ National Organization for Women**
1000 16th St. NW
Washington, DC 20036 (202)331-0066
**Concern(s):** feminism; empowerment; equal rights; law; pro-choice. The nation's largest organization solely devoted to advancing women's rights and a major leader in the fight against those who seek to outlaw abortion, vandalize clinics and terrorize patients and medical staff. NOW played a major role in abortion rights candidate's electoral victories in three states and organized two of the largest abortion rights marches in American history in a single year. Other issues include the Equal Rights Amendment, day care, health care, and violence against women. **Other Resources:** Publishes NATIONAL NOW TIMES and maintains a Legal Defense and Education Fund. **Contact(s):** Molly Yard (President).

**E ▸ National Outdoor Leadership School**
Box AA
Lander, WY 82520 (307)332-6973
**Concern(s):** environment; education. Teacher of wilderness skills and leadership. Wrote "Soft Paths," about minimum impact camping, as well as other books. To order "Soft Paths," contact Stackpole Books at (800) 732-3669. **Publisher:** Stackpole Books. **Member:** Co-op America.

**H ▸ National Parents Resource Institute For Drug Education**
Y00 Edgewood Ave., #1002
Atlanta, GA 30303 (404)651-2548
**Affiliation:** Robert W. Woodruff Volunteer Service Center. **Concern(s):** health; preventative medicine; drug/alcohol; volunteers. This organization uses discussion groups, panels, forums, lectures and any other media to try to help educate people on the dangers of drugs.

**E ▸ National Parks and Conservation Association**
1776 Massachusetts Ave. NW
Washington, DC 20036 (202)223-6722
**Concern(s):** environment; media; natural resources; acid rain; wildlife/endangered species; conservation; volunteers. Has been fighting - and winning - battles for the integrity and survival of the National Parks every years since. Now more than 50,000 members strong, the NPCA is still the only private, citizen-funded organization devoted to protecting, promoting, and improving all our National Parks. Works to protect the park system from acid rain, unwise development, raid on natural resources, and from overuse, as well as conservation of wildlife within those parks. Sponsors special outdoor events. **Other Resources:** Publishes NATIONAL PARKS magazine, and other materials. Internship available and volunteers needed. **Est.:** 1919. **Dues:** $25/yr. **Member:** Environmental Federation of America. (800)NAT-PARK. **Contact(s):** Paul C. Pritchard (President).

**☮ ▸ National Peace Institute Foundation**
1835 K St. NW
Washington, DC 20006 (202)223-1770
**Concern(s):** peace; media; politics; lobbying; conflict resolution. It works with local groups to promote conflict resolution and peace and sponsor events. Led the citizen effort in the formation of the US Institute of Peace. A leader in educating the public in these issues. Includes a national network of 5 affiliated regional councils; a computer conference to improve global information exchanges; development of an educational package consisting of five public TV programs dealing with all aspect of peace from the family to international issues. **Other Resources:** See DIRECTORY OF CONFLICT RESOLUTION RESOURCES and PEACE INSTITUTE REPORTER (periodicals). Also, Alliance for Our Common Future **Est.:** 1982. **Contact(s):** Kathleen J. Lansing (Acting Director), Thomas C. Westropp (Chairman). (800)237-3223. **Other:** Box 39994, Washington, DC 20077-5085.

**A ▸ National Pesticide Telecommunication Network**
Texas Tech University
Thompson Hall, Rm. S129
Lubbock, TX 79430 (806)743-3091
**Concern(s):** agriculture; health; pesticides; hazardous/toxic waste; consumer protection. Provides to the public vital information on pesticide use and toxicology. Hotline: (800)858-7378.

**H ▸ National Prevention Network**
444 N. Capitol St. NW, #520
Washington, DC 20001
**Concern(s):** health; preventative medicine; substance abuse. **Other Resources:** See NATIONAL PREVENTION NETWORK — DIRECTORY.

**☮ ▸ National Priorities Project (NPP)**
See NATIONAL PRIORITIES ACTION PACKET (directories).

**✍ ▸ National PTA**
700 Rush St.
Chicago, IL 60611 (312)787-0977
**Concern(s):** education; family.

J ▶ **National Puerto Rican Coalition**
1700 K St. NW
Washington, DC 20006 (202)223-3915
**Concern(s):** justice; diversity; minority rights. See DIRECTORY OF PUERTO RICAN ORGANIZATIONS.

P ▶ **National Rainbow Coalition**
2033 M St. NW
Washington, DC 20036 (202)728-1180
**Concern(s):** politics; peace; justice; third party; law; lobbying; peace dividend. A broad-based grassroots movement uniting people from any class, race, religion, region, sex, and sexual orientation. Founded by Rev. Jesse Jackson, its goal is to reduce US military spending and US-sponsored conflict in Central America and Middle East, and achieve democracy in South Africa; defend the rights of women, minorities, and lesbians and gays; and meet our nation's needs for education, housing, employment, health and child care, drug education, treatment and interdiction. **Est.:** 1984. **Contact(s):** Jack O'Dell, Patricia McGurk and Jesse Jackson, Founder.

E ▶ **National Recycling Coalition**
1101 30th St. NW, #305
Washington, DC 20007 (202)625-6406
**Concern(s):** environment; recycling; waste management. A coalition of recycling industries and groups that sponsors an annual conference and produces a list of relevant publications. **Other:** 45 Rockefeller Plaza, Room 2350, New York, NY 10020. (212)765-1800.

E ▶ **National Recycling Congress**
Box 10540
Portland, OR 97210
**Concern(s):** environment; recycling.

❂ ▶ **National Research Center**
National Association of Home Builders
400 Prince Georges Center Blvd.
Upper Marlboro, MD 20772 (301)249-4000
**Concern(s):** energy. Provides list of architects who design and contractors who build energy-efficient homes.

✌ ▶ **National Resistance Committee**
Box 42488
San Francisco, CA 94142 (415)824-0214
**Concern(s):** peace; anti-draft. The NRC organizes, encourages, and supports resistance to selective service registration, reinstatement of the draft, and "national youth service." Our activities include advocacy of non-registration and other forms of non-compliance, demonstrations, civil disobedience, lobbying, networking resisters and resistance groups, producing and distributing literature, and speaking at workshops and events. **Other Resources:** RESISTANCE NEWS (irregular), literature, electronic distribution of resource material via Peacenet, speakers/workshop facilitators Bureau, legal and counseling information and referrals. **Est.:** 1980. **E-Network:** PeaceNet. **ID:** 'mwehle'. **Contact(s):** Edward Hasbrouck, Matt Nicodemus (Organizers). (707)826-7033.

P ▶ **National Resource Center**
See guide, CIVILIAN CONGRESS (directories).

❂ ▶ **National Rural Electric Cooperative Association**
1800 Massachusetts Ave. NW
Washington, DC 20036 (202)857-9500
**Concern(s):** energy; agriculture; economics; consumer rights; rural communities; cooperatives. **Contact(s):** Bob Bergland.

T ▶ **National Sanctuary Defense Fund**
942 Market St., #706
San Francisco, CA 94102-4008 (415)362-8366
**Affiliation:** Nicaragua Interfaith Committee for Action. **Concern(s):** Third World; politics; peace; immigration; Central America. This fund helps support all those courageous individuals and groups that provide sanctuary to the political refugees from Third World countries, especially Central America. **Contact(s):** Penny Deleray (Administrator).

A ▶ **National Save the Family Farm Coalition**
80 F St. NW, #714
Washington, DC 20001
**Concern(s):** agriculture; family farms; rural communities. A coalition of 38 farm activists in different states fighting to establish federal policies on a local level designed to preserve small-scale and family farms.

T ▶ **The National Security Archive**
1755 Massachusetts Ave. NW, #500
Washington, DC 20036 (202)797-0882
**Concern(s):** Third World; justice; education; foreign policy; constitutional rights. A research institute, the Archive locates, acquires, organizes, and disseminates government documents pertinent to important issues of US defense, foreign intelligence, and international economic policy. The records are obtained through the freedom of Information act, declassification requests and legal suits, as well as through many other channels: government reports released without classification, donated record holdings, Congressional reports and Presidential Libraries. **Other Resources:** For orders or inquiries: Chadwyck-Healey,Inc., 1101 King St., Alexandria, VA 22314. Nonprofit. **Est.:** 1885. (703)683-4890.

$ ▶ **National Self-Help Resource Center**
1729-31 Connecticut Ave. NW
Washington, DC 20009 (202)387-0194
**Concern(s):** economics; politics; justice; community self-reliance; grassroots community organizing. A technical assistant and information broker for local citizen participation efforts. Referrals to community resource centers and neighborhood and community groups. **Other Resources:** See NETWORK NEWS. **Contact(s):** Wayne Alexander.

H ▶ **National Senior Citizens Law Center**
1815 H St. NW
Washington, DC 20006 (202)887-5280
**Concern(s):** health; seniors; victims' rights. A national legal services support center specializing in the legal problems of the elderly. The Center conducts litigation, administrative, and legislative advocacy on behalf of poor elderly clients. Provides technical assistance, training, and dissemination of information to legal services and nursing home ombudsmen on the state and local level. **Est.:** 1972.

A ▶ **National Sharecroppers Fund**
See RURAL ADVANCE newsletter.

🕊 ▶ **The National Society for Animal Protection**
100 N. Crooks Rd., #102
Clawson, MI 48017 (313)435-6655
**Concern(s):** environment; animal rights. The Society works to solve problems facing animals while simultaneously developing alternatives to eliminate animal and environmental exploitation in the future. They conduct campaigns to combat epidemic pet overpopulation, to protect Alaskan sea otters and American black bears, partnership programs with needy overseas humane societies, and increased involvement in Alaskan wildlife and environmental concerns. **Dues:** $25/yr.

✍ ▶ **National Society for Internships & Experiential Education**
See DIRECTORY OF PUBLIC SERVICE INTERNSHIPS; OPPORTUNITIES FOR THE GRADUATE, POST-GRADUATE, & MID-CAREER PROFESSIONAL; DIRECTORY OF UNDERGRADUATE INTERNSHIPS; DIRECTORY OF WASHINGTON INTERNSHIPS.

E ▶ **National Solid Waste Management Association**
1730 Rhode Island Ave. NW
Washington, DC 20036 (202)659-4613
**Concern(s):** environment; recycling.

E ▶ **The National Speleological Society**
Cave Ave.
Huntsville, AL 35810
**Concern(s):** environment; education; recreation. Speleology refers to the study of caves(as in spelunking).

D ▶ **National Student Campaign Against Hunger**
29 Temple Place
Boston, MA 02111 (617)292-4823
**Concern(s):** demographics; education; hunger; students. This campaign's purpose is to bring awareness to the hunger problem facing the Third World and this country. They do this by staging hunger strikes and publishing educational material. **Contact(s):** Leslie Samuelrich.

$ ▶ **National Taxpayers Union**
713 Maryland Ave. NE
Washington, DC 20002 (202)543-1300
**Concern(s):** economics; politics; government accountability; law; networking; taxation. NTU, through an annual analysis of congressional roll call votes, measures the performance of our nation's senators and representatives on spending issues. The NTU study is one of the few studies that does not play the "rating game." NTU is a nonpartisan group concerned with protecting the interests of the overburdened American taxpayer. It has helped to organize the most extensive, broadbased network of taxpayers in the US, representing 200,000 members interested in reducing taxes. **Other Resources:** Publishes newsletter, DOLLARS AND SENSE. **Est.:** 1969. **Contact(s):** Patrick J. Malloy (Executive Director), Jim Davidson (Chairman).

E ▶ **National Toxics Campaign Fund**
1168 Commonwealth Ave.
Boston, MA 02134 (617)232-0327
**Concern(s):** environment; health; hazardous/toxic waste; public health. A coalition of thousands of ordinary citizens, statewide consumers, organizations, environmental groups, family farmers, lawyers, businessmen and women, public health officials, scientists and educators working to implement citizen-based preventative solutions to the nation's toxics and environmental problems. It has offices in 8 states, a broad based toxic reduction program aimed at organizing and advocating local groups, and providing state and local legislators with technical assistance. **Other Resources:** See TOXIC TIMES newsletter; CITIZEN'S TOXICS PROTECTION MANUAL; ONCE IS NOT ENOUGH: A CITIZEN'S RECYCLING MANUAL; FIGHTING TOXICS: A MANUAL (directories). Publications List available. Citizens environmental laboratory. **Est.:** 1983. **E-Network:** Econet. **Member:** Environmental Federation of America. **Fax:** (617)232-3945. **Contact(s):** Gary Cohen (Executive Director).

E ▶ **National Trust for Historical Preservation**
1785 Massachusetts Ave. NW
Washington, DC 20036 (202)673-4000
**Concern(s):** environment; education; conservation; preservation. Serves as an national advocate and catalyst for historic preservation. Work includes: publishing, educating, litigating, lobbying and providing local preservation organizations with advisory services, grants and loans. It protects more than 75 historic properties nationwide. Encourages public participation in the preservation of culturally and historically significant American sites, buildings and objects. **Other Resources:** See HISTORIC PRESERVATION magazine and PRESERVATION NEWS newsletter; and SIGNS FOR MAIN STREET: GUIDELINES (directories).

J ▶ **National Urban League**
1111 14th St. NW
Washington, DC 20005 (202)898-1604
**Concern(s):** justice; urban; politics; discrimination; racism; minority rights; ethnic concerns. A national interracial, community service organization which uses the tools and methods of social work, economics, law, business management, and other disciplines to secure equal opportunities in all sectors of our society for Blacks and other minorities. It is also a nonpartisan organization. Mission is the elimination of racial discrimination and segregation in this country and achievement of parity for blacks and other minorities in every phase of American life. Nonprofit. **Contact(s):** John E. Jacob (President). (202)898-1611. 500 E. 62nd St., New York, NY 10021. (212)310-9000.

✌ ▶ **National War Tax Resistance Coordinating Committee**
Box 85810
Seattle, WA 98145 (206)522-4377
**Concern(s):** peace; politics; boycott. Coordinates local and regional actions planned around the country to focus attention on military spending and war tax resistance. The committee's purpose is to make the national war tax resistance movement more visibly and functionally cohesive. **Other Resources:** Campaigns, The Alternate Revenue Service, the Celebration of Conscience, and Standing Up For Peace Contests. See NETWORK NEWS newsletter; MORE THAN A PAYCHECK and WAR TAX MANUAL FOR COUNSELORS & LAWYERS (directories).

E ▶ **The National Water Center**
Route 3, Box 716
Eureka Springs, AR 72632 (501)253-9431
**Concern(s):** environment; water; hazardous/toxic waste; recycling. Gathers, distills, and disseminates information on water issues, emphasizing personal responsibility for human and hazardous wastes. "We all live downstream!" **Other Resources:** Revised and updated WE ALL LIVE DOWNSTREAM guidebook, $9. See AQUA TERRA journal. **Dues:** $10/yr. **Publisher:** Water Works Publishing. **Contact(s):** Charlisa Cato. (501)253-6866.

E ▶ **National Water Resources Association**
3800 N. Fairfax Dr., #4
Arlington, VA 22203 (703)524-1544
**Concern(s):** environment; water; natural resources. Encourages the nation to utilize wise management, conservation and beneficial water usage.

E ▶ **National Wildflower Research Center**
2600 FM 973 St. N.
Austin, TX 78725 (512)929-3600
**Concern(s):** environment; conservation; beautification. A private organization dedicated to conserving and replacing the regional beauty provided by North American wildflowers and other native plants. Aims to reestablish native plants in landscapes. **Other Resources:** See WILDFLOWER newsletter and WILDFLOWER JOURNAL. Catalog available, conducts seminars, and serves as a clearinghouse. **Contact(s):** David K. Northington (Executive Director), Carlton B. Lees (Vice President).

E ▶ **National Wildlife Federation's Conservation Summits**
1400 16th St. NW
Washington, DC 20036 (703)790-4371
**Affiliation:** National Wildlife Fund. **Concern(s):** environment; wild-

life/endangered species; recreation. The Summits provide great summer programs for adults, families, and educators at some of America's most spectacular sites. Enjoy: Scenic beauty; excellent nature programming; wildlife and plant ecology field trips; and Environmental Issues and Citizen Action Classes. **Fax:** (703)442-7332. (800)432-6564. **Contact(s):** Sheri Sykes (Coordinator).

### E ▶ National Wildlife Federation/Fund
1400 16th St. NW
Washington, DC 20036-2266    (202)797-6800
**Concern(s):** environment; conservation; resources; wildlife/endangered species. Private citizen organization promoting the wise use of natural resources. The Federation is composed of affiliate groups in nearly every state and territory. Influences state and national conservation policies with assistance from its affiliates and members through administrative, legislative and legal channels. Hunters are among some of their supporters. See, also, Resource Conservation Alliance; Institute for Conservation Leadership; NWF Conservation Summits; Wildlife Camp. **Other Resources:** See NATIONAL WILDLIFE, BACKYARD NATURALIST; INTERNATIONAL WILDLIFE, RANGER RICK and YOUR BIG BACKYARD (periodicals); ENVIRONMENTAL QUALITY INDEX; CONSERVATION DIRECTORY; TOXIC 500; NFW CONSERVATION DIRECTORY. Radio and TV shows. **Member:** Global Tomorrow Coalition. Hotline: (202)737-2024. **Contact(s):** Jay D. Hair (President).

### E ▶ National Wildlife Refuge Association
10824 Fox Hunt Lane
Potomac, MD 20854-1553    (507)454-5940
**Concern(s):** environment; wildlife/endangered species; wilderness; conservation; preservation. Organization dedicated to preserving and sustaining the National Wildlife Refuge System for future generations. Goals are: to protect the integrity of the NWRS; to increase public understanding and appreciation of the NWRS; to conduct education and information programs; to stimulate public and private decision-making and action to improve the quality of the NWRS; and to actively pursue projects benefiting the NWRS and America's wildlife populations. **Other Resources:** See BLUE GOOSE FLYER newsletter. **Contact(s):** Forrest A. Carpenter (President), Art Hughlett.

### F ▶ National Women's Health Network
1325 G St. NW (lower level)
Washington, DC 20005  (202)347-1140
**Concern(s):** feminism; health; nutrition; consumer protection. Established to challenge the abuses and inadequacies of our existing medical system. It testifies on behalf of women medical consumers at congressional hearings and pressures the federal regulatory agencies to respond to consumer needs; and to mobilize people to take action in their own communities. Supports Pro-Choice, safe sex, breast cancer prevention (reducing dietary fat intake), and safe drugs and medical devices. Whatever the female health problem, it is in the forefront. **Other Resources:** Publishes NETWORK NEWS newsletter. Also provides alerts, brochures and information service with membership. A $45 membership will buy you a copy of THE NEW OUR BODIES, OURSELVES, OR OURSELVES GROWING OLDER. **Est.:** 1975. **Dues:** $25+/yr. **Contact(s):** Olivia H. Cousins (Chair), Leslie Orloff

### ✍ ▶ National Women's History Project
7738 Bell Rd.
Windsor, CA 95492-8515
**Concern(s):** education; feminism; justice; diversity. Catalog features curriculum resources, reference books, publications for children, and other materials that focus on a multicultural approach to women's history.

### F ▶ National Women's History Project
7738 Bell Rd.
Windsor, CA 95492    (707)838-6000
**Concern(s):** feminism; education. Multi-cultural educational materials promoting the study of women's history. Teacher training and annual conference. **Other Resources:** Free catalog, wholesale and retail.

### F ▶ National Women's Political Caucus
1275 K St. NW
Washington, DC 20005  (202)898-1100
**Concern(s):** feminism; politics; sexism; lobbying. Established to win equal representation for women in government: economic equality, equal rates, responsible government, local political support and training of women. **Est.:** 1971.

### ☼ ▶ National Wood Energy Association
777 N Capitol St. NE., #805
Washington, DC 20002-4239    (202)408-0664
**Concern(s):** energy; solid fuel.

### E ▶ National Woodland Owners Association
374 Maple Ave. E
Vienna, VA 22180    (703)255-2300
**Concern(s):** environment; forestry; conservation. Nationwide independent association of small private woodland owners devoted entirely to non-industrial private forestry. NWOA is independent of the forest products industry and forestry agencies. It works with all organizations to promote non-industrial forestry and represents private landowners on wildlife, forests, and resource issues. Provides technical assistance. **Other Resources:** Newsletter, WOODLAND REPORT; see NATIONAL WOODLANDS MAGAZINE. **Est.:** 1983. **Dues:** $15/yr. **Contact(s):** Dr. Keith A. Argow (President/CEO).

### L ▶ National Writers Union
13 Astor Place
New York, NY 10003    (212)254-0279
**Concern(s):** labor; unions. Trade union for freelance writers bargaining for contracts, addressing grievances, and striving to establish a community of writers. Membership is open to writers who have published or are actively trying to publish their work. **Other Resources:** Free Brochure. **Contact(s):** Anne Wyville.

### L ▶ National Youth Work Alliance
1751 N St. NW
Washington, DC 20036  (202)785-0764
**Concern(s):** labor; education; jobs; volunteers; youth. A consortium of coalitions of youth service organizations, other community-based youth work groups and interested individuals and organizations. Referrals to state coalitions of youth workers, city youth workers' coalitions, and Washington, DC organizations serving youth. **Other Resources:** Publishes YOUTH ALTERNATIVES monthly. **Contact(s):** Tom McCarthy.

### 🕊 ▶ Native American Awareness Group
3370 'C' 34th St.
Boulder, CO 80301
**Concern(s):** peace; conflict resolution. Promotes international understanding and peace around the world.

### J ▶ Native American Policy Network
See NATIVE AMERICAN POLICY NETWORK DIRECTORY.

### J ▶ Native American Prisoners Rehabilitation Research Project
2848 Paddock Lane
Villa Hills, KY 41017
**Concern(s):** justice; education; criminal system; Native Americans. **Other Resources:** Publishes IRON HOUSE DRUM newsletter, for and by Native prisoners and their loved ones across North America. **Contact(s):** Little Rock Reed (Director).

### J ▶ Native American Rights Fund
See NARF LEGAL REVIEW/NCBL NOTES (periodicals).

### E ▶ Native Forest Council
Box 2171
Eugene, OR 97402    (503)688-2600
**Concern(s):** environment; politics; forests; lobbying. **Other Resources:** Publishes FOREST VOICE, a devastating indictment of logging techniques and government complicity. **Fax:** (503)461-2156.

### A ▶ Native Seeds/SEARCH
2509 N. Campbell Ave., #325
Tucson, AZ 85719
**Affiliation:** Southwestern Endangered Arid Land Resource Clearing House. **Concern(s):** agriculture; justice; environment; Native Americans; diversity; organic; farmlands; preservation; soil; subsistence; drylands. This organization's mission is to preserve traditional native crops of the Southwest and northern Mexico. It deals directly with native farmers, horticulturalists, and educators in striving to accomplish this. The staff is comprised of Indian and non-Indian ethnobotanists, educators, gardeners and students. It hopes to reintroduce the concepts and land management techniques of ancient and present-day native farmers to all interested Native Americans. **Other Resources:** Its quarterly publication, SEEDHEAD NEWS, features articles about the cultural and scientific aspects of native agriculture. It prints a Seedlisting biannually for the Spring and Fall, and its seeds are made available free to Native Americans. Nonprofit.

### H ▶ Natural Death Centre
20 Heber Rd.
London, NW2 England    (4481208 2853
**Concern(s):** health; spiritual; death/dying; interfaith. The Centre has been set up to help people explore their fears about dying in the context of a variety of attitudes to death in different cultures and religions. It serves as a resource not merely for the elderly but for people of all ages who are intrigued by this fascinating subject. **Other Resources:** "Living With Dying" group workshops and dinner discus-

sion series. **Est.:** 1991. **Fax:** (4481 452 6434. **Contact(s):** Josefine Speyer (Coordinator).

### A ▶ Natural Food Associates
Box 210
Atlanta, GA 30301
**Concern(s):** agriculture; health; organic; nutrition. A educational organization which teaches the values inherent in organic farming and natural food in America. **Other Resources:** See NATURAL FOOD AND FARMING magazine. Nonprofit.

### A ▶ Natural Food Institute
Box 185WMB
Dudley, MA 01570
**Concern(s):** agriculture; environment; health; organic; sustainability; hazardous/toxic waste; nutrition.

### A ▶ Natural Organic Farmers Association
15 Barre St.
Montpelier, VT 05602-3504  (802)223-7222
**Concern(s):** agriculture; health; organic. An association of consumers, gardeners, and diversified farmers who share a vision of local, organic agriculture. Through education and member participation, NOFA works together to strengthen agriculture in Vermont. Parent organization of Vermont Organic Farmers, a certification committee and also hosts an annual conference, holds numerous workshops, and publishes the quarterly NOFA-Notes. **Other Resources:** NOFA-NOTES. Nonprofit. **Est.:** 1971. **Dues:** $20/yr. **Member:** N.E., NOFA Regional Group; OFPANA; OFAC. **Contact(s):** Enid Wonnacott (Coordinator), Cherie Morse (Administration Assistant).

### E ▶ Natural Resource and Environmental Education Program
US Forest Service
Box 2417
Washington, DC 20013  (202)447-3957
**Concern(s):** environment; education; natural resources. Includes both basic environmental education activities and specific explorations about current issues affecting the management of natural resources. The program helps you better understand, and explain to others, the importance of natural resource management. .

### E ▶ Natural Resources Council of America
801 Pennsylvania SE, #410
Washington, DC 20003  (202)547-7553
**Concern(s):** environment; energy; natural resources; resource management. An organization comprised of over 65 national and regional organizations dedicated to the sound management of the world's natural resources. **Other Resources:** Conducts special projects and briefings, field trips and task forces. See NRCA NEWSletter. Publications list. See, also, Trust For the Future. Nonprofit. **Contact(s):** Andrea Yank (Executive Director).

### E ▶ Natural Resources Defense Council
40 West 20 St.
New York, NY 10011    (212)727-2700
**Concern(s):** environment; politics; health; natural resources; hazardous/toxic waste; conservation; lobbying. A membership organization dedicated to protecting natural resources and improving the quality of the human environment. NRDC combines legal action, scientific research and citizen education in an environmental protection program. Major work has been in the areas of energy policy and nuclear safety; toxic substances; air and water pollution; urban transportation; natural resources and conservation; and the international environment. **Other Resources:** See Mothers and Others for a Livable Planet; AMICUS JOURNAL; and NEWSLINE, a bimonthly newsletter; CITIZEN'S HANDBOOK ON GROUNDWATER PROTECTION. Publications list is also available. Nonprofit. **Dues:** $10/yr. **Member:** Environmental Federation of America. **Fax:** (212)727-1773. (800)648-NRDC. **Contact(s):** John Adams (Executive Director), Adrian DeWind (Chairman). **Other:** 1350 New York Ave. NW, #300, Washington, DC 20006 Justin R. Ward (202)783-7800.

### E ▶ Natural Rights Center
Box 90
Summertown, TN 38483(615)964-3992
**Affiliation:** Plenty USA. **Concern(s):** environment; justice. A public policy research, education, and litigation project dealing with issues concerning the environment and ecology. Its focus is on long-term trans-generational injuries whose full impacts are not immediately felt and are more difficult to remedy in the future. **Other Resources:** Newsletter. **Est.:** 1980. **Dues:** Donation. **Frequency:** 4/yr. **Pages:** 4-8. **Circ.:** 1.4M. **E-Network:** Econet. **ID:** 'Natlaw'. MCI Mail under A. Bates. **Contact(s):** Albert Bates (Director). **Other:** Plenty USA, Box 2306, Davis, CA 95617

### ✍ ▶ Natural Science for Youth Foundation
130 Azalea Dr.
Roswell, GA 30075    (404)594-9367

**Concern(s):** education; environment; childhood; youth. Provides counseling to community groups in the planning and development of environmental and natural science centers and museums and native animal parks which are designed particularly to meet the needs and interests of children and young people. **Other Resources:** Publishes DIRECTORY OF NATURAL SCIENCE CENTERS; NATURAL SCIENCE CENTER NEWS; OPPORTUNITIES BULLETIN. **Contact(s):** John Ripley Forbes (Founder/President), E. Ripley Forbes (Secretary).

E ◆ **The Nature Conservancy**
1815 N. Lynn St.
Arlington, VA 22209    (703)841-5300
**Concern(s):** environment; conservation; wildlife/endangered species; volunteers. An international organization committed to preserving biological diversity by protecting lands and wildlife and their ecosystems. Manages a system of over 1,100 nature sanctuaries and provides land protection in 50 states and 12 Latin American countries. **Other Resources:** Publishes NATURE CONSERVANCY magazine. Volunteer positions available. **Dues:** $15/yr. (800)628-6860. **Contact(s):** Frank D. Boren (President).

H ◆ **Naturopathy Institute**
See DIRECTORY OF ALTERNATIVE THERAPY SCHOOLS & COLLEGES.

D ◆ **Negative Population Growth**
16 E. 42nd St.
New York, NY 10017    (212)599-2020
**Concern(s):** demographics; population growth. An organization founded to inform Americans who believe that human numbers must be reduced if we are ever to put an end to mass starvation and suffering in this world. **Other Resources:** Newsletter, HUMAN SURVIVAL. Nonprofit. **Est.:** 1972. **Contact(s):** Donald W. Mann (President). **Other:** 210 The Plaza, Teanack, NJ 07666(201)837-3555.

T ◆ **Neighbor to Neighbor**
15 Dutch St., #500-B
New York, NY 10038-3799   (212)406-1440
**Concern(s):** Third World; peace; economics; boycott; corporate responsibility; socially-responsible investing; Central America. BOYCOTT EL SALVADORAN COFFEE — The boycott is a way to apply pressure to force a Congressional cutoff of all military-based aid and to have the El Salvadoran government negotiate an end to the war. Products: Maxwell House, Maxim, Yuban, Sanka, Folgers, High Point, Nescafe, Tasters Choice, Soca, Brava, Hills Bros., Chase and Sanborn, and MJB. **Other Resources:** To protest, write to: Alan MacDonald, CEO, Nestle Corp., 100 Manhattanville Rd., Purchase, NY 10577; J.G. Smole, CEO, Procter & Gamble, Fifth & Sycamore Sts., Cincy, OH 45202; Jahn M. Richman, CEO, General Foods, Kraft Ct., Glenview, IL 10003.

T ◆ **Neighbor to Neighbor**
2000 Massachusetts Ave.
Cambridge, MA 02140   (617)354-2210
**Concern(s):** Third World; justice; economics; foreign policy; boycott. A national organization committed to promoting a new US policy in Central America based on independence and equality. In January 1990, Neighbor to Neighbor will launch an international boycott of Salvadoran coffee as a vehicle to engage millions of Americans in cutting US funding for the death squad government in El Salvador.

P ◆ **Neighborhood Salon Association**
Fawkes Building
1624 Harmon Pl., #330
Minneapolis, MN 55403
**Concern(s):** politics; grassroots organizing. Utne Reader printed an article on Neighborhood Salons that caught on in a big way. This is it's result. Members receive a newsletter and are put in contact with others who want to participate in their area/bioregion. **Est.:** 1983. **Dues:** $12/yr. **Frequency:** 4/yr.

H ◆ **Neptune Society**
930 W. Alameda
Burbank, CA 93506-9939   (818)953-9995
**Concern(s):** health; environment; death/dying; conservation. A way to avoid the confusion and frustrations of costly funerals and preserve the environment as well. Call for an office near you.(818)845-2415.

T ◆ **The Network in Solidarity With the People of Guatemala**
1314 14th St. NW
Washington, DC 20005  (202)483-0050
**Concern(s):** Third World; politics; justice; foreign policy; Central America. Conducts projects and campaigns in the area of human rights, humanitarian aid, opposition to military aid, and public education concerning Guatemala.

T ◆ **Network of Educators Committees on Central America**
1118 22nd St. NW
Washington, DC 20037  (202)429-0137
**Concern(s):** Third World; education; justice; Central America.

✍ ◆ **Network, For Public School**
108 Little Patuyent Pky, #301
Columbia, MD 21044
**Affiliation:** National Committee for Citizens. **Concern(s):** education.

⚥ ◆ **Network, National Catholic Social Justice Lobby**
806 Rhode Island Ave. NE
Washington, DC 20018   (202)526-4070
**Concern(s):** peace; politics; spiritual; lobbying; faith. An organization that lobbies congressional representatives to enact laws providing economic justice for the poor and powerless, protecting human rights, and promoting disarmament. **Other Resources:** Publishes bi-monthly update of events on Capitol Hill, NETWORK newsletter. **Contact(s):** Nancy Sylvester (National Coordinator).

P ◆ **Networking Institute Inc.**
505 Waltham St.
East Newton, MA 02165 (617)965-3340
**Concern(s):** politics; future; economics; environment; health; media; networking; sustainability; research; analysis; ideation; computer networking; grassroots organizing. Books and periodicals which provide a wealth of information on how to network. Its aim is to create a sustainable future for the world by increase individual participation rather than hierarchy. **Other Resources:** See directory THE NETWORKING BOOK: PEOPLE CONNECTING WITH PEOPLE; NETWORKING Newsletter; NETWORKING JOURNAL; mailing list; computer networking systems. Also, TNI Multilogue. **Est.:** 1982. **Member:** Co-op America.

⚥ ◆ **Nevada Desert Experience**
Box 4487
Las Vegas, NV 89127-0487  (702)646-4814
**Concern(s):** peace; spiritual; anti-nuclear; test ban; interfaith; disarmament. A faith-based organization with Franciscan origins and scriptural values working to end nuclear weapons testing through a campaign of prayer, dialogue, and nonviolent direct action. "We see the Comprehensive Test Ban as a step toward disarmament." **Other Resources:** See newsletter, DESERT VOICES. Regular programs each year are Lenten Desert Experience and August Desert Witness. "We co-sponsor and assist other groups in programs at the Nevada Test Site." **Contact(s):** Peter J. Ediger, Mary H. Lehman (Co-directors).

A ◆ **New Alchemy Institute**
237 Hatchville Rd.
East Falmouth, MA 02536   (508)564-6301
**Concern(s):** agriculture; environment; energy; food production; solid waste; water; sustainability. Research and education projects on technologies for food, energy, water, waste and shelter systems that are environmentally sound and economically efficient. Offers education programs that provide practical information to gardeners, small-scale farmers and education institutions. **Other Resources:** See NEW ALCHEMY QUARTERLY. New Alchemy Institute Catalogue - books and products for ecological living. Nonprofit. **Est.:** 1969. **Dues:** $35/yr. **Contact(s):** Bill O'Neil (Public Information Coordinator).

⚥ ◆ **New Call To Peacemaking National Conference**
Box 1245
Elkhart, IN 46515    (219)294-7536
**Concern(s):** peace.

T ◆ **New Civilization**
16255 Ventura Blvd.
Encino, CA 91436-2354
**Concern(s):** Third World; environment; economics; future; ideation; development. "We invite inquiries from serious persons worldwide interested in the redesign of their 'villages' and thereby of our whole culture. We provide a package of books and corresponding centers for those who want them. We would like to make contact with thinkers in the 'developing countries' not yet destroyed by the Industrial Revolution."

$ ◆ **New Consumer, Ltd.**
52 Elswick Rd.
Newcastle upon Tyne, NE4 6JH England
91-272-1148
**Concern(s):** economics; alternative markets; socially-responsible investing; trade. An organization in Britain patterned after Co-op America. Educates the public about a just economy, and provides products and services from responsible businesses.

E ◆ **New England Wild Flower Society, Inc.**
'Garden in the Woods'
Hemenway Rd.
Framingham, MA 01701
**Concern(s):** environment; bioregionalism; conservation; preservation. A regional group that is dedicated to preserving the native plants of New England from destruction.

E ◆ **New Forests Fund**
731 8th St. SE
Washington, DC 20003  (202)547-3800
**Concern(s):** environment; forests.

✍ ◆ **New Horizons for Learning**
4649 Sunnyside North
Seattle, WA 98103    (206)547-7936
**Concern(s):** education; holism. International membership network that sponsors talks, workshops, seminars, conferences and a 16-page quarterly newsletter that can keep you up to date on the new reformers—and on how their ideas are faring in the profession. **Other Resources:** ON THE BEAM newsletter. Nonprofit. **Est.:** 1980. **Dues:** $25-250/yr.; with newsletter. **Contact(s):** Dee Dickinson.

P ◆ **New Jersey Citizen Action**
See guide, ORGANIZING FOR SOCIAL CHANGE.

S ◆ **New Jewish Agenda**
64 Fulton St., #1100
New York, NY 10038   (212)227-5885
**Concern(s):** spiritual; peace; justice; faith. Jews from a variety of backgrounds and affiliations committed to progressive human values and the building of a shared vision of Jewish life. Society can be changed and human cooperation can be achieved. Working for social progress not only reflects Jewish ideals, but enhances Jewish security. Its national platform upholds progressive Jewish values and affirms that the goals of peace and justice are attainable. Deals with issues such as women's rights, anti-Semitism, Israel, labor, etc. **Other Resources:** See AGENDA IN BRIEF newsletter.

$ ◆ **The New Road Map Foundation**
Box 15981
Seattle, WA 98115
**Concern(s):** economics; education; alternative consumer; trade. Educational organization concerned with the role of personal responsibility and personal initiative in effecting positive global changes. Believes that lasting change towards a humane, sustainable culture is rooted in personal responsibility for the needs and potentials of both ourselves and our larger community. Educational offerings focuses on personal finances, personal relationships and personal health. **Other Resources:** Transforming Your Relationship with Money and Achieving Financial Independence course. **Office:** 507 3rd Ave. Seattle, WA 98104-2355.

H ◆ **New Song Center for Bereaved Children and Those Who Love Them**
219 N. Siesta Lane, #101
Tempe, AZ 85281      (602)991-9132
**Concern(s):** health; education; death/dying; childhood. Helping children with grief through support for children and those who love them (ages 5-12). **Contact(s):** Gabriella Lawrence (President), Heather Devich (Coordinator). (602)966-1999. Kathy McAlister , Treasurer. (602)921-0433.

⚥ ◆ **New World Action**
Box 474
Berkeley, CA 94701
**Concern(s):** peace; environment; education; world order; youth; childhood; nonviolence; conflict resolution. World movement shifts from wars, pollution, waste, oppression, and poverty to caring for Human Family/biosphere to be launched anywhere by 3+ persons publicly shifting highest loyalty from nation, race, creed to world community harmonizing living forms. forms. "Shift" implies rejection of glorified nation, national sovereignty, security and defense, while encouraging child and youth refusal to cooperate with acts and institutions of destruction. Conceptualize New World.

E ◆ **New York Botanic Garden**
Bronx, NY 10458-5126
**Concern(s):** environment; research; wilderness. Researches tropical ethnobotany; plant cataloging. **Other Resources:** Home of the Garden Society who publish GARDEN.

E ◆ **New York Zoological Society**
New York Zoological Park
Bronx, NY 10460
**Affiliation:** Wildlife Conservation International. **Concern(s):** environment; wildlife/endangered species; conservation. Funds wildlife conservation projects. **Other Resources:** See WILDLIFE CONSERVATION magazine.

**♥ ♦ NGO Committee on UNICEF**
See Action for Children.

**T ♦ Nicaragua Information Center**
See NICARAGUA INFORMATION CENTER BULLETIN (periodicals).

**T ♦ Nicaragua Interfaith Committee For Action**
942 Market St., #709
San Francisco, CA 94102     (415)433-6057

**Concern(s):** Third World; justice; spiritual; peace; Central America; interfaith; conflict resolution. This organization wishes to end the distrust between our two countries through helping mend the destruction that our secret operations have caused. **Other Resources:** National Sanctuary Defend Fund, NICARAGUA UPDATE newsletter.

**T ♦ Nicaragua Network**
Pacific Southwest Region
Box 1004
Berkeley, CA 94701

**Concern(s):** Third World; education; peace; Central America. A national organization that coordinates material aid, sister relations, and education between the US and Nicaragua in order to promote solutions in Nicaragua and to strengthen the links between the peace, justice and farm movements. **Other Resources:** See NICARAGUA NETWORK NEWS letter.

**T ♦ Nicaragua Solidarity Network**
339 Lafayette St.
New York, NY 10012     (212)674-9499

**Concern(s):** Third World; politics; justice; Central America.

**$ ♦ Nippon Ecology Network**
Sudacho Towa Bldg. 5F
2-2 Kanda-Sudacho; Chiyoda-Ku
Tokyo, 101 Japan     03-3258-9121

**Concern(s):** economics; environment; trade; green consumer; socially-responsible investing; alternative markets. Formerly "The Citizens' Recycle Movement of Japan," Nippon Ecology Network works to create a sustainable future both as an environmental organization and as a green business. Current business activities include: organic food home delivery, environmentally-friendly product catalog, publishing, producing fleamarkets and other events.

**E ♦ Nisqually Delta Association**
Box 7444
Olympia, WA 98507

**Concern(s):** environment; wetlands. Trying to preserve their wetlands .

**P ♦ NORML (National Organization to Reform Marijuana Laws)**
1636 R St. NW
Washington, DC 20009     (202)483-5500

**Concern(s):** politics; justice; health; reform; legislative; lobbying; holism; criminal system. This organizations purpose is to legalize marijuana. **Other Resources:** Publishes a newsletter. See related group called HEMP.

**E ♦ North American Association for Environmental Education**
Box 400
Troy, OH 45373     (513)339-6835

**Concern(s):** environment; education; volunteers. A professional society of teachers, college and university faculty and students, governmental, media and nonprofit personal whose mission is the development of environmental education in all educational institutions, both formal and nonformal. **Other Resources:** Volunteers needed. Inquire. Nonprofit. **Dues:** $20/students; $35/regular. **Other:** 10178 Ashby Place, Fairfax, VA 22030 Edward J. McCrea (202)343-3895.

**E ♦ North American Bioregional Council**
Turtle Island Office
c/o Jacinta McCoy
Olympia, WA 98502

**Concern(s):** environment; bioregionalism. See POLLEN: A JOURNAL OF BIOREGIONAL EDUCATION; and Bioregional Clearinghouse (directories).

**E ♦ North American Bluebird Society**
Box 6295
Silver Springs, MD 20910     (301)384-2798

**Concern(s):** environment; wildlife/endangered species; preservation. Goals: To educate the public about the importance of three species of bluebird in North America and to preserve and increase these birds' populations. **Other Resources:** Speakers Bureau, monitors and reports on bluebird trails, and supplies nest box information for those interested in assisting.

**❁ ♦ North American Christian Peace Conference**
777 UN Plaza, #1
New York, NY 10017-3521     (516)223-1880

**Affiliation:** Global Christian Peace Conference. **Concern(s):** peace; justice; spiritual; disarmament; faith. An organization of churches, denominations, congregations, and individual Christians in the US and Canada devoted to peace, disarmament, human rights and social-economic justice. NACPC cooperates closely with other nongovernmental organizations and with the United Nations. NACPC has consultive status with the United Nations economic & social council and with many other agencies of the United Nations System. It is a component part of the global Christian Peace Conference. **Other Resources:** Newsletter. Nonprofit. **Est.:** 1958. **Dues:** $25/member; $100/donor. **Price:** $50/yr. **Fax:** (516)223-1880. **Contact(s):** Philip Oke (Executive Secretary). **Other:** Global Christian Peace Conference, 111 21 Prague 1, Jungmannova, Czeck Land.

**T ♦ North American Coalition for Human Rights in Korea**
See KOREA BI-WEEKLY REPORT.

**E ♦ North American Coalition on Religion and Ecology**
5 Thomas Circle NW
Washington, DC 20005     (202)462-2591

**Concern(s):** environment; spiritual; interfaith. An interfaith alliance designed to help the North American religious community enter into the environmental movement in the 1990s with more informed understanding, deeper commitment, and a dynamic sense of environmental service. NACRE's vision is embodied in the phrase "Caring for Creation." NACRE is seeking to develop an interdisciplinary approach whereby scientific disciplines can interact meaningfully with major environmental and ethical questions never before faced. **Other Resources:** Publishes ECO-LETTER. Provides press and fund-raising internships. Organizing the Intercontinental Conference on Caring for Creation and prepares resource materials to help houses of worship into environmental ministry. **Dues:** $25, $75/organization. **Contact(s):** Donald B. Conroy (Director).

**S ♦ The North American Conference on Christianity and Ecology**
444 Waller St.
Box 14305
San Francisco, CA 94114     (415)626-6064

**Concern(s):** spiritual; environment; education; faith; activism. This conference believes that Christ's message was one of environmental concern, that taught us to care and love nature. **Other Resources:** Newsletter, FIRMAMENT. **Contact(s):** Eleanor Rae (President), Frederick Krueger (Executive Secretary). **Other:** 1522 Grand Ave., St. Paul, MN 55105.

**❁ ♦ North American Coordinating Committee of Non-Governmental Organizations on the Question of Palestine**
Box 576
Cambridge, MA 02140

**Concern(s):** peace; justice; Third World; Mid-East; conflict resolution; diversity; indigenous peoples.

**A ♦ North American Farm Alliance**
Box 102
Covert, MI 49043-0102

**Concern(s):** agriculture; environment; politics; feminism; Third World; labor; peace; health; rural communities; sustainability; hazardous/toxic waste; hunger. A progressive coalition of farm organizers, union workers, and political and legal activists from across the US and Canada. NAFA's member groups have provided grassroots leadership to address the rural economic crisis in a broader context of global peace, social justice and ecological sustainability. NAFA is committed to building a new grassroots membership base of farmers, rural people and others who share these values. **Other Resources:** See NORTH AMERICAN FARMER newspaper. **Est.:** 1983. **Contact(s):** Ed Marks (Executive Director), Merle Hansen (President).

**E ♦ North American Lake Management Society**
Box 217
Merrifield, VA 22116

**Concern(s):** environment; education; preservation; water; land; wetlands; rivers. Goal: To prevent the premature destruction of lakes, ponds, reservoirs, impoundments and their watersheds through education and promoting a better understanding of these as ecological units. **Dues:** $25-$750/yr.

**E ♦ North American Loon Fund**
RR 4, Box 217
Meredith, NH 03253     (603)279-6163

**Concern(s):** environment; wildlife/endangered species; volunteers. Emphasizes study of loon populations and their habitat. Sponsors loon preservation, public education and research projects across the US and Canada. **Other Resources:** Volunteer programs offered through affiliates. **Dues:** $15/yr.

**✍ ♦ North American Montesorri Teachers' Association (NAMTA)**
2859 Scarborough Rd.
Cleveland Heights, OH 44118

**Concern(s):** education; childhood. An umbrella organization for the Montesorri movement in the US that publishes a quarterly journal, parent education booklets and videos, and materials on starting Montesorri programs in private and public settings. Sponsors conferences and publishes a directory of schools and teacher-training courses.

**E ♦ North American Native Fishes Association**
123 W. Airy Ave.
Philadelphia, PA 19119     (215)247-0384

**Concern(s):** environment; wildlife/endangered species; conservation; water. Goals: To encourage increased scientific appreciation and conservation of native fishes through observation, study, and research; to assemble and distribute information about native fishes; and, to bring together people interested in fishes that are native to this continent for scientific purposes or aquarium study. **Dues:** $11-15/yr.

**E ♦ North American Permaculture**
Box 573
Colville, WA 99114

**Concern(s):** environment; agriculture; economics; permaculture. NAP was formed to promote ecologically and economically designed systems called permacultures; to provide permaculture information; and to help build grassroots permaculture groups through information, referrals and networking. **Other Resources:** Members receive newsletters, permaculture referrals, and access to NAP research database. See ALTERNATOR newsletter and guide, PERMACULTURE: A PRACTICAL GUIDE FOR A SUSTAINABLE FUTURE (directories).

**✍ ♦ North American Students of Cooperation (NASCO)**
Box 7715
Ann Arbor, MI 48107     (313)663-0889

**Concern(s):** education; students. Actively creating cooperative housing for college students on college campuses. Also, helping with other student cooperatives, and publications on cooperatives. **Other Resources:** CAMPUS CO-OP DIRECTORY. Nonprofit. **Member:** Co-op America.

**H ♦ North American Vegetarian Society**
See VEGETARIAN VOICE newsletter.

**E ♦ North American Water Office**
Box 174
Lake Elmo, MN 55042-0174 (612)770-3861

**Concern(s):** environment; energy; water. An organization which educates people about solutions to environmental problems caused by society's waste streams. Publications, networks, and a service for investment advisors which ranks electric utilities by amount of pollution emitted. Call or write to find out how to apply financial incentives restructuring to utilities in your area. Nonprofit. **Member:** Co-op America. **Contact(s):** George Crocker.

**E ♦ North American Wildlife Foundation**
102 Wilmot Rd., #410
Deerfield, IL 60015     (708)940-7776

**Concern(s):** environment; agriculture; wildlife/endangered species; farming. Goals: To reverse the decline in North American wildlife populations through research, education and communication efforts. Research programs promote the prosperous coexistence of wildlife and farmers. **Other Resources:** Prairie Farming Program, student programs, research programs. **Dues:** $20+/yr.

**E ♦ North American Wildlife Park Foundation, Inc.**
Wolf Park
Battle Ground, IN 47920 (317)567-2265

**Concern(s):** environment; wildlife/endangered species; volunteers. Conducts research and public education on behalf of the wolf, offering opportunities for study to researchers, students and others interested in observing wolves. **Other Resources:** Educational outreach programs to school children; yearly Wolf Behavior Seminars for zoo and wildlife personnel, wolf and wolf hybrid owners and others; and publication of research data. Volunteers needed to raise animals, maintain facilities, etc. **Dues:** $10+/yr:$500/life.

E ♦ **North Carolina Botanical Gardens**
University of North Carolina
3375 Totten Center
Chapel Hill, NC 27599-3375 (919)967-2246
**Concern(s):** environment; education.

E ♦ **Northcoast Environmental Center**
879 9th St.
Arcata, CA 95521          (707)822-6918
**Concern(s):** environment; politics; activism; bioregionalism; lobbying. Informational and lobbying center of the California northcoast environment. **Other Resources:** See EcoNews newspaper. **Est.:** 1971. **Contact(s):** Tim McKay (Coordinator), Andy Alm

E ♦ **Northern Alaska Environmental Center**
218 Driveway
Fairbanks, AK 99701     (907)452-5021
**Concern(s):** environment; education; politics; preservation; wilderness; wildlife/endangered species; lobbying; law; volunteers; polar. Through education and action, NAEC is dedicated to protecting environment of north of the Alaska Range and works closely with government agencies on land-use issues such as the implementation of the Alaska Lands Act, Arctic National Wildlife Refuge, and oil and gas leasing. Currently working on wilderness designation for the coastal plain of ANWR and arctic development issues. **Other Resources:** Opportunities for research internships and a wide variety of volunteer projects. Inquire. Publishes the NORTHERN LINE(periodical). **Dues:** $25, $35/family, includes 4/yr. journal. **Fax:** (907)452-3100. **Contact(s):** Rex Blazer (Executive Director), Larry Landry (Associate Director).

J ♦ **Northern California Council of Churches**
See SEQUOIA (periodicals).

P ♦ **Northern California Greens**
Box 3727
Oakland, CA 94609
**Concern(s):** politics; Green.

E ♦ **Northern Sun Alliance**
See NORTHERN SUN NEWS and Mobilization for Survival.

E ♦ **Northshield**
Box 385
Ely, MN 55731          (218)365-3309
**Concern(s):** environment; education; water; wilderness; volunteers. An all-volunteer educational organization dedicated to preserving the clean water sources and wilderness in Minnesota. **Other Resources:** Quarterly publication. **Subscription:** $12/yr. **Member:** Co-op America.

A ♦ **Northwest Coalition for Alternatives to Pesticides**
Box 1393
Eugene, OR 97440          (503)344-5044
**Concern(s):** agriculture; pesticides. This group works hard to find the very best and effective alternatives to pesticides. **Other Resources:** See A JOURNAL OF PESTICIDE REFORM (periodicals).

H ♦ **Northwest Health Foundation**
See LIVING WELL (periodicals).

O ♦ **Northwest Nuclear Safety Campaign**
1914 N. 34th St., #407
Seattle, WA 98103          (206)547-3175
**Concern(s):** energy; anti-nuclear. Works to stop nuclear weapons plant pollution.

O ♦ **Northwest Power Planning Council**
850 SW Broadway, #1100
Portland, OR 97205          (503)222-5161
**Concern(s):** energy; efficiency; conservation. Developed Northwest Conservation and Electric Power plan which sets requirements for energy efficiency.

☷ ♦ **Nuclear Age Peace Foundation**
1187 Coast Village Rd.
Santa Barbara, CA 93108     (805)965-3443
**Concern(s):** peace; disarmament. A nonpartisan educational organization, the foundation is raising public awareness of the dangers of accidental nuclear war, which have not be diminished by arms control treaties, and is encouraging steps to reduce those risks. Also offers peace leadership awards. **Other Resources:** NUCLEAR ALERT newsletter, THE INTERNATIONAL ACCIDENTAL NUCLEAR WAR PREVENTION NEWSLETTER; Periodic Global Security Studies; WAGING

PEACE booklets designed to promote informed dialogue on critical issues facing humanity; Swackhamer Prizes Essay Contest. **Est.:** 1982. **Subscription:** $35/yr. **Contact(s):** David Krieger (President).

☷ ♦ **Nuclear Arsenal Project**
See NUCLEAR ARSENAL HANDBOOK (directories).

☷ ♦ **Nuclear Control Institute**
1000 Connecticut Ave. NW, #704
Washington, DC 20036   (202)822-8444
**Concern(s):** peace; energy; environment; health; anti-nuclear; hazardous/toxic waste. A private policy research center specializing in nuclear proliferation problems. **Contact(s):** Paul Leventhal (President), Alan Kuperman (Issues Director).

☷ ♦ **Nuclear Dialogue Project**
106 Fiztrandolph Rd.
Princeton, NJ 08540-7204   (609)924-1015
**Concern(s):** peace; environment; disarmament. A dynamic, innovative national peace organization which seeks to achieve true and lasting peace by bringing together people from widely different points of view to depolarize the disarmament discussion, to build consensus, and to seek mutually beneficial approaches to economic, environmental, and security issues. **Contact(s):** Rachel Findley.

☷ ♦ **Nuclear Free America**
1133 19th St. NW
Washington, DC 20036
**Concern(s):** peace; economics; boycott; corporate responsibility; socially-responsible investing; anti-nuclear. BOYCOTT LONG DISTANCE TELEPHONE Service — They have major nuclear weapons communications systems contracts. Products: AT&T, ITT, and MCI long distance telephone services. **Other Resources:** To protest, write to: AT&T, 550 Madison Ave., New York, NY 10022. (800) 222-0300; ITT, 320 Park Ave., New York, NY 10022. (800) 526-3000; MCI, 230 Shilling, Hunt Valley, MD 21031.

☷ ♦ **Nuclear Free America**
325 E. 25th Ave.
Baltimore, MD 21218     (301)235-3575
**Concern(s):** peace; environment; health; anti-nuclear; hazardous/toxic waste. A national clearinghouse and resource center for the grassroots Nuclear Free Zone movement. NFA has assisted thousands of individual organizations and communities in their efforts to create a Nuclear Free World. There are now over 3600 NFZs in 24 countries, making this the largest anti-nuclear movement in the world. The NFZ movement challenges communities to debate and decide their own role in the nuclear arms race, independent of Congress and the President. **Other Resources:** See newsletter, THE NEW ABOLITIONIST. Also; THE TOP 50 NUCLEAR WEAPONS CONTRACTORS; PROFILES OF THE TOP 50 NUCLEAR WEAPONS CONTRACTORS; NUCLEAR FREE ZONE REGISTRY (directories). **Est.:** 1982. **Contact(s):** Albert Donnay (Director).

E ♦ **Nuclear Information and Resource Service**
1424 16th St. NW, #601
Washington, DC 20036  (202)328-0002
**Concern(s):** environment; energy; health; hazardous/toxic; anti-nuclear; hazardous/toxic waste. A national clearinghouse and networking center for people concerned about nuclear power issues. Dedicated to sound, non-nuclear energy policy, it serves safe energy and environmental activists with reliable, accurate information, resources, and organizing assistance. Provides citizens with the information/tools necessary to challenge nuclear facilities/policies. Works to increase energy efficiency toward a sustainable, renewable energy future. Stop deregulation of radioactive waste. **Other Resources:** See THE NUCLEAR MONITOR, a newsletter and magazine, GROUND-SWELL; NIRS ALERT; publications list; NIRSNET (BBS) are available to members. Publishes an energy audit manual for towns and universities: TEACHER'S RESOURCE GUIDE. Internships offer $100-week. **Dues:** $20/yr. **Contact(s):** Michael Mariotte, Diane D'Arrigo.

☷ ♦ **Nuclear Information Center**
1431 Ocean Ave.
Santa Monica, CA 90401
**Concern(s):** peace; anti-nuclear. An organization that provides information on nuclear tests, weapons, and plants throughout the world. **Other Resources:** Sponsors The Global Walk.

☷ ♦ **Nuclear Weapons Freeze of Santa Cruz County**
See MONTHLY PLANET newspaper.

T ♦ **Nuevo Instituto de Centroamerica**
See newsletter, EL ESTILIANO and N.I.C.A.

☷ ♦ **The Nukewatch**
Box 2658
Madison, WI 53701-2658   (608)256-4146
**Affiliation:** Progressive Foundation. **Concern(s):** peace; environment; boycott; activism; nonviolence; civil disobedience; anti-nuclear. Originally chartered as The Progressive Foundation (still its legal name), Nukewatch broadened its agenda after federal government in 1979 abandoned its attempted censorship of The Progressive. It developed programs to promote formation of NFZ's, to encourage public and private disinvestment in major nuclear weapons contractors and facilitate direct citizen action against the nuclear threat. It heightens public awareness of the H-bomb in our midst, stimulating greater resistance to militarism. **Other Resources:** Programs—Missile Silo Campaign; Citizen's Action Guides; The H-bomb Truck Watch campaign; Invest In Peace; Protest and Resist. Newsletter, PEACE PLANTER and newspaper, NUKEWATCH PATHFINDER. Offers: maps, poster, T-shirts, postcards, NFZ kits. **Contact(s):** Samuel H. Day, Jr. (Co-director).

✍ ♦ **The Oasis Group**
Box 330094
Kahului, HI 96733          (808)877-8016
**Concern(s):** education; environment; media; broadcasting. Runs a children's gardening project in conjunction with local schools and a retail organic fertilizer company. Also sponsors an environmental radio program. **Member:** Co-op America.

✍ ♦ **Oberlin Student Co-operative Association**
Wilder Box 86
Oberlin, OH 44074
**Concern(s):** education; economics; students; cooperatives.

L ♦ **Occupational Safety and Health Law Center**
Box 280
Shepherdstown, WV 25443   (304)876-0511
**Concern(s):** labor; justice; health; occupational safety; reform.

E ♦ **Ocean Alliance**
Bldg. E, Fort Mason
San Francisco, CA 94123     (415)441-9570
**Concern(s):** environment; wildlife/endangered species; conservation. Organization working on conservation, education, advocacy and research to protect and understand whales and their habitat. Conservation and education organization working for the whales and their ocean habitat. **Other Resources:** See WHALE CENTER JOURNAL newsletter. Conducts Adopt-A-Gray-Whale program. **Contact(s):** Mark Palmer (Executive Director), Thomas Johnson (President).

E ♦ **Ocean Arks International**
1 Locust St.
Falmouth, MA 02540     (508)540-6801
**Concern(s):** environment; water. Fish, snails, plants, and trees are major parts of the septage treatment facility of the town of Harwich on Cape Cod engineered by John Todd. It has now been proven that high quality water can be produced from septage without the use of hazardous chemicals. **Other Resources:** See ANNALS OF EARTH (periodicals). **Contact(s):** John Todd.

A ♦ **Ocean View Farms**
3540 Overland Ave.
Los Angeles, CA 90034   (310)836-2171
**Concern(s):** agriculture; environment; organic; conservation; water; pesticides. An organic community garden group. "We give free workshops/demonstrations of composting to the public. Our aim is to grow vegetables and fruits without pesticides or poisons while conserving water." Nonprofit.

E ♦ **The Oceanic Society**
See Friends of the Earth. **Contact(s):** Curtis Clifton (Information Officer).

✈ ♦ **Oceanic Society Expeditions**
Fort Mason Center
Building E
San Francisco, CA 94939     (415)441-1106
**Affiliation:** Oceanic Society. **Concern(s):** education; Third World; travel; polar. Tours to Galapagos, Costa Rica, Belize, Alaska, Australia, Botswana, Indonesia, and more. Free schedule of trips. **Member:** Co-op America.

✈ ♦ **Odyssey Tours**
1821 Wilshire Boulevard, #550
Santa Monica, CA 90403   (310)453-1042
**Concern(s):** education; Third World; travel; development. Educational and cultural exchange trips to Asia. Travelers experience leadership training, community organizing or sacred adventure in China, Tibet, India and Nepal. **Contact(s):** Steve Goldsmith.

T ♦ **Office of the Americas**
See FOCUS newsletter.

### ✍ ◆ Office on Global Education

See MAKE A WORLD OF DIFFERENCE: CREATIVE ACTIVITIES FOR GLOBAL LEARNING (directories).

### L ◆ Oil, Chemical and Atomic Workers International Union

1126 16th St. NW
Washington, DC 20036    (202)223-5570

**Concern(s):** labor; unions. **Other:** Box 2812, Denver, CO 80201. Joseph M. Misbrener , President.

### ✍ ◆ The Ojai Foundation

Box 1620
Ojai, CA 93023    (805)646-8343

**Concern(s):** education; health; spiritual; transformation; holism. Situated on 40 acres of beautiful land in the Upper Ojai Valley, the Foundation was established as an educational institution. "Between 1979 and 1987, we undertook a bold educational experiment that brought together teachers from all over the world to participate in interdisciplinary and intercultural dialog, explore social and environmental issues, and engage in individual and group practice. In 1987, the Foundation School was established for students." Nonprofit. **Est.:** 1975.

### ✍ ◆ Omega Arts Network

Box 1227
Jamaica Plain, MA 02130    (617)522-8300

**Concern(s):** education; health; spiritual; transformation; holism. "We are working toward a major Transformational Arts Festival in 1992; the 200th anniversary of the discovery of America by Columbus, a time for artists to join together in the healing of the Earth." **Other Resources:** Database of over 600 "transformational/visionary/sacred artists." **Contact(s):** Saphira Linden (Founder). (617)522-4181.

### S ◆ Omega Institute

Lake Dr., RD 2, Box 377
Rhinebeck, NY 12572    (914)266-4301

**Concern(s):** spiritual; arts; health; psychology; transformation; literature; poetry; music. 250+ "programs in psychology, the arts, spirituality, and health with such renowned faculty as Thich Nhat Hanh, Anne Wilson Schaef, Rosanne Cash, Bernie Seigel, Gabrielle Roth, Deepok Chopra, Andre Codrescu, Ysaye Barnwell, and Philip Kapleau. Enjoy tennis, swimming, and hiking. Lakeside campus available for rentals. Call or send for information." **Other Resources:** Extensive catalog available. **Est.:** 1982. **Contact(s):** Elizabeth Lesser (Editor), Stephan Rechtschaffen (Founder/President). (914)266-8049.

### ☢ ◆ On Beyond War

222 High St.
Palo Alto, CA 94301    (415)328-7756

**Concern(s):** peace; education; disarmament; global understanding; volunteers. An educational movement providing concerned individuals with the opportunity to influence the most critical issue of our time: how to end war on the planet. There will always be conflict, but in the nuclear age it is imperative for humanity to learn to resolve its differences by means other than violence and war. It is now active throughout the US and in a number of other countries. Beyond War is now an active volunteer organization throughout the US and in a number of other countries. **Other Resources:** Publishes newsletter, BEYOND WAR. Nonprofit. **Contact(s):** Richard L. Rathburn (President).

### ☢ ◆ 1% For Peace

Box 658
Ithaca, NY 14851    (607)273-1919

**Concern(s):** peace; economics; education; economic conversion; peace dividend; global understanding. A new organization seeking a vast increase in funding for activities which promote understanding and cooperation among nations divided by cultural and ideological differences. One of its goals is to pass a law committing an amount equal to 1% of the defense budget for citizen and cultural exchanges and cooperative international ventures in science, business, the arts, education, and other fields. Nonprofit.

### ? ◆ One World

5772 E. Campo Walk
Long Beach, CA 90803

**Concern(s):** future; ideation. Seeks to pool the ideas and hearts of all people and all organizations to assist in world change.

### ✈ ◆ One World Family Travel Network

c/o Lost Valley Center
Box 111, 81868 Los Valley Lane
Dexter, OR 97431    (503)937-3351

**Concern(s):** education; networking; travel. A network linking travelers with socially responsible travel options. Membership includes a directory, periodic updates, and other support services. **Member:** Co-op America.

### J ◆ Operation PUSH

930 E. 50th St.
Chicago, IL 60615    (312)373-3366

**Concern(s):** justice; economics; boycott; corporate responsibility; socially-responsible investing; discrimination. Has weekly forums broadcasted on WGCI 1390AM. It encourages everybody to help make a change. BOYCOTT NIKE — Sells millions of dollars of merchandise to African-Americans without involving these companies or individuals in their operations. Products: All NIKE brand footwear and athletic wear. **Other Resources:** To protest, write to: NIKE Corp., 9000 S.W. Numbus Dr., Beaverton, OR 97005-7198. (503) 671-6453. **Dues:** $20/yr. **Contact(s):** Rev. Willie T. Barrow.

### E ◆ Operation Stronghold

Box 234
Chiloquin, OR 97624    (503)783-2345

**Concern(s):** environment; wildlife/endangered species; conservation; wilderness. Coalesces landowners into a voluntary organization which encourages the development of wildlife-potential private lands. A program led by the private sector which helps farmers, ranchers, timber producers and other landowners create vital reservoirs of water. **Contact(s):** Dayton Hyde (President).

### T ◆ Opportunity International

Box 3695
Oak Brook, IL 60522    (312)279-9300

**Concern(s):** Third World; development; hunger. Formerly the Institute for International Development, its purpose is to fight hunger at its root cause; unemployment. People in developing countries don't have food because they don't have jobs. OI creates jobs among the poor by sharing the business financing and know-how needed to create free enterprise opportunities for small family business.

### ☢ ◆ Oregon Peace Institute

921 SW Morrison
Portland, OR 97223

**Concern(s):** peace.

### A ◆ Organic Food Network

c/o American Fruitarian Society
1108 Regal Row
Austin, TX 78748    (512)280-5566

**Affiliation:** American Fruitarian Society. **Concern(s):** agriculture; organic. **Contact(s):** Ann Abbott.

### A ◆ Organic Foods Production Association of North America

Box 31
Belchertown, MA 01007

**Concern(s):** agriculture; environment; sustainability; natural resources. A trade association of farm organizations, processors and distributors who support the development of a sustainable agricultural system based on the stewardship of natural resources and the development, maintenance and protection of healthy agricultural soil. **Contact(s):** Marc Schwartz (President).

### A ◆ Organic Growers and Buyers Association

1405 Silver Lake Rd. NW
St. Paul, MN 55112-9301    (612)378-8335

**Concern(s):** agriculture; economics; health; organic; nutrition; alternative consumer.

### $ ◆ Organization for Economic Cooperation and Development

2001 L St. NW, #700
Washington, DC 20036    (202)785-6323

**Concern(s):** economics. US office. **Other Resources:** See DIRECTORY OF INTER-AMERICAN AND OTHER ASSOCIATIONS IN THE AMERICAS; DIRECTORY OF DEVELOPMENT RESEARCH AND TRAINING INSTITUTES IN AFRICA.

### P ◆ Organize Training Center

1095 Market St., #419
San Francisco, CA 94103    (415)552-8990

**Concern(s):** politics; economics; community self-reliance; grassroots organizing. Supports grassroots leaders and organizers throughout the US with training, consultation, and publications designed to help them gain the knowledge and skills needed to build and maintain strong community organizations of low- to middle-income people. OTC consults with local leaders to help them launch new organizing projects and each year OTC offers two 4-day workshops on community organizing. **Other Resources:** OTC publishes a variety of materials of interest to community organizers and leaders of community organizations, including THE ORGANIZER MAILING, a quarterly compilation of articles and reprints. **Est.:** 1973. **Frequency:** 4/yr. **Subscription:** $40, $50 organizations. **Price:** $12/ea. **Pages:** 80. **Publisher:** OTC. **Other Formats:** Prodigy under CSVF16A. **E-Network:** A.O.L. (America On-Line). **ID:** Reb Moshe. **Contact(s):** Mike Miller (Executive Director), Moshe Ben Asher (Staff Organizer).

### ☼ ◆ Orgone Biophysical Research Lab

Box 1395
El Cerrito, CA 94530    (510)526-5978

**Concern(s):** energy; environment; education; analysis; research; science. Devoted to replication of the Sex-Economic and Orgone Biophysical Research findings of the late Dr. Wilhelm Reich. Experimental drought-abatement and Desert-Greening programs, publications, educational activities and workshops. **Other Resources:** Annual, PULSE OF THE PLANET; Prospectus: "Drought Abatement Outreach Program"; Prospectus: "Desert Greening Program." educational workshops. Nonprofit. **Est.:** 1978. **Publisher:** Natural Energy Works. **Contact(s):** Dr. James DeMeo (Director). **Other:** Natural Energy Works, Box 864, El Cerrito, CA 94530.

### ✈ ◆ Our Developing World

13004 Paseo Presada
Saratoga, CA 95070    (408)376-0755

**Concern(s):** education; Third World; development; travel. A organization designed to bring the realities of the Third World to North Americans. Study tours focus on people and socio-economic development. Includes meetings with grassroots contacts. Nonprofit. (408)379-4431.

### ✍ ◆ Our Planet in Every Classroom

c/o World Federalist Association
UN Office, 777 UN Plaza
New York, NY 10017    (212)599-1320

**Affiliation:** World Federalist Association. **Concern(s):** education; peace; World order; United Nations. WFA began in Canada, where more than 50,000 posters have been distributed to classrooms in the past two years. It has since been taken to more than 20 other countries, including the Soviet Union and the US. In keeping with the spirit of the project, it is non-political and not for profit. The poster bears only the NASA image of the full Earth on a black background, with no words or border. .

### E ◆ Outdoor Industry Conservation Alliance

Box 88126, Public Affairs Dept.
Seattle, WA 98138-0126    (206)395-5955

**Affiliation:** Recreational Equipment, Inc.. **Concern(s):** environment; recreation; conservation. A group of companies working to raise money for environmental concerns. **Contact(s):** Wally Smith (President), Kathleen Beamer.

### E ◆ Outdoor Writers Association of America

2017 Cato Ave., #101
State College, PA 16801    (814)234-1011

**Concern(s):** environment; education; recreation. An international organization representing professional communicators who report and reflect upon America's diverse interests in the outdoors. More than 1700 members, they are writers, broadcasters, photographers, artists, and lecturers living and working in the US, Canada, Mexico, and other parts of the world. Dedicated to the preservation and promotion of the outdoors and outdoor recreation, effective communication of the numerous alternatives that face today's recreationist. **Other Resources:** Newsletter, OUTDOORS UNLIMITED. **Est.:** 1927. **Contact(s):** Sylvia G. Bashline (Executive Director).

### T ◆ Overground Railroad

See TELEGRAPH NEWS (periodicals).

### ✍ ◆ Overseas Development Council

1717 Massachusetts Ave. NW, #501
Washington, DC 20036    (202)234-8701

**Concern(s):** education; Third World; global understanding; development. Private organization engaged in comprehensive analysis of the economic and political issues of US-Third World interdependence. The Council is recognized as the major forum for the discussion of US relations with developing countries and as a source of timely analysis and innovative approaches to global problems. **Other Resources:** Publications catalog available. Nonprofit. **Fax:** (202)745-0067. **Contact(s):** John W. Sewell (President), Victor H. Palmieri (Chairman).

### ✈ ◆ Overseas Development Network

Box 1430
Cambridge, MA 02238    (617)868-3002

**Concern(s):** Third World; peace; travel; volunteer; education. This network of Third World students in the US is building links with their people at home and young people around the world. It has intern programs in Bangladesh, Zimbabwe, the Philippines, South and Central America and Appalachia. Some 70 student groups in the US provide workshops, meeting, and seminars to address fundamental issues of global poverty, injustice, and peace. Live, learn, and work with grassroots groups in many parts of the world. Other: Box 2306, Stanford, CA 94305.

**F ♦ Overseas Education Fund**
See Women, Law, and Development Network.

**T ♦ OXFAM America**
See OXFAM AMERICA NEWS letter.

**E ♦ P.O.L.I.T.E. (Permission Of Landowner In Order To Enter)**
Box 422
Sturgeon Bay, WI 54235 (414)743-6777
**Affiliation:** Whitetails Unlimited, Inc. **Concern(s):** environment; justice; wildlife/endangered species; civil liberties. Project that requires hunters to get the permission of the landowner before they enter the property to hunt.

**⚥ ♦ Pace Peace Center**
Pace University
78 N. Broadway
White Plains, NY 10603 (914)633-0005
**Concern(s):** peace; world order; international law; conflict resolution. Makes available a comprehensive legal frame of reference to world peace problems. It focuses on international law codification, strengthening of international courts and effective law enforcement through improved international organizations, arms control agreements, effective international sanctions, and protection through law of human rights and global resources. Cooperates with many other institutions in peace studies/educational activities. Funding is entirely dependent on contributions. **Contact(s):** Benjamin Ferencz (Executive Director).

**⚥ ♦ Pacific Peace Fund**
5516 Roosevelt Way NE
Seattle, WA 98105 (206)525-0025
**Concern(s):** peace.

**✍ ♦ Pacific Studies Center**
See GLOBAL ELECTRONICS newsletter.

**✍ ♦ Pacific University of Hawaii**
c/o Lao Valley Lodge
RR1, Box 518
Wailuku, HI 96793 (808)242-5555
**Concern(s):** education; arts; media; spiritual; activism; fine arts; culture; transformation; global understanding. The university will create an academic arm to train people in the use of arts and media for planetary transformation. Degrees will be offered at the Associate, Bachelors, Masters & Doctorate levels. **Contact(s):** Ed Elkin (Academic Dean).

**E ♦ Pacific Whale Foundation**
101 N. Kihei Rd.
Kihei, HI 96753 (808)879-8860
**Concern(s):** environment; wildlife/endangered species; oceans. Conducts field research worldwide and assists government and non-government agencies in developing conservation policies and plans for endangered marine life; involved with the scientific study of the ocean and its marine mammals; applies research findings to the preservation of the marine environment; sponsors education and conservation programs to enhance ecological awareness. **Other Resources:** Ocean Outreach Docents and marine debris clean-up fundraising. **Dues:** $15/student-$500/patron. (800)WHALE-11.

**E ♦ Pacific Yearly Meeting Committee on Unity With Nature**
See EARTH LIGHT magazine and Friends Committee on Unity with Nature.

**T ♦ Palestine Solidarity Committee**
Box 372, Peck Slip Station
New York, NY 10272 (212)964-7299
**Concern(s):** Third World; Mid-East; networking. An expanding national Palestinian organization.

**J ♦ Pan-American Indian Association and Adopted Tribal Peoples**
Box 244
Nocatee, FL 33864
**Concern(s):** justice; Third World; Native Americans; indigenous peoples.

**T ♦ Panos Institute**
1717 Massachusetts Ave. NW, #301
Washington, DC 20036-2001 (202)483-0044
**Concern(s):** Third World; health; environment; hunger; development; sustainability. An independent information and policy studies organization dedicated in working in partnership with others to raise public understanding of sustainable development. **Other Resources:** Magazine, Panoscope. Offices in Hungary, Paris and London. **E-Network:** Econet. **ID:** "panos". **Fax:** (202)483-3059. Telex: 490-000-8533PAN. **Contact(s):** Don Edwards (Executive Director).

**♿ ♦ Paralyzed Veterans of America**
7 Mill Brook Rd.
Wilton, NH 03086
**Concern(s):** health; justice; disabled's rights; disabled. One of its first legislative victories helped veterans purchase automobiles with special equipment. Continues to work for legislation to create federal standards for full access for all. Depends entirely on tax-deductible contributions. For the last 15 years it has distributed packages of greeting cards to raise money. **Other Resources:** Cosponsors the National Veterans Wheelchair Games, has 55 offices around the country to help veterans get the benefits for which they are entitled, and established the PVA/EPVA Center for Neuroscience and Regeneration Research of Yale University. Nonprofit. **Est.:** 1946. **Contact(s):** Victor S. McCoy, Sr. (President).

**⚥ ♦ Parenting in the Nuclear Age**
6501 Telegraph Ave.
Oakland, CA 94609 (510)658-7101
**Concern(s):** peace; family; education.

**⚥ ♦ Parents, Teachers and Students For Social Responsibility**
Box 517
Moretown, VT 05660 (802)229-0137
**Concern(s):** peace; education; politics; grassroots organizing; government accountability. Promotes a cherished American ideal that "we the people" are the government and those who hold public office are public servants. "We stress the necessity of being well-informed in order to make the decisions that will best care for the next generation. We recognize each individual's ability to make a difference and believe that the most effective way to teach young people about democracy is to practice it. We believe that the greatest health risk facing children today is nuclear war." **Other Resources:** Publishes newsletter, YOPPY and "The Dot Chart" **Contact(s):** Glenn W. Hawkes (Executive Director). (802)223-3409.

**? ♦ Parliament of Innovators**
14426 NE 16th Pl.
Bellevue, WA 98007 (206)641-5206
**Concern(s):** future; ideation. The Parliament was a major objective of the Soviet-American Citizens' Summit in Washington, D.C. in February 1988, to promote joint projects in education, cooperative entrepreneurship, medicine, health care, cooperation in space and other areas.

**⚥ ♦ Parliamentarians Global Action**
211 E. 43rd St., #1604
New York, NY 10017 (212)687-7755
**Concern(s):** peace; world order. Co-sponsored with the Movement of Non-Aligned Nations, a conference calling on all nations to accept compulsory jurisdiction of the World Court in time for the centennial of the first (1899) World Peace Conference at the Hague. **Contact(s):** Aaron Tovish (Executive Director).

**J ♦ Partisan Defense Committee**
Box 99, Canal Street Station
New York, NY 10013 (212)406-4252
**Concern(s):** justice; minority rights; racism; political prisoners. "A class-struggle, non-sectarian legal and social defense organization which champions cases and causes in the interest of the whole of the working people. This purpose is in accordance with the politcla views of the Sparticist League." **Other Resources:** A magazine, CLASS-STRUGGLE DEFENSE NOTES. **Contact(s):** Deborah Mackson (Executive Director), Paul Cooperstein (Secretary).

**E ♦ Partners For Livable Places**
1429 21st St. NW
Washington, DC 20036 (202)887-5990
**Concern(s):** environment; economics; conservation; social ecology; community self-reliance. Goal: To improve the quality of life in our nation's communities, primarily through conservation and sensitive development of the physical environment, and to encourage a greater public consciousness of those physical surroundings and the ecological and social consequences. Members stress the process of partnership between public and private sectors for cost-efficient use of resources and believe that livability of a community is determined by local decisions and local actions. **Other Resources:** Formerly National Coalition for Amenities. See LIVABILITY newsletter. **Est.:** 1977. **Dues:** $35/yr. **Fax:** (202)466-4845. **Contact(s):** Daniel McCahn (Information Officer).

**T ♦ Partners of the Americas**
1424 K St. NW, #700
Washington, DC 20005 (202)628-3300
**Concern(s):** Third World; hunger; development. Promotes economic and social development in the Western hemisphere. US states are "partnered" with Latin American countries, and citizens on both sides of the partnership work together to carry out development or educational projects at the grassroots level. Program areas include agricul-

ture, culture, helping the disabled, economic development, education, emergency preparedness, health, and sports. **Contact(s):** Martha Lewis, Alan Rubin.

**✍ ♦ Partnership for Service-Learning**
Intercultural Studies, Warren Wilson College
701 Warren Wilson College Rd.
Swannanoa, NC 28778 (704)298-3325
**Concern(s):** education; Third World; global understanding; development. Consortium of colleges, service agencies, churches and related organizations united to foster service-learning in American higher education. **Contact(s):** Virginia McKinley, Chris Ahrens

**☉ ♦ Passive Solar Industries Council**
2836 Duke St.
Alexandria, VA 22314 (703)823-3356
**Concern(s):** energy; politics; solar energy; lobbying.

**M ♦ Pate Institute For Human Survival**
30 Putnam Park Rd.
West Redding, CT 06896
**Concern(s):** media; peace; future; communications; conflict resolution; ideation. A Connecticut-based think tank on communications. **Contact(s):** Joan Dydo.

**♥ ♦ Pathfinder Fund**
9 Galen
Watertown, MA 02172-4501 (617)924-7200
**Concern(s):** family; feminism; demographics; environment; economics; hunger; population growth; family planning; empowerment; population. Family planning is directly responsible for improving the health of mothers and children, and helping women to control their childbearing and seek new options. Fewer people means less strain on fragile economies, and provides opportunity for more food, housing, energy, classrooms, jobs and improving the environment. Encourages innovative solutions to population problems and continues to direct the developing world's focus on family planning as a humane and pragmatic response. Nonprofit. **Est.:** 1957.

**⚥ ♦ Pax Christi USA**
348 E. 10th St.
Erie, PA 16503 (814)453-4955
**Affiliation:** Pax Christi International. **Concern(s):** peace; justice; spiritual; interfaith; lobbying; nonviolence. An interfaith international organization that contributes to building peace and justice by exploring and articulating the ideals of Christian nonviolence. They also strive to make this a part of their personal life and the structure of society. **Other Resources:** Publishes a pocket sized book, WORDS OF PEACE and newsletter, PAX CHRISTI USA. See, also, Center on Conscience and War. **Contact(s):** Bishop Thomas J. Gumbleton (National President), Mary Lou Kownacki, OSB (National Coordinator).

**T ♦ Pax World Foundation**
4400 E. West Hwy., #130
Bethesda, MD 20814 (301)657-2440
**Affiliation:** Pax World Fund. **Concern(s):** Third World; peace; hunger; development; conflict resolution. Promotes international understanding, reconciliation, and development by providing financial support for selected programs and projects. Third World activities emphasize meeting basic human needs through small-scale community-based initiatives. Other projects further peaceful relations among people through organizing Friendship Tours to troubled regions of the world, and through support of conflict resolution organizations.

**$ ♦ PACE of Philadelphia**
See GRASSROOTS ECONOMIC ORGANIZING (GEO) NEWSLETTER.

**✈ ♦ PCI Tours**
Rex Govorchin Association
8405 NW 53rd St. A108
Miami, FL 33166 (800)255-2508
**Concern(s):** environment; forests. Tours to Costa Rica, including sightseeing in San Jose and tropical rainforests. **Member:** Co-op America.

**⚥ ♦ Peace and Justice Coalition**
186 College St.
Burlington, VT 05401 (802)863-2345
**Concern(s):** peace; justice; demographics; world order; conversion; poverty; homelessness; activism; networking. "We are working for a world in which international conflicts are settled without war, and in which people treat each other with love, dignity, and justice. ...striving to end the threat of nuclear annihilation by promoting nuclear disarmament. ...to stop harmful US military and economic intervention in the affairs of other countries. We oppose violation of human rights." An educational organization representing 12+ Burlington area groups working to form a more trusting, empowered society. **Other Resources:** Central clearinghouse for information on peace activities, library, office support services, peace store, newsletter, PEACE AND

JUSTICE NEWS letter. Nonprofit. **Est.:** 1979. **Member:** Co-op America. **Contact(s):** Greg Guma (Coordinator). (802)863-8326.

### ☷♦ Peace Brigades International
PBI/USA, Box 1233
Harvard Square Station
Cambridge, MA 02238   (617)625-1786

**Concern(s):** peace; justice; conflict resolution; civil liberties; nonviolence. PBI sends unarmed peace teams invited into areas of violent repression or conflict to provide protective accompaniment to grassroots workers whose lives are threatened to foster reconciliation and peace dialogue and to education and train in nonviolence and human rights. **Other Resources:** Publishes a membership newsletter, PBI/USA REPORT. Nonprofit. **Est.:** 1981. **Frequency:** 12/yr. **Subscription:** $25/yr. includes newsletter. **Pages:** 18. **Circ.:** 1.2M. **E-Network:** PeaceNet. **ID:** 'pbiusa'. **Fax:** (617)876-8186. **Contact(s):** Mary MacArthur, John Lindsay-Poland (Coordinators). (415)564-9707.

### ☷♦ Peace Center of Marin
1024 Sir Francis Drake Blvd.
San Anselmo, CA 94960
**Concern(s):** peace.

### ☷♦ Peace Development Fund
Affiliation: Pacific Peace Fund. See PEACE DEVELOPMENTS and EXCHANGE PROJECT NEWSLETTER (periodicals).

### ☷♦ Peace Education Resource Center
2437 N. Grant Blvd.
Milwaukee, WI 53210   (414)445-9736
**Affiliation:** Milwaukee Peace Center. **Concern(s):** peace. **Contact(s):** Jacqueline Haessly.

### ☷♦ Peace Farm
See Red River Peace Network (RRPN).

### ☷♦ Peace Links
See PEACE LINKS - WOMEN AGAINST NUCLEAR WAR (periodicals).

### ☷♦ Peace Pac
110 Maryland Ave. NE
Washington, DC 20002   (202)543-4100
**Affiliation:** Council for a Liveable World. **Concern(s):** peace; politics; conflict resolution; disarmament; anti-nuclear; lobbying. A House of Representatives lobbying group for nuclear arms control. Supports anti-nuclear House candidates by raising campaign contributions. **Est.:** 1982. **Other:** 20 Park Plaza, Boston, MA 02116.

### ☷♦ Peace Resource Center
13 W. Figueroa
Santa Barbara, CA 93101-3203   (805)965-8583
**Concern(s):** peace.

### ☷♦ The Peace Resource Project
Box 1122
Arcata, CA 95521   (707)822-4229
**Concern(s):** peace; environment; activism. "...brings you a diversified selection of resources on peace/social justice/environmental issues, such as colorful adult & children's T-shirts, button, bumpers stickers, rubber stamps, posters, books, audiocassettes, and postcards. We strive to give excellent service." **Other Resources:** Recycled paper catalog. **Fax:** (707)822-6202.

### ☷♦ Peace Studies Unit
United Nations, #3235
New York, NY 10017   (212)963-1234
**Concern(s):** peace; Third World; United Nations. **Other Resources:** Publishes PEACE NOTES.

### ☷♦ Peace With Justice Week
777 UN Plaza
New York, NY 10017   (212)682-3633
**Concern(s):** peace; justice; education; politics; spiritual; interfaith; conflict resolution; lobbying; law; social justice. Sponsored by dozens of national organizations, this is an annual interfaith event held in mid-October that has grown into a major educational and organization vehicle for people of faith to make the linkages between issues of justice and peace clearer. Activities range from worship services to educational activities to legislative advocacy to Shalom Fairs.

### ☷♦ Peacemaker Movement
See PEACEMAKER (periodicals).

### ☷♦ Peacemakers International
Box 42488
San Francisco, CA 94142   (415)668-2956
**Concern(s):** peace; education; activism; conservation. Sponsors the Walking Rainbow for Service, Healing, Peacemaking and the

Greening of the Earth. **Contact(s):** Jane Jarlsberg, Pam Davis (707)523-1229.

### ✍♦ Peacemaking for Children
See PEACEMAKING FOR CHILDREN NEWSLETTER.

### ✐♦ PeaceWorks
Center for the Dances of Universal Peace
Box 626
Fairfax, CA 94930
**Affiliation:** Center for the Dances of Universal Peace. **Concern(s):** arts; peace; theater.

### ☷♦ The Pembina Institute
Box 7558
Drayton Valley, AL T0E 0M0 Canada
**Concern(s):** peace; education; conflict resolution. Publishes Peace Education News.

### M♦ PEN American Center
See AMERICAN RIGHT TO READ NEWSLETTER.

### E♦ Peninsula Conservation Foundation
See Harbinger Communications.

### E♦ Pennsylvania Resources Council
Box 88
Media, PA 19063-0088   (215)565-9131
**Concern(s):** environment; media; resources; conservation; recycling; computer networking; electronic democracy; BBS. Pennsylvania's oldest nonprofit organization, recognized nationally for its expertise in recycling, waste reduction and litter control. **Other Resources:** Publishes booklet on recycling and waste reduction for consumers — ALL ABOUT RECYCLING; the ENVIRONMENTAL SHOPPING HANDBOOK and provides a hotline, sells canvas shopping bags, and runs database/BBS (215) 892-9940. Also PRC NEWSLETTER. Nonprofit. **Est.:** 1939. **Office:** 25 West 3rd St. Media, PA 19063. Hotline: (800)468-6772. **Contact(s):** Ruth Becker (Executive Director).

### H♦ People Against Cancer
Box 10
Otho, IA 50569-0010   (515)972-4444
**Concern(s):** health; alternative consumer. Distributes educational materials concerning non-toxic alternative forms of cancer therapy and a wide range of literature including an international directory to alternative therapy centers; provides counseling services fot those seeking guidance regarding therapeutic alternatives. Nonprofit. **Contact(s):** Frank D. Wiewel (President).

### J♦ People Against Racist Terror (PART)
Box 10488
Burbank, CA 91510
See TURNING THE TIDE newsletter.

### E♦ People for Eldorado Mountain
Box 305
Eldorado Springs, CO 80025 (303)449-4532
**Concern(s):** environment.

### J♦ People for the American Way
2000 M St. NW, #400
Washington, DC 20036   (202)467-4999
**Concern(s):** justice; politics; spiritual; feminism; discrimination; pro-choice; reform. An organization which attempts to show the real American way, not the one some of the fundamentalists would have you believe. **Other Resources:** Press clips and FORUM newspaper. **Contact(s):** Arthur J. Kropp (President).

### ☛♦ People for the Ethical Treatment of Animals (PETA)
Box 42516
Washington, DC 20015-0516   (301)770-7444
**Concern(s):** environment; health; agriculture; animal rights; boycott; corporate responsibility; socially-responsible investing; green consumer; nutrition; alternative consumer. National animal protection organization with more than a quarter of a million members. It is dedicated to establishing the rights and improving the lives of all animals—by educating, changing lifestyles and exposing cruelty wherever it occurs. Seeks to educate policymakers and the public about issues involving the intense, prolonged and unjustifiable abuse of animals, and to promote an understanding of the inherent rights of sentient animals. **Other Resources:** See PETA NEWS and THE PETA GUIDE TO COMPASSIONATE LIVING AND ANIMAL LIBERATION (directories). Catalogue available. Hotline: (301)770-8980. **Contact(s):** Alex Pacheco (Chairman), Ingrid Newkirk (National Director). (301)770-8976 (catalog). BOYCOTT GILLETTE — They were found to be in violation of the Animal Welfare Act for inhumane and unnecessary animal testing. Loreal—They conduct cruel and

unusual animal testing. Carme—Sold to IRDC which was found guilty of six willful violations of laws preventing cruelty in animal testing. Other Resources: To protest, write to: Gillette, The Prudential Towers Bldg., Boston, MA 02199 (617) 421-7765. Loreal, c/o Cosmair, Guy Preleougne, 575 5th Ave. NY, NY 10017 (800) 631-7356. IRDC, Frances Wazeter, 900 Main St. Mattewan, MI 49071 (616) 638-3336. Office: 4928 Wyaconda Rd. Rocky Ridge, MD 21778.

### ☷♦ People For A Change
131 Mangels Ave.
San Francisco, CA 94131
**Concern(s):** peace; spiritual; feminism; justice; peace dividend; economic conversion; interfaith; sexism; social justice; minority rights A non-sectarian, multiracial, multi-cultural, progressive, political, educational, activist, subscription-based organization that believes in peaceful coexistence, conversion to a peace economy, environmental protection, economic justice, and a world free from war racism, sexism, and ageism. The are determined to make up in numbers what they lack in financial resources. **Other Resources:** Newsletter, PEOPLE FOR A CHANGE, BUILDING OURSELVES A BASE. **Dues:** $10/yr, half price to the nearly broke. **Contact(s):** George R. Fouke.

### ♿♦ People to People Committee for the Handicapped
See DIRECTORY OF ORGANIZATIONS INTERESTED IN PEOPLE WITH DISABILITIES.

### ☷♦ People's Anti-War Movement
See FIGHTING BACK newsletter.

### ☷♦ People's Assembly for the UN
301 E. 45th St.
'The Delegate', #20B
New York, NY 10017   (212)983-3353
**Affiliation:** International Network for a UN Second Assembly. **Concern(s):** peace; politics; United Nations; reform. Coalition of NGOs, individuals, seeking second chamber within UN system, for more direct representation of peoples: Arranges frequent seminars attracting people from many backgrounds. Nonprofit. **Est.:** 1975. **Contact(s):** Dr. Harry Lerner (Convenor).

### H♦ People's Medical Society
See DIAL 800 FOR HEALTH (directory).

### A♦ People, Food and Land Foundation
See National Land for People.

### E♦ The Peregrine Fund, Inc.
5666 West Flying Hawk Lane
Boise, ID 83709   (208)362-3716
**Concern(s):** environment; wildlife/endangered species; volunteers. Goal: The study and conservation of birds of prey and their habitat: Cooperates with government and non-governmental organizations, corporations and individuals to conserve biological diversity through investigations, training and education. Has established captive breeding and release programs in the US and assisted 34 other countries on six continents. **Other Resources:** Volunteers assist with all program area although primary focus is on providing tours to visitors. The Peregrine Falcon Recovery program and work in Mexico, Central America, Africa and Asia. **Dues:** $25-1000/yr.

### A♦ Permaculture Communications
See THE PERMACULTUTRE ACTIVIST (periodicals).

### A♦ Permaculture Drylands Institute
See Running Rain Society and guide, SUSTAINABLE LIVING IN DRYLANDS.

### A♦ Permaculture Institute of North America
4649 Sunnyside Ave. N, #305
Seattle, WA 98103-6900
**Concern(s):** agriculture; permaculture. Conducts scientific research in the area of agriculture.

### E♦ Permanent Charities Committee
11132 Ventura Blvd., #401
Studio City, CA 91604   (818)760-7722
**Concern(s):** environment; spiritual; media; activism; volunteers; philanthropy; press. Created to facilitate requests that charitable organizations make of the entertainment industry, PCC has donated over $80 million to more than 90 agencies throughout Southern California. PCC will have information about participating in its upcoming Earth Day Earth Walk to raise money for environmental groups.

### A♦ Pesticide Action Network
965 Mission St., #514
San Francisco, CA 94103   (415)541-9140
**Concern(s):** agriculture; environment; health; hazardous/toxic waste. Worldwide coalition of over 300 non-governmental organiza-

tions in more than 50 countries working to stop pesticide misuse and global pesticide proliferation. **Other Resources:** See PANNA OUT-LOOK, GLOBAL PESTICIDE MONITOR and DIRTY DOZEN CAMPAIGNER newsletters. **Fax:** (415)541-9253. **Contact(s):** Monica Moore (Executive Director).

**A ♦ Pesticide Watch**
1129 State St., #A
Santa Barbara, CA 93101 (805)564-1093
**Concern(s):** agriculture; environment; pesticides.

**M ♦ PEN American Center**
See AMERICAN RIGHT TO READ NEWSLETTER.

**T ♦ Philippine Resource Center**
See PHILIPPINE RESOURCE CENTER MONITOR (periodicals).

**T ♦ Philippine Workers Support Committee**
2252 Puna St.
Honolulu, HI 96817 (808)595-7362
**Concern(s):** Third World; labor; Philippines; foreign relations. A US labor-based network of chapters, committees and individuals united around the principle of supporting our sisters and brothers in the Philippines in their efforts to gain basic trade union and democratic rights. This Honolulu chapter acts as clearinghouse, coordinating center for the US network, and the main contact point with the Kilusang Mayo Uno, May First Movement, the leading nationalist democratic trade union center in the Philippines. **Other Resources:** Exposures to Philippine labor movement. Speakers, films, slides on Philippines, miscellaneous articles and research. KMY Correspondence subs ($15/year), bulletin of leading Philippine labor organizations. See PHILIPPINE LABOR ALERT. Nonprofit. **Est.:** 1984. **Dues:** $10, $25 unions, includes Alert. **Contact(s):** John Witeck (Coordinator).

**☛ ♦ Physicians Committee For Responsible Medicine**
Box 6322
Washington, DC 20015 (202)686-2210
**Concern(s):** health; environment; animal rights; alternative consumer; nutrition; preventive health. Nationwide network of physicians and others concerned with ethical and practical issues in medicine. It promotes the use of alternatives to animals in medical research, education and consumer products testing, preventative medicine and nutrition.

**⚕ ♦ Physicians For Social Responsibility (PSR)**
1000 16th St. NW, #810
Washington, DC 20036 (202)785-3777
**Concern(s):** peace; energy; education; disarmament; global understanding; anti-nuclear. National organization of over 12,000 doctors, medical students, and other health professionals. Produces studies and films and holds conferences on the dangers and medical effects of nuclear power and nuclear weapons. 153 chapters across the US. **Other Resources:** See PSR REPORTS (periodicals) and World Peace Camp for Teens. **Contact(s):** David Lewis (Director, Policy & Legislation).

**E ♦ Planet Drum Foundation**
Box 31251
San Francisco, CA 94131 (415)285-6556
**Concern(s):** environment; urban; bioregionalism; sustainability. An ecological, educational organization furthering the ideas of bioregionalism and urban sustainability through workshops, lectures, publications, and performances. **Other Resources:** See RAISE THE STAKES, news magazine. Book, A GREEN CITY PROGRAM FOR THE BAY AREA AND BEYOND; BIOREGIONAL DIRECTORY; also, Alaska Bioregional Network. Nonprofit. **Est.:** 1973. **Dues:** $20/yr.; $25 outside US; newspaper + 25% discounts. **Contact(s):** Peter Berg (Founder).

**E ♦ Planet Earth Foundation**
2701 1st Ave., #400
Seattle, WA 98121 (206)547-7000
**Concern(s):** environment. See Campaign to End Hunger. .

**⚕ ♦ Planetary Citizens**
325 North St.
San Francisco, CA 94103 (916)926-2241
**Concern(s):** peace; spiritual; education; activism; global understanding; world order. Founded by Norman Cousins, U Thant, and Donald Keys to assist in stimulating global awareness and a conscious identification with humanity as a whole, as stated in its motto, "ONE EARTH, ONE HUMANITY, ONE DEITY." The organization was predicated on the realization that adjustment of international relations and the achievement of global peace would require, above all else, emergence of a "global patriotism" or a sense of belonging to the human family, and the embracing of all its parts. **Other Resources:** See newsletters, PLANET EARTH and ONE FAMILY. **Est.:** 1974. **Contact(s):** Donald Keys (President), Norman Cousins (deceased) (Founder). (415)325-2939.

**M ♦ Planetary Consciousness**
3327 E. Broadway
Tucson, AZ 85716
**Concern(s):** media; multilogues. **Contact(s):** Joan Arnold.

**E ♦ Planetary Evolution Committee**
142 Spring St.
Newport, RI 02840 (401)848-5828
**Concern(s):** environment; peace; future; networking; analysis; research. A resource center consolidating the efforts of environmental and peace groups. **Other Resources:** Newsletter. **Dues:** $25/yr. **Member:** Co-op America.

**? ♦ Planetary Society**
65 N. Catalina Ave.
Pasadena, CA 91106 (818)793-5100
**Concern(s):** future; energy; education; environment; ideation; analysis; science; conservation; space. Attempts to increase human knowledge about the planets, including our own. It attempts to drum up more support both publicly and financially for space exploration. **Other Resources:** Publishes a magazine, PLANETARY REPORTER. **Contact(s):** Carl Sagan, Louis Freidman.

**E ♦ Planetary Survival Alliance**
Box 4844
San Luis Obispo, CA 93403 (805)549-9670
**Affiliation:** Greenpeace/Rainforest Action Network. **Concern(s):** environment; forests. **Contact(s):** Zaxa Masferrer.

**♥ ♦ Planned Parenthood Federation of America**
2010 Massachusetts Ave. NW
Washington, DC 20036 (202)785-3351
**Affiliation:** International Planned Parenthood Federation. **Concern(s):** family; demographics; feminism; health; population growth; family planning; counseling. The purpose of this organization is to serve a fundamental human right: The right to decide freely and responsibly when or whether to have a child. **Other Resources:** Directory. **Est.:** 1916. **Contact(s):** Faye Wattleton (President). (212)541-7800. **Other:** 810 Seventh Ave., New York, NY 10019.

**U ♦ Planners Network**
1601 Connecticut Ave. NW
Washington, DC 20009-1035 (202)234-9382
**Affiliation:** Institute for Policy Studies. **Concern(s):** urban; agriculture; future; ideation; planning; rural communities; development An association of professionals, activists, academics, and students involved in physical, social, economic, and environmental planning in urban and rural areas. **Other Resources:** Publishes a newsletter. **Contact(s):** Prentice Bowsher (Director).

**E ♦ The Planning and Conservation League**
909 12th St. #203
Sacramento, CA 95814 (916)444-8726
**Concern(s):** environment; wildlife/endangered species; conservation; forests; oceans/rivers. In 1988 this organization ran a successful campaign for Proposition 70, the California Wildlife, Coastal and Parks Initiative. More than 65% of the voters approved the initiative, which is purchasing and permanently protecting $776 million worth of critical natural and park lands, wildlife habitat, and key areas along the California coast. **Other Resources:** See Californians for Transportation Solutions and CALIFORNIA TODAY (periodicals). **Contact(s):** Dr. Gerald H. Meral (Executive Director). **Other:** 701 Ocean St., Santa Cruz, CA 95060. Gary Patton , President. (408)425-2202.

**E ♦ Plastics Recycling Institute**
Rutgers University, Bldg. 3529, Busch Campus
Center for Plastics Recycling Research
Piscataway, NJ 08855 (201)932-4402
**Concern(s):** environment; recycling. Promotes plastics collection and reuse through research and public education. **Other Resources:** PLASTICS & RECYCLING REPORT (periodicals).

**T ♦ Plenty USA**
Box 2306
Davis, CA 95617 (916)753-0731
**Concern(s):** Third World; demographics; agriculture; economics; hunger; community-self reliance; rural communities; indigenous peoples; development; networking. A development, education, and environmental organization working around the world in collaboration with groups and individuals in disadvantaged communities. Special focus on indigenous people and cross-cultural cooperation. Projects include small-scale agriculture, primary health care, micro-economic development, and village technology. Winner of The Right Livelihood Award. **Other Resources:** See PLENTY BULLETIN and Natural Rights Center. Nonprofit. **Est.:** 1974. **Circ.:** 3.5M. **Other Formats:** Peacenet/Econet, user name 'natlaw'. **E-Network:** MCI. **ID:** Plenty USA. **Contact(s):** Peter Schweitzer (Executive Director), Charles Haren (Program Director).

**✍ ♦ Point Foundation**
27 Gate Five Rd.
Sausalito, CA 94965 (415)332-1716
**Concern(s):** education; environment; global understanding; activism; research. Parent organization of The Whole Earth Institute. The Foundation's purpose is to collect practical information and disseminate it to the public. **Other Resources:** See Whole Earth Institute, The Well (BBS), THE WHOLE EARTH CATALOG on CD-ROM, and THE WHOLE EARTH REVIEW. **Member:** Co-op America. **Contact(s):** Richard Schuffler.

**P ♦ Political Research Associates**
678 Massachusetts Ave., #205
Cambridge, MA 02139 (617)661-9313
**Concern(s):** politics; justice; media; analysis; media watch; research; racism; discrimination. "An independent research institute which collects and disseminates information on right-wing political groups and trends. Centralized in our archives is a continuously-updated collection of over one hundred right-wing publications, including newspapers, magazines, newsletter, direct mail appeals, and books. We also maintain files on individuals, groups, and topics of interest to those researching the right-wing. Material in the file is drawn from both primary and secondary sources." **Other Resources:** Classes, speakers, research, and publications. Publishes A TOPICAL REPORT (a series), sample topic—"The Coors Connection", and monographs, sample titles — "Apartheid in our Living Rooms." "Nostalgia on the Right." Publications list available.

**M ♦ Politics and Government Multilogue**
3704 11 Ave. South
Minneapolis, MN 55407
**Concern(s):** media; politics; multilogues. **Contact(s):** Tom Ables.

**D ♦ Population and Environmental Psychology**
Office of Educational Dev., UAB School of Medicine
401 Community Health Services Building
Birmingham, AL 35294
**Affiliation:** American Psychological Association. **Concern(s):** demographics; environment; population growth. A small group of social scientists and design professionals having research, teaching, and practice interests in environment and population issues. Members include psychologists, sociologists, planners, architects, landscape architects, and interior designers. Quarterly newsletter and co-sponsor (with EDRA) of Environment and Behavior. **Contact(s):** James M. Richard, Jr.

**D ♦ Population Communication**
1489 E. Colorado Blvd., #202
Pasadena, CA 91106 (818)793-4750
**Concern(s):** demographics; population growth. An international, nongovernmental organization which was established to communicate population messages to national leaders and to actively explore solutions to the population problem. Nonprofit. **Est.:** 1977. **Fax:** (818)793-4791. **Contact(s):** Robert W. Gillespie (President).

**D ♦ Population Communications Services**
John Hopkins University
624 N. Broadway
Baltimore, MD 21205 (301)955-7666
**Concern(s):** demographics; Third World; feminism; population growth; family planning. Offers technical and financial assistance in population and family planning communication to agencies and organizations in developing countries. Established with support from the US AID, is designed to help develop greater public awareness of family planning and promote wider use of freely chosen contraceptive methods. **Other Resources:** See POPULATION REPORTS (periodicals). **Est.:** 1982.

**D ♦ The Population Council**
One Dag Hammarskjold Plaza
New York, NY 10017 (212)644-1300
**Concern(s):** demographics; health; family; population growth; family planning. An international organization that undertakes social science and biomedical research, advises and assists government and international agencies and disseminates information on population issues. It is committed to the enhancement of human welfare and works in 3 areas: biomedical research in the field of human reproduction to develop and improve contraceptive methods; social science research into causes of population change, their societal implications, technical assistance to family planning. **Other Resources:** Quarterly journal, POPULATION AND DEVELOPMENT REVIEW. Bimonthly journal, STUDIES IN FAMILY PLANNING. Nonprofit. **Est.:** 1952. **Contact(s):** George Zeidenstein.

**D ♦ Population Crisis Committee**
1120 19th St. NW, #550
Washington, DC 20036 (202)659-1833
**Concern(s):** demographics; environment; population growth. Pro-

motes international population and family planning programs through public education, policy analysis, liaison with international leaders and organizations. Provides funding for private family planning projects overseas. **Other Resources:** Publishes the HUMAN SUFFERING INDEX; MAJOR PRIVATE ORGANIZATIONS DIRECTORY; NONGOVERNMENTAL ORGANIZATIONS IN INTERNATIOANL POPULATION CRISIS COMMITTEE (directory). **Contact(s):** Larry Kegan, Edwin M. Martin

**D ▸ Population Environment Balance, Inc.**
1325 G St. NW, #1003
Washington, DC 20005-3104 (202)879-3000
**Affiliation:** Carrying Capacity Network. **Concern(s):** demographics; environment; family; population growth; family planning. Purpose is to impress upon the American public and policymakers the significant relationship between population growth and distribution in the US and our national well-being, and to champion a national commitment to a population policy that will foster a stable population, a strong economy, sustainable resource use, and an ecologically healthful environment for all Americans. Some current targets are: global warming, family planning, and local growth control. **Other Resources:** See ACTIVIST'S HANDBOOK (directories); BALANCE REPORT; HAVE YOU HEARD? (periodicals). Fact sheets, DATA sheets, and other reports and materials. Balance Clearinghouse offers publications, BALANCE ACTION ALERTS. **Dues:** $25/yr. **Contact(s):** Rose M. Hanes (Executive Director), Garrett Hardin (Honorary Chairman).

**T ▸ The Population Institute**
110 Maryland Ave. NE
Washington, DC 20002 (202)544-3300
**Concern(s):** Third World; environment; demographics; population growth. The world's largest independent, grassroots organization specializing in global population issues. It is primarily concerned with bringing the world's population into balance with its resources and environment, creating population stability and enhancing the quality of life. It seeks to draw attention to those developing countries where the problems of overpopulation are most critical by trying to convince their leaders that they must balance their populations with their resources. **Other Resources:** See POPLINE, a newsletter. Nonprofit. **Contact(s):** Werner Fornos (President).

**D ▸ Population Reference Bureau**
1875 Connecticut Ave. NW, #520
Washington, DC 20009 (202)483-1100
**Concern(s):** demographics; population growth. A private organization that publishes a variety of resources. Reports on the policy implications of current demographic trends. **Other Resources:** Publishes POPULATION BULLETINS; POPULATION TODAY MAGAZINE; annually updated WORLD POPULATION DATA SHEET; US Population Sheet wall charts; POPULATION HANDBOOK; POPULATION TRENDS AND PUBLIC POLICY reports. Nonprofit. **Est.:** 1929. **Contact(s):** Kim Crews, Art Haupt.

**D ▸ Population Resource Center**
1725 K St. NW, #1102
Washington, DC 20006 (202)467-5030
**Concern(s):** demographics; population growth. An organization committed to improving policymaking through the provision of balanced, objective analyses on the relationship of demographic trends to social and economic issues. Founded on the conviction that population is among a handful of basic factors that determine social and economic progress. The Center serves as a resource for policymakers in government, corporations, and the nonprofit sector on the relationship of demographic trends to social and economic issues. **Other Resources:** Population Facts in Brief, Population Focus, Population Summary. Nonprofit. **Est.:** 1975. **Contact(s):** Shelley Kossak. (202)546-5030. **Other:** 500 E. 62nd St., New York, NY 10021. Jane S. De Lung. (212)888-2820.

**T ▸ Population Services International**
1120 19th St. NW, #600
Washington, DC 20036 (202)785-0072
**Concern(s):** Third World; demographics; family; health; population growth; family planning; AIDS. A corporation that provides health and family planning products and services in developing countries. AIDS prevention education features prominently in many of their projects. Nonprofit. **Est.:** 1970. **Contact(s):** Richard A. Frank (President), Dana Hovig (Program Manager).

**? ▸ Post-Industrial Future Project**
Box 2699
Canmore, AB TOL OMO Canada
**Concern(s):** future; economics; ideation. **Contact(s):** Ruben Nelson.

**M ▸ Prairie Fire Organizing Committee**
See BREAKTHROUGH newsletter.

**A ▸ PrairieFire Rural Action**
See PRAIRIE JOURNAL (periodicals).

**✌ ▸ Presbyterian Church**
110 Maryland Ave. NE
Washington, DC 20002-1369 (202)543-1126
**Concern(s):** peace; justice; spiritual; faith; activism. This church is involved in many progressive aspects of today's problems. Whether the problem is international or inner in scope, they try to help. **Other Resources:** Presbytell, a telecommunications information disseminating tool; Presbyterian Hunger Project; Presbyterian Peacemaking Program; Presbyterian Women; see REPORT TO PRESBYTERIANS FROM WASHINGTON. Nonprofit. (800)872-3283. **Contact(s):** Jorge Lara-Braud.

**D ▸ Presbyterian Hunger Program**
100 Witherspoon
Louisville, KY 40202-1396 (502)569-5000
**Affiliation:** Presbyterian Church. **Concern(s):** demographics; hunger. Nonprofit. (800)872-3283. **Contact(s):** Diane Hockenbury. **Other:** Presbyterian Church, 110 Maryland Ave. NE, Washington, DC 20002.

**✌ ▸ Presbyterian Peace Fellowship**
See BREIFLY newsletter.

**S ▸ Presbyterian Peacemaking Program**
100 Witherspoon St.
Louisville, KY 40202-1396 (502)569-5784
**Affiliation:** Presbyterian Church. **Concern(s):** spiritual; family; peace; health; faith; conflict resolution; psychology. "Sometimes when we hear the word 'peacemaking' our thoughts turn to the global problems that are in todays headlines. This peacemaking deals with the problems at home and with oneself." This program tries to build communication with in the families, community and church. Has many resources available. Peacemaking is not just for nations but for all of us, including our inner selves. **Other Resources:** Pamphlets, books and videotapes. Nonprofit. (800)872-3283. **Contact(s):** Dick Walks. **Other:** Presbyterian Church, 110 Maryland Ave. NE, Washington, DC 20002.

**✌ ▸ Presbyterian Women**
100 Witherspoon
Louisville, KY 40202-1396 (502)569-5365
**Affiliation:** Presbyterian Church. **Concern(s):** peace; feminism; spiritual; activism; faith; empowerment. Nonprofit. **Contact(s):** Gladys Strachan. **Other:** Presbyterian Church, 110 Maryland Ave. NE, Washington, DC 20002

**♈ ▸ Primarily Primates**
Box 15306
San Antonio, TX 78212
**Concern(s):** environment; wildlife/endangered species; animal rights. **Contact(s):** Wallace W. Swett (President).

**J ▸ Prisoner Legal Services**
2 Catherine St.
Poughkeepsie, NY 12610
**Concern(s):** justice; prisons; criminal system. This organizations concentrates on prisoners' legal rights and the violations that are committed throughout the US Prison System.

**F ▸ Pro-Choice Task Force**
c/o All Saints Church
132 N. Euclid Ave.
Pasadena, CA 91101 (818)796-1172
**Affiliation:** All Saints Episcopal Church. **Concern(s):** feminism; spiritual; reform; interfaith; pro-choice. "The mission of the Force of the Church is to secure the right of procreative choice for all women. This right is consistent with the Judeo-Christian understanding of the empowerment of each person with the freedom to make choices and the responsibility for those choices. We believe that the preservation of this right is essential to the creation of a just and equitable society." **Other Resources:** Publishes newsletter, THE VOICE. Nonprofit. **Est.:** 1990. **Contact(s):** Joanne Parker, Ginny Heringer (818)783-4727.

**M ▸ Process Education**
3773 Marble Peak Place
Tucson, AZ 85718
**Concern(s):** media; education; multilogues. **Contact(s):** Philip E. Johnson.

**✌ ▸ Professionals' Coalition for Nuclear Arms Control**
1616 P St. NW, #320
Washington, DC 20036 (202)332-4823
**Concern(s):** peace; politics; disarmament; lobbying. A lobbying coalition of professionals committed to stopping the arms race, believing they have a special responsibility to do so. Supports initiatives that will halt the arms race and redefine national security to include arms control and reductions. Offers up-to-date information on legislation. Maintains an alert network. Created by Physicians for Social Responsibility, Lawyers Alliance for Nuclear Arms Control, and Union of Concerned Scientists and now boasts many professional organizations. **Other Resources:** Publishes newsletter, THE PROFESSIONAL and books, a CITIZEN LOBBYIST SKILLS MANUAL and a GUIDE TO NONPARTISAN VOTER EDUCATION. See, also, Legislative Strategies and Lobbying Network. Fact sheets on reordering the federal budget; booklet/BUILDING DOWN. **Est.:** 1984. **Fax:** (202)667-1760. **Contact(s):** David Cohen (President/Lobbyist), Victoria Almquist (Executive Director).

**H ▸ Program for Appropriate Technology in Health**
See DIRECTIONS (periodicals).

**$ ▸ Progressive Community Associates (PCA)**
Box 122
Athens, OH 45701
**Concern(s):** economics; environment; community self-reliance; intentional communities; social ecology. New, ecologically sensitive, human-scale community, Southeast Ohio near university. Private 5-acre tracts. Community land. Identification of shared interest groups. Participation in larger community via diverse educational outreach programs in appropriate technology, cooperative living, etc. Community-based institutions through participatory democracy. **Other Resources:** Discusses intentional community in a brochure. **Est.:** 1975.

**✍ ▸ Progressive Education**
See PROGRESSIVE PERIODICALS DIRECTORY.

**✌ ▸ Progressive Foundation**

See Nukewatch and NUKEWATCH PATHFINDER newspaper.

**P ▸ The Progressive Policy Institute**
316 Pennsylvania Ave. SE
Washington, DC 20003 (202)547-0001
**Concern(s):** politics. Mr. Shapiro was Governor Clinton's Presidential Campaign advisor. **Contact(s):** Robert Shapiro.

**✍ ▸ Progressive Science Institute**
Box 5335
Berkeley, CA 94705-335(510)654-1619
**Concern(s):** education; spiritual; energy; transformation; science. This institute is concerned with the fatalistic view of today's science. They do research into new approaches to scientific thought and philosophy. **Other Resources:** Publication, THE SCIENTIFIC WORLDVIEW. **Est.:** 1984. **Fax:** (510)864-3909. **Contact(s):** Glenn Borchardt (Director).

**✌ ▸ Progressive Student Network**
See PROGRESSIVE STUDENT NEWS letter, .

**T ▸ Project Abraco**
515 Broadway
Santa Cruz, CA 95060 (408)423-1626
**Affiliation:** Resource Center for Nonviolence. **Concern(s):** Third World; peace; conflict resolution. This project is so designed as to show and develop a greater sense of solidarity between the people of the US and Brazil. **Other Resources:** Newsletter, TERRA NOSSA.

**M ▸ Project Censored**
c/o Carl Jensen
Sonoma State University
Rohnert Park, CA 94928 (707)664-2149
**Concern(s):** media; journalism; censorship; media watch; responsibility. An annual national news media research project which explores and exposes important issues which have been overlooked, undercovered, or censored. Nominations of "censored" stories are due by November 1 of each year. The results are published annually in a book titled "Top 25 Censored Stories of the Year." See THE 10 BEST CENSORED STORIES. **Other Resources:** Classes, speakers, research, and publications. Publishes A TOPICAL REPORT (a series), sample topic—"The Coors Connection", and monographs, sample titles — "Apartheid in our Living Rooms." "Nostalgia on the Right." Publications list available. **Est.:** 1976. **Frequency:** Annual. **Price:** $10/ea. **Pages:** 88. **Publisher:** Censored Publications. **E-Network:** CompuServe. **ID:** Carl Jensen. **Fax:** (707)664-2505. **Contact(s):** Carl Jensen, PhD (Founder/Director), Mark Lowenthal (Research Associate). (707)664-2800.

**D ▸ Project Concern International**
Box 85322
San Diego, CA 92138 (619)279-9690
**Concern(s):** demographics; health; Third World; hunger; nutrition; public health. They place medical professionals in underserved area in the US and the Third World. **Office:** 3550 Afton Rd

⚛ ◆ **Project Minnesota**
See LEON NEWSLETTER.

F ◆ **Project on the Status and Education of Women**
Association of American Colleges
1818 R St. NW
Washington, DC 20009 (202)387-1300
**Affiliation:** Association of American Colleges. **Concern(s):** feminism.

T ◆ **Project South Africa**
260 Park Ave. S
New York, NY 10010 (212)533-8000
**Concern(s):** Third World; justice; South Africa. **Contact(s):** Walter Naegle (Executive Director).

J ◆ **Project Tandem**
2650 Marshland Rd
Wayzata, MN 55391
**Concern(s):** justice; spiritual; politics; interfaith; grassroots organizing; civil liberties. Promotes freedom of thought, conscience, and religion according to Article 18 of the Universal Declaration of Human Rights. Tandem conference activities are directed at shaping and promoting a methodology for the worldwide development of tolerance, understanding, and respect for diversity of religion. The three elements of the program include academic papers and concrete projects in social theory, international law, and grassroots organizing.

⚛ ◆ **Project Victory**
560 Oxford, #1
Palo Alto, CA 94306
**Concern(s):** peace; politics; conflict resolution. See GREAT TURNING: PERSONAL PEACE, GLOBAL VICTORY (directories). Nonprofit.
**Contact(s):** Craig Schindler.

P ◆ **Project Vote Smart**
129 NW 4th St #204
Corvallis, OR 97330 (800)786-6885
**Concern(s):** politics; voting. Four years in development, a nonpartisan organization that collects factual material on candidates for federal office, such as bios, campaign finances, and issue statements. This information is available verbally through their 800 number or in printed format through their 900 number for $3. (900)786-6885 in print.
**Contact(s):** Richard Kimball (President).

J ◆ **Promise the Children**
Unitarian Universalist Service Committee
130 Prospect St.
Cambridge, MA 02139-1813(617)868-6600
**Affiliation:** Unitarian Universalist Service Committee. **Concern(s):** justice; demographics; children; hunger; poverty. 50% of the poor are children, 13 million live in poverty, 5.5 million go to bed hungry every night, 1 million are homeless, and government housing programs have dropped 80% since 1980. Infants born in Jamaica, Panama and Chile have a greater chance of surviving to the age of one. This campaign has stimulated and helped organize programs in 28 states. Volunteer services include: tutoring, mentoring, breakfast, counselling teen-age mothers, field trips and job searches. **Other Resources:** Action kit includes—"Children in Crisis: the Challenge of the Decade," a background paper, and "Child Hunger in America." a briefing paper and strategy guide, updates and alerts. **Fax:** (617)868-7102.
**Contact(s):** Dr. Richard S. Scobie (Executive Director).

⚛ ◆ **Psychologists For Social Responsibility**
1841 Columbia Rd. NW, #209
Washington, DC 20009 (202)745-7084
**Concern(s):** peace; health; education; psychology; research. This coalition works to prevent the possibility of nuclear war and build a durable peace for future generations through research and public education. Supports and promotes alternatives that would reduce world tensions and create a psychologically favorable atmosphere for survival. **Other Resources:** Newsletter. **Contact(s):** Anne Anderson.

$ ◆ **Public Citizen**
2000 P St. NW., #605
Washington, DC 20036-0757 (202)833-3000
**Concern(s):** economics; environment; health; politics; labor; consumer rights; consumer protection; corporate responsibility; occupational safety. A citizen research, lobbying and litigation organization. Since its founding by Ralph Nader, it has fought for consumer rights in the market place, for safe products, and for a clean and healthy environment and workplace. **Other Resources:** Freedom of Information Clearinghouse; Critical Mass Energy Project; Congress Watch; Buyer's Up; Health Research Group. See also, periodical PUBLIC CITIZEN and PEOPLE & TAXES; POWER OF THE STATES and SPICES OF LIFE (directories). Nonprofit. **Est.:** 1971. **Fax:** (202)728-4095.
**Contact(s):** Ralph Nader (Founder). (202)785-3704. Ralph Nader Founder.

☺ ◆ **Public Citizen's Buyers Up**
Box 33757
Washington, DC 20033 (202)833-3000
**Affiliation:** Public Citizen. **Concern(s):** energy; resource management. A research and advocacy organization that monitors and reports on energy and environmental issues affecting consumers. "We conduct industry investigations, lobby for progressive legislation, publish various papers and reports, and also administer a group purchasing program for home heating oil in the metro Washington, DC, Philadelphia, and Baltimore areas." **Other Resources:** BUYERS UP NEWS - quarterly newsletter. **Est.:** 1983. **Office:** 2000 P St. NW Washington, DC 20036. **Fax:** (202)728-4095. **Contact(s):** Linda Beaver (National Director), Bess Bezirgan (Communications Director). (202)785-3704.

J ◆ **Public Concern Foundation**
See WASHINGTON SPECTATOR (periodicals).

H ◆ **Public Health Institute**
See Global Warming Watch.

E ◆ **Public Information Center**
Environmental Protection Agency
401 M St. SW
Washington, DC 20460 (202)475-7751
**Affiliation:** Environmental Protection Agency. **Concern(s):** environment. Drinking Water Hotline—(800)426-4791.

$ ◆ **The Public Interest**
1112 16th St. NW
Washington, DC 20036 (202)785-8555
**Concern(s):** economics; politics; policy. Established to increase the effectiveness of public interest advocates by providing public interest organizations and policymakers with reliable information on the economic aspects of public policy issues; to systematically involve economists in public policy formulation. **Est.:** 1972.

M ◆ **Public Interest Computer Association**
See PICA NEWS letter.

H ◆ **Public Voice for Food and Health Policy**
1001 Connecticut Ave. NW
Washington, DC 20036 (202)569-5930
**Concern(s):** health; agriculture; environment; nutrition; policy; hazardous/toxic waste. Seeks to advance consumer interests in natural food and health policy-making. Works closely with Congress, federal regulatory agencies, the food industry and the media. Promotes programs and legislation that aims toward a safer and more affordable, nutritious food supply. Addresses issues such as pesticide and chemical residues, contaminants, inspection, food labeling, agricultural subsidies and health policies for women and the rural poor. **Other Resources:** See ACTION ALERT bulletin. **Contact(s):** Ellen Haas (Executive Director).

T ◆ **Pueblo to People**
Box 366
Bolinas, CA 94924
**Concern(s):** Third World; economics; environment; trade; Latin America. An alternative trade organization. "We focus our efforts on craft and agricultural co-operatives of very low income women in Central America and Peru. Handmade cotton clothing and exquisite weavings from Guatemalan cooperatives. Peruvian sweaters. Nicaraguan and Peruvian coffee. Honduran cashews. Blankets, furniture, gifts. Building worker-owned co-ops in Latin America." **Other Resources:** Catalog. Nonprofit. **Est.:** 1979.

$ ◆ **Puget Sound Co-op Federation/Foundation**
521 Wall St.
Seattle, WA 98121
**Concern(s):** economics; cooperatives.

? ◆ **Quality Team Tracking Program**
Paul Revere Insurance Group
Worcester, MA 01613
**Concern(s):** future; ideation. A company "Quality Circle" program in which employees' ideas for improving their jobs are logged into a company-wide computer network and the "stealing" of ideas is encouraged. The company considers the program "a corporate revolution...vastly successful from a business viewpoint."

E ◆ **Quebec-Labrador Foundation – Canada (QLF)**
1822, rue Sherbrooke Ouest
Montreal, PQ H3H 1E4 Canada (514)933-7767
**Affiliation:** Quebec-Labrador Foundation Inc. (USA). **Concern(s):** environment; agriculture; economics; conservation; natural resources; wildlife/endangered species; water; oceans/rivers; sustainability; development; planning. The Atlantic Center is an umbrella term for QLF programs. Through a variety of projects, QLF works to build support for conservation of natural resources within cultural contexts. Broadly defined, the primary program areas are rivers and water-

sheds; wildlife and habitats; rural landscapes and community development. **Other Resources:** Publishes NEXUS at the Atlantic Center for the Environment. Nonprofit. **Est.:** 1963. **Dues:** $25/50/100/250/500. **Fax:** (514)931-6521. **Contact(s):** Nathalie Zinger (Director, Quebec Program). **Other:** QLF Newfoundland, Box 3, Nagle's Place, St. John's, NF A1B 272, Canada. Heather Griffin, Director-Newfoundland/Labrador. (709)754-5948.

✈ ◆ **Questers Tours and Travels**
257 Park Ave. S
New York, NY 10010 (212)673-3120
**Affiliation:** Environmental Defense Fund. **Concern(s):** education; Third World; travel; Latin America. Tours focusing on the natural history of a country or region in the Americas, Europe, Asia, and Africa.
**Member:** Co-op America.

✏ ◆ **Quixote Center**
See ROCINANTE (periodicals).

E ◆ **R.E.I. Adventures**
Box 88126
Seattle, WA 98138 (206)395-4375
**Concern(s):** environment; recreation. Adventure trips sponsored by the outdoor gear and clothing cooperative, Recreational Equipment International, R.E.I., the largest consumer co-op in the US, cofounded the Outdoor Conservation Alliance. **Member:** Co-op America.

E ◆ **Rachel Carson Council**
8940 Jones Mill Rd.
Chevy Chase, MD 20815(301)652-1877
**Concern(s):** environment; agriculture; health; hazardous/toxic waste; natural resources. An independent scientific organization seeking to advance Ms. Carson's cause and philosophy by promoting public interest and knowledge of our environment; encouraging enlightened conservation measures; and serving as a clearinghouse of information. The main focus is chemical contamination, especially the pesticide problem explored in her book, SILENT SPRING. Its impact on human and environmental health has broad effects on the economy, government, agricultural methods and industrial practices. **Contact(s):** Marjorie Smigel (Director), Shirley Briggs (Executive Director). (301)652-1827.

E ◆ **Radioactive Waste Campaign**
625 Broadway
New York, NY 10012 (212)677-1601
**Affiliation:** Environmental Action Coalition. **Concern(s):** environment; energy; health; hazardous/toxic waste; nuclear. This campaign is for the enactment and enforcement of laws that would control radioactive waste. **Other Resources:** See RWC WASTE PAPER, a periodical. **Contact(s):** Patrick J. Malloy (Executive Director).

E ◆ **Rails-To-Trails Conservancy**
1400 16th St. NW, #300
Washington, DC 20036 (202)797-5400
**Concern(s):** environment; recreation; conservation; volunteers. Organization dedicated to converting thousands of miles of abandoned railroad corridors to public trails for various activities; walking, bicycling, horseback riding, cross-country skiing, wildlife habitat and nature appreciation. **Other Resources:** Six month volunteer programs available from the national office for service in the local chapter offices. **Member:** Environmental Federation of America.
**Contact(s):** David G. Burnwell (President).

P ◆ **Rainbow Coalition**
**(See National Rainbow Coalition)**
**Concern(s):** politics; justice; peace; grassroots organizing; alternative party. See National Rainbow Coalition.

E ◆ **Rainforest Action Network**
450 Sansome St. #700
San Francisco, CA 94111 (415)398-4404
**Affiliation:** Earth Island Institute. **Concern(s):** environment; agriculture; economics; Third World; conservation; forests; global warming; boycott; development. Works to save the world's rainforests through direct action, grassroots organizing, facilitating communication between US and Third World organizers, spearheading public education projects, and organizing boycotts. BOYCOTT EMPIRE/BEROL PENCILS — Uses rainforest wood in some pencils. MITSIBUSHI CORP. — Import tropical rainforest woods into Japan for use. To Protest, write to: Robert T. Phillips, Empire/Berol Corp., Pencil St., Shelby TN 37160 (615) 684-4133. **Other Resources:** Publishes RAINFOREST ACTION NETWORK ALERT newsletter; WORLD RAINFOREST REPORT; and conducts boycotts. Also see, Planetary Survival Alliance.
**Contact(s):** Randall Hayes (Executive Director).

E ◆ **Rainforest Alliance**
270 Lafayette St., #512
New York, NY 10012 (212)941-1900
**Concern(s):** environment; education; conservation; preservation; forests. Dedicated to the conservation of the worlds tropical forests.

Organization uses education, facilitating public involvement, promoting cooperation, and research. **Other Resources:** Research, office management and special projects and events. **Other:** 295 Madison Ave., New York, NY 10017(212)599-5060.

**E ▶ The Rainforest Foundation**
1776 Broadway, 14th Fl.
New York, NY 10019 (212)581-9060
**Concern(s):** environment; justice; Third World; forests; indigenous people; development. During an '87 Brazilian tour, rock musicianSting witnessed the widespread burning, logging, mining, and ranching that is quickly leveling the pristine Amazon forest. This Foundation was created to aid in the preservation of this forest and indigenous people who live there. **Other Resources:** Goals: 1) preserve areas of the Amazon rainforest surrounding the last remaining Indian tribes; 2) promote worldwide awareness regarding the Amazon rainforest and the indigenous tribes living there; 3) promote environmental studies in the world. **Est.:** 1989. **Contact(s):** Sting, Jean-Pierre Dutilleux (Founders).

**E ▶ Rainforest Information Center**
1256 6th Ave.
San Francisco, CA 94122
**Concern(s):** environment; forests.

**E ▶ Raptor Center**
University of California - Davis
Veterinary Medicine
Davis, CA 95616 (916)758-8185
**Concern(s):** environment; wildlife/endangered species. Treats and rehabilitates injured raptors.

**E ▶ Rare Breeds Survival Foundation of America**
c/o Hyman L. Battle Jr.
280 Park Ave.
New York, NY 10017-1216 (212)856-6800
**Concern(s):** environment; wildlife/endangered species. This organization gives gifts, grants or loans to other organizations to help keep rare breeds from extinction. **Other:** 860 1 Ave., New York, NY (212)758-8019.

**✌ ▶ Real Peace Project**
4 Granville Rd
Lincoln, MA 01773
**Concern(s):** peace. **Contact(s):** Robert L. Miller.

**♿ ▶ Recording for the Blind**
20 Rosezel Rd.
Princeton, NJ 08540 (609)452-0606
**Concern(s):** media; health; education; responsibility; broadcasting; disabled; volunteers. An organization that provides free recordings of text books to the blind or other print-handicapped students and professionals. Reader-monitored teams produce tapes of textbooks at 29 RFB studios. **Other Resources:** Volunteers needed as readers. Nonprofit. **Est.:** 1948. **Contact(s):** Virginia Persing (Manager, Public Information).

**✌ ▶ Recreators For Social Responsibility**
309 Hawthorne Ave.
Palo Alto, CA 94301 (415)321-5113
**Concern(s):** peace; environment; anti-nuclear; recreation. Organization founded by recreational professionals concerned about nuclear and quality of life issues. **Est.:** 1984. **Contact(s):** Annie Head.

**✌ ▶ Red River Peace Network (RRPN)**
HCR2 Box 25
Panhandle, TX 79068 (806)335-1715
**Affiliation:** Peace Farm. **Concern(s):** peace; activism; networking; anti-nuclear. A network throughout Texas, New Mexico, Oklahoma, and Kansas of peace and justice activists. The Farm grew out of RRPN's concern over the Pantex plant near Amarillo, Texas. It organizes yearly peace camps and other educational events at the Farm. **Other Resources:** ADVOCATE (periodicals). **Contact(s):** Ellen Barfield, Jerry Stein (Treasurer). (806)335-1872.

**J ▶ Reforma (National Association to Promote Library Service to the Spanish Speaking)**
See REFORMA NEWSLETTER.

**S ▶ Reformed Church of America**
161 W. 12th
Holland, MI 49423 (616)396-8707
**Concern(s):** spiritual; faith. **Other Resources:** CITY GATE newsletter. Friendship Press and Bible Way. Curriculum available via RCA Distribution Center, 3000 Ivanrest SW, Grandville MI 49418; 616-538-3470 or try 800-828-8013. **Contact(s):** Betty Voskuil. **Other:** 475 Riverside Dr., New York, NY 10115. (212)870-3077.

**✏ ▶ Regional Organization of Theatres South**
See Alternate Roots.

**T ▶ Reinvesting in America**
261 W. 35th St., #1402
New York, NY 10001-1906 (212)629-8850
**Affiliation:** World Hunger Year. **Concern(s):** Third World; hunger. A campaign that gathers and disseminates information to grassroots groups about the most effective programs and policy proposals on hunger and poverty-related issues, will help national and local groups obtain better media coverage and funding for programs; and works with legislators so that the very best of these programs and policies become the basis of pilot projects and new legislation. **Contact(s):** Bill Ayres.

**J ▶ Religious Action**
See Leadership Conference on Civil Rights.

**F ▶ Religious Coalition For Abortion Rights**
100 Maryland Ave. NE
Washington, DC 20002 (202)543-7032
**Concern(s):** feminism; spiritual; justice; pro-choice; interfaith. Congress shall make no law respecting an establishment of religion or prohibiting the free exercise thereof." (First Amendment) A coalition of 35 faith groups with the potential to mobilize 33 million citizens to fight for religious and reproductive freedom. More than 100,000 of their followers rallied at the March for Women's Equality/Women's Lives. Pro-Choice is a religious issue with increasing pressure being put on the government to take sides. Anti-abortion laws violates the First Amendment. Hotline (202)543-0224.

**T ▶ Religious Task Force on Central America**
See CENTRAL AMERICA REPORT (periodicals).

**E ▶ Relocation Assistance & Information Network (RAIN)**
107 April Dr.
Camp Hill, PA 17011 (717)737-4324
**Concern(s):** environment; justice; health; hazardous/toxic waste. RAIN helps individuals, groups and communities mitigate hazardous waste and materials that contaminate their immediate environment. In cases where mandatory relocation is ordered, it seeks social justice to receive fair and equitable compensation for the victims. **Other Resources:** THE BACK POCKET RELOCATION HANDBOOK. **Est.:** 1987. **Contact(s):** Catharene Garula (Public Information Officer), Sam Garula

**H ▶ Remove Intoxicated Drivers (RID-USA)**
Box 520
Schenectady, NY 12301 (518)372-9624
**Concern(s):** health; substance abuse.

**E ▶ The Rene Dubos Center For Human Environments, Inc.**
100 E. 85th St.
New York, NY 10028 (212)249-7745
**Concern(s):** environment; social ecology. An organization founded by the late scientist-humanist, Rene Dubos, to foster knowledge and develop programs that create stable, pleasurable, profitable, and favorable environments for the health of the Earth and the continued growth of civilization. **Other Resources:** See DIRECTORY by same name. Publishes an occasional newsletter, THINKING GLOBALLY, ACTING LOCALLY. **Contact(s):** William R. Eblen (President), Ruth A. Eblen (Executive Director).

**✪ ▶ Renew America**
1400 16th St. NW, #710
Washington, DC 20036 (202)232-2252
**Affiliation:** Fund for Renewable Energy and the Environment. **Concern(s):** energy; environment; resources; natural resources; conservation; air pollution. An education and networking forum supported by concerned individuals and charitable foundations which is dedicated to the efficient use of all natural resources and the development of a safe and sustainable environment. **Other Resources:** Publishes the guides SUSTAINABLE ENERGY and COMMUNITIES AT RISK; the quarterly newsletter RENEW AMERICA REPORT; and a quarterly and annual STATE OF THE STATES. See Center for Renewable Resources. Nonprofit. **Contact(s):** Tina C. Hobson (Executive Director), Denis Hayes (Chairman). Ric Barrick , Legislative Hotline. (202)466-6880.

**✪ ▶ Renewable Fuels Association**
1 Massachusetts Ave. NW
Washington, DC 20001 (202)289-3835
**Concern(s):** energy; environment; renewable resources; conservation; preservation. This association promotes the use of renewable fuels as our only hope for a cleaner environment for tomorrow.

**E ▶ The Renewable Natural Resources Foundation**
5430 Grosvenor Lane
Bethesda, MD 20814 (301)493-9101
**Concern(s):** environment; natural resources. Objectives are: to advance the application of sound practices in managing and conserving natural resources; promote public education; foster coordination and cooperation among organizations in the field; and, to develop a Renewable Natural Resources Center. Believe the future vitality of the world is dependent on the conservation and replenishment of its renewable resources; the recycling of used resources; and the protection of wildlife from extinction. **Other Resources:** See Coastal Society and RENEWABLE RESOURCES JOURNAL. **Est.:** 1972. **Contact(s):** Robert Dwaine Day (Executive Director), Darlene S. Thompson (Administrative Assistant).

**M ▶ Reporters Committee for Freedom of the Press**
See NEWS MEDIA AND THE LAW (periodicals).

**F ▶ Reproductive Rights National Network**
17 Murray St.
New York, NY 10007 (212)267-8891
**Affiliation:** Health Policy Advisory Center. **Concern(s):** feminism; justice; empowerment; pro-choice. Established to organize women into local groups to promote feminine perspectives on reproductive rights. To educate and take action on these issues. Our goal is for all women, all people to have reproductive freedoms and self determination. **Other Resources:** Publishes HEATH/PAC BULLETIN. **Est.:** 1979.

**H ▶ Research Alternatives**
See HAZARD MONTHLY (periodicals).

**P ▶ Resist**
See RESIST newsletter.

**✌ ▶ Resource Center For Nonviolence**
515 Broadway
Santa Cruz, CA 95060 (408)423-1626
**Concern(s):** peace; energy; education; Third World; anti-nuclear; nonviolence; disarmament; volunteers. A volunteer center that works alongside affiliated political action groups in safe energy and nuclear disarmament issues. **Other Resources:** See newsletter, CENTER UPDATE; and Project Abraco. Workshops, study groups, speakers and films, class presentations for churches and public organizations. Internships available. New Society Bookstore on premises. **Contact(s):** Anita Heckman (Staff Member).

**E ▶ Resource Conservation Alliance**
1400 16th St. NW
Washington, DC 20036-2266 (202)797-6800
**Affiliation:** National Wildlife Federation. **Concern(s):** environment; resources; conservation.

**✍ ▶ Resources**
See ALTERNATIVE AMERICA directory.

**E ▶ Resources for the Future**
1616 P St. NW
Washington, DC 20036 (202)328-5000
**Concern(s):** environment; future; natural resources; global warming. Independent research organization specializing in natural resources and the environment. Research relies on the tools of economics and other social sciences as well as the natural sciences. Seeks to inform and improve policy debates on resource and environmental issues by disseminating its research. Maintains a nonpartisan, objective stance on all specific policy issues. Distributes research through books, articles, seminars and other means. **Other Resources:** See guide, SCARCITY AND GROWTH RECONSIDERED and newsletter, ANNUAL POLICY REVIEW. **Contact(s):** Robert W. Fri (President).

**E ▶ Restoring the Earth**
1713 C Martin Luther King Jr. Way
Berkeley, CA 94709 (510)843-2645
**Concern(s):** environment; conservation. Through influence on public opinion and public policy, it hopes to make repair of natural resources a high national priority, to galvanize a national restoration effort and to develop a broad national constituency for environmental renewal. Offers a community outreach and youth/schools program. Distributes pamphlets, slide/tape and multi-part documentary TV series on environmental restoration; video and audio tapes. Publishes news bulletin. **Other Resources:** See guide, REPAIR MANUAL FOR PLANET EARTH. **Contact(s):** John Berger.

**T ▶ Results**
236 Massachusetts Ave. NE, #300
Washington, DC 20002 (202)543-9340
**Concern(s):** Third World; politics; demographics; hunger; development; lobbying; law; volunteers. Rapidly expanding lobbying entity consisting of 100 groups in 46 states with branches in Canada, Australia, Great Britain and West Germany. US volunteers hold monthly meetings where letters to Congress and local newspaper editors are generated concerning domestic and global hunger. Conferences feature members of Congress and experts in various fields. Attempts to focus congressional attention on a wide range of issues from

support for primary health care to World Bank lending policies. **Est.:** 1980. **Contact(s):** Sam Harris (Director), Dorsey Lawson (Assistant Director).

**H ◆ Retreats International**
See DIRECTORY OF RETREAT HOUSES IN UNITED STATES AND CANADA.

**E ◆ Rhino Rescue USA, Inc.**
1150 17th St. NW, #400
Washington, DC 20036    (202)293-5305
**Concern(s):** environment; politics; wildlife/endangered species; law. Organization dedicated to save the rhino from extinction by funding rhino sanctuaries and research, organizing congressional hearings and working with the US State Department and international experts to end the trade of rhino horn. **Other Resources:** Contact office for local fundraising.

**$ ◆ Richard and Rhoda Goldman Fund**
1160 Battery St., #400
San Francisco, CA 94111    (415)788-1090
**Concern(s):** economics; philanthropy. A private foundation which reflects the founders' commitment to provide financial support to charitable organizations which enhance the quality of life, primarily in the San Francisco Bay area. It is interested in supporting programs which will have a significantly positive impact in a wide array of fields including: the elderly, environmental and civic affairs. **Contact(s):** Duane Silverstein (Executive Director).

**S ◆ Right Livelihood Awards Foundation**
Box 15072, S-10465
Stockholm, **Sweden**    +46 8 7020340
**Concern(s):** spiritual; future; philanthropy; invention. Also known as the Alternative Nobel Prize, these awards are bestowed in December in the Swedish Parliament for outstanding work of great benefit to humanity in the fields of Peace and Disarmament, Human Rights, Poverty Alleviation and Economic Development, Human Development and Environmental Regeneration and Conservation. **Other Resources:** Brochure and annual press release. Books, PEOPLE AND PLANET; REPLENISHING THE EARTH; FOR A FUTURE THAT WORKS; and TACKLING GLOBAL PROBLEMS FROM THE GRASSROOTS. **Est.:** 1980. **Contact(s):** Kepstin Bennett (Administrative Director).

**⚉ ◆ Riverside Church Disarmament Program**
475 Riverside Dr.
New York, NY 10115    (212)222-5900
**Concern(s):** peace; education; disarmament; anti-nuclear. This program sponsors and promotes education in action to reverse the arms race. **Other Resources:** Publishes a newsletter, DISARMING NOTES. **Est.:** 1978. **Contact(s):** Rev. Eric Kolbell.

**H ◆ Robert W. Woodruff Volunteer Service Center**
See National Parents Resource Institute For Drug Education.

**H ◆ Robinson Research Institute**
Yarrow Center, 1165 Yarrow Circle
Highland, UT 84003    (801) 756-7763
**Concern(s):** health; environment; preventative medicine; holism; research; nutrition. Conducts research on various herbs and their uses as homeopathic remedies. Information is not intended to be used as diagnosis, treatment, or mitigation of any disease condition. It provides a summary, "Herbs and Your Health," which is a guide to historical and traditional uses of herbs for the student of herbal lore and philosophy. A brochure is distributed free at local health food stores. **Price:** Free. **Pages:** 4. **Contact(s):** Loren C. Robinson (Founder).

**☺ ◆ Rocky Mountain Institute**
1739 Snowmass Creek Rd.
Old Snowmass, CO 81654-9199    (303)927-3851
**Concern(s):** energy; environment; agriculture; peace; politics; economics; natural resources; global warming; conservation; national security; appropriate technology; efficiency; resource management. The Lovins, Right Livelihood Award recipients, established this mountain retreat as a think tank for renewable energy. They promote community self-reliance, appropriate technology, conservation, and reduction on foreign energy fuel sources to insure national security. **Other Resources:** Publishes newsletter. Many resources available. SOFT ENERGY PATH: TOWARD A DURABLE PEACE is Amory Lovins best known book. See guides, PRACTICAL HOME ENERGY SAVINGS; BUSINESS OPPORTUNITY WORKBOOK; and RESOURCE-EFFICIENT HOUSING GUIDE. Nonprofit. **Est.:** 1982. **Contact(s):** Amory Lovins (President), Hunter Lovins (Vice-President). (303)927-3128.

**⚉ ◆ Rocky Mountain Peace Center**
1520 Euclid
Boulder, CO 80302    (303)443-3680
**Concern(s):** peace; justice; Third World; anti-nuclear; test ban. Organizes direct action protests against nuclear tests and the nuclear

arms race; also does Central America projects to stop human rights abuse in Nicaragua and El Salvador. **Other Resources:** See guide, COMMUNITIES FOR CONSERVATION AND ACTION: A MANUAL FOR BUILDING COMMUNITY.

**A ◆ Rodale Foundation, Press and Research Center**
Rodale Press
33 Minor St.
Emmaus, PA 18049    (215)967-5171
**Affiliation:** Rodale Institute. **Concern(s):** agriculture; environment; health; sustainability; nutrition. The Center develops, tests and publicizes new farming techniques that reduce the need for pesticides and chemical fertilizers. If you send a SASE to Organic Gardening's Reader Service, they can provide you with free lists of organic farming certification organizations, advice and information groups, a directory of resources on alternative agriculture, and an information packet on organic pest control—all developed for their Regeneration Gardener's Network. **Other Resources:** Publishes ORGANIC GARDENING; NEW FARM; and PREVENTION magazines. **Member:** Regeneration Gardeners Network. **Office:** 222 Main Emmaus, PA 18049. **Contact(s):** Robert Rodale (deceased) (President). **Other:** R.D. #1, Box 323, Kutztown, PA 19530. Linda Deitz

**A ◆ Rodale Institute**
Rodale Institute
222 Main St.
Emmaus, PA 18049    (215)967-5171
**Concern(s):** agriculture; environment; health; sustainability; hazardous/toxic wastes; nutrition; pesticides. **Other Resources:** See The NEW FARM magazine or Community Regeneration Project. **Contact(s):** James Morgan (Executive Director).

**T ◆ Roosevelt Center for American Policy Studies**
250 S. Wacker, #1250
Chicago, IL 60606-5834
**Concern(s):** Third World; politics; foreign policy. Study and research in non-scientific areas.

**M ◆ Roundtable Discussions**
6703 Pawtucket Rd.
Bethesda, MD 20817
**Concern(s):** media; ideation; multilogues. 208 people in 89 countries are on the mailing list of Roundtable, which sends each a suggested progressive topic for discussion each month and includes a seminal article on the topic. **Contact(s):** Jane Cole, Robert Cole.

**✍ ◆ Rowe Camp & Conference Center**
Kings Highway Rd.
Rowe, MA 01367    (413)339-4954
**Concern(s):** education; spiritual; politics; health; youth; faith; activism; transformation; networking; psychology. "Since 1924 we have been a progressive, open co-ed summer camp for teenagers and later pre-teens, singles and families. In the fall, winter and spring we offer weekend retreats with some of the finest leaders in the country in the areas of psychology, religion, politics, health, and fun." **Other Resources:** Weekends for ecological activists, peace workers, myths, dreams, goddesses, drumming, Wicca, music, gays, lesbians, art, intimacy, men's issues, writing and more. Nonprofit. **Est.:** 1924. **Other Formats:** Cheshire, sticky labels. **Labels:** 20M/negotiable. **Contact(s):** Doug Wilson, Prue Berry (Executive Directors). (413)339-4468.

**E ◆ The Ruffed Grouse Society**
1400 Lee Dr.
Corapolis, PA 15108    (412)262-4044
**Concern(s):** environment; wildlife/endangered species; land. Organization dedicated to improving the environment for the ruffed grouse, American woodcock and other forest wildlife. Organization has strong emphasis on creating and improving young forest habitat on public lands. **Other Resources:** Assists with local banquets and chapters. **Dues:** $20/yr.

**A ◆ Running Rain Society**
Box 74
Datil, NM 87821    (505)772-2634
**Affiliation:** Permaculture Drylands Institute. **Concern(s):** agriculture; environment; justice; drylands; permaculture; land; Native Americans. Its goals are research and education in drylands use: farming, restoration, and permaculture design, with special emphasis on marginal lands and Indian lands. "We consult on Permaculture projects specializing in water harvesting and alternative energy. Educational services can be provided for permaculture design courses and classes on a variety of subjects." **Other Resources:** Consulting work with Native American groups on land management issues. Nonprofit. **Est.:** 1988. **Dues:** $25/yr. **Contact(s):** Daniel Howell (Director), Karen Howell (Research Assistant). **Other:** Permaculture Drylands Institute, Box 27371, Tucson, AZ 85726.

**J ◆ Running Strong for American Indian Youth**
Christian Relief Services
632 S. Second St.
Raton, NM 87740-0670
**Affiliation:** Christian Relief Services. **Concern(s):** justice; education; spiritual; Native Americans; youth; diversity; minority rights; philanthropy; faith. Sponsors of the Pine Ridge Reservation Garden and Nutrition Program.

**A ◆ Rural Advancement Fund**
See RURAL ADVANCE newsletter.

**⚉ ◆ Rural Alliance For Military Accountability**
502 E. John St., #D
Carson City, NV 89706    (702)885-0166
**Affiliation:** Tides Foundation. **Concern(s):** peace; economics; politics; disarmament; government accountability; grassroots organizing. Supports and encourages rural citizens who are fighting to protect themselves and their communities from abuses of the US military. Promotes an integrated understanding of the role the military plays in our economic and political life. **Other Resources:** Publishes a quarterly newsletter called SKYGUARD. **E-Network:** Environet. **Fax:** (702)885-0167. **Contact(s):** Marla Painter (Executive Director), Juan Montes (Director of Programs).

**☺ ◆ Rural America, Inc.**
See COMMUNITY TRANSPORTATION REPORTER (periodicals).

**F ◆ Rural American Women, Inc.**
2439 Freyou Rd.
New Iberia, LA 70560-9338    (318)364-8000
**Concern(s):** feminism; agriculture; family farms; discrimination; empowerment/counselling; rural communities. A national organization working to bring visibility and recognition to the achievements and concerns of rural women. **Contact(s):** Judy Voehringer.

**A ◆ Rural Coalition**
2001 S St. NW, #500
Washington, DC 20009    (202)483-1500
**Concern(s):** agriculture; politics; economics; rural communities. **Contact(s):** Catherine Lerza.

**A ◆ Rural Economics Policy Program**
See COMMUNITY RESEARCHER'S GUIDE TO RURAL DATA (directories).

**D ◆ Rural Network**
Route 2, Box 150B
GazsMils, WI 54631
**Concern(s):** demographics; agriculture; economics; health; networking; rural relocation. For single people who are country-oriented and who value a healthy environment, some members already own land; some plan a move and are seeking congenial neighbors or a companion. **Other Resources:** Contact service and monthly newsletter, ADVOCATE, where readers exchange experiences, discuss problems, offer advice, invite visitors, etc. **Other:** Advocate/Rural Network, 6236 Borden Rd., Boscobel, WI 53805.

**A ◆ Rural Vermont**
See magazine, ORGANIC FARMER, THE DIGEST OF SUSTAINABLE AGRICULTURE.

**⚉ ◆ Sacramento Peace Center**
See BETWEEN THE LINES newspaper.

**⚉ ◆ Sacramento Religious Community for Peace**
See PeaceWorks newspaper.

**E ◆ The Sacred Earth Network, Inc.**
426 6th Ave.
Brooklyn, NY 11215    (718)768-8569
**Concern(s):** environment; peace; sustainability; East-West. An international confederacy focussing on the "inner" component of the environmental crisis and a resource for "cutting edge" information and assistance to international environmental grassroots initiatives. Seeks to foster an experiential awareness o Deep Ecology among both environmentalists and citizens which can serve as a foundation for problem-solving in all spheres of human influence; and initiate cooperative activities between US and Soviet environmentalists. **Other Resources:** Publishes newsletter in both English and Russian. Nonprofit. **Est.:** 1990. **Dues:** $25/yr. **Frequency:** 2/yr. **Subscription:** $10/yr. **Pages:** 6-8. **Circ.:** 2M. **E-Network:** Econet. **ID:** IGC: @"sen". **Fax:** (718)788-2554. **Contact(s):** Bill Pfeiffer (Director), Diane Depuydt (Associate Director). (212)924-2295.

**E ◆ The Sacred Earth Society**
Box 620883
San Diego, CA 92102
**Concern(s):** environment; spiritual; politics; transformation; activism; conservation; preservation. A spiritual, ecological, and political organization with the mission of bringing to the public the catastrophic

situation of our planet. "We use our magazine, the SACRED EARTH JOURNAL and television programs to do this. We believe that the earth is sacred, that the jungles, animals, and 'primitive' peoples must be saved and protected." **Other Resources:** THE SACRED EARTH JOURNAL. **Est.:** 1990. **Contact(s):** Eric Siegel (Founder/Chairman), Peter Sorensen (Founding Director).

**E ▸ Sacred Passage**
Drawer CZ
Bisbee, AZ 85603 (602)432-7353
**Concern(s):** environment; spiritual; education; transformation. A guided 11-day meditation and wilderness solo program for individuals with the belief that powerful environmental change comes from a profound personal experience of the basic insight of deep ecology. Training is available for guides and assistance on specific Sacred Passages.

**✪ ▸ Safe Energy Communication Council**
1717 Massachusetts Ave. NW, #LL215
Washington, DC 20036 (202)483-8491
**Concern(s):** energy; environment; global warming; anti-nuclear; renewables. A national coalition of environmental, energy, and public interest media organizations working to increase public awareness of the ability of energy efficiency and renewable energy to meet an increasing share of our nation's energy needs and also of the serious economic and environmental liabilities of nuclear power. **Other Resources:** Publishes a series of reports called MYTHbusters and PUBLIC MEDIA CENTER'S INDEX OF PROGRESSIVE FUNDERS. Produces widely distributed public service announcements. See Telecommunications and Research Action Center; and Public Media Center. Nonprofit. **Contact(s):** Scott Denman (Director), Mary O'Driscoll (National Press Coordinator).

**✈ ▸ Samantha Smith Center**
9 Union St.
Hallowell, ME 04347 (207)626-3415
**Concern(s):** education; peace; media; travel; childhood; youth; conflict resolution. Established to continue expanding our youth exchanges between the US and the USSR. "We are dedicated to fostering international cooperation, understanding, and communication between families and communities in the USSR and in the US. Through education, the media and youth exchange projects, we have played a role in dispelling the stereotypical myths about our two nations. The Center was named after the young peacemaker who so tragically died in a plane crash." Nonprofit. **Est.:** 1985. **Contact(s):** Jane G. Smith.

**E ▸ San Antonio Bioregional Research Group**
515 E. North Loop Rd.
San Antonio, TX 78216
**Concern(s):** environment; politics; research; bioregionalism.

**♈ ▸ San Diego Animal Advocates**
Box 813
Vista, CA 92083
**Concern(s):** environment; animal rights.

**✌ ▸ San Francisco Study Group for Peace**
See ThinkPeace newsletter.

**E ▸ San Luis Obispo County Earth Day Coalition**
See EARTH JOURNAL (periodicals).

**✍ ▸ Sandhill Farm**
See COMMUNITY BOOKSHELF under publishers.

**M ▸ Sane Education Fund**
5808 Greene St.
Philadelphia, PA 19144 (215)848-4100
**Concern(s):** media; education; press. Produces CONSIDER THE ALTERNATIVES. **Member:** Unitarian Universalist Peace Network.

**✌ ▸ Sane/Freeze**
1819 H St. NW, #1000
Washington, DC 20006-3603 (202)862-9740
**Concern(s):** peace; Third World; education; disarmament; anti-nuclear; intervention; militarism; test ban. The nation's largest grassroots peace organization working through public education, local organizing, direct action, and national lobbying, to cut military spending, abolish nuclear weapons, curb interventionist policies and reorder federal spending priorities. Resulted from the merger of SANE (The Committee for a Sane Nuclear Policy) and the National Nuclear Weapons Freeze Campaign. **Other Resources:** A syndicated radio program, "Consider the Alternatives" Publishes the GRASS ROOTS ORGANIZER, SANE World/Freeze Focus, flyers and pamphlets. See, SOCIALLY-RESPONSIBLE BUYER'S GUIDE. Nonprofit. **Est.:** 1987. **Contact(s):** Rev. William Sloane Coffin, Jr. (President), Nick Carter (Executive Director).

**E ▸ Save America's Forests**
4 Library Ct. SE
Washington, DC 20003 (202)544-9219
**Concern(s):** environment; forests. Coalition of forest reform groups and individuals around the country working to make management for ecological values the top priority for America's publicly-owned National Forests. **Other Resources:** Free brochure. **Member:** Co-op America.

**E ▸ Save Our Earth**
2008 1/2 Preuss Rd.
Los Angeles, CA 90034 (310)839-1976
**Concern(s):** environment; demographics; population growth. Publishes a small newsletter on various environmental issues particularly centering on the issue of over-population. Ms. Stansfield, the founder, was formerly with the Zero Population Growth chapter in Los Angeles and organized a pro-choice demonstration for the Pope when he visited the smog inferno. Her radical approach eventually got her expelled from ZPG. **Contact(s):** Elaine Stansfield (Director/Editor).

**E ▸ Save Our Streams Program**
1401 Wilson Blvd.
Level B
Arlington, VA 22209 (705)528-1818
**Affiliation:** Izaak Walton League of America. **Concern(s):** environment; oceans/rivers; volunteers. A river protection program of the Izaak Walton League of America, active in 37 states. SOS teaches volunteers to restore rivers through water quality monitoring, restoration practices and advocacy. The program provides kits, guide and computer listings of projects. **Other Resources:** Publishes quarterly, SPLASH. Splash subscription available with purchase of SOS kit for $6. Nonprofit. **Est.:** 1969. **Dues:** $20/yr. includes newsletter. **Fax:** (703)528-1836. **Contact(s):** Karen Firehock (Program Director), Eunice Groark (Monitoring Coordinator).

**J ▸ Save the Children**
54 Wilton Rd.
Westport, CT 06880 (203)226-7272
**Concern(s):** justice; demographics; health; children; hunger. A development agency dedicated to improving the quality of life and defending the rights of children, particularly in underprivileged communities. Perhaps you have seen Cliff Robertson or Sally Struthers on late night TV promoting their work. They remain legitimate, worthwhile, and effective. Nonprofit. **Member:** Co-op America. (800)243-5075;(800)257-2900. **Contact(s):** Andrea Williamson-Hughes. (203)221-4000.

**♈ ▸ Save the Dolphin Project**
Earth Island Institute
300 Broadway, # 28
San Francisco, CA 94133 (415)788-3666
**Affiliation:** Earth Island Institute. **Concern(s):** environment; wildlife/endangered species; preservation; animal rights. Devoted to ending the slaughter of dolphins by the tuna industry. Activities include: Research and dissemination of educational materials, coordination of a canned tuna boycott, identifying dolphin-safe tuna, lawsuit to force implementation of the Marine Mammal Protection Act. **Other Resources:** DOLPHIN ALERT newsletter. (800)3-DOLPHIN. **Contact(s):** David Phillips, Brenda Killian.

**E ▸ Save the Dunes Council, Inc**
Box 114
Beverly Shores, IN 46301 (219)879-3937
**Concern(s):** environment; economics; preservation; conservation; Great Lakes; air pollution. Preservation and the protection of Indiana Dunes for public use and enjoyment. Group works for better control of air, water, and waste pollution. Involved with shoreline erosion and shoreline policy affecting Lake Michigan. **Other Resources:** Concession Shops. **Dues:** $10/senior, $30/couple, $500/life.

**E ▸ Save the Earth**
4881 Topanga Canyon Blvd., #201
Woodland Hills, CA 91364 (818)833-2784
**Concern(s):** environment; research. A public benefit corporation dedicated to the expansion of environmental awareness in our society. Funds scientific research and educational programs designed to raise the public environmental consciousness. Nonprofit.

**E ▸ Save the Florida Panther**
Box 21112
Tampa, FL 33622-1112
**Concern(s):** environment; wildlife/endangered species.

**E ▸ Save the Manatee**
1101 Audubon Way
Martland, FL 32751 (800)342-1281
**Concern(s):** environment; wildlife/endangered species. Reports injured Manatees and educates people about protecting them. (Florida Only)

**E ▸ Save the Rainforest, Inc.**
Dodgeville High School
912 W. Chapel
Dodgeville, WI 53533
**Concern(s):** environment; forests. A student-teacher organization which provides information and updates about the rainforest free of charge. Anyone can write and be placed on the mailing list.

**E ▸ Save the Tallgrass Prairie, Inc.**
4101 W. 54th Terrace
Shawnee Mission, KS 66205
**Concern(s):** environment; wilderness. Tallgrass prairie park.

**E ▸ Save the Whales**
Box 2397
Venice, CA 90291 (310)392-6226
**Concern(s):** environment; education; wildlife/endangered species; oceans/rivers; childhood. Our purpose is to educate children and adults on marine mammals, their environment, and their preservation. It is beginning educational programs via a mobile unit (Whales on Wheels) which will bring lectures and hands-on materials (skeletal parts of marine mammals, baleen, pelts, visual aides, etc.) to schoolchildren. Beach cleanups combined with lectures are offered to schoolchildren (with an emphasis on underprivileged children) several times a year. **Other Resources:** Letter-writing campaign issues which are sent to members who want to be letter writers and members of general public. "Our office is an information source for public - we receive inquiries by phone and letter. We publish a quarterly newsletter." Nonprofit. **Est.:** 1977. **Office:** 1426 Main St. Venice, CA 90291. **Contact(s):** Maris Sidenstecker (Director).

**E ▸ Save-The-Redwoods**
114 Sansome St.
San Francisco, CA 94104 (415)367-2352
**Concern(s):** environment; energy; forests; conservation; resources. Objects: To rescue from destruction representative areas of our primeval forests; cooperate with the California State Park Commission, the National Park Service, and other agencies, in establishing Redwood parks and reservations; privately purchase Redwood groves; encourage a greater understanding of the need for primeval Redwood/Sequoia and other forests of America as natural objects of extraordinary value to present and future generations; and to support reforestation and conservation. **Other Resources:** Publishes a quarterly, SAVE-THE-REDWOODS BULLETIN. **Dues:** $10/yr. **Contact(s):** Bruce S. Howard (President), John B. Dewitt (Executive Director).

**E ▸ Scenic America**
216 7th St. SE
Washington, DC 20003 (202)546-1100
**Concern(s):** environment; urban; beautification; conservation. The only national conservation organization devoted to protecting America's scenic landscapes and cleaning up visual pollution. Scenic America provides information and technical assistance on billboard and sign control, scenic highways, tree protection and growth management. **Other Resources:** CITIZENS HANDBOOK ON CURBING ALCOHOL AND TOBACCO BILLBOARDS. HANDBOOK ON SCENIC HIGHWAYS; LEGAL HANDBOOK ON SIGN CONTROL, and newsletter, SIGN CONTROL NEWS. **Est.:** 1982. **Contact(s):** Sally Oldham (President), Hal Hickstar (Policy Director).

**E ▸ Scenic Shoreline Preservation Conference**
4623 More Mesa Dr.
Santa Barbara, CA 93110 (805)964-2492
**Concern(s):** environment; ocean/rivers; preservation.

**S ▸ School for Esoteric Studies**
40 E. 49th St., #1903
New York, NY 10017 (212)755-3027
**Concern(s):** spiritual; arts; transformation; culture. "Today one can discern a growing network of men and women all over the world who embody a vital spirit and are becoming an increasingly potent force for transformation in human affairs... A view of the deeper spiritual significance of this integrating group is offered in a 30-page booklet: BUILDING AND BRIDGING, the New Group of World Servers; it includes practical evidence of their work.".

**✍ ▸ School for Field Studies**
376 Hale St.
Beverly, MA 01915 (617)927-5339
**Concern(s):** education; environment.

**✈ ▸ School for International Training**
Kippling Rd.,Box 676
Brattleborough, VT 05301 (800)451-4465
**Affiliation:** Experiment in International Living. **Concern(s):** education; travel. "Accredited study abroad; senior college and graduate school. Prepares students for international/intercultural careers. Programs include: College Semester & Summer Abroad programs in 32

countries, many in developing nations. World Issues, a 2-year upper division bachelor's program. Includes overseas internship. M.A. in Teaching Languages for teachers of ESL, French, and Spanish. Master's in Intercultural Management." **Other Resources:** Publishes a quarterly newspaper, WORLD VIEW; Experiment in International Living. **Fax:** (802)254-6674. **Contact(s):** Marshall Brewer, Lani Wright (Counselors). (802)257-7751.

**T ▸ School of Interdisciplinary Study**
See INDIGENOUS WORLD (periodicals).

**✍ ▸ School of Living (SOL)**
Route 1, Box 185A
Cochranville, PA 19330
**Concern(s):** education; economics; agriculture; environment; decentralization; community self reliance; land trusts; permaculture; cooperatives. Explores options for decentralization, cooperative living, and land reform. SOL offers training conferences, financing for Community Land Trust (CLT) development, permaculture demonstrations, monetary and economic reform activities. It administers a regional CLT alliance for intentional communities, homesteaders, and other residential users wishing to place land in trust. **Other Resources:** See GREEN REVOLUTION newsletter. **Est.:** 1934.

**$ ▸ Schumacher Society**
RD3, Box 76
Great Barrington, MA 01230 (413)528-1737
**Concern(s):** economics; community self-reliance. Dedicated to the promotion and furtherance of a holistic and humanistic philosophy of economics put forward by the late Dr. F.W. Schumacher, author of SMALL IS BEAUTIFUL. **Other Resources:** Lectures and books, publishes magazine through Rodale Press, RESURGENCE. **Est.:** 1980. **Subscription:** Membership. **Contact(s):** Robert Swan.

**☮ ▸ Science for Peace**
University College
University of Toronto
Toronto, ON M5S 1A1 Canada
**Concern(s):** peace; energy; education; science; appropriate technology. Publishes the BULLETIN and other publications.

**✍ ▸ Science Resource Center**
See SCIENCE FOR THE PEOPLE (periodicals).

**✍ ▸ Scientists' Institute for Public Information**
355 Lexington Ave.
New York, NY 10017 (212)661-9110
**Concern(s):** education; media; journalism; science; media watch; responsibility. Works to improve public understanding of science and technology. Recognizing that most Americans get neatly all their information by turning on their TVs or radios, or opening the pages of a newspaper or magazine, SIPI seeks to bridge the gap between scientist and the media. **Other Resources:** Media Resource Service, The Videotape Referral Service, and SIPIscope, a newsletter. Nonprofit.

**✈ ▸ Sea Quest Expeditions**
Zoetic Research
Box 2424
Friday Harbour, WA 98250 (206)378-5767
**Concern(s):** education; environment; travel; recreation. Outdoor adventures in the Pacific Northwest, Mexico, and Florida led by environmental educators. Contributes to environmental groups. **Member:** Co-op America.

**E ▸ Sea Shepherd**
Box 7000-S
Redondo Beach, CA 92077 (310)373-6979
**Concern(s):** environment; wildlife/endangered species; oceans/rivers; volunteers. International all-volunteer conservation organization working to save whales, seals and dolphins. Operates educational programs and works to increase public awareness of the threats to marine mammals. **Other Resources:** SEA SHEPHERD LOG newsletter and Whale Hotline. **Dues:** Donation. Hotline: (310)543-2888. **Contact(s):** Paul Watson, Ben White (Director).

**E ▸ Sea Turtle Rescue Fund**
1725 DeSales St., #500
Washington, DC 20036 (202)737-3600
**Affiliation:** Center for Marine Conservation. **Concern(s):** environment; wildlife/endangered species. **Contact(s):** Mary Dele Donnely.

**D ▸ Second Harvest National Food Bank Network**
116 S. Michigan Ave., #4
Chicago, IL 60603-6001 (312)341-1303
**Affiliation:** Food for Survival. **Concern(s):** demographics; agriculture; Third World; food distribution; hunger. **Member:** National Food Bank Network. **Contact(s):** Pamela Heydt, Lucy Cabrera (Executive Director). **Other:** Food For Survival, Hunts Point Co-op, Box 10424, Chicago, IL 60610.

**☮ ▸ Section on Social Responsibility, Canadian Psychological Association**
c/o Craig Summers, Chair
Dept. of Psychology, Laurentian University
Sudbury, ON P3E 2C6 Canada (705)675-1151
**Affiliation:** Laurentian University. **Concern(s):** peace; health; feminism; justice; education; politics; Native Americans; indigenous peoples; anti-nuclear; militarism; psychology. This group of psychologists focuses on the professional contributions that we can make to political and social issues. Militarism and the sanity of nuclear deterrence have been continuing foci. Activities have also included feminism, mental health institutionalization and native rights. **Other Resources:** Publishes a newsletter. **Dues:** $8.56, $5.35 students (Canadian $). **E-Network:** Bitnet/Netnorth. **ID:** @nickel.laurentian.ca. **Member:** Section 2 of the Canadian Psychological Association. **Contact(s):** Craig Summers (Chair).

**A ▸ The Seed Corps**
Box 1705
Santa Rosa, CA 95402 (707)575-3707
**Concern(s):** agriculture; development.

**A ▸ The Seed Saver's Exchange**
RR 3, Box 239
Decorah, IA 52101 (319)382-3949
**Concern(s):** agriculture; development. Volunteer gardners growing rare, open-pollinated vegetables, fruits, and ornamental plants, and saving the seed to trade with other Exchange members. Nonprofit. **Contact(s):** Kent Whealey (Director).

**☮ ▸ Seeds of Peace**
2440 16th St.
Box 241
San Francisco, CA 94103 (415)420-1799
**Concern(s):** peace; disarmament; anti-nuclear; test ban. Established during the Great Peace March. Provides support to the Direct Action Community involved with ending the military build-up and proliferation of nuclear weapons, submarines and first strike capabilities. Major issues: the Comprehensive Test Ban Treaty and affordable housing for the homeless. Walks for nuclear disarmament, Nevada Test Site Actions and Homeless Marches have all contributed to their diversity.

**D ▸ Seeds: Christians Concerned About Hunger**
222 E. Lake Dr
Decatur, GA 30030 (404)378-3566
**Concern(s):** demographics; Third World; economics; spiritual; hunger; volunteers; faith. Its purpose is to end US and world hunger. It is committed to encouraging and enabling Christians to respond to the poor, not just with charity, but with Biblical justice. Seeds seeks a mature understanding of the spiritual, political, and economic realties that lie at the root of hunger. **Other Resources:** Publishes SEEDS magazine, SPROUT NEWSLETTER, and MAIN STREET AMERICA (book), THE THIRD WORLD (book), a hunger action handbook, and sends out information on volunteer opportunities. (800)537-9359.

**H ▸ Self-Help Clearinghouse**
See SELF-HELP SOURCEBOOKS (directories).

**J ▸ Senate Select Committee on Indian Affairs**
See FEDERAL PROGRAMS OF ASSISTANCE TO AMERICAN INDIANS directory.

**M ▸ SeniorNet**
Institute for the Future
2740 Sand Hill Rd.
Menlo Park, CA 94025-7097
**Concern(s):** media; politics; health; ideation; computer networking; seniors. A network of computer-using elders designed to facilitate sharing of interests and ideas and group responses to political issues.

**✈ ▸ SERVAS**
11 John St., #706
New York, NY 10038 (212)267-0252
**Concern(s):** education; peace; Third World; travel; development. A host and visitors network with offices in 100 different countries. You can set the limits on visits in your home from day visits to 2 or 3 days. And you can reach beyond the tourist attractions and get to know people of any of the member countries without cost to you. Peace, understanding and good will are the goal of this transnational network. **Other Resources:** Publishes SERVAS INTERNATIONAL NEWS newsletter. **Est.:** 1948. **Contact(s):** Randi Metsch-Ampel.

**L ▸ Service Employees International Union**
See UNION (periodicals).

**☮ ▸ Seth/Jane Roberts World Peace Network**
3868 Centinela Ave, #12
Los Angeles, CA 90066 (310)313-1162
**Concern(s):** peace; justice; environment; activism; animal rights. Based on the premise that all life is sacred, everything has consciousness, and we form our own reality. The Network's ultimate goal is implementation of the Codicils as outlined in the Jane Roberts' books, Psychic Politics, which offers a framework for a new world civilization. **Other Resources:** Peace Packet is available for a donation. Mystic art workshops as a bridge to other dimensions and development of the dream-art sciences toward implementation of the Codicils as presented in Jane Roberts philosophical works. **Est.:** 1988. **Contact(s):** Madelon Rose Logue (West Coast Coordinator), Dale Mann (East Coast Coordinator).

**H ▸ Seva Foundation**
108 Spring Lake Dr.
Chelsea, MI 48118 (313)475-1351
**Concern(s):** health; Third World; justice; demographics; development; disabled; indigenous peoples; Native Americans; homelessness. An international service organization and a network of people working to alleviate suffering. Seva's main activities are support of the Nepal Blindness Program and of Aravind Eye Hospital in Madurai, India. Seva is also working with Guatemalan villagers and with Gautemalan refugees in the south of Mexico. Through small seed grants and other assistance, Seva is a catalyst for a variety of service projects around the world. Here, Seva works with Native Americans and with the homeless. **Est.:** 1979. **Fax:** (313)475-5846. **Contact(s):** Joan Wolf (Special Project Coordinator), Judy Gallagher (Administrator). Ram Dass

**J ▸ Seventh Generation Fund**
See NATIONAL SELF-SUFFICIENCY (periodicals).

**D ▸ Share Our Strength (SOS)**
1511 K St. NW
Washington, DC 20005 (202)393-2925
**Concern(s):** demographics; hunger. **Contact(s):** Joann Shepherd.

**$ ▸ Shared Living Resource Center**
2375 Shattuck Ave.
Berkeley, CA 94704 (510)548-6608
**Concern(s):** economics; urban; environment; education; intentional communities; community self-reliance; social ecology; architecture. Promotion of shared living and the Village Cluster housing concept through; 1) Education and outreach about ecological and social benefits; 2) Profile and consultation sessions for individuals and groups to facilitate shared living; 3) Architectural and planning assistance for conversion of existing and construction of new shared living community housing. **Other Resources:** Newsletter, SHARED LIVING COMMUNITY. Information packets, consultation sessions. slide talk presentations, planning design and working drawings, workshops, presentations at panels and conferences, and library. Nonprofit. **Est.:** 1987. **Fax:** (510)549-9960. **Contact(s):** Ken Norwood (Executive Director), David Hawkins (Administrative Assistance).

**L ▸ Sheet Metal Workers International Association**
1750 New York Ave. NW
Washington, DC 20006 (202)783-5880
**Concern(s):** labor; unions. **Contact(s):** Edward J. Carlough (President).

**T ▸ SHARE Foundation**
See Going Home Campaign & SHARE INTERNATIONAL (periodicals).

**E ▸ Sierra Club**
404 C St. NE
Washington, DC 20002 (202)547-1141
**Concern(s):** environment; politics; education; conservation; lobbying. Purpose is to promote conservation of the natural environment by influencing public policy decisions. Also, to practice and promote the responsible use of the Earth's ecosystem and resources, and to educate and enlist humanity to protect and restore the quality of the natural and human environment. **Other Resources:** SIERRA magazine; NATIONAL NEWS REPORT; Sierra Club Legal Defense Fund; guides, GLOBAL WARMING; HANDBOOK FOR PEACE AND ENVIRONMENT; Nonprofit. **Dues:** $33, $15/student/senior. **Contact(s):** Mike McCloskey (Chairman). **Other:** 730 Polk St., San Francisco, CA 94109 Michael L. Fischer , Executive Director. (415)776-2211.

**E ▸ Sierra Club Legal Defense Fund**
2044 Fillmore St.
San Francisco, CA 94115 (415)567-6100
**Concern(s):** environment; politics; acid rain; water; law. A public interest law firm providing legal representation for national, regional, and local groups and individuals committed to protecting the environment. The Legal Defense Fund is involved in litigation to reduce acid rain and water pollution to safeguard national forests, parks, wilderness areas, and seashores. As a independent nonprofit organization, it makes the government enforce the laws and the companies obey them. Nonprofit. **Member:** Environmental Federation of America. **Contact(s):** Freder P. Sutherland (Executive Director). **Other:** 1531 P St. NW, Washington, DC 20005(202)667-4500.

**E ▶ Sierra Club Population Committee**
3550 West 6th St., #321
Los Angeles, CA 90020   (310)719-3083
**Concern(s):** environment; demographics; politics; population growth; lobbying; law. An organization that works at all levels to achieve global population stabilization through both educational and legislative advocacy programs that are strongly supported by grass roots activists.

**$ ▶ Sirius Community**
See BUILDERS OF THE DAWN (directories).

**E ▶ Siskiyou Action Project**
Box 13070
Portland, OR 97213   (503)249-2958
**Concern(s):** environment; forests; wildlife/endangered species. Encourages grassroots lobbying on legislation affecting forests. A dynamic network of people speaking out and taking a stand for our public forests. **Other Resources:** See, also, Siskiyou Regional Education Project. Nonprofit. **Contact(s):** Lou Gould.

**E ▶ Siskiyou Regional Education Project**
Box 13070
Portland, OR 97213   (503)249-2958
**Concern(s):** environment; forests; wildlife/endangered species. Grassroots organization educating the public about the crisis taking place in our country's forests. Lou Gould has spent 5 years visiting communities, bringing crucial information to schools, conferences, and public forums through a slide show and lecture. Additional supportive materials on the Siskiyous and the ancient forests of the Northwest are in the process of being developed. Contributions are tax-deductible. **Other Resources:** See also, Siskiyou Action Project. Nonprofit. **Contact(s):** Lou Gould.

**✈ ▶ Sister Cities International**
120 S. Payne St.
Alexandria, VA 22314   (703)836-3535
**Concern(s):** education; Third World; peace; justice; travel; development; hunger. **Contact(s):** Peter Loan.

**✍ ▶ Skagit Peace Education Fund**
Box 386
LaConner, WA 98257
**Concern(s):** education; peace.

**D ▶ Skiers Ending Hunger/Ski to End Hunger**
1701 University Ave. SE
Minneapolis, MN 55414 (612)331-SNOW
**Concern(s):** demographics; hunger; sports. A fundraising and educational organization which supports skiers in having their sport contribute to the end of hunger. Funds raised by Ski To End Hunger support several relief and development agencies doing work overseas and in America. **Contact(s):** Paul Thompson.

**A ▶ Small Farm Center**
UC Davis
Davis, CA 95616
**Concern(s):** agriculture; food production. Big on Fava beans.

**D ▶ Small Town Institute**
See SMALL TOWN (periodicals).

**✍ ▶ Smithsonian Institution**
1000 Jefferson Dr. SW
Washington, DC 20560   (202)357-1300
**Concern(s):** education; arts; science; research; analysis. An independent trust of the US, established for the increase and diffusion of knowledge among people. Mission accomplished by: Field investigations; the development of the national collections in natural history and anthropology and their preservation for study, reference, and exhibition; scientific research and publications, programs of national and international cooperative research, conservation, education, and training; answering inquiries from the public. **Other Resources:** Publishes the SMITHSONIAN Magazine. **Est.:** 1846. **Contact(s):** Robert McCormick Adams (Secretary), Robert Hoffmann (Assistant Secretary). (202)357-2939.

**☙ ▶ Snake River Alliance**
Box 1731
Boise, ID 83701   (208)344-9161
**Concern(s):** peace; environment; health; boycott; hazardous/toxic waste. Took on the weapons industry and the DOE, activists have been working for 10 years to expose the DOE's environmentally unsound practices in Idaho. Succeeded in stopping plutonium reactor refinery. An Idaho citizens' organization working for peace, the reversal of the arms race, and responsible solutions to nuclear waste. **Contact(s):** Elizabeth Paul.

**$ ▶ Social Investment Forum**
430 1st Ave. North, #204
Minneapolis, MN 55401 (612)333-8338

**Concern(s):** economics; socially responsible investment. "A national trade association of investment professionals and individuals developing and promoting the practice of socially responsible investing. The membership has over 750 members including institutional investors, mutual fund managers, technical analysts, foundation investors, and individual investors. Working Assets, Calvert Group, Dreyfus Third Century Fund, US Trust Company, Franklin Research & Development, South Shore Bank of Chicago, Investor Responsibility Resource Center, Scudder..." **Other Resources:** Coalition for Environmental Responsible Economics (CERES), a project that drew up the Valdez Principles. Newsletter; GUIDE TO SOCIALLY RESPONSIBLE INVESTING; information clearinghouse. See Franklin Research & Progressive Asset Management under business. **Member:** Co-op America. **Contact(s):** Joan M. Kanavich (Associate Director), John E. Schultz (President). **Other:** 711 Atlantic Ave., 5th Floor, Boston, MA 02111.

**P ▶ Social Movement Empowerment Project**
721 Shrader St.
San Francisco, CA 94117
**Concern(s):** politics; peace; nonviolence; civil disobedience. Strategies are being outlined and formalized for movement activists. **Other Resources:** See THE PRACTICAL STRATEGIST, newspaper format. Also, THE MAP TRAINING MANUAL.

**✍ ▶ Social Studies School Service**
1000 Culver Boulevard
Culver City, CA 90230
**Concern(s):** education. See GLOBAL EDUCATION BOOK CATALOG under publishers.

**P ▶ Socialist Labor Party**
See PEOPLE (periodicals).

**P ▶ Socialist Party USA**
516 W. 25th St., #404
New York, NY 10001   (212)691-0776
**Concern(s):** politics; alternative party; Democratic Socialism. "...historically worked long and hard for disarmament and the prevention of war, while contending that is only by abolishing the root economic causes of war will finally be ended..." Committed to fighting sexism and racism, "recognizes that the oppression of women pre-dates capitalism and will not automatically be ended by a transition to democratic socialism. ...considers itself a part of an international 'third force' opposed to Capitalism and Communism." Embraces all progressives. **Other Resources:** See THE SOCIALIST and MAY DAY! (periodicals). **Est.:** 1901.

**P ▶ Socialist Workers Party**
See MILITANT (periodicals).

**E ▶ Society For Ecological Restoration and Management**
1207 Seminole Highway
Madison, WI 53711   (608)262-9547
**Concern(s):** environment; conservation. Created to promote the development of ecological restoration both as a discipline and as a model for a healthy relationship with nature, and to raise awareness of the value and limitations of restoration as a conservation strategy. **Other Resources:** Publishes RESTORATION AND MANAGEMENT NOTES; and, SER NEWS. **Est.:** 1987. **Contact(s):** William Jordan III (Supervisor of Administration), John Rieger (President). (619)237-6754. (608)263-7885.

**E ▶ Society for Human Ecology**
See INTERNATIONAL DIRECTORY OF HUMAN ECOLOGISTS.

**S ▶ Society for Humanistic Judaism**
See HUMANISTIC JUDAISM magazine.

**T ▶ Society for International Development**
USA Chapters Committee
1401 New York Ave., #1100
Washington, DC 20005  (202)347-1800
**Affiliation:** Cooperative League of the USA. **Concern(s):** Third World; development; research; analysis. The world's largest and most geographically widespread association for people with an interest in international economic, political, and social development. Also serves as a network for individuals and organizations with a interest in international development. SID attracts people from all viewpoints in the development process, whether as practitioners, policymakers, researchers, or concerned citizens. **Other Resources:** See journal, DEVELOPMENT, and newsletter, COMPASS (periodicals). **Est.:** 1957. **Contact(s):** Enrique Iglesias (President), Nancy Swing (703)752-2710. 265 Rocky Run Rd., Falmouth, VA 22405.

**H ▶ The Society for the Psychological Study of Social Issues**
Box 1248
Ann Arbor, MI 48106-1248

**Affiliation:** American Psychological Association. **Concern(s):** health; peace; justice; psychology; research. As Division 9 of APA, it publishes the SPSSI Newsletter.

**L ▶ The Society for the Reduction of Human Labor**
RD #1, Box 416, Hopson Rd.
Dolgeville, NY 13329
**Concern(s):** labor; economics.

**H ▶ Society For Nutrition Education**
2000 Dennis Ave.
Silver Springs, MD 20902   (301)217-1701
**Concern(s):** health; education; consumer protection; nutrition. **Contact(s):** Mary Goodwin.

**J ▶ Society of American Archivists**
See NATIVE AMERICAN ARCHIVES: AN INTRODUCTION (directories).

**M ▶ Society of Professional Journalists**
See FREEDOM OF INFORMATION REPORT (periodicals).

**☙ ▶ Society of Professionals in Dispute Resolution**
c/o The American Arbitration Association
1730 Rhode Island Ave. NW, #509
Washington, DC 20036  (202)331-7073
**Affiliation:** American Arbitration Association. **Concern(s):** peace; conflict resolution. Sponsors research and work to increase public understanding of dispute resolution procedures.

**A ▶ Soil and Water Conservation Society**
7515 NE Ankeny Rd.
Ankeny, IA 50021-9764 (515)289-2331
**Concern(s):** agriculture; environment; soil; land; water; conservation; natural resources. Publishes a multitude of books and booklets on soil and water conservation. Produce children's cartoon booklets. **Other Resources:** See JOURNAL OF SOIL AND WATER CONSERVATION (periodicals). Nonprofit. **Est.:** 1945. **Dues:** $36/yr. (first time members) $44 (renewals). **Fax:** (515)289-1227. **Contact(s):** David R. Cressman (President), Tim Kautza (Director of Programs).

**A ▶ Soil Remineralization**
152 South St.
Northampton, MA 01060
**Concern(s):** agriculture; soil. **Contact(s):** Joanna Campe.

**☙ ▶ Sojourners Fellowship**
Box 29272
Washington, DC 20017  (202)636-3637
**Concern(s):** peace; spiritual; faith; anti-nuclear. A ministry of the Christian community that publishes Sojourners magazine. Emphasizes biblical perspective. Produces written materials and resources for churches on nuclear arms race and Christian response. **Other Resources:** See SOJOURNERS magazine. **Office:** 1321 Otis St. NE Washington, DC 20017. **Contact(s):** Jim Wallis.

**☀ ▶ Solar Box Cookers International**
1724 11th St.
Sacramento, CA 95814  (916)444-6616
**Concern(s):** energy; Third World; environment; solar; efficiency. An organization promoting solar cooking to benefit people and environments worldwide. Their handbook tells how to make and use a simple convenient solar cooker. These cookers are proving effective in the Third World. **Other Resources:** Other teaching tools include foldable demonstration cooker, research, information network, training workshops and consultation. Quarterly newsletter, SOLAR BOX JOURNAL. Handbook $5 in US. Free to institutions abroad. Nonprofit. **Est.:** 1987. **E-Network:** Econet. **Fax:** (916)447-8689. **Contact(s):** Beverly Blum (Executive Director), Kevin Coyle (Resources Coordinator).

**☀ ▶ Solar Electric Light Fund**
1739 Connecticut Ave. NW
Washington, DC 20009  (202)234-7265
**Concern(s):** energy; Third World; solar. Promotes brokers and facilitates solar rural electrification in developing countries. Nonprofit. **Contact(s):** Neville Williams.

**☀ ▶ Solar Energy Industries Association (SEIA)**
777 N. Capitol St. NE., #805
Washington, DC 20002  (703)524-6100
**Concern(s):** energy; environment; solar. A national trade association of manufacturers of solar equipment, contractors, and professionals in related areas. Principal activities include government affairs, publications, technical and economic research, and market data collection. It has 3 technology-specific divisions: photovoltaics, solar buildings products, and solar thermal power. As the major representative of the solar energy industry in the US, it provides support for and generation information to the public and the industry. **Other Resources:** Sponsorships of conferences and workshops. An annual conference/trade show is held during the first quarter of each year. See magazine,

SOLAR INDUSTRY JOURNAL, and directory, SOLAR ELECTRIC APPLIANCES. **Fax:** (202)408-8536. **Contact(s):** Scott Sklar (Executive Director), Roger Little (President). (202)408-0660.

**☼ ♦ Solar Energy Research Institute**
1617 Cole Blvd.
Golden, CO 80401-3393 (303)231-7676
**Concern(s):** energy; solar research. SERI is a federal government laboratory focusing on research and development for solar technologies. SERI can provide answers to general questions about solar energy. **Contact(s):** Dr. H. H. Hubbard (Director).

**☼ ♦ Solar Retrofit Consortium**
345 E. 56th St.
New York, NY 10022-5138 (212)355-0817
**Concern(s):** energy; solar.

**E ♦ Solid Waste Alternatives Project (SWAP)**
6930 Carroll Ave., #600
Tacoma Park, MD 20912 (301)891-1100
**Affiliation:** Environmental Action Foundation. **Concern(s):** environment; recycling. SWAP stands out as the leading environmental authority on plastic packaging and waste. **Other Resources:** Publishes WASTELINE, a quarterly newsletter.

**A ♦ Solutions Network**
See INTERNATIONAL PERMACULTURE SPECIES YEARBOOK (TIPSY) (diectories)

**J ♦ South & Meso American Indian Information Center (SAIIC)**
Box 28703
Oakland, CA 94604 (510)834-4263
**Concern(s):** justice; Native Americans; indigenous peoples; self-determination. Supports the struggles of Native Americans for self-determination in South and Central America, the Caribbean, and Mexico, by publishing a magazine, organizing conferences, urgent action bulletins, and organizing for 500 years of Native American Resistance. **Other Resources:** "We have a small library open to the public. We publish many special publications on various related issues and SAIIC Newsletter. We hold many public events and tours of South and Meso American Indian leaders. We also have a small library of videos." **Est.:** 1983. **E-Network:** PeaceNet. **ID:** 'saiic'. **Fax:** (510)834-4264. **Contact(s):** Nilo Cayuqueo (Coordinator), Peter Veilleux (Editor/office manager).

**T ♦ South North Communication Network**
See BARRICADA INTERNACIONAL (periodicals).

**✍ ♦ South Street Centre**
Box 227
Boulder Creek, CA 95006 (408)338-2540
**Concern(s):** education. Serves the homeschooling community. "We offer activities and classes for children, educational counseling and resources for families." **Other Resources:** "We are contracted by the local school district to provide programs for homeschoolers. **Est.:** 1987. **Contact(s):** Betsy Herbert, Estelle Fein (Co-directors).

**S ♦ Southern California Association for Philanthropy (SCAP)**
315 W. 9th St., #1000
Los Angeles, CA 90015-4210 (213)489-7307
**Concern(s):** spiritual; philanthropy. This new edition and primary source of data about charitable giving in Southern California is the only survey on the overall charitable giving of the region's most important corporations and foundations is now available for $15.

**T ♦ Southern California Ecumenical Council**
See EL RESCATE newsletter.

**✍ ♦ Southern California Library for Social Studies and Research**
See HERITAGE (periodicals).

**J ♦ Southern Christian Leadership Conference**
334 Auburn Ave. NE
Atlanta, GA 30312 (404)522-1420
**Concern(s):** justice; urban; demographics; peace; politics; spiritual; faith; minority rights; reform; lobbying; volunteers; nonviolence; racism; discrimination; poverty. Founded by the late Martin Luther King to give moral leadership and spiritual leadership toward mass involvement of people to the struggle against racial oppression. Advocates nonviolent direct action. Works through social and social work with the poor. **Other Resources:** Dozens of projects need volunteers. **Est.:** 1957. **Contact(s):** Dr. Joseph E. Lowery, Rev. Alford E. Love.

**J ♦ Southern Organizing Committee for Economic & Social Justice**
See SOUTHERN FIGHT-BACK (periodicals).

**J ♦ Southern Poverty Law Center**
1001 S. Hull St.
Montgomery, AL 36104 (205)264-0286
**Concern(s):** justice; education; racism; discrimination; minority rights. Established to define and defend through education and litigation the legal rights of poor people. **Other Resources:** Published KLANWATCH INTELLIGENCE REPORT for law enforcement officials. Other reports available to the public. See LAW REPORT (periodicals). **Est.:** 1971. **Contact(s):** Morris S. Dees, Jr.

**A ♦ Southwest Regional Permaculture Institute**
Box 1812
Santa Fe, NM 87504 (505)982-2063
**Concern(s):** agriculture; Third World; environment; urban; permaculture; sustainability; drylands; recycling; land use; development. The permaculture ethic: care of the Earth, care of all species, and recycling of excess. At the institute they truly live by this ethic. They are devoted to sustainable living systems in the drylands. They conduct research and analysis on dryland region throughout the world. **Other Resources:** See journal, SUSTAINABLE LIVING IN DRYLANDS. **Contact(s):** Scott Pittman (Director).

**T ♦ Southwest Research & Information Center**
Box 4524
Albuquerque, NM 87106 (505)262-1862
**Concern(s):** Third World; environment; economics; foreign policy; development; consumer rights; research. Offers educational and technical assistance on environmental, social, and consumer problems. **Other Resources:** Publishes THE WORKBOOK, a quarterly magazine. Nonprofit. **Est.:** 1971. **Member:** Co-op America.

**A ♦ Southwestern Endangered Arid Land Resource Clearing House**
See Native Seeds/SEARCH.

**✏ ♦ SPARC - Social and Public Art Resource Center**
685 Venice Blvd.
Venice, CA 90291 (310)822-9560
**Concern(s):** arts; urban; graphics; ethnic concerns. Neighborhood Pride: Great Walls Unlimited. The Center's thirteen year history is closely tied to the production of murals in the City of Los Angeles, For the last two years, with funding from the City of Los Angeles, we have commissioned 24 artists to paint mural with the City of Los Angeles through our Neighborhood Pride: Great Walls Unlimited program. We are currently seeking artists for mural projects. **Contact(s):** Alan Nakagawa (Community Coordinator). (310)822-9783.

**P ♦ Speak Truth to Power Project**
5115 S. A1A Highway
Melbourne Beach, FL 32951 (407)952-0600
**Affiliation:** Institute for Space and Security Studies. **Concern(s):** politics; energy; education; government accountability; space; science; research. Independent research and education on areas like: "Star Wars" "Peace Shield," KAL-007 shootdown, Challenger explosion, Contragate, nuclear testing, public exposure to radiation for toxic wastes, arms control treaty compliance, JFK's murder, MIAs in Southeast Asia, mistreatment of veterans, Tomkin Gulf to Persian Gulf - unnecessary wars. **Est.:** 1982. **Contact(s):** Dr. Robert M. Bowman (President).

**M ♦ Speech Communication Association**
See FREE SPEECH YEARBOOK (periodicals).

**♿ ♦ Spinal Associates**
See SPINAL NETWORK: THE TOTAL RESOURCE FOR THE WHEELCHAIR COMMUNITY (directories).

**S ♦ Spiritual Emergency Network**
250 Oak Grove Ave.
Menlo Park, CA 94025
**Affiliation:** Institute of Transpersonal Psychology. **Concern(s):** spiritual; health; transformation; counseling; holism.

**P ♦ Stanley Foundation**
See WORLD PRESS REVIEW magazine.

**☢ ♦ Stark County Peace Community**
225 Arlington Ave. SW
Canton, OH 44706-1136
**Concern(s):** peace. **Contact(s):** W. Harrington.

**H ♦ Stop Teenage Addiction to Tobacco (STAT)**
See TOBACCO AND YOUTH REPORTER newsletter.

**☢ ♦ Stop War Toys Campaign**
Box 1093
Norwich, CT 06360
**Concern(s):** peace; education; economics; boycott; childhood. A boycott of toy manufactures that produce toys that refer to violence or war. (508)744-3417.

**E ♦ StopStyro**
2180 Milvia St.
Berkeley, CA 94704 (510)644-6359
**Concern(s):** environment; waste management.

**E ♦ The Student Conservation Association, Inc.**
Box 550
Charlestown, NH 03603 (603)826-4301
**Concern(s):** environment; volunteers; conservation; students. A membership organization, offers partially/full expense-paid opportunities for adult volunteers to assist with the stewardship of US public lands and natural resources. "Position Listings" are available for the Resource Assistant Program (18 and older) and High School Program (16-18). **Other Resources:** See magazine, EARTH WORK; directory, STUDENT CONSERVATION ASSOCIATION CATALOG for volunteer job listings. Nonprofit. **Fax:** (603)826-7755. **Contact(s):** Wallace Eaton (Public Relations Director).

**$ ♦ The Student Environmental Action Coalition (SEAC)**
Box 1168
University of North Carolina
Chapel Hill, NC 27514-1168 (919)967-4600
**Concern(s):** economics; environment; education; justice; youth; corporate responsibility; sustainability. SEAC is a national network of over 1,000 student environmental groups. SEAC's goal is to show the interconnections between environmental and other social concerns, and to make corporations more accountable to the public. **Other Resources:** See newsletter, THRESHOLD. Nonprofit. **Est.:** 1988. **Dues:** $15, $25 group, $35 non-student. **E-Network:** Bitnet. **ID:** SEAC @ UNC.BITNET. **Contact(s):** J. Burger (National Office Representative), Eric Odell (Newsletter Editor).

**M ♦ Student Press Law Center**
See SPLC REPORT (periodicals).

**✍ ♦ Student Pugwash, USA**
1638 R St. NW, #32
Washington, DC 20009 (202)328-6555
**Concern(s):** education; labor; jobs; volunteers; students; science. An educational organization devoted to preparing students to better understand the social & ethical dimensions of science and technology. **Other Resources:** See NEW CAREERS, A DIRECTORY OF JOBS AND INTERNSHIPS IN TECHNOLOGY & SOCIETY. Nonprofit. **Contact(s):** Denise Nepveux.

**☢ ♦ Student/Teacher Organization to Prevent Nuclear War**
11 Garden St.
Cambridge, MA 02138 (617)492-8305
**Concern(s):** peace; anti-nuclear.

**✍ ♦ Students United for Peace**
See STUDENTS UNITED FOR PEACE NEWSLETTER.

**S ♦ Sunrise International Network**
Box 113
Warrenville, IL 60555
**Concern(s):** spiritual; education; transformation; global understanding. A global network of people who want to see "love" as central to all Earthly actions.

**P ♦ The Supreme Court Watch**
Nation Institute
72 Fifth Ave.
New York, NY 10011 (212)463-9270
**Affiliation:** Nation Institute. **Concern(s):** politics; justice; law; civil liberties. Evaluates the civil rights and liberties records of potential and actual nominees to the Supreme Court; issues major reports which carefully reviews judicial records; attorneys, law students, and citizens function as an independent organization. **Est.:** 1981. **Dues:** $25-250/yr.

**☂ ♦ SUPRESS - Students United Protesting Research on Sentient Subjects**
Box 1062
Pasadena, CA 91102 (818)584-0446
**Concern(s):** environment; animal rights.

**E ♦ Surfrider Foundation**
Box 2704 #86
Huntington Beach, CA 92647 (714)960-8390
**Concern(s):** environment; ocean/rivers. An organization established to protect and enhance the quality of the shoreline environment through conservation, research, and education. Surfriders is dedicated to preserving the natural state of our waves and beaches, improving recreational opportunities and assuring a clean and healthy marine environment for all people. After riding a black wave in 1988, they, with lawyer and EPA, indicted Humboldt County papermills in N. California on 100+ violations.

## U ▶ Survival News Service
See BURWOOD JOURNAL.

## ✽ ▶ Syracuse Peace Council
See PEACE NEWSLETTER.

## S ▶ Taft Group
See directories, AMERICA'S NEWEST FOUNDATIONS: THE SOURCE-BOOK ON RECENTLY CREATED PHILANTHROPIES; FUNDRAISER'S GUIDE TO HUMAN SERVICE FUNDING; NATIONAL DIRECTORY OF NONPROFIT ORGANIZATIONS; TAFT FOUNDATION REPORTER.

## L ▶ Tamiment Institute
See LABOR HISTORY (periodicals) and Tamiment Institute Library under directories section.

## T ▶ Task Force on Militarization in Asia and the Pacific/National Council of Churches
See ACTION ALERT and ASIA & PACIFIC UPDATE (periodicals).

## L ▶ Teamsters For a Democratic Union
Box 10128
Detroit, MI 48210
**Concern(s):** labor; politics; unions; planning; lobbying. A rank and file movement for referendum and democracy in the Teamsters Union. **Other Resources:** See newsletter, CONVOY DISPATCH.

## H ▶ Technology Management Group
See WORLDWIDE AIDS DIRECTORY.

## $ ▶ Tele-Effective Securities, Inc.
1106 2nd St., #183
Encinitas, CA 92024
**Concern(s):** economics; socially-responsible investing. Socially and economically conscious investment broker. Quality jumbo CDs at healthy, federally-insured banks and savings & loans. (800)3332-0852. **Contact(s):** Mary Mortenson.

## M ▶ Telecommunications Co-op Network
1333 H St. NW, #1155
Washington, DC 20005   (202)682-0949
**Concern(s):** media; telecommunications. Not-for-profit co-op that helps charitable organizations save money on communications costs, including long-distance and 800 service, fax, voice mail. Works with Co-op America organizational members. **Member:** Co-op America.

## ♿ ▶ Telecommunications for the Deaf, Inc.
See INTERNATIONAL TELEPHONE DIRECTORY OF TDD USERS.

## M ▶ Telecommunications Research and Action Center
1717 Massachusetts Ave. NW, #LL215
Washington, DC 20036   (202)462-2520
**Affiliation:** Safe Energy Communication Council. **Concern(s):** media; energy; telecommunications; research.

## ✽ ▶ Tellus Research Program
c/o Sara Shannon
Box 20170, Tompkin Station
New York, NY 10009   (212)674-1659
**Concern(s):** peace; environment; health; anti-nuclear; hazardous/toxic waste. Does a comprehensive study of all aspects of the nuclear industry on it effects of the habitability of the Earth and human health. **Other Resources:** Quarterly NUCLEAR HAZARDS and NUCLEAR CHRONICLE, writes articles for magazines and disseminates relevant information. Nonprofit. **Est.:** 1990. **Circ.:** 4M. **Fax:** (212)674-1659. **Contact(s):** Sara Shannon.

## E ▶ The Tennessee Initiative for Environmental Sensitivity in Construction
2704 12th Ave. South
Nashville, TN 37204   (515)297-2269
**Concern(s):** environment; economics; conservation; planning; alternative consumer. In order to provide alternative methods and materials that are safer and more environmentally sensitive for planners, architects, engineers, public officials and consumers when making critical building decisions, a new national coalition is forming to provide a catalog and to suggest workable and affordable alternatives. Attention given to the impact of the use and manufacture of construction products on the economy; and jobs to enable long-range planning. **Other Resources:** Resource Package available. **Contact(s):** Charles A. Howell III.

## E ▶ Terra
3751 N. Sawyer
Chicago, IL 60618   (312)463-8228
**Concern(s):** environment; health; agriculture; hazardous/toxic waste; anti-nuclear; pesticides. Working to end the policies and practices that degrade the environment and the quality of life for the peoples of the Americas. Present campaigns: stopping pesticide "Circle of Poison," passing Pesticide Export Reform Act and Stopping

trade deregulation under G.A.T.T. (focus on pesticides), stopping B.R.C. Classifying of nuclear waste. **Other Resources:** TERRA NEWSLETTER. **Est.:** 1989. **Dues:** $20/yr. includes newsletter. **E-Network:** Peacenet. **ID:** 'bgould'. **Member:** National Coalition Against Misuse of Pesticides; Pesticide Action Network. (312)509-1808. **Contact(s):** Phyllis Hasbrouck (Director), Susan Compernolle (Secretary). (312)262-4375. Bruce Gould, Treasurer. (708)869-4000.

## E ▶ Texas Committee on Natural Resources
5934 Royal Lane, #223
Dallas, TX 75230-3803   (214)368-1791
**Concern(s):** environment; energy; economics; education; health; resource management; natural resources; volunteers; air pollution; hazardous/toxic waste; wildlife/endangered species; water; transportation; forests; land use. This organization addresses environmental issues and promotes a quality environment. It is organized as an umbrella to numerous volunteer task forces and serves as a network for environmental education. **Other Resources:** Publishes CONSERVATION PROGRESS. **Contact(s):** Morine H. Kovick (Executive Director).

## $ ▶ The Other Economic Summit (TOES)
1442 Harvard St. NW
Washington, DC 20009   (202)667-4659
**Concern(s):** economics; environment; sustainability; community self-reliance. International non-governmental forum for bringing together groups and individuals who understand that prevailing economic theory and practice is destroying the planet and its peoples. TOES supporters share an interest in an economics that will create a socially just and environmentally sustainable society. Provides a meeting place for exchange of alternatives to the dismal economics of self-interest. Promotes appropriate scale and community-based development. Publishes books and a journal. **Other Resources:** TOES/NA NEWSLETTER. **Est.:** 1984. **Contact(s):** Larry Martin (Coordinator).

## S ▶ Theosophical Society in America
Box 270
Wheaton, IL 60189-0270   (708)668-1571
**Concern(s):** spiritual; education; interfaith; transformation; research; analysis. A world organization promoting the study of religion, philosophy, and science. Library with 12,000 volumes dealing with mysticism, religions, sciences, philosophy, and history of human race. **Member:** Co-op America.

## S ▶ Third Millenium Project
1611 N. Kent St., #610
Arlington, VA 22209-2111   (703)841-0048
**Affiliation:** Institute for 21st Century Studies. **Concern(s):** spiritual; future; ideation; faith. Purpose: "to give the world, on the occasion of the 2000th anniversary of the birth of Christ, a vision of how we Christians think God would like the planet Earth managed during the third millennium. It would include a detailed, country-by-country analysis of the likely future if present trends and policies continue, and of the possible future if nations pursue alternative policies." Nonprofit. **Contact(s):** Gerald O. Barney (Executive Director).

## S ▶ Third Universal Order
RFD 1, Box 120
Hampton, CT 06247
**Concern(s):** spiritual; peace; interfaith; conflict resolution. A world community of spirit friends composed of Buddhists, Jews, Moslems, Christians, Hindus, and all other religions is being initiated. The Order will help you link with other members for mutual support and friendship as well as to develop reverence for all life and respect for the whole human family.

## T ▶ Third World Resources/Data Center
See directories, AFRICA, ASIA AND PACIFIC; FOOD, HUNGER, AGRI-BUSINESS; HUMAN RIGHTS; LATIN AMERICA AND CARIBBEAN; MIDDLE EAST; THIRD WORLD RESOURCE DIRECTORY; THIRD WORLD STRUGGLES FOR PEACE AND JUSTICE; TRANSNATIONAL CORPORATIONS AND LABOR; and newsletter, THIRD WORLD RESOURCES: A QUARTERLY REVIEW.

## E ▶ Thorne Ecological Institute
5398 Manhattan Circle
Boulder, CO 80303   (303)499-3647
**Concern(s):** environment; education; natural resources; global understanding. Encourages the wise use of our natural resources by promoting the knowledge of ecological facts and principles through educational programs.

## E ▶ Threshold, Inc.
Drawer CU
Brisbee, AZ 85603   (602)432-7353
**Concern(s):** environment; education; wildlife/endangered species. Purpose is to improve mankind's understanding of and relationship to the environment, focusing on the development of ecological sound

alternatives for practical applications in society. **Other Resources:** See Tropical Forest Crisis Project.

## ✽ ▶ Tides Foundation
See Common Agenda Coalition; Institute for Global Communications; Rural Alliance for Military Accountability.

## T ▶ Tidewater Nicaragua Project Foundation
See newsletter under same name.

## E ▶ Timber Wolf
Sigurd Olson Environmental Institute
Northland College
Ashland, WI 54806   (715)682-4531
**Concern(s):** environment; education; wildlife/endangered species. A broad-based coalition of business, environmental and outdoors organizations dedicated to increasing public awareness and acceptance of the wolf in its native habitat and its ecological role. **Fax:** (715)682-1308. **Contact(s):** Mark R. Peterson (Director).

## M ▶ TNI Multilogue
505 Waltham
West Newton, MA 01265
**Affiliation:** Networking Institute. **Concern(s):** media; multilogues.

## H ▶ Tobacco Products Liability Project
School of Law, Northeastern University
400 Huntington Ave.
Boston, MA 02115   (617)437-2026
**Concern(s):** health; victims' rights; consumer protection; substance abuse. Lawyers litigation group on tobacco.

## ? ▶ Together Foundation for Global Unity
Box 9030
Jackson, WY 83001   (307)733-0626
**Concern(s):** future; politics; ideation; activism. Helps people with workable ideas get in touch with each other so they can put those ideas into action.

## ? ▶ Tomorrow Today: A Pavilion of Possibilities
Box 24252
Los Angeles, CA 90024-0252   (818)760-8996
**Concern(s):** future; ideation. "A museum of the future, designed to inspire and enable the human community to solve its critical problems." **Contact(s):** John Holmdahl.

## ✽ ▶ Topsfield Foundation
Route 169, Box 203
Pomfret, CT 06258   (203)928-2616
**Concern(s):** peace; media; education; activism; disarmament; East-West; research; national security; press. Operates the International Security news Clipping Service on issues related to arms control, military technology, and superpower relations. It goes to some 500 subscribers who are charged only for reproduction and mailing costs. **Other Resources:** See GRASSROOTS PEACE DIRECTORY and INTERNATIONAL SECURITY NEWS CLIPPING SERVICE (periodicals).

## L ▶ Trade Unionists for Action and Democracy
See LABOR TODAY (periodicals).

## T ▶ Trade-Aid, Inc.
5605 15th Ave. S
Minneapolis, MN 55417
**Concern(s):** Third World; economics; alternative consumer; development; alternative markets. **Contact(s):** Bette Schiller.

## ✾ ▶ Trans-Species Unlimited
Box 1553
Williamsport, PA 17703   (717)322-3252
**Affiliation:** Animal Rights Mobilization (ARM!). **Concern(s):** environment; animal rights. Animal rights activist group. **Other Resources:** See Animal Rights Mobilization (ARM!).

## ✑ ▶ Transaction Periodicals Consortium
Department 8010
Rutgers University
New Brunswick, NJ 08903
**Concern(s):** education.

## T ▶ Transafrica
545 8th St. SE, #200
Washington, DC 20003   (202)547-2550
**Concern(s):** Third World; justice; politics; development; hunger; Africa; lobbying; Caribbean; South Africa. This organization lobbies for foreign policy reform concerning Africa and the Caribbean. **Contact(s):** Niikwao Akuetteh.

## ? ▶ Transformation 2000
Box 1122
Del Mar, CA 92014
**Concern(s):** future; ideation; networking. Is building a network to turn conflict and scarcity to cooperation and abundance.

**E ▸ Transmissions Project**
725 Arizona, #108
Santa Monica, CA 90401 (310)451-1810
**Affiliation:** Friends of the United Nations Environmental Programme. **Concern(s):** environment; education; activism. See PERSONAL ACTION FOR THE EARTH (directories).

**✈ ▸ Travel Horizons**
Box 4410
Laguna Beach, CA 92652-4410 (714)752-9036
**Concern(s):** education; Third World; travel; development. Offers experiential and transformational travel programs worldwide, and arranges tours for groups. Also provides travel services for meetings, conferences and seminars. Newsletter available. **Contact(s):** Darryle Stafford (Editor).

**✈ ▸ Travellers Earth Repair Network (TERN)**
Box 1064
Tonasket, WA 98855 (509)486-4726
**Affiliation:** Friends of the Trees. **Concern(s):** education; environment; networking; travel; jobs; volunteers. Tourists can link up with local environmental programs of organic gardening, reforestation, erosion control and other projects to save the Earth.

**U ▸ TreePeople**
12601 Mulholland Dr.
Beverly Hills, CA 90210 (818)753-4600
**Concern(s):** urban; environment; politics; planning; forests; grassroots organizing. A problem-solving organization that fosters environmental stewardship by promoting personal involvement, community action and global awareness. Serving as a resource for citizens ready to take action, TreePeople pioneers citizen involvement in urban forestry and conducts Citizen Forester training classes to teach individuals how to re-green their neighborhoods. **Other Resources:** Publishes an inspirational book titled, THE SIMPLE ACT OF PLANTING A TREE. **Contact(s):** Andie Lipkis, Katie Lipkis (Co-founders).

**A ▸ Trees For Life**
1103 Jefferson
Wichita, KS 67203 (316)263-7294
**Concern(s):** agriculture; Third World; demographics; food production ; food distribution; hunger; development. Provides funding, management, and know-how to people in developing countries to plant and care for food-bearing and fuel trees, and place beehives, and fuel efficient stoves to fight world hunger. Based on the conviction that in this day and age of adequate resources, technology and know-how, there is no reason for large numbers of people to suffer the unnecessary pain of hunger and starvation. To fight hunger we must use a long-term approach. **Other Resources:** See LIFE LINES newsletter. Nonprofit. **Contact(s):** Balbir S. Mathur (Executive Director).

**T ▸ Trickle-Up Program**
54 Riverside Dr.
New York, NY 10024 (212)362-7958
**Concern(s):** Third World; economics; politics; development; grassroots organizing.

**E ▸ Tropical Forest Crisis Project**
Drawer CU
Brisbee, AZ 85603 (602)432-7353
**Affiliation:** Threshold, Inc.. **Concern(s):** environment; economics; wilderness. A fund to provide quick, creative assistance to critical environmental forest protection work in tropical countries.

**E ▸ Trout Unlimited**
501 Church St. NE
Vienna, VA 22180 (703)281-1100
**Concern(s):** environment; wildlife/endangered species; oceans/rivers; conservation. A membership organization of concerned anglers nationwide. TU's national office works with Congress and federal government agencies for the protection and wise management of America's fishing waters. Also active on state and local levels, monitoring pollution, fighting environmental abuse, preserving wild rivers, cleaning polluted waters and educating the public. TU is developing a national conservation network to enable rapid, effective response to threats to the resource. **Other Resources:** See TROUT MAGAZINE. **Contact(s):** Robert L. Herbst (Executive Director).

**E ▸ The Trust for Public Land**
116 New Montgomery
San Francisco, CA 94105 (415)495-4014
**Concern(s):** environment; economics; land trusts; conservation. Conserves land as a living resource for present and future generations. As a result-oriented organization, TPL works closely with urban and rural groups and government agencies to: 1) acquire and preserve open space to serve human needs; 2) share knowledge of nonprofit land acquisition processes; 3) pioneer methods of land conservation and environmentally sound land use. Since its founding, has protected nearly half a million acres of scenic recreational, urban, rural, and wilderness land. **Est.:** 1973. **Member:** Environmental Federation of America. **Contact(s):** Martin J. Rosen (President).

**$ ▸ Trust For the Future**
801 Pennsylvania Ave. SE, #410
Washington, DC 20003-2167 (202)547-7553
**Affiliation:** Natural Resources Council of America. **Concern(s):** economics; environment; conservation; land trusts. **Contact(s):** Andrea J. Yank (Executive Director). **Other:** 2704 12th Ave. S, Nashville, TN 37204

**$ ▸ Turtle Island Earth Stewards**
1420 NW Gilman Blvd., #2346
Issaquah, WA 98027
**Concern(s):** economics; politics; intentional communities; land trusts; grassroots, community organizing. Helps intentional communities place their land into public trusts which emphasize sustainable ecological stewardship of the land. TIES works with groups to build consensus, resolve conflicts, and run more effective meetings. **Other Resources:** Sponsors the Community Catalyst Project. **Est.:** 1981. **Member:** Fellowship for Intentional Community.

**E ▸ The 21st Century Society**
Box 357
Lawrence, KS 66044 (913)842-1943
**Concern(s):** environment; economics; future; politics; green consumer; cooperatives; networking; activism. A co-op organization networking for social and environmental policy change through activism. Funded through memberships and t-shirt sales. Would like to organize chapters in other states. **Other Resources:** Newsletter. **Member:** Co-op America. **Contact(s):** Leslie W. Blevins, Jr. (Executive Director), Denise Hamler (Publisher).

**☮ ▸ 20/20 Vision National Project (East)**
30 Cottage St.
Amherst, MA 01002 (413)549-4555
**Concern(s):** peace; environment; politics; disarmament; nonviolence; activism; lobbying; law; grassroots organizing. Publishes an action postcard every month identifying one issue and one action you can do at home to redefine America's priorities from militarism to the environment and human needs. The 20-minute monthly actions are usually to write a letter or make a phone call to a policy-maker facing a critical decision. **Other Resources:** "If we decide to work together, we will give you a guidebook for every Core Group member, an accounting system, software for managing your list of subscribers, promotional materials, camera-ready artwork, on-site training and ongoing support." **Est.:** 1986. **Dues:** $20+/yr. **Fax:** (413)549-0544. **Contact(s):** Lois Barber (Founder/President), Dick Mark (Executive Director). (202)728-1157. (413)253-2939.

**☮ ▸ 20/20 Vision National Project (West)**
1181 Solano Ave., #C
Albany, CA 94706 (800)DISARMS
**Concern(s):** peace; activism; analysis. **Contact(s):** Jeremy E. Sherman. **Other:** Box 5781, Carmel, CA 93921 David Albert (408)372-8918.

**M ▸ Union for Democratic Communications**
Box 1220
Berkeley, CA 94701
**Concern(s):** media; politics; future; communications; media watch; electronic democracy; ideation; international law; broadcasting; film; analysis. Communication serves as instruments of repression and domination or tools for human emancipation. Socially concerned organizations and individuals cannot remain indifferent to mass communication issues for a democratic society. It addresses issues in such areas as: mainstream media, grassroots communication strategies, military uses of new technologies, media and international law, the globalization of culture as reflected in mass-mediated forms and the limitations and failures of television. **Other Resources:** THE DEMOCRATIC COMMUNIQUE newsletter.

**$ ▸ Union for Radical Political Economics**
See periodicals for REVIEW OF RADICAL POLITICAL ECONOMICS.

**E ▸ The Union Institute**
440 E. McMilan St.
Cincinnati, OH 45206-1947 (513)861-6400
**Concern(s):** environment; education; politics. Offers PhD in Environmental Studies. Write them for the curriculum. **Other Resources:** See SOCIAL POLICY magazine.

**S ▸ Union of American Hebrew Congregations**
Religious Action Center
2027 Massachusetts Ave. NW
Washington, DC 20036 (202)387-2800
**Concern(s):** spiritual; peace; politics; faith; conflict resolution; lobbying. Under the auspices of the Commission on Social Action of Reform Judaism, a joint instrumentality of the Central Conference of American Rabbis and the Union of Hebrew Congregations with its affiliates. Conducts Chai/Impact, a grassroots network of committed Jews across nationwide who on the basis of religious convictions seek to enhance the quality of life in America and globally. Human survival depends on informed, reasoned effective social action. Chai=life (Hebrew). **Other Resources:** See Commission on Social Action of Reform Judaism. **Member:** Impact Network. **Contact(s):** Albert Vorspan (Director), Ed Rehfeld (Legal Assistant). **Other:** Religious Action Center, 838 Fifth Ave, New York, NY 10021. Rabbi David Saperstien (212)249-0100.

**✪ ▸ Union of Concerned Scientists**
26 Church St.
Cambridge, MA 02238 (617)547-5552
**Concern(s):** energy; peace; global warming; policy; anti-nuclear; disarmament. Scientists and other citizens concerned about the impact of advanced technology on society. Conducts independent research, public advocacy, and public-education activities focused on nuclear arms control, nuclear power safety, and national energy policy. **Other Resources:** Also books and reports, briefing papers, brochures and videos. See NUCLEUS and CATALYST newsletters; HOW YOU CAN FIGHT GLOBAL WARMING: AN ACTION GUIDE (directories). Nonprofit. **Member:** Environmental Federation of America. **Contact(s):** Howard Ris (Executive Director), Sean Meyer (Field Coordinator). **Other:** 1616 P St NW, Washington, DC 20036. (202)332-0900.

**M ▸ Unison Institute**
1731 Connecticut Ave. NW
Washington, DC 20009 (202)797-7200
**Concern(s):** media; telecommunications. A telecommunications system with environmental data. **Contact(s):** John Chelan.

**J ▸ Unitarian Universalist Association**
Department for Social Justice
100 Maryland Ave. NE
Washington, DC 20002 (202)547-0254
**Concern(s):** justice; politics; spiritual; faith; lobbying; government accountability; petition. A section of the denominations' Department for Social Justice that monitors public policy and legislative issues to provide information to UUA members and to represent the thrust of UUA general resolutions to the US Congress, the Executive branch, and other agencies of government; implements the public policy resolutions of the General Assembly through independent and collective advocacy and by training the UU's to register their views as concerned citizens. **Other Resources:** See WINDOW ON THE WORLD and UNITARIAN-UNIVERSALISTS IN SUPPORT OF SANCTUARY NEWSLETTER (periodicals). **Contact(s):** Robert Z. Alpern (Director).

**S ▸ Unitarian Universalist Association of Congregations**
25 Beacon St.
Boston, MA 02108-2800(617)742-2100
**Concern(s):** spiritual; peace; politics; education; faith; activism; grassroots organizing; lobbying. A membership of about 1,000 congregations serving adults and children in the US and Canada. This association represents the consolidation in 1961 of two older religious denominations, the Universalists, organized in 1793 and the Unitarians, organized in 1825. Beyond the local congregations, it provides area leadership and consultation, creates a religious education curriculum, spurs social action efforts and implements programs overseas and interfaith areas. UUA believes in freedom of belief. **Other Resources:** Produces pamphlets, devotional material, and the newspaper, the UNIVERSALIST WORLD; supports Beacon Press. **Est.:** 1961. **Fax:** (617)367-3237.

**☮ ▸ Unitarian Universalist Peace Network**
5808 Greene St.
Philadelphia, PA 19144 (215)843-2930
**Concern(s):** peace; spiritual; faith; anti-nuclear; networking. Primary task is "to provide the means by which UU congregations can become involved and remain active in peacemaking." Was created by a coalition of UU organizations desiring to express their concern about nuclear proliferation in a clear, effective manner. These organizations are the International Association for Religious Freedom, the UUA, the UU Service Committee, the UU Women's Federation, the UU Peace Fellowship, and the UU UN office. **Other Resources:** Numerous programs and resources available, including Action Alert Network briefs. See UNIPAX **Contact(s):** Stephanie R. Nichols, Rev. Carol W. Powers (Co-directors).

**D ▸ Unitarian Universalist Service Committee**
130 Prospect St.
Cambridge, MA 02139-1813(617)868-6600
**Concern(s):** demographics; justice; Third World; spiritual; hunger; discrimination; nonviolence; volunteers; faith. As the international headquarters, it coordinates a volunteer service corps for US volun-

teers within the Society and local community organizations dedicated to dealing with human rights, world hunger, institutional oppression and other social issues. From its struggle against fascism more than 50 years ago, it has consistently supported programs for peace, justice and human rights with campaigns in Africa and Central America, with an expanding focus on the Philippines. Works also with policy makers. **Other Resources:** Volunteers needed for projects, studies or general assistance. Publishes Service Committee News and maintains a Human Rights Education Department. Promise the Children campaign. See SERVICE COMMITTEE NEWS **Fax:** (617)868-7102. **Contact(s):** Director of Volunteer Programs.

### L ◗ United Automobile, Aerospace, Agricultural, Implement Workers of America

See SOLIDARITY (periodicals).

### J ◗ United Church of Christ Commission for Racial Justice
5113 Georgia Ave. NW
Washington, DC 20011 (202)291-1593
**Affiliation:** United Church of Christ. **Concern(s):** justice; urban; spiritual; faith; discrimination; racism; ethnic concerns; minority rights; racial tensions. As a national body of UCC, the General Synod has mandated that the Commission shall provide leadership in mobilizing membership for the church to work for justice and reconciliation among persons and groups, in the area of race, both within the Church and in society in general. The Commission, in cooperation with Operation Push and members of the Congressional Black Caucus, helped to establish the National Rainbow Coalition. **Other Resources:** Guides, TOXIC WASTES AND RACE IN THE US; and COUNCIL FOR HEALTH & HUMAN SERVICES—DIRECTORY SERVICES. Also, COURAGE IN THE STRUGGLE FOR PEACE AND JUSTICE, a periodical. **Contact(s):** Rev. Benjamin F. Chavis (Executive Director), Toni Killings (Director). **Other:** Office for Church in Society, 110 Maryland Ave., NE, Washington, DC 20002-5694 Jay Lintner , Director. (202)543-1517.

### L ◗ United Farm Workers Union
Box 62
Keene, CA 93531-9989 (805)822-5571
**Concern(s):** labor; agriculture; environment; health; hazardous/toxic waste; pesticides; farm workers; conservation. This is a union of farm workers. They strive to keep the work conditions with in the law. Child labor, dangerous work conditions, and low pay are among some of the major concerns of this union. **Other Resources:** See FOOD AND JUSTICE newsletter. **Contact(s):** Dolores Huerta, Cesar Chavez (Founder). (617)227-8260. **Other:** United Farmworkers of America, 8 Beacon St., Boston, MA 02186. Roberto DeLaCruz. (617)698-4940.

### T ◗ United Methodist Church
Department of Peace and World Order
777 UN Plaza
New York, NY 10017 (212)682-3633
**Affiliation:** General Board of Church & Society/Global Ministries. **Concern(s):** Third World; peace; justice; demographics; spiritual; faith; world order; development; militarism; social justice; foreign policy. This church conducts research, education and action on peace and development issues, UN affairs, militarism, economic justice, and US foreign policy. **Other Resources:** See ENGAGE/SOCIAL ACTION magazine and FAITHFUL WITNESS ON TODAY'S ISSUES (periodicals). **Contact(s):** Robert McClean (Director). **Other:** 475 Riverside Dr., #1502, New York City, NY 10115(212)870-3766.

### ☙ ◗ United Nations
1 United Nations Plaza
New York, NY 10017 (212)963-1234
**Concern(s):** peace; Third World; health; education; United Nations; conflict resolution; development. This world organization is still in its infancy. Even though it has existed for over 45 years, it has only now begun to have an affect on world problems. Though sometimes considered a puppet of the superpowers and large corporations this organization does some exceptional work in the fields of education, health, conservation, research, and conflict resolution. **Other Resources:** Many additional resources. Contact UN for specifics. See Legacy International; United Nations Environment Programme & Population Fund; periodicals, InterDEPENDENT and UN CHRONICLE; and under business The World Bank. Nonprofit. **Est.:** 1945.

### ☙ ◗ United Nations Association of the USA
485 5th Ave.
New York, NY 10017 (212)697-3232
**Concern(s):** peace; United Nations. This association conduct research and promotes public education about global issues. Works to encourage constructive US policy in the United Nations. **Other Resources:** See journal, InterDEPENDENT. **Est.:** 1965. (202)966-5393.

### ☙ ◗ United Nations Association of USA
1010 Vermont Ave. NW, #904
Washington, DC 20005 (202)347-5004
**Concern(s):** peace; United Nations; world order. A nonpartisan organization working in Washington, at UN Headquarters, and in thousands of communities across America to build public understanding of and support for international cooperation through the UN. Receives no financial support from the US government or the UN. It depends entirely upon private sources. **Other Resources:** THE INTERDEPENDENT, a news journal; UNA-USA Publications available. Nonprofit. **Contact(s):** Andy Rice, Edward C. Luck (President). **Other:** 485 Fifth Ave., New York, NY 10017-6104.

### ☙ ◗ United Nations Department for Disarmament Affairs
See DISARMAMENT (periodicals).

### E ◗ United Nations Environment Programme
North American Liaison Office
Room DC 2-0803, United Nations
New York, NY 10017 (212)963-8138
**Concern(s):** environment; peace; United Nations. Established by the UN General Assembly, it serves as an advocate for environmental management among UN agencies, regional, national, and NGO's. Areas of concentration are atmospheric issues, freshwater, oceans and coastal areas, land degradation, loss of biological diversity, hazardous and toxic chemicals. Activities include monitoring, assessments, training and technical cooperation, information and legal initiatives. **Other Resources:** June 5th, annual world environment day; Environmental Sabbath Day; UNEP NEWS; ENVIRONMENTAL EVENTS RECORD; STATE OF THE ENVIRONMENT REPORT; EXECUTIVE DIRECTORS ANNUAL REPORT; see directories section for ENVIRONMENTAL GUIDLELINES FOR WORLD INDUSTRY **Contact(s):** William H. Mansfield III (Deputy Executive Director). **Other:** UNEP Washington Office, 1889 F St. NW, Washington, DC 20006. Noel J. Brown , D.C. Chief (202)289-8456.

### D ◗ United Nations High Commissioner on Refugees
See REFUGEES (periodicals).

### ☙ ◗ UniteNations International Children's Fund UNICEF
See Global Forum of Spiritual and Parliamentary Leaders on Human Survival.

### D ◗ United Nations Population Fund
c/o United Nations Fund for Population Activities
220 E. 42nd St.
New York, NY 10017 (212)297-5000
**Affiliation:** United Nations Fund for Population Activities. **Concern(s):** demographics; environment; population growth. **Other Resources:** Publications and Audio-Visual Guide available, see UNITED NATIONS FILMS AND VIDEOS (media); INVENTORY OF POPULATION PROJECTS IN DEVELOPING COUNTRIES AROUND THE WORLD and POPULATION PROGRAMMERS AND PROJECTS GUIDE TO SOURCES(directories). **Contact(s):** Dr. Nafis Sadik (Executive Director).

### ☙ ◗ Unity-and-Diversity World Council
1010 S. Flower St., #401
Los Angeles, CA 90015-1428 (213)742-6832
Concern(s): peace; spiritual; justice; environment; world order; diversity. A worldwide coordinating body of individuals, groups, and networks-fostering the emergence of a new universal person and civilization based on unity-and-diversity among all peoples and all life. Other Resources: See SPECTRUM magazine and UNITY-AND-DIVERSITY WORLD DIRECTORY. Nonprofit. Est.: 1965 Dues: $25/yr. ind.; $40/yr. prof; $60/yr. org. Fax: (213)748-0679 Contact(s): Leland Stewart (Central Coordinator).

### ☙ ◗ Universal Organization For Peace
Box 41606
St. Petersburg, FL 33743
**Concern(s):** peace; world order. Promotes the recognition of and allegiance to world laws by governments and individuals. **Contact(s):** Mary L. McCall.

### A ◗ UC Sustainable Agriculture Research & Education Program
University of California
Davis, CA 95616 (916)752-7556
**Concern(s):** agriculture; education; research. **Contact(s):** Bill Liebhardt.

### ✈ ◗ University Research Expeditions Program
University of California
Berkeley, CA 94720 (510)642-6586
**Concern(s):** education; environment; energy; travel; appropriate technology; volunteers. Purpose: To promote public involvement in ongoing worldwide scientific research and educational activities in the environmental, natural, and social sciences. Current emphasis: Projects in cooperations with scientists from developing nations, focused on preserving the Earth's resources and improving people's lives. Members: 400 participants per year. Participants make a tax-deductible donation to the university to support the research and cover their expenses. **Other Resources:** Volunteer participants needed from all walks of life to serve 2 to 3 weeks as field assistants on research teams. Participants make a tax-deductible donation to the university to support the research and cover their expenses.

### ☙ ◗ Upstate Coalition Builders
87 Hillary Lane
Penfield, NY 14526 (716)385-1155
**Affiliation:** National Coalition Building Institutes. **Concern(s):** peace; justice; conflict resolution; diversity; racism; discrimination. Consultation and training in Upstate & Western New York in managing diversity, prejudice reduction and conflict resolution. **Est.:** 1989. **Contact(s):** Joyce S. Herman (Director). **Other:** National Coalition Building Institutes, 172 Brattle St., Arlington, MA 02174.

### U ◗ Urban Ecology
Box 10144
Berkeley, CA 94709 (510)549-1724
**Concern(s):** urban; environment; demographics; sustainability. Organization committed to the development of ecologically healthy and socially vital cities and towns. **Other Resources:** International Ecological City Conference; publishes newsletter which serves as a clearinghouse for urban restoration projects worldwide. **Contact(s):** Richard Register (President).

### U ◗ Urban Environment Foundation
1001 Connecticut Ave. NW
Washington, DC 20036 (202)331-8387
**Concern(s):** urban; environment; hazardous/toxic waste; sustainability.

### ☉ ◗ US Biomass Industries Council
1730 N. Lynn St., #610
Arlington, VA 22209 (703)524-6104
**Concern(s):** energy; environment; renewables. **Other Resources:** American Wind Energy Association; Solar Energy Industries Association.

### T ◗ US Catholic Conference
Department of Social Development & World Peace
3211 4th St. NE
Washington, DC 20017 (202)541-3000
**Concern(s):** Third World; demographics; peace; hunger; development; foreign policy; faith. Educates about the effect of US food policies on international development and the world food system through statements of Catholic clergy and educators, press releases, and consultations. Participates in interfaith and ecumenical food and development policy endeavors.

### D ◗ US Committee For Refugees
1025 Vermont Ave. NW
Washington, DC 20005 (202)347-3507
**Concern(s):** demographics; Third World; hunger; development; population; refugees; immigration. Provides information and education about refugees. Its sets itself the task of consulting with refugees and their government leaders, stimulating research on refugee problems, and working closely with American voluntary agencies. **Other Resources:** See UNITED STATES COMMITTEE FOR REFUGEES - DIRECTORY.

### U ◗ US Conference of Mayors
1620 I St. NW
Washington, DC 20006 (202)293-7330
**Concern(s):** urban; politics; economics; planning; community investment; inner city; transportation; sustainability; economic conversion. Mayors from all over the US have come together to draw up blueprints for repairing America's rapidly decaying infrastructure. Until the President is willing to prioritize funds for this venture, it is useless. **Other Resources:** See US Conference of Mayors AIDS Program; and LOCAL AIDS SERVICES: THE NATIONAL DIRECTORY.

### H ◗ US Conference of Mayors AIDS Program
1620 I St. NW
Washington, DC 20006 (202)293-7330
**Affiliation:** US Conference of Mayors. **Concern(s):** health; politics; education; public health; preventative medicine; AIDS. A national, nonpartisan organization representing over 800 mayors from cities with populations over 30,000. The Conference seeks to improve

communication and cooperation between cities on a number of issues, including AIDS. It provides grants to local, community-based organizations that conduct AIDS education programs. **Other Resources:** Publishes comprehensive directory of state and local AIDS services, local AIDS Services. **Contact(s):** Thomas Cochran (Executive Director).

### ○ ◆ US Export Council for Renewable Energy
Box 10095
Arlington, VA 22210    (703)524-6105
**Concern(s):** energy; environment; renewables.

### A ◆ US Farmers Association
See US FARM NEWS (periodicals).

### ⚡ ◆ US Institute of Peace
1550 M St. NW, #700
Washington, DC 20005   (202)457-1700
**Concern(s):** peace; education; nonviolence; analysis; conflict resolution. The root causes of conflicts are often overlooked or not understood in society's proclivity to use force and threats of force to maintain stability. Progressive organizations are more interested in the process of conflict resolution than in examining the deep seated precepts which bring on a specific conflict. The Institute has a grant program to aid researchers to examine specific historic incidents and cultural foundations which have led to peace threatening disagreements. **Other Resources:** Newsletter, the USIP JOURNAL; TV projects and a publication series, IN BRIEF. **Other:** 360 Lexington Ave., New York, NY 10017.

### A ◆ US National Committee For World Food Day
1001 22nd St. NW, #300
Washington, DC 20437   (202)653-2404
**Concern(s):** agriculture; demographics; health; food production; food distribution; hunger; poverty; nutrition. Purpose: To increase awareness, understanding and effective year-round action on farm/food/health/hunger issues. 400 member organizations, supports programs throughout US, a clearinghouse of information, and resource center supporting a broad coalition of entities in which people are helped to understand that food is linked to the community, national and global concerns as well as many other issues. Assists supporting organizations, local organizers and the general public. **Other Resources:** Publications, curriculum, audiovisuals available. World Food Day falls on October 16 every year. **Fax:** (202)653-5760. **Contact(s):** Patricia Young (National Coordinator).

### ⚡ ◆ US Peace Council
See PEACE AND SOLIDARITY (periodicals).

### H ◆ US Public Interest Research Group (USPIRG)
215 Pennsylvania Ave. SE
Washington, DC 20003   (202)546-9707
**Concern(s):** health; economics; environment; hazardous/toxic waste; consumer rights. See Working Group on Community Right-To-Know; Citizens Energy Project; CITIZEN AGENDA newsletter.

### ⚡ ◆ US-USSR Bridges for Peace
The Norwich Center
Box 710
Norwich, VT 05055    (802)649-1000
**Concern(s):** peace; politics; East-West; conflict resolution; lobbying; grassroots organizing. A coalition of over 50 educational civic, peace, and church groups working to build understanding between the people of the US and USSR through "citizen diplomacy." Initiated at the height of a resurgence in Cold War thinking, it has worked at challenging deeply-rooted enemy images between the US and USSR. **Other Resources:** Publishes biannual BRIDGES FOR PEACE NEWSLETTER; BUILDING BRIDGES: US-USSR - A HANDBOOK FOR CITIZEN DIPLOMATS, a "How to" book for the citizen diplomacy movement. Also US-USSR Bridges for Peace. **Est.:** 1983. **Contact(s):** Clinton Gardner (President).

### ✈ ◆ US-USSR Reconciliation Projects
Box 271
Nyack, NY 10960-0271   (914)358-4601
**Affiliation:** Fellowship of Reconciliation. **Concern(s):** education; peace; East-West; travel. Seeks to mutually increase the knowledge of the peoples of the US and USSR through mutual exchange programs. The organization wishes to strip the enemy image from the two countries and replace it of one of similar peoples. **Other Resources:** Conducts annual Volga and Mississippi River peace cruises, Journeys for Reconciliation, and US-Soviet Youth Quest.

### T ◆ US-Vietnam Friendship Association
See VIETNAM TODAY (periodicals).

### H ◆ Vegetarian Resource Group
See VEGETARIAN JOURNAL (periodicals).

### H ◆ Vegetarian Society Inc.
Box 34427
Los Angeles, CA 90034   (310)281-1907
**Concern(s):** health; education; nutrition. An educational organization dedicated to a healthier diet for person and planet. **Other Resources:** See VEGETARIAN LIVING newsletter. Nonprofit. **Contact(s):** Vic Rorsythe (President), Carla Romo (Vice President). (310)392-7735.

### ⚡ ◆ Veterans for Peace, Inc.
Box 3881
Portland, ME 04104   (207)797-2770
**Concern(s):** peace; education; economics; disarmament. A veterans educational organization working with others to educate the general public concerning (a) costs of war, (b) the arms race, (c) US foreign policy issues, and (d) the exigency of abolishing war as an instrument of international policy. Membership open to veterans of all eras. 57 Chapters nationally. **Other Resources:** See POINT and VFP JOURNAL (periodicals); Special Issue Journal, "Abolish War! - The Last Campaign." A treatise on the exigency of abolishing war as an instrument of international policy. **Est.:** 1985. **Circ.:** 2M. **E-Network:** PeaceNet. **ID:** 'vfphq'. **Fax:** (207)878-3618. **Contact(s):** Jerry Genesio (Executive Director).

### ⚡ ◆ Vietnam Veterans Against the War
See VETERAN (periodicals).

### M ◆ Viewers for Quality Television
28 Westwood Dr.
Hillsdale, MI 49242
**Concern(s):** media; film; responsibility; media watch.

### U ◆ Virginia Polytechnic Institute and State University
College of Architecture and Urban Studies
202 Cowgill Hall
Blacksburg, VA 24061
**Concern(s):** urban; architecture.

### ✈ ◆ Volunteer: The National Center
See DIRECTORY OF VOLUNTEER CENTERS.

### ✈ ◆ Volunteers for Peace Workcamps
43 Tiffany Rd.
Belmont, VT 05370    (802)259-2759
**Concern(s):** education; Third World; travel; development; volunteers. This organization coordinates Workcamps in the USA and mainly western and eastern Europe with some programs in the "Third World." Provides consultation and placement service for work camp hosts and volunteers, linking people with programs. An inexpensive and personal way to travel, live and work in a foreign country, best described as a fully internationalized short-term "peace corps." For students June-September opportunities to travel and promote goodwill. **Other Resources:** THE INTERNATIONAL WORKCAMPER Newsletter and THE INTERNATIONAL WORKCAMP DIRECTORY. Nonprofit. **Est.:** 1981. **Contact(s):** Peter Coldwell.

### A ◆ Volunteers in Technical Assistance (VITA)
1815 N. Lynn St., #200
Arlington, VA 22209-8438   (703)276-1800
**Concern(s):** agriculture; education; energy; economics; volunteers; science. An organization that provides technical information and assistance to developing countries. VITA has experts in renewable energy, agriculture, and business development that lend their time to solve technical problems for individuals and organizations around the world.

### ✎ ◆ Waldorf Schools
17 Hemlock Hill
Great Barrington, MA 01230
**Concern(s):** education; childhood. "Enlightening and informative, Ronald Kotzch's article about Waldorf education from Utne Reader September/October 1990 is now available as an eight-page, full-color reprint (includes the Editor's Note, a education resource guide, plus a current list of Waldorf schools in North America). Call for quantity discount information." **Other Resources:** Publishes a directory of Waldorf schools and offers teacher training.

### ⚡ ◆ War Resisters League
c/o Michael Marsh
339 Lafayette St.
New York, NY 10012   (212)228-0450
**Concern(s):** peace; education; economics; boycott; corporate responsibility; socially-responsible investing. BOYCOTT WAR TOYS — Such toys are a contradiction to efforts for world peace. **Other Resources:** See Alternative Revenue Service; guides, GUIDE TO WAR TAX RESISTANCE and ORGANIZERS' MANUAL (directories); periodicals, SPEW and NONVIOLENT ACTIVIST magazine. **Contact(s):** Michael Marsh.

### ⚡ ◆ War Resisters League
339 Lafayette St.
New York, NY 10012   (212)228-0450
**Concern(s):** peace; war tax revolt; disarmament. Works nonviolently to eliminate all war and the causes of war. It has local groups in many cities throughout the US and is part of the worldwide War Resisters International. National pacifist organization opposed to armaments, conscription, and war. Publishes newsletter and subscription magazine. Regional offices and local chapters. Also available 34-page Handbook for Nonviolent Action and the new Directory of Nonviolence Trainers. **Other Resources:** Publishes EVERYONE MAKES A DIFFERENCE, a pamphlet which describes 16 ways to start trying to change the world; an Organizer's Manual; GUIDE TO WAR TAX RESISTANCE MANUAL; NONVIOLENT ACTIVIST, newsletter & Literature list. **Est.:** 1923. **Contact(s):** Ralph DiGia, Charles Bloomstein, Nancy Sedgwick Heskett.

### T ◆ The Washington Office on Latin America
110 Maryland Ave. NE
Washington, DC 20002   (202)544-8045
**Concern(s):** Third World; spiritual; peace; faith; Latin America. This Church sponsored organization monitors legislation and policies that influence Latin America and reports on the latest developments and violation of human rights in that region. **Other Resources:** See LATIN AMERICA UPDATE (periodicals). **Est.:** 1974.

### E ◆ Washington Research Institute
See DOLPHIN NETWORK newsletter.

### ✈ ◆ Washington Trails Association
See SIGNPOST MAGAZINE.

### E ◆ Waste Oil Action
Box 134
Frankenmuth, MI 48734 (517)624-5536
**Concern(s):** environment; economics; boycott; corporate responsibility; socially-responsible investing; recycling. BOYCOTT CHEVROLET, CHRYSTLER, OLDSMOBILE, PONTIAC — They refuse to use recycled petroleum products in manufacture. **Other Resources:** To protest, write to: Lee Iacocca, Chrysler Corp., 12000 Chrysler Dr., P.O. Box 1919, Highland Park, MI 48288. (800) 992-1997. Robert Stempel, General Motors Corp., 3044 West Grand Blvd., Detroit, MI 48202. (313) 956-5252.

### E ◆ Water Center
See AQUA TERRA magazine and WE ALL LIVE DOWNSTREAM - A GUIDE TO WASTE TREATMENT THAT STOPS WATER POLLUTION; and NATIONAL WATER CENTER.

### ✎ ◆ Water Pollution Control Federation
601 Wythe St.
Alexandria, VA 22314   (703)684-2400
**Concern(s):** education; environment; science; water pollution. Primary purpose is to educate the population on the effects and control of water pollution. This federation does this by providing effective leadership and guidance to all constructive efforts. **Other Resources:** Technical periodicals, manual electronic information retrieval, conferences, government affairs and public education programs.

### ✈ ◆ Web of Life Foundation
Box 922223
Sylmar, CA 91392    (818)367-6324
**Concern(s):** environment; animal rights; vegetarian. "Networking compassion to heal the Planet." "Our interest is to inform, educate and network caring individuals and organizations. Although our concern extends to all living things, our database focuses mainly on Animal Rights/Protection organizations around the country. This information is supplied on a not-for-profit basis to anyone." Nonprofit. **Est.:** 1990. **E-Network:** CompuServe. **ID:** 705211201. **Fax:** (818)363-3258. **Contact(s):** Randy Ralston (Director).

### J ◆ Welfare Warriors
4504 N. 47th St.
Milwaukee, WI 53218   (414)444-0220
**Concern(s):** justice; feminism; family; welfare rights; children; child support; day care; discrimination; sexism. **Other Resources:** See WELFARE MOTHERS VOICE (periodicals). **Contact(s):** Pat Gowens (Founder).

### H ◆ The Wellness Community
1235 5th St.
Santa Monica, CA 90401-1401   (310)393-1415
**Concern(s):** health; self-help. A tax exempt organization, it is supported by individuals and organizations who believe that people with cancer who participate in their own recovery and who have friends, involvement, hope and enjoyment will substantially improve the quality of their lives and may enhance recovery. "Our supporters provide the environment and the facilities for such learning because we believe that it is devastating and debilitating for such people to feel alone, hopeless, helpless and without joy..." Nonprofit. **Contact(s):** Harold

H. Benjamin, Ph.D. (Executive Director).

### ✍ ◗ Westcoast Institute of Sacred Ecology & School of Geomancy
2816 9th St.
Berkeley, CA 94710
**Concern(s):** education; environment; spiritual; transformation.

### D ◗ Western Center on Law and Poverty
See CALIFORNIA AND NEVADA LSC LEGAL (directory).

### E ◗ Western Earth Support Co-op
Box 269
Westcliffe, CO 81252    (719)742-5305
**Concern(s):** environment; wilderness; activism. Active in protecting wilderness and educating the public about deep ecology. **Other Resources:** List of environmental job openings in Western North America. Nonprofit. **Member:** Co-op America.

### J ◗ Western Shoshone National Council
Box 68
Duckwater, NV 89314-0068 (702)863-0227
**Concern(s):** justice; environment; health; Native Americans; hazardous/toxic waste. The WSNC purpose is to unite all Western Shoshone interests into one entity, to foster and promote the formation of a Western Shoshone Nation negotiating team to undertake negotiations with the US for a legislative agreement confirming ownership of lands within the Western Shoshone ancestral territory and establishment of a formal Western Shoshone Government. **Other Resources:** Publishes WESTERN SHOSHONE NATION NEWSLETTER. **Fax:** (702)863-0301. **Contact(s):** Chief Raymond D. Yowell, Joel Freedman. (212)431-4899.

### E ◗ Whale Adoption Project
International Wildlife Coalition
Box 388
North Falmouth, MA 02556-0388
**Affiliation:** International Wildlife Coalition. **Concern(s):** environment; wildlife/endangered species. This project helps protect whales by adopting a whale. While you don't literally adopt a whale you do pledge money to help keep the species alive. **Office:** 634 North Falmouth Highway North Falmouth, MA 02556-0388. **Contact(s):** Dan Morast (Executive Director).

### E ◗ Whale Museum
Box 945
Friday Harbor, WA 98250    (206)378-4710
**Concern(s):** environment; wildlife/endangered species; oceans/rivers. Dedicated to furthering the knowledge, understanding and appreciation of the earth's wild species, especially cetaceans and other marine flora and fauna of Puget Sound and the San Juan archipelago. Private corporation funded through admissions, donations, memberships, private grants and its own programs and publications. **Other Resources:** Operates Adopt-An-Orca program.

### E ◗ Whitetails Unlimited, Inc.
Box 422
Sturgeon Bay, WI 54235 (414)743-6777
**Concern(s):** environment; education; wildlife/endangered species. This group supports programs which ensure the present and future well being of the white-tailed deer and its habitat. Also, educates the people on sound conservation practices. **Other Resources:** Projects, P.O.L.I.T.E. (Permission of Landowner in order to Enter) and D.E.E.R. (Developing Educational and Environmental Resources). **Dues:** $15/supporting.

### E ◗ The Whole Earth Institute
27 Gate Five Rd.
Sausalito, CA 94965    (415)332-1716
**Affiliation:** Point Foundation. **Concern(s):** environment; alternative consumer; green consumer; conservation; preservation; research. The research and development arm of the Foundation. With the continued help of generous supporters, the Institute is a way in which Point can branch into new arenas of exploration and information dissemination. Creating a comprehensive Whole Earth resource data bank, hosting innovative conferences, and sponsoring active, multidimensional research studies such as our exploration of the environmental restoration movement are but a few of the projects planned by them. **Other Resources:** The WELL, BBS; WHOLE EARTH CATALOG on CD-ROM only; WHOLE EARTH REVIEW; guide, FRINGES OF REASON; and SIGNAL, a business catalog of hi-tech communications items. Nonprofit. **Est.:** 1968. **E-Network:** The WELL. **ID:** Kerwit@Well. **Contact(s):** Kelly Teevan (Executive Director).

### ✍ ◗ Whole Language Umbrella
4848 N. Fruit St.
Fresno, CA 93705
**Concern(s):** education; labor; childhood; alternative; union. A confederation of teacher-support groups across the US and Canada. It

supports the application of whole language approaches in educational settings, and sponsors an annual conference, as well as publications. **Contact(s):** Debbie Manning.

### E ◗ Wilderness Expeditions
310 Washington Ave. SW
Roanoke, VA 24016    (703)342-5630
**Concern(s):** environment; forests. Tours of jungles in Peru, emphasizing jungle conservation in areas where rainforest ecosystems are rapidly being destroyed. Trips support rainforest preservation and Peruvian Children's Fund Orphanage. **Member:** Co-op America.

### E ◗ The Wilderness Society
900 17th St. NW
Washington, DC 20006  (202)833-2300
**Concern(s):** environment; wilderness; conservation. The purpose is to protect wildlands and wildlife along with safeguarding our public lands, national forests, wildlife refuges, national seashores, recreation areas and public domain lands. It believes that the public lands is the greatest treasure that we have to pass on to future generations. **Other Resources:** See National Forest Action Center; periodicals, WILDERNESS magazine and FOREST ISSUES BULLETIN. **Est.:** 1935. **Dues:** $15/new, $30/renewal. **Member:** Environmental Federation of America. **Contact(s):** George T. Frampton, Jr. (President).

### E ◗ Wilderness Watch, Inc.
Box 782
Sturgeon Bay, WI 54235 (414)743-1238
**Concern(s):** environment; sustainability. The purpose of this organization is to promote the sustained use of America's sylvan lands and waters.

### ✈ ◗ Wildland Journeys
3516 NE 155th St.
Seattle, WA 98155    (206)365-0686
**Concern(s):** education; Third World; travel; development. Worldwide nature and culture explorations in South America, Africa and Asia. Trips emphasize cross-cultural interactions and support conservation and community development projects. **Other Resources:** Free catalog. **Contact(s):** Kurt Kutay.

### E ◗ Wildlife Camp
1400 16th St. NW
Washington, DC 20036  (703)790-4369
**Affiliation:** National Wildlife Fund. **Concern(s):** environment; education; wildlife/endangered species; camping; outdoor recreation. This Camp is an opportunity for children ages 9 through 13 to develop an understanding of the natural world and begin to foster an attitude of environmental citizenship while participating in a camp setting. A delightful blend of nature study, games, hiking, swimming, exploring, and enjoyment of the beauty and grandeur of the environment. **Fax:** (703)442-7332. (800)432-6564. **Contact(s):** Susan Johnson (Manager, Youth Program).

### E ◗ Wildlife Conservation International
New York Zoological Park
Bronx, NY 10460    (212)364-7963
**Concern(s):** environment; wildlife/endangered species; volunteers. Purpose: To help preserve the Earth's biological diversity and valuable ecosystems. With 122 projects in 46 countries, WCI addresses conflicts between humans and wildlife and explores locally sustainable solutions. Current Emphasis: Tropical rainforests; African elephant and rhino. Tibetan plateau and conservation training. **Other Resources:** See New York Zoological Society; periodicals, WCI NEWS and ANIMAL KINGDOM magazine. 122 projects in 46 countries. Volunteer programs: Grants for graduate students and professionals in wildlife sciences upon proposal submission. **Dues:** $25/yr. **Member:** Global Tomorrow Coalition. (800)221-3333. **Contact(s):** George Schaller (Director), A. William Weber (Assistant Director for Conservation). (212)220-5090.

### E ◗ Wildlife Information Center
629 Green St.
Allentown, PA 18102    (215)434-1637
**Concern(s):** environment; wildlife/endangered species; conservation. Secures and disseminates wildlife conservation, education, recreation and scientific research information dealing with wildlife issues at the local, state, national and international level. Advocates wildlife protection and non-killing uses such as observation, photography and tourism. Distributes books, reports and factsheets; maintains clipping archive; issues action alerts. **Other Resources:** See WILDLIFE ACTIVIST, WILDLIFE CONSERVATION REPORTS, EDUCATIONAL HAWKWATCHER newsletters and WILDLIFE BOOK REVIEW. **Contact(s):** Donald S. Heintzelman (Executive Director).

### E ◗ Wildlife Management Institute
1101 14th St. NW, #725
Washington, DC 20005  (202)371-1808
**Concern(s):** environment; wildlife/endangered species; conserva-

tion; natural resources. Private scientific and educational organization dedicated to the restoration, sound management and wise use of natural resources in North America. WMI works cooperatively with government agencies, higher educational institutions, and private conservation organizations and individuals in the everyday crusade for improving management of North America's natural resources, especially wildlife. **Other Resources:** See OUTDOOR NEWS BULLETIN newsletter. **Contact(s):** Lawrence R. Jahn (President).

### E ◗ Wildlife Preservation Trust International
34th St. & Girard Ave.
Philadelphia, PA 19104  (215)222-3636
**Concern(s):** environment; wildlife/endangered species; conservation. Dedicated to the preservation of endangered species through protected breeding. By establishing coordinated programs for captive breeding, field studies, public education, professional training, and reintroductions into protected habitats, they are striving to preserve the precious biological diversity of our planet's lifeforms and environments; species and habitats that are being annihilated as you read this. **Contact(s):** William R. Konstant (Executive Director), Gerald M. Durrell (Founder, Honorary Chairman).

### E ◗ Wildlife Rescue League
1930 Hileman Rd.
Falls Church, VA 22043  (703)241-0028
**Concern(s):** environment; wildlife/endangered species. Or contact your state fish and game department or local humane agency.

### E ◗ The Wildlife Society
5410 Grosvenor Lane
Bethesda, MD 20814    (301)897-9770
**Concern(s):** environment; wildlife/endangered species. An international organization of professionals serving the resource management fields, especially wildlife ecology. Of primary interest is the interaction of all wildlife populations with their natural environments. Objectives of the Society are: to promote sound stewardship of wildlife resources and habitats; prevent human-induced environmental degradation; and increase awareness and appreciation of wildlife values. **Other Resources:** See THE WILDLIFER NEWSLETTER. **Contact(s):** Harry E. Hodgdon.

### E ◗ Williams Watershed Protection Agency
4495 Cedar Flat Rd.
Williams, OR 97544
**Concern(s):** environment; wetlands; water; oceans/rivers.

### M ◗ Wilmington College Peace Resource Center
Pyle Center, Wilmington College
Box 1183
Wilmington, OH 45177  (513)382-5338
**Concern(s):** media; peace; education; students; anti-nuclear. PRC provides easy access to a wide range of print and audio-visual peace education resources. Made available nationwide. Home of Hiroshima/Nagasaki Memorial of research materials on the 1945 atomic bombings. **Other Resources:** Catalog and quarterly newsletter of peace education resource information available by request. Nonprofit. **Est.:** 1975. **Contact(s):** Helen Wiegel (Director).

### ✈ ◗ Windhorse Touring and Trading
Box 7604
Missoula, MT 59807    (406)542-2110
**Concern(s):** education; environment; Third World; travel; volunteers. Leads educational trips to the Himalayas, including volunteer work projects in national parks, villages, and monasteries. **Member:** Co-op America.

### E ◗ The Windstar Foundation
2317 Snowmass Creek Rd.
Snowmass, CO 81654    (303)927-4777
**Concern(s):** environment; agriculture; environment; sustainability. A leader and catalyst for developing responsible action toward a sustainable future on a global scale. It was born in 1976 of the dream of two men, entertainer John Denver and educator Tom Crum. An educational organization, it believes individuals can make a difference in the world. **Other Resources:** Prints an article called "Windstar Vision" in WORLDWATCH magazine and guide, CREATING A HEALTHY WORLD. Nonprofit. **Est.:** 1976. **Fax:** (303)927-4779. **Contact(s):** Steve Blomeke (Executive Vice-President), John Denver (President).

### E ◗ Windsurfers for Clean Water
1125 W. California Ave.
Mill Valley, CA 94941    (415)772-3149
**Concern(s):** environment; water; ocean/rivers; recreation. Researches water quality in San Francisco Bay and Pacific Ocean, educates water recreators, and works with government and industry to clean the water. **Other Resources:** Newsletter, meeting, beach clean-ups. **Member:** Co-op America.

**Wisconsin Coordinating Council on Nicaragua**
Box 1534
Madison, WI 53701    (608)257-7230
**Concern(s):** peace; Third World; Central America. Coordinates sister-city and citizen diplomacy projects with Nicaragua. Sells a book on sister-cities: history, directory, and how-to. **Member:** Co-op America.

**Wise Woman Center**
Box 64
Woodstock, NY 12498    (914)246-8081
**Concern(s):** feminism; spiritual; health; holism; transformation; alternatives consumer. The Center exists to reweave the story cape of the ancients. Goddesses, goats, and green witches gather here for workshops, retreats, and apprenticeships in herbal medicine and woman spirit. The sacred ground, the fairy mound, the sister spiral, the ritual circle, and the amused muses musing museum await you. **Other Resources:** Catalog, $1. Books, WISE WOMAN HERBAL CHILDBEARING YEAR. 196 pages, $8.95. HEALING WISE: THE SECOND WISE WOMAN HERBAL, 312 pages, $11.95. Video WEEDS TO THE WISE, 1 hour, $40. **Est.:** 1981. **Contact(s):** Susun Weed (Founder), Sarah Evans (Coordinator). (914)658-8057.

**Witness for Peace**
Box 33273
Washington, DC 20033    (202)797-1160
**Concern(s):** Third World; peace; justice; foreign policy; volunteers; Central America; nonviolence; intervention. Supports the presence of long or short-term volunteers in the war zones of Nicaragua and works in the US to turn governmental policy from one of military intervention to one of justice, peace, and friendship with Nicaragua. The Long Term Witness Program builds on the testimony and moral authority of eyewitnesses who have stood nonviolently with the Nicaraguan people in war zones, in order to create a network of popular support in the US for a change in policy. **Other Resources:** Hotline and Video available. WITNESS FOR PEACE MAGAZINE and NEWSBRIEF. Hotline: (202)797-1531.

**Woman's Circle**
Box 712
El Prado, NM 87529    (505)758-7787
**Concern(s):** feminism; spiritual; environment; empowerment; recreation; transformation. The Circle is a 5 day retreat in the beauty of sacred Taos, New Mexico. The Circle is a process that focuses on empowerment, self-expression and experience. It is a coming together of women to explore, nurture and accept the unique woman in each of us in a safe and loving environment. While here you will have experiential trips to sacred areas, hot springs and mountain trails. **Contact(s):** JoDee Powers, Suzi Juarez.

**Women and Food Information Network**
1505 S. Broadway, #6
Champaign, IL 61801    (217)337-5418
**Concern(s):** agriculture; feminism; health; nutrition. **Contact(s):** Kate Cloud.

**Women and Foundations/Corporate Philanthropy**
141 5th Ave., #7
New York, NY 10010    (212)460-9253
**Concern(s):** feminism; economics; philanthropy. See DIRECTORY OF WOMEN'S FUNDS.

**Women Against Military Madness**
3255 Hennepin Ave. S, #125B
Minneapolis, MN 55408-9986    (612)827-5364
**Concern(s):** feminism; peace; empowerment; activism; rights. A grassroots citizens group, made up of individuals working for peace and justice. The organization prepares individuals and gives them support in their struggle for peace. "We are committed to working for non-violent management of world conflict. We have empowerment groups to facilitate action to demand policy and priority shifts of the US government." **Other Resources:** Newsletter. Tough Dove, puppet that educates kids about peace and justice. Low Income Mothers - grants money to women with children. Media Watch, holds media, local and national, accountable on peace & justice issues. Las Madres, Central America. Nonprofit. **Est.:** 1982. **Dues:** $30; lower income. **Member:** Minnesota Peace and Justice Coalition. **Fax:** (612)827-6433. **Contact(s):** Lucia Wilkes, Daniella Maus (Co-directors). (612)826-5365.

**Women Against Pornography**
321 W. 47th St.
New York, NY 10036    (212)307-5055
**Concern(s):** feminism; rape; discrimination; sexism. Seeks to educate the public about the connection between pornography and violence against women and discrimination practices.

**Women in Waste**
c/o Florence Thompson; Bresenhan, Thompson & Assoc.
Box 761
Bloomsburg, PA 17815
**Concern(s):** feminism; environment; recycling.

**Women Involved in Farm Economics**
HC Rt 1
Royal City, WA 99357
**Concern(s):** agriculture; feminism; economics. **Contact(s):** Alice Parker.

**Women Strike For Peace**
710 G St. SE
Washington, DC 20003    (202)544-2211
**Affiliation:** Women's International League for Peace & Freedom. **Concern(s):** peace; politics; feminism; law; anti-nuclear; test ban; disarmament. This project came into existence on Nov. 1, 1961 when 100,000 women in 60 cities across US came out of kitchens and jobs to protest against atmospheric nuclear tests which were poisoning the air and children's food. It made a significant contribution toward achieving the 1963 Partial Test Ban Treaty. "A comprehensive test ban is our unfinished goal. We campaign against the nuclear arms race through an on-going lobby-by-proxy, the Newsletter and other activities." **Other Resources:** Publishes STAR WARS: A BASIC PRIMER FOR THE LEGITIMATELY CONFUSED; and monthly, LEGISLATIVE ALERT. **Est.:** 1961. **Frequency:** 12/yr. **Subscription:** $10/yr. **Circ.:** 4M. **Circ.:** Edith Villastrigo (Legislative Director), Cynthia Johnson (Co-director). **Other:** Room 706, 145 S. 13th St., Philadelphia, PA 19107.

**Women to Women Communications**
See WOMEN FIGHT BACK (periodicals).

**Women USA Fund**
See Women's Foreign Policy Council.

**Women's Action Alliance**
See T.A.P.P. SOURCES: A NATIONAL DIRECTORY OF TEENAGE PREGNANCY PREVENTION.

**Women's Action for Nuclear Disarmament (WAND)**
305 7th St. SE
Washington, DC 20003    (202)543-8505
**Concern(s):** feminism; peace; disarmament. A citizens' organization founded by Helen Caldicott to empower women politically to direct US policies toward a world free of the threat of nuclear war and towards a stable peace by ending the nuclear arms race. Thousands of women have joined to learn more about the nuclear threat, educate others, and pressure elected officials to pull back from the nuclear brink. Provides speaker training workshops, organizes women across the nation to be effective grassroots lobbyists in Congress. **Other Resources:** WAND BULLETIN; FACTS FOR THE NUCLEAR AGE, articles from other sources, best lists of video, films, and other resources. Over 80 groups in 35 states. **Est.:** 1980. **Contact(s):** Beverly Droz (President), Diane Aronson (Director). (617)64306740. **Other:** 691 Massachusetts Ave., #204, Arlington, MA 02174

**Women's Alternative Economic Summit**
UN/NGLS
2 UN Plaza/DC2-1102
New York, NY 10017    (212)963-1234
**Concern(s):** feminism; environment; economics; empowerment; sexism. Formed as a result of the disastrous effects the global economic policies have on women. Since its formation, WAES has been promoting programs to further women's understanding of economics. Now it is proposing a women's summit to be convened in Vienna to precede and channel recommendations to the UN Commission on the Status of Women. **Est.:** 1985.

**Women's Center**
See HERA (periodicals).

**Women's Computer Literacy Center**
Box 68
Jenner, CA 95450    (707)632-5763
**Concern(s):** education; feminism; literacy. Computer training and education based on a unique holistic learning style, particularly appropriate for women. Author of The Women's Computer Literacy Handbook. **Member:** Co-op America.

**Women's Environment & Development Organization**
845 3rd Ave., 15th floor
New York, NY 10022    (212)759-7982
**Affiliation:** Women USA Fund. **Concern(s):** feminism; environment; Third World; foreign policy; law; population; pro-choice. Promotes women's equal participation in policymaking and leadership on environment, development and global security issues, from grassroots to international levels. Its 55-member Women's International Policy Action Committee, including women from every region of the world, is monitoring UNCED decisions, forming regional Women for a Healthy Planet centers and sponsoring grassroots Community Report Card project, enabling women to evaluate the real environmental and social justice health status of their communities. Formerly Women's Foreign Policy Council. **Other Resources:** Newsletter, NEWS & VIEWS, Declaration of Interdependence, Report Cards, video and audio tapes. Fax: (212)759-8647. Contact(s): Mim Kelber, Bella Abzug.

**Women's Information Exchange**
See NATIONAL WOMEN'S MAILING LIST (directories).

**Women's Institute For Free Press**
3306 Ross Place NW
Washington, DC 20008    (202)966-7783
**Concern(s):** justice; freedom of expression; civil liberties; constitutional rights.

**Women's International Coalition to Stop Making Radioactive Waste**
77 Homewood Ave.
Allendale, NJ 07401    (201)728-2593
**Concern(s):** feminism; peace; environment; health; nuclear; hazardous/toxic waste. This coalition attempts to expose the falsehoods of nuclear power. It does this through various educational means. **Other Resources:** Newsletter, NUCLEAR POWER IN CRISIS. **Contact(s):** Karen Westdyk (Director). (201)327-3914.

**Women's International League for Peace and Freedom**
1213 Race St.
Philadelphia, PA 19107    (215)563-7110
**Concern(s):** peace; politics; feminism; empowerment; activism; anti-nuclear; lobbying; nonviolence. An international organization stressing nonviolent solutions to domestic and international problems. Seeks to unite women in all countries who oppose war, exploitation, and oppression, stands for equality of all people in a world free of racism and sexism; the building of a constructive peace through world disarmament; and changing of government priorities to meet human needs. Conducts grassroots organizing by branches nationwide, national office in Philadelphia, a legislative office in Washington. **Other Resources:** Newsletters, LEGISLATIVE BULLETIN and PEACE AND FREEDOM. Hotlines: Arms Control—(202)543-0006; South Africa—(202)546-0408; Central America—(202)667-0990. See Women Strike For Peace. **Est.:** 1915. **Contact(s):** Ann Ivey (President). **Other:** Legislative Office, 710 G St., Washington, DC 20003 Isabel Guy, Legislative Director. (202)544-2211.

**Women's International Network**
187 Grand St.
Lexington, MA 02173
**Concern(s):** feminism; activism; sexism; discrimination; networking. This international network of women use networking to get the message out to governments, institutions, and the public on women's issues. **Other Resources:** Publishes WIN NEWS. **Contact(s):** Fran Hoskins.

**The Women's Jail Project**
Box 1592
Madison, WI 53701-1592    (608)251-6314
**Concern(s):** justice; feminism; prisons; political prisoners; reform; prisons; criminal system. While anti-nuclear activist Bonnie Urfer spent time in prison, she started this support project for women. Their newsletter portrays many important insights into the lives of women in prison and is vital testimony to the psychic waste that the system produces. **Other Resources:** Newsletter, THE INSIDER. **Subscription:** Donation. **Contact(s):** Bonnie Urfer, Jane Simonds (Co-Directors).

**Women's Legal Defense Fund**
1875 Connecticut Ave. NW
Washington, DC 20009    (202)986-2600
**Concern(s):** feminism; equal rights; law; sexism. A pro-bono group of female attorneys dedicated to the elimination of sex discrimination in the law and in the society as a whole. The Fund takes an active role in educating the public, the government, and the legislative community about widespread problems of sexism in this country. "Based on our legal expertise, our work with women's groups, and our services to female clients, we also provide a feminine voice before the courts and in the setting of public policy." **Other Resources:** See CUSTODY HANDBOOK (directories).

**Women's Peace Network**
See MADRE Speaks/MADRE Informa magazine.

**F ◆ Women's Project of the Association for Union Democracy**
500 State St.
Brooklyn, NY 11217      (718)855-6650
**Affiliation:** Association for Union Democracy. **Concern(s):** feminism; labor; empowerment; labor; workplace democracy; sexism. This is an ongoing project dedicated to fighting sexual discrimination in unions and on the job. Also, it develops leadership potential in women union members. **Other Resources:** Advocacy, organizational support, coalition-building with women's issues groups both in and out of unions. Supports women working and trying to get access to non-traditional jobs. Nonprofit. **Est.:** 1985. **Dues:** $25/yr. **Fax:** (718)855-6799. **Contact(s):** Brenda Bishop (Project Director), Susan Jennik (Executive Director).

**F ◆ Women's Research and Education Institute**
1700 18th St. NW, #400
Washington, DC 20009  (202)328-7070
**Concern(s):** feminism; education. **Other Resources:** Publications list.

**S ◆ Women's Technical Assistance Project**
See CHURCH FUNDING RESOURCE GUIDE (directories). .

**E ◆ Woods Hole Oceanographic Institute**
Woods Hole, MA 02543  (508)548-1400
**Concern(s):** environment; oceans/rivers; global warming. This organization focuses on marine science and the effects that civilization is having on the ocean environment. **Other Resources:** Publishes OCEANUS.

**F ◆ Woodswomen**
25 West Diamond Lake Rd.
Minneapolis, MN 55419 (612)822-3809
**Concern(s):** feminism; environment; recreation. Provides a wide variety of outdoor adventures for women of all ages. "Backed by over 13 years experience in guiding domestic and international trips, we offer bicycling, scuba, climbing, backpacking, trekking and much more!" **Other Resources:** Free brochure. **Member:** Co-op America.

**E ◆ Work on Waste, USA (W.O.W.)**
See W.O.W. Series of Video Tapes on the Solid Waste Crisis (media).

**L ◆ Workers' Solidarity Alliance**
See IDEAS AND ACTION newspaper.

**J ◆ Working Group on Community Right-To-Know**
215 Pennsylvania Ave. SE
Washington, DC 20003  (202)546-9707
**Affiliation:** US Public Interest Research Group. **Concern(s):** justice; constitutional rights; civil liberties.

**✍ ◆ World Affairs Council**
1726 M St. NW
Washington, DC 20036  (202)293-1051
**Concern(s):** education; politics; peace; Third World; world order; global understanding; foreign policy. Educational organization devoted to informing US citizens about foreign policy and global issues. **Est.:** 1949.

**✻ ◆ World Association for World Federation**
777 UN Plaza, 12th Fl.
New York, NY 10017      (212)599-1320
**Affiliation:** World Federalist Association. **Concern(s):** peace; justice; world order; United Nations. An international organization promoting peace and justice through world law and a strengthened United Nations, dedicated to eliminating the use of force in international relations. WAWF was founded in Montreaux, Switzerland in 1947. "We are now an international movement with members in over 30 countries and national organizations in about 15 countries." WAWF has its international secretariat in Amsterdam and a United Nations office here in New York. **Other Resources:** Publishes WORLD FEDERALIST NEWS, a newsletter. Reports on UN legal and institutional initiatives. **Est.:** 1947. **Frequency:** 3/yr. **Subscription:** $15/2 yrs for reports. **Pages:** 8. **Circ.:** 2M. **E-Network:** PeaceNet. **ID:** "worldfed". **Fax:** (212)599-1332. **Contact(s):** Jack Yost (UN Representative).

**A ◆ World Association of Soil and Water Conservation**
317 Marion Ave.
Volga, SD 57071-9140  (605)627-9309
**Concern(s):** agriculture; environment; soil; water; conservation. **Contact(s):** William C. Moldenhauer.

**✻ ◆ World Citizens Assembly**
110 Sutter St., #708
San Francisco, CA 94104-4023  (415)474-9773
**Concern(s):** peace; justice; education; world order; disarmament; global understanding. Provides services to globally-minded citizens,

---

linking information-gathering and strategy development and implementation, especially through contacts with the UN. **Other Resources:** publishes a newsletter WORLD CITIZEN. **Est.:** 1975. **Contact(s):** Douglas Mattern (President), Carl Caseboldt (Vice President). 145 E. 50th St., New York, NY 10022

**F ◆ World Conference on Religion and Peace**
777 UN Plaza
New York, NY 10017      (212)687-2163
**Concern(s):** feminism; justice; health; environment; battered women; children; seniors; substance abuse. Deals with issues such as children's rights, discrimination against and abuse of women, religious discrimination, drug abuse, aging, the family, indigenous people, the environment. **Other Resources:** Publishes RELIGION FOR PEACE; BRIDGES OF PEACE, WCRP/USA Newsletters, quarterly, WCRP REPORT. **Contact(s):** Rev. Nikkyo Niwano (Secretary General).

**E ◆ World Conservation Monitoring Centre/IUCN Commission on National Parks and Protected Areas**
See guide, UNITED NATIONS LIST OF NATIONAL PARKS AND PROTECTED AREAS.

**✻ ◆ World Constitution and Parliament Association**
1480 Hoyt St., #31
Lakewood, CO 80215      (303)233-3548
**Concern(s):** peace; world order. Working towards a World Constituent Assembly for late 90's. Has been trying to get governments to ratify the World Constitution drafted at the Association's second World Constituent Assembly in 1977. Delegates to the Assembly can be duly chosen representatives of cities, duly chosen representatives of organizations or just plain individuals, so long as they get 700 signatures on a pre-approved petition. Other restrictions may apply. **Other Resources:** Literature and Resources list available. **Contact(s):** Philip Isely (Secretary-General). (303)526-0463.

**S ◆ World Council of Churches**
475 Riverside Dr.
New York, NY 10115      (212)870-2533
**Concern(s):** spiritual; peace; justice; faith. Consists of 306 member churches throughout the world which are provided information and guidance regarding international problems. Assists in forming a Christian attitude on world issues. (212)870-2522.

**T ◆ World Crafts Council**
29 West 53 St.
New York, NY 10019
**Concern(s):** Third World; economics; development; alternative consumer.

**E ◆ World Environment Center**
419 Park Ave. S, #1404
New York, NY 10016      (212)683-4700
**Concern(s):** environment. An organization whose mission is to serve as a bridge between industry and governments aimed at strengthening environmental management and industrial safety worldwide through exchange of information and technical expertise. Provides international public recognition for outstanding industrial accomplishments. **Other Resources:** Publications include, NETWORK NEWS; CHLORINE SAFETY PAYS; POLLUTION PREVENTION PAYS. **Est.:** 1974. **Fax:** (212)683-5053.

**✻ ◆ World Federalist Association**
418 7th St. SE
Washington, DC 20003  (202)546-3950
**Affiliation:** World Association for World Federation. **Concern(s):** peace; world order. The oldest and largest organization working for the abolition of war and a healthful global environment through the establishment of just and enforceable world laws. An educational membership organization, part of a worldwide movement, which seeks to replace armed conflict as a way of settling international disputes. Goal: the abolition of war through a system based on world law, limited in accord with the principle of federalism, in which global institutions could resolve conflicts peacefully. **Other Resources:** News magazine, WORLD FEDERALIST. Brochures, pamphlets, and books available through WFA National Office. Projects: Campaign for UN Reform; and Our Planet in Every Classroom. **Contact(s):** Norman Cousins (deceased) (President), Walter Hoffmann (Executive Director). (800)428-3927.

**A ◆ World Food Institute**
45 Kildee Hall
Iowa State University
Ames, IA 50011
**Concern(s):** agriculture; Third World; health; food production; policy; development; hunger; nutrition. **Contact(s):** Janet Olson.

**? ◆ World Future Society**
4916 St. Elmo Ave.
Bethesda, MD 20814      (301)656-8274

---

**Concern(s):** future; ideation; analysis. An educational and scientific organization that serves as a neutral clearinghouse for ideas about the future, including forecasts, scenarios, and alternatives. **Other Resources:** See periodicals, THE FUTURIST; FUTURE SURVEY/FUTURE SURVEY ANNUAL; and FUTURE RESEARCH DIRECTORY. Holds occasional conferences; operates a futurist bookstore (catalog available). WORLD FUTURE STUDIES NEWSLETTER with directory issue. Nonprofit. **Est.:** 1966. **Dues:** $30/yr. **Fax:** (301)951-0394. **Contact(s):** Edward Cornish (President).

**✍ ◆ World Game Project (World Game Institute)**
University City Science Center
3508 Market St.
Philadelphia, PA 19104  (215)387-0220
**Concern(s):** education; global understanding. Has expanded Buckminster Fuller's world game, now covering every country and topic of global decision-making, using 150 data variables to give information to everyone which previously was only available to the power elite. **Contact(s):** Medard Gabel (Executive Director).

**S ◆ World Goodwill**
113 University Place
Box 722 Cooper Station
New York, NY 10276      (212)982-8770
**Affiliation:** Lucis Trust. **Concern(s):** spiritual; peace; justice; faith; conflict resolution. They seek to: aid in establishing right human relations, help mobilize the energy of goodwill everywhere in public opinion on the world, cooperate in the work of preparation for the reappearance of Christ (the "Coming One"), and educate world public opinion on the causes of world problems, so creating a thought forum of solution. **Other Resources:** The various activities and publications available through World Goodwill are listed in the "Reply Slip" included with each quarterly newsletter. **Est.:** 1932. **E-Network:** PeaceNet. **ID:** 'pcoles'. **Contact(s):** Ida Urso, Ph.D. (Director), Sarah McKechnie (President).

**✻ ◆ World Government Organizations Coalition**
774 Colusa Ave.
El Cerrito, CA 94530
**Concern(s):** peace; world order. **Contact(s):** Dr. Lucile Green.

**H ◆ World Health Organization**
See periodicals, WHO CHRONICLE; WORLD HEALTH; and WORLD HEALTH ORGANIZATION PUBLICATIONS CATALOG.

**✈ ◆ World Home Exchange Network**
878 30 Ave.
San Francisco, CA 94121      (800)SAY-WHEN
**Concern(s):** education; travel. Free travel accommodations made possible by first computerized exchange service.

**D ◆ World Hunger Education**
See WHO'S INVOLVED WITH HUNGER: AN ORGANIZATION GUIDE FOR EDUCATION AND ADVOCACY (directories).

**D ◆ World Hunger Year**
261 W. 35th St., #1402
New York, NY 10001-1906  (212)629-8850
**Concern(s):** demographics; Third World; feminism; hunger; poverty; homelessness; development. This organization does research on the hunger crisis in the world today. It attempts to disseminate information on hunger to the public by providing accurate facts on the subject to the media. **Other Resources:** See periodicals, HUNGERLINE and FOOD MONITOR; and project, Reinvesting in America Campaign.

**✍ ◆ World Information Systems**
Box 535
Cambridge, MA 02238
**Concern(s):** education; future; global understanding; planning; ideation.

**E ◆ World Nature Association, Inc.**
Box 673
Silver Springs, MD 20901      (301)593-2522
**Concern(s):** environment; education; conservation; global understanding. Purpose is to bring together naturalists to assist in the conservation and restoration of the natural world primarily outside the US. Supports education and research projects in conservation. **Dues:** $10, $20/family, $150/life.

**✻ ◆ World Neighbors**
5116 N. Portland Ave.
Oklahoma City, OK 73112      (800)242-6387
**Concern(s):** peace; conflict resolution.

**✻ ◆ World Order Models Project**
See ALTERNATIVES: SOCIAL TRANSFORMATION AND HUMANE GOVERNANCE (periodicals).

✈ ◆ **World Peace Camp for Teens**
RR2, Box 81
Lincolnville, ME 04849   (207)998-4777
**Affiliation:** Physicians for Social Responsibility; Samantha Smith Foundation. **Concern(s):** education; peace; youth; childhood; students; travel. (207)338-5165.

S ◆ **World Peace One**
5770 Pershing Ave.
St. Louis, MO 63112   (314)725-4241
**Concern(s):** spiritual; transformation. Helps people develop peaceful lifestyles using a "systems" approach: people are encouraged to make their own plan for creating peace in their lives. **Other Resources:** Publishes the PEACE PACT GUIDE. **Member:** Co-op America. **Other:** 7114 Idlewood, St. Louis, MO 63136.

✷ ◆ **World Peace Through Law Center**
1000 Connecticut Ave. NW, #800
Washington, DC 20036  (202)466-5428
**Concern(s):** peace; world order. Its major purpose is to persuade the nations of the world to accept more and more treaties and conventions, so as to expand the network of transnational law and legal institutions, thus fostering the development of a World of Peace with Justice in all areas of international contact of Peoples and nations. **Other Resources:** The WORLD JURIST, bulletin/newsletter. **Contact(s):** Charles S. Rhyne (World President).

✷ ◆ **World Peace University**
Box 10869
Eugene, OR 97440   (503)741-1794
**Concern(s):** peace; education; environment; media; activism; world order; broadcasting. Offers: 1) On campus Peace Studies Graduate Degree program, 2) Off campus workshops, courses and conferences, 3) Guided core peace study internships for credit, 4) Rain forest preservation through ownership projects, 5) Radio for Peace International providing global shortwave peace intercommunication 6) Integrated Ecology books and articles, 7) Internationally located branch campuses. **Other Resources:** Department of Integrated Ecology. Publishes a handbooks, HOW NATURE WORKS: REGENERATING KINSHIP WITH PLANET EARTH; and CONNECTING WITH NATURE. Newsletter. See, also, Radio for Peace (media). **Est.:** 1985. **Frequency:** 4/yr. **Price:** $11 w/postage. **Bulk:** 30% off/24. **Circ.:** 500. **E-Network:** Econet. **ID:** 'worldpeaceu'. **Fax:** (503)741-1279. **Contact(s):** Dr. Richard Schneider (Chancellor), Michael J. Cohen, Ed.D (Department Chair). (206)378-6313.

✷ ◆ **World Peacemakers Inc.**
2025 Massachusetts Ave. NW
Washington, DC 20036  (202)265-7582
**Concern(s):** peace; spiritual; transformation; conflict resolution; activism. This organization wishes to bring both inner and outer peace to the world by increasing one's knowledge of their inner selves and involvement in the world around them. **Other Resources:** See HANDBOOK FOR WORLD PEACEMAKERS GROUP (directories). **Contact(s):** Bill Price: (President).

✷ ◆ **World Policy Institute**
777 UN Plaza
New York, NY 10017   (212)490-0010
**Concern(s):** peace; Third World; justice; environment; politics; world order; natural resources; social justice; foreign policy; East-West; conflict resolution; intervention. Established to form practical alternatives to war, poverty, social justice, and ecological damage. The philosophy of the institute is that the system of competing nation-states must be transformed because it legitimizes violence, fosters social inequities, and encourages careless exploitation of planetary resources. **Other Resources:** See WORLD RESOURCES INSTITUTE PUBLICATIONS CATALOG, WORLD POLICY JOURNAL, and World Order Models Project; WORLD PEACE AND WORLD ORDER STUDIES: A CURRICULUM GUIDE. **Est.:** 1961. **Fax:** (212)986-1482.

T ◆ **World Population Society**
1333 H St. NW, #760
Washington, DC 20005  (202)898-1303
**Concern(s):** Third World; demographics; feminism; environment; family planning; population growth. An organization concerned with the crisis of over-population and the ways we can prevent it or slow it down. Promotes birth control and family planning.

✷ ◆ **World Priorities Inc.**
3013 Dumbarton Ave. NW
Washington, DC 20007  (202)965-1661
**Concern(s):** peace; justice; economics. **Contact(s):** Ruth Sivard (Director).

E ◆ **World Research Foundation**
15300 Ventura Blvd., #405
Sherman Oaks, CA 91403   (818)907-5483

**Concern(s):** environment; health; research; networking. An international health and environmental network. Offices are located in China, West Germany, England & US with libraries (open to the public) containing journals, periodicals and books (some dating to the 1600s) in all areas of health. Computers are connected to 500 databases encompassing 5,000 medical journals from 100 countries. WRF has an Advisory Board of 95 medical and scientific specialists. Call for information. We welcome donations. Nonprofit.

E ◆ **World Resources Institute**
1709 New York Ave. NW, #700
Washington, DC 20006  (202)638-6300
**Concern(s):** environment; Third World; natural resources; development. An independent, nonpartisan policy research center helping governments, private sector, international leaders and policymakers answer: How can societies meet human needs and nurture economic growth while preserving natural resources and environmental integrity? Aims to provide accurate information about global resources and environmental conditions, analysis of emerging issues and development of creative yet workable responses. **Other Resources:** Publishes reports, papers; sponsors seminars, conferences, briefings. Center for Environment & Development; NGO NETWORKER newsletter; COMMON PROPERTY RESOURCES (directories). **Member:** Global Tomorrow Coalition; Environmental Federation of America. **Contact(s):** James Gustave Speth (President), Rafe Pomerance (Senior Associate).

A ◆ **World Seed Fund**
c/o Abundant Life Seed Foundation
Box 772
Port Townsend, WA 98368  (206)385-5660
**Affiliation:** Abundant Life Seed Foundation. **Concern(s):** agriculture; development.

☂ ◆ **World Society for the Protection of Animals**
29 Perkins St., Box 109
Boston, MA 02130   (617)522-7000
**Concern(s):** environment; wildlife/endangered species; animal rights. An international organization of several hundred member humane societies in more than 60 countries. Maintains an international disaster relief fund to aid animals affected by man-made or natural disasters. If there is a need to enact protective legislation, or develop a humane education program, or investigate incidents of cruelty in the transport and slaughter of livestock, WSPA is there. (See Animals International). **Other Resources:** ANIMAL INTERNATIONAL magazine. **Office:** 29 Perkins St. Boston, MA 02130. **Contact(s):** John C. Walsh (President/Regional Director), Trevor Scott (Director General).

E ◆ **World Wildlife Fund**
1250 24th St. NW
Washington, DC 20037  (202)293-4800
**Affiliation:** Conservation Foundation. **Concern(s):** environment; wildlife/endangered species; conservation; biodiversity. The purpose of this foundation is to work worldwide to preserve endangered wildlife and wildlands by encouraging sustainable development and the preservation of biodiversity, particularly in the tropical forests of Latin America, Africa, Asia. **Other Resources:** See Conservation Foundation; National Celebration of the Outdoors; OFFICIAL WORLD WILDLIFE FUND GUIDE TO ENDANGERED SPECIES OF NORTH AMERICA (directories). **Dues:** $15/yr. **Member:** Global Tomorrow Coalition; Environmental Federation of America. **Contact(s):** Kathryn S. Fuller (President). (202)293-9211.

✷ ◆ **World Without War Council**
1736 Martin Luther King Jr. Way
Berkeley, CA 94709   (510)845-1992
**Concern(s):** peace; world order; disarmament. Challenges peace organization stereotypes even as it seeks alternatives to the Pentagon's. It focuses its work on the arenas in which non-governmental organizations seek to shape American purpose in world affairs. It is not a membership organization, but a kind of management consultant agency for enterprises that do not yet exist - enterprises essential to wise American leadership in progress toward a world that resolves international conflict without mass violence. **Other Resources:** WAR PEACE FILM GUIDE (media); guides, AMERICANS AND WORLD AFFAIRS; DIRECTORY OF NATIONAL ORGANIZATIONS DEALING WITH CENTRAL AMERICA; and PEACE ARCHIVES: A GUIDE TO LIBRARY COLLECTIONS; RAISING THE CURTAIN: A GUIDE TO INDEPENDENT ORGANIZATIONS. **Contact(s):** Robert Pickus (President).

✈ ◆ **WorldTeach**
Harvard Institute for International Development
1 Eliot St.
Cambridge, MA 02138-9611(617)495-5527
**Affiliation:** Phillips Brooks House Association. **Concern(s):** education; peace; travel; volunteers. Its volunteers worked in 5 countries in 1990-91: China, Costa Rica, Namibia, Poland, and Thailand, teaching math, English, and science in bustling cities, quiet towns, and rural

villages for one year internships. Volunteers pay fees to cover costs of participating in the program. The Project arranges the position which provides housing and a modest salary throughout the year. Since 1986 it has placed over 400 volunteers overseas. **Other Resources:** Call for brochure or application. Nonprofit. **Est.:** 1986. **Fax:** (617)495-1239.

E ◆ **Worldwatch Institute**
1776 Massachusetts Ave. NW
Washington, DC 20036  (202)452-1999
**Concern(s):** environment; Third World; natural resources; development. The purpose of this institute is to inform policy makers and the public about the interdependence of world economics and environmental support systems. **Other Resources:** Bimonthly magazine, WORLD WATCH, and papers alerting the people to the need to reduce the environmental degradation within the next decade. Annual guide to the world's condition, STATE OF THE WORLD.

F ◆ **Worldwide**
1331 H St. NW
Washington, DC 20005  (202)347-1514
**Concern(s):** feminism; environment; empowerment; natural resources; networking; sustainability. Helps women at all levels of society participate in the protection of the environment and in the management of natural resources. Goals are to establish a worldwide network of women concerned about environmental management and protection; to educate the public and policymakers about the vital links between women, natural resources, and sustainable development; to promote the inclusion of women and their environmental perceptions in the design and implementation of development policies. **Other Resources:** Publishes DIRECTORY OF WOMEN IN ENVIRONMENT; and newsletter, WORLDWIDE NEWS. Nonprofit. **Dues:** $35/yr. **Contact(s):** Joan Martin-Brown (Chairman), Cynthia R. Helms (President, Washington Forum).

✐ ◆ **Worldwise 2000**
1225 15th St. NW
Washington, DC 20005
**Concern(s):** education; global understanding; networking; conflict resolution. Education campaign for the last decade of this century. Will plan and carry out activities emphasizing global understanding, cooperation and responsibility. By working closely with existing organizations, coalitions and institutions it will help them reach larger audiences and expand their missions. Sharing resources, knowledge and technology, more people can become "worldwise." Will enlist support of elected officials in helping to create a world based on new ways of thinking and doing. **Contact(s):** Karen Mulhauser (Co-director), Nancy M. Yanofksy (202)363-2478.

F ◆ **WOMLAND (Women of Matriarchal Beliefs on Sacred Land)**
Box 55
Troy, ME 04987
**Concern(s):** feminism; economics; spiritual; environment; transformation; empowerment; land trusts. A spiritual organization committed to creating balance on Earth. To that end, it acquires and protects land, assuring access to it by current and future generations of women and children so that they may be restored to full empowerment and relationship with sacred Mother Earth. **Other Resources:** Bimonthly newsletter. Nonprofit. **Est.:** 1986. **Dues:** $60/yr. or $5/month. **Contact(s):** Chris of Conventree (Corresponding Secretary).

✐ ◆ **Wysong Institute**
See Wysong Corporation (business).

E ◆ **The Xerces Society**
10 SW Ash St., 3rd Fl.
Portland, OR 97204   (503)222-2788
**Concern(s):** environment; wildlife/endangered species; preservation. Butterfly and moth preservation. **Other Resources:** Magazine, WINGS: ESSAYS ON INVERTEBRATE CONSERVATION. **Fax:** (503)222-2763. **Contact(s):** Melody Mackey Allen (Executive Director).

A ◆ **Yankee Permaculture**
See INTERNATIONAL PERMACULTURE SOLUTIONS JOURNAL (periodicals) and TRIP (directories). .

✷ ◆ **Young and Teen Peacemakers**
See PEACE OF OUR MINDS (periodicals).

✐ ◆ **Young Naturalist Foundation**
See periodicals CHICKADEE and OWL.

✈ ◆ **Youth Ambassadors of America**
119 N. Commercial
Bellingham, WA 98225
**Concern(s):** education; peace; conflict resolution; travel.

✈ ◗ **Youth Environmental Society**
Box 441
Cranbury, NJ 08512
**Concern(s):** education; environment; activism; travel; youth.

♥ ◗ **Youth Policy Institute**
See AMERICAN FAMILY newsletter; STUDENT PRESS SERVICE NEWS REPORT; YOUTH POLICY (periodicals). **Other Resources:** FUTURE CHOICES, a triannual, $127/year, periodical.

E ◗ **Youths for Environment and Society**
346 Commerce St.
Alexandria, VA 22314    (703)549-3630
**Affiliation:** Legacy International. **Concern(s):** environment; Third World; education; sustainability; conservation; leadership; development; volunteers; travel. Focuses on environmental concerns, development and security. A voluntary, nonpolitical, international environmental organization dedicated to mobilizing young people (18-30) to assume leadership roles in environmental protection and sustainable development. Provides training for community action and public education, emphasis on leadership and promotion of cross-cultural understanding. YES groups worldwide with plans for USA chapters on campuses nationwide. Develops educational materials. **Contact(s):** Sureyya Ozkizilcik.

D ◗ **Zero Population Growth**
1400 16th St. NW, #320
Washington, DC 20036    (202)332-2200
**Concern(s):** demographics; environment; population growth. Advocates zero population growth, the point at which population size stays the same from year to year. A national organization, ZPG works to promote the advantages of achieving a sustainable balance of people, resources, and the environment, both in the US and worldwide. Works independently and in coalition with other organizations to represent members' concerns. Founded in the 60's by Paul Ehrlich. **Other Resources:** Publishes ZPG REPORTER, Action Alert Network, MEDIA TARGETS, bimonthly newsletter on media coverage, Teacher's PET project for educators and Newswatch, research library of articles in magazines & newspapers. **Dues:** $10/student/senior, $20/individual. **Contact(s):** Susan Weber (Executive Direstor).

E ◗ **Zoetic Research/Sea Quest Expeditions**
Box 2424
Friday Harbour, WA 98250    (206)378-5767
**Concern(s):** environment; ocean/rivers; wildlife/endangered species; polar. "Our name means 'endowed with life,' something you'll find in our biologist-led programs: participate in whale research, accredited outdoor classes; become intimate with the ocean and its creatures in safe, stable sea kayaks. Baja, Alaska, San Juan Island, Everglades, Dry Tortugas." **Member:** Co-op America.

✈ ◗ **Zoovival**
Box 15007-C11
Clearwater, FL 34629    (813)726-3385
**Concern(s):** education; environment; wildlife/endangered species; travel; jobs. Wildlife research/rescue expeditions. The ultimate foreign/US vacation. Help scientists study or relocate endangered plants and animals in doomed habitats. Own land at our wildlife refuges. Also, earn income at home saving rare species. **Other Resources:** Large information kit. **Member:** Co-op America. **Office:** 2340 S.R. 580, Building P-246 Clearwater, FL 34629. **Contact(s):** Gregory B. Cunningham.

---

# Special Thanks to:

*TRANET*

*Buzzworm*

*Invest Yourself Directory* by The Commission on Voluntary Service and Action

*Holistic Education  Review* and *Resource Guide*

# ② **Periodicals**

| | | | | | | | | | |
|---|---|---|---|---|---|---|---|---|---|
| A | = Agriculture | D | = Demographics | ☻ = Energy | ? | = Future | L | = Labor | S = Spiritual |
| ☛ | = Animal Rights | ♿ | = Disabled | E = Environment | G | = Gay/Lesbian | M | = Media | T = Third World |
| ✐ | = Arts | $ | = Economics | ♥ = Family | H | = Health | ✌ | = Peace | ✈ = Travel |
| ( | = Computers | ✍ | = Education | F = Feminism | J | = Justice | P | = Politics | U = Urban |

**J ▶ A.C.L.U. News**
1663 Mission St., 4th Fl.
San Francisco, CA 94103
**Affiliation:** American Civil Liberties Union. **Concern(s):** justice; civil liberties; freedom of expression. This periodical reports on violations of civil liberties from around the country and the efforts of people to combat them. The ACLU has recently been criticized for defending Nazis and KKK members as fundamentally critical to protecting the rights of all.

**L ▶ AALC Reporter**
1400 K St. NW, #700
Washington, DC 20005 (202)789-1020
**Affiliation:** African-American Labor Center/AFL-CIO. **Concern(s):** labor; justice; peace; jobs; minority rights; conflict resolution; unions. "Greater solidarity with labor in the Black community and more attention to that community's concerns within the labor movement are the goals. Reporting on cooperative work with groups such as the NAACP and on upcoming meetings on labor-Black issues is included in this newsletter." -C.C. **Est.:** 1965. **Frequency:** 6/yr. **Price:** Free. **Contact(s):** J. Sarr.

**✍ ▶ Access**
American Forum for Global Education
45 John St., #1200
New York, NY 10038 (212)732-8606
**Affiliation:** American Forum for Global Education. **Concern(s):** education; global understanding. A newsletter published with The Alliance for Education in Global and International Studies (AEGIS) and the International Exchange Association, Inc. (IEA).

**T ▶ Accion International Bulletin**
130 Prospect St.
Cambridge, MA 02139 (617)492-4930
**Affiliation:** Accion International. **Concern(s):** Third World; education; economics; development; hunger; community self-reliance; research. A quarterly update on the work of micro-enterprise assistance agencies throughout Latin America. The Bulletin provides background information on countries, statistics on programs, and case studies. **Est.:** 1970. **Fax:** (617)876-9509. **Contact(s):** Gabriela Romanow (Director of Communications), Elizabeth Rosenberg (Publications).

**T ▶ ACOA Action News**
198 Broadway
New York, NY 10038 (212)962-1210
**Affiliation:** American Committee on Africa. **Concern(s):** Third World; justice; Africa. "A little newsletter, this one is primarily a support organ for this committee. The work of the group is good and deserves support, but more comprehensive African freedom periodicals are available." -C.C. **Est.:** 1953. **Frequency:** 2/yr. **Subscription:** $5, $15 institution. **Price:** $.75/ea. **Contact(s):** Gail Hovey.

**A ▶ Acres USA, A Voice For Eco-Agriculture**
Box 9547
Kansas City, MO 64133 (816)737-0064
**Concern(s):** agriculture; environment; health; organic; hazardous/toxic waste; sustainability; pesticides. A journal about biological agriculture. Technology, economics, public policy and current events. Emphasizes producing quality food without using toxic chemicals. **Other Resources:** Send for free book catalog. **Frequency:** 12/yr. **Subscription:** $17/yr.; / $31/2 yrs; $45/3 yrs. **Price:** $2.30/ea. **Office:** 10008 East 60th Terrace, Kansas City, MO 64133.

**✌ ▶ Across Frontiers**
Box 2382
Berkeley, CA 94702
**Concern(s):** peace; East Europe. Newsletter of East European opposition. Covers important developments which are not covered elsewhere. **Frequency:** 4/yr. **Subscription:** $10/yr. **Price:** $2.50/ea.

**H ▶ Action Alert**
1001 Connecticut Ave. NW
Washington, DC 20036 (202)569-5930

**Affiliation:** Public Voice for Food and Health Policy. **Concern(s):** health; environment; agriculture; nutrition; hazardous/toxic waste; policy. Periodic bulletins on the food and health policies of the US government.

**T ▶ Action Alert**
475 Riverside Dr., #712
New York, NY 10115 (212)870-2922
**Affiliation:** Task Force on Militarization in Asia and the Pacific/ National Council of Churches. **Concern(s):** Third World; peace; spiritual; Third World; faith; activism; Asia; indigenous peoples. "A newsletter with several short news articles that cover the region in a pleasantly partisan manner." -C.C. **Est.:** 1977. **Frequency:** 4/yr. **Subscription:** Donation. **Price:** Free. **Contact(s):** Christopher Candland.

**E ▶ Action Bulletin**
Box 926
Arlington, VA 22216 (703)276-7070
**Affiliation:** Citizens Clearinghouse for Hazardous Wastes. **Concern(s):** environment; health; hazardous/toxic waste. "Tips on stopping careless transportation and storage of hazardous wastes are presented. A state-by-state news section on this subject, along with a complete resources section, makes this action bulletin a good source of information for curbing hazardous waste problems." -C.C. **Est.:** 1981. **Dues:** $15/yr. **Frequency:** 4/yr. **Subscription:** Membership. **Price:** $1/ea.

**✌ ▶ Action Linkage Networker**
5825 Telegraph Ave.
Oakland, CA 94609 (510)654-4819
**Affiliation:** Action Linkage. **Concern(s):** peace; networking; conflict resolution. "Networking by Action Linkage is commended for making a special contribution to global cultural change. 'Place to Link' and other components of this newsletter make it an essential aid to global cooperation." -C.C. **Est.:** 1986. **Dues:** $20/yr. **Frequency:** 12/yr. **Subscription:** Membership. **Price:** $.37/ea. **Contact(s):** Ann Weiser.

**P ▶ Activist Journal**
15 Dutch St., #500
New York, NY 10038-3708 (312)752-3562
**Affiliation:** Democratic Socialist of America, Youth Section. **Concern(s):** politics; health; justice; feminism; demographics; Democratic Socialism; sexism; poverty. Articles should be submitted on DOS or Mac disk, no longer than 1,500 words. Contributions are generally only accepted from members of the DSA Youth Section, though specialized contributors writing about current affairs, and student politics in particular, will be considered. We would like to receive books and magazines for review on: student and youth politics, foreign and domestic policy, urban poverty, national health insurance, racism, feminism, gay and lesbian issues, socialism. **Est.:** 1979. **Frequency:** 4/yr. **Subscription:** $8/yr. **Price:** $1/ea. **Pages:** 40. **Circ.:** 3M. **Contact(s):** J. Hughes (Editor).

**P ▶ ADA Today**
1511 K St. NW
Washington, DC 20005 (202)638-6447
**Affiliation:** Americans for Democratic Action. **Concern(s):** politics; law; analysis. "This is one of the oldest legislative public interest groups and is still active, though not a lone liberal voice in the wilderness as it was for many years in the Congress. It summarizes legislative moves and political developments." -C.C. **Est.:** 1947. **Frequency:** 4/yr. **Subscription:** $20/yr. **Price:** $5/ea. **Contact(s):** Donita Hicks.

**✌ ▶ ADPSR News**
225 Lafayette St., #205
New York, NY 10012 (212)431-3756
**Affiliation:** Architects, Designers, and Planners for Social Responsibility. **Concern(s):** peace; disarmament. "The planners are designing not only buildings but social progress campaigns under the auspices of this social action association. The primary goal of the eight-page newsletter is to help curb the nuclear arms race, but related points are discussed." - C.C. **Est.:** 1984. **Frequency:** 2-3/yr. **Subscription:** Donation. **Price:** Free. **Contact(s):** Kevin Gerard.

**✌ ▶ The Advocate**
HCR2 Box 25
Panhandle, TX 79068 (806)335-1715
**Affiliation:** Red River Peace Network. **Concern(s):** peace; justice; disarmament; anti-nuclear; nonviolence; civil disobedience; economic conversion. A journal for peace and justice published by the Peace Farm, a community working to end the nuclear arms race and address social concerns and located across the highway from the Pantex nuclear weapons plant, which is the final assembly point for all US nuclear warheads. **Frequency:** 3-6/yr. **Subscription:** $5/yr. **Price:** $1/ea. **Pages:** 16-24. **Circ.:** 2M. **Contact(s):** Ellen Barfield (Coordinator), Les Breeding (Editor). (806)376-1309.

**D ▶ Advocate**
Route 2, Box 150 B
GazsMils, WI 54631
**Affiliation:** Rural Network. **Concern(s):** demographics; agriculture; economics; health; networking; rural relocation. Questions, answers and comments from the Network. **Other Resources:** Contact service. **Price:** $1/sample.

**E ▶ Aerovironment**
1787 Columbia Rd. NW, 3rd Fl.
Washington, DC 20009 (202)387-1434
**Affiliation:** Institute for Transportation and Development Policy. **Concern(s):** environment; energy; transportation; planning. Newsletter. **Contact(s):** Paul McCready (Chairman).

**✍ ▶ AERO-Gram**
Alternative Education Resource Organization
417 Roslyn Rd.
Roslyn, NY 11577
**Concern(s):** education; childhood. Newsletter containing inside, up-to-date information on alternative schools and communities throughout the US and around the world. Edited by Jerry Mintz, who has been actively involved in alternative education for over 20 years. (He is also an independent consultant assisting parents and others wanting to start new alternative schools.)

**$ ▶ Affirms**
NextStep Publications
6340 34 Ave. SW
Seattle, WA 98126
**Concern(s):** economics.

**T ▶ Africa News**
Box 3851
Durham, NC 27702 (919)286-0747
**Affiliation:** Africa News Service. **Concern(s):** Third World; Africa. "Information addresses movements for improving society in Africa, with intense coverage of southern Africa. Liberation struggles, reform efforts and solidarity drives are all covered in this useful biweekly magazine." -C.C. Nonprofit. **Frequency:** 26/yr. **Subscription:** $30/yr.; $48 institution. **Circ.:** 3.5M. **Contact(s):** Reed Kramer.

**T ▶ Africa Recovery**
DPI Rm S0805
United Nations
New York, NY 10017 (212)963-6857
**Concern(s):** Third World; demographics; justice; Africa; development. This journal deals with the steps needed to bring about economic recovery to the continent of Africa. It attacks the World Bank by reporting its failure to face the problems of mounting debts, though it has positive things to say about its return to an investment policy based more on human need than profit.

**T ▶ Africa Report**
833 UN Plaza
New York, NY 10017 (212)949-5666
**Concern(s):** Third World; Africa. Well-researched articles by specialists, with photos, on current African affairs. **Contact(s):** Margaret A. Novicki (Editor).

**D ▸ African Farmer**
c/o The Hunger Project
1 Madison Ave.
New York, NY 10038 (212)532-4255
**Affiliation:** Hunger Project. **Concern(s):** demographics; Third World; hunger; Africa. Features the voices of small-scale farmers whose productivity is essential to ending hunger in Africa. The magazine is designed to foster a dialogue between farmers and the individuals who shape agricultural policy in Africa. Nonprofit. **Frequency:** 26/yr. **Pages:** 50-60. **Other:** 1388 Sutter St., San Francisco, CA 94109-5452.

**M ▸ Afterimage**
31 Prince St.
Rochester, NY 14607 (716)442-8676
**Affiliation:** Visual Studies Workshop. **Concern(s):** media; arts; culture; film. "Films, videos and photography are viewed from a people's perspective in this lively tabloid newspaper. "El Salvador on Film" was the cover story of one issue. Highly recommended for all involved with producing visual images." -C.C. **Est.:** 1972. **Frequency:** 10/yr. **Subscription:** $28, $32 institution. **Contact(s):** David Trend.

**P ▸ Against the Current**
7012 Michigan Ave.
Detroit, MI 48210
**Affiliation:** Center for Changes. **Concern(s):** politics; justice. "A journal focusing on movements for social and political change in the US and internationally. The magazine explores labor, feminist, environmentalist, race, and class issues from the perspective of 'Socialism from Below'. It is published in order to promote dialogue among activists, organizers, and serious scholars on the left." - C.W. **Frequency:** 6/yr. **Subscription:** $18/yr.; $25 institution. **Circ.:** 2.5M.

**P ▸ Agenda**
Agenda Publications
202 E. Washington #512
Ann Arbor, MI 48104
**Concern(s):** politics; education; grassroots organizing; networking; students. Since Ann Arbor is a college town, it goes beyond its community coverage to reflect some of the recent ferment on campuses across the country.

**S ▸ Agenda In Brief**
64 Fulton St., #1100
New York, NY 10038 (212)227-5885
**Affiliation:** New Jewish Agenda. **Concern(s):** spiritual; peace; justice; politics; faith. This newsletter deals with the issues that effect the New Jewish Agenda. It reports on developments, controversies and policies that the NJA attacks and issues pertaining to women's rights, Israel, anti-Semitism, labor and world Jewry.

**A ▸ Agriculture Employment Bulletin**
2607 T St.
Vancouver, WA 98861 (206)693-6439
**Concern(s):** agriculture; labor; jobs. Features guest-opinion and editorial articles on agricultural employment trends, job opportunities, resources, and helps. Contains 60-90 job listings per month in all areas of agriculture and agribusiness, including horticulture, research, extension, marketing, development, government, organic, sales, and more. Nation-wide listings. Job announcements are free to subscribing employers; position wanted announcements are free to individual subscribers. **Other Resources:** Resume assistance. Publishes brochures, flyers, reports, directories, business presentations, etc. **Est.:** 1989. **Frequency:** 26/yr. **Subscription:** $65, $80 nonprofit, $130 business. **Price:** $5/ea. **Pages:** 12-14. **Circ.:** 1M. **Publisher:** same. **Other Formats:** Listing of employers who placed job listings in the AE Bulletin in 1990. **Fax:** (206)693-6439. **Contact(s):** Brent Searle (Publisher/Editor), Jill Searle (Assistant Editor).

**E ▸ Ahbleza**
Southern Willamette Alliance
454 Willamette St.
Eugene, OR 97401
**Affiliation:** Southern Williamette Alliance. **Concern(s):** environment.

**H ▸ AIDS News**
POCAAN
814 NE 40th St.
Seattle, WA 98105
**Concern(s):** health; AIDS. A newsletter about personal responsibility and our multicultural bouillabaisse, not just AIDS. It is a comic book. **Contact(s):** Leonard Rifas.

**J ▸ AIM Magazine**
Box 20554
Chicago, IL 60620 (312)874-6184
**Concern(s):** justice; civil liberties. Short stories are the main attraction in this civil rights literary and cultural review. Black history, poetry, books, and national concerns are all dealt with in this functional periodical. Through the written word, to purge racism from the human blood stream and to encourage new writers to write. **Other Resources:** "Once a year we sponsor a short story contest. The 3 best are awarded $100. The best (two) receive $50. We also sponsor essay contests. Subject matter stem from top news items." **Est.:** 1974. **Frequency:** 4/yr. **Subscription:** $8/yr. **Price:** $2/ea. **Bulk:** 10% off/24. **Pages:** 48. **Circ.:** 7M. **Contact(s):** Ruth Apilado (Editor/Publisher), Dr. Myron Apilado (Managing Editor).

**J ▸ Akwesasne Notes**
Box 196, Via Rooseveltown
New York, NY 13655 (518)358-9531
**Affiliation:** Mohawk Nation. **Concern(s):** justice; cultural integrity; Native Americans. "For some 20 years this newspaper has effectively defended the rights and heritage of Native Americans. It is the best source of news for this nationalities group. All aspects of Indian life and related concerns are included. A high quality newspaper on Native issues in the US and Canada." - C.C. **Est.:** 1968. **Frequency:** 6/yr. **Subscription:** $15/yr. **Contact(s):** Doug George-Kanentiio.

**T ▸ Al Fajr Palestinian Weekly**
16 Cromwell St.
Hempstead, NY 11550
**Concern(s):** Third World; Mid-East. **Frequency:** Weekly. **Price:** $.50/ea.

**T ▸ Alert!: Focus on Central America**
Box 12056
Washington, DC 20005 (202)265-0890
**Affiliation:** Committee In Solidarity with People of El Salvador. **Concern(s):** Third World; Central America. "This newspaper is one of the most useful periodicals on Central America. The region from Belize to Nicaragua is covered, often with reporters from the front lines of conflict. Highly recommended." -C.C. **Est.:** 1983. **Frequency:** 10/yr. **Subscription:** $10/yr. **Price:** $.75/ea. **Contact(s):** Mike Zielinski.

**H ▸ Alive and Well on Planet Earth**
400 W. 43rd St.
New York, NY 10036 (212)967-2587
**Concern(s):** health; nutrition; vegetarian. Journal shows alternate lifestyles for meat eaters. Has great vegetarian recipes and facts on nutrition. **Frequency:** 6/yr.

**T ▸ Alliance Report**
Box 43208
Washington, DC 20010 (202)462-8197
**Affiliation:** National Alliance of Third World Journalists. **Concern(s):** Third World; media; journalism. "Journalists of color have united to advance effectively the cause of people's journalism for Third World countries. They are proudly partisan, publicizing the truth about South Africa and in the same issue exposing bias in Boston journalism. The 28-page issue reviews and covers the personalities and institutions of journalism in a professional style."-C.C. **Est.:** 1981. **Frequency:** 4/yr. **Subscription:** $10/yr. **Price:** $1/ea. **Pages:** 28. **Office:** 1419 V St. NW Washington, DC 20009. **Contact(s):** John Woodford.

**✏ ▸ Alternate Roots**
1083 Austin Ave. NE
Atlanta, GA 30307 (404)577-1079
**Affiliation:** Alternate Roots. **Concern(s):** arts; justice; environment; theater; culture; activism. A newsletter that reports on the mission of its parent organization by the same name. The newsletter reports on community-based performing art which is rooted in a particular community of place, tradition, or spirit. It is also committed to social and economic justice and the protection of the natural world. The newsletter also provides upcoming events list and a member directory. **Est.:** 1985. **Frequency:** 4/yr. **Price:** Free. **Other Formats:** Modem: (404) 577-7991). **Contact(s):** Kathie de Nobriga (Executive Director), Greg Carraway (Administrative Assistant).

**A ▸ Alternative Agriculture News**
9200 Edmonston Rd.
Greenbelt, MD 20770 (301)441-8777
**Affiliation:** Institute for Alternative Agriculture. **Concern(s):** agriculture; environment; sustainability. A newsletter that focuses on the actions of the Institute. Informative articles, newsbriefs, and tips on farming. **Frequency:** 12/yr.

**E ▸ Alternative Transportation News**
720 Brooks Ave.
Venice, CA 90291 (310)396-1527
**Affiliation:** Earthmind. **Concern(s):** environment; energy; transportation; conservation; preservation. Discusses alternative means of transportation and the implications that this would have for the environment. **Est.:** 1972.

**P ▸ Alternatives**
Journals Fulfillment Department
Butterworths, 80 Montvale
Stoneham, MA 02180
**Concern(s):** politics; justice; policy. **Frequency:** 4/yr. **Price:** $18/ea.

**P ▸ Alternatives: Social Transformation and Humane Governance**
475 Riverside Dr.
New York, NY 10025 (212)870-2391
**Affiliation:** World Order Models Project. **Concern(s):** politics; Third World; justice; policy; law; world order; grassroots organizing. "Alternatives is an international policy journal predicated on the principles of individual dignity, justice, and the right to participate in decision-making. It may be of interest to the scholar or theoretician in human relations." -C.C. **Est.:** 1975. **Frequency:** 4/yr. **Subscription:** $18, $36 institution. **Price:** $5.95/ea. **Contact(s):** Dhirubhai Sheth, Saul H. Mendlovitz

**E ▸ The Alternator**
The Alter Project
Slippery Rock University
Slippery Rock, PA 16057 (412)794-7397
**Affiliation:** NAP (North American Permaculture); The Alter Project. **Concern(s):** environment; energy; agriculture; education; permaculture; conservation; sustainability; appropriate technology; hazardous /toxic; pesticides; alterantives. ALTER = Alternative Living Technologies and Energy Research. This newsletter describes the general concerns of the Alter Project, the formal activity of the University which is non-petrochemical agriculture and alternative energy production. We have demonstration sites in both. Master's degree in sustainable systems. Three tracks: 1) Sustainable Agriculture; 2) Sustainable Natural Resource Management; 3) Built Environmental Allergy free - non toxic. **Frequency:** 4/yr. **Subscription:** $13/yr. **Pages:** 24. **Circ.:** 800. **Contact(s):** Dr. Robert A. Macoskey (Director), Mrs. Janie McFarland (Executive Secretary). (412)794-7322.

**J ▸ American Atheist**
Box 140195
Austin, TX 78714-0195
**Concern(s):** justice; politics; media; civil liberties; anti-authoritarian; activism; freedom of expression. "...focuses on subjects of particular concern or interest to Atheists: state/church separation and relations, religious history and criticism, the history of Atheism, and the Atheist lifestyle. It also reports on current Atheist activism." **Frequency:** 12/yr. **Subscription:** $25/yr. **Price:** Free sample. **Office:** 7215 Cameron Rd. #C Austin, TX 78752-2973.

**E ▸ The American Biology Teacher**
11250 Roger Bacon Dr., #19
Reston, VA 22090 (703)471-1134
**Affiliation:** National Association of Biology Teachers. **Concern(s):** environment; education; science. A nationally recognized journal that highlights research findings, innovative teaching strategies, laboratory exercises and reviews publications, computer programs and videos.

**✌ ▸ American Council for the UN University Newsletter**
4421 Garrison St. NW
Washington, DC 20016-4055 (202)686-5179
**Affiliation:** American Council for the UN University. **Concern(s):** peace; education; health; environment; economics; conflict resolution; nutrition; conservation. "Newsletter covers research conclusions, book announcements, conferences, and other activities of the United Nations University headquarter in Tokyo that administers a decentralized network of scholars on world problems in peace studies, nutrition, environment, technology, economics, and other areas of concern to the UN. The organization was established in 1975." - C.C. **Other Resources:** Seminars, information referrals to Americans and Canadians to UNCL information, WIP - Work in programs sent with newsletter - WIP is the publication from Tokyo. **Est.:** 1979. **Frequency:** 4/yr. **Subscription:** $25/yr. **Bulk:** 50% off/24. **Pages:** 16. **Circ.:** 5.5M. **Labels:** 5500. **E-Network:** Econet and Unison. **ID:** 'jglenn'. **Fax:** (202)289-4267. **Contact(s):** Jerome C. Glenn (Executive Director).

**D ▸ American Demographics**
Box 58184
Boulder, CO 80322-8184 (607)273-6343
**Affiliation:** American Demographics. **Concern(s):** demographics; media; economics; planning; analysis; research; trade; press. A magazine explicitly for business executives, market researchers, me-

dia and communications people, and public policy makers. Explains demographic trends and changes, and how to interpret the figures. "Writers should have clear understanding of specific population trends and their implications for business and planning." Perhaps not always progressive, but indispensable. **Est.:** 1978. **Frequency:** 12/yr. **Subscription:** $58/yr. **Price:** $5/ea. **Circ.:** 35M. **Contact(s):** Cheryl Russel (Editor-in-chief), Caroline Arthur (Managing Editor). **Other:** Box 68, Ithaca, NY 14851

**♥ ◆ American Family**
1221 Massachusetts Ave. NW
Washington, DC 20005  (202)638-2144
**Affiliation:** Youth Policy Institute. **Concern(s):** family; education; child support; day care; childhood. "National policy on families with a focus on child care is the subject of this newsletter. Related subjects such as the Head Start Program are found in this 24-page magazine." -C.C. **Est.:** 1979. **Frequency:** 11/yr. **Subscription:** $55/yr. **Price:** $6/ea. **Contact(s):** Lisa Herendeen.

**A ◆ American Farmland**
American Farmland Trust
1920 N St. NW, #400
Washington, DC 20036  (202)659-5170
**Affiliation:** American Farmland Trust. **Concern(s):** agriculture; economics; farmland. "...quarterly award-winning magazine of the American Farmland Trust (AFT). Compelling text and color photography present the latest information on the challenges confronting agricultural resources and the techniques being used to save them. A must for all who care about farmland." Nonprofit. **Dues:** $15/yr. **Frequency:** 4/yr. **Subscription:** Membership. **Member:** Global Tomorrow Coalition. **Contact(s):** Ralph E. Grossi.

**E ◆ American Forests**
1516 P St. NW
Washington, DC 20005  (202)667-3300
**Concern(s):** environment; forests. A magazine that presents the latest issues, lifestyles, how-to formulas, adventures and travel about forests, forestry, forest policy including nature guides. **Est.:** 1894. **Frequency:** 6/yr. **Subscription:** $24/yr. **Price:** $2.50/ea. **Pages:** 80. **Circ.:** 26M. **Contact(s):** Bill Rooney (Editor), Norah Deakin Davis (Managing Editor). **Other:** Box 2000, Washington, DC 20013

**⚹ ◆ American Friends Service Committee Newsletter**
2160 Lake St.
San Francisco, CA 94121
**Affiliation:** American Friends Service Committee. **Concern(s):** peace; justice; spiritual; militarism; anti-draft; activism; nonviolence; disarmament. interfaith. This newsletter reports on the activities of AFSC, a group founded by Quakers at the turn-of-the-century but now functioning as an interfaith organization. Their major issues is peace, disarmament, anti-draft, social justice and economic conversion.

**E ◆ American Hiker**
1776 Massachusetts Ave. NW
Washington, DC 20036  (202)833-8229
**Affiliation:** American Hiking Society. **Concern(s):** environment; recreation. A magazine of hiking and the outdoors, a voice in the halls of Congress that has federal land managers nationwide. **Frequency:** 4/yr. **Subscription:** $6/yr. **Price:** $1/ea. **Contact(s):** Louise Marshall (President).

**J ◆ American Indian Law Newsletter**
U.N.M. School of Law
1117 Stanford, NE, Box 4456
Albuquerque, NM 87102(505)277-5462
**Affiliation:** American Indian Law Center. **Concern(s):** justice; politics; Native Americans. "Legislative defense of Native American civil rights is promoted here. Legal strategies and congressional legislation affecting tribes and individual Indians are explained." -C.C. **Est.:** 1968. **Frequency:** 6/yr. **Subscription:** $20/yr. **Price:** $4.50/ea. **Contact(s):** Marc Mannes.

**A ◆ American Journal of Alternative Agriculture**
9200 Edmonston Rd., #117
Greenbelt, MD 20770  (301)441-8777
**Affiliation:** Institute for Alternative Agriculture. **Concern(s):** agriculture; environment; sustainability; family farms; farmland; food production/distribution. This journal reports on the alternative ways that exists for farmers to use. Alternatives to pesticides, government subsidies, etc. It provides an outlet for interdisciplinary research reviews and reports concerned with the development and improvement of low-input farming systems. Articles range from agronomy to agriculture policy and economics, by dedicated and leading scientists and research administrators. **Dues:** $30/yr. includes Journal and Newsletter. **Frequency:** 4/yr. **Contact(s):** Garth Youndberg (Editor).

**⚹ ◆ American Journal of International Law**
2223 Massachusetts Ave. NW
Washington, DC 20008  (202)265-4313
**Affiliation:** American Society of International Law. **Concern(s):** peace; justice; conflict resolution; international law. "Promotes resolution of international conflict through law and the legal process rather than might and force." -C.C. **Est.:** 1906. **Frequency:** 4/yr. **Subscription:** $50/yr. **Price:** $15.00/ea. **Contact(s):** Thomas M. Franck.

**H ◆ American Journal of Public Health**
1015 15th St. NW
Washington, DC 20005  (202)789-5600
**Affiliation:** American Public Health Association. **Concern(s):** health; public health. Covers all aspects of public health science and practice. **Contact(s):** Seiko Baba Brodbeck.

**L ◆ American Labor**
2000 P St. NW
Washington, DC 20036  (202)828-5170
**Affiliation:** American Labor Education Center. **Concern(s):** labor. "Each issue of this 8-page newsletter revolves around a theme. Strike strategy, press relations, job safety, and organizing techniques are four previous themes. Single and bulk copies of past issues can be ordered." -C.C. **Est.:** 1979. **Frequency:** Irregular. **Subscription:** $9.95/yr. **Price:** $1.65/ea. **Contact(s):** Matt Witt.

**P ◆ The American Prospect**
Box 7645
Princeton, NJ 08543-7645
**Concern(s):** politics; future. A new liberal political and social science magazine that is trying to reshape the liberal agenda. Deals with pressing national issues of the day and features such well noted writers as Robert Kuttner. Solution oriented. **Frequency:** 4/yr. **Subscription:** $25/yr.

**M ◆ American Right to Read Newsletter**
568 Broadway
New York, NY 10012   (212)255-4009
**Affiliation:** PEN American Center. **Concern(s):** media; justice; civil liberties; freedom of expression; censorship. "Censorship is fought with articles on issues such as book-banning attempts. Civil libertarians and library advocates will be interested." -C.C. **Est.:** 1970. **Frequency:** 4/yr. **Price:** Free. **Contact(s):** Harold Marcus.

**✎ ◆ The American Scholar**
1811 Q St. NW
Washington, DC 20009  (202)265-3808
**Concern(s):** arts; education; politics; science. Articles on science, politics, literature, the arts, etc. Book reviews. **Contact(s):** Joseph Epstein (Editor).

**J ◆ American Visions**
Box 51200
Boulder, CO 80321-1200
**Affiliation:** Membership Data Center. **Concern(s):** justice; politics; arts; diversity. "The Magazine of Afro-American Culture." **Frequency:** 6/yr. **Subscription:** $18/yr.

**✎ ◆ The American Voice**
332 West Broadway, #1215
Louisville, KY 40202   (502)562-0045
**Concern(s):** arts; literature. "...is one of the liveliest magazines to appear in the US in recent years... exceptional for its range and quality." - Frank Macshane. Stories, poems, and essays by daring new writers and such established writers as Kay Boyle, Chaim Potok, Doris Grumbach, Joy Harjo. "Impressive... ambitious." -Small Press. **Est.:** 1984. **Frequency:** 4/yr. **Subscription:** $12/yr. **Price:** $5/sample. **Contact(s):** Frederick Smock, Sallie Bingham.

**E ◆ Amicus Journal**
40 West 20 St.
New York, NY 10011   (212)727-2700
**Affiliation:** Natural Resource Defense Council. **Concern(s):** environment; health; natural resources; hazardous/toxic waste. The award-winning publication of the Council. Covers national and international environmental policy and has been called "The leading journal of environmental thought and opinion". Nonprofit. **Dues:** $10/yr. **Frequency:** 4/yr. **Subscription:** Membership. **Price:** $4/ea. **Fax:** (212)727-1773. **Contact(s):** Francesca Liman (Editor), Elizabeth Hansen (Assistant Editor). **Other:** Natural Resource Defense Council, 1350 New York Ave. NW, Washington, DC 20005.

**J ◆ Amnesty Action**
322 8th Ave.
New York, NY 10001   (212)807-8400
**Affiliation:** Amnesty International. **Concern(s):** justice. "Serious concerns about torture and rights violations of political prisoners are covered here. Emphasis is on prisoners of conscience adopted by the

sponsoring organization and on organizational news."-C.C. **Est.:** 1966. **Frequency:** 6/yr. **Subscription:** $25/yr. **Price:** $4/ea. **Contact(s):** Ron Lajoie.

**J ◆ Amnesty International Orange County Newsletter**
14 Autumn Hill Lane
Laguna Hills, CA 92653  (714)752-2297 (W)
**Affiliation:** Amnesty International. **Concern(s):** justice; political prisoners; capital punishment. An international organization dedicated to the immediate unconditional release of all prisoners of conscience, fair prompt trials for political prisoners and the abolishment of all torture and capital punishment. Prisoners of conscience are persons who have been imprisoned solely for their religion, political affiliations, race, etc., who have never used nor advocated the use of violence. Groups all over the world gather together to write letters on behalf of these prisoners. **Contact(s):** Sandra Gardner. (714)643-8221.

**P ◆ Anarchy**
Box 1446
Columbia, MO 65205-1446  (314)442-4352
**Concern(s):** politics; anti-authoritarian. "...is A Journal of Desire Armed! Neither left nor right, we're just uncompromisingly anti-authoritarian. We reject all ideology because we want to create a genuinely free alternative vision - radically cooperative and communitarian, ecological and feminist, spontaneous and wild - a liberatory vision free from the constraints of our own human self-domestication. For those who haven't given up on their most intimate and bold desires!" Nominated for UTNE READER's '90 Alternative Press Awards. **Est.:** 1980. **Frequency:** 4/yr. **Subscription:** $12/yr. **Price:** $2/ea. **Pages:** 44.

**H ◆ Anima, An Experimental Journal**
1053 Wilson Ave.
Chambersburg, PA 17201   (717)263-8303
**Concern(s):** health; spiritual; feminism; arts; transformation; psychology; research; analysis. "...celebrates the sources of our separate identity in the common soul of us all. Authors from the Teilhard Research Institute and the Foundation for Mind Research; anthropologists, musicologists, and philosophers explore frontiers of awareness between fields of conventional scholarship. Articles on Eastern religion, Jungian psychology, and human wholeness present a cross-cultural perspective centered on the question of creativity in a cultural source... a physical example of its themes." **Est.:** 1974. **Frequency:** 2/yr. **Subscription:** $9.95/yr. **Price:** $5.95/ea. **Bulk:** 40% off 24. **Pages:** 72. **Circ.:** 1M+. **Contact(s):** Harry Buck, Barbara D. Rotz.

**🐦 ◆ Animal Activist Alert**
2100 L St. NW
Washington, DC 20037  (202)452-1100
**Affiliation:** Humane Society of the US. **Concern(s):** environment; animal rights. A newsletter for members of the Action Alert Team which covers the Humane Society's actions throughout this country. **Frequency:** 4/yr. **Price:** Free.

**🐦 ◆ Animal Experiments Are a Dying Tradition**
Anti-Vivisection Society
801 Old York Rd., #204
Jenkintown, PA 19046-1685     (215)887-0816
**Affiliation:** Anti-Vivisection Society. **Concern(s):** environment; animal rights. "But some traditions die hard. Join us in our fight to end the exploitation of animals in research, testing and education, and find out why the use of animals in experiments is scientifically unsound as well as ethically objectionable." **Dues:** $10/yr. **Frequency:** 11/yr. **Subscription:** Membership.

**E ◆ Animal Kingdom**
New York Zoological Park
Bronx, NY 10460
**Affiliation:** Wildlife Conservation International. **Concern(s):** environment; wildlife/endangered species. A magazine with excellent coverage of international wildlife conservation. **Frequency:** 6/yr. **Subscription:** $14.95/yr.

**🐦 ◆ Animal's Agenda**
Box 6809
Syracuse, NY 13217   (203)452-0446
**Affiliation:** Animal Rights Network. **Concern(s):** environment; animal rights. A magazine providing a broad range of information about animals and environmental issues, providing a forum for discussion of problems and ideas. It seeks to reach people at all levels of consciousness and commitment to inspire a deep regard for and greater activism on behalf of animals and nature. Nonprofit. **Est.:** 1980. **Frequency:** 10/yr. **Subscription:** $22/yr. **Price:** $2.75/ea. **Bulk:** 45% off/24. **Pages:** 64. **Circ.:** 30M. **Publisher:** Animal Rights Network, Inc. **Labels:** 13000. **Office:** 456 Monroe Turnpike Monroe, CT 06468. **Fax:** (203)452-9543. **Contact(s):** Kim Bartlett (Editor).

### ☂ ♦ The Animal's Voice
3961 Landmark St.
Culver City, CA 90232

**Affiliation:** Compassion For Animals Foundation. **Concern(s):** environment; animal rights. "...the award-winning international magazine of animal defense issues. This nationally acclaimed animal rights magazine received mainstream recognition by being nominated for four consumer honors including the 1989 Magie Award for Best Overall issue in a social/political category. An aggressive, hard-hitting animal rights publication that offers you the most comprehensive and authoritative resource for animal defense issues." **Frequency:** 6/yr. **Subscription:** $18/yr. **Price:** $3/ea.

### ☂ ♦ Animalines
814 Castro St.
San Francisco, CA 94114   (415)826-7658

**Concern(s):** environment; education; animal rights; wildlife/endangered species. Addresses animal protection issues from an ecological perspective, viewing all beings as indispensable threads of a living tapestry - interconnected to each other and to all the natural processes that sustain life. It focuses on the need for humane education programs to present a larger and more unified vision, a vision capable of exciting young people and challenging their fertile minds. **Contact(s):** Edward S. Duvin (Editor).

### ☂ ♦ Animals
Massachusetts Society for the Prevention of Cruelty
to Animals
350 S. Huntington Ave.
Boston, MA 02130

**Affiliation:** Massachusetts Society for the Prevention of Cruelty to Animals. **Concern(s):** environment; animal rights; conservation; wildlife/endangered species. Informative, well-researched articles on animal welfare and pet care, conservation, international wildlife, and environmental issues affecting animals; no personal accounts or favorite pet stories.

### ☂ ♦ Animals International
Box 190
Boston, MA 02130

**Affiliation:** World Society for the Protection of Animals. **Concern(s):** environment; wildlife/endangered species; animal rights. Magazine.

### E ♦ Annals of Earth
10 Shanks Pond Rd.
Falmouth, MA 02540   (508)540-6801

**Affiliation:** Ocean Arks International. **Concern(s):** environment; sustainability. "Dedicated to cultural transformation and ecological sustainability. Philosophical and environmental issues come with earthy pragmatism. Edited by Nancy Jack Todd. Contributors include: Ralph Abraham, Wendell Berry, Wes Jackson, James Lovelock, Lynn Margulis, Dorian Sagan, Kirkpatrick Sale, William Irwin Thompson, John Todd, Nancy Jack Todd. Reports on the work of Ocean Arks and Lindisfarne Association." **Frequency:** 3/yr. **Subscription:** $15/yr.

### E ♦ Annual Policy Review
Resources for the Future
1616 P St. NW
Washington, DC 20036   (202)328-5025

**Affiliation:** Resources for the Future (National Center for Food & Agricultural Policy). **Concern(s):** environment; agriculture; natural resources; food production. Addresses a policy issue or set of issues in considerable depth.

### ✍ ♦ Anthropology and Humanism Quarterly
1703 New Hampshire Ave. NW
Washington, DC 20009   (504)388-5942

**Affiliation:** American Anthropological Association. **Concern(s):** education; justice. "Using humanistic thinking in their discipline, these anthropologists make the human endeavor the point of their work. Their publication is written in a down-to-earth style that the anthropology students as well as the professional will enjoy reading." **Est.:** 1974. **Frequency:** 4/yr. **Subscription:** $25/yr. **Price:** $2/ea. **Publisher:** Geoscience Publications. **Contact(s):** Miles Richardson. (202)232-8800.

### ♅ ♦ The Anti-Draft
731 State St.
Madison, WI 53703   (608)257-7562

**Affiliation:** Committee Against Registration and the Draft. **Concern(s):** peace; militarism; anti-draft. "This peace newsletter is the best national periodical on the military draft. Its draft focus is rounded with a useful literature list and articles on US military adventures." -C.C. **Est.:** 1979. **Frequency:** 6/yr. **Subscription:** $10/yr. **Price:** $1/ea. **Contact(s):** Gillam Kerley.

### T ♦ ANC Weekly News Briefing
801 Second Ave., #405
New York, NY 10017   (212)490-3487

**Affiliation:** African National Congress of South Africa. **Concern(s):** Third World; South Africa. "Democracy through majority rule in South Africa is advocated in the dozen-odd pages of this newspaper. A political solution to the problem of white minority rule over the Black South African majority is preferred." -C.C. **Est.:** 1981. **Frequency:** 26/yr. **Subscription:** $20/yr. **Price:** $1/ea.

### E ♦ Appalachia
299 Gunstock Hill Rd.
Gilford, NH 03246

**Affiliation:** Appalachian Mountain Club. **Concern(s):** environment; recreation; wilderness; conservation. Oldest mountaineering journal in the country covers nature, conservation, climbing, hiking, canoeing, and ecology. **Frequency:** 2/yr. **Contact(s):** Helen Howe (Poetry Editor).

### E ♦ Appalachian Trailway News Magazine
Box 807
Harpers Ferry, WV 25425   (304)535-6331

**Affiliation:** Appalachian Trail Conference. **Concern(s):** environment; preservation. This magazine reports on the preservation and management of the Appalachian Trail, a 2100 mile foot path and protective corridor, generally following the crest of the Appalachian Mountains for Maine to Georgia. **Est.:** 1925. **Circ.:** 23M. **Contact(s):** Judy Jenner (Editor), David N. Startzell (Executive Director).

### F ♦ Appeal
Box 1077, North B St.
Berkeley, CA 97409   (510)547-7251

**Affiliation:** Feminists for Reason. **Concern(s):** feminism. Magazine.

### H ♦ APA Eros
co/ J & K Burt
960 SW Jefferson Ave.
Corvallis, OR 97333

**Concern(s):** health; education. Reader-written newsletter about sex and relationships of all kinds.

### E ♦ Aqua Terra - Water Concepts for an Ecological Society
Route 3, Box 716
Eureka Springs, AR 72632   (501)253-9431

**Affiliation:** National Water Center. **Concern(s):** environment; water. "We are attempting to understand water as part of ourselves. As conscious individuals, we can control our own water. We ask people to submit stories of personal experiences realizing their water selves. Those with regard for water, who understand her and treat her as an ally will survive. This journal is a networking effort to get clean pure water in the coming millennium. Heal the waters!" **Other Resources:** WE ALL LIVE DOWNSTREAM - A GUIDE TO WASTE TREATMENT that stops water pollution. **Est.:** 1980. **Dues:** $10/yr. **Price:** $5.95/ea. **Bulk:** $5ea/24. **Pages:** 100. **Circ.:** 3M. **Publisher:** Water Works Publishing. **Contact(s):** Barbara Harmony (Coordinator), Jacqui Froelich (Editor). (501)253-6866.

### E ♦ Archives of Environmental Health
Heldref Publications
4000 Albemarle St. NW
Washington, DC 20016   (202)362-6445

**Concern(s):** environment; health; consumer protection; hazardous/toxic waste; public health. For 46 years, this noted journal has provided objective documentation of the effects of environmental agents on human health. In one single source Archives of Environmental Health: An International Journal brings together the latest research from such varying fields as epidemilology, toxicology, biostatistics, and biochemistry. In a field where today's certainty often becomes tomorrow's myth, this journal publishes new research with scientific integrity and rigorous methodology. **Frequency:** 6/yr. **Subscription:** $85/yr. **Price:** $14/ea. **Pages:** 64. **Circ.:** 2M. **Publisher:** Heldref Publications. **Contact(s):** Patricia McCready (Managing Editor).

### ✍ ♦ Arena Review
Department of Sociology
Boston College
Chestnut Hill, MA 02167

**Concern(s):** education; activism; research. **Frequency:** 4/yr. **Price:** $24/ea. **Contact(s):** Michael Malec.

### H ♦ Arizona Networking News
7121 E. Sahuaro Dr. So.
Scottsdale, AZ 85254   (602)951-1275

**Concern(s):** health; spiritual; preventative medicine; holism; transformation. A networking newspaper tabloid assisting those who are into holistic health and metaphysics. **Frequency:** 4/yr. **Subscription:** $10/yr. **Pages:** 24. **Circ.:** 70M. **Contact(s):** Joanne Henning Tedesco (Editor).

### ♅ ♦ Arms Control Reporter
2001 Beacon St.
Brookline, MA 02146

**Affiliation:** Institute for Defense and Disarmament Studies. **Concern(s):** peace. "Institutions may find this objective clipping service helpful in keeping up with the enormous number of articles on arms control talks and issues. Its cost and size make its use less feasible for most peace groups, whose money could be better spent elsewhere." -C.C. Newsletter. **Est.:** 1982. **Frequency:** 11/yr. **Subscription:** $297/yr. ($125 for local groups). **Price:** $27/ea. **Contact(s):** Chalmers Hardenbergh.

### ♅ ♦ Arms Control Today
11 Dupont Circle NW, #900
Washington, DC 20036   (202)797-6450

**Affiliation:** Arms Control Association. **Concern(s):** peace; disarmament. "This moderate periodical is not predictable on arms control issues. Indeed, one article takes the absurd position that it could be detrimental to arms control to have a complete missile test ban." -C.C. **Est.:** 1971. **Frequency:** 12/yr. **Subscription:** $25/yr. **Price:** $3/ea. **Contact(s):** Robert Travis Scott.

### ✍ ♦ Art Hazards News
Center for Safety in the Arts
5 Beekman St.
New York, NY 10038   (212)227-6220

**Affiliation:** Center for Occupational Hazards. **Concern(s):** arts; labor; health; occupational safety. A newsletter "interested only in articles related to health and safety issues in visual art, performing arts, and museums." **Est.:** 1978. **Frequency:** 10/yr. **Subscription:** $15/yr. **Price:** $1/ea. **Bulk:** 40% off/24. **Pages:** 4. **Contact(s):** Michael McCann (Editor).

### ✍ ♦ Art Works
815 16th St. NW, #301
Washington, DC 20006   (202)842-7880

**Affiliation:** Labor Heritage Foundation. **Concern(s):** arts; labor; culture; unions; graphics; fine arts; music. "A newsletter that reports on the activities of the Foundation. Well-written and illustrated, it seeks to involve art, i.e., music, paintings, graphics, back into the labor movement." -C.C. Nonprofit. **Est.:** 1984. **Dues:** $30/friend; $50/sponsor. **Frequency:** 2/yr. **Price:** Free. **Pages:** 4-6. **Fax:** (202)842-7838. **Contact(s):** Joe Glazer (Chairman), Joanne Delaplaine (Executive Director).

### ✍ ♦ Artifex
Archaeus Project
2402 University Ave.
St. Paul, MN 55114

**Concern(s):** arts. "A guide for the perplexed in this time of transition. From Jungian and other perspectives, articles discuss the symbolism of social, scientific, and religious ideas. Artifex has a small, quiet circulation, a subscription turnover of less than 5% annually, and a readability that will take you from cover to cover. New subscribers receive a free copy of Archaeus 5, a study of UFOs and the Self (an $8 value)." **Frequency:** 4/yr. **Subscription:** $20/yr.

### ✍ ♦ Artpaper
119 N. 4th St., #303
Minneapolis, MN 55401   (612)332-0093

**Concern(s):** arts; media; culture; philanthropy; activism; theater; film; film. "...an alternative journal on art and culture. Produced in Minnesota but with a national scope, Artpaper is irreverent, accessible, local, and polyphonic. More inclusive than most, and less uniform, we're the one art magazine truly devoted to the fullness and fun of cultural life outside the mainstream. Also, for artists' financial survival, Artpaper has the nation's most comprehensive listing of grants and competitions for visual artists." **Est.:** 1980. **Frequency:** 10/yr. **Subscription:** $18/yr. **Price:** $2.75/ea. **Circ.:** 10M. **Contact(s):** Lane Relyea (Editor), Vince Leo (Associate Editor).

### ✍ ♦ Artpolice
5228 43rd Ave. S
Minneapolis, MN 55417-2210   (612)331-1721

**Concern(s):** arts; media; politics; peace; environment; activism; graphics. Primarily a visual book by artists. "Though based in Minneapolis, we have regular contributions in several other North American cities. Our politics are pro-Earth and anti-war." **Frequency:** 3/yr. **Subscription:** $10/yr. **Bulk:** 50% off/24. **Pages:** 20. **Circ.:** 1M. **Office:** 25 University SE, #305 Minneapolis, MN 55414. **Contact(s):** Frank Gaard (Facilitator), Andy Baird (Political Officer). (612)379-8721.

**T ▶ Asia & Pacific Update**
475 Riverside Dr., #712
New York, NY 10115    (212)870-2922
**Affiliation:** Task Force on Militarization in Asia and the Pacific/ National Council of Churches. **Concern(s):** Third World; peace; Asia; Pacific/Pacific Rim; indigenous peoples. "This selection serves as a peace action alert with recommendations for reader action. It is a short one- or two-sheet bulletin on urgent Pacific peace and social issues." -C.C. **Est.:** 1981. **Frequency:** Irregular. **Price:** Free. **Contact(s):** Christopher Candland.

**T ▶ Asian Affairs: An American Review**
Heldref Publications
4000 Albemarle St. NW
Washington, DC 20016    (202)362-6445
**Concern(s):** Third World; economics; Asia; foreign policy; research; analysis. This journal focuses on US policy in Asia, as well as on the domestic politics, economics, and international relations of the Asian countries. Written primarily for readers wanting relevant information about a part of the world that is of vital importance to American interests, it is also a valuable resource for teachers, political analysts, and those involved in international business. The journal is published under the sponsorship of the Contemporary US-Asia Research Institute in N.Y. **Frequency:** 4/yr. **Subscription:** $60/yr.

**T ▶ Asian Rights Advocate**
1821 W. Cullerton
Chicago, IL 60608    (312)226-0675
**Affiliation:** Church Committee on Human Rights in Asia. **Concern(s):** Third World; justice; Asia; indigenous peoples. "Human rights for peoples in Asian countries are promoted. Rights violations in the Philippines and Korea get special attention." -C.C. **Est.:** 1980. **Frequency:** 11/yr. **Subscription:** $5/yr. **Price:** $.50/ea. **Contact(s):** Linda Jones.

**☞ ▶ ASPCA Report**
441 E. 92th St.
New York, NY 10128    (212)876-7700
**Affiliation:** American Society for the Prevention of Cruelty to Animals (ASPCA). **Concern(s):** environment; animal rights. The magazine that keeps you up to date on everything that's happening in the field of animal protection. Each issue also contains handy tips on training and caring for your companion animals, press clips from around the world on animal protection, updates on ASPCA legislation and litigation, and timely book reviews.

**P ▶ The Atlantic**
745 Boylston St.
Boston, MA 02116
**Concern(s):** politics; education; economics; arts; trade; literature. In-depth articles on public issues, politics, social sciences, education, business, literature, and the arts, with emphasis on information rather than opinion. **Contact(s):** William Whitworth (Editor).

**E ▶ Audubon**
National Audubon Society
950 Third Ave.
New York, NY 10022    (212)832-3200
**Concern(s):** environment; energy; conservation; preservation; wildlife/endangered species. "We are edited for people who delight in, care about and are willing to fight for the protection of wildlife, natural resources, and the global environment... We have recently shifted the emphasis away from nature appreciation and natural history and more toward environmental issues." Magazine. **Est.:** 1887. **Frequency:** 6/yr. **Price:** $4/ea. **Fax:** (212)755-3752. **Contact(s):** Les Line (Editor).

**E ▶ Audubon Activist**
950 3rd Ave.
New York, NY 10022    (212)832-3200
**Affiliation:** National Audubon Society. **Concern(s):** environment; politics; wildlife/endangered species; grassroots organizing. A news journal for members of the Audubon Society and environmentalists who want to take action on pressing environmental issues. It provides thorough reports on related news and tips on how to become involved. **Dues:** $20/yr. **Frequency:** 11/yr. **Subscription:** Membership.

**⚥ ▶ AUFP Newsletter**
116 Johnson
Highland Park, NJ 08904    (201)246-4007
**Affiliation:** Athletes United for Peace. **Concern(s):** peace; activism. "Many athletes are concerned about more than just speed and a good score. World peace is a concern in this occasional periodical, with a desire for reduction of both nuclear and conventional arms." -C.C. **Est.:** 1982. **Frequency:** 2/yr. **Price:** Free. **Contact(s):** Phil Shnick.

**E ▶ Backpacker Magazine**
Rodale Press
33 Minor St.
Emmaus, PA 18049
**Concern(s):** environment; health; recreation. Articles on self-propelled backcountry travel: backpacking, technique, kayaking/canoeing, mountaineering, nordic skiing, health, natural science. **Publisher:** Rodale Press. **Contact(s):** John Viehman (Executive Editor).

**$ ▶ Backwoods Home Magazine**
Box 2630
Ventura, CA 93002    (805)647-9341
**Concern(s):** economics; environment; agriculture; health; community self-reliance; alternative consumer. A magazine written for person who values independence, self-sufficiency and the planet on which they live. It offers "how to" articles on owner-built housing, alternative energy, gardening, health, self-employment, country living and other topics related to an environmentally-sound and self-reliant life style. **Frequency:** 6/yr. **Subscription:** $9.95/yr.

**E ▶ The Backyard Naturalist**
1400 16th St. NW
Washington, DC 20036-2266    (202)797-6800
**Affiliation:** National Wildlife Federation. **Concern(s):** environment. A biweekly column distributed to over 7,000 publications nationwide.

**M ▶ Bacon's Media Alerts**
332 S. Michigan Ave.
Chicago, IL 60604
**Concern(s):** media; press. **Publisher:** Bacon's Publishing Company.

**✐ ▶ Bad Haircut**
1055 Adams St. SE, #4
Olympia, WA 98501-4151
**Concern(s):** arts; culture. A vibrant publication which combines peace, human rights and environmental issues in a unique format of poetry, fiction, essays, interviews and art. Bad Haircut was founded with the hope that art with progressive themes can inspire others to work for a better world in their own individual ways; starting chain reactions that together will help influence our society as a whole. **Other Resources:** Besides BAD HAIRCUT (the magazine) we're trying to expand our publications to include postcards, one-time collections and possibly T-shirts. **Est.:** 1987. **Frequency:** Irregular. **Subscription:** $14/4 issues. **Price:** $4/ea. **Bulk:** Call. **Pages:** 35 to 100. **Circ.:** 2M. **Contact(s):** Kim Goforth, Ray Goforth (Editors/ Publishers).

**D ▶ Balance Report**
Population Environment Balance
1325 G St. NW, #1003
Washington, DC 20005    (202)879-3000
**Affiliation:** Population Environment Balance. **Concern(s):** demographics; population growth. Newsletter. **Frequency:** 6/yr. **Contact(s):** Rose M. Hanes (Executive Director), Garrett Hardin (Honorary Chairman).

**E ▶ Balance Wheel**
Association for Conservation Information
408 South Polk St.
Albany, MO 64402    (816)726-3677
**Affiliation:** Association for Conservation Information. **Concern(s):** environment; conservation; wildlife/endangered species; resources. Newsletter. Nonprofit. **Contact(s):** Rod Green (President).

**P ▶ Ballot Access News**
3201 Baker St.
San Francisco, CA 94123    (415)922-9779
**Affiliation:** Coalition for Free and Open Elections. **Concern(s):** politics; petition; leadership; reform; alternative party. "The struggle is for fair election laws for small political parties. Open election activists will appreciate this newsletter." -C.C. **Est.:** 1985. **Frequency:** 12/yr. **Subscription:** $6/yr. **Price:** Free. **Contact(s):** Richard Winger.

**T ▶ Barricada Internacional**
Barricada USA-G
Box 410150
San Francisco, CA 94141    (415)621-8981
**Affiliation:** South North Communication Network. **Concern(s):** Third World; foreign policy; Central America. Written and translated in Nicaragua, printed and distributed in San Francisco, CA. Provides first-hand news and analysis from perspective of Central Americans. Covers politics, economics, culture, popular movements, developments in the FSLN, human rights and more. Bilingual, English, and Spanish format. **Other Resources:** The South-North Communication Network is dedicated to providing a third-world perspective to the US public. In addition to distributing BARRICADA INTERNACIONAL, the network sponsors educational activities, lectures, and distributes other materials. **Frequency:** 12/yr. **Subscription:** $35/yr. **Price:**

$2.95/ea. **Bulk:** 40% off/24. **Pages:** 56. **Circ.:** 3.5M. **E-Network:** PeaceNet. **ID:** 'barricada'. **Contact(s):** Shelly Sherman (Administrative Director), Ruth Warner (Promotion).

**⚥ ▶ Base Conversion News**
222 View St., #C
Mountain View, CA 94041
**Affiliation:** Center for Economic Conversion. **Concern(s):** peace; economics; disarmament; economic conversion; peace dividend. This newsletter follows legislation regarding military base closings, networks information about what is being done with bases and installations that have already closed, and provides contact information regarding agencies that will assist local planners and community people respond to the impact of base closings.

**J ▶ Bayou La Rose**
c/o Arthur Miller
302 N. 'J' St. #3
Tacoma, WA 98403
**Concern(s):** justice; environment; labor; political prisoners; Native Americans; indigenous peoples; workplace democracy; criminal system; social justice. "This magazine covers prisons, native, environment and workplace issues... Highly recommended." -Prison News Service. **Contact(s):** Arthur Miller.

**L ▶ BC&T Report & News**
10401 Connecticut Ave.
Kensington, MD 20895    (301)933-8600
**Affiliation:** Bakery, Confectionary, & Tobacco Workers International Union. **Concern(s):** labor; politics; unions; lobbying. A monthly leadership newsletter published for members. **Frequency:** 12/yr. **Contact(s):** Carolyn J. Jacobson (Director of Public Relations).

**✐ ▶ Bear Essential News for Kids**
Box 26908
Tempe, AZ 85285
**Concern(s):** education; youth; global understanding; science. Educational and entertaining articles for children in grades K through 3 and 4 through 8, including: world news in kids' terms; unique school projects; profiles of interesting achievers; family entertainment; science; youth sports and health; bilingual and multicultural topics; hobbies/young careers; pets and pet care; cartoon humor; activities, trivia, or puzzles that are educational.

**E ▶ Bear News**
c/o Great Bear Foundation
Box 2699
Missoula, MT 59806    (406)721-3009
**Affiliation:** Great Bear Foundation. **Concern(s):** environment; wildlife/endangered species; conservation. "A newsletter for those concerned about the fate of the world's eight species of bears and the ecosystems they inhabit. Our quarterly tabloid, praised by wildlife biologists and conservationists, keeps you up to date on events that threaten bear survival. Anecdotes, analysis, impassioned advocacy, investigative reporting, sound biology." Nonprofit. **Frequency:** 4/yr. **Subscription:** $20/yr.

**E ▶ Befriending Creation**
608 E. 11th St.
Davis, CA 95616    (916)758-5407
**Affiliation:** Friends Committee on Unity with Nature. **Concern(s):** environment; spiritual; interfaith. Primarily a means of communication among Friends' (Quaker) Meetings, this newsletter is about our spiritual relations with the environment, and also a means of bringing news from the "outside" world to Friends on the environment and our spiritual interests in it. **Other Resources:** Membership, meetings, and conferences, other flyers and booklets. Nonprofit. **Est.:** 1985. **Dues:** Suggest $10 donation per yr. **Frequency:** 11/yr. **Subscription:** $15/yr. **Price:** $1.50/ea. **Pages:** 6. **Circ.:** 425. **E-Network:** Econet. **ID:** 'pymcun'. **Contact(s):** Chris Laning (Editor), Isabel Bliss (Clerk/Chair). (313)475-9976.

**H ▶ Behavioral Medicine**
Heldref Publications
4000 Albemarle St. NW
Washington, DC 20016    (202)362-6445
**Concern(s):** health; public health; psychology. Formerly Journal of Human Stress, an interdisciplinary journal of particular interest to physicians, psychiatrists, psychologists, nurses, educators, and all who deal with the close interaction of behavior and physical health. Carries reports of the latest research in psychoimmunology, stress, personality type, environmental stressors, workplace stress, and facing illness. Distinguished experts on the editorial board review all articles to maintain the highest standard of integrity. **Frequency:** 4/yr. **Subscription:** $38, $65 institution.

**J ▶ Berkeley Journal of Sociology**
458 A Barrows Hall, University of California
Berkeley, CA 94720

**Concern(s):** justice; feminism; demographics; education. Sociology and social work. **Frequency:** Annual. **Price:** $6/ea.

F ◗ **Berkeley Women's Law Journal**
2 Boalt Hall School of Law
University of California
Berkeley, CA 94720    (415)642-6263
**Concern(s):** feminism; justice; health; disabled's rights; gay/lesbian. "The journal is an interdisciplinary law journal focusing on the legal concerns of women, which are under-represented in traditional literature." Deals with feminist, gay/lesbian, and disability issues. **Est.:** 1985. **Frequency:** Annual. **Subscription:** $16, $35 institution. **Pages:** 300. **Circ.:** 500.

$ ◗ **Better Business**
235 E. 42nd St.
New York, NY 10017
**Concern(s):** economics; trade. Articles for small businesses, minority businesses, and businesses owned by women. **Contact(s):** John F. Robinson (Publisher).

☮ ◗ **Between the Lines**
Sacramento Peace Center
1917A 16th St.
Sacramento, CA 95814   (916)446-0787
**Affiliation:** Sacramento Peace Center. **Concern(s):** peace; feminism; justice; politics; activism. "A cooperative progressive newspaper dedicated to the diversity of local, grassroots activism. Our purpose is to provide a forum for the exchange of ideas and information and to assist the activist community in reaching a wider audience. It is edited and produced by a working collective operating democratically by consensus." **Subscription:** $10/yr.; $18/2 yrs.

☮ ◗ **Beyond War**
222 High St.
Palo Alto, CA 94301-1097   (415)328-7756
**Affiliation:** On Beyond War. **Concern(s):** peace; conflict resolution; anti-draft; anti-nuclear. Provides educational materials, both written and audio-visual. Publishes Beyond War newsletter.

E ◗ **Bicycle Guide**
711 Boylston St.
Boston, MA 02116
**Concern(s):** environment; recreation. "Our magazine covers all aspects of cycling from an enthusiast's perspective: racing, touring, sport riding, product reviews, and technical information. We depend on free lancers for touring articles, personality profiles, and race coverage." **Contact(s):** Theodore Costantino (Editor).

J ◗ **Bill of Rights in Action**
601 S. Kingsley Dr.
Los Angeles, CA 90005  (213)487-5590
**Affiliation:** Constitutional Rights Foundation. **Concern(s):** justice; constitutional rights; civil liberties; minority rights. "Civil liberties are defended, with direct references and quotes from the US Constitution, for the benefit of school students. Minority rights are often highlighted in this newsletter." -C.C. **Est.:** 1967. **Frequency:** 4/yr. **Subscription:** Free to educators. **Price:** Free. **Contact(s):** Marshall Croddy.

J ◗ **Bill of Rights Journal**
175 5th Ave.
New York, NY 10010   (212)673-2040
**Affiliation:** National Emergency Civil Liberties Committee. **Concern(s):** justice; constitutional rights; civil liberties; minority rights. "Activists on the front lines of defense of the Bill of Rights explain strategies for defending these basic rights. The magazine ranks with the ACLU periodical Civil Liberties in effectively organizing for these rights. Highly recommended." -C.C. **Est.:** 1951. **Frequency:** Annual. **Price:** $25/ea. **Contact(s):** Jeff Kisseloff.

A ◗ **Bio-Dynamics**
Box 550
Kimberton, PA 19475   (215)935-7797
**Affiliation:** Bio-Dynamic Farming and Gardening Association, Inc.. **Concern(s):** agriculture; organic. A corporation whose task is to advance the practices and principles of Biodynamic (B-D) agriculture. The association publishes this magazine as well as books, offers a biodynamic advisory service, supports training programs, sponsors conferences and lectures, funds research projects, and supplies biodynamic preparations. Nonprofit. **Frequency:** 4/yr. **Subscription:** $35/yr. **Circ.:** 1.5M. **Contact(s):** Roderick Shouldice (Administrative Director), Joel Morrow (Editor). (413)528-2944.

E ◗ **BioCycle: The Journal of Waste Recycling**
Box 351
Emmaus, PA 18049    (215)967-4135
**Concern(s):** environment; recycling. This magazine reports on composting/recycling and other related material as a main strategy to

reduce our dependence on landfills. Sister publication to In Business. **Frequency:** 12/yr. **Publisher:** The JG Press, Inc. **Office:** 18 S. Seventh St. Emmaus, PA 18049. **Contact(s):** Jerome Goldstein (Publisher).

E ◗ **Bird Watcher's Digest**
Box 110
Marietta, OH 45750
**Concern(s):** environment; wildlife/endangered species. Articles, words, for bird watchers: first-person accounts; how-to's, pieces on endangered species; profiles, and cartoons. **Contact(s):** Mary B. Bowers (Editor).

J ◗ **Black Child Advocate**
1463 Rhode Island Ave. NW
Washington, DC 20005  (202)387-1281
**Affiliation:** National Black Child Development Institute. **Concern(s):** justice; children; minority rights. "Special ideas are offered relating to Black children and youth, with emphasis on education and health. Legislation, regulations, public policy and advocacy all find a place in its editorial policy." -C.C. Magazine. **Est.:** 1974. **Frequency:** 4/yr. **Subscription:** $12.50/yr. **Price:** Donation. **Contact(s):** Sharon Dennis.

✍ ◗ **The Black Collegian**
1240 S. Broad St.
New Orleans, LA 70125
**Concern(s):** education; justice; students; diversity; minority rights. Articles on experiences of African-American students, careers, and how-to subjects. **Contact(s):** K. Kazi-Ferrouillet (Managing Editor).

J ◗ **Black Enterprise**
130 5th Ave.
New York, NY 10011   (212)242-8000
**Concern(s):** justice; economics; politics; education; arts; minority rights; trade; analysis; science; culture. Articles on money management, careers, political issues, entrepreneurship, high technology, and lifestyles for black professionals. Profiles. **Contact(s):** Earl Graves (Editor).

M ◗ **Black Film Review**
2025 I St. NW
Washington, DC 20006  (202)466-2753
**Concern(s):** media; justice; arts; film; diversity; minority rights. "Black-produced cinema and films of interest to Black people are the focus. It is the fanciest of the progressive film reviews and is full of social and ethnic themes." -C.C. **Est.:** 1985. **Frequency:** 4/yr. **Subscription:** $10, $20 institution. **Price:** $3/ea. **Publisher:** Sojourner Publications. **Contact(s):** David Nicholson.

J ◗ **Black Scholar**
Box 2869
Oakland, CA 94609    (510)547-6633
**Concern(s):** justice; minority rights; racism. "Anyone interested in the theory and practice of the Black civil rights movement will benefit from this well-written and exciting journal. Writers for The Black Scholar include some of the most struggle-tempered veterans as well as younger activists and intellectuals. It is a basic selection for its specialty." -C.C. **Est.:** 1969. **Frequency:** 6/yr. **Subscription:** $25, $35 institution. **Price:** $5/ea. **Contact(s):** Robert Chrisman.

☮ ◗ **Black Vet**
680 Fulton St.
Brooklyn, NY 11217    (718)935-1168
**Affiliation:** Black Veterans for Social Justice. **Concern(s):** peace; Third World; justice; racism; veterans. "The Black Vet speaks on the special problems of Third World veterans. Racism in the military was a recent typical topic in their newsletter." -C.C. **Est.:** 1988. **Frequency:** 6/yr. **Subscription:** $5/yr. **Price:** Donation. **Contact(s):** Oronde Takuma.

✐ ◗ **Bloomsbury Review**
1028 Bannock
Denver, CO 80204     (303)892-0620
**Concern(s):** arts; culture; literature. For the progressive literary buff, this is perhaps the finest review. This newspaper contains interviews, critiques, commentary, poetry, and book reviews from the very best in their fields. Nationwide circulation. **Frequency:** 6/yr. **Subscription:** $14/yr. **Price:** $3/ea. **Publisher:** Owaissa Communications. **Contact(s):** Tom Auer (Editor/Publisher), Marilyn Auer (Associate Editor).

E ◗ **Blue Goose Flyer**
10824 Fox Hunt Lane
Potomac, MD 20854-1553
**Affiliation:** National Wildlife Refuge Association. **Concern(s):** environment; wildlife/endangered species; wilderness; conservation; preservation. This newsletter examines the loss of the habitats of fowl and wildlife in the US. Ways that this can be prevented are also

discussed. **Frequency:** 4/yr.

H ◗ **Body & Soul**
Box 610
Carmichael, CA 95609   (916)944-4918
**Concern(s):** health; preventative medicine; nutrition; alternative consumer; holism. This newspaper supplies you with much information on alternative health care and the latest in vitamin therapies and related areas. The contributing writers are doctors and physicians from many fields. **Subscription:** $8.25/yr. (800)955-5066. **Contact(s):** Nick N. Dordevic (Publisher/Editor), Michael Arthur (Managing Editor).

✐ ◗ **Boston Review**
33 Harrison Ave.
Boston, MA 02111-2008(617)350-5353
**Concern(s):** arts; politics; culture. "Bimonthly publication of art and culture." Covers politics, poetry, fiction, all the arts and culture. **Est.:** 1975. **Frequency:** 6/yr. **Subscription:** $12, $15 institutions. **Price:** $2.50/ea. **Pages:** 40. **Circ.:** 10M. **Contact(s):** Margaret Ann Roth (Editor), Timothy Lewire (Managing Editor).

S ◗ **Both Sides Now**
Free People Press
Route 6, Box 28
Tyler, TX 75704      (214)592-4263
**Concern(s):** spiritual; economics; health; agriculture; peace; politics; energy; nonviolence; Green; anti-authoritarian; decentralization; appropriate technology; organic; transformation. "An Alternative Journal of New Age/Aquarian Transformations." Current events and think-pieces with an emphasis on spiritual/political synthesis. Issues revolve around nonviolence, pacifism, decentralization, green politics, human rights, social justice, alternative lifestyles & institutions, healing, economics, appropriate technology, organic farming, metaphysics & the occult, and anarchism. **Frequency:** Irregular. **Subscription:** 6/$3; $5/10. **Price:** $0.75ea., postpaid. **Bulk:** 66% off/100. **Pages:** 16-24. **Circ.:** 2M. **Contact(s):** Elihu Edelson (Editor).

E ◗ **Bottle/Can Recycling Update**
Box 10540
Portland, OR 97210
**Concern(s):** environment; recycling. Newsletter. **Contact(s):** Jerry Powell (Editor).

E ◗ **Boundary Waters Journal**
9396 Rocky Ledge Rd.
Ely, MN 55731
**Concern(s):** environment; recreation; natural resources; wilderness; wildlife/endangered species; ocean/rivers; bioregionalism. Articles on recreation and natural resources in Minnesota's Boundary Waters Canoe Area Wilderness and Ontario's Quetico Provincial Park. Regular features include canoe-route journals, fishing, camping, hiking, cross-country skiing, wildlife and nature; regional lifestyles, history, and events. **Contact(s):** Stuart Osthoff (Editor).

$ ◗ **Boycott Shell Bulletin**
900 15th St. NW
Washington, DC 20005  (202)842-7350
**Affiliation:** Boycott Shell Campaign. **Concern(s):** economics; Third World; boycott; South Africa. A bulletin that reports on the current environmental and human rights mishaps of Shell Oil. **Frequency:** 4/yr.

? ◗ **Brain/Mind Bulletin (see New Sense)**

T ◗ **Bread for the World**
802 Rhode Island Ave. NW
Washington, DC 20018  (202)269-0200
**Affiliation:** Bread for the World. **Concern(s):** Third World; demographics; spiritual; health; hunger; faith. "Stopping hunger in poor countries through progressive legislation as well as through charity is promoted. Christians and other interested folks may be sparked by the information in this little newsletter." -C.C. **Est.:** 1975. **Frequency:** 12/yr. **Subscription:** $15/yr. **Price:** Free. **Contact(s):** Lloyd Goodman.

☮ ◗ **Breakthrough**
475 Riverside Dr., #570
New York, NY 10115   (212)870-3290
**Affiliation:** Global Education Associates. **Concern(s):** peace; economics; education; global understanding; economic conversion. A magazine that covers peace, global culture, economics with articles written by some of the most thoughtful people writing today. (212)870-3291.

P ◗ **Breakthrough**
Prairie Fire Organizing Committee
Box 10422
San Francisco, CA 94114
**Affiliation:** Prairie Fire Organizing Committee. **Concern(s):** politics;

justice; alternative party; racism; discrimination; activism. A newsletter which emphasizes the Marxist outlook on society and reports ways to convert society to Marxism. A voice for militant Black liberation. "...takes and activist approach to theory. Always has interesting material." -Prison News Service. **Frequency:** Irregular. **Price:** $6/ea.

**Brethren Peace Fellowship Newsletter**
Box 455
New Windsor, MD 21776 (301)775-2254
**Concern(s):** peace; spiritual; Third World; demographics; faith; nonviolence; Mid-East; conflict resolution; capital punishment. Concerned with Christian peace education on issues related to nonviolence and war. Main focuses have been the Middle East conflict, Central America, draft counseling, Christian basis of pacifism, justice for the poor, abolition of the death penalty. **Est.:** 1967. **Frequency:** 6/yr. **Pages:** 4. **Circ.:** 740. **Contact(s):** Dale Aukerman (Coordinating Secretary).

**Bridges of Peace**
42 Francis Ave., #15
Cambridge, MA 02138
**Affiliation:** World Conference on Religion and Peace. **Concern(s):** peace; spiritual; education; interfaith; activism; youth; global understanding. A youth newsletter. **Contact(s):** Patrice Brodeur (WCRP Youth Moderator).

P **Bridging the Gap**
810 1st St. NE
Washington, DC 20002 (202)408-0034
**Affiliation:** Government Accountability Project (GAP). **Concern(s):** politics; health; labor; whistle-blowing; corporate responsibility; government accountability. USDA meat and poultry inspectors, workers at nuclear weapons facilities and power plants; many other "whistle-blowers" are covered along with helpful hints. This magazine exposes government and corporate fraud, waste and health threatening conditions of workers. Reports to the public about government and corporate whistle-blowers and local citizen groups; investigative services to state and local government bodies; legal education to law students pursuing public interest careers. Nonprofit. **Est.:** 1977. **Contact(s):** Louis Clark (Executive Director).

**Briefly**
Box 271
Nyack, NY 10960 (914)358-4601
**Affiliation:** Presbyterian Peace Fellowship. **Concern(s):** peace; spiritual; faith. "Members of Presbyterian denominations unite here in their longing for world peace. The newsletter includes upcoming events and theological discussions about Presbyterians and peacemaking." -C.C. **Est.:** 1944. **Frequency:** 4/yr. **Price:** Donation. **Contact(s):** Ralph Mould.

**Bucknell Review**
Bucknell University
Bucknell Hall
Lewisburg, PA 17837 (717)524-1184
**Concern(s):** arts; education; science. "An interdisciplinary book-journal, each issue devoted to a major theme or movement in humanities or sciences..." **Est.:** 1941. **Frequency:** 2/yr. **Subscription:** $36/yr. **Price:** $18/ea. **Pages:** 196. **Circ.:** 500.

E **Bulletin**
Box 2081
Gloucester, MA 01930-2081 (508)281-9209
**Affiliation:** Coastal Society. **Concern(s):** environment; oceans/rivers. Newsletter reports on the Coastal Society activities. It has inspiring articles that appeal to many people from different professions. Nonprofit. **Est.:** 1975. **Frequency:** 4/yr. **Subscription:** $25/yr. **Price:** $5/ea. **Bulk:** 10% off/24. **Pages:** 24. **Circ.:** 500. **Fax:** (508)281-9371. (508)281-9333. **Contact(s):** Thomas Bigford (Executive Director).

T **Bulletin of Concerned Asian Scholars**
3239 9th St.
Boulder, CO 80304 (303)449-7439
**Concern(s):** Third World; environment; Asia. An independent periodical on modern Asia, published regularly since 1968 when it began as a forum for opponents of the brutal US aggression in Southeast Asia. The BULLETIN is: free to dissent from establishment perspectives; anti-imperialist, progressive, and nonpartisan; illustrated and readable; international in editors, authors, and readers; referred by specialists and scholars. Nonprofit. **Est.:** 1968. **Frequency:** 4/yr. **Subscription:** $55/yr. institutions. **Price:** $5.50/ea. **Pages:** 72. **Circ.:** 1.6M. **Contact(s):** Bill Doub (Managing Editor), Jay Dillon (Editorial Assistant).

**Bulletin of Science Technology & Society**
Materials Research Lab
Pennsylvania State University
University Park, PA 16802
**Concern(s):** education; energy; environment; science.

**Bulletin of the Atomic Scientists**
6942 S. Kimbark
Chicago, IL 60637 (312)702-2555
**Affiliation:** Atomic Scientist Association. **Concern(s):** peace; environment; anti-nuclear; disarmament. "Probably the best known professional periodical on the nuclear arms race, particularly because of the famous clock on the cover telling us how close we are to nuclear holocaust. Since Hiroshima was leveled in 1945, the clock has been getting steadily closer to the final hour: midnight." -C.C. Founded by the concerned scientists who worked on the Manhattan Project, including Einstein and Oppenheimer. **Est.:** 1946. **Frequency:** 10/yr. **Subscription:** $30: $55/2 yrs. **Circ.:** 20M. **Contact(s):** Len Ackland.

**Bulletin of the Caucus on Social Theory and Art Education**
123 Education Building
Florida State University
Tallahassee, FL 32306 (904)644-5473
**Affiliation:** Caucus on Social Theory and Art Education. **Concern(s):** arts; culture. "Primarily read by art educators, this academic journal includes theoretical thesis on art and society. Practical applications of art theory and ideas for teaching social concerns in the art field find a place here." -C.C. **Est.:** 1980. **Dues:** $10/yr. **Frequency:** Annual. **Subscription:** Membership. **Price:** $6/ea. **Contact(s):** Tom Anderson.

U **Burwood Journal**
Box 41834
Los Angeles, CA 90041 (213)255-9502
**Affiliation:** Survival News Service. **Concern(s):** urban; education; agriculture; environment; economics; energy; spiritual; recycling; cooperatives; conservation; appropriate technology. "Focus: To educate city dwellers in realistic, practical ways to 'survive' (re, earthquake preparation, arrest crime, economic survival, city gardens, compost pits, alternative energy, wild foods, etc.)." Co-ops, credit unions, recycling, etc. Strong spiritual focus. Ways to walk lightly on the Earth and lower our impact on an individual level. **Other Resources:** Lectures, wild food outings, survival outings, classes. A small line of top quality products and books also available. Nonprofit. **Est.:** 1980. **Frequency:** 4/yr. **Subscription:** $8.50/yr. **Price:** $1/ea. **Pages:** 12. **Circ.:** 2.5M. **Publisher:** Survival News Service. **Contact(s):** Christopher Nyerges, Vernon Devans.

$ **Business Ethics**
914 7th St., #3
Santa Monica, CA 90403 (310)395-4416
**Concern(s):** economics; corporate responsibility; socially-responsible investing; community investment; land trusts; trade. Magazine about ethics in corporations and business. Contains profiles and real-life problems and solutions to ethical dilemmas in business. As we pass from the me decade to the we decade where decency and caring about people and the planet prevail, those businesses that show they care about their employees, their customers, their shareholders, their suppliers and their community will thrive. Includes new paradigm examples as well as inspiring articles. **Frequency:** 6/yr. **Subscription:** $49/yr. **Member:** Co-op America. **Contact(s):** John Raatz (Publisher/Editor).

D **The Business of Ending Hunger**
The Hunger Project
1388 Sutter St.
San Francisco, CA 94109-5452 (415)928-8700
**Affiliation:** Hunger Project. **Concern(s):** demographics; hunger. A quarterly newsletter for the service clubs, corporations, and businesses working to make ending hunger a priority. Nonprofit. **Frequency:** 4/yr.

$ **Buyer's Market**
Box 19367
Washington, DC 20036 (202)833-3000
**Affiliation:** Public Citizen. **Concern(s):** economics; consumer education. Ralph Nader's consumer advisory, an 8-page monthly newsletter packed full of useful techniques and tactics to improve your buying skills. A Resources section on the back page of each advisory will offer free publications and other references should you wish to dig deeper into a topic and come out even further ahead in the marketplace.

E **Buzzworm**
Box 6853
Syracuse, NY 13217-7930 (303)442-1969
**Concern(s):** environment; media; conservation; journalism. "As an independent magazine reporting on national and international issues Buzzworm strives to offer balanced and comprehensive coverage of the challenges facing the world so that the general reader may thoughtful and actively respond. None of Buzzworm's shareholders are large corporations or special interest groups and the magazine is not affiliated in any way with any environmental or political organizations." **Other Resources:** EARTH JOURNAL directory. Many descriptions used in Macrocosm were derived from Buzzworm with permission. **Est.:** 1988. **Frequency:** 12/yr. **Subscription:** $18/yr. **Price:** $5/ea. **Office:** 2305 Canyon Blvd. #206 Boulder, CO 80302. (800)825-0061. **Contact(s):** Joseph E. Daniel (Editor/Publisher), Elizabeth Darby Junkin (Managing Editor).

J **CALC Report**
198 Broadway
New York, NY 10038 (212)964-6730
**Affiliation:** Clergy and Laity Concerned. **Concern(s):** justice; politics; peace; interfaith; grassroots organizing. "Peace and justice through local grassroots action are featured in this little magazine. People from all faiths have united in CALC to struggle for social justice, with news of this movement reflected here. The report is highly recommended for all those interested in a religious basis for social action."-C.C. **Est.:** 1965. **Dues:** $20/yr. **Frequency:** 6/yr. **Subscription:** Membership. **Price:** Donation. **Contact(s):** Roger Powers.

E **California**
11601 Wilshire Blvd., #400
Los Angeles, CA 90025
**Concern(s):** environment; economics; politics; education; urban; arts; bioregionalism; conservation; trade; analysis; childhood; ethnic concerns; culture. Features, with a California focus, on politics, business, environmental issues, ethnic diversity, travel, style, fashions, restaurants, the arts, and sports. Service pieces, profiles, and well-researched investigative articles. **Contact(s):** Rebecca Levy (Managing Editor).

J **California Prisoner**
1909 6th St.
Sacramento, CA 95814
**Concern(s):** justice; prisons; political prisoners; capital punishment; criminal system. **Frequency:** 6/yr. **Price:** $20/ea.

**Callaloo**
Dept. of English
University of Virginia
Charlottesville, VA 22903
**Concern(s):** arts; Third World; literature; Caribbean; Africa. Fiction and poetry by, and critiques on Afro-American, Caribbean, and African artists and writers. **Contact(s):** Charles H. Rowell (Editor).

E **Calypso Dispatch**
930 W. 21st St.
Norfolk, VA 23517 (804)627-1144
**Affiliation:** Cousteau Society. **Concern(s):** environment; ocean/rivers. This newsletter reports on the activities of the Cousteau Society and the problems facing the ocean environment of the world. **Frequency:** 12/yr. **Fax:** (804)627-7547. **Contact(s):** Jean-Michel Cousteau, C.L.S. Merriam (Research/Communications).

E **Calypso Log**
930 W. 21st St.
Norfolk, VA 23517 (804)627-1144
**Affiliation:** Cousteau Society. **Concern(s):** environment; oceans/rivers. A full-color bimonthly magazine - sent to all members of The Cousteau Society - that features reports on society expeditions and environmental issues, interviews with leading thinkers, photography by the Cousteau team and much more. **Dues:** $20/yr. **Frequency:** 6/yr. **Subscription:** Membership. **Fax:** (804)627-7547. **Contact(s):** Jean-Michel Cousteau (Editorial Director), Mary Batten (Editor).

M **Camera Obscura: A Journal of Feminism & Film Theory**
University of Rochester
R Rhees Library
Rochester, NY 14627
**Concern(s):** media; feminism; arts; politics; film; culture. This journal covers film, political and feminist theory, pop culture, video and photography. **Est.:** 1976. **Frequency:** 3/yr. **Subscription:** $14, $28 institution. **Price:** $6, $10 institutions. **Pages:** 180. **Circ.:** 3M. **Publisher:** John Hopkins University Press. **Contact(s):** Janet Bergstrom (Editor).

$ **Campaign Report**
76 Summer St.
Boston, MA 02110 (617)338-5783
**Affiliation:** National Jobs with Peace Campaign. **Concern(s):**

economics; peace; demographics; justice; budget; peace dividend; economic conversion; welfare rights. A national effort to redirect federal funds from military spending toward pressing domestic needs, such as housing, day care, education, health care, transportation, environmental protection and other socially useful industries. Local campaigns work to bring together diverse constituencies - civil rights, labor, peace, and low income - around a common agenda. They work around a variety of local issues, including welfare reform, economic conversion, housing, voting. Newsletter. **Frequency:** 2/yr. **Pages:** 20. **Circ.:** 20M. **Contact(s):** Regina Eddy (Managing Director), Michael Brown (Program Director).

### ✌ ▶ CARD News Service
731 State St.
Madison, WI 53703    (608)257-7562

**Affiliation:** Committee Against Registration and the Draft. **Concern(s):** peace; militarism; anti-draft. "This news service is the best source of news about registration and the draft. Both national news on the problem and grassroots news from CARD chapters are featured."-C.C. **Est.:** 1986. **Frequency:** 6/yr. **Subscription:** $10/yr. **Price:** $2/ea. **Contact(s):** Gillam Kerley.

### T ▶ CARECEN Speaks
3112 Mt. Pleasant St. NW
Washington, DC 20010    (202)328-9799

**Affiliation:** Central American Refugee Center. **Concern(s):** Third World; justice; Central America; refugees; immigration. "Refugees from the genocide in Guatemala and the death squads of El Salvador find hope in this newsletter. It does a good job as a networking tool in bringing together refugees from the region and those wanting to help them."-C.C. **Est.:** 1984. **Frequency:** 6/yr. **Subscription:** $10/yr. **Price:** $1/ea. **Contact(s):** Minor Sinclair.

### T ▶ Caribbean Labour
Box 122
Glen Oaks Station, NY 11004    (718)898-3601

**Affiliation:** Caribbean Workers Council. **Concern(s):** Third World; labor. "Workers' rights and union organizing are agitated for, usually bimonthly. Workers of Puerto Rico, Jamaica, and other Caribbean countries find a voice here."-C.C. **Est.:** 1986. **Frequency:** Irregular. **Subscription:** $3/yr. **Price:** $1/ea. **Contact(s):** Paul N. Tennessee.

### T ▶ Caribbean Newsletter
Box 20392, Parkwest Station
New York, NY 10025

**Affiliation:** Friends for Jamaica. **Concern(s):** Third World; Caribbean. Caribbean Newsletter covers current news and analysis on political, economic, and social conditions in the English-speaking Caribbean. It is published by the Friends for Jamaica Collective. **Est.:** 1981. **Frequency:** 6/yr. **Subscription:** $10/yr. **Price:** $2/ea. **Circ.:** 500.

### D ▶ Carrying Capacity News/FOCUS
1325 G St. NW, #1003
Washington, DC 20005    (202)879-3044

**Affiliation:** Carrying Capacity Network (CCN). **Concern(s):** demographics; environment; population. This newsletter provides the long and short of the carrying capacity problems facing the US. They contain articles, reviews, and resources to help activists, policymakers, educators, and the public better understand the urgent and multi-faceted nature of the carrying capacity crisis. Nonprofit. **Est.:** 1991. **Dues:** $35, organizations $50-80. **Frequency:** 4/yr. **Subscription:** $20/yr. **Pages:** 20. **Circ.:** 1M. **E-Network:** Econet. **ID:** 'smabley'. **Fax:** (202)879-3019. **Contact(s):** Stephen M. Mabley (Network Coordinator).

### M ▶ Cartoons by Bulbul
Box 4100
Mountain View, CA 94040    (415)961-5709

**Concern(s):** media; arts. "Bulbul's monthly packet of about 16 cartoons is drawn for reprint by periodicals. Most of his social justice creations focus on labor concerns, but other concerns such as peace and environment are also sketched." -C.C. **Est.:** 1976. **Frequency:** 12/yr. **Subscription:** Depends on circulation of periodical. **Publisher:** Arachne Publishing. **Contact(s):** Bulbul.

### ✐ ▶ Catalyst
Atlanta-Fulton Public Library
1 Margaret Mitchell Square
Atlanta, GA 30303-1089

**Concern(s):** arts; literature. Newsletter with fiction and poetry by southern writers, primarily black writers. **Frequency:** 2/yr.

### ✌ ▶ Catalyst
1616 P St. NW, #310
Washington, DC 20036    (202)332-0900

**Affiliation:** Union of Concerned Scientists. **Concern(s):** peace; environment; politics; anti-nuclear; grassroots organizing; law. "Scien-

tists concerned about nuclear weapons and power publicize this newsletter to promote a future free of nuclear problems. News on treaty negotiations, legislation, and grassroots efforts is all part of the package." -C.C. **Est.:** 1970. **Frequency:** 6/yr. **Subscription:** Donation. **Price:** Free. **Contact(s):** Charles Monfort.

### J ▶ Catalyst: A Socialist Journal of Social Services
Box 1144
New York, NY 10025    (718)784-6160

**Affiliation:** Institute of Social Service Alternatives. **Concern(s):** justice; economics; education. "Liberal arts disciplines from a pro-cooperative perspective are the angle here. In the studies of these professionals and scholars, meeting human needs is considered more important than the profit motive." -C.C. **Est.:** 1976. **Frequency:** 4/yr. **Subscription:** $15/yr. **Price:** $4/ea. **Contact(s):** Judy Zangwill.

### T ▶ Catalyst: Economics for a Living Earth
64 Main St.
Montpelier, VT 05602    (802)223-7943

**Affiliation:** Institute for Gaean Economics. **Concern(s):** Third World; economics; justice; socially-responsible investing; alternative consumer; indigenous peoples; alternative markets; development. Opportunities to support grassroots, decentralized projects here and in the Third World with loans, investments and donations. This is the networking newsletter covering social responsibility, new economic models and projects, for people who want their money to make a difference, with a focus on native peoples. Focuses on small businesses, worker-ownership, co-ops, responsive (and usually small) publicly traded companies, nonprofits, local currency, appropriate technology, and alternative banks. **Other Resources:** Projects include, Grassroots Corporate Action Campaign, Green Mountain Biodiversity Project; All Species Project. See INVESTING FROM THE HEART newsletter. Resource Guide available. **Frequency:** 4/yr. **Subscription:** $25/yr. **Member:** Co-op America. **Contact(s):** Susan Meeker-Lowry.

### ✌ ▶ Catholic Peace Fellowship Bulletin
339 Lafayette St.
New York, NY 10012    (212)673-8990

**Affiliation:** Catholic Peace Fellowship. **Concern(s):** peace; spiritual; faith; militarism. "This fellowship acted as a harbinger of the peace fellowships of other religious denominations. It continues to serve as a positive example for the others and sparks activism for peace in the Church of Rome."-C.C. **Est.:** 1965. **Frequency:** 3/yr. **Subscription:** Donation. **Price:** Free. **Contact(s):** Bill Ofenloch.

### A ▶ Catholic Rural Life
National Catholic Rural Life Conference
4625 NW Beaver Dr.
Des Moines, IA 50310

**Concern(s):** agriculture; environment; spiritual; land; rural communities; faith. Each issue focuses on a theme relating ethics and the land. **Frequency:** 5/yr.

### D ▶ Catholic Worker
36 E. 1st St.
New York, NY 10003    (212)254-1640

**Affiliation:** Catholic Worker Movement. **Concern(s):** demographics; justice; spiritual; faith; poverty; grassroots organizing. "This little tabloid is published to promote action and greater concern for the poor and disadvantaged. It is meant to work within the grassroots of the Catholic Church for social justice for the homeless, farm-workers, peace, and women clergy."-C.C. **Est.:** 1933. **Frequency:** 8/yr. **Price:** Free. **Contact(s):** Robbie Gamble. (212)473-8973. **Other:** 55 E. 3rd St., New York, NY 10003.

### ✌ ▶ CCCO News Notes
2208 South St.
Philadelphia, PA 19146    (215)545-4626

**Affiliation:** Central Committee for Conscientious Objectors. **Concern(s):** peace; anti-draft. "Pacifists concerned about the military draft and military service learn from this newsletter how to note officially their objection on principle to war. News of the organization and sister groups appears also."-C.C. **Est.:** 1949. **Frequency:** 4/yr. **Price:** Free. **Contact(s):** Robert A. Seeley.

### F ▶ CDF Reports
122 C St. NW, 4th Fl.
Washington, DC 20001    (202)628-8787

**Affiliation:** Children's Defense Fund. **Concern(s):** feminism; justice; child support; children; welfare rights; day care. "Better social programs for disadvantaged children instead of more money for the Pentagon are advocated in these reports. Whether needing more assistance because they are poor, handicapped or children of color, these children will find a voice in this progressive periodical."-C.C. **Est.:** 1979. **Frequency:** 12/yr. **Subscription:** $29.95/yr. **Price:** Donation. **Contact(s):** Virginia Witt.

### T ▶ CENSA's Strategic Report
2288 Fulton St., #103
Berkeley, CA 94704    (510)540-5006

**Affiliation:** Center for Study of Americas. **Concern(s):** Third World; agriculture; Central America; development. "Agricultural assistance for Nicaragua by CENSA and current analysis of relations between the US and Central America are key parts of this newsletter. Each report focuses on one aspect of Central America and makes a concrete contribution to the solidarity movement."-C.C. **Est.:** 1985. **Frequency:** 3-5/yr. **Subscription:** $10/yr. **Price:** $2.50/ea. **Contact(s):** Roger Burbach.

### M ▶ Censorship News
2 W. 64th St.
New York, NY 10023    (212)873-6500

**Affiliation:** American Ethical Union. **Concern(s):** media; arts; justice; civil liberties; censorship; freedom of expression. Newsletter. **Publisher:** National Coalition Against Censorship.

### ✍ ▶ The Centennial Review
312 Linton Hall
Michigan State University
East Lansing, MI 48824-1044

**Concern(s):** education; science. Articles on sciences, humanities, and interdisciplinary topics. **Contact(s):** R.K. Meiners (Editor).

### ✌ ▶ Center for Peace and Conflict Studies Newsletter
Wayne State University
5229 Cass, #101
Detroit, MI 48202    (313)577-3453

**Affiliation:** Center for Peace and Conflict Studies. **Concern(s):** peace; education; students. "This university's peace education program is a refreshing alternative to the usual college ROTC courses. Most of the quarterly's four pages are devoted to updates on center projects."-C.C. **Est.:** 1974. **Frequency:** 4/yr. **Price:** Free. **Contact(s):** Lawrence Rosinger.

### A ▶ Center for Rural Affairs Newsletter
Box 405
Walthill, NE 68067    (402)846-5428

**Affiliation:** Center for Rural Affairs. **Concern(s):** agriculture; family farms; rural communities; bioregionalism. Concerned about the role of public policy in the decline of family farms and rural communities, this newsletter provokes public thought about social, economic and environmental issues affecting rural America, especially the Midwest and Plains regions. **Frequency:** 12/yr.

### L ▶ Center for Socialist History Interbulletin
2633 Etna St.
Berkeley, CA 94704    (510)843-4658

**Affiliation:** Center for Socialist History. **Concern(s):** labor; politics; education. "The history of workers' and people's movements, as well as a radical perspective on general US history, is the point. Although it utilizes a rather academic style, it could be useful to both the general public and the scholar in getting an alternative view of past events."-C.C. **Est.:** 1981. **Frequency:** Irregular. **Subscription:** $10/4. **Price:** $2.50/ea. **Contact(s):** Ernest Haberkern.

### J ▶ Center Focus
3700 13th St. NE
Washington, DC 20017    (202)635-2757

**Affiliation:** Center of Concern. **Concern(s):** justice; Third World; peace; spiritual; faith; social justice; foreign policy development; analysis. This newsletter focuses on many issues of social justice and policy. In-depth analysis is one refreshing point of this little in size; powerful in scope newsletter. **Frequency:** 6/yr. **Contact(s):** Peter J. Henriot, James Hug (Executive Director). (202)635-2757.

### ✌ ▶ Center Update
515 Broadway
Santa Cruz, CA 95060    (408)423-1626

**Affiliation:** Resource Center For Nonviolence. **Concern(s):** peace; education; Third World; nonviolence. This newsletter reports on the current happenings at the Center, along with program announcements, book reviews and current periodical availability at their bookstore/library. **Frequency:** 4/yr. **Contact(s):** Steve Belling.

### T ▶ Central America Bulletin
347 Dolores St., #327
San Francisco, CA 94410    (415)255-2003

**Affiliation:** Central America Research Institute. **Concern(s):** Third World; Central America. "Each month, events of Central America are featured, along with efforts in the US to promote independence in the region. All Central American countries are included with emphasis on El Salvador, Guatemala, and Nicaragua."-C.C. **Est.:** 1981. **Frequency:** 12/yr. **Subscription:** $15, $20 institution. **Price:** $1/ea. **Contact(s):** Arnon Hadar.

**T ◆ Central America Monitor**
464 19th St.
Oakland, CA 94612    (510)835-4692
**Affiliation:** Data Center. **Concern(s):** Third World; Central America. "Reprinted are news articles from the range of news and opinion periodicals (Guardian to National Review) on Costa Rica, El Salvador, Guatemala, Honduras, and Nicaragua. This collection of reprints provides a balanced view of the region."-C.C. **Est.:** 1985. **Frequency:** 24/yr. **Price:** Donation. **Contact(s):** Bill Berkowitz.

**T ◆ Central America NewsPak**
Box 2327
Austin, TX 78768    (512)476-9841
**Affiliation:** Central American Resource Center. **Concern(s):** Third World; Central America. "A compilation of current news articles from some 10 US and Mexican newspapers, the NewsPak is the best objective source of news on Central America. The New York Times and the Christian Science Monitor are typical reprint sources. For the breadth of its reprints, this compilation is highly recommended."-C.C. **Est.:** 1986. **Frequency:** 26/yr. **Subscription:** $38/yr. **Price:** Free. **Contact(s):** Luz Guerra.

**T ◆ Central America Report**
1747 Connecticut Ave. NW
Washington, DC 20009    (202)387-7652
**Affiliation:** Religious Task Force on Central America. **Concern(s):** Third World; spiritual; faith; militarism; intervention. "Walking alongside our brothers and sisters in Central America" has been the purpose of this group's newspaper for about ten years now. It is a first choice for people of faith working for democracy in the region."-C.C. **Est.:** 1980. **Frequency:** 6/yr. **Subscription:** $6/yr. **Price:** $1/ea. **Contact(s):** Margaret Swedish.

**T ◆ Central American Refugee Defense Newsletter**
14 Beacon St., #506
Boston, MA 02108    (617)227-9727
**Affiliation:** Central American Refugee Defense Fund. **Concern(s):** Third World; justice; refugees; immigration. "Both political and economic refugees from deadly conditions in Central America find a friend here. Most refugees come from Guatemala and El Salvador, but immigrants from other countries of the region are also defended."-C.C. **Est.:** 1982. **Frequency:** 4/yr. **Subscription:** $10/yr. **Price:** Free. **Contact(s):** Daniel Katz.

**D ◆ Central Park**
Box 1446
New York, NY 10023    (212)496-7671
**Concern(s):** demographics; peace; feminism; Third World; arts; culture. "A 'journal of the arts & social theory,' this 100-odd-page magazine has presented photo and written essays on topics like the homeless, apartheid, feminism, and world peace. Avant garde in style, this cultural magazine welcomes all progressives to share their literary creations with its readers."-C.C. **Est.:** 1980. **Frequency:** 2/yr. **Subscription:** $9, $10.50 institution. **Price:** $5/ea. **Contact(s):** Stephen-Paul Martin, Richard Royal, Eve Ensler.

**T ◆ Challenge: A Journal of Faith and Action in Central America**
1470 Irving St. NW
Washington, DC 20010    (202)332-0292
**Affiliation:** Ecumenical Program on Central America & the Caribbean (EPICA). **Concern(s):** Third World; politics; Central America; volunteers. A journal that depicts the works of many brave volunteers working in Central America to change the society there along with the actions of the church there and here in the US. **Est.:** 1968. **Frequency:** 3/yr. **Subscription:** $10/yr. **Price:** $3.50/ea. **Pages:** 16. **Circ.:** 2M. **Labels:** 5000. **Fax:** (202)332-1184. **Contact(s):** Minor Sinclair.

**✍ ◆ Change**
Heldref Publications
4000 Albemarle St. NW
Washington, DC 20016    (202)362-6445
**Concern(s):** education; politics; economics. Well-known and respected as an opinion magazine dealing with contemporary issues in higher learning, the award winning Change spotlights trends, provides new insights, and analyzes the implications of educational programs. Aritlces cover influential institutions and individuals, new teaching methods, finances, governance, and public policy. **Frequency:** 6/yr. **Subscription:** $23, $45 institutions.

**F ◆ Changing Men, Issues in Gender, Sex & Politics**
306 N. Brooks St.
Madison, WI 53715    (608)256-2565
**Affiliation:** National Organization for Men Against Sexism. **Concern(s):** feminism; peace; men's liberation; nonviolence. The nation's only men's magazine for men and women alike. Addressing the problems, dynamics, & joys of change in relationships in the 1990's. Appeals to the reader who is ready to confront & explore personal growth. In depth analysis, poetry, sports, history, fiction, and much more. Provides updated listings of men's groups & events across the nation. A must for those who study gender, feminism, or the men's movement! **Est.:** 1979. **Frequency:** 2/yr. **Subscription:** $24/2 yrs; $40 institution. **Price:** $6/ea. **Bulk:** 10% off/24. **Pages:** 64. **Circ.:** 4M. **Date Publ.:** 11/90. **Publisher:** Feminist Men's Publications. **Labels:** 4000. **Contact(s):** Peter Bresnick (Business Manager), Rick Cote (Editor). (608)256-3965.

**✍ ◆ Changing Schools**
Colorado Options in Education
Box 191
Lakewood, CO 80226
**Concern(s):** education; childhood. A newsletter/journal on alternative schools, including public school programs.

**$ ◆ Checkbook**
806 15th St. NW
Washington, DC 20005    (202)347-7823
**Affiliation:** Center for the Study of Services. **Concern(s):** economics; consumer rights. A magazine that studies and rates service firms.

**☢ ◆ Chemical Weapons Convention Bulletin**
Center for National Policy
317 Massachusetts Ave. NE
Washington, DC H9H 3L4    (202)546-9300
**Affiliation:** Center for National Policy. **Concern(s):** peace; environment; health; hazardous/toxic waste.

**E ◆ Chesapeake Bay Magazine**
1819 Bay Ridge Ave.
Annapolis, MD 21401
**Concern(s):** environment; Chesapeake Bay. A magazine with mechanical and how-to articles on boating, fishing, conservation in Chesapeake Bay. **Contact(s):** Jean Waller (Editor).

**✍ ◆ Chickadee**
The Young Naturalist Foundation
56 The Esplanade, #306
Toronto, ON M5E 1A7 Canada
**Affiliation:** Young Naturalist Foundation. **Concern(s):** education; environment; youth; childhood. Animal and adventure stories, for children ages 3 to 8. Also puzzles, activities, and observation games. **Contact(s):** Catherine Ripley (Editor).

**♥ ◆ Child Care ActioNews**
330 7th Ave, 18th Fl.
New York, NY 10001    (212)239-0138
**Affiliation:** Child Care Action Campaign. **Concern(s):** family; day care. Better quality, expanded day care is promoted in the eight pages of this newspaper. While the short-term goal is improvement of current day care facilities, the final goal is a "national system of quality, affordable child care."-C.C. **Est.:** 1983. **Dues:** $20/yr. **Frequency:** 6/yr. **Subscription:** Membership. **Price:** Donation. **Contact(s):** Barbara Reisman.

**✍ ◆ Childhood - The Waldorf Perspective**
c/o Nancy Aldrich
Route 2, Box 2675
Westford, VT 05494
**Concern(s):** education; health; homeschooling; holism. A journal that explores holistic and spiritual alternatives in parenting, schooling, and home schooling with a focus on the Waldorf view of child development. On family life, cooperative initiatives, curriculum, imaginative play, the wonder of the natural world, story-telling, music, artistic work, handwork, handicrafts, festivals, reviews, resources, networking. Nurturing the magical time of childhood. **Frequency:** 4/yr. **Subscription:** $20/yr. **Price:** $5/sample. **Contact(s):** Nancy Aldrich.

**☛ ◆ Children and Animals**
2100 L St. NW
Washington, DC 20037    (202)452-1100
**Affiliation:** Humane Society of the US. **Concern(s):** environment; education; animal rights. Magazine for teachers of pre-K-6th grade pupils.

**☢ ◆ Children's Campaign for Nuclear Disarmament Newsletter**
14 Everit St.
New Haven, CT 06511    (203)787-5262
**Affiliation:** Children's Campaign for Nuclear Disarmament. **Concern(s):** peace; education; disarmament; childhood. "Youth worried about nuclear war can feel better by doing some of the things suggested in this newsletter. These include letter writing to US representatives and rallies for peace."-C.C. **Est.:** 1981. **Frequency:** 4/yr. **Price:** Donation. **Contact(s):** Donald Joughlin.

**H ◆ Children's Digest**
1100 Waterway Blvd.
Box 567
Indianapolis, IN 46202
**Concern(s):** health; education; nutrition; youth. Health publication for preteens. Informative articles, and fiction (especially realistic, adventure, mystery and humorous), with health, safety, exercise, nutrition, sports, or hygiene as theme. Historical and biographical articles. Poetry activities. **Contact(s):** Elizabeth Rinck (Editor).

**✍ ◆ Children's Environments**
NYU Graduate School & Univ. Ctr.
33 W. 42nd St.
New York, NY 10036    (212)944-2335
**Affiliation:** Children's Environments Research Group. **Concern(s):** education; childhood. **Frequency:** 4/yr.

**✍ ◆ Children's Surprises**
Box 236
Chanhassen, MN 55317
**Concern(s):** education; youth. "Activities for today's kids and parents." Educational activities, puzzles, games in reading, language, math, science, cooking, music, and art. Articles about history, animals, and geography. **Contact(s):** Peggy Simenson, Jeanne Palmer (Editors).

**T ◆ Chile Newsletter**
Box 3620
Berkeley, CA 94703    (510)845-9398
**Affiliation:** Casa Chile. **Concern(s):** Third World; South America. "The problems of the people of Chile under the dictatorship of General Pinochet are presented. Solidarity with these repressed people and the actions of the US toward that country are also noted."-C.C. **Est.:** 1981. **Frequency:** 6/yr. **Subscription:** $10/yr. **Price:** Donation. **Contact(s):** Vanessa Whang.

**S ◆ Christian *New Age Quarterly**
Box 276
Clifton, NJ 07011-0276
**Affiliation:** Bethaheva's Concern. **Concern(s):** spiritual; faith; reform. "A bridge supporting dialogue between New Agers and Christians. In a cooperative spirit of mutual appreciation, we clarify both the differences and common ground of Christianity and the New Age Movement. A lively journal with columns and features, we consistently offer high quality writing, sound scholarship, and the sparkle of plain, good fun." **Est.:** 1989. **Frequency:** 4/yr. **Subscription:** $12.50/yr. **Price:** $3.50/ea. **Pages:** 20. **Publisher:** Bathsheva's Concern. **Contact(s):** Catherine Groves (Publisher/Editor).

**S ◆ Christian Century**
407 S. Dearborn St.
Chicago, IL 60605    (312)427-5380
**Concern(s):** spiritual; politics; justice; faith. Liberal Christian magazine published for clergy and laity. "We use articles dealing with social problems, ethical dilemmas, political issues, international affairs, and the arts, as well as the theological and ecclesiastical matters. We focus on concerns that arise at the juncture between church and society." **Contact(s):** James M. Wall (Editor).

**J ◆ Christianity and Crisis**
537 W. 121st St.
New York, NY 10027    (212)662-5907
**Concern(s):** justice; demographics; peace; spiritual; faith; activism. "This Protestant opinion magazine is designed to inspire a greater commitment to social concerns activities. It is a top choice in the field of general topic religious activist periodicals, and deserves to be read by all Christians concerned about the human condition."-C.C. **Est.:** 1941. **Frequency:** 19/yr. **Subscription:** $24, $30 institution. **Price:** $1.75/ea. **Contact(s):** Leon Howell.

**☢ ◆ Christopher News Notes**
12 E. 48th St.
New York, NY 10017    (212)759-4050
**Affiliation:** Christophers. **Concern(s):** peace; spiritual; faith. "You may have heard the Christophers' public service ads for peace on your local TV or radio. The same type of positive ideas for personal and world peace make up this pleasant religious-inspired pamphlet series."-C.C. **Est.:** 1945. **Frequency:** 10/yr. **Price:** Free. **Contact(s):** Joseph R. Thomas.

**J ◆ Church and State**
8120 Fenton St.
Silver Springs, MD 20910    (301)589-3707
**Affiliation:** Americans United for Separation of Church and State. **Concern(s):** justice; spiritual; politics; constitutional rights; civil liberties. "The US Constitution requires separation of the state and the church, and promoting this is the purpose of the magazine. Both government control of religions and government subsidies to religions, such as tax credits for church school education, are opposed."-

C.C. **Est.:** 1948. **Frequency:** 11/yr. **Subscription:** $10/yr. **Price:** $1/ea. **Contact(s):** Joseph L. Conn.

**J ▸ Church Women ACT**
110 Maryland Ave. NE
Washington, DC 20002 (202)544-8747
**Affiliation:** Church Women United. **Concern(s):** justice; feminism; spiritual; faith; law. "This one-sheet legislative newsletter reflects the concerns of the interdenominational women's group. It covers the range of social concerns issues."-C.C. **Est.:** 1985. **Frequency:** Irregular. **Subscription:** Donation. **Price:** Free.

**J ▸ The Churchman**
1074 23rd Ave. N
St. Petersburg, FL 33704 (813)894-0097
**Concern(s):** justice; peace; spiritual; faith. "We hope that this 'oldest religious journal' publishes for many more years with its commitment to social justice within and outside the church. If you like your respect for God mixed with some down-to-earth humanism, you will like The Churchman. It is ecumenical, peace-loving and concerned about life on Earth."-C.C. **Est.:** 1804. **Frequency:** 9/yr. **Subscription:** $10/yr. **Price:** Free. **Publisher:** Churchman Co. **Contact(s):** Edna Ruth Johnson.

**S ▸ Churchwoman**
Church Women United
475 Riverside Dr.
New York, NY 10115 (212)870-2347
**Affiliation:** Church Women United. **Concern(s):** spiritual; feminism; demographics; peace; politics; faith. A magazine committed to the empowerment of women and works for global justice and peace. Goals are: to deepen our understanding of what it means to be Christian women of faith in today's world; to develop a visible ecumenical community; to work for a just, caring and peaceful society; to use responsibly Earth's resources...our intelligence, time, energy and money. Focuses on vital issues: food, shelter, health, education, work, justice, peace, human rights, environment and family stability. **Contact(s):** Doris Anne Younger (General Director), Claire Randall

**✏ ▸ Cineaste**
Box 2242
New York, NY 10009 (212)982-1241
**Concern(s):** arts; media; film. "US and foreign films are reviewed from a left perspective in this thick tabloid. Interviews and biographical profiles complement a fine film selection."-C.C. **Est.:** 1967. **Frequency:** 4/yr. **Subscription:** $13/yr. **Price:** $4/ea. **Publisher:** Cineaste Publishers. **Office:** 200 Park Ave. S New York, NY 10003.

**E ▸ CIPA: Complete List of Books and Reports in Print**
Box 189040
Sacramento, CA 95818 (916)442-2472
**Affiliation:** California Institute of Public Affairs (CIPA)/Claremont Colleges. **Concern(s):** environment; sustainability; natural resources. This is an independent statewide organization working for a better understanding of the character, problems, and future awareness of the world as interdependent through focusing on sustainable development and natural resource protection in California. This is their book and report list. **Est.:** 1969. **Frequency:** 2/yr. **Price:** Free. **Contact(s):** Thaddeus C. Trzyna (Editor).

**J ▸ The Circle**
1530 E. Franklin Ave.
Minneapolis, MN 55404
**Concern(s):** justice; Native Americans. Newspaper featuring news and commentary from the Upper Midwest Native American community, accompanied by national news and perspectives. **Frequency:** 12/yr. **Subscription:** $12/yr.

**E ▸ CITES Ark**
3705 Cardiff Rd.
Chevy Chase, MD 20815(301)654-3150
**Affiliation:** Convention on International Trade in Endangered Species of Wild Fauna and Flora (CITES). **Concern(s):** environment; wildlife/endangered species. This magazine reports on illegal importation of wildlife and fauna into the US and the ways that it is being combated. **Frequency:** 4/yr.

**P ▸ Citizen Action News**
1300 Connecticut Ave. NW, #401
Washington, DC 20036 (202)857-5153
**Affiliation:** Citizen Action. **Concern(s):** politics; health; environment; consumer protection; grassroots organizing. Newsletter. **Frequency:** 4/yr. **Contact(s):** Heather Booth.

**$ ▸ Citizen Agenda**
215 Pennsylvania Ave. SE
Washington, DC 20003 (202)546-9707
**Affiliation:** US Public Interest Research Group. **Concern(s):** economics; consumer rights. "This newsletter promotes consumer actions and research in the spirit of Ralph Nader, who sparked the group's formation. Campus chapter news and ideas on national consumer campaign needing support find a place here also."-C.C. **Est.:** 1983. **Dues:** $25/yr. **Frequency:** 4/yr. **Subscription:** Membership. **Contact(s):** Melinda Upton, Kathleen Traphagon

**P ▸ Citizen Participation**
Tufts University
Medford, MA 02155 (617)628-5000
**Affiliation:** Lincoln Filene Center for Citizenship. **Concern(s):** politics; demographics; justice; grassroots organizing; housing; poverty. "Grassroots organizing for social concerns issues such as housing and voting rights is the purpose of this newspaper, In depth analysis of the issues is interspersed with practical suggestions for action, providing an effective editorial mix."-C.C. **Est.:** 1979. **Frequency:** 4/yr. **Subscription:** $12/yr. **Price:** $3/ea. **Contact(s):** Stuart Langton.

**U ▸ City Limits**
40 Prince St.
New York, NY 10012-9801 (212)925-9820
**Concern(s):** urban; justice; demographics; health; education; feminism; citizen activism; housing; health care; job creation; day care. For 15 years, an award-winning magazine has provided news, investigative reports and analysis of such critical issues as housing and homelessness, health care, job creation, day care, the urban environment, community reinvestment and more. **Est.:** 1976. **Frequency:** 10/yr. **Subscription:** $15/yr. **Price:** $2/ea. **Bulk:** 33% off/24. **Pages:** 24-32. **Circ.:** 3M. **Publisher:** City Limits Community Information Service, Inc.. **Fax:** (212)966-3407. **Contact(s):** Doug Turetsky (Editor), Lisa Glazer (Associate Editor). Andrew White, Senior editor.

**J ▸ Civil Liberties**
132 W. 43rd St.
New York, NY 10036 (212)944-9800
**Affiliation:** American Civil Liberties Union. **Concern(s):** justice; civil liberties; freedom of expression. "Individual rights are staunchly defended in this tabloid of one of the world's best known civil liberties groups. Organizational activities such as court briefs, chapter news, et al., are emphasized. The ACLU is a politically neutral rights group which tends to be more of an activist social change group."-C.C. **Est.:** 1927. **Dues:** $20/yr. **Frequency:** 4/yr. **Subscription:** Membership. **Price:** $5/ea. **Pages:** 12. **Circ.:** 275M. **Contact(s):** Ari Korpivaara.

**J ▸ Civil Liberties Alert**
122 Maryland Ave. NE
Washington, DC 20002 (202)544-1681
**Affiliation:** American Civil Liberties Union, DC. **Concern(s):** justice; civil liberties; freedom of expression; capital punishment; criminal system. "This newsletter describes new legislation needing support or defeat, on issues of concern to the ACLU. Such issues range from free speech to the death penalty, with voting records documented."-C.C. **Est.:** 1978. **Frequency:** 4/yr. **Subscription:** Donation. **Price:** Free. **Contact(s):** Sherille Ismail.

**J ▸ Civil Liberties Review**
Box 2047
Olathe, KS 66061 (913)829-0609
**Concern(s):** justice; media; civil liberties; freedom of expression; censorship. Focuses on issues of due process before the law, opposes repressive legislation, champions freedom of speech, of the press, and open debate of ALL issues. The basic concern is for rights of individuals. **Subscription:** $6/yr. **Pages:** 2. **Circ.:** 600. **Contact(s):** Laird Wilcox (Editor).

**☮ ▸ Civilian-Based Defense: News & Opinions**
Box 31616
Omaha, NE 68131 (402)558-2085
**Affiliation:** Civilian-Based Defense Association. **Concern(s):** peace; politics; nonviolence; civil disobedience; grassroots organizing. Attempts to widen the defense debate through articles as well as announcements of meetings and conferences around the world. **Frequency:** 6/yr. **Contact(s):** Melvin G. Beckman, Philip D. Bogdonoff.

**J ▸ Class-Struggle Defense Notes**
Partisan Defense Committee
Box 99, Canal Street Station
New York, NY 10013 (212)406-4252
**Affiliation:** Partisan Defense Committee. **Concern(s):** justice; minority rights; racism; political prisoners. **Contact(s):** Deborah Mackson (Executive Director), Paul Cooperstein (Secretary).

**E ▸ Clean Water Action News**
1320 18th St. NW, #300
Washington, DC 20036 (202)457-1286
**Affiliation:** Clean Water Action. **Concern(s):** environment; health; hazardous/toxic waste; waste management; water. "Water pollution by industry and governments is opposed here. Whether it is exotic toxic waste chemicals in our oceans or everyday household sewage in the nearest river, it is an unnecessary evil, this newsletter believes."-C.C. **Est.:** 1971. **Frequency:** 4/yr. **Subscription:** $24, $40 institution. **Price:** Donation. **Contact(s):** Zev Remba.

**$ ▸ Clean Yield**
Box 1880
Greensboro Bend, VT 05842 (802)533-7178
**Affiliation:** Clean Yield Group. **Concern(s):** economics; socially-responsible investing. A stockmarket newsletter for socially concerned investors. Profiles publicly traded companies, comments on the current stock market climate, and reports on developments in the ethical investment movement. "Principles and profits working together." **Frequency:** 12/yr. **Subscription:** $85/yr.; $100 business. **Price:** $3/sample. **Pages:** 8. **Member:** Co-op America.

**✍ ▸ The Clearing House**
Heldref Publications
4000 Albemarle St. NW
Washington, DC 20016 (202)362-6445
**Concern(s):** education. Each issue has a variety of articles for teachers and administrators of middle schools and junior and senior high schools. It includes experiments, trends, and accomplishments in courses, teaching methods, administrative procedures and school programs. Articles deal in a forthright manner with important controversial issues. Special monthly features include "Speaking Out," which offer points of view on educational trends, "Innovations in the Classroom." **Frequency:** 6/yr. **Subscription:** $40/yr.

**E ▸ Clearinghouse Bulletin**
1325 G St. NW, #1003
Washington, DC 20005 (202)879-3044
**Affiliation:** Carrying Capacity Network. **Concern(s):** environment; demographics; energy; activism; population growth; conservation; natural resources; networking. This bulletin provides activists with essential information on environmental, population and resource issues along with the linkages among them from a carrying capacity perspective. It highlights the efforts of organizations dealing with these issues. **Est.:** 1990. **Dues:** $35/yr.; $80/organization. **Frequency:** 6/yr. **Subscription:** Membership. **Pages:** 8-12. **Circ.:** 2.5M. **E-Network:** Econet. **ID:** 'smabley'. **Fax:** (202)879-3019. **Contact(s):** Stephen M. Mabley (Network Coordinator).

**J ▸ Clearinghouse Review**
407 S. Dearborn, #400
Chicago, IL 60605 (312)939-3830
**Affiliation:** National Clearinghouse for Legal Services. **Concern(s):** justice; criminal system; social justice. "Legal information for Legal Services lawyers and paralegals is provided. Other legal workers using the law for advancing human needs will find it useful."-C.C. **Est.:** 1975. **Frequency:** 4/yr. **Subscription:** $75/yr. **Price:** $6/ea. **Contact(s):** Lucy Mass.

**E ▸ Climate Alert**
324 4th St. NE
Washington, DC 20002 (202)547-0104
**Affiliation:** Climate Institute. **Concern(s):** environment; global warming. This newsletter covers issues relating to global warming and stratospheric ozone depletion. It has well written and informative articles on the issues relating to this global phenomenon. Nonprofit. **Est.:** 1986. **Dues:** $95/yr. **Frequency:** 10/yr. **Fax:** (202)547-0111. **Contact(s):** Nancy Wilson (Editor).

**L ▸ CLUW News**
15 Union Square W
New York, NY 10003 (212)242-0700
**Affiliation:** Amalgamated Textile & Clothing Workers Union. **Concern(s):** labor; feminism; unions; equal pay; sexism. "CLUW and their newsletter have done more than anyone else in bringing women's issues to the labor movement's agenda. From equal pay to paid maternity leave, all concerns of female workers are presented."-C.C. **Est.:** 1975. **Dues:** $20/yr. **Frequency:** 6/yr. **Subscription:** Membership. **Contact(s):** Diane Curry.

**$ ▸ The Co-op America Quarterly**
2100 M St. NW, #403
Washington, DC 20063 (202)872-5307
**Affiliation:** Co-op America. **Concern(s):** economics; environment; peace; energy; alternative consumer; cooperatives. A magazine that covers emerging, hopeful alternatives to "business as usual" and offers practical strategies and resources for using, buying, and investing power to create a new economy. CAQ envisions an economy based

on peace and justice, cooperation, and a healthy environment. Formerly Building Economic Alternatives, the organization was established in 1982. **Other Resources:** Many of the descriptions found in Macrocosm were contributed and reprinted from their yearly directory of members that is included with a subscription. Nonprofit. **Est.:** 1985. **Dues:** $20/yr. **Frequency:** 4/yr. **Subscription:** $20/yr. **Price:** $2/back issue. **Bulk:** 50% off/24. **Pages:** 40-56. **Circ.:** 60M. **Fax:** (202)223-5821. **Contact(s):** Cindy Mitlo (Editor), Alex Levin (Editorial Assistant).

### E ▶ Coastal Reporter
Sandy Hook
Highlands, NJ 07732    (201)291-0055
**Affiliation:** American Littoral Society. **Concern(s):** environment; ocean/rivers. This newsletter publishes scientific and popular material, reports on special activities for scuba divers and underwater photographers. A periodical for the professional and amateur interested in the conservation and study of coastal habitat and wildlife. **Frequency:** 4/yr. **Contact(s):** D. W. Bennett (Executive Director).

### E ▶ Coastwatch
Box 826
Provincetown, MA 02657    (617)487-3622
**Affiliation:** Center for Coastal Studies. **Concern(s):** environment; wildlife/endangered species; oceans/rivers. This newsletter shows activities of the center to save the coastal environment and the whales. It has informative articles on the destruction of the coast by pollution and other means. **Frequency:** 6/yr.

### H ▶ Collation
National Citizens Coalition for Nursing Home Reform
1224 M St. NW
Washington, DC 20005    (202)393-2018
**Affiliation:** National Citizens Coalition for Nursing Home Reform. **Concern(s):** health; consumer protection; seniors. "Better health and living conditions at nursing homes are advocated in this triannual review. Scores of short pieces and reviews cover the field in detail, and form a good information and action resource for activists and other concerned folks." -C.C. **Est.:** 1977. **Frequency:** 3/yr. **Subscription:** $35/yr. **Price:** $10/ea. **Contact(s):** Elma Holder.

### P ▶ Collective Voice
3255 Hennepin Ave. S., #245
Minneapolis, MN 55408
**Concern(s):** politics; justice; demographics; grassroots organizing; racism; homelessness; gay/lesbian. A magazine for the Upper Midwest activist. **Frequency:** 6/yr. **Subscription:** $15/yr.

### ✍ ▶ College Teaching
Heldref Publications
4000 Albemarle St. NW
Washington, DC 20016    (202)362-6445
**Concern(s):** education. The unique, interdisciplinary journal that support faculty members in their often-overlooked role as teachers. It's a journal with practical ideas, successful methods, and new programs for faculty development. A lively page, The Quick Fix, brings you a simple technique or an idea that works. For all teachers and for administrators concerned with faculty development - this journal brings inspiration and excitement back to college teaching! **Frequency:** 4/yr. **Subscription:** $42/yr.

### M ▶ Columbia Journalism Review
Columbia University
New York, NY 10027    (212)280-5595
**Affiliation:** Graduate School of Journalism. **Concern(s):** media; journalism; broadcasting. "This review serves as the journalism review of record, the 'bible' of newspaper, television, and radio criticism. Where the St. Louis Journalism Review is more practical for, and is produced for, working journalists and media activists on the local level, it concentrates on the journalism student, academia, and the national journalism community."-C.C. **Est.:** 1962. **Frequency:** 6/yr. **Subscription:** $16/yr. **Price:** $2.50/ea.

### E ▶ Columbiana
Chesaw Route
Box 83-F
Oroville, WA 98844
**Concern(s):** environment. **Frequency:** 4/yr. **Price:** $7.50/ea.

### P ▶ Columbus Free Press
209 S. High St., #203
Columbus, OH 43215    (614)228-5796
**Concern(s):** politics; alternative party. A magazine of articles, art, photos, cartoons, interviews, satire, criticism, news items and reviews. It has a loosely Left perspective. "Nothing which might offend on the basis of race and sex. Must have local application." **Est.:** 1970. **Frequency:** 12/yr. **Subscription:** $10 /yr. **Price:** $1/ea. **Pages:** 12. **Circ.:** 15M. **Publisher:** Duane Jager. **Contact(s):** Duane Jager (Publisher/Editor).

### ✐ ▶ The Comics Journal
7563 Lake City Way
Seattle, WA 98115
**Concern(s):** arts; literature; graphics. "This scrappy monthly guide covers the best and the worst in contemporary and classic comics: comic books, strips, cartoons, 'graphic novels', and more. Recent interviews include Ralph Steadman, Jules Feiffer, and Lynda Barry." **Est.:** 1976. **Frequency:** 12/yr. **Subscription:** $18/yr. **Price:** $3.50/ea. **Circ.:** 10M. **Contact(s):** Gary Groth.

### S ▶ Commentary
165 E. 56th St.
New York, NY 10022    (212)751-4000
**Affiliation:** American Jewish Committee. **Concern(s):** spiritual; Third World; faith; Middles East. Articles on contemporary issues, Jewish affairs, social sciences, community life, religious thought, cultural. Serious fiction; book reviews. **Contact(s):** Norman Podhoretz (Editor).

### S ▶ Common Boundary Magazine
7005 Florida St.
Chevy Chase, MD 20815(301)652-9495
**Concern(s):** spiritual; health; psychology; holism; transformation. The Common Boundary: Between Spirituality and Psychotherapy publishes this magazine and holds an annual conference for those interested in the spiritual aspects of psychotherapy and the psychological dimensions of spiritual growth. Also "kindred spirit" network groups are formed across the country to discuss these issues. The magazine and conference have featured Robert Bly, Ram Dass, James Hillman, Stephen Levine, Thich Nhat Hanh, Alice Walker, Matthew Fox, and Marion Woodman. **Other Resources:** A $500 award is given annually to the outstanding psychospiritual thesis or dissertation. Topics include Shamanism, expressive arts, meditation, contemplation, ecofeminism, co-dependency, bodywork, and dreams. **Est.:** 1980. **Frequency:** 6/yr. **Subscription:** $19/yr. **Price:** $3.95/ea. **Bulk:** 30% off/24. **Pages:** 50. **Circ.:** 20M. **Contact(s):** Charles Simpkinson, Ph.D (Publisher), Grace Ogden (Advertising Manager). (301)652-9495.

### P ▶ Common Cause Magazine
Box 220
Washington, DC 20077-1275    (202)833-1200
**Affiliation:** Common Cause. **Concern(s):** politics; economics; justice; energy; government accountability; grassroots organizing; activism; lobbying; reform; municipal; foreign policy; budget; constitutional rights; conservation; corporate responsibility. Focuses on national issues and features investigative articles, in-depth interviews, legislative updates, and Action Alerts explaining issues and suggesting lobbying actions member might take. **Office:** 2030 M St. NW Washington, DC 20036. **Contact(s):** Fred Wertheimer (President).

### F ▶ Common Ground
Box 313
Buffalo, NY 14213
**Concern(s):** feminism. **Frequency:** 12/yr. **Subscription:** $14/yr.

### S ▶ Common Ground
See directories for COMMON GROUND: RESOURCES FOR PERSONAL TRANSFORMATION.

### ☺ ▶ Common Sense on Energy and our Environment
Box 215
Morrisville, PA 19067    (215)736-1153
**Concern(s):** energy; environment. "...the newsletter for independent thinkers who refuse to let their environmental agenda be set by others. It is the only newsletter that explores all aspects of the scientific, technical, economic, and political components of energy and environmental issues." **Frequency:** 12/yr. **Subscription:** $29/yr. **Contact(s):** Jason Blank Makansi, Kristina Blank Makansi.

### A ▶ Common Sense Pest Control Quarterly
Box 7414
Berkeley, CA 94707    (510)524-2567
**Affiliation:** Bio Integral Resource Center. **Concern(s):** agriculture; environment; health; hazardous/toxic waste; pesticides. This newsletter provides information on least-toxic methods for managing any pests found in homes or gardens, including insects, weeds, plant diseases and rodents. Nonprofit. **Est.:** 1984. **Dues:** $30, $50 institutions. **Frequency:** 4/yr. **Subscription:** $30, $50 institution. **Price:** $8/ea. **Circ.:** 2.5M. **Fax:** (510)524-1758. **Contact(s):** Irene Juniper (Manager).

### P ▶ Commonwealth Report
15 Dutch St., #500
New York, NY 10038    (312)962-0390
**Affiliation:** Democratic Socialists of America. **Concern(s):** politics; Democratic Socialism. "Devoted to covering: the intersection of

politics and public opinion; how Americans think and talk about issues; social trends and political strategies, insider reports from the field." **Frequency:** 10/yr.

### $ ▶ Communities: Journal of Cooperation
Route 1, Box 155-M
Rutledge, MO 63563    (816)883-5543
**Affiliation:** Foundation for Personal and Community Development. **Concern(s):** economics; intentional communities; cooperatives; community self-reliance. Since its inception, this magazine has been the periodical focusing on the dynamic and richly diverse world of intentional communities. It chronicles both what is happening in the movement and how communities foster social experimentation that is crucial for a culture in crisis. **Other Resources:** Co-published the 1990/91 DIRECTORY OF INTENTIONAL COMMUNITIES. **Est.:** 1973. **Frequency:** 4/yr. **Subscription:** $18/yr. **Price:** $5/ea. **Bulk:** 40% off/24. **Pages:** 64. **Circ.:** 1.2M. **Publisher:** Communities Publication Cooperative. **Labels:** 1200. **E-Network:** MCI Mail. **ID:** QUEST. **Contact(s):** Laird Schaub (Business Manager), Charles Betterton (Managing Editor). (815)256-2245.

### $ ▶ Community Change
1000 Wisconsin Ave. NW
Washington, DC 20007    (202)342-0519
**Affiliation:** Center for Community Change. **Concern(s):** economics; urban; politics; community self-reliance; grassroots organizing. "Community organizing in the neighborhoods of our country is covered in this newsletter- from red-lining to inner-city improvement campaigns. Tips on improving organizational effectiveness also help make this a basic organizer's tool."-C.C. **Est.:** 1987. **Frequency:** 4/yr. **Subscription:** $20/yr. **Price:** Free. **Contact(s):** Ann Roberts, Tim Saasta, Allen Fishbein.

### $ ▶ Community Economics
57 School St.
Springfield, MA 01105    (413)746-8660
**Affiliation:** Institute for Community Economics (ICE). **Concern(s):** economics; community self-reliance; land trusts; community investment; socially-responsible investing. News stories and updates on the nation-wide Community Land Trust network, creating perpetually affordable homes on community-owned land. Provides information on Community Loan Funds and options for safe, direct investment by socially-concerned individuals and institutions in credit-starved low-income communities. This newsletter provides case examples of people empowering themselves to combat injustice, and reports on affordable housing policy. **Other Resources:** COMMUNITY LAND TRUST HANDBOOK. **Dues:** $15/yr. **Frequency:** 4/yr. **Subscription:** Membership. **Price:** $1/ea. **Pages:** 16-24. **Circ.:** 7M. **Labels:** 7000. **Fax:** (413)746-8862. **Contact(s):** Kirby White (Editor), Lisa Berger (Production/Design).

### P ▶ Community Endeavor News
240-B Commercial St.
Nevada City, CA 95959    (916)265-0824
**Concern(s):** politics; environment; justice; grassroots organizing. "Planetary News Advocating Personal Involvement." **Fax:** (916)265-6903. **Contact(s):** Susan Lukasha (Publisher).

### ✐ ▶ Community Murals Magazine
Box 65
Berkeley, CA 94701
**Concern(s):** arts; fine arts; graphics. **Contact(s):** Jane Norling.

### $ ▶ Community Service Newsletter
1901 Hannah Branch Rd.
Burnsville, NC 28714    (704)675-4262
**Concern(s):** economics; labor; politics; community self-reliance. Ernest Morgan, Vol. 38 No. 4: Employee Stock Ownership (ESOP) plans which give more control over production to the workers; the Universal Stock Ownership Plan (USOP) which would distribute part ownership of the growth of all American corporations to the citizens; a tax on money to redirect investments away from speculation and into productive facilities; encouragement in co-ops and credit unions; and a value system stemming rampant materialism and growth.

### ☺ ▶ Community Transportation Reporter
725 15th St. NW, #900
Washington, DC 20005    (202)628-1480
**Affiliation:** Rural America, Inc./Community Transportation Association Of America. **Concern(s):** energy; agriculture; environment; transportation; rural communities. This periodical deals with rural transportation and ways that it can be successfully implemented. **Frequency:** 12/yr. **Price:** $45/ea. (202)628-2537.

### T ▶ Compass
1401 New York Ave., #1100
Washington, DC 20005    (202)347-1800
**Affiliation:** Society for International Development, USA Chapters Committee. **Concern(s):** Third World; development. This newsletter

focuses on the economic policies prevailing from capitals all around the world today. It can be seen as a compass to guide people to the politically correct frame of mind. **Frequency:** 4/yr. **Contact(s):** Enrique Iglesias (President), Nancy Swing (703)752-2710. 265 Rocky Run Rd., Falmouth, VA 22405

### E ♦ Compendium Newsletter
Box 35473
Los Angeles, CA 90035   (310)559-9160
**Affiliation:** Educational Communications. **Concern(s):** environment; education. This newsletter covers local to international news, calendar of events, correspondence group targets, materials and resources, book reviews, and more on environmental issues. **Frequency:** 6/yr. **Subscription:** $20/yr. **Pages:** 20. **Contact(s):** Nancy Pearlman (Executive Producer), Anna Harlowe (Associate Director). (310)559-9160.

### F ♦ Complete Woman
1165 N. Clark
Chicago, IL 60610
**Concern(s):** feminism; health. Articles with how-to sidebars, giving practical advice to women on careers, health, personal relationships, etc. Inspirational profiles of successful women. **Contact(s):** Susan Handy (Senior Editor).

### E ♦ Compost Patch Ideas
306 Coleridge Ave.
Altoona, PA 16602   (814)946-9291
**Concern(s):** environment; spiritual; peace; politics; transformation; recycling. An educational center that sees itself as a catalyst in the present transition from the modern worldview to what could be called the ecological worldview, a transformation in which the earth is reenchanted and sacralized. Our newsletter is about individuals and groups that are imagining this new worldview. We also offer a lending library of books and periodicals that pertain to these concerns and a clearinghouse for ideas on the waste and toxics crisis. **Circ.:** 1M. **Publisher:** Compost Patch, Inc. **E-Network:** Econet. **ID:** 'clieden'. **Contact(s):** Charles Leiden (President).

### ⚙ ♦ Conflict Management and Peace Science
Uris Building #476
Cornell University
Ithaca, NY 14853
**Affiliation:** International Peace Science Society. **Concern(s):** peace. "Academic in nature with an abundance of footnotes, this journal could be useful for the peace scholar. Its goal is international relations based on discussions, not fighting." -C.C. **Est.:** 1974. **Frequency:** Irregular. **Subscription:** $20/yr. **Price:** $10/ea. **Contact(s):** Manas Chatterji.

### ⚙ ♦ Conflict Resolution Notes
7514 Kensington St.
Pittsburgh, PA 15221   (412)371-1000
**Affiliation:** Conflict Resolution Center International, Inc. **Concern(s):** peace; media; conflict resolution; computer networking. Newsletter. **Dues:** $20/yr. **Subscription:** Membership. **Fax:** Yes. **Contact(s):** Paul Wahrhaftig.

### P ♦ Congress Watcher
215 Pennsylvania Ave. SE
Washington, DC 20003-0757   (202)546-4996
**Affiliation:** Congress Watch/Public Citizen. **Concern(s):** politics; economics; law; consumer rights. "A Ralph Nader-initiated project, this selection probes all aspects of Washington affairs. HOW A BILL BECOMES A LAW is an example of the informative type of basic article that non-aligned citizens might find informative."-C.C. **Est.:** 1979. **Frequency:** 6/yr. **Subscription:** $8/yr. **Price:** Donation. **Contact(s):** Jane Stone.

### H ♦ Connecting the Dots
Box 949
Felton, CA 95018   (408)423-4069
**Affiliation:** EarthSave. **Concern(s):** health; environment; energy; agriculture; nutrition; renewables; natural resources; animal rights. This newsletter reports on healthier and wiser environmental food choices of people, better conservative use of our natural resources and non-polluting energy supplies. **Contact(s):** John Robbins.

### F ♦ Connexions
4228 Telegraph Ave.
Oakland, CA 94609
**Concern(s):** feminism; education; global understanding. "We want to go beyond merely providing facts and information—as directly as possible—women's writing generally unavailable in the US, we will be helping women here understand and connect with the experiences and viewpoints of women in other parts of the world... We hope that [it] willbe one step towards building an international women's movement." **Est.:** 1981. **Frequency:** 4/yr. **Subscription:** $15/ yr.; $24 institutions. **Pages:** 32. **Circ.:** 3M.

### ⚙ ♦ Connexions Digest—A Social Change Sourcebook
427 Bloor St. West
Toronto, ON M5S 1X7 Canada   (416)960-3903
**Affiliation:** Connexions Information Services, Inc. **Concern(s):** peace; environment; justice; feminism. A journal of information and ideas about social, environmental and economic alternatives. No charge for listing events in the Network News section. Provides information and services for activists, voluntary, and nonprofit groups, and for all those seeking reliable and up-to-date information about social concern issues. Primarily focuses on Canada, or international issues of concern to Canadians. Articles, events, projects, activities, and information about other resources. **Other Resources:** The CONNEXIONS ANNUAL. Mailing lists of organizations, libraries, and individuals interested in environmental, peace and women's and social justice materials are available. Consulting services on how to organize and desktop publishing services. Nonprofit. **Frequency:** 4/yr. **Subscription:** $25/yr. includes Annual. **Bulk:** 40% off/24. **Pages:** 56. **Circ.:** 2M. **Labels:** 11000. **Contact(s):** Ulli Diemer (Editor), Karl Andur (Computer Systems).

### F ♦ Conscience
1436 U St. NW, #301
Washington, DC 20009-3916   (202)638-1706
**Affiliation:** Catholics For Free Choice. **Concern(s):** feminism; spiritual; demographics; pro-choice; faith; family planning; reform; population growth. A journal of pro-choice Catholic opinion. Circulation includes members of Congress, librarians, clergy, and journalists. Focuses on ideas and values, it takes a leading role in bringing the ethical discussion on reproductive rights and other issues into the public arena. CFFC, a national educational organization, supports the right to legal reproductive health care, especially to family planning and abortion. It also works to reduce the incidence of abortion and to increase women's programs. **Est.:** 1973. **Frequency:** 6/yr. **Subscription:** $25/yr. **Circ.:** 10M. **Labels:** 5000. **Fax:** (202)332-7995. **Contact(s):** Denise Shannon (Communications Director), Frances Kissling (President).

### ⚙ ♦ Conscience and Military Tax Campaign
4534 1/2 University Way NE
Seattle, WA 98105   (206)547-0952
**Affiliation:** Conscience and Military Tax Campaign. **Concern(s):** peace; anti-draft; militarism; war tax revolt. This newsletter reports on taxes and how they are used to fuel the military machine in this country. Also, on the ways this is being combated by people and the Campaign. **Est.:** 1979.

### E ♦ Conscious Choice
Box 14431
Chicago, IL 60614   (312)281-1177
**Concern(s):** environment; health; spiritual; holism; nutrition. A magazine dealing with the environment, natural foods, holistic health, and spirituality. **Frequency:** 4/yr. **Member:** Co-op America.

### E ♦ The Conscious Consumer
Box 51
Wauconda, IL 60084   (708)526-0522
**Concern(s):** environment; economics; alternative consumer; green consumer. One of a spate of new green consumer newsletters, launched by a senior editor of Consumers Digest magazine. **Contact(s):** John F. Wasik.

### $ ♦ Consumer Action News
693 Mission St., #403
San Francisco, CA 94105   (415)777-9635
**Affiliation:** Consumer Action. **Concern(s):** economics; health; consumer rights; consumer protection. "Although California consumer affairs are emphasized, the points raised are applicable to consumer rights throughout the nation. Utility problems and credit card billing rights are typical of the moderate features in this tabloid." -C.C. **Est.:** 1971. **Frequency:** 8-10/yr. **Subscription:** $25/yr. **Price:** Donation. **Contact(s):** Mike Heffer.

### T ♦ Consumer Health Perspectives
200 Park Ave. S
New York, NY 10003   (212)777-8210
**Affiliation:** American Council for Voluntary International Action. **Concern(s):** Third World; economics; hunger; development.

### H ♦ Consumer Reports
Consumers Union of the United States
256 Washington St.
Mount Vernon, NY 10553   (914)667-9400
**Affiliation:** Consumers Union of the United States. **Concern(s):** health; economics; consumer protection; consumer rights. Magazine. **Other:** HBox CS 2010-A, Mt. Vernon, NY 10551

### $ ♦ Consumer's Voice
6048 Ogontz Ave.
Philadelphia, PA 19141   (215)424-1441
**Affiliation:** Consumers Education & Protection Association (CEPA). **Concern(s):** economics; health; consumer rights; consumer protection. "Strongly advocating the rights of consumers, this periodical pulls no punches in exposing manufacturers' negligence and sometimes purposely bad products. It goes beyond the product reviews of most consumers periodicals, and gives ideas on stopping shoddy merchandise and obtaining reimbursement where appropriate."-C.C. **Est.:** 1966. **Frequency:** 6/yr. **Subscription:** $6/yr. **Price:** Free. **Contact(s):** Lance Haver.

### $ ♦ Consumers Digest
5705 N. Lincoln Ave.
Chicago, IL 60659
**Concern(s):** economics; health; consumer rights. Articles on subjects of interest to consumers: products and services, automobiles, travel, health, fitness, consumer legal affairs, and personal money management. **Contact(s):** John Manos (Editor).

### ✍ ♦ Contact II Magazine
Box 451, Bowling Green Station
New York, NY 10004
**Concern(s):** arts; poetry; literature. "Poetry and book reviews make up the bulk of this well-written literary magazine. Subjects range from the excitement of change in Central America to the despondency of the homeless in this country. This is one of the most exciting literary magazines published today." -C.C. **Est.:** 1976. **Frequency:** 2/yr. **Subscription:** $8, $14 institution. **Price:** $7/ea. **Publisher:** Contact II Publications. **Contact(s):** J.G. Gosciak, Maurice Kenny.

### ✍ ♦ Contemporary Literature
7141 Helen C. White Hall
University of Wisconsin
Madison, WI 53706
**Concern(s):** arts; literature. "...specializes in interviews with both established and rising poets and novelists, and articles on all forms of 20th-century literature. Featuring recent interviews with Cynthia Ozick, Rosellen Brown, Chaim Potok, and John Barth." **Est.:** 1960. **Frequency:** 4/yr. **Subscription:** $20, $47 institution. **Circ.:** 2M. **Contact(s):** L. S. Dembo.

### P ♦ Contragate Alert
8773 Venice Blvd.
Los Angeles, CA 90034   (310)287-1556
**Affiliation:** Christic Institute. **Concern(s):** politics; justice; peace; Third World; government accountability. An alert published by the Christic Institute to keep their followers and the public up to date on the groundbreaking issues and news events surrounding the Iran-Contra connection involving government officials, and the trade of guns for drugs. **Other Resources:** See CONVERGENCE newsletter. **Contact(s):** Sara Nelson (Executive Director).

### P ♦ Convergence
8773 Venice Blvd.
Los Angeles, CA 90034   (310)287-1556
**Affiliation:** Christic Institute. **Concern(s):** politics; justice; peace; Third World; environment; spiritual; international law; national security; government accountability; anti-nuclear; interfaith. A magazine on faith and politics. "We cover Law, Human Rights, International Affairs, Government Secrecy and Radiation Hazards." **Frequency:** 4/yr. **Subscription:** $25/yr. **Price:** $6.25/ea. **Pages:** 14. **Circ.:** 50M. **Other Formats:** Internet, user name - 'christic@igc.org'. **E-Network:** PeaceNet. **ID:** 'christic'. **Fax:** (202)462-5138. **Contact(s):** Andrew Lang (Editor), Sara Nelson (Director).

### L ♦ Convoy Dispatch
Box 10128
Detroit, MI 48210   (313)842-2600
**Affiliation:** Teamsters for a Democratic Union. **Concern(s):** labor; unions. "These truck-driving rank-and-file Teamster activists support fair, unrigged union election. They oppose national union domination and mob influence of local affiliates." -C.C. Newsletter. **Est.:** 1976. **Frequency:** 9/yr. **Subscription:** $25/yr. **Price:** $1/ea. **Contact(s):** Frank De Pirro.

### $ ♦ Cooperative Action
Box 8032
Ann Arbor, MI 48107   (313)663-3624
**Affiliation:** Michigan Alliance of Cooperatives. **Concern(s):** economics; labor; cooperatives. Monthly newsletter for the Alliance working on behalf of over 2000 cooperative businesses in Michigan. **Frequency:** 12/yr. **Subscription:** $35/yr. **Office:** 273 E. Liberty Plaza Ann Arbor, MI 48104. **Contact(s):** Ebba Hierta (Executive Director).

### $ ♦ Cooperative Grocer
Box 597
Athens, OH 45701   (800)878-7333

**Concern(s):** economics; cooperatives. Bimonthly magazine for and about food cooperatives. **Other Resources:** Free sample issue. **Frequency:** 6/yr. **Member:** Co-op America. (614)448-7333.

**$ ◆ Cooperative Housing Bulletin**
1614 King St.
Alexandria, VA 22314   (703)549-5201
**Affiliation:** National Association of Housing Cooperative. **Concern(s):** economics; community self-reliance; housing coop. This bulletin focuses on housing cooperatives across the country and documents the joys and pitfalls of this arrangements. Nonprofit. **Est.:** 1950. **Dues:** Sliding scale based on type of membership. **Frequency:** 6/yr. **Subscription:** $35/yr. **Pages:** 20-24. **Circ.:** 25M. **Fax:** (703)549-5204. **Contact(s):** Pamela M. St. Clair (Deputy Director), Herbert J. Levy (Director).

**$ ◆ Corporate Examiner**
475 Riverside Dr., #566
New York, NY 10115   (212)870-2295
**Affiliation:** Interfaith Center for Corporate Responsibility. **Concern(s):** economics; corporate responsibility. "This newspaper reports on policies and practices of the major US corporations with regard to women, the environment, foreign affairs, labor and consumers are featured. Most monthly issues cover the social impact of corporations and the application of social criteria to investments in these corporations." -C.C. **Est.:** 1971. **Frequency:** 10/yr. **Subscription:** $35/yr. **Price:** $3.50/ea. **Contact(s):** Diane Bratcher.

**⚉ ◆ Council for a Livable World Newsletter**
110 Maryland Ave. NE
Washington, DC 20002  (202)543-4100
**Affiliation:** Council for a Livable World. **Concern(s):** peace; disarmament. "Preventing nuclear war is the goal. Legislative action toward this end is promoted in the newsletter's pages." -C.C. **Est.:** 1962. **Frequency:** 12/yr. **Subscription:** Donation. **Price:** Free. **Contact(s):** Jerome Grossman (Chairman), John Isaacs (President). **Other:** 20 Park Plaza, Boston, MA 02116. Wayne Jaquith , Boston Director. (617)542-2282.

**⚉ ◆ Council on Economic Priorities Research Report**
30 Irving Place, 9th Fl.
New York, NY 10211-0194  (212)420-1133
**Affiliation:** Council on Economic Priorities. **Concern(s):** peace; environment; economics; consumer rights; alternative consumer; boycott; green consumer; boycott. A public interest research organization with a nationwide memberships. CEP seeks to promote corporate social responsibility and international peace. This newsletter addresses such topics as socially responsible investing, US-Soviet relations, arms control, and the environment. Nonprofit. **Est.:** 1969. **Frequency:** 12/yr. **Subscription:** $25/yr. **Price:** $2/ea. **Bulk:** $.50ea/24. **Pages:** 6. **Contact(s):** Jacqueline Gelman (Marketing Director), Marci Soulakis (Marketing Assistant).

**D ◆ Country Journal**
Box 8200
Harrisburg, PA 17105
**Concern(s):** demographics; agriculture; environment; rural relocation; rural communities. Portrays country living for people who live in rural areas or are thinking about relocating there. Discusses issues affecting these areas and includes how-to's and photo essays. **Est.:** 1974. **Frequency:** 6/yr. **Price:** $3/ea. **Circ.:** 320M. **Contact(s):** Peter V. Fossel (Editor).

**F ◆ Country Woman**
Box 643
Milwaukee, WI 53201
**Concern(s):** feminism. Profiles of country women, inspirational, reflective pieces. Personal-experience, nostalgia, humor, service-oriented articles, original crafts, and how-to features of interest to country women. **Contact(s):** Kathy Pohl (Managing Editor).

**E ◆ Countryside**
1700 Broadway
New York, NY 10019   (212)903-5190
**Concern(s):** environment. Recycling, wildlife protection, tree planting, and letter writing campaigns are among concerns which will be featured. This magazine is in search of demonstrations of successful environmental-related projects. **Publisher:** Hearst Corporation. **Contact(s):** Trudy Balch.

**⚉ ◆ Courage in the Struggle for Justice and Peace**
105 Madison Ave.
New York, NY 10016   (212)682-5656
**Affiliation:** United Church of Christ. **Concern(s):** peace; justice; feminism; spiritual; faith; activism. "Local and national social concerns are promoted for members of the Church (no relation to the similarly-named fundamentalist denomination). Solutions to the earthly evils of racism, sexism, and militarism are suggested." -C.C. **Est.:** 1985.

**Frequency:** 12/yr. **Price:** Free. **Contact(s):** Reverend Paul Sherry (President).

**⚉ ◆ CovertAction Information Bulletin**
Box 34583
Washington, DC 20043  (202)331-9763
**Concern(s):** peace; politics; CIA; international law; foreign policy. A quarterly journal dedicated to exposing the illegal activities of US intelligence agencies, including the CIA, FBI, NSA, and others. Particular focus on secret intervention and subversion of democratic movements at home and abroad. All stories are thoroughly documented. **Est.:** 1978. **Frequency:** 4/yr. **Subscription:** $17/yr.; $32 institution. **Price:** $5/ea. **Bulk:** 20% off/24. **Pages:** 64. **Circ.:** 7M. **Publisher:** C.A. Publications. **E-Network:** MCI. **ID:** 'covert'. **Office:** 1500 Massachusetts Ave. NW Washington, DC **Contact(s):** Rich Ray, Lou Wolf (Editors). (202)331-9763.

**⚉ ◆ CPSR Newsletter**
Box 717
Palo Alto, CA 94301  (415)322-3778
**Affiliation:** Computer Professionals for Social Responsibility. **Concern(s):** peace; anti-nuclear. "Computer uses to promote social justice issues are explained and promoted by these professionals. Their newsletter is concerned about the increasing use of computers to advance the arms race and about inadvertent missile-launching by computer." -C.C. **Est.:** 1983. **Frequency:** 4/yr. **Subscription:** $30/yr. **Price:** Free. **Contact(s):** Gary Chapman.

**✐ ◆ Cream City Review**
Box 413, University of Wisconsin
Milwaukee, WI 53201
**Concern(s):** arts; literature; graphics. "We serve a national audience interested in diverse writing (in terms of style, subject, genre) and writers known and newly published writers of fiction, poetry, and essays are featured, along with B&W artwork and a debate among 3 or more writers on a contemporary literary issue." **Contact(s):** Kit Pancoast (Editor).

**S ◆ Creation Spirituality**
Box 9216
Oakland, CA 94616
**Concern(s):** spiritual; environment; transformation; faith. Applies Creation Spirituality to the personal, social, and ecological issues of our day with reverence, humor and prophetic analysis. A magazine that is about an "Earthy spirituality for an evolving planet"... The ideas of Matthew Fox and this tradition. **Frequency:** 6/yr. **Contact(s):** Matthew Fox (Editor-in-chief), Dan Turner (Editor).

**J ◆ Crime and Social Justice**
Box 40601
San Francisco, CA 94140   (415)550-1703
**Affiliation:** Crime and Social Justice Association. **Concern(s):** justice; labor; urban; prisons; capital punishment; poverty; unemployment; reform; criminal system. "Criminal justice topics such as prison conditions, the death penalty, and the root causes of crime are included. This newsletter is the only journal in its field exposing poverty and joblessness as key causes of criminal activity, and advocating rehabilitation instead of punishment as a solution." -C.C. **Est.:** 1974. **Frequency:** 4/yr. **Subscription:** $50/yr. **Price:** $12.50/ea. **Contact(s):** Gregory Shank.

**J ◆ Crisis**
Crisis Publishing Co.
260 5th St., 6th Floor
New York, NY 10016   (212)481-4100
**Affiliation:** National Association for the Advancement of Colored People. **Concern(s):** justice; civil liberties; racism; diversity. "A mainstream coffee table style magazine, The Crisis has increased its coverage of Black culture and economic advancement. It is the only original civil rights periodical still publishing, and still makes an important, though less militant, contribution to civil rights." -C.C. **Est.:** 1910. **Frequency:** 10/yr. **Subscription:** $6/yr. **Price:** $2/ea. **Circ.:** 400M. **Contact(s):** Fred Beauford (Editor).

**✐ ◆ Critical Inquiry**
Wieboldt Hall
1050 E. 59th St.
Chicago, IL 60637
**Concern(s):** arts; culture; music. Critical essays that offer a theoretical perspective on literature, music, visual arts, and popular culture. No fiction, poetry, or autobiography. **Publisher:** University of Chicago Press. **Contact(s):** W. J. T. Mitchell (Editor).

**D ◆ Critical Sociology**
Department of Sociology
University of Oregon
Eugene, OR 97403   (503)686-5039
**Affiliation:** Insurgent Sociologist. **Concern(s):** demographics; justice; economics; alterantives. "Militant sociologists unite to write on

alternative theories and applications of their social science discipline. Reform of society, moving from an emphasis on private property to a new concern for human needs, is their commitment." -C.C. **Est.:** 1969. **Frequency:** 3/yr. **Subscription:** $15, $25 institution. **Price:** $5/ea. **Contact(s):** Val Burris.

**✐ ◆ Critique: Studies in Contemporary Fiction**
Heldref Publications
4000 Albemarle St. NW
Washington, DC 20016  (202)362-6445
**Concern(s):** arts; literature. In closely focused critical essays on contemporary fiction, it presents the first serious, detailed discussion of the fiction of our time - Bellow in the fifties, Barth and Hawkes in the sixties, Pynchon and Vonnegut in the seventies. Many first bibliographies also appear. Authors critiqued are from any country and usually have yet to develop a widespread reputation. **Frequency:** 4/yr. **Subscription:** $39/yr.

**P ◆ Cross Country Currents**
512 79th Terrace, #203
St. Petersburg, FL 33702   (716)693-8632
**Concern(s):** politics. Prints nonpartisan political and social commentary primarily consisting of subscriber contributions, to "broaden the base of our democratic dialogue by offering a vehicle to creative and courageous individuals."

**T ◆ Cuba Update**
124 W. 23rd St.
New York, NY 10011   (212)242-0559
**Affiliation:** Center for Cuban Studies. **Concern(s):** Third World; Caribbean. "The progress of the advancement of Cuban society and relations between Cuba and other nations are featured. Interesting perspectives of Cuban barrios, workplaces, and culture find space here." -C.C. **Est.:** 1978. **Frequency:** 6/yr. **Subscription:** $15/yr. **Price:** $2.50/ea. **Contact(s):** Sandra Levinson, Jane Franklin.

**A ◆ The Cultivar**
Agroecology Program
University of California
Santa Cruz, CA 95064   (408)459-4140
**Affiliation:** Agroecology Program/UCSC. **Concern(s):** agriculture; environment; economics; sustainability; organic; social ecology. Published by a research and education group working toward the development of ecological, socially, and economically sustainable agricultural systems. On the UCSC campus, the Program manages the 25-acre Farm and 4-acre Garden, which are open to the public. This newsletter invites questions, comments, and suggestions for future articles. Current and back issues are available free of charge. **Frequency:** 2/yr. **Contact(s):** Martha Brown.

**E ◆ The Cultivator**
RFD 2 Box 330
Brooks, ME 04921   (207)722-3112
**Affiliation:** Conservatory for Nature Culture. **Concern(s):** environment; demographics; agriculture; health; bioregionalism; hunger; poverty; food production; food distribution; nutrition. Forum on regional and inter-regional issues that touch on the politics of environment and food. Priorities given to hopeful solutions rather than doom and gloom outlook. Poetry, short stories as well as timeless "news" articles welcome. Stirring up old (through quotes and historical references), adding new (with current articles and observations), exploring regional self-reliance, bioregional philosophy and common sense. Emphasis on links between economic situations and global food politics. **Other Resources:** "Food For All" provides workshops and counseling in food and nutrition, natural and bioregional eating and philosophies of consumption. "We cater large gatherings and help facilitate sharing of food between growers and the needy." **Est.:** 1975. **Frequency:** 3/yr. **Subscription:** $6/yr. **Price:** $2/ea. **Bulk:** 40% off/24. **Pages:** 32-48. **Circ.:** 1M. **Publisher:** Little Letterpress/Robin Hood Books. **Contact(s):** Diana Prizio, Kip Penny (Editors).

**✐ ◆ Cultural Democracy**
Box 7591
Minneapolis, MN 55407  (217)498-8497(H)
**Affiliation:** Alliance for Cultural Democracy. **Concern(s):** arts; justice; culture; activism; Native Americans; diversity. Culture is an essential human need and each person and community has a right to a culture or cultures of their choice; all communities should have equitable access to the material resources of the commonwealth for their cultural expression; cultural values and policies should be decided in public debate with the guaranteed participation of all communities; the government does not have the right to favor one culture over another. This magazine's goal is to express fully this conviction. **Dues:** $25-40/yr. **Frequency:** 4/yr. **Subscription:** Membership. **Price:** $3/ea. **Bulk:** $2.50ea/24. **Pages:** 24. **Circ.:** 1M. **Publisher:** Inkworks Press. **Office:** Sangamon State University Springfield, IL 62794-9243. **Contact(s):** Ron Sakolsky (Editorial Coordinator). (217)786-6310.

J ▸ **Cultural Survival Quarterly**
53-A Church St.
Cambridge, MA 02138 (617)495-2562
**Affiliation:** Cultural Survival. **Concern(s):** justice; Third World; diversity; Native Americans; indigenous peoples. The Quarterly has addressed issues of both immediate and long-term concern to indigenous peoples throughout the world. It serves to inform the general public and policy makers in the US and abroad to stimulate action on behalf of tribal people and ethnic minorities. Involved with controversial project with NRDC to negotiate deal between Amazonian natives and Conoco. Nonprofit. **Est.:** 1976. **Frequency:** 4/yr. **Subscription:** $45/yr. **Pages:** 80. **Circ.:** 18M. **Contact(s):** Jason W. Clay (Editor), Leslie Baker (Associate Editor).

A ▸ **Culture and Agriculture**
Box 231, Rutgers University
Human Ecology Dept, Cook College
New Brunswick, NJ 08903
**Concern(s):** agriculture; environment; social ecology. **Frequency:** 4/yr. **Price:** $10/ea.

✌ ▸ **Culture Concrete**
2141-C Mission St., #305
San Francisco, CA 94110-9839
**Concern(s):** peace; intervention; militarism. This magazine first got its start during the Gulf war as an anti-war publication. Now it covers all issue pertaing to Arab culture and media coverage. Nonprofit. **Frequency:** 4/yr. **Subscription:** $16/yr.

? ▸ **Current**
Heldref Publications
4000 Albemarle St. NW
Washington, DC 20016 (202)362-6445
**Concern(s):** future; ideation; analysis. A unique journal that compiles the new thinking on today's perplexing problems. The editors of this far-reaching publication search through a flood of printed material to bring you the significant new ideas of the day. The timely articles in Current often come from unusual sources and are chosen without any particular bias; they define problems and suggest solutions. **Frequency:** 12/yr. **Subscription:** $25, $50 institutions.

F ▸ **Daughters of Sarah: The Magazine for Christian Feminists**
Box 411179
Chicago, IL 60641 (312)736-3399
**Concern(s):** feminism; spiritual; faith. A magazine that claims to be Ms. and Mother Jones for Christian feminists. **Frequency:** 6/yr. **Subscription:** $18/yr. **Price:** $3/yr. **Pages:** 40. **Circ.:** 6.5M. **Publisher:** Associated Church Press & Small Magazine Publishing Group. **Office:** 3801 N. Keeler Chicago, IL 60641. **Contact(s):** Reta Finger (Editor).

M ▸ **Deadline**
10 Washington Pl.
New York University
New York, NY 10003 (212)998-7960
**Affiliation:** Center for War, Peace, and the News Media. **Concern(s):** media; peace; disarmament; media watch. Bulletin reports on the issues as they are from Washington, not as some of the misinformation of the mainstream press says they are.

P ▸ **Decentralize!**
Box 1608
Washington, DC 20013-1608
**Concern(s):** politics; feminism; environment; decentralization; Green; bioregionalism; anti-authoritarian; nonviolence; alternative party. "Short letters and news items on nonviolent decentralist networking and strategy." **Est.:** 1986. **Frequency:** 4/yr. **Subscription:** $4/yr. **Price:** $1/ea. **Pages:** 6. **Circ.:** 500. **Contact(s):** Carol Moore (Editor).

E ▸ **Defenders**
1244 19th St. NW
Washington, DC 20036 (202)659-9510
**Affiliation:** Defenders of Wildlife. **Concern(s):** environment; wildlife/endangered species; conservation. A magazine that provides "provocative, in-depth coverage of major US and foreign wildlife conservation issues. It is beautifully illustrated with outstanding color photography." **Frequency:** 6/yr. **Subscription:** $20/yr. **Price:** $3/ea.

✌ ▸ **Defense Monitor**
1500 Massachusetts Ave. NW
Washington, DC 20005 (202)862-0700
**Affiliation:** Center for Defense Information. **Concern(s):** peace; disarmament. "This newsletter is unusual in that its staffers come from a background in the military and intelligence, and share a desire for a secure but reduced defense. Statistics and calm, studied reasoning take precedence over the emotion often displayed in other"peace publications, which suits its audience just fine."-C.C. **Est.:** 1972. **Frequency:** 10/yr. **Subscription:** $25/yr. **Price:** $1/ea. **Contact(s):** David Johnson.

H ▸ **Delicious!**
1301 Spruce St.
Boulder, CO 80302 (303)939-8440
**Affiliation:** New Health Communications. **Concern(s):** health; holism; alternative consumer; nutrition. Delicious! magazine is designed to educate consumers about healthy living. It features a natural health and beauty department, natural food recipes and the latest research on vitamins, herbs and homeopathy. Its contents should not be used as medical advice. **Frequency:** 8/yr. **Subscription:** $17/yr. **Publisher:** New Health Communications, Inc. **Contact(s):** Frank J. Lampe (Managing Editor).

M ▸ **Democratic Communique**
Speech Dept.
University of Oregon
Eugene, OR 97403 (503)686-4171
**Affiliation:** Union for Democratic Communications. **Concern(s):** media; journalism. "Progressive public access to the media is the goal of this newsletter. The Union for Democratic Communications was formed to facilitate the work of journalists and concerned citizens in this field."-C.C. **Est.:** 1975. **Frequency:** 6/yr. **Subscription:** $10/yr. **Price:** $2/ea. **Contact(s):** Janet Wasko.

P ▸ **Democratic Left**
15 Dutch St., #500
New York, NY 10038 (212)962-0390
**Affiliation:** Democratic Socialists of America. **Concern(s):** politics; grassroots organizing; Democratic Socialism. "The magazine of the largest democratic socialist grouping in the country, it should be on the basic list of all social activists. Some news of organizational affairs is included, but is only a fraction of the informative variety of news and feature articles. The pages have featured the thought of US Congress member Ron Dellums, international union presidents and authors such as Irving Howe. The views of rank-and-file activists are also given space here, in this effective alliance."-C.C. **Est.:** 1973. **Frequency:** 8/yr. **Subscription:** $8, $15 institution. **Price:** $1.50/ea. **Contact(s):** Barbara Ehrenrich.

P ▸ **Democratic Socialist REPORT & REVIEW**
2121 Waylife Ct.
Alva, FL 33920 (813)728-3159
**Concern(s):** politics; Democratic Socialism. "Democracy through socialism is promoted here, with the belief that we can have both. This proposed system is set forth as an alternative to the current economic system and also as an alternative to communism."-C.C. **Est.:** 1984. **Frequency:** 26/yr. **Subscription:** $15/yr. **Price:** Free. **Contact(s):** Robert E. Schlichter.

✌ ▸ **Desert Voices**
Box 4487
Las Vegas, NV 89127-0487 (702)646-4814
**Affiliation:** Nevada Desert Experience. **Concern(s):** peace; environment; spiritual; anti-nuclear; test ban; interfaith. The newsletter of the Nevada Desert Experience, a group dedicated to halting nuclear weapons production and testing. They have an ongoing vigil and protest at the Nevada Test Site near Las Vegas , Nevada. They welcome letters, articles, announcements of coming events, poetry or humorous pieces. Nonprofit. **Contact(s):** Mary Lehman, Peter Ediger (Co-directors).

✐ ▸ **Design Spirit**
438 3rd St.
Brooklyn, NY 11215 (718)768-9756
**Concern(s):** arts; urban; architecture. A magazine concerned with the impact of art and architecture, craft and design on human and environmental well-being. Its scope ranges from the design elements within individual dwelling places, to broader topics such as city planning issues. Contributors are international as is the subscriber and distribution network. **Other Resources:** The publication includes a regular department: RESOURCE ROUNDUP which is a free listing of other organizations and resources in related work. Calendar is also a regular included department, listing specific events, workshops, and classes. **Est.:** 1989. **Frequency:** 4/yr. **Subscription:** $16/yr. **Price:** $4.95/ea. **Bulk:** 40% off/24. **Pages:** 72. **Circ.:** 3M subs, 4M news stands. **Fax:** (718)768-9756. **Contact(s):** Suzanne Koblentz-Goodman (Editor/Publisher), Cara M. Brownell (Circulation/Subscriptions).

T ▸ **Development**
1401 New York Ave., #1100
Washington, DC 20335 (202)347-1800
**Affiliation:** Society for International Development, USA Chapters Committee. **Concern(s):** Third World; development. **Contact(s):** Enrique Iglesias (President), Nancy Swing. (703)752-2710. **Other:** 265 Rocky Run Rd., Falmouth, VA 22405

T ▸ **Development Update**
IDS, Box 980
Chicago, IL 60690
**Affiliation:** IDS. **Concern(s):** Third World; education; peace; environment; development; alternative markets; indigenous peoples; global understanding. Monitors the impact of tourism and development on Third World countries.

T ▸ **Developments**
c/o International Voluntary Services (IVS)
1424 16th St. NW, #204
Washington, DC 20036 (202)387-5533
**Affiliation:** International Voluntary Services (IVS). **Concern(s):** Third World; development; volunteers; hunger. This newsletter informs the public of IVS activities. **Est.:** 1988. **Fax:** (202)387-4234. **Contact(s):** Suzanne Beane Stafford (Interim Executive Director), Andrea Brock (Director, Communications).

E ▸ **Digit News**
45 Inverness Dr. East
Englewood, CO 80112 (303)790-2345
**Affiliation:** Diget Fund. **Concern(s):** environment; wildlife/endangered species. A newsletter focusing on the programs of The Digit Fund, a nonprofit organization started by Diane Fossey in Rwanda, Africa, to protect and study endangered mountain gorillas and their environment. The publication includes reports from researchers, international events supporting conservation and news of the speaker's bureau and school curriculum. Nonprofit. **Est.:** 1979. **Frequency:** 4/yr. **Subscription:** $30, $10 students. **Pages:** 8. **Circ.:** 14M. **Fax:** (303)790-4066. **Contact(s):** Dianne Hitchingham (Managing Director).

J ▸ **Dimensions: A Journal of Holocaust Studies**
823 UN Plaza
New York, NY 10017 (212)490-2525
**Affiliation:** Anti-Defamation League of B'nai B'rith. **Concern(s):** justice; racism; diversity; discrimination. "Never again will a blight of humanity such as the Holocaust occur if these human rights activists can possibly stop it. Anti-semitism and other forms of bigotry are strongly opposed."-C.C. **Est.:** 1985. **Frequency:** 3/yr. **Subscription:** $12/yr. **Price:** $5/ea. **Contact(s):** Dennis V. Klein.

H ▸ **Directions**
4 Nickerson St.
Seattle, WA 98109-1699
**Affiliation:** Program for Appropriate Technology in Health. **Concern(s):** health; disabled; consumer protection.

A ▸ **Dirty Dozen Campaigner**
Box 610
San Francisco, CA 94101 (415)541-9140
**Affiliation:** Pesticide Action Network. **Concern(s):** agriculture; environment; health; hazardous/toxic waste; pesticides. This newsletter attempts to list the 12 greatest abusers of pesticides in the nation. **Frequency:** 3/yr.

♿ ▸ **Disability Rag**
Box 145
Louisville, KY 40201 (502)459-5343
**Concern(s):** justice; health; welfare rights; disabled rights; disabled. "Citizens with disabilities will have equal access to all jobs and facilities, if these advocates win their goals. They work for more aids such as wheelchair ramps and against employment discrimination."-C.C. **Est.:** 1980. **Frequency:** 6/yr. **Subscription:** $12/yr.; $20 individuals. **Price:** $2/ea. **Circ.:** 5M. **Publisher:** Advocado Press. **Contact(s):** Mary Johnson.

✌ ▸ **Disarmament**
United Nations (UN)
Rm S-3150F
New York, NY 10017 (212)963-4272
**Affiliation:** UN, Department for Disarmament Affairs. **Concern(s):** peace; disarmament. "Some dozen features on world arms control grace each issue, with such formats as bibliographers, opinion articles, scholarly pieces, news reports, and a calendar of upcoming official disarmament events."-C.C. **Est.:** 1978. **Frequency:** 4/yr. **Subscription:** $24/yr. **Price:** $6/ea. **Contact(s):** Jennifer Mackby.

✌ ▸ **Disarming Notes**
475 Riverside Dr.
New York, NY 10115 (212)222-5900
**Affiliation:** Riverside Church Disarmament Program. **Concern(s):** peace; disarmament. Newsletter. **Contact(s):** Rev. Eric Kolbell.

P ▸ **Dissent**
521 5th Ave.
New York, NY 10017 (212)687-0890
**Affiliation:** Foundation for Study of Independent Social Ideas.

**Concern(s):** politics. "Noted author Irving Howe does a great job of editing and writing for Dissent, a rather scholarly but effective and accurate social democratic journal. One of the more widely circulated such journals, and is found in many college libraries and larger public libraries. 'Join some of the sharpest minds around to debate the prospects for a unified Germany, the perils and promises of market socialism, Paul Goodman's relevance for the nineties, the prospects for socialism, and whether it's time.'" -C.C. **Est.:** 1954. **Frequency:** 4/yr. **Subscription:** $18, $15 student, $21 institution. **Price:** $5/ea. **Contact(s):** Irving Howe, Michael Walter.

H ▶ **Doctor-Patient Studies**
5627 S. Drexel
Chicago, IL 60637 (312)752-3562
**Affiliation:** Center for Health Administration Studies. **Concern(s):** health; public health. This newsletter "generally accepts only contributions of articles and books related to research on the doctor-patient relationship, health care and medicine, medical ethics, and medical sociology. We publish hundreds of short reviews/abstracts." The Center has been around since 1955. **Est.:** 1990. **Frequency:** 6/yr. **Subscription:** $12/yr. **Price:** $2/ea. **Pages:** 20. **Circ.:** 200. **Publisher:** University of Chicago. **Contact(s):** J. Hughes.

M ▶ **Documents to the People**
8304 Tomlinson Ave.
Bethesda, MD 20817
**Affiliation:** American Library Association Government Documents Roundtable. **Concern(s):** media; education; journalism; press; media watch. "Cataloging government documents and facilitating their use by libraries are the purposes of this librarians' tool. It also reports on ways to safeguard the right of the public to have easy access to these public records." -C.C. **Est.:** 1972. **Frequency:** 6/yr. **Subscription:** $15/yr. **Price:** $3/ea. **Contact(s):** Joe Jaros.

$ ▶ **Dollars and Sense**
One Summer
Somerville, MA 02143 (212)691-5722
**Affiliation:** National Taxpayers Union. **Concern(s):** economics; labor; politics. "The US economy and its effects on workers and on the economies of other nations are the bottom line of this newsletter. Dollars and Sense presents economic issues in a popularly-written style intelligible to the lay person." -C.C. **Other Resources:** BULLETIN OF ECONOMIC AFFAIRS. Nonprofit. **Est.:** 1974. **Frequency:** 10/yr. **Subscription:** $42/yr. institution. **Price:** $2/ea. **Circ.:** 8.5M.

▶ **Dolphin Alert**
Earth Island Institute
300 Broadway # 28
San Francisco, CA 94133 (415)788-3666
**Affiliation:** Save the Dolphin Project. **Concern(s):** environment; animal rights; wildlife/endangered species; oceans. This newsletter provides information, tools and resources to help the public to understand the tuna/dolphin problem and become more active in efforts to stop the slaughter. Presents ways that people are already helping the campaign, Save the Dolphin Project, and provides a detailed " What you can do" section. **Other Resources:** Videos, brochures, bumperstickers, petitions and much more. Nonprofit.

E ▶ **Dolphin Log**
The Cousteau Society
8440 Santa Monica Blvd.
Los Angeles, CA 90069
**Affiliation:** Cousteau Society. **Concern(s):** environment; education; wildlife/endangered species; ocean/rivers; youth. "Available to family members of the Cousteau Society, is a spectacularly illustrated, award-winning, bimonthly magazine which introduces young readers to life in and around the sea. Its fascinating stories, facts, games, and experiments can be shared by the entire family. Articles on a variety of topics related to our global water system: marine biology, ecology, natural history, and water-related stories, for children aged 7 to 15." **Dues:** $28/yr. **Frequency:** 6/yr. **Subscription:** Membership. **Contact(s):** Pamela Stacey (Editor-in-chief), Jean-Michel Cousteau (Editorial Director).

E ▶ **Dolphin Net**
3220 Sacramento St.
San Francisco, CA 94115 (415)931-0948
**Affiliation:** Dolphin Network. **Concern(s):** environment; wildlife/endangered species. This newsletter is filled with news from the surprisingly broad network of people and organizations concerned with protecting the dolphins, the threat of drift nets, animal assisted therapy, and the Heinz and StarKist policies to can tuna caught by only dolphin safe methods. A project of the Washington Research Institute. Nonprofit. **Subscription:** $15/yr.

P ▶ **Dossier**
c/o Prevailing Winds Research
Box 23511
Santa Barbara, CA 93121 (805)566-8016
**Affiliation:** Prevailing Winds Research. **Concern(s):** politics; demographics; peace; Third World; economics; health; CIA; government accountability; corporate responsibility; Mid-East; national security; crime; poverty; AIDS; public health. A compendium of important articles and speeches on current affairs from John Judge, John Stockwell, Barbara Honegger, Daniel Sheehan, Tony Avergan, Bo Gritz, and others. The Washington Drug Cartel, poverty, S&L Rip-off, CIA, media, AIDS, and fascism's degenerative influence on US politics and foreign policy. Transcripts of the Other Americas Radio shows, Noam Chomsky, David Barsamian, and much more. Materials that you are not likely to find in your local paper or hear about on TV news. **Frequency:** 6/yr. **Subscription:** $75/yr. **Pages:** c100.

▶ **Draft Notices**
Box 15195
San Diego, CA 92115 (619)272-5718
**Affiliation:** Committee Oppose to Militarism and the Draft. **Concern(s):** peace; militarism; anti-draft. "Military adventurism in places such as Grenada and Central America is of concern to these folks, as well as the obvious issues of registration and the draft. The writing is informative, is easy to read and nicely compliments information in the earlier listed CARD News Service." -C.C. **Est.:** 1980. **Frequency:** 6/yr. **Subscription:** $10/yr. **Price:** $1/ea. **Contact(s):** Rick Jahnkow.

S ▶ **The Dreamweaver**
Box 150692
Fort Worth, TX 76108
**Concern(s):** spiritual; feminism; environment; transformation. A publication dedicated to all positive life paths! **Frequency:** 12/yr. **Subscription:** $10/yr. **Price:** $1/ea. **Contact(s):** Ladyhawk.

P ▶ **DSA Green News**
1608 N. Milwaukee, #403
Chicago, IL 60647
**Concern(s):** politics; environment; Democratic Socialism; social ecology. Agrees with Murray Bookchin's position that the "bio-centric" position depicts humans as a cancerous growth in the natural system, one that should be eliminated, but disagrees with the anti-spirit position of the Old Left and suggests that Bookchin's faith that all social ills will be cured by a single panacea, does not fit with the facts. While there is interrelatedness among current problems, they still have to be considered and solved separately as well as wholistically. **Contact(s):** James Hughes (Editor).

E ▶ **Ducks Unlimited**
1 Waterfowl Way
Long Grove, IL 60047 (312)438-4300
**Affiliation:** Ducks Unlimited. **Concern(s):** environment; wildlife/endangered species; conservation; wetlands. A magazine that reports on the efforts of activists to save the wetlands from destruction. Also, is concerned with wrongful hunting of waterfowl, but, is supportive of hunting. **Contact(s):** Matthew B. Connolly, Jr. (Executive Vice President).

▶ **Dynamic**
235 W. 23rd St.
New York, NY 10011 (212)989-4994
**Affiliation:** Communist Party/USA, YCL, USA. **Concern(s):** arts; media; labor; politics; culture; music; film; alternative party. "Movies, music and movements for basic social change are typical topics in this Marxist youth newspaper. It is the forefront with its promotion of college campus shanties against apartheid, the movement against drugs and strong support of labor." -C.C. **Est.:** 1983. **Frequency:** 6/yr. **Subscription:** $4/yr. **Price:** $.25/ea. **Contact(s):** Elena Mora.

E ▶ **E Magazine**
Box 6667
Syracuse, NY 13217 (203)854-5559
**Concern(s):** environment. Covers topical environmental issues in lively 4-color magazine format. A serious, independent, magazine for the concerned general public, the growing thousands of grassroots activists and veteran environmentalists. Regular features include: Key issues and campaigns; industry and consumer products trends; interviews with leading advocates and thinkers; reviews of books, films, videos; and ecological principals to live by. **Frequency:** 6/yr. **Subscription:** $20/yr. **Price:** $3.50/ea. **Pages:** c72. **Publisher:** Earth Action Network, Inc. **Office:** 28 Knight St. Norwalk, CT 06851. **Contact(s):** Doug Moss (Editor/Publisher). (800)825-0061.

M ▶ **E-News**
Box 691624
Los Angeles, CA 90069
**Concern(s):** media. Environmental video magazine (news) which selects products that fit their "waste-watch" criteria.

J ▶ **The Eagle**
Box 579MO
Naugatuck, CT 06670 (203)274-7853
**Concern(s):** justice; health; environment; arts; Native Americans; poetry; substance abuse; self-help; preventative medicine; nutrition. a volunteer staff publishing materials about "American Indians or on issues of importance to Indians, i.e. environment, diabetes, alcoholism, etc." **Est.:** 1981. **Frequency:** 6/yr. **Subscription:** $20/yr. **Price:** $2/ea. **Pages:** 28. **Circ.:** 5M. **Contact(s):** Jim Roaix (Managing Editor), Karen Cooper (Poetry Editor).

▶ **Early Education and Development**
39 Pearl St.
Brandon, VT 05733-1007
**Concern(s):** education; childhood. A quarterly professional journal for those involved in educational and preschool services to children and their families. Emphasizes the implications of current research on child development for early education and daycare programs, special needs programs, and other practical educational problems.

E ▶ **Earth Day 2000**
116 New Montgomery, #530
San Francisco, CA 94105 (800)727-8619
**Affiliation:** Earth Day Resources. **Concern(s):** environment; energy; sustainability; activism; efficiency; renewables; recycling. Focuses on Green consumer issues, etc. Nonprofit. **Dues:** $20/yr. **Contact(s):** Jeff Goldwasser (Editor).

S ▶ **Earth Ethics/Evolving Values for an Earth Community**
4006 Chestnut Pl.
Alexandria, VA 22311 (301)855-1064
**Affiliation:** Green Fire Foundation. **Concern(s):** spiritual; environment; agriculture; transformation. Examines the moral dimension of the environmental crisis, provoking discussion of the fundamental values that make up the dominant world view and pointing the way to a world view more in line with the reality of the Earth. Nonprofit. **Est.:** 1989. **Frequency:** 4/yr. **Subscription:** $10/yr. **Price:** $2.50/ea. **Bulk:** 40% off/24. **Pages:** 16. **Circ.:** 5M. **Fax:** (202)331-8986. **Contact(s):** Sara Ebenreck (Editor), Thomas S. Barrett (Publisher). (202)463-7456.

E ▶ **Earth First!**
Box 5176
Missoula, MT 59806 (406)728-8114
**Concern(s):** environment; peace; activism; civil disobedience; wildlife/endangered species; forests. "The radical environmental journal" with extensive environmental news and sometimes controversial opinions. Supports "direct action" to protect the environment. It advocates no compromise in defense of wilderness and biodiversity. **Est.:** 1970. **Frequency:** 8/yr. **Subscription:** $20/yr. **Price:** $3/ea. **Pages:** 40. **Circ.:** 15M. **E-Network:** Econet. **ID:** 'earthfirst'.

E ▶ **Earth Island Journal**
300 Broadway, #28
San Francisco, CA 94133 (415)788-3666
**Affiliation:** Earth Island Institute. **Concern(s):** environment. A magazine reporting international environmental news and the activities of Institute. Purpose: To examine the fundamentals of our ecological crisis, act as an early warning system to identify issues and respond quickly and directly. "Local news from around the world", eyewitness accounts from the environmental frontlines—from Moscow to Malaysia—with global eco-news and exposes you'll find no where else. Special focus is on marine life and rainforests. **Dues:** $25/yr. **Frequency:** 4/yr. **Subscription:** Membership. **Price:** $3/ea. **Contact(s):** David R. Brower (Chairman), David Phillips (Co-director).

E ▶ **Earth Journal**
Box 423
Cayucos, CA 93430 (805)995-2468
**Affiliation:** San Luis Obispo County Earth Day Coalition. **Concern(s):** environment; demographics; peace; justice; social ecology; social justice. Purpose: To provide a forum for the discussion of environmental, peace, and justice issues, both local and global; to raise awareness of humankind's impact on the planet, past to future, and to encourage people to review habits and make lifestyle changes to cause the least impact on the planet and non-human species; to educate ourselves and the public about environment, peace, and justice issues. It is designed to have a widespread appeal; to be a voice and a tool for the concerned public. **Est.:** 1990. **Frequency:** 12/yr. **Subscription:** $15/yr. **Price:** Free. **Pages:** 20. **Circ.:** 10M. **E-Network:** EcoNet. **ID:** 'earthjournal'. **Member:** International Earth Day. **Contact(s):** Terri Dunivant (Editor/Publisher), Zeke Turley (Manager). **Other:** San Luis Obispo County Earth Day Coalition, Box 1810, San Luis Obispo, CA 93406.

**E ▶ Earth Light**
608 East 11th St.
Davis, CA 95616 (916)758-5407
**Affiliation:** Pacific Yearly Meeting Committee on Unity With Nature. **Concern(s):** environment; spiritual; interfaith. A magazine of insight, inspiration, and information on the spiritual basis of the concern we share for our environment and our planet. Articles, stories, poetry, and art on the spiritual-environmental connection from a variety of heritages and viewpoints are welcome, including the Biblical and the radical. The Committee was formed in 1985. **Other Resources:** Annual conferences, assistance to Quaker Meetings within our region in furthering environmental/spiritual concerns. **Est.:** 1990. **Frequency:** 4/yr. **Subscription:** $15/yr. **Price:** $5/ea. **Pages:** 20. **Circ.:** 600. **E-Network:** Econet. **ID:** 'pymcun'. **Office:** 684 Benicia Santa Rosa, CA 95409. **Contact(s):** Chris Laning (Editor), Chuck Orr (Committee Chairman). (619)436-8346. **Other:** Pacific Yearly Meeting Committee on Unity With Nature, 1915 Montgomery Ave., Cardiff, CA 92007.

**E ▶ Earth News**
Box 1620
Agoura Hills, CA 91376 (818)597-8733
**Concern(s):** environment; economics; activism. Environment-oriented newsletter informing and educating the public about how they can take responsibility for themselves and teaching them how they can make a difference. Nonprofit. **Est.:** 1990. **Contact(s):** Lisa Goldman (Editor), Dale Hallcom (Publisher). **Other:** 5126 Clareton Dr., #200, Agoura Hills, CA 91301.

**H ▶ Earth Star**
Box 337
West Somerville, MA 02144 (617)623-2040
**Affiliation:** Whole Life Times. **Concern(s):** health. A magazine of natural and healthful living. **Frequency:** 6/yr. **Member:** Co-op America.

**E ▶ Earth Work**
Student Conservation Association
Box 550
Charlestown, NH 03603 (603)826-4301
**Affiliation:** Student Conservation Association, Inc.. **Concern(s):** environment; education; conservation; volunteers; students; jobs. A monthly magazine for and about conservation professionals, present and future. Includes job listings, career insights, profiles, interviews, and think pieces. The Association has been operating since 1957. **Other Resources:** Programs for student and adult volunteers to assist with stewardship of our public lands and natural resources. Nonprofit. **Est.:** 1991. **Dues:** $15+/yr. **Frequency:** 12/yr. **Subscription:** $29.95/yr. **Price:** $6/ea. **Pages:** 36. **Circ.:** 10M. **Publisher:** Student Conservation Association. **Fax:** (603)826-7755. **Contact(s):** Linda Rounds (Circulation Director), Scott D. Izzo (President).

**E ▶ Earth's Advocate**
ECOSLO
Box 1014
San Luis Obispo, CA 93406
**Concern(s):** environment; recycling. Newspaper.

**✐ ▶ Earth's Daughters**
Box 622, Station C
Buffalo, NY 14209 (716)837-7778
**Concern(s):** arts; feminism; literature; graphics; fine arts. Fiction, poetry, and B&W photos or drawings. "Finely crafted work with a feminist theme." "We are a feminist arts periodical." **Est.:** 1971. **Frequency:** 2-4/yr. **Subscription:** $12/3, $20/3 institutions. **Price:** $4/sample. **Bulk:** 35% off/24. **Pages:** 50.

**E ▶ Earthkeeping Environmental Quarterly**
Box 604
Dallas, PA 18612-0604 (707)696-4200
**Concern(s):** environment; agriculture. **Contact(s):** Greg Howells (Publisher).

**E ▶ The Earthwise Consumer**
Box 1506
Mill Valley, CA 94942 (415)383-5892
**Concern(s):** environment; health; green consumer. This newsletter has articles on healthy and happy living. Stresses natural ways of healing and living. Has informative articles and helpful advice. **Frequency:** 8/yr. **Contact(s):** Deborah Lynn Dadd (Editor).

**✌ ▶ East-West Outlook**
109 11th St. SE
Washington, DC 20003 (202)546-1700
**Affiliation:** American Committee on US-Soviet Relations. **Concern(s):** peace; disarmament; conflict resolution; East-West. "Detente and discussion between the US and the socialist countries are promoted. These are recommended as a positive alternative to military and economic conflict."-C.C. **Est.:** 1977. **Frequency:** 6/yr. **Subscription:** $12/yr. **Price:** $2/ea. **Contact(s):** Jeanne Mattison.

**T ▶ ECHO Development Notes**
17430 Durrance Rd.
North Fort Myers, FL 33917
**Affiliation:** Educational Concerns for Hunger Organization (ECHO). **Concern(s):** Third World; demographics; agriculture; spiritual; hunger; poverty; faith; food production; food distribution. An interdenominational Christian group which provides practical agricultural information and distributes seed of underexploited food, forage and reforestation plants to development workers and missionaries working with small Third World farmers. This is its technical bulletin, filled with useful, agricultural "how-to's" and networks this information to ninety countries worldwide.

**E ▶ ECO**
101 Transit St.
Providence, RI 02906 (401)351-1211
**Concern(s):** environment; urban; economics; permaculture; architecture; planning. The objective of this newsletter is to promote a complimentary, ecological synthesis of design practices and our natural surroundings. **Est.:** 1989. **Contact(s):** Eva Anderson.

**E ▶ Ecocurrents**
540 Allen St.
Syracuse, NY 13210-2204 (315)442-9007
**Affiliation:** Ecoropa. **Concern(s):** environment; networking. Critical presentations of current trends in the field of ecology. Closer ties between the European and American Greens may come from this new publication. The editors of this newsletter previously sent us Ecoropa from Europe. Now they've moved to the the US and will continue building up a worldwide Green Network. **Other Resources:** Affiliation is at this address in Europe: 42 Rue Sorbier, Paris, 75020 France. **Pages:** 4. **Circ.:** 600. **Contact(s):** Matthias Finger (Professor).

**E ▶ EcoCultural Perspectives**
4545 N. 36th St., #120
Phoenix, AZ 85018 (602)956-4996
**Concern(s):** environment. Formerly Tucson Lifeline. **Contact(s):** Julie Noterman (Editor).

**E ▶ ECO-Letter**
5 Thomas Circle NW
Washington, DC 20005 (202)462-2591
**Affiliation:** North American Conference on Religion and Ecology. **Concern(s):** environment; spiritual; interfaith. Bimonthly on religion and ecology, featuring articles on "my greening," homiletic tips, contacts for local action, environmental practices and liturgies, articles of substance. Diane Sherwood, editor. **Frequency:** 6/yr. **Contact(s):** Donald B. Conroy (President), Diane Sherwood.

**E ▶ The Ecologist**
55 Hayward St.
Cambridge, MA 02140
**Concern(s):** environment; economics. Forward-looking journal of the post-industrial age. Stresses connections between economic and environmental issues and their implications. Founded by renowned British ecological thinker, Edward Goldsmith. One of the first periodicals to recognize the concept of global ecology and to take a stance on the critical environmental issues of today. **Est.:** 1969. **Frequency:** 6/yr. **Subscription:** $30, $25/students, $65/institution. **Price:** $6/ea. **Publisher:** MIT Press Journals.

**E ▶ Ecolution**
4344 Russell Ave.
Los Angeles, CA 90027 (213)662-5207
**Affiliation:** Eco-Home Network. **Concern(s):** environment; urban; sustainability; architecture; planning. The newsletter of the Network, founded in 1984, a membership organization affiliated with the Eco-Home Demonstration Home, a model of ecological living in the city. Network membership provides access to resources to help members create more ecologically sound and energy efficient lifestyles. **Other Resources:** Information packets - xeriscaping; water conservation and grey water systems; recycling; organic gardening; composting. Workshops - Recycling; Composting. Resource Center with library and bookstore. Tours are available. **Est.:** 1985. **Dues:** $20, $25 family, $50 institution/business. **Frequency:** 4/yr. **Subscription:** Membership. **Price:** $1/ea. **Pages:** 18. **Circ.:** 1.5M. **Contact(s):** Julia Russell (Founder/Executive Director), Bob Walter (President). (213)388-5338.

**E ▶ Econews**
879 9th St.
Arcata, CA 95521
**Affiliation:** Northcoast Environmental Center. **Concern(s):** environment. The purpose of this newsletter is to disseminate information and lobby in favor of the northcoast environment of California. **Frequency:** 12/yr. **Subscription:** $18/yr. **Contact(s):** Tim McKay (Coordinator), Andy Alm

**L ▶ Economic Notes**
80 E. 11th St., #634
New York, NY 10003 (212)473-1042
**Affiliation:** Labor Research Association. **Concern(s):** labor; economics; jobs; analysis. "A first choice for readers interested in labor economics from a workers' viewpoint. As a news and opinion review, it does a great job of explaining the how and why of labor/capital relations."-C.C. **Est.:** 1932. **Frequency:** 6/yr. **Subscription:** $20/yr. **Price:** $3/ea. **Contact(s):** Greg Tarpinian.

**P ▶ EcoSocialist Review**
1608 N. Milwaukee, 4th Fl.
Chicago, IL 60647 (312)752-3562
**Affiliation:** Environmental Community of Democratic Socialists of America. **Concern(s):** politics; environment; socialism. "We review books and magazines for analysis and review from an ecosocialist perspective on topics such as ecology, toxics, transportation, electoral politics, socialism, military policy, worker safety, Canada and Mexico, Third World development. We publish short reviews." **Est.:** 1987. **Frequency:** 4/yr. **Subscription:** $8/yr. **Price:** $1/sample. **Pages:** 16. **Circ.:** 1M. **E-Network:** Bitnet. **ID:** 'dsa@sam.spc.uchicago.edu'. **Contact(s):** J. Hughes (Editor).

**E ▶ EDF Letter**
257 Park Ave. S
New York, NY 10010 (212)505-2100
**Affiliation:** Environmental Defense Fund. **Concern(s):** environment; economics; lobbying. This leading national, NY-based organization with over 100,000 members, links science, economics and law to create innovative, economically viable solutions to today's environmental problems. This is their newsletter. Nonprofit. **Frequency:** 4/yr. **Subscription:** $20/yr. **Circ.:** 135M. **Contact(s):** Norma Watson (Editor), Tim Connor (Assistant).

**E ▶ Edges Magazine**
577 Kingston Rd.
Toronto, ON M4E 1R3 Canada (416)691-2316
**Affiliation:** Canadian Institute of Cultural Affairs. **Concern(s):** environment; economics; justice; politics; spiritual; education; health; holism; transformation. Documents a whole system transition by: creating Earth consciousness at the grassroots level; changing the equations of economics on a planetary scale; breaking down boundaries in the wake of evolutionary forces; exploring partnerships for transformation of old-style relations; taking charge of our own learning processes; underlining the inner healing power of the body; highlighting new images of social change; and, putting a human face on the environmental crisis. **Contact(s):** Brian Stanfield (Editor).

**E ▶ Educational Hawkwatcher**
629 Green St.
Allentown, PA 18102 (215)434-1637
**Affiliation:** Wildlife Information Center. **Concern(s):** environment; education; wildlife/endangered species; conservation. Newsletter.

**E ▶ The Egg, a Journal of Eco-Justice**
Center for Religion, Ethics & Social Policy
Anabel Taylor Hall, Cornell University
Ithaca, NY 14853 (607)255-9240
**Affiliation:** Eco-Justice Project. **Concern(s):** environment; justice; spiritual; interfaith. Links the issues of ecology and justice, offers an ethical framework with a theologically spiritual undergirding and a long-range global perspective, and stresses the connections in protecting and liberating both Earth and people. Its articles help you understand and tackle social and environmental injustice. **Other Resources:** The "Untangling the Waste Knot" Program. A traveling education program, giving an eye-opening overview of the solid waste crisis. Shalom Connections, Keeping and Healing the Creation; conferences, workshops, lecture programs. **Est.:** 1981. **Frequency:** 4/yr. **Subscription:** $10/yr. **Pages:** 20. **Circ.:** 3M. **Publisher:** IT Publishing. **Contact(s):** Mary Jeanette Ebenhack (Eco-Justice Project Executive Director), William E. Gibson (Editor). (607)255-4225. Rhoda Meador , Circulation/Marketing Manager.

**T ▶ El Estiliano and N.I.C.A.**
Box 1409-CO
Cambridge, MA 02238 (617)497-7142
**Affiliation:** Nuevo Instituto de Centroamerica. **Concern(s):** Third World; justice; Central America. "Life in Esteli, Nicaragua, is narrated in the Institute's newsletter. Fascinating anecdotes about solidarity efforts for development, and the destructive contra attacks against these efforts, are included."-C.C. **Est.:** 1984. **Frequency:** 6/yr. **Subscription:** Donation. **Price:** Free. **Contact(s):** Beverly Treumann.

**E ▸ El Paisano**
Box 4294
Palm Springs, CA 92263
**Affiliation:** Desert Protective Council, Inc. **Concern(s):** environment; wilderness. Newsletter reports on the Desert Protective Council and their activities. **Contact(s):** Bill Neill.

**T ▸ El Rescate**
2675 W. Olympic Blvd.
Los Angeles, CA 90006 (213)387-0460
**Affiliation:** Southern California Ecumenical Council. **Concern(s):** Third World; justice; refugees. "Defense of human rights in Central America and refugees' rights in the US is the purpose of the newsletter. It documents particular incidents of torture and disappearances and suggests ideas for action."-C.C. **Est.:** 1980. **Frequency:** 12/yr. **Subscription:** Donation. **Price:** Free.

**E ▸ El Tecolote**
Box 40037
San Francisco, CA 94140
**Affiliation:** National Audubon Society, San Francisco Chapter. **Concern(s):** environment; wildlife/endangered species. This newsletter reports on the wildlife, especially birds, of the bay area. Informative articles and great photos fill this tiny regional newsletter.

**E ▸ The Elmwood Newsletter**
Box 5765
Berkeley, CA 94705 (510)845-4595
**Affiliation:** Elmwood Institute. **Concern(s):** environment; spiritual; transformation. A creative compendium of systematic thinking, the newsletter facilitates the shift from a patriarchal, mechanistic worldview to an ecological one, with authors such as Fritjof Capra, Riane Eisler, Hazel Henderson, Daniel Ellsberg, and Frances Moore Lappe, focusing on new paradigm solutions to today's global problems. Offers a good introduction to the philosophical and spiritual dimensions of today's ecological movement. **Frequency:** 4/yr. **Subscription:** $25/yr. **Price:** $2/ea. **Pages:** 16. **Circ.:** 1M. **Fax:** (510)845-1439. **Contact(s):** Shana Penn (Editor).

**❂ ▸ Energy Unlimited**
Box 493
Magdelena, NM 87825-0493
**Concern(s):** energy. This newsletter presents non-conventional technology for the researcher, inventor, and the layman." **Est.:** 1978. **Subscription:** $96/yr. **Price:** $6/ea. **Pages:** 48. **Circ.:** 500. **Contact(s):** Rhetta Jacobson.

**❂ ▸ Energy Update**
236 Massachusetts Ave. NE
Washington, DC 20002 (202)543-6060
**Affiliation:** National Consumer Law Center. **Concern(s):** energy; consumer. Newsletter. **Contact(s):** Charles Hill.

**P ▸ Engage/Social Action**
United Methodist Church Board of Church & Society
777 UN Plaza
New York, NY 10017 (212)682-3633
**Affiliation:** United Methodist Church Board of Church & Society. **Concern(s):** politics; justice; spiritual; faith; activism. "Serves as the key periodical promoting a range of social concerns issues within and outside the Methodist Church. There will often be a number of articles on one theme, with shorter pieces and reviews completing the magazine."-C.C. Nonprofit. **Est.:** 1973. **Frequency:** 11/yr. **Subscription:** $10/Donation. **Contact(s):** Lee Ranck (Editor).

**$ ▸ Entrepreneur**
2392 Morse Ave.
Irvine, CA 92714
**Concern(s):** economics; trade. Articles for established and aspiring independent business owners, on all aspects of running a business. **Contact(s):** Rieva Lesonsky (Editor).

**$ ▸ Entrepreneurial Woman**
2392 Morse Ave.
Irvine, CA 92714
**Concern(s):** economics; feminism; trade. Profiles of female entrepreneurs; how-to's on running a business, and pieces on coping as a woman owning a business. **Contact(s):** Rieva Lesonsky (Editor).

**H ▸ Environ**
c/o Wary Canary Press
Box 2204
Fort Collins, CO 80522 (303)224-0083
**Concern(s):** health; environment; hazardous/toxic waste; preventative medicine; holism; social ecology; self-help; nutrition; consumer protection. Current health/ecology magazine offering reviews, op/ed columns, toxic alerts, "environing" tips, resource and consumer alternatives with emphasis on use reduction and proliferation of environmental toxics not only nurtures human health, but enhances total global ecology. A thinking readers environmental health advisor called "the best resource currently available for keeping up with the changing world of products, companies, and research in environmental health," —Carol Venolia. **Other Resources:** Publishes WARY CANARY periodical. **Frequency:** 4/yr. **Subscription:** $15/yr.; $27/2 yrs. **Price:** $4/ea. **Pages:** 40. **Publisher:** Wary Canary Press. **Contact(s):** Suzanne Randegger, Ed Randegger (Co-Publishers/Editors).

**E ▸ Environment**
4000 Albemarle St., NW
Washington, DC 20016 (202)362-6445
**Affiliation:** Helen Dwight Reid Educational Foundation. **Concern(s):** environment. A forum for critical analysis and interpretation of issues concerning the physical, biological, and social environment. This magazine offers an integrated view of the many aspects of environmental management at both the regional and global levels. All subjects in environmental science and policy are treated objectively, intelligently, and authoritatively. **Est.:** 1956. **Frequency:** 10/yr. **Subscription:** $24, $48 institution. **Price:** $4.50/ea. **Pages:** 48. **Circ.:** 16M. **Publisher:** Helen Dwight Reid Educational Foundation. **Contact(s):** Barbara T. Richman (Managing Editor).

**E ▸ Environmental Action Magazine**
6930 Carroll Ave., #600
Tacoma Park, MD 20912 (301)891-1100
**Affiliation:** Environmental Action Foundation. **Concern(s):** environment; energy; politics; activism; grassroots organizing. Environmental news and analysis. Lively, timely and chock-full of information on the major environmental issues facing the US. More than a magazine, your subscription supports the grassroots and national activism of Environmental Action. **Est.:** 1970. **Dues:** $25/yr. **Frequency:** 6/yr. **Subscription:** Membership. **Price:** $2.50/ea. **Bulk:** 40% off/24. **Pages:** 36. **Circ.:** 20M. **Publisher:** EA Inc. **Contact(s):** Barbara Ruben, Hawley Truax (Co-editors).

**E ▸ Environmental Ethics**
Department of Philosophy
University of Georgia
Athens, GA 30602
**Concern(s):** environment; spiritual; transformation. "An Interdisciplinary Journal Dedicated to the Philosophical Aspects of Environmental Problems" is one of the leading forums for serious philosophical work in environmental philosophy. The articles are scholarly, yet accessible. Leading writers have contributed to its pages. **Est.:** 1979. **Frequency:** 4/yr. **Subscription:** $18/yr. **Price:** $6/back issues.

**E ▸ The Environmental Forum**
Environmental Law Institute
1616 P St. NW, #200
Washington, DC 20036 (202)328-5150
**Affiliation:** Environmental Law Institute. **Concern(s):** environment; law. **Other Resources:** Publishes ENVIRONMENTAL LAW REPORTER, NATIONAL WETLANDS NEWSLETTER, and a definitive reference titled LAW OF ENVIRONMENTAL PROTECTION, and many other reports and books. Nonprofit. **Contact(s):** J. William Futrell (President).

**E ▸ Environmental Health Monthly**
Box 926
Arlington, VA 22216 (703)276-7070
**Affiliation:** Citizens Clearinghouse for Hazardous Wastes, Inc.. **Concern(s):** environment; health; hazardous/toxic waste. A periodical that deals with the health of the environment. Focuses on the damages done by the government and industries from hazardous and toxic wastes. **Frequency:** 12/yr. **Contact(s):** Lois Gibbs (Executive Director).

**E ▸ Environmental Law Reporter**
Environmental Law Institute
1616 P St. NW, #200
Washington, DC 20036 (202)328-5150
**Affiliation:** Environmental Law Institute. **Concern(s):** environment; law. Reports on new legislation, proposed and enacted, that effects the environment today. It also reports on the improvement of institutional ability to implement existing law. **Other Resources:** Publishes THE ENVIRONMENTAL FORUM, NATIONAL WETLANDS NEWSLETTER, and a definitive reference titled LAW OF ENVIRONMENTAL PROTECTION, and many other books and reports. Nonprofit. **Est.:** 1969. **Contact(s):** J. William Futrell (President), Barry Breen (Editor). (202)328-5002.

**E ▸ Environmental Opportunities**
Box 4957
Arcata, CA 95521-4957 (707)839-4640
**Affiliation:** Environmental Studies Department/Antioch, New England. **Concern(s):** environment; jobs. This newsletter comprehensively lists job openings throughout the US in a variety of areas such as administrative biology, fisheries, wildlife, horticulture, nature centers, outdoor and environmental education, organizations, research, teaching, etc. as well as seasonal positions and internships. **Frequency:** 12/yr. **Subscription:** $44/yr. **Price:** $4.50/ea. **Pages:** 12-16. **Circ.:** 4M. **Fax:** (707)822-7727. **Contact(s):** Sanford Berry (Editor).

**E ▸ Environmental Update**
218 D St. SE
Washington, DC 20003 (202)544-2600
**Affiliation:** Environmental Policy Institute. **Concern(s):** environment; politics; conservation; lobbying. Newsletter. **Member:** Global Tomorrow Coalition. **Contact(s):** Michael S. Clark (President).

**✌ ▸ Episcopal Peace Fellowship Newsletter**
1317 G St. NW
Washington, DC 20005 (408)252-1998
**Affiliation:** Episcopal Peace Fellowship. **Concern(s):** peace; spiritual; faith. "Even the more well-off Episcopalians are working for a peaceful world. The recent election of a liberal bishop to head the national Episcopal Church has encouraged Church activists."-C.C. Nonprofit. **Est.:** 1939. **Dues:** $25, $35 couple, $5 limited income. **Frequency:** 4/yr. **Subscription:** Donation. **Price:** Free. **Circ.:** 3M. **E-Network:** PeaceNet. **ID:** 'epf'. **Fax:** (202)393-3695. (408)252-3181. **Contact(s):** Ann P. McElroy (Chair), Mary H. Miller (Executive Secretary). (202)783-3380.

**S ▸ The Episcopalian**
1716 Spruce St.
Philadelphia, PA 19107
**Affiliation:** Evangelical Ministries. **Concern(s):** spiritual; faith. Magazine. .

**S ▸ EroSpirit**
Box 35160
Albuquerque, NM 87176(505)897-1443
**Concern(s):** spiritual; transformation. Chronicles the emergence of the New Paradigm and is dedicated to personal, social and planetary transformation through love, the balance of masculine and feminine polarities, and personal integrity. **Frequency:** 6/yr. **Subscription:** $24/yr. **Price:** $4.50/ea. **Bulk:** $3ea/24. **Pages:** 12. **Circ.:** 700. **Contact(s):** Julian Spalding (Publisher).

**E ▸ ESP News**
10 Lombard St., #250
San Francisco, CA 94111 (415)433-1000
**Affiliation:** Conservatree Paper Co.. **Concern(s):** environment; economics; alternative consumer; trade. This newsletter reports on "Environmentally Sound Products" available to consumers from the Conservatree Paper Company. **Est.:** 1976. **Pages:** 4. **Contact(s):** David Assman (Vice-President).

**E ▸ Everyone's Backyard**
Box 926
Arlington, VA 22216 (703)276-7070
**Affiliation:** Citizens Clearinghouse for Hazardous Wastes (CCHW). **Concern(s):** environment; health; hazardous/toxic waste. A journal for the Grassroots Movement for Environmental Justice. It is written for and by people organizing to fight toxic polluters, dumpers, and operators with practical information/scientific information in plain language and tactical tips on how to fight to win. Founded by Lois Gibbs. **Frequency:** 6/yr. **Subscription:** $25/yr. **Pages:** 16. **Circ.:** 20M. **Office:** 2315 Wilson Blvd. Arlington, VA 22201. **Contact(s):** Lois Gibbs (Founder).

**E ▸ Everything Natural**
Box 279
Forest Knolls, CA 94933 (415)663-1685
**Concern(s):** environment. Newsletter. **Contact(s):** Debra Lynn Dadd.

**E ▸ Exchange**
1017 Duke St.
Alexandria, VA 22314 (703)683-7778
**Affiliation:** Land Trust Alliance. **Concern(s):** environment; economics; agriculture; politics; conservation; land use; wilderness; land trusts; resource management; policy. Subjects include: Land protection and management, legal matters and policy developments. This is the only periodical that covers one of the fastest growing movements in conservation—local and regional land trusts. **Other Resources:** NATIONAL DIRECTORY OF CONSERVATION LAND TRUSTS. **Frequency:** 4/yr. **Subscription:** $30/yr.

**P ▸ Exchange Project Newsletter**
Box 270
Amherst, MA 01004 (413)256-8306
**Affiliation:** Peace Development Fund. **Concern(s):** politics; peace; grassroots organizing. "A periodic publication about ideas on improving social change organizing are the attraction. Organizing tips

as well as organizing resource materials are reviewed."-C.C. **Est.:** 1984. **Frequency:** 4/yr. **Price:** Free. **Contact(s):** Judy Kavasik.

**M ▸ Extra!**
130 W. 25th St., 8th Fl.
New York, NY 10001 (212)633-6700
**Affiliation:** Fairness & Accuracy In Reporting. **Concern(s):** media; politics; media watch; electronic democracy; press; government accountability. This newsletter offers well-documented criticism in an effort to correct media bias. In particular, Extra! scrutinizes media practices that slight public interest and minority viewpoints, writing articles on bias, media mergers, censored news, press/state cronyism and right-wing inroads into the media. **Est.:** 1986. **Frequency:** 8/yr. **Subscription:** $30/yr.; $40 institution. **Bulk:** 25% off/24. **Pages:** 20. **Circ.:** 100M. **Contact(s):** Jeff Cohen (Executive Director), Tiffany Devitt (202)332-FAIR.

**✐ ▸ F.U.T.U.R.E. Newsletter**
F.U.T.U.R.E.
Box 228
Butte, ND 58723 (701)626-7360
**Concern(s):** arts; environment; spiritual; agriculture; culture; alternative; music; transformation; organic. Calendar of 30-60 coming alternative culture events worldwide, including music and art festivals, conferences on creative change, preventive medicine, spiritual/psychological subjects, alternative forms of energy, gatherings of organic farmers and gardeners, barterers, and others. North American events are listed for the five weeks following date of issue; foreign events are given two to three months in advance. Articles in various subject areas of alternative culture, metaphysics, and health. **Other Resources:** Arranged chronologically. **Frequency:** 12/yr. **Subscription:** $15/yr. **Price:** $2/ea. **Contact(s):** Serena Dossenko (Editor).

**✐ ▸ Factsheet Five**
6 Arizona Ave.
Rensselaer, NY 12144-4502 (518)479-3707
**Concern(s):** arts; media; press; culture. A guide to the very small press, focused mainly on magazines with circulation 15,000 or less but including independent music, books, video, software, and networking news from a variety of sources.All topics are covered, with approximately 1000-1500 short reviews & abstracts in every issue. Not everything we cover is progressive. (Warning: Expect listings from Neo-Nazis, sadists, vivisectionists, and other unpalatable misfits as well. An education, for sure.) **Other Resources:** Mr. Gunderloy is most recently doing a magazine called "'zine" which offers analysis of alternative magazines. **Frequency:** 6/yr. **Price:** $3/ea. **Bulk:** $1.80ea/24. **Pages:** 112. **Contact(s):** Mike Gunderloy (Editor).

**S ▸ Faithful Witness on Today's Issues**
777 UN Plaza
New York, NY 10017 (212)682-3633
**Affiliation:** United Methodist Church Department of Peace and World Order. **Concern(s):** spiritual; justice; peace; faith. A series of booklets which builds on the premise that "faithful witness" involves constant grappling with current issues in light of Biblical and theological reflection. They are designed to stimulate thought, discussion and further study on a number of complex, sometimes controversial, social issues—contain valid General Conference resolutions, as printed in the Book of Resolutions 1988 with related statements on Social Principles.

**♥ ▸ Family Day Care Bulletin**
725 15th St. NW
Washington, DC 20005 (202)347-3300
**Affiliation:** Children's Foundation. **Concern(s):** family; day care. "Better child care is advocated here, with the benefit of the experience of the Foundation. Stories on home-based care predominate, with tips on care of children and on positive legislation for home-care providers."-C.C. **Est.:** 1977. **Frequency:** 4/yr. **Subscription:** $10, $15 institution. **Price:** $2.50/ea. **Contact(s):** Kay Hollestell.

**A ▸ Family Farm Networker**
110 Maryland Ave. NE, #509
Washington, DC 20002 (800)424-7290
**Affiliation:** Interfaith Impact for Justice and Peace. **Concern(s):** agriculture; economics; spiritual; family farms; interfaith. Newsletter. .

**F ▸ Family Planning Perspectives**
2010 Massachusetts Ave. NW, 5th Fl.
Washington, DC 20036 (202)296-4012
**Affiliation:** Alan Guttmacher Institute. **Concern(s):** feminism; demographics; pro-choice; population growth. This journal focuses on the responsible ways couples can plan having children. Also provides information to teens on birth control and the legislation being put in place to take away peoples rights to choice.

**♈ ▸ The Farm Report**
Box 30654
Bethesda, MD 20824
**Affiliation:** Farm Animal Reform Movement (FARM). **Concern(s):** environment; health; agriculture; vegetarian; animal rights. This newsletter is the Voice of FARM - the Farm Animal Reform Movement. FARM seeks to end animal suffering on farms by promoting awareness of the harm caused by agribusiness to our health (human and non-human), environment, resources, and economy. **Est.:** 1981. **Frequency:** 4/yr. **Price:** Free. **Pages:** 4-8. **Circ.:** 20M.

**A ▸ Farming Uncle International Journal**
c/o Franqui
2917 Grand Concourse, #CN
Bronx, NY 10468
**Concern(s):** agriculture. Poultry, bees, goats, gardening, fruit, nutrition, recipes, etc. Articles from many sources. Lists approximately 100 specialized plants and animal journals and clubs. Information free. A sporadic "Periodical for Natural People and Mother Nature Lovers." Devoted to Holistic Living,...Whole Health, Ecology, Social Responsibility...peace, love and nonviolence...a magazine for homesteaders." **Est.:** 1977. **Subscription:** $5/yr. **Contact(s):** Louis Toro (Editor/Publisher), A. Louis Franqui (Assistant Editor/Manager).

**✌ ▸ FAS Public Interest Report**
307 Massachusetts Ave. NE
Washington, DC 20002 (202)546-3300
**Affiliation:** Federation of American Scientists. **Concern(s):** peace; politics; anti-nuclear; lobbying. "Some 5,000 scientists have united to support this lobby for peace and reduction of nuclear arms. All scientists and those interested in science in the public interest will find it beneficial to subscribe."-C.C. **Est.:** 1947. **Frequency:** 10/yr. **Subscription:** $25, $50 institution. **Price:** Donation. **Contact(s):** Jeremy J. Stone.

**✌ ▸ Fellowship Magazine**
Box 271
Nyack, NY 10960 (914)358-4601
**Affiliation:** Fellowship of Reconciliation. **Concern(s):** peace; justice; spiritual; interfaith; militarism; nonviolence. "The Fellowship is one of the oldest existing peace organizations, and an early advocate of nonviolent resistance to the violence of war. It supports conscientious objection to military service for religious reasons and works for peace around the world with its affiliates in other countries. This is its religious and pacifist journal containing news items and provocative articles related to peace and justice concerns."-C.C. **Frequency:** 8/yr. **Contact(s):** Virginia Baron.

**F ▸ Feminist Bookstore News**
Box 882554
San Francisco, CA 94188 (415)626-1556
**Concern(s):** feminism; education.. A trade magazine for feminist bookstores and Women-in-Print movement. Features more than 100 pages of articles on the practical and political aspects of feminist bookselling and over 250 reviews and announcement of new books. **Est.:** 1976. **Frequency:** 6/yr. **Subscription:** $60/yr. **Price:** $6/ea. **Pages:** 100+. **Circ.:** 600. **Office:** 456 14th St., #6 San Francisco, CA 94103. **Fax:** (415)626-8970. **Contact(s):** Carol Seajay (Publisher).

**F ▸ Feminist Collections**
112 A Memorial Library
728 State St.
Madison, WI 53706 (608)263-5754
**Concern(s):** feminism. "Publishes on topics such as feminist publishing, book selling and distribution; feminist issues and librarianship; and resources for feminist research." **Est.:** 1980. **Frequency:** 4/yr. **Subscription:** $23, $43 institution. **Price:** $5/ea. **Pages:** 30. **Circ.:** 1.4M. **Contact(s):** Susan Searing, Linda Shult (Editors).

**F ▸ Feminist Studies**
Women's Studies Program
University of Maryland
College Park, MD 20742 (310)454-2363
**Concern(s):** feminism; family. A journal that covers aspects in all fields of women's studies on feminism, sexuality, family and human relations. Also reports on significant works by women authors. **Est.:** 1972. **Frequency:** 3/yr. **Subscription:** $45/yr. **Price:** $16/ea. **Pages:** 250. **Circ.:** 7M. **Contact(s):** Claire Moses (Editor/Manager).

**F ▸ Feminist Teacher**
442 Ballantine Hall
Indiana University
Bloomington, IN 47405
**Concern(s):** feminism; education. **Frequency:** 3/yr. **Price:** $12/ea.

**P ▸ Fifth Estate**
Box 02548
Detroit, MI 48202
**Concern(s):** politics; anti-authoritarian. Emphasis on serious theoretical articles, in-depth debate, and support for militant opposition to all governments, corporations, and bureaucracies. "...in a class of its own as and anti-authoritarian paper." - Prison News Service. **Frequency:** 4/yr. **Price:** $7/ea.

**J ▸ Fighting Back**
Box 1819, Madison Square Station
New York, NY 10159 (212)741-0633
**Affiliation:** All-Peoples Congress; People's Anti-War Movement. **Concern(s):** justice; politics; minority rights. "Militant campaigns for rights of people of color, women, and gays are headlined. The draft, imperialism, and poor people's struggles are just three more of the many concerns agitated about by this newsletter."-C.C. **Frequency:** 4/yr. **Subscription:** $5/yr. **Price:** $.25/ea. **Office:** 146 W. 25th St. New York, NY 10001. **Contact(s):** Gavrielle Gemma.

**F ▸ Fighting Woman News**
11438 Z Cronridge Dr
Owings Mills, MD 21117(301)363-4919
**Concern(s):** feminism; health; empowerment. "Our audience is composed of adult women actually practicing martial arts with an average experience of 4+ years... Our material is quite different from what is found in newsstand martial arts publications... Our readership is knowledgeable and critical. Also feminist." **Frequency:** 4/yr. **Subscription:** $10, $15 institution. **Price:** $3/ea. **Pages:** 24. **Circ.:** 4M. **Contact(s):** Franci Sreinburg (Editor).

**S ▸ Firmament**
444 Waller St.
Box 14305
San Francisco, CA 94114 (415)626-6064
**Affiliation:** North American Conference on Christianity and Ecology. **Concern(s):** spiritual; environment; faith; social ecology; acid rain; global warming; transformation. The newsletter of Christian ecology where Christians for the Earth can read of the relationship between the teachings of Christ and ecology. Oil spills, DDT, acid rain, CO2 buildup, destruction of the ozone layer and a host of other environmental desecrations are witness to man's desertion of God's covenant and with calendars and newsbriefs it gives readers guidance on actions, films, publications and retreats, and ideas to restores the Earth's sanctity. **Frequency:** 4/yr. **Contact(s):** Eleanor Rae (President), Frederick Krueger (Executive Secretary). **Other:** NACCE, 309 E. Front St. #200, Traverse City, MI 49684.

**J ▸ First Principles**
122 Maryland Ave. NE, #207R
Washington, DC 20002 (202)544-5380
**Affiliation:** Center for National Security Studies. **Concern(s):** justice; politics; civil liberties; law; government accountability. "Legislation and judicial decisions are of concern in this newsletter. Typical articles are on government snooping, the Freedom of Information Act, and national security vis-a-vis civil liberties."-C.C. Jointly funded by the ACLU and Fund for Peace. Nonprofit. **Est.:** 1974. **Frequency:** 4/yr. **Subscription:** $15/yr.; $10 students. **Circ.:** 3.5M. **Contact(s):** Ann Profizich.

**E ▸ Fish and Wildlife Reference Service Newsletter**
5430 Grosvenor Lane, #110
Bethesda, MD 21087
**Affiliation:** Fish and Wildlife Reference Service. **Concern(s):** environment; wildlife/endangered species. A listing of new research in fish and wildlife management and includes notes about upcoming meetings and tips on retrieving information. The Service provides copies of reports as well as literature searches. **Frequency:** 4/yr. **Price:** Free.

**✐ ▸ Five Fingers Review**
Box 15426
San Francisco, CA 94115
**Concern(s):** arts; activism; literature; poetry. Socially aware fiction, nonfiction, and poetry that address concerns of the day in surprising ways. Published once or twice a year.

**P ▸ The Flight of the Eagle**
Box 1026
Loveland, CO 80539
**Affiliation:** Human Party. **Concern(s):** politics; alternative party. Motto: "Where there is no vision, the people perish...A New Party...A New Manner of Thinking...For a New America." A newsletter reporting the progress of a campaign to establish a new party (The Human Party) in America on a spiritual/humanitarian foundation. Edited by Dr. Larry Holden, intended future US presidential candidate for the year 2000. Insightful and provocative essays and commentary concerning enlightened spiritual political action. Focus on inward change prior to outward action. **Other Resources:** Newsletter published under auspices of campaign for A New America - a "living organism" dedicated to deep, fundamental social/political change based on inward transformation and to the creation of the Human Party. **Est.:** 1981. **Frequency:** 6/yr. **Subscription:** Donation. **Pages:** 6-8. **Circ.:** 400.

**Contact(s):** Dr. Larry Holden.

**T ◈ Focus**
1227 4th St.
Santa Monica, CA 90401     (310)451-2428
**Affiliation:** Office of the Americas. **Concern(s):** Third World; justice; Central America; indigenous peoples; development; intervention; self-determination. "The Focus newsletter is concentrating on Central America during this period of change there. The sponsoring group plays an active part in the movement for self-determination in that region, and reports on its work there."-C.C. **Est.:** 1974. **Frequency:** 4/yr. **Price:** Donation.

**✍ ◈ Focus**
156 5th Ave., #600
New York, NY 10010-7002   (212)242-0214
**Affiliation:** American Geographical Society. **Concern(s):** education; env global understanding. This magazine attempts to focus on different geographical issues each month. It gives the reader great information on geography, which is something Americans lag on. .

**D ◈ Food and Hunger Notes**
21 S. 12th St.
Akron, PA 17501     (717)859-1151
**Affiliation:** Mennonite Central Committee. **Concern(s):** demographics; Third World; spiritual; faith; hunger. "Basic solutions to world hunger and farm problems are presented by the Mennonite church report. Hunger policy improvements and food distribution to drought- and poverty-stricken areas are both seen as necessary solutions."-C.C. **Est.:** 1860. **Frequency:** 6/yr. **Subscription:** $5/yr. **Price:** Donation. **Contact(s):** Art Meyer, Jocele Meyer.

**L ◈ Food and Justice**
Box 62
La Paz, CA 93531-9989 (805)822-5571
**Affiliation:** United Farm Workers, AFL-CIO. **Concern(s):** labor; economics; health; unions; hazardous/toxic waste; boycott. "The frequent table grape boycotts by the farmworkers and children's deaths caused by cancer from pesticides are typical features. Profiles of volunteers helping the farmworkers are also an important part of Cesar Chavez' magazine."-C.C. **Est.:** 1984. **Frequency:** 12/yr. **Subscription:** $5/yr. **Price:** Donation. **Contact(s):** Cesar Chavez.

**T ◈ Food First Development Report**
145 9th St.
San Francisco, CA 94103     (415)864-8555
**Affiliation:** Institute for Food & Development Policy. **Concern(s):** Third World; agriculture; demographics; nutrition; development. "Increased US government efforts for social development in underdeveloped nations are the focus of this journal. New and improved legislation on Third World development is advocated."-C.C. **Est.:** 1987. **Frequency:** 4-5/yr. **Subscription:** $24/yr. **Price:** $6/ea. **Contact(s):** Ann Kelly.

**T ◈ Food First News**
145 9th St.
San Francisco, CA 94103     (415)864-8555
**Affiliation:** Institute for Food and Development Policy. **Concern(s):** Third World; agriculture; demographics; hunger; development; food production; food distribution; policy. "The Food First folks founded this newsletter to publicize their efforts and others' to have more tax dollars spent for fighting hunger instead of for war. This selection covers hunger news, and nicely complements their previous listing, which offers longer analysis."-C.C. **Est.:** 1975. **Frequency:** 4/yr. **Subscription:** Donation. **Price:** Free. **Contact(s):** Frances Moore Lappe, Marilyn Borchadt; Joseph Collins.

**A ◈ The Food Irridiation Alert!**
Food & Water, Inc.
225 Lafayette St., #612
New York, NY 10012     (800)EAT-SAFE
**Affiliation:** National Coalition to Stop Food Irradiation, Inc.. **Concern(s):** agriculture; environment; health; organic; hazardous/toxic waste; nutrition. Food Irradiation destroys vitamins, enzymes, and creates new products, some of them toxic, in food. Radioactive materials used are hazardous to workers and surrounding communities. At NCSFI, we are committed to safe food and to safe, healthy conditions for food industry workers, their families, and neighboring residents. **Frequency:** 4/yr. **Subscription:** $25/yr. **Bulk:** $.50ea/24. **Circ.:** 2.5M. **Contact(s):** Mary Carroll Randall (Administrator).

**D ◈ Food Monitor**
261 W. 35th St., #1402
New York, NY 10001-1906 (212)629-8850
**Affiliation:** World Hunger Year. **Concern(s):** demographics; Third World; hunger; poverty; homelessness; policy. An excellent general resource about political, economic and social relations, decisions and policies that determine food production, financing and distribution which result in or affect malnutrition throughout the US and the world.

Exists to inform the general public, the media and policymakers on the extent and the causes of hunger in the US and abroad.

**D ◈ Foodlines; A Chronicle of Hunger and Poverty in America**
1875 Connecticut Ave. NW
Washington, DC 20009 (202)986-2200
**Affiliation:** Food Research and Action Center. **Concern(s):** demographics; justice; health; politics; nutrition; welfare rights; Medicare; national health; hunger; poverty; policy. "The purpose of this selection goes beyond the right to adequate nutrition and government food programs and also covers assaults by welfare budget slashers who would cut other social welfare programs. Nutrition programs for seniors, children, and low-income folks are the essence of Foodlines, however, which is published for the beneficiaries as well as for the program advocates. Provides information on issues concerning low-income Americans"-C.C. **Est.:** 1979. **Frequency:** 12/yr. **Subscription:** $20/yr. **Price:** Donation. **Contact(s):** Cecilia Perry.

**J ◈ Ford Foundation Letter**
320 E. 43rd St.
New York, NY 10017
**Affiliation:** Ford Foundation. **Concern(s):** justice; feminism; children. This foundation's long standing interest in improving child-care services set a norm by which other child care programs are measured. Yet, they fail to face the central problem of an economic system which requires the break up or break down of families to meet the demands of industries for cheap labor which necessitates both parents working to meet the family needs. Newsletter.

**✇ ◈ Foreign Affairs**
58 E. 68th St.
New York, NY 10021-5984  (212)734-0400
**Affiliation:** Council of Foreign Relations. **Concern(s):** peace; Third World; politics. "...publishes groundbreaking articles on all aspects of global politics and economics, and is the leading forum through which international leaders communicate their views. Articles cover a wide range of topics, from nuclear winter to environmental hazards to Perestroika to US-China relations following the sobering events in Tiannamann Square." **Frequency:** 5/yr. **Subscription:** $32/yr. **Fax:** (617) 523-2067.

**P ◈ Foreign Policy**
Box 2104
Knoxville, IA 50197-2104    (212)764-4050
**Concern(s):** politics; Third World; peace; education; foreign policy; intervention; law; government accountability. Previews events—elections, legislation, negotiations, diplomatic visits—that will shape the foreign policy news in the coming month. "For two decades...the source of perspectives and background necessary for a true understanding of what's happening in the world." **Other:** 729 7th Ave., New York, NY 10019.

**P ◈ Foreign Policy Magazine**
2400 N St. NW
Washington, DC 20037  (202)862-7940
**Affiliation:** Arms Control Association. **Concern(s):** politics; Third World; foreign policy. This magazine promotes public support of arms control through the press; works to foster an improved relationship between nations by creating a better understanding of foreign policy; and keeps its readers abreast of important legislative developments.

**E ◈ Forest & Conservation History**
701 Vickers Ave.
Durham, NC 27701     (919)682-9319
**Affiliation:** Forest History Society. **Concern(s):** environment; forests; conservation. Features original articles, essays on new trends, and timely book reviews as well as reports of new research. The Society is an organization of scholars, foresters, industrialists, conservationists and scientists who appreciate the significance of our forest heritage. **Est.:** 1957. **Frequency:** 4/yr. **Subscription:** $25/yr.

**E ◈ Forest Watch**
CHEC
14417 SE Laurel
Oak Grove, OR 97267     (503)652-7049
**Affiliation:** Cascade Holistic Economic Consultants. **Concern(s):** environment; forests. This magazine reports on public forest planning and management providing technical information for forestry conservation groups. **Contact(s):** Randall O'Toole (Director, Forest Economist), Jeffrey St. Clair (Editor).

**J ◈ Forum**
1460 Broadway
New York, NY 10036    (202)462-4777
**Affiliation:** People for the American Way Action Fund. **Concern(s):** justice; media; civil liberties; censorship; constitutional rights. "Book burnings and other forms of censorship are positively un-American, say People for the American Way. This paper inspires us to help protect

our Constitutional liberties."-C.C. **Est.:** 1979. **Dues:** $25/yr. **Frequency:** 4/yr. **Subscription:** Membership. **Price:** Donation. **Contact(s):** Matthew Freeman.

**✇ ◈ Forum**
Educators for Social Responsibility
23 Garden St.
Cambridge, MA 02138   (617)492-1764
**Affiliation:** Educators for Social Responsibility. **Concern(s):** peace; education; conflict resolution; militarism; disarmament; students. "Teaching peace in the schools is facilitated through teaching aids, conference news, and a bibliography of print and video selections. This magazine also suggests ways of working for peace in the larger community."-C.C. **Est.:** 1983. **Frequency:** 4/yr. **Subscription:** $20/yr. **Price:** $5/ea. **Contact(s):** Tony Wagner.

**✇ ◈ The Fourth R**
525 Amity St.
Amherst, MA 01002     (413)545-2462
**Affiliation:** National Association for Mediation in Education (NAME). **Concern(s):** peace; education; conflict resolution. This newsletter is edited and published for NAME at the Mediation Project at the University of Massachusetts. The magazine reports one way that educators and people are trying to give a subduing influence to education. Has reviews of books, tapes, and audio materials for education. Great articles on home education. Nonprofit. **Est.:** 1984. **Dues:** $30; $50/organization. **Subscription:** Membership. **Contact(s):** Annette Townley (Executive Director), Rachel Goldberg (Project Assistant).

**P ◈ Fourth World Review**
24 Abercorn Place
London, NW8 England    071 286 4366
**Concern(s):** politics; economics; alternative party; community self-reliance; grassroots organizing; decentralization. The Fourth World refers to the world of small nations and small communities. Global problems have become unsolvable because of giantism. "We seek a new world order based on the human scale and the right of small communities to determine their own pattern of life." **Other Resources:** Academic Inn Dinner/Discussion; Fourth World Assemblies; Institute of Social Inventions. FAX: 071 289 9081 (Attn: 4th World). **Est.:** 1966. **Frequency:** 6/yr. **Subscription:** Donation. **Price:** $2/ea. **Pages:** 32. **Circ.:** 2M. **Contact(s):** John Papworth (Editor), Nicholas Albery (Director). 081 208 2853.

**J ◈ The Franciscan Worker**
Franciscan Workers of Junipero Serra
715 Jefferson St.
Salinas, CA 93905     (408)757-3838
**Affiliation:** Franciscan Workers of Junipero Serra. **Concern(s):** justice; demographics; spiritual; labor; faith; hunger; homelessness; farmworkers. Soup kitchens, farmworkers and homelessness are their issues. Tax deductible gifts can be donated to their admirable cause. Newsletter. Nonprofit. **Est.:** 1982. **Subscription:** Donation. **Pages:** c12.

**J ◈ Free Inquiry**
Box 5
Buffalo, NY 14215-0005 (716)834-2921
**Affiliation:** Council for Democratic & Secular Humanism. **Concern(s):** justice; media; civil liberties; censorship. "Countering religious fundamentalists, the humanist scholars who write and support this 48-page magazine are dedicated to defending 'freedom and secularism in the contemporary world.' Each issue contains about 10 articles, usually by teachers."-C.C. **Est.:** 1980. **Frequency:** 4/yr. **Subscription:** $20/yr. **Price:** $3.75/ea. **Contact(s):** Paul Kurtz (Editor), Tim Madigan (Executive Editor).

**M ◈ Free Speech Yearbook**
5105 Backlick Rd.
Building E
Annandale, VA 22003    (703)650-0533
**Affiliation:** Speech Communication Association. **Concern(s):** media; justice; journalism; civil liberties. "Each year First Amendment questions considered of key importance by the association are presented in scholarly footnoted papers, in journal form. Journalism students and scholars will appreciate it."-C.C. **Est.:** 1973. **Frequency:** Annual. **Subscription:** $10/yr. **Price:** $10/ea. **Contact(s):** Stephen Smith.

**$ ◈ Free Spirit**
Box 486, Station J
Toronto, ON M4J 4Z2 Canada
**Concern(s):** economics; justice; feminism; future; intentional communities; ideation. This newsletter is dedicated to the idea that life should be lived as if it is worth living. Explorations into alternative lifestyles, sexuality, ecology, and economic alternatives. **Est.:** 1989. **Frequency:** 12/yr. **Subscription:** $8/yr. **Price:** $1/ea.

✍ ▶ **Free Spirit: News & Views on Growing Up**
Free Spirit Publishing, Inc.
400 First Ave. N., #616
Minneapolis, MN 55401
**Concern(s):** education; health; psychology; youth. Nonfiction related to the lives of teens and preteens (school, peer relationships, family, health, etc.). Annual cartoon and writing contests for kids. Readers are 10- to 14-years-old. **Publisher:** Free Spirit Publishing, Inc.

J ▶ **The Freedom of Information Report**
The Society of Professional Journalists
53 W. Jackson Blvd., #731
Chicago, IL 60604-3610 (312)922-7424
**Affiliation:** Society of Professional Journalists. **Concern(s):** justice; media; politics; economics; government accountability; censorship; constitutional rights; corporate responsibility. **Fax:** (312)922-7668.

P ▶ **Freedom Socialist**
New Freeway Hall
5018 Rainier Ave., South
Seattle, WA 98118
**Concern(s):** politics; alternative party. Newsletter of Marxist theory. **Frequency:** 4/yr. **Price:** $5/ea.

J ▶ **Freedom to Read Foundation News**
50 E. Huron St.
Chicago, IL 60611 (312)944-6780
**Affiliation:** American Library Association and the Freedom to Read Foundation. **Concern(s):** justice; media; censorship; press; journalism; responsibility. "These folks favor access to the range of opinion in the literature of our libraries. Book banning is opposed."-C.C. **Est.:** 1972. **Dues:** $25/yr. **Frequency:** 4/yr. **Subscription:** Membership. **Price:** $6.25/ea. **Contact(s):** Judith F. Krug.

J ▶ **Freedom Writer**
Box 589
Great Barrington, MA 01230 (413)274-3786
**Concern(s):** justice; media; spiritual; censorship; civil liberties; constitutional rights. "The separation of church and state is championed in this national newsletter. Fundamentalists of the right and religion in the schools are opposed."-C.C. **Est.:** 1984. **Frequency:** 10/yr. **Subscription:** $10/yr. **Price:** Free. **Contact(s):** Barbara Simon, Skipp Porteous.

J ▶ **Freedomways**
799 Broadway, #542
New York, NY 10003 (212)477-3985
**Affiliation:** Freedomways Association. **Concern(s):** justice; politics; minority rights; diversity; constitutional rights; grassroots organizing. "Stimulating in form and educational in essence, it reviews the civil rights movement, national and international. Cultural reviews, inspiring features and an outstanding book notes section make it a foremost review in its field."-C.C. **Est.:** 1961. **Frequency:** 4/yr. **Subscription:** $7.50/yr. **Price:** $2/ea. **Contact(s):** Esther Jackson.

$ ▶ **The Freeman**
Foundation for Economic Education
Irvington-on-Hudson
New York, NY 10533 (914)591-7230
**Affiliation:** Foundation for Economic Education. **Concern(s):** economics; politics. Articles on economic, political, and moral implications of private property, voluntary exchange, and individual choice. **Contact(s):** Brian Summers (Senior Editor).

A ▶ **Fresh Connections**
Box 1070
Captain Cook, HI 96704 (808)328-9044
**Affiliation:** Adaptations. **Concern(s):** agriculture; environment; organic; permaculture; sustainability. A newsletter designed to connect producers and users of all types of plants in Hawaii. It solicits articles from executive chefs, nursery owners, growers, landscapers, herbal medicinal practitioners, permaculturalists, and others about fresh produce, fruits, organic techniques, medicinal & ornamental plants, and suburban gardening. The purpose of the publication is to develop communication, marketing, and a sense of creating a sustainable, ecological & humanistic-oriented economy. **Other Resources:** Mainly an organic farm, organizes local growers and markets. Group was organized in 1980. **Est.:** 1990. **Frequency:** 4/yr. **Subscription:** $15/yr. **Price:** $2/ea. **Pages:** 8. **Circ.:** 1M. **E-Network:** PeaceNet/ConflictNet. **ID:** 'adaptions'. **Contact(s):** Tane Dotta (Publisher).

S ▶ **Friends Journal**
1501 Cherry St.
Philadelphia, PA 19102 (215)741-7277
**Affiliation:** American Friends Service Committee. **Concern(s):** spiritual; peace; justice; faith. "The quaker viewpoints on peace, justice, society, and the spirit are included here. It will be of interest to Quakers and their friends. From personal experience on the West Bank to finding a new mythology, from exploring reactions to abortion to matters of war tax resistance, Friends Journal provides a Quaker approach."-C.C. **Est.:** 1955. **Frequency:** 12/yr. **Subscription:** $18/yr. **Price:** $1.50/ea. **Publisher:** Friends Publishing Corp. **Contact(s):** Vinton Deming.

☮ ▶ **Friends of Peace Pilgrim Newsletter**
43480 Cedar Ave.
Hemet, CA 92344 (714)927-7678
**Affiliation:** Friends of Peace Pilgrim. **Concern(s):** peace; spiritual; interfaith; volunteers. "Overcome evil with good, falsehood with truth, hatred with love." Volunteers continue to keep the message of Peace Pilgrim alive through this newsletter. Nonprofit. **Frequency:** 3-4/yr.

F ▶ **Frontiers: A Journal of Women Studies**
Women's Studies Program
Box 325, University of Colorado
Boulder, CO 80309
**Concern(s):** feminism. This journal has articles, poetry, stories and book reviews in every issue that links academic and popular sides of feminist concerns. **Est.:** 1975. **Frequency:** 3/yr. **Subscription:** $16, $33 institution. **Contact(s):** Charlotta Hensley (Editor).

P ▶ **Frontline**
Box 2809
Oakland, CA 94609 (510)843-7495
**Concern(s):** politics; alternative party. "Well-known radical journalist Irwin Silber is a key writer and editor of this theoretical Leninist journal. He is typical of the quality and experience of writers for Frontline."-C.C. Marxist. **Est.:** 1979. **Frequency:** 23/yr. **Subscription:** $20, $25 institution. **Price:** $.75/ea. **Publisher:** Line of March Publications. **Contact(s):** Max Elbaum; Irwin Silber, Ellen Kaiser.

J ▶ **Full Disclosure**
Box 8275
Ann Arbor, MI 48107 (313)747-7027
**Concern(s):** justice. "The right to know how our government operates and the right to personal privacy are typical topics in the 20 pages of the Full Disclosure newspaper. Applications of the Freedom of Information Act are also updated."-C.C. **Est.:** 1984. **Frequency:** 12/yr. **Subscription:** $18/yr. **Price:** $2/ea. **Bulk:** 50% off/24. **Pages:** 12-16. **Circ.:** 7M. **Other Formats:** is directory of Electronic Surveillance Equipment Suppliers. **Contact(s):** Lynn Johnston, Glenn Roberts

✏ ▶ **The Funny Times, Inc.**
3108 Scarborough Rd.
Cleveland, OH 44118-4050 (216)371-8600
**Concern(s):** arts; media; politics; press; graphics; culture. A monthly humor newspaper featuring political humor and social commentary in writing and cartoons. **Frequency:** 12/yr. **Contact(s):** Susan Wolpert.

E ▶ **Future Survey/Future Survey Annual**
5413 Webster Rd.
LaFayette, NY 13083 (315)677-9278
**Affiliation:** World Future Society. **Concern(s):** environment; future. Abstracts and critical comments on recent books, reports, and articles (selected from newspapers, magazines, and journals) on world futures, international economics, defense and disarmament, energy, environment, and resources, food and agriculture, society and government, the US economy, work, cities/housing/transportation, crime and justice, health, families and education, communications, science and technology, and methods to shape the future. **Other Resources:** FUTURE SURVEY is published by the World Future Society (4916 St. Elmo Ave., Bethesda, MD 20814) which also publishes a bimonthly magazine, THE FUTURIST, and a quarterly journal, FUTURES RESEARCH QUARTERLY + catalog to "The Futurist Bookstore." **Est.:** 1979. **Dues:** $30/yr. (including subscription to FUTURIST). **Frequency:** 12/yr.+ annual. **Subscription:** $66/yr. **Price:** $6.50/survey; $25/annual. **Pages:** 16; c200/annual. **Contact(s):** Michael Marien (Editor), Edward Cornish (Publisher). (301)656-8274.

? ▶ **Futurific Magazine**
280 Madison Ave.
New York, NY 10016 (212)684-4913
**Concern(s):** future; ideation; invention. "We report on what is coming in all areas of life from international affairs to the arts and sciences. Readership cuts across all income levels and includes leadership, government, corporate and religious circles." Nonprofit. **Est.:** 1976. **Frequency:** 12/yr. **Price:** Sample/$5+SAE. **Circ.:** 10M. **Publisher:** Futurific, Inc. **Contact(s):** Balint Szent-Miklosy (Editor-in-Chief).

? ▶ **The Futurist**
4916 St. Elmo Ave.
Bethesda, MD 20814-5089 (301)656-8274
**Affiliation:** World Future Society. **Concern(s):** future; ideation. A bimonthly magazine of forecasts, trends, and ideas about the future. Issues frequently covered include agriculture, computers, demographics, ecology, economics, education, energy, health, transportation, and values. **Frequency:** 6/yr. **Subscription:** $36/yr. **Price:** $4.50/ea. **Pages:** 60. **Circ.:** 30M. **Fax:** (301)951-0394. **Contact(s):** Edward Cornish (Editor), Timothy H. Williard (Managing Editor).

E ▶ **Garbage**
435 9th St.
Brooklyn, NY 11215 (718)788-1700
**Concern(s):** environment; energy; economics; recycling; resource management; waste management; alternatives consumer; green consumer; renewables. The first independently published environmental magazine not funded by a membership or nonprofit group. It is dedicated to exploring the truth about environmental issues and taking a thorough look at the option, stressing a sense of responsibility yet never losing its sense of humor. Wants us to understand that concern and action in favor of the environment can start in our own homes and everyday lives. **Frequency:** 6/yr. **Subscription:** $21/yr. **Price:** $4.95/ea. **Contact(s):** Patricia Moore (Editor/Publisher).

A ▶ **Garden**
The Garden Society
Botanical Garden
Bronx, NY 10458
**Affiliation:** Garden Society. **Concern(s):** agriculture; environment. Articles on botany, horticulture, ecology, agriculture. **Contact(s):** Karen Polyak (Editor).

E ▶ **Garden Doctor**
1684 Willow
Denver, CO 80220
**Concern(s):** environment; agriculture. "The Rolls Royce of gardening newsletters".

✏ ▶ **Gauntlet**
309 Powell Rd.
Springfield, PA 19064 (215)328-5476
**Concern(s):** arts; justice; literature; censorship; freedom of expression. "An annual that tackles censorship with controversial censored work, art that caused its ban in Canada, lively commentary, satire and original fiction. Bold, unrelenting, irreverent, Gauntlet challenges even First Amendment purists to free expression. #1 features Ray Bradbury, Isaac Asimov, Harlan Ellison, George Carlin, Andres Serrano." **Frequency:** Annual. **Subscription:** $16/2 yrs. **Price:** $8.95/ea. **Pages:** 112.

M ▶ **GBH/The Members' Magazine**
376 Boylston St.
Boston, MA 02116
**Concern(s):** media; broadcasting; film. Member magazine for WGBH, Boston's public TV and radio stations. Articles based on WGBH programming, written in first- or third-person. **Contact(s):** Jack Curtis (Managing Editor).

H ▶ **Genetic, Social, and General Psychology Monographs**
Heldref Publications
4000 Albemarle St. NW
Washington, DC 20016 (202)362-6445
**Concern(s):** health; psychology. Publishes articles of monograph length that make an outstanding contribution to the field of psychology. Articles may deal with the biological as well as the behavioral and social aspects of psychology and may present a series of research studies, a new theory, or an in-depth criticism of an existing theory. Notable articles include "Children's Conceptions of Shadow Phenomena" and "Normative Conformity and Racial Prejudice in South Africa." **Frequency:** 4/yr. **Subscription:** $65/yr.

A ▶ **geneWATCH**
Council for Responsible Genetics
19 Garden St.
Cambridge, MA 02138
**Affiliation:** Council for Responsible Genetics. **Concern(s):** agriculture; agriculture; biotechnology; science. "Devoted exclusively to examining the social, political, and ethical impacts of new genetic technologies. Takes neither the uncritical 'gee whiz' approach of the mainstream science press nor the short-sighted 'how do we turn a profit on this' approach of the business press. CRG is a non-profit organization dedicated to insuring that biotechnology is developed safely and in the public interest."-C.W. Nonprofit. **Frequency:** 6/yr. **Subscription:** $24/yr.; $30 institute. **Pages:** 12. **Circ.:** 1M.

✍ ▶ **The Geographical Review**
156 5th Ave., #600
New York, NY 10010-7002 (212)242-0214
**Affiliation:** American Geographical Society. **Concern(s):** education; environment; global understanding.

**✍ ◗ Gleanings**
40 S. Fullerton Ave.
Montclair, NJ 07042  (201)783-7616
**Affiliation:** Global Learning. **Concern(s):** education; justice; economics; childhood. "This newsletter is a networking tool including upcoming conferences and seminars on justice issues in the schools, and short review of publications on these issues. Children and youth benefit from it, since it helps advance such concerns in the schools."-C.C. **Est.:** 1975. **Frequency:** 4/yr. **Subscription:** $2/yr. **Price:** Free. **Contact(s):** Paula Gotsch.

**P ◗ Global Communities**
Institute for Policy Studies
1601 Connecticut Ave. NW
Washington, DC 20009  (202)234-9382
**Affiliation:** Institute for Policy Studies. **Concern(s):** politics; peace; municipal; foreign policy; interantional law. This magazine covers the wide range of foreign policy initiatives launched from city halls around the nation, including sister city programs, nuclear free zones, international trade development, divestment, human rights, and more. Originally published by Center for Innovative Diplomacy as the BULLETIN OF MUNICIPAL FOREIGN POLICY, founded by Larry Agran. **Frequency:** 4/yr. **Subscription:** $15/yr. **Price:** $3/ea. **Pages:** 60. **Circ.:** 10M.

**✍ ◗ Global Electronics**
222B View St.
Mountain View, CA 94041  (415)969-1545
**Affiliation:** Pacific Studies Center. **Concern(s):** education; science. "Military and corporate technology across the world, electronics included, is covered by this newsletter. The effect of this technology is explained with a concern for the problems it can cause people."-C.C. **Est.:** 1982. **Frequency:** 12/yr. **Subscription:** $10/yr. **Price:** $1/ea. **Contact(s):** Lenny Siegal.

**✍ ◗ Global Perspectives**
Augsburg College
731 21 Ave. South
Minneapolis, MN 55454  (612)330-1159
**Affiliation:** Center for Global Education. **Concern(s):** education; justice; Third World; global understanding; hunger; development. This newsletter attempts to introduce readers to conditions in the rest of the world such as poverty and injustice. It also examines the root causes of these problems and how Americans can play an active role in this change both here and abroad. **Est.:** 1982. **Frequency:** 4/yr. **Fax:** (612)330-1695. **Contact(s):** Mavis Anderson, Joan Moline (Coordinators).

**A ◗ Global Pesticide Monitor**
Box 610
San Francisco, CA 94101  (415)541-9140
**Affiliation:** Pesticide Action Network. **Concern(s):** agriculture; environment; health; pesticides; hazardous/toxic waste. This newsletter reports on violations with pesticides throughout the world. Informative articles on alternatives to pesticides. **Frequency:** 3/yr.

**E ◗ Global Releaf Report**
Box 2000
Washington, DC 20013  (202)667-3300
**Affiliation:** American Forestry Association. **Concern(s):** environment; forests; conservation; global warming. Newsletter. **Frequency:** 4/yr. **Contact(s):** R. Neil Sampson (Executive Director).

**⚙ ◗ Global Report**
218 E. 18th St.
New York, NY 10003  (212)475-1077
**Affiliation:** Center for War/Peace Studies. **Concern(s):** peace; United Nations; world order. This newsletter focuses on the global problems of today. Problems such as economics, human rights, the environment, and international conflict are discussed in this quarterly newsletter. **Est.:** 1977. **Frequency:** 4/yr. **Subscription:** $20/yr. **Pages:** 4. **Contact(s):** Richard Hudson (Executive Director).

**S ◗ Gnosis, A Journal of Western Inner Traditions**
Box 14217 SD
San Francisco, CA 94114
**Concern(s):** spiritual; interfaith. "Steering between the closed-minded skeptics and 'true believers', this magazine explores Western spiritual traditions in articles, interviews, and reviews. Jewish, Christian, Islamic, Hermetic, and Occult beliefs (and their offshots and heresies) are discussed from non-sectarian and thought-provoking viewpoints. Unique and very readable, with lively reader feedback and fascinating illustration." **Frequency:** 4/yr. **Subscription:** $15/yr.

**⚙ ◗ God and Caesar**
Commission on Home Ministries
Box 347
Newton, KS 67114
**Affiliation:** General Conference Mennonite Church. **Concern(s):**

peace; spiritual; war tax revolt; militarism; interfaith. A newsletter that shares information, questions, and convictions on war taxes. **Frequency:** 4/yr.

**$ ◗ Good Money**
Box 363
Worcester, VT 05682  (802)223-3911
**Affiliation:** Good Money Publications, Inc.. **Concern(s):** economics; socially-responsible investing. This newsletter provides columns and features of interest to ethically and socially concerned investors on socially responsive companies (domestic and foreign), socially-screened funds, how companies respond to social issues, SRI groups and organizations worldwide, and how investors can make profitable investments while respecting their principles. **Frequency:** 6/yr. **Subscription:** $75/yr. **Pages:** 12. **Circ.:** 600. **Member:** Co-op America. **Contact(s):** Ritchie Lowry (President), Steven Helm (Director of Research).

**M ◗ Granta**
250 W. 57th St., #1203
New York, NY 10107  (212)246-1313
**Concern(s):** media; arts; politics; culture; journalism; literature. "Granta is a mass marketed paperback magazine co-published with Penguin Books, devoted to contemporary literature and political discussion." **Est.:** 1979. **Frequency:** 4/yr. **Subscription:** $32/yr. **Price:** $9.95/ea. **Pages:** 256. **Circ.:** 100M. **Publisher:** Grant Publications, Ltd.. **Contact(s):** Bill Bufford (Editor).

**P ◗ Grassroots**
Box 9586
Charlotte, NC 28299  (704)332-3090
**Affiliation:** Grassroots Leadership. **Concern(s):** politics; demographics; labor; grassroots organizing; poverty. "Singer Si Kahn is the director of the sponsoring group, which seeks to empower folks by telling them about better techniques for building their groups. His inspiring style for organizing poor and working people is reflected in the upbeat Grassroots newsletter."-C.C. **Est.:** 1986. **Frequency:** 2/yr. **Price:** Donation. **Contact(s):** Tema Okun.

**$ ◗ Grassroots Economic Organizing (GEO) Newsletter**
Box 5065
New Haven, CT 06525  (203)389-6194
**Affiliation:** PACE of Philadelphia. **Concern(s):** economics; politics; labor; environment; workplace democracy; grassroots organizing; green consumer; cooperatives. A forum for exchange and collaboration for all groups concerned to create and nourish a grassroots, democratically controlled economy—progressive labor activists, worker-owned enterprises, community-based economic empowerment, or environmental justice groups. Provides timely information on funding sources, marketing strategies, clean technological alternatives, as well as a "clipping service" of some 40 publications with implications for grassroots economic development. **Other Resources:** Formerly CHANGING WORK magazine. Nonprofit. **Est.:** 1991. **Frequency:** 4-6/yr. **Subscription:** $19.95/yr. **Price:** $4/ea. **Bulk:** 20% off 24. **Pages:** 8-12. **Circ.:** 500+. **Contact(s):** Len Krimerman (Editorial coordinator), Frank Lindenfeld (Co-editor). (203)785-8714.

**P ◗ Grassroots Fundraising Journal**
Box 11607
Berkeley, CA 94601
**Concern(s):** politics; economics; activism; grassroots organizing; fundraising. This is a newsletter covering grassroots fundraising for activist and nonprofit organizations. Includes book excerpts, how-to's, and personal experience stories on fundraising. **Est.:** 1981. **Frequency:** 6/yr. **Subscription:** $20/yr. **Price:** $3/sample. **Circ.:** 3M. **Contact(s):** Kim Klein, Lisa Honig (Partners).

**✈ ◗ Great Expeditions**
Box 8000-411
Sumas, WA 98295-8000
**Concern(s):** education; travel. "Budget travel advice, free ads to subscribers, and reports about hiking, climbing, boating and living around the world. This magazine offers insightful articles on budget travel, cross-cultural contact, trekking, socially responsible tourism in Asia, Africa, Latin America. Hard-to-find info on destinations and cultures untouched by mass tourism." **Other Resources:** "Subscribers receive free travel companion ads, free use of an information exchange and a copy of 33 WAYS TO SAVE ON TRAVEL, an information guide to money-saving travel tips." **Frequency:** 6/yr. **Subscription:** $18/yr. **Price:** $3/sample. **Contact(s):** Craig Henderson (Editor).

**E ◗ The Green Consumer Letter**
c/o Tilden Press
1526 Connecticut Ave. NW
Washington, DC 20036-1049  (800)955-4733

**Concern(s):** environment; economics; green consumer. "...the authoritative, independent voice of environmentally safe shopping, written by Joel Makower, author of THE GREEN CONSUMER. Full of investigations, product and company information, money- and Earth-saving tips." "Innovative, irreverent,"-LA Time Newsletter. **Other Resources:** Also publishes THE GREEN BUSINESS LETTER for $97 a year. **Frequency:** 12/yr. **Subscription:** $27/yr. **Price:** $3/ea. **Contact(s):** Joel Makower (Publisher).

**E ◗ Green Earth Observer**
Box 327
El Verano, CA 93428  (707)935-7257
**Affiliation:** Green Earth Foundation. **Concern(s):** environment; spiritual; education; transformation. A newsletter reporting on research, education, and dissemination of information that fosters and contributes to the healing and harmonizing of the relationships between humanity and nature. Also has interesting books on the New Age. Organizations and periodicals are also listed. Nonprofit. **Est.:** 1989. **Frequency:** 4/yr. **Subscription:** $25/yr.; $15/low income. **Pages:** 8. **Circ.:** 1M. **E-Network:** Peacenet/Econet. **ID:** 'rmetzner'. **Contact(s):** Ralph Metzner (Editor), Martha Katt (Production).

**S ◗ Green Egg**
Box 1542
Ukiah, CA 95482
**Affiliation:** Church of all Worlds. **Concern(s):** spiritual; environment; activism; transformation. A magazine focusing on shamanism, Goddess lore, psychic development, environmental activism, suppressed history, and alternative sexuality. "The official journal of the Church of All Worlds, a Neo-Paganism Religion dedicated to the celebration of all life, the maximal actualization of human potential, and the realization of ultimate individual freedom and personal responsibility in harmonious eco-psychic relationship with the total Biosphere of Holy Mother Earth. Thou art Goddess!" **Frequency:** 4/yr. **Subscription:** $13/yr. **Contact(s):** Otto Zell (Editor), Morning Glory Zell.

**E ◗ Green Letter**
Box 30208
Kansas City, MO 64112  (816)931-9366
**Affiliation:** Green Committees of Correspondence. **Concern(s):** environment; politics; justice; economics; feminism; peace; decentralization; nonviolence; men's liberation; sustainability. A newsletter that reports on value-based politics of the local Green parties in the Kansas City and Missouri area. The newsletter is distributed to its members free of charge. **Est.:** 1984. **Frequency:** 4/yr. **Subscription:** Membership. **Price:** Free. **Contact(s):** Jim Richmond (Coordinator).

**E ◗ Green Letter, in Search of Greener Times**
Box 14141
San Francisco, CA 94114  (415)548-1801
**Affiliation:** Green Committees of Correspondence. **Concern(s):** environment; politics; Green. A magazine dedicated to building an effective green movement that transforms this society into one which honors green values. News and analysis, especially of the Greens in the US and the Green Committees of Correspondence, a national network of grassroots groups, a forum for reporting on the activities of the international Green Movement. **Frequency:** 4/yr. **Subscription:** $20/yr. **Price:** $3/ea. **Bulk:** Call. **Pages:** 50. **Contact(s):** George Franklin (Collective Member), Margo Adair (415)861-6838.

**E ◗ Green Living Magazine**
WEN, Freepost
London, EC1B IZT **England**
**Concern(s):** environment; future; economics; Green; invention; green consumer. This magazine features the "Green Home," the model home of the future. Room by room, you will see how you can use a variety of natural products to create a safe environment. Practical suggestions are also given on how to be "Green" and how to safeguard the Earth.

**E ◗ Green Marketalert**
345 Wood Creek Rd.
Bethlehem, CT 06751  (203)266-7209
**Concern(s):** environment; economics; green consumer; trade; alternative consumer. This newsletter tracks the business impacts of green consumerism. Covers corporate strategies, regulation, marketing/advertising, green consumer surveys, products/packaging, international developments and more. Also provides resources for implementing green business strategies. **Frequency:** 12/yr. **Subscription:** $295, $145, nonprofit. **Contact(s):** Carl Frankel.

**P ◗ Green Politics**
Box 372
West Lebanon, NH 03784  (802)295-1544
**Affiliation:** Left Green Network. **Concern(s):** politics; arts; alternative party; Green; poetry. The quarterly discussion journal of the Left

Green Network. Complaints have arisen that the Network tends to be male, undemocratic, and aggressive. They have succeeded in dominating the Green Party and alienting key feminists. **Other Resources:** Publishes monthly, LEFT GREEN NOTES; quarterly, DISCUSSION JOURNAL.

**E ▸ Green Prints**
Box 1355
Fairview, NC 28730
**Concern(s):** environment. An offshoot of MOTHER EARTH NEWS, it is a new quarterly on the human side of gardening covering the wide range of emotions which come from gardening through reprinting the classic and discovering new poets and essayists who experience the special ties the gardener feels for the Earth and its inhabitants. **Frequency:** 4/yr.

**$ ▸ Green Revolution**
Box 42663
Tucson, AZ 85733 (602)577-2187
**Affiliation:** School of Living. **Concern(s):** economics; community self-reliance; community investment. This newsletter has been called "the Grandmother of the counter-culture" and provides leading edge articles and information on self-reliance, community development and social transformation. Talks about decentralized and cooperative solutions to our problems. Based on the work of Ralph Borsodi. **Est.:** 1934. **Frequency:** 4/yr. **Pages:** 8. **Circ.:** 900. **Contact(s):** Thomas H. Greco, Jr. (President), Ginny Green (Clerk).

**E ▸ The Green Sheet**
Box 247
Skaneateles, NY 13152 (315)685-8295
**Concern(s):** environment; economics. A newsletter listing organizations and businesses offering environmental alternatives. **Frequency:** 6/yr. **Publisher:** The Green Being Co. **Contact(s):** Tony Colella.

**E ▸ Green Synthesis**
1507 Le Grande Ter.
San Pedro, CA 90732 (310)833-2633
**Affiliation:** Green Committees of Correspondence. **Concern(s):** environment; bioregionalism; social ecology. A newsletter and journal for social ecology, deep ecology, bioregionalism, eco-feminism, and the green movement. **Publisher:** League for Educational Democracy. **Contact(s):** Bob Koelher.

**✍ ▸ Green Teacher**
McKeever Environmental Learning Center
RD 3, Box 121
Sandy Lake, PA 16145
**Affiliation:** Centre for Alternative Technology (England). **Concern(s):** education; environment; energy; childhood; science. Published by the Centre, it focuses on environmental education, organic and ecological principals, renewable energy, peace education.

**D ▸ Greener Pastures Gazette**
Box 1122
Sierra Madre, CA 91025 (818)355-1670
**Affiliation:** Greener Pastures Institute. **Concern(s):** demographics; urban; agriculture; rural relocation; rural communities. The newsletter for those searching for countryside Edens where the Good Life still exists. The Institute tries to help people to leave unfulfilling and ecologically destructive lifestyles in large metropolitan areas for more harmonious lives in more rural settings, nationwide, and to a lesser extent overseas. We counsel on vocational change, self-sufficiency, place awareness, etc. **Other Resources:** Brochure available on request. **Frequency:** 4/yr. **Subscription:** $22/yr. **Price:** $3/ea. **Bulk:** $1.25ea/24. **Pages:** 6. **Circ.:** 1.5M. **Fax:** (818)440-9471. **Contact(s):** William L. Seavey (Publisher), Laurel Gillesse (Art Director).

**E ▸ Greenpeace Magazine**
1436 U St. NW
Washington, DC 20009 (202)462-1177
**Affiliation:** Greenpeace, USA. **Concern(s):** environment; peace; energy; politics; health; animal rights; ocean/rivers; wildlife/endangered species; nonviolence; civil disobedience; anti-nuclear; polar; corporate responsibility; government accountability; hazardous/toxic waste. "Nonviolent direct action is a key tactic of Greenpeace in defending human and animal rights at sea and on land. Petitions, rallies, and direct interference against nuclear weapons ships and whaling expeditions are some ways this group fights the good fight. The magazine is slick and well-written, and will probably move you to action on these issues."-C.C. **Est.:** 1980. **Frequency:** 6/yr. **Subscription:** $20/yr. **Price:** $1.50/ea. **Contact(s):** Andre Carrothers, Daphne Wysham (Editors).

**P ▸ Grey City Journal**
5627 S. Drexel
Chicago, IL 60637 (312)752-3562
**Concern(s):** politics; arts; activism; analysis; culture. "We are an independent progressive newspaper, printed as part of the Friday issue of the University of Chicago newspaper, THE MAROON. We generally accept the copy only from University community writers, but would be interested in printing progressive cartoon strips from contributors. We would like to receive books and magazines for review on all aspects of arts, culture and politics: we are very broad. We also publish reviews." **Est.:** 1982. **Frequency:** Weekly. **Subscription:** $30/yr. **Price:** $1/ea. **Pages:** 4. **Circ.:** 35M. **Publisher:** Chicago Maroon. **Contact(s):** J. Hughes (Editor).

**✍ ▸ Grit**
208 W. 3rd St.
Williamsport, PA 17701
**Concern(s):** education; youth. Articles with photos on young people involved in unusual hobbies, occupations, athletic pursuits, and personal adventures. **Contact(s):** Joanne Decker (Assignment Editor).

**✌ ▸ Ground Zero**
16159 Clear Creek Rd., NW
Poulsbo, WA 98370 (206)779-6673
**Concern(s):** peace; civil disobedience; nonviolence; anti-nuclear. A faith-based core community maintains a long-term nonviolent campaign against the neighboring Trident Submarine base. Weekly leafleting, vigils, and nonviolent direct actions have taken place since 1978. This newsletter contains insights from the teachings of Gandhi, M.L. King, D. Day and Jesus applied to today's world. **Est.:** 1982. **Frequency:** 4/yr. **Subscription:** $10/donation. **Circ.:** 10M. **Contact(s):** Karol Schulkin, Renee Krisko (Core Members). (206)697-1470.

**✪ ▸ Groundswell**
1424 16th St. NW, #601
Washington, DC 20036 (202)328-0002
**Affiliation:** Nuclear Information and Resource Service. **Concern(s):** energy; environment; health; anti-nuclear; hazardous/toxic waste. "Nuclear energy is the primary concern, with other environmental issues covered as well. If you are active in opposing your area nuclear power plant or construction site, you will want to subscribe to this magazine."-C.C. **Est.:** 1978. **Frequency:** 4/yr. **Subscription:** $20/yr. **Price:** Free. **Contact(s):** Michael Mariotte.

**$ ▸ Groundswell**
2000 Century Plaza, #238
Columbia, MD 21044 (301)740-1177
**Affiliation:** Common Ground USA. **Concern(s):** economics; politics; monopolies. A newsletter, that like its parent group, focuses on the causes of today's problems not the symptoms. The newsletter also wants to help identify those with special privileges and monopolies TO abolish them. **Est.:** 1985. **Frequency:** 6/yr. **Subscription:** $12/yr. **Price:** $2/ea. **Bulk:** 40% off/24. **Pages:** 8. **Circ.:** 3M. **Contact(s):** Hanno Beck (Executive Director), Steven Cord (Chief Operating Officer).

**✍ ▸ Growing Without Schooling**
2269 Massachusetts Ave.
Cambridge, MA 02140 (617)864-3100
**Concern(s):** education; childhood. Magazine. **Frequency:** 6/yr. **Publisher:** Holt Associates, Inc. **Member:** Co-op America.

**P ▸ The Guardian**
24 W. 25th St.
New York, NY 10010 (212)691-0404
**Affiliation:** Institute for Independent Social Journalism. **Concern(s):** politics; justice; environment. "A famed 'independent radical newsweekly' is easily the best left-of-center periodical in the US. From the cultural coverage to the international news from the frontlines of the struggle, it certainly is the newspaper of record for left activists and scholars. It regularly summarizes the positions of key groups on questions of popular interest, even those groups with which it does not necessarily agree. A controversial 'Opinions' section permits a diverse range of analysis of strategies."-C.C. **Frequency:** 46/yr. **Subscription:** $33.50/yr.; $55 institution. **Circ.:** 20M. **Contact(s):** Ellen Davidson.

**J ▸ Guild Practitioner**
Box 673
Berkeley, CA 94701 (510)848-0599
**Affiliation:** Meiklejohn Peace Institute. **Concern(s):** justice; politics; law; petition; constitutional rights; government accountability; reform. "This highly recommended journal of the country's most progressive lawyers' association covers issues in a little more depth than the group's newspaper, reviewed above. Background analyses on Supreme Court nomination policy, legal strategy for social change movement causes, and ideas for democraticizing the legal process are representative of the features included."-C.C. **Est.:** 1936. **Frequency:** 4/yr. **Subscription:** $20/yr. **Price:** $2/ea. **Contact(s):** Ann Fagan Ginger, David Christiano.

**J ▸ Habitat World**
Habitat & Church Sts.
Americus, GA 31709-3498 (912)924-6935
**Affiliation:** Habitat for Humanity International. **Concern(s):** justice; demographics; Third World; poverty; hunger; homelessness; development; housing. "Folks donating their labor to build houses for the poor are the impetus behind this newsletter. The World is the national link and networking tool for hundreds of groups of people doing this in communities across the US and in several foreign countries."-C.C. **Est.:** 1984. **Frequency:** 6/yr. **Price:** Free. **Contact(s):** Geoff Van Loucks.

**✐ ▸ Harper's Magazine**
Box 7511
Red Oak, IA 51591-0511 (212)614-6500
**Concern(s):** arts; education; media; politics; justice; feminism; literature; culture. A good mainstream publication of fiction and non-fiction for the well-educated, socially-concerned person who is active in community and political affairs. **Frequency:** 12/yr. **Subscription:** $18/yr. **Office:** 666 Broadway New York, NY 10012.

**E ▸ Harrowsmith Country Life**
The Creamery
Ferry Rd.
Charlotte, VT 05445
**Concern(s):** environment; agriculture. "America's highly acclaimed country-living magazine of gardening, fine food, the home, the environment and issues that affect the quality of our lives and the world around us. ...literate, handsomely illustrated and full of ideas that will challenge, provoke and inspire you as an involved gardener, homeowner and creative cook." **Frequency:** 6/yr. **Subscription:** $14.97/yr. **Price:** $3/ea. **Contact(s):** Tom Rawls (Editor).

**J ▸ Harvard Women's Law Journal**
Publications Office
Harvard Law School
Cambridge, MA 02138 (617)495-3726
**Concern(s):** justice; feminism. "We are a law review which deals with law related [issues]; [including] legal histories, literary, and sociological perspectives on the law as it effects women and feminism." **Frequency:** Annual. **Subscription:** $10/yr. **Price:** $11/ea. **Pages:** 350. **Circ.:** 900. **Contact(s):** Suzanne Goldbert (Editor-in-chief).

**D ▸ Have You Heard?**
Population Environment Balance
1325 G St. NW, #1003
Washington, DC 20005-3104 (202)879-3000
**Affiliation:** Population Environment Balance. **Concern(s):** demographics; environment; population growth; conservation; sustainability. A humorous, "short takes" newsletter, focusing on US population and environmental issues. **Dues:** $25/yr. **Frequency:** 4/yr. **Subscription:** Membership. **Circ.:** 10M.

**S ▸ Haversack**
Box 408676
Chicago, IL 60640 (312)728-5850
**Affiliation:** Franciscans. **Concern(s):** spiritual; justice; demographics; faith. "Franciscans working for basic social change started this newsletter to make the religious order more socially concerned, and to present ideas for individual involvement in social issues."-C.C. **Est.:** 1976. **Frequency:** 6/yr. **Subscription:** $8/yr. **Price:** $1.50/ea. **Contact(s):** Athena Calogeras.

**H ▸ Hazard Monthly**
966 Hungerford Dr.
Rockville, MD 20850-1714
**Affiliation:** Research Alternatives. **Concern(s):** health; environment; hazardous/toxic waste.

**✌ ▸ Headline Series**
Foreign Policy Association
729 7th Ave.
New York, NY 10019 (212)764-4050
**Affiliation:** Foreign Policy Association. **Concern(s):** peace; politics; Third World; education; foreign policy; intervention; global understanding. Publications series by recognized scholars, journalists and other experts, providing background on a broad range of world areas and topics, and special publications on problems debated by the nation's policymakers.

**H ▸ Health and Development**
Box 189
Dallastown, PA 17313
**Concern(s):** health; justice; economics; consumer rights; consumer protection; alternative consumer. A magazine about growth, social security, donor policies, entrepreneurs, and property rights.

**E ▶ Health and Environment Digest**
2500 Shadywood Rd.
Orono, MN 55331        (612)471-9292
**Affiliation:** Freshwater Foundation. **Concern(s):** environment; health; water; land; public health. Medically accurate information on key health issues related to water, land, and air quality. Monthly newsletter with the most up-to-date information on the health effects of environmental contaminants. Provides an overview of current research, new methodologies, and summaries of emerging health concerns related to environmental contaminants. The Foundation's mission is to help keep water usable for human consumption. Nonprofit. **Contact(s):** Barbara Scott Murdock (Editor).

**H ▶ Health Advocate**
2639 S. LaCienega Blvd.
Los Angeles, CA 90034      (310)204-6010
**Affiliation:** National Health Law Program. **Concern(s):** health; politics; law. "Legal and legislative aspects of health care policy find attention in this quarterly. This Legal Services funded newsletter focuses most frequently on local and state health care programs and rulings."-C.C. **Est.:** 1969. **Frequency:** 4/yr. **Subscription:** $15/yr. **Price:** Free. **Contact(s):** Jane St. John.

**H ▶ Health Facts**
237 Thompson St.
New York, NY 10012      (212)674-7105
**Affiliation:** Center for Medical Consumers. **Concern(s):** health; politics; economics; government accountability; corporate responsibility; consumer protection. "Another public interest consumer health periodical, this one deals both with advocacy issues such as a more effective FDA and with simple personal health issues. These personal health consumer issues include physician/patient relations, unnecessary surgeries and like topics."-C.C. **Other Resources:** Free medical library. **Est.:** 1976. **Frequency:** 4/yr. **Subscription:** $35/yr. **Price:** $5/ea. **Contact(s):** Mary Ann Napoli.

**H ▶ Health Foods Business**
567 Morris Ave.
Elizabeth, NJ 07208
**Concern(s):** health; economics; nutrition; preventative medicine; trade. Articles profiling health food stores. Shorter pieces on trends, research findings, preventive medicine, alternative therapies. Interviews with doctors and nutritionists. **Contact(s):** Gina Geslewitz (Editor).

**H ▶ Health Letter Newsletter**
2000 P St. NW, #605
Washington, DC 20036-0757      (202)872-0320
**Affiliation:** Health Research Group. **Concern(s):** health; politics; labor; consumer protection; alternative consumer; government accountability; corporate responsibility; occupational safety. "Information from tightly sealed government and industry files on health issues, as well as information on common health problems, is explained monthly. From aspirin deaths to X-ray safety - this newsletter will eventually cover it all."-C.C. **Est.:** 1985. **Frequency:** 12/yr. **Subscription:** $18/yr. **Price:** $1.50/ea. **Contact(s):** Sidney M. Wolfe.

**H ▶ Health Science**
Box 30630
Tampa, FL 33630
**Concern(s):** health; labor; preventative medicine; occupational safety. The philosophy of this newsletter is to educate the people on the physiology and lifestyle practices that insure health, happiness, peace and prosperity for everyone, everywhere. **Frequency:** 6/yr. **Subscription:** $25/yr. **Contact(s):** Mark A. Huberman (President), James Michael Lennon (Editor).

**H ▶ Health-Care Revue**
44 Broadway
Greenlawn, NY 11740
**Concern(s):** health; justice; disabled; seniors; disabled's rights. **Publisher:** Equal Opportunity Publishers, Inc.

**H ▶ Health/PAC Bulletin**
17 Murray St.
New York, NY 10007      (212)267-8890
**Affiliation:** Health Policy Advisory Center. **Concern(s):** health. "Health policy is examined with an eye toward promoting increased national health programs, concerns of health care workers and better local medical care. The quality news notes, book reviews, and short articles on health care make it a first choice in its field."-C.C. **Est.:** 1968. **Frequency:** 4/yr. **Subscription:** $35/yr. **Price:** $5/ea. **Contact(s):** Joe Gordon.

**E ▶ HEC News**
1001 Connecticut Ave. NW, #827
Washington, DC 20036      (202)331-8387
**Affiliation:** Human Environment Center. **Concern(s):** environment;

urban; economics; conservation; youth. This newsletter reports on the activities of the Center. Current focus is the expansion of youth conservation programs. **Frequency:** 4/yr.

**H ▶ Hemlock Quarterly**
Hemlock Society
Box 11830
Eugene, OR 97440
**Affiliation:** Hemlock Society. **Concern(s):** health; death/dying. "Magazine is concerned exclusively with right-to-die issues, particularly active voluntary euthanasia for the terminally ill or seriously incurably ill." Nonprofit. **Est.:** 1980. **Frequency:** 4/yr. **Subscription:** $20/yr. **Price:** Free sample. **Pages:** 180. **Contact(s):** Derek Humphry.

**F ▶ HERA**
Box 354
Binghamton, NY 13902
**Affiliation:** Women's Center. **Concern(s):** feminism.

**H ▶ The Herb Quarterly**
Box 548
Boiling Springs, PA 17007
**Concern(s):** health; nutrition. Articles on herbs: practical uses, cultivation, gourmet cooking, landscaping, herb tradition, medicinal herbs, crafts ideas, unique garden designs, profiles of herb garden experts, practical how-to's for the herb businessperson. **Contact(s):** Linda Sparrowe (Editor).

**H ▶ HerbalGram**
Box 201660
Austin, TX 78720      (512)331-8868
**Affiliation:** American Botanical Council and Herb Research Foundation. **Concern(s):** health; alternative consumer; preventative medicine. This newsletter covers most aspects of herbs and medicinal plants: research reviews, extensive in-depth monographs on single herbs, media coverage, legal and regulatory news, conference reports, books, calendar, networking, much more. No commercial advertising. Beautiful full color artwork. Collector quality! **Other Resources:** Reprints of "Classic" Botanical Articles from scientific journals. 8-page Booklets on individual herbs (most popular). Nonprofit. **Est.:** 1983. **Frequency:** 4/yr. **Subscription:** $25/yr. **Price:** $5.95/ea. **Pages:** 56. **Circ.:** 6.5M. **Publisher:** American Botanical Council. **Fax:** (512)331-1924. **Contact(s):** Mark Blumenthal (Executive Director/Editor), Margaret Wright (Circulation Manager).

**F ▶ Heresies: A Feminist Publication on Art and Politics**
Box 1306, Canal St. Station
New York, NY 10013      (212)227-2108
**Concern(s):** feminism; justice; arts; media; sexism; racism; film; theater; poetry; minority rights; diversity. A collectively edited journal of fiction, nonfiction; poetry; art; the visual arts; photography. "All issues are thematic... Since racism comes up everywhere, everyday, in all kinds of situations, used and discussed by everyone, everywhere." **Est.:** 1976. **Frequency:** 2/yr. **Subscription:** $23 individual; $33 institution. **Price:** $6.75/ea. **Pages:** 96. **Circ.:** 8M. **Office:** 280 Broadway New York, NY 10007.

**✍ ▶ Heritage**
6120 S. Vermont Ave.
Los Angeles, CA 90044      (213)759-6063
**Affiliation:** Southern California Library for Social Studies and Research. **Concern(s):** education; media; politics; justice; research. "People's movements are archived in this important library, with news of the institution noted in their quarterly report. Selections from their collections are noted as well as news on the state of the library. A donation will put you on their mailing list."-C.C. **Est.:** 1982. **Frequency:** 4/yr. **Subscription:** Donation. **Price:** Free. **Contact(s):** Sarah Cooper.

**E ▶ High Country News**
Box 1090
Paonia, CO 81428
**Affiliation:** High Country Foundation. **Concern(s):** environment; energy. Articles on environmental issues, public lands management, energy, and natural resource issues; profiles of western innovators; pieces on western politics. Poetry. B&W photos. **Contact(s):** Betsy Marston (Editor).

**✎ ▶ High Performance**
1641 18th St.
Santa Monica, CA 90404-3807      (310)315-9383
**Concern(s):** arts; media; culture; theater; music; film. A magazine about contemporary art such as performance, experimental dance/theater/music, video, and multi-media projects. "Performing arts productions are reviewed quarterly from a socially concerned perspective. Individual theater performances as well as new music and film festivals are among areas reviewed."-C.C. **Est.:** 1977. **Frequency:** 4/yr. **Subscription:** $20 USA; $24 Canada. **Price:** $6/ea. **Pages:** 88.

**Circ.:** 25M. **Publisher:** Astro Artz. **Contact(s):** Steven Durland (Editor).

**P ▶ Highlander Reports**
Route 3, Box 370
New Market, TN 37820      (615)933-3443
**Affiliation:** Highlander Research & Education Center. **Concern(s):** politics; justice; demographics; peace; education; grassroots organizing; minority rights; racism; self-determination; poverty. "Grassroots community organizing is taught at Highlander for empowerment of working and poor people. Rosa Parks and Dr. Martin Luther King, Jr., were inspired here, and the center continues to inspire common people to organize more effectively for themselves, their neighbors, and their environment."-C.C. **Est.:** 1932. **Frequency:** 4/yr. **Subscription:** $5/yr. **Price:** Free. **Contact(s):** Miles Horton.

**E ▶ Historic Preservation**
1785 Massachusetts Ave. NW
Washington, DC 20036      (202)673-4000
**Affiliation:** National Trust for Historical Preservation. **Concern(s):** environment; conservation; preservation. Magazine. **Frequency:** 6/yr.

**✍ ▶ Holistic Education Review**
39 Pearl St.
Brandon, VT 05733      (802)247-8312
**Concern(s):** education; childhood. The premier journal of leading-edge approaches in education. Covers innovative methods, cultural and social issues, education for peace and justice, global and environmental education, learning styles, rites of passage, and much more. Insightful essays and book reviews. The magazine that offers a unified vision of the future of education to today's teachers and parents. Highly acclaimed by readers and critics alike. **Other Resources:** Publishes books on holistic education. **Est.:** 1988. **Frequency:** 4/yr. **Subscription:** $26/yr. **Price:** $7/ea. **Pages:** 64. **Circ.:** 2.5M. **Publisher:** Holistic Education Press. **Contact(s):** Charles Jakiela (Publisher).

**✍ ▶ Home Education Magazine**
Box 1083
Tonasket, WA 98855      (509)486-1351
**Concern(s):** education; alternative; childhood. A magazine for homeschooling parents. Articles on all aspects of homeschooling, several regular columnists, major book exerpts, interview with homeschooling personalities, new, information, resources, reviews, and much more. An invaluable homeschooling resource! **Other Resources:** Publishes directory, catalog, and books, including books from other publishers. **Est.:** 1983. **Frequency:** 6/yr. **Price:** $4.50/ea. **Pages:** 56. **Circ.:** 5.2M. **Publisher:** Home Education Press. **Contact(s):** Mark Hegener (Publisher), Helen Hegener (Managing Editor).

**✍ ▶ Home Education Researcher**
School of Education
Seattle Pacific University
Seattle, WA 98119
**Concern(s):** education; homeschooling. "A quarterly journal seeking and disseminating research on home education. Annotated bibliography lists over 350 references. Also publishes scholarly papers on home schooling, comparing its results to conventional schooling."

**☯ ▶ Home Magazine**
5900 Wilshire Blvd., 15th Fl.
Los Angeles, CA 90036
**Concern(s):** energy; solar; conservation. Articles of interest to homeowners: architecture, remodeling, decorating, how-to's, project ideas, landscaping, taxes, insurance, conservation, and solar energy. **Contact(s):** Joseph Ruggiero (Editor).

**☯ ▶ Home Power Magazine**
Box 130
Hornbrook, CA 96044      (916)475-3179
**Concern(s):** energy; environment; solar; wind; hydrogen. A magazine of home-made electricity. It deals with power made from sun, wind, and water sources. "We publish factual & technical information about small scale application of renewable, non-polluting energy sources." It covers photovoltaics, micro-hydro, bio-mass, inverters, batteries, energy-efficient appliances, electric vehicles and more. Written by people who use renewable energy now - in their homes and business. **Other Resources:** "We are currently branching out into book publishing. We are now working on our first project called HEAVEN'S FLAME by Joe Radabaugh. This booklet is on using and building solar cookers." **Est.:** 1987. **Frequency:** 6/yr. **Subscription:** $10/yr. **Price:** $3.50/ea. **Bulk:** 50% off/24. **Pages:** 100. **Circ.:** 10M. **Publisher:** Home Power Inc. **Office:** 1000 Copco Rd. Ashland, OR 97520. **Contact(s):** Karen Perez (Business Manager), Richard Perez (Editor/CEO/Publisher).

## ☉ ◆ Home Resource Magazine
Box 12061
Boulder, CO 80303    (303)449-6126

**Concern(s):** energy; agriculture; environment; education; solar; renewables; efficiency; conservation; appropriate technology. A magazine that deals with issues relevant to the housebuilder, such as solar, energy conservation, gardening and related topics. **Est.:** 1984. **Frequency:** 6/yr. **Subscription:** $22/yr. **Price:** $3.75ea. **Pages:** c80. **Circ.:** 30M.

## D ◆ Homewords
1830 Connecticut Ave. NW
Washington, DC 20009  (202)462-7551

**Affiliation:** Homelessness Information Exchange. **Concern(s):** demographics; hunger; homelessness; poverty; networking. Newsletter.

## ✍ ◆ Hopscotch
Box 1292
Saratoga Springs, NY 12866

**Concern(s):** education; family; literature; poetry; youth; childhood. Articles, fiction, and short poetry for girls ages 6 to 12. "We believe young girls deserve the right to enjoy a season of childhood before they become young adults; we are not interested in such topics as sex, romance, cosmetics, hairstyles, etc." **Frequency:** 6/yr. **Contact(s):** Donald P. Evans (Editor).

## A ◆ Horticulture
Statler Bldg.
20 Park Plaza, #1229
Boston, MA 02116

**Concern(s):** agriculture; horticulture. Authoritative, well-written articles on all aspects of gardening. **Contact(s):** Deborah Starr (Articles Editor).

## E ◆ Hortideas
Rt. 1, Box 302
Gravel Switch, KY 40328

**Concern(s):** environment; beautification. Monthly newsletter on gardening and horticulture.

## ☛ ◆ HSUS News
2100 L St. NW
Washington, DC 20037  (202)452-1100

**Affiliation:** Humane Society of the US. **Concern(s):** environment; animal rights. Magazine. **Frequency:** 4/yr.

## E ◆ Hug the Earth Publications
42 Greenwood Ave.
Pequannock, NJ 07440

**Concern(s):** environment; spiritual; transformation. "We publish broadsides, and a one-time only journal on land & life." Writers include Gary Snyder, Charles Olson, Flavia Alaya, Ken Lumpkin, E. Durling Merrill, et al. **Other Resources:** Publishes A JOURNAL OF LAND AND LIFE. Features poetry, art, criticism, reviews, letters, on the environment and place in literature. **Est.:** 1980. **Contact(s):** Kenneth Lumpkin (Editor).

## H ◆ The Human Ecologist
Box 66637
Chicago, IL 60666    (312)665-6575

**Affiliation:** Human Ecology Action League. **Concern(s):** health; environment; social ecology; nutrition; hazardous/toxic waste; preventative medicine. This newsletter provides information and current news on food allergies, chemical sensitivities, ecological illness, and related subjects in these regularly featured departments: consumer file; pesticide update; books and reviews; trading post; letters; and news.

## H ◆ Human Ecology Forum
Cornell University
1150 Comstock
Ithaca, NY 14853-0998

**Concern(s):** feminism; social justice; racism; sexism; discrimination; equal rights; public health. This magazine is well written and provides a forum for issues to be presented from the social impact view. **Frequency:** 4/yr.

## $ ◆ The Human Economy Newsletter
Box 14, Department of Economics
Mankato State University
Mankato, MN 56001    (507)389-5325

**Affiliation:** Human Economy Center. **Concern(s):** economics; networking. "New directions in economic thought and action" - an information exchange newsletter, with essays and book reviews, for people working towards a new kind of economics. **Member:** Co-op America.

## J ◆ Human Rights Internet Reporter
c/o Human Rights Centre, University
of Ottawa, 57 Louis Pasteur
Ottawa, ON K1N 6N5 Canada    (613)564-3492

**Affiliation:** Human Rights Internet. **Concern(s):** justice; Third World. The most current, comprehensive reference tool in the human rights field. Every issue is fully indexed and cross-referenced by subject, by geographic focus, and by organization. A specialized index on vocabulary was developed to meet the needs of human rights advocacy organizations and scholars. Includes Commentary, a Calendar, news of major developments, Fact-Finding Missions, reports about human rights defenders, NGOs, inter-governmental organizations, and much more. **Other Resources:** Accompanied by a Master List of organizations, publication, and indexing language. Publishes a multitude of directories in addition to the Reporter. **Frequency:** 4/yr. **Subscription:** $50/yr, $75 institution. **Fax:** (613)564-4054.

## J ◆ Human Rights Quarterly
701 W. 40th St., #275
Baltimore, MD 21211

**Concern(s):** justice; Third World; peace; conflict resolution; racism; United Nations; research; analysis. This journal reports on international human rights issues as pertaining to the United Nations' Universal Declaration of Human Rights. **Frequency:** 4/yr.

## T ◆ Human Rights Watch
1522 K St. NW
Washington, DC 20005  (202)371-6592

**Affiliation:** Human Rights Watch. **Concern(s):** Third World; justice. This newsletter is concerned with Third World human rights issues and is meant to assist human rights and legislative activists. **Dues:** $20/donation. **Other:** 485 5th Ave., New York, NY 10017. **Contact(s):** Aryeh Neier, Executive Director. (212)972-8400.

## D ◆ Human Survival
Negative Population Growth
16 E. 42nd St.
New York, NY 10017    (212)599-2020

**Affiliation:** Negative Population Growth. **Concern(s):** demographics; environment; population growth. This newsletter advises current activities and events and developments concerning population, resources, and the environment. **Frequency:** 3/yr. **Contact(s):** Donald W. Mann (President).

## J ◆ Humanist
Box 146
Amherst, NY 14226    (716)839-5080

**Affiliation:** American Humanist Association. **Concern(s):** justice; politics; education; economics. "Thomas Jefferson and Isaac Asimov are two examples of humanists sometimes mentioned in the columns of this attractive magazine. Their philosophy of putting individuals in the material world over future pie-in-the-sky is the philosophy of the humanist. For those wanting to know more about humanism, The Humanist magazine is the best source."-C.C. **Est.:** 1941. **Frequency:** 6/yr. **Subscription:** $18/yr. **Price:** $3/ea. **Contact(s):** Lloyd Morain.

## S ◆ Humanistic Judaism
28611 W. Twelve Mile Rd.
Farmington Hills, MI 48018  (313)478-7610

**Affiliation:** Society for Humanistic Judaism. **Concern(s):** spiritual; justice; demographics; faith. "This magazine is the Jewish equivalent of the Christians' Churchman. Social concerns, Jewish-Christian relations, and of course, Judaism and the human condition are typical topics."-C.C. **Est.:** 1969. **Frequency:** 4/yr. **Subscription:** $15/yr. **Price:** $5/ea. **Contact(s):** Bonnie Cousens, Ruth Feldman.

## J ◆ Humanitas International Newsletter
Box 818
Menlo Park, CA 94026

**Affiliation:** Humanitas International Human Rights Committee. **Concern(s):** justice; Third World; peace. Coverage of human rights issues. **Frequency:** 4/yr. **Contact(s):** Jim Wake.

## ✍ ◆ Humpty Dumpty's Magazine
1100 Waterway Blvd.
Box 567
Indianapolis, IN 46206

**Concern(s):** education; health; youth. General-interest publication with an emphasis on health and fitness for children ages 4 to 6. Easy-to-read fiction, some with health and nutrition, safety, exercise, or hygiene as theme; humor and light approach preferred. No-cook recipes using healthful ingredients. **Contact(s):** Christine French Clark (Editor).

## T ◆ Hunger Notes
1889 F St. NW
Washington, DC 20006  (202)289-3812

**Affiliation:** International Fund for Agricultural Development.

## D ◆ [continued]
**Concern(s):** Third World; demographics; agriculture; hunger; poverty; homelessness; food production; food distribution. "Background articles on developing countries' aid needs are followed by listings of resources and programs to fulfill these needs. Such resources include private and government relief agencies, and solidarity efforts such as the Quest for Peace."-C.C. **Est.:** 1976. **Frequency:** 6/yr. **Subscription:** $15, $40 institution. **Price:** $3/ea. **Contact(s):** Patricia Kutzner (Executive Director).

## D ◆ The Hunger Project Papers
1388 Sutter St.
San Francisco, CA 94109-5452    (212)532-4255

**Affiliation:** Hunger Project. **Concern(s):** demographics; Third World; education; hunger; development. A series of analytical papers on issues related to hunger and development published periodically in this report presenting technical and professional analysis of subjects related to ending hunger. Nonprofit. **Frequency:** 26/yr.

## D ◆ Hungerline
261 W. 35th St., #1402
New York, NY 10001    (212)629-8850

**Affiliation:** World Hunger Year. **Concern(s):** demographics; Third World; feminism; hunger; poverty; homelessness; development. This newsletter provides hunger-related stories, statistics and analyses for use by print and broadcast journalists, hunger activists and congressional offices. It's Media Speakers Bureau offers leading experts on the problems of hunger and poverty for radio and TV shows, as well as speeches to colleges, civic, religious and other concerned groups. **Frequency:** 12/yr.

## ✑ ◆ Hungry Mind Review
1648 Grand Ave.
St. Paul, MN 55105    (612) 699-2610

**Concern(s):** arts. **Fax:** (613)564-4054

## J ◆ huracan
Box 7591
Minneapolis, MN 55407

**Concern(s):** justice; Native Americans; activists. Small newspaper devoted to challenging the 1992 quincentenary clebrations. Chronicles various protest activities. **Frequency:** 4/yr. **Subscription:** $15/yr.

## ✑ ◆ Hurricane Alice: A Feminist Quarterly
207 Lind Hall
207 Church St. SE
Minneapolis, MN 55455

**Concern(s):** arts; feminism. Articles, fiction, essays, interviews, and reviews, with feminist perspective. **Contact(s):** Martha Roth.

## ☉ ◆ Hydata-News & Views
5410 Grosvenor Ln, #220
Bethesda, MD 20814-2192  (301)493-8600

**Affiliation:** American Water Resources Association. **Concern(s):** energy; environment; water; resources. A newsletter dealing with the research in hydroelectric power and other uses for water.

## ☉ ◆ Hydrogen Today
219 S. Siesta Lane, #101
Tempe, AZ 85281    (602)921-0433

**Affiliation:** American Hydrogen Association. **Concern(s):** energy; environment; hydrogen; solar; appropriate technology. Newsletter reports on transition from fossil fuels to solar hydrogen technologies including fuel cells. It believes that there is an information gap that exists within the scientific and educational community, industry, the political establishment, the media, and the public. It further reports on the transition from the fossil depletion economy, to a renewable solar-hydrogen economy that will last forever. **Other Resources:** Publications list available. **Est.:** 1990. **Frequency:** 6/yr. **Subscription:** $30, $15 senior/student. **Price:** $3/ea. **Pages:** 10. **Circ.:** 2.5M. **Fax:** (602)967-6601. **Contact(s):** Roy McAlister (President), Bob Liden (Editor).

## H ◆ Hygienic Community Network News (HCN)
Box 7972
Santa Cruz, CA 95061

**Concern(s):** health; vegetarian. Reports on efforts of people to network together into forming a natural hygiene community. **Contact(s):** Paul Newey, Helen J. Story.

## F ◆ Hypatia
10th & Morton Sts.
Bloomington, IN 47405  (618)692-0803

**Concern(s):** feminism; arts; spiritual; transformation. A journal that covers a wide variety of issues expressing the feminist philosophy and arts. **Frequency:** 3/yr. **Subscription:** $20, $40 institution. **Price:** $10, $20/ea. **Bulk:** 40% off/24. **Pages:** 180. **Circ.:** 1M. **Publisher:** Indiana University Press (Journals Manager). **Office:** Box 1437, Southern Illinois University, Edwardsville, IL 62026.

**U ▸ IBF News**
4887 Columbia Dr. S
Seattle, WA 98108-1919 (206)767-3927
**Affiliation:** International Bicycle Fund. **Concern(s):** urban; energy; education; economics; environment; alternative; transportation; development; planning; travel; recreation. This newsletter covers issues of transportation planning, economic development, safety education and international understanding relating to bicycle and bicycle trailer projects. Nonprofit. **Est.:** 1982. **Frequency:** 2/yr. **Pages:** 2+. **Circ.:** 8M. **Contact(s):** David Mozer (Editor).

**F ▸ Icarus Review**
Box 50174
Austin, TX 78763 (512)477-2269
**Concern(s):** feminism; men's liberation. This review publishes short stories, poems, myths and personal essays concerning men's issues in relationship and recovery. **Est.:** 1989. **Frequency:** 2/yr. **Subscription:** $6/yr. **Price:** $3/ea. **Pages:** 50. **Circ.:** 500. **Contact(s):** Mark Lawrence (Editor).

**ICE Melter Newsletter**
Box 26577
Philadelphia, PA 19141 (215)635-1122
**Affiliation:** Interfaith Coalition on Energy. **Concern(s):** energy; spiritual; interfaith; conservation. This newsletter discusses ways in which people can conserve energy and practice environmental stewardship. The newsletter does not try to exclude any religions beliefs or practices. Nonprofit. **Est.:** 1980. **Frequency:** 4/yr. **Subscription:** $20/yr. **Price:** $5/ea. **Bulk:** 50% off/24. **Pages:** 12. **Circ.:** 10M. **Contact(s):** Andrew Rudin (Project Coordinator).

**T ▸ IDAF News Notes/Focus in Southern Africa**
Box 17
Cambridge, MA 02138 (617)491-8343
**Affiliation:** International Defense and Aid Fund for Southern Africa. **Concern(s):** Third World; justice; South Africa; Africa. "People wishing to donate money or other resources for the survival and advancement of the South African majority can learn how here. Details on the people's struggle there are mentioned as well in this newspaper."-C.C. **Est.:** 1982. **Frequency:** 4/yr. **Subscription:** $8/yr. **Price:** $1/ea. **Contact(s):** Geoffrey Wisner.

**L ▸ Ideas and Action**
Box 40400
San Francisco, CA 94140
**Affiliation:** Workers' Solidarity Alliance. **Concern(s):** labor; economics; workplace democracy; worker ownership; cooperatives; unions. A newspaper chronicling direct action, solidarity, and rank-and-file management of workers' struggles, working towards a new social system based on collective management of the economy by all working people. **Frequency:** 4/yr. **Price:** $6/ea.

**Ideas and Information About Development Education**
c/o International Development Conference
1401 New York Ave. NW, #1100
Washington, DC 20005 (202)638-3111
**Affiliation:** International Development Conference. **Concern(s):** education; global understanding. This newsletter presents news and views on educating Americans about developing countries and international economic, environmental, and social problems. Published jointly with InterAction and the American Forum on Global Education. Conference was established in 1951. **Est.:** 1986. **Frequency:** 4/yr. **Subscription:** $10/yr. **Pages:** 12. **Circ.:** 2M. **Fax:** (202)638-1374. **Contact(s):** Andrew E. Rice (Editor).

**J ▸ IFCO News**
402 W. 145th St.
New York, NY 10031 (212)926-5757
**Affiliation:** Interreligious Foundation for Community Organization. **Concern(s):** justice; demographics; spiritual; interfaith; poverty. "The programs of the social justice groups receiving IFCO assistance are summarized by this newsletter. Longer background features on conditions in areas being served are included. Technical, fundraising and group development advice is offered to these groups by IFCO."-C.C. **Est.:** 1968. **Frequency:** 4/yr. **Subscription:** $15, $20 institution. **Price:** $.25/ea. **Contact(s):** Gail Walker.

**$ ▸ IMPACT**
2001 S St. NW, #410
Washington, DC 20009 (202)328-7700
**Affiliation:** Center for Auto Safety. **Concern(s):** economics; health; consumer rights; consumer protection. This newsletter reports on auto & highway safety work of Center for Auto Safety. It covers safety litigation, auto defects, lemon laws, recalls, federal & state investigations, secret warranties, and fuel economy stories. **Frequency:** 6/yr. **Subscription:** $60, $30 media. **Circ.:** 1.2M. **Contact(s):** Debra Barclay (Editor). (202)328-7700.

**In Brief**
72 Franklin St., #402
Boston, MA 02110 (617)542-0265
**Affiliation:** American Jewish Congress Task Force on Nuclear Disarmament. **Concern(s):** peace; spiritual; faith; anti-nuclear; disarmament. "New national legislation for a nuclear arms freeze is an important part of this Jewish perspective on nuclear weapons. Israel's part in the nuclear arms race could, however, be better covered."-C.C. **Est.:** 1982. **Frequency:** 6/yr. **Subscription:** $6/yr. **Price:** Free. **Contact(s):** Sheila Decter.

**E ▸ In Context, a Quarterly of Humane Sustainable Culture**
Box 11470
Bainbridge, WA 98110 (206)842-0216
**Affiliation:** Context Institute. **Concern(s):** environment; economics; education; sustainability. Explores practical pathways to a positive future with a whole-systems perspective and emphasis on solutions, each issue goes deeply into a timely theme to serve up fresh thinking and workable approaches to current human problems. Past themes in this magazine: climate change, caring for families, transforming education, the ecology of the media, sustainability: the state of the art, earth/spirit, global warming, educational innovations, and consumption. '91 Alternative Press Award Winner. **Other Resources:** Consulting services. **Est.:** 1983. **Frequency:** 4/yr. **Subscription:** $18/yr. **Price:** $5/ea. **Bulk:** $2.50ea/24. **Pages:** 64. **Circ.:** 6M. **Other Formats:** MCI Mail. **E-Network:** Peacenet/Econet. **ID:** 'incontext'. **Fax:** (206)842-5108. **Contact(s):** Robert Gilman (Editor/Publisher), Alan Atkisson (Executive Editor).

**P ▸ In These Times**
1912 Debs Ave.
Mt. Morris, IL 61054 (312)772-0100
**Affiliation:** Institute for Public Affairs. **Concern(s):** politics; Democratic Socialism; alternative party. "The leading national, independent Democratic Socialist newspaper, its viewpoint is far from the Marxist left, however, with frequent discussions of strategies for working within the Democratic Party. It covers labor and women's movements well."-C.C. **Est.:** 1976. **Frequency:** 41/yr. **Subscription:** $34.95/yr. **Price:** $1/ea. **Circ.:** 130M. **Contact(s):** James Weinstein. (800)435-0715.

**In Touch**
528 Hennepin Ave., #704
Minneapolis, MN 55403 (612)339-4944
**Affiliation:** Illusion Theater Prevention Program. **Concern(s):** education; arts; health; feminism; childhood; AIDS; rape/sexual abuse; child abuse; theater. A newsletter published by the Theater that keeps its followers abreast of its activities concerning sex education of children. Utilizes drama and various other forms of performing arts to convey messages about AIDS and issues of sexual abuse.

**M ▸ The Independent**
625 Broadway, 9th Fl.
New York, NY 10012 (212)473-3400
**Affiliation:** Foundation for Independent Video/Film. **Concern(s):** media; arts; politics; broadcasting; film. "Independent filmmakers from all over are creating fascinating works on topics that rarely show up in the mainstream. The results surface at film festivals or occasionally on public television. The best guide to this underground film world is THE INDEPENDENT. It maintains a world view that preserving film and the access are important determinants to a culture. By presenting visions of what's beyond the movie screen and TV set, assures us that truth will be always shown." **Frequency:** 10/yr. **Price:** $35/ea.

**Independent Energy**
Alternative Sources of Energy, Inc.
107 S. Central Ave.
Milaca, MN 56353
**Affiliation:** Alternative Sources of Energy, Inc. **Concern(s):** energy; renewables; solar. This newsletter covers alternative energy technologies, primarily in power applications, and reports on industry, government, markets and regulatory affairs. It has a specific section devoted to photovoltaics. **Est.:** 1979. **Frequency:** 10/yr.

**Independent Living**
44 Broadway
Greenlawn, NY 11740
**Affiliation:** Independent Living Research Utilization. **Concern(s):** health; justice; disabled; disabled's rights. Articles addressing lifestyles of persons who have disabilities. Possible topics: home health care, travel, sports, cooking, hobbies, family life, and sexuality. **Other Resources:** See ANNOTATED REGISTRY OF INDEPENDENT LIVING PROGRAMS and DIRECTORY OF INDEPENDENT LIVING PROGRAMS. **Publisher:** Equal Opportunity Publishers, Inc. **Contact(s):** Anne Kelly (Editor).

**Index on Censorship**
485 5th Ave.
New York, NY 10017 (212)972-8400
**Affiliation:** Fund For Free Expression. **Concern(s):** arts; justice; literature; censorship; freedom of expression; poetry; graphics. "Censorship here and abroad is fought in a dozen or so pieces on writers' suppression by government agencies. It's a rather informal newsletter that often includes poetry and cartoons on free speech."-C.C. **Est.:** 1972. **Frequency:** 10/yr. **Subscription:** $30/yr. **Price:** $3/ea.

**J ▸ Indian Report**
245 2nd St. NE
Washington, DC 20002 (202)547-6000
**Affiliation:** Friends Committee on National Legislation. **Concern(s):** justice; demographics; politics; spiritual; interfaith; Native Americans; welfare rights; law; policy. "The Quakers' support of Native American rights is given in these eight pages. Housing, child welfare and economic well-being are some aspects of Indian treaty rights and self-determination protected through suggested new legislation."-C.C. **Est.:** 1978. **Frequency:** 4/yr. **Subscription:** Donation. **Price:** Free. **Contact(s):** Cindy Darcy, Retta Swartzendruber

**J ▸ Indigenous Women**
Box 174
Lake Elmo, MN 55042
**Concern(s):** justice; family; feminism; Native Americans. A new Magazine dedicated to the issues and concerns of Native American women. **Frequency:** 2/yr. **Subscription:** $10/yr.

**T ▸ Indigenous World**
School of Interdisciplinary Study
Miami University
Oxford, OH 45056
**Affiliation:** School of Interdisciplinary Study. **Concern(s):** Third World; justice; self-determination; diversity; indigenous peoples; Native Americans.

**T ▸ Indochina Issues**
318 4th St. NE
Washington, DC 20002 (202)547-5075
**Affiliation:** Indochina Project. **Concern(s):** Third World; justice; peace; Asia; foreign policy; development. "An analytical journal of commentary on developments in that vital area of the world. Southeast Asia vis-a-vis the US is the subject, with each number of the newsletter focusing on a specific aspect of the region. It could serve to supplement the Southeast Asia Chronicle, a more complete selection in the area."-C.C. Nonprofit. **Est.:** 1979. **Frequency:** 10/yr. **Subscription:** $20/yr.

**T ▸ Indochina Newsletter**
2161 Massachusetts Ave.
Cambridge, MA 02140 (617)497-5273
**Affiliation:** Asia Resource Center. **Concern(s):** Third World; development; Asia; foreign policy. Looks at developments in Vietnam, Laos, and Cambodia, and US policy toward those countries. Provides critique and perspective generally not available to the US public in the mainstream media. Draws links between US policies in other parts of the world. Nonprofit. **Est.:** 1979. **Frequency:** 6/yr. **Subscription:** $13/yr. **Price:** $1 + postage. **Bulk:** 25% off/24. **Pages:** 4-10. **Circ.:** 750. **Contact(s):** Paul Shannon (Editorial Board). **Other:** Asia Resource Center, Box 15275, Washington, DC 20003.

**L ▸ Industrial Worker**
1095 Market St., #204
San Francisco, CA 94103 (415)863-WOBS
**Affiliation:** Industrial Workers of the World. **Concern(s):** labor; environment; unions; forests. Rank and file labor union newspaper. Direct action, direct democracy and on the job action builds worker power as a force in the movement for change. Judi Bari has been a frequent contributing writer. **Est.:** 1905. **Frequency:** 12/yr. **Subscription:** $12/yr. **Price:** $.50/ea. **Bulk:** 50% off/24. **Pages:** 12. **Circ.:** 5M.

**$ ▸ INFACT News**
310 E. 38th St. , #301
Minneapolis, MN 55401 (612)825-6837
**Affiliation:** INFACT. **Concern(s):** economics; peace; justice; education; boycotts; corporate responsibility; government accountability; anti-nuclear; militarism; budget; children. "This newsletter beats Nestles, making that corporation more concerned about proper use of their infant formula. They continue their efforts for children and others, currently targeting companies that contribute to nuclear weapons production, in particular GE."-C.C. **Other Resources:** See INFACT (GE Boycott). **Est.:** 1977. **Frequency:** 2/yr. **Price:** Free. **Contact(s):** Nancy Cole.

**E ▸ INFORM Reports**
381 Park Ave. S, #1301
New York, NY 10016 (212)689-4040

**Affiliation:** INFORM. **Concern(s):** environment; health; natural resources; hazardous/toxic waste; public health. A newsletter that identifies and reports on practical actions for the protection and conservation of natural resources and public health. Its current research focuses on such critical environmental issues such as hazardous waste reduction, garbage management, urban air pollution, and land and water conservation. Nonprofit. **Est.:** 1974. **Dues:** $25/yr. **Frequency:** 4/yr. **Subscription:** $25/yr. **Pages:** 6. **Circ.:** 1.6M. **Fax:** (212)447-0689. **Contact(s):** Jerri McDermott (Associate Director/Communications), Joanna Underwood (President).

### ✍ ▶ Information Bulletin
70 Washington Sq., S
New York, NY 10012    (212)998-2633
**Affiliation:** Elmer Holmes Bobst Library, NYU. **Concern(s):** education; labor; justice; media; constitutional rights; unions; civil rights; discrimination; self-determination. "The Bobst Library contains collections relating to people's and labor history. The Bulletin often focuses on a single aspect of the library, with descriptions of their collections and donations policy."-C.C. **Est.:** 1981. **Frequency:** Irregular. **Subscription:** Donation. **Price:** Free. **Contact(s):** Dorothy Swanson.

### ☙ ▶ Inforum
803 N. Main St.
Goshen, IN 46526    (219)534-3402
**Affiliation:** Fourth Freedom Forum Inc.. **Concern(s):** peace; national security. A newsletter that discusses ways to create and maintain international security. **Frequency:** 4/yr. (800)233-6786. **Contact(s):** Marc Hardy (Executive Director).

### E ▶ Inner Voice
Box 11615
Eugene, OR 97440    (503)484-2692
**Affiliation:** Association of Forest Service Employees For Environmental Ethics. **Concern(s):** environment; forests; conservation; whistleblowers; wildlife/endangered species. A newspaper covering public land issues and info on the free speech rights of federal employees. "We publish articles on National Forests written by Forest Service employees who practice true stewardship on public lands." **Other Resources:** Local chapters on national forests; education; speaking; support of free speech rights of federal employees. Nonprofit. **Est.:** 1989. **Dues:** $20/yr. **Frequency:** 6/yr. **Subscription:** $20/yr. **Price:** Free. **Pages:** 12-16. **Circ.:** 15M. **Contact(s):** Tom Ribe (Editor).

### M ▶ Inter Nation
72 5th Ave.
New York, NY 10011    (212)242-8400
**Affiliation:** Nation. **Concern(s):** media; politics; Third World; press. "This news packet consists of one investigative feature story on international politics. It is intended primarily as a news service for periodicals."-C.C. **Est.:** 1987. **Frequency:** 12/yr. **Subscription:** Depends on circulation of subscribing periodical. **Price:** Call. **Contact(s):** George Black.

### D ▶ Interaction
Global Tomorrow Coalition
1325 G St. NW, #915
Washington, DC 20005-3104    (202)628-4016
**Affiliation:** Global Tomorrow Coalition. **Concern(s):** demographics; environment; energy; future; hunger; sustainability. A newsletter focusing on issues related to sustainable development. .

### ☙ ▶ The InterDependent
1010 Vermont Ave. NW, #904
Washington, DC 20005    (202)347-5004
**Affiliation:** United Nations Association of the USA. **Concern(s):** peace; world order; United Nations. Journal that focuses on the need for international interdependence. Believes that this can only be accomplished by more dependence on the United Nations. **Frequency:** 6/yr. **Contact(s):** Andy Rice. **Other:** 485 Fifth Ave., New York, NY 10017.

### ✈ ▶ International Employment Hotline
Box 3030
Oakton, VA 22106    (703)620-1972
**Concern(s):** education; labor; jobs; travel. This newsletter reveals the latest developments in international employment. Scores of exciting current jobs offer comfortable overseas living for both the temporary traveler and the career-minded. Since 1980 the HOTLINE has covered thousands of jobs in over 100 countries. Readers also receive information on how to get into the world's most prestigious international organizations. Also provides international job hunting advice. **Other Resources:** "We carry specialty books on working overseas." **Est.:** 1980. **Frequency:** 12/yr. **Subscription:** $36/yr. **Pages:** 8. **Circ.:** 5M. **Fax:** (703)620-1973. **Contact(s):** Will Cantrell (Editor).

### E ▶ International Environmental Affairs: Journal for Research & Policy
17 1/2 Lebanon
Hanover, NH 03755
**Concern(s):** environment; conservation; policy; global warming; oceans/rivers; forests. Academic journal concerned with global environmental policies. It addresses all environmental and conservation issues including local climate change, ozone depletion, conservation of species, ocean management, desertification, and others.

### F ▶ International Family Planning Perspectives
2010 Massachusetts Ave. NW, 5th Fl.
Washington, DC 20036    (202)296-4012
**Affiliation:** Alan Guttmacher Institute. **Concern(s):** feminism; demographics; Third World; pro-choice; population growth; family planning. This journal, like its US counterpart, focuses on family planning. This one only broadens its scope to cover the developing world.

### T ▶ International Health & Development
1120 Vermont Ave. NW, #610
Washington, DC 20005    (202)835-9056
**Affiliation:** Institute of International Health and Development. **Concern(s):** Third World; health; demographics; economics; development; public health. An educational magazine devoted to examining public health and development policies affecting developing nations; provides a forum for debate on existing governmental and private programs; encourages policy makers in the field to explore alternative ways of meeting the pressing health and economic needs of developing nations. Nonprofit. **Frequency:** 4/yr. **Subscription:** $24/yr. **Price:** $6/ea. **Pages:** 32. **Circ.:** 20M. **Other Formats:** Fax: (202) 452-1269. **Contact(s):** Graciela D. Testa (Editor), Paul Dietrich (Publisher).

### L ▶ International Labor Reports
Box 5036
Berkeley, CA 94705
**Concern(s):** labor; unions. **Frequency:** 6/yr. **Price:** $28/ea.

### ✈ ▶ International Living
824 E. Baltimore St.
Baltimore, MD 21202
**Concern(s):** education; labor; economics; travel; jobs; socially-responsible investing. This newsletter contains short pieces and features, with useful information on investing, shopping, travel, employment, education, real estate, and lifestyles overseas. **Contact(s):** Kathleen Peddicord (Editor).

### A ▶ The International Permaculture Solutions Journal
7781 Lenox St.
Jacksonville, FL 32221
**Affiliation:** Yankee Permaculture. **Concern(s):** agriculture; environment; sustainability; organic; permaculture. Stresses SOLUTIONS to the global environment crisis through personal choices. Topics ranging from sustainable food systems, economic systems, the Forest Ecosystem Rescue Network, and allied themes. Bill Mollison, Bill McLarney, Michael Crofoot, Thelma Snell, James Duke and Dan Hemenway will be among the contributing writers. Letters and book review largely reader-written. **Frequency:** Irregular. **Subscription:** $25/yr. **Pages:** 24. **Circ.:** 1M. **Contact(s):** Dan Hemenway (Editor/Publisher), Cynthia Baxter (Associate Editor).

### J ▶ International Review of Third World Culture and Issues
Box 1785
Palm Springs, CA 92263
**Concern(s):** justice; Third World; Africa; South Africa; discrimination; racism; minority rights; diversity. "Civil rights for people of color in the US and abroad are advocated. Black, Hispanic, and political prisoner news is of particular importance in this stimulating magazine."-C.C. **Est.:** 1979. **Frequency:** 4/yr. **Subscription:** $10/yr. **Price:** $2.50/ea. **Contact(s):** Joe Beaver, Ray Maestas.

### ☙ ▶ International Security News Clipping Service
Route 169, Box 203
Pomfret, CT 06258    (203)928-2616
**Affiliation:** Topsfield Foundation. **Concern(s):** peace; media; education; activism; disarmament; East-West; research; national security; press. This newsletter sends out information on the military and other governmental activities. It sends out these articles throughout this newsletter to other periodicals for reprint. You only have to pay for what you reprint.

### ○ ▶ International Solar Energy Intelligence Report
BPI, 951 Pershing Dr.
Silver Springs, MD 20910
**Concern(s):** energy; solar; wind. A newsletter covering all aspects of solar energy with a special concentration of photovoltaics and wind power. Regular features include articles on solar energy economics,

business, technology, and international, federal, state and local regulations. Other features include new publications, solar energy events calendar, contract opportunities and grants awarded. Articles are received from correspondents worldwide. **Est.:** 1975. **Frequency:** Weekly.

### E ▶ International Wildlife
8925 Leesburg Pike
Vienna, VA 22184    (703)790-4000
**Affiliation:** National Wildlife Fund. **Concern(s):** environment. A magazine with short-feature articles that make nature - and human use and stewardship of it - understandable and interesting. **Contact(s):** Jan Boysen (Associate Editor).

### ☙ ▶ The International Workcamper Newsletter
43 Tiffany Rd.
Belmont, VT 05730    (802)259-2759
**Affiliation:** Volunteers for Peace International Workcamps. **Concern(s):** peace; Third World; education; East-West; global understanding; volunteers. The newsletter reports on volunteer workcamps throughout the world. It also provides you with information for registering for the work programs. **Frequency:** Annual. **Price:** Free. **Contact(s):** Peter Coldwell (Director).

### ✍ ▶ Interracial Books for Children Bulletin
1841 Broadway
New York, NY 10023    (212)757-5339
**Affiliation:** Council on Interracial Books for Children. **Concern(s):** education; justice; arts; discrimination; racism; culture. "Book reviews, of course, are the main point here, but this review covers related areas as well. Movie stereotypes, teaching methods, and both suitable and negative selections from culture and education are described as well."-C.C. **Est.:** 1967. **Frequency:** 8/yr. **Subscription:** $16, $24 institution. **Price:** $4/ea. **Contact(s):** Bradford Chambers.

### E ▶ Interspecies Newsletter
Interspecies Communication, Inc.
273 Hidden Meadow Lane
Friday Harbor, WA 98250
**Affiliation:** Interspecies Communication, Inc.. **Concern(s):** environment; education; arts; wildlife/endangered species; social ecology. This quarterly newsletter is sustained by membership subscriptions. It reports on the ongoing work of IC which functions primarily to help humans re-establish their emotional ties with the natural world. Nonprofit. **Est.:** 1978. **Dues:** $25/yr-$1,000 lifetime.

### J ▶ Into the Night
1980 65th St., #3D
Brooklyn, NY 11204
**Concern(s):** justice; political prisoners; activism. "This is a newsletter for freedom for political prisoners held in the US. Although sometimes handwritten and sloppy in format, it serves to supply news not available elsewhere on incarcerated activists."-C.C. **Est.:** 1987. **Frequency:** 12/yr. **Subscription:** $25, $35 institution. **Price:** Free. **Contact(s):** D. Stokes.

### ? ▶ Invent!
3201 Corte Madeira, #304
Camarillo, CA 93012    (805)484-9786
**Affiliation:** Inventors Workshop International Educational Foundation. **Concern(s):** future; ideation; invention. This magazine focuses on new inventions across the country and world. It seeks to help make the climate more acceptable for inventors to show their inventions and invent. Nonprofit. **Est.:** 1971. **Frequency:** 6/yr. **Subscription:** $35/yr. **Price:** $5/ea. **Circ.:** 20M+. **E-Network:** Inventnet. **Fax:** (805)388-3097. **Contact(s):** Alan Arthur Tratner (President).

### $ ▶ Investing from the Heart
64 Main St.
Montpelier, VT 05602    (802)223-7943
**Affiliation:** Catalyst (Institute for Gaean Economics). **Concern(s):** economics; Third World; socially-responsible investing; alternative consumer; development; alternative markets. Putting our Earth, our values, peace and justice, back into our economic lives are the main goals of this newsletter. Gives descriptions of models that can empower us to regain community and cooperation. Lots of knowledge on the rainforest opportunity. **Frequency:** 6/yr.

### A ▶ The IPM Practitioner
Box 7414
Berkeley, CA 94707    (510)524-2567
**Affiliation:** Bio-Integral Resource Center. **Concern(s):** agriculture; environment; pesticides; preservation. Monitors the field of integrated pest management applied to agriculture, landscape, structural, medical, range, veterinary, and forest settings. Highlights practical methods and products. Nonprofit. **Est.:** 1978. **Dues:** $25, $50 institution. **Frequency:** 10/yr. **Subscription:** $25, $50 institution. **Pages:** 24. **Circ.:** 3M. **Fax:** (510)524-1758. **Contact(s):** Irene Juniper (Manager).

## ☢ ◗ IPPNW Report
126 Rogers St.
Cambridge, MA 02142   (617)868-5050

**Affiliation:** International Physicians for the Prevention of Nuclear War. **Concern(s):** peace; disarmament; anti nuclear. "The international equivalent of Physicians for Social Responsibility works to use the prestige of and trust in doctors to stop nuclear weapons worldwide. Conferences, publications, and studies are means to the end, which is nuclear disarmament."-C.C. **Est.:** 1982. **Frequency:** 3/yr. **Subscription:** $15/yr. **Price:** Free. **Contact(s):** Peter Zheutlin.

## ☢ ◗ IPRA Newsletter
Antioch College
795 Livermore
Yellow Springs, OH 45387   (513)767-6444

**Affiliation:** International Peace Research Association. **Concern(s):** peace; education; environment; feminism; Third World; media; conflict resolution; militarism; research; development. Reports on scholarly research and peace development work by country and region. Lists peace resources and includes calendar. Nonprofit. **Est.:** 1965. **Dues:** $30, $15 low income. **Circ.:** @1.3M. **E-Network:** PeaceNet. **ID:** 'antiochcol'. **Fax:** (513)767-1891. **Contact(s):** Paul Smoker (Secretary General).

## J ◗ Iron House Newsletter
See Native American Prisoners Rehabilitation Research Project.

## S ◗ Israel Horizons
150 5th Ave., #911
New York, NY 10011   (212)255-8760

**Concern(s):** spiritual; Third World; justice; politics; Mid-East; faith. "The magazine is a progressive/socialist zionist periodical dealing with progressive forces in Israel, specifically Mapam and the Kibbutz Artzi Federation—but not exclusively these groups. We also deal with problems facing the world Jewish community from a progressive/socialist zionist perspective." **Frequency:** 4/yr. **Subscription:** $15/yr. **Price:** $3.50/ea. **Pages:** 32. **Circ.:** 3M. **Fax:** (212)627-1287. **Contact(s):** Arieh Lebowitz (Editor).

## J ◗ Issues and Concerns
Box 1986
Indianapolis, IN 46206   (317)353-1491

**Affiliation:** Disciples of Christ (Christian Church). **Concern(s):** justice; politics; political prisoners; activism. "The political prisoner of the month, a dozen or so news briefs and a list of resources are standard bimonthly features are included in this newsletter. Letter-writing is particularly encouraged to save the lives and health of prisoners of conscience."-C.C. **Est.:** 1983. **Frequency:** 6/yr. **Subscription:** Donation. **Price:** Free. **Contact(s):** Paul Wilson.

## H ◗ Issues in Radical Therapy
1404 Wicklow
Boulder, CO' 80303

**Affiliation:** Cooperative Power. **Concern(s):** health; psychology. "Psychological therapy theories from a humanist viewpoint are offered in this journal. Past influences in the articles have come from thinkers such as Freud, Fanon, and Marx."-C.C. **Est.:** 1975. **Frequency:** Irregular. **Subscription:** $9, $20 institution. **Price:** $3/ea.

## ✐ ◗ Itchy Planet
Box 45831
Seattle, WA 98145   (206)322-6838

**Concern(s):** arts; environment; peace; health; culture. "A magazine of amusing funnies on such subjects as TV, nuclear winter and AIDS give us a chance to laugh about the problems we work month in and month out to solve. It also is a comics review, with short descriptions and ordering information on socially concerned funnies."-C.C. **Est.:** 1988. **Frequency:** 4/yr. **Subscription:** $9/yr. **Price:** $2.25/ea. **Publisher:** Fantagraphics Books. **Contact(s):** Leonard Rifas.

## ✍ ◗ Jack and Jill
Box 567
Indianapolis, IN 46206

**Concern(s):** education; health; youth. Articles for 6- to 8-year-olds, on sports, fitness, health, safety, exercise. Features on history, biography, life in other countries, etc. Short poems, games, puzzles, projects, recipes, photos.

## T ◗ Jewish Affairs
235 W. 23rd St., 7th Fl.
New York, NY 10011   (212)989-4994

**Concern(s):** Third World; justice; spiritual; faith; self-determination; Mid-East; discrimination. "Like most other Jewish periodicals, this journal crusades against anti-Semitism. It is different from them, however, in its strong support for Palestinian equality in the Middle East and for the two peoples living together with self-determination for Palestine."-C.C. **Est.:** 1970. **Frequency:** 6/yr. **Subscription:** $6/yr. **Price:** $1.25/ea. **Contact(s):** Herbert Aptheker.

## S ◗ Jewish Currents
Morris U. Schappes
22 E. 17th St., #601
New York, NY 10003   (212)924-5740

**Concern(s):** spiritual; politics; feminism; labor; Third World; peace; faith; Mid-East. "Articles of Jewish interest, progressive politics, Black-Jewish relations,… reviews of books, records, plays, films, events… lively style, hard facts, secular p.o.v., pro-Israel/non-Zionist." Covers issues pertinent also to feminism, civil rights, and labor history. Nonprofit. **Est.:** 1946. **Frequency:** 12/yr. **Subscription:** $20/yr. **Price:** $2/yr. **Pages:** 48. **Circ.:** 5M.

## S ◗ Jewish Vegetarians Newsletter
Box 1463
Baltimore, MD 21203   (301)366-VEGE

**Affiliation:** Jewish Vegetarians of North America. **Concern(s):** spiritual; health; environment; vegetarian; animal rights; faith. This magazine covers issues related to Judaism and vegetarianism, including health, ethics, food, economics, animal rights, ecology, and world hunger. The magazine also has poetry, interviews, cartoons, reviews, letters, news item, non-fiction. Nonprofit. **Est.:** 1983. **Dues:** $24/yr. **Frequency:** 4/yr. **Subscription:** $12/yr. **Pages:** 16. **Circ.:** 800. **Other Formats:** Cheshire/self-adhesive/mag tape. **Contact(s):** Charles Stahler, Debra Wasserman. (301)366-8343.

## L ◗ Job Seeker
Dept. A, Route 2, Box 16
Warrens, WI 54666   (608)378-4290

**Concern(s):** labor; environment; jobs. Specializes in environmental and natural resource vacancies nationwide. Two issues per month lists employment opportunities from private, local, state, and federal employers. **Est.:** 1988. **Frequency:** 26/yr. **Subscription:** $60/yr. **Price:** $3.35/ea. **Pages:** 16. **Circ.:** 1.7M. **Contact(s):** Becky Potter (Editor).

## L ◗ Jobs Impact Bulletin
815 16th St. NW, #301
Washington, DC 20006   (202)842-7816

**Affiliation:** Full Employment Action Council/AFL-CIO. **Concern(s):** labor; politics; economics; jobs; unions. "These folks know that no unemployment is acceptable, and have many suggestions for moving towards full employment. New bills in Congress, minority youth and new resources are typical article subjects."-C.C. **Est.:** 1981. **Frequency:** 10/yr. **Subscription:** $20/yr. **Price:** Free. **Contact(s):** J. Scott.

## ✐ ◗ Journal of Arts Management and Law
Heldref Publications
4000 Albemarle St. NW
Washington, DC 20016   (202)362-6445

**Concern(s):** arts; labor; justice; economics; politics. Covers the often-neglected areas of policy, law, management, marketing, finance, law, management, marketing, finance, labor relations,. and technology in the performing and visual arts. The articles, interviews, and legal analysis are essential for managers, lawyers, teachers, and trustees in the arts, as well as for law, arts, and business libraries. The annual special issues have become authoritative resources; among them: VOLUNTEERS IN THE ARTS and SOCIAL RESPONSIBILITY IN THE ARTS. **Frequency:** 4/yr. **Subscription:** $45/yr.

## ✍ ◗ Journal of Career Planning & Employment
62 Highland Ave.
Bethlehem, PA 18017

**Concern(s):** education; students. Articles on topics related to career planning, placement, recruitment, and employment of new college graduates.

## ☢ ◗ Journal of Conflict Resolution
275 S. Beverly Dr.
Beverly Hills, CA 90212

**Concern(s):** peace; Third World; conflict resolution. **Publisher:** Sage Publications, Inc.

## ✍ ◗ Journal of Educational Research
Heldref Publications
4000 Albemarle St. NW
Washington, DC 20016   (202)362-6445

**Concern(s):** education; research; childhood; youth; students. The Journal has contributed to the advancement of educational practice in elementary and secondary schools. Authors experiment with new procedures, evaluate traditional practices, replicate previous research for validation, and perform other work central to understanding and improving the education of today's students and teachers. A valuable resource for teachers, counsellors, supervisors, administrators, and educational researchers. **Est.:** 1920. **Frequency:** 6/yr. **Subscription:** $55/yr.

## E ◗ Journal of Environmental Education
Heldref Publications
4000 Albemarle St. NW
Washington, DC 20016   (202)362-6445

**Concern(s):** environment; education; research; analysis. This is a vital research journal for everyone teaching about the environment. Each issue features case studies of relevant projects, evaluation of new research, and discussion of public policy and philosophy in the area of environmental education. **Frequency:** 4/yr. **Subscription:** $47/yr. **Price:** $11.75/ea. **Pages:** 40. **Circ.:** 1M. **Publisher:** Heldref Publications. **Contact(s):** Marilyn Millstone (Managing Editor).

## E ◗ Journal of Environmental Health
720 S. Colorado Blvd.
South Tower, #970
Denver, CO 80222   (303)756-9090

**Affiliation:** National Environmental Health Association. **Concern(s):** environment; health; economics; consumer protection; recycling. "Health professionals may appreciate this scholarly collection of analyses on the environment vis-a-vis the law, new consumer products, waste, etc." -C.C. In-depth analysis and global perspectives on key issues, NEHA news, an Information Exchange, EH update (short news items, research briefs, announcements, educational and employment opportunities in classified section plus regular columns, etc). **Est.:** 1938. **Frequency:** 6/yr. **Subscription:** $40/yr. **Price:** $7/ea. **Contact(s):** Ida Frances Marshall.

## E ◗ Journal of Environmental Quality
677 S. Segoe Rd.
Madison, WI 53711

**Affiliation:** American Society for Agronomy. **Concern(s):** environment; agriculture; economics; health; hazardous/toxic wastes; global warming; water; pesticides. This journal reports on the dangers of pollution to the environment as dealing with agriculture. **Frequency:** 4/yr.

## ✍ ◗ Journal of Experiential Education
University of Colorado
Box 249
Boulder, CO 80309   (303)492-1547

**Affiliation:** Association for Experiential Education. **Concern(s):** education. A professional journal for people involved in the experiential education field. The journal contains articles, research papers, book reviews, and an idea notebook. Topics include: Community service, adventure programming, environmental education, ethics, leadership, cultural journalism, internships, the creative arts, multi-cultural education, living history, leadership development, management training, adult education, and experiential education in the schools. **Other Resources:** Publish a number of books and directories as well as a monthly jobs clearinghouse. The Association was founded in 1973. Nonprofit. **Est.:** 1978. **Dues:** $35-$50, $125 organization. **Frequency:** 3/yr. **Subscription:** $25/free for members. **Price:** $8/ea. **Pages:** 65. **Circ.:** 1.8M. **Fax:** (303)492-7090. **Contact(s):** Marla Riley (Office Manager), Dan Garvey (Executive Director).

## H ◗ Journal of Group Psychotherapy, Psychodrama and Sociometry
Heldref Publications
4000 Albemarle St. NW
Washington, DC 20016   (202)362-6445

**Concern(s):** health; psychology; counseling. Published in cooperation with the American Society of Group Psychotherapy and Psychodrama, this quarterly features articles on the application of action methods to the fields of psychotherapy, counseling, and education. Action techniques include psychodrama, role playing, and social skills training. The journal, founded by J.L. Moreno, publishes reviews of the literature, case reports, and theoretical articles with practical application. **Frequency:** 4/yr. **Subscription:** $50/yr.

## H ◗ Journal of Health Politics, Policy & Law
Duke University Press
6697 College Station
Durham, NC 27708   (919)684-2173

**Concern(s):** health; politics; national health. Focuses on the initiation, formulation, and implementation of health policy. Scholars, policymakers, and practitioners in political science, economics, public administration, law, medicine, and ethics analyze the relations between government and health - as they are now and as they ought to be. **Frequency:** 4/yr. **Subscription:** $36, $66 institution. **Price:** $17/ea. **Circ.:** 2M. **Publisher:** Duke University Press. **Contact(s):** James Morone (Editor), Deborah Stone (Book Review Editor).

## ☼ ◗ Journal of Hydrogen
219 S. Siesta Lane, #101
Tempe, AZ 85281   (602)921-0433

**Affiliation:** American Hydrogen Association. **Concern(s):** energy; environment; hydrogen; solar; appropriate technology; efficiency;

water; resource management. A journal reporting on transition from fossil fuels to solar hydrogen technologies including fuel cells. Strives to fill the information gap that exists within the scientific and educational community, industry, the political establishment, the media, and the public. It further reports on the transition from the fossil depletion economy, to a renewable solar-hydrogen economy that will last forever. **Est.:** 1990. **Frequency:** 4/yr. **Price:** $3/ea. **Circ.:** 2.5M. **Fax:** (602)967-6601. **Contact(s):** Harry Braun.

**T ▶ Journal of Palestine Studies**
Box 25697, Georgetown Station
Washington, DC 20007 (202)342-3990
**Affiliation:** Institute for Palestine Studies. **Concern(s):** Third World; peace; Mid-East. "Articles on the Arab-Israeli conflict and on the survival of the Palestinians are written in a scholarly but unfootnoted style. Both the current situation in the Middle East and historical events are analyzed."-C.C. **Est.:** 1971. **Frequency:** 4/yr. **Subscription:** $24, $36 institution. **Price:** $6/ea. **Pages:** 200+. **Circ.:** @4.5M. **Fax:** (202)342-3927. **Contact(s):** Dr. Hisham Sharabi.

**E ▶ Journal of Pesticide Reform**
Box 1393
Eugene, OR 97440 (503)344-5044
**Affiliation:** Northwest Coalition for Alternatives to Pesticides. **Concern(s):** environment; agriculture; health; hazardous/toxic waste; pesticides. "Slashing the use of pesticides on crops and using safer chemicals when pesticides are necessary are the objectives. The editor is concerned with both farmworkers and consumers, and recommends ways people can have pesticide use cut."-C.C. **Est.:** 1979. **Frequency:** 4/yr. **Subscription:** $12, $20 institution. **Price:** $3/ea. **Contact(s):** Dr. Mary O'Brien.

**H ▶ Journal of Polymorphous Perversity**
Box 1454, Madison Square Station
New York, NY 10159 (212)689-5473
**Concern(s):** health; psychology. It is a humorous and satirical journal of psychology and psychiatry that The Wall Street Journal called "a social scientist's answer to Mad Magazine." Boldly going where other journals have feared to tread, JPP has brought its readers such hilarious articles as "The Etiology and Treatment of Childhood" and "Psychotherapy of the Dead." **Frequency:** 2/yr. **Subscription:** $9.75/yr. **Office:** 20 Waterside Plaza New York, NY 10010.

**✏ ▶ Journal of Popular Film and Television**
Heldref Publications
4000 Albemarle St. NW
Washington, DC 20016 (202)362-6445
**Concern(s):** arts; media; broadcasting; film. Reflecting interest in popular culture studies, the JOURNAL treats commercial films and television in the broadest sense. Its editors at the Popular Culture Center, Bowling Green State University, seek thoughtful articles on stars, director, producers, studios, networks, genres, series, and the audience. Filmographies, bibliographies, book reviews, and illustrated essays on theory and criticism and regular features. **Frequency:** 4/yr. **Subscription:** $24, $48 institution.

**✍ ▶ The Journal of Psychohistory**
Box 401
New York, NY 10024 (212)799-2294
**Affiliation:** Institute of Psychohistory. **Concern(s):** education; health; psychology. "...is a controversial scholarly quarterly called 'a fresh point of view' by the New York Times. Articles include 'The Gulf Crisis as Human Sacrifice', 'The Unconscious Origins of Bush's Popularity', 'The Masochism of Japanese Workers', 'The History of Child Assault' and 'The Recession as a Cleansing Fantasy'." **Other Resources:** Also publishes handbook for psychohistorians. Publishers list available. **Est.:** 1973. **Frequency:** 6/yr. **Subscription:** $48, $95 organization. **Price:** $10/ea. **Circ.:** 3M. **Contact(s):** Lloyd DeMause (Editor), Kenneth Adams (Associate Editor). **Other:** 2315 Broadway, New York City, NY 10024.

**H ▶ Journal of Psychology: Interdisciplinary and Applied**
Heldref Publications
4000 Albemarle St. NW
Washington, DC 20016 (202)362-6445
**Concern(s):** health; psychology. Publishes a variety of research and theoretical articles in the field of psychology, with an emphasis on articles that integrate divergent data and theories, explore new avenues for thinking and research or present criticisms of the present status of the behavioral disciplines. Notable articles include "Psychological Aspects of Components of Pain," "Prejudice and Neurotic Symptomatology Among White "South Africans" and "The Emotions of Professional Writers." **Frequency:** Annual. **Subscription:** $80/yr.

**E ▶ Journal of Soil and Water Conservation**
7515 NE Ankeny Rd.
Ankeny, IA 50021-9764 (515)289-2331
**Affiliation:** Soil and Water Conservation Society. **Concern(s):** environment; land; water; conservation; natural resources. The JSWC is a multidisciplinary journal that serves as a forum for the discussion of land and water issues. It features authoritative general interest articles, research reports, editorial viewpoints, commentary, and news of current events. Nonprofit. **Est.:** 1945. **Dues:** $30 (first time members) $44 - renewals. **Frequency:** 6/yr. **Subscription:** $30/yr. **Price:** $7.50/ea. **Pages:** 8. **Circ.:** 12M. **Fax:** (515)289-1227. **Contact(s):** Max Schnepf (Editor).

**T ▶ Journal of Third World Studies**
Box 1232
Americus, GA 31709
**Concern(s):** Third World; justice; politics.

**F ▶ Journeymen**
513 Chester Turnpike
Candia, NH 03034
**Concern(s):** feminism; men's liberation. A newsletter exploring men's issues, spirituality, and sexuality. "A real alternative to the growing number of mainstream men's magazines... You'll find intelligent, sensitive writing on issues related to men.. A much needed link for those involved in th rising men's movement."-Utne Reader **Frequency:** 4/yr. **Subscription:** $24/yr.

**✍ ▶ Joyful Child**
Box 5506
Scottsdale, AZ 85261
**Concern(s):** education; health; spiritual; transformation; childhood; psychology. A magazine designed to awaken self-esteem, love, peace, and joy in children as well as adults. Emphasizes that joy is the "true essence" of humanity but needs to be cultivated more carefully in this society.

**$ ▶ Jubilee Partners Report**
Box 68
Comer, GA 30629 (404)783-5131
**Affiliation:** Jubilee Partners. **Concern(s):** economics; justice; demographics; cooperatives; community self-reliance; minority rights. "Their long-standing promotion of interracial communities and cooperative housing makes their newsletter one worth reading and supporting."-C.C. **Est.:** 1979. **Frequency:** 4/yr. **Price:** Free. **Contact(s):** Don Mosley.

**M ▶ Jump Cut**
Box 865
Berkeley, CA 94701 (510)658-4482
**Affiliation:** Jump Cut Association. **Concern(s):** media; arts; film; culture. "Jump Cut, like Cineaste, is a left film newspaper. Both are excellent, but this is a little sharper in its focus on social concerns videos and movies, with more attention given to specialized documentaries."-C.C. **Est.:** 1974. **Frequency:** 2-3/yr. **Subscription:** $14/yr. **Price:** $4/ea.

**E ▶ Kagenna**
Box 4713
Cape Town, 8000 South Africa
**Concern(s):** environment; politics; Third World; South Africa; Green. A magazine published by a cooperative about "Green" values: ecology, politics, culture. The only Green issues magazine in South Africa. Nonprofit. **Frequency:** 4/yr.

**♿ ▶ Kaleidoscope**
326 Locust St.
Akron, OH 44302 (216)762-9755
**Concern(s):** health; arts; disabled; poetry; graphics; fine arts. "We publish lively, energetic, well-crafted fiction, poetry, and visual arts related to the experience of disability. Also critical essays and book reviews, photo essays, interviews, personal experience narrative. Established writers/artists featured alongside new, promising writers. No bias as to style, but openly hostile to the sentimental and the trite. We are responsive to originality of thought and innovative treatment of subject." **Frequency:** 2/yr. **Subscription:** $9, $12 institute. **Price:** $4.50/ea. **Bulk:** %20 off/24. **Pages:** 56-64. **Circ.:** 2M. **Publisher:** Kaleidoscope Press. **Contact(s):** Darshan C. Perusek (Editor).

**E ▶ Katuah**
Box 638, Katuah Province
Leicester, NC 28748 (704)683-1414
**Concern(s):** environment; agriculture; bioregionalism; permaculture. A journal devoted to the Southern Appalachian area. It regards the region as an ecologically whole system that provides habitat, life support, and relationship to a whole range of life forms - wildlife, plant life, as well as the human. "We explore how we humans can live in a dynamic, participatory way with the rest of the life community here in these mountains." Themes included Habitat & Biodiversity, Children, The Black Bear, On Death & Dying, and Preserving the Wilderness. Nonprofit. **Est.:** 1983. **Frequency:** 4/yr. **Price:** $1.50/yr. **Pages:** 33. **Contact(s):** Scott Bird.

**A ▶ KCSA Newsletter**
Box 588, Hwy 271S
Poteau, OK 74953-0588 (918)647-9123
**Affiliation:** Kerr Center for Sustainable Agriculture, Inc. (KCSA). **Concern(s):** agriculture; environment; sustainability; social ecology. The KCSA Newsletter is a free monthly publication printed on recycled paper. This newsletter deals with agricultural related topics ranging from sustainability to reform. It is well written and informative. **Est.:** 1986. **Frequency:** 12/yr. **Price:** Free. **Pages:** 4. **Circ.:** 5M. **Fax:** (918)647-8712. **Contact(s):** Heidi C. Carter (Education Coordinator), Teresa A. Maurer (Associate Program Director).

**E ▶ Keep Tahoe Blue**
League to Save Lake Tahoe
Box 10110
South Lake Tahoe, CA 95731 (916)541-5388
**Affiliation:** League to Save Lake Tahoe. **Concern(s):** environment; water. Informs on efforts to protect Lake Tahoe's incomparable beauty from ever-present threats of degradation. **Dues:** $35/yr. **Frequency:** 4/yr. **Subscription:** Membership.

**✍ ▶ Kids Face**
Box 158254
Nashville, TN 37215
**Concern(s):** education; environment; peace; youth; students; activism; sustainability; conservation; childhood. An ambitious newspaper started by kids, for kids, stressing positive solutions to today's problems in the environment. Its goal is to build a better and more peaceful world, and most of all a sustainable future.

**🐾 ▶ Kind News**
2100 L St. NW
Washington, DC 20037 (202)452-1100
**Affiliation:** Humane Society of the US. **Concern(s):** environment; education; animal rights; students. Four-page newspaper for students.

**P ▶ Kindred Spirits Journal**
Box 542
Lewisburg, PA 17837 (717)398-7383
**Affiliation:** Kindred Spirits. **Concern(s):** politics; environment; peace; Green. "A wing of the Green movement leaning toward political and social change, not just tilling our wastes into the garden. They go beyond decentralism to concern about the contras and nuclear issues. This is definitely one of the best Green periodicals published in this country."-C.C. **Est.:** 1986. **Frequency:** 4/yr. **Subscription:** $5/yr. **Price:** $1.25/ea. **Contact(s):** Michel Ochs.

**J ▶ Klanwatch Intelligence**
Box 548
Montgomery, AL 36195-5101
**Concern(s):** justice; racism; discrimination; diversity. This newsletter keeps track of the Klan and Nazi's actions in the US. It achieves this through article contributions from people throughout the nation. An interesting thing about this monthly is it not only tells you about the Klans activities but how to combat them. **Frequency:** 12/yr. **Pages:** 8.

**A ▶ Koinonia Newsletter**
Route 2
Americus, GA 31709 (912)924-0391
**Affiliation:** Koinonia Partners. **Concern(s):** agriculture; justice; environment; demographics; fair housing; social ecology. "Koinonia Farm made efforts toward fair housing and integration long before it was popular. They continue today in their farm-based efforts toward harmony with land and with people."-C.C. **Est.:** 1942. **Frequency:** 5/yr. **Subscription:** Donation. **Price:** Free. **Contact(s):** Liz Holler.

**T ▶ Korea Bi-weekly Report**
110 Maryland Ave. NE
Washington, DC 20002 (202)546-4304
**Affiliation:** North American Coalition for Human Rights in Korea. **Concern(s):** Third World; Asia. "Support for human rights in Korea and a more equitable US policy vis-a-vis North and South Korea are promoted. This report serves as a news bulletin on Korea."-C.C. **Est.:** 1982. **Frequency:** 26/yr. **Subscription:** $15/yr. **Price:** Free. **Contact(s):** Pharis Harvey.

**E ▶ L.A. Resources**
18822 Beach Blvd., #202
Huntington Beach, CA 92648 (714)963-7697
**Affiliation:** Community Resource Publications. **Concern(s):** environment; health; spiritual; holism; transformation. New Age magazine with articles dealing with health, self-help, environmental concerns, spiritual growth, new psychology and ways to better one's life through non-traditional modes. Seminars, workshops on effective advertising and marketing for New Age entrepreneurs. 11th year in Los Angeles. Largest circulation New Age publication in L.A. **Est.:** 1981. **Fre-**

quency: 4/yr. **Subscription:** $10/yr. **Price:** Free. **Pages:** 72. **Circ.:** 130M. **Publisher:** Community Resource Publications. **Fax:** (714)963-4796. **Contact(s):** Earl Bell (Operations Manager).

**M ▸ L.A. Weekly**
2140 Hyperion Ave.
Los Angeles, CA 90027
**Concern(s):** media; justice; environment. Los Angeles' prime alternative newsweekly. **Frequency:** Weekly. **Subscription:** $46/yr.

**L ▸ Labor Center Reporter**
2521 Channing Way, #300
Berkeley, CA 94720 (510)642-0323
**Affiliation:** Labor Center - Institute of Industrial Relations. **Concern(s):** labor; health; occupational safety. "The Center's one-sheet newsletter seems to cover mainly occupational health. It could be useful to union activists."-C.C. **Other Resources:** Labor Occupational Health Program MONITOR. **Est.:** 1979. **Frequency:** 26/yr. **Subscription:** $15/yr. **Price:** $15/ea. **Contact(s):** Bruce Poyer.

**L ▸ Labor History**
17 Washington Sq. S
New York, NY 10012 (212)998-2638
**Affiliation:** Tamiment Institute. **Concern(s):** labor; unions. "The historical information in this journal makes it a useful tool for strategists in the labor movement. Labor organizers and organizing drives of past years are covered, with valuable lessons to be learned from these studies."-C.C. **Est.:** 1960. **Frequency:** 4/yr. **Subscription:** $21, $29 institution. **Price:** $8/ea. **Contact(s):** Dan Leab.

**L ▸ Labor Notes**
7435 Michigan Ave.
Detroit, MI 48210 (313)842-6262
**Affiliation:** Labor Education and Research Project. **Concern(s):** labor; unions. "This little newsletter provides useful tidbits on national union and international labor issues. Both the rank-and-file and labor officials will find the information of interest."-C.C. For union activists containing news of labor struggles often not available elsewhere. **Est.:** 1979. **Frequency:** 12/yr. **Subscription:** $10, $20 institution. **Price:** Free. **Contact(s):** Jim Woodward.

**L ▸ Labor Occupational Health Program Monitor**
2521 Channing Way
Berkeley, CA 94720 (510)642-5507
**Affiliation:** Labor Occupational Health Program. **Concern(s):** labor; education; unions; occupational safety. "The Monitor is part of a labor education program to educate workers on how to avoid job hazards. A resource section is included."-C.C. **Other Resources:** LABOR CENTER REPORTER. **Est.:** 1974. **Frequency:** 4/yr. **Subscription:** $10/yr. **Price:** $2.50/ea. **Contact(s):** Eugene S. Darling.

**T ▸ Labor Report on Central America**
Box 28014
Oakland, CA 94604 (510)272-9951
**Affiliation:** Labor Network on Central America. **Concern(s):** Third World; labor; Central America. "Unity between workers of the US and of Central America is promoted to stop US intervention. Solidarity delegations to help the people of Nicaragua are an important part of the periodical."-C.C. **Est.:** 1985. **Frequency:** 6/yr. **Subscription:** $5/yr. **Price:** Free. **Contact(s):** Al Weinrub.

**L ▸ Labor Research Review**
3411 W. Diversey, #PE
Chicago, IL 60647 (312)278-5418
**Affiliation:** Midwest Center for Labor Research. **Concern(s):** labor; unions. "Ideas and strategy on how to put the "movement" back in the labor movement are included, along with pages from labor history. This title is recommended for all labor activists."-C.C. **Est.:** 1982. **Frequency:** 2/yr. **Subscription:** $12/yr. **Price:** $7/ea. **Contact(s):** Jack Metzgar.

**L ▸ Labor Today**
7917 S. Exchange, #211
Chicago, IL 60617 (312)933-4900
**Affiliation:** Trade Unionists for Action and Democracy. **Concern(s):** labor; unions. "It is the recommended first choice for rank-and-file labor activists. Union democracy, organizing drives and articles on past and present workers' struggles are among the many topics covered. Its attractive layout and popular writing style are just two reasons workers read it for ideas on advancing their interests."-C.C. **Est.:** 1962. **Frequency:** 4/yr. **Subscription:** $6.50/yr. **Price:** $1.75/ea. **Contact(s):** Debbie Albano.

**L ▸ Labor World**
102 E. Boone Ave.
Spokane, WA 99202
**Concern(s):** labor.

**G ▸ Lambda Book Report**
Lambda Rising, Inc.
1625 Connecticut Ave. NW
Washington, DC 20009 (202)462-7924
**Concern(s):** justice; gay/lesbian. "...a book review magazine dedicated to promoting the latest in gay and lesbian books. If you read gay and lesbian books, you need Book Report. Find out about every new book in every new issue. Experience provocative essays, revealing interviews, in-depth reviews and more! Leavitt, Maupin, Lorde, Baldwin, Schulman...with Book Report you're in the best of company." **Frequency:** 6/yr. **Subscription:** $15/yr. **Price:** $3/ea. **Circ.:** 20M. **Contact(s):** Jane Troxell (Editor), Page Maccubbin (Publisher).

**☮ ▸ LANAC Newsletter**
43 Charles St., #3
Boston, MA 02114 (617)227-0118
**Affiliation:** Lawyers Against Nuclear Arms Control. **Concern(s):** peace; politics; disarmament; law. "Stopping nuclear weapons through the legal system is the goal. Legislative action is also a priority of this lawyers' professional newsletter."-C.C. **Est.:** 1981. **Frequency:** 6/yr. **Subscription:** $30/yr. **Price:** $5/ea. **Contact(s):** Alan Sherr.

**E ▸ Land Letter**
1800 N. Kent, #1129
Arlington, VA 22209-2109
**Concern(s):** environment; agriculture; health; conservation; hazardous/toxic waste; wildlife/endangered species; forest; land; policy. Information service covering the full spectrum of federal policies affecting the nation's private and public lands. Coverage includes: agriculture, budget and finance, coastal zone, endangered species, energy and minerals, fish & wildlife, forests, hazardous wastes, the EPA, parks & recreation, public lands (BLM), tax policy, pollution, water resources, wetlands and wild & scenic rivers. Three-in-one reporting system includes Monthly News Reports; Special Reports & Index; and Status Reports. **Publisher:** W.J. Chandler and Associates. **Contact(s):** Jim Howe (Managing Editor). (202)783-7762.

**A ▸ The Land Report**
2440 E. Water Well Rd.
Salina, KS 67401 (913)823-5376
**Affiliation:** Land Institute. **Concern(s):** agriculture; environment; sustainability. This newsletter contains reports on the technological and environmental breakthroughs which will help the Earth sustain life. **Contact(s):** Wes Jackson, Dana Jackson

**A ▸ The Land Stewardship Newsletter**
14758 Ostlund Trail North
Marine, MN 55047 (612)433-2770
**Affiliation:** Land Stewardship Project. **Concern(s):** agriculture; environment; health; education; farm policy; sustainability; soil; organic; conservation; vegetarian; resources; land. The mission is to foster an ethic of stewardship toward soil and water resources and to promote the development and implementation of more sustainable methods of agriculture. An educational program working for public policy changes that will lead to the development of a sustainable agricultural system. It also provides a lively forum where vegetarians and meat-eaters duke it out. **Other Resources:** LAND NOTES, a column on land ethics provided to local newspapers. Nonprofit. **Est.:** 1982. **Frequency:** 4/yr. **Subscription:** $20/yr. **Price:** $5/ea. **Bulk:** 80% off/24. **Pages:** 18. **Circ.:** 5M. **Contact(s):** Ron Kroese (Executive Director), Patrick Moore (General Manager).

**E ▸ Land/LEAF**
3368 Oak Ave.
Stevens Point, WI 54481 (715)344-6158
**Affiliation:** Land Educational Association Foundation. **Concern(s):** environment. "Functional and mimeographed, LandLEAF includes a number of environmental articles. Topics in one issue include irradiated foods, no nukes news and mining pollution."-C.C. **Est.:** 1974. **Frequency:** 4/yr. **Subscription:** $10/yr. **Contact(s):** Gertrude Dixon.

**T ▸ Latin America Update**
110 Maryland Ave. NE
Washington, DC 20002 (202)544-8045
**Affiliation:** Washington Office on Latin America. **Concern(s):** Third World; justice; Latin America. "Brazil, Chile, and Peru are three South American nations whose current affairs are covered, along with news from all the hot spots of Central America. Democracy and human rights issues are the concerns."-C.C. **Est.:** 1974. **Frequency:** 6/yr. **Subscription:** $14, $25 institution. **Price:** $2.50/ea. **Contact(s):** David Holiday.

**T ▸ Latin American Perspectives**
Box 5703
Riverside, CA 92517 (714)787-5508
**Concern(s):** Third World. "Scholarly analysis and discourse on social theory south of the border is the topic. The essays are meticulously researched and worth taking the time to read."-C.C. **Est.:** 1974. **Frequency:** 4/yr. **Subscription:** $28, $72 institution. **Price:** $7.95/ea. **Publisher:** Sage Publications. **Contact(s):** Ronald H. Chilcote.

**H ▸ Law Report**
400 Washington Ave.
Montgomery, AL 36195 (205)264-0286
**Affiliation:** Southern Poverty Law Center. **Concern(s):** health; political prisoners; racism; discrimination; minority rights. "Legal assistance for people of color and poor folks is advocated here. Discouraging the Ku Klux Klan and defending political prisoners are of special importance to the Center."-C.C. **Est.:** 1985. **Frequency:** 6/yr. **Subscription:** Donation. **Price:** Free. **Contact(s):** Morris S. Dees, Jr..

**☮ ▸ Lawyers' Committee on Nuclear Policy Newsletter**
225 Lafayette St., #513
New York, NY 10012 (212)334-8044
**Affiliation:** Lawyers' Committee on Nuclear Policy. **Concern(s):** peace; politics; anti-nuclear; conflict resolution; law. "Legal strategy to stop nuclear weapons is discussed in this professional periodical. Action in the courts and in the halls of Congress is advocated as a way lawyers can help in this struggle for survival." -C.C. **Est.:** 1981. **Dues:** $35/yr. **Frequency:** 5/yr. **Subscription:** Membership. **Price:** Free. **Contact(s):** David Birman (Executive Director).

**$ ▸ Left Business Observer**
250 W. 85th St.
New York, NY 10024 (212)874-4020
**Concern(s):** economics; politics; analysis. Economics and business are the topics analyzed in one of the few left-of-center business newsletters. The stock market, world trade and corporate misadventures are documented. Articles include: living stands, government policy, trade, debt, development, financial markets, Eastern Europe and USSR, limitations of conventional economic categories and statistics. "A salutary antidote to the economic mush in mainstream periodicals." -Alexander Cockburn. **Est.:** 1986. **Frequency:** 12/yr. **Subscription:** $20, $50 institution. **Price:** $2.50/ea. **Bulk:** 30% off/24. **Pages:** 8. **Circ.:** 2.5M. **Labels:** 2500. **E-Network:** PeaceNet. **ID:** 'lbo'. **Contact(s):** Doug Henwood (Editor/Publisher), Christine V. Bratton (Associate Publishers).

**✎ ▸ Left Curve**
Box 472
Oakland, CA 94604 (510)763-7193
**Concern(s):** arts; politics; culture; anarchism/anti-authoritarian. An artist produced magazine that addresses the problems of cultural forms emerging from the crises of modernity that strive to be independent from the control of dominant institutions. We publish original work by individuals, as well as cultural work that are integral, organic parts of emancipatory movements. **Frequency:** Irregular. **Subscription:** $18/yr. **Price:** $7/ea. **Bulk:** $5ea/24. **Circ.:** 1M. **Office:** 410 Webster St. Oakland, CA 94604. **Contact(s):** Csaba Polony (Editor).

**P ▸ Left Green Notes**
Box 372
West Lebanon, NH 03784 (802)295-1544
**Affiliation:** Left Green Network. **Concern(s):** politics; alternative party; Green. An organizing bulletin. **Frequency:** 12/yr.

**$ ▸ Lemon Times**
2001 S St. NW, #410
Washington, DC 20009 (202)328-7700
**Affiliation:** Center for Auto Safety. **Concern(s):** economics; health; consumer rights. A newsletter for CAS members. Includes articles such as tips for using small claims court, lemon lawyers for members, defect alerts, publication notices, major CAS actions. Includes annual report. **Frequency:** 4/yr. **Subscription:** $15/yr. **Price:** Membership. **Pages:** 5. **Circ.:** 12M. **Publisher:** Center for Auto Safety. **Contact(s):** Debra Barclay (Editor).

**E ▸ Leon Newsletter**
Project Minnesota
7455 S. Sarah Lake Dr.
Rockford, MN 55373
**Affiliation:** Project Minnesota. **Concern(s):** environment.

**M ▸ The Letter Exchange**
Box 6218
Albany, CA 94706 (510)526-7412
**Concern(s):** media; education; multilogues. A magazine devoted to conversation through the mail. Personal listings by subscribers (no Singles Ads) are grouped by topic, ranging from Art, Contemporary Issues and Daily Life to Politics, Religions, Women's Interests and Writing. A free forwarding service for all initial letters is included. **Est.:** 1981. **Frequency:** 3/yr. **Subscription:** $18/yr. **Price:** $8/ea.

**Pages:** 36. **Circ.:** 2.5M. **Contact(s):** Steve Sikora (Editor/Publisher).

**P ◆ Libertarian Labor Review**
Box 2824, Station A
Champaign, IL 61820
**Concern(s):** politics; labor; anti-authoritarian. Independent Anarcho-Syndicalist journal. LLR reports on syndicalist movements around the world, and offers a forum for discussion of the North American anarchist and later movements. **Other Resources:** Pamphlets and reprints on related issues. Continues WOBBLE and SELF-MANAGEMENT NEWSLETTER. **Est.:** 1986. **Frequency:** 2/yr. **Subscription:** $5/yr. **Price:** $2.75/ea. **Bulk:** 50% off/24. **Pages:** 46. **Contact(s):** Jeff Stein.

**P ◆ Liberty**
Box 1167
Port Townsend, WA 98368   (206)385-5097
**Concern(s):** politics; justice; arts; third party; ideation; culture; freedom of expression; censorship. "A provocative libertarian journal of culture, politics and ideas. Every issue features challenging and exciting articles and reviews taking on anything from the American Empire to the artistic establishment, from the War on Drugs to the new campus censorship... plus other challenging and fun reading for those who value freedom!" **Est.:** 1987. **Frequency:** 6/yr. **Subscription:** $19.50/yr. **Price:** $4/ea. **Pages:** 72-80. **Circ.:** 4.5M. **Contact(s):** R.W. Bradford, Stephen Cox.

**M ◆ Lies of Our Times**
145 W. 4th St.
New York, NY 10012   (212)254-1061
**Affiliation:** Institute for Media Analysis, Inc.. **Concern(s):** media; politics; media watch; responsibility; government accountability. A magazine of media criticism focusing on misinformation, disinformation, and propaganda in the major print and broadcast organizations. It covers subjects which are ignored as well as hypocrisies, misleading emphases, and hidden premises; the biases which systematically share reporting. **Other Resources:** Books, monographs, conferences, and publications list/catalog available. **Est.:** 1990. **Frequency:** 11/yr. **Subscription:** $24/yr. **Price:** $3/ea. **Bulk:** 30% off/24. **Pages:** 24+. **Circ.:** 10M. **Publisher:** Sheridan Square Press. **E-Network:** PeaceNet. **ID:** 'instmedia'. **Fax:** (212)254-9598. MCI Mail: IMA. **Contact(s):** Ellen Ray (Executive Director), William Schaap (Managing Editor).

**A ◆ Life Lines**
1103 Jefferson
Wichita, KS 67203   (316)263-7294
**Affiliation:** Trees For Life. **Concern(s):** agriculture; environment; Third World; food production; hunger; development; forests. A newsletter that gives updates on the current environmental problems of today's forests and aims at educating the public about the linkage of trees and world hunger. **Frequency:** 4/yr.

**J ◆ Lifelines**
1325 G St. NW
Washington, DC 20005   (202)347-2411
**Affiliation:** National Coalition to Abolish the Death Penalty. **Concern(s):** justice; capital punishment. "The death penalty is seen by this coalition as a violation of one's basic human rights. Reasons it is wrong and campaigns to stop it are included."-C.C. **Est.:** 1981. **Frequency:** 6/yr. **Subscription:** $10/yr. **Price:** Free. **Contact(s):** Leigh Dingerson.

**F ◆ Lilith**
250 W. 57th St., #2432
New York, NY 10107   (212)757-0818
**Concern(s):** feminism; spiritual; politics; faith. "Named for the woman who predated Eve, Lilith magazine looks at Jewish life through a feminist filter and speaks out on Jewish feminist concerns to the general women's movement. Read about politics, history, 'JAP'-baiting, feminist family dynamics, the Jewish stake in reproductive freedom, and much, much more." **Frequency:** 4/yr. **Subscription:** $14/yr.; $20 institutions. **Publisher:** Lilith Publications Inc.

**✐ ◆ Limbic Plus**
Jenzen Kelly Associates, Inc.
32260 88th Ave.
Lawton, MI 49065
**Concern(s):** education; health; psychology; childhood. A bimonthly newsletter about the educational implications of recent research on the brain, consciousness, and learning. Includes features on life-long learning, educational resources, exemplary teachers, and more.

**T ◆ Links**
Box 407, Audubon Station
New York, NY 10032
**Affiliation:** Central America Health Rights Network. **Concern(s):** Third World; health; justice; economics; Central America; racism. A

magazine that shows the links between economics, racism, and underdevelopment in the Third World. **Frequency:** 4/yr. **Subscription:** $30/yr.

**✍ ◆ The Lion and the Unicorn**
Brooklyn College
English Dept.
Brooklyn, NY 11210
**Concern(s):** education; youth. Articles offering criticism of children's and young adult books, for teachers, scholars, artists, and parents. **Contact(s):** Geraldine DeLuca, Roni Natov (Editors).

**✍ ◆ Listen Magazine**
Pacific Press Publishing
Box 7000
Boise, ID 83707
**Concern(s):** education; health; psychology. Articles providing teens with "a vigorous, positive, educational approach to the problems arising out of the use of tobacco, alcohol, and other drugs." **Publisher:** Pacific Press Publishing. **Contact(s):** Lincoln Steed (Editor).

**F ◆ Listen Real Loud**
American Friends Service Committee
1501 Cherry St.
Philadelphia, PA 19102
**Affiliation:** American Friends Service Committee, Nationwide Women's Program. **Concern(s):** feminism. "Intended to promote communication and debate among regional, national, overseas staff, and committee members, as well as to expand the dialogue with movement with whom, AFSC engages."-C.W. **Dues:** $10-20/yr. suggested donation. **Frequency:** 4/yr. **Pages:** 24.

**$ ◆ Little Free Press**
Route 2, Box 137
Cushing, MN 56443
**Concern(s):** economics; politics. "Articles, etc. to focus on a better economic system for the world and total freedom for each individual." This newsletter seeks to find solutions to world problems. **Est.:** 1969. **Frequency:** 6/yr. **Subscription:** Gratis only. **Price:** Free/SASE. **Pages:** 6. **Circ.:** 2M. **Contact(s):** Ernest Mann (Editor-Publisher).

**U ◆ Livability**
1429 21st St. NW
Washington, DC 20036   (202)887-5990
**Affiliation:** Partners for Liveable Places. **Concern(s):** urban; arts; feminism; environment; health; architecture; culture; planning; conservation; elderly; family; youth. A newsletter that focuses on the amenities of a city. These amenities are in six categories: cultural planning, heritage and cultural tourism, animation, natural and scenic resources, profit by design, and community image. Additional focus on human issues or social equity (i.e., elderly, family, and youth). The newsletter helps the individual or group develop cultural strategies on social issues. **Dues:** $35/yr. **Frequency:** 2/yr. **Fax:** (202) 466-4845. **Contact(s):** Daniel McCahan (Information Officer).

**✍ ◆ Live and Learn**
13731 Ventura Blvd.
Sherman Oaks, CA 91423   (818)995-7121
**Concern(s):** education. A magazine dedicated to the gentle overthrow of the school system, and to the implementation of 21st Century learning systems to affect the future of education on our planet.

**E ◆ Live Wild or Die**
Box 13765
Portland, OR 97213
**Concern(s):** environment; politics; anti-authoritarian. Newspaper.

**H ◆ Living Well**
7935 216 St. NW, #E
Edmonds, WA 98020
**Affiliation:** Northwest Health Foundation. **Concern(s):** health.

**☸ ◆ LNAC Almanac**
Box 60552
Pasadena, CA 91106   (818)799-6193
**Affiliation:** Librarians for Nuclear Arms Control. **Concern(s):** peace; education; disarmament; anti-nuclear; test ban. "Librarians can be militant too, when they have an issue they feel strongly about. The issue of nuclear survival is effectively covered in their professional newsletter with update on nuclear treaties, legislation, and ideas for personal action. As one would expect, there is an informative reading list of books, pamphlets, and suggested articles."-C.C. **Est.:** 1984. **Frequency:** 4/yr. **Subscription:** $10/yr. **Price:** Donation. **Contact(s):** Victoria Musmann.

**E ◆ Log Cabin**
Box 881
Med Lake, WA 99022
**Concern(s):** environment. Back-to-the-land network newsletter. Members share doings, interests, tips and make contacts. **Price:** $1/

sample.

**P ◆ Love and Rage**
Box 3, Prince St. Station
New York, NY 10012
**Concern(s):** politics; justice; feminism; anti-authoritarian; minority rights; discrimination; racism; sexism. "A revolutionary anarchist monthly with news coverage from around North America. Their prison coverage is provided by the New York Anarchist Black Cross."-Prison News Service. Supplies an equal amount of "love" with articles like "black skinheads speaking-out against sexism", and other tempered and realized material. Though angry, much of the material in this newsletter is surprisingly even-handed. Represents the youth wing of the anarchist movement.

**✍ ◆ Love and Rockets**
7563 Lake City Way
Seattle, WA 98115
**Concern(s):** arts; media; graphics. "Los Bros. Hernandez revolutionary comic magazine, contains exploits of emblematic L.A. punkettes Maggie and Hopey, and the continuing saga of Palomar, that 'Central American Dogpatch'. Sexy, fantastic, down-to-earth, and exquisitely drawn." **Est.:** 1976. **Frequency:** 4/yr. **Subscription:** $10/yr. **Price:** $2.25/ea. **Pages:** 30. **Circ.:** 18M. **Contact(s):** Gary Groth.

**♥ ◆ Loving More Journal**
Box 6306
Captain Cook, HI 96704-6306   (808)929-9691
**Concern(s):** family. Focused on group marriage and other forms of multiple-adult "committed relationships". Includes personal accounts, member letters, newsbrief related to the lifestyle. Also contains member network related resources and annual conference information. Practical tips and support for those in the lifestyle. **Other Resources:** Support for local groups (networking and materials); lifestyle primer (book); phone line consultation service; annual conference. Nonprofit. **Est.:** 1984. **Dues:** $25-$60/yr. **Frequency:** 4/yr. **Subscription:** Membership. **Price:** $4 (back issues). **Pages:** 14. **Circ.:** 600. **Publisher:** Polyfidelitous Educational Productions. **E-Network:** The Well. **ID:** 'pepsyn'. **Member:** Co-op America. **Contact(s):** Ryam Nearing (Director/Editor), B. Northrop (Operations/Graphics).

**T ◆ Lucha/Struggle**
New York Circus Collective
Box 37, Times Square Station
New York, NY 10108   (212)928-7600
**Concern(s):** Third World; justice; demographics; spiritual; Latin America; immigration; faith; foreign policy. Analysis and theological reflection on current situation in Latin America. It also reports on US response, both government and popular to the situations that develop in these regions. It covers Latin American history, liberation theology, US foreign policy and immigration, labor and economic issues. **Est.:** 1976. **Frequency:** 6/yr. **Subscription:** $10/yr. **Bulk:** 40% off/24. **Pages:** 40. **Office:** 900 Riverside Dr. New York, NY 10032. **Fax:** (212)928-2757.

**L ◆ Machinist**
1300 Connecticut Ave. NW
Washington, DC 20036   (202)857-5200
**Affiliation:** International Association of Machinists & Aerospace Workers. **Concern(s):** labor; justice; unions. "On workers' rights and human rights, this union is one of the most progressive, a perspective that is reflected in the pages of their popularly-written magazine. Unionists and sympathizers will enjoy reading it monthly."-C.C. **Est.:** 1946. **Frequency:** 12/yr. **Subscription:** $3/yr. **Price:** $.25/ea. **Contact(s):** Dean Ruth.

**S ◆ Magical Blend Magazine**
Box 11303
San Francisco, CA 94101   (415)673-1001
**Concern(s):** spiritual; health; transformation. "We accept the premise that a new world view is being born. Whether this birth is to be an easy or difficult one will depend largely upon the individual. The aim of this newsletter is to chart the course of this transformation, to assist the individual and contribute to the birthing process. We attempt to explore many alternative possibilities." **Frequency:** 4/yr. **Subscription:** $14/yr. **Price:** $3.95/ea. **Pages:** 120. **Circ.:** 45M. **Publisher:** Magical Blend Inc.. **Office:** 25 Taylor St., #624 San Francisco, CA 94102. **Contact(s):** Michael Langeview (Publisher), Valerie Brona (Administrative Assistant). (415)673-1002.

**A ◆ Maine Organic Farmer & Gardner**
RR 2, Box 595A
Lincolnville, ME 04849   (207)622-3118
**Affiliation:** Maine Organic Farmer & Gardner Association. **Concern(s):** agriculture; environment; organic; farmland; sustainability. "...promotes and encourages sustainable agriculture and environmentally sound living. Our primary focus is organic farming, gardening and forestry., but we also deal with local, national and

international agriculture. food and environmental issues." Nonprofit. **Frequency:** 6/yr. **Price:** $2/sample. **Circ.:** 10M. **Contact(s):** Jean English (Editor). **Other:** Box 2176, Augusta, ME 04330.

**P ▸ The Maine Progressive**
21 McKeen St.
Brunswick, ME 04011 (207)725-7675
**Affiliation:** Invert. **Concern(s):** politics; economics; peace; networking; grassroots organizing. An alternative voice for people committed to achieving a democratic society in which everyone can live in dignity and peace. "We are an alternative to mainstream newspapers with informative articles and networking people by advertising events, jobs, etc. dedicated for social change." **Est.:** 1986. **Frequency:** 12/yr. **Price:** $.90/ea. **Pages:** 28. **Circ.:** 5M. **Labels:** 3000. **Contact(s):** Selma Sternlieb (Editor), Larry Dansinger (Bulletin & Calendar Office). (207)827-3107. **Other:** Invert, Box 110, Stillwater, ME 04489.

**T ▸ MADRE Speaks/MADRE Informa**
121 W. 27th St.
New York, NY 10001 (212)627-0444
**Affiliation:** MADRE/Women's Peace Network. **Concern(s):** Third World; justice; family; feminism; Central America; development. "Ways you can help work with mothers and children of Central America are explained in MADRE's bilingual magazine. Poetry, prose, and straight feature articles explain freedom and human rights movements of that region from a mother's perspective."-C.C. **Est.:** 1984. **Frequency:** 3-4/yr. **Subscription:** $10/yr. **Price:** Donation. **Contact(s):** Maria Dolores Hajosy.

**J ▸ MALDEF Newsletter**
634 S. Springs St., 11th Fl.
Los Angeles, CA 90014 (213)629-2512
**Affiliation:** Mexican American Legal Defense and Education Fund. **Concern(s):** justice; minority rights. "MALDEF plays a role for Chicanos similar to the role the NAACP plays for Blacks. Civil rights advancement through legislation, legal actions and other means is provided to make life for these Hispanics better and more fair."-C.C. **Est.:** 1973. **Frequency:** 3/yr. **Subscription:** Donation. **Price:** Free. **Contact(s):** Alicia Maldonado, Antonia Hernandez (President).

**F ▸ MAN!**
1611 W. 6th St.
Austin, TX 78703 (512)477-9595
**Affiliation:** Austin Men's Center. **Concern(s):** feminism; men's liberation. Encourages men and women to deepen their journeys in recovery by presenting ideas, feelings and experiences that enhance, excite and heal by utilizing the message of the men's and recovery movements to everyone. Through understanding and trust we might break the patterns imposed on us as children and recover and nurture our inner child and raise healthier children and better the world. **Frequency:** 4/yr. **Subscription:** $10/yr. **Price:** $4/ea. **Contact(s):** John Lee (Publisher), Lyman Grant (Managing Editor).

**A ▸ Manna**
1701 University Ave. SE, #202
Minneapolis, MN 55414 (612)331-1099
**Affiliation:** International Alliance for Sustainable Agriculture. **Concern(s):** agriculture; Third World; sustainability; development. Newsletter. **Frequency:** 6/yr.

**E ▸ Marine Bulletin**
Box 23298
Savannah, GA 31403 (912)234-8062
**Affiliation:** National Coalition for Marine Conservation. **Concern(s):** environment; ocean/rivers. This bulletin reports on the coalitions effort to save the oceans, fish, and the marine environment. Informative articles. **Est.:** 1973. **Frequency:** 6/yr. **Contact(s):** Ken Hinman (Executive Director).

**P ▸ Master Switch Weekly**
New Studium Generale, Box 623
Maidenhead
Berkshore, SL6 8XJ England
**Concern(s):** politics; future; grassroots organizing; ideation; invention; networking; leadership. Has been formed to promote "continuous public domain innovation," using temporary " expert networks" to help individuals and small groups "independently and in combination to exercise, test and expand their joint powers of creativity, enterprise and leadership."

**P ▸ The Match**
Box 3488
Tucson, AZ 85722
**Concern(s):** politics; anti-authoritarian. "We criticize authoritarian institutions and remedies for social problems. This magazine advocates freedom from coercion as a way of living that leads to fewer crimes and oppressions." **Est.:** 1969. **Frequency:** 4/yr. **Subscription:** $10/yr. **Price:** $2.50/ea. **Pages:** 40-80. **Circ.:** 1.7M.

**F ▸ Matrix Women's Newsmagazine**
108 Locust St., #14
Santa Cruz, CA 95060 (408)426-3512
**Concern(s):** feminism; justice; empowerment; gay/lesbian; sexism. Matrix, the largest feminist newspaper in the West, is a spirited monthly newspaper that features lively articles, news, reviews, poetry, artwork, columns, and cartoons by women. Due to economic hard times, publication ceased January 1992. The staff invites interested parties to pick up the torch. **Est.:** 1977. **Frequency:** 12/yr. **Subscription:** $14/yr. **Pages:** 24-32. **Circ.:** 25M. **Contact(s):** Elizabeth Baldwin (Editor), Karla Schultz (Co-Publishers). Tracey Jefferys-Renault, Publisher.

**E ▸ Mattole Restoration Newsletter**
4062 Wilder Ridge Rd
Garberville, CA 95440-4613
**Affiliation:** Mattole Restoration Council. **Concern(s):** environment; conservation; preservation. This newsletter gives the current information on the efforts to restore the watrershed area around the salmon grounds.

**S ▸ Mature Years**
Box 801
Nashville, TN 37202
**Concern(s):** spiritual; health; seniors; faith. "Our purpose is to help people understand and use the resources of the Christian faith in dealing with specific opportunities and problems related to aging," writes Mr. Downall. "Articles on social issues, ecological concerns, travel, nostalgia, health, human interest, religion, international affairs, and humor. Our readers (age 55+) are as active as possible, eager to know places and ways in which they can contribute their ideas and experience." **Contact(s):** Donn C. Downall (Editor).

**P ▸ May Day!**
5502 W. Adams Blvd.
Los Angeles, CA 90016
**Affiliation:** Socialist Party, USA. **Concern(s):** politics; Democratic Socialism. "This discussion journal of democratic socialism covers similar topics with a similar perspective to those of Socialist Review. May Day!'s cultural and social change coverage is more concise and limited than the others, but can serve to complement it."-C.C. **Est.:** 1981. **Frequency:** 4/yr. **Subscription:** $10/yr. **Price:** $2.50/ea. **Contact(s):** Robert E. Schlichter.

**M ▸ Media & Values**
Fort Mason Center
1962 South Shenandoah St.
Los Angeles, CA 90034
**Affiliation:** Center for Media and Values. **Concern(s):** media; media watch. "This 24-page magazine reflects on and recommends action for better quality media. It takes a strong stand against violence, prejudice and militarism. It's the most action-oriented journalism review in the US and is recommended to all favoring better print and electronic media."-C.C. Nonprofit. **Est.:** 1977. **Frequency:** 4/yr. **Subscription:** $30/yr. **Price:** $5/ea. **Pages:** 24-30. **Circ.:** 15M. **Contact(s):** Elizabeth Thoman (Executive Director).

**M ▸ Mediactive**
Alternative Media Information Center
39 W. 14th St.
New York, NY 10011 (212)929-2663
**Affiliation:** Media Network. **Concern(s):** media; politics; film; grassroots organizing. "Visual media, including slide shows, videos and films, are reviewed here. In addition, ways of using these resources in community and social concerns organizing are explained."-C.C. Articles on the latest trends in the field of alternative media. **Est.:** 1985. **Frequency:** 4/yr. **Subscription:** $10/yr. **Price:** Free. **Contact(s):** Diana Agosta.

**H ▸ Medical Abstracts Newsletter**
Box 2170
Teaneck, NJ 07666 (201)836-5030
**Concern(s):** health. Medical Abstracts Newsletter provides consumers with summaries of the latest medical breakthroughs and discoveries, abstracted from over 150 scientific journals. **Est.:** 1981. **Frequency:** 12/yr. **Subscription:** $24.95/yr. **Contact(s):** Toni L. Goldfarb (Publisher).

**H ▸ Medical Self-Care**
Box 701
Providence, RI 02901 (401)351-4320
**Concern(s):** health; preventative medicine; alternative consumer. A magazine promoting wellness and alternative health practices. **Frequency:** 6/yr. **Price:** $15/ea. **Contact(s):** Carole Pisarczyk.

**S ▸ Meditation Magazine**
6801 Lindley Ave.
Reseda, CA 91335 (818)343-4998
**Concern(s):** spiritual; peace; transformation. Explores and promotes meditation as a consciousness-expanding activity and to be a reference for organizations who share our vision of creating a harmonious world through thought and action. "We believe the purpose of meditation includes the nurturing of individual and group spiritual awareness." **Contact(s):** Tricia Harbula, Patrick Harbula (Editors).

**F ▸ Men's Council Journal**
Box 4795
Boulder, CO 80306 (303)444-3473
**Concern(s):** feminism; environment; men's liberation. Focuses on the ritualistic aspects of manhood and men's liberation. **Frequency:** 4/yr. **Subscription:** $15/yr. **Pages:** 28. **Circ.:** 10M. **Contact(s):** James Bzura, Tom deMers (Co-editors).

**E ▸ Mendocino Commentary**
Box 1222
Fort Bragg, CA 95437 (707)964-6528
**Affiliation:** Mendocino Environmental Center. **Concern(s):** environment; peace; justice. Peace and environmental paper servicing the Mendocino County area. **Est.:** 1975. **Dues:** $15/yr. **Price:** Free. **Office:** 366 N. Main Fort Bragg, CA 95437. **Contact(s):** Marco McClean (Editor/Typesetter).

**E ▸ The Mendocino Country Environmentalist**
Box A
Ukiah, CA 95482 (707)459-5490
**Affiliation:** Mendocino Environmental Center. **Concern(s):** environment; peace; justice; activism. This newspaper contains frequent articles on offshore oil drilling, Judi Bari and Earth First!, war protests, and food and justice isssues. **Est.:** 1981. **Frequency:** 20/yr. **Subscription:** $20/yr. **Office:** 160 W. Stanley St. Ukiah, CA 95482. **Contact(s):** Richard W. Johnson, Jr.

**✍ ▸ Mentor**
Box 4382
Overland Park, KS 66204 (913)362-7889
**Concern(s):** education. This newsletter seeks to promote and encourage the art and practice of mentoring: passing on knowledge, value, and skills to recreate a sense of community so missing in our lives. **Other Resources:** Sponsors two writing contests, The Mentor Award for supporting and promoting mentoring through the written word and the Mentor Essay Contests for High School Seniors. **Est.:** 1989. **Frequency:** 4/yr. **Subscription:** $20/yr. **Price:** $5/ea. **Bulk:** $3/ea. (5+). **Pages:** 12. **Circ.:** 200. **Contact(s):** Maureen Waters (Editor/Publisher).

**✍ ▸ Merlyn's Pen, The National Magazine of Student Writing**
Box 1058, Dept. WR
East Greenwich, RI 02818
**Concern(s):** education; youth; students. Short stories, reviews, travel pieces, and poetry. **Contact(s):** James Stahl (Editor).

**P ▸ Mesechabe**
7712 Cohn, #2
New Orleans, LA 70118 (504)861-8832
**Affiliation:** Mesechabe Foundation and Center for Gulf South History & Culture. **Concern(s):** politics; environment; art; Green; culture; bioregionalism. A magazine about reinhabitation and the Green Movement in the Mississippi River Watersheds and the Northern coast of the Gulf of Mexico. Each issues emphasizes bioregional art and culture, Green Politics and economics, and networking throughout the bioregions. **Est.:** 1988. **Frequency:** 4/yr. **Subscription:** $12/yr. **Price:** $3/ea. **Pages:** 32. **Circ.:** 5-600. **Contact(s):** John Clark, Stephen Duplantier (Editors). **Other:** Center for Gulf South History & Culture, 7725 Cohn St., New Orleans, LA 70118

**E ▸ Message Post: Portable Dwelling Info Letter**
Box 190-MAC
Philomath, OR 97370
**Concern(s):** environment; agriculture; media; press; alternatives For long-period camping; or living in tent, tipi, wickiup, cave, van, trailer, boat, remote cabin, etc. This newsletter contains stories of experiences, candid product reports, tips and contacts. **Other Resources:** Also offers the Light Living Packet of plans and reports: shelters, conveniences and comforts easily improvised most anywhere; simple shower, ovenless baking, insulated tipi, etc. 104p. $2 each. **Frequency:** 6/yr. **Subscription:** $5/6 issues. **Price:** $1/sample. **Pages:** 12. **Circ.:** 2M.

**U ▸ Metro Ministry Newsletter**
5700 S. Woodlawn
Chicago, IL 60637 (312)643-7111
**Affiliation:** Institute on the Church in Urban Society. **Concern(s):** urban; demographics; justice; labor; spiritual; hunger; poverty; home-

lessness; unemployment; interfaith. "Support of local congregations and ministers with urban ministries is found here. Suggested focus of such ministries includes helping surrounding communities fight hunger, homelessness, and joblessness."-C.C. **Est.:** 1985. **Frequency:** 4/yr. **Subscription:** $8/yr. **Price:** $2/ea. **Contact(s):** Clinton Stockwell.

**T ▸ Middle East Report**
1500 Massachusetts Ave. NW, #119
Washington, DC 20005 (202)223-3677
**Affiliation:** Middle East Research & Information Project. **Concern(s):** Third World; Mid-East. This magazine provides and analysis of the political economy and US involvement in the Mid-East. **Est.:** 1945. **Frequency:** 6/yr. **Subscription:** $45/yr. **Pages:** 48. **Circ.:** 6.2M. **Fax:** (202)223-3604. **Contact(s):** Esther Merves.

**P ▸ Militant**
14 Charles Ln.
New York, NY 10014 (212)242-5530
**Affiliation:** Socialist Workers Party. **Concern(s):** politics; labor; Third World; alternative party. "The official paper of the Socialist Workers Party, this selection promotes the ideas of the late Leon Trotsky. This group is noteworthy as the largest Trotskyist grouping, and their periodical could interest people who want a popularly written periodical with a Trotskyist perspective."-C.C. **Est.:** 1928. **Frequency:** 50/yr. **Subscription:** $45/yr. **Contact(s):** Douglas Jemess.

**✌ ▸ Militarism Resource Project News**
Box 13416
Philadelphia, PA 19101 (215)386-4875
**Affiliation:** Militarism Resource Project. **Concern(s):** peace; justice; anti-draft. "The primary focus of the Project's newsletter is military life for members of the military. The rights of draftees are included, as well as discussion on the debate over money for human needs versus military spending."-C.C. **Est.:** 1983. **Frequency:** 4/yr. **Subscription:** $20/yr. **Price:** Donation. **Contact(s):** Harold Jordan.

**✐ ▸ Mini-Mag**
1827 Haight St., #208
San Francisco, CA 94117
**Concern(s):** arts; education; feminism; health; music. Fiction and nonfiction, humor, fillers, and poetry. "Broad areas of interest are: mystical-metaphysical, art, music, interviews/profiles of noteworthy people, education, computers, women's issues, and health." **Contact(s):** Dan Blacharski (Editor).

**✐ ▸ Minnesota Review**
Dept. of English
SUNY-Stony Brook
Stony Brook, NY 11794 (516)420-2050
**Concern(s):** arts; poetry. "for those across the country wanting 'committed fiction, poetry, essays and reviews.' Based on the quality of its writers and pieces, it is clearly among the top five literary magazines in the US."-C.C. **Est.:** 1964. **Frequency:** 2/yr. **Subscription:** $7, $14 institution. **Price:** $4/ea.

**✍ ▸ Minority Engineer**
44 Broadway
Greenlawn, NY 11740
**Concern(s):** education; labor; justice; students; science; minority rights; discrimination. Articles for college students on career opportunities in engineering fields, techniques of job hunting; developments in and applications of new technologies. Interviews. Profiles. **Publisher:** Equal Opportunity Publishers, Inc. **Contact(s):** James Schneider (Editor).

**J ▸ Minority Rights Group**
c/o Cultural Survival
53 Church St.
Cambridge, MA 02138 (617)495-2562
**Affiliation:** Minority Rights Group. **Concern(s):** justice; minority rights. "Each issue focuses on one group that is a minority in its country. These objective reports serve to document the status of these groups and cover both new refugees from other countries and natives who are not in the majority."-C.C. **Est.:** 1965. **Frequency:** 6/yr. **Subscription:** $15.80/yr. **Price:** $3.95/ea. **Contact(s):** Sue Roff.

**J ▸ Minority Trendsletter**
Center for Third World Organizing
3861 Martin Luther King Jr. Way
Oakland, CA 94609
**Affiliation:** Center for Third World Organizing. **Concern(s):** justice; Third World; minority rights. **Frequency:** 4/yr. **Subscription:** $20/yr.

**✐ ▸ Mississippi Mud**
Mud Press
1336 SE Marion St.
Portland, OR 97202 (503)236-9962
**Concern(s):** arts; literature; graphics. "The big magazine for the big issues of the day. 'Subversion, short stories, poetry, weird art and just plain genius'-Seattle's The Rocket... 'A brash, gutsy outlet for unsanitized writing'-Seattle Weekly... 'Intellectual mayhem, a welcome remedy for the malaise of literary pretension'-Eugene, Oregon's What's Happening." **Frequency:** 4/yr. **Subscription:** $19/yr. **Price:** $6 postpaid. **Pages:** 44. **Circ.:** 1.5M. **Contact(s):** Joel Weinstein (Editor).

**✌ ▸ Mobilizer**
Mobilization for Survival
45 John St., #811
New York, NY 10038 (212)385-2222
**Affiliation:** Mobilization for Survival. **Concern(s):** peace; energy; Third World; environment; justice; grassroots organizing. "'Abolish nuclear weapons and power; stop military intervention; meet human needs; reverse the arms race' have been the points of unity for this magazine since its inception. It is a top choice among periodicals making the necessary link between these related issues in an exciting, easy-to-read manner. National demonstrations and local group public actions are a favorite topic here."-C.C. **Est.:** 1977. **Contact(s):** John Miller.

**H ▸ Modern Maturity**
American Association of Retired Persons
3200 E. Carson
Lakewood, CA 90712
**Concern(s):** health; economics; seniors. Articles for older readers on careers and the work place; human interest; practical information on living (health, technology, housing, food, etc.); investments, financial and legal matters; personal relationships; consumer topics; and fiction. "Happenings" (updates on historical events), short verse, humor, and regionals. **Contact(s):** Ian Ledgerwood (Editor).

**E ▸ Monday Developments**
Interaction
1717 Massachusetts Ave. NW
Washington, DC 20036 (202)667-8227
**Affiliation:** Interaction. **Concern(s):** environment; justice; jobs; volunteers. Has an extensive listing of employment opportunities with humanitarian and environmental organizations in the US and abroad. It also contains up-to-the-minute news of interest to the 120 private volunteer agencies that are members of Interaction.

**J ▸ Monitor**
Box 50469
Atlanta, GA 30302 (404)221-0025
**Affiliation:** Center for Democratic Renewal. **Concern(s):** justice; racism; discrimination; minority rights. "Fighting bigoted violence and curbing the influence of racist hate groups are the purposes. Formerly published by the National Anti-Klan Network, this newsletter is concerned about hate groups across the US."-C.C. **Est.:** 1968. **Frequency:** 6/yr. **Subscription:** $15, $25 institution. **Price:** $3/ea. **Contact(s):** Lynora Williams.

**E ▸ Mono Lake Newsletter**
Box 29
Lee Vining, CA 93541 (619)647-6595
**Affiliation:** Mono Lake Committee. **Concern(s):** environment; water; rivers; preservation; conservation. Partially funded by the Mono Lake Foundation, a nonprofit organization dedicated to studying and protecting the Mono Lake watershed. Material contained in this newsletter may be quoted or reproduced for review, news reporting, educational purposes or related nonprofit uses. Nonprofit. **Frequency:** 4/yr. **Subscription:** $20/yr. **Pages:** 20. **Circ.:** 18M. **Publisher:** Mono Lake Committee/Kutsavi Press. **Contact(s):** Lauren Davis (Editor).

**✍ ▸ Montesorri Life**
American Montesorri Society
150 5th St.
New York, NY 10011 (212)924-3209
**Affiliation:** American Montesorri Society. **Concern(s):** education; childhood. "An in-depth magazine about the Montesorri movement in the US. **Other Resources:** The Society also supervises teacher-training and accreditation of schools; sponsors workshops and conferences.

**✌ ▸ Monthly Planet**
Box 8463
Santa Cruz, CA 95061 (408)429-8755
**Affiliation:** Nuclear Weapons Freeze of Santa Cruz County. **Concern(s):** peace; conflict resolution. "Conflict resolution through discussion rather than through military force is promoted in the Foundation's newsletter. Meetings and efforts of the sponsoring group are a regular part, with meetings of other groups also mentioned."-C.C. **Est.:** 1983. **Frequency:** 11/yr. **Subscription:** $15/yr. **Price:** Free. **Contact(s):** John Govsky.

**P ▸ Monthly Review**
122 W. 27th St., 10th Fl.
New York, NY 10001 (212)691-2555
**Affiliation:** Monthly Review Foundation. **Concern(s):** politics; analysis; alternative party. "Footnoted and intellectual, this small, independent Marxist journal uses Marxist thought to critique contemporary conditions. Now some 40 years old, this journal is one of the more popular theoretical journals of its genre."-C.C. **Est.:** 1949. **Frequency:** 11/yr. **Subscription:** $25/yr. **Contact(s):** Paul Sweezy, Harry Magdoff (Co-editors).

**✪ ▸ Mother Earth News**
80 5th St.
New York, NY 10011 (212)337-6787
**Concern(s):** energy; health; environment; economics; efficiency; alternative markets; nutrition. How-to magazine on home business, alternative energy systems, home building, home retrofit and home maintenance, seasonal cooking, gardening and crafts. **Frequency:** 6/yr. **Price:** $3/sample.

**P ▸ Mother Jones**
1663 Mission St.
San Francisco, CA 94107-8249 (415)558-8881
**Affiliation:** Foundation for National Progress. **Concern(s):** politics; justice; economics; environment; labor; civil liberties; workplace democracy. "Provides investigative reports, national and international news, and progressive perspectives in politics, culture, and current controversies, It reports on subjects that matter the most: civil liberties, media censorship, national politics, social issues, peace and disarmament, and the environment."-C.W. **Est.:** 1976. **Frequency:** 6/yr. **Subscription:** $24/yr. **Pages:** 78. **Circ.:** 110M. **Contact(s):** Adam Hochschild (Editor).

**♥ ▸ Mothering**
Box 1690
Santa Fe, NM 87504 (505)984-8116
**Concern(s):** family; feminism; environment; conservation. It serves the healing of our Mother Earth through the healing of mothers - both the inner healing of mothers themselves and the healing of the act of mothering whether done by men or by women. This magazine celebrates the experience of mothering and fathering as something worthy of one's best efforts due to the immense importance of parenting in healthy child development. We recognize parents as the experts and wish to provide truly helpful information on which parents can base informed choices. **Other Resources:** Please see list of back issues, books, and videos currently available. **Est.:** 1979. **Frequency:** 4/yr. **Subscription:** $22/yr. **Price:** $5.95/ea. **Pages:** 148. **Circ.:** 60M. **Office:** 515 Don Gasper Sante Fe, NM 87504. **Fax:** (505)986-8335. **Contact(s):** Peggy O'Mara (Publisher/Editor), Joe Bala Zuccarello (General Manager/Circulation).

**J ▸ Movement Support Network News**
666 Broadway
New York, NY 10012 (212)614-6464
**Affiliation:** Center for Constitutional Rights. **Concern(s):** justice; politics; political prisoners; government accountability; CIA; reform. An anti-repression project in cooperation with the National Lawyers' Guild, Freedom Now! National Campaign for Amnesty and Human Rights for Political Prisoners c/o Movement Support Network which does work in the area of grand juries, government spying and repression. This is their newsletter. **Frequency:** 4/yr. **Contact(s):** Morton Stavis (President), Patricia Maher (Executive Director).

**✐ ▸ Moving Out**
Box 21249
Detroit, MI 48221
**Concern(s):** arts; feminism. Poetry, fiction, articles, and art by women.

**✐ ▸ Mr. Cogito**
U.C. Box 627, Pacific University
Forest Grove, OR 97116 (503)226-4135
**Concern(s):** arts; poetry. A magazine on human rights, Eastern Europe - various political-social themes in poetry, e.g., Arab/Muslim World, Human Rights, Eastern Europe, Central America, American Indian contests. **Other Resources:** Mr. Cogito Press has published such books as Joe Napora's TO RECOGNIZE THIS DYING, Ann Chandonnet's CANOEING IN THE RAIN, POEMS FOR MY ALERT-ATHABASCAN SON, Patrick W. Gray's SPRING COMES TO ARNET, Baranczak's UNDER MY OWN ROOF, Krynicki's CITIZEN R.K. Nonprofit. **Est.:** 1973. **Frequency:** Irregular. **Price:** $3/ea. **Bulk:** 50% off/24. **Pages:** 28. **Circ.:** 500. **Publisher:** Mr. Cogito Press. **Contact(s):** John M. Gogol, Robert A. Davies (Co-editors). **Other:** 2518 N.W. Savier St., Portland, OR 97210.

**F ▸ Ms.**
Box 57132
Boulder, CO 80322-7132 (212)551-9595

**Concern(s):** feminism. Articles relating to women's roles and changing lifestyles; feminist analysis of domestic and international news; profiles, health, art and culture, books and reviews, metaphysics, feminist classics, and general interest. **Frequency:** 12/yr. **Subscription:** $45/yr. **Contact(s):** Robin Morgan (Editor). **Other:** Lang Communications, Inc., One Times Square, New York, NY 10036.

✌ ▸ **MSRRT Newsletter**
4645 Columbus Ave. S.
Minneapolis, MN 55407 (612)541-8572
**Affiliation:** Minnesota Library Association Social Responsibilities Roundtable. **Concern(s):** peace; justice; environment; labor; arts. Peace and justice news, commentary and resource listings for the library community and interested others. Emphasis is on annotations of alternative periodicals: radical, Native American, criminal justice, African American, gay/lesbian, Latino, Asian American, feminist, peace, international human rights, ecology, labor, counterculture arts, etc. **Other Resources:** Programs at annual conferences of Minnesota Library Association. Information services about social justice issues. **Est.:** 1988. **Frequency:** 10/yr. **Subscription:** $15/yr. **Price:** S.A.S.E. **Pages:** 16. **Circ.:** 250. **Date Publ.:** 12/90. **Publisher:** payable to MLA/MSSRT. **Fax:** (612)541-8600. **Contact(s):** Chris Dodge (Editor/publisher), Jan DeSirey (Co-editor). (612)823-1214.

$ ▸ **Multinational Monitor**
Box 19405
Washington, DC 20036 (202)387-8030
**Affiliation:** Essential Information. **Concern(s):** economics; politics; Third World; monopolies; lobbying; development. "Ralph Nader inspired the founding of the Monitor, which keeps tabs on the manipulations and misdeeds of multi-national corporations. It serves to give both current news on these companies and ways citizens can fight their abuses. It is a top choice periodical in the field. Frequently focuses on the Third World."-C.C. **Est.:** 1979. **Frequency:** 12/yr. **Subscription:** $22/yr. **Price:** $2.50/ea. **Contact(s):** John Richard.

E ▸ **MYTHbusters**
1717 Massachusetts Ave. NW, #LL215
Washington, DC 20036 (202)483-8491
**Affiliation:** Safe Energy Communication Council. **Concern(s):** environment; energy; anti-nuclear. A series of reports debunking the myths of nuclear power. Produces widely distributed public service announcements. Nonprofit. **Contact(s):** Scott Denman (Director), Mary O'Driscoll (National Press Coordinator).

P ▸ **NAN Bulletin**
1651 Fuller St. NW
Washington, DC 20009 (202)332-7766
**Affiliation:** National Association of Neighborhoods. **Concern(s):** politics; economics; grassroots organizing; community self-reliance. A bulletin that reports on the issues and actions of the National Association of Neighborhoods. It also helps educate fellow members on the issues that are affecting their neighborhood. **Est.:** 1975. **Frequency:** 12/yr. **Contact(s):** Stephen Glaude (Executive Director).

P ▸ **NAN Displacement Reporter**
1651 Fuller St. NW
Washington, DC 20009 (202)332-7766
**Affiliation:** National Association of Neighborhoods. **Concern(s):** politics; economics; grassroots organizing; community self-reliance. This bulletin promotes the neighborhood movements and brings to light the issues that are of the most importance to the neighborhoods. It also discusses the techniques used to solve these problems. **Frequency:** 12/yr. **Contact(s):** Stephen Glaude (Executive Director).

J ▸ **NARF Legal Review/NCBL Notes**
1506 Broadway
Boulder, CO 80302 (303)447-8760
**Affiliation:** Native American Rights Fund. **Concern(s):** justice; Native Americans. "The legal front of the movement for American Indian self-determination is the focus. All aspects of independence for these people are covered."-C.C. **Est.:** 1970. **Frequency:** 4/yr. **Price:** Free. **Contact(s):** Susan Aikeketa.

P ▸ **The Nation**
72 5th Ave.
New York, NY 10011 (212)242-8400
**Concern(s):** politics; economics; justice; labor; Third World; law; consumer rights; civil liberties; foreign policy; monopolies. A 127-year-old progressive newsweekly that is firmly committed to reporting the issues of labor, national politics, business, consumer affairs, environmental politics, civil liberties, and foreign affairs. **Other Resources:** A news clipping service called INTER NATION. **Est.:** 1865. **Frequency:** 47/yr. **Subscription:** $44/yr.; $75/2 yrs. **Price:** $3/ea. **Circ.:** 85M. **Publisher:** Hamilton Fish, III. **Fax:** (212)463-9712. **Other:** Box 10763, Des Moines, IA 50340-8563.

H ▸ **The Nation's Health**
1015 15th St. NW
Washington, DC 20005 (202)789-5600
**Affiliation:** American Public Health Association. **Concern(s):** health; public health. Reports policy issues and government activities within executive agencies and the Congress. **Contact(s):** Seiko Baba Brodbeck.

J ▸ **National Black Law Journal**
405 Hilgard
Los Angeles, CA 90024 (310)825-7941
**Concern(s):** justice; minority rights; reform. "Similar in purpose to NCBL Notes, this selection covers the genre in a more academic way. Landmark cases concerning equal opportunity, voters' rights and other legal concerns of peoples of color are analyzed."-C.C. **Est.:** 1971. **Frequency:** 3/yr. **Subscription:** $25/yr. **Price:** $25/ea. **Contact(s):** George Brown.

$ ▸ **National Boycott News**
c/o Institute for Consumer Responsibility
Box 95770
Seattle, WA 98115-2770 (206)523-0421
**Affiliation:** Institute for Consumer Responsibility. **Concern(s):** economics; boycott. Each dollar you spend is a vote in favor of a corporation or organization, its products or services, and its policies and practices. A magazine that reports on consumer-oriented boycotts designed to influence those policies and practices. Nonprofit. **Est.:** 1985. **Frequency:** Irregular. **Subscription:** 4/$10; $20 nonprofit; $40 corporations. **Price:** $3/ea. **Pages:** 196. **Circ.:** 8M. **Office:** 6506 28th Ave. NE Seattle, WA 98115. **Contact(s):** Todd Putnam (President), Timothy Muck (Secretary-Treasurer). (206)524-7726.

✍ ▸ **National Coalition News**
58 Schoolhouse Rd.
Summertown, TN 38483(615)964-3670
**Affiliation:** National Coalition of Alternative Community Schools. **Concern(s):** education. Keep up with what's happening around the Coalition and throughout the growing international alternative education network. Regular reports from the NCACS Board and National Office, articles from member schools, relevant reprints from other sources, letters from around the world, updates on legal battles over educational freedom, book reviews, resources for educators, writings by students, plus an active environmental section. Subscriptions available to parents, teachers, and students at NCACS. Nonprofit. **Est.:** 1975. **Frequency:** 4/yr. **Subscription:** $20; $10 to members. **Circ.:** 1.7M. **Publisher:** NCACS. **Contact(s):** Michael Traugot (Office Coordinator), Mary Ellen Bowen (News Editor).

A ▸ **National Gardening Magazine**
180 Flynn Ave.
Burlington, VT 05401
**Concern(s):** agriculture; horticulture. Articles, seed-to-table profiles of major crops; firsthand reports from experienced gardeners in this country's many growing regions; easy-to-follow gardening techniques; garden food recipes; coverage of fruits, vegetables, and ornamentals. **Contact(s):** Warren Schultz (Editor).

✍ ▸ **National Geographic Magazine**
17 & M St. NW
Washington, DC 20036 (202)857-7000
**Affiliation:** National Geographic Society. **Concern(s):** education; environment; environment; wildlife/endangered species; global understanding. First-person articles on geography, exploration, natural history, archeology, and science. Half staff written, half written by recognized authorities and published authors. **Frequency:** 12/yr.

✍ ▸ **National Geographic World**
1145 17th St. NW
Washington, DC 20036
**Concern(s):** education; youth; global understanding. Picture magazine for young readers, ages 8 and older. Proposals for picture stories only. No unsolicited manuscripts. **Contact(s):** Pat Robbins (Editor).

E ▸ **National News Report**
730 Polk St.
San Francisco, CA 94109 (415)923-5668
**Affiliation:** Sierra Club. **Concern(s):** environment. "Club activities and interests are the topic of this newsletter. It serves to bring the national environmental concerns community up to date more frequently, in between issues of the more feature-oriented Sierra magazine."-C.C. **Est.:** 1969. **Frequency:** 27/yr. **Subscription:** $15/yr. **Price:** Free. **Contact(s):** Anthony Antico.

F ▸ **National NOW Times**
1000 16th St. NW
Washington, DC 20036 (202)331-0066
**Affiliation:** National Organization for Women. **Concern(s):** feminism; politics; justice. "NOW has become the primary organization of choice (no pun intended) for people interested in defending and advancing the rights of women. The NOW Times does a great job of speaking for the women's movement as well as other public interest issues. This basic newspaper helps in national coalitions and demonstrations for labor and civil rights, in addition to playing a part in working for world peace."-C.C. **Est.:** 1968. **Frequency:** 6/yr. **Subscription:** $25/yr. **Price:** Donation. **Contact(s):** Sheri O'Dell.

E ▸ **National Parks**
1776 Massachusetts Ave. NW
Washington, DC 20036 (202)223-6722
**Affiliation:** National Parks and Conservation Association. **Concern(s):** environment; natural resources; wildlife/endangered species; conservation. A magazine dedicated exclusively to the preservation and promotion of US national parks through various forms of media in the school systems. Utilizing spectacular photography and incisive writing, this magazine explores the entire park system, from great natural parks and historical areas to wildlife activities and critical conservation issues. **Est.:** 1919. **Frequency:** 6/yr. **Subscription:** $25/yr. **Contact(s):** Paul C. Pritchard (President), Michael Strutin (Senior Editor).

J ▸ **The National Prison Project Journal**
ACLU Foundation
1875 Connecticut Ave. NW, #410
Washington, DC 20009
**Affiliation:** National Prison Project. **Concern(s):** justice; criminal system. "A project which seeks to strengthen and protect the rights of adult and juvenile offenders; to improve overall conditions in correctional facilities by using existing administrative, legislative, and judicial channels; and to develop alternatives to incarceration."-C.W. **Frequency:** 4/yr. **Subscription:** $25/yr.; $2 prisoners. **Pages:** 20. **Circ.:** 650.

J ▸ **National Self-Sufficiency**
Box 10
Forestville, CA 95436
**Affiliation:** Seventh Generation Fund. **Concern(s):** justice; Native Americans. "Single theme newsletter promoting tribal independence from the US government. Topics include civil rights, mineral rights, and general freedom for Native Americans."-C.C.

P ▸ **The National Voter**
League of Women Voters
1730 M St. NW
Washington, DC 20036 (202)429-1965
**Affiliation:** League of Women Voters. **Concern(s):** politics; feminism. A magazine featuring in-depth coverage of timely national issues on the league's agenda and accounts of grassroots action and lobbying nationwide. **Contact(s):** Nancy M. Newman (President), Grant P. Thompson (Executive Director).

E ▸ **National Wetlands Newsletter**
Environmental Law Institute
1616 P St. NW, #200
Washington, DC 20036 (202)328-5150
**Affiliation:** Environmental Law Institute. **Concern(s):** environment; politics; law; wetlands. A newsletter designed to serve scientists, policy makers, planners and conservationists at all levels of government and throughout the private sector. Features articles on the most recent developments in science, law, policy and regulation of wetlands, floodplains and coastal water resources. Nonprofit. **Frequency:** 6/yr. **Subscription:** $48/yr. **Contact(s):** J. William Futrell (President).

E ▸ **National Wildlife**
8925 Leesburg Pike
Vienna, VA 22184 (703)790-4510
**Affiliation:** National Wildlife Federation. **Concern(s):** environment; wildlife/endangered species; natural resources. "Our purpose is to promote the wise use of the nation's natural resources and to conserve and protect wildlife and its habitat. Our magazine reaches a broad audience that is largely interested in wildlife conservation and nature photography. We avoid too much scientific detail and prefer anecdotal, natural history material." **Est.:** 1963. **Frequency:** 12/yr. **Circ.:** 950M. **Contact(s):** Bob Strohm (Editor-in-chief), Mark Wexler (Editor).

E ▸ **National Woodlands Magazine**
374 Maple Ave. E
Vienna, VA 22180 (703)255-2700
**Affiliation:** National Woodland Owners Association. **Concern(s):** environment; forestry; conservation. It is devoted to reporting on the efforts to keep the forests non-industrialized. **Frequency:** 12/yr.

✎ ▸ **Native Arts Update**
ATLATL
402 W. Roosevelt
Phoenix, AZ 85003

**Concern(s):** arts. Newsletter.

### J ◆ Native Nations
175 5th Ave., #2245
New York, NY 10010
**Concern(s):** justice; Native Americans. New magazine features Native American news, quincentenary information, commentary, arts coverage, and film and book reviews. **Frequency:** 12/yr. **Subscription:** $20/yr.

### J ◆ Native Peoples Magazine, The Arts and Lifeways
1833 N. 3rd St.
Phoenix, AZ 85004          (602)252-2236
**Concern(s):** justice; arts; Third World; Native Americans; indigenous peoples. "The primary purpose of this magazine is to offer a sensitive portrayal of the arts and lifeways of native peoples of the Americas." Book excerpts, nostalgia, history, interviews, personal experiences, and photo features. **Est.:** 1987.

### J ◆ Native Self-Sufficiency
Box 10A, 6450 1st St.
Forestville, CA 95436
**Concern(s):** justice; environment; Native Americans. In-depth reporting on political and social issues affecting North American peoples from a Native perspective. This newsletter looks at ways of combining the best of Native values to preserve culture and environment for today and the future. **Frequency:** 4/yr. **Subscription:** $8/yr.

### A ◆ Natural Food and Farming
Box 210
Atlanta, GA 30301
**Affiliation:** Natural Food Associates. **Concern(s):** agriculture; health; education; organic; nutrition; preventative medicine; sustainability. Expect to find articles on health, nutrition, prevention medicine, environmental illnesses, organic farming, food preservation, sustainable agriculture, vitamins and minerals, and recipes galore in this magazine. **Dues:** $20/yr.; $55/3yrs; $300/life. **Frequency:** 12/yr. **Subscription:** Membership.

### H ◆ Natural Health
17 Station St., Box 1200
Brookline, MA 02147-0001  (800)666-8576
**Concern(s):** health; agriculture; environment; spiritual; organic; holism; transformation. "Provides a practical and information guide for leading a full, healthy, and harmonious life. It examines a wide range of complementary ideas: traditional and modern, Oriental and Occidental, intuitive and scientific, visionary and practical, and looks with care at frontiers and new ideas as well as at the wisdom of thinkers and cultures from the past. In this context, it explores the way natural foods, holistic health, alternative medicine, organic agriculture, deep ecology, and a balanced approach. **Other Resources:** Formerly EAST WEST: THE JOURNAL OF NATURAL HEALTH & LIVING. **Frequency:** 12/yr. **Subscription:** $18/yr.

### H ◆ Natural Health World
1920 N. Kilpatrick
Portland, OR 97217
**Concern(s):** health; spiritual; transformation; nutrition. This magazine deals with issues relevant to the "New Age" person. From health controversies to nutritional recipes you will be able to find it in this periodical. **Frequency:** 12/yr.

### ✍ ◆ Natural History Magazine
79th & Central Park W.
New York, NY 10024       (212)769-5100
**Affiliation:** American Museum of Natural History. **Concern(s):** education. "...translates the natural sciences into spectacular color photography and truly absorbing reading. From archeology to zoology, from inner man to outer space, its articles are both fascinating and easy to understand. A unique combination of visual beauty and scientific accuracy that explores, explains, defines, and depicts." **Est.:** 1900. **Frequency:** 12/yr. **Subscription:** $22/yr. **Contact(s):** Alan Ternes (Editor-in-chief).

### H ◆ Natural Living Newsletter
Box 849, Madison Sq. Station
New York, NY 10159
**Concern(s):** health; environment.

### E ◆ The Naturalist
De Young Press
Box 7252
Spencer, IA 51301
**Concern(s):** environment. Magazine.

### E ◆ Nature Conservancy
1815 N. Lynn St.
Arlington, VA 22209      (703)841-5300

**Concern(s):** environment; conservation; wildlife/endangered species. A magazine that documents the crises facing the rare and endangered species of this planet. It also focuses on how their habitat and ecosystem is effected and endangered. **Other Resources:** Izaak Walton League of America; Bio-Energy Council. (800)872-1899.

### ✍ ◆ Nature, Society, and Thought (NST)
University of Minnesota, Rm.148 Tate
116 Church St. SE
Minneapolis, MN 55455
**Concern(s):** education; environment. **Frequency:** 4/yr. **Subscription:** $15/yr.

### L ◆ NCL Bulletin
815 15th St. NW, #516
Washington, DC 20005  (202)639-8140
**Affiliation:** National Consumers League. **Concern(s):** labor; economics. "This group's bulletin is a first choice consumers selection because of its linking of consumers' and workers' issues. The NCL is the oldest such group and has lasted because of effective coverage of such topics. Highly recommended."-C.C. **Est.:** 1899. **Frequency:** 6/yr. **Subscription:** $20, $100 corporation. **Price:** $4/ea. **Contact(s):** Linda Golodner.

### $ ◆ NCLC Reports (National Consumer Law Center)
11 Beacon St.
Boston, MA 02108
**Affiliation:** National Consumer Law Center. **Concern(s):** economics; energy; consumer rights. Newsletter.

### M ◆ NCTV News
Box 2157
Champaign, IL 61824
**Affiliation:** National Coalition on Television Violence. **Concern(s):** media; economics; media watch; responsibility; boycott. This newsletter lists television shows, networks, and advertisers who are targeted for excessive violence. **Frequency:** 4/yr. **Contact(s):** Thomas Radecki, M.D. (Chairperson & Research Director).

### U ◆ Neighborhood Caretaker
1522 Grand Ave., #4C
St. Paul, MN 55105
**Concern(s):** urban; health; education; Third World; drugs; inner city; crime; substance abuse; seniors; conflict resolution; job training; Africa. For those who are looking for breakthrough methods and models for urban areas, this newsletter summarizes material from groups working on multidisciplinary approaches to neighborhood disorders: the gap between poor and middle class, adult illiteracy, job skills neglect, abandoned elders, alcoholism and depression and more. A unique information and networking tool for individuals and groups looking for collaborative and empowering methods. Worldwide focus with special focus on Africa. **Frequency:** 10/yr. **Contact(s):** Burt Dyson, Elizabeth Dyson (Editors).

### $ ◆ The Neighborhood Works
2125 W. North Ave.
Chicago, IL 60647          (312)278-4800
**Affiliation:** Center for Neighborhood Technology. **Concern(s):** economics; environment; energy; labor; politics; conservation; community self-reliance; grassroots organizing; worker ownership; community investment. "This newsletter covers environmental, economic development, energy, and affordable housing issues from a neighborhood point of view. It describes local approaches to meeting basic human needs: recycling, energy conservation, worker ownership, neighborhood reinvestment, community gardening. What's working in neighborhoods around the country?" **Est.:** 1978. **Frequency:** 8/yr. **Subscription:** $25/yr. **Price:** $3.50/ea. **Contact(s):** Mary O'Connell.

### J ◆ Network
806 Rhode Island Ave. NE
Washington, DC 20018  (202)526-4070
**Affiliation:** Network, National Catholic Social Justice Lobby. **Concern(s):** justice; politics; spiritual; faith; lobbying. This network attempts to influence Congress at the local level to enact laws that protect human rights internationally. This is an update on event on Capitol Hill. **Est.:** 1971. **Frequency:** 6/yr.

### F ◆ Network News
c/o National Women's Health Network
1325 G St. NW (lower level)
Washington, DC 20005  (202)347-1140
**Affiliation:** National Women's Health Network. **Concern(s):** feminism; health; nutrition; consumer protection. This newsletter with timely updates and in-depth reports on medical issues that affect women—in language all can understand. You will find information about osteoporosis, birth control, breast cancer, AIDS and other health

concerns, as well as book reviews, resources and schedules of upcoming conferences. **Other Resources:** Publishes NETWORK NEWS. **Est.:** 1975. **Dues:** $25+/yr. **Frequency:** 6/yr. **Subscription:** Membership. **Contact(s):** Olivia H. Cousins (Chair), Leslie Orloff.

### $ ◆ Network News
1729-31 Connecticut Ave. NW
Washington, DC 20009  (202)387-0194
**Affiliation:** National Self-Help Resource Center. **Concern(s):** economics; politics; justice; community self-reliance; grassroots community organizing. Newsletter. **Frequency:** 6/yr. **Contact(s):** Wayne Alexander.

### ❀ ◆ Network News
National War Tax Resistance Coordinating Committee
Box 85810
Seattle, WA 98145          (206)522-4377
**Affiliation:** National War Tax Resistance Coordinating Committee. **Concern(s):** peace; politics; war tax revolt. A newsletter for war tax resistance activists, counselors, and attorneys printed by the National War Tax Resistance Coordinating Committee, a clearinghouse and resource center for the conscientious war tax resistance movement in the US. **Other Resources:** Flyers, posters, a legal manual, slide show. **Est.:** 1982. **Frequency:** 6/yr. **Subscription:** $10/yr. **Price:** $.60/ea. **Contact(s):** Carolyn Stevens (Coordinator).

### E ◆ The Networker
Box 8731
Missoula, MT 59807        (406)721-5420
**Concern(s):** environment; bioregionalism; forests; wildlife/endangered species; wetlands. The quarterly newsletter of the Alliance for the Wild Rockies—a bioregional alliance of 110+ conservation organizations and businesses working to protects wildlands, wildlife habitat, and water quality in Montana, Idaho, Wyoming, Oregon, Washington, Alberta, and British Columbia. The Networker covers developments in federal lands, legislation, endangered species, forest management, and grassroots organizing. **Est.:** 1988. **Frequency:** 4/yr. **Subscription:** $15/yr. **Price:** Free. **Pages:** 24. **Circ.:** 3M. **Fax:** (406)721-5912. **Contact(s):** Mike Bader (Executive Director), Cass Chinske (President, Board of Directors).

### L ◆ Networking Newsletter
Provident Press
RR2 Box 233A
Monson, ME 04464
**Affiliation:** Backcountry Homeworker's Exchange. **Concern(s):** labor; feminism; economics; homeworkers. The Networking Newsletter has free ads for members and brief news clips of interest to women who work at home.

### ❀ ◆ The New Abolitionist
325 E. 25th St.
Baltimore, MD 21218      (301)235-3575
**Affiliation:** Nuclear Free America. **Concern(s):** peace; politics; disarmament; anti-nuclear; grassroots organizing. The New Abolitionist is the newsletter of Nuclear Free America, an international clearinghouse and resource center for Nuclear Free Zones (NFZs). It reports on local, national, and international NFZ campaigns and initiatives. **Frequency:** 4/yr. **Subscription:** $15/yr. **Pages:** 14. **Circ.:** 5M. **Publisher:** Nuclear Free America. **Contact(s):** Albert Donnay (Editor).

### H ◆ New Age Journal
342 Western Ave.
Brighton, MA 02135        (617)787-2005
**Concern(s):** health; education; economics; spiritual; holism; transformation. Articles on social change, environmental issues, personal growth, natural foods, holistic/alternative health, parenting and business. "Resources for New Age Living" is a special directory section of 25+ published as part of each issue. **Frequency:** 6/yr. **Pages:** 5. **Publisher:** Rising Star Associates. **Contact(s):** Jonathan Adolph (Senior Editor), Lisa Yane (Assistant Editor).

### M ◆ New Age Retailer
c/o Duane Sweeney
Box 224
Greenbank, WA 98253-0489(206)678-7772
**Concern(s):** media; press. A major review newsletter for New Age booksellers. **Contact(s):** Duane Sweeney (Editor).

### E ◆ The New Alchemy Quarterly
237 Hatchville Rd.
East Falmouth, MA 02536  (508)564-6301
**Affiliation:** New Alchemy Institute. **Concern(s):** environment; agriculture; sustainability; food production. This newsletter promotes sustainable agricultural systems that restore ecological balance and helps neighborhoods feed themselves. "Located on a 12-acre farm on Cape Cod, we have a range of research, education, and network-

ing programs that enhance environmental integrity and human well-being." **Other Resources:** New Alchemy Institute Catalogue - Books and products for Ecological Living ($3). Nonprofit. **Est.:** 1969. **Dues:** $35/yr. **Frequency:** 4/yr. **Subscription:** Membership. **Circ.:** 3M. **Contact(s):** Bill O'Neill (Public Information Coordinator).

**E ◆ The New Catalyst**
Box 99
Lillooet, BC V0K 1V0 Canada

**Concern(s):** environment; politics; peace; justice; Green; bioregionalism. The Fourth World, European Greens and Permaculture as well as news from the bioregions are included. West Canada's only rural-based review of art and opinion cover key issues and ideas of the 90's: The Environment; Local Control; Your Food and Water Quality; Regional Arts and Cultures; Green Politics; Bioregionalism; Eco-feminism; Native Rights; the Peace Movement; and more.

**E ◆ The New Crucible: A Magazine About Man and His Environment**
RR 1, Box 76
Stark, KS 66775-9802

**Concern(s):** environment. Aspires to be a magazine of understanding. "We will call attention to environmental factors and include here the social and psychological environment which is crucial to understanding the continuing argument between environment and heredity, and perhaps more honestly, the combination of the two." **Est.:** 1964. **Frequency:** 12/yr. **Subscription:** $24/yr. **Price:** $5/ea. **Bulk:** 40% off/24. **Pages:** 100. **Publisher:** Mary De Young - De Young Press. **Contact(s):** Garry De Young (Editor), Mary De Young (Publisher).

**F ◆ New Directions For Women**
108 W. Palisade Ave.
Englewood, NJ 07631

**Concern(s):** feminism; politics. The leading feminist news in the country, progressive and political feminist journalism at its best. Nonprofit. **Frequency:** 6/yr. **Subscription:** $12/yr.; $20 institution. **Pages:** 28.

**⚙ ◆ The New Economy**
National Commission for Economic Conversion & Disarmament
Box 15025
Washington, DC 20003 (202)544-5059

**Affiliation:** National Commission for Economic Conversion & Disarmament. **Concern(s):** peace; economic conversion; disarmament. This newsletter covers ways in which our economy could be converted from a war time stance to a peace time one. Reports on ways in which the government and organizations are trying to achieve this and the ways they are not. **Frequency:** 4/yr. **Office:** 1801 18th St. NW Washington, DC 20009. **Contact(s):** Seymour Melman (Program Director), Jonathan Feldman (National). (202)462-0091.

**✎ ◆ New England Review**
Middlebury College
Middlebury, VT 05753

**Concern(s):** arts; literature; poetry. Fiction, nonfiction, and poetry of varying lengths. "National, international, literary, political, effectively radical writing." **Contact(s):** T. R. Hummer (Editor), Devon Jersild (Associated Editor).

**L ◆ New Equity**
Box 1477
East Arlington, MA 02174-0022 (413)545-4875

**Affiliation:** 18. **Concern(s):** labor. "Workers' social democratic ownership of workplaces is a key focus here, with increased worker control of enterprises owned by others covered too. Workers wanting to reform private enterprise relations will find this journal useful. Formerly Workplace Democracy."-C.C. **Est.:** 1973. **Frequency:** 4/yr. **Subscription:** $18, $36 institution. **Price:** $5/ea. **Contact(s):** Julie Melrose, Rob Okun.

**A ◆ The New Farm**
Rodale Institute
222 Main St.
Emmaus, PA 18049

**Affiliation:** Rodale Institute. **Concern(s):** agriculture; environment; health; hazardous/toxic waste; nutrition; trade; pesticides; organic. This magazine is geared for the commercial farmer who wishes to become organic. It advocates responsible organic farming methods and practices. **Frequency:** 8/yr.

**T ◆ New Internationalist Magazine**
Box 1143, Lewiston
New York, NY 14092

**Concern(s):** Third World; politics; feminism; environment; peace; demographics; Green; Socialism; reform. This magazine focuses on one key global issue — debt, climate, Soviet Union, cars, Peru — every month. Winner of the Alternative Magazine awards - Best

International coverage. Originates in Britain and reports on world poverty, rich vs. poor, and current debates on the radical changes necessary to meet human basic needs. Issues have included: radical lifestyles, fear and violence, race in South Africa, the sexes, recycling, Sandanistas, religion, justice, socialism, and food. **Other Resources:** Employee cooperative. Free sample issues available. Also, Third World calendar, almanac, cards, recycled wrapping paper. Wholesale and retail. **Frequency:** 12/yr. **Subscription:** $36/yr.; $50 institutions. **Member:** Co-op America. **Contact(s):** Sue Shaw, Richard Swift, Co-editor. (416)588-6478.

**P ◆ New Left Review**
113 E. Centre St.
Nutley, NJ 07110

**Concern(s):** politics; alternative party. **Frequency:** 6/yr. **Subscription:** $28/yr. **Contact(s):** B. de Boer.

**☢ ◆ New Manhattan Project Newsletter**
15 Rutherford Pl.
New York, NY 10003 (212)598-0964

**Affiliation:** American Friends Service Committee. **Concern(s):** peace; disarmament. "The Quakers' concern about the nuclear arms race is reflected in this four-page newsletter. News, events, and issues are included."-C.C. **Est.:** 1978. **Frequency:** 6/yr. **Subscription:** $10/yr. **Price:** Free. **Contact(s):** Jenny Knight.

**P ◆ New Options**
Box 19324
Washington, DC 20036 (202)745-7460

**Concern(s):** politics; peace; environment; decentralization; networking. An intriguing "post-liberal and post-socialist" newsletter which investigates new ideas and approaches that go beyond those of the traditional left or right. Each issue reinterprets national and international news, looks critically at social change groups, political books, and includes an extremely high-energy "Forum" in which these new ideas are debated by readers. Reports on new possibilities with regards to creating a peaceful, just and decentralized world. Good networking and book reviews. **Other Resources:** No longer in print, but back issues are still available. **Contact(s):** Mark Satin (Editor).

**M ◆ New Pages**
Box 438
Grand Blanc, MI 48439 (313)743-8055

**Concern(s):** media. News, articles, and essays concerning alternatives in print and media. Resources, bibliographies, contact lists of social/economic/political change groups. Reviews books and periodicals from independent publishers. "The Magazine for Info-Maniacs": reviews alternative press books and periodicals and comments on the alternative press scene." -Craig Canan. **Other Resources:** Directory of distributors & mailing lists for US libraries and bookstores. **Est.:** 1981. **Frequency:** 3/yr. **Subscription:** $12/yr. **Price:** $5/ea. **Bulk:** 50% off/24. **Pages:** 80+. **Circ.:** 5M. **Fax:** (313)743-2730. **Contact(s):** Casey Hill (Publisher).

**E ◆ New Paradigm Digest**
c/o Earthtrends
1118 5th #1
Santa Monica, CA 90403 (310)393-2670

**Affiliation:** Earthtrends. **Concern(s):** environment; economics; trade; alternative consumer; green consumer. Earthtrends publishes New Paradigm Digest, a bi-monthly review of emerging social and business trends leading to a sustainable world. **Subscription:** $48, $96 for corporation. **Contact(s):** Jeff Hutner (Editor).

**P ◆ New Patriot**
202 S. State St., #1420
Chicago, IL 60604

**Concern(s):** politics; justice. Restoring America's revolution", elevates Nader, Jesse Jackson, Michael Harrington, Maggie Kuhn, John Conyers, Eleanor Smeal and others to the levels of Paine, Jefferson, Abe Lincoln, and Sojourner Truth and other early liberationists. Rossen, a two-time veteran, served as an advisor for the Students for a Democratic Society. This magazine includes important history lessons about the development of democracy in this country and elsewhere. **Frequency:** 6/yr. **Subscription:** $14.95/yr. **Contact(s):** John Rossen (Publisher/Editor).

**P ◆ New Perspectives Quarterly**
10951 W. Pico Blvd., #202
Los Angeles, CA 90064

**Concern(s):** politics; economics; justice. Diverse viewpoints exploring new ideas from important thinkers. **Frequency:** 4/yr. **Subscription:** $25/yr.

**✍ ◆ New Political Science**
Department of Political Science
Columbia University
New York, NY 10027 (212)581-5282

**Affiliation:** Caucus for a New Political Science. **Concern(s):** edu-

cation; politics. "More progressive uses for political science theories are suggested in these footnoted, scholarly pieces. This group is striving to extend the boundaries of discussion for the study of politics."-C.C. **Est.:** 1978. **Frequency:** 4/yr. **Subscription:** $20, $40 institution. **Price:** $5.50/ea. **Contact(s):** Florindo Velpacchio.

**P ◆ New Politics**
Box 98
Brooklyn, NY 11231

**Concern(s):** politics; alternative party. **Frequency:** 6/yr. **Subscription:** $28/yr.

**H ◆ New Realities**
Heldref Publications
4000 Albemarle St. NW
Washington, DC 20016 (202)362-6445

**Concern(s):** health; spiritual; holism; psychology. Designed for today's inquisitive readers, with topics ranging from holistic health to personal enhancement. From nutrition to creativity. From higher consciousness to ESP. From the tested to the unknown. And the messages, the lessons, and the meanings you'll find in this magazine will empower you at work, at home, at every level of relationship with the world around you by using the power of imagery, triggering an addiction curing experience, developing and using intuition. **Frequency:** 6/yr. **Subscription:** $23, $28 institutions.

**P ◆ The New Republic**
1220 19th St. NW
Washington, DC 20036 (202)331-7494

**Concern(s):** politics; Third World; peace; environment; arts; media. A liberal to left, intellectual magazine that comments on public affairs and the arts. Many excellent writer, tends to be pro-Israel and sometimes neo-conservative. **Frequency:** 48/yr. **Subscription:** $69.97/yr. **Circ.:** 100M.

**P ◆ New River Free Press**
Box 846
Blacksburg, VA 24060

**Concern(s):** politics. **Frequency:** 12/yr. **Subscription:** $4/yr.

**? ◆ New Sense (now Brain/Mind Bulletin)**
Interface Press
Box 42211
Los Angeles, CA 90042 .(213)223-2500

**Concern(s):** future; health; spiritual; education; psychology; ideation; science; research; transformation; holism; analysis. A newsletter "married to the art and poetry now known to illuminate the scientific quest" integrating scientific findings with promising leads and ideas in other arenas, providing practical tools for clarifying interrelationships between disciplines. "The dead horse in this case is the reductionist, linear paradigm that has dominated Western thought...Nature is biased toward evolution, spirit and imagination. It's time for the hidden agenda of sensible people to become the cultural mandate." **Other Resources:** Founder, Marilyn Ferguson, authored AQUARIAN CONSPIRACY and THE BRAIN REVOLUTION. Her new book, THE NEW COMMON SENSE: Secrets of the Visionary Life, is slated for early next year. **Est.:** 1975. **Frequency:** 12/yr. **Subscription:** $35/yr, $50 institution. **Price:** $3.75/ea. **Bulk:** Inquire. **Pages:** 4. **Circ.:** 10M. (800)553-MIND. **Contact(s):** Marilyn Ferguson (Founder/Executive Editor).

**J ◆ New Times**
738 Higuera St.
San Luis Obispo, CA 93401 (805)546-8208

**Concern(s):** justice; politics; environment; arts. Considered one of the best small city community newsweeklies, similar to the LA weekly. **Frequency:** Weekly. **Contact(s):** Steve Moss (Editor).

**$ ◆ New Wealth**
Box 9844
Santa Fe, NM 87504 (505)986-1401

**Affiliation:** Community Economic and Ecological Development Institute. **Concern(s):** economics; environment; education; health; agriculture; intentional communities; social ecology; bioregionalism; land trusts; holism; sustainability. This journal is devoted to reporting on the new wealth of communities, cooperation. Through cooperation communities can establish new economic interdependencies with other communities. **Frequency:** Annual. **Contact(s):** David Mulligan.

**F ◆ New Woman**
240 W. 37th. St.
New York, NY 10018 (212)947-2591

**Concern(s):** feminism; empowerment. Self-help/inspirational articles, on psychology, sex, relationships, money, careers. Travel features, with personal discovery angle. Lifestyle, health, and fitness features. Profiles of celebrities, business women. **Contact(s):** Karen Walden (Editor).

## J ◆ New World Times
625 Ashbury St. #14
San Francisco, CA 94117

**Concern(s):** justice; Native Americans. "A platform for the rebirth of the American Indian—their cry for justice and an end to genocide, NWT is a politically aware and environmentally focused tabloid newspaper offering an outlet for activists movements and the work of pioneering artists, whose words spill from our pages uncensored." **Frequency:** 4/yr. **Subscription:** 10/yr. **Pages:** 40.

## ✐ ◆ New York Review of Books
Box 940
Farmingdale, NY 11737

**Concern(s):** arts; media. Very intellectual left-wing political and literary newspaper. **Frequency:** 22/yr. **Subscription:** $37.50/yr.

## J ◆ New York University Review of Law & Social Change
110 W. 3rd St.
New York, NY 10012    (212)998-6370

**Affiliation:** NYU School of Law. **Concern(s):** justice; reform; criminal system; social justice. "Where the HRI Reporter focuses primarily on international cases, the NYU review is concerned more with US human rights issues. It is edited primarily for legal professionals and socially concerned law students."-C.C. **Est.:** 1969. **Frequency:** 4/yr. **Subscription:** $12/yr. **Price:** $5/ea. **Contact(s):** Milo Mumgaard, Carol Clifford.

## T ◆ News & Views
845 3rd Ave.
New York, NY 10022    (212)759-7982

**Affiliation:** Women's Environment & Development Organization. **Concern(s):** Third World; feminism; politics; foreign policy; sexism; discrimination; lobbying; law. This newsletter reports on legislation and foreign policy decisions that affect women here and around the world. **Frequency:** 12/yr. **Fax:** (212)759-8647. **Contact(s):** Mim Kelber.

## L ◆ News and Letters
59 E. Van Buren, #707
Chicago, IL 60605

**Concern(s):** labor. **Frequency:** 10/yr. **Subscription:** $2.50/yr.

## $ ◆ News from Aprovecho
80574 Hazeltine Rd.
Cottage Grove, OR 97424    (503)942-9434

**Affiliation:** Aprovecho Institute. **Concern(s):** economics; environment; health. This newsletter is deliberately produced by hand and hopes to plant the seeds and provide inspiration that will reach many more people. The articles are reader written. It came together without a formal theme, common threads run through most of its contents: Elements of a vision for remaking society so that our lives are more human, natural, ecological, and sustainable. Whether in food or agriculture, housing, cross-cultural understanding, how-to's, human relations, it offers alternatives. **Frequency:** 5/yr. **Subscription:** $15/yr. **Pages:** 6. **Circ.:** 500. **Contact(s):** Linda Smiley.

## M ◆ News Media and the Law
1735 I St. NW
Washington, DC 20006    (202)466-6313

**Affiliation:** Reporters Committee for Freedom of the Press. **Concern(s):** media; justice; press; constitutional rights; civil liberties. "The First Amendment of the Bill of Rights is defended by these reporters, with the emphasis on legal defense. This is a useful periodical for investigative reporters and civil libertarians working for a free press."-C.C. **Est.:** 1977. **Frequency:** 4/yr. **Subscription:** $20/yr. **Price:** $5/ea. **Contact(s):** Jane E. Kirtley.

## T ◆ News Notes
Maryknoll Justice and Peace
Maryknoll, NY 10545    (914)941-7590

**Affiliation:** Maryknoll Justice and Peace Office. **Concern(s):** Third World; spiritual; Africa; Central America; hunger; faith. "Liberation theology is the doctrine these dedicated missionaries subscribe to, as they help Third World countries to be self-sustaining and self-determining. From the battle areas of Central America to the famine-stricken areas of Africa, these women and reports on conditions in those places in this colorful, slick, TV Guide-size magazine."-C.C. **Est.:** 1976. **Frequency:** 6/yr. **Subscription:** $10/yr. **Price:** Donation.

## J ◆ Newsbriefs
330 7th Ave., #10N
New York, NY 10001    (212)629-6170

**Affiliation:** Lawyers Committee for International Human Rights. **Concern(s):** justice. "Defense of victims of human rights abuses, often pro bono, is the point. Deportations and foreign violations are typical topics in Newsbriefs."-C.C. **Est.:** 1986. **Dues:** $30/yr. **Frequency:** 4/yr. **Subscription:** Membership. **Price:** $7.50/ea. **Contact(s):** Mitchell Hartman.

## H ◆ Newservice
Box 21126
Phoenix, AZ 85036-1126

**Affiliation:** Do It Now Foundation. **Concern(s):** health. Newsletter. **Frequency:** 6/yr. **Subscription:** $20/yr.

## ✍ ◆ Newsletter of Americans for the University of UNESCO
Box 18418
Asheville, NC 28814

**Concern(s):** education.

## M ◆ Newsletter on Intellectual Freedom
50 E. Huron St.
Chicago, IL 60611    (312)944-6780

**Affiliation:** Intellectual Freedom Commission of the American Library Association. **Concern(s):** media; justice; civil liberties; censorship; freedom of expression. "For years librarians and civil libertarians have depended on this important periodical for information for fighting censorship. Articles on book-banning attempts and pertinent legislation, and general articles on the subject, make this a periodical every concerned librarian and reader will want to consider adding to his or her reading list."-C.C. **Est.:** 1952. **Frequency:** 6/yr. **Subscription:** $25/yr. **Price:** $5/ea. **Contact(s):** Judith F. Krug.

## P ◆ Newsweek
444 Madison Ave.
New York, NY 10022    (800)631-1040

**Concern(s):** politics; media. Mainstream liberal news magazine.

## E ◆ Nexus
39 S. Main St.
Ipswich, MA 01938    (508)356-0038

**Affiliation:** Atlantic Center for the Environment. **Concern(s):** environment; urban; future; activism; networking. This periodical helps build links between our culture and the environmental problems facing it. Nonprofit. **Est.:** 1963. **Dues:** $25-$500/yr. **Pages:** 12-20. **Circ.:** 6M. **E-Network:** Econet. **ID:** 'atantictr'. **Fax:** (508)356-7322. **Contact(s):** Brent Mitchell (Director/Conservation & Communications).

## T ◆ NGO Networker
1709 New York Ave. NW, #700
Washington, DC 20006    (202)638-6300

**Affiliation:** World Resources Institute. **Concern(s):** Third World; environment; agriculture; hunger; development/relations; foreign policy; air pollution; biotechnology. Provides information and a bulletin board for many private voluntary organizations working in relief and development. **Frequency:** 4/yr.

## T ◆ Nicaragua Information Center Bulletin
Box 1004
Berkeley, CA 94701    (510)549-1387

**Affiliation:** Nicaragua Information Center. **Concern(s):** Third World; Central America. "News of improvements in Nicaraguan society, contra destruction and US Congressional action make this newsletter a good source of information on that country. Suggestions for action are also helpful."-C.C. **Est.:** 1983. **Frequency:** 6/yr. **Subscription:** Donation. **Price:** Free.

## T ◆ Nicaragua Network News
1247 E St. SE
Washington, DC 20003    (202)544-9355

**Affiliation:** Nicaragua Network. **Concern(s):** Third World; Central America. "Probably the one best source of news from the front lines on struggle of the Nicaraguan people. Sister city projects, material aid campaigns and peace and development efforts are just a few topics included."-C.C. **Est.:** 1987. **Frequency:** 6/yr. **Subscription:** $10/yr. **Price:** Free. Hotline: (202)223-6422. **Contact(s):** Linda Clements.

## T ◆ Nicaragua Update
942 Market St., #706
San Francisco, CA 94102-4008    (415)433-6057

**Affiliation:** Nicaragua Interfaith Committee for Action. **Concern(s):** Third World; spiritual; interfaith. "Solidarity of clergy and laity with the people of Nicaragua is organized through this periodical. The other countries of the region are also featured."-C.C. **Est.:** 1979. **Frequency:** 6/yr. **Subscription:** $12/yr. **Price:** Donation. **Contact(s):** Janine Chagoya.

## E ◆ NIRS Alert
1424 16th St. NW, #601
Washington, DC 20036    (202)328-0002

**Affiliation:** Nuclear Information & Resource Service. **Concern(s):** environment. "Proposed regulations and new legislation concerning nuclear power are noted. The hope is that readers will use the information either to keep the plants shut down or to make them less unsafe."-C.C. **Est.:** 1975. **Frequency:** 12/yr. **Subscription:** $20/yr. **Price:** Donation.

## J ◆ NLADA Cornerstone
1625 K St. NW, 8th Fl.
Washington, DC 20006    (202)452-0620

**Affiliation:** National Legal Aid & Defender Association. **Concern(s):** justice; welfare rights. "Ensuring the right to decent legal representation for poor people is the goal. Legal rulings on tenant, welfare, and other basic rights are noted."-C.C. **Est.:** 1977. **Frequency:** 5/yr. **Subscription:** $20/yr. **Price:** $5/ea.

## A ◆ NOFA-Notes
15 Barre St.
Montpelier, VT 05602-3504    (802)223-7222

**Affiliation:** Natural Organic Farmers Association. **Concern(s):** agriculture; health; organic. This newsletter focuses on organic farming practices and the activities of organic farmers. Nonprofit. **Est.:** 1971. **Dues:** $20/yr. **Frequency:** 4/yr. **Subscription:** Membership. **Pages:** varies. **Contact(s):** Enid Wonnacott (Coordinator), Cherie Morse (Administration Assistant).

## F ◆ No Longer Silent
Box 3582
Tucson, AZ 85722

**Concern(s):** feminism; demographics; pro-choice; family planning; empowerment; population growth; battered women. A magazine of anarchy and feelings. Inside there are collages, clippings, statistics on battered women, notes on the black flag, and first person screams of anger and concern. A less intellectual than usual approach that has room for life and poetry. **Price:** $1.50/ea. **Contact(s):** Eliza Blackweb.

## J ◆ Nolo News
950 Parker St.
Berkeley, CA 94710    (510)549-1976

**Affiliation:** NOLO Press. **Concern(s):** justice; economics; reform; civil liberties; self-determination; taxation. Articles on legal topics of interest to self helpers and general public— also lawyer jokes. **Est.:** 1980. **Frequency:** 4/yr. **Subscription:** $7/yr. **Price:** $2/ea. **Publisher:** Nolo Press. **Contact(s):** Ralph Warner, Steve Elias (Associate Publisher). (510)549-2001.

## T ◆ Nommo
308 Westwood Plaza #112 C
Los Angeles, CA 90024

**Concern(s):** Third World; politics; justice; Africa; South Africa; anti-authoritarian; political prisoners. "This is the magazine of the African Students at UCLA with a revolutionary perspective and an interest in prison struggle."-Prison News Service.

## P ◆ The Nonviolent Activist
War Resisters League
339 Lafayette St.
New York, NY 10012    (212)228-0450

**Affiliation:** War Resisters League. **Concern(s):** politics; feminism; peace; economics. A magazine with political analysis from a pacifist perspective, feature articles, and information relating to nonviolence, feminism, disarmament, international issues, resistance to registration & draft, war tax resistance, counter-recruitment and more. **Other Resources:** Review & resource listings included. **Frequency:** 8/yr. **Subscription:** $15, $25 institution. **Price:** $1.50/ea. **Bulk:** Call. **Pages:** 24. **Circ.:** 16M. **Publisher:** War Resisters League. **Contact(s):** Ruth Benn (Editor), David McReynolds.

## ✺ ◆ Nonviolent Sanctions
1430 Massachusetts Ave., 6th Fl.
Cambridge, MA 02138    (617)876-0311

**Affiliation:** Albert Einstein Institution. **Concern(s):** peace; politics; nonviolence; activism. This newsletter supports work on the strategic uses of nonviolent sanctions in relation to problems of political violence. Independent and nonsectarian, it does not endorse political candidates and is not an advocate of any political organization. Nonprofit. **Est.:** 1983. **Frequency:** 4/yr. **Subscription:** $5/yr. **Price:** $2/ea. **Pages:** 8. **Circ.:** 1M. **Fax:** (617)876-0837. **Contact(s):** Roger S. Powers (Editor).

## ✺ ◆ North American Christian Peace Conference Newsletter
777 UN Plaza, #1
New York, NY 10017-3521    (516)223-1880

**Affiliation:** North American Christian Peace Conference. **Concern(s):** peace; justice; spiritual; disarmament; faith. Reports on the activities of the North American Christian Peace Conference and its parent organization, the "Global Christian Peace Conference." It is not only limited to North America but the world in its reporting. **Other Resources:** See listing under organizations. Nonprofit. **Est.:** 1958. **Dues:** $25; $100/donor. **Subscription:** Membership. **Fax:** (516)223-1880. **Contact(s):** Philip Oke (Executive Secretary).

**A ▸ The North American Farmer**
Box 102
Covert, MI 49043-0102
**Affiliation:** North American Farm Alliance. **Concern(s):** agriculture; politics; Third World; labor; environment; feminism; eco ; health; hazardous/toxic waste; hunger; sustainability; rural communities; family farms. "Family farmers are supported in the 8 pages of this tabloid newspaper. Networking and coalition-building with other groups for family farms are key goals."-C.C. Provides news and analysis to the movement for progressive family farm agriculture in the US, Canada and other countries. **Est.:** 1984. **Frequency:** 12/yr. **Subscription:** $10/yr. **Price:** $1/ea. **Contact(s):** Carol Hodne.

**✐ ▸ North American Review**
University of Northern Iowa
Cedar Falls, IA 50614 (319)266-8487
**Concern(s):** arts; environment; poetry; literature; culture. Poetry, fiction, articles, reviews, long-poems, and nonfiction with an environmental theme. **Est.:** 1815. **Frequency:** 4/yr. **Subscription:** $14/yr. **Price:** $4/ea. **Pages:** 72. **Circ.:** 5M. **Contact(s):** Robley Wilson. (319)273-2681.

**J ▸ Northeast Indian Quarterly**
300 Caldwell Hall
Cornell University
Ithaca, NY 14853 (607)255-1923
**Affiliation:** American Indian Program, Cornell University. **Concern(s):** justice; environment; politics; Native Americans. The work of poets and artists working in a Native tradition, appealing to anyone who has a genuine interest about how the indigenous perspective can affect today's issues and how Native peoples can take the lead in developing a new philosophy toward the environment that can translate into public policy. Magazine. **Frequency:** 4/yr. **Subscription:** $15/yr. **Bulk:** 40% off/24. **Pages:** 50. **Circ.:** 850. **Publisher:** American Indian Program - Cornell University. **Contact(s):** Jose Barrero (Editor), Susan Dixon (Managing Editor). (607)255-4308.

**H ▸ Northeast Transcultural Health Newsletter**
Katahdin AHEC
1 Coburn Hall
Orono, ME 04469
**Concern(s):** health.

**E ▸ Northern Lights**
Box 8084
Missoula, MT 59807-8084
**Concern(s):** environment. Thoughtful articles about the contemporary West. Occasional fiction. "We're open to virtually any subject as long as it deals with our region (the Rocky Mountains) in some way." **Contact(s):** Donald Snow (Editor).

**E ▸ The Northern Line**
Northern Alaska Environmental Center
218 Driveway
Fairbanks, AK 99701
**Affiliation:** Northern Alaska Environmental Center. **Concern(s):** environment; polar. Environmental news of Arctic and Interior Alaska. Nonprofit. **Dues:** $25/yr. **Frequency:** 4/yr. **Subscription:** Membership. **Contact(s):** Marie Beaver (Editor/Development Coordinator), Trudy Heffernan (Office Manager).

**☮ ▸ Northern Sun News**
1519 E. Franklin Ave.
Minneapolis, MN 55404 (612)874-1540
**Affiliation:** Mobilization for Survival. **Concern(s):** peace; energy; Third World; environment; justice; anti-nuclear; disarmament; volunteers. Northern Sun Alliance is a volunteer-based membership organization formed to halt the spread of nuclear plants and weapons. It demands the development of community-controlled, renewable sources of energy, supports the principal of self-determination for people, and promotes a world view of society based on cooperation and equality. **Est.:** 1977. **Frequency:** 11/yr. **Price:** Free. **Bulk:** Call. **Pages:** 12-16. **Circ.:** 15M. **Publisher:** same. **Contact(s):** Henry Fieldseth (Coordinator).

**E ▸ Northwest Conservation: News and Priorities**
c/o Greater Ecosystem Alliance
Box 2813
Belsingham, WA 98227 (206)671-9950
**Affiliation:** Greater Ecosystem Alliance. **Concern(s):** environment; conservation; bioregionalism. G&E promotes protection of biological diversity through the conservation of greater ecosystems. "Since these concepts are relatively new, our work requires education, research, and advocacy. Our efforts to sustain biodiversity focus on conserving the greater North Cascades, Selkirk, Olympic and Central Cascades, ecosystems." Newsletter. **Other Resources:** Publication, FOREVER WILD. Nonprofit. **Est.:** 1989. **Dues:** $15/yr. **Frequency:** 4/yr. **Subscription:** $15/yr. **Pages:** 16. **Circ.:** 600. **Fax:** (206)671-8429. **Contact(s):** Mitch Friedman (Executive Director), Mary Cutbill (Office Manager).

**E ▸ Not Man Apart**
Friends of the Earth
218 D St. SE
Washington, DC 20003 (202)544-2600
**Affiliation:** Friends of the Earth. **Concern(s):** environment. "Friends is one of the most progressive and effective environmental groups. Both activists and inquisitive citizens will enjoy the mix of action news and information articles."-C.C. Magazine.

**E ▸ NRCA News**
801 Pennsylvania Ave. SE, #410
Washington, DC 20003 (202)547-7553
**Affiliation:** Natural Resources Council of America. **Concern(s):** environment; natural resources. A newsletter that reports on the actions and efforts of the Natural Resources council of America.

**E ▸ NRDC Newsline**
40 West 20th St.
New York, NY 10011-4211 (212)727-2700
**Affiliation:** Natural Resources Defense Council. **Concern(s):** environment; energy; demographics; wilderness; population growth; conservation; natural resources; wildlife/endangered species. This newsletter of the Natural Resources Defense Council focuses on many issue facing our planet today. These topics include rainforests, AIDS, overpopulation, and many more. **Est.:** 1981. **Frequency:** 5/yr. **Subscription:** $10/yr. **Fax:** (212)727-1773. **Contact(s):** Susan Henriksen (Editor). **Other:** 1350 New York Ave. NW, Washington, DC 20005(202)783-7800.

**☮ ▸ Nuclear Alert**
1187 Coast Village Rd.
Santa Barbara, CA 93108 (805)965-3443
**Affiliation:** Nuclear Age Peace Foundation. **Concern(s):** peace; disarmament. A newsletter that raises public awareness of the dangers of accidental nuclear war. Encourages steps to reduce those risks through informative and controversial articles. **Est.:** 1982. **Subscription:** $35/yr. **Contact(s):** David Krieger (President).

**✪ ▸ Nuclear Chronicle**
c/o Sara Shannon
Box 20170, Tompkin Station
New York, NY 10009 (212)674-1659
**Affiliation:** Tellus Research Program. **Concern(s):** energy; peace; anti-nuclear. A comprehensive discussion of all aspects of nuclear industry as it affects the habitability of the Earth and human health. It includes resources and reviews. Nonprofit. **Est.:** 1990. **Frequency:** 4/yr. **Price:** Donation. **Pages:** 8. **Circ.:** 4M. **Fax:** (212)674-1659. **Contact(s):** Sara Shannon.

**✪ ▸ Nuclear Power in Crisis**
77 Homewood Ave.
Allendale, NJ 07401 (201)327-3914
**Affiliation:** Women's International Coalition to Stop Making Radioactive Waste. **Concern(s):** energy; environment; peace; politics; anti-nuclear; social ecology; appropriate technology; government accountability; corporate responsibility. This newsletter exposes deceit and corruption behind the nuclear power/weapons/space program. Development of clean free energy (electro-gravitic-magnetic). Promotes the philosophy of "voluntary simplicity" which was espoused by Duane Elgin in his book by the same title. **Frequency:** 26/yr. **Subscription:** $10/yr. **Price:** Free. **Pages:** 2. **Circ.:** 1.5M. **Contact(s):** Larry Bogart (Coordinator), Karen Westdyk (Director). (201)728-2395.

**☮ ▸ The Nuclear Resister**
Box 43383
Tucson, AZ 85733 (602)323-8697
**Concern(s):** peace; anti-nuclear; activism. A comprehensive newsletter chronicle of anti-nuclear and anti-war civil disobedience focusing on providing support for the women and men imprisoned as a result of such actions. Also a clearinghouse and networking center for information about nonviolent direct action in the anti-nuclear movement. **Other Resources:** Compilation of annual statistics on incidence of protest arrests on nuclear issues. Available for interviews and public speaking, and can refer speakers in local areas on issues related to anti-nuclear resistance. **Est.:** 1980. **Frequency:** Every 6 weeks. **Subscription:** $18/10 issues. **Price:** Free sample. **Pages:** 8. **Circ.:** 1M. **Contact(s):** Jack Cohen-Joppa, Felice Cohen-Joppa (Editors/Publishers).

**☮ ▸ Nuclear Times**
401 Commonwealth Ave.
Box 351, Kenmore Station
Boston, MA 02215
**Concern(s):** peace; future; environment; justice; economics; conflict resolution; economic conversion; peace dividend; ideation. A magazine examining the impact of military policies on human rights, the environment, and economic justice. Reports on the new thinking that will bring real security to our world—development of a sustainable global economy, building ecological societies, designing alternatives to military solutions in conflict resolution, and creating a demilitarized world. **Other Resources:** Nuclear issues, grassroots actions, and activism. **Frequency:** 4/yr. **Contact(s):** Richard Healey (Executive Director), Leslie Fraser (Editor). (617)266-1193. **Other:** 298 Fifth Ave., Room 512, New York, NY 10001.

**☮ ▸ Nucleus**
26 Church St.
Cambridge, MA 02238 (617)547-5552
**Affiliation:** Union of Concerned Scientists. **Concern(s):** peace; energy; disarmament; anti-nuclear. Scientists present facts arguing against nuclear weapons and for peace. From one of the largest and most effective of the professional groups working to end the nuclear arms race, it covers energy policy, national security, and in general, the impact of technology on society. **Other Resources:** Books, reports, briefing papers, videos, educational curricula. **Est.:** 1969. **Frequency:** 4/yr. **Subscription:** $15/yr. **Price:** Donation. **Pages:** 8-12. **Circ.:** 80M. **Fax:** (617)864-9405. **Contact(s):** Steven Krauss (Senior Editor), Warren Leon (Director of Public Education).

**☮ ▸ Nukewatch Pathfinder**
Box 2658
Madison, WI 53701-2658 (608)256-4146
**Affiliation:** Progressive Foundation. **Concern(s):** peace; environment; boycott; civil disobedience; nonviolence; anti-nuclear. This newsletter details events, actions, and ideas relating to nuclear disarmament campaigns in the US and abroad. **Other Resources:** See Nukewatch under organizations. **Frequency:** 6/yr. **Contact(s):** Samuel H. Day, Jr., Bonnie Urfer (Co-directors).

**H ▸ Nutrition Action Healthletter**
1875 Connecticut Ave. NW, #300
Washington, DC 20009-5728 (202)332-9110
**Affiliation:** Center for Science in the Public Interest. **Concern(s):** health; agriculture; nutrition; organic. This newsletter covers information on food additives, labeling, and organic agriculture. Nonprofit. **Est.:** 1971. **Dues:** $20/yr. **Frequency:** 10/yr. **Subscription:** $20/yr. **Price:** $2/ea. **Pages:** 16. **Circ.:** 250M. **Fax:** (202)265-4954. **Contact(s):** Richard Layman (Marketing Director).

**☮ ▸ NVC Newsletter**
Friends Peace Committee
1501 Cherry St.
Philadelphia, PA 19102
**Affiliation:** Friends Peace Committee. **Concern(s):** peace; spiritual; interfaith.

**☮ ▸ Objector**
Box 42249
San Francisco, CA 94142 (415)552-6433
**Affiliation:** Central Committee for Conscientious Objectors. **Concern(s):** peace; politics; justice; education; activism; anti-draft. "The CCCO promotes opposition to military service and covers related issues such as war taxes in their newsletter. The draft is a key concern."-C.C. **Est.:** 1980. **Frequency:** 9/yr. **Subscription:** $15/yr. **Price:** $2/ea. **Contact(s):** Ann Wrixon.

**L ▸ Occupational & Health Magazine**
Stevens Publishing
225 N. New Rd., Box 7573
Waco, TX 76714
**Concern(s):** labor; health; occupational safety.

**E ▸ Ocean Magazine**
Friends of the Earth
218 D St. SE
Washington, DC 20003 (202)544-2600
**Affiliation:** Friends of the Earth. **Concern(s):** environment; ocean/rivers. "Maintaining the world's seas and oceans as safe resources for plants, sea creatures and humans is the goal. Preservation of ocean species and chemically safe water are key points."-C.C. **Est.:** 1987. **Frequency:** 12/yr. **Subscription:** $15/yr. **Price:** Donation. **Contact(s):** John G. Catena.

**E ▸ Oceans Policy News**
1709 New York Ave. NW, #700
Washington, DC 20006 (202)347-3766
**Affiliation:** Council on Ocean Law. **Concern(s):** environment; ocean/rivers. This newsletter deals with important policy decisions that are taking effect in our nation and world today. It also reports on the actions of the Council. **Frequency:** 12/yr. **Contact(s):** Lee A. Kimball (Executive Director). (202)347-3766.

**F ▸ Off Our Backs**
2423 18th St. NW, 2nd Fl.
Washington, DC 20009 (202)234-8072

**Concern(s):** feminism. National feminist news journal dedicated to showcasing women's struggle in the work place along with the home. "Consider ourselves a radical feminist news journal, with complete coverage of national and international news about women. Free to prisoners." **Frequency:** 12/yr. **Subscription:** $15, $30 institution. **Price:** $2/ea. **Bulk:** 40% off/5. **Pages:** 36. **Circ.:** 22M. **Contact(s):** Carol Anne Douglas.

**E ▸ The Official RPG Reporter**
American Recycling Market
Box 577
Ogdensburg, NY 13669 (800)267-0707
**Affiliation:** American Recycling Market. **Concern(s):** environment; economics; recycling; green consumer. A newsletter focusing on the recycled products industry. **Est.:** 1985. **Frequency:** 12/yr. **Subscription:** $75/yr. **Fax:** (315)471-3258. **Contact(s):** Mike Fraser.

**E ▸ Olympic Ancient Forest Report**
Box 950
Port Townsend, WA 98368 (206)385-4214
**Concern(s):** environment; forests. Newsletter.

**? ▸ Omni**
1965 Broadway
New York, NY 10023-5965 (212)496-6100
**Concern(s):** future; energy; environment; education; ideation; science. This magazine covers "all branches of science with an emphasis on the future: What will this discovery or technique mean to us next year, in five years, or even by the year 2010? People want to know, want to understand what scientists are doing and how scientific research is affecting their lives and their future. It publishes articles about science in language that people can understand. We seek very knowledgeable science writers who are ready to work with scientists and futurists."

**☮ ▸ On Gogol Boulevard**
62-151 1st Ave.
New York, NY 10003 (718)499-7720
**Concern(s):** peace; activism; East-West. Networking bulletin for activists East and West. Nonprofit. **Subscription:** $5/4 issues. **Contact(s):** Bob McGlynn, William Falk

**J ▸ On Guard**
175 5th Ave., #808
New York, NY 10010 (212)777-3470
**Affiliation:** Citizen Soldier. **Concern(s):** justice; peace. "The military should respect the rights of its members" is the precept of these soldiers. Atomic veterans and peace activists in the military are two constituencies featured."-C.C. Nonprofit. **Est.:** 1975. **Frequency:** 4-5/yr. **Subscription:** $10/yr. **Price:** $.50/ea. **Contact(s):** Tod Ensign.

**✍ ▸ On the Beam**
New Horizons for Learning
4649 Sunnyside North
Seattle, WA 98103
**Affiliation:** New Horizons for Learning. **Concern(s):** education. "...is the journal of New Horizons for Learning, a nonprofit, international network of educators and others interested in education reform. On the Beam contains leading-edge research and strategies, reports on successful education innovations and on influential international conferences. Subscribers receive three 16-page issues yearly plus notification of NHFL-sponsored events." Nonprofit. **Dues:** $20/yr. **Frequency:** 3/yr. **Subscription:** Membership.

**F ▸ On the Issues: The Journal of Substance for Progressive Women**
Box 3000, Dept. OTI
Denville, NJ 07834 (718)275-6020
**Concern(s):** feminism; politics; health; environment; empowerment; activism; animal rights. "For ideas and opinions too controversial for the mainstream media, this magazine discusses feminism, politics, health, social reform, animal rights, ecology, global humanism, and more with thoughtful, unexpurgated insight. Kate Millet, Rep. Pat Schroeder, Andrea Dworkin, Flo Kennedy, Petra Kelly, and others." **Frequency:** 4/yr. **Subscription:** $14.75/yr.; $24.75 institutions. **Pages:** 44. **Circ.:** 50M. **Office:** 97-77 Queens Blvd. Forest Hills, NY 11374. **Contact(s):** Merle Hoffman (Editor-in-Chief), Beverly Lowy (Managing Editor).

**✍ ▸ On the Line**
616 Walnut
Scottdale, PA 15683-1999
**Concern(s):** education; arts; environment; youth; poetry; childhood. Weekly paper for 10- to 14-year-olds. Uses nature and how-to articles, fiction, poetry, puzzles, cartoons. **Contact(s):** Mary Clemens Meyer (Editor).

**J ▸ On Watch**
1168 Union, #201
San Diego, CA 92101 (619)233-1701
**Affiliation:** National Lawyers Guild Military Law Task Force. **Concern(s):** justice; peace; anti-draft. "The rights of citizens vis-a-vis the military are the point. Legal draft resistance and rights of service people and veterans are also covered. The half dozen articles cover in depth the concerns of this task force. Anyone working in the area of GI or draft rights will benefit."-C.C. **Est.:** 1977. **Frequency:** 6/yr. **Subscription:** $10, $15 institution. **Price:** $1.50/ea. **Contact(s):** Kathleen Gilbert, Charles T. Bumer

**☮ ▸ One Family**
325 North St.
San Francisco, CA 94103 (916)926-2241
**Affiliation:** Planetary Citizens. **Concern(s):** peace; environment; education; activism; world order. This newsletter reports on the group Planetary Citizen. It contains information on how the group is trying to educate the people and stimulate their curiosity into a common world government. **Contact(s):** Norman Cousins (deceased) (Chairman), Donald Keys (President).

**P ▸ One Person's Impact**
Box 751
Westborough, MA 01581 (508)366-0146
**Concern(s):** politics; economics; environment; education; environment; activism; grassroots organizing. Dedicated to teaching about environmental and social responsibility. Newsletter, special reports, workshops and lectures, information network. "Our goal is to convince others to believe what we are convinced is true - that all life is connected and every person - at home, at work, at play - can make a difference." **Other Resources:** Information network to subscribers, special reports such as CHANGING DIAPERS; ONE KID'S IMPACT; EARTH YEAR ACTION GUIDE. **Est.:** 1989. **Frequency:** 6/yr. **Subscription:** $24, $100 corporations. **Pages:** 8. **Circ.:** 1.5M. **Contact(s):** Maria Valenti (President/Publisher).

**P ▸ Onionhead**
Arts on the Park, Inc.
115 N. Kentucky Ave.
Lakeland, FL 33801
**Concern(s):** politics; arts; culture. Short stories, essays, and poetry on provocative social, political, and cultural observations and hypotheses.

**P ▸ The Open Road**
Box 6135, Station G
Vancouver, BC V6R 4G5 Canada
**Affiliation:** Vancouver News Group. **Concern(s):** politics; feminism; environment; justice; anti-authoritarian; Green; political prisoners. Deals with all popular struggles that possess an anti-authoritarian slant. Feminism, community organizing, prisons, ecology, and much more. **Est.:** 1976. **Frequency:** 3/yr. **Subscription:** $25/yr. institutions. **Price:** $1.50/ea.

**$ ▸ Opportunity Evaluation Newsletter**
Box 150
Logan, UT 84321
**Concern(s):** economics. Lists current business opportunities available to the public giving an objective appraisal and other information to help you know which, if any, are for you.

**✏ ▸ Option**
2345 Westwood Blvd., #2
Los Angeles, CA 90064
**Concern(s):** arts; music. "The top all-around music mag in the states today"-Whole Earth Catalog. "A valuable service for anyone not satisfied with the standard music press"-Trouser Press Record Guide. "Covers an immense variety of music"-Utne Reader. "Reviews of hundreds of albums and cassettes each issue"-New York Times. "A vibrant report on new frontiers of music"-Library Journal. "Excellent"-Rolling Stone. **Frequency:** 6/yr. **Subscription:** $15/yr.

**✍ ▸ Options in Learning**
AllPIE
Box 59
East Chatham, NY 12060 (518)392-6900
**Affiliation:** Alliance for Parental Involvement in Education. **Concern(s):** education; childhood. A newsletter of the Alliance, offering parents information about educational options, resources, book and product reviews, support, and encouragement. **Other Resources:** Book and Resources Catalog; workshops, speakers, conferences, pamphlets, and referral service. Nonprofit. **Est.:** 1989. **Dues:** Donation - $20/yr. **Frequency:** 4/yr. **Subscription:** $5-20/donation. **Pages:** 16. **Contact(s):** Seth Rockmuller, Katherine Houk (Co-editors).

**P ▸ Oral History of the American Left**
70 Washington Square S
New York, NY 10012 (212)998-2630
**Affiliation:** Elmer Holmes Bobst Library, NYU. **Concern(s):** politics; education. "This occasional bulletin on oral history notes holdings in their library and similar collections in other institutions. History of radicals and worker activists of the past predominates, with current activists often included."-C.C. **Est.:** 1981. **Frequency:** Irregular. **Subscription:** Donation. **Price:** Free. **Contact(s):** Paul Buhle. (212)998-2505.

**S ▸ Orange County Resources**
18822 Beach Blvd., #202
Huntington Beach, CA 92648 (714)963-7697
**Affiliation:** Community Resource Publications. **Concern(s):** spiritual; health; environment; transformation; holism. New Age magazine with articles dealing with health, self-help, environmental concerns, spiritual growth, new psychology and a way to better ones ways through non-traditional modes. Oldest and largest circulation New Age magazine in Orange County. **Other Resources:** Seminars/workshops on effective advertising and marketing for New Age entrepreneurs. **Est.:** 1984. **Frequency:** 4/yr. **Subscription:** $10/yr. **Price:** Free. **Pages:** 72. **Circ.:** 130M. **Publisher:** Community Resource Publications. **Contact(s):** Earl Bell (Operations Manager).

**A ▸ Organic Farmer, The Digest of Sustainable Agriculture**
15 Barre St.
Montpelier, VT 05602 (802)223-7222
**Affiliation:** Rural Vermont. **Concern(s):** agriculture; health; organic; sustainability. This digest gives helpful information on how to farm organically. It also reports on the dangers of using non-organic methods to farm.

**A ▸ Organic Gardening**
Rodale Press
33 Minor St.
Emmaus, PA 18049
**Concern(s):** agriculture. Organic gardening techniques.

**A ▸ Organic Gardening with Bountiful Gardens**
5798 Ridgewood Rd.
Willits, CA 95490
**Affiliation:** Ecology Action. **Concern(s):** agriculture; organic. This periodical shows inventive ways of gardening for the pro or novice. **Contact(s):** John Jevons.

**A ▸ Organic Times**
1301 Spruce St.
Boulder, CO 80302 (303)939-8440
**Affiliation:** New Health Communications. **Concern(s):** agriculture; organic. A magazine dedicated to providing its readers with up-to-date information of interest to the organic products industry, including legislation, events and innovations in production, certification, distribution and marketing. Facilitates communication among the trade and serves as a catalyst for the growth of the market. **Publisher:** New Health Communications, Inc. **Fax:** (303)939-9559. **Contact(s):** Stephen M. Hoffman (Editor), Frank J. Lampe (Managing Editor).

**J ▸ The Organizer**
11 John St.
New York, NY 10038 (212)406-3330
**Affiliation:** National Alliance Against Racist & Political Repression. **Concern(s):** justice; constitutional rights; racism; discrimination; justice; political prisoners. "Political prisoners in the US and police brutality are key fightback concerns featured here. Where many human rights groups worry mainly about rights abuses in Asia or Africa, the Alliance fights for human rights in our own backyard. The Organizer is commended for its useful resource and action recommendations."-C.C. **Est.:** 1973. **Frequency:** 6/yr. **Subscription:** $7/yr. **Price:** Free. **Contact(s):** Kay Anderson (Editor).

**P ▸ The Organizer**
739 8th St. SE
Washington, DC 20003 (202)547-9292
**Affiliation:** Institute for Social Justice. **Concern(s):** politics; grassroots organizing. Reports on community organizations nationwide. **Frequency:** 4/yr. (202)547-9292.

**E ▸ Orion**
Myrin Institute
136 E. 64th St.
New York, NY 10021 (212)758-6475
**Affiliation:** Myrin Institute. **Concern(s):** environment; justice; energy; arts; health; social ecology. This magazine's aim "is to characterize conceptually and practically our responsibilities to the earth and all forms of life, and to explore the ethic of humane stewardship; to advance the notion that effective stewardship comes from feelings of respect and admiration for the Earth: foster and nurture what we have

come to revere; to help us deepen our personal connection with the natural world as a source of enrichment and inner renewal." Special section focuses on a theme. **Est.:** 1982. **Frequency:** 4/yr. **Subscription:** $14/yr. **Price:** $4/ea. **Pages:** 64. **Circ.:** 10M. **Contact(s):** George K. Russell (Editor).

T ♦ **The Other Israel**
4816 Cornell Ave.
Downers Grove, IL 60515    (312)969-7584
**Affiliation:** Israeli Council for Israeli-Palestinian Peace. **Concern(s):** Third World; peace; conflict resolution; Mid-East. "The Other Israel is the newsletter of the Israeli opposition to the government mistreatment of the Palestinians. Reports from the scene in Israel and Jordan accurately document excesses there and advocate reconciliation."-C.C. **Est.:** 1983. **Frequency:** 6/yr. **Subscription:** $30/yr. **Price:** Free. **Contact(s):** Adam Keller.

✍ ♦ **Other Networks**
Box 14066
Philadelphia, PA 19123  (215)922—0227
**Affiliation:** Public Interest Media Project. **Concern(s):** education; conflict resolution; networking. For people who want to learn about networking. Written for and by people interested in networking. **Other Resources:** Publishes newsletter, OTHER NETWORKS. Nonprofit. **Frequency:** 4/yr. **Subscription:** $25/yr. **Contact(s):** Stan Pokras (Editor-in-chief).

⚉ ♦ **The Other Side**
300 W. Apsley St.
Philadelphia, PA 19144  (215)849-2178
**Concern(s):** peace; justice; Third World; eth faith; Native Americans; indigenous peoples. "This attractive magazine promotes Christian concern about peace and justice issues. Both ministers and laity contribute to the articles, from the front lines in El Salvador to the Indian reservations of the Southwest. Its easy-going style makes it a joy to read and learn from."-C.C. **Est.:** 1965. **Frequency:** 10/yr. **Subscription:** $19.75/yr. **Price:** $3/ea. **Contact(s):** Mark Olson.

E ♦ **The Otter Raft**
Box 221220, Dept. D
Carmel, CA 93922    (408)625-3290
**Affiliation:** Friends of the Sea Otter. **Concern(s):** environment; wildlife/endangered species; oceans; preservation. This newsletter covers the actions of the Friends of the Sea Otter. It also spotlights the troublesome things in our society that are endangering these creatures and their habitat. **Dues:** $15/yr; $100/life. (408)373-2747.

D ♦ **Our Common Future**
299 King Ave.
Columbus, OH 43201    (614)424-6203
**Affiliation:** Hunger and Development Coalition of Central Ohio. **Concern(s):** demographics; environment; Third World; hunger; development. This newsletter reports on the actions of HADCCO, who are working collectively on issues related to the survival of our planet and all of its inhabitants. It also reports on legislation taking place that will hamper the survival of this fragile Earth, book reviews, and helpful organizations that can help you make a difference. Nonprofit. **Est.:** 1986. **Dues:** $25, $100 organization. **Subscription:** $10/yr. **Contact(s):** Marilyn Welker (Program Coordinator).

J ♦ **Our Struggle/Nuestra Lucha**
2827 Catania Way
Sacramento, CA 95826  (916)361-9072
**Affiliation:** Latino Commission, Democratic Socialists of America. **Concern(s):** justice; politics; minority rights; Democratic Socialism. "Common concerns of the Hispanic rights movement and democratic socialism are conveyed in Our Struggle. Economic democracy, equality, and self-determination in the nations south of the border and in the barrios of this country are demanded."-C.C. **Est.:** 1983. **Frequency:** 4-5/yr. **Subscription:** $10/yr. **Price:** Donation. **Contact(s):** Duane Campbell.

✍ ♦ **Out West**
10522 Brunswick Rd.
Grass Valley, CA 95945  (916)477-9378
**Concern(s):** arts; environment; literature; recreation; culture. "Roving journalist Chuck Woodbury roams the West's blue highways by 'porta-newsroom' writing about whatever he discovers along the way. 'Delightful', said USA Today. Featured by all TV networks, LA Times, Washington Post, People. This magazine explores two laners, eat at EAT, laugh at funny signs - in 'the newspaper that roams'." **Est.:** 1988. **Frequency:** 4/yr. **Subscription:** $6/yr. **Price:** $2.50/ea. **Pages:** 40. **Circ.:** 10M. **Contact(s):** Chuck Woodbury.

E ♦ **Outdoor America**
1401 Wilson Blvd
Arlington, VA 22209    (703)528-1818
**Affiliation:** Izaak Walton League. **Concern(s):** environment; education; wilderness; conservation; resources; wildlife/endangered spe-

cies; recreation A magazine about natural resource conservation issues and outdoor recreation, especially fishing, hunting, and camping. Nonprofit. **Est.:** 1922. **Frequency:** 4/yr. **Contact(s):** Jack Lorenz (Executive Director).

E ♦ **Outdoor News Bulletin**
1101 14th St. NW, #725
Washington, DC 20005  (202)371-1808
**Affiliation:** Wildlife Management Institute. **Concern(s):** environment; wildlife/endangered species; conservation; resources. This bulletin reports on the combined efforts of the Wildlife Management Institute, the government, schools, and progressive individuals to improve the natural resource management of this country especially wildlife. **Frequency:** 26/yr.

✎ ♦ **Outdoors Unlimited**
2017 Cato Ave., #101
State College, PA 16801  (814)234-1011
**Affiliation:** Outdoor Writers Association of America. **Concern(s):** arts; environment; education; recreation; literature; journalism. A newsletter that allows the exercise of the writing craft at the same time is expresses its appreciation for the outdoors. Nonprofit. **Est.:** 1927. **Frequency:** 12/yr. **Contact(s):** Carol Kersavage (Editor).

E ♦ **Outside**
Mariah Publication Corp.
1165 N. Clark St.
Chicago, IL 60610    (312)951-0990
**Concern(s):** environment; recreation; preservation. "...a monthly national magazine for active, educated, up-scale adults who love the outdoors and are concerned about its preservation." Material concerns outdoor sports and expeditions, how-to's, the environment, interviews, book excerpts and much more." **Contact(s):** John Rasmus (Editor), Mark Bryant (Managing Editor).

✍ ♦ **Owl**
The Young Naturalist Foundation
56 The Esplanade, #306
Toronto, ON M5E 1A7 **Canada**
**Affiliation:** Young Naturalist Foundation. **Concern(s):** education; environment; youth; science; childhood. Articles for children ages 8 to 12 about animals, science, people, technology, new discoveries, activities. **Contact(s):** Deborah Pearson (Editor).

T ♦ **OXFAM America News**
115 Broadway
Boston, MA 02116    (617)482-1211
**Affiliation:** OXFAM America. **Concern(s):** Third World. "News of the developing countries and programs that Oxfam sponsors is carried in this newsletter. African, Asian, and South American self-help development projects are featured."-C.C. **Est.:** 1977. **Frequency:** 3/yr. **Subscription:** Donation. **Price:** Free. **Contact(s):** Tim Johnson.

E ♦ **P3 (Planet Three)**
Box 52
Montgomery, VT 05470
**Concern(s):** environment; education; childhood. Great kids environmental magazine. **Frequency:** 6/yr. **Contact(s):** Randi Hacker (Editor).

⚉ ♦ **Pacific Bulletin**
Box 3148
Auckland Central, New Zealand
**Concern(s):** peace; Third World; anti-nuclear; indigenous peoples. "A typical article might explain the detrimental effects of nuclear weapons detonations on the Marshall Islands, independence of Pacific islands and nations from the US, and reduction of nuclear weapons there are also regularly promoted. Formerly located in Hawaii."-C.C. **Est.:** 1981. **Frequency:** 6/yr. **Contact(s):** Roman Bedur.

⚉ ♦ **Palestine Focus**
Box 27462
San Francisco, CA 94127
**Concern(s):** peace; Mid-East. **Frequency:** 6/yr. **Subscription:** $10/yr.

⚉ ♦ **Palestine Perspectives**
9522A Lee High
Fairfax, VA 22031
**Concern(s):** peace; Mid-East. **Frequency:** 6/yr. **Subscription:** $15/yr.

T ♦ **Panascope**
1717 Massachusetts Ave. NW, #301
Washington, DC 20036-2001    (202)483-0044
**Affiliation:** Panos Institute. **Concern(s):** Third World; hunger; development; sustainability. The magazine which reports about debt, drought, famine, and education in the Third World, from a Third World perspective. **Frequency:** 6/yr. **Subscription:** $30/yr.

**Contact(s):** Don Edwards (Executive Director).

S ♦ **Parabola**
Parabola Books
666 Broadway
New York, NY 10012  (212)505-6200
**Concern(s):** spiritual; arts; health; education; interfaith; literature; film; psychology; substance abuse. "A unique quarterly journal bringing together scholars in literature, mythology, comparative religion, and popular culture to probe the mythic underpinnings of contemporary life. Includes articles, interviews, stories and folktales, book and film reviews focused around a theme: Addiction, The Creative Response, The Sense of Humor." **Est.:** 1975. **Frequency:** 4/yr. **Subscription:** $20/yr. **Price:** $6/ea. **Pages:** 128. **Circ.:** 36M. **Publisher:** Parbola Books. **Contact(s):** Rob Baker (Editor), Joseph Kulin (Executive Publisher).

H ♦ **Parenting**
Box 56861
Boulder, CO 80322
**Concern(s):** health; education; psychology; child care. Articles on education, health, fitness, nutrition, child development, psychology, and social issues for parents of young children. **Frequency:** 10/yr. **Subscription:** $18/yr. **Office:** 501 2nd St. San Francisco, CA 94107. **Contact(s):** David Markus (Editor).

M ♦ **Parenting for Peace & Justice Newsletter**
4144 Lindell, #122
St. Louis, MO 63031    (314)533-4445
**Affiliation:** Institute for Peace & Justice. **Concern(s):** media; feminism; peace; spiritual; conflict resolution; interfaith. "Raising children nonviolently, and teaching them to relate to others likewise, are explained by the Fords. Both parents and educators will find ideas for developing peaceful ways of relating - for our children and for ourselves."-C.C. **Est.:** 1970. **Frequency:** 6/yr. **Subscription:** $15/yr. **Price:** $1/ea. **Contact(s):** James Ford, Nanette Ford

♥ ♦ **Parents**
685 3rd Ave.
New York, NY 10017    (212)878-8700
**Concern(s):** family; health; education; psychology; child care. Articles on parenting, family, women's and community issues, etc. Informal style with quotes from experts. **Other Resources:** Parents magazine book club. (800)727-3682. **Contact(s):** Ann Pleshette Murphy (Editor).

⚉ ♦ **Pax Christi USA**
348 E. 10th St.
Erie, PA 16503    (814)453-4955
**Affiliation:** Pax Christi USA. **Concern(s):** peace; spiritual; interfaith; faith; disarmament; nonviolence. "Catholics and others join here to suggest ways for peace through disarmament and justice. Nonviolence is the method for their vision of world peace."-C.C. **Est.:** 1972. **Frequency:** 4/yr. **Subscription:** $10/yr. **Price:** $.50/ea. **Contact(s):** Mary Lou Kownacki.

A ♦ **PANNA Outlook**
965 Mission St., #514
San Francisco, CA 94103    (415)541-9140
**Affiliation:** Pesticide Action Network. **Concern(s):** agriculture; environment; hazardous/toxic wastes. This newsletter reports on the actions of the Network. Articles on alternatives to pesticides, violators of pesticide use, and legislative information. **Frequency:** 6/yr.

⚉ ♦ **Peace & Change**
Center for Peaceful Change
Kent State University
Kent, OH 44242    (216)672-3143
**Affiliation:** Center for Peaceful Change. **Concern(s):** peace. "This academic journal delves into the theory of peace and peaceful change. A couple of typical articles deal with analysis of the European peace movement; comparison of the peace movement today and forty years ago."-C.C. **Est.:** 1972. **Frequency:** 4/yr. **Subscription:** $15, $21 institution. **Price:** $4.50/ea. **Contact(s):** Dennis P. Carey.

⚉ ♦ **Peace and Democracy News**
Box 1640, Cathedral Station
New York, NY 10025    (212)666-5924
**Affiliation:** Campaign for Peace and Democracy. **Concern(s):** peace; labor; Third World; justice; feminism; East-West; disarmament. Bulletin of the Campaign, linking democratic activists from the Western peace movement and the Eastern European and Soviet human rights movement. It covers issues of peace and disarmament, social justice, human rights, labor, feminism, as inseparable from the perspective that they are inseparable from democracy and one another. Nonprofit. **Est.:** 1984. **Frequency:** 2/yr. **Subscription:** $10, $15 institution. **Price:** $5/ea. **Bulk:** 50% off/24. **Pages:** 48-64. **Circ.:** 6M. **Fax:** (212)662-5892. **Contact(s):** Joanne Landy (Director), Gail Danek-er (Editor).

**F ▸ Peace and Freedom**
710 G St. SE
Washington, DC 20003 (202)544-2211
**Affiliation:** Women's International League for Peace and Freedom. **Concern(s):** feminism; peace; politics; activism; lobbying. "The WILPF is one of the most important groups in the peace movement and their effectiveness is reflected in their inspiring magazine. The articles, over a year's time, will touch on almost every aspect of the peace movement, from peace and feminism to local peace events in Smalltown, USA. Highly recommended newsletter for all interested in working for peace."-C.C. **Est.:** 1915. **Frequency:** 6/yr. **Subscription:** $10/yr. **Office:** 1213 Race St. Philadelphia, PA 19107. **Contact(s):** Isabel Guy (Legislative Director), Anne Ivey (President). (215)563-7110.

**✌ ▸ Peace and Justice Newsletter**
186 College St.
Burlington, VT 05401 (802)863-8326
**Affiliation:** Peace and Justice Coalition. **Concern(s):** peace; justice; world order; conversion. A Burlington coalition newsletter encouraging co-operative ways consistent with the concepts of peace, food and justice, working for fundamental social change through mutual support and collective action. **Frequency:** 10/yr. **Contact(s):** Greg Guma (Coordinator).

**✌ ▸ Peace and Solidarity**
11 John St., #804
New York, NY 10038 (212)989-1194
**Affiliation:** US Peace Council. **Concern(s):** peace. "Militant and cross-cultural, this peace group brings together labor, people of color, students, and others into one united effort for world peace. Independence and self-determination for all nations are also key ideas promoted in this inspiring newsletter. A first choice for activists."-C.C. **Est.:** 1978. **Dues:** $10/yr. **Frequency:** 12/yr. **Subscription:** Membership. **Price:** Free. **Contact(s):** Michael Myerson.

**✌ ▸ Peace Chronicle**
George Mason University
4400 University Dr.
Fairfax, VA 22030 (703)323-2806
**Affiliation:** Consortium on Peace Research Education and Development (COPRED). **Concern(s):** peace; volunteers; jobs. This newsletter covers the latest developments and activities in peace research and conflict resolution, provides news from COPRED's 13 working groups and business activities, as well as announcements of recent publications and resources, job openings, internships, conferences and other events. **Frequency:** 6/yr. **Pages:** 26-32. **Circ.:** 700. **Contact(s):** Maire A. Dugan (Editor), David A. Cianto (Production).

**✌ ▸ Peace Conversion Times**
200 N. Main St., #M-2
Santa Ana, CA 92701 (714)547-6282
**Affiliation:** Alliance for Survival. **Concern(s):** peace; economics; renewables; disarmament; peace dividend; economic conversion. A newsletter that reports on ways that military budgets can and should be converted to peaceful purposes such as education, revitalizing the economy, and social welfare. Nonprofit. **Est.:** 1980. **Frequency:** 6/yr. **Subscription:** Free. **Pages:** 8. **Circ.:** 7M. **Fax:** (714)547-6322. **Contact(s):** Marion Pack (Executive Director), Jeannie Bernstein (President of Board).

**✌ ▸ Peace Developments**
44 N. Prospect St.
Box 270
Amherst, MA 01004 (413)256-8306
**Affiliation:** Peace Development Fund/Pacific Peace Fund. **Concern(s):** peace; fundraising. "Assistance in organizing projects for peace by giving financial grants is summarized in the funding groups' quarterly reports. The reports give donors specifics on where their dollars go, and give those seeking grants an idea of what type of projects are likely to win grant approval."-C.C. **Est.:** 1983. **Frequency:** 4/yr. **Subscription:** Donation. **Price:** Free. **Contact(s):** Meg Gage.

**✌ ▸ Peace Education Newsletter**
Box 1153
Miami Beach, FL 33119
**Concern(s):** peace. **Contact(s):** Fran Schmidt.

**✌ ▸ PEACE in Action**
Box 244
Arlington, VA 22210 (703)528-2758
**Affiliation:** Foundation for PEACE. **Concern(s):** peace. "A profile of a peace activist deserving to be emulated opens each issue. Several strategizing features and a dozen or so regular articles round out this tool for peace. Recommended."-C.C. **Est.:** 1985. **Frequency:** 6/yr. **Subscription:** $25/yr. **Price:** $4/ea. **Contact(s):** James L. Roush.

**✌ ▸ Peace Institute Reporter**
1835 K St. NW
Washington, DC 20006 (202)223-1770
**Affiliation:** National Peace Institute Foundation. **Concern(s):** peace; media; politics; conflict resolution; lobbying. Newsletter. **Frequency:** 6/yr. **Contact(s):** Kathleen J. Lansing (Acting Director), Thomas C. Westropp (Chairman). (800)237-3223.

**✌ ▸ Peace Links - Women Against Nuclear War**
747 8th St. SE
Washington, DC 20003 (202)544-0805
**Affiliation:** Peace Links. **Concern(s):** peace. "Women against nuclear war have banded together for peace between US citizens and the Soviets through people-to-people encounters and local organizing. They have had some difficulty, however, in moving beyond a white, middle-class constituency."-C.C. **Est.:** 1985. **Frequency:** 4/yr. **Subscription:** Donation. **Price:** Free. **Contact(s):** Beth Bumpers.

**✌ ▸ The Peace Magazine**
736 Bathurst St.
Toronto, ON M5S 2R4 Canada
**Concern(s):** peace.

**✌ ▸ Peace Newsletter**
924 Burnet Ave.
Syracuse, NY 13203 (315)472-5478
**Affiliation:** Syracuse Peace Council. **Concern(s):** peace; justice; social justice; economic conversion. "For people in Central or Upstate New York, it is invaluable as a source for news and events of the movement for peace and justice. For others, it can provide continuing examples of how one community attempts to combine theory with practice. In other words, it is a journal of local activism with a liberationist nonviolent slant!" Adheres to the "myth of objective journalism." **Est.:** 1936. **Frequency:** 6/yr. **Subscription:** $10/yr. **Price:** $.75/ea. **Pages:** 20. **Circ.:** 5M. **Contact(s):** JoAnn Stack (Coordinator).

**✌ ▸ Peace of our Minds**
RD 1-H, Box 171
West Edmeston, NY 13485
**Affiliation:** Young and Teen Peacemakers. **Concern(s):** peace. "A forum by kids, for kids. Encourages young people (ages 8 to 18) to explore their roles as peacemakers. They write about cultural, ethnic, and familial differences as well as challenges of physical disabilities. Kid-to-Kid column is a question- and-answer forum for kids to explore issues of concern." **Frequency:** 5/yr. **Subscription:** $10/yr.

**✌ ▸ The Peace Planter**
1127 University Ave.
Madison, WI 53701 (608)256-4146
**Affiliation:** Nukewatch/The Progressive Foundation. **Concern(s):** peace; boycott; anti-nuclear. This progressive periodical keeps readers informed of which companies and products to boycott due to their involvement in the nuclear industry. Also reports on the activities of the organization. **Frequency:** 12/yr. **Contact(s):** Samuel H. Day, Jr. (Co-director).

**✌ ▸ Peace Progress**
Box 3282
Huntsville, AL 35810 (205)534-5501
**Affiliation:** International Association of Educators for World Peace. **Concern(s):** peace; education; disarmament. "School teachers and other educators can get ideas on organizing for world peace and nuclear disarmament, and for educating for peace in the schools."-C.C. **Est.:** 1974. **Dues:** $35/yr. **Frequency:** Annual. **Subscription:** Membership. **Price:** Donation. **Contact(s):** P. Achava Amrung.

**✌ ▸ Peace Review**
2439 Birch St. , #8
Palo Alto, CA 94306 (415)328-5477
**Concern(s):** peace; Third World; foreign policy. The international quarterly of world peace. A new magazine which presents the best writing on peace research from around the world, carefully edited for the general reader, with reports from peacemaking in the field, and reviews of many new books appearing on the topic. For Profit. **Est.:** 1989. **Frequency:** 4/yr. **Subscription:** $24/yr. **Price:** $6/ea. **Bulk:** 25% off/24. **Pages:** 48. **Circ.:** 900. **Publisher:** Peace Review Publications Inc.. **E-Network:** PeaceNet. **ID:** 'preview'. **Fax:** (415)328-7518. **Contact(s):** John L. Harris (Editor).

**✌ ▸ Peace Tax Fund Newsletter**
2121 Decatur Pl. NW
Washington, DC 20008 (202)483-3751
**Affiliation:** National Campaign for a Peace Tax Fund. **Concern(s):** peace; economics; war tax revolt; taxation; peace dividend. "The goal is a law permitting people morally opposed to war to have the military part of their taxes allocated to peacemaking. The newsletter does a great job of promoting that view."-C.C. **Est.:** 1972. **Dues:** $25/yr. **Frequency:** 4/yr. **Subscription:** Membership. **Price:** Free. **Contact(s):** Steve Tracy.

**✌ ▸ Peace Times**
9523 Jasper Ave.
Edmonton, AL T5H 3V2 Canada (403)429-3659
**Concern(s):** peace; activism. Nonprofit. **Frequency:** Weekly. **Subscription:** $50/yr. **Price:** $.25/ea. **Bulk:** 40% off/24. **Pages:** c12. **Circ.:** 3M. **E-Network:** Econet. **ID:** web:'tooker'. **Fax:** (403)425-5767. **Contact(s):** David Boroditsky (Publisher), Tooker Gomberg (Editor).

**✌ ▸ The Peacebuilder**
610 Ethan Allen Ave.
Takoma Park, MD 20912 (301)891-2997
**Affiliation:** American Peace Network. **Concern(s):** peace; education; activism; conflict resolution; global understanding. This newsletter has one purpose in mind: Abolish War! This periodical accomplishes this by reporting on steps towards peace and informative articles on things that may retard the abolishment of war. **Est.:** 1985. **Frequency:** 4/yr. **Price:** $2.50/ea. **Circ.:** 6M. **E-Network:** PeaceNet. **Fax:** (301)891-2997. **Contact(s):** Peter Zuckerman (President).

**E ▸ Peaceful Pieces**
Box 6469
Boise, ID 83707 (208)345-6709
**Affiliation:** Boise Peace Quilt Project. **Concern(s):** environment; peace; politics; social justice; disarmament; grassroots organizing. "What can ordinary people who are concerned about the environment, nuclear disarmament, and social justice, do to help avert disaster? We are a group of people living in Boise, ID, who decided to wage peace from a quilting frame. We call our work the Boise Peace Quilt Project, and our newsletter, 'Peaceful Pieces'." Good grass roots material. **Est.:** 1983. **Frequency:** 2/yr. **Subscription:** $6/yr. **Price:** $3/ea. **Circ.:** 600. **Contact(s):** Lyn McCollum (Editor), Heidi Read (Business Manager). (208)378-7168. **Other:** Boise Peace Quilt Project, 1110 Warm Springs Ave., Boise, ID 83712.

**✌ ▸ Peacemaker**
Box 627
Garberville, CA 95440 (707)826-1377
**Affiliation:** Peacemaker Movement. **Concern(s):** peace. "Personal stories by and about peacemakers make this periodical a unique and inspiring selection for participants in the peace movement. The usual calendar notices section and resource reviews are also included."-C.C. **Est.:** 1948. **Frequency:** 12/yr. **Subscription:** $3/yr. **Price:** $.50/ea. **Contact(s):** Victoria Serra.

**✍ ▸ Peacemaking for Children Newsletter**
2437 N. Grant Blvd.
Milwaukee, WI 53210
**Affiliation:** Peacemaking for Children. **Concern(s):** education; peace; childhood.

**✌ ▸ The Peacemonger**
7365 Valle Ave.
Atascadero, CA 93422 (805)461-1955
**Concern(s):** peace; justice; environment. Magazine. **Frequency:** 12/yr. **Contact(s):** Eric Greening (Editor), Nathan Koren (Publisher).

**✌ ▸ The Peacemonger**
Rains Box 250
Stanford, CA 94305
**Concern(s):** peace; justice. Published by a group of graduate students from Stanford University, this newspaper does not claim to be the "voice" of Students for Peace or any other organization. "We welcome letters and contributions from all our readers, subject only limited to space. What's so funny about peace, love, and understanding?" **Frequency:** 12/yr. **Contact(s):** David Porter, Martha Otis.

**✌ ▸ PeaceWork**
2161 Massachusetts Ave.
Cambridge, MA 02140 (617)661-6130
**Affiliation:** American Friends Service Committee. **Concern(s):** peace; spiritual; activism; nonviolence; interfaith. "A New England Peace and Social Justice Newsletter" published by the regional office of the AFSC. Eclectic emphasis on empowerment journalism, many listings of events, resources, campaigns, etc. Eyewitness reports of nonviolent actions. Serves activist community nationwide, with frequent reader participation/dialogue. **Other Resources:** Free sample; 20-year anthology available. Nonprofit. **Frequency:** 11/yr. **Subscription:** $10/3rd class; $15/first class. **Price:** $1/ea. **Pages:** 16. **Circ.:** 2M. **E-Network:** Peacenet. **Fax:** (617)354-2832. **Contact(s):** Pat Farren (Editor), Jeanne Gallo (Executive Secretary).

**T ▸ PeaceWorks**
Sacramento Religious Community for Peace
Box 163078
Sacramento, CA 95816 (916)456-2616

**Affiliation:** Sacramento Religious Community for Peace. **Concern(s):** Third World; peace; justice; spiritual; interfaith. A newspaper reporting on Third World triumphs in self sufficiency, homelessness, schools , jails, the Gulf War, and anything having to do with peace or economic/social justice. Nonprofit. **Dues:** $50, $30 low income. **Frequency:** 10-11/yr. **Subscription:** $15/yr, free to members.

L ♦ **The People**
914 Industrial Ave.
Palo Alto, CA 94303    (415)494-1532
**Affiliation:** Socialist Labor Party. **Concern(s):** labor; economics; politics; alternative party. "For about 100 years, this newspaper has promoted the social and economic theories of Daniel DeLeon. Recently it changed its boring old-style format to a more exciting and better-written tabloid format. Marxist content."-C.C. **Est.:** 1891. **Frequency:** 26/yr. **Subscription:** $4/yr. **Price:** Free. **Contact(s):** Robert Bills.

$ ♦ **People & Taxes**
Public Citizen
2000 P St. NW, #605
Washington, DC 20036-0757    (202)833-3000
**Affiliation:** Public Citizen. **Concern(s):** economics; peace. "Here is the definitive journal of progressive tax reform, started by Ralph Nader. It tells who really benefits from most tax breaks, how our tax laws work, and how citizens can work to reform them."-C.C. **Est.:** 1972. **Frequency:** 12/yr. **Subscription:** $10/yr. **Price:** $1/ea. **Contact(s):** Ruth Simon.

M ♦ **People for the American Way Press Clips**
2000 M St. NW, #400
Washington, DC 20036-3307    (202)467-4999
**Affiliation:** People For the American Way. **Concern(s):** media. "Several press clippings for each of several topics are reprinted to summarize issues of concern to organization members. Defending separation of church and state and other constitutional rights are frequent focuses."-C.C. **Contact(s):** Arthur J. Kropp (President).

⚥ ♦ **People For A Change, Building Ourselves A Base**
131 Mangels Ave.
San Francisco, CA 94131
**Affiliation:** People For A Change. **Concern(s):** peace; economics; feminism; demographics; justice; politics; peace dividend; economic conversion; social justice; racism; sexism. This newsletter envisions a world free from racism, sexism, and ageism where humans live in peaceful coexistence. Favors economic conversion to a peacetime economy, environmental protection, socio-economic justice and working for a world without war. world free from war racism, sexism, and ageism. The are determined to make up in numbers what they lack in financial resources. **Dues:** $10/yr, half price to the nearly broke. **Contact(s):** George R. Fouke.

P ♦ **People's Daily World**
239 W. 23rd St.
New York, NY 10011    (212)924-2523
**Concern(s):** politics; labor; peace; Third World; alternative party; activism; unions. "This new product, resulting from the merger of the People's World on the West Coast with the Daily World, is the most socially-concerned daily paper in the US. It is published Tuesday through Saturday, with a special weekend edition also available. The price is a bargain for this Marxist paper featuring a well-packaged mix of culture, labor, and other news of people's movements across the US and around the world."-C.C. **Est.:** 1986. **Frequency:** Daily. **Subscription:** $15/yr. **Price:** $.25/ea. **Publisher:** Long View Publishing Co. **Contact(s):** Barry Cohen.

P ♦ **People's Tribune**
Box 3524
Chicago, IL 60654    (312)772-2779
**Concern(s):** politics; labor; justice; arts; media; alternative party. "Scientific socialism is the philosophy used to explain events of the day to its readers. Concerns of labor, ethnics, and cultural workers are all featured in this incisive, well-written newspaper."-C.C. **Est.:** 1974. **Frequency:** 26/yr. **Subscription:** $10, $15 institution. **Price:** $.25/ea. **Contact(s):** Luis Rodriguez.

P ♦ **People's World**
1819 10th St.
Berkeley, CA 94710
**Concern(s):** politics; alternative party; Democratic Socialism. A weekly socialist rag from the Bay area. Extremely valuable if you want to find out what is going on under the headlines of mainstream press.

T ♦ **Periodic Reports from CARECEN**
3112 Mt. Pleasant St. NW
Washington, DC 20010    (202)328-9799
**Affiliation:** Central American Refugee Center. **Concern(s):** Third

World; justice; Central America. "Refugees from Central America should be able to live safely in their own countries, these folks believe. If they must flee their homes in order to live, the US should embrace them as it does immigrants from other countries, say these reports."-C.C. **Est.:** 1986. **Frequency:** 8/yr. **Subscription:** $20/yr. **Price:** $3/ea. **Contact(s):** Minor Sinclair.

A ♦ **The Permaculture Activist**
Box 3630
Kailua-Kona, HI 96745
**Affiliation:** Permaculture Communications. **Concern(s):** agriculture; environment; urban; permaculture; sustainability; rural communities. In-depth articles on how to design and implement permaculture systems in a variety of environments, rural & urban; small-scale self-reliance to regional/global reforestation; news from regional permaculture groups around North America; educational programs, demonstration projects, and how you can get involved. This newsletter is the best North American source for permaculture information, news, and articles calendar of design courses. **Frequency:** 4/yr. **Subscription:** $16/yr. **Price:** $4/ea. **Bulk:** $.75ea/24. **Pages:** 24. **Circ.:** 1M. **Contact(s):** Guy Baldwin (Editor/Publisher).

M ♦ **Perpetual Notions Newsletter**
Box 6298
Laguna Niguel, CA 92677
**Concern(s):** media; politics; media watch; responsibility; government accountability. A journal which will publish all the news that is left out of the mass media. By accepting no advertising it will be able to print the news which the multinational corporate advertisers keep out of the press and off the airwaves of NBC, CBS and ABC. The 8-page monthly newsletter will cover the unprinted political news (e.g. the Contra-cocaine pipeline) as well as information on personal growth.

📖 ♦ **Person-Centered Review**
Sage Publications
2111 West Hillcrest Drive
Newberry Park, CA 91320
**Concern(s):** education; health; psychology; childhood. A quarterly journal devoted to the continued development of Carl Rogers' person-centered approach to the fields of education, psychotherapy, supervision, and human development. Encourages critical reflection on theory and practice, innovations in therapy and education, and further research; contains news of conferences, training, and associations.

P ♦ **Perspectives on Political Science**
Heldref Publications
4000 Albemarle St. NW
Washington, DC 20016    (202)362-6445
**Concern(s):** politics; analysis; reform. This contains close to 100 reviews of new books in the ever-changing fields of government, politics, internal affairs, and political thought. These books are reviewed by outstanding specialists 1-12 months after publication. Also included are major articles covering innovations or rethinking traditions in teaching techniques. Occasional symposia issues address the state of the art in political science and public policy. **Other Resources:** Formerly PERSPECTIVE and TEACHING POLITICAL SCIENCE. **Est.:** 1990. **Frequency:** 4/yr. **Subscription:** $35, $75 institution.

S ♦ **Perspectives on Science and Christian Faith**
Box 668
Ipswich, MA 01938
**Affiliation:** American Scientific Association. **Concern(s):** spiritual; education; energy; environment; faith; science.

E ♦ **Pesticides and You**
National Coalition Against the Misuse of Pesticides
701 E St. SE
Washington, DC 20003    (202)543-5450
**Affiliation:** National Coalition Against the Misuse of Pesticides. **Concern(s):** environment; health; hazardous/toxic waste. "Natural insecticides are recommended as replacements for unnecessary toxic ones, such as DDT. Related land issues also find a place here."-C.C. **Est.:** 1981. **Frequency:** 5/yr. **Subscription:** $20, $100 institution. **Price:** Free. **Contact(s):** Jay Feldman (National Coordinator).

🐾 ♦ **PETA News**
Box 42516
Washington, DC 20015    (301)770-7444
**Affiliation:** People for the Ethical Treatment of Animals (PETA). **Concern(s):** environment; education; politics; animal rights; lobbying. This newsletter and organization was formed to educate policy makers and the public about the issues involving the intense, prolonged, and unjustifiable abuse of animals, and to promote an understanding of the inherent rights of sentient animals to be treated with respect and kindness. **Frequency:** 6/yr. **Subscription:** $15/yr. **Price:** Free. **Bulk:** Free. **Pages:** 20. **Circ.:** 300M. **Office:** 4980 Wyaconda Rd. Rockville, MD 20852. (Outreach Department).

T ♦ **Philippine Labor Alert**
2252 Puna St.
Honolulu, HI 96817    (808)595-7362
**Affiliation:** Philippine Workers Support Committee. **Concern(s):** Third World; labor; Philippines; foreign relations. A bulletin of Philippine Workers Support Committee, a US National Network of chapters doing solidarity work for and with the Kilusang Mayo Uno (May 1st Movement) and Philippine labor. Chapters in Honolulu, SF Bay Area, New York, Boston, and Chicago. **Est.:** 1984. **Frequency:** 4/yr. **Subscription:** $7/yr. **Price:** $2/ea. **Pages:** 12. **Circ.:** 1.5M. **Contact(s):** John Witeck (Coordinator).

T ♦ **Philippine Resource Center Monitor**
Box 40090
Berkeley, CA 94704
**Affiliation:** Philippine Resource Center. **Concern(s):** Third World; Asia. Reports on developments in the Philippines as well as US policies and relations with that area. **Frequency:** 10/yr. **Subscription:** $15/yr.

☼ ♦ **Photovoltaic Insider's Report**
1011 W. Colorado Blvd.
Dallas, TX 75208
**Concern(s):** energy; solar. This illustrated newsletter reports the latest advance in worldwide photovoltaic technology. Descriptions and abstracts of recent photovoltaic patents are included. Covering the field from materials to market, it contains current information on R&D, new products and systems, applications, industry news and trends, market development, and procurement opportunities. **Est.:** 1982. **Frequency:** 12/yr.

✏ ♦ **Pig Iron**
Box 237
Youngstown, OH 44501    (216)783-1269
**Concern(s):** arts; poetry. "Each annual issue focuses on a single topic such as humor, labor, the Third World and science fiction. Poetry, prose, and art alternate to create a flowing, often progressive, social commentary."-C.C. **Est.:** 1973. **Frequency:** Annual. **Subscription:** $7/yr. **Price:** $2.50/ea. **Publisher:** Pig Iron Press. **Contact(s):** Jim Villani; Rose Sayre, Nate Leslie (Editors).

M ♦ **PICA News**
666 Pennsylvania Ave. SE
Washington, DC 20003    (202)544-9234
**Affiliation:** Public Interest Computer Association. **Concern(s):** media; planning; computer networking. "Socially-concerned computer users with extra money may want to access PICA News. It is designed to help groups better utilize computer use."-C.C. **Est.:** 1984. **Frequency:** 10/yr. **Subscription:** $30/yr. **Price:** $3/ea.

⚥ ♦ **Planet Earth**
325 North St.
San Francisco, CA 94103    (916)926-2241
**Affiliation:** Planetary Citizens. **Concern(s):** peace; environment; spiritual; education; global understanding; holism; activism; world order. This magazine tries to stimulate global awareness and a conscious identification with humanity as a whole. It reports on how people are coming together in a sense of "global patriotism" and working to bring others into the fold. **Contact(s):** Donald Keys (President), Norman Cousins (deceased) (Founder).

U ♦ **Planning**
1313 E. 60th St.
Chicago, IL 60637    (312)955-9100
**Affiliation:** American Planning Association. **Concern(s):** urban; agriculture; economics; planning; land use; analysis. Reports on America's communities, describing national trends, local successes, and professional techniques relevant to city planning. Stories focus on all aspects of land use, from saving farmland to recycling abandoned industrial sites. Communities of all sizes are covered in this magazine: small towns, suburbs, and big cities. **Frequency:** 12/yr. **Subscription:** $40/yr. **Circ.:** 25M. **Contact(s):** Sylvia Lewis (Editor).

L ♦ **Plant Shutdowns Monitor**
464 19th St.
Oakland, CA 94612    (510)835-4692
**Affiliation:** Data Center. **Concern(s):** labor; economics. "A parts plant in Detroit relocating, without notice, to South Korea would be a typical cause for concern in this periodical. It is basically an article reprint service for unions and others concerned about runaway shops' negative effects on the workers and economy of the old workplace."-C.C. **Est.:** 1983. **Frequency:** 12/yr. **Subscription:** $300/yr. **Price:** $10/ea. **Contact(s):** Tracy Helser.

E ▸ **Plastics & Recycling Report**
Rutgers University, Bldg. 3529, Busch Campus
Center for Plastics Recycling Research
Piscataway, NJ 08855 (201)932-4402
**Affiliation:** Plastics Recycling Institute. **Concern(s):** environment; recycling. Offers news on research activities and information on products made from recycled plastic.

✏ ▸ **Plays, The Drama Magazine for Young People**
120 Boylston St.
Boston, MA 02116
**Concern(s):** arts; theater. One-act plays, skits, creative dramatic material, suitable for school productions at junior high, middle, and lower grade levels. Plays with one set preferred. Uses comedies, dramas, satires, farces, melodramas, dramatized classics, folktales, fairy tales, and puppet plays. **Contact(s):** Elizabeth Preston (Managing Editor).

A ▸ **Plenty Bulletin**
Box 2306
Davis, CA 95617 (916)753-0731
**Affiliation:** Plenty USA. **Concern(s):** agriculture; environment; justice. "Plenty promotes the relief and development efforts of the Farm, a large cooperative community. An ambulance service in the Bronx and soybeans for protein in Guatemala are two key projects."-C.C. **Est.:** 1974. **Frequency:** 4/yr. **Subscription:** $10/yr. **Price:** Free. **Circ.:** 3.5M. **Other Formats:** Peacenet/Econet, user name 'natlaw'. **E-Network:** MCI Mail. **ID:** 'plentyusa'. **Contact(s):** Peter Schweitzer.

✏ ▸ **Poetry: San Francisco Quarterly**
Fort Mason Center
Building D
San Francisco, CA 94123 (415)621-3073
**Concern(s):** arts; poetry. "As a 'quarterly of bold and compassionate poetry,' it does a great job of giving us a nice mix of past poets, such as Whitman and Dickinson, and present poets' social commentary writings. At least two dozen poems are published in each of the 16-page tabloid issues."-C.C. **Est.:** 1985. **Frequency:** 4/yr. **Subscription:** $5/yr. **Price:** $1.50/ea. **Contact(s):** Herman Berlandt.

✌ ▸ **Point**
Box 1314
Jamaica Plain, MA 02130 (617)524-7207
**Affiliation:** Smedley D. Butler Brigade, Veterans for Peace. **Concern(s):** peace; veterans; nonviolence. "A vanguard veterans' newsletter that seeks to act as point men did in Vietnam - to walk in advance of others in order to be the first to find trouble. Veteran Brian Wilson is mentioned as a vet to emulate, as he sought to stop an arms train by lying on the track."-C.C. **Est.:** 1986. **Frequency:** 4/yr. **Subscription:** $5/yr. **Price:** Free. **Contact(s):** Barry Brodsky.

P ▸ **Point of View**
1004 Pennsylvania Ave. SE
H2-344 House Annex II
Washington, DC 20515 (202)675-6730
**Affiliation:** Congressional Black Caucus Foundation. **Concern(s):** politics; justice; lobbying; minority rights. Magazine that focuses on issues that primarily deal with blacks. The magazine focuses on all issues from the Black point of view. **Frequency:** 4/yr. **Contact(s):** Julian C. Dixon (President), Ron V. Dellums (Chairman). (202)226-7790.

P ▸ **Political Affairs**
235 W. 23rd St.
New York, NY 10011 (212)989-4994
**Affiliation:** Communist Party USA. **Concern(s):** political; labor; peace; justice; alternative party. "Labor, racism, peace, and culture are four favorite topics here, with regular contributors including Gus Hall, Henry Winston, and Herbert Apthekier. The CPUSA publishes this monthly to explain the basis of its views and actions on the above topics and myriad other concerns, which makes it important in understanding their actions aimed at changing American society."-C.C. **Est.:** 1921. **Frequency:** 12/yr. **Subscription:** $10, $15 institution. **Price:** $1/ea. **Contact(s):** Michael Zagarell.

✏ ▸ **Political Pix**
Box 804
Norwich, VT 05055
**Concern(s):** arts; politics; graphics; government accountability. Cartoons for thoughtful people. Each week Pix delights its subscribers with dozens of editorial cartoons fresh from the pens of superb artistic thinkers. Keep your finger on the pulse of contemporary political events and get a variety of potent views that you do not ordinarily see. Insights with a bite.

✍ ▸ **Pollen: Journal of Bioregional Education**
103 Gibson Lane
Wilder, KY 41076
**Affiliation:** North American Bioregional Council. **Concern(s):** education; environment; childhood; bioregionalism. Promotes a bioregional perspective in education—the recognition that "humans must establish a new respectful relationship with nature and recover a sense of place." This ecological approach emphasizes diversity and decentralization, relevant to both the content and process of education.

T ▸ **Popline**
110 Maryland Ave. NE
Washington, DC 20002 (202)544-3300
**Affiliation:** Population Institute. **Concern(s):** Third World; environment; demographics; population growth. A news and feature service provided to more than 2,100 daily newspapers worldwide, correspondents in 159 countries and US policymakers. It explores, analyzes, and evaluates facts and public policies relating to the problem of world overpopulation. The Population Institute is a non-governmental public education organization, supported by private funds and does not seek or receive US government grants. Nonprofit. **Contact(s):** Werner Fornos (President).

D ▸ **Population and Development Review**
One Dag Hammarskjold Plaza
New York, NY 10017 (212)644-1300
**Affiliation:** Population Council. **Concern(s):** demographics; Third World; population growth; development. This journal reports on the population increases in the world and the ways that they are being combated. It also reports on the development that this growth is causing and the effects that it is having. **Frequency:** 4/yr. **Contact(s):** George Zeidenstein.

D ▸ **Population Bulletin**
Population Reference Bureau
1875 Connecticut Ave. NW, #520
Washington, DC 20009 (202)482-1100
**Affiliation:** Population Reference Bureau. **Concern(s):** demographics; population growth. In-depth reports by experts analyzing world and national demographic trends. Widely used by universities, businesses, individuals, and the media. The Bureau has been established since 1929. Nonprofit. **Est.:** 1956. **Frequency:** 4/yr. **Subscription:** $45/yr. **Price:** $7/ea. **Pages:** 50. (800)877-9881(orders). **Contact(s):** Mary Kent (Editor).

E ▸ **Population Newsletter**
666 Pennsylvania Ave. SE, 2nd floor
Washington, DC 20003 (202)547-9009
**Affiliation:** National Audubon Society Population Program. **Concern(s):** environment; demographics; feminism; population; population growth; family planning. Reports on the Program's activities. In addition it has informative articles that report on ways to help curb the population explosion. This newsletter is not for the birds! **Frequency:** 6/yr. **Contact(s):** Patricia Baldi (Director).

T ▸ **Population Reports**
624 N. Broadway
Baltimore, MD 21205 (301)955-7666
**Affiliation:** John Hopkins University, Population Communications Services. **Concern(s):** Third World; population. Helps promote family planning in Third World countries and promote free choice in contraceptive methods.

D ▸ **Population Today**
Population Reference Bureau
1875 Connecticut Ave. NW, #520
Washington, DC 20009 (202)483-1100
**Affiliation:** Population Reference Bureau. **Concern(s):** demographics; population growth. A magazine with a wide variety of population trends in the US and around the world, from new census and survey reports, to conferences, software, and book reviews, to features on important domestic and international population issues. The Bureau was founded in 1929. Nonprofit. **Est.:** 1973. **Dues:** $45/yr. **Frequency:** 12/yr. **Subscription:** $45/yr. **Price:** $2/ea. **Fax:** (202)328-3937. (800)877-9881(orders). **Contact(s):** Susan Kalish (Editor).

$ ▸ **Portable Dwelling Newsletter**
Box 190-MU
Philomath, OR 97370
**Concern(s):** economics; environment; recreation. For long-period camping; or living in tent, tipi, wickiup, cave, van, trailer, boat, remote cabin, etc. Plans for shelters, conveniences and comforts easily improvised most anywhere: simple shower, portable faucet, ovenless baking, insulated tipi, and others. Plus candid product reports, tips, contacts. It interweaves "primitive" and "space age" tech for comfort, lightness, low cost. Shelters and conveniences easily improvised anywhere: city, farm, mountains, travelling. **Other Resources:** Formerly the MESSAGE POST. **Frequency:** Irregular. **Subscription:** $5/yr. **Price:** $1/ea. **Pages:** 16. **Circ.:** 1.2M. **Publisher:** Light Living Library.

✌ ▸ **Positive Alternatives**
222 C View St.
Mountain, CA 94041 (415)968-8798
**Affiliation:** Center for Economic Conversion. **Concern(s):** peace; economics; economic conversion. Formerly the Plowshare Press, the voice of the Conversion movement — the movement to shift resources and talent from military to socially and environmentally useful activities. The publication covers local, regional, and national efforts and includes news reports, analysis, interviews, and book reviews. **Frequency:** 4/yr. **Subscription:** $25/yr. **Circ.:** 4M. **Contact(s):** Michael Closson (Director).

D ▸ **Post Amerikan**
Box 3452
Bloomington, IL 61701
**Concern(s):** demographics; agriculture; rural communities. **Frequency:** 6/yr. **Subscription:** $6/yr.

E ▸ **Powerline**
6930 Carroll Ave., #600
Tacoma Park, MD 20912 (301)891-1100
**Affiliation:** Environmental Action Foundation. **Concern(s):** environment. "The economic and environmental effects of nuclear power are the chief topic. Electric rates, nuclear accidents and waste management are specifically covered."-C.C. **Est.:** 1975. **Frequency:** 6/yr. **Subscription:** $20, $30 institution. **Contact(s):** Christina Nichols.

P ▸ **The Practical Strategist**
721 Shrader St.
San Francisco, CA 94117
**Affiliation:** Social Movement Empowerment Project. **Concern(s):** politics; peace; nonviolence; civil disobedience. Major emphasis is placed on believing in and recognizing activist movement successes. Another emphasis is on recognizing the many roles of social activists and working with them rather than charging that others are on the wrong track. Four roles are characterized by this newspaper: "the citizen", "the rebel", "the social change agent", and "the reformer". **Other Resources:** See also, THE MAP TRAINING MANUAL. **Price:** $2/ea.

H ▸ **Practitioner Resources Newslogue**
3906 W. Ina Rd., #200-345
Tucson, AZ 85741 (602)744-7887
**Concern(s):** health; holism; alternative consumer. This Newslogue is a newsletter developed for the healing arts practitioner: filled with tips, techniques, and suggestions for a successful practice and a balanced life. Topics include marketing, personal development, insurance updates, tax information, and more. The catalog features business products and tools: books on practice management, partnership, marketing, business software, video cassettes, and specialty items. **Other Resources:** Sponsors workshops on practice management. Nonprofit. **Est.:** 1991. **Frequency:** 3/yr. **Price:** Free. **Fax:** (602)744-7887. **Contact(s):** Cherie Sohnen-Moe (Co-director).

J ▸ **The Pragmatist, A Utilitarian Approach**
A Utilitarian Approach
Box 392
Forest Grove, PA 18922
**Concern(s):** justice; economics; taxation; civil liberties. "..presents practical proposals for saving every person thousands in taxes by opening up government monopolies and services to competition. Examines beliefs and legislation that hinder individual lifestyle choices." **Frequency:** 6/yr. **Subscription:** $10/yr. **Price:** $3/ea. **Pages:** 16. **Circ.:** 1.8M. **Contact(s):** Jorge E. Amador (Editor).

A ▸ **Prairie Journal**
PrairieFire Rural Action
550 11th St., #200
Des Moines, IA 50309
**Affiliation:** PrairieFire Rural Action. **Concern(s):** agriculture; environment; family farms; rural communities News and feature articles on the organization's work and key issues concerning farm and rural advocacy. Nonprofit. **Dues:** $35/yr. **Frequency:** 4/yr. **Circ.:** 500.

A ▸ **Prairie Naturalist**
Box 8238
Grand Forks, ND 58202
**Concern(s):** agriculture; rural communities.

A ▸ **Prairie Paper**
825 M St., #101
Lincoln, NE 68508 (402)477-0825
**Concern(s):** agriculture; rural communities.

E ▸ **Preservation News**
1785 Massachusetts Ave. NW
Washington, DC 20036 (202)673-4000

**Affiliation:** National Trust for Historical Preservation. **Concern(s):** environment; conservation. Newsletter. **Frequency:** 12/yr.

**⚐ ▶ Preventing School Failure**
Heldref Publications
4000 Albemarle St. NW
Washington, DC 20016  (202)362-6445
**Concern(s):** education. Preventing School Failure is the journal for educators and parents seeking strategies for promoting the success of students with learning and behavior problems. It spotlights examples of programs and practices that are helping children. Practical and specific articles in Preventing School Failure are written by teachers, teacher educators, and parents. Frequent special sections include: "Frankly Speaking," "Getting It Together," and "On the Horizon." **Frequency:** 4/yr. **Subscription:** $35, $52 institution.

**H ▶ Prevention**
Rodale Press
33 Minor St.
Emmaus, PA 18049
**Affiliation:** Rodale Foundation. **Concern(s):** health; nutrition. This longtime established health magazine tackles a wide variety of problems. Its uniqueness lies in the fact that the majority of its writers are health professionals.

**E ▶ Prime Times**
Grote Deutsch & Co.
2802 International Lane, #120
Madison, WI 53704
**Concern(s):** environment; health; economics; psychology; consumerism; seniors. Articles on travel, environment, science, health, human interest, regional interest, humor, family, retirement, consumerism, and psychology are used by Prime Times. "No nostalgia, sentimentalized fiction, or stereotyping." Readers of the quarterly are 50+ years old with diverse interests. **Contact(s):** Rod Clark (Executive Editor).

**⚐ ▶ Priority Parenting**
Box 1793
Warsaw, IN 46580  (219)453-3864
**Concern(s):** education; child raising; families. "To support the way you nurture your family." Theme issues on single parenting, handling holidays, pregnancy loss, older kids, etc. Feedback and resource listings. This newsletter supports and encourages parents to follow their hearts and instincts and not society's dictates. **Other Resources:** Parent's reference book called NOT ON THE NEWSSTANDS, a guide to over 125 little known parenting publications. **Est.:** 1984. **Frequency:** 12/yr. **Subscription:** $14/yr. **Price:** $2/ea. **Bulk:** 50% off/24. **Pages:** 20. **Circ.:** 250. **Contact(s):** Tamra Orr (Editor).

**J ▶ Prison News Service**
Box 5052, Station A
Toronto, ON M5W 1W4 Canada
**Affiliation:** Bulldozer Collective. **Concern(s):** justice; peace; political prisoners; Native Americans; indigenous peoples; minority rights; social justice; reform; criminal system; prisons. A newspaper focusing chiefly on political prisoners in America and Canada, but not exclusively. Special concern for Native and ethnic peoples. Questions the wisdom and authority of our justice systems and the conditions in which prisoners are kept. Written almost entirely by prisoners, it delivers a perspective of the underclass and other disenfranchised found in no other periodical. **Subscription:** $10 donation/prisoners free.

**J ▶ Prisoners' Legal News**
c/o Paul Wright, #930783
Box 5000, HC-63
Clallum Bay, WA 98326
**Concern(s):** justice; reform; criminal system; social justice. "'Working to Extend Democracy to All' is produced by Washington State prisoners. It details recent court cases of relevance to prisoners, as well as informative articles."-Prison News Service. **Other:** Box 1684, Lake Worth, FL 33460.

**J ▶ Privacy Journal**
Box 15300
Washington, DC 20003  (202)547-2865
**Concern(s):** justice. "If you think that computers and governments have too much information on you, then you will like this newsletter. Incorrect information in local credit bureau files was the subject of a particularly comprehensive article in a recent issue."-C.C. "An independent monthly newsletter on privacy in a computer age." **Est.:** 1974. **Frequency:** 12/yr. **Subscription:** $109/yr. **Contact(s):** Robert Ellis Smith.

**✐ ▶ Processed World**
41 Sutter St., #1829
San Francisco, CA 94104  (415)751-7365

**Affiliation:** Bay Area Center for Art & Technology. **Concern(s):** arts; media; culture. "The award-winning BAD ATTITUDE magazine caustically covers the Underside of the Information Age: Unique incisive analysis, wild graphics, biting satire, great poetry and fiction." "Processed World has shown that rethinking the relationship between labor and liberation is as simple as opening your eyes and describing what you see."-Village Voice **Est.:** 1980. **Frequency:** 2/yr. **Subscription:** $15/2 yrs. **Pages:** 64. **Circ.:** 4M.

**⚙ ▶ The Professional**
1616 P St. NW, #320
Washington, DC 20036  (202)332-4823
**Affiliation:** Professionals' Coalition for Nuclear Arms Control. **Concern(s):** peace; politics; disarmament; lobbying. This newsletter provides insightful analysis of congressional activities and specific actions that citizen lobbyists can take to influence pending legislation. **Est.:** 1984. **Contact(s):** Victoria Almquist.

**⚙ ▶ Progress**
Box 2309
La Jolla, CA 92038  (619)454-3343
**Affiliation:** Mothers Embracing Nuclear Disarmament (MEND). **Concern(s):** peace; feminism; anti-nuclear; disarmament. Quarterly newsletter with regular communique and practical information and ideas for personal actions one can take to help make our world more peaceful. Nonprofit. **Contact(s):** Maureen Pecht King (Executive Director).

**P ▶ The Progressive**
Box 421
Mt. Morris, IL 61054-0421  (608)257-4626
**Concern(s):** politics; justice; civil liberties; activism; grassroots organizing. A magazine of opinion and social commentary. "For 80 years, [it] has been a leading voice of dissent in America." **Frequency:** 12/yr. **Subscription:** $30/yr. **Office:** 409 E. Main St. Madison, WI 53703. **Contact(s):** Erwin Knoll (Editor), Joy E. Wallin

**A ▶ A Progressive Grocer**
Four Stamford Forum
Stamford, CT 06901
**Concern(s):** agriculture; economics; trade. Articles related to retail food operations; ideas for successful merchandising, promotions, and displays. **Contact(s):** Michael J. Sansolo (Manager Editor).

**P ▶ Progressive Review**
1739 Connecticut Ave. NW
Washington, DC 20009  (202)232-5544
**Concern(s):** politics; analysis. "The Review has impressive coverage from the nation's capital on national and international concerns. An alternative newspaper 20 years ago, it has evolved into a small magazine consisting of short pieces on interesting social and cultural issues. Highly recommended."-C.C. **Est.:** 1966. **Frequency:** 9/yr. **Subscription:** $13/yr. **Price:** $1/ea. **Contact(s):** Sam Smith.

**⚙ ▶ Progressive Student News**
Box 1027
Iowa City, IA 52244  (319)351-8041
**Affiliation:** Progressive Student Network. **Concern(s):** peace; Third World; economics; education; justice; South Africa; divestments; boycott; human rights. "This networking tool serves to spread ideas and success stories of student organizing around peace and freedom issues. "Study and struggle" is the Network's slogan. They feel that campus democracy and demands for divestment of investments in South African are important concerns."-C.C. **Est.:** 1980. **Frequency:** 5/yr. **Subscription:** $6/yr. **Price:** Free. **Contact(s):** Bruce Nestor.

**⚙ ▶ Promoting Enduring Peace**
Box 5103, 112 Beach Ave.
Woodmont, CT 06460  (203)878-4769
**Concern(s):** peace. "Each packet consists of a number of reprinted articles on peace concerns from the progressive press. The packets are meant to be samples from which you may choose to order copies in bulk for distribution just for the price of the postage. It is a unique service."-C.C. **Est.:** 1952. **Frequency:** 4/yr. **Subscription:** Free (postage for bulk copies). **Contact(s):** Howard Frazier, Alice Frazier.

**M ▶ Propaganda Review**
c/o Media Alliance
Bldg. C, Fort Mason Ctr.
San Francisco, CA 94123
**Affiliation:** Media Alliance. **Concern(s):** media; politics; media watch; government accountability. Surveys and documents the "propaganda environment" through analysis of the US government, corporatiosn, institutions, the media, and politicians.

**E ▶ Protecting Children**
American Humane Association
Box 1266
Denver, CO 80201  (303)695-0811

**Affiliation:** American Humane Association. **Concern(s):** environment; feminism; justice; animal rights; child abuse. "Preventing child abuse is the point of this newsletter. The pieces in its 24 pages effectively present ideas on stopping mistreatment - whether by parents or outside the home environment."-C.C. **Frequency:** 4/yr. **Subscription:** $5/yr. **Price:** $2/yr. **Office:** 1984 **Contact(s):** Kathryn Bond.

**⚙ ▶ PSR Reports**
1000 16th St. NW, #810
Washington, DC 20036  (202)785-3777
**Affiliation:** Physicians for Social Responsibility. **Concern(s):** peace; health; energy; education; disarmament; global understanding; anti-nuclear.

**H ▶ Psychologists for Social Responsibility Newsletter**
1841 Columbia Rd. NW. #209
Washington, DC 20009  (202)745-7084
**Affiliation:** Psychologists for Social Responsibility. **Concern(s):** health; peace. "The psychologists' counterpart to the PSR selection listed above analyzes peaceful ways of conflict resolution. Talking, instead of violence, is suggested as an alternative to the arms race; nuclear weapons in particular."-C.C. **Est.:** 1982. **Frequency:** 4/yr. **Subscription:** $35/yr. **Price:** $1.50/ea. **Contact(s):** Anne Anderson.

**F ▶ Psychology of Women Quarterly**
Department of Education & Counseling
University of Kentucky; 237 Dickey Hall
Lexington, KY 40506-0017
**Affiliation:** American Psychological Association. **Concern(s):** feminism; health; psychology. Academic journal that discusses issues pertaining to women's psychology. **Est.:** 1976. **Frequency:** 4/yr. **Subscription:** $32/yr. **Price:** $20/ea. **Pages:** 128. **Contact(s):** Judith Warell (Editor).

**$ ▶ Public Citizen**
2000 P St. NW., #605
Washington, DC 20036-0757  (202)833-3000
**Affiliation:** Public Citizen. **Concern(s):** economics; health; environment; consumer rights; corporate responsibility. "Nader's Raiders advocate better-quality products and corporate and government reform in this thick newspaper. Citizen involvement in these issues is recommended to reform the system and make it work better. Investigative reports and articles of timely political interest on consumer rights, health and safety, environmental protection, safe energy, tax reform, and government and corporate accountability."-C.C. **Est.:** 1980. **Dues:** $20/yr. **Frequency:** 6/yr. **Subscription:** Membership. **Price:** $2/ea. **Contact(s):** Catherine Baker.

**L ▶ Public Employee**
1625 L St. NW, #1115
Washington, DC 20036  (202)452-4800
**Affiliation:** American Federation of State, County, and Municipal Employees. **Concern(s):** labor. "This magazine is a popularly written voice of labor, of interest to the general public as well as union members. AFSCME banners are often seen at national demonstrations, indicating that their interests go beyond unionism."-C.C. **Est.:** 1959. **Frequency:** 12/yr. **Subscription:** $5/yr. **Price:** Free. **Contact(s):** Marshall O. Donley Jr.

**J ▶ The Public Eye Magazine**
14 Beacon St., #407
Boston, MA 02108
**Affiliation:** Civil Liberties Committee, Massachusetts National Lawyers Guild. **Concern(s):** justice; politics; civil liberties; government accountability; CIA. A magazine covering government intelligence, abuse, right-wing spying, and harrassment of progressives. **Frequency:** 4/yr.

**⚐ ▶ Public Interest Report**
307 Massachusetts Ave. NE
Washington, DC 20002  (202)546-3300
**Affiliation:** Federation of American Scientists. **Concern(s):** education; politics. "Recommendations for educational and legislative action are presented in this scientists' social action newsletter. Resources on these ideas and reduction of nuclear weapons are regular parts of the reports."-C.C. **Est.:** 1946. **Frequency:** 12/yr. **Subscription:** $12.50/yr. **Price:** $1.25/ea. **Contact(s):** Jeremy Stone.

**⚐ ▶ Public School Montessorian**
230 10th Ave. South
Minneapolis, MN 55415
**Concern(s):** education; childhood. Examines the application of Montesorri education in public school settings. Addresses issues of child development, teacher preparation, public education policies, and more. A good resource for non-Montesorri trained parents and educators who want to understand Montessori

principles. **Frequency:** 4/yr. **Subscription:** $12/yr. **Price:** $20 parent groups (20 copies).

### M ▸ Publisher's Weekly
Box 1979
Marion, OH 43302 (800)842-1669

**Concern(s):** media; arts; literature; press. PW "has been keeping authors informed about the business of books for over 100 years. Each issue gives you a broad and colorful overview of all that's new and newsworthy in the field [of] book design and manufacturing. News of people in the field. Bookselling and marketing. The international scene. Media tie-ins. Calendars of upcoming events. Convention reports, advance reviews of approximately 100 hardcover and paperback books. Industry trends and prospects." **Subscription:** $119, $97/writers.

### E ▸ Pulse of the Planet
Box 1395
El Cerrito, CA 94530 (510)526-5978

**Affiliation:** Orgone Biophysical Research Lab. **Concern(s):** environment; energy; education; science; analysis; research. An Environmental & Geophysical Journal focused upon the bioenergetic research findings of Dr. Wilhelm Reich. Global surveys of biological, atmospheric and geophysical events and anomalies for each week of the year, plotted on world maps. Articles and notes on new developments in Bioenergetic Research. **Frequency:** Annual. **Subscription:** $20/yr. **Price:** $20/ea. **Bulk:** 40% off/24. **Pages:** 100. **Circ.:** 1M. **Publisher:** Natural Energy Works. **Contact(s):** Dr. James DeMeo (Director/Editor).

### ✪ ▸ The PV Network News
2303 Cedros Circle
Santa Fe, NM 87505 (505)473-1067

**Concern(s):** energy; solar. A solar electric and DC systems user newsletter. One issue is Solar Electricity Today, a directory listing 600+ books, catalogs, magazines, newsletters, dealers, mail order shops, and manufacturers of PV and related equipment. This issue is $7 alone. A 4-issue subscription for $15 gets 3 issues of how-to information and Solar Electricity Today. **Other Resources:** VHS videos. PV Places is 2 hours of visiting PV installations in the west, water pumping, houses (including a utility disconnect) RV's, offices and studios. Short Course in PV is nearly 4 hours of classroom. Tapes are not broadcast quality. **Est.:** 1980. **Frequency:** 4/yr. **Subscription:** $15/yr. **Pages:** 8. **Circ.:** 200. **Labels:** 1200. **Contact(s):** A. D. Paul Wilkins (Editor/publisher).

### ✪ ▸ PV News
c/o PV Energy Systems, Inc.
Box 290
Casanova, VA 22308

**Affiliation:** PV Energy Systems. **Concern(s):** energy; solar; alternative. This newsletter reports the latest research and industrial developments in photovoltaics. Coverage of international events is quite detailed. Issues regularly contain editorial commentaries, meeting notices, and bibliographic citations for new PV publications. **Est.:** 1981. **Frequency:** 12/yr.

### S ▸ Quaker Service Bulletin
1501 Cherry St.
Philadelphia, PA 19102 (215)864-0204

**Affiliation:** American Friends Service Committee. **Concern(s):** spiritual; peace; justice; faith; social justice. "The Friends' Committee ranks with the Unitarian Universalists' Service Committee in their wide-ranging efforts for social justice and concerns across the globe, with their programs explained in their fine bulletin."-C.C. **Est.:** 1919. **Frequency:** 3/yr. **Subscription:** $5/yr. **Price:** Donation. **Contact(s):** Diane Shandor.

### H ▸ Quality Care Advocate
National Citizens Coalition for Nursing Home Reform
1224 M St. NW
Washington, DC 20005 (202)393-2018

**Affiliation:** National Citizens Coalition for Nursing Home Reform. **Concern(s):** health; consumer protection. "Nursing homes should be enjoyable places to live, not warehouses for the elderly, says this newsletter. Suggestions are made for improvement of individual facilities and for legislation raising the standards of all nursing homes."-C.C. **Est.:** 1986. **Frequency:** 6/yr. **Subscription:** $25/yr. **Price:** Free. **Contact(s):** Janet Wells.

### S ▸ Quest
Theosophical Publishing House
Box 270
Wheaton, IL 60189 (312)668-1571

**Concern(s):** spiritual; transformation; psychology. "A metaphysical magazine, with articles on philosophy, comparative religion, science, arts, psychology, and powers latent in [hu]man[s]." **Est.:** 1988. **Subscription:** $14/yr. **Price:** $3.95/ea. **Pages:** 96. **Circ.:** 40M. **Contact(s):** William Metzger.

### ✏ ▸ Quixote
1812 Marshall
Houston, TX 77098 (713)529-7944

**Affiliation:** Quixote Collective. **Concern(s):** arts; activism. "This leftist literary journal looks for the humorous side to oppression, imperialism, and other social ills. There is an abundance of poetry, including some translations of Latin American poems."-C.C. **Est.:** 1966. **Frequency:** 12/yr. **Subscription:** $20/yr. **Price:** $2/ea. **Contact(s):** Melissa Bondy.

### E ▸ R.A.C.H.E.L'S Hazardous Waste News
Environmental Research Foundation
Box 73700
Princeton, NJ 08543-3541

**Affiliation:** Environmental Research Foundation. **Concern(s):** environment; energy; hazardous/toxic waste; waste management. News and resources for the movement for environmental justice. Information for citizens fighting toxics in their communities. Important technical information summarized into language that anyone can understand — so the powers that be don't hold a monopoly on information. This newsletter contains short and direct articles; designed for the busy activist. **Other Resources:** R.A.C.H.E.L. (Remote Access Chemical Hazards Electronic Library) under media section. **Frequency:** Weekly. **Subscription:** $25/yr. **Pages:** 2. **Contact(s):** Abbi Allen (Office Manager), Peter Montague (Editor). **Other:** Environmental Research Foundation, Box 73700, Washington, DC 20056-3700.

### P ▸ Radical America
One Summer St.
Somerville, MA 02143 (617)628-6585

**Affiliation:** Radical America Collective. **Concern(s):** politics; justice; alternative party; Democratic Socialism. "It was the harbinger of the many New Left journals that flowered in the 1960s and 1970s. Today it is not only the oldest of this type of journal, but ranks with Socialist Review as the best. This independent journal exerts much influence on the democratic left with its articles, properly balanced between historical perspective and topical strategy."-C.C. **Est.:** 1967. **Frequency:** 6/yr. **Subscription:** $15/yr. **Price:** $3.95/ea. **Contact(s):** Kim Westheimer.

### ✍ ▸ Radical History Review
70 Washington Square S, 10th Fl.
New York, NY 10012 (212)464-5108

**Affiliation:** Mid-Atlantic Radical Historians' Organization (MARHO). **Concern(s):** education; justice; politics; feminism; research. Written in jargon-free English, RHR examines the ways hierarchies of all types have been constructed and reconstructed. Issues of race, class, and gender regularly inform political critiques of history and history writing. RHR also offers review essays and analyses of the uses and abuses of history in the popular media, history museums and other public forums. Nonprofit. **Est.:** 1975. **Dues:** $24, $20 students. **Frequency:** 3/yr. **Subscription:** $24, $20 students. **Price:** $5/ea. **Pages:** varies. **Circ.:** 1.8M. **Publisher:** Cambridge University Press. **Contact(s):** David Nasaw.

### ✍ ▸ Radical Teacher
Box 102
Cambridge, MA 02142 (617)492-3468

**Affiliation:** Boston Women's Teachers' Group. **Concern(s):** education; feminism. "A discussion of sex roles in alternative schools typifies their progressive/feminist perspective. These teachers believe that nonauthoritarian, student-centered teaching is best." -C.C. "A Socialist and Feminist Journal on the Theory and Practice of Teaching." **Est.:** 1975. **Frequency:** 3/yr. **Subscription:** $8, $11 institution. **Price:** $3/ea. **Contact(s):** Susan O'Malley. **Other:** Box 1160, Pauma Valley, CA 92061.

### ? ▸ Rain
Box 30097
Eugene, OR 97403-1097

**Concern(s):** future; energy; economics; environment; education; agriculture; politics; ideation; sustainability; science; appropriate technology; community self-reliance; family farms. "In this magazine we look for socially just, radically democratic, and ecologically sound alternatives to the dominant corporate, status scene. We examine in detail the workings, origins, and reasons for success behind actions taken by communities around the world. By concentrating on what has already happened, ideas and methods that have really worked, Rain searches for a sustainable future." **Est.:** 1974. **Frequency:** 4/yr. **Subscription:** $20/yr. **Price:** $5/ea. **Contact(s):** Danielle Janes, Greg Bryant (Co-editors).

### S ▸ Rainbow City Express
Box 8447
Berkeley, CA 94707

**Concern(s):** spiritual; feminism; environment; health; transformation; psychology. Accounts of spiritual awakening, Kundalini activation, archetypal stirrings, collective consciousness/evolution of consciousness, women's spirituality, reincarnation/Karma, ecological concerns and creative self-expression, and many related topics. Our magazine's goal has been to provide a peaceful forum for the sharing of disparate experiences/viewpoints. **Other Resources:** STARRY ARCHERS GAZETTE, a network/society/quarterly newsletter for Sagittarians and other creative souls interested in creative sharing and growth. **Est.:** 1988. **Frequency:** 4/yr. **Subscription:** $24/yr. **Price:** $6/ea. **Bulk:** 40% off/24. **Pages:** 65. **Circ.:** 1M. **Contact(s):** Helen B. Harvey (Editor/Publisher).

### E ▸ Rainforest Action Network Alert
450 Sansome St., #700
San Francisco, CA 94111-3315 (415)398-4404

**Affiliation:** Rainforest Action Network. **Concern(s):** environment; Third World; conservation; forests; global warming; development; boycott. This newsletter focuses on the nightmarish destruction taking place against the rainforests of the world and the actions being taken to stop them. **Frequency:** 12/yr. **Contact(s):** Randall Hayes (Executive Director).

### E ▸ Raise the Stakes
Box 31251
San Francisco, CA 94131 (415)285-6556

**Affiliation:** Planet Drum Foundation. **Concern(s):** environment; urban; bioregionalism; urban sustainability. Newspaper. See Foundation. **Dues:** $20/yr.; $25 outside US; 25% discounts. **Frequency:** 2/yr. **Price:** $4/ea. **Pages:** 16. **Circ.:** 2M. **Contact(s):** Kari Carter (Editorial/Production), Judy Goldhaft (Production/Director).

### E ▸ Ranger Rick
1400 16th St. NW
Washington, DC 20036 (202)797-6800

**Affiliation:** National Wildlife Federation. **Concern(s):** environment; education; wildlife/endangered species; conservation; youth; recreation. Articles on wildlife, conservation, natural sciences, and kids in the outdoors, for 6- to 12-year-olds. Nature-related fiction and science fiction welcome. Games, crafts, poems, and puzzles. **Contact(s):** Gerald Bishop (Editor).

### ✪ ▸ re news digest
861 Central Parkway
Schenectady, NY 12309 (518)372-1799

**Concern(s):** energy; environment; renewables; solar; conservation; wind; transportation; appropriate technology.. This news service informs about the latest in solar, photovoltaics, conservation, geothermal, research biomass, wind power, wave power, energy policy, and all forms of renewable energy. They read over more than 80 publications and give their readers the essential details. Calender of conferences included. Looseleaf. **Frequency:** 12/yr. **Subscription:** $60 yr; $97/2 yrs. **Pages:** 8. **Contact(s):** Sandra Oddo (Editor/Publisher).

### E ▸ Re: Sources
6930 Carroll Ave., #600
Tacoma Park, MD 20912 (301)891-1100

**Affiliation:** Environmental Task Force. **Concern(s):** environment. "Consists of a collection of features, a bibliography and a resources directory. In addition, there is a section of brief notes on sundry environmental points."-C.C. **Est.:** 1980. **Frequency:** 4/yr. **Subscription:** $16/yr. **Price:** $4/ea. **Contact(s):** Morgan Gopnik.

### ♿ ▸ RE: view
Heldref Publications
4000 Albemarle St. NW
Washington, DC 20016 (202)362-6445

**Concern(s):** education; health; disabled; children; youth. Formerly Education for the Visually Handicapped, it interests all persons concerned with services for visually handicapped children, youth and adults, including those who are multihandicapped and/or deaf-blind. Articles deal with useful practices, research findings, investigations, professional experiences, and controversial issues in education, rehabilitation teaching and counseling, orientation and mobility, and other services for the visually handicapped. **Frequency:** 4/yr. **Subscription:** $40/yr.

### ✪ ▸ Real Goods News
966-M Mazzoni St.
Ukiah, CA 95482

**Affiliation:** Real Goods Trading Co.. **Concern(s):** energy; environment; renewables; efficiency; alternative markets. A newsletter of the Real Goods Trading Co., who publish the catalogue Real Good Alternative Energy Sourcebook. **Frequency:** 3/yr. **Subscription:** $20/yr. **Circ.:** 150M. **Contact(s):** John Schaeffer (Proprietor), Eileen Enzla (Manager).

### P ▸ Realist
Box 1230
Venice, CA 90294 (310)392-5848

**Concern(s):** politics. "After a 10-year hiatus, The Realist is back, albeit in newsletter format instead of the former magazine. Satire continues to be the forte, with Paul Krassner's irreverent creation poking fun at all staid convention. Krassner continues his '60s participation in the Free Speech Movement with this outrageously funny publication in the tradition of Lenny Bruce." -C.C. **Est.:** 1958. **Frequency:** 4/yr. **Subscription:** $8/yr. **Price:** $2/ea. **Contact(s):** Paul Krassner (Editor/Publisher).

**S ⬥ Reality Change**
Box 7786
Austin, TX 78713-7786  (512)479-8909
**Affiliation:** Austin Seth Center. **Concern(s):** spiritual; transformation. Our magazine's purpose is to enhance human dignity everywhere by teaching a philosophy that empowers people to achieve positive life changes with love, fun, and awareness. It publishes articles that relate how individuals put these ideas into practice in their daily lives. Nonprofit. **Est.:** 1984. **Dues:** $50/yr. **Frequency:** 4/yr. **Subscription:** $18/yr. **Price:** $5.95/ea. **Bulk:** 40% off/24. **Pages:** 68. **Circ.:** 600. **Other Formats:** None. **Labels:** 2000. **Contact(s):** Maude Cardwell (Director & President), David Millican (Vice President). (512)477-3423.

**P ⬥ Reason**
Box 526
Mt. Morris, IL 61054    (310)392-0443
**Concern(s):** politics; justice; demographics; economics. "Deals with social, economic and political issues, supporting both individual liberty and economic freedom. ...political sophisticated analysis, solid reporting, and excellent writing" from a liberal-libertarian perpective. **Frequency:** 11/yr. **Subscription:** $19.95/yr. **Office:** 2716 Ocean Park Ave., #1062 Santa Monica, CA 90405.

**⬥ RECON**
Box 14602
Philadelphia, PA 19134
**Concern(s):** peace. This newsletter exposes Pentagon activity worldwide. Clarifies shady military events.

**E ⬥ Recycle!**
c/o Earth Care Paper Inc.
4601 Hammersleu Rd.
Madison, WI 53714    (608)277-2920
**Affiliation:** Earth Care Paper Co. **Concern(s):** environment; recycling. Addresses issues related to recycling in all sectors, including paper, oil, batteries. The journal's articles are written entirely by William C. Burns, Director of Environmental Affairs at Earth Care. Earth Care also devotes 15% of its direct mail catalog to environmental education. It supplies recycled paper products for consumers and businesses in the US, Canada, Japan, and Finland. **Other Resources:** Educational materials on a wide range of recycling issues for both adults and children. The company also has an extensive fund raising program for schools and other groups. **Est.:** 1982. **Frequency:** 2/yr. **Subscription:** Free with any order. **Price:** $2/ea. **Circ.:** 600M. **Contact(s):** William C. Burns (Director/Environmental Affairs), Carol T. Moseson (Director of Marketing).

**✎ ⬥ Red Bass**
216 Charter
New Orleans, LA 70130  (504)522-7158
**Concern(s):** arts; culture; poetry. "Individual issues often concentrate on a theme, with the prose, essays, interviews, reviews, and poetry revolving around the theme. It is undoubtedly the best literary review published in the South today." -C.C. **Est.:** 1983. **Frequency:** Irregular. **Subscription:** $10, $15 institution. **Price:** $4/ea. **Publisher:** Red Bass Productions. **Contact(s):** Jay Murphy.

**E ⬥ Reflections**
Box 368
Duncan Falls, OH 43734
**Concern(s):** environment; education; wildlife/endangered species; conservation; youth. "A National Magazine Publishing Student Writing." Fiction and nonfiction, poetry, any length. "Our magazine goes into K through 12th grades of schools and general offices. The purpose is to encourage writing." **Frequency:** 2/yr. **Contact(s):** Dean Harper (Editor).

**M ⬥ Reforma Newsletter**
c/o Elaine Valenzuela
Main Library, Box 27470
Tucson, AZ 85726
**Affiliation:** Reforma (National Association to Promote Library Service to the Spanish Speaking). **Concern(s):** media. "Libraries should have more books, periodicals, and audio media in Spanish, says Reforma. Some progress has been made in New York and Miami, but more efforts should be made - especially in the Southwest, with its large Hispanic population." -C.C. **Est.:** 1982. **Frequency:** 4/yr. **Subscription:** $20, $35 institution. **Price:** $5/ea. **Contact(s):** Elaine Valenzuela.

**D ⬥ Refugees**
UN High Commissioner on Refugees
1718 Connecticut Ave. NW
Washington, DC 20009  (202)387-8546
**Affiliation:** United Nations High Commissioner on Refugees. **Concern(s):** demographics; refugees; immigration.

**P ⬥ Regardie's**
1010 Wisconsin Ave. NW, #600
Washington, DC 20007  (202)342-0410
**Concern(s):** politics. Profiles and investigations of the "high and mighty" in the DC area: "We require aggressive reporting and imaginative, entertaining writing." **Contact(s):** Brian Kelly (Editor).

**☸ ⬥ Religion for Peace**
777 UN Plaza
New York, NY 10017    (212)687-2163
**Affiliation:** World Conference on Religion and Peace. **Concern(s):** peace; spiritual; justice; conflict resolution; interfaith. "Officials of churches and synagogues join together here to promote the peace and justice purposes of the United Nations. Disarmament, equitable resource distribution and self-determination are some ideas promoted." -C.C. **Other Resources:** See also WCRP/USA REPORT. Nonprofit. **Est.:** 1963. **Frequency:** 3/yr. **Subscription:** $10/yr. **Contact(s):** John B. Taylor (Editor), Norma U. Levitt (President).

**S ⬥ Religious Humanism**
Box 278
Yellow Springs, OH 45387  (513)324-8130
**Affiliation:** Fellowship of Religious Humanists. **Concern(s):** spiritual; interfaith. "This cross-religious humanist journal nicely complements the Christian-humanist and Jewish-humanist ones. Genetics, situation ethics, and science and religion are typical topics." -C.C. **Est.:** 1963. **Frequency:** 4/yr. **Subscription:** $10/yr. **Price:** $2.50/ea. **Contact(s):** Paul Beattie, Lucina Beattie.

**S ⬥ Religious Socialism**
45 Thornton St.
Roxbury, MA 01908    (617)427-3953
**Affiliation:** Democratic Socialists of America — Religion & Socialism Commission. **Concern(s):** spiritual; reform; interfaith. "There is no contradiction between being a believer and being a socialist, says the DSA. The social gospel is promoted as a good way of putting religion to use here on Earth." -C.C. **Est.:** 1977. **Frequency:** 4/yr. **Subscription:** $5/yr. **Price:** $1.50/ea. **Contact(s):** John C. Cort.

**E ⬥ Renew America Report**
Renew America
1400 16th St. NW, #710
Washington, DC 20036  (202)232-2252
**Affiliation:** Renew America. **Concern(s):** environment; energy; natural resource; conservation; resource management. A newsletter featuring articles and columns relating current issues to the development of a sustainable society. **Frequency:** 4/yr. **Subscription:** $25/yr. **Pages:** 16. **Circ.:** 7M. **Contact(s):** Ric Barrick (Director of Communication), Norma Rogers

**◉ ⬥ Renewable Resources Journal**
5430 Grosvenor Lane
Bethesda, MD 20814    (301)493-9101
**Affiliation:** Renewable Natural Resources Foundation. **Concern(s):** energy; renewable resources. This journal reports on renewable natural resources and public policy alternatives. **Est.:** 1972. **Contact(s):** W. Watson Fenimore (Associate Editor).

**P ⬥ Report from the Capital**
200 Maryland Ave. NE
Washington, DC 20002  (202)544-4226
**Affiliation:** Baptist Joint Committee on Public Affairs. **Concern(s):** politics; spiritual; law; faith. Magazine. **Frequency:** 10/yr.

**P ⬥ Report from the Hill**
League of Women Voters
1730 M St. NW
Washington, DC 20036  (202)429-1965
**Affiliation:** League of Women Voters. **Concern(s):** politics; feminism. Newsletter. **Contact(s):** Nancy M. Newman (President), Grant P. Thompson (Executive Director).

**T ⬥ Report on Guatemala**
Box 28594
Oakland, CA 94604    (510)835-0810
**Affiliation:** Guatemala News and Info Bureau. **Concern(s):** Third World; justice; Central America. "This report is a top source for social progress news from that Central American country. Peasant cooperative efforts, the reform movement, US military aid, and the death squads are all featured." -C.C. **Est.:** 1978. **Frequency:** 6/yr. **Subscription:** $10, $15 institution. **Price:** $1.25/ea. **Contact(s):** Daniele Rossdeutscher.

**T ⬥ Report on Science and Human Rights**
1333 H St. NW
Washington, DC 20005  (202)326-6790
**Affiliation:** American Association for the Advancement of Science. **Concern(s):** Third World; justice; education; South America. "Terror by Uruguay's military physicians and psychiatric abuses here in the US are topics that give an idea of the thrust of this selection. It shows scientists' concern for human rights at home and abroad." -C.C. **Est.:** 1978. **Frequency:** 4/yr. **Subscription:** Free. **Contact(s):** K. Hannibal.

**P ⬥ Report to Presbyterians from Washington**
110 Maryland Ave. NE
Box 52
Washington, DC 20002  (202)543-1126
**Concern(s):** politics; justice; demographics; spiritual; education; faith; lobbying; law. "Social justice legislative efforts needing support are summarized in this newsletter. Presbyterians interested in working with others from their denomination on such issues will want to subscribe." -C.C. **Est.:** 1979. **Frequency:** 6/yr. **Subscription:** $3/yr. **Price:** Free. **Contact(s):** George A. Chauncey.

**A ⬥ The Reporter**
100 Maryland Ave. NE, #500A
Washington, DC 20002  (202)544-5750
**Affiliation:** American Agricultural Movement. **Concern(s):** agriculture; politics; law. Newspaper that reports on legislation dealing with the US agricultural community. Very informative. **Frequency:** 12/yr.

**☸ ⬥ Reporter for Conscience' Sake**
1601 Connecticut Ave. NW
Washington, DC 20009  (202)483-4510
**Affiliation:** National Interreligious Service Board of Conscientious Objectors. **Concern(s):** peace; spiritual; interfaith; anti-draft.

**P ⬥ Resist**
One Summer St.
Somerville, MA 02143    (617)623-5110
**Affiliation:** Resist. **Concern(s):** politics; justice; anti-authoritarian; philanthropy. "One or two feature articles on "resisting illegitimate authority," combined with a report on recent grants by Resist to social change groups, make up the 8-page newsletter. Typical articles may cover dissidents in the US or other countries and their democratic actions." -C.C. **Est.:** 1967. **Frequency:** 10/yr. **Subscription:** $7.50, $15 institution. **Contact(s):** Tatiana Schreiber.

**J ⬥ Resistance News**
Box 42488
San Francisco, CA 94142    (415)524-4778
**Affiliation:** National Resistance Committee. **Concern(s):** justice; politics; social justice. "Non-cooperation with illegitimate authority is explained here. A broad range of social justice concerns is touched upon in this periodical." -C.C. **Est.:** 1980. **Frequency:** Irregular. **Subscription:** $5/yr. **Price:** Free. **Contact(s):** Fred Moore, Matt Nicodemus

**T ⬥ Resource Center Bulletin**
Box 4506
Albuquerque, NM 87196 (505)842-8288
**Affiliation:** Inter-Hemispheric Resource Center. **Concern(s):** Third World; development; hunger; foreign policy. "Resource materials, mostly on the Third World, are included here. One or two articles, as well as the resources, are included in each 4-page issue." -C.C. **Est.:** 1984. **Frequency:** 4/yr. **Subscription:** $5/yr, $7.50 foreign. **Price:** $1.50/ea. **Pages:** c8. **Circ.:** 3.5M. **Contact(s):** Tom Barry.

**E ⬥ Resource Recycling**
Box 10540
Portland, OR 97210    (503)227-1319
**Concern(s):** environment; recycling. A journal that covers issues of recycling of paper, plastic, metals and glass. Technical and non-opinionated. Likes regional articles and is expanding issues on composting. **Est.:** 1982. **Frequency:** 12/yr. **Subscription:** $27/yr. **Circ.:** 8.5M. **Fax:** (503)227-6135. **Contact(s):** Jerry Powell (Editor). (800)277-1427.

**✈ ⬥ Responsible Traveling**
2 Kensington Rd.
San Anselmo, CA 94960 (415)843-5506 (H)
**Affiliation:** Center for Responsible Tourism. **Concern(s):** education; travel. This newsletter reports quarterly on the activities of the Center. It provides networking information for those organizations and individuals wanting to travel responsibly. **Frequency:** 4/yr. **Subscription:** $10/donation. **Circ.:** 2M. **Contact(s):** Virginia T. Hadsell (Executive Director), Betty Stott (Office Manager). (415)258-6594.

**$ ⬥ Responsive Philanthropy**
2001 S St. NW, #620
Washington, DC 20009  (202)387-9177

**Affiliation:** National Committee for Responsive Philanthropy. **Concern(s):** economics; alternative consumer. "If you feel guilty about your million dollars and want to give some of it to public interest groups, this periodical is for you. Working- and middle-class folks can also gain ideas on more effectively fulfilling our social responsibility."-C.C. **Other Resources:** Newsletter. **Est.:** 1977. **Frequency:** 4/yr. **Subscription:** $25/yr. **Contact(s):** Robert Bothwell.

### E ♦ Resurgence
Rodale Press
33 Minor St.
Emmaus, PA 18049

**Affiliation:** Schumacher Society. **Concern(s):** environment; spiritual; conservation. This magazine represents the best of British "green" thinking. It is more than an environmental magazine, it has articles on a wide range of themes, including ecology, conservation, sustainability, education, new science, small scale economics and politics. **Frequency:** 6/yr. **Subscription:** $32/yr. **Pages:** 64. **Publisher:** Rodale Press. **Contact(s):** Satish Kumar (Editor).

### P ♦ Rethinking Marxism
Box 85
Newton Center, MA 02159

**Concern(s):** politics; alternative party. Marxism. **Frequency:** 4/yr. **Subscription:** $24/yr.

### ✍ ♦ Rethinking Schools
Box 93371
Milwaukee, WI 53202    (414)265-6217

**Concern(s):** education; justice; peace; urban; conflict resolution; childhood; diversity; Native Americans. An independent educational journal/newspaper published by educators in Milwaukee area public schools. Examines a wide scope of problems in today's education, including urban social problems, standardized testing, reading methods, and many issues of interest to parents as well as educators. **Other Resources:** Publishes magazine, RETHINKING COLUMBUS. Nonprofit. **Est.:** 1986. **Frequency:** 6/yr. **Subscription:** $10/yr.; $15 institutions. **Pages:** 24. **Office:** 1001 E. Keefe Milwaukee, WI 53212. **Contact(s):** Bob E. Peterson.

### $ ♦ Review of Radical Political Economics
c/o Department of Economics
University of California
Riverside, CA 92521

**Affiliation:** Union for Radical Political Economics. **Concern(s):** economics; politics. A substantial, scholarly journal considering economics from a radical perspective. **Frequency:** 4/yr. **Subscription:** $60/yr. **Pages:** 309. **Circ.:** 3M.

### S ♦ ReVision: The Journal of Consciousness and Change
Heldref Publications
4000 Albemarle St. NW
Washington, DC 20016   (202)362-6445

**Concern(s):** spiritual; energy; interfaith; science; transformation; reform. This is an international journal that makes possible an interdisciplinary dialogue between modern science and mysticism. Its goal is to provide a bridge between the ancient and the modern, between nations, cultures, races, and religions. The articles in ReVision cut across many disciplines and areas of study, including philosophy, psychology, comparative religion, cultural anthropology, thanatology, neuropsysiology, astro- and subatomic physics, biology, social sciences, and the arts. **Frequency:** 4/yr. **Subscription:** $24, $35 institution.

### E ♦ Ridge Review
Box 90
Mendocino, CA 95460-0090

**Concern(s):** environment; economics; agriculture. The best information and analysis available about life on the Northern California Coastal Ridges. Our magazine takes a long term view at institutions and the social and economic practices that shape our lives. Each issue is dedicated to a different topic such as Agriculture, Housing, Media, Fairs, Water, Money, and Justice. Over 30 topics. **Frequency:** 4/yr. **Subscription:** $10/yr. **Price:** $3/ea. **Bulk:** $1.80ea/24. **Pages:** 60. **Circ.:** 3.5M. **Publisher:** Ridge Times Press. **Contact(s):** Jim Tarbell, Judy Tarbell (Publisher/Editors).

### J ♦ Rights
175 5th Ave.
New York, NY 10010    (212)673-2040

**Affiliation:** National Emergency Civil Liberties Committee. **Concern(s):** justice; civil liberties. "This magazine contains features defending our liberties under the Bill of Rights, such as the freedoms of speech, religion, and assembly. In addition to publication of the magazine, the group brings cases to trial in defense of these rights."-C.C. **Est.:** 1953. **Frequency:** 6/yr. **Subscription:** $7.50/yr. **Price:** $1/ea. **Contact(s):** Jeff Kisseloff.

### H ♦ RNA Advisor
3636 Medical Dr., #101
San Antonio, TX 78229   (800)842-8101

**Concern(s):** health; labor; jobs; occupational safety. Employment advisor for RN's around the US. Besides job openings, it also reports on abuse of nurses, job hazards, and innovative nursing practices. **Price:** Free. **Publisher:** Chrysalis Publishing Company. **Contact(s):** John Flemming.

### E ♦ Robin Newsletter
7781 Lenox St.
Jacksonville, FL 32221

**Affiliation:** Forest Ecosystem Rescue Network (FERN). **Concern(s):** environment; agriculture; forests; permaculture. News from the FERN and SOLUTIONS Networks. A forum for dialogue on issues, strategies and the evolution of permaculture design providing publicity for other groups with similar interests. The Tree Bank, a FERN program, is a strategy for saving the temperate forests. Once a year they stage a "Fate of Our Forests" conference. **Est.:** 1984. **Dues:** $16.50 US, $18 foreign. **Frequency:** Irregular. **Subscription:** Membership. **Bulk:** 10% off/24. **Publisher:** Yankee Permaculture. **Labels:** 20000. **Contact(s):** Dan Hemenway, Cynthia Baxter (Coordinators).

### S ♦ Rocinante
Box 5206
Hyattsville, MD 20782    (301)699-0042

**Affiliation:** Quixote Center. **Concern(s):** spiritual; Third World; justice; faith. "Features reports on projects of the Quixote Center, a Catholic social concerns group. These projects include humanitarian aid to Nicaragua, racial and economic justice efforts, and increased democracy in the church."-C.C. **Est.:** 1976. **Frequency:** 4/yr. **Subscription:** Donation. **Price:** Free. **Contact(s):** D. Pomerleau.

### ◉ ♦ Rocky Mountain Institute Newsletter
1739 Snowmass Creek Rd.
Old Snowmass, CO 81654-9199

**Affiliation:** Rocky Mountain Institute. **Concern(s):** energy; environment; agriculture; natural resources; global warming; conservation. Reports on the Institute's important work in the area of energy, water, security and local economic renewal. Pioneers in the least-cost method of planning.

### P ♦ Roll Call: The Newspaper of Capitol Hill
900 2nd St. NE
Washington, DC 20002   (202)289-4900

**Concern(s):** politics. Factual, breezy articles with political or Congressional angle; Congressional historical and human-interest subjects; political lore; political satire and humor. **Contact(s):** James K. Glassman (Editor-in-chief).

### A ♦ Rural Advance
2124 Commonwealth Ave.
Charlotte, NC 28205    (704)334-3051

**Affiliation:** Rural Advancement Fund/National Sharecroppers Fund. **Concern(s):** agriculture; labor; media; farm policy; farm workers; press; family farms. "Farmers, farmworkers, and sharecroppers all have a voice in this newsletter. Conditions of farm work and the struggle to save the family farm are key focal points."-C.C. **Est.:** 1937. **Frequency:** 4-5/yr. **Price:** Free. **Contact(s):** Cary Fowler.

### E ♦ Ruralite
Box 558
Forest Grove, OR 97116

**Concern(s):** environment; health; rural communities. Articles of interest to a primarily rural and small-town audience in Oregon, Washington, Idaho, Nevada, northern California, and Alaska. "Think pieces" affecting rural/urban interests, biographies, local history and celebrations, self-help, etc. Humorous articles and animal pieces. No fiction or poetry. No sentimental nostalgia.

### E ♦ RWC Waste Paper
625 Broadway, 2nd Fl.
New York, NY 10012    (212)473-7390

**Affiliation:** Radioactive Waste Campaign. **Concern(s):** environment; energy; peace; health; hazardous/toxic waste; anti-nuclear. "Transportation and storage of nuclear by-products are the focus. Dangerous transfer of these wastes on our highways and the expensive storage required for thousands of years indicate that these problems should be treated by stopping nuclear power and weapons."-C.C. **Est.:** 1979. **Frequency:** 4/yr. **Subscription:** $8/yr. **Price:** $1/ea. **Contact(s):** Steven Becker.

### E ♦ The Sacred Earth Journal
Box 620883
San Diego, CA 92102

**Affiliation:** Sacred Earth Society. **Concern(s):** environment; spiritual; politics; transformation; alternative party; interfaith. A forum for free thought and unique concepts for saving our Mother Earth. The

views expressed are from all extremes of the political spectrum. Spirituality, from all religious perspectives and scientific analysis. Also "Tools of Empowerment" are presented. **Est.:** 1990. **Frequency:** 4/yr. **Subscription:** $15/yr. **Price:** $1.50/ea. **Bulk:** 25% off/24. **Pages:** 20. **Circ.:** 4M. **Publisher:** Paul Wade for the Sacred Earth Society. **Contact(s):** Eric Siegel (Founder/Chairman), Paul Wade (Publisher/Editor). (619)563-6230.

### F ♦ The Sacred Path
Box 570394
Tarzana, CA 91357

**Affiliation:** Men's Center Of Los Angeles. **Concern(s):** feminism; men's liberation. Newsletter. **Contact(s):** Jim Takacs (Editor).

### A ♦ Safe Food Action
1875 Connecticut Ave. NW
Washington, DC 20009   (202)332-9110

**Affiliation:** Americans for Safe Food/Center for Science in the Public Interest. **Concern(s):** agriculture; health; environment; hazardous/toxic waste. Newsletter. **Frequency:** 4/yr.

### A ♦ The Safe-Food Gazette
1875 Connecticut Ave. NW
Washington, DC 20009   (202)332-9110

**Affiliation:** Americans for Safe Food/Center for Science in the Public Interest. **Concern(s):** agriculture; health; environment; nutrition; consumer protection; hazardous/toxic wastes. Newsletter.

### F ♦ Sage: A Scholarly Journal on Black Women
c/o SWEP, Box 42741
Atlanta, GA 30311-0741 (404)681-3643

**Concern(s):** feminism; justice; arts; literature; diversity; minority rights; racism; sexism. Reports on black women's studies, Afro American and women's literature. Provides an interdisciplinary forum, promotes feminist scholarship, and disseminates new knowledge about Black women to a broad audience. **Other Resources:** Ask for extension 360. **Frequency:** 2/yr. **Subscription:** $15, $25 institution. **Price:** $8/ea. **Pages:** 72. **Circ.:** 2M. **Contact(s):** Patricia Bell Scott (Editor).

### J ♦ SAIIC Newsletter (South & Meso American Indian Information Center Newsletter)
Box 28703
Oakland, CA 94604    (510)834-4263

**Concern(s):** justice; Native Americans; indigenous peoples. SAIIC's goals are to promote peace and social justice for Indian People: 1) by providing information to the general public in North America, Europe, and to human rights and solidarity organizations regarding the struggles for survival and self- determination of Indian peoples of South and Meso America; 2) by facilitating exchange and promoting direct communication and understanding between native peoples. **Other Resources:** SAIIC's projects and programs include: 1) publication of the Newsletters in Spanish and English, as well as other special publications; 2) Indian Visitor Program; 3) human rights advocacy; 4) 500 Years of Resistance project; 5) Indian Women's Project; **Est.:** 1983. **Frequency:** 4/yr. **Subscription:** $15/yr.; $30/outside US. **Bulk:** $35/2. **Pages:** 26-40. **Circ.:** 4M. **E-Network:** PeaceNet. **ID:** 'saiic'. **Fax:** (510)834-4264. **Contact(s):** Nilo Cayuqueo (Coordinator), Peter Veilleux (Editor/office manager).

### M ♦ St. Louis Journalism Review
8380 Olive Blvd.
St. Louis, MO 63132    (314)991-1699

**Concern(s):** media; media watch; press; responsibility. A Critique of St. Louis metropolitan affairs, print and broadcast media by working journalists in the St. Louis area. Also covers news and developments not covered by the mass media. Critique of media: press, broadcasting, TV, cable, advertising, P.R. communications. Independent, investigative journal evaluating local, regional, and national news. Content of direct interest both to general public/media community. **Est.:** 1970. **Frequency:** 12/yr. **Subscription:** $25/yr. **Price:** $2/ea. **Bulk:** 50% off/24. **Pages:** 26. **Circ.:** 6.5M. **Contact(s):** Charles L. Klotzer (Editor/Publisher).

### ✍ ♦ SAMISDAT
456 Monroe Turnpike
Monroe, CT 06468    (203)452-0446

**Concern(s):** arts; environment; justice; peace; literature; poetry; culture. Founded toward the end of the Vietnam War, this magazine knows the real war never ended. We're still fighting - for the needs of the planet, human rights, and the rights of animals, with stories, poems, reviews, and critical commentary. **Other Resources:** "We do some related chapbook publishing." **Est.:** 1973. **Frequency:** Annual. **Subscription:** $15/yr. (includes books). **Price:** $3/ea. **Pages:** 50. **Circ.:** 300. **Contact(s):** Merritt Clifton (Editor/Publisher).

### ✍ ♦ San Fernando Poetry Journal
18301 Halstead St.
Northridge, CA 91325    (818)349-7080

**Concern(s):** arts; poetry. "This review goes beyond the regional by presenting an outlet for poetry about national concerns of war and peace, justice and freedom. The peace-related poetry in particular makes the journal a top selection in its specialty."-C.C. **Est.:** 1980. **Frequency:** 4/yr. **Subscription:** $10/yr. **Price:** $3/ea. **Publisher:** Kent Publications. **Contact(s):** Richard Cloke.

P ◆ **San Francisco Bay Guardian**
520 Hampshire St.
San Francisco, CA 94110    (415)255-3100
**Concern(s):** politics; environment; arts. An urban newsweekly specializing in investigative, consumer and lifestyle reporting for a sophisticated, urban audience. **Frequency:** weekly. **Contact(s):** Bruce Brugmann (Editor/Publisher).

� ◆ **SANE World/Freeze Focus**
1819 H St. NW, #1000
Washington, DC 20006-3603    (202)546-7100
**Affiliation:** SANE/Freeze. **Concern(s):** peace. "SANE and the Nuclear Freeze Campaign have merged, producing one of the largest and most effective peace organizations. This marriage is producing a nice combination of articles on local peace organizing and national rallies and lobbying drives. This publication (and organization) is recommended to anyone concerned about peace."-C.C. **Dues:** $25/yr. **Frequency:** 4/yr. **Subscription:** Membership. **Price:** $5/ea. **Contact(s):** Richard Samuel West.

✐ ◆ **The Santa Cruz Comic News**
Box 8543
Santa Cruz, CA 95061    (408)426-0113
**Concern(s):** arts; politics; graphics. "This Planet's First Cartoon Newspaper." **Est.:** 1984. **Frequency:** 24/yr. **Subscription:** $21.95/yr./ $20 out of state. **Contact(s):** Thom Zajac (Editor), Mark Zepezauer (Associate Editor).

✐ ◆ **Sassafras**
Box 26004
Alexandria, VA 22313    (703)922-2800
**Affiliation:** People's Music/Freedom. **Concern(s):** arts; music. "Promotion of progressive folk music and networking among concerned musicians of all types is the purpose. News of festivals, concerts, and conferences also makes it a good networking tool."-C.C. **Est.:** 1980. **Frequency:** 2/yr. **Subscription:** $5-$25/yr. **Price:** Donation. **Contact(s):** Marsha Lee Cutting. (703)941-0086.

E ◆ **Save Our Earth**
2008 1/2 Preuss Rd.
Los Angeles, CA 90034 (310)839-1976
**Concern(s):** environment; demographics; population; population growth. This newsletter reports on the overpopulation problem and ways to help solve it. **Contact(s):** Elaine Stansfield (Director/Editor).

E ◆ **Save the Whales**
Box 2397
Venice, CA 90291    (310)392-6226
**Affiliation:** Save the Whales. **Concern(s):** environment; education; wildlife/endangered species; oceans/rivers; childhood. Newsletter. Nonprofit. **Est.:** 1977. **Office:** 1426 Main St. Venice, CA 90291. **Contact(s):** Maris Sidenstecker (President).

E ◆ **Save-The-Redwoods Bulletin**
114 Sansome St.
San Francisco, CA 94104    (415)367-2352
**Affiliation:** Save-The-Redwoods. **Concern(s):** environment; energy; forests; conservation; resources. This bulletin reports on lobbying efforts in the halls of Washington and state capitals to save the redwoods. Also it details efforts of the logging industry to derail these efforts and continue on their destructive paths. **Contact(s):** Bruce S. Howard (President), John B. Dewitt (Executive Director).

✐ ◆ **Science and Nature**
53 Hickory Hill
Tappan, NY 10983    (914)359-2283
**Affiliation:** Dialectics Workshop. **Concern(s):** education; research. "Natural scientists look at socialist philosophy as it applies to their fields. The 160 pages of each issue of the journal cover the range of disciplines."-C.C. **Est.:** 1978. **Frequency:** Annual. **Subscription:** $6.50/yr. **Price:** $6.50/ea. **Contact(s):** Lester Talkington.

✐ ◆ **Science and Society**
#4331, John Jay College
CUNY, 445 W. 59th St.
New York, NY 10019
**Concern(s):** education; energy; agriculture; analysis; science. **Frequency:** 4/yr. **Subscription:** $15/yr.

✐ ◆ **Science for the People**
897 Main St.
Cambridge, MA 02139    (617)547-0370

**Affiliation:** Science Resource Center. **Concern(s):** education; health; consumer protection; occupational safety; science. "Positive and negative applications of science for human needs versus military needs and the profit motive are discussed. Medical research, occupational health, psychology applications are covered."-C.C. **Est.:** 1969. **Frequency:** 6/yr. **Subscription:** $12/yr. **Price:** $2/ea.

✐ ◆ **The Scientific Worldview**
Box 5335
Berkeley, CA 94705    (510)654-1619
**Affiliation:** Progressive Science Institute. **Concern(s):** education; energy; science. An outline of the scientific philosophy that will develop during the last half of the Industrial-Social Revolution. From the viewpoint of environmental determinism, the author criticizes classical mechanism as fatalistic and modern systems philosophy as solipsistic.

✐ ◆ **The Scientist**
1133 15th St. NW
Washington, DC 20015 (202)857-0355
**Affiliation:** American Association for the Advancement of Science. **Concern(s):** education; energy; science. "A behind-the-scenes look inside labs, and into the boardrooms of the fast changing world of science. Provides current news, topical opinion, research developments, and professional guidance in each and every issue." **Other Resources:** This periodical also reports on job openings for scientists worldwide. **Frequency:** 24/yr. **Subscription:** $58/yr.

E ◆ **Sea Frontiers/Sea Secrets**
4600 Rickenbacker Causeway
Key Bisqane
Miami, FL 33149-9900    (305)361-4888
**Affiliation:** International Oceanographic Foundation. **Concern(s):** environment; ocean/rivers; conservation. Illustrated articles on scientific advances related to the sea, biological, physical, chemical, or geological phenomena, ecology, conservation, etc., written in a popular style for lay readers. **Other Resources:** Books available. Nonprofit. **Est.:** 1953. **Frequency:** 6/yr. **Contact(s):** Jean Bradfisch (Executive Editor), Edward T. Foote II (President).

E ◆ **Sea Shepherd Log**
Box 7000-S
Redondo Beach, CA 90277 (310)373-6979
**Affiliation:** Sea Shepherd. **Concern(s):** environment; wildlife/endangered species; oceans/rivers. This newsletter details the adventures of Sea Shepherd, a radical activist group that sails the seas and protests anything that might endanger the animals living within. **Frequency:** 12/yr.

E ◆ **Sea Wind**
94 Station, #645
Higham, MA 02043    (617)749-5387
**Affiliation:** International Marinelife Alliance. **Concern(s):** environment; wildlife/endangered species; oceans/rivers. This bulletin reports on the alliances efforts to educate the public on the wise use and harvest of the seas natural resources. **Frequency:** 4/yr. **Fax:** (617)749-6544. **Contact(s):** Dr. Vaughn R. Pratt.

✐ ◆ **Seattle's Child**
Box 22578
Seattle, WA 98122
**Concern(s):** education; family; children. Articles of interest to parents, educators, and childcare providers for children under 12, plus investigative reports and consumer tips on issues affecting families in the Puget Sound region. **Contact(s):** Ann Bergman (Editor).

$ ◆ **Seedling**
1807 2nd St., Studio 2
Santa Fe, NM 87501    (505)986-1401
**Affiliation:** Community Economic and Ecological Development Institute. **Concern(s):** economics; environment; intentional communities; social ecology; bioregional. A newsletter reporting on the progress of CEED's intentional community, Pangea. **Est.:** 1988. **Frequency:** 4/yr. **Price:** Membership. **Contact(s):** David Mulligan, Jim Cummings (Editor).

D ◆ **Seeds Magazine**
222 E. Lake Dr
Decatur, GA 30030    (404)378-3566
**Affiliation:** Seeds: Christians Concerned About Hunger. **Concern(s):** demographics; spiritual; hunger; faith. Seeds magazine is a first rate general information source on every aspect of hunger issues. An educational ministry and a network of Christians concerned about this issue. (800)537-9359.

H ◆ **Self-Help Reporter**
25 W. 43rd St., #620
New York, NY 10036    (212)642-2929
**Affiliation:** Graduate School & University Center of CUNY. **Concern(s):** health; psychology; alternative consumer; holism; self-help; research; counseling. The newsletter has been covering the

growth of the self-help movement — the self-help ethos with its emphasis on empowerment, self-determination and mutuality; self-help group activities around the country; and research outcomes about the effectiveness of self-help. Its audience includes both professionals and laypeople involved in self-help. The newsletter reports self-help group activities, theoretical underpinnings, and new trends in this burgeoning area. **Est.:** 1976. **Frequency:** 4/yr. **Subscription:** $10/yr. **Pages:** 8. **Circ.:** 1M. **Publisher:** National Self-Help Clearinghouse. **Contact(s):** Audrey Gartner (Executive Director), Frank Riessman (Director). (212)642-2944.

H ◆ **Senior Citizens News**
925 15th St. NW
Washington, DC 20005    (202)624-9500
**Affiliation:** National Council of Senior Citizens. **Concern(s):** health; seniors; national health; medicare "One of the most progressive seniors' organizations, and this is reflected in their newspaper. Social security cutbacks, Medicare, and other concerns of older citizens are featured."-C.C. **Est.:** 1962. **Frequency:** 12/yr. **Subscription:** $10/yr. **Price:** $1/ea. **Contact(s):** Theresa McKenna.

H ◆ **Senior Magazine**
3565 S. Higuera St.
San Luis Obispo, CA 93401
**Concern(s):** health; seniors. Personality profiles and health articles and book reviews of interest to senior citizens of California.

J ◆ **Sequoia**
942 Market, #707
San Francisco, CA 94102    (415)434-0672
**Affiliation:** Northern California Council of Churches. **Concern(s):** justice; Third World; politics; peace; environment; spiritual; interfaith. "Although published by California churches, Sequoia's beat is the world, with Third World news as likely as news of the churches social concerns work in California. Its subtitle, 'the church at work,' reflects the social responsibility of the church promoted in this periodical."-C.C. **Est.:** 1979. **Frequency:** 6/yr. **Subscription:** $12/yr. **Price:** $2/ea. **Contact(s):** Janet Burks, Paul Burks

✈ ◆ **SERVAS International News (magazine)**
11 John St.
New York, NY 10038    (212)267-0252
**Affiliation:** SERVAS USA. **Concern(s):** education; travel.

J ◆ **Service Committee News**
78 Beacon St.
Boston, MA 02108    (617)742-2120
**Affiliation:** Unitarian Universalist Service Commission. **Concern(s):** justice; spiritual; faith; hunger; social justice. "Among the most militant in defending peace and working for justice across the globe. Their newsletter goes beyond the usual religious charity to promotion of self-help and social change to eliminate the causes of hunger and injustice."-C.C. **Est.:** 1939. **Dues:** $25/yr. membership. **Frequency:** 4/yr. **Contact(s):** Leora Zeitlin.

D ◆ **The Shadow**
Box 20298
New York, NY 10069    (212)921-4317
**Concern(s):** demographics; justice; homelessness. "An activist/anarchist paper based on squatters struggles in New York. Of particular interest to anyone from NYC, but its excitement is infectious."-Prison News Service. **Office:** 265 W. 37th. St. New York, NY 10018.

✐ ◆ **Shalom - The Jewish Peace Letter**
Box 271
Nyack, NY 10960    (914)358-4601
**Affiliation:** Jewish Peace Fellowship. **Concern(s):** peace; environment; spiritual; faith. Members are a diverse group of people, religious and secular Jews from all traditions and branches of Judaism. All believe deeply that Jewish ideals and experience provide inspiration for a nonviolent way of life. We strive to build a social order that will utilize the resources of human ingenuity for the benefit of all, in which our concern for the future will be shown by respect for the precious resources of the Earth. Newsletter. **Frequency:** 4/yr. **Subscription:** $5/yr. **Bulk:** Negotiable. **Pages:** 8. **Circ.:** 3.5M. **Contact(s):** Joyce Bressler (Staffperson), Rabbi Philip Bentley (President).

S ◆ **Shaman's Drum**
Box 430
Willits, CA 95490
**Concern(s):** spiritual; transformation. This superbly-produced magazine can be regarded as the central focus and forum for the revival of interest in shamanism in our time. **Subscription:** $15/yr. **Contact(s):** Timothy White (Editor).

T ◆ **SHARE International Foundation**
6530½ Sepulveda Blvd.
Van Nuys, CA 91411-1394
**Concern(s):** Third World; justice; hunger; human rights; self-deter-

mination. This newsletter's premise: "Everyone has the right to a standard of living adequate for the health and well-being of himself and his family, including food, clothing, housing and medical care and necessary social services, and the right to security in the event of unemployment, sickness, disability, widowhood, old age or other lack of livelihood in circumstances beyond their control."—Universal Declaration of Human Rights, Article 25. Nonprofit. **Frequency:** 10/yr. **Pages:** 24.

**E ▸ Share the Earth Newsletter**
Box 831
Boulder, CO 80306 (303)444-6430
**Affiliation:** Jim Morris T-Shirts Catalog. **Concern(s):** environment; politics; activism; conservation; animal rights; wildlife/endangered species. A newsletter of the Jim Morris T-Shirts company that has a unusual twist: It actually doesn't promote the company. Instead it puts out useful and informative information about the problems facing our society today. **Est.:** 1978. **Frequency:** 4/yr. **Subscription:** $5/yr. **Pages:** 8. **Publisher:** Mountain Media and Graphic Center. **Contact(s):** Jim Morris (Founder/Editor).

**$ ▸ Shared Living Community**
2375 Shattuck Ave.
Berkeley, CA 94704 (510)548-6608
**Affiliation:** Shared Living Resource Center. **Concern(s):** economics; urban; environment; education; intentional communities; community self-reliance; social ecology; architecture. Newsletter. **Est.:** 1990. **Frequency:** 4-6/yr. **Subscription:** $15-25/yr. **Pages:** 8. **Circ.:** 1.3M. **Fax:** (510)549-9960. **Contact(s):** Ken Norwood (Executive Director), David Hawkins (Administative Assistance).

**✍ ▸ Sharing Space**
Box 271
Nyack, NY 10960 (914)358-4601
**Affiliation:** Fellowship of Reconciliation (CCRC). **Concern(s):** education; conflict resolution. This newsletter serves as a support system for teachers and others who are using the CCRC (Children's Creative Response to Conflict) insights in working with children. Readers and CCRC staff share new ideas, techniques and activities. **Frequency:** 3/yr. **Subscription:** $5/yr. **Price:** $1/ea. **Pages:** 12. **Contact(s):** Paula Cuth Conner.

**♈ ▸ Shelter Sense**
2100 L St. NW
Washington, DC 20037 (202)452-1100
**Affiliation:** Humane Society of the US. **Concern(s):** environment; animal rights. A newsletter for animal-control and animal-shelter personnel.

**J ▸ Shelterforce**
439 Main St.
Orange, NJ 07050 (201)678-3110
**Affiliation:** National Housing Institute. **Concern(s):** justice; demographics; economics; housing; tenant rights; cooperatives. "Tenant rights and fair housing are the organizing points. Articles written by activists in co-ops, apartments and projects across the US explain how you can organize with others for good quality affordable housing."-C.C. **Est.:** 1975. **Frequency:** 6/yr. **Subscription:** $15, $25 institution. **Price:** $3/ea. **Contact(s):** Woody Widrow.

**D ▸ A Shift in the Wind**
The Hunger Project
1 Madison Ave.
New York, NY 10010 (212)532-4255
**Affiliation:** Hunger Project. **Concern(s):** demographics; hunger. The world's largest circulation newspaper on the subject of hunger (approximately 2 million households throughout the world). Nonprofit. **Contact(s):** Jean Holmes (Executive Director).

**S ▸ SHMATE**
Box 4228
Berkeley, CA 94704
**Concern(s):** spiritual; Third World; justice; faith. "A journal of politics, culture, and the arts, with emphasis of a progressive Jewish approach, literature, and action; special issues on single subjects e.g. humor, Holocaust resistance, gay and lesbian Jews, Jewish identity, the political and social right, the farm crisis, Gypsies/Roma, gays and the Holocaust, Israel and Palestine, pornography..." **Est.:** 1982. **Frequency:** 4/yr. **Subscription:** $15; $25 institutions. **Price:** Sample $3; $6.50 institutions. **Circ.:** 3M.

**✐ ▸ Shoe Tree**
215 Valle del Sol Dr.
Santa Fe, NM 87501
**Affiliation:** National Association for Young Writers. **Concern(s):** arts; education; literature; poetry; youth; childhood. Fiction, nonfiction, and poetry by writers ages 6 to 14. "We are looking for writing with a strong voice." **Contact(s):** Sheila Cowing (Editor-in-chief).

**E ▸ Sierra**
730 Polk St.
San Francisco, CA 94109 (415)923-5544
**Affiliation:** Sierra Club. **Concern(s):** environment; politics; education; conservation; lobbying. "Enjoying the outdoors is primary with Sierra, with the love for natural beauty reflected in the sympathetic editorial policy in favor of keeping the outdoors unexploited and natural. If you want a slick, full color outdoors magazine, Sierra is a good choice."-C.C. **Est.:** 1893. **Frequency:** 6/yr. **Subscription:** $35/yr. **Fax:** (415)776-4868. **Contact(s):** Jonathan King (Editor-in-chief).

**E ▸ Sign Control News**
216 7th St. SE
Washington, DC 20003 (202)546-1100
**Affiliation:** Scenic America. **Concern(s):** environment; conservation; beautification. Summary of news, legal decisions, and other developments regarding sign control, view protection and other aesthetic regulations. Provides an articulate, informed voice for those who believe it is not necessary to sacrifice the character of our communities or the beauty of our landscape for America to grow economically. Stands up against the billboard industry and others responsible for visual pollution. **Other Resources:** Publishes newsletter, SIGN CONTROL News. Books, factsheets and reprints also available. Nonprofit. **Dues:** $20/yr. **Frequency:** 6/yr. **Subscription:** Membership. **Pages:** 8. **Contact(s):** Edward T. McMahon, Joan Moody (Communications Director).

**✈ ▸ Signpost Magazine**
Washington Trails Association
1305 Fourth Ave., #512
Seattle, WA 98101 (206)625-1367
**Affiliation:** Washington Trails Association. **Concern(s):** education; environment; recreation; travel. "Editorial comment heavily weighted for Pacific Northwest backpackers, ski tourers, snow shoers, etc.," and related activities. Trail and road conditions and places to go in Washington State and elsewhere. **Est.:** 1975. **Frequency:** 12/yr. **Subscription:** $25/yr. **Price:** $2.50/ea. **Pages:** 40. **Circ.:** 3.3M. **Contact(s):** Ann Marshall (Editor).

**F ▸ Signs: Journal of Women in Culture & Society**
207 E. Duke Building
Duke University
Durham, NC 27708 (919)684-2783
**Concern(s):** feminism; education; arts; literature; empowerment. A journal of theoretical and historical issues concerning women in all areas of society. It has essays and book reviews. **Est.:** 1975. **Frequency:** 4/yr.. **Subscription:** $29, $21 students, $58 institution. **Contact(s):** Jean O'Barr (Editor).

**E ▸ Silent Sports**
717 10th St.
Box 152
Waupaca, WI 54981
**Concern(s):** environment; recreation. Upper Midwest monthly on bicycling, cross-country skiing, running, canoeing, hiking, backpacking, and other "silent" sports; articles. **Frequency:** 12/yr.

**✐ ▸ Sing Heavenly Muse! Women's Poetry & Prose**
Box 13320
Minneapolis, MN 55414
**Concern(s):** arts; feminism; poetry. Short stories, essays, and poetry.

**✐ ▸ Sing Out! Magazine**
Box 5253
Bethlehem, PA 18015 (215)865-5366
**Concern(s):** arts; music. A "journal covering traditional, contemporary, and ethnic folk music. Each issue features complete lead sheets to 20 songs with feature articles, interviews, reviews, news, festival listings, instrumental 'teach-ins', and regular columns by founder Pete Seeger and other prominent artists in the folk world covering issues ranging from children's music to performing artists' issues to storytelling and more." **Est.:** 1950. **Frequency:** 4/yr. **Subscription:** $15/yr. **Price:** $3.75/ea. **Pages:** 100. **Publisher:** Sing Out Corp. **Contact(s):** Mark D. Moss.

**✍ ▸ Sipapu**
23311 County Rd. 88
Winters, CA 95694 (916)662-3364
**Concern(s):** education; peace; Third World. "Social concerns publications on topics such as peace, culture, and the Third World are reviewed in this selection. Occasional interviews with progressive writers and editors and other fine features, make Sipapu a top selection in its genre."-C.C. "A newsletter for librarians, collectors, and others interested in the alternative press." **Est.:** 1970. **Frequency:** 2/yr. **Subscription:** $8/yr. **Price:** $4/ea. **Pages:** 24. **Circ.:** 400. **Contact(s):** Noel Peattie (Editor/Publisher).

**M ▸ SIPIscope**
355 Lexington Ave.
New York, NY 10017 (212)661-9110
**Affiliation:** Scientists' Institute for Public Information. **Concern(s):** media; education; environment; health; science; media watch; AIDS. A newsletter focusing on media coverage of science, technology, environment, and health. Each issue contains narrative and interviews of scientists, policy-makers, and media people and has a particular focus — recent issues have been on: "New Realities in National Security"; "Report From the Cutting Edge" (new science developments for TV reporters); "A Successful TV Science Show: Who's Got the Answer?"; "Covering AIDS: It's Not Just Another Story." **Frequency:** 4/yr. **Subscription:** $25/free to working journalists. **Pages:** 28. **Circ.:** 8M. **Other Formats:** Media Resource Service-(800)223-1730. **Contact(s):** Jay Letto (Assistant Editor), Fred Jerome (Editor).

**✍ ▸ The Skeptical Inquirer**
Box 229
Buffalo, NY 14215 (716)834-3222
**Concern(s):** education; science. "A breath of fresh air, separating the fact from the fiction in the flood of occultism and pseudoscience on the scene today. Each issue features authors such as Carl Sagan, Isaac Asimov, Martin Garnder, and James Randi on all aspects of the paranormal. Are you curious? Magazine articles are about science facts, either the fringes or the mainstream, from a skeptical point of view. In-depth reports, facts, and figures on what scientists and organizations claim and what is fact." **Frequency:** 4/yr. **Subscription:** $25/yr. **Fax:** (716)834-0841. **Contact(s):** Paul Kurtz.

**E ▸ Skipping Stones: A Multicultural Children's Quarterly**
Box 3939
Eugene, OR 97403-0939
**Concern(s):** environment; education; youth. A multi-ethnic children's magazine that encourages cooperation, creativity and a celebration of cultural and environmental richness. Acts as a playful forum for communication among children from different lands and backgrounds, accepting writings and art from children everywhere and in all languages. An English translation accompanies the original text. **Other Resources:** Provides pen-pals for children. **Est.:** 1988. **Frequency:** 4/yr. **Subscription:** $20/institution. **Price:** $3.75 + postage. **Bulk:** 40% off/24. **Pages:** 32. **Circ.:** 2.5M. **Contact(s):** Arun N. Toke (Publication Manager), Amy Klauke (Associate Editor).

**A ▸ Small Farm Advocate**
Box 405
Walthill, NE 68067 (402)846-5428
**Affiliation:** Center for Rural Affairs. **Concern(s):** agriculture; family farms; rural communities; bioregionalism. "Family farms are promoted to continue the traditional means of food production in order to curb corporations' increasing domination over farming. Stories of folks saving their homesteads and successfully continuing food production are included."-C.C. **Frequency:** 4/yr. **Subscription:** $10, $15 institution. **Price:** $3/ea. **Contact(s):** Nancy L. Thompson.

**M ▸ Small Press Review**
Box 100
Paradise, CA 95967
**Concern(s):** media; press; journalism. News pieces and reviews about small presses and little magazines. **Contact(s):** Len Fulton (Editor).

**D ▸ Small Town**
The Small Town Institute
Box 517
Ellensburg, WA 98926
**Affiliation:** Small Town Institute. **Concern(s):** demographics; economics; environment; arts; planning; housing. The voice of small town America. Articles on planning, preservation, attracting industry, housing, shopping malls, central business district improvement and other matters of interest to small communities. **Other Resources:** PROMOTING THE ARTS IN SMALL COMMUNITIES is available for $6. **Dues:** $30/yr. **Frequency:** 6/yr. **Subscription:** Membership.

**✍ ▸ Smithsonian Magazine**
900 Jefferson Dr. SW, #1310C
Washington, DC 20560 (202)786-2900
**Affiliation:** Smithsonian Institute. **Concern(s):** education; arts; analysis; research; science. The official magazine of the Institution, presents current news within the context of a larger background and provides regular coverage each month of every subject area of the Smithsonian Museums; art, history, science and technology. **Frequency:** 12/yr. **Contact(s):** Don Moser (Editor).

**H ▸ Smoking and Health Review**
2013 H St. NW
Washington, DC 20006 (202)659-4310

**Affiliation:** Action on Smoking and Health. **Concern(s):** health; hazardous/toxic; preventative medicine; public health. "Limiting air pollution from tobacco smoke is a key goal - from the eating places to the work places. Nonsmokers' rights and health dangers from smoking are central aspects of the ASH people."-C.C. **Est.:** 1967. **Frequency:** 4/yr. **Subscription:** Donation. **Price:** Free.

P ◆ **Social Anarchism: A Journal of Practice & Theory**
2743 Maryland Ave.
Baltimore, MD 21218    (301)243-6987
**Concern(s):** politics; environment; economics; feminism; anti-authoritarian; intentional communities; Green; alternative party. Deals with subjects such as anarchism, feminism, ecology, Green politics and culture, and communitarianism. **Frequency:** 2/yr. **Subscription:** $10/4 issues. **Price:** $3/ea. **Bulk:** 40% off/24. **Pages:** 96. **Contact(s):** Howard J. Ehrlich (Editor).

$ ◆ **Social Concept**
1266 Boulevard
New Haven, CT 06511    (617)435-2450
**Concern(s):** economics; analysis. "This academic journal covers social sciences from a socially concerned perspective. Deep thinkers will get into its analysis of capital and social development."-C.C. **Est.:** 1983. **Frequency:** 2/yr. **Subscription:** $12, $25 institution. **Price:** $7/ea. **Contact(s):** David Levine.

J ◆ **Social Justice Review**
3835 Westminster Pl.
St. Louis, MO 63108    (314)371-1653
**Concern(s):** justice; politics; economics; spiritual; social justice; faith. Publishes scholarly articles on socioeconomic, religious, social, intellectual and political problems from a progressive Catholic angle. **Est.:** 1908. **Contact(s):** Rev. John H. Miller (Editor).

J ◆ **Social Justice: A Journal of Crime, Conflict & World Order**
Box 40601
San Francisco, CA 94140    (415)550-1703
**Affiliation:** Global Options. **Concern(s):** justice; peace; economics; feminism; urban; conflict resolution; sexism; racism; civil liberties; discrimination; analysis; criminal system; self-determination. Combines authoritative analysis on global issues (human rights, peaceful resolution of interstate conflict, state terrorism, sovereignty and self-determination) with domestic policy concerns such as civil liberties, and reducing crime as well as race and gender discrimination, and utilizes an inter-disciplinary approach. Nonprofit. **Est.:** 1974. **Frequency:** 4/yr. **Subscription:** $30/yr.; $68 institutions. **Price:** $10/ea. **Bulk:** 20% off/24. **Pages:** 180. **Circ.:** 3.5M. **Labels:** 1500. **Fax:** (510)528-4731. **Contact(s):** Gregory Shank (Managing Editor).

J ◆ **Social Policy**
25 W. 43rd St., #620
New York, NY 10036    (212)642-2929
**Affiliation:** Union Institute. **Concern(s):** justice; politics; education; social justice; foreign policy. "Since 1970 we have been covering key progressive political and social movements as they develop. Articles have led the way in school reform, rethinking human services, debates on voter registration, and we continue to break fresh ground with a renewed committment to community organizing. It reports on contemporary social thought, policy issues and action. It covers the range of foreign policy, the human services, economics, and more." **Est.:** 1970. **Frequency:** 4/yr. **Subscription:** $20/yr. **Price:** $5/ea. **Pages:** 64. **Circ.:** 3M. **Publisher:** The Union Institute. **Fax:** (212)719-2488. **Contact(s):** Audrey Gartner (Managing Editor), Frank Riessman (Co-editor). (212)642-2944.

S ◆ **Social Questions Bulletin**
76 Clinton Ave.
Staten Island, NY 10301  (718)273-4941
**Affiliation:** Methodist Federation for Social Action. **Concern(s):** spiritual; justice; faith. "Greater social awareness within the Methodist church and more effective social action in society are the goals. Concerns include stopping sexism, racism, and militarism, and encouraging more peaceful relations among ourselves and among nations."-C.C. **Est.:** 1910. **Frequency:** 6/yr. **Subscription:** $10/yr. **Price:** $2/ea. **Contact(s):** George D. McClain.

P ◆ **Socialism and Democracy**
33 W. 42nd St.
New York, NY 10036    (212)790-4300
**Concern(s):** politics; analysis; alternative party; reform; Democratic Socialism. It interprets historical and current development from a socialist point of view. **Frequency:** 2/yr. **Subscription:** $8/yr. **Price:** $4/ea. **Bulk:** 40% off/24. **Pages:** 200. **Circ.:** 500. **Contact(s):** Michael E. Brown, Frank Rosengarten.

P ◆ **The Socialist**
5502 W. Adams Blvd.
Los Angeles, CA 90016  (213)939-8281
**Affiliation:** Socialist Party USA. **Concern(s):** politics; Democratic Socialism. "As the organ of the Socialist Party USA founded in 1901, our magazine provides news and editorials from a democratic socialist/feminist perspective." Covers a wide range of topics. Nonprofit. **Est.:** 1976. **Dues:** $15/yr-low income; $40/yr. regular; $75/yr-high income. **Frequency:** 10/yr. **Subscription:** $5/yr. **Pages:** 12. **Circ.:** 1.5M. **Publisher:** State Committe, Socialist Party of California. **Member:** Mobilization for Survival, COFOE, others. **Contact(s):** Charles Curtiss (Editor).

P ◆ **Socialist Action**
3435 Army St., #308
San Francisco, CA 94110
**Concern(s):** politics; analysis; alternative party. **Frequency:** 12/yr. **Subscription:** $8/yr.

P ◆ **Socialist Review**
2940 16th St.
San Francisco, CA 94103-3664
**Affiliation:** Center for Social Research and Education. **Concern(s):** politics; alternative party. For 20+ years, SR has been one of the leading journals of the US, providing an unparalleled forum for debate, analysis, and strategy. It has consistently presented daring and engaging work on feminist politics, democratic movements, organizing strategies, and radical perspectives on US politics and culture. **Est.:** 1970. **Frequency:** 4/yr. **Subscription:** $24/yr. **Price:** $7/ea. **Bulk:** 10% off/24. **Pages:** 204. **Fax:** (415)547-3733. **Contact(s):** Leslie A. Kauffman (Executive Editor), Elizabeth Toledo (Publisher).

$ ◆ **Socioeconomic Newsletter**
Airport Rd.
White Plains, NY 10604
**Concern(s):** economics; justice; social justice.

S ◆ **Sojourners**
Box 29272
Washington, DC 20017  (202)636-3637
**Affiliation:** Sojourners Fellowship. **Concern(s):** spiritual; Third World; peace; faith; nonviolence. "20 years ago, a Christian-based community in DC began publishing this magazine to promote an early type of 'liberation theology' through similar communities and individual church laity. The cultural coverage is tops in the progressive religious periodicals community, and the general coverage includes social action at national denominations' conventions as well as in the local congregation."-C.C. **Est.:** 1971. **Frequency:** 10/yr. **Subscription:** $27/yr. **Pages:** 52. **Circ.:** 40M. **Contact(s):** Jim Wallis, Joe Roos

☺ ◆ **Solar Industry Journal**
777 N. Capitol St. NE., #805
Washington, DC 20002  (202)408-0660
**Affiliation:** Solar Energy Industry Association. **Concern(s):** energy; solar; alternative. Reports new, events, and political developments that affect the entire solar industry. Regular features include information on new products, press releases, and interesting solar prize projects from the industry. Also, America's leading labs for solar research report on their most current work each Quarter. **Est.:** 1990. **Dues:** $25/yr. **Frequency:** 4/yr. **Subscription:** Membership. **Pages:** 37. **Fax:** (202)408-8536. **Contact(s):** Scott Sklar (Publisher).

☺ ◆ **Solar Today**
2400 Central Ave., #B-1
Boulder, CO 80301    (303)443-3130
**Affiliation:** American Solar Energy Society. **Concern(s):** energy; environment; solar; efficiency. A magazine which shows alternative forms of energy, especially solar. Reports on current activities of the country and world in converting to the most abundant form of free energy we have. **Frequency:** 6/yr.

L ◆ **Solidarity (UAW)**
8000 E. Jefferson
Detroit, MI 48214    (313)926-5791
**Affiliation:** United Automobile, Aerospace, Agricultural, Implement Workers of America. **Concern(s):** labor. "Those wanting to keep up with the labor movement through easy reading might wish to subscribe to this popularly written magazine. It covers auto workers' concerns, of course, but also features topical stories on other aspects of life in the US."-C.C. **Est.:** 1955. **Frequency:** 12/yr. **Subscription:** $5/yr. **Price:** Free. **Contact(s):** Dave Elsila.

T ◆ **Solidarity/Solidaridad**
24 E. Wall St.
Bethlehem, PA 18018  (215)868-6271
**Affiliation:** Committee in Solidarity with Latin American Nonviolent Movements. **Concern(s):** Third World; Latin America. "Linking nonviolent social movements of Latin America with those in the US is the function. Spanish language issues alternate with English issues."-C.C. **Est.:** 1982. **Frequency:** 4/yr. **Subscription:** $5/yr. **Price:** Free. **Contact(s):** Margaret D. Wilde.

✐ ◆ **Sound Choice**
Box 1251
Ojai, CA 93023
**Concern(s):** arts; music. "Music the mass media can't let you hear": rock, folk, ethnic, electronic and other genres. This magazine includes interviews, scene, reports, and gear. **Price:** $2.50/sample.

T ◆ **South Asia Bulletin**
Department of History
Southern University of New York
Albany, NY 12222    (518)462-2450
**Concern(s):** Third World; education; Asia; development. "South Asia Bulletin is a bi-annual magazine focusing on the social and economic issues of that region. Issues often concentrate on a special topic, such as political economy, colonialism, and women in development."-C.C. **Est.:** 1981. **Frequency:** 2/yr. **Subscription:** $10, $20 institution. **Price:** $7/ea. **Contact(s):** Vasant Kaiwar.

E ◆ **South Carolina Wildlife**
Box 167
Columbia, SC 29202
**Concern(s):** environment; recreation; wildlife/endangered species. Articles with regional outdoor focus; conservation, natural history, wildlife, and recreation. Profiles, how-tos. **Contact(s):** John E. Davis (Editor).

T ◆ **Southeast Asia Chronicle**
538 7th St. SE
Washington, DC 20003  (202)547-1114
**Affiliation:** Asia Resource Center. **Concern(s):** Third World; South East Asia. "Objective support of freedom movements across the region is offered through features on current concerns there. The magazine is recommended as the best source of information on all the countries in that part of the world."-C.C. **Est.:** 1965. **Frequency:** Irregular. **Subscription:** Donation. **Price:** $2.50/ea. **Contact(s):** Jacqui Chagnon, Roger Rumpf

T ◆ **Southern Africa Perspectives**
Africa Fund
198 Broadway
New York, NY 10038    (212)962-1210
**Affiliation:** Africa Fund. **Concern(s):** Third World; South Africa; Africa. "This magazine features analysis about South Africa and the liberated states of Angola, Zimbabwe, and Mozambique, among others. Repression in South Africa and efforts toward freedom are topics usually included."-C.C. **Frequency:** 12/yr. **Subscription:** $10, $18 institutions. **Price:** $1.25/ea. **Contact(s):** Jennifer Davis.

✍ ◆ **Southern Exposure**
Box 531
Durham, NC 27702    (919)688-8167
**Affiliation:** Institute for Southern Studies. **Concern(s):** education; justice; analysis; social justice; minority rights. "Each issue revolves around a theme, which might be media, culture, labor, economics, civil rights, or any other subject of importance to the people's public interest in the Southern US. The issues are carefully compiled to stand on their own and are often kept for future re-reading and reference."-C.C. Nonprofit. **Est.:** 1973. **Frequency:** 4/yr. **Subscription:** $16, $20 institution. **Price:** $5/ea. **Circ.:** 7.5M. **Contact(s):** Bob Hall, Eric Bates (Editor).

J ◆ **Southern Fight-Back**
Box 811
Birmingham, AL 35201  (205)776-7874
**Affiliation:** Southern Organizing Committee for Economic & Social Justice. **Concern(s):** justice; politics; labor; demographics; grassroots organizing; racism; discrimination; poverty. "Race issues, the labor movement, the environment and poor people's concerns are all noted in Southern Fight-Back. The periodical is a fine vehicle for regional organizing, promoting rallies, demonstrations, voting, and other methods of achieving social and economic well-being for people in the region it covers."-C.C. **Est.:** 1975. **Frequency:** 4/yr. **Subscription:** $5/yr. **Price:** Free. **Contact(s):** Anne Braden.

☺ ◆ **Space and Security News**
5115 S. A1A Highway
Melbourne Beach, FL 32951 (407)952-0600
**Affiliation:** Institute for Space and Security Studies. **Concern(s):** energy; peace; politics; space; security; government accountability. This newsletter exposes the danger of "Star Wars" weapons in space. SASN has become a powerful independent voice for the military, economic, environmental, health-care, and legal/political security of the American people. It exposes government lies (KAL-007, Challenger, Contragate, nuclear testing, MIAs, treaty compliance, JFK's

murder, etc.). The Institute was created in 1982. Nonprofit. **Est.:** 1984. **Frequency:** 4/yr. **Subscription:** $25/yr. **Price:** $10/ea. **Bulk:** 75% off/24. **Pages:** 16. **Circ.:** 10M. **Contact(s):** Dr. Robert M. Bowman (President).

### S ◆ Spectrum
1010 S. Flower St., #401
Los Angeles, CA 90015  (310)839-0758
**Affiliation:** Unity & Diversity World Council. **Concern(s):** spiritual; education; arts; holism; interfaith. This magazine seeks to promote the integration of knowledge. Has a spiritual orientation. Numerous book reviews. "Articles, interviews, reviews, and letters on religion, spirituality, philosophy, social sciences, and the arts. **Frequency:** 4/yr. **Subscription:** $8/yr. **Price:** $2/ea. **Pages:** 24. **Bulk:** 20% off/24. **Contact(s):** Louis K. Acheson (Editor). (213)742-6832.

### ☯ ◆ Spew
War Resisters League
339 Lafayette St.
New York, NY 10012  (212)228-0450
**Affiliation:** War Resisters League. **Concern(s):** peace; environment; justice. As in the 60's, the students are disgusted with the state of our environment and adult inaction in reducing racism, militarism, pollution, crime, and other human abuses.

### E ◆ Splash - Save Our Streams
1401 Wilson Blvd.
Level B
Arlington, VA 22209  (705)528-1818
**Affiliation:** Izaak Walton League of America. **Concern(s):** environment; oceans/rivers. A newsletter of Izaak Walton Save Our Streams Project, it is available with the purchase of a S.O.S. adoption kit. It allows all of its articles to be reprinted at no charge as long as Splash and the League are credited. and computer listings of projects. Nonprofit. **Est.:** 1969. **Dues:** $20/national dues. **Frequency:** 4/yr. **Subscription:** $6/yr. **Pages:** 8. **Circ.:** 3.8M. **Date Publ.:** 9/90. **Fax:** (703)528-1836. **Contact(s):** Karen Firehock (Program Director), Eunice Groark (Monitoring Coordinator).

### M ◆ SPLC Report
1735 I St. NW
Washington, DC 20006  (202)466-5242
**Affiliation:** Student Press Law Center. **Concern(s):** media; justice; freedom of expression; constitutional rights; censorship.

### J ◆ Spotlight
980 N. Fair Oaks Ave.
Pasadena, CA 91103-3097  (818)791-1978
**Affiliation:** American Friends Service Committee (Pacific SW Region). **Concern(s):** justice; peace; spiritual; immigration; nonviolence; interfaith; volunteers. This newsletter provides an in-depth look at some of the programs conducted by the Pacific Southwest Region of the American Friends Service Committee. Most of these activities are carried out by committee members and volunteers. Please contact the office if you would like to know more about these programs or to get involved. **Frequency:** 2/yr. **Fax:** (818)791-2205. **Contact(s):** Linda A. Lotz (Director of Programs).

### E ◆ The Spotted Owl Report
California Dept. of Forestry & Fire Protection
Box 94426
Sacramento, CA 94244-2460
**Concern(s):** environment; wildlife/endangered species. **Contact(s):** Raul Tuazon (HCP Team Leader).

### ✐ ◆ Spring
English Department, Box u-25
University of Connecticut
Storrs, CT 06268
**Concern(s):** arts; health; culture; psychology. "A Journal of Archetype and Culture" featuring writers such as: James Hillman, Patricia Berry, Charles Boer, Edward Casey,... **Est.:** 1941. **Subscription:** $30/yr. **Price:** $12.50/ea., $15 institutions. **Pages:** 200. **Circ.:** 1.8M. **Contact(s):** Charles Boer, Ross Miller.

### H ◆ Sproutletter
Box 62
Ashland, OR 97520  (503)488-2326
**Concern(s):** health; nutrition; vegetarian. An organic vegetarian food newsletter, it has covered live food, indoor food gardening, nutrition, vegetarianism, holistic health. Includes regular columnists, sprout basics, sprout recipes, tips, resources, product and book reviews. **Est.:** 1980. **Frequency:** 4/yr. **Subscription:** $17/yr. **Price:** $3/ea. **Bulk:** 40% off/24. **Pages:** 14. **Circ.:** 3M. **Publisher:** Sprouting Publications. **Contact(s):** Michael Linden (Owner).

### S ◆ Starlight Times
Box 4313
River Edge, NJ 07661  (201)489-2222
**Concern(s):** spiritual; health; transformation.

### E ◆ State of the States
Renew America
1400 16th St. NW, #710
Washington, DC 20036  (202)232-2252
**Affiliation:** Renew America. **Concern(s):** environment; energy; natural resource; conservation; resource management. This newsletter ranks each state's policies and programs on environmental issues. **Frequency:** 4/yr. **Subscription:** $25/yr. **Pages:** 16. **Circ.:** 7M. **Contact(s):** Ric Barrick (Director of Communication).

### ☯ ◆ The Stone & Sling
1205 County Route 60
Rexville, NY 14877  (607)225-4592
**Concern(s):** peace; environment; anti-nuclear. Essays, poems, etc., on environmental defense, wilderness, and sense of place, with an emphasis on the nuclear waste issue and what can be done about it on the local level. "Our focus is the Susquehanna/Allegheny headwaters region but we strive for the universal." **Frequency:** 6/yr. **Pages:** 6. **Circ.:** 250. **Contact(s):** Walt Franklin (Editor/Publisher).

### ✐ ◆ Stone Soup
Children's Art Foundation
Box 83
Santa Cruz, CA 95063
**Concern(s):** arts; children. "A collection of fiction, poetry, and art by children. This magazine is printed on quality paper, with color art throughout and an Activity Guide in every issue, it provides a forum for serious young writers and artists who have something to say about their lives. Frequent features include art by Soviet children and writing by Navajo children." **Frequency:** 6/yr. **Subscription:** $20/yr.

### S ◆ Story Friends
Mennonite Publishing House
Scottsdale, PA 15683
**Concern(s):** spiritual; education; arts; poetry; youth; childhood; faith. Stories for 4 to 9-year olds, on Christian faith and values in everyday experiences. Poetry. **Publisher:** Mennonite Publishing House. **Contact(s):** Marjorie Waybill (Editor).

### $ ◆ Strategic Planning & Review
World Bank
1818 H St. NW, Rm S-12-011
Washington, DC 20433  (202)477-1234
**Affiliation:** World Bank. **Concern(s):** economics; analysis; planning.

### L ◆ Struggle
Box 13261
Detroit, MI 48213  (313)824-6258
**Affiliation:** Detroit Branch, Marxist-Leninist Party, USA. **Concern(s):** labor; education; jobs; literacy; unions; alternative party. "Worker's culture is the attraction in this incisive literary review. Short stories, poetry, debate on the role of literature in the labor movement and readers' letters combine to make Struggle a literary tool for the workers' control."-C.C. **Est.:** 1985. **Frequency:** 4/yr. **Subscription:** $6/yr. **Price:** $1.50/ea. **Contact(s):** Tim Hall.

### ✍ ◆ Student Anti-Apartheid Movement Newsletter
Africa Fund
198 Broadway
New York, NY 10038  (212)962-1210
**Affiliation:** Africa Fund. **Concern(s):** education; Third World; justice; activism; South Africa. "Imitation shanty towns and university divestment of stocks in companies doing business in South Africa are frequently mentioned as ideas needing promotion. With the current upsurge in activism on campuses in solidarity with the victims of apartheid, this newsletter should be a favorite."-C.C. **Est.:** 1979. **Frequency:** 6/yr. **Price:** Free. **Contact(s):** Joshua Nessen.

### M ◆ Student Press Service News Report
1221 Massachusetts Ave. NW, #B
Washington, DC 20005  (202)638-2144
**Affiliation:** Youth Policy Institute. **Concern(s):** media. "SPS is a national news service for high school and college newspapers. The news items are written by youth ages 17 to 26 and focus on national concerns."-C.C. **Est.:** 1979. **Frequency:** 18/yr. **Subscription:** $49/yr. **Price:** $3/ea. **Contact(s):** Lynne Banks.

### ✍ ◆ Students United for Peace Newsletter
630 14th St., #6
Sacramento, CA 95814  (916)447-3696
**Affiliation:** Students United for Peace. **Concern(s):** education; Third World; activism; Central America; South Africa. "Nuclear disarmament, Central America, and South Africa are three concerns in this

inspiring newsletter. Ideas for working on peace around these and other areas are expounded."-C.C. **Est.:** 1985. **Frequency:** 6/yr. **Subscription:** $5/yr. **Price:** Free. **Contact(s):** Craig Usher, Emily Murdock

### D ◆ Studies in Family Planning
One Dag Hammarskjold Plaza
New York, NY 10017  (212)644-1300
**Affiliation:** Population Council. **Concern(s):** demographics; feminism; population growth; family planning. This journal discusses ways that people can help control the explosive population growth by family planning. **Frequency:** 6/yr. **Contact(s):** George Zeidenstein.

### ✐ ◆ Sulfur
210 Washtenaw
Ypsilanti, MI 48197-2526  (313)483-9787
**Concern(s):** arts; health; literature; psychology. "The big, umbrella magazine of the 80's: literature (Ginsberg, Artaud, Vallejo), art (Golub, Kitaj), psychology (Hillman, Giegerich), archival materials (Pound, Olson); writing that roadtests the language, art criticism, book reviews." "To put it simply the writers published in Sulfur are the ones I continue to read"-Gary Snyder. **Est.:** 1981. **Frequency:** 2/yr. **Subscription:** $12, $17 institute. **Price:** $7/ea. **Pages:** 200. **Contact(s):** Clayton Eshleman.

### S ◆ The Sun
107 N. Robertson St.
Chapel Hill, NC 27516  (919)942-5282
**Concern(s):** spiritual; transformation. In interviews, essays, fiction, and poetry, this magazine asks a lot of its readers: self-honesty, thoughtfulness, the willingness to live with questions instead of answers. Some of the writer's are well-known, others are unknown: what they share is passion and intelligence, a faith in the power of love, an acknowledgment of the great mystery and the great truth in all of us, which words can only hint at, but oh such lovely hints... **Other Resources:** Anthologies available. **Frequency:** 12/yr. **Subscription:** $15/6 issues, $30/yr. **Publisher:** The Sun Publishing Co. **Contact(s):** Sy Safransky (Editor).

### ☯ ◆ Surviving Together: A Journal on Soviet-American Relations
1601 Connecticut Ave. NW, #301
Washington, DC 20009  (202)387-3034
**Affiliation:** Institute for Soviet-American Relations. **Concern(s):** peace; East-West; disarmament. Chronicles the many and diverse activities in Soviet-American relations. It reports on current events, exchanges, joint projects, public education, health and the environment. The journal provides a forum for very different points of view and exposes the reader to the complex nature of relations between the Soviet and American governments and between the peoples. Subscriptions: $15 students/teachers/seniors; $25; $35 libraries and organizations. **Other Resources:** HANDBOOK OF ORGANIZATIONS INVOLVED IN SOVIET-AMERICAN RELATIONS 1990; profiles 313 nonprofit organizations active in Soviet-American activities with an appendix including relevant government offices in US & USSR, trade resources, and school exchanges. Nonprofit. **Est.:** 1983. **Frequency:** 3/yr. **Price:** $10/ea. **Bulk:** $5ea/24. **Pages:** 100. **Circ.:** 4M. **E-Network:** PeaceNet. **ID:** 'isar'. **Fax:** (202)667-3291. **Contact(s):** Eliza Klose (Executive Director), Anne L. Hunt (Co-editor). John Sturino , Systems Coordinator.

### A ◆ Sustainable Living in Drylands
Box 1812
Santa Fe, NM 87504  (505)982-2063
**Affiliation:** S.W. Regional Permaculture Institute. **Concern(s):** agriculture; Third World; environment; urban; permaculture; sustainability; recycling; land use; development. A Permaculture journal devoted to sustainable living systems in drylands. Interest is international — covering agro-forestry, agriculture, urban strategies, housing, village formation, and Third World solutions. The journal espouses the Permaculture ethic: care of the Earth, care of all species, and recycling of excess. **Frequency:** 4/yr. **Subscription:** $25/yr. **Price:** $2.50/ea. **Bulk:** $1.50ea/24. **Pages:** 12. **Circ.:** 1.8M. **Office:** 1300 Luisa, #24 Sante Fe, NM 87501. **Contact(s):** Scott Pittman (Director).

### ✐ ◆ Talkin' Union
Box 5349
Takoma Park, MD 20912  (301)270-8412
**Concern(s):** arts; music. "This magazine concentrates on workers' culture, specializing in poetry, short stories, photos, and songs by everyday workers. Music is the key feature, with the words and music of the songs often printed."-C.C. **Est.:** 1981. **Frequency:** Irregular. **Subscription:** $7.50, $12 institution. **Price:** Donation. **Contact(s):** Saul Schniderman.

**E ▸ Talking Leaves**
1430 Willamette, # 367
Eugene, OR 97401 (503)342-2974
**Affiliation:** Cascadia Bioregion. **Concern(s):** environment; peace; spiritual. A volunteer staff assembles this newspaper about deep ecology and spiritual activism. **Contact(s):** Carolyn Moran (Publisher/Editor), Harriet Kofalk (Associate Editor).

**T ▸ Telegraph News**
722 Monroe
Evanston, IL 60202 (312)328-0772
**Affiliation:** Overground Railroad. **Concern(s):** Third World; justice; demographics; Central America; refugees; immigration. "Lodging and safe transport of Central American refugees are promoted in the tradition of the Underground Railroad, through which this country's slaves were helped to freedom. These courageous folks work with others in the sanctuary movement to save these peasants from El Salvador and Guatemala."-C.C. **Est.:** 1983. **Frequency:** 6/yr. **Subscription:** Donation. **Price:** Free. **Contact(s):** Mary Jude Postel, David Janzen.

**M ▸ Telemedium**
120 E. Wilson St.
Madison, WI 53703 (608)257-7712
**Affiliation:** National Telemedia Council. **Concern(s):** media; broadcasting; film. "Promoting better television and radio is the function of this newsletter. The key means to this goal is their critical evaluation of programming, toward a media-wise society."-C.C. **Est.:** 1953. **Dues:** $20/yr. **Frequency:** 4-6 yr. **Subscription:** Membership. **Price:** $2/ea. **Contact(s):** Marieli Rowe, Celeste Kirk.

**M ▸ The 10 Best Censored Stories**
c/o Project Censored
Sonoma State University
Rohnert Park, CA 94928 (707)664-2148
**Affiliation:** Project Censored. **Concern(s):** media; justice; responsibility; media watch. "The top 10 censored stories of the previous year are capsulized in this paper. A combination of journalism review and bibliographic listing, this annual is an innovative approach to constructive media criticism." -C.C. **Est.:** 1976. **Frequency:** Annual. **Price:** Free. **Contact(s):** Carl Jensen.

**S ▸ The Ten Directions**
Zen Center of Los Angeles
923 South Normandie Ave.
Los Angeles, CA 90006
**Concern(s):** spiritual. Personal, social, political, and ecological problems from a Zen perspective. **Frequency:** 2/yr. **Subscription:** Donation. **Pages:** 48. **Circ.:** 10M.

**E ▸ Terra Newsletter**
3751 N. Sawyer
Chicago, IL 60618 (312)463-8228
**Affiliation:** Terra. **Concern(s):** environment; health; hazardous/toxic waste. It attempts to report on the things that are presently degrading the environment and ways to stop these things. These things include pesticides, nuclear waste, and other hazardous material. **Est.:** 1989. **Member:** National Coalition Against Misuse of Pesticides; Pesticide Action Network. **Contact(s):** Phyllis Hasbrouck (Director), Susan Compernolle (Secretary). (312)262-4375.

**T ▸ Terra Nossa**
515 Broadway
Santa Cruz, CA 95060 (408)423-1626
**Affiliation:** Project Abraco. **Concern(s):** Third World; peace; conflict resolution. This newsletter reports on the current developments with the Project Abraco. It further reports on the greater sense of solidarity the project has created among the peoples of Brazil and the US.

**☮ ▸ The Test Banner**
Box 26725
Las Vegas, NV 89126 (702)386-9834
**Affiliation:** American Peace Test. **Concern(s):** peace; disarmament; nonviolence; civil disobedience; anti-nuclear. A newsletter focusing on international nuclear weapons testing and the grassroots efforts to stop it. The publication educates about effects of nuclear testing; health, environmental and economic. Nonviolent Civil Resistance is also focus of the Test Banner. **Other Resources:** Testing Alert Hotline (702) 386-9831. Recording of latest nuclear test info. Testing Alert Network: Subscribers ($25/year) are called after every nuclear test worldwide; many participants activate phone trees or vigils in local communities. **Est.:** 1986. **Dues:** None. **Frequency:** 4/yr. **Subscription:** $10/donation. **Pages:** 16-20. **Circ.:** 11M. **Contact(s):** Debra Richardson, David Solnit.

**E ▸ Texas Monthly**
Box 1569
Austin, TX 78767
**Concern(s):** environment; education; economics; politics; arts; childhood; trade; analysis; culture. Features and departments on art, architecture, food, education, business, politics, etc. "We like solidly researched pieces that uncover issues of public concern, reveal offbeat and previously unreported topics, or use a novel approach to familiar topics." **Frequency:** 12/yr. **Contact(s):** Gregory Curtis (Editor).

**✎ ▸ The Original Art Report (TOAR)**
Box 1641
Chicago, IL 60690 (312)588-6897
**Concern(s):** arts; media; theater; music; film; culture. TOAR is the rational voice - commentary and analysis - of the politics, economics, and socio-philosophical conditions found in the visual arts condition. **Est.:** 1967. **Frequency:** Irregular. **Subscription:** $15.50/yr. **Price:** $1.25/ea. **Bulk:** 20% off/24. **Pages:** 6-8. **Contact(s):** Frank Salantrie (Editor/Publisher).

**✍ ▸ Thinking Families**
605 Worcester Rd.
Towson, MD 21204
**Concern(s):** education; family; youth; childhood. Articles on the social, intellectual, and physical development of elementary school children. **Contact(s):** Marjory Spraycar (Editor).

**☮ ▸ ThinkPeace**
486 41st St. , #3
Oakland, CA 94609 (510)654-0349
**Affiliation:** San Francisco Study Group for Peace. **Concern(s):** peace; health. "A newsletter about personal experiences of peace workers illustrating ways to avoid burnout, to increase peace in our daily lives, and to promote world peace. Peacemaking techniques are also addressed."-C.C. **Est.:** 1985. **Frequency:** 6/yr. **Subscription:** $15/yr. **Price:** $.50/ea., sample free. **Contact(s):** David Martinez.

**T ▸ third world**
Rua da Gloria, 122, Gr. 105
Rio de Janiero
RJ -, Brazil (021)242-1957
**Concern(s):** Third World; Latin America; Asia. "Published as a step towards establishing a New International Information Order. It contains information on and analysis of the conditions and aspirations of emerging nations. Separate editions are published in Spanish and Portuguese." Excellent Third World coverage. **Frequency:** 6/yr. **Subscription:** $9/yr. **Price:** $2/ea. **Pages:** 65. **E-Network:** Geonet. **ID:** 'terceiro-mundo'. (021)252-7440. **Contact(s):** Bill Hinchberger (Editor, English), Andrea Moutinho (Business Manager). (021)222-1370.

**T ▸ Third World Resources: A Quarterly Review of Resources From and About The Third World**
464 19th St.
Oakland, CA 94612-9761 (510)835-4692
**Affiliation:** Third World Resources/Data Center. **Concern(s):** Third World. Each issue of this newsletter contains a four-page guide to organizations and their print and audiovisual resources: (Spring) ASIA AND PACIFIC, (Summer) AFRICA, (Fall) LATIN AMERICA AND THE CARIBBEAN, (Winter) the MIDDLE EAST, providing educators and activists with up-to-date, annotated materials from all Third World areas. **Frequency:** 4/yr. **Subscription:** $10/yr.; $30/yr. organizations. **Price:** $2.50/ea. **Bulk:** Call. **Pages:** 24. **Circ.:** 1.5M. **Other Formats:** Geonet, user **ID:** 'geo2:tfenton'. **E-Network:** Peacenet. **ID:** 'tfenton'. **Contact(s):** Thomas P. Fenton, Mary J. Heffron (Compilers/Editors). (510)536-1876.

**L ▸ This Time**
Box 10
Orland, ME 04472
**Affiliation:** H.O.M.E., Inc. (Homeworkers Organized for More Employment). **Concern(s):** labor; homeworkers. Newsletter.

**M ▸ 3-2-1- Contact**
Children's Television Workshop
1 Lincoln Plaza
New York, NY 10023 (212)595-3456
**Affiliation:** Children's Television Workshop. **Concern(s):** media; education; film; science; children. Entertaining and informative articles for 8- to 14-year-olds, on all aspects of science, computers, scientists, and children who are learning about or practicing science. **Contact(s):** Jonathan Rosenbloom (Editor).

**✎ ▸ The Threepenny Review**
Box 9131
Berkeley, CA 94709
**Concern(s):** arts; media; politics; music; theater; broadcasting; film. Essays on books, theater, film, dance, music, art, television, and politics. **Frequency:** 4/yr. **Contact(s):** Wendy Lesser (Editor).

**✍ ▸ The Threshold**
Box 1168, University of North Carolina
Chapel Hill, NC 27514-1168 (919)967-4600
**Affiliation:** Student Environmental Action Coalition (SEAC). **Concern(s):** education; environment; students; networking. SEAC is searching for interested parties and inviting other student organizations to join their environmental coalition. This is their newsletter. "With the newsletter we can let you know what is happening nationally and regionally, and you can let us know what you are doing. To that end we are looking for submissions to print." **Other Resources:** Formerly NETWORK NEWS. **Dues:** $35, $15 students. **Frequency:** 8/yr. **Subscription:** $25/yr.

**E ▸ The Tide**
8205 Santa Monica Blvd., #1-308
West Hollywood, CA 900465912 (213)654-3453
**Concern(s):** environment; politics; law. The Tide is a fast and easy way to stay informed about environmental legislation, and to have monthly correspondence with your elected representatives in Washington. The Tide is a personalized, monthly newsletter. Each issue contains lists of major legislation pending in the senate and House on which postcards are available. We do not sell our mailing lists to junk mail people or use them for any other purpose other than Tide. **Frequency:** 12/yr. **Subscription:** $24/yr. **Contact(s):** Scott D. Silverman (Editor).

**T ▸ Tidewater Nicaragua Project Foundation Newsletter**
3916 Shell Rd
Hampton, VA 23669
**Affiliation:** Tidewater Nicaragua Project Foundation. **Concern(s):** Third World; justice; Central America. "This group's people-to-people assistance is noted in this quarterly newsletter. Updates on Nicaragua and news of humanitarian and development aid for that poor nation are the topics."-C.C. **Est.:** 1984. **Frequency:** 4/yr. **Subscription:** Donation, $8 institution. **Price:** Free. **Contact(s):** Judy Tazewell.

**$ ▸ Tightwad Gazette**
RR1, Box 3570
Leeds, ME 04263
**Concern(s):** economics; environment; social ecology; sustainability; conservation; recycling. These people live on what other people throw out. This newsletter is their way of sharing ideas on how to recycle and encourage others to do so. There are treasures in those dumpsters. The trick it to stop is from getting to the dumps.

**P ▸ Tikkun Magazine**
5100 Leona St.
Oakland, CA 94169
**Affiliation:** Institute for Labor and Mental Health. **Concern(s):** politics; health; spiritual; lobbying; faith; psychology. Ecology movements can't win until they address the daily life pains that create a psychological, spiritual, and ethical crisis in the lives of most Americans. Until people transcend their "surplus powerlessness" they will agree with ecologists, but do nothing. TIKKUN addresses the strategies for overcoming that powerlessness and reframing politics and culture in a way that might make ecological victory possible. **Frequency:** 6/yr. **Subscription:** $30/yr. **Price:** $5/ea. **Pages:** 96. **Circ.:** 40M. **Contact(s):** Michael Lerner (Editor). **Other:** Subsciptions, Box 332, Mt. Morris, IL 61054-0332.

**H ▸ Tobacco and Youth Reporter**
Box 60658
Longmeadow, MA 01116 (413)567-2070
**Affiliation:** Stop Teenage Addiction to Tobacco (STAT). **Concern(s):** health; economics; substance abuse; boycott. Great newsletter about protesting tobacco companies. **Contact(s):** Joe Tye.

**$ ▸ TOES/NA Newsletter**
Department of Ecology
University of Maine
Orono, ME 04469 (207)972-9877
**Affiliation:** The Other Economic Summit (TOES). **Concern(s):** economics; feminism; trade; empowerment. This newsletter reports on the activities that take place during The Other Economic Summit. It also reports on the issues that this summit finds of paramount importance. **Contact(s):** Susan Hunt.

**T ▸ Toward Freedom**
209 College
Burlington, VT 05401 (802)658-2523
**Concern(s):** Third World; peace; United Nations; South Africa. "A Progressive Perspective on World Events". A newsletter on nonaligned movement and developing nations, UN, and South Africa; and most recently the new Europe. **Est.:** 1952. **Frequency:** 8/yr. **Subscription:** $20/yr.

## E ▶ Toxic Times

1168 Commonwealth Ave., 3rd Fl.
Boston, MA 02134       (617)232-0327

**Affiliation:** National Toxics Campaign Fund. **Concern(s):** environment; health; hazardous/toxic waste. "Toxic waste is a topic most of us would rather sweep under the carpet. After all, who wants to contemplate the cumulative health effects of the thousands and thousands of chemical compounds we come into contact with each day? Yet toxic pollution will affect many of our lives. That's what makes this newsletter important; it offers useful information on detecting toxic dangers in your community as well as news (both bad and good) about toxic cleanup efforts nationally." **Frequency:** 4/yr. **Subscription:** $15/yr. **Contact(s):** Gary Cohen (Policy Director), John O'Connor (Executive Director).

## F ▶ Tradeswoman

Box 40664
San Francisco, CA 94140      (415)821-7334

**Concern(s):** feminism; labor; equal rights/ pay. "Tradeswoman magazine is aimed at women working in non-traditional blue collar jobs. We deal with subjects such as labor, affirmative action, employment and networking." **Est.:** 1981. **Frequency:** 4/yr. **Subscription:** $25/yr. **Price:** $3.50/ea. **Pages:** 50-70. **Circ.:** 2M.

## ? ▶ Trajectories

Permanent Press
Box 700305
San Jose, CA 95170

**Concern(s):** future; spiritual; peace; demographics; energy; ideation; analysis; transformation; poverty. "My goals are: Abolition of poverty and war; increase in human intelligence and emotional stability; space colonization and longevity; unleashing higher potentials in every brain. Robert Anton Wilson's Newsletter Trajectories is available through writing to Permanent Press. Trajectories is for you if you are deeply interested in space... Nanotechnology and artificial intelligence... Parapsychology... Longevity... the new brain machines... the Aquarian Conspiracy." **Contact(s):** Robert Anton Wilson (Writer/Psychologist).

## ✪ ▶ TRANET

Box 567
Rangeley, ME 04970

**Concern(s):** energy; Third World; peace; environment; appropriate technology; self-reliance; networking. TRANET's Newsletter-Directory is an abstracting service and networking tool. It provides short briefs on publications, programs, projects, and peoples involved in environmental, peace, human rights, feminist, humanistic economy, and other A & T (Alternative & Transformational) movements. It is unique in its worldwide coverage with news and contact information of Alternative Japan, Alternative Europe, and news from the Third World. 200+ members who contribute to the exchange of information. **Other Resources:** TRANET also helps third world nations develop appropriate technology libraries and provides a networking clearinghouse to help its members link with one another. **Est.:** 1976. **Frequency:** 6/yr. **Subscription:** $30/yr. **Price:** $5/ea. **Pages:** 16. **Circ.:** 2M. **E-Network:** Earthnet. **ID:** 'ellisb'. **Contact(s):** Peter Thibeault (President), William N. Ellis (General Coordinator). (207)864-2252.

## ✽ ▶ Transcontinental Peace Newsletter (TPN)

Heidland 9
Fisherhude, 2802 Germany  (049)4293-1264 or 65

**Concern(s):** peace. TPN is published several times a year and can be subscribed to free of charge. It is not copyright protected. If quoted they only ask that you use it as the source, refer to its address, that it is free and send them a copy of the reprint. TPN is a useful list of news items from the European front on issues of peace and disarmament that should interest all American readers. English. **Other Resources:** Formerly TRANSANTLANTIC PEACE NEWSLETTER (TPN). **E-Network:** PeaceNet/GreenNet. **Fax:** (049)4293-1337. **Contact(s):** Dr. Burkhard Luber.

## S ▶ Transformation Times

Box 425
Beavercreek, OR 97004 (503)632-7141

**Concern(s):** spiritual; environment; transformation. This magazine is dedicated to expanding awareness of physical, mental, and spiritual resources. "We believe that an awareness of these resources will enable a transformation of planetary consciousness to one of unity and love. We gladly accept display ads, articles, classified ads, calendar information and other material that is in keeping with this intention. Write for a copy of display advertising rates or writers guidelines." **Est.:** 1983. **Frequency:** 10/yr. **Subscription:** $8/yr. **Pages:** 30. **Circ.:** 8M. **Publisher:** Life Resources Publications. **Contact(s):** Connie L. Faubel (Editor), E. James Faubel (Managing Editor).

## T ▶ Transition

2001 Evans Rd
Cary, NC 27513

**Concern(s):** Third World; justice; Africa; minority rights; indigenous peoples. Promotes the idea of free ideas and social change at an international level. Writers such as Carlos Fuentes and Kincaid; disussions as wide-range as Mandela, Mapplethorpe, Rushdie. A valuable voice from the African community. **Frequency:** 4/yr. **Subscription:** $24/yr.

## ✈ ▶ Transitions Abroad: The Guide To Learning, Living, and Working

18 Hulst Rd.
Amherst, MA 01002      (413)256-0373

**Concern(s):** education; Third World; economics; travel; networking. An established resource guide to international work, study, and socially responsible travel. Each bimonthly issue focuses on one area of the world. Departments include Socially Responsible Travel and Third World Focus. Emphasis is on social change through global education and networking. **Other Resources:** 1) International Resource Guides on work, study, living and alternative travel abroad. 2) TRANSITIONS ABROAD EDUCATIONAL TRAVEL DIRECTORY (annual, in July). **Est.:** 1977. **Frequency:** 6/yr. **Price:** $6.95/ea. **Bulk:** 50% off/24. **Pages:** 64. **Circ.:** 21M. **Publisher:** Transitions Publishing. **Fax:** (413)256-0373. **Contact(s):** Clay Hubbs, Ph.D. (Editor/Publisher), Lisa Aciukewicz (Assistant Editor/Publisher).

## T ▶ Transnational Perspectives

Case Posta 161
Geneva, 16 Switzerland

**Concern(s):** Third World; politics; economics; environment; justice. TP takes a "longer view of world politics," analyzing political, economic, and cultural forces now transforming the international system. One of the voices advocating policies of compassion and cooperation. A well put together magazine that does appear to duplicate other efforts. Excellent articles and book reviews from all over globe. 3 aims: Pacific settlement of disputes, reduction of violence; New possibilities for cooperative, transformative action, especially through UN; and Ecology. **Other Resources:** Occasional seminars, symposia on specific world issues, such as Non-Proliferation of Nuclear Weapons. **Est.:** 1974. **Frequency:** 3/yr. **Subscription:** $15/yr. **Price:** $5/ea. **Pages:** 48. **Circ.:** 5M. **Contact(s):** Rene Wadlow (Editor), Pierre Porret (Associate Editor).

## ✈ ▶ Travel Smart

Communications House, Inc.
Dobbs Ferry, NY 10522   (914)693-4208

**Concern(s):** education; travel. "A monthly newsletter for people who travel at least once a year. 'Most up-to-date guidance available'-New York Times... 'Pulls no punches'-Newsweek. Info on best current travel deals, ten-plus pages. Readers get discounts on all travel (cruises, tours, international airfare). Includes four free reports on surviving air crash, travelling healthy, avoiding rip-offs, saving travel dollars." **Est.:** 1976. **Frequency:** 12/yr. **Subscription:** $37/yr. **Price:** SASE #10 w/3 stamps=Free. **Contact(s):** H.J. Teison (Editor/Publisher).

## E ▶ Tree Song

Box 31087
Seattle, WA 98103

**Concern(s):** environment; education; forests. This newsletter's primary concerns are educating the public about the deforestation of our forests and how we can prevent it.

## E ▶ Treetop Panorama

Rural Route 1, Box 160
Payson, IL 62360

**Concern(s):** environment. "Choosing subject categories has not been easy as Treetop Panorama covers much ground. It is imaginative, good natured and down-to-earth." **Est.:** 1983. **Frequency:** 4/yr. **Subscription:** $8/4 issues. **Price:** $2/ea. **Pages:** 32. **Circ.:** 1M. **Contact(s):** Jared Scarborough (Editor).

## F ▶ Tribune

International Women's Tribunal
777 UN Plaza
New York, NY 10017      (212)687-8633

**Affiliation:** International Women's Tribunal. **Concern(s):** feminism; Third World. A United Nations newsletter which deals with women's issues on an international and socioeconomic level. **Est.:** 1976. **Frequency:** 4/yr. **Subscription:** $8/yr.

## S ▶ tricycle

Box 3000
Denville, NJ 07834-9877

**Concern(s):** spiritual; arts; environment; A Buddhist magazine which in its first issue featured an interview between Spalding Gray and the Dalai Lama, poetry by Gary Snyder, articles on AIDS, politics and film from a Buddhist perspective. **Frequency:** 4/yr. **Subscription:** $20/yr.

## F ▶ Trivia

Box 606
N. Amherst, MA 01059

**Concern(s):** feminism; justice; sexism; discrimination. "...a leading journal of feminist thought, publishing critical essays, reviews, translations, experimental prose. #15 features a radical critique of New Age thought, articles on sexual subordination and the Nazi State, feminism and S/M, and lesbian separatist theater." Says The Literary Magazine Review: "Its position in the culture of literary publishing cannot be overstated." **Frequency:** 3/yr. **Subscription:** $14/yr. **Contact(s):** Lisa Weil (Editor).

## E ▶ Tropicus

1015 18 St. NW, #1000
Washington, DC 20036  (202)429-5660

**Affiliation:** Conservation International. **Concern(s):** environment; conservation; wildlife/endangered species; forests. A newsletter that reports on the activities of Conservation International. It also has interesting articles on what is happening in the tropical regions of the world. Nonprofit. **Frequency:** 4/yr. **Price:** Membership. **Contact(s):** Russell A. Mittermeier (President), Peter A. Seligmann (Chairman).

## H ▶ True Food

Box 87
Woodstock, NY 12498

**Concern(s):** health; nutrition. "Goldbecks' newsletter for the concerned consumer and cook. It features the best - and worst - of new supermarket and natural foods by brand name, food fads and politics, 'White Lies' (ad deception), 'True Stories' (famous guest writers), humor, Wholefoods Cuisine, and more East West dubbed the Goldbecks 'the guiding lights of wholefoods'. Free Goldbeck cookbook to new subscribers." **Frequency:** 4/yr. **Subscription:** $14/yr.

## J ▶ Turning the Tide

Box 1990
Burbank, CA 91507      (818)509-3435

**Affiliation:** People Against Racist Terror (PART). **Concern(s):** justice; feminism; education; media; urban; racism; discrimination; sexism; gay/lesbian; political prisoners; pro-choice; minority rights; racial tensions; ethnic concerns; diversity. A youth-oriented anti-racist newsletter based in L.A. with a national distribution and network. It exposes organized neo-nazi groups, KKK, and random racist, sexist, anti-semitic, and homophobic violence. Educates in support of liberation and self-determination. Provides a forum for discussion of issues facing anti-racist organizers, contact lists of anti-racist groups nationally and locally. "We support outreach, self-organization, and education of young people." **Other Resources:** Research reports on projects of the racist right: links of neo-nazis to English only, Anti-Abortion movements; exposes of racists in the anti-war movement, racist use of TV, etc. **Est.:** 1988. **Frequency:** 6/yr. **Subscription:** $5, $10 institution. **Price:** $1/ea. **Bulk:** $.50ea/24. **Pages:** 10. **Circ.:** 1M. **E-Network:** CompuServe. **ID:** 71277, 1625. **Member:** Center for Democratic Renewal, John Brown Anti-Klan Network. Message (213)461-3127. **Contact(s):** Michael Novick (Editor).

## ✍ ▶ Turnstile

175 5th Ave., #2348
New York, NY 10010

**Concern(s):** arts; literature; poetry. "This eclectic multi-cultural volume features the best new fiction, non-fiction, poetry, and art. Includes interviews with renowned authors: T. Coarghessan Boyle, Salman Rushdie and Jane Smiley. 1989 CCLM award recipient." "A good deal of pleasure" -Library Journal. **Est.:** 1986. **Frequency:** 4/yr. **Subscription:** $22/yr. **Price:** $6.50/ea. **Pages:** 128. **Circ.:** 2M.

## E ▶ 21st Century Society Newsletter

Box 357
Lawrence, KS 66044      (913)842-1943

**Affiliation:** 21st Century Society. **Concern(s):** environment; future; economics; politics; sustainability; ideation; reform. "Working to unite and become strong, proactive influence for worldwide environmental, social and political transformation. We must not GIVE up hope. We must share a Global Interdependent Vision of Earth." **Frequency:** 4/yr. **Member:** Co-op America. **Contact(s):** Leslie W. Blevins, Jr. (Executive Director), Denise Hamler (Publisher).

## ? ▶ 2000 / The Millennium Magazine

1431 Ocean Ave., #516
Santa Monica, CA 90401      (310)458-4448

**Concern(s):** future; politics; arts; ideation; planning; reform; culture. "The winds of change are beginning to blow like never before. We see the transformation of civilization on Earth into a harmonious whole, with the year 2000 as a symbolic 'Fulcrum of the Epoches.' Our publication is a synergetic mix of science, politics, art, philosophy, ecology, education, entertainment and everything that strongly influences our world's future." **Frequency:** Irregular. **Subscription:** $10/yr. **Price:** $2/ea. **Bulk:** $1.75ea/24. **Pages:** 20. **Circ.:** 1M. **Contact(s):** Peter Sorensen (Publisher/Editor), Greg Wright (Co-editor). (818)784-0325.

✌ ▸ **UN Chronicle**
United Nations
Rm A-3317
New York, NY 10017 (212)963-1234
**Affiliation:** United Nations. **Concern(s):** peace; United Nations. "Summaries of key countries' views on topics under discussion in the UN are published in the chronicle. Students and debaters of world controversies will find this record of interest."-C.C. **Est.:** 1975. **Frequency:** 11/yr. **Subscription:** $14/yr. **Price:** Donation. **Contact(s):** B. Menon.

P ▸ **Unclassified**
ANSECA
2100 M St. NW, #607
Washington, DC 20037
**Concern(s):** politics; peace; CIA. Ex-CIA, FBI, etc.

E ▸ **Underwater Naturalist**
Sandy Hook
Highlands, NJ 07732
**Affiliation:** American Littoral Society. **Concern(s):** environment; conservation. The bulletin of the Society, "a national coastal conservation organization. Articles, field notes, book reviews on such topics at wetlands, estuarine water quality, underwater photography, sharks, coral reefs, beaches. Lots of membership activities. **Dues:** $25/yr, includes subscription. **Frequency:** 4/yr.

T ▸ **Unidad Borinquena**
160 W. Lippincott
Philadelphia, PA 19133 (215)634-4443
**Affiliation:** National Congress for Puerto Rican Rights. **Concern(s):** Third World; justice; Caribbean. "Independence for Puerto Rico from the US is the key concern. Treatment of Puerto Ricans both in the US and in their country is highlighted, in hopes the reader will take personal action in defense of their rights."-C.C. **Est.:** 1982. **Frequency:** 4/yr. **Subscription:** $7/yr. **Price:** $2/ea. **Contact(s):** Joan Blaustein.

L ▸ **Union**
1313 L St. NW
Washington, DC 20005 (212)898-3200
**Affiliation:** Service Employees International Union. **Concern(s):** labor; unions. "A bimonthly magazine of service workers and one of the more socially concerned official periodicals of national unions. Concerns of workers in other industries, as well as general social concerns, such as peace and aging, are included in this attractive selection."-C.C. **Est.:** 1987. **Dues:** $132/yr. **Frequency:** 6/yr. **Price:** Free. **Contact(s):** Tim Johnson.

L ▸ **Union Democracy Review**
500 State St.
Brooklyn, NY 11217 (718)855-6650
**Affiliation:** Association for Union Democracy. **Concern(s):** labor; unions; civil liberties. A newsletter dedicated to covering Union Democracy issues. AUD is a civil liberties and advocacy organization dedicated solely to the cause of advancing democracy in the US and Canada labor unions since 1969. "Teamsters for a Democratic Union and local union elections are typical topics briefly covered in this newsletter. Each issue concludes with an enlightening resource reviews section."-C.C. **Other Resources:** Advice, referrals, legal support and advocacy. Nonprofit. **Est.:** 1973. **Dues:** $25/yr. **Frequency:** 6/yr. **Subscription:** $10/yr. **Price:** $1.50/ea. **Circ.:** 3M. **Fax:** (718)855-7699. **Contact(s):** Susan M. Jennik (Executive Director), Brett Nair (Office Manager).

✌ ▸ **UNIPAX**
172 Pleasant St.
Laconia, NH 03246 (603)524-6488
**Affiliation:** Unitarian Universalist Peace Fellowship. **Concern(s):** peace; spiritual; faith. "This newsletter prints items of interest to all peace advocates as well as news of the UU Peace Fellowship and its members."-C.C. **Est.:** 1984. **Frequency:** Irregular. **Subscription:** Donation. **Price:** Free. **Contact(s):** Helen H. Dick.

D ▸ **Unitarian-Universalists in Support of Sanctuary Newsletter**
4831 E. 22nd St.
Tucson, AZ 85711 (602)748-1551
**Affiliation:** Unitarian-Universalist Church of Tucson. **Concern(s):** demographics; Third World; justice; spiritual; faith; refugees. "Unitarian-Universalists have the largest number of individual congregations that have declared themselves a sanctuary to Central American refugees. Their newsletter can be useful to anyone interested in this issue, since it covers the broad movement, not just efforts in their denomination."-C.C. **Est.:** 1986. **Dues:** $10/yr. **Frequency:** 4/yr. **Subscription:** Membership. **Price:** Free. **Contact(s):** David Johnson.

T ▸ **Update**
ICC Building
Georgetown University
Washington, DC 20057 (202)687-5676
**Affiliation:** Central American Historical Institute. **Concern(s):** Third World; Central America. "Current and past history of the people and governments of Central America is reviewed. Charts and graphs are sometimes used to illustrate the points in this newsletter."-C.C. **Est.:** 1982. **Frequency:** 12/yr. **Subscription:** $27, $50 institution. **Price:** $.75/ea. **Contact(s):** Betsy Cohn.

✍ ▸ **The Urban Review**
Fulfillment Department; Agathon Press, Inc.
49 Sheridan Ave.
Albany, NY 12210 (212)741-3087
**Concern(s):** education; urban; planning; ethnic concerns; urban; students; youth; childhood. "...provides a forum for communication among urban educators, scholars, administrators, and all others concerned with improving public education in urban communities. The journal publishes original reports on important empirical studies and theocratical essays that examine the basic issues confronting urban schools." **Est.:** 1966. **Frequency:** 4/yr. **Subscription:** $22, $44 institution. **Price:** $12.50/ea. **Pages:** 64. **Publisher:** Plenum Publishing Corporation. **Contact(s):** David E. Kapel (Editor), William T. Pink.

J ▸ **US Anti-Apartheid Newsletter**
1501 Cherry St.
Philadelphia, PA 19102 (215)241-7168
**Affiliation:** American Friends Service Committee. **Concern(s):** justice; South Africa. "Upcoming conferences and demonstrations are noted here, as are resources promoting human rights and majority rule in Southern Africa. Accounts of events in that region also contribute to making this newsletter one of the most useful periodicals on the freedom movement there."-C.C. **Est.:** 1986. **Frequency:** 4/yr. **Subscription:** $10/yr. **Price:** Free. **Contact(s):** Jerry Herman.

A ▸ **US Farm News**
Box 496
Hampton, IA 50441 (515)456-4470
**Affiliation:** US Farmers Association. **Concern(s):** agriculture. "For about 40 years this group has been working for preservation of family farms, peace, and trade with other countries, and related issues. US Farm News is the best source of articles on progressive topics written from a farmer's perspective."-C.C. **Est.:** 1952. **Frequency:** 12/yr. **Subscription:** $5/yr. **Price:** $1/ea. **Contact(s):** F. W. Stover.

✍ ▸ **US Kids**
245 Long Hill Rd.
Middletown, CT 06457
**Concern(s):** education; science. Articles and fiction on issues related to kids ages 5 to 10, fiction, true life adventures, science and nature topics. Real-world focus; no fantasy. **Contact(s):** Gabriel Davis (Editor).

E ▸ **US Water News**
230 Main St.
Halstead, KS 67056
**Concern(s):** environment; water; oceans/rivers. Newsletter.

✌ ▸ **USIP Journal**
1550 M St. NW , #700
Washington, DC 20005 (202)457-1700
**Affiliation:** US Institute of Peace. **Concern(s):** peace; nonviolence; analysis; conflict resolution. This journal is geared to show the causes of conflict and educate people on them so they are not repeated. **Other**: 360 Lexington Ave., New York, NY 10017

M ▸ **Utne Reader**
Fawkes Building
1624 Harmon Pl.
Minneapolis, MN 55403 (612)338-5040
**Concern(s):** media; arts; literature; press. "This Readers Digest-style magazine indeed features 'the best of the alternative press,' as their subtitle suggests. Most articles are reprinted from more mainstream alternatives such as Mother Jones and The Progressive Review. Happily, though, an increasingly number are appearing from more activist-oriented papers such as The Guardian and Greenpeace. It is enthusiastically recommended for all who like to read - for the pleasure and information contained in this basic magazine."-C.C. **Est.:** 1983. **Frequency:** 6/yr. **Subscription:** $18/yr. **Price:** $4/ea. **Contact(s):** Eric Utne, J. Walljasper

H ▸ **Vegetarian Journal**
Box 1463
Baltimore, MD 21203 (301)366-VEGE
**Affiliation:** Vegetarian Resource Group. **Concern(s):** health; environment; vegetarian; nutrition; animal rights. Addresses issues of health, animal rights, and ecology. Nonprofit. **Frequency:** 6/yr. **Subscription:** $20/yr. **Pages:** 36. **Circ.:** 17M. **Contact(s):** Charles Stahler.

H ▸ **Vegetarian Living**
Box 34427
Los Angeles, CA 90034 (310)392-7735
**Affiliation:** Vegetarian Society, INC. **Concern(s):** health; nutrition; vegetarian. A newsletter devoted to Vegetarian Living, giving recipes and hints for those converting to vegetarian ways. Nonprofit. **Est.:** 1948. **Dues:** $25/yr. **Frequency:** 12/yr. **Office:** 2401 Lincoln Blvd Santa Monica, CA 90405. **Contact(s):** Vic Rorsythe (President), Carla Romo (Vice President). (714)648-0145.

H ▸ **Vegetarian Times**
Box 446
Mt. Morris, IL 61054-9894 (312)848-8100
**Concern(s):** health; vegetarian; nutrition. "Magazine covers all aspects of vegetarianism." **Frequency:** 12/yr. **Subscription:** $24.95/yr. **Price:** $3/ea. **Pages:** 80. **Circ.:** 165M. **Contact(s):** Sally Cullen (Editor), Paul Obis.

H ▸ **Vegetarian Voice**
Box 72
Dolgeville, NY 13329
**Affiliation:** North American Vegetarian Society. **Concern(s):** health; economics; environment; politics; vegetarian; nutrition; animal rights; activism; alternative markets. This tabloid style newspaper reports on every aspect of vegetarianism known or unknown. Not only does it deal with food it also deals with animal rights, cruelty free products, and political activism. **Frequency:** 4/yr. **Subscription:** $12/yr.

E ▸ **Vermont Life**
61 Elm St.
Montpelier, VT 05602
**Concern(s):** environment; bioregionalism. Articles about Vermont subjects only. **Contact(s):** Tom Slayton (Editor-in-chief).

E ▸ **Vermont Vanguard Press, Statewide Weekly**
Vanguard Publishing
87 College St.
Burlington, VT 05401 (802)864-0506
**Concern(s):** environment; arts; politics; economics; community self-reliance. A weekly alternative paper dedicated to Vermont politics, environment, arts, etc. **Est.:** 1978. **Frequency:** Weekly. **Circ.:** 25M. **Contact(s):** Joshua Mamis (Editor).

✌ ▸ **The Veteran**
Box 408594
Chicago, IL 60640 (312)761-8248
**Affiliation:** Vietnam Veterans Against the War. **Concern(s):** peace; Third World; veterans; Central America; intervention. "The sponsoring group, VVAW, played a strategic role in opposing the Vietnam War from within the military, and they continue their good work today. Stopping another Vietnam situation in Central America and veterans' rights are issues regularly addressed."-C.C. **Est.:** 1969. **Frequency:** 4/yr. **Subscription:** $6/yr. **Price:** $.50/ea. **Contact(s):** Pete Zastrow.

✌ ▸ **Veteran Affairs News**
Box 2745
Bangor, ME 04402 (207)947-9819
**Affiliation:** Forgotten Families. **Concern(s):** peace; politics; justice; Third World; foreign policy; national security; CIA; government accountability; veterans; prisoners; Asia; Native Americans. Designed to inform the public on current events of interest to the US Veteran. Articles represent news released from the US Veterans Administration, the American League of Families which handles the MIA-POW situation in Southeast Asia, and Forgotten Families which handles issues concerning Covert Operations of the US and how those operations affect the American family, and the Bureau of Indian Affairs, among other services and information centers around the country. **Est.:** 1990. **Frequency:** 4/yr. **Subscription:** $20/yr. **Price:** $5/ea. **Pages:** 12. **Circ.:** 25M. **Fax:** (207)945-6499. **Contact(s):** Sherry Sullivan (President/Investigator).

✌ ▸ **Veterans For Peace Journal**
Box 3881
Portland, ME 04104 (207)797-2770
**Concern(s):** peace; education; economics; disarmament; conflict resolution; economic conversion. A journal dedicated to educating the

public over many issues that affect our countries economic, social, and foreign relations. These issues are the costs of war and the arms race, foreign policy, and abolishing war as a tool for foreign policy. Regular features include: President's Message, Project Reports, Essays, Book Reviews, VFP Chapter Directory. **Est.:** 1985. **Frequency:** 4/yr. **Subscription:** $15/yr. **Price:** $5/ea. **Bulk:** 20% off/24. **Pages:** 34. **Circ.:** 3M. **E-Network:** PeaceNet. **ID:** 'vfphq'. **Fax:** (207)797-2770. **Contact(s):** Jerry Genesio (Executive Director).

**J ▸ Victimology: An International Journal**
2333 N. Vernon St.
Arlington, VA 22207 (703)536-1750
**Concern(s):** justice; feminism; victims' rights; reform; children; child abuse; rape/sexual abuse; battered women; volunteers. "We are the only magazine specifically focussing on the victim, on the dynamics of victimization; for social scientists, criminal justice professionals and practitioners, social workers and volunteer and professional groups engaged in prevention of victimization and in offering assistance to victims of rape, spouse abuse, child abuse, incest, abuse of the elderly, natural disasters, etc." **Frequency:** 4/yr. **Price:** $5/sample. **Circ.:** 2.5M. **Contact(s):** Emilio C. Viano (Editor-in-chief).

**T ▸ Vietnam Today**
Box 5043
San Francisco, CA 94101
**Affiliation:** US-Vietnam Friendship Association. **Concern(s):** Third World; Asia. "Friendship between the people of Vietnam and the US is the purpose of Vietnam Today. Economic, cultural, and social exchanges between the former enemies are promoted. Material aid for the people of Vietnam is also solicited by this newsletter."-C.C. **Est.:** 1979. **Frequency:** 4/yr. **Subscription:** $6/yr. **Price:** $1/ea. **Contact(s):** Beatrice Eisman.

**P ▸ Village Voice**
Box 1905
Marion, OH 43306 (212)475-3300
**Concern(s):** politics; justice; environment; peace; arts; media; feminism. A newspaper dealing with current or controversial topics. **Frequency:** Weekly. **Subscription:** $44.20/yr. **Office:** 842 Broadway New York, NY 10003. **Contact(s):** Michael Caruso (Features Editor).

**E ▸ Vision**
9 West Broad St.
Stamford, CT 06902 (203)323-8987
**Affiliation:** Keep America Beautiful. **Concern(s):** environment; recycling; conservation; beautification. This newsletter reports on the many projects of Keep America Beautiful. **Frequency:** 4/yr.

**F ▸ The Voice**
c/o All Saints Church
132 N. Euclid Ave.
Pasadena, CA 91101 (818)796-1172
**Affiliation:** Pro-Choice Task Force. **Concern(s):** feminism; spiritual; religious reform; interfaith; family planning; pro-choice. This newsletter informs the community on the pro-choice candidates and issues, and to actually participate in the political process and expand membership on the Task Force to include all men and women committed to pro-choice and who have an interest in participating. Nonprofit. (213)681-9441.

**✍ ▸ A Voice For Children**
Box 4143
Sante Fe, NM 87502
**Affiliation:** The Fifteeth Street School Foundation. **Concern(s):** education; childhood; holism. "Its purpose is to provide educators and parents with information which may by useful as they address recent national critiques of public education. Its intent is to speak with a positive voice for children", in the tradition of Summerhill. **Frequency:** 3/yr. **Contact(s):** Edward M. Jones (Editor).

**J ▸ Voice of Reason Newsletter**
Box 6656
Silver Springs, MD 20906 (301)598-2447
**Affiliation:** Americans for Religious Liberty. **Concern(s):** justice; spiritual; freedom of expression; interfaith. Regularly informs readers about new threats to basic rights, sectarian intrusion into public education, how much your taxes are being used for sectarian purposes. It also keeps readers up to date on what is being done about church-state separation violations. **Other Resources:** Free with a membership to ARL. **Est.:** 1981. **Frequency:** 4/yr. **Subscription:** $10/yr. **Price:** Free. **Contact(s):** Edd Doerr.

**✐ ▸ Voices**
478 W. MacArthur Blvd.
Oakland, CA 94609 (510)428-9191
**Affiliation:** Redwood Records Cultural & Educational Fund. **Concern(s):** arts; music. "Angela Davis helped found Redwood Records Company; Holly Near is the president of RRCEF, a fund established to promote cross-cultural understanding. Voices details the group's activities and reports on items of interest to members."-C.C. **Est.:** 1982. **Dues:** $20/yr. **Frequency:** 2/yr. **Subscription:** Membership. **Price:** Donation.

**☮ ▸ Voices for Peace**
4816 Cornell Ave.
Downers Grove, IL 60515 (312)969-7584
**Affiliation:** America-Israel Council for Israeli-Palestinian Peace. **Concern(s):** peace; Third World; conflict resolution; Mid-East. "Peace between the Israelis and the Palestinians through mutual recognition is promoted here. Voices does not side with either party, but urges dialogue between Israel and the Palestinians' organization."-C.C. **Est.:** 1982. **Dues:** $18/yr. **Frequency:** Irregular. **Subscription:** Membership. **Price:** Free. **Contact(s):** Mary Appelman.

**H ▸ Voluntary Service in Action**
Commission on Voluntary Service and Action
Box 11Z-COY
New York, NY 10009 (212)468-8624
**Affiliation:** Commission on Voluntary Service and Action. **Concern(s):** health; justice; environment; volunteers; occupational safety; victims' rights; conservation. Voluntary service in action, designed for the growing numbers of people active in, interested in, or simply curious about full-time voluntary service. Magazine articles "from the field," photos, editorial, advice for the volunteer organizer. Contributing correspondent, advertiser, distributor inquiries welcome. The Commission was one of the first NGO established by the UN in 1946. **Other Resources:** INVEST YOURSELF: THE CATALOGUE OF VOLUNTEER OPPORTUNITIES, A GUIDE TO ACTION. **Est.:** 1988. **Frequency:** 4/yr. **Subscription:** $14/yr. **Price:** $4/ea. **Bulk:** 20% off/24. **Pages:** 96. **Circ.:** 5M. **Contact(s):** Susan Angus (Editor), Jim Rosenberg (Circulation). (212)974-2405.

**E ▸ The Walking Magazine**
9-11 Harcourt
Boston, MA 02116
**Concern(s):** environment; health; recreation. Magazine articles on fitness, health, equipment, nutrition, travel and adventure, famous walkers, and other walking-related topics. **Contact(s):** Bradford Ketchum (Editor).

**$ ▸ Wall Street Green Review**
24861 Alicia Pkwy, #C-293
Laguna Hills, CA 92653 (714)588-9863
**Affiliation:** SRI Advisors. **Concern(s):** economics; environment; socially-responsible investing; toxic/hazardous waste; recycling; trade; corporate responsibility. This newsletter tracks business and financial news of companies in the hazardous and solid waste industries, as well as alternative resource companies involved in recycling, renewable energy, and other non-polluting technologies for environmental development. **Contact(s):** David L. Brown (Publisher).

**F ▸ WAND Bulletin**
305 7th St. SE
Washington, DC 20003 (202)543-8505
**Affiliation:** Women's Action for Nuclear Disarmament (WAND). **Concern(s):** feminism; peace; disarmament. **Other Resources:** WAND BULLETIN; FACTS FOR THE NUCLEAR AGE, articles from other sources, best lists of video, films, and other resources. 80 groups in over 35 states. **Est.:** 1980. **Frequency:** 4/yr. **Contact(s):** Beverly Droz (President), Diane Aronson (Director). (617)64306740. **Other:** 691 Massachusetts Ave., #204, Arlington, MA 02174

**☮ ▸ WarChild Monitor**
Box 487
Eureka Springs, AR 72632 (501)253-8900
**Concern(s):** peace; education; conflict resolution; nonviolence; youth. Challenges society's institutions and practices glorifying and enhancing war in the mind of the child. It informs and educates the public on the militarization of children and how they are the victim's of all conflicts in the end. **Contact(s):** Richard Parker, Ph. D. (Director), Samuel Hilburn (Associate Director).

**H ▸ The Wary Canary**
c/o Wary Canary Press
Box 2204
Fort Collins, CO 80522 (303)224-0083
**Concern(s):** health; environment; holism; preventative medicine; self-help; psychology; consumer protection; social ecology; hazardous/toxic waste. A networking national newsletter providing info about preventive self-care and recovery in environmentally or chemically induced illness, toxic response syndromes (TRS) and allergies. An exchange of information between/for/about "Wary Canaries" who act as early warning signals of toxic products, conditions, or materials. Reports on non-traditional treatments and detoxing methods, physical/psychological approaches to wellness; and consumer actions for responsible laws, regulations and products. **Other Resources:** Also publishes ENVIRON MAGAZINE. **Frequency:** 4/yr. **Subscription:** $20/yr. **Pages:** 16-20. **Publisher:** Wary Canary Press. **Contact(s):** Ed Randegger, Suzanne Randegger

**P ▸ Washington Insight**
1023 15th St. NW, #500
Washington, DC 20005 (202)789-1011
**Affiliation:** National Association of Evangelicals. **Concern(s):** politics. Newsletter.

**F ▸ Washington Memo**
2010 Massachusetts Ave. NW, 5th Fl.
Washington, DC 20036 (202)296-4012
**Affiliation:** Alan Guttmacher Institute. **Concern(s):** feminism; demographics; pro-choice; population growth. This memo focuses on the legislation and lobbying efforts that are trying to strip men and women of their right to choice and responsible birth control.

**P ▸ The Washington Monthly**
1611 Connecticut Ave. NW
Washington, DC 20009
**Concern(s):** politics. Magazine with investigative articles on politics, government and the political culture. **Contact(s):** Charles Peters (Editor).

**P ▸ Washington Newsletter**
245 2nd St. NE
Washington, DC 20002 (202)547-6000
**Affiliation:** Friends Committee on National Legislation. **Concern(s):** politics; spiritual; peace; Third World; law; interfaith; activism; disarmament; foreign policy. "The Friends publish one of the best periodicals containing recommendations on new legislation needing support. Their well-known activism on progressive issues is reflected in this excellent selection."-C.C. **Est.:** 1943. **Frequency:** 11/yr. **Subscription:** $20/yr. **Price:** Free. **Contact(s):** Laura Petroff, Alison Oldham (Legal Action Coordinator). (202)547-4343.

**E ▸ Washington Post Magazine**
1150 15th St. NW
Washington, DC 20071
**Concern(s):** environment; economics; justice; politics; arts; bioregionalism; analysis; trade; culture; minority rights. Personal-experience essays, profiles, and general-interest pieces on business, arts and culture, politics, science, sports, education, children, relationships, behavior, etc. Articles should be of interest to people living in Washington, DC area. **Publisher:** The Washington Post. **Contact(s):** Linton Weeks (Managing Editor).

**T ▸ Washington Report on the Hemisphere**
724 9th St. NW
Washington, DC 20001 (202)393-3322
**Affiliation:** Council on Hemispheric Affairs. **Concern(s):** Third World; Latin America. "Pluralistic institutions in Latin America are promoted in this group's newsletter. It shares the progressive perspective of other listings here, but the price will prevent most individuals and groups from subscribing."-C.C. **Est.:** 1980. **Frequency:** 26/yr. **Subscription:** $105, $165 institution. **Price:** $1/ea. **Contact(s):** Laurence R. Birnj.

**P ▸ Washington Reports**
2 W. 64th St.
New York, NY 10023 (212)873-6500
**Affiliation:** American Ethical Union. **Concern(s):** politics; justice; law; reform; civil liberties. "Legislation covering the relations between churches and the public is analyzed in this newsletter. Prayer in the public schools and other violations of the separation of church and state in legislation are opposed."-C.C. **Est.:** 1976. **Frequency:** 10/yr. **Subscription:** $7.50/yr. **Price:** Donation. **Contact(s):** Barb Pequet, Herb Blinder

**P ▸ Washington Spectator**
Box 20065
London Terrace Station
New York, NY 10011 (212)741-2365
**Affiliation:** Public Concern Foundation. **Concern(s):** politics. "Tristram Coffin's perspective and commentary are offered in this four-page opinion newsletter. His perceptive thoughts fall squarely on target with in-depth analysis on subjects of interest to progressives in the nation's capital."-C.C. **Est.:** 1974. **Frequency:** 22/yr. **Subscription:** $10/yr. **Price:** $.50/ea. **Contact(s):** Tristram Coffin.

**E ▸ Wasteline**
6930 Carroll Ave., #600
Tacoma Park, MD 20912 (301)891-1100
**Affiliation:** Environmental Action Foundation. **Concern(s):** environment; recycling; conservation. A quarterly newsletter of the Solid Waste Alternatives Project focusing on waste reduction and recycling. **Other Resources:** See Environmental Action Foundation. **Sub-**

**scription:** $10/yr. **Publisher:** Environmental Action, Inc. **Contact(s):** Ruth Caplan (Executive Director), Nicholas A. Fedoruk (Director).

E ▶ **Water Resources Bulletin**
5410 Grosvenor Ln, #220
Bethesda, MD 20814-2192 (301)493-8600
**Affiliation:** American Water Resources Association. **Concern(s):** environment; water; resources. This bulletin reports on the shape of our waterways and hydroelectric power research. Informs you of breakthroughs in research and legislation.

P ▶ **Ways & Means**
Center for Policy Alternatives
1875 Connecticut Ave. NW
Washington, DC 20009 (202)387-6030
**Affiliation:** Center for Policy Alternatives. **Concern(s):** politics; justice; economics; grassroots organizing. "Progressive city and state government is the goal of this newsletter. Policy changes in favor of human needs, progressive taxation, and equitable distribution of services are all covered."-C.C. **Est.:** 1976. **Frequency:** 4/yr. **Subscription:** $15/yr. **Price:** $1.50/ea. **Contact(s):** Sandra Martin.

E ▶ **WCI News**
New York Zoological Park
Bronx, NY 10460 (212)220-5090
**Affiliation:** Wildlife Conservation International. **Concern(s):** environment; wildlife/endangered species; conservation.

☮ ▶ **WCRP/USA Newsletter**
777 UN Plaza
New York, NY 10017 (212)687-2163
**Affiliation:** World Conference on Religion and Peace. **Concern(s):** peace; spiritual; justice; interfaith. "Clergy and laity interested in working for world peace publish this report on the sponsoring group's activities. It is primarily a group organ."-C.C. **Other Resources:** See also RELIGION FOR PEACE newsletter. **Dues:** $25/yr. **Frequency:** 3/yr. **Subscription:** $10/yr. **Contact(s):** William F. Vendley (Editor), Norma U. Levitt (President).

E ▶ **Weatherwise**
Heldref Publications
4000 Albemarle St. NW
Washington, DC 20016 (202)362-6445
**Concern(s):** environment; climate. America's only popular magazine devoted to weather, shares this experience with the reader. It captures the power, beauty, and excitement of the ever-changing elements in vibrant color photographs and crisp, well-written articles. Weatherwise is published in association with the American Meteorological Society. **Frequency:** 6/yr. **Subscription:** $25, $42 institution.

J ▶ **Welfare Mothers Voice**
4504 N. 47th St.
Milwaukee, WI 53218 (414)444-0220
**Affiliation:** Welfare Warriors. **Concern(s):** justice; feminism; family; demographics; welfare rights; children; child support; day care; discrimination; sexism; housing; social justice. Bilingual paper. **Contact(s):** Pat Gowens (Founder).

J ▶ **Western Shoshone Nation Newsletter**
Box 140068
Duckwater, NV 89314-0068 (702)863-0227
**Affiliation:** Western Shoshone National Council. **Concern(s):** justice; environment; health; Native Americans; hazardous/toxic waste. This newsletters purpose is to report on all Western Shoshone interests from negotiating with the US for a legislative agreement confirming ownership of lands within the ancestral territory to the establishment of a Western Shoshone Government with full sovereignty. The newsletter also reports on nuclear power and testing on their lands and violations against Mother Earth. **Frequency:** 4/yr. **Subscription:** Donation. **Price:** Free. **Pages:** 12. **Fax:** (702)863-0301. **Contact(s):** Chief Raymond D. Yowell.

E ▶ **Whalenews**
Box 2639
San Pedro, CA 90731-0943 (310)548-6279
**Affiliation:** American Cetacean Society. **Concern(s):** environment; wildlife/endangered species. This newsletter reports on the Cetacean Society and its actions to save the whales. Also reports on the whaling industry and the attempts to fight them.

E ▶ **Whalewatch**
International Wildlife Coalition
Box 388
North Falmouth, MA 02556
**Affiliation:** International Wildlife Coalition. **Concern(s):** environment; wildlife/endangered species. This newsletter reports on efforts to save the whales from the enactment of legislation to ban whaling and other detrimental activities to environment. **Frequency:** 4/yr. **Member:** International Wildlife Coalition.

E ▶ **Whalewatcher**
Box 2639
San Pedro, CA 90731-0943 (310)548-6279
**Affiliation:** American Cetacean Society. **Concern(s):** environment; wildlife/endangered species. This journal reports on the many exciting things whales do and how you can help save them. Beautiful photos of these great mammals. **Frequency:** 4/yr.

M ▶ **What Is To Be Read**
1736 Columbia Rd. NW, #202
Washington, DC 20009 (202)387-1753
**Affiliation:** Corporate Economic News Service. **Concern(s):** media; education. "Twenty or so books are reviewed in each issue of this newsletter. Subjects range from land use and urban reform to 'Prisoners of the American Dream.'"-C.C. **Est.:** 1984. **Frequency:** 6/yr. **Subscription:** $25/yr. **Price:** Donation. **Other Formats:** Available on 5.25/3.5 floppies for IBM WordPerfect. **Contact(s):** Henry Leland.

☮ ▶ **When the People Lead...**
3268 Sacramento St.
San Francisco, CA 94115 (415)346-1875
**Affiliation:** Center For US-USSR Initiatives. **Concern(s):** peace. "Our philosophy, 'When the people lead, the leaders will follow,' undergirds all our programs. We go directly to citizens to assess issues, stimulate ideas and work toward solutions." **Frequency:** 4/yr. **Contact(s):** Sharon Tennison (President).

J ▶ **Whispering Wind Magazine**
8009 Wales St.
New Orleans, LA 70126
**Concern(s):** justice; Native Americans. Magazine devoted to preserving Native American customs. Excellent guide for finding and making traditional dress, crafts, and powwows. **Frequency:** 6/yr. **Subscription:** $16/yr.

H ▶ **WHO Chronicle**
Box 5284
New York, NY 10249 (212)963-6132
**Affiliation:** World Health Organization, UN. **Concern(s):** health; public health; United Nations. "The UN's efforts for the improvement of world health are the main subject area covered. This chronicle serves as the journal of record for actions promoting world health, includes summaries of the group's books and pamphlets and is available in other major languages besides English. For a WHO periodical published for the general public, see listing for World Health."-C.C. **Est.:** 1947. **Frequency:** 6/yr. **Subscription:** $10/yr. **Price:** Free.

E ▶ **Whole Earth Review**
27 Gate Five Rd.
Sausalito, CA 94965 (415)332-1716
**Affiliation:** Point Foundation. **Concern(s):** environment; economics; alternative consumer; green consumer. The Review, which does not take ads, is the successor publication to the best-selling Whole Earth Catalogs, Whole Earth Review gives its readers access to information useful in their daily lives, access to new ideas, and access to a community of education that works, individual by individual, to make the future a better place to visit. Formerly CoEvolution Quarterly. **Other Resources:** Books; CD-ROM (The Electronic Whole Earth Catalog). The WELL - Electronic conferencing network. Cyberthon - a 24-hour adventure in virtual reality. The Hackers' Conference. Whole Earth Institute. Nonprofit. **Est.:** 1968. **Frequency:** 4/yr. **Subscription:** $27/yr.; $35 institution. **Price:** $6/ea. **Pages:** 144. **Circ.:** 50M. **Publisher:** Point Foundation. **E-Network:** The WELL. **ID:** Kerwit@Well. **Contact(s):** Kelly Teevan (Executive Director).

H ▶ **Wholistic Living News**
Association for Wholistic Living
Box 16346
San Diego, CA 92116
**Affiliation:** Association for Wholistic Living. **Concern(s):** health; holism.

✎ ▶ **Wide Open Magazine**
Wide Open Press
116 Lincoln St.
Santa Rosa, CA 95401 (707)545-3821
**Concern(s):** arts; health; environment; poetry; self-help. "We prefer short poems with a punch, maximum 16 lines and we will consider all styles and forms." Deals with contemporary issues in writing, self-help and solutions to current problems facing humanity. **Est.:** 1984. **Frequency:** 4/yr. **Subscription:** $24/yr. **Price:** $6/sample. **Pages:** 80. **Contact(s):** Clif Simms, Lynn L. Simms (Co-editors).

E ▶ **Wildbird**
Box 6050
Mission Viejo, CA 92690
**Concern(s):** environment; wildlife/endangered species. Features and columns, words, for field birders and garden birders. "No pieces on taming wild birds." **Contact(s):** Tim Gallagher (Managing Editor).

E ▶ **Wilderness**
900 17th St. NW
Washington, DC 20006 (202)833-2300
**Affiliation:** Wilderness Society. **Concern(s):** environment; recreation. Periodical focusing on the problems facing our national parks, shorelines, and recreation areas. **Est.:** 1935.

E ▶ **Wildlife Activist**
629 Green St.
Allentown, PA 18102 (215)434-1637
**Affiliation:** Wildlife Information Center. **Concern(s):** environment; wildlife/endangered species; conservation. Newsletter.

E ▶ **Wildlife Conservation**
629 Green St.
Allentown, PA 18102 (215)434-1637
**Affiliation:** New York Zoological Society. **Concern(s):** environment; education; wildlife/endangered species; science; conservation. Through its unique blend of exploration, adventure and scientific excellence it inspires appreciation for, and understanding of, the world's natural heritage of wildlife and habitats. This magazine reflects the conservation commitment of its internationally respected publisher. **Frequency:** 6/yr. **Subscription:** $11.95/yr.

✍ ▶ **Wildlife Education**
3590 Kettner Blvd.
San Diego, CA 92101 (619)299-0114
**Concern(s):** education; environment; wildlife/endangered species. **Fax:** (619)299-0114. **Contact(s):** Linda C. Wood (Managing Editor).

E ▶ **Wildlife News**
1717 Massachusetts Ave. NW
Washington, DC 20036 (202)265-8394
**Affiliation:** African Wildlife Foundation. **Concern(s):** environment; wildlife/endangered species. Newsletter. **Subscription:** $15/yr.

E ▶ **The Wildlifer**
5410 Grosvenor Lane
Bethesda, MD 20814
**Affiliation:** Wildlife Society. **Concern(s):** environment; wildlife/endangered species; conservation. This newsletter reports on human induced degradation of animal habitats and the interaction of wildlife with their natural habitats. **Frequency:** 6/yr.

☮ ▶ **Wilmington College Peace Resource Center Newsletter**
Pyle Center
Box 1183
Wilmington, OH 45177 (513)382-5338
**Affiliation:** Wilmington College Peace Resource Center. **Concern(s):** peace; education; students. A tool to help concerned individuals and groups find useful peace education resources from a wide variety of sources, and to provide information about peace-related activities. Nonprofit. **Est.:** 1975. **Frequency:** 4/yr. **Price:** Donation. **Pages:** 6. **Circ.:** 2M. **Contact(s):** Helen Wiegal (Director, PRC).

☮ ▶ **WILPF Program and Legislative Action Bulletin**
1213 Race St.
Philadelphia, PA 19107 (215)563-7110
**Affiliation:** Women's International League for Peace and Freedom (WILPF). **Concern(s):** peace; economics. Covers latest information on organizing work and legislation relating to disarmament, ending US intervention, racial justice, women's rights, budget priorities and other peace and justice issues. Provides timely grassroots action and lobbying suggestions. **Frequency:** 6/yr. **Subscription:** $10/yr. **Price:** $2/ea. **Bulk:** 50% off/24. **Pages:** 8. **Circ.:** 900. **Publisher:** WILPF. **Contact(s):** Jerilyn Bowen (Program Director), Isabel Guy (Legislative Director).

✪ ▶ **Wind Energy Weekly**
777 N. Capitol St. NE., #805
Washington, DC 20002 (202)408-8988
**Affiliation:** American Wind Energy Association. **Concern(s):** energy; environment; wind; renewables. A newsletter informing the reader about regulatory and policy issues related to the use of wind energy at the state, federal, and international level; wind technology improvements; trade news; environmental issues of interest to the wind industry. **Est.:** 1974. **Frequency:** Weekly. **Subscription:** $225/yr. **Pages:** 4+. **Circ.:** 400. **E-Network:** Econet. **ID:** 'awea'. **Fax:** (202)408-8536. MCI MAIL: AWEA. **Contact(s):** Randy Swisher (Executive Director), Mike Marvin (Director, Government Affairs).

**✪ ▶ WindLetter**
777 N. Capitol St. NE., #805
Washington, DC 20002 (202)408-8988
**Affiliation:** American Wind Energy Association. **Concern(s):** energy; environment; wind; renewables. News of association events/activities, news of legislative affairs, and small turbines articles. **Est.:** 1974. **Frequency:** 12/yr. **Subscription:** $35/yr. **Pages:** 4+. **Circ.:** 500. **E-Network:** Econet. **ID:** 'awea'. **Fax:** (202)408-8536. MCI Mail: AWEA. **Contact(s):** Randy Swisher (Executive Director), Mike Marvin (Director of Government Affairs).

**☮ ▶ Window on the World**
777 UN Plaza, #7D
New York, NY 10017 (212)986-5165
**Affiliation:** Unitarian Universalist, UN Office. **Concern(s):** peace; United Nations. "Supporting the programs of the UN and expanding its influence are the purposes of WINDOW OF THE WORLD. The Unitarian Universalists have been some of the most consistent supporters of the UN, and continue their commitment in this selection."-C.C. **Est.:** 1971. **Frequency:** 8/yr. **Subscription:** $25/yr. **Price:** Free. **Contact(s):** Sue Nichols, Vernon Nichols.

**E ▶ Wings: Essays on Invertebrate Conservation**
The Xerces Society
10 SW Ash St.
Portland, OR 97204 (503)222-2788
**Affiliation:** Xerces Society. **Concern(s):** environment; conservation; wildlife/endangered species. This is a membership magazine intended for the general reader; it is illustrated with full-color photographs of invertebrates, and features articles by leading scientists and conservationists. The Society began in 1971. **Other Resources:** 4th of July Butterfly Count - volunteers do population readings; 2) Atala, published occasionally - scientific journal; 3) Butterfly Gardening: Creating Summer Magic in Your Garden (members only); 4) The Common Names of North American Butterflies Nonprofit. **Est.:** 1987. **Dues:** $25, $15 student/seniors, $50 supporter. **Frequency:** 3/yr. **Subscription:** Membership. **Price:** $2.50/ea. **Pages:** 16. **Contact(s):** Mary Troychak (Editor).

**F ▶ Wingspan**
Box 1491
Manchester-By-the-Sea, MA 01944 (617)282-3521
**Concern(s):** feminism; health; men's liberation; psychology. The key to its national impact is the 585 individual, volunteer distributors who receive bulk shipments of 50-3,500 free and distribute them to local men's groups, therapists, body workers, health food stores, etc. Seeding the community helps spawn men's work and men's groups. Newspaper. **Frequency:** 4/yr. **Subscription:** 50 free to men's organizations, etc. **Price:** Donation. **Pages:** c16. **Circ.:** 110M. **Fax:** (301)268-2368. **Contact(s):** Bob Frenier (Publisher), Chris Harding (Editor). (301)267-6923.

**D ▶ The Witness**
Box 359
Ambler, PA 19002 (215)643-7067
**Affiliation:** Episcopal Church. **Concern(s):** demographics; justice; spiritual; interfaith; poverty; discrimination; racism; housing. "This magazine covers issues of interest to religious folks of all denominations, not just Episcopalians. The poor and those discriminated against are of special concern, with peace questions also being treated here."-C.C. **Est.:** 1917. **Frequency:** 12/yr. **Subscription:** $15/yr. **Price:** $1.50/ea. **Publisher:** Episcopal Church Publisher Co. **Contact(s):** Mary Lou Suhor.

**T ▶ Witness for Peace**
Box 567
Durham, NC 27702 (919)688-5049
**Affiliation:** Witness for Peace. **Concern(s):** Third World; spiritual; interfaith; Central America. "This 16-page magazine gives more in-depth coverage of the group's concerns than their NEWSBRIEF previously reviewed. The group's humanitarian and protest efforts regarding Central America as well as efforts of others, are noted."-C.C. **Est.:** 1983. **Frequency:** 6/yr. **Subscription:** $25/yr. **Price:** Free. **Circ.:** 40M. **Contact(s):** Ron Steif.

**T ▶ Witness for Peace Newsbrief**
Box 567
Durham, NC 27702 (919)688-5049
**Affiliation:** Witness for Peace. **Concern(s):** Third World; spiritual; interfaith; Central America. "Solidarity delegations to Nicaragua, El Salvador, and other Central American nations are the primary purpose of this newsletter. With a grassroots religious base in the churches and synagogues, frequent brigades of opponents to US military aid help with development projects in war zones and legislative action."-C.C. **Est.:** 1983. **Frequency:** 6/yr. **Subscription:** $10/yr. **Price:** Free. **Contact(s):** Ron Steif.

**F ▶ The Woman Activist**
2310 Barbour Rd.
Falls Church, VA 22043
**Concern(s):** feminism; politics; activism; law; lobbying. This bulletin reports on legislation from Washington that affects women.

**F ▶ Womanews**
Box 220, Village Station
New York, NY 10014 (212)674-1698
**Concern(s):** feminism; empowerment. New York's only feminist newspaper dealing with women's issues. "We are a monthly publication with an events calendar, classifieds, reviews of books, movies, music, health, and sports. We have display advertising, letter section, national, and international newsbriefs." **Est.:** 1979. **Frequency:** 10/yr. **Subscription:** $15/yr. **Price:** $1.25/ea. **Pages:** 22. **Circ.:** 6.5M. **Contact(s):** Diana Corzen (Office Manager).

**F ▶ Women & Therapy**
Haworth Press, Inc.
75 Griswold St.
Binghampton, NY 13904
**Concern(s):** feminism; health; psychology. "...the only professional journal that focuses entirely on the complex interrelationship between women and the therapeutic experience. The journal is devoted to descriptive, theoretical, clinical, and empirical perspectives on the topic of women and therapy. Women comprise the overwhelming majority of clients in therapy. Yet there has been little emphasis on this area in the training of therapists or in the professional literature. Women & Therapy is designed to fill this void." **Frequency:** 4/yr. **Subscription:** $32/yr. **Price:** Free sample. **Pages:** 120. **Circ.:** 1M. **Publisher:** Haworth Press.

**F ▶ Women and Health**
117 Saint John's Pl.
Brooklyn, NY 11217
**Concern(s):** feminism; health. A multidisciplinary journal presenting the most current scholarly information on the entire spectrum of women's health. **Publisher:** Hayworth Press Inc. **Contact(s):** Dr. Jeanne Mager Stellman (Editor).

**F ▶ Women Against Military Madness Newsletter**
3255 Hennepin Ave. S, #125B
Minneapolis, MN 55408-9986 (612)827-5364
**Affiliation:** Women Against Military Madness. **Concern(s):** feminism; peace; empowerment; activism; rights. A newsletter that shows the fallacies of the current US government policies and demonstrates how women and men can effectively change those policies. Nonprofit. **Est.:** 1982. **Dues:** $30; lower income. **Frequency:** 12/yr. **Subscription:** Membership. **Pages:** 6. **Circ.:** 2.8M. **Labels:** 2800. **Member:** Minnesota Peace and Justice Coalition. **Fax:** (612)827-6433. **Contact(s):** Lucia Wilkes (Director-Co), Daniella Maus (Co-director). (612)826-5365.

**✐ ▶ Women Artists News**
300 Riverside Dr.
New York, NY 10025 (212)666-6990
**Concern(s):** arts; feminism; activism; sexism. "...chock full of articles, reviews, visuals and is accurately named. Exhibition reviews and short profiles of women artists constitute its feature section. Strong points include regular, detailed reporting panels, coverage of alternative space exhibitions, often slighted in other magazines; listings; and special feature... WAN feels like news from the front. The lives and careers of women artists are particularly hard, and this magazine conveys that sense of struggle..."-New Art Examiner. **Est.:** 1972. **Frequency:** 4/yr. **Price:** $3/ea. **Pages:** 50. **Publisher:** Midmarch Arts Press. (212)865-5509.

**F ▶ Women Fight Back**
Box 161775
Cupertino, CA 95016
**Affiliation:** Women to Women Communications. **Concern(s):** feminism; justice. A new periodical that contains women's personal experience in the primary areas of our society: military; education; big business; business ownership and employment; legislation and government programs; crime and the criminal justice system; religion, the church, and membership organizations; health products and the health treatment industry. **Est.:** 1992. **Frequency:** 12/yr. **Subscription:** $36/yr. **Bulk:** 100/$50.

**$ ▶ Women in Business**
9100 Ward Parkway
Box 8728
Kansas City, MO 64114-0728
**Affiliation:** American Business Women's Association. **Concern(s):** economics; feminism; trade. Publication of the American Business Women's Association, for career women from 25 to 55 years old; no profiles. **Contact(s):** Wendy Myers (Editor).

**F ▶ Women Library Workers Journal**
c/o McFarland & Company Inc.
Box 611
Jefferson, NC 28640 (919)246-4460
**Concern(s):** feminism; education; sexism; equal rights; law; students. WLW Journal provides information for the development and empowerment of women, particularly women in librarianship. It generates an international forum for candid articles and news items focused on current issues - sexism, pay equity, wrongful stereotypes, literacy, advocacy, censorship, and others. An extensive section involves a critical examination of books. **Frequency:** 4/yr. **Subscription:** $18/yr. **Price:** $7/ea. **Pages:** 32. **Circ.:** 500. **Publisher:** McFarland & Company Inc. **Contact(s):** Rhonda Herman (Business Manager), Caroline Mahla (Assistant to the Business Manager). (919)246-4460.

**F ▶ Women of Power**
Box 827
Cambridge, MA 02238-0827
**Concern(s):** feminism; spiritual; politics; empowerment; transformation. A magazine of feminism, spirituality, and politics. Fiction and nonfiction, poetry. **Frequency:** 4/yr. **Subscription:** $26/yr. **Contact(s):** Char McKee (Editor).

**F ▶ Women's Agenda**
1500 Massachusetts Ave. NW
Washington, DC 20005 (202)862-0700
**Affiliation:** Center for Defense Information. **Concern(s):** feminism; peace; politics; EQUAL RIGHTS; disarmament; lobbying. This newsletter provides a medium for the expression of women's views on the military and other aspects of national security. The Agenda also promotes women's involvement in national security decisions. It also provides information to other women's groups and women on national security events. **Est.:** 1985. **Contact(s):** Rear Admiral Gene R. LaRocque (Director).

**F ▶ Women's Press**
1009 Morro St. # 201
San Luis Obispo, CA 93401-3227 (805)466-9154
**Affiliation:** Women's Resource Center. **Concern(s):** feminism. A monthly newsletter that includes Women's Resource Center news; a calendar of local events and groups; book reviews; national news; and general information of interest to women. It is also a forum for creative writing, letters and poetry. **Frequency:** 12/yr. **Subscription:** $7/yr. **Pages:** 8. **Circ.:** 1.5M. **Contact(s):** Jo Ernest (Coordinator), Joan Costello (President). (805)772-1790.

**F ▶ Women's Research Network News**
Sara Delano Roosevelt Memorial House
47-49 East 65th St.
New York, NY 10021 (212)570-5001
**Affiliation:** National Council for Research on Women. **Concern(s):** feminism; labor; jobs. Includes News from the Council; Member Centers; International Centers; Caucuses; Publications and Resources; Upcoming Events; Job Opportunities; and Opportunities for Research, Study, and Affiliation as well as other news of interest to women's research, action, policy, and funding communities. **Frequency:** 4/yr. **Subscription:** $35, $100 institution. **Fax:** (212)570-5380. **Contact(s):** Debra L. Schultz (Editor).

**F ▶ Women's Review of Books**
Wellesley College
828 Washington
Wellesley, MA 02181-8255
**Affiliation:** Center for Research on Women. **Concern(s):** feminism. A newspaper that reviews books by women that are about women. It is essential for the librarian in obtaining and keeping abreast of quality reading material for their feminist collections. **Frequency:** 11/yr. **Subscription:** $16/yr.; $30 institution. **Circ.:** 12M.

**F ▶ Women's Rights Law Reporter**
Rutgers Law School
15 Washington St.
Newark, NJ 07102
**Concern(s):** feminism; politics; sexism; discrimination; equal rights. This journal reports on aspects of law that affect women. **Frequency:** 4/yr. **Subscription:** $20/yr.

**✍ ▶ Women's Studies International Forum**
Pergamon Journals, Inc
Fairview Park
Elmsford, NY 10523
**Concern(s):** education; feminism. **Frequency:** 4/yr. **Subscription:** $25/yr. **Publisher:** Pergamon Journals, Inc.

**F ◆ Women's Studies Quarterly**
City University of NY
311 E. 94th St.
New York, NY 10128    (212)360-5790
**Concern(s):** feminism; education. "News, issues, events in women's studies;" anything that promotes non-sexist learning at all levels of education. **Est.:** 1972. **Frequency:** 6/yr. **Subscription:** $25, $35 institutions. **Pages:** 150. **Publisher:** The Feminist Press.

**F ◆ Women: a cultural view**
c/o Oxford University Press Business Office
2001 Evans Rd.
Cary, NC 27513
**Concern(s):** feminism; arts; education; literature; culture. From the Native American women's movement to feminism, rapper women, feminist men and feminism, film theory, poetry, history and much more. **Frequency:** 3/yr. **Subscription:** $32/yr.; $70 institutions.

**⚙ ◆ Work in Progress**
1911 Kenbar Ct.
McLean, VA 22101    (703)241-1815
**Affiliation:** American Council for UN University. **Concern(s):** peace; education. "Work in Progress provides a sampling from publications, reports, working papers and other resources of the UN University. The dozen full-page features in each issue reflect the concern of the UN for social and economic justice around the world."-C.C. **Est.:** 1979. **Frequency:** 3/yr. **Subscription:** Free. **Price:** Donation. **Contact(s):** John Fenton.

**E ◆ The Workbook**
Box 4524
Albuquerque, NM 87106 (505)262-1862
**Affiliation:** Southwest Research & Info Center. **Concern(s):** environment; energy; agriculture; justice; feminism; networking. "A useful magazine that is a basic networking tool, not only for people of the Southwest, but for the entire country. It is basically a collection of resource reviews, with a particularly fine press review section. A typical piece might deal with a dangerous aspect of nuclear power. Each issue contains a feature article and 25 or more pages of 'Sources of Information' in more than two dozen subject categories. Publications listed are mostly from small press or alternative sources."-C.C. Nonprofit. **Est.:** 1974. **Frequency:** 4/yr. **Subscription:** $12, $25 institution. **Price:** $3.50/ea. **Pages:** 48. **Circ.:** 3.5M. **Fax:** (505)262-1864. **Contact(s):** Kathy Cone Newton (Editor).

**L ◆ Workers World**
46 W. 21st St.
New York, NY 10010    (212)255-0352
**Concern(s):** labor; justice; politics; feminism; civil liberties; gay/lesbian; prisons; criminal system; minority rights; unions. "One of the oldest radical leftist newspapers in the US, this tabloid is particularly noteworthy for its coverage of prisoners' issues and the gay liberation movement. In addition, it has useful features on labor, peace, and women's movements, and on movements of people of color. This popularly written selection reflects the view of the Workers World Party, which is in the forefront of domestic social change movements."-C.C. **Est.:** 1959. **Frequency:** Weekly. **Subscription:** $10/yr. **Price:** $.50/ea. **Publisher:** W.W. Publishers. **Contact(s):** Deirdre Griswold.

**L ◆ Workers' Democracy**
Box 24115
St. Louis, MO 63130    (314)727-8554
**Concern(s):** labor. "Increased workers' input and even control in the workplace are promoted quarterly. Aspects covered range from quality control circles to the controversial question of workers' representatives on the company's board of directors."-C.C. **Est.:** 1981. **Frequency:** 4/yr. **Subscription:** $6, $12 institution. **Price:** $1.50/ea. **Publisher:** Workers' Democracy Press. **Contact(s):** Don Fitz.

**✐ ◆ Working Classics**
298 9th Ave.
San Francisco, CA 94118    (415)387-3412
**Concern(s):** arts; literature. "Progressive literature is presented, both prose and poetry. Labor, peace, and economic justice are typical subjects in this selection, which nicely complements the Mill Hunk Herald." -C.C. **Est.:** 1981. **Frequency:** 4/yr. **Subscription:** $10, $20 institution. **Price:** $3/ea. **Publisher:** Red Wheelbarrow Press. **Contact(s):** David Joseph.

**F ◆ Working Mother**
Lang Communication
230 Park Ave.
New York, NY 10169
**Concern(s):** feminism; economics. Articles that help women in their task of juggling job, home, and family. "We like humorous pieces that solve or illuminate a problem unique to our readers." **Publisher:** Lang Communication.

**? ◆ Working Papers for a New Society**
186 Hampshire St.
Cambridge, MA 02139
**Concern(s):** future; planning; ideation. **Frequency:** 6/yr.

**L ◆ Working People's News**
496A Hudson St., #K-54
New York, NY 10014
**Concern(s):** labor. **Frequency:** 12/yr. **Subscription:** $10/yr.

**F ◆ Working Woman**
230 Park Ave.
New York, NY 10169    (212)551-9500
**Concern(s):** feminism; economics. Articles on business and personal aspects of the lives of working women. (800)234-9675. **Contact(s):** Kate White (Editor-in-chief).

**⚙ ◆ World Affairs**
Heldref Publications
4000 Albemarle St. NW
Washington, DC 20016    (202)362-6445
**Concern(s):** peace. Published by the American Peace Society since 1834, World Affairs is the oldest journal of international affairs in the US. Its articles illuminate issues involved in international conflict, and its special issues bring together divergent views and analyses of important topics. Special issues include those devoted to: religion and democracy, the World Court, disinformation, and resistance movements. **Frequency:** 4/yr. **Subscription:** $28, $35 institutions.

**$ ◆ World Business Academy Perspectives**
433 Airport Blvd., #416
Burlingame, CA 94010    (415)342-2387
**Affiliation:** World Business Academy. **Concern(s):** economics. A newsletter with a focus on process, values and spirit in the corporate world that makes it more truly "radical" than its socialist counterparts. **Est.:** 1987. **Contact(s):** John Renesch (Managing Director), Rinaldo Brutoco (Co-founder).

**⚙ ◆ World Democracy News**
1835 K St. NW
Washington, DC 20006-1552    (202)223-1770
**Affiliation:** Alliance for our Common Future. **Concern(s):** peace; world order. Quarterly newsletter on Federalism and working democracy, including news of organizations involved in environment, development, population, and other global issues. **Member:** World Government Organizations Coalition. **Contact(s):** Rick Wicks, Tom Ehrenzeller.

**T ◆ World Development**
UN Development Program
1 UN Plaza
New York, NY 10017    (212)906-5000
**Concern(s):** Third World; development.

**T ◆ World Development Forum**
The Hunger Project
1 Madison Ave.
New York, NY 10010    (212)532-4255
**Affiliation:** Hunger Project. **Concern(s):** Third World; demographics; development; hunger. A twice-monthly report of facts, trends and opinion in international development published as a public service. Nonprofit. **Frequency:** Twice 12/yr. **Contact(s):** Peggy Streit.

**T ◆ World Eagle**
64 Washburn Ave.
Wellesley, MA 02181    (617)235-1415
**Concern(s):** Third World; energy; demographics; population growth; hunger. Publishes a monthly 32-page social studies resource on topics such as global hunger, energy, population, trade, and military expenses.

**⚙ ◆ World Federalist News**
c/o WAWF
777 UN Plaza, 12th Fl.
New York, NY 10017    (212)599-1320
**Affiliation:** World Association for World Federation. **Concern(s):** peace; environment; world order; United Nations. This newsletter presents a unique source of information and opinion on global issues, world integration and the strengthening of world institutions. Your paid subscription helps support the collection and dissemination of this information. Additional contributions are needed and much appreciated. **Frequency:** 8/yr. **Subscription:** $15/yr.; $10/students, seniors. **Pages:** 8. **E-Network:** PeaceNet. **ID:** "worldfed". **Contact(s):** Jack Yost (Director).

**⚙ ◆ World Friends**
Box 560
Hicksville, NY 11802    (212)737-6952
**Concern(s):** peace. Newsletter with listings of people all over the world, who are looking for pen-friends, research colleagues, travel contract, singles matchmaking. "World Peace - through communication." **Member:** Co-op America.

**⚙ ◆ World Goodwill Newsletter**
113 University Place
Box 722 Cooper Station
New York, NY 10276    (212)982-8770
**Affiliation:** World Goodwill. **Concern(s):** peace; spiritual; faith; conflict resolution. This newsletter reports on the activities of its Organization. This newsletter also lists available periodicals from the parent organization. Good informative articles on the activities of World Goodwill. **Est.:** 1932. **Frequency:** 4/yr. **Price:** Free. **Circ.:** 18M. **E-Network:** PeaceNet. **ID:** 'pcoles'. **Contact(s):** Ida Urso, Ph.D. (Director), Sarah McKechnie (President).

**H ◆ World Health**
525 23rd St. NW
Washington, DC 20037    (202)861-3200
**Affiliation:** World Health Organization, UN. **Concern(s):** health; public health. "Popularly written and dealing with nutrition and other personal health problems, this magazine is enjoyed by the public around the world in several of the major languages. Disease control and primary health care are typical features."-C.C. **Est.:** 1958. **Frequency:** 10/yr. **Subscription:** $12.50/yr. **Price:** Free. **Contact(s):** John Bland.

**H ◆ World Hunger Action Newsletter**
15 Rutherford Pl.
New York, NY 10003    (212)598-0963
**Affiliation:** American Friends Service Committee. **Concern(s):** health; Third World; hunger; development; nutrition. "Food issues, including development, crops and hunger, are featured from a global perspective. Details on the issues, recommended legislation and a resource section are included."-C.C. **Est.:** 1976. **Frequency:** 12/yr. **Subscription:** $5/yr. **Price:** Donation. **Contact(s):** Dee Anne Dodd.

**⚙ ◆ The World Jurist**
1000 Connecticut Ave. NW, #800
Washington, DC 20036    (202)466-5428
**Affiliation:** World Peace Through Law Center. **Concern(s):** peace; world order. A bulletin that reports on the efforts to get a transnational law set up. **Contact(s):** Charles S. Rhyne (World President).

**⚙ ◆ World Peace News**
1F Adrian Court
Peekskill, NY 10566
**Affiliation:** American Movement for World Government. **Concern(s):** peace; world order. Newsletter. **Frequency:** 4/yr. **Contact(s):** R.W. Harrington (President).

**⚙ ◆ World Peace News**
777 UN Plaza
New York, NY 10017    (212)963-1234
**Concern(s):** peace; United Nations; world order. Newspaper focusing on UN, world government developments; major forum for exchange of ideas of individuals here and abroad; convenes annual seminar on UN, global issues. **Contact(s):** Thomas Liggett (Editor).

**⚙ ◆ World Policy Journal**
777 UN Plaza
New York, NY 10017    (212)490-0010
**Affiliation:** World Policy Institute. **Concern(s):** peace; Third World; justice; environment; politics; world order; natural resources; social justice; foreign policy; East-West; conflict resolution; intervention. A progressive international affairs quarterly which coverage includes security policy, US-Soviet relations, international trade and economic policy and developments in Latin America, Asia, and Africa. **Frequency:** 4/yr. **Subscription:** $23/yr. **Circ.:** 8.5M. **Contact(s):** Terri Coar (Promotion Director), Adrienne Edgar (Editor).

**P ◆ World Press Review**
Subscription Department
Box 1997
Marion, OH 43305    (800)669-1002
**Affiliation:** Stanley Foundation. **Concern(s):** politics; Third World; education; media; global understanding; foreign policy; media watch. "...published as a nonprofit educational service to foster the international exchange of information. The magazine is composed of material excerpted from the press outside of the US. Articles are subject to translation and editing. Photo selections, captions are by the editors..." Nonprofit. **Frequency:** 12/yr. **Subscription:** $24.97/yr. **Price:** $2.95/ea. (212)889-5155. **Other:** Stanley Foundation, The, 200 Madison, Office of Publications, New York, NY 10016.

**E ◆ World Rainforest Report**
300 Broadway, #28
San Francisco, CA 94133    (415)398-4404

**Affiliation:** Rainforest Action Network. **Concern(s):** environment; forests. "The decreasing percentage of the Earth's surface covered by rainforests is causing environmental problems. Surface problems, such as erosion and the danger to animal species, as well as atmospheric problems, are explained, along with suggestions on action."-C.C. **Est.:** 1985. **Frequency:** 4/yr. **Subscription:** $20/yr. **Price:** $1/ea. **Contact(s):** Denise Voelker.

E ♦ **The World Rivers Review**
  301 Broadway, #B
  San Francisco, CA 94133    (415)986-4694
**Affiliation:** International Rivers Network. **Concern(s):** environment; ocean/rivers. Newsletter. **Frequency:** 6/yr. **Contact(s):** Phil Williams (Executive Director).

E ♦ **World Wastes**
  6255 Barfield Rd.
  Atlanta, GA 30328
**Concern(s):** environment; recycling. Case studies of refuse haulers, landfill operators, resource recovery operations, and transfer stations, with solutions to problems in field. **Contact(s):** Bill Wolpin (Editor/Publisher), Allison Baer (Associate Editor).

E ♦ **World Watch**
  1776 Massachusetts Ave. NW
  Washington, DC 20036    (202)452-1999
**Affiliation:** Worldwatch Institute. **Concern(s):** environment; sustainability. Ay magazine that offers in-depth coverage of international environmental issues. They keep you fully informed of global problems and ways we can work towards a sustainable society. **Frequency:** 6/yr. **Subscription:** $15/yr.

F ♦ **Worldwide News**
  1331 H St. NW
  Washington, DC 20005    (202)347-1514
**Affiliation:** Worldwide. **Concern(s):** feminism; environment; empowerment; natural resources; networking; sustainability. This newsletter features information on individuals, events, projects, studies, and reports that affect women, the environment, and natural resources. **Frequency:** 6/yr. **Contact(s):** Joan Martin-Brown (Chairman), Cynthia R. Helms (President, Washington Forum).

✐ ♦ **The Writer**
  120 Boylston St.
  Boston, MA 02116
**Concern(s):** arts; media; literature; journalism. Articles and excellent resources for journalists, poets, novelists and others. This magazine offers practical articles for writers on how and where to market manuscripts in various fields of interest. **Other Resources:** Many of the descriptions that appear in Macrocosm USA were supplied with permission from THE WRITER. We thank them for all the good work. **Est.:** 1887. **Frequency:** 12/yr. **Subscription:** $24.75/yr. **Publisher:** The Writer, Inc. **Contact(s):** Sylvia K. Burack (Editor/Publisher).

☮ ♦ **Wyoming, The Hub of the Wheel**
  The Willow Bee Publishing House
  Box 9
  Saratoga, WY 82331
**Concern(s):** peace; arts; poetry; literature. Fiction and nonfiction, poetry. "An international literary/art magazine devoted to peace, the human race, positive relationships, and the human spirit and possibilities. **Publisher:** The Willow Bee Publishing House. **Contact(s):** Dawn Senior (Managing Editor).

✐ ♦ **Yellow Silk: Journal of Erotic Arts**
  Verygraphis
  Box 6374
  Albany, CA 94706
**Concern(s):** arts; literature; fine arts; graphics; poetry. What do excellent literature, fine arts, and Eros have in common? This profusely illustrated, four-color quarterly: stunning to eye, ear, mind, and heart, as well as those regions most erotic works aim at solely. Editorial policy: "All persuasions; no brutality." O. Henry Short Story Award winner; upcoming anthology from Crown Publishing. **Frequency:** 4/yr. **Subscription:** $24/yr. **Publisher:** Verygraphis.

H ♦ **Yoga Journal**
  2054 University Ave.
  Berkeley, CA 94704    (510)841-9200
**Concern(s):** health; holism. Magazine about yoga and healthful living. Also, yoga calendar, videotape. **Frequency:** 6/yr. **Member:** Co-op America.

☮ ♦ **Yoppy**
  Box 517
  Moretown, VT 05660    (802)229-0137
**Affiliation:** Parents, Teachers and Students For Social Responsibility. **Concern(s):** peace; education; childhood. A newsletter inspired by

Dr. Seuss book, Horton Heas a Who, a story about each person's ability to make a difference. **Frequency:** 4/yr. **Contact(s):** Glenn W. Hawkes (Executive Director). (802)223-3409.

♿ ♦ **Young and Alive**
  4444 S. 52nd St.
  Lincoln, NE 68506
**Concern(s):** education; health; justice; disabled; disabled's rights. Feature articles for blind and visually impaired young adults, on adventure, biography, camping, health, hobbies, and travel. Photos. **Contact(s):** Richard Kaiser (Editor).

P ♦ **Your Washington Ethical Action Office Reports**
  2 W. 64th St.
  New York, NY 10023    (212)873-6500
**Affiliation:** American Ethical Union. **Concern(s):** politics; peace; justice; law; social justice. "Monthly newsletters outline pending legislation and events concerning peace and social justice issues. Readers are given specific action to take on each issue."-C.C. **Est.:** 1981. **Frequency:** 12/yr. **Subscription:** $7.50/yr. **Price:** Donation. **Contact(s):** Herb Blinder, Barb Pequet.

J ♦ **Youth Law News**
  1663 Mission St., 5th Fl.
  San Francisco, CA 94103    (415)543-3307
**Affiliation:** National Center for Youth Law. **Concern(s):** justice; civil liberties; reform; juvenile; children. "Offers expertise to the legal services community on issues affecting children and youth. Legislation and court action are recommended to improve the quality of life for youth." -C.C. **Est.:** 1982. **Frequency:** 6/yr. **Subscription:** $15, $25 institution. **Price:** $1.50/ea. **Contact(s):** Marcia Henry.

✍ ♦ **Youth Policy**
  1221 Massachusetts Ave. NW, #B-1
  Washington, DC 20002  (202)638-2144
**Affiliation:** Youth Policy Institute. **Concern(s):** education; youth. "Features, updates, and events come together to make this a useful package of information for people concerned about youth and youth services. The institute's ideas for youth programs are moderate in substance, making the periodical attractive to all, regardless of political philosophy."-C.C. Also includes FUTURE CHOICES (3 issues), and YOUTH RECORD (24 issues) **Est.:** 1979. **Frequency:** 9/yr. **Subscription:** $127/yr. **Pages:** 84. **Circ.:** 1.1M. **Contact(s):** Andrew Schwartz.

P ♦ **Z Magazine**
  150 W. Canton St.
  Boston, MA 02118    (617)236-5878
**Affiliation:** Institute for Social & Cultural Communications. **Concern(s):** politics; justice; peace; environment; activism; ideation; analysis. "This magazine is an entertaining collection of political and social commentary from a progressive perspective, aiming "to assist activist efforts to attain a better future." Special columns devoted to music, art, sports, and book reviews help make the cultural coverage of special interest. Top writers such as Noam Chomsky, David Dellinger and Manning Marable give promise to the future of this new political magazine."-C.C. **Est.:** 1987. **Frequency:** 11/yr. **Subscription:** $25, $35 institution; $18 low-income. **Pages:** 96. **Circ.:** 21M. **Contact(s):** Lydia Sargent.

J ♦ **Zenger**
  Box 3323
  Madison, WI 53703    (608)251-0036
**Concern(s):** justice; politics; drugs; CIA; government accountability; criminal system. "...independent and does not speak for or promote any particular organization or ideology. We don't trust anyone and neither should you." Issues in this paper range from hemp to government plots. **Pages:** 8-12. **Contact(s):** Jackson Clubb (Editor), Ben Masel (Associate Editor).

H ♦ **Zillions**
  Consumers Union of the United States
  256 Washington St.
  Mt. Vernon, NY 10553
**Affiliation:** Consumers Union of the United States. **Concern(s):** health; education; economics; consumer rights; consumer protection. Articles on consumer education (money, product testing, health, etc.), for children, preteens, and young teens. "We are the Consumer Reports for kids." **Frequency:** 6/yr. **Contact(s):** Jeanne Kiefer.

E ♦ **Zoo Life**
  11661 San Vincente Blvd., #402
  Los Angeles, CA 90049
**Concern(s):** environment; conservation. Articles on the work zoos and aquariums are doing in the fields of animal conservation and education. **Frequency:** 4/yr. **Contact(s):** Audrey Tawa (Editor).

# ③ **Media, Computers & Other Sources**

| | | | | | |
|---|---|---|---|---|---|
| A = Agriculture | D = Demographics | ✿ = Energy | ? = Future | L = Labor | S = Spiritual |
| 🖎 = Animal Rights | ♿ = Disabled | E = Environment | G = Gay/Lesbian | M = Media | T = Third World |
| ✐ = Arts | $ = Economics | ♥ = Family | H = Health | ✾ = Peace | ✈ = Travel |
| ℂ = Computers | 🖎 = Education | F = Feminism | J = Justice | P = Politics | U = Urban |

### 🖎 ♦ Action For Children's TV
20 University Rd.
Cambridge, MA 02138   (617)876-6620
**Concern(s):** education; media; media watch; childhood; responsibility. A national consumer organization working to improve broadcast practices relative to children through education, research, and legal action. ACT tries to increase the diversity and eliminate the commercial abuses of children's programming. Our ultimate goal is obtaining the widest possible variety of entertainment, education, and information programming designed for the child in specific age groups, offered without commercials. Nonprofit. **Est.:** 1968.

### ♥ ★ Adoption
Alternative Media Information Center
39 W. 14th St.
New York, NY 10011   (212)929-2663
**Affiliation:** Media Network. **Concern(s):** family; justice; media; children; film. A guide to 22 film titles on different aspects of adoption including disabled children, older children and single parent adoption. **Contact(s):** Don Derosby (Executive Director).

### J ★ An Advocate's Guide to the Media
Children's Defense Fund
122 C St. NW
Washington, DC 20001   (202)628-8787
**Affiliation:** Children's Defense Fund. **Concern(s):** justice; media; politics; demographics; feminism; health; education; hunger; responsibility; press; film; children; child abuse; nutrition; childhood. **Contact(s):** Marian Wright-Edelman (Executive Director).

### D ♦ Affiliated Media Foundation Movement - AMFM
1024 Elysian Fields
New Orleans, LA 70117 (504)943-5713
**Concern(s):** media; politics; demographics; electronic democracy; broadcasting; grassroots organizing; poverty. A national association of community organizations, churches, unions, and broadcast facilities committed to using media as an organizing tool for low income communities. "We have operations in Little Rock, Dallas, New Orleans, Salinas, Atlanta, Des Moines, Shreveport, and nationally distributed radio programming." **Other Resources:** Publication, Open Channels. Assistance to low income communities in applying for FCC licenses, garnering community support, and developing the grassroots fundraising to put community stations on the air. **Est.:** 1977. **Frequency:** 4/yr. **Subscription:** $5/donation. **Price:** $1/ea. **Pages:** 4-8. **Circ.:** 200. **Fax:** (504)944-7078. **Contact(s):** Michelle Healy (Executive Director), Mac England (Station Manager). (501)372-6119.

### M ♦ Agenda Project
Countdown 2001
110 N. Payne St.
Alexandria, VA 22314   (703)684-4735
**Concern(s):** media; future; education; ideation; electronic democracy; computer networking; BBS. An electronic network being planned to link educators and high school students to facilitate sharing of experiences, information, and knowledge about how to create the best possible 21st century. **Est.:** 1989.

### ✐ ♦ Alternate Roots
1083 Austin Ave., NE
Atlanta, GA 30307   (404)577-1079
**Affiliation:** Regional Organization of Theatres South. **Concern(s):** arts; justice; environment; theater; culture; activism. A membership organization based in the Southeast USA whose mission is to support the creation and presentation of original, community-based performing art which is rooted in a particular community of place, tradition, or spirit. It is also committed to social and economic justice and the protection of the natural world. Publishes newspaper. **Other Resources:** Artistic development (workshops, residencies), communication/networking (publications), audience development (tour subsidy, Performance Festival). Publishes a workbook, HELP YOURSELF: A CULTURAL WORKBOOK ON ALTERNATIVE CULTURAL DEVELOPMENT and newspaper. **Est.:** 1976. **Frequency:** 4/yr. **Price:** Free.

**Other Formats:** Modem: (404) 577-7991; call first). **Contact(s):** Kathie de Nobriga (Executive Director), Greg Carraway (Administrative Assistant).

### M ♦ Alternative Media Information Center
See Media Network.

### M ♦ Alternative Press Syndicate
Box 775, Madison Square Station
New York, NY 10159
**Concern(s):** media; press. Promotes the alternative press and informs the public about media issues. **Est.:** 1966.

### M ♦ Alternative Radio
1814 Spruce St.
Boulder, CO 80302   (303)444-8788
**Concern(s):** media; broadcasting. Makes available in tape or transcript form speeches and debates presented at various institutions throughout the US by many progressive-radical superstars. Public Radio commonly uses this audio material. **Contact(s):** David Barsamian.

### M ♦ Alternative Views
Box 7279
Austin, TX 78713   (512)477-5148
**Concern(s):** media; film.

### ℂ ♦ Alternatives: The Computer Bulletin Board Dedicated to Progressive Social Change
1224-555 St. Mary Ave.
Winnepeg, MB R3C 3X4 Canada
**Concern(s):** media; future; politics; BBS; computer networking; ideation; electronic democracy. A communications network for discussion of issues and ideas.

### ℂ ♦ Alternet
2025 Eye St. NW, #1118
Washington, DC 20006  (202)887-0022
**Affiliation:** Institute for Alternative Journalism. **Concern(s):** media; BBS; journalism; press. Alternative news wire service. Quarterly dues will get you an index every month and you can purchase articles for reprint. **Contact(s):** Margaret Ingell (Executive Director).

### 🖎 ♦ Americans Dialogue
8033 Sunset Blvd., #967
Los Angeles, CA 90046
**Concern(s):** education; media; broadcasting. Established expressly for the purpose of producing educational radio programming. It is distributed nationally via NPR Satellite & the Pacifica Program Service and now airs on approximately 60 stations. Cassettes available for a donation. **Est.:** 1986. **Contact(s):** Robert Foxworth.

### 🖎 ♦ Animal Rights
154 Newbury St., #24
Peabody, MA 01960   (617)535-4203
**Concern(s):** environment; media; animal rights; activism. A syndicated program that showcases animal rights violations throughout this country and abroad. This program also reports on the positive things happening in the struggle for animals rights.

### T ★ Apartheid and South Africa
Alternative Media Information Center
39 W. 14th St.
New York, NY 10011   (212)929-2663
**Affiliation:** Media Network. **Concern(s):** Third World; media; justice; demographics; environment; Africa; film. A guide with descriptions of 40 recommended films on apartheid, anti-apartheid resistance, South Africa, Namibia, Angola, Mozambique, and Zimbabwe. **Contact(s):** Don Derosby (Executive Director).

### ✐ ♦ Artist Equity Association
Box 86244
Los Angeles, CA 90086-0244   (213)620-0201
**Concern(s):** arts; peace; justice; culture; conflict resolution; freedom of expression; censorship. An aesthetically nonpartisan organization for professional visual artists. The only such national organization working to improve conditions for all artists. Founded by visual artists,

and conceived as a means to improve artists' conditions and protect artists' rights and interests through a program of professional services, legislative representation, and communications. **Other Resources:** "We are planning an exchange of art with the Soviet artists, and we are the organization that built the Goddess of Democracy. The most important reason of our existence is to guarantee the artists' right to free expression." Nonprofit. **Est.:** 1947. **Contact(s):** Charles Sherman (President). (213)655-1900.

### ✐ ♦ Artists For Peace, Food, and Justice
Box 4923
Des Moines, IA 50306   (515)967-6865
**Concern(s):** arts; peace; justice; education; activism; culture. A network of visual and performing artists who assist groups in using the arts for peace and justice work. Membership open to anyone who wants to help. **Contact(s):** Phil Carver.

### T ★ Asian American Media Reference Guide
Asian Cine-Vision, Inc.
32 E. Broadway
New York, NY 10002   (212)925-8685
**Concern(s):** Third World; media; film; Asia. Producers, directors, and distributors of more than 1,000 films or videotapes produced by or featuring Asians and Asian Americans. Arranged alphabetically by title; indexed by subject, category, producer/director, distributor, and ethnic group. Data includes: Name, address, and phone of producer, director, and distributor; title and synopsis of film, language used, length and format, rental and purchase prices. **Frequency:** Irregular. **Price:** $19.95/ea. + $2 shipping. **Pages:** 120. **Date Publ.:** 8/89. **Publisher:** Asian CineVision, Inc. **Fax:** (212)925-8157. **Contact(s):** Bill Gee (Editor).

### M ♦ The Association for Responsible Communication - ARC
ARC International Headquarters
25000 Glen Ivy Rd.
Corona, CA 91719   (714)737-5584
**Concern(s):** media; economics; media watch. Responsible communication is not an imposition of one set of values over another. It is a stance of personal integrity about what is communicated, both as a professional communicator and as a human being. Members are aware of the influence our live and our communication have on the world. We sponsor forums and events in which the nature of this responsibility comes into sharper focus, exploring its practical implications in all forms of media.

### M ♦ Association of Independent Video Filmmakers
Foundation For Independent Video & Film
625 Broadway
New York, NY 10012   (212)473-3400
**Affiliation:** Foundation For Independent Video & Film. **Concern(s):** media; labor; union; film. A national trade association for individual film & video producers—effective national representation of membership to government, industry and general public (AIVF); FIVF a nonprofit tax-exempt foundation for promoting individual video and film. It sponsors workshops, seminars, screenings, and publishes a monthly magazine. Nonprofit. **Est.:** 1974.

### M ♦ Basic Assumptions Productions
60 E. 12th St. , #4H
New York, NY 10003   (212)995-0535
**Concern(s):** media; future; film. Future crises are set in current events which seem to be harmless if viewed in isolation but if looked at holistically may reveal the future. This theme is being explored by Steven Borns in a Documentary Film on Crashes Coming. Borns is looking for more stories about episodes which foreshadowed future crashes. **Contact(s):** Steven Borns.

### ℂ ♦ BBS Bible USA
Box 104
Collegeville, PA 19426
**Concern(s):** media; electronic democracy; computer networking; BBS. Approximately 8,500 public computer bulletin board systems classified by area code and indexed by product/service with company name, address or location, phone, requirements for admission, and

description of system. **Frequency:** Annual. **Price:** $26.95/ea. **Pages:** c90. **Date Publ.:** 2/91. **Contact(s):** Thomas W. Bubeck (Publisher).

E◆ **Biosphere Films**
4 W. 105th St., #6A
New York, NY 10025
**Concern(s):** environment; media.

☸◆ **Bringing Bad Things to Light**
INFACT
Box 3223
South Pasadena, CA 91031   (818)799-9133
**Affiliation:** INFACT. **Concern(s):** peace; media; economics; boycott; film. A video about GE.

M◆ **Bullfrog Films**
Oley, PA 19547      (800)543-3764
**Concern(s):** media; film.

T◆ **California Newsreel**
149 Ninth St., #420
San Francisco, CA 94103   (415)621-6196
**Concern(s):** Third World; media; film; South Africa. A video distributor specializing in social change videos and films. Through their Southern African Media Center Apartheid materials are available. **Other Resources:** Write for catalogs.

M◆ **Cambridge Documentary Films**
Box 385
Cambridge, MA 02139
**Concern(s):** media; film.

E◆ **Canadian Film Institute**
See SWITCHING ON TO THE ENVIRONMENT, a media guide.

T◆ **CARE Film Unit**
660 1st Ave.
New York, NY 10016   (212)686-3110
**Concern(s):** Third World; media; demographics; agriculture; hunger; film. This unit films documentary style videos on the problems of the world. (Public Relations). (212)979-6265.

T★ **Central America**
Alternative Media Information Center
39 W. 14th St.
New York, NY 10011   (212)929-2663
**Affiliation:** Media Network. **Concern(s):** Third World; media; justice; demographics; environment; Central America; film. A guide with descriptions of 40 films on Nicaragua, El Salvador, Guatemala, Grenada and the conflicts in the region. **Contact(s):** Don Derosby (Executive Director).

♥★ **Child Abuse and Neglect and Family Violence Audiovisual Catalog**
Clearinghouse on Child Abuse and Neglect Information
Box 1182
Washington, DC 20013   (703)821-2086
**Affiliation:** Clearinghouse on Child Abuse and Neglect Information. **Concern(s):** family; media; feminism; justice; child abuse; children; film. Distributors of over 300 films, videotapes, filmstrips with tapes, and audiovisual packages about child abuse and family violence. Arranged alphabetically by title; indexed by product, subject, and distributor name. Categories include title, name of producer, distributor name and address, description of materials, including length, format, and price. **Frequency:** Irregular. **Price:** $20/ea. **Pages:** 160. **Date Publ.:** 2/90. **Office:** 8201 Greensboro Dr. McLean, VA 22103.

✍◆ **Children's Television Workshop**
One Lincoln Plaza
New York, NY 10023   (212)496-5300
**Concern(s):** education; media; film; broadcasting; childhood. Produces educational television and video programs for children. **Other Resources:** See 3-2-1-CONTACT under periodicals. **Member:** Co-op America. (212)595-3456.

M◆ **The Cinema Guild Film & Video Catalog**
1697 Broadway
New York, NY 10019   (212)246-5522
**Affiliation:** Cinema Guild. **Concern(s):** media; arts; film. This guild is one of America's leading distributors of independently produced films and videotapes. Predominantly a source of award-winning documentaries, our collection focuses on such areas as: African Studies, Anthropology, Arts, Asian Studies, Chicano Studies, Media Studies, Environmental Studies, Latin American Studies, Mideast Studies, Women's Issues, Urban Studies, etc. The films and videos deal with current political, social, and cultural issues of relevance. **Other Resources:** Special subject flyers. "We sell/rent our videos/films to

schools, libraries, universities, community groups, businesses, church groups, etc. We publish an annual catalog of our collection and frequent collection updates with new titles." **Est.:** 1975. **Fax:** (212)246-5525. **Telex:** 238790 NYK. **Contact(s):** Judith Trojan (Director Promotion), Gary Crowdus (President).

☸◆ **Civilized Defense Plan**
803 N. Main St.
Goshen, IN 46526
**Affiliation:** Fourth Freedom Forum. **Concern(s):** media; peace; film. A book written by Brembeck that is also in video version. "An international businessman who is convinced that the security of nations is far more attainable through trade agreements than the arms race. His premise is a compelling one—this is more just a McDonald's in Moscow. Brembeck proposes a plan to eliminate all weapons of mass destruction, and redefine the balance of power in economic rather than military terms." — Big Books from Small Presses. **Contact(s):** Marc A. Hardy (Executive Director), Howard S. Brembeck (President).

♥◆ **Clearinghouse on Child Abuse and Neglect Information**
Box 1182
Washington, DC 20013   (703)821-2086
**Concern(s):** family; media; feminism; child abuse; battered women; film; criminal system. Distributors of over 300 films, videotapes, filmstrips with tapes, slides with tapes, and audiovisual packages about child abuse and neglect and family violence. **Other Resources:** See CHILD ABUSE AND NEGLECT AND FAMILY VIOLENCE AUDIOVISUAL CATALOG. **Frequency:** Irregular. **Price:** $20/ea. **Pages:** 160. **Date Publ.:** 2/90. **Office:** 8201 Greensboro Dr. McLean, VA 22201.

ℂ◆ **The Cleveland Free-Net**
319 Wickenden Building
Cleveland, OH 44106
**Affiliation:** Community Telecomputing Laboratory. **Concern(s):** media; computer networking; electronic democracy; BBS. A free BBS conducted for the residents of Cleveland, Ohio.

M◆ **CNN (Cable News Network)**
One CNN Center
Box 105366
Atlanta, GA 30348-5366
**Concern(s):** media; broadcasting; journalism; electronic democracy. A 24-hour newschannel started by TBS in 1980. This station provides the most up-to-date news on events and has rewritten TV journalism taking it to new heights. **Other Resources:** HEADLINE NEWS, also known as CNN2. **Est.:** 1980. **Fax:** (404)827-1593. **Contact(s):** Ted Turner (Founder/CEO).

ℂ◆ **Communications & Computer Multilogues**
Box 14066
Philadelphia, PA 19123
**Concern(s):** media; multilogues; computer networking. **Contact(s):** Stan Pokras.

J★ **Community Issues**
Alternative Media Information Center
39 W. 14th St.
New York, NY 10011   (212)929-2663
**Affiliation:** Media Network. **Concern(s):** justice; media; economics; demographics; urban; discrimination; racial tensions; housing; film; racism; gentrification; planning; inner city. A guide to 48 film titles on community issues such as: neighborhood development, gentrification and displacement housing, race relations, and tenant organizing. **Contact(s):** Don Derosby (Executive Director).

ℂ◆ **Community Memory Project**
Box 996
Berkeley, CA 94701
**Concern(s):** media; future; ideation; BBS. A two-way "people's computer network" providing terminals in several public locations where people can exchange ideas (and barter services, tap into community information, etc.).

ℂ◆ **Community Telecomputing Laboratory**
See Cleveland Free-Net.

☸ℂ **ConflictNet**
3228 Sacramento St.
San Francisco, CA 94115
**Affiliation:** Institute For Global Communications. **Concern(s):** media; peace; future; computer network; networking; BBS; conflict resolution. A computer network devoted entirely to the concepts of Conflict Resolution. **Other Resources:** EcoNet, PeaceNet, HomeoNet, and gateways to countless others.

✍ℂ **Connected Education, Inc.**
92 Van Cortlandt Park South, #6F
Bronx, NY 10463      (212)549-6509

**Affiliation:** Electronic Information Exchange System. **Concern(s):** media; education; computer networking; electronic democracy; BBS. In 1988, in conjunction with the New School for Social Research, it awarded the first Master's degree earned entirely via computer. Some 400 students from 26 states as well as countries in Europe, Middle East, Asia, & South America, have attended Connect Ed's on-line campus housed at EIES. **Est.:** 1986.

☸ℂ **Connecting with Nature (WORLDPEACEU)**
Box 10869
Eugene, OR 97440      (503)741-1794
**Concern(s):** media; peace; education; environment; activism; world order; broadcasting; BBS. This BBS offers information on World Peace Universities Peace Studies Graduate Degree program, 2. Off campus workshops, courses and conferences, 3. Guided core peace study internships for credit, 4. Rain forest preservation through ownership projects, 5. Radio for Peace International providing global shortwave peace intercommunication 6. Integrated Ecology books and articles, 7. Internationally located branch campuses. The BBS is located on ECONET. (Conference Worldpeaceu) **Other Resources:** Department of Integrated Ecology. **Est.:** 1985. **Frequency:** 4/yr. **Subscription:** $11 w/postage. **Bulk:** 30% off/24. **Circ.:** 500. **E-Network:** Econet. **ID:** 'worldpeaceu'. **Fax:** (503)741-1279. **Contact(s):** Dr. Richard Schneider (Chancellor), Michael J. Cohen, Ed.D (Department Chair). (206)378-6313.

E◆ **Conservation Film Service**
408 E. Main St.
Box 776
League City, TX 77574-0776
**Concern(s):** environment; media; conservation; film.

M◆ **Coronet Film and Video**
108 Wilmot Rd.
Deerfield, IL 60015      (800)621-2131
**Concern(s):** media; film.

$◆ **Corporate Economic News Service**
See WHAT IS TO BE READ (periodicals).

✏◆ **Creative Resources Guild**
Box 3397
Santa Monica, CA 90408      (310)390-1470
**Concern(s):** arts; media; peace; environment; justice; film; theater; theater; graphics; music; culture; broadcasting; film. An association of artists, entertainers, visionaries, and healers who are interested in pursuing their talents and skills to help heal the world. "We have produced: Heal The Earth Music & Arts Festival; Spirit of Peace Gathering at the Peace Park; Whole Life Expo Entertainment; networking meetings, concerts, urban shamanic ceremonies." **Other Resources:** See CRG RESOURCE DIRECTORY. Offers a subsidy fund for performers and an audio-visual referral library. **Est.:** 1988. **Frequency:** Annual. **Price:** $7.50/ea. **Date Publ.:** Every June. Events: (310)285-3495. **Contact(s):** John Tibayan (Executive Director), Karin Wilson (Board Secretary).

M★ **CRG Resource Directory**
Box 3397
Santa Monica, CA 90403
**Affiliation:** Creative Resource Guild. **Concern(s):** media; arts; peace; environment; theater; broadcasting; film. Art, Entertainment & Media for a Better World. Our purpose is to improve the world and the quality of life by promoting the creating of more socially conscious, spiritual, and humanitarian productions in the mass media and the world arena (TV, film, radio, recordings, books, publications, theater, concerts, public media events). **Other Resources:** Many of the descriptions found in Macrocosm were reprinted with permission from the Executive Director of Creative Resources Guild. Many thanks for their contributions and good work! **Frequency:** Annual. **Price:** $7.50/ea. **Bulk:** $6.50ea/24. **Pages:** 40. **Circ.:** 1M. **Date Publ.:** 6/91. **Contact(s):** John Tibayan (Executive Director), Sandra Reid (Public Relations).

ℂ◆ **DataNet**
Institute for Security and Cooperation in Outer Space
1314 Massachusetts Ave. NW
Washington, DC 20005   (202)462-8886
**Affiliation:** Institute for Security and Cooperation in Outer Space. **Concern(s):** media; energy; future; ideation; space; BBS; computer networking; electronic democracy. A computer network for "sharing [of] ideas and suggestions on space-related issues."

M◆ **Deep Dish TV, The First National Satellite Access Network**
339 Lafayette St.
New York, NY 10012   (212)473-8933
**Concern(s):** media; film. If you have your own TV dish antenna or are on cable you can tune in programs on the unification of Korea, the elections in Nicaragua, the environmental crisis, martial law

in Taiwan... These programs are produced by independent activists in all parts of the world and made available free of charge through your local public access stations. Call Deep Dish for programs and request programs to your station. A satellite network linking access producers, programmers, videomakers, activists, people. **Other Resources:** Programs shown on more than 300 cable channels nationwide. Staff can help plan national distribution of your film.

**M ◆ Direct Cinema Ltd.**
Box 69589
Los Angeles, CA 90060  (800)345-6745
**Concern(s):** media; arts; film.

**M★ Directory of Information and Referral Services in the United States and Canada**
Alliance of Information & Referral Systems
Box 3546
Joliet, IL 60434
**Affiliation:** Alliance of Information & Referral Systems. **Concern(s):** media; broadcasting; press. About 650 social service information and referral agencies with two or more staff members who have the primary assignment to provide information; includes Call for Action radio broadcasting stations and Federal Information Centers. Arranged and indexed geographically; with agency name, address, phone, hours and days of operation, director, operating organization, population and area served, type of service, funding source, whether a directory is published, classification system used. **Frequency:** Irregular. **Price:** $22.50/ea. +$2.50 shipping. **Pages:** 230. **Date Publ.:** Spring 1987. **Labels:** 41. **Contact(s):** Linda Lewis (Editor).

**& ( Direct Link/REACH**
617 7th Ave.
Fort Worth, TX 76104
**Affiliation:** Center for Computer Assistance.. **Concern(s):** health; media; disabled; electronic democracy. The Center for Computer Assistance to the Disabled (C-CAD) online through METRO: (817)429-5327 as well as through the in print newsletter C-CAD works to build electronic cottages for the disabled.

**⊛★ Disarmament**
Alternative Media Information Center
39 W. 14th St.
New York, NY 10011  (212)929-2663
**Affiliation:** Media Network. **Concern(s):** peace; media; disarmament; anti-nuclear. Directory and up-date of selected media on the arms race and nuclear disarmament. **Contact(s):** Don Derosby (Executive Director).

**E ◆ Earth Watch Video Production**
729 West Center, #310
Pocatello, ID 83204  (208)233-4147
**Concern(s):** environment; media; arts; film. Producing globally-ecologically and culturally relevant TV programming dubbed into any language necessary, and the message distributed by broadcasting - satellite uplink/downlink cablecasting or group networking with VHS, Beta or 3/4" tape format program cassettes. **Contact(s):** Barry John Heidt (Producer/Director).

**E ◆ Earthvision**
1810 Oak St., #6
Santa Monica, CA 90405  (310)285-8269
**Concern(s):** environment; media; education; press. An umbrella organization dedicated to, 1) produce a series of commercials that offer solutions to the worlds problems while marketing a humanitarian product, and, 2) building alternative methods of education and communication. **Other:** 39-23 48th St., Sunnyside, NY 11104. (718)898-7390.

**E ( EcoLinking, Everyone's Guide to Online Information**
Peach Pit Press
2414 Sixth St.
Berkeley, CA 94710  (510)548-4393
**Concern(s):** environment; media; BBS; computer networking. This reference guide provides useful information for the beginner to the expert in successfully computer-networking community. Information on computer set-up, online services, and various environmental BBS's. **Price:** $18.95/ea. **Fax:** (510)541-5991. **Contact(s):** Don Ritner (Author).

**E ◆ Econews**
Box 35473
Los Angeles, CA 90035-0473
**Affiliation:** Educational Communications, Inc.. **Concern(s):** environment; media; broadcasting; film. Two-time Emmy nominated television series highlighting timely issues regarding the quality of the environment. Worldwide, national, and local environmental issues are discussed from various viewpoints by distinguished guests. **Other Resources:** Videocassette can be purchased or rented from Educa-

tional Communications. Write for brief catalog. **Contact(s):** Nancy Pearlman (Executive Producer), Anna Harlowe (Associate Director).

**E ( EcoNet**
18 De Boom St.
San Francisco, CA 94107  (415)923-0900
**Affiliation:** Institute for Global Communications. **Concern(s):** media; environment; electronic democracy; computer networking; BBS. It is an international, computer based communication system committed to serving organizations and individuals who are working for environmental preservation and sustainability. Most importantly, it is a community of persons using the network for information sharing and collaboration with the intent of enhancing the effectiveness of all environmentally orientated programs. **Other Resources:** PeaceNet, HomeoNet, ConflictNet, and gateways to countless others. **E-Network:** Econet. **Contact(s):** Bill LeLand (Director).

**✍ ( Ed-Line**
National School Public Relations Association
1501 Lee Highway
Arlington, VA 22209  (703)528-5840
**Concern(s):** education; future; media; ideation; BBS. The news and information network of the NSPRA, running on The Source. Includes a database called "Classroom Ideas" - "updated weekly, contains bright ideas and tips for teachers to use in the classroom" - and a database called "Ed Exchange" - "a bulletin board feature through which any subscriber can post a question, comment (and request responses)."

**T ◆ El Salvador Media Project**
335 W. 38th St.
New York, NY 10018  (212)714-9118
**Concern(s):** Third World; media; Central America. **Other:** 2886 Mission St., San Francisco, CA 94110. (415)824-6695.

**( ◆ Electronic Information Exchange System (EIES)**
New Jersey Institute
Newark, NJ 07102
**Concern(s):** media; education; electronic democracy; computer networking; BBS. The home of many projects, including the Virtual Classroom, Connect Ed, and Carinet. EIES2 is the only truly tailorable computer conferencing software currently on the market. **Other Resources:** See Connected Education, Inc.

**( ◆ ElfNet**
Alivesystems
Box 6844
Malibu, CA 90264-0369 (310)317-1411
**Concern(s):** media; future; ideation; BBS. A bulletin board for members of the Network for Social Invention which facilitates "evolving global intelligence." An "affable brain system" for "the leading future-creators of Planet Earth." **Other Formats:** MCI Mail, user name - 2154406@mcimail.com. **E-Network:** Peacenet. **ID:** 'fjeffrey'. Telex: 650-215-4406 MCI. **Contact(s):** Francis Jeff.

**M ◆ Empowerment Project**
1653 18th St., #3
Santa Monica, CA 90404
**Concern(s):** media; politics; peace; Third World; nonviolence; civil disobedience; film; activism. A media resource center for independent videographers, filmmakers and activists working on progressive projects of social, political, and artistic importance. Facilities are provided for video production, post-production, duplication, screenings, events and workshops. Temporary office space with a computer system is available for graphics, publishing, mailings, and database uses; and, support for project development, fundraising and promotion, and distribution assisting independents. **Other Resources:** Subsidized access to the facility is provided for select approved projects. Produced videos COVER-UP and DESTINATION NICARAGUA. Catalogue available. Tax-exempt. **Fax:** (310)453-4347.

**E ◆ Environment Today**
c/o National Public Radio
2025 M St. NW
Washington, DC 20036-3309  (202)797-6800
**Affiliation:** National Wildlife Federation. **Concern(s):** environment; media; wildlife/endangered species; broadcasting. Radio show hosted by Jay D. Hair, President of the NWF on NPR. (202)822-2000.

**E ◆ Environmental Directions**
Box 35473
Los Angeles, CA 90035-0473
**Affiliation:** Educational Communications, Inc. **Concern(s):** environment; media; film. This nation's longest running half-hour interview show on the environment continues to be in the forefront of presenting the problems and solutions about the ecological crisis. Tapes can be purchased or rented through Educational Communications, Inc. **Other Resources:** Over 700 shows on videocassette. Write for brief catalog. **Contact(s):** Nancy Pearlman (Executive Producer), Anna

Harlowe (Associate Director).

**E ◆ Environmental Film Festival**
1026 W. Colorado Ave.
Colorado Springs, CO 80904
**Concern(s):** media; environment; film.

**E ◆ Environmental Media Association**
10536 Culver Blvd.
Culver City, CA 90232  (310)559-9334
**Concern(s):** environment; media; arts; broadcasting; film; forests; conservation. The planet's fragile ecological balance is seriously threatened. The public must be alerted to the need for action and inspired to respond. The entertainment industry can take a lead in this effort. Films, TV programs and music have a unique ability to infuse the popular culture with a particular message. The industry can educate and motivate the public to confront environmental problems and take decisive steps towards their solution. EMA serves a clearinghouse for environmental expertise. **Contact(s):** Lauren McMahon (Executive Director).

**E ◆ Environmental News Service**
3505 West 15th Ave.
Vancouver, BC V6R 2Z3 Canada  (604)732-4000
**Concern(s):** environment; media; telecommunications; electronic democracy; broadcasting; press. A global environmental news daily of the world's first international news agency dedicated exclusively to environmental issues. Our daily publication presents a global perspective on a myriad of subjects such as oceans, toxins, climate, health, species survival, wilderness, agriculture, law, water, scientific developments. products, services and politics. A Weekly Journal ($58), Daily Fax ($215), and an Electronic Newsline($55/year). **Other Resources:** Provides Weekly Updates, Electronic News Service, Environmental Information Packages, Radio News and Features. **Frequency:** Daily/weekly. **Subscription:** $215, $58/yr. $60, $18 per quarter. **E-Network:** Econet. **ID:** web:'ens'. **Fax:** (604)732-4400. **Contact(s):** Jim Crabtree (Managing Editor), Sunny Lewis (Publisher/Editor).

**E ◆ Environmental Viewpoints**
Box 35473
Los Angeles, CA 90035-0473
**Affiliation:** Educational Communications, Inc.. **Concern(s):** environment; media; education; broadcasting. Radio magazine show (interviews, commentary music, etc.) which can be heard twice a month on KXLU, 88.9 FM at 11 PM on Sunday in the Los Angeles area. Guests are welcome in the studio and over the telephone. Calendar items are also announced. **Contact(s):** Nancy Pearlman (Producer/Host).

**J ◆ Facets Multimedia**
See HUMAN RIGHTS FILM GUIDE. .

**M★ FAIR Resource Lists**
Fairness & Accuracy in Reporting
130 W. 25th St., 8th Fl.
New York, NY 10001  (212)633-6700
**Affiliation:** Fairness & Accuracy in Reporting. **Concern(s):** media; politics; economics; media watch; journalism; press; responsibility; corporate responsibility; government accountability. A mini-directory of resources, general media factoids, and alternative press contacts with addresses and phone numbers. **Fax:** (212)727-7668. **Contact(s):** Jeff Cohen (Executive Director). (202)332-FAIR.

**M ◆ Fax Alert Service**
1325 G St. NW, #1003
Washington, DC 20005  (202)879-3044
**Affiliation:** Carrying Capacity Network. **Concern(s):** media; environment; peace; demographics; press; telecommunications; population growth. Relays to subscribers urgent calls for action from a variety of sources addressing carrying capacity issues which demand immediate action such as resource conservation, energy, population, development, and economic and related social issues in the US. Nonprofit. **Est.:** 1989. **Dues:** $35, $50-80 organization. **Price:** $25/yr. **Fax:** (202)879-3019. **Contact(s):** Stephen M. Mabley (Network Coordinator).

**M ◆ Film and Video Catalog**
New Day Films
121 W. 27th St.
New York, NY 10001  (212)645-8210
**Affiliation:** New Day Films. **Concern(s):** media; film. This catalog is the result of a cooperative of independent filmmakers who are distributing films and videos about social change. **Fax:** (212)505-1567.

**M ▶ Film Distribution Center**
Box 8293
Kirkland, WA 98034-0293
**Concern(s):** media; film.

**M ▶ Filmmakers Library**
124 E. 40th St.
New York, NY 10016    (212)808-4980
**Concern(s):** media; film.

**J★ Films for Humanities, Inc.**
Box 2053
Princeton, NJ 08543-2053    (800)257-5126
**Concern(s):** justice; media; environment; demographics; film. A film company that specializes in films and videos dealing in humanitarian causes around the world. Films and videos are available for purchase or on a rental basis.

**☯★ Films for Peace and Justice**
c/o Donnelly/Colt
Box 188
Hampton, CT 06247    (203)455-9621
**Concern(s):** peace; justice; media; film. A guide to 150+ movies with themes of peace and justice, including feature films and documentaries. Includes stunning photographs from 54 films, plus a list of 112 films and video distributors and resources on films and videos. Introductions by Ed Asner and Ruby Dee. Originally published as War Resisters League 1987 Peace Calender. **Price:** $3.50/wirebound. **Pages:** 75. **Fax:** (203)455-9597. **Contact(s):** Clay Colt, Kate Donnelly, Ann Melnick (Editors).

**M★ Films For a Peaceful Planet**
Complexe Guy-Favreau, East Tower
Room 102, 200 Dorchester Blvd. W.
Montreal, QC H2Z 1X4 Canada
**Affiliation:** National Film Board of Canada. **Concern(s):** media; arts; education; peace; justice; film; childhood. This resource guide divides into two parts: animation films and documentaries. An index lists films as to grade level, themes, interest, and subject area. A wide variety for peace education, includes animation and documentaries. Topics: war, nuclear, women, human rights, prejudice, conflict resolution, development, and attitudes.

**M ▶ Films Incorporated**
5547 N. Ravenswood Ave.
Chicago, IL 60640    (800)323-4222
**Concern(s):** media; film.

**M ▶ Florida Films**
Box 13712, 925 NW 25th Ave.
Gainesville, FL 32604
**Concern(s):** media; environment; film; wildlife/endangered species.

**M ▶ Foundation For Independent Video & Film**
See INDEPENDENT (periodicals) and Association of Independent Video Filmmakers.

**ℂ ▶ Fulcrum: The R & D Network for the Development of Human Systems**
School of Business and Economics
Sonoma State University
Rohnert Park, CA 94928 (707)664-2377
**Concern(s):** media; future; ideation; electronic democracy; computer networking; BBS. This "electronic think tank" facilitates collaborative interaction among individuals, groups and institutions. Fulcrum functions via electronic mail through an inter-university consortium called Edunet (which uses GTE Telenet's Telemail conferencing system). **Est.:** 1981. **E-Network:** GTE Telent's Telemail. **ID:** 'edunet'. **Contact(s):** Saul Eisen (Administrator).

**S C★ Fund Raising Management - Non-Profit Software Package Directory Issue**
Hoke Communications, Inc.
224 7th St.
Garden City, NY 11530
**Concern(s):** spiritual; media; economics; fundraising; philanthropy; trade; computer networking. List of suppliers of computer software designed for use in the field of nonprofit fund raising. **Publisher:** Hoke Communications, Inc.

**M ▶ Gaia Communications**
8205 Santa Monica Bl. #1-180
Los Angeles, CA 90046    (800)964-3434
**Concern(s):** media; economics; environment; press; alternate consumer. This communications business provides advertising through media outlets for companies who are making products that are environmentally sound and useful. This company has developed successful publicity campaigns for environmental nonprofit organizations and businesses both locally and nationally. "We specialize in

media relations, including planning and implementing campaigns, press conferences, media mailings, and special events." **Est.:** 1990. **Contact(s):** Janet Bridges, Catherine Leach.

**E ▶ Gaia Institute**
1047 Amsterdam Ave.
New York, NY 10025
**Concern(s):** environment; media; education; animal rights; broadcasting; film; wildlife/endangered species. Founded as a television connection—to educate a wider public about our Earth and other life with whom we share. Through television, it is introducing a global awakening to an ecological world view in a developing, positive social movement with role model leaders. Has produced a multi-faceted Animal Rights series. Each year it brings the Festival for the Earth and Animals to cable television. Produces Animalwatch, an ambitions multi-faceted series for mainstream TV. Nonprofit. **Contact(s):** Mary de la Valette (President). **Other:** Box 852, South Lynnfield, MA 01940.

**S ▶ Gaia Video Company**
1122 S. Roxbury Dr.
Los Angeles, CA 90035
**Concern(s):** spiritual; media; environment; transformation; film. Produces videos of workshops, seminars, lectures, ritual ceremonies, pilgrimages, thinking leaders' portraits, etc., aimed at the people who are eager to enter a holistic world and transform our patriarchal society into a "partnership society". **Contact(s):** Noelle Imparato (Producer:).

**ℂ ▶ GEMNET**
Chestnut Hill College
Germantown & Northwestern Avenues
Chestnut Hill, PA 19118-2695    (215)248-1150
**Affiliation:** Global Information Motivators. **Concern(s):** media; computer networking; BBS. Founded and run by educators, this educational computer communication and information network strives to increase student global literacy and computer literacy and computer literacy at the same time. Using it helps to prepare students for careers in the globally-connectedtechnical job market while increasing their understanding of world issues and information. Nonprofit. **Contact(s):** Wayne Jacoby (President).

**E ℂ Global Action Network**
Box 819
Ketchum, ID 83340
**Affiliation:** Global Environment Project Institute. **Concern(s):** environment; media; electronic democracy; computer network; BBS. Its primary goal is to set up a computerized bulletin board with extensive information on pending environmental legislation. Has now joined forces with Econet and operates independently of GEPI. **Other Resources:** Guide, ECOTEAM WORKBOOK. **Contact(s):** Deborah Shimkus (Executive Director).

**$ ℂ Global Business Network**
5900-H Hollis St.
Emeryville, CA 94608
**Concern(s):** economics; media; future; BBS; trade; computer networking; electronic; democracy. Operates an ongoing computer teleconference generating "adaptive scenarios" relative to global business conditions, trends, challenges, activities. **Fax:** (510)547-8510.

**T ℂ ▶ The Global Electronic University**
Box 382
Niantic, CT 06357
**Concern(s):** Third World; media; future; education; ideation; BBS; electronic democracy. This project, in development, will considerably enlarge electronic/satellite communication among different nations, institutions, organizations, and individuals - in particular between the "First World" and "Third World." **E-Network:** EIES computer net 1703. **Contact(s):** Parker Rossman.

**ℂ ▶ Global Information Motivators**
See GEMNET.

**? ℂ Global Suggestion Box for Ideas to Promote Global Harmony**
California Lutheran University
60 W. Olsen Rd.
Thousand Oaks, CA 91360-2787    (213)466-8091
**Concern(s):** future; media; ideation; electronic democracy; computer networking; BBS. Prof. Woetzel made this proposal in 1986, plus a parallel proposal for a Center for the Study of Ideas with offices in the US, East Germany and China: "Individuals would be encouraged to send in ideas that would be placed on computers and perhaps become the subjects of seminars. Conferences would be held to encourage nations to try the best ideas." The Center will "coordinate proposals from the West, East, and Third World and examine them for possible implementation." **Est.:** 1986. 2315 Alcyona Dr., Los Ange-

les, CA 90068.

**ℂ ▶ Global Systems Analysis and Simulation (GLOSAS) Project**
Global Information Services
43-23 Colden St.
Flushing, NY 11355-3998
**Concern(s):** future; education; ideation; electronic democracy; computer networking; BBS. GLOSAS, combining global teleconferencing and computer conferencing, simulation and game systems, computer bulletin boards and other telecommunicational media, seeks to construct a "Globally Distributed Decision Support System" to help decision-makers deal with interwoven problems: "Mind-empowerment tools to help people do better thinking." Promotes the exchange of university courses electronically around the world. **Other Resources:** A number of courses promoted by this transcultural educational initiative are already on-line around the Pacific Rim and the Japanese Broadcasting Corporation taking active roles. A directory of electronic courses is being developed. Nonprofit. **E-Network:** GLOSAS.

**☯ ▶ Global Vision TV & Radio**
1017 S. Van Ness
San Francisco, CA 94110
**Concern(s):** peace; media; arts; broadcasting; film. A weekly half-hour television program that highlights the efforts of people presenting choices for a positive global future. The show also features musicians and artists who are committed to peace and social justice. These radio programs are carried by National Public Radio. Our shows have been on the air now for two years. **Contact(s):** Azarra (TV & Radio Producer/Arts Correspondent).

**$ ▶ Goodfellow Publisher' Representatives**
2054 University Ave., #302
Berkeley, CA 94704    (510)548-1680
**Concern(s):** economics; media; environment; trade; press. Sells advertising for several national magazines dealing with health, the environment, social issues, and spirituality. Services free to advertiser. **Member:** Co-op America.

**M★ Green Gems**
Alternative Media Information Center
39 W. 14th St.
New York, NY 10011    (212)929-2663
**Affiliation:** Media Network. **Concern(s):** media; environment; energy; agriculture; education; film; sustainability. A guide to 40 film titles on the environmental and energy issues including toxics, agriculture, land and water, and nuclear issues. **Contact(s):** Don Derosby (Executive Director).

**M★ Green Mountain Post Films Bulletin/Catalogue**
Box 229
Turners Falls, MA 01376(413)863-4754
**Affiliation:** Green Mountain Post Films. **Concern(s):** media; arts; peace; environment; energy; politics; justice; activism; film. Summaries of the group's films, with ordering information, comprise the bulletin, there are about two dozen films listed in each issue. Peace, nuclear war and ways to prevent such war are major categories of subjects. Offers social issues films and videos on war and peace, ecology, energy, health, justice, and the law, human/civil rights, politics, and the arts. **Other Resources:** "We generally offer one page descriptions of each film/video. Sometimes a study guide is available. We also produce films for other organizations." **Est.:** 1975. **Frequency:** Irregular. **Price:** $2, free to organizations. **Pages:** 8-16. **Circ.:** 40M. **Labels:** 100. **Contact(s):** Charles Light (Producer/Distribution), Daniel Keller (Producer).

**E ▶ Green Newsline**
Box 384, 150 Hamakua Dr.
Kailua, HI 96734    (808)261-3776
**Concern(s):** environment; media; politics; telecommunications; press; law. Nationwide telephone environmental news service available 24-hours a day by a "900" number. Weekly world weather watch, environmental legislation news through Touch Tone News (TM). **Est.:** 1991. (900)988-0023 ext. 878. **Contact(s):** Gary Hickling, R. Alan Campbell (Founder).

**J ℂ HandsNet**
819 1/2 Pacific Ave., #2
Santa Cruz, CA 95060-4433
**Concern(s):** justice; media; demographics; computer networking; electronic democracy; BBS. Provides news, resources, and information on hunger, homeless, housing and poverty-related issues as well as e-mail and information exchange among its subscribers nationwide.

**✍ ℂ Holistic Education Community Network**
The Institute for Educational Studies
4202 Ashwoody Trail
Atlanta, GA 30319

**Affiliation:** Institute for Educational Studies. **Concern(s):** education; media; health; ideation; computer networking; electronic democracy; networking; holism; BBS. Interested in evolving a global electronic community of holistic education professionals which models new possibilities for enhancing our creativity and effectiveness. Also working to link up like minds in order to create a critical mass for reconstructing education. **Other Resources:** See Global Alliance for Transforming Education.

**H C   HomeoNet**
3228 Sacramento St.
San Francisco, CA 94115
**Affiliation:** Institute For Global Communications. **Concern(s):** health; media; education; computer network; networking; BBS. A computer network devoted entirely to the health and holistic professions. **Other Resources:** EcoNet, PeaceNet, ConflictNet, and gateways to countless others.

**J ★  Human Rights Film Guide**
Facets Multimedia
1517 W. Fullerton Ave.
Chicago, IL 60614       (800)331-6197
**Affiliation:** Facets Multimedia. **Concern(s):** justice; media; labor; indigenous peoples; civil liberties; capital punishment; film; refugees; freedom of expression; civil liberties. Distributors of 400+ films and videotapes concerned with human rights and related issues, including refugees, freedom of speech, labor, indigenous peoples, economic relations, assassination, and the death penalty. Classified by subject and indexed geographically or by title, geographical subject/distributor name. Distributor name: address, phone, title, description of subject coverage, length of film, format in which available (16 mm, VHS, black and white or color, etc.), name of director. **Other Resources:** Includes bibliography. **Price:** $6.95 + 55ß shipping. **Pages:** 115. **Date Publ.:** 1985. **Fax:** (312)929-5437. (800)331-6197. **Contact(s):** Anne Gelman, Milos Stehlik (Editors).

**M ♦  Icarus Films**
153 Waverly Place
New York, NY 10014       (212)727-1711
**Concern(s):** media; arts; film.

**? C   IdeaNet**
14161 Riverside Dr., #3
Sherman Oaks, CA 91423-2363    (818)784-0325
**Affiliation:** Action Linkage Network. **Concern(s):** future; media; electronic democracy; computer networking; ideation; BBS. An effort to link up and coordinate the efforts of as many of the world's ever-expanding group of Idea-Gathering Organizations ("IGO's") as possible and so give every good new idea whose creator wishes to share it through a universally-known forum for speedy, wide dissemination, with credit. **Other Resources:** An Idea "Task Force" is being started on the international (but mostly North American) Action Linkage Network. Get involved and contact the founder for more information or a list of important IGO's. **Est.:** 1985. **Contact(s):** Gregory Wright (Director/Founder).

**M ♦  Institute for Alternative Journalism**
See Alternet.

**C ♦   Institute for Global Communications**
3228 Sacramento St.
San Francisco, CA 94115    (415)923-0900
**Affiliation:** Tides Foundation. **Concern(s):** media; peace; environment; health; Third World; electronic democracy; computer networking; BBS. IGC supports several international social-change computer networks, all using the same host computer and conferencing software. It is home of PeaceNet, EcoNet, ConflictNet and HomeoNet, and is linked to networks all over the world. Nonprofit. **Contact(s):** Geoff Sears (Executive Director).

**M ♦  International Documentary Association**
1551 S. Robertson Blvd.
Los Angeles, CA 90035
**Concern(s):** media; film. A membership organization dedicated to promoting the documentary form, supporting the efforts of non-fiction film and video makers around the world, and increasing public appreciation and demand for documentary programs. IDA works to encourage and expand opportunities for the production, distribution, and exhibition of documentary film and video. Nonprofit.

**E ♦   International Wildlife Film Festival**
Rankin Hall
University of Montana
Missoula, MT 58912
**Concern(s):** environment; media; education; wildlife/endangered species; film.

**F ♦   ISIS International**
See POWERFUL IMAGES: A WOMAN'S GUIDE TO AUDIOVISUAL RESOURCES.

**M ♦  Jump Cut Association**
See JUMP CUT (periodicals).

**M ♦  KAB: It's More Than a Slogan**
9 W. Broad St.
Stamford, CT 06902       (203)323-8987
**Affiliation:** Keep America Beautiful. **Concern(s):** media; environment; recycling; conservation; beautification film. Video. .

**✍ ♦  Kids' Internationally Distributed Superstation (KIDS)**
33 Wren Valley
Eureka, MO 63025       (314)993-KIDS
**Concern(s):** education; media; future; ideation; youth; film; networking; childhood. Solicits youngsters' ideas for TV programs and program segments, and in the course of its programs (possibly to begin in 1989?) will promote children's brainstorming sessions to generate solutions to global problems. **Contact(s):** Nancy Joyce.

**✍ ♦  Kids' Network**
National Geographic Society
17 & M Sts.
Washington, DC 20036   (202)857-7000
**Affiliation:** National Geographic Society. **Concern(s):** education; media; global understanding; telecommunications. A telecommunications-based geography curriculum.

**P ♦   KPFA-FM94**
2207 Shattuck Ave.
Berkeley, CA 94704
**Affiliation:** Pacific Foundation. **Concern(s):** politics; media; arts; justice; broadcasting; music; literature. Listener-sponsored Pacifica Radio with programs devoted to environment, minorities, politics, literature, music of all sorts, etc. **Other Resources:** Program Guide magazine with articles. For Profit. **Est.:** 1949. **Dues:** $45, $25 low income. **Contact(s):** Marcie Lockwood (Assistant Manager), Richard Wolinsky (Folio Editor).

**✎ ♦  Ladyslipper Inc.**
613 Vickers Ave.
Durham, NC 27701
**Concern(s):** arts; feminism; music; empowerment. World's largest distributor of recordings by women. Catalog/resource guide contains over 2,000 annotated titles. **Contact(s):** Laurie Fuchs.

**$ ♦   The Last Word**
Box 178
Blue Hill, ME 04614    (207)374-9913
**Concern(s):** economics; trade; fundraising. Public relations, advertising, fund raising, event production, research, and trend consulting for socially and environmentally responsible companies and organizations. **Member:** Co-op America.

**✎ ♦  Living Stage Theater Company**
6th & M Ave. SW
Washington, DC 20024   (202)554-9066
**Concern(s):** arts; justice; theater; minority rights; children. Social outreach company is a leading improvement children/people's theater working with the forgotten people of our community - children, youth, physically and/or mentally disabled people, imprisoned people, and seniors. **Contact(s):** Kelly Jerome (Production Coordinator).

**J ♦   Lucis Productions**
Lucis Trust
Box 722
Cooper Station, NY 10276
**Affiliation:** Lucis Trust. **Concern(s):** justice; media; film. Video on Right Human Relations, Josette Allan.

**M ♦  Master Video**
7322 Ohms Lane
Edina, MN 55439
**Concern(s):** media; film.

**M ♦  Media Action Research Center**
475 Riverside Dr.
New York, NY 10115    (212)865-6690
**Concern(s):** media. **Other Resources:** MEDIA & VALUES, periodical. (212)663-8900.

**P ♦   Media for Social Change: A Resource Guide for Community Groups**
c/o Connexions
427 Bloor St. West
Toronto, ON M5s1X7 Canada    (416)960-3903
**Affiliation:** Connexions. **Concern(s):** politics; media; networking; press; film; activism. A public relations handbook for community workers and social change activists. Shows how to write a news release, hold a press conference, create public service announcements, create your own low-cost newsletters, posters, or videos.

**Other Resources:** Consulting and desktop publishing services. **Est.:** 1975. **Price:** $9.95/ea. **Contact(s):** Cynthia Dunham (Editor).

**M ♦  Media Network**
Alternative Media Information Center
39 W. 14th St.
New York, NY 10011    (212)929-2663
**Affiliation:** Alternative Media Information Center. **Concern(s):** media; Third World; justice; demographics; environment; energy; urban; film. The information center is operated to provide comprehensive computerized database evaluations of outstanding social, political, cultural and environmental films and videotapes. Thousands of titles cross-indexed into hundreds of subject areas. **Other Resources:** See the following media guides: THIRD WORLD ORGANIZING; CENTRAL AMERICA; APARTHEID AND SOUTH AFRICA; DISARMAMENT; GREEN GEMS; COMMUNITY ISSUES; REPRODUCTIVE RIGHTS; ADOPTION; SAFE PLANET; and a magazine, MEDIACTIVE. Also, NFCB NEWS. **Contact(s):** Don Derosby (Executive Director).

**M ♦  Media Resource Service**
Scientists' Institute for Public Information
355 Lexington Ave.
New York, NY 10017    (800)223-1730
**Affiliation:** Scientists' Institute for Public Information. **Concern(s):** media; education; health; journalism; science. A free telephone referral service funded by foundation grants and media associations, maintains a database of science, technology and health experts' addresses and phone numbers who have agreed to speak with the media on issues within their areas of expertise. **Est.:** 1980. (212)661-9110.

**M ♦  Media Watch**
1803 Mission St.
Santa Cruz, CA 95060
**Concern(s):** media; media watch.

**P C   Meta Network**
2000 N. 15th St., #103
Arlington, VA 22201
**Affiliation:** Metasystems Design Group, Inc. **Concern(s):** politics; media; future; peace; Third World; computer networking; BBS; electronic democracy; leadership. An on line international think-tank of leaders and change agents who discuss such issues as development in leadership, management, and human development theory; cross-cultural communication; and the potential for new communications technologies in politics and organizations. Metasystems Design also markets the Caucus conferencing software.

**C ♦   Metasystems Design Group, Inc.**
See Meta Network.

**E ♦   Mushalko's Radiophonic Lab**
2462 Stoneleigh Ct.
Dublin, OH 43017-9014
**Concern(s):** environment; media; broadcasting. No-hype advertising, writing, and audio production services for radio. Also a radio science show educating listeners about modern environmental problems. **Other Resources:** Free cassette tape of show. **Member:** Co-op America.

**♨ ♦  National Film Board of Canada**
1251 Avenue of the Americas
New York, NY 10020    (212)586-5131
**Concern(s):** peace; justice; media; conflict resolution; global understanding; film. See Films for a Peaceful Planet. **Other:** 111 E. Wacker Dr., #113, Chicago, IL 60601.

**M ♦  National Telemedia Council**
See TELEMEDIUM (periodicals).

**J ★  Nationwide Black Radio Directory**
CDE
Box 310551
Atlanta, GA 30331
**Concern(s):** justice; media; broadcasting; diversity. About 500 Black-owned radio stations, broadcasting firms, radio stations with Black programming, college radio stations, syndicated radio shows, music organizations, music publications, and other music and broadcasting companies with strong Black influence or ownership. **Frequency:** Annual. **Price:** $50/ea. + $2.50 shipping. **Pages:** c35. **Circ.:** 5M. **Date Publ.:** Fall 1990. **Publisher:** CDE. **Contact(s):** Charles Edwards (Publisher).

**E ♦   Nature NewsBreak**
1400 16th St. NW
Washington, DC 20036-2266    (202)797-6800
**Affiliation:** National Wildlife Federation. **Concern(s):** media; environment; broadcasting. Daily 60-second radio program bringing conservation to 12 million people each week.

## E ♦ NatureScope

National Wildlife Federation
1400 16th St. NW
Washington, DC 20036-2266     (703)790-4360
**Affiliation:** National Wildlife Federation. **Concern(s):** environment; media; education; conservation; childhood. Naturescope is the National Wildlife Federation's creative education series dedicated to inspiring in children an understanding and appreciation of the natural world while developing the skills they will need to make responsible decisions about the environment. The award-winning science and environmental activity series is designed for educators who work with children in grades K-8. Nonprofit. **Dues:** $20/yr. **Member:** N.E. NOFA regional group, OFPANA, OFAC. **Fax:** (703)442-7332. **Contact(s):** Barbara Pitman (Director).

## E ♦ Network Earth

Turner Broadcasting System
One CNN Center
Atlanta, GA 30348     (404)874-9696
**Affiliation:** Planet Live, Inc. **Concern(s):** environment; media; economics; demographics. Originally Earthbeat, a weekly TV magazine series about the underreported side of global crisis—the inventive solutions to challenges of environment and economy, hunger and health, social justice and international relations. First show aired October 15, 1989. Presently, Network Earth can be viewed every Sunday at 11PM ET and 8PM PT and focuses primarily on environment issues. Narrated by George Log. **Other Resources:** Facilitates the Network Earth Forum, a Bulletin Board Service on CompuServe. **Est.:** 1989. **E-Network:** CompuServe. **Fax:** (404)881-1799. **Contact(s):** J.J. Ebaugh (Founder/CEO).

## ℂ ♦ New Computerized World Information Service

World Information Clearing Centre
Box 58
1211 Geneva, 20 Switzerland     022 798 5162
**Concern(s):** media; future; film; electronic democracy; computer networking; ideation; BBS. Exchange information on global problems in brief and lively ways through video, visual and computer technologies.

## M ♦ New Day Films

See FILM AND VIDEO CATALOG.

## M ♦ New Dimensions Radio and Tapes

Box 410510
San Francisco, CA 94141-0510     (415)563-8899
**Concern(s):** media; broadcasting. Produces and distributes national radio series called "New Dimensions," which airs on 200 radio stations, and features interviews with thinkers, social innovators, and visionaries. **Other Resources:** Tape programs for sale. Write for free bimonthly newsletter. **Contact(s):** Justine Toms.

## E ♦ New Era Media

425 Alabama St.
San Francisco, CA 94110
**Concern(s):** environment; media; arts; broadcasting; music; film. Distributor/publisher of visual music and narrative nature videos for appreciation, relaxation, inspiration and education. Subjects include ecology, dolphins, birds, the rainforest, national parks and outer space. Representing Children's Television Workshop, Malibu Video, Marine Mammal Fund, Miramar, Nature Science Network, Peter Roberts, Sea Studios and Wilderness Video.

## M ♦ New Voices

4704 Overbrook
Bethesda, MD 20816     (301)656-7244
**Affiliation:** Public Interest Video Network. **Concern(s):** media; Third World; education; development; film. **Contact(s):** Arlen Slobodow (Executive Director).

## M ♦ New Yorker Films

16 W. 61st St.
New York, NY 10023     (212)247-6110
**Concern(s):** media; film.

## ☉ ℂ NIRSNET

1424 16th St. NW, #601
Washington, DC 20036     (202)328-0002
**Affiliation:** Nuclear Information and Resource Service. **Concern(s):** energy; media; environment; health; computer network; anti-nuclear; hazardous/toxic waste; BBS. A computer BBS containing up-to-date information on every nuclear power plant in the country; technical assistance such as expert advice in interpreting and surmounting government regulations that discourage citizen participation in nuclear issues; regulatory and legislative alerts, letting you know about major events—in time to do something about them; and an information clearinghouse, a wide selection of information on nuclear power. Available at cost to NIRS members.

## ✐ ♦ NOVA Transcripts

Box 322
Boston, MA 02134
**Affiliation:** Public Broadcasting System. **Concern(s):** media.

## T ♦ The Other America's Radio

Box 85
Santa Barbara, CA 93102
**Concern(s):** Third World; media; broadcasting. "Our primary concern is to increase the scope and integrity of information available regarding Central & South America, covert actions and the environment. We strive to provide in-depth information unavailable elsewhere. Our programs draw upon the expertise of policymakers, policy analysts, and those who live and work in the regions covered. Currently we are the only independent broadcast group regularly producing such work." Received in the US and worldwide. **Other Resources:** Tapes available from Prevailing Winds Research publications. See Publishers. **Contact(s):** Eric Schwartz (Producer).

## M ♦ Pacific Foundation

See Pacifica Radio and KPFA-FM94.

## ℂ ♦ The Pacific Telecommunications Council

1110 University Ave, #308
Honolulu, HI 96826     (808)941-3789
**Concern(s):** media; computer networking; BBS; Third World; Pacific/Pacific Rim; telecommunications. Serves as a regional telecommunications organization which brings together in a single forum both the providers and users of communication services, as well as policy makers, lplanners, scientists and academicians. The council is the only NGO especially designed to embrace members from all countries that play a role in the development and beneficial use of telecommunications in the Pacific hemisphere. Nonprofit. **Est.:** 1980. **Contact(s):** Richard Barber (Executive Director), James G. Savage (Assistant Director).

## P ♦ Pacifica Cassette Tapes Catalogue

3729 Cahuenga Blvd. W
North Hollywood, CA 91604-3504
**Affiliation:** Pacifica Foundation/Radio. **Concern(s):** politics; media; justice; feminism; environment; peace; broadcasting; EQUAL RIGHTS. This catalogue offers Pacifica Radio Archive's best selling tapes. The Archive is the oldest collection of public radio programs in the US. These 30,000 recordings, made by Pacifica and independent producers since 1949, represent a wide range of perspectives on many areas, including African-American history, the women's movement, contemporary philosophy, arms control, and the environment. Nonprofit. **Est.:** 1949. **Frequency:** Irregular. **Price:** Free. **Fax:** (818)985-8802. **Contact(s):** Bill Thomas (Director), Karole Selmon (Cassette Assistant).

## P ♦ Pacifica Radio

2207 Shattuck Ave.
Berkeley, CA 94704
**Affiliation:** Pacific Foundation. **Concern(s):** media; arts; broadcasting; music; literature. A public radio station that disseminates a wide variety of perspectives in many areas such as: African-American History, the women's movement, contemporary philosophy, arms control, and the environment. **Est.:** 1949. **Fax:** (818)985-8802. **Contact(s):** Bill Thomas (Director).

## P ★ Pacifica Radio Archive Catalog

3729 Cahuenga Blvd. W
North Hollywood, CA 91604-3504 (818)506-1077
**Affiliation:** Pacifica Foundation. **Concern(s):** politics; media; broadcasting; culture. "Twice each year the Pacifica Radio Group publishes an updated listing of recordings of their choice broadcasts. There is no charge, but donations to help with expenses are appreciated."-C.C. **Est.:** 1972. **Frequency:** 2/yr. **Price:** Free. **Other Formats:** WELL under 'ppspra'. **E-Network:** PeaceNet. **ID:** 'pp-spacific'. **Fax:** (818)985-8802. **Contact(s):** Bill Thomas (Director).

## M ♦ Paper Tiger Television

339 Lafayette St.
New York, NY 10012     (212)420-8196
**Concern(s):** media; broadcasting. See Deep Dish TV Network. (212)420-9045.

## M ♦ PBS Video

1320 Braddock Pl.
Alexandria, VA 22314     (800)424-7963
**Affiliation:** Public Broadcasting System. **Concern(s):** media; film. **Contact(s):** Bruce Christensen (President).

## ⚵ ★ Peace Education Resources Catalog: Audio-Visuals

Pyle Center
Box 1183
Wilmington, OH 45177
**Affiliation:** Wilmington College Peace Resource Center. **Concern(s):** peace; media; education; conflict resolution; anti-nuclear; global understanding; film. Videotapes, films and slideshows on peacemaking, conflict resolution; nonviolence, nuclear war, Hiroshima/Nagasaki, environment, global education. Resources for elementary to adult. Nonprofit. **Est.:** 1975. **Frequency:** 1-2/yr. **Price:** Donation. **Pages:** 20. **Contact(s):** Helen Weigel (Director. PRC).

## ⚵ ♦ Peace Films Inc.

1524 Yale St., #4
Santa Monica, CA 90404
**Concern(s):** peace; media; film. **Contact(s):** Cathy Zheutlin (President).

## ⚵ ♦ Peace Through The Airwaves

University of the Air
Box 1143
Arleta, CA 91331     (818)365-3262
**Concern(s):** peace; media; broadcasting.

## ⚵ ♦ Peaceful Warrior Productions

13601 Ventura Blvd., #209
Sherman Oaks, CA 91423     (818)784-7550
**Concern(s):** media; broadcasting; film. A company committed to altering the content of the images that go out around the world in television and film from this town. "Globally, we are connected by the news/information/entertainment mediums. By introducing consciousness into these forms we will change the world." **Contact(s):** Levar Burton.

## ⚵ ♦ Peacemakers Television

Box 521
Los Angeles, CA 90053
**Concern(s):** media; arts; environment; peace; broadcasting; film; poetry; music. Provides broadcast videocassettes promoting global peace, justice, environmental stability, and spiritual growth. Formats include interviews, speeches, documentaries, musicians, and poets. **Other Resources:** Distribute a free copy of STEPS TO INNER PEACE upon request. **Est.:** 1987. **E-Network:** Peacenet. **ID:** 'jowen'. **Contact(s):** John Owen, Madeleine Schwab (Producers).

## ⚵ ℂ PeaceNet

3228 Sacramento St.
San Francisco, CA 94115
**Affiliation:** Institute For Global Communications. **Concern(s):** media; peace; education; computer network; networking; BBS. A computer-based communications and information-sharing system providing electronic mail, conferences, BBS's, databases, Telex, Fax, and gateway services to help you gather, organize and share valuable up-to-date and comprehensive information about issues like peace, nuclear weapons, the arms race, arms control, Central America, environmental protection, international development, apartheid, social justice, human rights, and more. Peacenet is accessible if you have a computer and a modem. **Other Resources:** EcoNet, HomeoNet, ConflictNet, and gateways to countless others. **E-Network:** PeaceNet.

## ⚵ ♦ Peaceworks

991 Terrace 49
Los Angeles, CA 90042
**Concern(s):** peace; media; broadcasting; film. A weekly television series that explores new ways of thinking and new ways of acting that lead us into a world where Peace Works - without weapons and without violence to our beautiful planet. Distributed in Los Angeles since 1986 and nationally via the Catholic Telecommunications Network of America. **Contact(s):** Nancy Campeau (Producer). (213)254-1836.

## ✍ ★ Pennsylvania State University Audiovisual Services

Division of Media and Learning Resources
Special Services Building
University Park, PA 16802     (814)865-6314
**Concern(s):** media; education. Over 1,400 rental and 400 social science videos and films for sale. **Other Resources:** Catalog is called, PERSPECTIVES ON FILM AND VIDEO.

## ✐ ♦ Performing and Fine Artists for World Peace

Box 261
Lihue, HI 96766     (808)241-3626
**Concern(s):** arts; peace; environment; justice; activism; disarmament; preservation; conservation; culture; fine arts. Presents concerts, art exhibits, and children's festivals that focused on the theme of peace. These presentations have addressed such issues as human and native rights, hunger and homelessness, environmental preservation, and disarmament. We were designated as a Peace Messenger by the United Nations in 1987. **Other Resources:** "We wish to establish the International Week of Peace on Kauii in September 1991. We will be presenting our fourth Annual Intervention Day of Peace with

opening on Sept. 13." **Est.:** 1986. **Dues:** $10+/yr. **Contact(s):** Howard Shapiro (Director).

### E♦ Planet Live, Inc.
See Network Earth.

### F★ Powerful Images: A Woman's Guide to Audiovisual Resources
ISIS International
Box 25711
Philadelphia, PA 19144
**Affiliation:** ISIS International. **Concern(s):** feminism; media; Third World; demographics; film. List of about 250 producers and distributors of feminist audiovisual materials, with special emphasis on the Third World. Data include company name, address, phone, and description of audiovisual, including content, length, and subject. **Frequency:** Irregular. **Price:** $12/ea.; payment must accompany order. **Date Publ.:** 1986. **Contact(s):** Maria Eugenia Jelincic (Editor).

### S♦ Presbytell
100 Witherspoon St.
Louisville, KY 40202     (800)872-3283
**Affiliation:** Presbyterian Church. **Concern(s):** media; spiritual; education; peace; justice; economics; faith; conflict resolution; telecommunications. This is the voice-line of the Presbyterian Church. It offers General Assembly information, the Weekender, Presbyterian Headline News, Online counseling, and voice mail. A wide range of progressive concerns aimed at finding social solutions. Nonprofit.

### M♦ Prime Time Communications
210 Medio Dr.
Los Angeles, CA 90049     (310)472-3477
**Concern(s):** media. Ex-Newsweek-CBS journalist Karl Fleming likes to help people with worthy goals to effectively market and present their messages on TV, in print, in speeches and presentations. Emphasis on media and presentation skills. **Contact(s):** Karl Fleming (President).

### ✍♦ The Producers Consortium
Box 291929
Los Angeles, CA 90029     (818)985-4157
**Concern(s):** education; media; arts; spiritual; film; transformation; culture. An educational media production company with emphasis on transformational, progressive programs that inform, entertain, and inspire audiences in subjects ranging from the arts, culture, the environment, the humanities, science, metaphysics and philosophy. **Other Resources:** Co-productions, live events, workshops, screenings, lectures, production services for other nonprofits. Nonprofit. **Est.:** 1987. **E-Network:** Compuserve. **ID:** '177000,1441'. **Contact(s):** Christopher Toussaint (Executive Director), Greg Wright (Secretary). (818)784-0325.

### ( ♦ Public Electronic Network (PEN)
Information Systems Department
1685 Main St.
Santa Monica, CA 90401
**Concern(s):** media; politics; computer networking; electronic democracy; municipal; BBS. Established to provide Santa Monica residents free electronic mail and conferencing. Users can also communicate directly with city government. **Est.:** 1989.

### M♦ Public Interest Media Project
See Other Networks.

### M♦ Public Interest Video Network
4704 Overbrook
Bethesda, MD 20816     (301)656-7244
**Concern(s):** media; Third World; film; foreign policy. Media center serving public interest community needs. PIVN serves nationwide TV and radio audiences by producing and distributing programs with an independent viewpoint. Programs are available for sale or rental in 3/4," beta or VHS format. provides complete AV services and expertise to help nonprofit public organizations educate the public, develop more active and stronger constituencies, and develop more widespread and comprehensive media literacy. **Other Resources:** Produces New Voices Project and World View Series. **Contact(s):** Arlen Slobodow (Executive Director), Patrick Esmonde-White.

### M♦ Public Media Center
25 Scotland
San Francisco, CA 94133     (415)885-0200
**Affiliation:** Safe Energy Communications Council. **Concern(s):** media; responsibility; film; press. A public interest advertising agency/media resource center which primarily works with other nonprofit, public interest/advocacy organizations in gaining media access through training. **Other Resources:** PUBLIC MEDIA CENTER'S INDEX OF PROGRESSIVE FUNDERS DIRECTORY. Nonprofit.

### ( ♦ Public-Access Xanadu(TM) or PAX(TM)
Mindful Press
3020 Bridgeway #295
Sausalito, CA 94965
**Concern(s):** media; electronic democracy; computer networking; press; BBS. A proposed world-wide instantaneous publishing system for every kind of text, graphics, audio, film and computer data; a repository into which anyone may place material to be published; freedom of the press brought to the computer screen in a new, clarifying system of order. PAX has special rights to the use of Autodesk's Xanadu software for the universal publishing repository. Some 25 years in the making, a "universal electronic publishing network" which will operate on "hypertext". **Other Resources:** Videos, books, and T-shirts are available on the subject of this project in progress.

### M♦ Pyramid Films
Box 1048, 2801 Cole Ave.
Santa Monica, CA 90406-1048     (800)421-2304
**Concern(s):** media; film.

### ( ♦ R.A.C.H.E.L. (Remote Access Chemical Hazards Electronic Library)
Box 73700
Washington, DC 20056-3700     (202)328-1119
**Affiliation:** Environmental Research Foundation. **Concern(s):** media; environment; health; hazardous/toxic; computer networking; electronic democracy; press; BBS. RACHEL is a fully indexed on-line database. The database includes one Coast Guard's CHRIS Manual (Chemical Hazard Response Information System), re New Jersey Dept. of Health Fact Sheet on 1,100 toxic chemicals and over 6 years' worth of NEW YORK TIMES articles on the environment abstracted for easy access. **Other Resources:** There is no user charge. To sign up, write E.R.F. requesting a password. See CITIZEN'S TOXIC WASTE AUDIT MANUAL (directories). **Est.:** 1981. **Price:** $40/yr. **Office:** 1432 U St. NW Washington, DC 20009. **Contact(s):** Robbin Zeff (Associate Director), Maria Pellerano (Director of Finance).

### ✇♦ Radio For Peace International
Box 88
Santa Ana, Costa Rica
**Affiliation:** World Peace University. **Concern(s):** media; Third World; peace; broadcasting; Latin America. A short-wave station (7.375 Mhz) which broadcasts worldwide, seven days a week, to provide practical information and insights into all aspects of world peace. A joint project of World Peace University, Oregon, and University of Peace in Costa Rica, dedicated to broadcasting programs to increase understanding about conflict resolution, sustainable development, elimination of world hunger, peace education, environmental conservation, social justice and other cross-cultural issues. **Other Resources:** Airs peace oriented programming internationally in English and Spanish. Nonprofit. **E-Network:** Econet. **ID:** "worldpeaceu". **Fax:** (503)741-1279. **Other:** Radio for Peace, Box 10869, Eugene, OR 97440. Dr. F. Richard Schneider, Chancellor.

### G♦ RadioWest
Box 38327
Los Angeles, CA 90038
**Concern(s):** justice; gay/lesbian; media; broadcasting. An organization of independent producers. Produces THIS WAY OUT for the gay and lesbian community. Nonprofit.

### E( RecycleLine
American Recycling Market
Box 577
Ogdensburg, NY 13669     (800)267-0707
**Affiliation:** American Recycling Market. **Concern(s):** environment; media; recycling; green consumer; BBS. An online information service for the recycling industry. Instant access to over 20,000 markets, 2,500 certified recycled products. DataBank, Traders Classified Service, Resource Library, and Electronic Mailroom. **Est.:** 1985. **Fax:** (315)471-3258. **Contact(s):** Mike Fraser.

### ✎♦ Redwood Records
6400 Hollis, #8
Emeryville, CA 94608     (510)428-9191
**Concern(s):** arts; education; music; culture. An organization dedicated to bringing progressive ideas and culture to people through music and educational work. "Music that Rocks the Boat!" **Other Resources:** See VOICES (periodicals). Nonprofit. **Contact(s):** Cynthia Frenz.

### J★ Reel Change: A Guide to Social Issue Films
New York Zoetrope
838 Broadway
New York, NY 10003     (212)254-8235
**Concern(s):** media; peace; environment; justice; health; film. 300+ distributors of 16mm films on social issues, including disarmament, nuclear freeze, environmental concerns, racial and sexual justice, and occupational health and safety; publishers of film-related books and periodicals. Arranged alphabetically with name and address. For publisher's entries include publication title, publisher name, and address. Principal content of publication is annotated filmography of over 500 16mm films, videotapes, and slide shows. **Frequency:** Irregular. **Price:** $6.95/ea. **Date Publ.:** 1979. **Publisher:** New York Zoetrope. (800)CHAPLIN.

### F★ Reproductive Rights
Alternative Media Information Center
39 W. 14th St.
New York, NY 10011     (212)929-2663
**Affiliation:** Media Network. **Concern(s):** feminism; demographics; media; film; family planning; pro-choice. Guide to 60 film titles on topics such as reproductive health; childcare; birth control; gay and teenage sexuality; single mothers; and attacks on women's rights. **Contact(s):** Don Derosby (Executive Director).

### J♦ Results Education Fund
4801 Kona Kove Way
Yorba Linda, CA 92686-2110
**Concern(s):** jsutice; media; demographics; Third World; hunger; development; film. Makes videos on hunger and development issues available to the public for the cost of postage. **Contact(s):** Greer Malone.

### E★ Safe Planet
Alternative Media Information Center
39 W. 14th St.
New York, NY 10011     (212)929-2663
**Affiliation:** Media Network. **Concern(s):** environment; media; education; energy; acid rain; global warming; renewables; film. If you, or your group, wants to start a discussion of agricultural policy, acid rain, global warming, alternative energy, or any of the other environmental concerns of the age you can find a film to get things started. Safe Planet, a 40-page guide, costs $11.50, provides detailed information on over 80 new films and videos on environmental topics. **Price:** $11.50/ea. **Pages:** 40.

### H♦ Sageline
Maui, HI     (800)999-4454
**Affiliation:** Executive Office on Aging, Governor's Office. **Concern(s):** health; media; telecommunications; seniors; self-help. Hawaii's free telephone service where older adults can get quick, understandable answers on health, finances, housing, medical care, legal problems, leisure activities and more. 24-hours a day, 7 days a week, call for a free brochure. Great idea!

### E( Save the Planet
c/o Software Excitement
Box 3072; 6475 Crater Lake Highway
Central Point, OR 97502 (800)444-5457
**Concern(s):** media; environment; energy; demographics; economics; politics; electronic democracy. The program is user friendly and very professionally designed. Topics include fossil fuel combustion, population. increases, forest destruction, the "greenhouse effect", environmental organizations, recycling ideas, energy saving tips, environmental investing and shopping guidelines. A built-in letter writing utility complete with names and addresses of all US Senators and Representatives. Writing letters is fully automated; just fill in the body of your letter or retrieve text from saved topic. **Other Resources:** Requires CGA of better.

### ✍★ Sexuality Education: A Resource Book
Garland Publishing Co.
136 Madison Ave.
New York, NY 10016     (212)686-7492
**Concern(s):** media; feminism; education; film. List of suppliers of audiovisual materials for use in sexuality education. Principal content is essays describing ways to plan and implement sexuality education programs. Data include company name, address, and phone. **Price:** $47/ea. **Pages:** 450. **Date Publ.:** 1989. **Publisher:** Garland Publishing Co. **Fax:** (212)889-9399. (800)627-6273. **Contact(s):** Carol Cassell, Pamela M. Wilson (Editors).

### M♦ Skylink Satellite Communications, Inc.
953 N. Highland Ave.
Los Angeles, CA 90038
**Concern(s):** media; electronic democracy; broadcasting; film. A customized satellite delivery service designed to meet the needs of distributors of recorded or live events. Skylink founders have handled the distribution of over 7,000,000 programs on tape and film to TV stations. In July 1985, the Skylink team designed the worldwide satellite delivery of the historic Live Aid Concert, seen by over two billion people around the world under the auspices of Synat, the former name of Skylink Satellite Communications, Inc. **Contact(s):** Jim Tuverson, Jr. (President).

**ℂ ▶ Some Things Special**
28 Eagle St.
Freedonia, NY 14063
**Concern(s):** media; environment; economics; computer networking; alternative markets; BBS. Compuserve's nationwide electronic marketing section of the "Electronic Mall" for green products. **E-Network:** CompuServe. **ID:** Electronic Mall Section. **Contact(s):** Dan Valone, Dot Valone.

**✐ ▶ Steven Bergman Enterprises**
Box 481
Carmel Valley, CA 93924     (408)659-3259
**Concern(s):** arts; health; music; psychology. Provides musical and educational audio cassettes which "enhance the well-being of the planet." **Contact(s):** Brandy.

**H ▶ The Strecker Group**
1216 Wilshire Blvd.
Los Angeles, CA 90017
**Concern(s):** media; health; AIDS; public health; film. Distributes videotapes on the theory of AIDS virus origins. (800)548-3198. **Contact(s):** Dr. Robert Strecker.

**✐ ▶ Sundance**
780 West Layton Ave.
Salt Lake City, UT 84104     (800)422-2770
**Concern(s):** arts; environment; culture; activism. "When you purchase something from our catalog… your purchase also helps support Sundance programs for new talent and development in the arts and effort to enhance and preserve our environment." **Other Resources:** Sundance Summer Theatre, Sundance Cottage Retreats. **Est.:** 1969. **Fax:** (801)973-4989. **Contact(s):** Robert Redford (Founder). (801)225-4107.

**E★ Switching on to the Environment**
150 Rideua St.
Ottawa, ON K1N 5X6 Canada     (613)232-6727
**Affiliation:** Canadian Film Institute. **Concern(s):** media; environment; Third World; development; air pollution; acid rain; film. Lists 100+ films on environmental and development concerns. They are available internationally, appeal to a general audience, are suitable for broadcast, and are useful to educators investigating global issues. Air pollution, acid rain, wetlands, and wildlife are among the subjects treated.

**H ▶ There is a Solution**
23505 Crenshaw Blvd., #201
Torrance, CA 90505
**Concern(s):** media; health; broadcasting; substance abuse; counseling. A twice-weekly live radio call-in show which explores the problems of addictions, compulsions, and unfulfilling relationships and offers hope through examples and solutions. Guests include authors, speakers, and members of various Anonymous programs. "As host, I also keep my anonymity and share my recovery of over 14 years in Alcohol Anonymous and over 13 in Overeaters Anonymous. Currently air Sunday at 9PM on KIEV 870-AM and Monday at 7PM on the Cable Radio Network (CRN)." **Other Resources:** CRN is heard on many cable systems throughout California and in several other states. **Fax:** (310)534-8827. **Contact(s):** Larry W. (Producer/Host).

**T★ Third World Organizing**
Alternative Media Information Center
39 W. 14th St.
New York, NY 10011     (212)929-2663
**Affiliation:** Media Network. **Concern(s):** media; Third World; justice; demographics; environment; Native Americans; minority rights; indigenous peoples; activism; film. A guide to the best films and videotapes on issues affecting Asian, Black, Latino, and Native American communities, selected from hundreds of titles by a panel of civil rights activists and media professionals. More than 80 titles listed, with evaluative descriptions, length, format, producer, price and distributor. Topics include civil rights; education, health, immigration, work, militarism and housing. Also section on other media resources. **Contact(s):** Don Derosby (Executive Director).

**M ▶ This Way Out**
Box 38327
Los Angeles, CA 90038   (213)469-5907
**Affiliation:** RadioWest. **Concern(s):** media; activism; media watch. A project of RadioWest, a nonprofit organization of individual producers. Nonprofit. (310)854-2616.

**M ▶ Turner Broadcasting System**
One CNN Center
Box 105366
Atlanta, GA 30348-5366
**Concern(s):** media; broadcasting; journalism; electronic democracy. This once back water independent station has become the alternative network for people who want entertainment, sports, culture,

news and information. TBS sponsors many environmental, peace, and progressive projects. **Other Resources:** CNN, 24-hour newschannel; WTBS, 24-hour variety channel; TNT, 24-hour classic move channel; Network Earth, a environmental show and BBS on Compuserve; Captain Planet, an environmental superhero children's television show. **Fax:** (404)827-1593. **Contact(s):** Ted Turner (Founder/CEO).

**✍ ▶ United Nations Films & Videos**
United Nations
Room S-845
New York, NY 10017     (212)963-1234
**Concern(s):** education; media; politics; environment; justice; energy; United Nations; natural resources; film. Many UN productions may be borrowed via public libraries. Topics include economic concerns, human settlements, environment and resources, political affairs, and UN. **Other Resources:** Provides list of various distributors of various productions concerning related issues. **Other:** University of Illinois, Film Center, 1325 S. Oak St., Champaign, IL 61820.

**✍ ▶ University of the Air**
Box 1143
Arleta, CA 91331
**Concern(s):** media; education; global understanding; broadcasting. The program will be a two semester university curriculum on Peace and Development broadcast to more than 30 countries. Almost 30 academic courses have been taped for broadcast. Students will be expected to keep up with the course work, write the assigned papers and will receive a "Diplomat-Generalist" certificate on successful completion.

**E ▶ US Environmental Film Festival**
243 Santa Monica Place
Santa Monica, CA 90401     (310)576-0818
**Concern(s):** media; environment; film. Organizes film showings at various events.

**✍★ The Video Project 1992 Catalog: Films and Videos for a Safe and Sustainable World**
5332 College Ave., #101
Oakland, CA 94606     (510)655-9050
**Affiliation:** Video Project. **Concern(s):** media; environment; peace; Third World; Central America; sustainability; film. Our primary purpose: to provide quality, affordable educational video and film programs on the issues and ideas critical to our future. Over 100 documentaries, including 25 new titles since our last catalog. An excellent collection of documentaries "for a safe and sustainable world." **Other Resources:** Individual membership program, starting at $35 per year, entitles members to $10 rentals and 20% discount on most programs. Nonprofit. **Est.:** 1983. **Frequency:** 2/yr. **Price:** Free. **Pages:** 32. **Fax:** (510)655-9115. **Contact(s):** Steve Ladd (Executive Director).

**M ▶ The Videotape Referral Service**
Scientists' Institute for Public Information
355 Lexington Ave.
New York, NY 10017     (800)223-1730
**Affiliation:** Scientists' Institute for Public Information. **Concern(s):** media; education; health; journalism; film; science. Serves as a go between, providing television reporters with access to videotape sources, not with the tapes themselves. SIPI will not store or transmit videotapes, but will refer journalists to the producers of the tapes they need and do all the leg to track it down. **Est.:** 1980. (212)661-9110.

**M ▶ Visions**
Visions Productions
Box 931555
Los Angeles, CA 90093
**Concern(s):** media; spiritual; future; health; film; transformation; ideation; holism. A cable TV program designed to enlighten the public and enrich studies of advancing consciousness. Guests on Visions reflect studies in parapsychology, futurism, ancient and modern methods of holistic health, and the development of human potential. Contact Valli Aman to be on the Visions mailing list for programming details in the Group W Century Cable or American Cable areas. **Contact(s):** Valli Aman (Host).

**M ▶ Visual Studies Workshop**
See AFTERIMAGE newspaper.

**E★ The W.O.W. Series of Video Tapes on the Solid Waste Crisis**
Route 2, Box 322
Canton, NY 13617
**Affiliation:** Work on Waste, USA (W.O.W.). **Concern(s):** environment; media; waste management; film. WOW No.16: "Waste Management as if the Future Mattered." In this fast-paced 60-minute VHS videotape, Dr. Paul Connet puts our trash problem into the larger

context of global pollution and our resource crises. He illustrates the positive alternatives incineration - source separation, reuse, recycling, composting, toxic removal. 48 page booklet to included. Cost: 30.00. Videos generally run 30-60 minutes at a cost of $25-30. **Publisher:** Video-Active Productions. **Contact(s):** Roger Bailey, Dr. Paul Connett **Other:** 92 Judson St., Canton, NY 13617

**✍★ The War Peace Film Guide**
World Without War Publications
1736 Martin Luther King Way
Berkeley, CA 94709
**Affiliation:** World Without War. **Concern(s):** media; peace; world order; film. Offers annotated descriptions and evaluations of 287 war peace films, plus program aids and other resources. **Date Publ.:** 1980. **Publisher:** World Without War Publications. **Contact(s):** John Dowling.

**ℂ ▶ The WELL (Whole Earth 'Lectronic Link)**
27 Gate Five Rd.
Sausalito, CA 94966     (415)332-1716
**Affiliation:** Whole Earth Institute. **Concern(s):** media; computer networking; electronic democracy; BBS. A computer BBS that offers low-cost access to a unique communications tool. The WELL is divided into conferences that cover a wide range of topics in both general-interest and technical areas (Books, Parenting, Writers, Macintosh, etc.). It's a place where professionals and personal interactions overlap, weaving a tapestry of interactivity that approaches a village-like quality in an electronic environment. Nonprofit. **Est.:** 1968. **Subscription:** $8/month. **Price:** $3/hour online. **E-Network:** The WELL (415) 332-6106. **ID:** Kerwit@Well. **Contact(s):** Kelly Teevan (Executive Director). (415)332-4335.

**J ▶ White Buffalo Multi-Media**
Box 73
Woodstock, NY 12498     (914)246-9995
**Concern(s):** media; justice; Native Americans; film. Draws on years of slide/multi-screen production to present the wisdom of native cultures, many of them speaking directly to our current world situation. Now these multi-media programs are being adapted to the video format, beginning with a documentary on the "Great Law of Peace of the Iroquois". **Contact(s):** Nathan Koenig (President), Scott Anderson (Office Manager).

**S ▶ Whole Life Radio Network KFOX-93.5**
123 W. Torrance Blvd., #102
Redondo Beach, CA 90277     (310)374-9796
**Concern(s):** media; arts; spiritual; broadcasting; transformation. First "New Age" radio station in Los Angeles. 9am-4pm every morning weekday airs New Age/metaphysical/human potential/holistic/consciousness talk/philosophy, and advice. 1pm-3pm Monday shows features many of the top New Age speakers who appear at the Expos and around the world, such as Ram Dass, Timothy Leary, Dennis Weaver, John Robbins and Terry Cole Whittaker are interviewed live with callings from the audience. **Contact(s):** Richard Greene, Dee Riggs (Co-hosts).

**M ★ Xchange Television**
440 W. Main St.
Wyckoff, NJ 07481
**Concern(s):** media; broadcasting; film.

**✍ ▶ Young Artists United (YAU)**
7095 Hollywood Blvd., #499
Hollywood, CA 90028     (310)281-7515
**Concern(s):** media; arts; activism. A nonpartisan group of entertainment industry professionals who donate their time and talents to community activism and to promoting social awareness among today's youth on issues ranging from substance abuse, to safe sex, to the importance of education. YAU's members acknowledge and accept responsibility to create positive role models for young people through public service announcements, national speakers, educational forums and community outreach projects. Nonprofit.

*Special Thanks to:* **Creative Resources Guild** for permission to use some of the descriptions from their directory.

# ④ **Publishers & Publications Lists**

| | | | | | | |
|---|---|---|---|---|---|---|
| A = Agriculture | D = Demographics | ☺ = Energy | ? = Future | L = Labor | S = Spiritual |
| ☛ = Animal Rights | ♿ = Disabled | E = Environment | G = Gay/Lesbian | M = Media | T = Third World |
| ✐ = Arts | $ = Economics | ♥ = Family | H = Health | ♆ = Peace | ✈ = Travel |
| ( = Computers | ✐ = Education | F = Feminism | J = Justice | P = Politics | U = Urban |

**T ♦ Accion International Publications List**
130 Prospect St.
Cambridge, MA 02139 (617)492-4930
**Affiliation:** Accion International. **Concern(s):** Third World; economics; community self-reliance; development; community investment. Primarily a private organization that works with local affiliate organizations in 13 countries to reduce poverty through micro-enterprise assistance. It has a free quarterly bulletin, annual report, and other general information Nonprofit. **Est.:** 1974. **Fax:** (617)876-9509. **Contact(s):** Elizabeth Rosenberg (Publications), Gabriela Romanow (Communications).

**P ♦ Advocate Press**
441 Chapel St.
New Haven, CT 06511 (203)777-0900
**Concern(s):** politics; education; arts; graphics; grassroots organizing. Commercial printing business featuring graphic design and typesetting. Also publishes books and pamphlets related to history at the grassroots.

**A ♦ agAccess**
Box 2008
Davis, CA 95617 (916)756-7177
**Concern(s):** agriculture; sustainability; research. Supplies all available agricultural and horticultural books. It also performs specialized research and information retrieval services in sustainable agriculture and supplies farmers, universities, and agricultural professionals worldwide. **Other Resources:** Agricultural & horticultural books, a free mail-order book catalog, and book publishing. It has a retail store in Davis. **Est.:** 1984. **Publisher:** agAccess. 603 4th St., Davis, CA 95616

**E ♦ Alaska Northwest Books**
22026 20th Ave. S.E.
Bothell, WA 98021
**Concern(s):** environment; education; travel; wilderness; wildlife/endangered species; polar. Nonfiction, with an emphasis on the natural world and the history of Alaska, Western Canada, and Pacific Northwest; travel books; biographies; cookbooks; field guides; guidebooks. **Contact(s):** Maureen Zimmerman (Manager).

**♆ ♦ The Albert Einstein Institution Publications List**
1430 Massachusetts Ave., 6th Fl.
Cambridge, MA 02138 (617)876-0311
**Affiliation:** Albert Einstein Institution. **Concern(s):** peace; nonviolence. The Institution disseminates research on the history, characteristics, and potential application of nonviolent sanctions through books, monographs, conference reports, and a newsletter. **Est.:** 1983. **Fax:** (617)876-0837. **Contact(s):** Roger Powers (Publications Coordinator).

**✐ ♦ The Alliance for Parental Involvement in Education (AllPIE) Book & Resources Catalog**
Box 59
East Chatham, NY 12060-0059 (518)392-6900
**Affiliation:** Alliance for Parental Involvement in Education, Inc.. **Concern(s):** education; family; childhood. Books and resources to empower parents with respect to the education of their children. Books on public, private homeschooling, special education, educational enrichment, etc. **Other Resources:** Newsletter, Referral Service, Workshops, Conferences. Nonprofit. **Est.:** 1989. **Frequency:** 4/yr. **Price:** Free. **Pages:** 8. **Contact(s):** Seth Rockmuller (President), Katharine Houk (Executive Director).

**☺ ♦ American Council for an Energy-Efficient Economy Publication List**
1001 Connecticut Ave. NW, #535
Washington, DC 20036 (202)429-8873
**Affiliation:** American Council for an Energy-Efficient Economy. **Concern(s):** energy; environment; efficiency; air pollution; conservation. See listing under Organizations. **Contact(s):** Robert Socolow (Chairman), Arthur Rosenfeld

**☺ ♦ American Wind Energy Association Publication List**
777 N. Capitol St. NE., #805
Washington, DC 20002 (202)408-8988
**Affiliation:** American Wind Energy Association. **Concern(s):** energy; environment; wind; renewables. Description and cost information for all publications relating to wind energy technology. **Est.:** 1974. **E-Network:** Econet. **ID:** 'awea'. **Fax:** (202)408-8536. MCI Mail: AWEA. **Contact(s):** Randy Swisher (Executive Director), Mellissa Williams (Office Manager).

**✐ ♦ AMOK**
Box 875112
Los Angeles, CA 90878
**Concern(s):** arts; culture; literature. "World's Weirdest Books! 3,000 controversial titles: Magick, Bizarre Sex, Psychedelics, Mayhem, Sleaze, Exotica, Conspiracy, Suppressed Information. Comprehensive coverage of Situationism, Anarchism, Noam Chomsky. Hate literature, Blaxpoitation and Noir fiction, Robert Anton Wilson, Dada, and more." "A wonderful conspectus of that other literature that exists light years away from mainstream publishing"-J.G. Ballard. **Other Resources:** Large catalog available. **Price:** $8.95/ea.

**E ♦ Annual Environmental Sourcebook**
Island Press
Box 7
Covelo, CA 95428 (202)232-7933
**Concern(s):** environment. The most complete catalog of books on the environment. Over 180 hard-to-find books from organizations across the country. Also, vital reference books that deal with a wide range of ecology issues. **Frequency:** Annual. **Price:** $2/refundable. **Publisher:** Island Press. Order: (800)828-1302. **Contact(s):** Charles C. Savitt (President).

**H ♦ Aries Rising Press**
Box 29532
Los Angeles, CA 90029
**Concern(s):** health; education; AIDS. Distributes books by Dr. Alan Cantwell, theorist/researcher of the origins of the AIDS virus.

**S ♦ Aurora Press**
Box 573
Santa Fe, NM 87504 (505)989-9804
**Concern(s):** spiritual; health; psychology; death/dying; transformation. "...pioneers books that catalyze personal growth, balance and improve the quality of life. Titles include: COMING HOME - A Guide to Dying at Home with Dignity. UNINVITED GUESTS - A Documented History of UFO Sightings, ALIEN ENCOUNTERS & COVER-UPS, and titles by Rudhyar, Haich & Chia." **Other Resources:** Free catalog. **Est.:** 1982.

**E ♦ Backcountry Publications**
Div. of the Countryman Press, Inc.
Box 175
Woodstock, VT 05091
**Concern(s):** environment; recreation. Regional guidebooks on hiking, walking, canoeing, bicycling, mountain biking, cross-country skiing, and fishing. **Contact(s):** Carl Taylor (Editor).

**☺ ♦ Ballinger Publishing Co.**
Rt 3, Box 20B
Hagerstown, MD 21740 (800)638-3030
**Concern(s):** energy; justice; environment; health. Reference and professional books on energy, social and behavioral sciences, criminal law and justice, psychology, housing and real estate, health policy, and administration business, finance and economics. **Other Resources:** Free book catalog. Published ENERGY: THE NEXT 20 YEARS by Hans H. Landsberg; and, PEACE RESOURCE BOOK (1988).

**F ♦ Beacon Press**
25 Beacon St.
Boston, MA 02108
**Concern(s):** feminism; justice; spiritual; education; environment; global understanding; diversity. General nonfiction: women's studies; liberal religion; Asian, African-American, Jewish, and Native American

studies; gay and lesbian issues; philosophy; and current affairs. Series include: Black Women Writers and Asian Voices (fiction series); Night Lights (multi-cultural children's books); Concord Library (environmental series); Men and Masculinity Series (nonfiction) and the Barnard New Women Poets Prize Winner Series. **Other Resources:** Published GLOBAL ECOLOGY HANDBOOK. **Contact(s):** Lauren Bryant (Senior Editor).

**S ♦ Bear & Company, Inc.**
Drawer 2860
Santa Fe, NM 87504-2860 (505)983-9868
**Concern(s):** spiritual; health; environment; transformation; Native American. Publisher of 60+ nonfiction New Age "books to celebrate and heal the earth...that will help transform our culture philosophically, environmentally, and spiritually." Topics: ecology, Native American spirituality and personal planetary healing. **Other Resources:** Free catalog. SACRED PLACES by J. Swan; ISLANDS OUT OF TIME by William I. Thompson; VIBRATIONAL MEDICINE by Dr. R. Gerber; CRYING FOR A DREAM by R. Erdoes. PROFILES IN WISDOM: NATIVE ELDERS SPEAK ABOUT THE EARTH by S. McFaddene. **Contact(s):** Barbara Clow (Editor).

**✐ ♦ Bergin & Garvey**
670 Amherst Rd.
Granby, MA 01033 (413)253-9980
**Concern(s):** education; feminism; birth. Paulo Freire's works, including THE POLITICS OF EDUCATION and others; THE MORAL AND SPIRITUAL CRISIS IN EDUCATION by David Purpel; EDUCATION AND THE AMERICAN DREAM; and other social-political studies of education; anthropological approaches to childbirth; and other subjects. **Other Resources:** An imprint of the Greenwood Publishing Group. **Est.:** 1977. **Contact(s):** Sophy Craze.

**M ♦ Big Books from Small Presses**
Upper Access Books
Box 457
Hinesburg, VT 05461 (800)356-9315
**Concern(s):** media; arts; literature; journalism; press. "This is our third catalogue, and like the others, it doesn't include a single best-seller from a big publisher. We select only small-press books. The principal criterion is quality, not popularity. We're gratified by the enthusiastic response we've received from you, and from other discriminating readers throughout the US, Canada and around the world. You've proven that there is a substantial market for books outside the lowest denominator of mass appeal. Thanks!" **Other Resources:** An extraordinary selection of nonfiction books, many of which are hard to find in bookstores. 350 titles, including many for children. **Date Publ.:** 1991. **Contact(s):** Lisa & Steve Carlson, Gay Muller

**E ♦ Binford & Mort Publishing**
1202 N.W. 17th Ave.
Portland, OR 97209
**Concern(s):** environment. Books on subjects related to the Pacific Coast and the Northwest. **Contact(s):** J.F. Roberts (Editor).

**✐ ♦ Blue Bird Publishing**
1713 E. Broadway, #306
Tempe, AZ 85282 (602)982-9003
**Concern(s):** education; homeschooling. Specializes in reference and home education books. "The home schooling population in the US is exploding. We have a strong market for anything that can be targeted to this group. Other books concern current social issues." **Est.:** 1985. **Contact(s):** Cheryl Gorder (Publisher).

**H ♦ Book Publishing Company**
Box 99
Summertown, TN 38483 (615)964-3571
**Concern(s):** health; justice; environment; agriculture; vegetarian; gardening; Native Americans. Community-owned company specializing in books on vegetarian cooking, alternative health, Native Americans, ecology, and gardening. **Contact(s):** Bob Holzapfel.

M ➧ **Bookpeople Inc.**
2929 Fifth St.
Berkeley, CA 94710 (510)632-4700
**Concern(s):** media; press. Distributes large and small press books, as long as it fits their liberal to radical criteria. **Other Resources:** Publishes catalog semi-annually as well as monthly, THE BOOKPAPER. Call (800) 624-4466 (CA) or (800) 227-1516 (outside CA).

M ➧ **Bookslinger**
502 N. Prior Ave.
St. Paul, MN 55104 (800)397-2613
**Concern(s):** media; press. Represents 180+ independent small press publishers in all areas of the progressive movement. Catalog available with quarterly updates as well as BOOKSLINGER BIBLIOPHILE.

E ➧ **Bootstrap Press**
6 Valley Trail
Croton-On-Hudson, NY 10521
**Affiliation:** Intermediate Technology Development Group of North America. **Concern(s):** environment; economics; justice; politics. Publishes a wide variety of topics from economics to the environment. **Other Resources:** Published AFTER THE CRASH, by Guy Dauncey, and TOES Books.

✏ ➧ **Borgo**
Box 2845
San Bernadino, CA 92406
**Concern(s):** arts; justice; demographics; politics; literature; culture. "We publish and distribute scholarly books in the Humanities and Social Sciences for the library and academic markets. All of our books are published in open-ended, monographic series, including: THE MILFORD SERIES: POPULAR WRITERS OF TODAY; Stokvis Studies in HISTORICAL CHRONOLOGY AND THOUGHT; I.O. Evans Studies in the PHILOSOPHY AND CRITICISM OF LITERATURE; Clipper Studies in the American Theater; Borgo BioViews; Bibliographies of Modern Authors; etc." **Contact(s):** Robert Reginald.

E ➧ **Boxwood Press**
183 Oceanview Blvd.
Pacific Grove, CA 93950 (408)375-9110
**Concern(s):** environment; demographics. A publishing company specializing in ecology, natural history, animals, plants, and human ecology. **Est.:** 1952. **Fax:** (408)375-0430. **Contact(s):** Ralph Buchsbaum (President).

F ➧ **Branden Publishing Co.**
17 Station St., Box 843
Brookline Village, MA 02145
**Concern(s):** feminism; education. Novels, biographies, and autobiographies. Especially books by or on women. Also considers queries on history, computers, business, performance arts, and translations. **Contact(s):** Adolph Caso (Editor).

S ➧ **Brethren Press**
1451 Dundee Ave.
Elgin, IL 60120 (312)742-5100
**Affiliation:** Church of the Brethren. **Concern(s):** spiritual; faith. Publishes many books dealing with critical ethical and social issues. **Est.:** 1897. **Contact(s):** Jeanne Donovan (Acting Assistant Book Editor).

✍ ➧ **Bright Ring Publishing**
Box 5768
Bellingham, WA 98227 (206)734-1601
**Concern(s):** education. Books for parents, teachers, and children which encourage creative, independent thinking. Suitable for ages 2 to 12. **Other Resources:** Free brochure, wholesale and retail. **Contact(s):** Mary Ann Kohl.

✍ ➧ **Brown Publishing Co.**
Box 539
Dubuque, IA 52001
**Concern(s):** education; spiritual; childhood; faith. Has published COOPERATIVE LEARNING, COOPERATIVE LIVES: A Sourcebook of Learning Activities for Building a Peaceful World and distributes curriculum guides on global education and American social issues published by the Center for Learning. Also offers an extensive catalog of books on Catholic religious education, including works on peace education from a religious perspective.

A ➧ **C. Olson & Company**
Box 5100
Santa Cruz, CA 95063-5100 (408)458-3365
**Concern(s):** agriculture; economics; community self-reliance; food production; food distribution. "Promoting food self-sufficiency through establishing community food tree nurseries for public distribution to yards and public lands." Looks to publish books that will sell in natural food and independent book stores that promotes a lifestyle that has less negative impact on the environment. **Est.:** 1975. **Contact(s):** C.L. Olson.

E ➧ **Capra Press**
Box 2068
Santa Barbara, CA 93120 (805)966-4590
**Concern(s):** environment. "A general trade press with a focus on the West." Topics include self-help, animals, biographies, art/architecture, gardening, language/literature, natural history/environment, regional, and sociology. Recently published Edward Abbey's BLACK SUN. **Est.:** 1969. **Contact(s):** Noel Young.

H ➧ **Celo Books**
1901 Hannah Branch Rd.
Burnsville, NC 28714 (702)675-4925
**Concern(s):** health; death/dying; seniors. "We publish books on death and dying education, aging, and grieving." **Est.:** 1962.

M ➧ **Celo Valley Books**
346 Seven Mile Ridge Rd.
Burnsville, NC 28714 (704)675-5918
**Concern(s):** media; press. Book production for people wishing to self-publish a book. One percent of profits donated to the charity of the client's choice.

H ➧ **Center for Auto Safety Publications Brochure**
Center for Auto Safety
2001 S St. NW. #410
Washington, DC 20009 (202)328-7700
**Affiliation:** Center for Auto Safety. **Concern(s):** health; consumer protection. See THE LEMON BOOK. CAS Publications Brochure lists Books, Periodicals, Reports & Information, Auto Defect Packets, Fuel Economy Publications, Consumer Action Guides and Arbitration Manuals. 100+ items available. **Other Resources:** The publications brochure from the Center for Auto Safety is free with a self-addressed, stamped envelope sent to CAS Publications Dept. Please include SASE with each request. **Est.:** 1970. **Contact(s):** Debra Barclay (Communications Director).

M ➧ **Channing L. Bete Co.**
200 State Rd.
South Deerfield, MA 01373 (800)628-7733
**Concern(s):** media; education; spiritual; economics; health; press. A scriptographical publishing company that deals with educational and informative material from the fields of religion, education, business and industry, community service, and health. **Other Resources:** Publications lists are available by topic. **Frequency:** 2/yr. **Fax:** (413)665-6671. **Contact(s):** Marie Bete (Assistant Publisher). (413)665-7611.

E ➧ **Chelsea Green Publishing Co.**
Route 113, Box 130
Post Mills, VT 05058 (802)333-9073
**Concern(s):** environment; politics; education. Fiction and nonfiction on natural history, biography, history, politics, and travel. "Emphasis on nonfiction: nature, biography, travel, outdoors, serious fiction (literary)." **Contact(s):** Ian Baldwin, Jr. (Editor), Michael Moore (Associate Editor).

E ➧ **Cheshire Books**
4532 Cherryvale Ave.
Soquel, CA 95073 (415)321-2449
**Concern(s):** environment; energy; arts; wind; efficiency. "We are now publishing material from the writing public at large, and authors are invited to submit manuscripts in fields of art, architecture, energy and the environment, and science. Most recent books are THE WIND POWER BOOK, THE ECOLOGY OF FREEDOM, and THE DAY AFTER MIDNIGHT." **Est.:** 1976. **Contact(s):** Michael Riordan.

E ➧ **Chicago Review Press**
814 N. Franklin St.
Chicago, IL 60610
**Concern(s):** environment; education; travel; youth. Nonfiction: project books for young people ages 10 to 18, anthropology, travel, nature, and regional topics. Published VOLUNTEER VACATIONS, a guide. **Contact(s):** Linda Matthews (Editor).

✏ ➧ **Children's Book Press**
Attn: Donna Fitch
1339 61st St.
Emeryville, CA 94608
**Concern(s):** arts; education; justice; literature; childhood; graphics; global understanding; diversity; children. "Progressive prize-winning full-color picture books for children. Bilingual and all-English tales from Nicaragua, Mexico, Central America, Southeast Asia, Puerto Rico, and the African-, Native-, Mexican-American, are among communities in North America. Features ethnic illustrations by fine artists." **Other Resources:** Receive our catalog for two years. **Est.:** 1975. **Price:** $2/ea. **Contact(s):** Harriet Rohmer.

✏ ➧ **City Lights Review**
261 Columbus Ave.
San Francisco, CA 94133
**Concern(s):** arts; media; literature. "City Lights bookstore is a great deal more than a place to purchase books. It's a cultural crossroads where several generations of writers, activists, and visionaries have gathered to trade ideas and gain inspiration. It is a great deal more than a place to read poems. Its pages feature the likes of Noam Chomsky, Alexander Cockburn, Susan Griffin, and the late Edward Abbey. The poetry, fiction, and criticism publishes focuses of our social and political landscape." **Frequency:** Irregular. **Subscription:** $9.95/yr. **Contact(s):** Lawrence Ferlinghetti.

✍ ➧ **Community Bookshelf**
Route 1, Box 155-MAC
Rutledge, MO 63563 (816)883-5543
**Affiliation:** Sandhill Farm. **Concern(s):** education; feminism; environment; economics; peace; community self-reliance; intentional communities; cooperatives; rural communities. A mail-order bookstore specializing in books on intentional community, co-ops, and other aspects of joyous alternative lifestyles and politics (e.g. feminism, ecology). "We are cooperatively run by Sandhill Farm, a small rural intentional community in northeastern Missouri. We enjoy the quality of staying small and try to answer each order quickly and personally." **Other Resources:** Free 10-page catalog available upon request. **Contact(s):** Rebecca S. Krantz, Laird Schaub

H ➧ **Compcare Publishers**
2415 Annapolis Lane
Minneapolis, MN 55441
**Concern(s):** health; family; psychology; substance abuse. Adult nonfiction; young adult nonfiction: books on recovery from addictive/compulsive behavior; emotional health; growth in personal, couple, and family relationships. **Contact(s):** Margaret Marsh (Manager).

✍ ➧ **CRISES Catalog**
1716 SW Williston Rd.
Gainesville, FL 32608 (904)335-2200
**Concern(s):** education; media; justice; environment; press. Publishes a descriptive catalog. (Planned, 1992) It will be publishing a library book-selection tool reviewing titles overlooked or misrepresented by CHOICE, LIBRARY JOURNAL, etc. To be supported by subscriptions. 150+ titles listed, organized into 24 subject areas. Most publications are interdisciplinary. Nonprofit. **Est.:** 1991. **Price:** $5/ea. **Pages:** c50. **Date Publ.:** 7/91. **Publisher:** CRISES Press, Inc.. **Contact(s):** Charles Willett (President), Lisa Barr (Secretary).

F ➧ **Crossing Press**
Box 1048
Freedom, CA 95019 (408)722-0711
**Concern(s):** feminism; health; spiritual; justice; transformation; nutrition; alternative consumer. Publisher of books on health, New Age, feminist, women's and men's studies, gay & lesbian, health (alternative solutions), new age spirituality, and cookbooks with a nutritional leaning. **Other Resources:** Partners receive newsletters and participate in special events and workshops. See ABC's for 21st Century project and EDUCATOR'S GUIDE: AN AGENDA FOR THE 21ST CENTURY. **Est.:** 1971. **Frequency:** Annual. **Price:** Catalog free. **Circ.:** 6M. **Member:** Co-op America. **Fax:** (408)722-2749. **Contact(s):** Denis Hayes (Marketing Director), John Gill (Editor/Owner). (800)777-1048.

✏ ➧ **Dawn Horse Press**
Box 3680
Clearlake, CA 95422
**Concern(s):** arts; education; literature; literacy. Publisher of progressive books and magazines. Publishes THE LAUGHING MAN; The Alternative to Scientific Materialism and RELIGIOUS PROVINCIALISM, a magazine, deals with issues of spirituality, sexuality, and health. **Est.:** 1972. **Contact(s):** Carolyn Lee (Editor).

✍ ➧ **Dawn Publications**
14618 Tyler Foote Rd.
Nevada City, CA 95959
**Concern(s):** education; spiritual; environment; childhood; transformation. Publishes books "helping people experience a sense of unity and harmony with all life...a deeper sensitivity and appreciation for the natural world." Titles: SHARING NATURE WITH CHILDREN, LISTENING TO NATURE, and SHARING THE JOY OF NATURE- all by Joseph Cornell, and CREATIVE NATURE VISUALIZATIONS by Garth Gilchrist.

J ➧ **The Denali Press**
Box 021535
Juneau, AK 99802-1535 (907)586-6014
**Concern(s):** justice; peace; Third World; refugees; minority rights; Native Americans; indigenous peoples. This press produces reference and scholarly books. Books range from a study of Alaska place names to resources for Hispanics but are centered most broadly on ethnic

and minority populations and refugees. **Est.:** 1986. **Fax:** (907)463-6780. **Contact(s):** Alan Edward Schorr (Editorial Director/Publisher).

### ✍ ◆ Department of State Publications
Publications Department
Bureau of Public Affairs
Washington, DC 20520   (202)647-6575
**Affiliation:** Bureau of Public Affairs. **Concern(s):** education. Government publications on various topics from social services, drug abuse, environmental or educational. Send for publications list.

### ✈ ◆ Dillon Press
242 Portland Ave. S.
Minneapolis, MN 55415
**Concern(s):** education; Third World; environment; travel; youth. Juvenile nonfiction: International festivals and foods, Third World countries and US States, major world cities, world geography/places of interest, environmental topics, contemporary and historical biographies for elementary and middle-grade levels, unusual or remarkable animals. **Contact(s):** Tom Schneider (Senior Editor), Lisa Erskine (Nonfiction editor).

### E ◆ Earthtrends
1118 5th St., # 1
Santa Monica, CA 90403   (310)393-2670
**Concern(s):** environment; media; economics; health; trade; alternative consumer; press. Represents green publishers including ADVERTISING AGE, BUSINESS ETHICS, EarthKeeping ENVIRONMENTAL QUARTERLY, EcoSource, Foresight Institute, GREEN MARKETING REPORT, THE GREEN CONSUMER LETTER & GREEN BUSINESS LETTER. **Other Resources:** Earthtrends also publishes NEW PARADIGM DIGEST, a bi-monthly review of emerging social and business trends leading to a sustainable world.

### E ◆ EarthWorks Press
1790 5th St.
Berkeley, CA 94710   (510)841-5866
**Concern(s):** environment; economics. Publisher of Environmental Books. List includes the #1 best-selling 50 SIMPLE THINGS YOU CAN DO TO SAVE THE EARTH, 50 SIMPLE THINGS KIDS CAN DO TO SAVE THE EARTH, THE RECYCLERS' HANDBOOK, and much more.

### $ ◆ EMC Corp.
300 York Ave.
St. Paul, MN 55101
**Concern(s):** economics; consumer. Vocational, career, and consumer education textbooks.

### ✍ ◆ Encyclopedia Brittanica Educational Corporation
310 S. Michigan Ave.
Chicago, IL 60604   (312)347-7000
**Concern(s):** education. Still one of the best reference libraries for your student at home or college.

### ✍ ◆ Enslow Publishers
Box 777
Hillside, NJ 07205
**Concern(s):** education; science; youth; childhood. Nonfiction books for young people. Areas of emphasis are children's and young adult books for ages 10-16 in areas of science, social studies, and biography. Other specialties for young people are reference books for all ages and easy reading books for teenagers. **Contact(s):** R.M. Enslow, Jr. (Editor/Publisher).

### ✍ ◆ ETC Publications
700 East Vereda Sur
Palm Springs, CA 92262-1608   (619)325-5352
**Concern(s):** education; future. "Considers timely topics in all nonfiction areas." Subjects pertain to educational management, futuristics and gifted education. Also publishes textbooks. **Est.:** 1972. **Contact(s):** Dr. Richard W. Holstrop (Senior Editor), LeeOna Holstrop (Editorial Director).

### $ ◆ Facts On File Publications
460 Park Ave. S
New York, NY 10017   (212)683-2244
**Concern(s):** economics; health; arts; trade; science. Reference and trade books on nature, business, science, health, language, history, the performing arts, etc. **Contact(s):** Gerard Helferich (Associate Publisher).

### E ◆ Falcon Press Publishing Co. Inc.
Box 1718
Helena, MT 59624   (800)582-BOOK
**Concern(s):** environment; education; wilderness; recreation; travel. Outdoors, wilderness, recreation, adventure travel. **Contact(s):** Michael S. Sample, Bill Schneider

### E ◆ Feline Press
Box 7219
Gainesville, FL 32605
**Concern(s):** environment; forests. Publishes RAINFORESTS: A Guide to Research and Tourist Facilities at Selected Tropical Forest Sites in Central and South America. **Price:** $21.95+1.50 shipping.

### F ◆ The Feminist Press
City University of New York
311 E. 94th St.
New York, NY 10128
**Concern(s):** feminism; peace. Reprints of significant "lost" fiction, memoirs, autobiographies, or other feminist work from the past; biography; original anthologies for classroom adoption; handbooks; bibliographies. "We are especially interested in international literature and the theme of women and peace." **Contact(s):** Florence Howe (Publisher).

### F ◆ Firebrand Books
1230 Ave. of the Americas
New York City, NY 14850
**Concern(s):** feminism; justice; gay/lesbian. Feminist and lesbian fiction and nonfiction. **Contact(s):** Nancy K. Bereano (Editor).

### P ◆ Four Walls Eight Windows
Box 548
New York, NY 10014   (212)463-0316
**Concern(s):** politics; arts; literature. A small press specializing in avant-garde literature and progressive politics. Publishes about 10 books a year. Unusual and thought-provoking books in all areas of concern. **Other Resources:** Free catalog, wholesale and retail. **Frequency:** 4/yr. **Office:** 39 W. 14th New York, NY 10018. (800)835-2246(ext. 123). **Contact(s):** John Oakes. (212)206-8965.

### ✍ ◆ Free Spirit Publishing
400 First Ave. N., #616
Minneapolis, MN 55401-1724   (612)338-2068
**Concern(s):** education; childhood; youth. "...offers you, and the young people in your life, the best in learning and life-style materials. Topics/titles include: THE KID'S GUIDE TO SOCIAL ACTION (foreword by Ted Danson), STRESS MANAGEMENT FOR TEENS, PLAYING SMART: A Parent's Guide to Enriching Offbeat Learning Activities for Ages 4-14." **Other Resources:** Catalog. **Est.:** 1983. **Price:** $1/ea. **Fax:** (612)337-5050. Order: (800)735-7323.

### S ◆ Friends United Press
101 Quaker Hill Dr.
Richmond, IN 47374
**Concern(s):** spiritual; faith. Nonfiction and fiction on Quaker history, biography, and Quaker faith experience. **Contact(s):** Ardith Talbot (Editor).

### S ◆ Friendship Press
Box 37844
Cincinnati, OH 45222-0844
**Affiliation:** National Council of Churches. **Concern(s):** spiritual; faith. Published the guide, MAKE A WORLD OF DIFFERENCE: Creative Activities for Global Learning. **Other:** 475 Riverside Dr., #772, New York, NY 10115

### E ◆ Fulcrum Publishing
350 Indiana St., #510
Golden, CO 80401   (303)277-1623
**Concern(s):** environment; economics; politics; travel; trade. Publishes books on nature and the environment, gardening, travel, self-help, history, business and politics. Mostly sells to bookstores. "We are focusing on nature narratives, American history, current issues, the environment, and self help." Other office locations in Concord, Massachusetts and Arlington, Virginia.

### E ◆ Gaia Catalog Co. & Bookstore
1400 Shattuck Ave., #15
Berkeley, CA 94709   (510)548-4172
**Concern(s):** environment; feminism; spiritual; music; literature; transformation. "Spirituality, ecology & multicultural arts for people with a global conscience. Books on eco-feminism & healing rituals, environmental resources & ecology for children, women's spirituality & the men's movement. Listen to the sound of the Earth speaking from Gregorian chanting to the drumming of Olatunji & Mickey Hart. Travel the world with handcrafted drums, masks, clothing & jewelry." **Other Resources:** Store and color catalog ($2) with books on ecological living, mediation music, goddess figurines, jewelry, "for renewing our connection to the Earth." **Frequency:** 2/yr.

### J ◆ Garret Park Press
Box 190
Garret Park, MD 20896   (301)946-2553
**Concern(s):** justice; feminism; education; labor; jobs; minorities.

Publishes an impressive array of directories and guidebooks with minorities and women on topics pertaining to career, education, finances and many other concerns. **Contact(s):** Robert Calvert, Jr.

### ✍ ◆ Global Education Book Catalog
10200 Jefferson Blvd.
Box 802
Culver City, CA 90232-0802 (800)421-4246
**Affiliation:** Social Studies School Service. **Concern(s):** education; media; global. For more than 20 years, SSSS has provided educators with the highest quality supplementary materials and the convenience of one-source ordering. This catalog represents our best effort to offer you a wide range of opinions on key topics across the curriculum: area studies, cross-cultural studies, world geography, and international issues. (310)839-2436.

### ✍ ◆ Graham-Conley Press
1936 E. Belmont Dr.
Tempe, AZ 85284   (602)491-1177
**Concern(s):** education. "Our primary market is libraries. We are publishers of reference books, guides, directories, handbooks, and computer software. Our most recent publication is a microcomputer indexing program and manual." **Est.:** 1982. **Contact(s):** Ellen Conley.

### E ◆ Green Perspectives
Box 111
Burlington, VT 05402
**Affiliation:** Green Program Project. **Concern(s):** environment; politics; Green. A publications list of ecological and Green publications.

### J ◆ Greenwood Press
88 Post Rd. West
Westport, CT 06881
**Concern(s):** justice; politics; demographics. Publishes significant directories and guides with the Social Scientist in mind.

### ✍ ◆ Harbinger House
2802 N. Alvernon Way
Tucson, AZ 85712   (602)326-9595
**Concern(s):** education; health; media; psychology; youth; childhood. Adult nonfiction focusing on social issues and personal growth; very little adult fiction. Children's picture books; stories for middle readers; nonfiction (Natural History Series). "Books of Integrity for Children and Adults." **Fax:** (602)326-8684. (800)759-9945. **Contact(s):** Zdenek Gerych (Editor-in-chief), Jeffrey H. Lockridge (Children's Books Editor).

### F ◆ Haworth Press Inc.
101 W. 31 St. W
New York, NY 10001   (212)563-4240
**Concern(s):** feminism; health. Publisher of WOMEN AND HEALTH (a periodical) and a series of books on women's health. Titles include HEALTH CARE OF THE FEMALE ADOLESCENT; HEALTH NEEDS OF WOMEN AS THEY AGE; EMBRYOS; ETHICS AND WOMENS RIGHTS; among others.

### H ◆ Health Communications, Inc.
3201 S.W. 15th St.
Deerfield Beach, FL 33442
**Concern(s):** health; psychology; substance abuse; self-help. Books on self-help recovery for adults and juveniles. **Contact(s):** Marie Stilkind (Editor).

### ✍ ◆ Heath & Company, D.C.
125 Spring St.
Lexington, MA 02173
**Concern(s):** education. Textbooks for schools and colleges. Professional books (Lexington Books Div.). Software and related educational material. **Contact(s):** Vince Duggan.

### E ◆ Hemingway Western Studies Series
Boise State University
1910 University Dr.
Boise, ID 83725
**Concern(s):** environment; arts; politics. Nonfiction relating to the Inter-Mountain West (Rockies) in areas of history, political science, anthropology, natural sciences, film, fine arts, literary history or criticism. **Contact(s):** Tom Trusky (Editor).

### S ◆ Herald Press
616 Walnut Ave.
Scottsdale, PA 15683   (412)887-8500
**Affiliation:** Mennonite Publishing House. **Concern(s):** spiritual; faith. Nonprofit. **Est.:** 1941.

### ✍ ◆ Hollowbrook Publishing, Inc.
Box 757
Wakefield, NH 03872   (603)522-3338
**Concern(s):** education; Third World; peace; feminism; spiritual. A

book publisher who publishes progressive academic books on topics such as nuclear weapons control, Third World politics, aspects of feminism, and Buddhism. For a catalog of our books please send $1.00 for postage and handling. **Fax:** (603)522-6305. **Contact(s):** Wyatt Benner (Book Editor).

### ✍ ▶ Holt Associates, Inc.
2269 Massachusetts Ave.
Cambridge, MA 02140 (617)864-3100

**Concern(s):** education; childhood. Books and materials for children and adults learning outside of school. **Other Resources:** Bimonthly magazine - GROWING WITHOUT SCHOOLING. Free catalog for self-addressed envelope with stamp enough for two ounce-mail.

### ✍ ▶ Home Education Press
Box 1083
Tonasket, WA 98859-1083 (509)486-1351

**Concern(s):** education; homeschooling. Publishes books on home schooling and alternative education, including ALTERNATIVE IN EDUCATION, THE HOME SCHOOL READER, ThHE HOME SCHOOL PRIMER. Also publishes HOME EDUCATION magazine. **Other Resources:** Free catalog of home schooling books—60 titles. Publishes GUIDE TO RESOURCES IN HOLISTIC EDUCATION, an extensive and excellent directory of alternative educators, periodicals, organizations, books and publishers for the educator and parent. **Contact(s):** Mark Hegener, Helen Hegener

### ♿ ▶ Human Policy Press Catalogue
Box 127, University Station
Syracuse, NY 13210 (315)443-3851

**Affiliation:** Center on Human Policy. **Concern(s):** health; education; justice; disabled; disabled's rights. An independent press started by the Center on Human Policy in 1974 to promote positive attitudes towards people with disabilities. In the 1990s, the press continues as a strong voice for the full integration of people with disabilities in the community. Goal: to improve society's literacy about disabilities by demonstrating that the greatest obstacles faced by people with disabilities are socially imposed. Nonprofit. **Est.:** 1974. **Frequency:** Annual. **Bulk:** 20% off/24. **Fax:** (315)443-4338. **Contact(s):** Julie Ann Racino (Managing Director), Rachael Zubal (Publications Coordinator). **Other:** 200 Huntington Hall, Syracuse, NY 13244

### H ▶ Humanics Publications
1482 Mescaslin St. NW
Atlanta, GA 30309 (800)874-8844

**Concern(s):** health; education; psychology; holism; self-help. "...provides to the reader books of value that inspire one to new awareness in self-worth and wellness. It's New Age imprint presents innovative topics on personal growth, wellness, modern Taoism, as well as children's books. Our books involve the reader in a quest for new realities. Works of high literary merit. Health, psychology, sociology, education, business, New Age, general self-help, teacher's resources, and educational guides." **Other Resources:** Send for free catalog. **Contact(s):** Robert Grayson Hall (Executive Editor), Gary B. Wilson (President). (404)874-2176.

### H ▶ IBS Press, Inc.
744 Pier Ave.
Santa Monica, CA 90405 (800)234-6485

**Concern(s):** health; nutrition; death/dying; holism; AIDS; psychology; self-help. "A pioneer in areas of Self-Help, Psychology, Grief Recovery, Death/Dying, Spiritual Psychology, and AIDS Education/Awareness. Hospices, doctors, therapists, nurses, ministers and many other turn to us for books which inspire, uplift, and deepen their understanding of life and death." **Other Resources:** Catalog available. **Fax:** (310)314-8268. (310)450-6485.

### E ▶ Idea House Publishing Co.
2019 Delaware Ave.
Wilmington, DE 19806 (302)571-9570

**Concern(s):** environment; economics; forests. Its first book: THE SOUL OF ECONOMIES. Plans to plant trees to make up for paper use, and guarantee that the paper companies they use cut no virgin forests.

### H ▶ Impact Publishers
Box 1094
San Luis Obispo, CA 93406 (805)543-5911

**Concern(s):** health; education; psychology; self-help; youth; childhood. "Practical, affordable self-help books on relationships, personal growth, families, communities, and health, by expert professionals in the human services. Conversational style, free of sexism, racism, ageism, and jargon. Since 1970, millions of satisfied readers have recommended 'books with impact' to friends in need." **Other Resources:** Free catalog.

### ✍ ▶ Independent Publishers Group
814 N. Franklin St.
Chicago, IL 60610 (800)888-4741

**Concern(s):** education; politics; arts. "Thirty of the most innovative and acclaimed small presses in the country are represented in its catalog. Here are hundreds of books on politics and current affairs, art, dance, theater, domestic and foreign travel, music, photography, myth, children's activity books, and much more." **Other Resources:** Catalog. **Est.:** 1987.

### ✐ ▶ Indiana University Press
10th and Morton Sts.
Bloomington, IN 47405

**Concern(s):** arts; justice; culture; music. Scholarly nonfiction, especially cultural studies, archaeology, and anthropology, etc.

### T ▶ Indonesia Publications
7538 Newberry Lane
Lanham-Seabrook, MD 20706 (301)552-4465

**Concern(s):** Third World; justice; peace; foreign policy; Pacific/Pacific Rim. Produces and markets internationally a range of periodicals and books on contemporary Indonesia, governments, academics, the mass media, and libraries. It is currently facilitating the establishment of a new independent organization which will conduct monitoring, resources, and advocacy on a broad range of dominant Indonesian issues, including politics, human rights, economics, the environment and social problems. **Fax:** (301)552-3251. **Contact(s):** John MacDougall (Editor).

### H ▶ Inner Traditions International
One Park St.
Rochester, VT 05767 (802)767-3174

**Concern(s):** health; eth alternative consumer; holism; psychology. "For fifteen years, it has published quality books on alternative health and healing, bodywork, esoteric philosophy, metaphysics, Eastern and Western mystery traditions, and self-development. Here are more than 200 titles to help you achieve personal health and spiritual growth." **Other Resources:** Free illustrated catalog. **Est.:** 1975. **Contact(s):** Ehud C. Sperling (President/Publisher), Leslie Kolket (Managing Editor).

### M ▶ Institute for Media Analysis - Publications List
145 W. 4th St.
New York, NY 10012 (212)254-1061

**Affiliation:** Institute for Media Analysis. **Concern(s):** media; politics; media watch; responsibility; government accountability. A list of publications that are concerned with media and government responsibility and accountability. Nonprofit. **Fax:** (212)254-9598.

### ✍ ▶ Interaction Book Company
7208 Cornelia Dr.
Edina, MN 55435

**Concern(s):** education. Publishes books, videos, films, and monographs on the cooperative learning methods developed by David and Roger Johnson at the Universtiy of Minnesota. Includes theory, research, and practical application of cooperative learning.

### ✈ ▶ Intercultural Press
Box 700
Yarmouth, ME 10021 (207)846-5168

**Concern(s):** education; travel. "...any book with an international or domestic intercultural, multicultural or cross-cultural focus, i.e., a focus on the cultural factors in personal, social, political or economic relations. Our books are published for educators in the intercultural field, business people who ar involved with international business, and anyone else who works in an international occupation or has had intercultural experience." **Contact(s):** David S. Hoopes (Editor-in-chief), Margaret D. Pusch.

### P ▶ International Publishers
239 W. 23rd St.
New York, NY 10011 (212)366-9816

**Concern(s):** politics; media; education; labor. "Books on world affairs, socialism, labor, culture, and philosophy are all reviewed in this selection. All books and pamphlets by this publisher promote basic social change. It is worth buying a book from their catalog just to be put on their book review mailing list."-C.C. **Other Resources:** BOOK NEWSLETTER. **Est.:** 1970. **Frequency:** 2/yr. **Subscription:** Free to customers. **Contact(s):** B. Smith.

### E ▶ Island Press
1718 Connecticut Ave. NW, #300
Washington, DC 20009 (202)232-7933

**Concern(s):** environment; conservation. Serves the worldwide community of environmental professionals with state-of-the-art books on conservation and the environment. **Other Resources:** Publishes 30 titles per year, distributes books of other publishers. Publications list available. Publishes the yearly ANNUAL ENVIRONMENTAL SOURCEBOOK, a free catalog. See, also, Center for Resource Economics. **Est.:** 1978. **Fax:** (202)234-1328. **Contact(s):** Charles Savitt (President/Publisher), Will Farnam (Marketing Director). **Other:** Box 7, Covelo, CA 95428 Elizabeth Mook

### E ▶ Johnson Books, Inc.
1880 S. 57th Court
Boulder, CO 80301

**Concern(s):** environment; education; recreation; travel. Nonfiction: environmental subjects, archaeology, geology, natural history, astronomy, travel guides, outdoor guidebooks, fly fishing, regional. **Contact(s):** Rebecca Herr (Editor Director).

### S ▶ Jossey-Bass Inc.
350 Sansome St.
San Francisco, CA 94104

**Concern(s):** spiritual; volunteers; philanthropy. Published BY THE PEOPLE: A History of Americans and Volunteers, and THE THIRD AMERICA, covering all aspects of the nonprofit sectors of the US.

### ✍ ▶ Knowledge Systems, Inc.
7777 W. Morris St.
Indianapolis, IN 46231 (317)244-8806

**Concern(s):** education; spiritual; health; transformation; holism. Catalog provides books and other resources for those seeking ways to understand and act creatively in our constantly changing times. Topics: understanding the times, relevant life-styles, creative transitions, healthy boundaries, financial independence, cultural patterns, healing experience, planetary peace, inventive learning, future consciousness, systems creativity, sacred life, and classic roadmaps. **Other Resources:** Adult non-fiction books which are listed in the GUIDEBOOK FOR THE 90'S with a triangle at the beginning of the description of the book. **Est.:** 1986. **Frequency:** 2/yr. **Subscription:** $4/yr. **Price:** $2/ea. **Bulk:** 50% off/24. **Pages:** 33. **Circ.:** 15M. **Date Publ.:** 4/91. **Labels:** 75. **Fax:** (317)248-1503. (800)999-8517. **Contact(s):** Marcia Knight (Marketing), Margaret Lazear (Editor). David Speicher , President.

### $ ▶ Kumarian Press
630 Oakwood Ave., #119
West Hartford, CT 06110-1529 (203)953-0214

**Concern(s):** economics; politics; peace; demographics; education.

### H ▶ Leading Edge Review
Box 24068
Minneapolis, MN 55424 (612)929-9534

**Concern(s):** health; spiritual; transformation. A New Age bookstore newsletter which previews 50 of the latest New Age books and cassettes. It is published quarterly and purchased by bookstores throughout the country, which in turn, distribute them free to customers. **Contact(s):** Sheila Grams (Writer/Publisher).

### ✍ ▶ The Learning Works, Inc.
Box 6187
Santa Barbara, CA 93160 (800)235-5767

**Concern(s):** education; environment. Publishes innovative and creative books for children (6-16). Environmental books include EARTH BOOK FOR KIDS: Activities to Help Heal the Environment, MY EARTH BOOK: Puzzles, Projects, Facts & Fun, ANIMAL ECOGRAMS, GARBAGE GAMES, COMPREHENSION COLLECTION (endangered wildlife). Series books "Birds, MAMMALS, FISHES and REPTILES.

### ✈ ▶ Lonely Planet
112 Linden St.
Oakland, CA 94607

**Concern(s):** education; travel. "The leading publisher of guides for the independent traveler. With over 100 titles in print, It's travel survival kits, shoestring guides, walking guides, and phrasebooks provide practical information for a range of travel styles and budgets to destinations all over the world. New titles cover Vietnam, Laos, and Cambodia, Iceland, Greenland, and the Faroe Islands, and Kenya." **Other Resources:** Newsletter/booklist Free.

### ❂ ▶ Lorien House
Box 1112
Black Mountain, NC 28711 (704)669-6211

**Concern(s):** energy; appropriate technology. Introduced the world to solar energy in 1974 with the first technical, hands-on-book (still available), and is continuing research with an eye to future books in solar and other technological answers to this world's problems. **Other Resources:** Please write for annual price list. **Est.:** 1969. **Contact(s):** David A. Wilson (Owner/President).

### F ▶ McFarland & Co.
Box 611
Jefferson, NC 28940 (919)246-4460

**Concern(s):** feminism; media; peace; politics; environment; economics. Published many of the books listed in Macrocosm, particularly reference books of a progressive nature. Write or call for a free catalog.

### ♥ ▶ Meadowbrook Press
18318 Minnetonka Blvd.
Deephaven, MN 55391

**Concern(s):** family; feminism; education; youth; childhood; birth.

Upbeat, useful books on pregnancy, childbirth and parenting, travel, humor, children's activities, 60,000 words.

**S ◆ Mennonite Publishing House**
See Herald Press.

**H ◆ Metamorphous Press**
Box 10616
3249 N.W. 29th Ave.
Portland, OR 97210
**Concern(s):** health; economics; psychology; youth; trade. Business, education, health, how-to, humor, performance arts, psychology, sports and recreation, and women's topics. Also children's books that promote self-esteem/self-reliance. "We select books that provide the tools to help people improve their lives and the lives of those around them." **Contact(s):** Gene Radeka (Acquisitions Editor).

**F ◆ Midmarch Arts Press**
300 Riverside Dr.
New York, NY 10025    (212)666-6990
**Concern(s):** feminism; arts. Publishes books on women's art history, resources and biographies. Organizes and coordinates international conferences on arts and women, and exhibitions, as well as maintaining an archive on women artists. **Other Resources:** Send for publications list. See WHOLE ARTS DIRECTORY, and GUIDE TO WOMEN'S ART ORGANIZATIONS & DIRECTORY FOR THE ARTS. **Est.:** 1972.

**✈ ◆ Moon Publications**
722 Wall St.
Chico, CA 95928    (916)345-5473
**Concern(s):** education; press; travel. Portable travel guides with maps, illustrations, and subject/place names index.

**✍ ◆ Mountain Meadows Press**
Box 447
Kooskia, ID 83539
**Concern(s):** education; family; homeschooling. Has published THE INTERACTIVE PARENT: How to Help Your Child Survive and Succeed in the Public Schools by Dr. Linwood Laughy; HOME SCHOOL: Taking the First Step by Borg Hendrickson, and other books on home education and parental involvement.

**E ◆ The Mountaineers Books**
306 Second Ave. W.,
Seattle, WA 98119
**Concern(s):** environment; recreation; travel. Nonfiction, noncompetitive aspects of outdoor sports such as mountaineering, backpacking, canoeing, kayaking, bicycling, skiing. Field guides, regional histories, biographies of outdoor people; accounts of expeditions. **Contact(s):** Margaret Foster-Finan (Editor-Manager).

**E ◆ Namchi United Enterprises**
Box 33852, Station D
Vancouver, BC V6J 4L6 Canada    (604)736-6931
**Concern(s):** environment. Publisher of environmental information guide - GOOD PLANETS ARE HARD TO FIND! **Contact(s):** Ronald M. Bazar.

**E ◆ The Nature Book Society Catalogue**
RBC/NBS
Box 10852
Des Moine, IA 50336-0875
**Concern(s):** environment; education. A fine offering of books for the nature lover. **Other Resources:** Catalog.

**E ◆ The Nature Library**
150 Nassau St., #1020
New York, NY 10038-1516    (212)608-3327
**Concern(s):** environment; education. A publications list available.

**E ◆ Naturegraph Publishers**
Box 1075
Happy Camp, CA 96039
**Concern(s):** environment; health; justice; land; holism; Native Americans. Nonfiction: Native American culture, natural history, outdoor living, land and gardening, holistic learning and health, Indian lore, crafts, and how-to. **Contact(s):** Barbara Brown (Editor).

**E ◆ New Alchemy Institute Catalogue**
237 Hatchville Rd.
East Falmouth, MA 02536    (508)564-6301
**Affiliation:** New Alchemy Institute. **Concern(s):** environment; agriculture; sustainability. A catalogue of books and products for ecological living. **Est.:** 1969. **Contact(s):** Bill O'Neill (Public Information Coordinator).

**F ◆ New Books on Women and Feminism**
University of Wisconsin
112 A Memorial Library
Madison, WI 53706    (608)263-5754

**Concern(s):** feminism; education. "A subject-arranged, indexed bibliography of new titles in women's studies, listing books and periodicals." **Frequency:** 4/yr. **Subscription:** $20, $38 institution. **Price:** $2.75 sample. **Pages:** 75. **Circ.:** 1.5M. **Contact(s):** Susan Searing, Carolyn Wilson

**H ◆ New Health Communications**
See DELICIOUS! and ORGANIC TIMES (periodicals).

**J ◆ New Humanity Press**
Box 215
Berkeley, CA 94701
**Concern(s):** justice; peace; economics; social justice. "Our slant is looking for the 'truth', however we find it, and looking to improve our uniquely human condition, with a view to universal justice and peace-seeking harmony for all life everywhere." **Est.:** 1986.

**H ◆ New Idea Press, Inc.**
Box 13683
Boulder, CO 80308-3683    (303)666-5242
**Concern(s):** health; education; substance abuse; psychology; childhood. "Publishes popular health, psychology, social change and self-help books aimed at paraprofessionals and general readership. Marketing methods include sales through nonprofit organizations. Innovative, unorthodox and controversial approaches welcome." Presently looking for manuscripts on addiction (physiological basis), and children's books on mental illness and grieving. **Est.:** 1985. **Contact(s):** Martha Gorman (Editor).

**S ◆ New Leaf Distributing Co.**
5425 Tulane Dr. SW
Atlanta, GA 30336    (404)691-6996
**Concern(s):** spiritual; health; transformation; holism. Employee-owned wholesale distributor of New Age and wholistic books and materials. **Contact(s):** Richard Bellezza.

**◉ ◆ New Science Library**
Shambhala Publications, Inc.
300 Massachusetts Ave.
Boston, MA 02115
**Concern(s):** energy; environment; education; spiritual; science; transformation. **Other Resources:** Publications list available.

**F ◆ New Seed Press**
Box 9488
Berkeley, CA 94709
**Concern(s):** feminism; arts; education; racism; sexism; childhood. "We are a small feminist collective committed to publishing non-sexist, non-racist stories for children which actively confront issues of sexism, racism, classism. We are currently soliciting manuscripts with active female characters who take responsibility for themselves and their lives, stories that challenge assumptions about the inferiority of women." Fiction and the arts. **Est.:** 1972.

**E ◆ New Society Publishers**
4527 Springfield Ave.
Philadelphia, PA 19143-0582    (215)382-6543
**Concern(s):** environment; peace; justice; Third World; nonviolence; ecology; development; planning; worker ownership. The nation's only trade publishing house specifically dedicated to producing resources, promoting fundamental social change through nonviolent action. "We produce books on peace, ecology, human rights, development and Third World issues, worker self-management, nonviolent forms of childcaring, etc." **Est.:** 1981. **Contact(s):** David H. Albert (Direct Marketing Manager), T. L. Hill (Marketing Manager).

**$ ◆ New Worlds Press**
Box 56
Terre Haute, IN 47808    (812)232-6323
**Concern(s):** economics; politics; justice. Published THE WORLD'S WASTED WEALTH: THE POLITICAL ECONOMY OF WASTE by J.W. Smith. "We are twice as rich as we realize, we are wasting half our wealth. Turning only a part of that wasted production towards building tools for the Third World could eliminate world poverty in only 45 years and actually cost nothing. That wealth is currently wasted anyway." An excellent in-depth overview of the economic waste inherent in all sectors of American economics. **Other Resources:** J.W. Smith is starting The Institute for Economic Democracy, see organizations. THE WORLD'S WASTED WEALTH 2 is due to be out January, 1993. **Contact(s):** Ralph Hansen (Executive Director).

**⚙ ◆ NewSage Press**
Box 41029
Pasadena, CA 91114-8029    (818)795-0266
**Concern(s):** peace; justice; feminism. Committed to publishing books of quality in content as well as production. Publishes books that "touch people's lives, and breaks through stereotypes and statistics to humanize humanity." Our specialty is photo essay books. **Contact(s):** Maureen Michelson (Publisher). **Other:** 1341 E. Colorado Blvd., #205, Pasadena, CA 91106

**J ◆ Nolo Press**
950 Parker St.
Berkeley, CA 94710    (510)549-2001
**Concern(s):** justice; politics; economics; labor; reform; discrimination; social justice; civil liberties. Publisher of books and software that help people undertake legal tasks without lawyers. **Other Resources:** Quarterly Newsletter-NOLO NEWS, with articles on legal topics of interest to self helpers and the general public—also, Lawyer Jokes. **Est.:** 1971. **Contact(s):** Steve Elias (Associate Publisher).

**⚘ ◆ Ocean Tree Books**
Box 1295
Santa Fe, NM 87504    (505)983-1412
**Affiliation:** Friends of Peace Pilgrim. **Concern(s):** peace; future; spiritual; education; transformation; global understanding. Publishes "books for making peace in a changing world." Our Peacewatch Edition titles include: Gandhi's SEVEN STEPS TO GLOBAL CHANGE, PEACE PILGRIM, VICTORIES WITHOUT VIOLENCE, and Mikhail Gorbachev's A ROAD TO THE FUTURE. Functions also as a service, ethical/spiritual, and future-oriented, and is the source of Barbara Marx Hubbard's monumental work of spiritual futurism, THE BOOK OF CO-CREATION, and her introductory work, HAPPY BIRTHDAY PLANET EARTH. **Other Resources:** An annual catalog and an occasional newsletter titled BLOSSOMS AND BRANCHES which contains reflections of personal commentary, news of forthcoming books, and reports on the "walking with a purpose" pilgrimage tradition, travels & discovery. Nonprofit. **Est.:** 1983. **Frequency:** Irregular. **Subscription:** Donation. **Bulk:** 40% off/24. **Publisher:** Ocean Tree Books. **Labels:** 790. **Contact(s):** Richard Polese (Director). **Other:** Friends of Peace Pilgrim, 43480 Cedar Ave., Hemet, CA 92344.

**⚘ ◆ One World Publishing**
Box 423
Notre Dame, IN 46556
**Concern(s):** peace; spiritual; world order; transformation. Promotes themes, ideas presented in book, ONE WORLD: The Approach to Permanent Peace on Earth and the General Happiness of Mankind. **Contact(s):** John Kiang (Director).

**S ◆ Orbis Books Bulletin**
Maryknoll
New York, NY 10545    (800)258-5838
**Concern(s):** spiritual; media; justice; Third World; development; interfaith. "The Maryknoll Missionaries' social justice books are reviewed every 6 months in these pages. Liberation theology, hunger, the social gospel and Third World development are a few topics reviewed for the publisher's customers. Publishes all of Third World Resources' books."-C.C. **Est.:** 1960. **Frequency:** 2/yr. **Price:** Free. **Publisher:** Orbis Books.

**F ◆ Oryx Press**
4041 N. Central Ave.
Phoenix, AZ 85004-1483    (602)54-6156
**Concern(s):** feminism; justice; health. Publishes significant directories and guides on children's and women's issues, substance abuse and other health issues. **Est.:** 1975. **Contact(s):** Susan Slesinger (Editorial Vice President).

**E ◆ Outdoor Books**
The Nature Library
150 Nassau St., #1020
New York, NY 10038-1516    (212)608-3327
**Concern(s):** environment; recreation. A free catalog of useful guides for those who love the outdoors, camping, hiking or nature walking.

**H ◆ Oxford University Press**
200 Madison Ave.
New York, NY 10016    (212)679-7300
**Concern(s):** health; arts; education; literature; science. Authoritative books on literature, history, philosophy, etc.; college textbooks, medical, and reference books. (800)451-7556.

**✍ ◆ Pantheon Books**
See Schocken Books.

**S ◆ Parallax Press Catalog**
Box 7355
Berkeley, CA 94707    (510)525-0101
**Concern(s):** spiritual; interfaith; transformation. "Books and tapes by Thich Nhat Hanh and others on mindful awareness and social responsibility. Titles include: BEING PEACE, THE SUN MY HEART, MOON BAMBOO. Other new books: IN THE FOOTSTEPS OF GANDHI: Interviews with Spiritual Social Activists, including Dalai Lama, Desmond Tutu, Ram Dass, Joanna Macy, Joan Baez, and Gary Snyder."

**✍ ◆ Parent Child Press**
Box 767
Altoona, PA 16603

**Concern(s):** education; feminism; family; childhood. Publishes books and other materials dedicated to enhancing early learning. Titles include PEACEFUL CHILDREN, PEACEFUL WORLD: THE CHALLENGE OF MARIA MONTESORRI, A Parents Guide to the Montessorri Classroom, TUTORING IS CARING: You Can Help Someone To Read and other books, pamphlets, and slides on parenting and Montessorri education. Produces posters, prints, and activities to encourage art appreciation by young children.

✍ ♦ **Parenting Press, Inc.**
Box 75267
Seattle, WA 98115    (206)364-2900
**Concern(s):** education; family; youth; child care. Publisher of books to help improve the competence of parents and children, as well as to provide a work environment that supports family life. Promotes cooperative approaches.

T ♦ **Path Press**
53 W. Jackson Blvd.
Chicago, IL 60604
**Concern(s):** Third World; Africa; indigenous peoples. Quality books by and about African-Americans and Third-World peoples. **Contact(s):** Herman C. Gilbert (Editor).

☙ ♦ **Peace Education Resources Catalog: BOOKS**
Pyle Center
Box 1183
Wilmington, OH 45177    (513)382-5338
**Affiliation:** Wilmington College Peace Resource Center. **Concern(s):** peace; education; conflict resolution; anti-nuclear; global understanding. Books, curriculum materials, cassette tapes, and posters on peacemaking, conflict resolution, nonviolence, nuclear war, Hiroshima/Nagasaki. Resources for all ages. Nonprofit. **Est.:** 1975. **Frequency:** 1-2/yr. **Subscription:** Donation. **Pages:** 20. **Contact(s):** Helen Wiegel (Director, PRC).

☙ ♦ **Peace Press**
540 Pacific Ave.
Santa Rosa, CA 95404
**Concern(s):** peace.

✍ ♦ **Plenum Publishing Corp.**
233 Spring St.
New York, NY 10013    (212)620-8000
**Concern(s):** education; justice; energy; science. Trade nonfiction on science, social science, and humanities. Also publishes a wide variety of Journals on these subjects. **Other Resources:** Published GLOBAL ALERT: THE OZONE POLLUTION CRISIS by Jack Fishman and Robert Kalish. **Est.:** 1947. **Contact(s):** Linda Greenspan Regan (Senior Editor).

☙ ♦ **Plowshares Press, Inc.**
139 Raritan Ave.
Highland Park, NJ 08904    (201)937-9222
**Concern(s):** peace; environment. A worker-managed union print shop which accepts work only from nonprofit or public-interest organizations and individuals working for peace, justice, and a safe planet. Nonprofit.

✍ ♦ **Porter Sargent Publishing, Inc.**
11 Beacon St., #1400
Boston, MA 02108    (617)523-1670
**Concern(s):** education. "Handbook Series and Special Education Series offers standard, definitive reference works in private education and writings and texts in special education." The Extending Horizon Series is an outspoken, unconventional series that presents topics of importance in contemporary affairs and the social sciences." **Other Resources:** Published THE DIRECTORY FOR EXCEPTIONAL CHILDREN. **Est.:** 1914.

P ♦ **Prevailing Winds Research**
Box 23511
Santa Barbara, CA 93121    (805)566-8016
**Concern(s):** politics; demographics; peace; Third World; economics; health; CIA; government accountability; corporate responsibility; Mid-East; national security; crime; poverty; AIDS; public health. The works of John Judge, John Stockwell, Barbara Honegger, Daniel Sheehan, Tony Avergan, Bo Gritz, and others, in reprints or tapes. Read or hear about the Washington Drug Cartel, poverty, the S & L Rip-off, the CIA, the media, or AIDS. Audio tapes of the Other Americas Radio shows, Noam Chomsky, David Barsamian, and much more. **Other Resources:** See DOSSIER (periodicals).

✍ ♦ **Publications Exchange**
8306 Mills Dr., #241N
Miami, FL 33183    (305)387-0853
**Concern(s):** education; Third World; global understanding. Latest in Cuban books and magazines now available through direct importer and sent by US mail. Write or call for free brochure.

H ♦ **Pyramid Books New-Age Collection**
133 W. 72nd St.
New York, NY 11209    (800)621-6015
**Concern(s):** health; spiritual; arts; holism; transformation; music. "Beautiful four-color catalog features hundreds of New Age books plus a large selection of New Age music and self-help tapes - metaphysical jewelry - natural quartz points, pyramids and spheres, healing stones - sculptures, gifts, and tarot decks. Pyramid Books is the largest and most complete New Age catalog." **Pages:** 32. **Publisher:** Pyramid Books.

S ♦ **Quest Books**
306 W. Geneva Rd.
Box 270
Wheaton, IL 60189-0270
**Affiliation:** Theosophical Publishing House. **Concern(s):** spiritual; health; interfaith; holism; transformation. "Major established publisher with books and tapes on astrology, yoga, psychism, holistic health, occultism, Eastern mysticism, comparative religion, and nature." **Other Resources:** Color catalog. **Contact(s):** Shirley Nicholson (Senior Editor).

H ♦ **R & E Publishing**
Box 2008
Saratoga, CA 95070    (415)494-1112
**Concern(s):** health. A wide variety of self-help, how-to, and health books, generally with a progressive slant. **Est.:** 1967. **Contact(s):** R. Reed (Publisher).

✍ ♦ **Resource Publications, Inc.**
160 E. Virginia St., #290
San Jose, CA 95112    (408)286-8505
**Concern(s):** education; family. Books with emphasis on cooperative activities and communal celebrations, both for families and for educators. Recent titles include LEARNING TO LIVE TOGETHER AT HOME AND IN THE WORLD and MAKING ART TOGETHER STEP-BY-STEP. **Est.:** 1973. **Contact(s):** William Burns (Publisher), Kenneth Guentert (Editorial Director).

✍ ♦ **Richard C. Owen Publishers, Inc.**
135 Katonah Ave.
Katonah, NY 10536    (800)336-5588
**Concern(s):** education; childhood. Reading programs and classroom materials fully devoted to a child-centered, meaning-centered, Whole Language approach—including "Ready to Read", the innovative national reading program of New Zealand. Also offers a large selection of professional and staff development titles to acquaint educators with Whole Language theory methods, as well as in-service workshops. **Other Resources:** Publishes the quarterly newsletter TEACHERS NETWORKING: THE WHOLE LANGUAGE NEWSLETTER.

✍ ♦ **Robert Briggs Associates**
400 Second St., #108
Lake Oswego, OR 97034-3127
**Concern(s):** education. Publisher of pamphlets and books by notable intellectuals.

H ♦ **Rodale Press**
33 E. Minor St.
Emmaus, PA 19098
**Concern(s):** health; environment. Books on health, gardening, homeowner projects, cookbooks, inspirational topics, pop psychology, woodworking, natural history. **Contact(s):** Pat Corpora.

✍ ♦ **Scarecrow Press**
Box 656
Metuchen, NJ 08840    (201)548-8600
**Concern(s):** education; justice; spiritual; arts; media. "Emphasis on reference books, scholarly monographs, some professional textbooks. Dominant subject ares include: Cinema, women, minorities, music, literature, library science, social work, parapsychology." **Est.:** 1950. **Contact(s):** Norman Horrocks (Vice President, Editorial), Barbara Lee (Senior Editor).

☼ ♦ **Schocken Books**
201 E. 50th St.
New York, NY 10022    (212)751-2600
**Affiliation:** Pantheon Books. **Concern(s):** energy; environment; feminism; education; arts; spiritual. General nonfiction: Judaica, women's-studies, education, art history. Also, published RAINBOOK: Resources for Appropriate Technology.

✍ ♦ **Seven Locks Press**
Box 27
Cabin John, MD 20818    (301)320-2130
**Concern(s):** education; Third World; community. "Books that promise to enlighten public policy; also books of regional interest that are entertaining." Biography, textbook, and reference. Published ENTANGLING ALLIANCES: How the Third World Shares Our Lives, and CITIZEN DIPLOMATS. "Literate, intelligent, socially conscious men and women are our readers." **Other Resources:** Free book catalog. **Est.:** 1975. **Contact(s):** James McGrath (President/Publisher).

E ♦ **Sierra Club Books**
730 Polk St.
San Francisco, CA 94109    (415)776-2211
**Concern(s):** environment; education; recreation; youth; conservation. Nonfiction: environment, natural history, the sciences, outdoors and regional guidebooks; nature photography; juvenile fiction and nonfiction. Published HANDBOOK FOR PEACE AND ENVIRONMENT.

P ♦ **South End Press**
116 Botolph St.
Boston, MA 02115    (617)266-0629
**Concern(s):** politics. A collective that has published over 150 nonfiction books covering a wide range of progressive political topics. Nonprofit. Box 7816, Edison, NJ 08818-7916.

H ♦ **Spring Publications, Inc.**
Box 222069
Dallas, TX 75222    (214)943-4093
**Concern(s):** health; psychology. "Jungian background but critical reflection on Jungian tradition; intellectual but neither academic nor New Age." **Contact(s):** James Hillman (Editor), Mary Helen Sullivan (Managing Editor).

H ♦ **St. Martin's Press**
175 5th Ave.
New York, NY 10010    (212)674-5151
**Concern(s):** health; spiritual; transformation. Publishes books and distributes books from small presses. Gardening, do-it-yourself, personal transformation, health, etc. Retail and wholesale.

E ♦ **Stackpole Books**
Box 1831, Dept. Coop
Harrisburg, PA 17105    (800)READ-NOW
**Concern(s):** environment; recreation; wilderness. It has published outdoor books, nature guides, and how-to books for over 60 years. Featuring the guide SOFT PATH on the minimum impact approach to understanding, preserving, and enjoying our natural resources, from the wilderness professionals of the National Outdoor Leadership School (NOLS).

M ♦ **Steve Davis Publishing**
Box 190831
Dallas, TX 75219    (214)954-4469
**Concern(s):** media; press. Reference material that attempts to take a fresh approach to timely topic and offers the reader helpful information. Published THE WRITER'S YELLOW PAGES. **Other Resources:** Book catalog for SASE. **Est.:** 1982. **Contact(s):** Steve Davis (Publisher).

E ♦ **Stillpoint Publishing International Inc.**
Box 640
Walpole, NH 03608    (603)756-9281
**Concern(s):** environment; spiritual; activism; transformation. Publishing goal is to provide insightful information and practical tools to help reshape lives, to reflect universal values that honor humanity, the Earth, and the sacred. **Est.:** 1983. **Fax:** (603)756-9282. **Contact(s):** Gisela Rank (Associate Director of Publicity), Von Braschler (Marketing Director).

E ♦ **Stone Wall Press, Inc.**
1241 30th St. NW.
Washington, DC 20007
**Concern(s):** environment; conservation; wildlife/endangered species. Publishing a small, select list of conservation, natural history, and "outdoor" books since 1972. Titles include WILDLIFE EXTINCTION, PLANT EXTINCTION: A Global Crisis, VANISHING FISHES OF NORTH AMERICA, COYOTES. Send self-addressed stamped enveloped for free brochure. **Est.:** 1972. **Contact(s):** H. Wheelwright (Publisher).

H ♦ **Strawberry Hill Press**
2595 15th Ave.
San Francisco, CA 94127
**Concern(s):** health; Third World. Nonfiction: biography, autobiography, history, cooking, health, how-to philosophy, performance arts, and Third World. **Contact(s):** Carolyn Soto (Editor).

✍ ♦ **Sudbury Valley School Press**
2 Winch St.
Framington, MA 01701
**Concern(s):** education; childhood. A series of books and booklets that describe day-to-day life at an innovative alternative school, and the radical child-rearing philosophy that guides it. Current titles: FREE AT LAST, THE SUDBURY VALLEY SCHOOL EXPERIENCE, and CHILD REARING.

**E ◆ Sunstone Publications**
RD 3, Box 100A
Cooperstown, NY 13326 (607)547-8207
**Concern(s):** environment; agriculture; spiritual. Books on personal growth, planetary healing, and exploring the sky, including THE EARTH STEWARD'S HANDBOOK. Also, flower presses and other nature products.

**E ◆ Survival News Service**
Box 42152
Los Angeles, CA 90042 (213)255-9502
**Concern(s):** environment; urban; economics; energy; justice; crime; recycling; cooperatives; appropriate technology. Publishes BURWOOD JOURNAL and books on recycling, urban survival, plants, wild foods, thinking and Native Americans, generally their own material. **Contact(s):** Christopher Nyerges, Vernon Devans.

**◢ ◆ SUNY Press**
State University Plaza
Albany, NY 12246-0001
**Concern(s):** education. Current catalog NEW VISIONS FOR A DISTINGUISHED PROFESSION...EDUCATION includes several titles of interest, including EDUCATION, MODERNITY, AND FRACTURED MEANING by Donald W. Oliver.

**◢ ◆ Tarcher, Inc., Jeremy P.**
5858 Wilshire Blvd.
Los Angeles, CA 90036
**Concern(s):** education; spiritual; health; feminism; psychology; transformation. General nonfiction: psychology, spirituality, creativity, personal development, health and fitness, women's concerns, science for the layperson, etc. **Contact(s):** Jeremy P. Tarcher (Editor-in-chief).

**◢ ◆ Teachers College Press**
Teachers College, Columbia University
1234 Amsterdam Ave.
New York, NY 10027 (212)678-3929
**Concern(s):** education; peace; holism; childhood. A long list of significant titles includes books by Douglas Sloan, and important writer in holistic education, and Betty Reardon on peace education. **Other Resources:** Free book catalog. **Contact(s):** Carol L. Saltz (Director).

**P ◆ Telos**
431 E. 12th St.
New York, NY 10009 (212)228-6479
**Concern(s):** politics; arts; culture; literature. A journal that deals with left-wing politics and philosophy and literary criticism. Publishes about 2 books a year. **Est.:** 1968. **Subscription:** $26, $60 institution. **Price:** $7.50. $15 institution. **Pages:** 256. **Circ.:** 3.5M. **Publisher:** Telos Press. **Contact(s):** Paul Piccone.

**E ◆ Ten Speed Press**
Box 7123
Berkeley, CA 94707 (510)845-8414
**Concern(s):** environment; health; recreation; jobs; self-help. Self-help and how-to on careers, recreation, etc.; natural science, history, cookbooks. "We publish trade books." **Contact(s):** Mariah Bear (Editor).

**S ◆ Theosophical Publishing House**
See Quest Books.

**E ◆ Tilden Press**
1526 Connecticut Ave. NW
Washington, DC 20036 (202)332-1700
**Concern(s):** environment. Publishes THE GREEN CONSUMER and THE GREEN CONSUMER NEWSLETTER to help people lead more environmentally sound lives. (800)955-4733.

**T ◆ Touch the Future: An Agenda for Global Education in America**
Interaction
1717 Massachusetts Ave. NW
Washington, DC 20036 (202)667-8227
**Affiliation:** Interaction. **Concern(s):** Third World; education; development; hunger. A publications brochure available. **Contact(s):** Dr. Peter J. Davies. 200 Park Ave. South, New York, NY 10003. (212)777-8210.

**◢ ◆ University of Arizona Press**
1230 N. Park Ave., #102
Tucson, AZ 85719
**Concern(s):** education; justice; Third World; science; Native Americans; Latin America. Scholarly nonfiction: anthropology, history, the sciences, natural history, American Indian and Latin American studies, regional or national topics, books of personal essays. **Contact(s):** Gregory McNamee (Senior Editor), Barbara Beatty (Acquiring Editor).

**J ◆ University of Minnesota Press**
2037 University Ave., S.E.,
Minneapolis, MN 55414
**Concern(s):** justice; Third World; arts; minority rights; culture; analysis. Fiction: minority and Third World. Nonfiction: media studies, literary theory, philosophy, cultural criticism, regional titles. **Contact(s):** Terry Cochran (Editor-in-chief).

**◢ ◆ University of the Trees Press**
Box 66
Boulder Creek, CA 95006
**Concern(s):** education; holism; childhood. Learning materials for teaching the whole child, including step-by-step books full of photos and illustrations, and tapes that teach children visualization and meditation.

**◢ ◆ University Press of America**
4720 Boston Way
Lanham, MD 20706 (301)459-3366
**Concern(s):** education; justice; politics; spiritual. College/graduate level textbooks of a scholarly nature concerned with the following topics: environment, economics, business, psychology, political science, Black and African studies, philosophy, religion, sociology, music, art, literature, drama and education. **Est.:** 1975. **Contact(s):** James E. Lyons.

**◢ ◆ US Government Books Catalog**
US Government Printing Office
Stop: SM
Washington, DC 20401 (202)783-3238
**Concern(s):** education; politics. Lists hundreds of useful and popular books and subscriptions published by the Government. Government books on research, census information, business, medicine, law, and regulations, statistics, foreign trade, manufacturing, science, and more. **Publisher:** US Government Printing Office.

**F ◆ Volcano Press**
Box 270
Volcano, CA 95689
**Concern(s):** feminism; health; arts; education; justice; youth; battered women. Woman-owned publisher of books on women's health and social issues, domestic violence, art books, and children's books. **Other Resources:** Free catalog, wholesale and retail.

**E ◆ Wellington Press**
Route 7, Box 1256
Tallahassee, FL 32308
**Concern(s):** environment; peace; economics. Books and games related to peace, the environment, personal finances, and philosophy. **Other Resources:** Free brochure, wholesale and retail.

**P ◆ West End Press**
Box 27334
Albuquerque, NM 87125
**Concern(s):** politics. "Politically progressive material favored." **Est.:** 1976.

**◢ ◆ Westview Press**
5500 Central Ave.
Boulder, CO 80301 (303)444-3541
**Concern(s):** education. Books concern a wide variety of progressive issues aimed at the college level. Published a guide: TO CELBRATE: Reshaping Holidays.

**E ◆ Wildlife Book Review**
629 Green St.
Allentown, PA 18102 (215)434-1637
**Affiliation:** Wildlife Information Center. **Concern(s):** environment; wildlife/endangered species; conservation.

**$ ◆ William Morrow & Co., Inc.**
1350 Avenue of the Americas
New York, NY 10105 (212)261-6500
**Concern(s):** economics; politics. Published MEGATRENDS 2000, by John Naisbitt/Pat Aburdene. **Est.:** 1926. **Contact(s):** James D. Landis (Publisher), Andrew Ambraziejus (Managing Editor).

**◢ ◆ Williamson Publishing Company Inc.**
1110 North 8th Ave., #C
Gainesville, FL 32601 (802)425-2102
**Concern(s):** education; health; feminism; economics; childhood. "Our areas of concentration are children's activity books, people oriented business and psychology books, women's issues, cookbooks, international marketing, gardening, small-scale livestock raising, family housing (all aspects), health and education." **Est.:** 1983.

**H ◆ Wilshire Book Co.**
12015 Sherman Rd.
North Hollywood, CA 91605 (818)765-8579
**Concern(s):** health; psychology. Psychological self-help with strong motivational messages. Adult fables. **Contact(s):** Melvin Powers (Editor-Director).

**F ◆ Wingbow Press**
2929 Fifth St.
Berkeley, CA 94710
**Concern(s):** feminism; health; psychology. Nonfiction: women's interests, health, psychology. **Contact(s):** Randy Fingland (Editor).

**☙ ◆ Word Works**
2888 Bluff St., #405
Boulder, CO 80301 (303)449-9059
**Concern(s):** peace. Nonfiction book production: editing, laser printing, publisher search service. Recent title, ALTERNATIVE SECURITY: Living Without Nuclear Deterrence. **Other Resources:** Free brochure.

**H ◆ Workman Publishing Co.**
708 Broadway
New York, NY 10003 (212)254-5900
**Concern(s):** health. Mid-size publisher and distributor of books and calendars: health, humor and gift, hobbies and crafts, cooking, travel. **Est.:** 1969.

**H ◆ World Health Organization Publications Catalogue**
World Health Organization
49 Sheridan Ave.
Albany, NY 12210
**Affiliation:** World Health Organization. **Concern(s):** health; public health. This catalogue provides bibliographic data for all publications officially issued by the WHO since its establishment in 1948. Well over 2,000 books and reports are included, representing more than four decades of effort to support international health work through the provision of objective, validated information. **Est.:** 1948. **Pages:** 294.

**M ◆ Yankee Books**
Box 1248, 62 Bayview St.
Camden, ME 04843
**Concern(s):** media; environment; press; bioregionalism. Books relating specifically to New England: cooking, crafts, environmental issues; also gardening, nature, humor, popular history books. **Contact(s):** Linda Spencer (Senior Editor).

**◢ ◆ The Zephyr Press**
3316 N. Chapel Ave.
Box 13448-C, Dept.
Tucson, AZ 85732-3448 (602)322-5090
**Concern(s):** education; environment; childhood; students; youth; global understanding. "Cutting-edge materials for innovative education. Here's your source for teaching materials that make a difference. Books, games, tapes, and other resources for—Global Awareness, Self-Awareness, Whole Language, Invention & Architecture, Whole-Brain Learning, Math & Science, Arts & Humanities, and Thinking Skills." Fantastic curriculum material for teachers. Relevant books, curriculum guides, and networking information. **Other Resources:** Has introduced a large line of learning packets and publishes a biannual newsletter and a catalog. **Frequency:** Annual. **Pages:** 127.

# ⑤ Businesses & Catalogues

## A♦ Abundant Life
Box 772
Port Townsend, WA 98368  (206)385-5660
**Affiliation:** World Seed Fund. **Concern(s):** agriculture; Third World; alternative markets; green consumer. A mail order seed company that deals with a variety of seeds from trees to vegetables. Seeds are open pollinated not hybrids. Thousands of free packets of seed are sent to Third World groups. Send a list of your special interests. **Other Resources:** Catalog, Bookstore, and gallery. **Fax:** (206)385-4874. **Contact(s):** Forest Shomer.

## ✎♦ Acorn Designs
5066 Mott Evans Rd.
Trumansburg, NY 14886(607)387-3424
**Concern(s):** arts; environment; peace; recycling. Recycled paper with wildlife and peace graphics; stationery, notepads, t-shirts, totes, bumper stickers. Implements the "Green Tax", a convenient way for consumers to pay for environmental restoration, education and nonviolent direct action. **Other Resources:** Free catalog. Retail and wholesale. **Member:** Co-op America.

## P★ Action Resource Guide
Box 597996
Chicago, IL 60659  (312)764-5752
**Affiliation:** Soapbox Junction Ltd.. **Concern(s):** politics; economics; fundraising; alternative markets; grassroots organizing. A pro-activism and street education coalition produces this catalog containing products from over 80 activist organizations. The items are books, posters, stickers, magazines, and many other items from a variety of special interest groups. "Our policy is to accept anyone into the coalition that sends a request." **Est.:** 1990. **Frequency:** 2,3/yr. **Subscription:** $3/yr. **Price:** $1/ea. **Bulk:** 50% off/24. **Pages:** 8-24. **Circ.:** 10M. **Contact(s):** Ashley Owens (President).

## ☼♦ Adamson Design
1015 Gayley Ave., #1228
Los Angeles, CA 90024  (310)208-6606
**Concern(s):** energy; urban; transportation. Alternate propulsion company. Architectural, industrial, environmental.

## H♦ Advanced Medical Nutrition
Box 5012
Hayward, CA 94545  (510)783-6969
**Concern(s):** health; nutrition; alternative consumer. Mail order house that deals with vitamins, nutrition and dietary concerns with health and healing. **Office:** 2247 National Ave. Hayward, CA 94545.

## E♦ Aeroscopic IAQ
5245 San Fernando Rd.-West
Los Angeles, CA 90039  (213)245-3024
**Concern(s):** environment; health; pollution; hazardous/toxic waste. Provides remediation services, specializing in fire, flood, and chemical incidents involving pesticides, fumigants, paints, adhesives, building materials. Dedicated to environmental hygiene, "we offer Hygi-Flo activated carbon filters for odor and pollution control, Dust Arrestor renewable electrostatic dust filters, localized air purification equipment, HVAC upgrading for pollution control & HVAC cleaning services." **Est.:** 1958.

## ☙♦ AIKI Works
Box 7845
Aspen, CO 81612  (303)925-7099
**Concern(s):** peace; economics; justice; conflict resolution; trade; victims' rights. Provides workshops and corporate training on conflict resolution using the principles of the martial art of Aikido. It is the work of Thomas Crum, author of THE MAGIC OF CONFLICT (Simon & Schuster, 1987) and other resource materials. **Est.:** 1986. **Fax:** (303)925-4532. **Fax:** (716)924-2799. **Contact(s):** Thomas Crum (President), Judith Warner (Administrator). (716)924-7302.

## H♦ Air Control Technologies/Summit Environmental
22647 Ventura Blvd., #239
Woodland Hills, CA 91364  (818)893-8584
**Concern(s):** health; environment; air pollution; hazardous/toxic waste. A company whose purpose is to create healthy working and living environments by eliminating toxins or other airborne contaminants which are known to cause illness. "We treat and remediate sick homes, create toxin-free interiors, design and build homes and workplaces free of indoor air pollution." (818)594-4143.

## $♦ Albion Financial Associates
2550 9th St., #318
Berkeley, CA 94710  (510)486-8333
**Concern(s):** economics; socially-responsible investing. **Contact(s):** Bonnie Albion.

## E♦ Alcoa Recycling Co., Inc.
1501 Alcoa Bldg.
Pittsburgh, PA 15219  (412)553-4645
**Concern(s):** environment; recycling. Offers advice on where and how to recycle aluminum cans and publishes a step-by-step guide to setting up a can collection program or full scale center.

## ☼★ Alternative Energy Retailer
Box 2180
Waterbury, CT 06722  (203)755-0158
**Concern(s):** energy; economics; trade; alternative consumer market; conservation. "We are a trade publication for the solid fuel industry. The appliances these folks produce help the little guy reduce the greenhouse effect by improving efficiency. We're a resource catalog." Feature articles for retailers of alternative energy products: wood, coal, and fireplace products and services. Interviews with successful retailers, stressing the how-to. B&W photos. **Frequency:** 12/yr. **Subscription:** $32/yr. **Price:** $3/ea. **Circ.:** 14M. **Contact(s):** Ed Easley (Editor).

## T♦ Alternative Gift Markets
HCR 6682
Lucerne Valley, CA 92356  (619)248-7106
**Concern(s):** Third World; justice; economics; alternative markets; development; hunger. "Presents for the homeless, the sick and the hungry; God's Family in Need; Medicine, food, water, shelter, livestock and education; Gifts for our planet and for people facing disasters; Presents that nourish self-dignity and well-being; Unique gifts that build peace and understanding in our global village." They collect donations for a large variety of worthy causes. **Other Resources:** ALTERNATIVE GIFT CATALOG. **Frequency:** Annual. **Office:** 9656 Palomar Trail, Lucerne Valley, CA 92356.

## T♦ Alternative Trading News
611 W. Wayne St.
Fort Wayne, IN 46802  (219)422-1650
**Affiliation:** Friends of the Third World. **Concern(s):** Third World; economics; demographics; environment; poverty; alternative markets; trade; green consumer; Central America. A small, national organization involved in "alternative trading": seeking to effect positive social change through marketing of ecologically sound, nonviolent, cooperatively produced products along with educational information, e.g., "we market coffee from Nicaraguan co-ops with information on the US trade embargo which promotes independence from the economics of apartheid." Marketing is done by volunteers, individuals or groups across the US. **Other Resources:** Catalog. **Dues:** $5, $10/yr. groups. **Frequency:** 4/yr. **Circ.:** 20M. **Contact(s):** Jim Goetsch (Administrator).

## ↞♦ Amberwood
Route 1, Box 206
Milner, GA 30257  (404)358-2991
**Concern(s):** economics; health; environment; alternative consumer; vegetarian; animal rights. You can be assured that none of the products available through this company have caused the exploitation, suffering or death of any animal. Since 1977 they have had a special interest in the problems of the wild burro by providing a permanent home "Amberwood Sanctuary". This was made possible with donations and purchases of Amberwoods wide range of animal-free products. **Other Resources:** Send for a free catalog. **Est.:** 1977.

## $♦ American Capital Strategies
3 Bethesda Metro Center, #350
Bethesda, MD 20814  (301)951-6122
**Concern(s):** economics; labor; worker ownership. Employee-owned investment banking firm specializing in ESOP (employee stock ownership plan) transactions. **Other Resources:** Free brochure. **Member:** Co-op America.

## E★ American Recycling Market, Inc.
Box 577
Box 577
Ogdensburg, NY 13669  (800)267-0707
**Concern(s):** environment; economics; recycling; green consumer. **Other Resources:** Publishes THE OFFICIAL RECYCLED PRODUCTS GUIDE, THE OFFICIAL RPG REPORTER, and runs RecyleLine, a BBS database. **Est.:** 1985. **Fax:** (315)471-3258. **Contact(s):** Mike Fraser.

## $♦ Amy Domini - Loring, Wolcott, & Coolidge
230 Congress St.
Boston, MA 02110  (617)523-6531
**Concern(s):** economics; socially-responsible investing. Amy Domini, co-author of "Ethical Investments," manages trusts with social criteria. **Member:** Co-op America.

## ✐♦ Animal Town Cooperative Ventures Catalog
Box 485
Healdsburg, CA 95448-0485(800)445-8642
**Affiliation:** Animal Town Company. **Concern(s):** education; environment; wildlife/endangered species; childhood. A mail order company offering cooperative games, books, and playthings for children that emphasize the environment. "We strive to educate others to being environmentally responsible and stress family togetherness through our products." **Est.:** 1976. **Frequency:** 2/yr. **Contact(s):** Ken Kolsbun, Jann Kolsbun.

## H♦ Applied Ergonomics
13734 39th Ave. NE
Seattle, WA 98125-3810  (206)361-1890
**Concern(s):** health; labor; occupational safety. "Ergonomics" is the relationship between the body and the work environment. Injury-prevention programs and recovery strategies. **Other Resources:** Free brochure available. **Member:** Co-op America.

## A♦ Arrowhead Mills, Inc.
Box 2059
Hereford, TX 79045  (806)364-0730
**Concern(s):** agriculture; health; environment; economics; alternative consumer; nutrition; organic; green consumer. Producers of fine organic grains and legumes.

## T♦ Artesanias Indigenas
7200 Sarah
St. Louis, MO 63143  (314)644-3722
**Concern(s):** Third World; economics; cooperatives; Latin America. Sells products made by cooperatives and Indian communities in Ecuador: wool and cotton clothing, hats, bags, and tapestries. Wholesale only. **Member:** Co-op America.

## E♦ Artful Solutions
618 Kenbrook Dr., Dept. CW1
Silver Spring, MD 20902
**Concern(s):** environment; green consumer. Catalog.

## E♦ Ashdun Industries, Inc.
400 Sylvan Ave.
Englewood Cliffs, NJ 07632  (201)569-3600
**Concern(s):** environment; recycling. Marketer & distributor of CARE (Consumer Action to Restore the Environment) household paper & cleaning products, stationery, cat litter, coffee filters & trash segregation bags. Also markets under Envirocare, Project Green, Enviroquest, AWARE & S.A.F.E. (Sound Alternatives for the Environment) brands nationally. (800)544-1892.

**E ♦ Atlantic Recycled Paper Co.**
Box 11021
Baltimore, MD 21212 (301)323-2676
**Concern(s):** environment; recycling. "100% recycled copier paper, printing paper, envelopes, computer paper, legal pads, notepads, loose-leaf paper, fax paper; paper towels, napkins, facial tissue, toilet paper, paper plates, bags & gift wrap." **Other Resources:** Catalog available. **Price:** $1/ea. **Office:** 332 Rossiter Ave. Baltimore, MD 21212. **Contact(s):** Daniel Jerrems.

**D ♦ Avon Hills Consumer Housing Coop, Inc.**
1400 Drexelgate Pkwy.
Rochester Hills, MI 48063 (313)652-0800
**Concern(s):** demographics; economics; housing; cooperatives. Offers quality, affordable housing to low and moderate income families. **Member:** Co-op America.

**♥ ♦ Baby Works**
11725 NW West Rd.
Portland, OR 97229 (503)645-4349
**Concern(s):** family; economics; environment; green consumer. Various style cotton diapers that rival throwaway diapers. Also, training pants, all-night pants, and many related items. Catalog. (800)422-2910. **Contact(s):** Paula.

**♥ ♦ Babykins International, Inc.**
#4-3531 Jacombs Rd.
Richmond, BC V6V 1Z8 Canada (604)270-6116
**Concern(s):** family; environment; economics; alternative consumer; green consumer. Manufacturer of high quality, environmental baby products, cotton diapering system (patented) & related products such as blankets, cloths, and changing pads. Supplier to retail, diaper services & hospitals.

**✈ ♦ Backroads Bicycle Touring**
1516 5th St., #H99
Berkeley, CA 94710 (800)245-3874
**Concern(s):** education; environment; energy; recreation; travel; transportation. "Call for our award-winning 70-page catalog featuring bicycling vacations in North America, Europe, Asia, and the Pacific. Find out why over 75% of all Backroads guests in 1990 were return customers or referred by their friends."

**$ ♦ Bank Credit Card OBSERVER**
342 Wall St.
Princeton, NJ 08204 (800)847-7378
**Concern(s):** economics; socially-responsible investing.

**A ♦ Barclay Recycling**
75 Ingram Dr.
Toronto, ON M6M 2M2 Canada (416)240-8227
**Concern(s):** agriculture; environment; recycling. This company has been providing the means, with its product The Soilsaver, to recycle kitchen and yard waste into valuable compost for over 11 years. Over 300,000 people have chosen the Soilsaver to compost their kitchen and yard waste.

**E ♦ Baubiologie's Hardware Catalog**
1199 Forest Ave. #125
Pacific Grove, CA 93950 (408)372-8626
**Concern(s):** environment; economics; alternative markets; green consumer. Healthful alternatives in building, decorating, gardening and home maintenance. Non-toxic products and meters for testing various forms of contamination.

**A ♦ Beneficial Insectary**
14751 Oak Run Rd.
Oak Run, CA 96069
**Concern(s):** agriculture; environment; organic. "We produce beneficial insects for biological pest control." Catalog.

**✈ ♦ Biological Journeys**
1696 Ocean Dr.
McKinleyville, CA 95521 (800)548-7555
**Concern(s):** education; environment; wildlife/endangered species; travel; recreation. A Natural history vacation with Biological Journeys offers something special for everyone. They have several winter and spring trips featuring whales and dolphins in the waters off the Baja peninsula. **Other Resources:** Save the Whales will receive a $100 if you mention them upon making reservations.

**E ♦ Blue rhubarb, inc.**
Old Creamery Rd.
Harmony, CA 93435 (800)926-1017
**Concern(s):** energy; economics; green consumer. Maker of the EcoSac(TM) Shopping System and other environmentally-friendly products, shares 10% of their pre-tax profits to help organizations that are working to restore and maintain the health of the planet. Products are available wholesale and retail.

**H ♦ The Body Shop**
45 Horsehill Rd.
Hanover Technical Center
Cedar Knolls, NJ 07927-2003
**Concern(s):** health; environment; economics; animal rights; alternative consumer. Offers innovative and effective products for your skin and hair. "We are environmentally conscious, use naturally based ingredients in minimal packaging, and we're against animal testing. Our products are honest and straight-forward -- and they smell great!" **Other Resources:** Free catalog. **Member:** Co-op America. **Contact(s):** Anita Roddick (Founder).

**✈ ♦ Boreal Birding & Nature Tours**
Box 1224
Banff, AL T0L 0C0 Canada (403)762-5190
**Concern(s):** education; environment; wildlife/endangered species; travel. 100+ species of birds, Great Grey, Boreal & Hawk Owls, 21 species of warblers, whooping crane nesting sites. Timber wolves, wood buffalo, moose, deer & bear, in a unique mosaic of wildlife habitats. The lodge, located in a spectacular wilderness, features photographic safaris and tours for the beginner.

**A ♦ Bountiful Gardens**
5798 Ridgewood Rd.
Willits, CA 94590
**Concern(s):** agriculture; organic. Catalog of a wide variety of organic seeds.

**E ♦ Brush Dance**
218 Cleveland Court
Mill Valley, CA 94941 (415)389-6228
**Concern(s):** environment; arts; recycling; green consumer; graphics. Designs and distributes recycled paper products and environmental gifts through a mail order catalog and to retailers. Cards, wrapping paper, stationery with messages and designs that connect us to each other and our Earth. **Other Resources:** Children's art contest to protect the rainforest. **Est.:** 1989. **Frequency:** 4/yr. **Contact(s):** Mark Lesser (President), Lee Klinger Lesser (Vice President).

**✈ ♦ Budget Europe**
Box 8401-LP
Ann Arbor, MI 48107 (313)668-0529
**Concern(s):** education; energy; travel; recreation; transportation. Inexpensive self-reliant travel in Europe, bike trips for novices and pros, trains, buses, hitching, hostels, camping. Updated each spring. Also conducts bike tours (ask). Information free.

**$ ♦ Calvert Group**
4550 Montgomery Ave.
Bethesda, MD 20814 (301)951-4814
**Concern(s):** economics; socially-responsible investing; alternative markets. Offers the nation's first and largest family of socially and environmentally responsible mutual funds. Calvert Social Investment Fund, offering stock bond, money market and balanced investment options, Calvert-Ariel Growth Fund and Calvert-Ariel Appreciation Fund have proven that enlightened investors can profit while pooling resources to encourage positive change. **Est.:** 1976. **Fax:** (301)754-7820. (301)951-4801. **Contact(s):** Steven J. Schueth (Vice President), Reed Gligorovic (Product Coordinator). (301)952-4815.

**$ ♦ The Catalyst Group**
139 Main St., #606
Brattleboro, VT 05301 (802)254-8144
**Concern(s):** economics; environment; energy; trade; recycling; cooperatives; networking. A networking and consulting company promoting socially concerned businesses and investment practices. Provides detailed reports tailored to clients' specific criteria. Consults with private investors to help them make informed decisions and work efficiently with their advisors. Financial and consulting services to businesses involved in the environmental market, especially waste management, energy control and production, ESOPs, and co-ops. **Member:** Co-op America. **Contact(s):** Blake Ross.

**H ♦ Chem-Free Exterminating Alternatives**
1711 E. 20th St.
Signal Hill, CA 90806 (800)833-7773
**Concern(s):** health; environment; hazardous/toxic waste; pesticides. "The safe and responsible option in termite control! We apply a patented forced air heating process that kills termites employing a full saturation technique. When it concerns the health of your family, it is the answer in safe termite eradication. Chemical free. Toxic free. Pollutant free." (310)985-3114.

**A ♦ Chemfree Environment**
16763 Hymus Blvd.
Kirkland, QC Canada (514)630-4400
**Concern(s):** agriculture; environment; pesticides. Biological insecticide for gardens and commercial agriculture. (800)833-7773 (USA). **Contact(s):** Gary Shepard.

**A ♦ Cherry Hill Cannery, Inc.**
Barre-Montpelier Rd.
Mail Route 1
Barre, VT 05641 (802)479-2558
**Concern(s):** agriculture; economics; health; cooperatives; nutrition; organic. A worker-owned cooperative making natural and organic foods: maple syrup, apple butter, assorted fruit sauces - over 120 items. **Other Resources:** Free catalog. **Member:** Co-op America.

**✍ ♦ Child's Work, Child's Play**
Center for Applied Psychology
3rd Fl., 441 N. 5th St.
Philadelphia, PA 19123
**Concern(s):** education; health; childhood. A catalog addressing the mental health needs of children and their families through play. **Other Resources:** Catalog is free.

**$ ♦ Chrysalis Money Consultants**
21 Linwood St.
Arlington, MA 02174 (617)648-0776
**Concern(s):** economics; urban; socially-responsible investing. Assists with financial and lifeplanning, such as vocational development, ethical investment, joint ownership, managing inherited wealth, and resolving family conflict. **Member:** Co-op America.

**E ♦ Clean Earth Solutions**
15061 Encanto Dr.
Sherman Oaks, CA 91403 (818)986-5110
**Concern(s):** environment; education; recycling. Recycles usable items to make functional and educational toys. **Member:** Co-op America.

**$ ♦ Clean Yield Group**
Box 1880
Greensboro Bend, VT 05842 (802)533-7178
**Concern(s):** economics; socially-responsible investing. A family of financial management and research publications dedicated to serving the socially responsible investor. **Other Resources:** See CLEAN YIELD newsletter. **Contact(s):** Rian Fried.

**E ♦ A Clear Alternative**
8707 West Lane
Magnolia, TX 77355
**Concern(s):** environment; economics; alternative markets; green consumer. Mail order catalog for alternatives to todays products. **Contact(s):** Lu Ann Matarelli.

**E ♦ Co-Aqua**
2369 Bourne Ave.
St. Paul, MN 55108 (612)647-0694
**Concern(s):** environment; labor; cooperatives; water; analysis. Consulting cooperative providing information on environmentally sound uses and management of water resources. **Member:** Co-op America.

**$ ♦ Co-op Alumni Association**
250 Rainbow Lane
Richmond, KY 40475 (606)623-0695
**Concern(s):** economics; cooperatives; unions. An association of co-op members continuing to develop cooperatives and credit unions. Publishes "Cooperative/Credit Union Dictionary," listing names and addresses of all co-ops and credit unions in the US. **Member:** Co-op America.

**$ ♦ Co-op America Alternative Catalog**
2100 M St. NW, #310
Washington, DC 20063 (202)872-5307
**Affiliation:** Co-op America. **Concern(s):** economics; environment; health; cooperatives; alternative markets; socially-responsible investing; corporate responsibility; green consumer; alternative consumer. This is a catalog of Co-op America's "socially responsible" products. Products are from small business; some are volunteer-run groups. Not all are co-ops, but all of them are in some way "socially responsible." It is our goal to direct the consumer to these businesses and develop an alternative market. Natural fiber clothing; third world crafts, safe household cleansers, jewelry and more. **Other Resources:** Many of the descriptions that are found in Macrocosm USA were furnished by Co-op America. Many thanks to all their good work and contributions to this project. **Price:** $1/ea. **Pages:** 16. **Date Publ.:** Every Fall. **Contact(s):** Jyotsna Sreenivasar.

**$ ♦ Co-op Resources & Service Project (CRSP)**
3551 White House Place
Los Angeles, CA 90004
**Concern(s):** economics; cooperatives; community investment; trade; socially-responsible investing; community investment; community self-reliance. Education, training, and development for all kinds of cooperatives. Sponsors a local barter system, a revolving loan fund, the Ecological Urban Village, the Shared Housing Network. **Other**

**Resources:** Newsletter. **Subscription:** $10/yr. **Member:** Co-op America.

### $ ♦ Common Good Loan Fund
1320 Fenwick Lane, #600
Silver Springs, MD 20910    (301)565-0053
**Concern(s):** economics; socially-responsible investing. Makes loans to intermediaries which support low-income housing, worker-owned cooperatives, and women & minority owned businesses. Information available for investors and borrowers. **Member:** Co-op America.

### $ ♦ Community Capital Bank
111 Livingston St.
Brooklyn, NY 11201
**Concern(s):** economics; environment; trade; community investment. A community development bank whose funds are dedicated to housing and small businesses in low to moderate income neighborhoods.

### $ ♦ Community Economic and Ecological Development Institute (CEED)
1807 2nd St., Studio 2
Santa Fe, NM 87501    (505)986-1401
**Concern(s):** economics; environment; health; arts; socially-responsible investing; culture. Helps local community create a socially responsible culture: sales of crafts and ecological products, revolving loan fund, healing arts center, "business incubator," and more. **Other Resources:** See periodicals for SEEDLING newsletter and NEW WEALTH journal. Nonprofit. **Member:** Co-op America.

### T ♦ Community Products, Inc.
RD#2, Box 1950
Montpelier, VT 05602    (802)229-1840
**Concern(s):** Third World; environment; socially-responsible investing; forests. Makes "Rainforest Crunch," a cashew and Brazil nut buttercrunch candy. Buys its nuts directly from forest peoples and donates 40% of its profits to rainforest preservation organizations. **Member:** Co-op America. **Contact(s):** Martha Broad.

### E ♦ Community Recycling and Resource Recovery
9189 De Garmo St.
Sun Valley, CA 91352    (213)875-0587
**Concern(s):** environment; recycling; waste management. Commercial and industrial recycling programs. Waste processing and recyclable material recovery at our Material Recovery Facility. Waste paper conversion into paper pulp under name of Reprocell(TM). Manufacture of pulp products including liquid and oil absorbent, hydroseeding and erosion control materials.

### ☌ ♦ The Compassionate Consumer
Box 27
Jericho, NY 11753    (718)445-4134
**Concern(s):** environment; economics; animal rights; alternative consumer. Mail order sales of cruelty-free products - cosmetics, body care, cleaners. **Member:** Co-op America.

### ☌ ♦ Compassionate Shopper
Beauty Without Cruelty
175 W. 12th St., #16G
New York, NY 10011    (212)989-8073
**Concern(s):** economics; environment; alternative markets; animal rights; green consumer. Catalog.

### E ♦ Confab Companies
2301 Dupont Dr., #150
Irvine, CA 92715    (714)955-2690
**Concern(s):** environment; economics; alternative markets; recycling; green consumer. "Today's Choice" has environmental products in the paper towel, bath tissue, facial tissue, napkins, feminine hygiene pads & baby wipe categories. Its product claims include non-dioxin bleaching process on all products and insuring, whenever possible, products are made from recycled materials and are recyclable.

### E ♦ Conservation Concepts
932 W. 9th St.
Upland, CA 91786
**Concern(s):** environment; water; conservation. Conservation is no longer an option, it's a social responsibility. Conservation Concepts shows you how to meet the mandated water cutbacks with the newest technology in water conservation - The Flush and Save System.

### E ♦ Conservatree Paper Co.
10 Lombard St., #250
San Francisco, CA 94111    (415)433-1000
**Concern(s):** environment; forestry; conservation; recycling. Produces environmentally sound papers for bulk (4 cartons or more) for users. Recommends other sources for small quantity users. The country's largest wholesaler specializing exclusively in recycled paper. Information Services also assist in the writing of recycled paper legislation on a local, state, and federal level. **Other Resources:**

Greeline Membership Program and ESP NEWS. **Est.:** 1976. **Fax:** (415)391-7890. **Contact(s):** David Assmann (Vice President). (800)522-9200.

### $ ♦ Consumers United Insurance Company
2100 M St. NW, #207
Washington, DC 20063    (202)872-5390
**Concern(s):** economics; health; labor; trade; national health; worker ownership; socially-responsible investing; Medicare. Worker-owned insurance company offering health and life insurance to members of nonprofits and cooperatives. Invests premiums in community development. Underwriter for Co-op America health insurance. Offers Healthstar Major Medical; Medicare supplement; Lifestar Term Life; and, Tax-deferred Annuity. **Member:** Co-op America. (800)255-4432. **Contact(s):** Jim Gibbons. (800)424-9711. (202)872-5709.

### $ ♦ Cooperative Fund of New England
108 Kenyon St.
Hartford, CT 06105    (203)523-4305
**Concern(s):** economics; labor; socially-responsible investing; community investment; cooperatives. Put your money into co-ops. This community loan fund takes investments from individuals and groups ($1,000 minimum) and lends it to coops in New England. As a socially responsible investment CFNE is safe - no investor has lost dollars. As a financier of co-ops, AFNE is a valuable resource as bank credit availability tightens. Donations are also gratefully accepted. **Est.:** 1975. **Contact(s):** Rebecca Dunn (Executive Director).

### $ ♦ Creative Financial Concepts
3701 Old Court Rd., #21
Baltimore, MD 21208    (301)484-7077
**Concern(s):** economics; socially-responsible investing. Socially responsible investment advisor and broker. Donates 10% of gross revenue to nonprofits. **Member:** Co-op America.

### E ♦ Cyclean
2000 S. Church
Georgetown, TX 78626    (512)863-4117
**Concern(s):** environment; urban; recycling; conservation. Recycles asphalt pavement, saving landfill space, eliminating the need to quarry new rock, and saving oil and money. Used by City of Los Angeles, among others. **Member:** Co-op America.

### T ♦ The Daily Planet
Box 522
Berkeley, CA 94701    (800)858-2665
**Concern(s):** Third World; economics; peace; alternative markets; East-West. "The world's most unusual catalog, wasn't content just bringing you funky, timely gifts like rainforest cookies, recycled crafts, Dan Quayle miscellany and cool t-shirts. So we put Russian Dressing, our emporium of Eastern Bloc memorabilia, on the flipside. 2 catalogs in 1! 10% of the proceeds to with-it nonprofits." **Price:** $1/ea.

### E ♦ DataPrompt, Inc.
Box 4627
Carson, CA 90749    (213)778-0522
**Concern(s):** environment; economics; recycling. "'A' certified by Cordoba as a small, disadvantaged minority company. We extend the life of laser printer toner cartridges, save you 50% and eliminate 5 lbs. of solid waste from our landfills. Our low prices include recycling toner cartridges, preventative maintenance, computerized scheduling, delivery and 200% unconditional guarantee."

### L ♦ David Appalachian Crafts
Box 2, Highway 404
David, KY 41616    (606)886-2377
**Concern(s):** labor; economics; alternative markets. Store selling traditional mountain crafts: patchwork quilts, oak split baskets, chairs, toys. **Member:** Co-op America.

### L ♦ Democratic Workplaces
Box 6365
Hartford, CT 06106    (203)951-4496
**Concern(s):** labor; economics; cooperatives; workplace democracy. Consulting service to assist organizations in creating and strengthening democratic workplaces. **Member:** Co-op America.

### L ♦ Deva Lifewear
Box WX92, 303 E. Main St.
Burkittsville, MD 21718-0438    (800)222-8024
**Concern(s):** labor; economics; homeworkers; cooperatives. "...a network of friends and neighbors who hand craft a unique collection of elegantly simple clothes for women and men. We work at home in the Maryland countryside, fashioning our creations one at a time. We choose to work in a cottage industry setting because it allows us to integrate our work with our lives. Our aim is to use natural fiberwear that lets you move freely and function naturally...Every garment bears the name of the stitcher who crafted it for you." **Other Resources:** Catalog. **Est.:** 1978. **Fax:** (301)663-3560.

### $ ♦ Diarchy Development
Box 1715
Boston, MA 02130    (617)522-6673
**Concern(s):** environment; economics; trade; socially-responsible investing. A financing, marketing, and management consulting firm that promotes long-term economic, social, and environmental responsibility.

### E ♦ Direct Mail Press
9335 Fraser Ave.
Silver Springs, MD 20910    (301)585-7077
**Concern(s):** environment. Founded by an environmentalist. Prints letters, brochures, booklets, envelopes, in quantities of 1,000 or more. Committed to promoting recycled paper.

### E ♦ Direct Marketing Association
See Preference Service.

### ✎ ♦ Down to Earth Design
6116 N. Central, #305
Dallas, TX 75206    (214)361-7750
**Concern(s):** arts; economics; graphics; alternatives markets. Advertising design- brochures, logos, ads, publications, packaging design, specialty items - for the alternative marketplace. **Member:** Co-op America.

### A ♦ Dubose Natural Farm
Route 4, Box 358
Blanco, TX 78606
**Concern(s):** agriculture; environment; organic.

### H ♦ E.L. Foust Co. Inc.
Box 105
Elmhurst, IL 60126    (800)225-9549
**Concern(s):** health; environment; air pollution; hazardous toxic. For over 15 years our customers have enjoyed relief from indoor air pollution in their homes, offices, and cars. If you suspect you suffer from indoor contamination or from the growing concern over "Sick Building Syndrome," call us!

### P ♦ Earth Cards
Conari Press
1339 61st St.
Emeryville, CA 94608    (510)596-4040
**Concern(s):** politics; environment; activism; lobbying. A booklet of addressed perforate cards for busy activists to send to politicians on environmental topics. **Contact(s):** Susan Fassberg (Designer).

### E ♦ Earth Care Catalog
Box 14140, Dept. FR
Madison, WI 53714    (608)277-2900
**Affiliation:** Earth Care Paper Company. **Concern(s):** environment; conservation; forests; recycling; green consumer; alternative markets. Products made from recycled paper including note cards, stationery, gift wrap, copy paper, computer and printing paper. Catalog includes short news items on recycling legislation in various regions of the country, and the environmental and political implications of irresponsible waste disposal. Offers holiday and special occasion cards, along with stationery featuring wildlife and nature designs. **Other Resources:** Free catalog, wholesale and retail. See RECYCLE! (periodicals). **Price:** Free. **Member:** Co-op America. **Office:** 100 S. Baldwin Madison, WI. **Contact(s):** John Magee.

### E ♦ The Earth Flag Company
Box 108
Middleville, NJ 07855    (201)579-7889
**Concern(s):** environment; economics. The Earth Flag, with a picture of the earth taken from space against a dark blue background, in three sizes. Nontoxic dyes. **Other Resources:** Free color brochure. **Member:** Co-op America. **Contact(s):** John Sanbonmatsu. (800)421-FLAG.

### E ♦ Earth Guide
1202 E. Maryland Ave.
Phoenix, AZ 85014    (602)956-4996
**Concern(s):** environment; economics; alternative consumer; green consumer. Coupon book for ecological products and services. **Other Resources:** Catalog. **Contact(s):** Julie Noterman (Editor).

### E ♦ Earth Pride
490 E. Main St.
Lake Zurich, IL 60047    (708)540-6770
**Concern(s):** environment; economics; trade; animal rights; hazardous/toxic waste; conservation. Offers the opportunity to build a successful business while saving the environment. It features a catalog of over 100 products which are environmentally safe and part of everyday life. Products can be sold full or part-time without paperwork, inventory, or collecting money. Environmentally sound products for home or office. Cruelty-free personal care products, household cleaners, post-consumer recycled paper. **Other Resources:** Catalog.

361

**Price:** $1/ea. **Pages:** 24. **Contact(s):** Tim Dern.

E ◆ **Earth Rescue Corp.**
1320 Hook Dr.
Middletown, OH 45042 (800)543-1922
**Concern(s):** environment; economics; recycling. "With its divisions Ribbon Rescue & Laser Rescue, reduces, reuses & recycles all plastic printer ribbons and laser cartridges. As a manufacturer of new plastic cartridges for over a decade, we have been part of the 'problem' for our environment...now we are the solution also."

T ◆ **Earth Sounds**
2822 Kinney Dr.
Walnut Creek, CA 94595(510)273-2409
**Concern(s):** Third World; arts; music; development; alternative markets. Our musical instruments are made in small villages in Southern Mexico from non-endangered natural products. Bamboo rain sticks, day turtles, fish and dove ocarinas, bean pod shakers, mini-gourd maracas and baby tambourines imitate the natural sounds of the Earth.

$ ◆ **Earth Tools**
9754 Johanna Place
Shadow Hills, CA 91040 (800)825-6460
**Concern(s):** economics; environment; green consumer; alternative markets. A thoughtful catalog of ecologically-correct products.

✍ ◆ **EarthAlert**
Box 20790
Seattle, WA 98102
**Concern(s):** education; environment; childhood. An entertaining and provocative new board game for the 90's. Players try to conserve oxygen while competing in four challenging categories: True/False, Roleplays, Q&A, Definitions. At EarthAlert's Recycle Centers, players participate in planet-saving activities.

H ◆ **Earthrise**
Box 1196
San Raphael, CA 94915 (415)485-0521
**Concern(s):** health; agriculture; economics; environment; green consumer; conservation. Green superfoods may become a major health supplement trend of the 90's. Popular demand has risen dramatically for spirulina and chlorella algae, and barley and wheat grass. Ecologically grown green foods boost health and energy from the cellular level up. They are naturally more absorbable than chemical vitamin supplements. This company provides a wide array of vitamins and these food supplements. **Other Resources:** Catalog. **Est.:** 1979. **Fax:** (415)485-0955. **Contact(s):** Robert Henrikson (President).

H ◆ **Earthsong**
Box 263
Little Falls, NJ 07424
**Concern(s):** health; economics; alternative consumer; organic. Mail order herbs. **Other Resources:** Catalog.

E ◆ **EarthSeals for Gaia**
Box 8000
Berkeley, CA 94707 (510)845-8977
**Concern(s):** environment; education; activism; global understanding. Stickers of the Earth as seen from space produced for organizations and individuals. They can be purchased for a suggested price of $1/6, $25/200, or $100 /roll and can be personalized with your group, organization, or periodicals name on the back. Seals are printed with ink that is gentle to the environment and are not waterproof. Prices are treated as Donations. Trades welcome. **Other Resources:** Other items are: posters, Earth Flag, pins and various other Earth merchandise. Call after 12 noon P.S.T. For Profit. **Est.:** 1988. **E-Network:** Econet. **ID:** 'phoffman'. **Contact(s):** Paul C. Hoffman (Catalyst).

✈ ◆ **Easy Going Travel**
1400 Shattuck Ave.
Berkeley, CA 94709 (510)843-3533
**Concern(s):** education; Third World; environment; travel; alternative markets; recreation. A retail outlet that supplies everything for the traveler except the tickets. A resource for travel guides and books on cultural and geographic background for world destinations. "We have a worldwide selection of maps. We also stock dual voltage appliances, electrical converters, luggage, health and water purification devices, money belts, and much more." **Other Resources:** Sponsors a weekly lecture series on current topics of interest to travelers. Topics range from socially responsible travel/ecotourism to demonstrations of how to pack carry-on luggage. **Est.:** 1980. (800)233-3533. **Contact(s):** Thelma Elkins (Owner). (510)843-6725.

E ◆ **Ecco Bella**
6 Provost Square, #602 CWA
Caldwell, NJ 07006 (201)226-5799
**Concern(s):** environment; health; animal rights; green consumer. "Products for an ecological lifestyle, The best non-toxic household and pet products, beautiful fragrances, aromatherapy skin care, all-natural personal care, recycled paper, cruelty-free cosmetics, and more! Fast delivery and 100% guaranteed We send beautiful gift baskets anywhere in the US." **Other Resources:** 32-page catalog available. Wholesale and retail. "We donate 10% of the profits to worthwhile environmental and animal protection groups." **Est.:** 1988. **Frequency:** 4/yr. **Price:** Free. **Pages:** 32. **Circ.:** 1,000M. **Fax:** (201)226-0991. (800)888-5320(not NJ). **Contact(s):** Sally Malanga (Sales Office). (800)888-5320.

☉ ◆ **Eco Solar**
2401 Lincoln Blvd., 2nd Fl.
Santa Monica, CA 90405 (310)392-7813
**Concern(s):** energy; environment; agriculture; economics; solar; recycling; forests; community self-reliance; efficiency; appropriate technology. Helps communities learn sustainable technology for community self-sufficiency. Specific projects include: water management sewer treatment, organic farming, solar energy, recycling, reforestation, composting, and resource-efficient housing.

E ◆ **Eco Solutions**
433 14th St. S.
Moorhead, MN 56560 (218)236-7374
**Concern(s):** environment; urban. Marketing firm which helps individuals, businesses, and cities with practical solutions to environmental problems such as safe food, water conservation, buying recycled products, composting and gardening, energy conservation, and wildlife preservation. It focuses on waste reduction (garbage prevention), the only long-term solution to the waste glut and pollution problems. Our work includes public education, consulting, research, and project development. **Est.:** 1988. **Contact(s):** Lilias Jones (Chairman).

E ◆ **Eco-Pack Industries, Inc.**
7859 S. 180th St.
Springbrook Bldg. #3
Kent, WA 98032 (206)251-0918
**Concern(s):** environment; economics; alternative markets; green consumer. This industry manufactures Quadra-Pak, an environmental-friendly alternative to petroleum based packing materials made from unbleached kraft paper. Quadra-Pak is recycled and biodegradable, and is naturally antistatic. It also offers surprise packing protection with its expanding and interlocking characteristics. **Other Resources:** Pledges 1% of its company's profit to reforestation. **Contact(s):** John Ratzenberger, Johnny Parker (Founders).

☉ ◆ **EcoAlternatives**
Box 69
San Clemente, CA 92674 (714)498-2373
**Concern(s):** energy; environment; recycling; water; efficiency. Over 400 eco-friendly goods for everyday use via mail order and their environmental general store located in Laguna Beach. They also make over one dozen of their own products. Some products include: biodegradable and nontoxic heavy-duty cleaners, drain degreaser/odor control, plant bug repellent, compost activator, canvas shopping bags, efficient fluorescent lightbulbs. **Other Resources:** Retail mail order catalog and wholesale prices available. **Member:** Co-op America. **Contact(s):** Francine Newman, Sheryl Nevitt **Other:** 231 Ocean Ave., Laguna Beach, CA 92651

H ◆ **Ecodex, Inc.**
One Aaron Rd.
Lexington, MA 02173 (617)862-3440
**Concern(s):** health; environment; hazardous/toxic waste. Tests homes and schools for indoor air and water quality. Also sells a home radon test kit which is approved by the EPA and recyclable. **Member:** Co-op America.

E★ **Ecologue**
International Environment Group
Box 71NA, 71 Sargent Camp Rd.
Peterborough, NH 03458
**Concern(s):** environment; economics; green consuemr; alternative consumer. "Environmental Catalogue and Consumer's Guide for a Safe Earth." Educational as well as a practical shopping guide. Various chapters inform you on what you can do to help make the world a more ecologically-correct place to live. **Price:** $18.95/ea. **Contact(s):** Bruce Anderson (Editor).

E ◆ **Ecosource**
Box 1656
Sebastopol, CA 95473 (707)829-7957
**Concern(s):** environment; education; alternative markets; recycling; green consumer. "Products for a safer, cleaner world": Recycled paper goods, water and air purification systems, biodegradable household cleaners, energy-efficient lighting, recycling systems, non-toxic paints and building supplies, safe pet and garden product books and much more. **Other Resources:** Environmental consulting and counselling. Catalog available. **Est.:** 1990. **Frequency:** 3-4/yr. **Date Publ.:** 10/90. **Fax:** (707)829-7312. (800)274-7040. **Contact(s):** Cliff Schumaker (Owner), Steve Lett (Research/Development Director). (707)829-3506. Margot Olmstead , Marketing Director.

✈ ◆ **Ecotour Expeditions**
Box 1066
Cambridge, MA 02238 (617)876-5817
**Concern(s):** education; environment; Third World; travel; forests. Expeditions in the Pantanal and rainforests of Ecuador and Brazil. Small groups travel by vessel or overland into pristine wilderness areas to observe plant and animal life. Guided by scientists, the trips are informed and exciting adventures. **Other Resources:** Free brochures. **Member:** Co-op America.

E ◆ **EcoWorks, Inc.**
2326 Pickwick Rd.
Baltimore, MD 21207 (301)448-1820
**Concern(s):** environment; energy; efficiency; anti-nuclear. A manufacturer and distributor of ecological and nuclear-free products, including ecological light bulbs and mercury-free batteries, packaged in recycled materials. Contributes 10% of its profits, 1% For Peace and other organizations working for a nuclear-free world. **Contact(s):** Albert Donnay. (301)448-3319.

✍ ◆ **Educational Spectrums Catalog**
Box 1014
Placerville, CA 95667-1014
**Concern(s):** education.

$★ **The Electronic Whole Earth Catalog**
Point Foundation
27 Gate Five Rd.
Sausalito, CA 94965
**Concern(s):** economics; environment; education; alternative markets. Only available on CD-ROM. More than 2500 entries on a wide variety of subjects, from sea kayaking to digital electronics. Extensively illustrated with over 2000 digitized images. Includes excerpts from some 400 entries from books on tape to birdcalls. Retails for $149.95. HyperCard is included free with order. Macintosh users only. Information: (415) 492-3200. Technical Support: (415) 492-3500. **Publisher:** Broderbund Software.

$ ◆ **Emerging Public Issues Corporation**
First Interstate Bank Center
6301 Gaston Ave., #344
Dallas, TX 75214 (214)821-1968
**Concern(s):** economics.

$ ◆ **The Employee Partnership Fund**
230 Park Ave., #1455
New York, NY 10169
**Affiliation:** Keilin and Bloom. **Concern(s):** labor; economics; worker ownership; workplace democracy.

☉ ◆ **Energy Auditor & Retrofitter**
2124 Kittredge, #95
Berkeley, CA 94704
**Concern(s):** energy; efficiency; conservation.

⚘ ◆ **Enlightened Living**
Box 1256
Sebastopol, CA 95473 (800)233-7309
**Concern(s):** peace; environment; education; activism; fundraising. This company produces the widely known "All One People" series of products. This product simply put is global conscience raising pictures of the Earth which gives a sense of one. **Other Resources:** Products available on T-Shirts, Sweatshirts, Posters, Buttons, and Magnets. **Contact(s):** Steven Ehli (President).

$ ◆ **EnviroMedia, Inc.**
756 Gilman St.
Berkeley, CA 94710 (510)526-3900
**Concern(s):** economics; environment; green consumer; corporate responsibility; alternative markets. "We are a group of small companies providing product development and marketing management services to environmental and other socially beneficial clients. " **Fax:** (510)526-9255. **Contact(s):** Gil Friend.

E ◆ **Environmental Awareness Products**
3600 Goodwin Rd.
Ionia, MI 48846 (800)255-9737
**Concern(s):** environment; economics; alternative markets. "Started to market items that would extend the voices of the Earth to those who longed to hear them and into places where they are seldom heard or remembered. We try to do this as faithfully as possible by offering products whose message, quality, beauty, simplicity, and value are congruent with the voices they represent. We are confident you will find these products a joy to see, hear and wear." Primarily cotton t- & sweat

shirts, sterling jewelry, and accessories. **Other Resources:** Catalog. **Est.:** 1985. **Price:** $2/ea.

### E ◗ Environmental Business Brokers Co.
6160 S. Syracuse Way, #310
Englewood, CO 80111    (303)771-3160
**Concern(s):** economics; environment; trade; analysis. Provides brokerage, financial, and business planning services for environmental industries. **Contact(s):** William L. Skufca.

### E ◗ Environmental Concerns
Box 1656
Sebastopol, CA 95473-1656
**Concern(s):** environment; economics; appropriate technology. Good environmental products catalogue. Some excellent items (lightbulbs, recycled paper) and some scare-tactic, yuppie-maintenance stuff. Use with care and selectivity. **Pages:** 32.

### $ ◗ Environmental Federation of California
2401 Lincoln Blvd., 2nd Fl.
Santa Monica, CA 90405    (310)452-3502
**Concern(s):** economics; environment; community investment. EFC conducts payroll deduction plans -- in public and private workplaces - to benefit 40+ nonprofit groups working to protect and preserve California's unique environment, urban and rural. One gift through your company's charitable campaign supports the efforts of all our member agencies.

### E ◗ Environmental Products
Box 25001
Anaheim, CA 92825    (714)997-3090
**Concern(s):** environment; recycled/solid waste. 100% recycled plastic products made from comingled waste including picnic tables, benches, trash receptacles, composters, sandboxes, fencing, decking, birdfeeders, window planters, landscape timber, lumber, car stops and speed bumps. Products won't splinter, crack, or rot. Graffiti and carvings are easily removed. Works like wood with ordinary tools, yet doesn't deplete our forests!

### $ ◗ Ethical Investments, Inc.
430 1st Ave. N., #204
Minneapolis, MN 55401    (612)339-3939
**Concern(s):** economics; socially-responsible investing. Socially responsible investment counseling and asset management for business and individuals. **Member:** Co-op America.

### T ◗ Exotic Gifts
Box 842
Hermosa Beach, CA 90254    (310)374-2570
**Concern(s):** Third World; economics; feminism; Asia; cooperatives; alternative markets. Imports and sells clothing made by cooperatives and destitute women's groups in Bangladesh and India. **Member:** Co-op America.

### A ◗ F.U.T.U.R.E. Organics, Inc.
Box 228
Butte, ND 58723    (701)626-7360
**Concern(s):** agriculture; environment; health; economics; nutrition; alternative consumer; organic; family farms. A family-owned organic farm, grain distributor, processor, and consultant. Custom blending of grains. Also, monthly newsletter with international calendar of ecological/energy events. **Member:** Co-op America. **Contact(s):** Serena Dossenko.

### ☯ ◗ Fafco Solar Heating Systems
26631 Cabot Rd., #B
Laguna Hills, CA 92653    (800)274-3638
**Concern(s):** environment; economics; solar; appropriate technology. The oldest and largest manufacturer of solar heating systems and has a unique domestic hot water system. Fafco distributes its products through authorized distributors. Revco Solar Engineering, Inc., and Solar Unlimited, with a total of 26 years solar experience, represent Fafco in the L.A. and Orange County areas. **Est.:** 1969. (714)367-0740.

### E ◗ Fallen Empire
66 Commercial St.
Malden, MA 02148    (800)367-0151
**Concern(s):** economics; Third World; alternative markets. "Junk mail...? doesn't make us any happier than it does you. Catalog companies are big culprits in the useless killing of trees. We are a catalog company. Fully 1/4 of every tax dollar goes to supporting non-American military forces. We say, conspiratorially, let's spend this money on American education. We'll try..." replacing trees, $5 credit to anyone mailed 2 catalogs, finding decent recycled paper, and using soy based inks. Sells clothes, household items, and various accessories.

### ✍ ◗ Family Pastimes
Rural Route #4
Perth, ON K7H 3C6 Canada
**Concern(s):** education; environment; childhood. Games stressing cooperative play, some with environmental themes. **Contact(s):** Jim Deacove, Ruth Deacove

### L ◗ Far Reaches Catalog
Box 151
Curlew, WA 99118    (509)779-4967
**Concern(s):** labor; economics; trade; cooperatives; alternative markets. Provides a marketing outlet for cottage industries in the Pacific Northwest: soap, lotions, and oils, toys, jewelry, pottery, moccasins, candles, batik and tie-dye, etc. **Other Resources:** Catalog, $1. Retail and wholesale. **Member:** Co-op America.

### $ ◗ Financial Alternatives
1514 McGee St.
Berkeley, CA 94703    (510)527-5604
**Concern(s):** economics; environment; politics; law; trade; socially-responsible investing. Formulates environmentally supportive legislation and other concepts which can be presented at The Other Economic Summit (TOES). Major thought is being given as to how to surmount the media hurdle which isolated the new economists from the media at the last TOES. **Other Resources:** Micro and mini business consulting and financing; personal finance; socially responsible investing. **Member:** Co-op America. **Contact(s):** Richard Register, Roger Pritchard.

### $ ◗ Financial Network Investment
605 1st Ave., #505
Seattle, WA 98104    (206)292-8483
**Concern(s):** economics; socially-responsible investing; trade. Certified financial planners specializing in socially responsible investing. Identifies specific social and financial objectives of individuals and businesses, and develops an investment strategy to meet each client's needs. **Member:** Co-op America. **Contact(s):** Kathleen Kendziorski, Jessica Greenway

### $ ◗ Financing Ozark Rural Growth & Economy (FORGE)
Box 269
Jasper, AR 72641    (501)446-2211
**Concern(s):** economics; agriculture; environment; community investment; organic; food production; rural communities. A host bank allows members to pool money to back loans primarily for local projects related to organic agriculture. **Contact(s):** Laurie Cook.

### $ ◗ First Affirmative Financial Network
410 N. 21st St., #203
Colorado Springs, CO 80904 (800)422-7284
**Concern(s):** economics; socially-responsible investing. Nationwide investment firm specializing in socially responsible investments. Co-op America's partner in providing financial services to our members. **Other Resources:** Offers a cassette tape, Socially Responsible Investing. **Member:** Co-op America. **Contact(s):** Ed Winslow, Scott Flora (719)636-1045.

### $ ◗ First Nations Financial Project
69 Kelley Rd.
Falmouth, VA 22405    (703)371-5615
**Concern(s):** economics; community investment; land trusts. **Contact(s):** Rebecca Adamson.

### $ ◗ FMA International
101 West St.
Hillsdale, NJ 07642    (201)358-1212
**Concern(s):** economics. Socially responsible and holistic businesses for sale (i.e., New Age promotion company, holistic spa, alternative magazine distributor, etc.). National and international broker of socially/environmentally responsible businesses. **Contact(s):** Nathan Battalion.

### E ◗ The Forest Trust
Box 519
Sante Fe, NM 87504-0519 (505)983-8992
**Concern(s):** environment; economics; forests; conservation; resource management; land trusts; community investment; rural communities. Provides resource protection strategies and land management services to conservation organizations, landowners, rural communities and public agencies. Seeks to improve national forest management, economic development in rural communities, land trusts and management of private lands through increasing the value, integrity, resilience and productivity of forest and range ecosystems.

### H ◗ 4 The Planet, Inc.
1391 6th St., #143
Sarasota, FL 34236    (813)365-1068
**Concern(s):** health; environment; hazardous/toxic waste. Sells a

unique line of environmental and consumer friendly, petro-free cleaners for the environmentally aware and chemically sensitive. These cruelty-free, concentrated, naturally derived products out-perform traditional hazardous cleaners; others are undergoing final testing. 2% of gross sales are donated to nonprofit environmental organizations.

### $ ◗ Franklin Insight
711 Atlantic Ave.
Boston, MA 02111    (617)423-6655
**Concern(s):** economics; environment; justice; socially-responsible investing; green consumer. A monthly investment advisory service that informs concerned investors about economic trends and companies that make a positive impact on society and the environment while exhibiting a potential for good financial rewards. **Other Resources:** INVESTING FOR A BETTER WORLD is its monthly newsletter. **Dues:** $195/yr. for complete service. **Subscription:** $19.95/yr. for newsletter. (800)548-5684.

### $ ◗ Franklin Research & Development Corporation
711 Atlantic Ave.
Boston, MA 02111    (617)423-6655
**Affiliation:** Social Investment Forum. **Concern(s):** economics; socially-responsible investing. Socially responsible investment advisor and newsletter publisher. **Member:** Coalition for Environmentally Responsible Economics. **Contact(s):** Diane Mills.

### $ ◗ Freedom Environmental Fund
c/o Beer, Stearns & Co.
1 Federal Plaza
Boston, MA 02110-2082(800)333-2327
**Affiliation:** Beer, Stearns & Co.. **Concern(s):** economics; socially-responsible investing. **Contact(s):** Theodore Ketterer.

### ✈ ◗ Friendship Tours
1905 E. Orangeburg Ave.
Modesto, CA 95355    (209)577-1514
**Concern(s):** education; Third World; travel. A woman-owned company dedicated to alternative travel. Custom-designed tours of small groups allow village visits and person-to-person exchanges. Owner has traveled to more than 80 countries. **Member:** Co-op America. **Contact(s):** Jo Taylor.

### T ◗ From The Rainforest
270 Lafayette St., #1103
New York, NY 10012    (212)219-8260
**Concern(s):** Third World; environment; agriculture; economics; forests; Asia; South America; alternative markets. An environmental food company which assists people defending the world's rainforests through direct contributions and by providing markets for their products. The product line contains a wide variety of mixed nuts and preservative free dried fruits from Brazil and Southeast Asia, packaged in recycled paper with vegetable based inks. (800)Earth-96.

### $ ◗ Gales Creek Insurance Service
2724 SW Macadam Ave.
Portland, OR 97201    (503)227-0491
**Concern(s):** economics. Specializes in serving the nonprofit community with insurance products: liability, property, and employer-employee benefits. Free information. **Member:** Co-op America.

### A ◗ Gardener's Supply
128 Intervale Rd.
Burlington, VT 05401    (802)863-4535
**Concern(s):** agriculture; environment; organic. "America's #1 catalog of innovative, environmentally safe gardening products. The most complete selection of seed-starting supplies, season extenders, organic fertilizers and pest controls, ingenious hand tools, watering systems, power equipment, greenhouses, and more." **Other Resources:** Free catalog, wholesale and retail. An employee-owned company. **Contact(s):** Paul Conrad.

### ✍ ◗ A Gentle Wind
Box 3103
Albany, NY 12203-0103 (518)482-0412
**Concern(s):** education; arts; childhood; music. Recorded music and stories for children with themes of sharing and caring for each other and the planet. Free catalog. Nonprofit. **Price:** Free. **Pages:** 10. **Contact(s):** Jill Person (President). (518)436-0391.

### E ◗ Gift Shopping For A Better World
30 Irving Place
New York, NY 10003    (212)420-1133
**Affiliation:** Council on Economic Priorities. **Concern(s):** environment; economics; peace; politics; consumer rights; alternative markets; green consumer. From the publishers of Shopping For A Better World, a catalog of socially-responsible gift ideas, mostly consumer-oriented books. **Contact(s):** Alice Tepper Marlin (President), Myra Alperson (Director for Social Responsibility). (800)U-CAN-HELP.

**E ◆ Glade Chemicals**
7302 East Helm Dr., #1002
Scottsdale, AZ 85260    (602)991-2725
**Concern(s):** environment; hazardous/toxic waste. Biodegradable, nontoxic chemicals for industrial cleaning and maintenance. Call for free fact sheets. **Member:** Co-op America.

**$ ◆ The Global Resource Bank**
126 SE 3rd St.
Hallandale, FL 33009    (305)458-7941
**Concern(s):** economics; environment; socially-responsible investing; trade. This Bank is a politically democratic economics solution to the world's problems. Its charter creates a global cooperative that produces economic freedom as it restores the environment. The enterprise empowers the individual, implements a General Agreement for Free Trade, matches demand with supply relieves the world of debt and furnishes its own start up funds. **Other Resources:** Publishes BANK NEWSLETTER quarterly. **Est.:** 1985. **E-Network:** Econet. **ID:** 'jpozzi'. **Fax:** (305)458-0426.

**$ ◆ Good Money Publications, Inc.**
Box 363
Worcester, VT 05683-0363    (800)535-3551
**Concern(s):** economics; socially-responsible investing. Up-to-date information for socially concerned investors and financial professionals. **Other Resources:** Newsletter, GOOD MONEY, $75 a year, handbook, and information services. Free brochure. **Member:** Co-op America. (802)223-3911.

**M ◆ Grass Roots Press, Inc.**
401 1/2 W. Peace St.
Raleigh, NC 27603    (919)828-2364
**Concern(s):** media; arts; press; graphics. Small offset print shop established with the primary goal of serving the progressive community's printing needs. **Member:** Co-op America. **Contact(s):** Gary Cappy.

**L ◆ The Great Alaska Catalog**
5750 Glacier Highway, #A3
Juneau, AK 99801    (907)780-4442
**Concern(s):** labor; economics; trade; homeworkers; alternative markets. Provides market for cottage industries, artists, and musicians throughout Alaska: jewelry, t-shirts, food, children's books, videos, cassette tapes. Retail only. **Other Resources:** Catalog, $1. **Member:** Co-op America.

**E ◆ Green Cross Certification Co.**
1611 Telegraph Ave., #111
Oakland, CA 94612
**Concern(s):** environment; economics; trade; recycling; hazardous/ toxic waste; preservation. Certifies specific claims that represent significant steps to reduce solid and toxic wastes, conserve energy and protect precious natural resources, like forests and clean water. Its certification standards are among the nation's toughest and are designed to encourage manufacturers to stay at the forefront of environmental change.

**E ◆ The Green Planet**
Box 15, 57 Lincoln St.
Newton, MA 02161    617-3-EARTH-1
**Concern(s):** environment; economics; green consumer; alternative markets. "Products for a Better World" is an environmental store based in the Greater Boston area. "We donate 10% of our profits to organizations working to solve environmental problems. Currently we're also marketing washable Lunch Bags and color-it yourself Rainforest posters." **Other Resources:** Catalog available.

**✈ ◆ Green Tortoise Adventure Travel**
Box 24459
San Francisco, CA 94124    (415)821-0803
**Concern(s):** education; economics; energy; travel; alternative markets; transportation. Alternative bus company running remodeled sleeper coaches to beautiful places at bargain prices, including Alaska, Mexico and cross country. **Contact(s):** Eric Gerrick.

**L ◆ Happy Home**
Route 1, Box 14A
Mathias, WV 26812    (304)897-5468
**Concern(s):** labor;economics; cooperatives; alternative markets. A crafts cooperative making and selling dolls, stuffed animals, Christmas decorations, wood crafts, quilted items, clothing, and so forth. **Other Resources:** Catalog. **Member:** Co-op America.

**$ ◆ The Hartman Group**
1280 Bison, #B-9550
Newport Beach, CA 92660    (714)644-2540
**Concern(s):** economics; environment; trade; alternative markets; green consumer. A social marketing firm specializing in the environment, ecology, children and the mature market. **Contact(s):** Mark Sten.

**☺ ◆ Healthful Hardware Catalog**
207 16th St., #B
Pacific Grove, CA 93950    (408)372-8626
**Concern(s):** energy; economics; alternative markets.

**H ◆ Healthy House Catalog**
4115 Bridge Ave., #104
Cleveland, OH 44113    (216)961-4646
**Affiliation:** Environmental Health Watch. **Concern(s):** health; environment; hazardous/toxic; alternative consumer. A catalog of products for your home that addresses the problems of indoor pollution. **Member:** Co-op America. **Contact(s):** Stuart Greenberg. (800)222-9348.

**☺ ◆ Heart Interface**
811 1st Ave. S
Kent, WA 98032    (206)859-0640
**Concern(s):** energy; renewables; efficiency. "Unplug from the power company. The new Olympian inverter/charger provides 3,000 watts of silent AC power from a battery bank. When generator or utility power is available, it turns into a 100 amp battery charger. Automatic switchover makes back-up power system for pellet stoves, lights, etc. Perfect for use with solar, wind or hydro systems." **Other Resources:** Call or send for free color brochure.

**✍ ◆ Hearthsong, Inc.**
400-A Morris St.
Sebastopol, CA 95472    (707)829-0900
**Concern(s):** education; economics; childhood; alternative markets. Toys you'll feel good about giving! Spring and summer fun with kites, craft kits, non-toxic art materials, nature projects, and many new and traditional toys and games. It's excellent service has resulted in our second consecutive selection for Parents' Choice Foundation Seal of Approval. All our products are unconditionally guaranteed. **Pages:** 48. **Contact(s):** Barbara Kane. (800)325-2502.

**H ◆ Herbalist & Alchemist, Inc.**
Box 458
Bloomsbury, NJ 08804-0458    (201)479-6679
**Concern(s):** health; alternative consumer; holism. Organic and wild herbal extracts, Chinese herbs, books about herbal medicine. **Other Resources:** Catalog, $1. Retail and wholesale. **Member:** Co-op America. **Contact(s):** Betzy Bancroft. (201)545-1979.

**♿ ◆ High Cotton Co.**
39 Broadway
Asheville, NC 28801    (704)253-1138
**Concern(s):** economics; health; feminism; cooperatives; empowerment; disabled. Woman-owned company making futons, cloth bags for groceries and luggage, and handmade furniture using domestic raw materials. Employs visually impaired people in manufacture and sales. **Member:** Co-op America.

**✈ ◆ High Country Adventures**
15990 Mill Creek Rd.
Frenchtown, MT 59834    (406)443-2842
**Concern(s):** education; environment; wilderness; recreation; travel. Oldest backpacking outfitter in the country. Guided backpacking trips in Montana and Wyoming, emphasizing sensitivity to wilderness, environmental education, and history. **Member:** Co-op America.

**H ◆ Historical Remedies**
122 S. Wabasha St.
St. Paul, MN 55107    (612)224-9344
**Concern(s):** health; environment; holism; alternative consumer. Provides a practical method of natural wellness with Homeopathic Medicine. These are offered open stock, in prepacked displays and in medicine kits developed to meet the needs of specific consumer groups.

**H ◆ Homeopathy: Medicine for the 21st Century**
Homeopathic Educational Services
2124 Kittredge St.
Berkeley, CA 94704    (510)649-0294
**Affiliation:** Homeopathic Educational Services. **Concern(s):** health; education; holism; alternative consumer. The most comprehensive catalog of homeopathic information available. Books, tapes, and medicines. "Homeopathy cures a larger percentage of cases than any other method of treatment." - Gandhi. **Office:** 2036 Blake St. Berkeley, CA **Fax:** (510)649-1955. Order: (800)359-9051.

**✍ ◆ Hugs for the Heart**
Box 85
Rainbow Lake, NY 12976
**Concern(s):** education; homeschooling. Offers a catalog listing games, books, puzzles, recordings, and other learning materials that encourage self-esteem, imagination, global and ecological awareness, and fun. Also, books on home schooling and sensitive child rearing.

**$ ◆ ICA Revolving Loan Fund**
58 Day St., #203
Somerville, MA 02144    (617)629-2700
**Concern(s):** economics; labor; worker ownership; workplace democracy; cooperatives. Provides financing and financial packaging assistance to worker-owned firms, with a focus on firms that have a significant employment impact. **Other Resources:** Business and financial consulting services for employee-owned firms and community-based companies. Also, financing for community-based businesses. **Member:** Co-op America. **Contact(s):** Katherine Gross.

**J ◆ Ikwe Marketing Collective**
Rt. 1, Box 286
Ponsford, MN 56575    (218)573-3411
**Concern(s):** justice; economics; feminism; agriculture; Native Americans; organic. Certified organic natural like wild rice, native American baskets, beadwork, quilts marketed by Native American women. Nonprofit. **Member:** Co-op America.

**✏ ◆ Indianapolis Arts Cooperative**
6841 S. Tibbs Ave.
Indianapolis, IN 46217    (317)881-1811
**Concern(s):** arts; economics; cooperatives. Provides services to small arts groups and individual artists at cost. **Member:** Co-op America.

**L ◆ Industrial Cooperative Association**
58 Day St., #203
Somerville, MA 02144    (617)629-2700
**Concern(s):** labor; economics; cooperatives; workplace democracy; worker ownership. Support services for employee-owned firms and companies considering a transition to employee ownership. Financial and technical assistance. **Other Resources:** Publications list available. **Member:** Co-op America.

**L ◆ InDios Co-op**
Box 901
Indiantown, FL 34956    (407)597-3838
**Concern(s):** labor; economics; education; cooperatives; worker ownership; community investment. A cooperative of former migrant workers which makes clergy shirts. Profits are used for salaries, and to educate members in accounting, managing, and marketing skills. **Member:** Co-op America.

**✈ ◆ Information Consulting Associates**
See DIRECTORY OF INTERCULTURAL EDUCATION NEWSLETTERS.

**☺ ◆ Integral Energy Systems**
105A Argall Way
Nevada City, CA 95959    (916)265-8441
**Concern(s):** energy; environment; solar; wind; renewable; recycling; appropriate technology. Alternative energy products for homes: solar panels, wind and water power, composting toilets, woodstoves, and more. Call for a free energy analysis. Our 105-page guidebook/ catalog has it all! Solar-electric, wind, hydropower, hot water, solar pumping. Complete systems. **Other Resources:** Publishes a INTEGRAL ENERGY NEWS. **Price:** $4/ea., refundable on purchase. **Member:** Co-op America. **Fax:** (916)265-6151. **Contact(s):** John Hill.

**$ ◆ Inter-American Development Bank**
Environmental Management Committee
1300 New York Ave. NW
Washington, DC 20577    (202)623-1000
**Affiliation:** Environmental Management Committee. **Concern(s):** economics; Third World; environment; development. **Contact(s):** Enrique Iglesias (President), Ed Farnworth

**H ◆ Inter-Natural**
See PURE PRODUCTS FOR PERSONAL CARE AND NATURAL HEALING CATALOG.

**E ◆ International Environment Consultants**
21533 Arcos Dr.
Woodland Hills, CA 91364    (818)716-7208
**Concern(s):** environment; energy; economics; air pollution; efficiency; resource management; transportation. TMZ Fuel enhancement system increases mpg 4-6 miles, reduces engine wear and hydrocarbon emissions 150-300% at idle. Clearbrook water filters awarded Gold Seal by Water Quality Assoc. Highest rating for quality removing more harmful pollutants than most other brands. Air filters high efficiency, HEPA certified. This consulting firm will have all the answers.

**✈ ◆ International Expeditions**
1776 Independence Ct.
Birmingham, AL 35216    (305)361-4697
**Concern(s):** education; environment; travel; recreation. Natural history expeditions to 30 destinations worldwide. Emphasis on environmental awareness and resource conservation. **Member:** Co-op America.

## H ♦ Internatural

Box 463, Baker Hill Rd.
South Sutton, NH 03273 (603)927-4776

**Concern(s):** health; environment; green consumer; holism. Publishes pure products for personal care and natural healing catalog. **Contact(s):** Sol Solomon.

## E ♦ Invincible

Box 13054
Phoenix, AZ 85002

**Concern(s):** environment; economics; green consumer; alternative markets. Merchandise for/of the environment.

## ✍ ♦ IRI Group, Inc.

200 E. Wood St., #255
Palatine, IL 60067

**Concern(s):** education; health. Instructional Resource Catalog lists books and materials on cooperative learning, whole language, critical and creative thinking skills, and the STARS substance abuse program.

## T ♦ Jacaranda Imports

Box 340087
Hartford, CT 06314-0087 (203)246-3914

**Concern(s):** Third World; health; Africa; disabled. Works with sheltered workshop in Africa employing handicapped people to make jewelry using semi-precious stones and traditional African beads. Wholesale and retail. **Other Resources:** Color brochure, $2. **Member:** Co-op America.

## ☯ ♦ Jade Mountain Import-Export Co.

Box 4616
Boulder, CO 80306 (800)442-1972

**Concern(s):** energy; environment; solar; wind; appropriate technology. "One of the world's largest selections of energy saving and appropriate technology products - solar electric, energy-efficient lighting, water saving, recycled paper products, demand water heaters, ecology products, hydro and wind generators, solar toys, and much more! One-year 80-page newsletter/catalog subscription. Call toll-free number for more information." **Contact(s):** Steve Troy.

## E ♦ Jim Morris Environmental T-Shirts Catalog

Box 831
Boulder, CO 80306 (303)444-6430

**Concern(s):** environment; economics; arts; alternative markets; green consumer; graphics. A company that produces and sells environmental T-shirts with highly stylized professional graphics and logos. **Other Resources:** Publishes a newsletter, SHARE THE EARTH; resource list; and an environmental book review list. **Est.:** 1978. **Contact(s):** Jim Morris (Founder/President).

## E ♦ The John Rossi Company

259 Washburn Rd.
Briarcliff Manor, NY 10510 (914)941-1752

**Concern(s):** environment; economics; green consumer; recycling; forests; conservation; alternative markets. Manufactures products from recycled newspaper: notepads, blank books, gift and home products. **Contact(s):** John Rossi.

## T ♦ Jubilee Crafts

6117 Germantown Ave.
Philadelphia, PA 19144 (215)849-0808

**Concern(s):** Third World; economics; justice; alternative markets; trade; development. An organization dedicated to providing an alternative market for Third World crafts while educating Americans about injustices surrounding the craftmakers' lives. "We are committed to helping those in the Third World raise their standards of living and be paid a fair market price for the goods of their labor. Each purchase from this catalog helps us to fulfill our mission." Nonprofit. **Contact(s):** Lila McCalla.

## L ♦ Keilin and Bloom

See Employee Partnership Fund.

## T ♦ Kemp Krafts

275 Main St.
Winooski, VT 05405 (802)655-9563

**Concern(s):** Third World; justice; economics; environment; recycling. Marketing for craftspeople. Sells Afro-American greeting cards, maple products, "nuclear free" light bulbs, wooden toys, reusable grocery bags, jewelry from South African cooperative. **Other Resources:** Free catalogs. **Member:** Co-op America.

## ☛ ♦ Kettle Care Products

1145 2nd Ave. E
Kalispell, MT 59901 (406)756-3485

**Concern(s):** health; environment; green consumer; animal rights. Herbal products not tested on animals; bath herbs, lotions, oils, as well as potpourri and "sleep and dream" pillows. **Other Resources:** Free catalog. **Member:** Co-op America.

## H ♦ L & H Vitamins

37-10 Crescent St.
Long Island City, NY 11101 (800)544-2598

**Concern(s):** health; economics; nutrition; alternative consumer; preventative medicine. A catalog of a wide variety of vitamins and natural herbs. (718)937-7400(NY). **Contact(s):** John Rao.

## ✐ ♦ Larry Fox & Co.

Box 729
Valley Stream, NY 11582 (516)791-7929

**Concern(s):** arts; graphics. Custom imprinted items for business and organizations. Also, free catalog of in-stock items for consciousness-raising. Discounts to Co-op America members. **Member:** Co-op America.

## ✈ ♦ Laughing Heart Adventures

Box 669
Willow Creek, CA 95573 (916)629-3516

**Concern(s):** education; environment; health; holism; recreation; travel. Canoe outings in western US and Mexico. Guides educate canoeists on the natural and human history of the region, and the stars. Also, stress reduction, holistic health, primitive land skills. **Member:** Co-op America.

## ☯ ♦ Lehman's Non-Electric Catalog

Box 41, 4779 Kidron Rd.
Kidron, OH 44636 (216)857-5441

**Concern(s):** energy; economics; alternative markets; appropriate technology. "Our hardware was founded and built upon an unusual premise—to supply the unique needs of America's largest Amish community. Items we stock are not found in the world at large. We believe they retain a valid usefulness in spite of those who say they're 'outdated' and 'obsolete'. Serving such a distinctive community also means Old World policies of fair price and satisfaction at any cost are an essential part of our day-to-day operations." Highly recommended. **Est.:** c1960.

## ☯ ♦ Leslie Manufacturing

RR #1, Box 286
Lawrence, KS 66044 (913)842-1943

**Concern(s):** energy; environment; recycling; conservation; renewables. Developing and manufacturing products which offer a "waste-to-energy" concept which avoids depletion of the Earth's resources. Invented the "Black Jack Firebox," which burns waste materials for heat. **Member:** Co-op America.

## $ ♦ Linda Q. Perrin & Associates

123 S. 53rd St.
Omaha, NE 68132 (402)556-3318

**Concern(s):** economics; fundraising. Helps organizations with fundraising. **Member:** Co-op America. **Contact(s):** Linda Perrin.

## ☛ ♦ Lion and Lamb Cruelty-free Products, Inc.

29-28 41st Ave., #813
Long Island City, NY 11101 (800)252-6288

**Concern(s):** environment; economics; health; animal rights; alternative markets; alternative consumer; green consumer. A mail order company that has 800+ different products ranging from makeup, health care, cleaning supplies and personal hygiene materials. All products are certified cruelty free. No animal testing, and most are formulated from natural ingredients. **Other Resources:** Free catalog available on request. 10% off to "not-for-profits." **Fax:** (718)361-5806.

## E ♦ Lowans & Stephens Environmental Products & Services

R.R. No. 1
Caledon East, ON L0N 1E0 Canada (519)941-6499

**Concern(s):** environment; health; hazardous/toxic waste; green consumer. Consulting and builders of nontoxic houses; also starting environmental products store. **Contact(s):** Ed Lowans Jr.

## F ♦ LYDIA - A Women's Cooperative Interchange

1257 E. Siena Heights Dr.
Adrian, MI 49221 (517)265-5135

**Concern(s):** feminism; economics; cooperatives; planning; networking. A voluntary association of women interested in the cooperative workplace. Sponsors annual exchange forums and other co-op gatherings. **Member:** Co-op America.

## T ♦ Marketplace: Handwork of India

1461 Ashland Ave.
Evanston, IL 60201 (708)328-4011

**Concern(s):** Third World; feminism; health; economics; disabled; cooperatives; Asia; empowerment. An organization helping unskilled women, handicapped people in India. 100% cotton clothing features patchwork and embroidery accents. **Other Resources:** Free catalog for self-addressed, stamped business envelope. Nonprofit. **Member:** Co-op America.

## $ ♦ Message Check Corporation

Box 3206-85
Seattle, WA 98114 (206)324-7792

**Concern(s):** economics; environment; activism. Message Check -- the originator of socially responsible money. Personal bank checks endorsed by Greenpeace, Audubon, PETA, and other national organizations working for a better world. Accepted in all US financial institutions. Messages include "Let the Oceans Live," "Stop Animal Testing," "Protect Habitats" and more. Each order generates a contribution. Free samples.

## T ♦ Mission Traders

705 N. Carolina Ave. SE
Washington, DC 20003 (202)546-3040

**Concern(s):** Third World; trade; economics; development. Imports and sells handcrafted items from developing countries: baskets, jewelry, paintings, wooden ware, clothing, from artisan cooperatives and income generating projects. **Member:** Co-op America. **Contact(s):** Karen Getman, Sue Kilgore

## ✍ ♦ The Montessori Shop

Box 1162
Arcata, CA 95521

**Concern(s):** education; homeschooling. Offers an extensive catalog of learning materials based on Maria Montessori's "prepared environment" for the child from birth through age 14. Also lists children's tools for household chores, music and art materials, and books for adults. Detailed descriptions aid in planning home school curricula. **Contact(s):** Michael Olaf.

## ✈★ Moon Travel Handbooks

722 Wall St.
Chico, CA 95928 (800)345-5473

**Concern(s):** education; travel. Travel handbooks to Asia, the Pacific, Canada, and the US advocate socially responsible, culturally aware tourism. The practical travel information, accommodations, and activities. **Other Resources:** Travelers can order Moon's free catalog, TRAVEL MATTERS, containing valuable travel tips. **Member:** Co-op America.

## ☛ ♦ My Brother's Keeper

211 S. 5th St.
Richmond, IN 47374-5400 (317)962-5079

**Concern(s):** economics; environment; alternative markets; animal rights. A catalogue that features products from 30 "cruelty-free" companies. Includes make-up, soaps, household products, baby and pet items. **Contact(s):** Denise Daugherty-Cooke.

## $ ♦ N.B.A. Credit Union

3807 Otter St.
Briston, PA 19007 (215)788-2000

**Concern(s):** economics; community investments. Financial institution which serves its member-investors through home, car, and other consumer loans. Checking and savings accounts, national ATM card. Nonprofit. **Member:** Co-op America. (800)441-0878.

## $ ♦ National Association of Community Development Loan Funds

Box 40085
Philadelphia, PA 19106-5085 (215)923-4754

**Concern(s):** economics; socially responsible investment. Connects socially concerned investors with community development loan funds which offer the opportunity to invest in low-cost housing and job creation projects in low-income communities. **Member:** Co-op America.

## E ♦ National Association of Diaper Services

2017 Walnut St.
Philadelphia, PA 19103 (215)569-3650

**Concern(s):** environment; health; economics; trade; alternative consumer market. Serves as the national trade association of the professional diaper service industry. Its member services deliver natural cotton diapers, professionally processed and treated with bacteriostatic agents to help prevent diaper rash, to nearly three-quarters of a million babies each year.

## $ ♦ National Cooperative Bank

1630 Connecticut Ave. NW
Washington, DC 20009 (202)745-4600

**Concern(s):** economics; alternative consumer; cooperatives. **Contact(s):** Tena Kemp, Thomas S. Condit.

## $ ♦ National Federation of Community Development Credit Unions

59 John St., #903
New York, NY 10038 (212)513-7191

**Concern(s):** economics; community investments. Will help you find a community development credit union near you. **Member:** Co-op America.

## ☼ ◆ Native Self-Sufficiency Center
RD 1, Box 375
Cold Brook, NY 13324   (315)845-8310
**Concern(s):** energy; economics; architecture; community self-reliance. Minority-owned,providing supplies and advice on building your own energy-efficient log home. Nonprofit. **Member:** Co-op America.

## H ◆ The Natural Choice
1365 Rufina Circle
Santa Fe, NM 87501   (800)621-2591
**Concern(s):** health; environment; hazardous/toxic; holism; recycling. "A leading catalog with over 300 of the most advanced and best in environmentally safe products: Non-toxic paints, stains & wood preservatives, natural health, bodycare & colognes, herbal remedies, healthy footware, recycled paper, cleaners, pet care, fertilizers, organic seeds, and more."

## H ◆ Natural Energy Works
Box 864
El Cerrito, CA 94530
**Concern(s):** health; environment; global warming; hazardous/toxic wastes. Books by Wilhelm Reich, James DeMeo, and others on the subject of Life Energy, Low Level Radiation, Electromagnetic pollution. Unusual devices for sale from EM field meter, GM Counter, Fitzroy Crystal Stormglass Barometer, Computer Radiation Shields, etc. **Est.:** 1986.

## E ◆ Natural Lifestyle Supplies
16W Lookout Dr.
Asheville, NC 28804
**Concern(s):** environment; health; economics; green consumer; animal rights; nutrition; alternative markets. Natural, organic foods, home, body, both, pet and environmental products. (800)752-2775.

## H ◆ Natural Pet Care
All the Best Pet Care
2713 East Madison
Seattle, WA 98112   (800)962-8266
**Concern(s):** health; alternative markets. "Catalog of the healthiest natural pet foods, safe, effective flea control, nutritional supplements that correct skin problems and strengthen the immune system." **Est.:** 1985. **Pages:** c24. **Contact(s):** Susan Moss, Ira Moss (Owners). (206)329-1417.

## ✈ ◆ Nature Quest
Drawer CZ
Bisbee, AZ 85603   (602)432-7353
**Concern(s):** education; environment; wilderness; travel; recreation. "A guided wilderness solo experience that could have a deeply moving effect on you and your life. Now offers solos in southern Baja California by the ocean, mainland Mexico, southern Arizona's Chiricahua Mountains, the Rocky Mountains of southern Colorado, and near the Lost River in West Virginia's Appalachian Mountains." **Contact(s):** John P. Milton.

## A ◆ The Natursoil Company
1015 W. Saint Germain, #400
Saint Cloud, MN 56301
**Concern(s):** agriculture; environment; recycling. Attractive cedar compost bins and new "Super-Charger" compost aeration mat for a self-aerating pile is an improved system for converting yard waste into rich compost in only thirty days with little or no turning. Write for free information on mail order, dealer, municipal and fundraising programs.

## A ◆ Necessary Trading Company
8131 Main St.
New Castle, VA 24127   (800)447-5354
**Concern(s):** agriculture; environment; organic; pesticides; food production. Safe and natural fertilizers and pest controls for homeowners, gardeners, and farmers. **Other Resources:** Catalog, $2 refundable with order. **Member:** Co-op America. **Contact(s):** Bill Wolf. (703)864-5103.

## $ ◆ New Alternatives Fund
295 Northern Blvd.
Great Neck, NY 11021   (516)466-0808
**Concern(s):** economics; energy; solar; socially-responsible investing; appropriate technology. A mutual fund concentrating on solar and alternative energy investment. Excludes weapons, South Africa, and nuclear power. **Other Resources:** "We will make available a prospectus that changes little from year to year for investors. We issue semi-annual reports to shareholders of our progress." **Est.:** 1982. **Contact(s):** Seurd (Vice President), Maurice (President).

## A ◆ The New American Food Company
2833 Duke Homestead Rd.
Durham, NC 27705
**Concern(s):** agriculture; economics; health; alternative consumer; organic. **Contact(s):** Walker Pruitt.

## $ ◆ New Land Trust
Box 263, Plumadore Rd.
Saranac, NY 12981
**Concern(s):** economics; environment; land trusts.

## ☼ ◆ New Millennium Technologies
Box 1049
Boulder, CO 80306   (800)488-2088
**Concern(s):** energy; economics; trade; alternative markets; efficiency; conservation. Energy-efficient computers, printers, fax machines, anti-radiation screens and low emission monitors. Computer, printer, copier, fax, telephone, modem, and scanner all in one efficient unit. Environmentally appropriate office equipment and office products, recycled fax paper, sticky notes, etc. (303)444-1476.

## $ ◆ Niche Marketing Services
See SEVENTH GENERATION CATALOG.

## A ◆ Nichols Garden Nursery Inc.
1190 N. Pacific Highway
Albany, OR 97321   (503)928-9280
**Concern(s):** agriculture; environment; family farms; forests. A family-owned seed and nursery business for over forty years which brings people closer to nature through gardening. Hard-to-find varieties. **Other Resources:** Free catalog. **Member:** Co-op America.

## E ◆ Northern Sun Merchandising
2916 East Lake Ave.
Minneapolis, MN 55406   (612)729-2001
**Concern(s):** environment; economics; alternative markets; green consumer. **Contact(s):** Scott Cramer.

## ✐ ◆ Northland Poster Collective
1613 East Lake St.
Minneapolis, MN 55407
**Concern(s):** arts; labor; peace; culture; activism; graphics. World-changing art of the labor, peace and justice movements. (800)627-3082.

## ✍ ◆ Not Ltd...
6219 Rockcliff Dr.
Hollywood, CA 90068   (310)396-3135
**Concern(s):** education; environment; childhood. Presents products committed to the enhancement of human life..."Peace Pebbles," a peaceful conflict resolution game and a new approach to a timeless tradition. Island Press, renowned for its library of books for better conservation and management. B.Y.O.B., environmentally compatible products with style for home and office. **Publisher:** Island Press. (800)347-WICK.

## E ◆ One Source
164 N. Blackston #1492
Fresno, CA 93701
**Concern(s):** energy;economics; environment; intentional communities; green consumer; alternative markets. This catalog is open to alternative communities and others who are striving to establish a social system based on biospheric integrity and personal development. The products listed as well as the process of manufacture must strive to be resource conserving, recyclable, biodegradable, and reduce waste to a minimum.

## T ◆ One World Trading Co.
Box 310
Summertown, TN 38483
**Concern(s):** Third World; labor; Central America. An organization marketing clothing made by Mayan artisans - colorful woven designs for adults and children. **Other Resources:** Catalog, $1. Retail only. Nonprofit. **Member:** Co-op America.

## A ◆ Organic Farms, Inc.
10726B Tucker St.
Beltsville, MD 20705   (800)222-6244
**Concern(s):** agriculture; health; organic; nutrition; alternate consumer. A grower and distributor providing information on where to buy organically grown food and a nationwide listing of organic restaurants. **Contact(s):** Joseph Dunsmoor (President).

## ✐ ◆ Orr Enterprises
Box 1717, Dept. CC
Monrovia, CA 91017
**Concern(s):** arts; environment; economics; green consumer; recycling; conservation; trees; alternative markets. Wildlife notecards on recycled paper. Original artwork.

## T ◆ Orrin International Trade Co.
3738 W. Whatespear Ave.
Chicago, IL 60647   (312)486-0422
**Concern(s):** Third World; economics; energy; peace; trade; alternative markets; East-West; appropriate technology. Market research has shown a demand for appropriate technologies. Orrin is now identifying small scale manufacturers who would like to use their international expertise and export alternative energy products to the Third World and Eastern Europe.

## E ◆ Out-Of-The-Dumps, Inc.
Box 70
Mt. Rainier, MD 20712
**Concern(s):** environment; economics; trade; recycling. Provides brokerage services and recycling consulting for companies involved with recyclable materials.

## A ◆ Outpost Natural Foods
100 East Capitol Dr.
Milwaukee, WI 53212-1206
**Concern(s):** agriculture; economics; health; alternative consumer; nutrition; organic; trade. A large natural food store. **Other Resources:** Publishes a monthly magazine/catalog. **Contact(s):** Art Blair.

## ✐ ◆ Papier Tiger
1800 Arch St.
Berkeley, CA 94789   (510)601-1138
**Concern(s):** arts; environment; economics; alternative markets; recycling; green consumer. Top quality design on 100% post-consumer, unbleached recycled paper. Dedicated to continually renewing the recycling movement in products and education.

## T ◆ Paraclete Society International
1132 SW 13th Ave.
Portland, OR 97205   (503)274-5434
**Concern(s):** Third World; economics; socially-responsible investing; trade; Central America; jobs; cooperatives; rural communities. Helps rural co-ops in Mexico and Guatemala with start-up loans and technical and marketing assistance. Sells products from these co-ops, returning 70% to producers. **Other Resources:** Catalog, $1. **Member:** Co-op America.

## $ ◆ The Parnassus Fund
244 California St.
San Francisco, CA 94111   (415)362-3505
**Concern(s):** economics; socially responsible investment. A socially-conscious mutual fund with the primary objective of long-term growth of capital, achieved by investing in companies that appear to be undervalued, and that meet social criteria requirements. **Member:** Co-op America. (800)999-3505. **Contact(s):** Jerome L. Dodson (President), Andrew Robinson. (800)999-3505.

## ☙ ◆ Pathways Associates
1640 School St., #105
Moraga, CA 94556-1123   (510)631-0112
**Concern(s):** peace; justice; activism. Develops programs that help individuals take a more active role in issues of global concern. Resource materials on citizen diplomacy, human rights, alternative security. **Member:** Co-op America.

## $ ◆ Pax World Fund
224 State St.
Portsmouth, NH 03801   (603)431-8022
**Affiliation:** Pax World Foundation. **Concern(s):** economics; socially-responsible investing. A no-load, diversified mutual fund investing only in companies producing life-supportive goods and services. Invests in companies, exercising pollution control, producing sustainable goods and services, not weapons production, with fair employment practices and promoting some international development. **Member:** Co-op America. (800)767-1729. **Contact(s):** Linda Werner.

## ✍ ◆ Peace Works, Inc.
3812 N. 1st St.
Fresno, CA 93726   (209)435-8092
**Concern(s):** education; peace; activism. Sells "Give Peace a Chance," a game invented by a child that challenges players to think about global interdependence while maintaining the cultural diversity of other countries. Also, t-shirts, tapes, posters, video. **Other Resources:** Free catalog. **Member:** Co-op America. **Contact(s):** Roberta Alexander.

## ☙ ◆ Peacemaker, Inc.
1348 Commerce Lane
Santa Cruz, CA 95060   (408)429-6000
**Concern(s):** peace; economics; alternative markets. **Contact(s):** Gary Scott.

## ✍ ◆ Pendle Hill
338 Plush Mill Rd.
Wallingford, PA 19086-6099 (215)566-4507
**Concern(s):** education; spiritual; interfaith; community. Quaker-directed ecumenical adult education center for religious and social concerns. Weekend conferences, resident program, pamphlets and books. **Other Resources:** Free catalog and brochures. Nonprofit. **Member:** Co-op America.

**$ ◆ Peter D. Kinder & Co.**
Kinder, Lydenberg, Domini & Co.
7 Dana St.
Cambridge, MA 02138   (617)547-7479
**Concern(s):** economics; environment; socially-responsible investing; green consumer. Prepares social analysis of over 1,000 companies. Provides the Social Index, a benchmark index of 400 companies that have passed social screens. **Member:** Co-op America.
**Contact(s):** Peter D. Kinder (President).

**☼ ◆ Planetary Solutions**
Box 1049
Boulder, CO 80306   (800)488-2088
**Concern(s):** energy; environment; economics; alternative markets; efficiency; conservation. A home products resource catalog. Low-flow devices, drip-irrigation systems, compact fluorescent lights, hot water heaters, refrigerators, solar panels, paints and finishes, home-remodeling products. Also automotive products: non-petroleum oils and lubricants, emissions reduction and fuel-efficiency devices and the best advice. **Other Resources:** Catalog available.

**✍ ◆ The Playmill of Maine**
RFD 3, Box 89
Dover-Foxcroft, ME 04426   (207)564-8122
**Concern(s):** education; feminism; childhood; family. It's work is to help bring the material world of children into alignment. Through the empowerment of children, healing the Earth gets a radical boost. Our children's projects, Toys for Peace and the World Dolphin Project for Children, use our wooden toys and accessories as deep symbols of peace and ecological awareness. Our job is to bring the dolphins' message through the toys to the hearts and minds of children so they can spread the word. (Write for Info). (207)564-7702.

**T ◆ Plowsharing Crafts**
6301-A Delmar
St. Louis, MO 63130   (314)863-3723
**Concern(s):** Third World; economics; alternative markets.
**Contact(s):** Rich Howard-Williams.

**E ◆ Preference Service**
11 W. 42nd St. , Box 3861
New York, NY 10163-3861   (212)768-7277
**Affiliation:** Direct Marketing Association. **Concern(s):** environment; economics; alternative consumer; conservation. Send your name and address to this service, which will remove your personal data from further mass mail lists. Unfortunately, to stop junk mail you are currently receiving, you must write every company to tell them to stop. **Other:** Direct Marketing Association, 11 W. 42nd St., New York City, NY 10036.

**$ ◆ Prentiss Smith & Co. Inc.**
103A Main St.
Brattleboro, VT 05301   (802)254-2913
**Concern(s):** economics; socially responsible investment. Investment management services for socially and environmentally concerned individuals and institutions. **Other Resources:** Free brochure. **Member:** Co-op America.

**H ◆ Preventic's, Inc.**
Box 3027
Kansas City, MO 64112   (800)888-4866
**Concern(s):** health; preventative; nutrition. "Established by a doctor to reduce vitamin costs for his patients. Now he's passing these savings on to you. 'We offer service with a smile! Sold by doctors, these are the finest quality vitamins available, and 80% of our formulas are hypoallergenic. You'll receive a free bimonthly newsletter that helps you help yourself. You can call us when you have questions and our trained staff will be happy to assist you.'"

**$ ◆ Progressive Asset Management**
1814 Franklin St., 9th Fl.
Oakland, CA 94612   (510)834-3722
**Affiliation:** Social Investment Forum. **Concern(s):** economics; socially-responsible investing. A full service, national investment brokerage firm specializing in socially and environmentally responsible investing. Provides access to all major investment vehicles; full range of socially and environmentally responsible investment opportunities; experienced, innovative financial consultants; comprehensive, diversified portfolio management. Offers low-income housing tax-credit investments that funnels taxes away from military. **Other Resources:** Besides low income housing tax-credit, PAM conducts frequent seminars on environmental investing, charitable remainder trusts and socially responsible investment alternatives. **Est.:** 1987. **Dues:** $100/yr. **Fax:** (510)836-1621. (800)527-8627. **Contact(s):** James Nixon, Eric Leenson (Chief Financial Officer).

**P★ Progressive Resources For Grassroots Organizing & Fundraising**
c/o Donnelly/Colt
Box 188
Hampton, CT 06247   (203)455-9621
**Concern(s):** politics; economics; grassroots organizing; fundraising. "Until we have a clean environment, an end to Apartheid and US intervention, a woman's right to choose, freedom and equality for women, gays and people of color, and peace and justice around the world, we'll be producing resources to [assist] those ends." Send for a free catalog. **Other Resources:** T-shirts, buttons, stickers, posters, postcards, union-made, in-stock and custom printing. **Price:** $1/ea. **Publisher:** Donnelly/Colt. **Fax:** (203)455-9527. **Contact(s):** Clay Colt, Kate Donnelly

**$ ◆ Progressive Securities**
5200 SW Macadam St., #350
Portland, OR 97201   (503)224-7828
**Concern(s):** economics; socially-responsible investing. Specializes in assisting concerned individual and institutional investors with a full range of socially responsible investments. "We offer financial services that provide competitive returns while investing in companies making a positive impact on the world through their products, services, and business ethics." **Other Resources:** Publishes a small quarterly newsletter. **Est.:** 1983. **Contact(s):** Carsten Henningsen (President), Wendy Jean Mitchell (Office Manager).

**$ ◆ Project Now Inc.**
Box 3970
Rock Island, IL 61201   (309)793-6931
**Concern(s):** economics; labor; education; socially-responsible investing; community investments; jobs; seniors; youth. Helps low-income people in Illinois with: business start-up, revolving loans, scholarships, Head Start, weatherization, health clinic, senior citizen employment, and more. Nonprofit. **Member:** Co-op America.

**T ◆ Pueblo to People**
1616 Montrose
Houston, TX 77006-1240   (713)523-1197
**Concern(s):** Third World; economics; trade; Central America; cooperatives. Works directly with Central American craft cooperatives, providing technical assistance, distribution vehicles and product development. **Other Resources:** Catalog of clothing, food, gifts available. Nonprofit. **Member:** Co-op America.

**$ ◆ Puget Sound Co-op Federation/Foundation**
4201 Roosevelt Way NE
Seattle, WA 98105   (206)632-4559
**Concern(s):** economics; trade; cooperatives. A trade association of cooperatively-owned businesses in Washington state. Helps existing small businesses and co-ops with expansion and crises, and assists in starting co-ops. **Member:** Co-op America.

**H ◆ Pure Products for Personal Care & Natural Healing**
Box 680, Shaker St.
Sutton, NH 03273
**Affiliation:** Inter-Natural. **Concern(s):** health; environment; agriculture; green consumer; alternative consumer; organic.

**☼ ◆ PV Energy Systems**
See PV NEWS.

**✐ ◆ Quad Left Graphics**
2 Church St.
Burlington, VT 05401   (802)658-4267
**Concern(s):** arts; economics; graphics. Graphic design for nonprofit and progressive organizations. Donates a portion of profits to peace groups and other politically progressive groups. **Member:** Co-op America.

**✈ ◆ R.E.I. (Recreational Equipment International)**
Box 88127, Dept. #N1029
Seattle, WA 98138   (800)426-4840
**Concern(s):** environment; education; travel; recreation; economics; cooperatives. Quality gear, clothing, accessories, and adventure tours for outdoor enthusiasts. Largest US consumer cooperative, it actively supports environmental programs through contributions to the Outdoor Alliance and volunteer work. **Other Resources:** Free catalog. Satisfaction guaranteed. **Member:** Co-op America.

**☛ ◆ RAGE**
Box 86837
Portland, OR 97206   (503)257-0278
**Concern(s):** environment; animal rights. Environmental and animal rights T-shirts.

**T ◆ Rainbow World Imports**
1043 69th Ave.
Philadelphia, PA 19126   (215)927-4686
**Concern(s):** Third World; economics; alternative markets; Central America; Asia. Imports clothing and other items from Guatemala, Nepal, and Tibetan refugees. **Member:** Co-op America.

**T ◆ RainForest Essentials, Ltd.**
12233 W. Olympic Blvd., #255
West Los Angeles, CA 90064
**Concern(s):** Third World; environment; economics; alternative markets; indigenous peoples; green consumer. Quality body care products with ingredients that are harvested from tropical rain forests. 40% of the profits are returned to Cultural Survival, a nonprofit organization, to be spent solely on rainforest projects that directly benefit the people who live there.

**☼★ Real Goods Alternative Energy Sourcebook**
966-M Mazzoni St., #4B
Ukiah, CA 95482   (800)762-7325
**Affiliation:** Real Goods Trading Company. **Concern(s):** energy; environment; solar; science; appropriate technology. The most complete work on independent power production ever assembled. Nine chapters on everything you need to disconnect from the utility company — solar, electric, wind, hydro, propane refrigeration, instantaneous water heating, composting and low flush toilets. The Sourcebook is $10 refundable on the first $100 order. **Other Resources:** Solar panels and other alternative energy products, do-it-yourself housing kits, 12-volt appliances, books, music, toys - anything for the new pioneer! **Price:** $10/ea. **Bulk:** $6ea/24. **Pages:** 420. **Member:** Co-op America. **Contact(s):** John Schaeffer (Proprietor), Eileen Enzla (Manager). (707)468-9214.

**E ◆ Recycle America**
18500 VonKarmen Ave.
Irvine, CA 92715   (714)474-2311
**Concern(s):** environment; economics; recycling. Recycle America, a Waste Management of North America service, is the nation's largest provider of collection and processing services for recyclable materials, serving commercial businesses and municipalities across the US and Canada.

**A ◆ Redwood City Seed Co.**
Box 361
Redwood City, CA 94064
**Concern(s):** agriculture; organic. Available by mail, a great selection of non-hybrid organics.

**T ◆ Resource Catalog**
Center of Concern
3700 13th St. NE
Washington, DC 20017   (202)635-2757
**Affiliation:** Center of Concern. **Concern(s):** Third World; economics; demographics; justice; Africa; fundraising. A form of raising money and helping people in Africa. A project of the Coalition for Peace in the Horn of Africa. Nonprofit. **Contact(s):** Peter J. Henriot, James Hug.

**E ◆ Resources Conservation**
Box 71
Greenwich, CT 06836   (203)964-0600
**Concern(s):** environment; energy; water; efficiency; conservation. Manufactures bathroom fixtures, including energy and water saving devices, and European-styled replacement parts for tub and shower. **Other Resources:** Free catalog. **Member:** Co-op America. (800)243-2862.

**J ◆ Riptide Communications**
666 Broadway
New York, NY 10012   (212)260-5000
**Affiliation:** Center for Constitutional Rights. **Concern(s):** justice; media; constitutional rights. Public Relations firm for the Center. **Contact(s):** Kathy Engel.

**☼ ◆ Rising Sun Enterprises**
Box 586
Snowmass, CO 81654   (303)927-8051
**Concern(s):** energy; economics; alternative markets.

**S ◆ Roots & Wings**
16607 Barberry , #C2
Southgate, MI 48195   (313)285-3679
**Concern(s):** spiritual; health; transformation; psychology. Dedicated to re-membering our connection. Individual and group programs through the Transpersonal HypGnosis Center. **Other Resources:** Extensive selection of transformational resources - 80 page catalog, $1. **Member:** Co-op America.

**E ◆ ROS Recycled Office Supply**
Box 15055
San Luis Obispo, CA 93406  (805)544-5457
**Concern(s):** environment; economics; green consumer; alternative markets. A complete line of recycled office products including computer paper, copier paper, file folders and Post-Its; also custom printing of letterhead, newsletters and brochures. In association with GDP Enterprises, ROS offers consultation on and implementation of a full line of waste and energy management systems. **Contact(s):** Sandi Sigurdson.

**E ◆ Rural Praxis, Inc.**
66 Orange Rd.
Warwick, MA 01364  (508)544-8521
**Concern(s):** environment; economics; fundraising; natural resources; land; conservation; analysis. Consultants in land use, environmental protection, and economic development. Grant-writing services for nonprofits. Produces educational materials such as World Bank, a board game. **Member:** Co-op America.

**✍ ◆ S.E.E. Global Contrast**
7632 Topanga Canyon Blvd. , #207
Canoga Park, CA 91304  (818)773-3044
**Concern(s):** education; arts; environment; recycling; graphics. Company's goal is to reach a broad audience, especially kids, through promotional and educational materials delivering a message that recycling and saving the environment can be exciting and fun. "We created the cartoon character: Thammy The Reagle Recycling Eagle - The Most Wanted #1 Public Hero!, for this purpose."

**L ◆ Samuel J. Greenberg Co.**
260 Grant St.
New Holland, PA 17557  (717)355-9297
**Concern(s):** labor; economics; environment; alternative markets; green consumer. Sells fabric to Amish and old-order communities. Also, cloth-fitted diapers made by Mennonites. Retail and wholesale. **Member:** Co-op America.

**$ ◆ Sand County Venture Fund**
MHK Ventures, Inc.
Palo Alto, CA 94301  (415)324-4414
**Concern(s):** economics; environment; trade; socially-responsible investing. Supports and maintains a venture capital fund with equity for environmental companies. **Contact(s):** Michael Hall Kieschnick.

**☢ ◆ Sandia National Laboratories (SNLA)**
Solar Energy Department
Box 5800
Albuquerque, NM 87185
**Concern(s):** energy; solar; research. "Implements the array and balance-of-systems (BOS) development, concentrator research, and systems tests subprograms of the federal photovoltaic program. This development effort is directed toward reducing the cost and performance of array and power conditioning subsystems to competitive levels as PV module prices also decrease. Concentrator research is directed at reducing the cost of PV modules through the concentration of sunlight." Also, caters to nuclear interests. **Contact(s):** Lynn Billman, Gary Cook.

**E ◆ Save the Rainforest Shopping Bags**
604 Jamie St.
Dodgeville, WI 53533  (608)935-9435
**Concern(s):** environment; economics; green consumer; alternative markets. Silk screened bags with frog design, are the size of a regular shopping bag and have handles. They can be sold for school fundraising projects. If the use of these bags can be popularized they can help reduce waste in our communities.

**☢ ◆ SaveEnergy Co.**
2410 Harrison St.
San Francisco, CA 94110  (415)824-6010
**Concern(s):** energy; environment; appropriate technology; efficiency; conservation. "Easy-to-use products for the home and garden. Now you can save energy and resources without sacrificing lifestyle. For instance, one new bulb replaces an ordinary incandescent and saves 55 gallons of oil over its lifetime. The same bulb uses only a quarter of the energy that a regular incandescent would. The catalog includes lights, timers, solar and recycling products, gift ideas and more."

**$ ◆ Self-Help Credit Union**
413 E. Chapel Hill St.
Box 3619C
Durham, NC 27702-3619  (919)683-3016
**Affiliation:** Center for Community Self-Help. **Concern(s):** economics; urban; demographics; community self-reliance; housing; empowerment; cooperatives; community investment. Provides financing for home ownership, minority and women owned businesses, and cooperatively-run businesses in North Carolina. Anyone can join - federally insured deposit accounts. **Member:** Co-op America.

**T ◆ SERRV Self-Help Handcrafts**
500 Main St.
Box 365
New Windsor, MD 21776  (301)635-6464
**Affiliation:** Church of the Brethren. **Concern(s):** Third World; economics; spiritual; consumer; alternative; faith. Administered by the Church's General Board, Elgin, Illinois. Its purpose is to promote the social and economic progress of people in developing regions of the world by purchasing and marketing their handcrafts in a just and direct-as-possible manner. **Other Resources:** Resale and wholesale catalog. Nonprofit. **Member:** Co-op America. **Contact(s):** Linda Jacobson.

**T ◆ Seva Catalog**
108 Spring Lake Dr.
Chelsea, MI 48118  (800)223-SEVA
**Concern(s):** Third World; economics; alternative markets. "Branch out in your gift giving. Trees, food, water, training, sight and medical care for people around the world are a few examples from the Seva Foundation 'Gifts of Service' Catalog. When you give tax-deductible gifts in the names of friends, they receive a personalized card describing the service project." Nonprofit.

**E ◆ Seventh Generation Catalog**
126 Intervale Rd.
Burlington, VT 05401  (800)456-1197
**Affiliation:** Niche Marketing Services. **Concern(s):** environment; economics; water; recycling; alternative markets; green consumer. Catalog of recyclable products offers consumers a way to help both present and future generations protect themselves and their precious environment. It contains a wide variety of biodegradable household products. There are also products such as home radon tests, water-saving faucets, stationery made from recycled newsprint and other items that will safeguard and preserve the environment. **Price:** $2/ea. **Pages:** 48. **Contact(s):** Alan Newman (President), Jeffrey Hollender (Chairperson). (800)456-1177. 10 Farrell St., South Burlington, VT 05403.

**H ◆ Shaklee Corp.**
444 Market St.
San Francisco, CA 94111  (415)954-3000
**Concern(s):** health; economics; nutrition; preventative medicine. **Other Resources:** Catalog.

**☢ ◆ Signal**
27 Gate 5 Rd.
Sausalito, CA 94965  (415)332-1716
**Affiliation:** Whole Earth Institute. **Concern(s):** energy; appropriate technology; electronic democracy; computer networking. Signal: Communication Tools for the Information Age is a 240-page catalog covering everything hi-tech, low-tech, and no-tech related to human communications, from speaking, acting, and drawing to satellite TV, computer networks, music synthesizers and beyond, with our usual how-to-use-it, where-to-find-it reviews. Nonprofit. **Pages:** 240. **E-Network:** The WELL. **ID:** Kerwit@Well. **Contact(s):** Kelly Teevan (Executive Director).

**P ◆ Soapbox Junction Ltd.**
See ACTION RESOURCE GUIDE under business.

**$ ◆ Social Banking Programs**
14 Elliot St.
Brattleboro, VT 05301  (802)257-0211
**Concern(s):** economics; environment; trade; socially-responsible investing. Assists banks in developing socially responsible lending programs. Helped Vermont National Bank's design its loan fund. **Contact(s):** James Valliere.

**$ ◆ Social Responsibility Investment Group**
The Candler Building
127 Peachtree St., NE, #6
Atlanta, GA 30303  (404)577-3635
**Concern(s):** economics; socially-responsible investing. Registered investment advisor on socially-screened portfolios of financial securities for individuals and institutions with a $200,000 minimum account size. **Member:** Co-op America. **Contact(s):** Bruce Gunter.

**$ ◆ Sohnen-Moe Associates**
3906 W. Ina , #200-264
Tucson, AZ 85741  (602)744-0094
**Concern(s):** economics; trade. A full service personal and professional development company. "We offer consulting and training to individuals and mainly small to medium-sized businesses. We provide tools and techniques for empowering people in business." **Other Resources:** See guide, BUSINESS MASTERY. **Est.:** 1978. **Price:** $19.95/ea. **Bulk:** 40% off/24. **Pages:** 256. **Publisher:** Sohnen-Moe Associates. **Labels:** 1200. **Fax:** (602)744-7887. **Contact(s):** Cherie Sohnen-Moe (President).

**☢ ◆ Solar Car Corporation**
1300 Lake Washington Rd.
Melbourne, FL 32935  (407)254-2997
**Concern(s):** energy; solar; renewables; appropriate technology. Develops, manufactures and markets solar electric, solar hybrid and alternative fueled vehicles, including stretch vans, offering practical transportation for urban use as commuter cars, utility vehicles and mass transit purposes. The company also offers solar electric boats, vehicle components and modules for retrofit builders and suppliers.

**☢ ◆ Solar Power Wagon**
ISD
600 15th St.
Newport Beach, CA 92663  (714)650-7042
**Concern(s):** energy; solar; appropriate technology. Pre-manufactured mobile photovoltaic (solar) power generating stations with optional gas, diesel or propane powered back-up generators and battery charging systems.

**$ ◆ South Shore Bank**
71st and Jeffrey Blvd.
Chicago, IL 60649  (312)753-5636
**Concern(s):** economics; socially-responsible investing; community investment. Full-service bank, pioneer of community reinvestment. All accounts support housing rehab, small business, and education in disinvested neighborhoods. National ATM card. Minimum investment: $100. **Member:** Co-op America.

**$ ◆ SRI Advisors**
24861 Alicia Parkway, #C-293
Laguna Hills, CA 92653  (714)588-9863
**Concern(s):** economics; Third World; environment; socially-responsible investing; South Africa; Asia. Socially responsible investment strategies and portfolio management for individuals and organizations. An SEC-registered investment advisor specializing in socially and environmentally responsible money management. In addition to traditional financial analysis, screens against nuclear energy, weapons manufacturing, South Africa, China, environmental pollution and favors companies that offer value to society and support positive social and environmental progress. **Other Resources:** See WALL STREET GREEN REVIEW newsletter. **Contact(s):** David L. Brown.

**✏ ◆ Steeleworks**
Box 18889
Philadelphia, PA 19119  (215)242-4107
**Concern(s):** arts; graphics. Distributes the work of artist Sara Steele in the form of cards, calendars, posters, t-shirts, etc. Also offers product development and marketing consulting to nonprofit organizations, socially conscious businesses and cultural institutions. **Contact(s):** Sara Steele.

**T ◆ Stephanie Schuster, Inc.**
345 W. 35th, #14
New York, NY 10001  (212)947-3900
**Concern(s):** Third World; feminism; trade; Latin America. Designer hand-knit women's sweaters made by women working at home in Uruguay. Embroidered shirts and other items. Wholesale only. **Member:** Co-op America.

**E ◆ Stewart's Greenline**
189 E. 28th Ave.
Vancouver, BC V5V 3R1 Canada  (800)665-1506
**Concern(s):** environment; economics; green consumer; alternative markets. Wholesaler/reseller of environmental products. **Other Resources:** An environmental directory of over 3000 businesses who cater to ecological concerns, $9.95. **Contact(s):** Don Rankin.

**☢ ◆ Sun Watt/Skyheat Association**
RFD Box 751
Addison, ME 04606  (207)497-2204
**Concern(s):** energy; solar; conservation; appropriate technology. Manufacturers solar electric products in an alternative energy workshop, including hybrid modules for both electricity and hot water, and solar battery rechargers. **Other Resources:** Free brochure, wholesale and retail. **Member:** Co-op America.

**✏ ◆ Syracuse Cultural Workers Project**
Box 6367
Syracuse, NY 13217  (315)474-1132
**Concern(s):** arts; culture. A publisher and distributor of calendars, posters, and cards that address the issues of social concern and human liberation. **Member:** Co-op America.

**☮ ◆ Tax Resistor's Penalty Fund**
Box 25
N. Manchester, IN 46962
**Concern(s):** peace; politics; economics; war tax revolt; economic conversion; peace dividend.

**T ♦ Thread of Hope**
Route 1, Box 1162
Lopez, WA 98161      (206)468-3497
**Concern(s):** Third World; economics; cooperatives; trade; Central America. Formed a weaving cooperative in Guatemala, and imports shawls and men's shirts made by the 300 weavers. **Member:** Co-op America.

**E ♦ Tire Retread Information Bureau**
26555 Carmel Rancho Blvd., #3
Carmel, CA 93923      (408)625-3247
**Concern(s):** environment; recycling. Retreaded tires for cars, trucks, airplanes, buses and emergency vehicles. "Retreading is the highest and best use for a worn tire." Retreading is Recycling.

**E ♦ Traditionals, Inc.**
4515 Ross Rd.
Sebastopol, CA 95472   (707)823-8911
**Concern(s):** environment; recycling. Envision products are the result of decades Fort Howard has spent developing the most advanced recycling technology in the world. Fort Howard and Traditionals are proud to offer you Envision - paper products that can help you do your part... to make a world of difference.

**✈ ♦ Travel Collaborative**
c/o Omni Travel on Arrow
14 Arrow St.
Cambridge, MA 02138   (617)628-2667
**Concern(s):** education; travel; networking. Cooperatively-run full service travel agency. Provides services for Co-op America's Travel Links and participates in the 1% for Peace program. **Member:** Co-op America.

**♿ ♦ Treekeepers**
249 S. Highway 101, #518
Solano Beach, CA 92075    (619)481-6403
**Concern(s):** justice; environment; disabled's rights; recycling; forests. Cotton shopping bag. Bag display stands for stores are made by the Association of Retarded Citizens. Wholesale and retail. **Member:** Co-op America.

**A ♦ Tucson Cooperative Warehouse**
350 S. Toole Ave.
Tucson, AZ 85701      (602)884-9951
**Concern(s):** agriculture; health; nutrition; organic; food distribution. A member-owned natural foods distributor serving the Southwest. Pricelist contains over 4,000 items with an emphasis on natural/ organic products. **Member:** Co-op America.

**L ♦ Twin Oaks Hammocks**
Route 4, Box 169
Louisa, VA 23093      (703)894-5125
**Concern(s):** labor; economics; cooperatives; intentional communities; alternative markets. An income-sharing community of 80 people living and working together. Makes and sells oak-and-rope hammocks and hammock chairs, wholesale and retail. **Member:** Co-op America.

**T ♦ UGAN (Union des Artisans du Nord)**
3327 18th St. NW
Washington, DC 20010   (202)328-6834
**Concern(s):** economics; Third World; trade; cooperatives; Africa. US representative of a cooperative of 400 African craftspeople skilled in weaving, crochet, hand-painted fabrics, pottery, wood carving, and bronze casting. **Member:** Co-op America.

**☼ ♦ Upstate Eco-Logic**
29 Drake Rd.
Newfield, NY 14867
**Concern(s):** energy; recycling; conservation. Company providing products for waste reduction, energy conservation, and recycling.

**☸ ♦ Valley Light Center**
1509 Ranch Rd.
Weed, CA 96094      (916)938-3772
**Concern(s):** peace; economics; arts; environment; activism; graphics; culture; alternative. Mail-order catalog with peace and environmental themes: books, tapes, posters, incense, rubber stamps, beeswax candles in a variety of colors. **Member:** Co-op America.

**♦ Vermont Land Trust**
5 Thomas Hill
Woodstock, NY 50309
**Concern(s):** economics; agriculture; land trusts; family farms. Alternative financial strategies are used for land trust projects to help preserve family farms.

**$ ♦ Vermont National Bank**
Box 804
Brattleboro, VT 05302   (800)544-7108

**Concern(s):** economics; socially-responsible investing. Full-service bank with socially-responsible fund - accounts include checking with interest, CD, and IRA. Money supports affordable housing, farming, environmental projects, small business development. Co-op America Visa Card. Funds in these accounts are covered by FDIC. **Member:** Co-op America. **Contact(s):** John Hashhagen, Jr. (President). (802)257-7151.

**A ♦ The Walnut Acres Organic Farms**
Penns Creek
Middleburgh, PA 17862 (717)837-0601
**Concern(s):** agriculture; health; organic; nutrition. Organic farm selling products through a mail-order catalog: cereals, baking mixes, jams, nut butters, pasta, canned vegetables and soups, as well as cooking and food processing supplies. **Other Resources:** CATALOG OF WHOLE FOODS FOR HEALTHFUL LIVING. **Est.:** 1946. **Member:** Co-op America. (800)344-9025. **Contact(s):** Paul Keene (Editor), Carolyn Straub (800)433-3998.

**A ♦ Waste Not**
1720 E. Garry Ave., #109
Santa Ana, CA 92715   (714)863-7133
**Concern(s):** agriculture; environment; economics; recycling; water. Carries an innovative breakthrough for kitchen waste separation and recycling. The Kitchen Compost installs under the sink to an existing home disposer and will collect viable organic matter while discharging "clean" water into the sewer line. Also carries water saving devices.

**E ♦ We Care**
77-725 Enfield Lane, #120
Palm Desert, CA 92260   (619)360-3838
**Concern(s):** environment. Quality household cleaners, recycled paper, games, books, videos, diapers, compact fluorescent bulbs, water savers and more! Our EarthPac gift packs make it easy to get a friend started, too! **Contact(s):** Jim Lichtman. (800)356-4430.

**E ♦ Webster Industries**
58 Pulaski St.
Peabody, MA 01960      (508)532-2000
**Concern(s):** environment; recycling. Manufacturer and distributor of recycled plastics products. Webster's Renew and heavier gauge Good Sense bags have received Green Cross certification for their respective 80% and 50% recycled plastics content, 24% of which is post-consumer.

**☼ ♦ Westgate Enterprises**
2407 Wilshire Blvd., #221
Santa Monica, CA 90403   (310)447-5891
**Concern(s):** energy; environment; economics; health; alternative consumer; efficiency. Distributor of complete line of long-life, full-spectrum (sunlight-simulating) incandescent, fluorescent and halogen lights. These lights relieves eye strain, fatigue and SAD (seasonal depression), shows true color and increases productivity. **Other Resources:** Free catalogue. (310)478-1954.

**E ♦ Whale Gifts Collection**
Box 810
Old Saybrook, CT 06475 (800)227-1929
**Affiliation:** Center for Marine Conservation. **Concern(s):** environment; conservation; fundraising. "A full-color catalog presented by the Center for Marine Conservation, contains decorative items, educational products, prints, and sculptures. Proceeds are used to fund marine conservation efforts." Nonprofit. **Pages:** 48.

**E ♦ White Industries**
100 Visionary Way
Fishers, IN 46038      (317)849-6830
**Concern(s):** environment; energy; global warming; transportation. Goal: to "green up" the automotive industry. For years, White has been a leader in protecting the Earth's ozone through the development of equipment to recycle the refrigerant in automotive air conditioners. Now the company is expanding to address a broad range of environmental issues in the auto industry.

**☛ ♦ Without Harm**
4605 Pauli Dr.
Manlius, NY 13104      (315)682-8346
**Concern(s):** environment; economics; green consumer; animal rights; alternative markets. Alternative cruelty-free products. **Contact(s):** Nancy Pedersen.

**$ ♦ Women's World Banking (WWB)**
8 West 40th St., 10th Fl.
New York, NY 10018      (212)768-8513
**Concern(s):** feminism; community investments; empowerment. A global network of 46 local affiliates in 38 countries with another 50 affiliates soon to be formed. Their capital funds are now valued at $10,000,000. The most impressive figure of all is a loan loss rate of 1.5% on 56,000 loans. **Other Resources:** Publishes

WWB NEWS, has developed a Management Institute, and a WWB Affiliate Exchange Program. **Contact(s):** Nancy Barry (President).

**$ ♦ The Worker Owned Network**
50 S. Court St.
Athens, OH 45701      (614)592-3854
**Concern(s):** economics; socially-responsible investing; worker ownership; jobs. Helps low-income people start their own worker-cooperative businesses in Southeast Ohio. Businesses started so far include: a restaurant, machine shop, health care, and craft shop. **Member:** Co-op America.

**$ ♦ Working Assets**
230 California St., #500
San Francisco, CA 94111   (415)989-3200
**Concern(s):** economics; environment; trade; socially-responsible investing. "Its VISA is the only credit card that works for the environment, peace, human rights, and economic justice... at no extra cost to you! Five cents goes to groups like Amnesty International, Rainforest Action Network, and Oxfam America. We know you have other cards, so we'll waive the fee for six months, then just $20 a year at 17.5% APR." (800)522-7759.

**$ ♦ Working Assets Funding Service**
230 California St., #500
San Francisco, CA 94111   (415)788-0777
**Affiliation:** Working Assets. **Concern(s):** economics; socially-responsible investing. Provides Working Assets credit cards, phone service and travel service, all of which are donation-linked products supporting progressive nonprofit organizations working for peace, human rights, hunger and the environment. Member of Co-op America. **Other Resources:** See TOOLS FOR PRACTICAL IDEALISTS - A Guide. **Member:** Co-op America. (800)522-7759. **Contact(s):** Carolyn Berner.

**$ ♦ Working Assets Long Distance Program**
230 California St., #500
San Francisco, CA 94111   (800)669-8585
**Affiliation:** Working Assets. **Concern(s):** economics; environment; fundraising; activism; trade. "Now there's an easy way to support progressive nonprofits... at no cost to you! Working Assets Long Distance donates 1% of your charges to groups like Amnesty International, Rainforest Action Network, and Oxfam America, while giving you high quality service and low rates through an arrangement with US Sprint. Put your principles on the line. Call to sign up or send for information." (800)522-7759.

**$ ♦ Working Assets Money Fund**
230 California St., #400
San Francisco, CA 94111   (800)533-3863
**Affiliation:** Working Assets. **Concern(s):** economics; socially-responsible investing. "How to earn good money while helping to clean up the environment, fight apartheid, improve higher education, support family farms, slow the arms race and encourage renewable energy."

**$ ♦ World Bank**
1818 H St. NW
Washington, DC 20433   (202)477-1234
**Affiliation:** United Nations. **Concern(s):** economics; Third World; trade; development. A United Nations lending institution involved with massive projects throughout the world. Though some projects are much needed, many have dubious results especially in the Third World. It has not totally been able to avoid the manipulations of large corporations and superpower interests. **Other Resources:** World Bank Publications are available at the following address: Department 0552, Washington DC, 20073-0552. Guide, DEVELOPMENT DATA BOOK, and periodical, STRATEGIC PLANNING & REVIEW.

**$ ♦ World Peace by Nina Grand**
111 East 14th St., #225
New York, NY 10003      (212)533-5967
**Concern(s):** economics; Third World; labor; trade; cooperatives; Central America; development; jobs. Works with Mayan weavers in Guatemala to make and sell clothing. **Member:** Co-op America.

**A ♦ Worm's Way**
3151 S. Highway, #446
Bloomington, IN 47401   (800)274-9676
**Concern(s):** agriculture; organic; family farms. "...is a unique company which offers an extensive selection of hydroponic and organic gardening supplies. They feature high-intensity indoor lighting systems, complete hydroponic systems, and a comprehensive stock of organic garden accessories. Distributors of earthworm castings, bat and seabird guano." **Other Resources:** Catalog. **Price:** $2/ea.

**✍ ♦ The Wright Group**
10949 Technology Place
San Diego, CA 92127

**Concern(s):** education. An extensive catalog of Whole Language materials, including The Story Box, a large number of reading series, and materials for parents and educators. Catalog includes The Whole Idea, a Whole Language newsletter with the latest information on Whole Language theory, research, and practice, Also offers teacher training.

H ▶ **WSA Community Pharmacy**
    341 State St.
    Madison, WI 53703    (608)251-3308
**Concern(s):** health; economics; worker ownership; holism; alternative consumer; nutrition; preventative medicine. Worker-collective pharmacy selling prescriptions, herbs, vitamins, homeopathy, health and beauty aids. Retail only. **Other Resources:** Mail order catalog, $1. **Member:** Co-op America.

H ▶ **Wysong Corporation**
    1880 N. Eastman Rd.
    Midland, MI 48640    (517)631-0009
**Affiliation:** Wysong Institute. **Concern(s):** health; education; environment; economics; preventative medicine; corporate responsibility. Along with its nonprofit Wysong Institute it produces a variety of products and educational materials emphasizing health prevention and ecological fiduciary responsibility. The winner of new product, environmental and in-house day care facility awards. Nonprofit.

E ▶ **Zellerbach, A Mead Co.**
    4000 E. Union Pacific
    Los Angeles, CA 90023   (213)262-6131
**Concern(s):** environment; recycling. Products which are environmentally safe. Offers our consumers a wide variety of recycled products such as: paper, chemicals and water conservation systems.

# Special Thanks to:

*Co-op America Quarterly* for their cooperation in compiling many of the business listings in this section. **Macrocosm USA, Inc**. is a member of **Co-op America** and encourages other groups and individuals to join.

# ⑥ References: Directories, Guides, et al.

| | | | | | | |
|---|---|---|---|---|---|---|
| A = Agriculture | D = Demographics | ☢ = Energy | ? = Future | L = Labor | S = Spiritual | |
| ☂ = Animal Rights | ♿ = Disabled | E = Environment | G = Gay/Lesbian | M = Media | T = Third World | |
| ✐ = Arts | $ = Economics | ♥ = Family | H = Health | ☙ = Peace | ✈ = Travel | |
| ℂ = Computers | ✍ = Education | F = Feminism | J = Justice | P = Politics | U = Urban | |

**♿▶ Academy of Dentistry for the Handicapped-Referral/Membership Roster**
211 E. Chicago Ave., 16th Fl.
Chicago, IL 60611
**Affiliation:** Academy of Dentistry for the Handicapped. **Concern(s):** health; disabled. 500 dentists, dental hygienists, and other professionals specializing in treatment of handicapped persons; international coverage. **Frequency:** Annual. **Price:** $35/ea. **Pages:** 50. **Labels:** 75. **Contact(s):** Dr. Paul Van Ostenberg (Executive Director).

**♿▶ Accent on Living - Buyers Guide**
Accent Special Publications
Box 700
Bloomington, IL 61702
**Concern(s):** health; disabled. 400+ manufacturers and distributors of products for disabled persons, ranging from wheelchairs to bowling ball pushers and talking calculators. **Frequency:** Biennial. **Pages:** 150. **Date Publ.:** 12/89; 12/91. **Publisher:** Cheever Publishing, Inc. **Contact(s):** Betty Garee (Editor).

**☙▶ Access: A Security Information Service**
1730 M St. NW, #605
Washington, DC 20036  (202)785-6630
**Concern(s):** peace; Third World; education; education; disarmament; conflict resolution; budget; national security. A non-advocacy clearinghouse of information on international security and peace issues, it connects people needing information with the most appropriate sources on issues like arms control, regional conflicts, and military spending. Provides issue briefs and many directories, an inquiry service for specific questions, a speaker referral service, a resource brief providing overviews of issues like conventional arms control and US covert activities, lists of sources and much more. **Other Resources:** See AN INTERNATIONAL DIRECTORY OF INFORMATION ON WAR, PEACE, AND SECURITY. GRASSROOTS PEACE DIRECTORIES—LOWER MIDWEST; MID ATLANTIC;NEW ENGLAND; NORTHWEST & PACIFIC RIM; SOUTH; UPPER MIDWEST; WESTERN STATES. See also, SEARCH FOR SECURITY, a directory. Nonprofit. **Contact(s):** Mary E. Lord (Executive Director).

**E▶ The Acid Rain Foundation - Directories**
1410 Varsity Dr.
Raleigh, NC 27606  (919)828-9443
**Affiliation:** Atmospheric Impact Research Center, NCSU. **Concern(s):** environment; recycling; acid rain; forests. Directories about Acid Rain and air pollution issues, includes the following publications: ACID RAIN: A HANDBOOK FOR STATES AND PROVINCES, ACID RAIN IN MINNESOTA, MINNESOTA LAWS AND ACID DEPOSITON, ECOSYSTEMS, and INTERNATIONAL DIRECTORY OF ACID DEPOSITION RESEARCHES, ACID PRECIPITATION DIGEST, and many more. Goals: To raise public awareness, supply educational resources, and support research. **Dues:** $35/yr. **Member:** Global Tomorrow Coalition. **Contact(s):** Harriett S. Stubbs, Ph.D (Executive Director), Joane Harer (Administrative Assistant).

**S▶ Activist Guide to Religious Funders**
Center for Third World Organizing
3861 Martin Luther King, Jr. Way
Oakland, CA 94609
**Affiliation:** Center for Third World Organizing. **Concern(s):** spiritual; feminism; justice; philanthropy; activism; interfaith. Does your organization need dollars? Do you provide: (1) needed services, (2) organize for social justice, or (3) advocate for women, minorities or immigrants? You may be eligible for funding from over $12 million granted by religious organizations each year. Find out if you qualify with this Guide to over 80 little known sources of funding from the religious community. Classified by religious denomination with name, address, phone and geographical area served. **Frequency:** Biennial. **Price:** $25/ea. **Pages:** 90. **Date Publ.:** 6/91. **Fax:** (510)654-5863. **Contact(s):** Gary Delgado (Editor).

**D▶ Activist's Handbook**
Population Environment Balance
1325 G St. NW, #1003
Washington, DC 20005-3104  (202)879-3000
**Affiliation:** Population Environment Balance. **Concern(s):** demographics; environment; politics; population growth. This guide provides in-depth explanation of population stabilization objectives, organizing techniques, and practical suggestions for activists ranging from local growth control issues to achieving national population stabilization. **Date Publ.:** 1989.

**J▶ Adoption Directory**
Gale Research Inc.
835 Penobscot Building
Detroit, MI 48226-4094  (800)877-GALE
**Concern(s):** justice; family; children. Adoption agencies, national and state agencies and associations involved in adoption and foster parents programs, adoption agencies and orphanages overseas that place children directly with US families; appendixes list state agencies that are sources for birth and marriage records and US immigration offices. Arranged geographically. Also includes bibliography, glossary, each state chapter begins with a survey of adoption laws and regulations; also discussion of adoption requirements outside US. **Price:** $55/ea. **Pages:** 450. **Date Publ.:** 8/89. **Publisher:** Gale Research Inc. **Fax:** (313)961-6241. **Telex:** (810)221-7086. **Contact(s):** Ellen Paul (Editor).

**♿▶ AFB Directory of Services for Blind and Visually Impaired Persons in the United States**
15 W. 16th St.
New York, NY 10011
**Concern(s):** health; disabled; volunteers. About 1,500 government and national voluntary agencies and other organizations, and schools for blind and visually impaired persons; all were established through local, state, or federal legislation. **Frequency:** Irregular. **Price:** $39.95/ea. + $4.50 shipping. **Pages:** 475.

**J▶ Affirmative Action Register**
Affirmative Action, Inc.
8356 Olive Blvd.
St. Louis, MO 63132  (800)537-0655
**Affiliation:** Affirmative Action, Inc.. **Concern(s):** justice; labor; minority rights; disabled rights; jobs. Each issue has 300 positions at a professional level (most requiring advanced study) available to minorities, veterans, and the handicapped; listings are advertisements placed by employers with affirmative action programs. **Frequency:** 12/yr. **Pages:** 50. **Circ.:** 55M. **Fax:** (314)997-1788. **Contact(s):** Warren H. Green (Editor).

**T▶ Africa: a Directory of Resources**
Third World Resources
464 19th St.
Oakland, CA 94612-9761  (510)536-1876
**Affiliation:** Third World Resources/Data Center. **Concern(s):** Third World; Africa. For postage and handling, add $1.50 for North America and $3.00 for foreign air mail. **Price:** $12.95/ea. **Pages:** 160. **Date Publ.:** Fall 1987. **Publisher:** Orbis Books. **Other Formats:** Geonet, user **ID:** 'geo2:tfenton'. **E-Network:** Peacenet. **ID:** 'tfenton'. **Contact(s):** Thomas P. Fenton, Mary J. Heffron (Compilers/Editors).

**J▶ Africa: Human Rights Directory & Bibliography**
c/o Human Rights Centre, University
of Ottawa, 57 Louis Pasteur
Ottawa, ON K1N 6N5 Canada  (613)564-3492
**Affiliation:** Human Rights Internet. **Concern(s):** justice; Third World; peace; Africa. Describes 150 organizations in Africa concerned with human rights and social justice, and organizations outside the continent focused on African human rights issues. Each entry contains information about the origin, purposes and activities of the groups; address, telephone, and names of executive officers; publications and appeals; and where an organization has been represses, the nature and extent. A bibliography of 1,000 annotated entries, the first one of Africa. **Dues:** 50% off to members. **Price:** $35/ea. **Date**

**Publ.:** 1989. **Fax:** (613)564-4054.

**H▶ Age Care Sourcebook: A Resource Guide for the Aging and Their Families**
Simon & Schuster, Inc.
20 Old Tappan Rd.
Old Tappan, NJ 07675
**Concern(s):** health; seniors; Medicare. 600+ state and local agencies that provide information or assistance for the care of the elderly. Principal content is a resource guide for adult children having to care for their aging parents, including information on financial planning, retirement housing, medical care, and wills. **Price:** $10.95/ea. **Date Publ.:** 8/87. **Publisher:** Simon & Schuster, Inc. **Contact(s):** Jean Crichton.

**H▶ Aging Myths: Reversible Causes of Mind and Memory Loss**
McGraw-Hill, Inc.
1221 Avenue of the Americas
New York, NY 10020
**Concern(s):** health; disabled; seniors; psychology. List of organizations that are concerned with the problems of mental dysfunction in the elderly. Principal content is discussion of reversible causes of this mental dysfunction. **Price:** $17.95/ea. **Publisher:** McGraw-Hill, Inc. **Contact(s):** Siegfried Kra.

**H▶ AIDS Information Resources Directory**
American Foundation for AIDS Research
5900 Wilshire Blvd. 2nd Fl., E. Satellite
Los Angeles, CA 90036
**Affiliation:** American Foundation for AIDS Research. **Concern(s):** health; AIDS. Classified by type of product, lists organizations providing educational material and products such as brochures, posters, and audiovisual materials, designed to fight the spread of AIDS. Categories include organization name, address, material or product, and reviewer's comments. **Price:** $10/ea. **Pages:** 195. **Date Publ.:** 1990. **Contact(s):** Trish A. Halleron, Janet I. Pisaneschi (Editors).

**H▶ AIDS Information Sourcebook**
Oryx Press
2214 N. Central at Encanto
Phoenix, AZ 85004
**Concern(s):** health; AIDS. Organizations providing information about AIDS; coverage includes Canada. Also includes chronology of the AIDS epidemic; bibliography of recent publications. Arranged geographically and indexed by organization name. **Frequency:** Annual. **Pages:** 85. **Date Publ.:** 6/90. **Publisher:** Oryx Press. **Fax:** (602)253-2741. **Contact(s):** H. Robert Malinowsky (Editor).

**H▶ AIDS: Public Policy Dimensions**
United Hospital Fund of New York
55 5th Ave.
New York, NY 10003  (212)645-2500
**Affiliation:** United Hospital Fund of New York. **Concern(s):** health; AIDS. About 150 national and local organizations offering AIDS programs and related services. Principal contents are articles resulting from a conference on AIDS held in NY City in January '86 and cosponsored by the United Hospital Fund of NY and the Institute for Health Policy Studies, UCSF. Analyzes AIDS social impact.

**E▶ Alaska Conservation Directory**
c/o Alaska Conservation Foundation
430 W. 7th Ave., #215
Anchorage, AK 99501  (907)276-1917
**Affiliation:** Alaska Conservation Foundation. **Concern(s):** environment; conservation; polar. Full listings for 85 Alaska-based conservation groups. **Price:** $15/ea. **Date Publ.:** 3/90. **Contact(s):** Jim Stratton (Editor).

**H▶ Alcoholism Information & Treatment Directory**
American Business Directories, Inc.
5711 S. 86th Circle
Omaha, NE 68127
**Concern(s):** health; substance abuse; psychology. 12,345 entries

geographically arranged with name, address, phone, size of advertisement, and first year of appearance in Yellow Pages. Compiled from telephone company "Yellow Pages," nationwide. Mailing labels and 3x5 cards. **Frequency:** Annual. **Publisher:** American Business Directories, Inc. **Fax:** (402)331-1505.

### ☼ ♦ All Things Nuclear
3930 Franklin Ave.
Los Angeles, CA 90027  (310)390-3898
**Affiliation:** Federation of Scientists. **Concern(s):** energy; environment; peace; anti-nuclear; hazardous/toxic waste; disarmament. Subjects: The Road to the Bomb; A Technical Review; Nuclear Reactors; Nuclear Weapons; Targeting Nuclear Bombs; The Arms Race; The Physical Effects of Nuclear Explosions; What Would a Nuclear War mean? Nonmilitary Applications of Radioactive Materials Ways to Peace. Reactors; fission/fusion/neutron bombs; plutonium-240 problem; directed nuclear explosions; nuclear weapons accidents; what rad. and rem mean; radioactive fallout; arms race; steps toward peace; shock wave effect. **Price:** $24/ea. **Bulk:** $14ea/24. **Pages:** 303. **Date Publ.:** 1990. **Office:** 3318 Colbert Ave.#200, Los Angeles, CA 90066. **Contact(s):** James C. Ware (Chairman), Sheldon Plotkin (Board Member).

### ⚐ ♦ All-in-One Guide to European-Atlantic Organizations
The European-Atlantic Movement Publications
18 Leylands Ave.
Bradford, BD9 5QW England
**Concern(s):** peace; volunteers; East-West. Approximately 35 inter-governmental and voluntary organizations concerned with Western co-operation. Data include organization name, address, description of body. **Frequency:** Irregular. **Price:** 50 British pence. **Date Publ.:** 1985.

### J ♦ Alliance For Cultural Democracy Membership Directory
Box 7591
Minneapolis, MN 55407
**Affiliation:** Alliance for Cultural Democracy. **Concern(s):** justice; arts; politics; diversity; discrimination; Native peoples; culture; grassroots organizing; activism; minority rights; networking. Includes the names, addresses, phone numbers, and areas of interest of 272 cultural activists. Areas include: arts administration, cultural organizer, political activist, networker, healer therapist, crafts person, video multimedia, radio, writer, dance, community center, theater, storyteller, music, film, mail art, photography, publications, visual arts, and education. **Frequency:** 2/yr. **Pages:** 42. **Date Publ.:** 1990. **Contact(s):** Ron Sakolsky.

### P ♦ The Almanac of American Politics
National Journal
1730 M St. NW
Washington, DC 20036  (202)857-1400
**Concern(s):** politics. Lists members of Congress with biographies, religious affiliation, description of states and districts, committee memberships, office address, phone number, voting records. **Publisher:** National Journal. (800)424-2921.

### ⚐ ♦ An Alternative Almanac for Educators
Living Education Resource Network
1554 Hayes Drive
Manhattan, KS 66502
**Affiliation:** Living Education Resource Network. **Concern(s):** education.

### ⚐ ♦ Alternative America
Resources
Box 1067, Harvard Square Station
Cambridge, MA 02238
**Affiliation:** Resources. **Concern(s):** education; economics; environment; energy; feminism; appropriate technology; intentional communities; activism. A directory of 12,000+ alternative, progressive, innovative, experimental groups and organizations for sources of jobs/career opportunities, and a travel guide to social, cultural, political and ecological experiments. It is broken into three parts: geographical by zip code with name, address, and telephone, plus one or more descriptive words; alphabetical listing of names; and, alphabetical listing of names. Included is about 1,000 foreign names. A great book for the traveling activist. **Frequency:** Annual. **Pages:** 250. **Date Publ.:** Every July. **Other Formats:** Magnetic tape; diskette; 3x5's; rolodex; 8 1/2 x 11 (33 up). **Fax:** (617)288-2999. **Contact(s):** Richard Gardner (Editor).

### ⚐ ♦ Alternative Community History Archive (ACHA)
427 Bloor St. West, #205
Toronto, ON M5S1X7 Canada
**Concern(s):** education; media; peace; environment; justice; feminism. In working for social change and alternatives, there is great value

in remembering what others have done and thought. ACHA seeks to preserve our community's "alternative" history, especially in the form of published materials. **Est.:** 1988.

### ⚏ ♦ Alternative Defense Project
Fund for Peace
345 E. 46th St.
New York, NY 10017  (212)661-5900
**Affiliation:** Fund for Peace. **Concern(s):** peace; national security. Explores alternative world security systems and encourages public and official discussion of Star Wars (SDI). **Contact(s):** James F. Tierney.

### T ♦ An Alternative Directory of South Asian Non-Governmental Organizations
Fourth World Press
202 Gillies Lane
Norwalk, CT 06854
**Concern(s):** Third World; Asia; volunteers. 425+ individuals and organizations in the nonprofit sector, and nongovernmental and private voluntary organizations in India, Bangladesh, Nepal, Pakistan, and Sri Lanka. Classified by topic or issue addressed by organization. **Frequency:** Irregular. **Pages:** 55. **Publisher:** Fourth World Press. **Contact(s):** Todd Nachowitz (Editor).

### M ♦ Alternative Library Literature, A Biennial Anthology
McFarland & Company, Inc.
Box 611
Jefferson, NC 28640
**Concern(s):** media; education; press. Passionate, unusual, refreshing? Yes, especially when some of the not-exactly-run-of-the-mill-LibSci-sources are considered: Feminist Teacher, Bulletin of the Atomic Scientists, UAW Ammo, Briarpatch, New Pages, Library Outreach Reporter, People's Daily World and more; 65 articles all told, covering such diverse topics as Work, Women, Nukes/Peace, Audio/Visuals and Censorship. Interspersed throughout are cartoons by Bert Dodson, Luna Ticks, bulbul, Joe Grant, Paul Hass and Jim Buckett. Index. **Frequency:** Biennial. **Pages:** 396. **Date Publ.:** 1990. **Contact(s):** Sanford Berman, James P. Danky (Co-editors).

### M ♦ Alternative Press Annual
Temple University Press
Broad & Oxford Sts.
Philadelphia, PA 19122  (215)787-8787
**Concern(s):** media; press. List of alternative press newspapers and magazines. Arranged alphabetically with name and address. Excerpts from articles appearing in the periodicals and representative of the alternative press during the year covered. This volume supersedes "Alternative Papers," and is the last in a series of four on this topic. **Date Publ.:** 1/88. **Publisher:** Temple University Press. **Contact(s):** Michael Ames (Editor-in-Chief), Patricia J. Case.

### M ♦ Alternative Press Index
Box 33109
Baltimore, MD 21218  (301)243-2471
**Affiliation:** Alternative Press Center. **Concern(s):** media; arts; justice; politics; press; culture; minority rights; alternative party. A subject index to over 350 alternative and radical periodicals. Each issue contains over 12,000 citations and includes book reviews, film reviews, and record reviews. The format is easy-to-understand. The topics covered include: Native Americans, Blacks, Women, the Left, Gays & Lesbians, New Age politics and more. A collective. **Frequency:** 4/yr. **Circ.:** 1M. **Other Formats:** Mailing labels available. **Office:** 1443 Gorsuch Ave. Baltimore, MD 21218. **Contact(s):** Peggy D'Adamo, Liz O'Lexa.

### ⚐ ♦ Alternative Press Publishers of Children's Books: A Directory
Cooperative Children's Books Center
Box 5288
Madison, WI 53705
**Affiliation:** Cooperative Children's Books Center. **Concern(s):** education; media; press. Nearly 140 alternative presses currently active in children's book publishing, and their distributors; coverage includes Canada. **Frequency:** Biennial. **Pages:** c75. **Contact(s):** Kathleen Horning (Editor).

### ✐ ♦ Alternative Publications: A Guide to Directories, Indexes, Bibliographies and Other Sources
McFarland & Company, Inc.
Box 611
Jefferson, NC 28640
**Concern(s):** arts; media; literature; research; journalism. "Useful bibliographic information... appropriate for university libraries and large public libraries"-Booklist/RBB; "entries give the title, author or editor, publisher, place of publication, date, size, number of pages, price, type of binding and an evaluative annotation"-American Librar-

ies; "of central importance"-Sipapu. This is the work of the American Library Association's Social Responsibilities Round Table Task Force on Alternatives in Print. Contains bibliographies and index. **Other Resources:** Formerly, FIELD GUIDE TO ALTERNATIVE MEDIA by ALA '84. A great list of video resources and where to send for catalogs. Unfortunately publications promoting pederasty and gay porn are listed, which make no sense next to third world issues. **Price:** $14.95/ea. **Pages:** 96. **Publisher:** McFarland & Company, Inc. **Contact(s):** Cathy Seitz Whitaker (Editor).

### ⚐ ♦ Alternatives in Education
Home Education Press
Box 1083
Tonasket, WA 98855
**Concern(s):** education; homeschooling. A guide to the alternatives to public and the traditional private school systems. Includes articles, essays resources on alternative schools, home schooling, Waldorf education, Montessori, apprenticeships, tutoring, alternative colleges and higher education, correspondence schools, learning centers and educational cooperatives. **Price:** $8.75/ea. **Bulk:** 50% off/24. **Pages:** 120. **Date Publ.:** 10/90. **Publisher:** Home Education Press. **Contact(s):** Helen Hegener (Managing Editor).

### ✈ ♦ Alternatives to the Peace Corps: Gaining Third World Experience
Institute for Food & Development Policy
145 9th St.
San Francisco, CA 94103  (800)888-3314
**Affiliation:** Institute for Food & Development Policy. **Concern(s):** education; Third World; peace; development; travel; volunteers. A booklet offering 50+ foreign service organizations (excluding the Peace Corps) that offer long or short-term volunteer service or travel opportunities in developing countries. **Frequency:** Irregular. **Pages:** 50. **Date Publ.:** Spring 1990. **Fax:** (415)864-3909.

### H ♦ Alzheimer's Disease Treatment Facilities and Home Health Care Programs
Oryx Press
4041 N. Central Ave.
Phoenix, AZ 85012
**Concern(s):** health; disabled; seniors. **Price:** $74.50/ea. **Pages:** 545. **Date Publ.:** 10/89. **Publisher:** Oryx Press.

### H ♦ Ambulatory Maternal Health Care and Family Planning Services
Professional Education Department
1275 Mamaroneck Ave.
White Plains, NY 10605
**Concern(s):** health; feminism; family; family planning; birth. List of professional organizations concerned with family planning and new-born care. Principal content is a guide for health care professionals on providing maternal health care and family planning services. **Price:** $1/ea. **Publisher:** Professional Education Department. **Contact(s):** F. E. F. Barnes (Editor).

### S ♦ America's Newest Foundations: The Sourcebook on Recently Created Philanthropies
The Taft Group; Gale Research Inc.
12300 Twinbrook Parkway, #450
Rockville, MD 20852  (800)888-TAFT
**Affiliation:** Taft Group. **Concern(s):** spiritual; philanthropy. 2,600+ private, corporate, and community foundations created since 1980 that provide grants to charitable organizations. **Frequency:** Annual. **Price:** $130/ea. **Pages:** c700. **Date Publ.:** 2/91. **Publisher:** Gale Research Inc. **Fax:** (301)816-0811. **Contact(s):** Susan E. Elnicki (Editor).

### H ♦ American Academy of Psychiatrists in Alcoholism & Addiction - Membership Directory
AAPAA
Box 376
Greenbelt, MD 20770
**Affiliation:** American Academy of Psychiatrists in Alcoholism & Addiction. **Concern(s):** health; substance abuse; psychology. About 800 member psychiatrists and psychiatric-medical residents concerned with alcohol and drug abuse. **Frequency:** Annual. **Price:** $50/ea. **Pages:** 70. **Date Publ.:** 5/91. **Labels:** 100.

### ♿ ♦ American Annals of the Deaf
Convention of American Instructors of the Deaf
Box 3163
Columbia, MD 21045
**Affiliation:** Convention of American Instructors of the Deaf. **Concern(s):** health; disabled. Education, supportive, rehabilitation, research, and information programs and services focusing on the deaf

and aurally handicapped, classified by type of organization or service. **Frequency:** Annual. **Price:** $22.50/ea. **Date Publ.:** Summer. **Fax:** (202)651-5708. **Contact(s):** Dr. William N. Craig, Dr. Helen B. Craig (Editors).

## ✐ ◆ American Association for Music Therapy - Membership Directory
Box 27177
Philadelphia, PA 19118
**Affiliation:** American Association for Music Therapy. **Concern(s):** arts; health; music; psychology. Approximately 530 music therapists and 130 students, with names alphabetically arranged and addresses geographically arranged. **Frequency:** Annual. **Price:** $15/ea. **Pages:** 40. **Date Publ.:** 3/90. **Labels:** 75. **Fax:** (800)461-3634. **Contact(s):** Marcia Broucek (Executive Director).

## ✐ ◆ American Board of Examiners in Psychodrama, Sociometry, and Group Psychotherapy - Directory
1734 P St. NW
Washington, DC 20036  (202)483-0514
**Affiliation:** American Board of Examiners in Psychodrama, Sociometry, and Group Psychotherapy. **Concern(s):** arts; health; drama; psychology. 300+ certified psychodramatists providing services, training, and consultation in psychodrama, sociometry, and group psychotherapy. **Frequency:** Annual. **Pages:** 20. **Date Publ.:** 8/90. **Contact(s):** Dale Richard Buchanan (Executive Director).

## H ◆ American Cancer Society Cancer Book
Doubleday & Company, Inc.
666 5th Ave.
New York, NY 10103
**Concern(s):** health; preventative medicine. List of about 135 cancer organizations, centers, information and support services and programs. Principal content of publication is information about the detection and prevention of cancer. **Price:** $22.50/ea. **Date Publ.:** 9/86. **Publisher:** Doubleday & Company, Inc. **Contact(s):** Arthur I. Holleb, MD.

## ✐ ◆ American Dance Therapy Association - Membership Directory
American Dance Therapy Association
2000 Century Plaza, #108
Columbia, MD 21044
**Affiliation:** American Dance Therapy Association. **Concern(s):** arts; health; theater; psychology. 1,100 listings geographically arranged with names, addresses, and career information. **Frequency:** Annual. **Price:** $5/ea. **Pages:** 50. **Date Publ.:** 2/91. **Contact(s):** Patricia Gardner (Office Manager).

## H ◆ American Holistic Medical Association - Directory of Members
4101 Lake Boone Trail, #201
Raleigh, NC 27607
**Affiliation:** American Holistic Medical Association. **Concern(s):** health; holism; alternative consumer. 550 doctors of medicine and other health practitioners who practice or are interested in holistic medicine. **Frequency:** Annual. **Price:** $7.25/ea. **Pages:** 80. **Circ.:** 1M. **Date Publ.:** 6/90. **Contact(s):** Tracey Weller (Business Manager).

## J ◆ The American Indian Index - A Directory of Indian Country, USA
Arrowstar Publishing
10134 University Park Station
Denver, CO 80210-0134
**Concern(s):** justice; Native Americans. **Contact(s):** Greg W. Frazier (Editor).

## J ◆ American Indian Index: A Directory of Indian Country USA
Arrowstar Publishing
10134 University Park Station
Denver, CO 80210
**Concern(s):** justice; Native Americans. 6,000+ Native American Indian and Eskimo tribes, social service organizations and agencies, newspapers, and traders. Classified by type of organization, then geographical. **Frequency:** Irregular. **Price:** $21/ea. **Pages:** c325. **Date Publ.:** 1990. **Publisher:** Arrowstar Publishing. **Contact(s):** R.J. Punley (Senior Editor).

## J ◆ American Indian Reference Book
Earth Art, Inc.
Box 166
Fulton, MI 49052
**Concern(s):** justice; Native Americans. Craft shops; pow-wows, festivals, and dances; federal reservations; schools, and other organizations involved with American Indians. **Frequency:** Irregular. **Price:**

$9.95/ea. **Pages:** 310. **Date Publ.:** 1990. **Publisher:** Earth Art, Inc. **Contact(s):** Cal Noell (Owner).

## H ◆ American Society of Clinical Hypnosis— Membership Directory
American Society of Clinical Hypnosis
2250 E. Devon, #336
Des Plaines, IL 60018
**Affiliation:** American Society of Clinical Hypnosis. **Concern(s):** health; holism; psychology. 4,200 physicians, dentists, and psychologists who use hypnosis. **Frequency:** Biennial, odd yrs. **Price:** $10/ea. **Pages:** 165. **Fax:** (708)297-3309.

## F ◆ American Women Writers: A Critical Reference Guide from Colonial Times to the Present
Continuum Publishing Co.
370 Lexington Ave.
New York, NY 10017  (800)638-3030
**Concern(s):** feminism. In four volumes, about 1,000 American fiction writers, poets, writers in the social sciences, magazine and newspaper writers, and others, including a considerable number of contemporary figures. Listings are essentially critical bibliographies and include an evaluation of the importance of the author's work, a bibliography and biographical information. **Pages:** 500-600/vol. **Date Publ.:** 10/91. **Publisher:** Continuum Publishing Co. **Contact(s):** Lina Mainiero, Langdon Lynne Faust (Editors).

## ✼ ◆ Americans and World Affairs (A Guide to Organizations and Institutions in Northern California)
World Without War Council
1736 Martin Luther King Way
Berkeley, CA 94709
**Affiliation:** World Without War Council. **Concern(s):** peace.

## ✼ ◆ An International Directory of Information on War, Peace, and Security
Ballinger Publishing
c/o HarperCollins, 2350 Virginia Ave.
Hagerstown, MD 21740  (800)638-3030
**Affiliation:** ACCESS: A Security Information Service. **Concern(s):** peace; media; national security; international law; press. 650+ organizations in 60 countries that provide information on issues of international security and peace and 175 related publications. **Other Resources:** Multilingual vocabulary aid for foreign-language organization names and periodical titles. **Frequency:** Triennial. **Pages:** 240. **Date Publ.:** 1991. **Publisher:** Ballinger Publishing Co. **Contact(s):** William H. Kincade, Priscilla B. Hayner (Co-editors).

## ☛ ◆ Animal Organizations and Services Directory
Animal Stories Publisher
16787 Beach Blvd.
Huntington Beach, CA 92647
**Concern(s):** environment; animal rights. **Publisher:** Animal Stories Publisher. **Contact(s):** Kathleen A. Reece.

## ✼ ◆ Annotated Bibliography for Teaching Conflict Resolution in Schools
National Association for Mediation in Education (NAME)
525 Amity St.
Amherst, MA 01002  (413)545-2462
**Affiliation:** National Association for Mediation in Education (NAME). **Concern(s):** peace; education; conflict resolution; students. This booklet lists articles, bibliographies, books, audio-visual materials & curricula manuals on conflict resolution materials for use in grades K-12. **Frequency:** 12/yr. **Subscription:** Free with membership to NAME.

## ♿ ◆ Annotated Registry of Independent Living Programs
Independent Living Research Utilization
3400 Bissonnet, #101
Houston, TX 77005
**Affiliation:** Independent Living Research Utilization. **Concern(s):** health; disabled. 160+ independent living service facilities for people with disabilities Similar to "Directory of Independent Living Programs (see separate entry), but lists fewer programs in greater detail. **Frequency:** Irregular. **Price:** $12.50/ea. **Pages:** 330. **Contact(s):** Margaret Nosek.

## S ◆ Annual Register of Grant Support: A Directory of Funding Sources
National Register Publishing Company; Macmillan, Inc.
3004 Glenview Rd.
Wilmette, IL 60091
**Concern(s):** spiritual; philanthropy. 2,800+ current grant programs

offered by government agencies, private foundations, educational and professional associations, corporations, unions, church groups and other organizations; special emphasis on programs offering grants to individual for study, travel, etc. Classified by subject area or grant purpose (e.g., special populations, humanities, international affairs, etc.) **Other Resources:** Also includes guide to writing a proposal. **Frequency:** Annual. **Pages:** c1,140. **Date Publ.:** 9/90. **Publisher:** National Register Publishing Company; Macmillan, Inc. **Fax:** (708)441-2264.

## ✍ ◆ APT for Libraries
CRISES Press, Inc.
1716 SW Williston Rd.
Gainesville, FL 32608  (904)335-2200
**Concern(s):** education; media; justice; environment; press. A news annual selection tool in the social and environmental sciences for public and college libraries. Essential to fill the gaps left by government, corporations, and media and to build well-balanced collections. Over 100 thought-provoking books and journals excluded from mainstream publishing, marketing, and reviews. Nonprofit. **Est.:** 1991. **Frequency:** Annual. **Subscription:** $12/yr.; $20/3 yrs. **Pages:** c50. **Date Publ.:** 7/91. **Publisher:** CRISES Press, Inc. **Contact(s):** Charles Willett (President), Lisa Barr (Secretary).

## S ◆ ARIS Funding Reports
Academic Research Information System (ARIS)
2940 16th St., #314
San Francisco, CA 94103
**Concern(s):** spiritual; education; philanthropy. Grant and fellowship programs of private organizations and federal government agencies. Published in three editions: "Creative Arts and Humanities Report," "Social and Natural Sciences Report," and "Biomedical Sciences Report." Each issue includes 125-200 listings. Classified by broad subject area. **Frequency:** Every six weeks. **Pages:** c45. **Publisher:** Academic Research Information System (ARIS). **Fax:** (415)558-8135. **Contact(s):** Betty L. Traynor (Editor).

## T ◆ Asia and Pacific: A Directory of Resources
464 19th St.
Oakland, CA 94612-9761  (510)536-1876
**Affiliation:** Third World Resources/Data Center. **Concern(s):** Third World; Asia; Pacific/Pacific Rim. For postage and handling, add $1.50 for North America and $3.00 for foreign air mail. Please, order from Third World Resources. **Price:** $12.95/ea. **Pages:** 160. **Date Publ.:** Spring 1986. **Publisher:** Orbis Books. **Other Formats:** Geonet. **Use ID:** 'geo2:tfenton'. **E-Network:** Peacenet. **ID:** 'tfenton'. **Contact(s):** Thomas P. Fenton, Mary J. Heffron (Compilers/Editors).

## ✍ ◆ Asian Studies Newsletter
Association for Asian Studies, Inc. (AAS)
204 S. State St., 1 Lane Hall
Ann Arbor, MI 48109
**Affiliation:** Association for Asian Studies, Inc. (AAS). **Concern(s):** education; media; Third World; Asia. Lists of publishers and producers of Asian studies publications, films, slides, and videos; conferences and meetings on Asian affairs; museums displaying Asian art and artifact exhibits; universities and other institutions offering academic programs, grants, fellowships, and employment opportunities in Asian studies. **Frequency:** 5/yr. **Subscription:** Members only. **Fax:** (313)665-3801. **Contact(s):** Carol M. Hansen (Editor).

## H ◆ Ask Your Doctor, Ask Yourself
Schiffer Publishing, LTD
1469 Morstein Rd.
West Chester, PA 19380
**Concern(s):** health; preventative medicine; alternative consumer; self-help. List of about 40 health care organizations involved in medical self-care, arranged alphabetically by name with address. **Price:** $10.95/ea. **Date Publ.:** 4/86. **Publisher:** Schiffer Publishing, LTD. **Fax:** (215)344-9765. **Contact(s):** Annette Thornhill.

## ♿ ◆ Assistive Technology Sourcebook
RESNA; 1101 Connecticut Ave. NW
Suite 700
Washington, DC 20036  (202)857-1199
**Affiliation:** RESNA. **Concern(s):** health; justice; disabled; disabled's rights. List of suppliers of equipment for the handicapped, as well as publishers of material pertinent to independent living for the handicapped. Principal content of publication is information about selecting appropriate equipment for recreation, leisure, education, and personal mobility. **Frequency:** Irregular. **Price:** $60/ea., prepaid. **Date Publ.:** 3/90. **Fax:** (202)775-2625. **Contact(s):** Alexandra Enders.

☮ ◆ **Association for Commuter Transportation -
Membership Directory**
1776 Massachusetts Ave. NW, #521
Washington, DC 20036
**Affiliation:** Association for Commuter Transportation. **Concern(s):** energy; urban; economics; transportation; alternative markets. About 1,200 corporations or public agencies operating car, van, or bus pools or promoting ride-sharing as alternative commuting method; includes suppliers dealing in van pool equipment and services, and others. **Frequency:** Annual. **Subscription:** Members only. **Pages:** 50. **Date Publ.:** Fall 1990. **Contact(s):** Sandra Spence (Editor).

S ◆ **Association for Creative Change within
Religious and Other Social Systems - Directory**
Association for Creative Change
Box 1022
Clemson, SC 29633
**Affiliation:** Association for Creative Change. **Concern(s):** spiritual; faith. 500 member consultants, trainers, and educators in the fields of religion, applied behavioral development, and organizational development in the US, Canada, and abroad. **Frequency:** Irregular. **Subscription:** Members only. **Pages:** c30. **Date Publ.:** 4/88. **Contact(s):** Wanda Meade, Katherine Goree (Editors).

H ◆ **Association of Halfway House Alcoholism
Programs of North America (AHHAP) -
Membership Directory**
786 E. Seventh St.
St. Paul, MN 55106
**Affiliation:** Association of Halfway House Alcoholism Programs of North America (AHHAP). **Concern(s):** health; demographics; substance abuse; homelessness. About 600 alcoholism programs, arranged geographically. **Frequency:** Annual. **Price:** $6/ea. **Pages:** 40. **Date Publ.:** 1/91. **Contact(s):** Ken Schonlau.

✐ ◆ **Association of Hispanic Arts News - Directory
of Hispanic Arts Organizations Section**
Association of Hispanic Arts (AHA)
173 E. 116th St.
New York, NY 10029    (212)860-5445
**Affiliation:** Association of Hispanic Arts (AHA). **Concern(s):** arts; dance, music, theater, visual arts List of art organizations offering performances and exhibits by Hispanic artists in the northeastern US, especially New York. Covers dance, music, theater, and visual arts classified by discipline. **Other Resources:** Formerly, Association of Hispanic Arts. **Frequency:** 4/yr. **Subscription:** Free.

✈ ◆ **Association of International Colleges and
Universities - Directory**
International University Press
1301 S. Noland Rd.
Independence, MO 64055
**Affiliation:** Association of International Colleges and Universities. **Concern(s):** education; students; travel. About 1,500 individuals, organizations, and institutions active in international education. **Frequency:** Annual. **Price:** $250/ea. **Pages:** 100. **Circ.:** 1M. **Date Publ.:** 1/91. **Publisher:** International University Press. **Contact(s):** Dr. John Wayne Johnston (Editor).

E ◆ **AVR Teacher's Resource Guide for Solid Waste
and Recycling**
Association of Vermont Recyclers
Box 1244
Montpelier, VT 05601
**Affiliation:** Association of Vermont Recyclers. **Concern(s):** environment; recycling. Information and materials on solid waste and recycling. In addition to evaluating material collected from curricula around the country, a number of Vermont teachers contributed their own favorite activities. The result is a resource guide with information, resources, and inter-disciplinary activities for teachers of grades K-12. **Other Resources:** Also publishes a newsletter, OUT OF THE DUMPS. **Pages:** 340.

$ ◆ **Barter Associations, Organizations &
Businesses in the United States**
Barter Publishing
Box 570213
Houston, TX 77257
**Concern(s):** economics; trade. Microfiche containing association or company names and addresses. **Frequency:** Triennial. **Price:** $19.95/ea. **Date Publ.:** 1990. **Publisher:** Barter Publishing. **Contact(s):** A. Doyle.

F ◆ **Battered Women's Directory**
Box E-94, Earlham College
Richmond, IN 47374
**Concern(s):** feminism; battered women. 2,000+ shelters, hotlines,

YWCA's, hospitals, mental health services, legal service agencies, and other organizations and agencies which offer services to abused wives in the US and abroad; includes listings of many educational resources on the problem. **Frequency:** Irregular. **Pages:** 285. **Date Publ.:** 8/85. **Other Formats:** Diskette. **Contact(s):** Terry Mehlman, Betsy Warrior (Compiler).

E ◆ **Bay Area Green Pages, The Local Handbook
for Planet Maintenance**
Green Media Group
Box 11314
Berkeley, CA 94701
**Affiliation:** Green Media Group. **Concern(s):** environment; economics; green consumer; volunteers. An environmental guide to green resources and businesses pertinent to the San Francisco Bay Area. **Contact(s):** Stephen C. Evans (Editor), Eric Ingersoll (Publisher).

✍ ◆ **Bear's Guide to Non-traditional College
Degrees**
Mendocino Book Co.
9301 N. Highway One, #1425
Mendocino, CA 95460
**Concern(s):** education; students. **Publisher:** Mendocino Book Co. **Contact(s):** Dr. John Bear.

$ ◆ **The Better World Investment Guide**
c/o Council on Economic Priorities
30 Irving Place, 9th Fl.
New York, NY 10211-0194    (800)U-CAN-HELP
**Affiliation:** Council on Economic Priorities. **Concern(s):** economics; environment; peace; socially-responsible investing; consumer rights; alternative markets; boycott; green consumer; boycott. Provides in-depth profiles of 100 major corporations, and discusses in detail the behavior behind their ratings. Also traces the history of ethical investing, profiles the leading socially screened funds, and offers a compendium of ethical investing options. Nearly everything you need to know in order to become an informed consumer and empowered investor. **Dues:** $35/yr. **Contact(s):** Alice Tepper Marlin (President), Myra Alperson (Director for Social Responsibility).

E ◆ **Beyond 25 Percent: Material Recovery Comes
of Age**
2425 18th St. NW
Washington, DC 20009    (202)232-4108
**Affiliation:** Institute for Local Self-Reliance. **Concern(s):** environment; economics; urban; conservation; resources; recycling; community self-reliance; planning; sustainability. Report. **Contact(s):** Neil Seldman (President), David Morris (Director).

✈ ◆ **Bicycling in Africa**
International Bicycle Fund
4887 Columbia Drive S
Seattle, WA 98108-1919    (206)767-3927
**Affiliation:** International Bicycle Fund. **Concern(s):** education; energy; health; travel; transportation. A handbook for bicycling in Africa. It includes: cross-cultural information, information on health and wellness, accommodation in Africa, selecting an itinerary, insurance, the weather, selecting a bike, planning an itinerary and more. Nonprofit. **Price:** $14.95/ea. **Bulk:** 40% off/24. **Pages:** 196. **Contact(s):** David Mozer (Author).

P ◆ **Biographical Dictionary of Neo-Marxism**
Greenwood Press, Inc.
88 Post Rd. W
Westport, CT 06881
**Concern(s):** politics; alternative party; activism. Over 200 neo-Marxist thinkers and activists, worldwide. Also includes articles on ten groups, periodicals, and movements deemed by the author as influential to the neo-Marxist movement. **Price:** $55/ea. **Pages:** 465. **Date Publ.:** 1985. **Publisher:** Greenwood Press, Cong. Information Serv. **Contact(s):** Robert A. Gorman (Editor).

E ◆ **Bioregional Bibliography**
c/o Kirkpatrick Sale
113 W. 11th St.
New York, NY 10011    (212)989-5098
**Affiliation:** Hudson Bioregional Council. **Concern(s):** environment; bioregionalism. **Contact(s):** Kirkpatrick Sale.

E ◆ **Bioregional Clearinghouse**
Turtle Island Office c/o Jacinta McCoy
1333 Overhulse Rd NE
Olympia, WA 98502
**Affiliation:** North American Bioregional Council. **Concern(s):** environment. Will provide information on bioregional organizations in any area as well as on other actions of the NABC and the planning for the NABC IV to be held in the Gulf of Maine bioregion. **Other:** Box 159, Petrolia, CA. Seth Zuckerman.

E ◆ **The Bioregional Directory**
Planet Drum
Box 31251
San Francisco, CA 94131    (415)285-6556
**Affiliation:** Planet Drum. **Concern(s):** environment; bioregionalism. A directory of bioregional groups that comes out in Planet Drum's newspaper, RAISE THE STAKES.

J ◆ **Black Americans Information Directory**
Gale Research Inc.
835 Penobscot Building
Detroit, MI 48226-4094 (800)877-GALE
**Concern(s):** justice; urban; politics; ethnic concerns; minority rights; networking; grassroots organizing; diversity. Information sources on a variety of aspects of Black American life and culture, including national, state, and local organizations; publishers of newspapers, periodicals, newsletters, and other publications and videos; television and radio stations; traditionally Black colleges and universities; library collections; museums and other cultural institutions; grants and scholarships; Black studies programs and research centers; federal and state government agencies. Black religious organizations. **Price:** $69.50/ea. **Pages:** 425. **Date Publ.:** 10/89. **Publisher:** Gale Research Inc. **Fax:** (313)961-6241. **Telex:** (810)221-7086. **Contact(s):** Darren L. Smith (Editor).

J ◆ **Black Resource Guide**
501 Oneida Pl. NW
Washington, DC 20011  (202)291-4373
**Concern(s):** justice; urban; politics; ethnic concerns; minority rights; networking; grassroots organizing; diversity. 3,000+ organizations especially relevant to or comprised primarily of Black Americans, including adoption agencies, business, bar associations, colleges, public administrators, book publishers, church denominations, financial institutions, hospitals, museums, embassies and consulates, and others: includes Blacks in federal elected and appointed positions; individuals chosen for their prominence in athletics, entertainment, and politics. Classified by line of business or activity. **Frequency:** Annual. **Price:** $50/ea. + $1.50 shipping. **Pages:** 285. **Circ.:** 25M. **Date Publ.:** 1/91. **Labels:** 150. **Contact(s):** R. Benjamin, Jacqueline L. Johnson (Publishers).

H ◆ **The Book of TLC**
219 W. 106th St., #3W
New York, NY 10025
**Concern(s):** health; environment. A manual on health and wellness with a section on healing and restoring the environment. **Contact(s):** Debra Derella, Ivan Cheren.

M ◆ **Books on Trial: A Survey of Recent Cases**
National Coalition Against Censorship
2 W. 64th St.
New York, NY 10023
**Affiliation:** National Coalition Against Censorship. **Concern(s):** media; justice; censorship. List of about 25 attorneys who have participated in school district book censorship litigation. Main content is narrative reporting of litigation surrounding attempts at censorship of published works, with recent decisions indexed by state and banned books indexed by author. **Frequency:** Irregular. **Price:** $5/ea. **Contact(s):** Leanne Katz (Executive Director).

$ ◆ **Builders of the Dawn**
Baker Rd.
Shutesbury, MA 01072
**Affiliation:** Sirius Community. **Concern(s):** economics; intentional communities. 90+ alternative communities cited for being progressive and innovative in such fields as alternative energy, biodynamic gardening, and spiritual and holistic programs. The authors lived in various alternative communities for over 23 years between them and have co-founded a community themselves based on the Findhorn model. The benefits and problems are explored and innovative approaches to governance, economics, bonding and ethics. **Other Resources:** Includes 120 photos. **Frequency:** Irregular. **Pages:** 375. **Date Publ.:** 1986. **Publisher:** Book Publishers, The. **Contact(s):** Corrine McLaughlin, Gordon Davidson (Co-authors).

☣ ◆ **Building Bridges: US-USSR - A Handbook for
Citizen Diplomats**
US-USSR Bridges for Peace
Box 710
Norwich, VT 05055
**Affiliation:** US-USSR Bridges for Peace. **Concern(s):** peace; conflict resolution; East-West. **Office:** Norwich Center **Contact(s):** Clinton Gardner (Editor).

**P ▶ Building Municipal Foreign Policies: An Action Handbook for Citizens and Local Elected Officials**
c/o Institute For Policy Studies
1601 Connecticut Ave. NW
Washington, DC 20009 (202)234-9382
**Affiliation:** Center for Innovative Diplomacy (retired). **Concern(s):** politics; peace; national security; municipal; government accountability. **Contact(s):** Michael H. Shuman.

**✍ ▶ Bureau of Indian Affairs Higher Education Grant People**
Office of Indian Education Programs
18th & C Sts. NW; Dept. of Interior
Washington, DC 20240 (202)208-3711
**Affiliation:** Bureau of Indian Affairs. **Concern(s):** education; justice; Native Americans. Offices of the higher education program with office name, name of contact, address, and phone number. **Frequency:** Annual. **Subscription:** Free. **Date Publ.:** 10/90. **Fax:** (202)343-1312.

**? ▶ Business Environmental Lending Library**
Earth Day International
800 Yates St.
Victoria, BC V8W 1L9 Canada (604)382-1990
**Affiliation:** Earth Day International. **Concern(s):** future; environment; energy; economics; ideation; networking; planning; appropriate technology; trade; alternative markets. "Locally administered, readily accessible information banks, each containing material describing environmental products and services offered by hundreds and potentially thousands of companies." Eventually information will be stored on computer disk. Many regions and countries need greater accessibility to environmental technologies. By creating a mutually beneficial relationship between business interests and environmental needs, related businesses can be propelled to the "cutting edge". **Other Resources:** Send for free brochure. **Fax:** (604)382-1660.

**$ ▶ Business Mastery**
3906 W. Ina, #200-264
Tucson, AZ 85741
**Affiliation:** Sohnen-Moe Associates. **Concern(s):** economics; trade. A business and planning guide for creating a fulfilling thriving business and keeping it successful! Make a quantitative shift in your relationship to your business with this comprehensive guide that balances practical business skill with a humanistic approach. Topics include: marketing and promotion, client retention, goal setting, practice management, public speaking, networking, and more. **Est.:** 1988. **Price:** $19.95/ea. **Bulk:** 40% off/24. **Pages:** 256. **Labels:** 1200. **Fax:** (602)744-7887. **Contact(s):** Cherie Sohnen-Moe (President).

**$ ▶ Business Opportunities Workbook, Implementing Economic Renewal Projects**
Rocky Mountain Institute/Economic Renewal Program
1739 Snowmass Creek Rd.
Old Snowmass, CO 81654-9199
**Affiliation:** Rocky Mountain Institute/Economic Renewal Program. **Concern(s):** economics; energy; agriculture; environment; community self-reliance; community investment; renewables; appropriate technology. Booklet documenting the ways small cities and towns have been reinvigorating their economies "from within"—without chasing smokestacks or pushing growth-for-growth's sake. Other casebooks available on energy and food.

**E ▶ Business Recycling Manual**
c/o Island Press
Box 7
Covelo, CA 95428 (202)232-7933
**Affiliation:** INFORM and Recourse Systems. **Concern(s):** environment; economics; recycling; waste management; corporate responsibility. The first complete guide to every business's recycling needs. This manual walks recycling managers through the program development process, from gathering data to conducting waste audits, and from marketing recyclables to monitoring and evaluating recycling programs. Worksheets, illustrations, appendixes, glossary, bibliography. **Price:** $92/binder. **Pages:** 196. **Date Publ.:** 1991. **Publisher:** INFORM. Order: (800)828-1302.

**J ▶ California and Nevada LSC Legal**
3535 W. Sixth St., 2nd Fl.
Los Angeles, CA 90020
**Affiliation:** Western Center on Law and Poverty. **Concern(s):** justice; demographics; poverty; housing.

**E ▶ California Co-op Directory**
California Department of Conservation
1020 N St.
Sacramento, CA 95814
**Affiliation:** California Department of Conservation. **Concern(s):** environment; economics; conservation; cooperatives.

**E ▶ California Environmental Directory**
Box 189040
Sacramento, CA 95818
**Affiliation:** California Institute of Public Affairs (CIPA)/Claremont Colleges. **Concern(s):** environment. The book gives addresses and phone numbers and concise descriptions of each organization's purposes, activities, and publications. Descriptions of the major groups are quite detailed and list branch offices. Many lesser-known but important groups are listed. **Price:** $25/ea. w/letterhead + $2 shipping otherwise $40. CA + 6.5%. **Other Formats:** Fax: (916) 442-2478. **Contact(s):** Thaddeus C. Trzyna (Editor).

**E ▶ California Toxics Directory**
Box 189040
Sacramento, CA 95818
**Affiliation:** California Institute of Public Affairs (CIPA)/Claremont Colleges. **Concern(s):** environment; health; hazardous/toxic waste; public health. 400+ entries include address, phone number, key contact person, purposes and activities as they relate to hazardous materials, and publications issued. Descriptions of organizations are often quite detailed and run several hundred words. **Price:** $20/ea. + $2 shipping CA + 6.5%. **Date Publ.:** 1990. **Contact(s):** Thaddeus C. Trzyna (Editor).

**F ▶ Campus Gang Rape: Party Games?**
Association of American Colleges
1818 R St. NW
Washington, DC 20009 (202)387-1300
**Affiliation:** Association of American Colleges. **Concern(s):** feminism; education; students; rape/sexual abuse. List of about 10 publishers and organizations concerned with gang rape on college campuses and discussions on this growing problem. **Price:** $3/ea., prepaid. **Date Publ.:** 8/85. **Other Formats:** Microfiche from Eric Document Reproduction Service, Computer Microfilm Corp., 3900 Wheeler Ave., Alexandria, VA 22304. **Contact(s):** Julie K. Ehrhart, Bernice R. Sandler.

**☝ ▶ Careers Working With Animals**
Humane Society of the US
2100 L St. NW
Washington, DC 20037 (202)452-1100
**Affiliation:** Humane Society of the US. **Concern(s):** environment; animal rights. A guide about work pertaining to animals. **Contact(s):** Guy R. Hodge.

**H ▶ Caring for Alzheimer's Patients: A Guide for Family & Health Care Providers**
Plenum Publishing Corporation
233 Spring St.
New York, NY 10013 (212)620-8000
**Concern(s):** health; disabled; seniors. About 5 organizations that provide information and resources concerning Alzheimer's disease support groups, hospitals, and other caregiving organizations. Principal context of publication is description of Alzheimer's disease and treatment. **Price:** $22.95/ea. **Date Publ.:** 8/89. **Publisher:** Plenum Publishing Corporation. **Fax:** (212)463-0742. **Contact(s):** Dr. Gary D. Miner et al. (212)741-6680.

**H ▶ Caring for the Mentally Impaired Elderly: A Family Guide**
Henry Holt & Company
115 W. 18th St.
New York, NY 10011 (212)633-0605
**Concern(s):** health; disabled; seniors. In appendixes - list of resources to aid mentally impaired elderly, including publications, institutions, and other sources of information. **Price:** $12.95/ea. **Date Publ.:** 1989. **Publisher:** Henry Holt & Company. **Contact(s):** Florence Safford.

**H ▶ Caring for the Sick**
Facts on File, Inc.
460 Park Ave. S
New York, NY 10016 (212)683-2244
**Concern(s):** health; disabled; seniors; alternative consumer. List of about 10 health care organizations that provide assistance or information in the field of home health care. Principal content is information on basic nursing care, first aid, and possible activities for the stay-at-home patient. **Price:** $18.95/ea. **Publisher:** Facts on File, Inc. **Contact(s):** Ellen Lagal (Editor).

**⚖ ▶ Carl Rogers Peace Project Directory**
1125 Torrey Pines Rd.
La Jolla, CA 92037
**Affiliation:** Carl Rogers Peace Project. **Concern(s):** peace. Organizational directory.

**✍ ▶ Centsitivity**
Center for Non-Traditional Education
1804 Vernon St. NW
Washington, DC 20009 (202)462-6333
**Affiliation:** Center for Non-Traditional Education. **Concern(s):** education.

**F ▶ Changing Men, Issues in Gender, Sex, and Politics - Resource Directory**
Feminist Men's Publications
306 N. Brook St.
Madison, WI 53715
**Affiliation:** National Organization for Men Against Sexism. **Concern(s):** feminism; sexism; men's liberation. Directory section in each issue covering resources, groups, events, etc., related to issues of interest to the men's movement. **Frequency:** 2-3/yr. **Price:** $4.50/ea. **Publisher:** Feminist Men's Publications. **Contact(s):** Rick Cote, Michael Biernbaum.

**S ▶ Charitable Organizations of the US**
Gale Research Inc.
835 Penobscot Building
Detroit, MI 48226-4094 (800)877-GALE
**Concern(s):** spiritual; philanthropy. 1,000 organizations in the US actively soliciting funds from the public to support their charitable programs and activities. **Frequency:** Biennial. **Price:** $139.50/ea. **Pages:** c1,000. **Date Publ.:** 1990. **Publisher:** Gale Research Inc. **Fax:** (313)961-6241. **Telex:** (810)221-7086. **Contact(s):** Doris Morris Maxfield (Editor).

**E ▶ Chesapeake Citizen Directory**
6600 York Rd., #100
Baltimore, MD 21403
**Affiliation:** Alliance for the Chesapeake Bay, Inc.. **Concern(s):** environment; agriculture; water; land use; resource management; rivers; wetlands; policy; pesticides; sustainability; Chesapeake Bay. Provides non-biased, non-technical information about Bay progress to the public. Key issues of concern: agriculture, education, fisheries, land use/development, research & monitoring, river protection, sediment pollution, sewage treatment, water quality, wetlands. **Price:** $10/ea. **Contact(s):** Frances H. Flanigan (Executive Director).

**♥ ▶ Child Find Photo Directory of Missing Children**
Child Find of America, Inc.
Box 277
New Paltz, NY 12561
**Affiliation:** Child Find of America, Inc.. **Concern(s):** family; justice; demographics; child abuse; children; criminal system. About 570 children reported as missing in the US arranged chronologically by date of birth and indexed alphabetically by name. Data in each child includes photograph, description, date of birth, date abducted or disappeared, location where last seen. Sometimes referred to as "National Directory of Missing Children." **Other Resources:** (800)A-WAY-OUT, a non-governmental contact for parents who want to return a kidnapped child. **Frequency:** Irregular. **Price:** $1.50/ea. **Pages:** 60. **Date Publ.:** 1988.

**✍ ▶ Child Sexual Abuse Prevention: How To Take The First Steps**
c/o Network Publications
1700 Mission St. #203
Santa Cruz, CA 95061
**Affiliation:** Illusion Theater. **Concern(s):** education; family; media; health; child abuse; preventive; rape/sexual abuse; theater; psychology; childhood. An eight-step guide on how to prevent and detect child sexual abuse. Includes hundreds of contacts and resources in media, curriculum, guides, books and more. It explains how to set up community prevention programs and offers practical hands on advice for working with the media, faith communities, schools, and local agencies. Though originally published in 1983, it still explains the elements of organizing a prevention program that is relevant today. **Date Publ.:** 1986. **Contact(s):** Cordelia Anderson, M.A. (Director/Editor). **Other:** Illusion Theater, 528 Hennepin Ave. #704, Minneapolis, MN 55403. (612)339-4944.

**H ▶ Children and Adolescents with Mental Illness: A Parents' Guide**
Woodbine House
5615 Fishers Lane
Rockville, MD 20852 (800)842-7323
**Concern(s):** health; justice; counseling; psychology; children; youth. List of organizations and facilities providing information and services

for families with mentally ill children. Principal content of publication is a discussion of mental illness in children and adolescents, including chapters on symptoms, diagnosis, therapy and hospitalization, education, long-term treatment and planning, and teenage suicide. **Price:** $12.95/ea. **Date Publ.:** 1988. **Publisher:** Woodbine House. **Contact(s):** Evelyn McElroy (Editor).

**H ▶ Choices: Realistic Alternatives in Cancer Treatment**
Avon Books
105 Madison Ave.
New York, NY 10016    (800)238-0658
**Concern(s):** health; consumer protection. Chapter title "Where to Get Help," which lists American Cancer Society offices, National Cancer Institute research study groups, cancer treatment centers, and other organizations and associations of assistance to cancer patients and their families in the US, Canada, and Europe. Research and treatment programs may also include some indication of the emphasis. **Frequency:** Irregular. **Date Publ.:** 1987. **Publisher:** Avon Books. **Fax:** (212)532-2172. **Contact(s):** Marion Morra, Eve Potts.

**S ▶ The Church Funding Resource Guide**
Women's Technical Assistance Project
733 15th St. NW, #510B
Washington, DC 20005    (202)638-0449
**Affiliation:** Women's Technical Assistance Project. **Concern(s):** spiritual; feminism; labor; economics; jobs; philanthropy; fundraising. **Price:** $54.10/ea.

**⚛ ▶ Citizen Diplomats: Americans Ending the Cold War**
Independent Publishers Group
814 N. Franklin St.
Chicago, IL 60610    (312)337-0747
**Concern(s):** peace; East-West; conflict resolution; anti-nuclear; nonviolence. Includes 100-page comprehensive resource guide listing the activities and addresses of hundreds of groups and individuals practicing citizen diplomacy. Profiles important citizen diplomats such as Armand Hammer, Samantha Smith, and Dr. Bernard Lown. **Price:** $16.95/ea. **Pages:** 448. **Publisher:** Seven Locks Press. **Fax:** (312)337-5985. Order: (800 888-4741. **Contact(s):** Gale Warner, Michael Shuman (Authors).

**E ▶ Citizen's Directory For Water Quality Abuses**
1401 Wilson Blvd.
Arlington, VA 22209
**Affiliation:** Izaak Walton League of America. **Concern(s):** environment; water. Contains a telephone directory listing the environmental agency telephone numbers for reporting pollution emergencies or obtaining information about streams and water quality as well as a guide to recognizing water pollution. You can obtain a list of your state's water control board as well as other listings of places to contact to report water pollution problems. **Price:** $2/ea. **Pages:** 16. **Date Publ.:** 9/89. **Contact(s):** Karen Firehock (Coordinator), Eunice Groark (Project Assistant).

**E ▶ Citizen's Guide to Global Issues**
Global Tomorrow Coalition
1325 G St. NW, #915
Washington, DC 20005-3104    (202)628-4016
**Affiliation:** Global Tomorrow Coalition. **Concern(s):** environment; peace; politics. **Contact(s):** Don Lesh (President), Walter Corson.

**E ▶ A Citizen's Handbook on Groundwater Protection**
Natural Resources Defense Council
40 West 20 St.
New York, NY 10011    (212)727-2700
**Affiliation:** Natural Resources Defense Council. **Concern(s):** environment; water. **Date Publ.:** 1984. **Contact(s):** Wendy Gordon.

**E ▶ A Citizen's Toxic Waste Audit Manual, A Tool for People Fighting Toxic Waste**
Greenpeace
1017 W. Jackson
Chicago, IL 60607
**Affiliation:** Rachel's Hazardous Waste News & Greenpeace. **Concern(s):** environment; energy; peace; hazardous/toxic waste. If you live near a factory that generates hazardous waste, or near an existing or proposed hazardous waste disposal facility, you will find this manual to be a useful resource. You can: Identify and rank sources of hazardous waste; fight off polluting facilities that are proposed; assemble a waste audit, exposing polluters and pressing for source reduction of waste; identify the hazards posed by 100's of different types of toxics; and, compile and publish the information.

**E ▶ The Citizen's Toxics Protection Manual**
National Toxics Campaign
37 Temple Place
Boston, MA 02111
**Affiliation:** National Toxics Campaign. **Concern(s):** environment; health; hazardous/toxic waste; public health. .

**E ▶ A Citizens' Guide to Plastics in the Ocean: More Than A Litter Problem**
Center for Marine Conservation
1725 DeSales NW, #500
Washington, DC 20036    (202)429-5609
**Affiliation:** Center for Marine Conservation. **Concern(s):** environment; ocean/rivers; wildlife/endangered species; waste management. **Contact(s):** Kathryn J. O'Hara, Suzanne Iudicello & Rose Bierce.

**P ▶ Civilian Congress**
2361 Mission St., #238
San Francisco, CA 94110    (415)695-1597
**Affiliation:** National Resource Center. **Concern(s):** politics; justice; constitutional rights; voting. "Active-duty military officers are constitutionally forbidden to serve in the US Congress. Civilian Congress says this exclusion should be enforced in order to ensure a Congress independent of the military. National Resource Center which serves as a catalyst for research and education regarding federal constitutional rights, provides assistance to voter/plaintiffs who litigate to defend their constitutional right to a civilian congress. Monitors press coverage of congress and assists writers."-C.C. **Est.:** 1964. **Frequency:** Annual. **Price:** $12/ea. **Date Publ.:** 1991. **Publisher:** Civilian Congress. **Contact(s):** Jack Fitch, Josef Brinckmann.

**E ▶ Clean Team Manual**
Keep America Beautiful
9 W. Broad St.
Stamford, CT 06902
**Affiliation:** Keep America Beautiful. **Concern(s):** environment; solid waste/recycling; conservation; beautification. Instruction handbook with business and industrial adaptation for solid waste recycling, conservation, and beautification.

**✍ ▶ Clearinghouse For Community-Based Free Standing Educational Institutions**
1804 Vernon St. NW
Washington, DC 20009    (202)462-6333
**Affiliation:** Association for Community Based Education. **Concern(s):** education. A national membership organization for alternative educational institutions, the Clearinghouse has a directory of community-based groups involved in adult and community education. Involved in setting up programs and developing training that may be utilized by community groups.

**T ▶ Clearinghouse on Development Communications**
1815 N. Ft. Myer Dr.
Arlington, VA 22209
**Concern(s):** Third World; development.

**$ ▶ Co-op America Organizational Member Directory**
2100 M St. NW, #310
Washington, DC 20063    (800)424-2667
**Affiliation:** Co-op America. **Concern(s):** economics; Third World; environment; cooperatives; alternative markets; socially-responsible investing; corporate responsibility; green consumer; trade. A directory of Co-op America's organizational members. Most are small business; some are volunteer-run groups. Not all are co-ops, but all of them are in some way "socially responsible." Goal: to direct the consumer to these businesses. 400+ nonprofit public interest groups, cooperatives, small alternative type businesses, and other members. **Other Resources:** This is a special issue that appears yearly in CO-OP AMERICA'S QUARTERLY. Many of the descriptions that appear in Macrocosm were reprinted by permission from Co-op America. Special thanks to all their great assistance and good work! **Frequency:** Annual. **Price:** $1/ea. **Pages:** 16. **Date Publ.:** Every Fall. **Contact(s):** Jyotsna Sreenivasar, Cindy Mitlo (Editor).

**♿ ▶ College and Career Programs for Deaf Students**
Gallaudet Research Institute
800 Florida Ave. NE
Washington, DC 20002    (202)651-5460
**Affiliation:** Gallaudet Research Institute. **Concern(s):** justice; health; students; disabled; disabled's rights. About 155 post-secondary institutions offering special services for deaf students arranged geographically and indexed by career field. **Frequency:** Biennial. **Price:** $12.95/ea. **Pages:** 150. **Contact(s):** Brenda W. Rawlings.

**$ ▶ Colorado Directory**
Colorado Community College
1391 N. Speed Blvd., # 600
Denver, CO 80204
**Affiliation:** Colorado Community College. **Concern(s):** economics; environment; cooperatives.

**S ▶ Common Ground: Resources for Personal Transformation**
Common Ground
305 San Anselmo Ave.
San Anselmo, CA 94960 (415)549-4900
**Affiliation:** Common Ground. **Concern(s):** spiritual; arts; health; transformation; music; holism; nutrition; preventative medicine; psychology. Music schools, art instructors, educational programs, conferences and festivals, natural and health food restaurants and suppliers, medicine and dentistry professionals who emphasize preventive health care, holistic health practitioners; individuals engaged in psychology, and psychic healing/arts; retreat sites, camps, hot springs, and inns; publications, book publishers, and other sources of materials; gyms, dance studios, yoga instructors; palmists and astrologists. Arranged by topic. **Frequency:** 4/yr. **Price:** $4/ea. **Pages:** 130. **Circ.:** 80M. **Fax:** (415)459-4974. **Contact(s):** Bah'Uddin Alpine (Publisher).

**E ▶ Common Property Resources**
World Resources Institute
1709 New York Ave. NW, #700
Washington, DC 20006    (202)638-6300
**Affiliation:** World Resources Institute. **Concern(s):** environment; energy; natural resources; conservation. **Date Publ.:** 1988.

**⚛ ▶ A Common Sense Guide to Peace**
Oceana Publications
75 Main St.
Dobbs Ferry, NY 10522
**Concern(s):** peace; world order. Approaches the subject of peace and security alternatives with a special focus on the need for international legal structures. **Publisher:** Oceana Publications. **Contact(s):** Benjamin Ferencz.

**$ ▶ Communities - Directory of Intentional Communities Issue**
Communities Publication Cooperative
126 Sun St.
Stelle, IL 60619
**Concern(s):** economics; intentional communities. About 240 known active intentional communities or communes arranged alphabetically by community name with address, year established, number of members, number of acres, style of organization, details of religion, diet, form of group government, sexual relationships predominating, and whether new members are desired. Brief descriptions of each group are given in a separate section. Formerly published in cooperation with "Green Revolution Magazine." **Frequency:** Irregular. **Price:** $12/ea. **Date Publ.:** 4/90. **Publisher:** Communities Publication Cooperative. **Contact(s):** Charles Betterton.

**E ▶ Communities at Risk**
Renew America
1400 16th St. NW, #710
Washington, DC 20036 (202)232-2252
**Affiliation:** Renew America. **Concern(s):** environment; energy; health; hazardous/toxic waste; renewables. **Contact(s):** Albert J. Fritsch (Author).

**E ▶ Communities for Conservation and Action: A Manual for Building Community**
Rocky Mountain Peace Center
1520 Euclid
Boulder, CO 80302
**Affiliation:** Rocky Mountain Peace Center. **Concern(s):** environment; energy; economics; agriculture; peace; sustainability; community self-reliance; appropriate technology; renewables; conservation. **Date Publ.:** 1988.

**D ▶ A Community Researcher's Guide To Rural Data**
c/o Island Press
Box 7
Covelo, CA 95428    (202)232-7933
**Affiliation:** Rural Economics Policy Program/The Aspen Institute. **Concern(s):** demographics; agriculture; environment; rural communities; housing; population growth. This book is a comprehensive manual intended for those less familiar with statistical data on rural America. It identifies a wealth of data sources such as decennial census of population and housing, population reports and surveys, and labor market information. Charts and index. **Price:** $19.95ea. **Pages:** 93. **Publisher:** Island Press. Order: (800)828-1302. Priscilla Salant (Author).

**E ♦ The Complete Guide to Environmental Careers**
Island Press
1718 Connecticut Ave. NW, #300
Washington, DC 20009 (800)828-1302
**Affiliation:** CEIP Fund. **Concern(s):** environment; jobs; volunteers. This book presents the essential information needed to plan any career search; hobby outlook, salary levels, volunteer and internship opportunities and entry requirements in the field. Gives readers an overview of the environmental field, as well as examples of the actual projects, jobs, and opportunities available. In-depth interviews detail the day-to-day responsibilities of more than 100 professionals in all fields of the environment. **Price:** $14.95 paper; $24.95 cloth. **Pages:** 328. **Date Publ.:** 1989. **Publisher:** Island Press.

**E ♦ Compost Patch, Inc.**
306 Coleridge Ave.
Altoona, PA 16602 (814)946-9291
**Concern(s):** environment; spiritual; peace; politics; transformation; recycling. An educational entity that strives to share ideas about innovative and imaginative individuals, groups, and communities that are moving beyond our industrial, mechanized, and patriarchal paradigms that are consuming and exploiting the planet. Focus is on the resource (waste) issue. "We are a clearinghouse to these types of issues. A newsletter tells of these positive ideas and how people can help. We also offer a lending library and information packets. Write for a sample newsletter." **Other Resources:** Newsletter, COMPOST PATCH IDEAS. "We provide education about composting, recycling, and other ecological matters. We also sell books and other publications and materials related to our concerns." **Est.:** 1985. **E-Network:** Econet. **ID:** 'cleiden'. **Contact(s):** Charles Leiden (Director).

**☙ ♦ A Concerned Citizen's Guide to National Security**
Box 2309
La Jolla, CA 92038
**Affiliation:** Mothers Embracing Nuclear Disarmament (MEND). **Concern(s):** peace; feminism; anti-nuclear; disarmament; national security. A pamphlet which assists in understanding the nuclear arms issue and explains how you can take an active role in the effort to reduce the risk of nuclear war. Nonprofit. **Contact(s):** Maureen Pecht King (Executive Director).

**P ♦ The Congressional Directory: Environment**
Environmental Communications
6410 Rocklidge Drive, #203
Bethesda, MD 20817
**Concern(s):** politics; environment; law. Includes short biographies of each member of Congress along with listings of the member's top aide on environmental issues. Biographies of some of the staffers are also included, along with lists of each committee and sub-committee dealing with environmental issues, an index which tells which committees handle which issues, congressional district maps, and so forth. **Publisher:** Environmental Communications.

**P ♦ Congressional Staff Directory**
Box 62
Mt. Vernon, VA 22121
**Concern(s):** politics; law. Lists members of Congress, committees, subcommittees, administration, over 2,700 staff biographies, office addresses, and phone numbers.

**✍ ♦ Connecting with Nature: The World Peace University Field Guide**
World Peace University
Box 10869
Eugene, OR 97440 (503)741-1794
**Affiliation:** World Peace University. **Concern(s):** education; environment; alternative. Achieve responsible fun, growth, and livelihoods. Utilize new, teachable, self-empowering, local outdoor activities: ethics, imageries, identifications, writings, reinforcements, gestalts, ecologies and physics. Catalyze lasting personal and global health by reawakening 53 biological senses which globally organize, balance, and regenerate Mature within and without. **Other Resources:** Training guidebooks, workshops, courses, and networking available. Nonprofit. **Est.:** 1985. **Price:** $11/ea. **Bulk:** 30% off/24. **E-Network:** Econet. **ID:** 'worldpeaceu'. **Fax:** (603)741-1279. **Contact(s):** Dr. Michael Cohen (Chairman, Integrated Ecology), Dr. Richard Schneider (Chancellor).

**E ♦ The Connexions Annual: A Social Change Sourcebook**
Connexions Information Services, Inc.
427 Bloor St. West, #568
Toronto, ON M5S 1X7 Canada (416)960-3903
**Affiliation:** Connexions Information Services, Inc.. **Concern(s):** environment; peace; environment; justice; feminism; politics; networking. A sourcebook describing 2,700+ groups, mostly Canadian, pursuing positive solutions to environmental, social, and international

problems. 16 chapters cover peace, international development, Native Peoples, Women and other topics. Listings include address, phone, contact, name, year founded, acronym, organizational structure, number of members and staff, types of resources, activities and services, primary interest, purposes and goals. Detailed subject and geographical indices. **Other Resources:** See MEDIA FOR SOCIAL CHANGE, a media guidebook; and CONNEXIONS DIGEST. **Est.:** 1975. **Frequency:** Annual. **Price:** $17.95 Canadian dollars. **Bulk:** 40% off/24. **Pages:** c224. **Circ.:** 2M. **Labels:** 11000. **Contact(s):** Ulli Diemer (Editor), Elizabeth Wall (Associate Editor).

**$ ♦ The Conscientious Investor's Guide to Socially-Responsible Mutual and Money Market Funds**
c/o Interfaith Center for Corporate Responsibility
475 Riverside Dr. # 566
New York, NY 10115 (212)870-2295
**Affiliation:** Interfaith Center for Corporate Responsibility. **Concern(s):** economics; spiritual; peace; politics; environment; Third World; interfaith; corporate responsibility; alternative markets; divestment; socially-responsible investing; boycott; anti-nuclear; economic conversion; peace dividend; boycott; South Africa; land trusts. This guide challenges the financial institutions and corporations by identifying those involved with nuclear weapons production, investment in South Africa, and Star Wars, and other issues counterproductive to peace, economic justice, and stewardship of Earth. **Other Resources:** INVESTMENT SERVICES & DIRECTORY OF ALTERNATIVE INVESTMENTS. **Contact(s):** Tim Smith.

**☀ ♦ Consumer Guide to Home Energy Savings**
American Council for an Energy-Efficient Economy
1001 Connecticut Ave. NW, #535
Washington, DC 20036 (202)429-8873
**Affiliation:** American Council for an Energy-Efficient Economy. **Concern(s):** energy; conservation. A guide to different devices and ways to save energy around the home. Packed full of information and helpful products that you can really use. **Contact(s):** Liz Burke (Chairman).

**$ ♦ Consumer Sourcebook**
Gale Research Inc.
835 Penobscot Building
Detroit, MI 48226-4094 (800)877-GALE
**Concern(s):** economics; health; environment; consumer rights; corporate responsibility; consumer protection. Approximately 7,300 federal, state, and city agencies providing aid and information to the consumer in such areas as consumer finance, health, safety, environmental concerns, corporate responsibility, product safety and reliability, etc.; NGO's, centers, institutes, etc., active in consumer issues. Special articles that offer tips and recommendations on subjects of consumer interest. **Frequency:** Biennial. **Price:** $185/ea. **Pages:** 530. **Date Publ.:** 6/89. **Publisher:** Gale Research Inc. **Fax:** (313)961-6241. **Telex:** (810)221-7086. **Contact(s):** Shawn Brennan (Editor).

**H ♦ A Consumer's Dictionary of Food Additives**
Crown Publishers, Inc.
201 E. 50th St.
New York, NY 10022 (212)572-2568
**Concern(s):** health; consumer protection; nutrition; alternative consumer; hazardous/toxic. "Definitions for the Layman of Ingredients Harmful and Desirable Found in Packaged Foods, with Complete Information for the Consumer." **Date Publ.:** 1978. **Publisher:** Crown Publishers, Inc.. **Contact(s):** Ruth Winter (Author).

**$ ♦ Consumer's Resource Handbook**
Consumer Handbook Information Center
Pueblo, CO 81009
**Affiliation:** Consumer Handbook Information Center. **Concern(s):** economics; consumer rights; corporate responsibility. 2,000+ corporate consumer contacts, automobile manufacturers corporate contact. Better Business Bureau offices, industry third-party dispute resolution programs, trade associations, state and local consumer protection officers, and other federal and state agencies commissioned to handle consumer complaints. **Frequency:** Biennial. **Subscription:** Free. **Pages:** 100. **Date Publ.:** 10/90. **Publisher:** US Office of Consumer Affairs.

**H ♦ Consumers' Guide to Hospitals**
Consumers Checkbooks
806 15th St. NW, #925
Washington, DC 20005 (202)347-7283
**Affiliation:** Consumers Checkbook. **Concern(s):** health; consumer protection. Almost 6,000 acute-care hospitals, arranged geographically with name, address, description of services, advanced teaching programs for doctors, university affiliation, and death rate statistics. **Pages:** 200. **Date Publ.:** 1991. **Publisher:** Consumers Checkbooks. **Contact(s):** Robert Krughoff (Editor).

**P ♦ The Contact Directory: Local Action on Global Issues**
Global Tomorrow Coalition
1325 G St. NW, #915
Washington, DC 20005 (202)628-4016
**Affiliation:** Global Tomorrow Coalition. **Concern(s):** politics; environment; energy; grassroots organizing.

**M ♦ The Contemporary Social Issues: A Bibliographic Series**
Reference & Research Services
511 Lincoln St.
Santa Cruz, CA 95060 (408)426-4479
**Concern(s):** media; education; politics; press. A bibliography of periodicals, books, pamphlets, activist organizations and government publications concerned with a wide variety of pertinent and progressive contemporary social issues. Each bibliography contains approximately 500 entries with complete citations. **Est.:** 1982. **Frequency:** 4/yr. **Subscription:** $45/yr. **Price:** $15/ea. **Bulk:** 20% off/24. **Pages:** 55. **Publisher:** Reference & Research Services. **Contact(s):** Joan Nordquist (Editor).

**E ♦ Contemporary World Issues**
ABC-CLIO
130 Cremona Dr. Box 1911
Santa Barbara, CA 93116-9939
**Concern(s):** environment; demographics; education; energy. Each reference book gives an excellent overview of each issue..tells you where to find out more... and how to get actively involved. Books will include the following: Adult Literacy/Illiteracy in the US; Environmental Hazards; Human Rights; American Homelessness; Nuclear Energy Policy; World Hunger; Space Exploration; Abortion; Public Schooling in America. Most have yet to be published yet. If you promise to buy the whole series of 11, it will cost you $405, prices subject to change. **Price:** $45/ea. **Publisher:** ABC-CLIO.

**E ♦ Controlling Nonpoint-Source Water Pollution, A Citizen's Handbook**
National Audubon Society
950 3rd Ave.
New York, NY 10022 (212)546-9100
**Affiliation:** Conservation Foundation; National Audubon Society. **Concern(s):** environment; water. **Contact(s):** Nancy Richardson Hansen, Hope M. Babcock & Edwin H. Clark II

**$ ♦ Cooperative Communicators Association - Membership Roster**
Cooperative Communicators Association
c/o Forrest Bradley, 2263 E. Bancroft
Springfield, MO 65804
**Affiliation:** Cooperative Communicators Association. **Concern(s):** economics; labor; cooperatives. Nearly 350 cooperative members involved in improving and enhancing communication in and about cooperatives. Classified by type of membership and indexed alphabetically. Nearly 350 cooperative members involved in improving and enhancing communication in and about cooperatives. **Frequency:** Annual. **Subscription:** Members only. **Pages:** 90. **Date Publ.:** 9/90. **Contact(s):** Forrest Bradley (Editor).

**$ ♦ Corporate Environmental Data Clearinghouse**
198 Broadway
New York, NY 10003 (212)420-1133
**Affiliation:** Council on Economic Priorities. **Concern(s):** economics; politics; environment; monopolies; corporate responsibility; lobbying. Comprehensive reports on major US companies and their environmental record. Coverage includes: Products and technologies; Lobbying and political issues; Environmental impacts; Legal and regulatory issues, all covering at least 5 years of data. It monitors current environmental literature and government data; and sends questionnaires to companies being followed. Information is digested and verified, then assembled into comprehensible and easy-to-use reports on each company. **Other Resources:** Prices are reasonable and on a sliding scale. CEP publishes SHOPPING FOR A BETTER WORLD, the annual guide to company social responsibility. Nonprofit. **Est.:** 1969. **Fax:** (212)420-0988. **Contact(s):** Jonathan Schorsch (Director), Robert Pubovits (Research Assistant).

**$ ♦ The Corporation Responsibility Monitor**
Data Center
464 19th St.
Oakland, CA 94612
**Affiliation:** Data Center. **Concern(s):** economics; labor; corporate responsibility; jobs. The entire publication is devoted to "causes and effects of the permanent or temporary elimination of jobs due to plant closings, cutbacks in services, and runaway shops." Comprised of press clippings, it deals with many specific local situations as well as general conditions. Includes a directory section, with information

accessible by company, location, industry, and number of workers affected. **Other Resources:** Data also available through computerized search service. **Frequency:** 12/yr. **Pages:** 100. **Contact(s):** Tracy Helser (Editor).

H ▶ **Council for Health & Human Service Ministries - Directory Services**
1905 Olde Homestead Lane
Lancaster, PA 17601 (800)822-4476
**Affiliation:** United Church of Christ. **Concern(s):** health; justice; spiritual; welfare rights; faith; children; social justice. About 200 social welfare agencies, retirement homes, children's residential homes, hospitals, and other facilities affiliated with the United Church of Christ. **Frequency:** Annual. **Price:** $2/ea. **Pages:** 90. **Date Publ.:** Spring 1991. **Fax:** (717)299-9981. **Contact(s):** Rev. Robert M. Glasgow (Consultant for Public Information).

U ▶ **Council for Urban Economic Development (CUED) - Directory**
1730 K St. NW, #915
Washington, DC 20006 (202)223-4735
**Affiliation:** Council for Urban Economic Development. **Concern(s):** urban; economics; politics; community self-reliance; planning; inner city; ethnic concerns. Approximately 1,000 economic development professionals working in local and state governments; private sector professionals and corporations; local and community development corporations; neighborhood and manpower groups. **Price:** $100/ea. **Pages:** 100. **Circ.:** 1.6M. **Date Publ.:** 1/90. **Contact(s):** Cynthia Vaugh (Editor).

F ▶ **The Courage to Heal: A Guide for Women Survivors of Child Sexual Abuse**
HarperCollins
10 E. 53rd
New York, NY 10022 (800)242-7737
**Concern(s):** feminism; health; child abuse; rape/sexual abuse; psychology; counseling; empowerment. List of organizations and support groups that provide assistance to women who were sexually abused as children; also includes publications dealing with child sexual abuse. This is primarily a recovery guide for women who were sexually abused as children. **Frequency:** Irregular. **Price:** $16.95/ea. **Date Publ.:** 2/90. **Publisher:** Harper Collins. **Contact(s):** Janet Goldstein (Senior Editor).

E ▶ **Creating a Healthy World: 101 Practical Tips for Home and Work**
Windstar Foundation
Box 286
Snowmass, CO 81654 (800)669-4777
**Affiliation:** Windstar Foundation. **Concern(s):** environment; health; energy; hazardous/toxic waste; recycling. The EarthPulse series provides practical tips for helping create a healthier environment. In addition, the handbooks contain background information to clarify how following these tips improves environmental health and the quality of our lives. It also includes resources which direct readers to additional information or products that can help them make more ecologically sound choices. Examples of tips found in the handbooks: Everyday Chemicals, Energy, and Recycling. **Contact(s):** Susan Hassol, Beth Richman.

E ▶ **Creating Our Future**
1640 Francisco St.
Berkeley, CA 94703-1217
**Concern(s):** environment; education; youth. This manual includes: tree planting, recycling, boycotts, how to organize student action groups, how to do mailings and flyers, use the media, and plan and carry-out projects. Contact COF for the latest "How to" manual. **Other Resources:** See listing under organization. **Price:** $5/ea. **Bulk:** 40% off/24. **Pages:** 60. **Contact(s):** Sat San Tokh Singh Khalsa (Director), Elizabeth Wharton.

✌ ▶ **Creating Peace: A Positive Handbook**
Larry Langdon Publications
5155 Nectar Way
Eugene, OR 97405
**Concern(s):** peace. Lists of peace organizations, publications, research groups, etc., interspersed with commentary on peace ideas and activities (communications, travel, national politics, etc.). Classified by area of activity. **Pages:** 65. **Date Publ.:** 11/82. **Publisher:** Larry Langdon Publications. **Contact(s):** Larry Langdon.

E ▶ **Creating Successful Communities, A Guidebook to Management Strategies**
Island Press
1718 Connecticut Ave. NW, #300
Washington, DC 20036 (800)828-1302
**Concern(s):** environment; agriculture; land; ocean/rivers; wetlands; rural communities; sustainability. **Date Publ.:** 1989. **Publisher:** Island Press. **Contact(s):** Stephen F. Harper, Luther Propst (Editors).

J ▶ **Crime in America: Historical Patterns and Contemporary Realities**
Garland Publishing Co.
136 Madison Ave.
New York, NY 10016 (212)686-7492
**Concern(s):** justice; urban; media; criminal system; press; inner city; prisons; political prisoners; juvenile. "An Annotated Bibliography". List of organizations conducting criminology research. Principal content of publication is information on books and periodicals on criminology. **Price:** $44/ea. **Publisher:** Garland Publishing Co. **Contact(s):** Francesco Cordasco, David N. Alloway.

♥ ▶ **Current Issues in Day Care**
Oryx Press
4041 N. Central Ave.
Phoenix, AZ 85012-3330
**Concern(s):** family; day care. **Publisher:** Oryx Press.

♥ ▶ **Custody Handbook**
Women's Legal Defense
1875 Connecticut Ave. NW
Washington, DC 20009 (202)986-2600
**Affiliation:** Women's Legal Defense. **Concern(s):** family.

H ▶ **Dealing Creatively with Death: A Manual of Death Education and Simple Burial**
Celo Press
1901 Hannah Branch Rd.
Burnsville, NC 28714
**Affiliation:** Continental Association of Funeral and Memorial Societies in the United States. **Concern(s):** health; death/dying. "Directory of Funeral and Memorial Societies" covering about 175 local societies concerned with simplifying funerals through pre-planning; societies are members of the Association in the US and the Memorial Society Association of Canada. Geographically arranged with society name, address, and phone. Includes information to help the consumer plan a funeral without the assistance of a memorial society and on organizing a society. **Frequency:** Irregular. **Date Publ.:** 1988. **Publisher:** Celo Press. **Contact(s):** Ernest Morgan.

✐ ▶ **DeSirey-Dodge Archives/DeSirey-Dodge Peace Post**
4645 Columbus Ave. S
Minneapolis, MN 55407
**Concern(s):** arts; peace; justice; media; culture; social justice. International mail art archive including artists' books, artists' stamps, xerography, collage, exhibit documentation, stickers, buttons, audio tapes, zines, radical pamphlets and periodicals, postcards, rubber stamps, etc. **Other Resources:** Information services about mail art and social justice issues. **Est.:** 1988. **Contact(s):** Chris Dodge (Archivist/mail artist), Jan DeSirey.

✍ ▶ **Development Data Book**
Social Studies School Service
1000 Culver Blvd.
Culver City, CA 90230
**Affiliation:** World Bank. **Concern(s):** education; economics; Third World; demographics; global understanding; development; students; World Bank. This booklet uses maps, charts, graphs, and short texts to present raw material to students to help explain Third World problems of poverty, population, trade, GNP, and education. Teaching level could run from grades 6 to 12.

$ ▶ **Development Directory**
Omnigraphics, Inc.
645 Griswold, 24th Fl.
Detroit, MI 48226
**Concern(s):** economics; Third World; development. Organizations, foundations, academic institutions, government agencies, professional associations, and firms pursuing research and development interests worldwide. Geographically arranged; indexed by subject. **Frequency:** Irregular. **Price:** $95/ea. **Pages:** 300. **Date Publ.:** 1990. **Publisher:** Omnigraphics, Inc. **Contact(s):** Pamela Korsmeyer (Editor), George Ropes.

H ▶ **Dial 800 for Health**
People's Medical Society
462 Walnut St.
Allentown, PA 18102 (800)624-8773
**Affiliation:** People's Medical Society. **Concern(s):** health. Health related organizations providing toll-free numbers, classified and indexed by subject. **Price:** $4/ea. **Pages:** 70. **Date Publ.:** 1987. **Contact(s):** Mike Rooney (Director of Projects).

D ▶ **Dictionary of Demography: Biographies**
Greenwood Press, Inc.
88 Post Rd. W
Westport, CT 06881
**Concern(s):** demographics; spiritual; environment; population growth; philanthropy; immigration; family planning; pro-choice. 3,360+ persons (living and deceased) in 99 countries who have contributed scholarship or political or intellectual influence in matters of population, including family policy, birth control, abortion, or migration, or who are presently working with population data and policymaking. **Price:** $125/ea. **Pages:** 1100. **Date Publ.:** 1985. **Publisher:** Greenwood Press, Inc. **Contact(s):** William Petersen, Renee Petersen (Editors).

E ▶ **Dictionary of Environmental Science and Technology**
c/o Island Press
Box 7
Covelo, CA 95428 (202)232-7933
**Concern(s):** environment; energy. Provides students and general readers with a working knowledge of the scientific and technical terminology associated with environmental studies and appraisals of current issues. In addition to the comprehensive text, the book has many useful diagrams tables, a list of resources addresses, and a guide to further reading. Tables, charts, graphs, appendix. **Price:** $33/paper. **Pages:** 399. **Publisher:** Island Press. Order: (800)828-1302. **Contact(s):** Andrew Porteous.

H ▶ **Different Drummer: Homosexuality in America**
Silver Burdett Press
190 Sylvan Ave.
Englewood Cliffs, NJ 07632 (800)843-3464
**Concern(s):** health; AIDS. List of resource centers that provide information on AIDS. Principal content is information on and discussion of homosexuality. **Price:** $11.29/ea. **Pages:** 115. **Date Publ.:** 4/86. **Publisher:** Simon and Schuster. **Fax:** (201)461-8178. **Contact(s):** Elaine Landau.

✍ ▶ **Directories in Print**
Gale Research Inc.
835 Penobscot
Detroit, MI 48226-4094 (800)877-GALE
**Concern(s):** education; research. This is the "big daddy" of them all. If you can lift to read it you will find listings for almost 15,000 business and industrial directories, professional and scientific rosters, biographical dictionaries, directory databases, directory issues of periodicals, and other lists and guides. Includes US directories that have national or multi-state coverage as well as many directories published outside of the US. Through this source you will find almost everything that has ever been documented. **Other Resources:** Many of the descriptions in Macrocosm were derived from DIRECTORIES IN PRINT, with permission from Gale Research, Inc., for the reference section of this database. Many thanks to the Permissions Department! **Frequency:** Annual. **Pages:** 2150. **Publisher:** Gale Research Inc. **Other Formats:** Magnetic tapes. **Fax:** (313)961-6241. Telex: (810)221-7086. **Contact(s):** Charles B. Montney (Editor).

♿ ▶ **Directory for Exceptional Children**
Porter Sargent Publishers, Inc.
11 Beacon St.
Boston, MA 02108
**Concern(s):** education; health; justice; disabled; children; child abuse; disabled's rights. 2,600+ public and private schools, clinics, and treatment centers for children and young adults with emotional, developmental, and organic disabilities; includes lists of governmental and private agencies, associations, etc. **Frequency:** Biennial. **Pages:** 1400. **Circ.:** 6M. **Date Publ.:** 1/90. **Publisher:** Porter Sargent Publishers, Inc. **Labels:** 400.

H ▶ **Directory of Adult Day Care in America**
National Institute of Adult Daycare
600 Maryland Ave. SW, West Wing 100
Washington, DC 20024
**Affiliation:** National Institute of Adult Daycare. **Concern(s):** health; seniors. Nearly 850 adult day care centers in the US; 40 state adult day care associations, arranged geographically. **Frequency:** Irregular. **Price:** $19.95/ea. **Pages:** 150. **Date Publ.:** Summer 1990. **Contact(s):** Ruth Von Behren, Ph.D.

✍ ▶ **Directory of African and Afro-American Studies in the United States**
African Studies Association, Credit Union Building
Emory University
Atlanta, GA 30322
**Affiliation:** African Studies Association. **Concern(s):** education; Third World; Africa. About 625 institutions offering programs in African and Afro-American studies; about 300 other institutions have briefer

listings. **Frequency:** Irregular. **Price:** $20/ea. + $2 shipping. **Pages:** c275. **Date Publ.:** 1991. **Contact(s):** Hamit M. Rana (Editor).

**J ▸ Directory of African American Religious Bodies**
Howard University School of Divinity Research Center
1400 Shepherd St. NE
Washington, DC 20017 (202)686-2255

**Concern(s):** justice; spiritual; interfaith; minority rights. Approximately 900 African American religious denominations; resource and service agencies that serve the African American community; religious educational institutions, research organizations, and professional religious organizations; African American colleges and universities founded by religious bodies; African American religious scholars. **Pages:** c400. **Date Publ.:** 1990. **Publisher:** Howard University Press. **Fax:** (202)686-2255. **Contact(s):** Dr. Wardell J. Payne (Research Director).

**♿ ▸ Directory of Agencies and Organizations Serving Deaf-Blind Individuals**
Helen Keller National Center
111 Middle Neck Rd.
Sands Point, NY 11050

**Affiliation:** Helen Keller National Center. **Concern(s):** health; disabled. Approximately 440 public and private agencies that provide programs and services for deaf-blind persons. Arranged geographically. **Frequency:** 1987/last. **Price:** $15/ea. **Pages:** 200. **Fax:** (516)944-7302.

**T ▸ Directory of Agencies Assisting Cooperatives in Developing Countries**
426 Via Cristoforo Colombo
Rome, 00145 Italy 6 5782610

**Concern(s):** Third World; economics; development; cooperatives. About 300 governmental and nongovernmental development assistance organizations; worldwide coverage; also includes cooperative training courses available to students from developing countries outside their own countries. **Frequency:** Triennial. **Price:** Free. **Other Formats:** Telex: 61181 FOODAGRI ROME. **Fax:** 6 5782610. **Contact(s):** Vittoria Zaffarano (Editor).

**✍ ▸ Directory of Alternative Therapy Schools & Colleges**
Naturopathy Institute
Box 56
Malverne, NY 11565

**Affiliation:** Naturopathy Institute. **Concern(s):** education; health; holism. Schools and college offering courses in alternative methods of healing: naturopathy, homeopathy, nutrition, massage, radionics, color therapy, herbology, etc. **Frequency:** Biennial. **Price:** $25/ea. **Pages:** 45. **Contact(s):** Edgar A. Kinon, N.D..

**✍ ▸ Directory of American Youth Organizations**
Free Spirit Publishing, Inc.
123 N. 3rd St., #716
Minneapolis, MN 55401

**Concern(s):** education; youth. 400+ organizations for young people covering a variety of interests, including sports, religion, conservation, careers, political activities, hobbies and social activities, science and technology, and global/peace issues. Formerly published by Father Flanagan's Boys Home. **Frequency:** Biennial. **Price:** $16.95/ea. **Pages:** 155. **Date Publ.:** 1991. **Publisher:** Free Spirit Publishing, Inc.. **Fax:** (612)337-5050. **Contact(s):** Judith Erickson.

**S ▸ Directory of Building and Equipment Grants**
Research Grant Guides
Box 4970
Margate, FL 33063

**Concern(s):** spiritual; philanthropy. Approximately 540 foundations; and about 30 government agency-sponsored programs offering building, renovation, and equipment grants to nonprofit organizations. **Frequency:** Biennial. **Price:** $37.50/ea. **Pages:** c200. **Date Publ.:** 1/91. **Publisher:** Research Grant Guides. **Contact(s):** Richard M. Eckstein (Editor).

**T ▸ Directory of Central America Organizations**
Central America Resource Center
Box 2327
Austin, TX 78768

**Affiliation:** Central America Resource Center. **Concern(s):** Third World; demographics; justice; Central America; refugees; immigration. About 1,050 organizations concerned with aspects of Central American life, including legal aid and sanctuary for refugees, human rights, and community education. **Frequency:** Irregular. **Price:** $10/ea. **Pages:** 330. **Date Publ.:** 1987. **Other Formats:** Diskette, $750. **Labels:** 50. **Contact(s):** William Pope (Adminstrator).

**J ▸ Directory of Child Abuse**
1033 N. Fairfax, #200
Alexandria, VA 22314

**Affiliation:** National Center for the Protection of Children. **Concern(s):** justice; family; children; child abuse; criminal system.

**F ▸ Directory of Child Day Care Centers**
Oryx Press
2214 N. Central at Encanto
Phoenix, AZ 85004 (800)457-6799

**Concern(s):** feminism; day care. Licensed day care facilities for children; state day care center licensing agencies. Published in four volumes covering northeastern, north central, western and southern US; each volume contains about 13,000 entries. **Frequency:** Annual. **Pages:** 430-530. **Publisher:** Oryx Press. **Fax:** (602)253-2741.

**$ ▸ Directory of Collectives (West Coast Directory of Collectives)**
The InterCollective

**Affiliation:** InterCollective. **Concern(s):** economics; cooperatives. Approximately 365 collectives, cooperatives, and grassroots organizations in California, Washington, Oregon, Alaska, and British Columbia. Arranged geographically. **Other Resources:** Brief articles related to collectives, cooperatives, and grassroot organizations. Cover title, DIRECTORY OF COLLECTIVES. Not deliverable at previous address. No forwarding address supplied. **Frequency:** Irregular. **Price:** $4/ea., postpaid (current edition). **Pages:** 120. **Date Publ.:** 1989.

**✍ ▸ Directory of Colleges and Universities with Accredited Social Work Degree Programs**
Council on Social Work Education
1600 Duke St.
Alexandria, VA 22314

**Affiliation:** Council on Social Work Education. **Concern(s):** education; students. 465+ institutions in North America with undergraduate and graduate programs in social work education accredited by the Council. **Frequency:** Annual. **Pages:** 40. **Date Publ.:** 6/90. **Labels:** 60. **Fax:** (703)683-8099. **Contact(s):** Nancy Randolph (Director of Accreditation).

**U ▸ Directory of Community Organizations—Chicago**
One E. Superior
Chicago, IL 60611

**Affiliation:** Institute of Urban Life. **Concern(s):** urban; economics.

**☮ ▸ Directory of Conflict Resolution Resources**
c/o COPRED; George Mason University
4400 University Drive
Fairfax, VA 22030 (800)23PEACE+

**Affiliation:** National Peace Institution Foundation; COPRED. **Concern(s):** peace; conflict resolution. A National Peace Institution Foundation and COPRED collaboration. Current plans call for listing mediation services, education, and training opportunities, associations and groups in the field, and resource materials (videotapes, periodicals, bibliographies, etc.). Publication scheduled for fall 1990. **Date Publ.:** Fall 1990. **Contact(s):** Cliff McCarth.

**H ▸ Directory of Counseling Services**
International Association of Counseling Services
5999 Stevenson Ave., 3rd Fl.
Alexandria, VA 22304

**Affiliation:** International Association of Counseling Services. **Concern(s):** health; education; counseling; psychology. About 200 accredited services in the US and Canada concerned with psychological, educational, and vocational counseling, including those at college and universities, community and technical colleges, and public and private agencies. **Frequency:** Annual. **Pages:** 245. **Date Publ.:** 9/90. **Contact(s):** Nancy E. Roncketti (Administrative Officer).

**T ▸ Directory of Development Research and Training Institutes in Africa**
Organization for Economic Cooperation & Development
2001 L St. NW, # 700
Washington, DC 20036 (202)785-6323

**Affiliation:** Organization for Economic Cooperation & Development. **Concern(s):** Third World; economics; Africa; development. Nearly 500 organizations engaged in research and training in the fields of economic and social development in Africa. Both English and French are used in text. **Frequency:** Irregular. **Pages:** 260. **Date Publ.:** 1987. **Fax:** (202)785-0350.

**E ▸ Directory of Environmental Investing**
Environmental Economics
1026 Irving St.
Philadelphia, PA 19107 (215)935-7168

**Concern(s):** environment; economics; socially-responsible investing; green consumer. An annual publication that profiles leading and emerging companies in the environmental services field. Looks at the regulatory setting in which this industry operates, competitive challenges, and the peculiar problems and opportunities within this dynamic and fast-growing sector of the economy. **Other Resources:** Updated quarterly. **Price:** $62.50 ppd.

**E ▸ Directory of Environmental Organizations**
Box 35473
Los Angeles, CA 90035

**Affiliation:** Educational Communications. **Concern(s):** environment; education; research. Alphabetical list of more than 4,000 names, addresses, and telephone numbers of international, national, state, regional, and local organizations concerned with environmental issues. Most comprehensive listing for Southern California groups — large and small. Also includes entries for nature centers, businesses, governmental agencies, and educational institutions. Compiled by volunteers. **Frequency:** Annual. **Price:** $30/ea. **Date Publ.:** 1991. **Other Formats:** Available on diskettes or labels for $200, PC or AppleWorks diskettes. Zip code index to alphabetical directory; $10. Send $2 for shipping on all orders. **Contact(s):** Nancy Pearlman (Executive Producer), Anna Harlowe (Associate Director).

**H ▸ Directory of Episcopal Facilities for the Elderly**
Episcopal Society for Ministry on Aging
323 Wyandotte St.
Bethlehem, PA 18015

**Affiliation:** Episcopal Society for Ministry on Aging. **Concern(s):** health; spiritual; seniors; faith. About 100 hospitals, nursing homes, retirement homes, and other facilities for the aging sponsored by the Church. **Frequency:** Triennial. **Price:** $3/ea. + $1 shipping. **Pages:** 85. **Date Publ.:** 9/85.

**H ▸ Directory of Facilities Obligated to Provide Uncompensated Services**
Department of Health and Human Services
5600 Fishers Ln, #11-03
Rockville, MD 20857

**Affiliation:** Department of Health and Human Services. **Concern(s):** health; public health. About 2,975 hospitals and other health care facilities that are obligated to provide some uncompensated services to patients as payment for loans disbursed through the Public Health Service under the Hospital Survey and Construction Act of 1946. **Frequency:** Annual. **Subscription:** Free. **Pages:** 125. **Date Publ.:** 1/91.

**♥ ▸ Directory of Family Planning Grantees, Delegates, and Clinics**
Family Life Information Exchange
Dept. of Health & Human; Box 30436
Bethesda, MD 20814

**Affiliation:** Family Life Information Exchange. **Concern(s):** family; health; family planning; public health. About 4,500 family planning clinics and recipients of grants funded by Title X of the Public Health Service Act through the Department of Health and Human Services. **Frequency:** Irregular. **Subscription:** Free. **Pages:** 170. **Date Publ.:** 10/87. **Fax:** (301)907-8906.

**✍ ▸ Directory of Financial Aids for Minorities**
Reference Service Press
1100 Industrial Rd., #9
San Carlos, CA 94070

**Concern(s):** education; justice; minority rights. 2,000+ financial aid programs and awards available to members of minority groups; includes scholarships, fellowships, loans, grants, awards, and internships; state government agencies with related information. **Frequency:** Biennial. **Price:** $45/ea. + $2.50 shipping. **Pages:** c525. **Date Publ.:** 1/91. **Publisher:** Reference Service Press. **Fax:** (415)594-0743. **Contact(s):** Gail Ann Schlachter (Editor).

**S ▸ Directory of Foundation Funding Sources**
Center for Non-Traditional Education
1804 Vernon St. NW
Washington, DC 20009 (202)462-6333

**Affiliation:** Association for Community Based Education. **Concern(s):** spiritual; economics; education; philanthropy. About 45 foundations with interests in funding community based education programs. Arranged alphabetical, indexed by average grant size, interest, other area of interest. **Frequency:** Irregular. **Price:** $15/ea. **Pages:** c90. **Date Publ.:** 1/87. **Contact(s):** Joan Eads (Editor).

**J ◆ Directory of Hispanic Organizations**
Philip Morris Companies, Inc.
120 Park Ave., 24th Fl.
New York, NY 10017
**Concern(s):** justice; urban; ethnic concerns; minority rights; networking; diversity. Approximately 160 Hispanic organizations arranged alphabetically and indexed by organization name, geography, and subject. **Frequency:** Biennial. **Subscription:** Free. **Pages:** c95. **Date Publ.:** 9/89. **Publisher:** Philip Morris Companies, Inc. **Fax:** (212)907-5396.

**H ◆ Directory of Holistic Medicine and Alternative Health Care Services in the US**
Health Plus Publishers
Box 22001
Phoenix, AZ 85028
**Concern(s):** health; holism. Nearly 1,100 health professionals, such as osteopaths, other physicians, nurses, chiropractors, dentists, nutrition consultants, clinics, and health centers involved in holistic medicine; associations, foundations, and schools and institutes that have courses in holistic medicine. Geographically arranged. **Frequency:** Biennial. **Pages:** 265. **Date Publ.:** Spring 1990. **Publisher:** Health Plus Publishers. **Contact(s):** Shirley Linde, Donald J. Carrow (Editors).

**H ◆ Directory of Hotlines and Crisis Intervention Centers**
Covenant House, c/o Patricia Connors
346 W. 17th St.
New York, NY 10011    (212)727-4000
**Affiliation:** Council on International Educational Exchange. **Concern(s):** health; counseling. About 1,070 crisis intervention and hotline programs arranged geographically and indexed by subject. **Frequency:** Irregular. **Price:** $35/ea.+$4 shipping. **Pages:** 230. **Date Publ.:** 1986. **Publisher:** Covenant House. **Contact(s):** John P. Myers (Editor).

**♿ ◆ Directory of Independent Living Programs**
Independent Living Research Utilization
3400 Bissonnet, #101
Houston, TX 77005
**Affiliation:** Independent Living Research Utilization. **Concern(s):** health; disabled. 350+ independent living programs that serve disabled people. Similar to "Annotated Registry of Independent Living Programs" but lists more programs in less detail. TDD number: (713) 666-0643. Arranged geographically with program name, address telecommunications Device for the Deaf (TDD) number, name of executive director. Quarterly updates. **Frequency:** Annual. **Pages:** 40. **Date Publ.:** 1/91. **Other Formats:** Diskette. **Contact(s):** Laurel Richards (Editor).

**U ◆ Directory of Information Resources in Housing and Urban Development**
HUD User
Box 6091
Rockville, MD 20850    (800)245-2691
**Affiliation:** Department of Housing & Urban Development. **Concern(s):** urban; demographics; housing. About 115 national organizations involved in housing and urban development issues; 40 databases, arranged by separate alphabetical sections for organizations and databases with entries for organizations. **Frequency:** Irregular. **Pages:** 90. **Date Publ.:** 5/86.

**$ ◆ Directory of Intentional Communities**
c/o Sandhill Farm
Route 1, Box 155-M
Rutledge, MO 63563    (804)361-1417
**Concern(s):** economics; intentional communities. Most comprehensive, accurate, easy-to-use directory of North American communities ever compiled. Over 325 listed, plus 50 on other continents. Maps, extensive cross-reference charts, and fully indexed. Also 40 articles about community living, and listings for more than 200 alternative resources. **Other Resources:** Also the publishers of COMMUNITIES JOURNAL. Nonprofit. **Dues:** $16-40/yr. **Frequency:** Biennial. **Bulk:** 40% off/24. **Pages:** 312. **Date Publ.:** 11/90; 1/93. **Labels:** 29. **E-Network:** MCI. **ID:** Quest. **Contact(s):** Laird Schaub (Business Manager), Geoph Kozeny (Database Coordinator). **Other:** Geoph Kozeny, c/o 1531 Fulton St., San Francisco, CA 94117.

**T ◆ Directory of Inter-American and Other Associations in the Americas.**
O.A.S. Bookshop
17th & Constitution Aves. NW
Washington, DC 20002  (202)458-3000
**Affiliation:** Organization of American States. **Concern(s):** Third World; Latin America; development. Cultural, informative, professional, and semiprofessional associations in Latin America; also includes fellowships and studies programs. **Other:** Organization of American States, 17th & Constitution Sts., Washington, DC 20006.

**✈ ◆ Directory of Intercultural Education Newsletters**
Information Consulting Associates
185 Kenneth St.
Hackensack, NJ 07601
**Affiliation:** Information Consulting Associates. **Concern(s):** education; travel. 190+ newsletters concerned with travel and intercultural education at all levels. **Pages:** 100. **Date Publ.:** 1/87. **Contact(s):** Muriel Wall (Editor).

**E ◆ The Directory of National Environmental Organizations**
US Environmental Directories
Box 65156
St. Paul, MN 55165
**Concern(s):** environment; conservation. Lists addresses and descriptions of over 500+ non-governmental environmental and conservation organizations in alphabetical order. Most of the organizations listed are national in scope, a few are regional but have national significance, and others are international and important nationally. Includes subject index with over 40 major environmental subject areas. Third edition. **Est.:** 1984. **Frequency:** 2-3 yrs. **Price:** $54/ea. **Pages:** 159. **Date Publ.:** Fall 1991. **Publisher:** US Environmental Directories. **Labels:** 54. **Contact(s):** John C. Brainard, Roger N. McGrath (Co-editors).

**♿ ◆ Directory of National Information Sources on Handicapping Conditions and Related Services**
Government Printing Office
Washington, DC 20402   (202)783-3238
**Affiliation:** National Institute of Disability & Rehabilitative Services. **Concern(s):** health; justice; disabled; disabled rights. Approximately 400 major national organizations which disseminate information on disabilities and services for disabled persons. **Frequency:** Irregular. **Price:** $17/ea. **Pages:** 350. **Publisher:** Government Printing Office. **Contact(s):** Inez Marie Fitzgerald.

**T ◆ Directory of National Organizations Dealing With Central America**
World Without War Council
1736 Martin Luther King Way
Berkeley, CA 94709
**Affiliation:** World Without War Council. **Concern(s):** Third World; peace; world order; Central America. **Contact(s):** Rich Tada.

**L ◆ Directory of National Unions & Employee Associations**
US Department of Labor's Bureau of Labor Statistics
710 N. Capitol St. NW
Washington, DC 20402
**Affiliation:** US Dept. of Labor's Bureau of Labor Statistics. **Concern(s):** labor; unions. **Publisher:** Government Printing Office.

**F ◆ Directory of National Women's Organizations**
Sara Delano Roosevelt Memorial House
47-49 East 65th St.
New York, NY 10021    (212)570-5001
**Affiliation:** National Council for Research on Women. **Concern(s):** feminism. This Directory (2nd edition), first published in the mid-80's, will contain indexed descriptions of diverse US national women's organizations and groups that include research centers and discipline caucuses, policy and activist organizations, foundations, government agencies, library and archives, political action committees and unions, sororities and religious groups, and other national organizations devoted to women's issues. **Date Publ.:** Possibly Fall 1991. **Fax:** (212)570-5380.

**E ◆ Directory of North American Fisheries and Aquatic Scientists**
5410 Grosvenor Lane
Bethesda, MD 20814-2199
**Affiliation:** American Fisheries Society. **Concern(s):** environment; wildlife/endangered species.

**H ◆ Directory of Nurse-Midwifery Practices**
American College of Nurse-Midwives
1522 K St. NW, #1000
Washington, DC 20005  (202)289-0171
**Affiliation:** American College of Nurse-Midwives. **Concern(s):** health; feminism; birth; holism. About 600 nurse and midwifery practices. **Frequency:** Annual. **Price:** $10/ea. **Fax:** (202)289-4395. **Contact(s):** Deborah R. Timmons.

**♿ ◆ Directory of Organizations Interested in People with Disabilities**
People to People Committee for the Handicapped
1020 Ashton Rd.
Ashton, MD 20861
**Affiliation:** People to People Committee for the Handicapped. **Concern(s):** health; justice; disabled; disabled's rights. About 100 organizations that provide assistance or support for persons with disabilities; state employment security agencies and vocational rehabilitation agencies; about 40 additional organizations concerned with the problems of the handicapped. Compiled in cooperation with Disabled American Veterans and the President's Committee on Employment of People With Disabilities. **Frequency:** Every four yrs. **Subscription:** Free. **Pages:** 70. **Contact(s):** David L. Brigham (Chairman).

**♿ ◆ Directory of Organizations Serving People with Disabilities**
Commission on Accreditation of Rehabilitation Facilities
101 N. Wilmot Rd., #500
Tucson, AZ 85711
**Affiliation:** Commission on Accreditation of Rehabilitation Facilities. **Concern(s):** health; education; disabled; childhood; counseling. About 2,600 organizations offering more than 7,200 hospital-based and outpatient medical rehabilitation, spinal cord injury and chronic pain management programs; brain injury, work hardening, infant and early childhood development programs; vocational evaluation, work adjustment, occupational skill training, job placement; work, services, personal & social adjustment services, etc. **Frequency:** Annual. **Price:** $25/ea. **Pages:** 175. **Date Publ.:** 1/91.

**H ◆ The Directory of Organizations, Associations, Self Help Groups & Hotlines for Mental Health & Human Services Professionals**
Haworth Press, Inc.
10 Alice St.
Binghamton, NY 13904  (607)722-5857
**Concern(s):** health; justice; counseling; psychology; self-help. "and Their Clients"; includes agencies, hotlines, and organizations providing information and services to children, youth, minorities, the handicapped, senior citizens, families of the mentally retarded, homeless, women, and others with special social or emotional needs. Includes agency, hotline, or organization name, address, phone. **Price:** $24.95/ea. **Pages:** 165. **Publisher:** Haworth Press, Inc. **Fax:** (607)772-1424. **Contact(s):** Robert L. Barker (Editor).

**☸ ◆ Directory of Peace Studies Programs**
c/o Center for Conflict Resolution
4400 University Drive
Fairfax, VA 22030
**Affiliation:** Consortium on Peace Research, Education & Development (COPRED). **Concern(s):** peace; conflict resolution; volunteers; jobs; students. This annotated, comprehensive directory of peace studies and conflict resolution programs in colleges and universities provides information about the goals and objectives of the programs, course requirements, course titles, internships, faculty backgrounds, seminars, conferences, student groups, and research projects. More than 220 listed. **Frequency:** Annual. **Price:** $15/ea. **Bulk:** 20% off/24. **Pages:** 78. **Date Publ.:** 8/90; 8/91. **Contact(s):** David Cianto (Compiler).

**U ◆ Directory of Private Fair Housing Organizations**
United States Commission on Civil Rights
Department of Urban Development
Washington, DC 20425  (202)376-8128
**Affiliation:** Department of Urban Development. **Concern(s):** urban; justice; demographics; economics; minority rights; housing; ethnic concerns; discrimination. 1,500+ private fair housing organizations offering counseling and legal assistance to minorities who are victims of discrimination or are searching for fair housing in their area; 160 community housing resource boards (CHRB) funded by the Department of Urban Development. **Pages:** 175. **Date Publ.:** 1986.

**J ◆ Directory of Public Interest Legal Internships/ The NAPIL Fellowships Guide**
National Association of Public Interest Law
1118 22nd St. NW
Washington, DC 20036  (202)466-3686
**Affiliation:** National Association for Public Interest Law (NAPIL). **Concern(s):** justice; politics; students; jobs; volunteers. Annual editions include detailed information on hundreds of summer internships and post-graduate fellowships with poverty law, civil rights, consumer and environmental groups. **Contact(s):** Michael Caudell-Feagan, Sue Schreiber.

## ✍ ▶ Directory of Public Service Internships: Opportunities for the Graduate, Post-Graduate & Mid-Career Professional

National Society for Internships & Experiential Education
3509 Haworth Dr.
Raleigh, NC 27609          (919)787-3263
**Affiliation:** National Society for Internships & Experiential Education.
**Concern(s):** education; labor; jobs; volunteers. **Date Publ.:** 1979.
**Contact(s):** Jane C. Kendall, Elizabeth Y. Coppedge (Editors).

## T ▶ Directory of Puerto Rican Organizations

National Puerto Rican Coalition
1700 K St. NW, #500
Washington, DC 20006  (202)223-3915
**Affiliation:** National Puerto Rican Coalition. **Concern(s):** Third World; Caribbean. About 60 local and national organizations in the US interested in programs and issues affecting the Puerto Rican community. **Fax:** (202)429-2223.

## ✍ ▶ Directory of Research Grants

Oryx Press
2214 N. Central at Encanto
Phoenix, AZ 85004          (800)457-6799
**Concern(s):** education; research; science. 4,000+ research grants available from government, business, foundation, and private sources. **Other Resources:** BBS: DIALOG Information Services and SDC Information Services under title 'GRANTS," updated monthly. **Frequency:** Annual. **Price:** $110/ea. **Pages:** c1,340. **Date Publ.:** 1/91. **Publisher:** Oryx Press. **Other Formats:** Computer printout. **Fax:** (602)253-2741.

## ♿ ▶ Directory of Residential Centers for Adults with Developmental Disabilities

Oryx Press
2214 N. Central Ave.
Phoenix, AZ 85004          (800)457-6799
**Concern(s):** health; disabled. **Price:** $78.50/ea. **Pages:** 305. **Date Publ.:** 12/88. **Publisher:** Oryx Press.

## ♿ ▶ Directory of Resources for Adults with Disabilities

Office of Vocational & Adult Education, Department of Education
400 Maryland Ave. SW
Washington, DC 20202  (202)401-3550
**Affiliation:** Department of Education. **Concern(s):** health; disabled. Over 95 federal and non-federal agencies and programs, associations, clearinghouses, foundations, and other resources for educators working with disabled adults. **Frequency:** Irregular. **Subscription:** Free. **Pages:** 125. **Other Formats:** Microfiche from National Technical Information Service, Springfield, VA 22161 (703) 487-4780; $6.95. **Contact(s):** William R. Langner (Education Program Specialist).

## H ▶ Directory of Resources for Aging, Gerontology, and Retirement

Media Marketing Group
Box 611
DeKalb, IL 60115
**Concern(s):** health; seniors. Federal, state, and local government agencies and organizations involved in gerontological studies. **Other Resources:** Formerly published by Minnesota Scholarly Press. **Frequency:** Biennial. **Price:** $75/ea. **Pages:** 400. **Publisher:** Media Marketing Group. **Contact(s):** Marcia LaSota (Editor).

## H ▶ Directory of Retreat Houses in United States and Canada

Retreats International
Box 1067
Notre Dame, IN 46556
**Affiliation:** Retreats International. **Concern(s):** health; justice. About 600 retreat houses arranged geographically. **Frequency:** Annual. **Price:** $10/ea. **Pages:** 50. **Date Publ.:** 1/91. **Contact(s):** Thomas W. Gedeon SJ, (Executive Director).

## ✍ ▶ Directory of Selected Early Childhood Programs

Office & Department of Special Education Programs
Dept. of Education; 400 Maryland Ave. SW, MES
Washington, DC 20202  (202)401-3550
**Affiliation:** Department of Special Education Programs. **Concern(s):** education; health; justice; childhood; disabled; disabled's rights. 235+ projects in educational research, personnel preparation, and handicapped children's services sponsored by government agencies, universities, and other organizations and funded under the Handicapped Children's Early Education Program and the

National Institute for Disability and Rehabilitation Research; other divisions of the Office of Special Education Programs. Prepared by the National Early Childhood Technical Assistance System, University of North Carolina-Chapel Hill. **Frequency:** Annual. **Subscription:** Free. **Other Formats:** Microfiche and photocopy from ERIC Document Reproduction Service, Computer Mircofilm Corp. **Contact(s):** Marcia J. Decker (Managing Editor).

## H ▶ Directory of Services for the Widowed in the United States and Canada

Widowed Persons Service; AARP
601 E St. NW
Washington, DC 20004  (202)434-2277
**Affiliation:** American Association of Retired Persons. **Concern(s):** health; psychology; death/dying; counseling. About 500 associations, clubs, and agencies offering counseling and other forms of assistance to widows and widowers. Arranged geographically. **Frequency:** Annual. **Subscription:** Free to libraries and public service organizations. **Pages:** 80. **Date Publ.:** 8/90. **Contact(s):** Carrie Bacon (Editor).

## J ▶ Directory of Special Programs for Minority Group Members: Career Information Services, Employment Skills Banks, Financial Aid Sources

Garrett Park Press
Box 190F
Garrett Park, MD 20896
**Concern(s):** justice; minority rights. About 2,000 private and governmental agencies offering financial aid, employment assistance, and career guidance programs for minorities. **Frequency:** Irregular. **Price:** $27/ea., prepaid; $30/billed. **Pages:** 300. **Date Publ.:** 1990. **Publisher:** Garrett Park Press. **Contact(s):** Willi L. Johnson (Editor).

## $ ▶ Directory of State and Local Consumer Organizations

Consumer Federation of America
1424 16th St. NW, #604
Washington, DC 20036  (202)387-6121
**Affiliation:** Consumer Federation of America. **Concern(s):** economics; consumer rights. About 550 nonprofit, nongovernmental, nonpartisan state and local groups engaged in consumer advocacy. Compiled in conjunction with the Food Marketing Institute. **Pages:** 55. **Date Publ.:** 1987.

## E ▶ Directory of State Environmental Agencies

Environmental Law Institute
1616 P St. NW, #200
Washington, DC 20036  (202)939-3800
**Affiliation:** Environmental Law Institute. **Concern(s):** environment; politics. **Contact(s):** Kathryn Hubler, Timothy Henderson (Editors).

## H ▶ Directory of Suicide Prevention/Crisis Intervention Agencies in the United States

American Association of Suicidology
2459 S. Ash
Denver, CO 80222
**Affiliation:** American Association of Suicide. **Concern(s):** health; psychology. About 600 suicide prevention and crisis intervention centers arranged geographically. **Frequency:** Annual. **Price:** $15/ea. **Pages:** 60. **Date Publ.:** 10/90. **Contact(s):** Julie Perlman (Executive Officer).

## ✍ ▶ Directory of Undergraduate Internships

National Society for Internships & Experiential Education
3509 Haworth Dr.
Raleigh, NC 27609          (919)787-3263
**Affiliation:** National Society for Internships & Experiential Education.
**Concern(s):** education; labor; jobs; students; volunteers. **Date Publ.:** 1981. **Contact(s):** Debra L. Mann, Grace Hooper (Editors).

## H ▶ Directory of US-Based Agencies Involved in International Health Assistance

National Council for International Health
1701 K St. NW, #600
Washington, DC 20006  (202)833-0070
**Affiliation:** National Council for International Health. **Concern(s):** health; feminism; family; demographics; Third World; population growth; family planning; nutrition; hunger; volunteers. 400+ private voluntary organizations, universities, civic groups, professional associations, and other groups which have health, nutrition, and population/family planning programs in developing countries. **Frequency:** Irregular. **Price:** $35/ea.+$2 shipping. **Pages:** 200. **Date Publ.:** 1991. **Fax:** (202)833-0075. **Contact(s):** Dr. Antoinette Brown.

## ✈ ▶ Directory of Volunteer Centers

Volunteer: The National Center
1111 N. 19th St., #500
Arlington, VA 22209
**Affiliation:** Volunteer: The National Center. **Concern(s):** education; volunteers; travel. Approximately 375 member bureaus and centers. **Frequency:** Annual. **Price:** $5/ea. **Date Publ.:** Spring 1991. **Contact(s):** Dennis Barnett (Director/Volunteer Center Development).

## ✍ ▶ Directory of Washington Internships

National Society for Internships & Experiential Education
3509 Haworth Dr.
Raleigh, NC 27609          (919)787-3263
**Affiliation:** National Society for Internships & Experiential Education.
**Concern(s):** education; labor; jobs; volunteers; students. **Date Publ.:** 1981. **Contact(s):** Debra L. Mann, Grace Hooper (Editors).

## F ▶ The Directory of Women Entrepreneurs, A National Source Book

c/o Wind River Publishing
Box 450827, North Lake Branch
Atlanta, GA 30345
**Concern(s):** feminism; economics. 2,700+ "women-owned businesses are listed nationally. Included are local, federal and private sources which offer assistance to women entrepreneurs by means of loan programs and technical training. Information about numerous networking association and organization is supplied. Listings contain company name, address and telephone number, year founded and founder(s) name(s), number of employees, primary business. S.I.C. code and key officers."-WLW Journal.

## F ▶ Directory of Women in Environment

Worldwide
1331 H St. NW
Washington, DC 20005  (202)347-1514
**Affiliation:** Worldwide. **Concern(s):** feminism; environment. **Contact(s):** Joan Martin-Brown (Chairman), Cynthia R. Helms (President, Washington Forum).

## F ▶ A Directory of Women's Funds

Women and Foundations/Corporate Philanthropy
141 5th St. #7
New York, NY 10010          (212)460-9253
**Affiliation:** Women and Foundations/Corporate Philanthropy.
**Concern(s):** feminism; spiritual; philanthropy.

## H ▶ Directory of Women's Health Care Center

Oryx Press
2214 N. Central at Encanto
Phoenix, AZ 85004          (800)457-6799
**Concern(s):** health; feminism; birth; family planning; empowerment. 200+ women's health care facilities and organizations arranged geographically. **Price:** $42.50/ea. **Pages:** 145. **Date Publ.:** 4/89. **Publisher:** Oryx Press. **Fax:** (602)253-2741. **Telex:** (910)951-1333 ALANET.

## F ▶ Directory of Women's Media

Sara Delano Roosevelt Memorial House
47-49 East 65th St.
New York, NY 10021          (212)570-5001
**Affiliation:** National Council for Research on Women. **Concern(s):** feminism; media. "To aid networking and increase communication among women nationally and internationally," covers every area of media-related professions including an international listing of women in media with address and statements of purpose. A descriptive interantional listing of 1,000+ periodicals, presses, publishers and other media by, for, and about women. **Other Resources:** Formerly called INDEX/DIRECTORY OF WOMEN'S MEDIA, and published by the Women's Institute for Freedom of the Press. **Frequency:** Annual. **Price:** $30/ea. **Pages:** 120. **Date Publ.:** Fall 1991. **Fax:** (212)570-5380.

## D ▶ Dirt Rich, Dirt Poor

Institute for Policy Studies
1601 Connecticut Ave. NW
Washington, DC 20009  (202)234-9382
**Affiliation:** Institute for Policy Studies. **Concern(s):** demographics; justice; poverty. **Contact(s):** Joe Belden.

## E ▶ Dirty Dozen

6930 Carroll Ave., #600
Tacoma Park, MD 20912          (301)891-1100
**Affiliation:** Environmental Action Foundation. **Concern(s):** environment; law. An annual report of the worst environmental voting records in Congress.

**⚔♦ Disarmament Directory for California**
Harbinger
50 Rustic Lane
Santa Cruz, CA 95060
**Concern(s):** peace; disarmament. **Publisher:** Harbinger.

**⚔♦ The Disarmer's Handbook of Military Technology and Organizations**
Viking Penguin
625 Madison Ave.
New York, NY 10022
**Concern(s):** peace; disarmament. A concise guide to modern weapons and war theory. **Date Publ.:** 1983. **Publisher:** Viking Penguin. **Contact(s):** Andrew Wilson.

**F♦ Displaced Homemaker Program Directory**
Displaced Homemakers Network
1411 K St. NW, #930
Washington, DC 20005   (202)628-6767
**Affiliation:** Displaced Homeworkers Network. **Concern(s):** feminism; family; counseling. 1,000+ counseling and career assistance centers for women who are (primarily) widowed, divorced, separated, or abandoned after full-time careers as wives and mothers. **Frequency:** Annual. **Pages:** 80. **Date Publ.:** 9/90. **Fax:** (202)628-0123. **Contact(s):** Rubie G. Coles (Deputy Director).

**E♦ Dolphin Data Base**
Box 9925
College Station, TX 77842
**Concern(s):** environment; wildlife/endangered species. Facilitation of peaceful co-existence and research between humans and Cetaceans (dolphins and whales) and other co-inhabitants of the planet. Clearinghouse providing a descriptive directory of others attempting to do the same and/or offering opportunities for others.

**E♦ Drinking Water: A Community Action Guide**
c/o Concern, Inc.
1794 Columbia Rd.
Washington, DC 20009   (202)328-8160
**Affiliation:** Concern, Inc. **Concern(s):** environment; water; conservation. General introduction to the complex issues of water management and protection with guidelines for public participation. Nonprofit. **Est.:** 1970. **Price:** $4/ea. **E-Network:** Econet. **Contact(s):** Susan Boyd (Executive Director), Burks Lapham (Chairman).

**H♦ Drug, Alcohol, and Other Addictions: A Directory of Treatment Centers and Prevention Programs Nationwide**
Oryx Press
2214 N. Central at Encanto
Phoenix, AZ 85004   (800)457-6799
**Concern(s):** health; substance abuse.18,000 federal, state, and local addiction treatment programs including public and private centers, geographically arranged by state. **Price:** $45/ea. **Pages:** 785. **Date Publ.:** 12/90. **Publisher:** Oryx Press. **Fax:** (602)253-2741.

**M♦ Earth Communications Office - ECO**
1925 Century Park East, #2300
Los Angeles, CA 90067
**Concern(s):** media; education; peace; environment; childhood; youth. "By incorporating environmental themes in TV shows, motion picture, music, art and literature, we can help create a climate of environmental concern. This can build a base of support for the many environmental organizations and leaders, thereby accelerating the rate at which environmental progress is achieved. We must focus attention on reaching children, as they are our greatest hope." **Other Resources:** "We organize a flow of interesting speakers on a variety of environmental issues, seminars; small salon-type meetings; provide written information, and act as a clearinghouse/databank." **Fax:** (310)785-0107. **Contact(s):** Bonnie Reiss (Executive Director).

**E♦ Earth Journal - Environmental Almanac and Resource Directory**
Buzzworm
2305 Canyon Blvd., Suite 206
Boulder, CO 80302   (303)442-1969
**Concern(s):** environment. Documents all areas of environmental concern. **Price:** $9.95/ea. **Date Publ.:** 1993. **Contact(s):** Joseph E. Daniel (Edito-in-Chief), Ilana Kotin (Editor).

**H♦ Earth Star**
Box 110
Temple, NH 03084
**Affiliation:** Whole Life New England. **Concern(s):** health; holism; preventative. About 500 preventive and holistic health practitioners and schools. **Price:** $2.50/ea. **Circ.:** 180M. **Publisher:** Earth Star Press, Inc. **Fax:** (617)628-1719.

**$♦ The Economics As If The Earth Really Mattered: A Catalyst Guide to Socially Conscious Investing**
New Society
Box 582
Santa Cruz, CA 95061   (800)333-9093
**Concern(s):** economics; socially-responsible investing. "...offers hundreds of ways to invest in building an economy consistent with life-affirming values. Shareholder actions, socially responsible investment and loan funds, small-scale investing, alternative exchange systems - tools for revitalization." Hundreds of names/addresses, resource lists. "The whole machine of the alternative economy of America."-Kirkpatrick Sale. **Other Resources:** A true primer of Gaean economics. Includes resource list and bibliographies. **Date Publ.:** 1988. **Publisher:** New Society. **Contact(s):** Susan Meeker-Lowry.

**E♦ Ecopreneuring**
c/o Island Press
Box 7
Covelo, CA 95428   (202)232-7933
**Concern(s):** environment; economics; green consumer; recycling. "The Complete Guide To Small Business Opportunities." Covers opportunities in recycling, energy conservation, personal care products, safe food, and investment services. Offers practical information, including market size, growth potential, and capital requirements. Directory of resources and index. **Price:** $17.95 paper; $34.95 cloth. **Pages:** 308. **Date Publ.:** 1991. **Publisher:** John Wiley & Sons. **Order:** (800)828-1302. **Contact(s):** Stephen J. Bennett (Author).

**E♦ Ecoteam Workbook**
Global Action Plan for the Earth
449A Route 28A
West Hurley, NY 12491
**Affiliation:** Global Action Plan for the Earth. **Concern(s):** environment. Lists 15 quantifiable goals & suggestions on how to meet them.

**✍♦ Educating for Global Responsibility: Teacher-Designed Curricula For Peace Education K-12**
Teachers College Press
1234 Amsterdam Ave.
New York, NY 10027   (212)678-3292
**Concern(s):** education; peace; youth; students. **Date Publ.:** 1987. **Publisher:** Teachers College Press. **Contact(s):** Betty Reardon (Editor).

**A♦ Education and Training Opportunities**
National Agricultural Library
Beltsville, MD 20705   (301)344-3755
**Affiliation:** Alternative Farming Systems Information Center. **Concern(s):** agriculture; education; permaculture; farmlands; conservation; organic; sustainability. The first edition has some 75 entries, mostly university courses, but has some notable gaps such as TIPSY, Farallone Institute, Frank P. Graham Farm, etc. But, the authors invite input for the next edition.

**✍♦ Educational Materials in Planning**
American Planning Association
1776 Massachusetts Ave. N.W.
Washington, DC 20036   (202)872-0611
**Affiliation:** American Planning Association. **Concern(s):** education; urban; environment; planning; land use.

**✍♦ Educator's Guide: An Agenda for the 21st Century**
Countdown 2001
110 N. Payne St.
Alexandria, VA 22314
**Affiliation:** ABC's For the 21st Century Project. **Concern(s):** education; future; demographics; ideation; students. This guide includes lesson plans, resource directories on peace, environment, education, ethics, development, and population. It is offered through Countdown 2001's "ABC's For the 21st Century Project." Instructional packages on various topics sell for $17 per unit. $85 includes guide and 6 packages. Nonprofit. **Price:** $17.95/ea. **Contact(s):** Sherry L. Schuller, Ph.D. (President).

**✍♦ Elmer Holmes Bobst Library (NYU)**
See ORAL HISTORY OF THE AMERICAN LEFT and INFORMATION BULLETIN (periodicals).

**S♦ Encyclopedia of Associations: National Organizations of the US**
Gale Research Inc.
835 Penobscot Building
Detroit, MI 48226-4094 (800)877-GALE
**Concern(s):** ethics; philanthropy; volunteer. Approximately 22,000 nonprofit membersip United States organizations of national scope divided into 18 classifications. **Price:** Volume 1, "National Organizations of the United States," $305; volume 2, "Geographic and Executive Index," $250; "Encyclopedia of Associations...Supplement," $295. **Frequency:** Annual. **Pages:** 3,650/2 vols. **Date Publ.:** 7/90. **Publisher:** Gale Research, Inc. **Other Formats:** CD-ROM as part of "Gale GlobalAccess Association"; magnetic tape; diskette. **Labels:** Custom printout. **Fax:** (313)961-6421. **Telex:** (810)221-7086. **Contact(s):** Deborah M. Burek (Editor).

**S♦ Encyclopedia of Associations: Regional, State, and Local Organizations**
Gale Research Inc.
835 Penobscot Building
Detroit, MI 48226-4094 (800)877-GALE
**Concern(s):** spiritual; philanthropy; volunteer. Series of five volumes, each containing over 9,000 listings for American associations limited in activity to regional, state, and local levels. Does not duplicate entries in "Encyclopedia of Associations," which covers national organizations. Five regions: Great Lakes, Northeastern, Southern and Mid-Atlantic, South Central and Great Plains, and Western states. **Frequency:** Biennial. **Pages:** c700 per vol. **Date Publ.:** 5/90. **Publisher:** Gale Research Inc. **Other Formats:** CD-ROM as part of 'Gale Global Access: Association'; magnetic tape; diskette. **Fax:** (313)961-6241. **Telex:** (810)221-7086. **Contact(s):** Susan Boyles Martin (Editor).

**H♦ Encyclopedia of Drug Abuse**
Facts on File, Inc.
460 Park Ave. S
New York, NY 10016   (212)683-2244
**Concern(s):** health; substance abuse. Directories of government agencies and private organizations concerned with medical, legal, biological, and social facets of drug abuse. Principal content is 1,000 entries on drugs and drug abuse and appendixes listing drug street language providing statistics, and summarizing drug control laws. **Price:** $40/ea. **Publisher:** Fact on File, Inc. **Contact(s):** Robert O'Brien, Sidney Cohen.

**H♦ Encyclopedia of Health Information Sources**
Gale Research Inc.
835 Penobscot Building
Detroit, MI 48226-4094 (800)877-GALE
**Concern(s):** health. 13,000+ sources of information of interest to health care personnel, such as publications, health organizations, research centers and institutes, databases, and government agencies. **Frequency:** Irregular. **Price:** $155/ea. **Pages:** 490. **Date Publ.:** 1987. **Publisher:** Gale Research Inc. **Fax:** (313)961-6241. **Telex:** (810)221-7086. **Contact(s):** Paul Wasserman (Editor).

**H♦ Encyclopedia of Public Affairs Information Sources**
Gale Research Inc.
835 Penobscot Building
Detroit, MI 48226-4094 (800)877-GALE
**Concern(s):** health; demographics; environment; feminism; justice; birth control. Associations, publications, and databases providing information about 300 public affairs topics such as the environment, welfare, capital punishment, birth control, housing, poverty, smoking., etc. **Price:** $145/ea. **Pages:** 300. **Date Publ.:** 1988. **Publisher:** Gale Research Inc. **Fax:** (313)961-6241. **Telex:** (810)221-7086. **Contact(s):** James R. Kelly, Desier L. Vikor, Paul Wasserman (Editors).

**H♦ Encyclopedia of Senior Citizens Information Sources**
Gale Research Inc.
835 Penobscot Building
Detroit, MI 48226-4094 (800)877-GALE
**Concern(s):** health; seniors. About 13,500 associations, federal agencies, research institutes, databases, and publications providing information or services of interest to senior citizens. **Price:** $155/ea. **Pages:** 500. **Date Publ.:** 1991. **Publisher:** Gale Research Inc. **Fax:** (313)961-6241. **Telex:** (810)221-7086. **Contact(s):** Yvonne Lev, Paul Wasserman, Barbara Koehler (Editors).

**?♦ Encyclopedia of Social Inventions**
The Institute for Social Inventions
20 Heber Rd.
London, NW2 6AA England   081 208 2853
**Affiliation:** Institute for Social Inventions. **Concern(s):** future; ideation; invention. Over 500 of the best and most imaginative (mainly non-technological) ideas and projects for tackling social problems are described by social inventors from around the world. Covers the theory and history of social innovations, and how best to promote them. It makes vital reading for professional or students or concerned citizens wanting new and unusual perspectives (some inspired and futuristic,

some more immediately feasible) in any of this volume's many broad subject areas. **Other Resources:** 1000 pound prize for best idea. Publishes SOCIAL INVENTIONS JOURNAL. **Frequency:** Annual. **Price:** $40/ea. **Contact(s):** Nicholas Albery (Editor), Valerie Yule (Publisher).

### ✍ ◆ Encyclopedia of the US Military
Harper & Row
10 E. 53rd St.
New York, NY 10010    (212)207-7000
**Concern(s):** education; peace; politics; Third World. Includes over 2,000 definitions of US military terms, weapons, equipment, organizations and treaties. Primary reference tool for journalists and activists. **Publisher:** Harper & Row.

### ? ◆ The Encyclopedia of World Problems and Human Potential
c/o K.G. Saur
175 5th Ave.
New York, NY NW2 6AA
**Concern(s):** future; ideation. This $200 volume (postpaid from K.G. Saur) identifies 10,233 world problems and 14,176 available tools for combating these problems. **Publisher:** K.G. Saur.

### D ◆ Ending Hunger: An Idea Whose Time Has Come
The Hunger Project
1388 Sutter St.
San Francisco, CA 94109-5452    (212)532-4255
**Affiliation:** Hunger Project. **Concern(s):** demographics; Third World; hunger. The definitive resource book on the issue of hunger widely used in schools and universities. Nonprofit. **Pages:** 430. **Date Publ.:** 1990. **Publisher:** Praeger Publishers. **Contact(s):** David Laws (Staff Writer), Anne-Marie Jensen (Domestic Hunger).

### ☀ ◆ Energy Resource Directory
Washington State Energy Office
809 Legion Way SE
Olympia, WA 98504
**Affiliation:** Washington State Energy Office. **Concern(s):** energy.

### E ◆ Environmental Disputes
c/o Island Press
Box 7
Covelo, CA 95428    (202)232-7933
**Concern(s):** environment; grassroots organizing; lobbying. Environmental Dispute Settlement is a set of procedures for settling disputes over environmental policies without litigation. This is particularly appealing in an era of increasing conflicts and public pressure to give citizens a stronger voice in decisions. "Community Involvement In Conflict Resolution" Index. **Price:** $22.95 paper; $34.95 cloth. **Pages:** 275. **Date Publ.:** 1990. **Publisher:** Island Press. Order: (800)828-1302. **Contact(s):** James E. Crowfoot, Julia M. Wondolleck (Authors).

### E ◆ Environmental Grantmakers Directory
Environmental Grantmakers Association
1290 Avenue of the Americas, #3450
New York, NY 10104    (212)373-4260
**Affiliation:** Environmental Grantmakers Association. **Concern(s):** environment; philanthropy; fundraising. Full page descriptions and mailing contacts for 150 grantmakers. Third Edition. **Date Publ.:** 1991.

### $ ◆ Environmental Guidelines for World Industry
International Chamber of Commerce, UNEP
Room DC 2-0803, United Nations
New York, NY 10017    (212)963-8139
**Affiliation:** United Nations Environment Programme. **Concern(s):** economics; environment; peace; United Nations; trade.

### E ◆ Environmental Organization Directory
Environmental Protection Agency
1200 6th Ave., Stop MD-108
Seattle, WA 98101
**Affiliation:** Environmental Protection Agency. **Concern(s):** environment. **Other:** EPA, JFK Bldg. #2203, Boston, MA 02203.

### E ◆ Environmental Periodicals Bibliography
International Academy of Santa Barbara
Environmental Studies Institute, 800 Garden
Santa Barbara, CA 93101    (805)965-5010
**Affiliation:** Environmental Studies Institute. **Concern(s):** environment; media; press. Available on CD-ROM. A huge database of this index journal is available to Econet users for customized searches. The database consists of citations to "environmentally oriented" periodicals—over 460 journal titles dateing back to 1972. Can conduct fee-based searches via email. **E-Network:** Econet. **ID:** "iasb". **Contact(s):** Mickey Flacks.

### E ◆ Environmental Politics
Congressional Quarterly
1414 22nd St. NW
Washington, DC 20037    (202)887-8500
**Concern(s):** environment.

### E ◆ Environmental Quality Index
1400 16th St. NW
Washington, DC 20036-2266    (202)797-6800
**Affiliation:** National Wildlife Federation. **Concern(s):** environment; natural resources. Annual subjective assessment of the state of natural resources and quality of life in America. **Frequency:** Annual.

### J ◆ Equal Rights Amendment: An Annotated Bibliography of the Issues
Greenwood Press, Inc.
88 Post Rd. W
Westport, CT 06881
**Concern(s):** justice; civil liberties. List of publishers of about 700 books, articles, government publications, and ERIC documents following the efforts to ratify the Equal Rights Amendment between 1975 and 1985, as well as organizations on record as supporting or opposing the ERA. **Price:** $29.95/ea. **Date Publ.:** 11/86. **Publisher:** Greenwood Press. **Contact(s):** Renee Feinberg.

### F ◆ The Equal Rights Handbook
Center for Partnership Studies
Box 51936
Pacific Grove, CA 93950
**Affiliation:** Center for Partnership Studies. **Concern(s):** feminism; justice; EQUAL RIGHTS; men's liberation. **Contact(s):** Riane Eisler (Co-director).

### T ◆ Ethnic Information Sources of the United States
Gale Research Inc.
835 Penobscot Building
Detroit, MI 48226-4094    (800)877-GALE
**Concern(s):** Third World; demographics; justice; diversity; press; film; minority rights. Non-print and print sources of information about ethnic groups representing more than 90 countries, regions, and language groups; includes associations, fraternal and religious organizations, tourist offices, festivals, fairs, libraries, museums, periodicals, book dealers, and sources of audiovisual materials. Omits Blacks, American Indians, and Eskimos, who are considered to be well-covered elsewhere. Arranged by ethnic group. **Frequency:** Irregular. **Price:** $175/ea. **Pages:** c1,400. **Date Publ.:** 8/83. **Publisher:** Gale Research Inc.. **Fax:** (313)961-6241. Telex: (810)221-7086. **Contact(s):** Paul Wasserman, Alice E. Kennington (Editors).

### E ◆ Everyone's Guide to Toxics in the Home
Greenpeace
1436 U St.
Washington, DC 20009    (202)462-1177
**Affiliation:** Greenpeace. **Concern(s):** environment; health; hazardous/toxic waste.

### S ◆ Facts on Grants: A Report on Grantmaking of the Charles Stewart Mott Foundation
Charles Stewart Mott Foundation
Mott Foundation Building, No. 1200
Flint, MI 48502
**Affiliation:** Charles Stewart Mott Foundation. **Concern(s):** spiritual; philanthropy. About 350 grants awarded in the fiscal year prior to publication arranged in separate sections for grants over and under $15,000, then in topical categories (youth employment, minority higher education, environment, arts, community education programs, economic revitalization). **Frequency:** Annual. **Subscription:** Free. **Pages:** c300. **Date Publ.:** 6/91. **Contact(s):** Judy Samelson (Director of Communications).

### H ◆ Family Planning Information Centers
American Business Directories, Inc.
5711 S. 86th Circle
Omaha, NE 68127
**Concern(s):** health; feminism; family planning. 4,870 listings arranged geographically and derived from the "Yellow Pages." **Frequency:** Annual. **Publisher:** American Business Directories, Inc. **E-Network:** Online Information Network. **Fax:** (402)331-1505.

### ♥ ◆ Family Resources Database
National Council on Family Relations
3989 Central Ave. NE, #550
Minneapolis, MN 55421
**Affiliation:** National Council on Family Relations. **Concern(s):** family; health; psychology; counseling. "Human Resource Bank," a directory of psychologists, sociologists, researchers, family life educators, marriage and family therapists, and other professionals who can

be contacted by the general public. Database consists mainly of citations of over 1,000 journal articles, abstracts, books, audiovisual materials, programs, services, and other resources available to researchers and professionals involved in family studies and related fields. **Other Resources:** BRS Information Technologies, DIALOG Information Services, Executive Telecom System, Inc., Bureau of National Affairs Human Resource Information Network. **Frequency:** 12/yr. updates. **Date Publ.:** 1979. **Fax:** (612)781-9348. **Contact(s):** Rocky M. Ralebipi (Director).

### A ◆ The Farms of Tomorrow
c/o Island Press
Box 7
Covelo, CA 95428    (202)232-7933
**Affiliation:** Biodynamic Farming and Gardening Association. **Concern(s):** agriculture; community self-reliance; community investment; family farms; development; preservation; sustainability; organic. "Community Supported Farms, Farm Supported Communities" (CSA—Community Supported Agriculture) is built upon the solid foundation of organic and biodynamic cultivation, but it focuses on the social and economic conditions that make farming possible. Includes a list of resources and contacts for those interested in initiating a CSA farm. **Price:** $12/paper. **Pages:** 169. **Date Publ.:** 1990. Order: (800)828-1302. **Contact(s):** Trauger M. Groh, Steven S.H. McFadden (Authors).

### J ◆ Federal Programs of Assistance to American Indians
Senate Select Committee on Indian Affairs
United States Senate
Washington, DC 20510
**Affiliation:** Senate Select Committee on Indian Affairs. **Concern(s):** justice; Native Americans. Programs "specifically designed to benefit Indian tribes and individuals... Indians or Indian tribes as eligible beneficiaries, and...(programs) deemed to be of special interest to Indians." **Frequency:** Irregular. **Subscription:** Free. **Pages:** c300. **Date Publ.:** 1988. **Contact(s):** Richard S. Jones.

### F ◆ Feminist Periodicals: A Current Listing of Contents
University of Wisconsin System Memorial Library
Women's Studies Librarian; #112A, 728 State St.
Madison, WI 53706
**Affiliation:** University of Wisconsin System. **Concern(s):** feminism; media; press. 100+ periodicals of national or midwestern readership focusing on women's issues, particularly from a feminist standpoint. **Frequency:** 4/yr. **Pages:** 110. **Contact(s):** Susan E. Searing, Ingrid Markhardt (Editors).

### A ◆ The Fertile Soil
c/o Island Press
Box 7
Covelo, CA 95428    (202)232-7933
**Concern(s):** agriculture; organic; sustainability. "A Grower's Guide to Organic and Inorganic Fertilizers". A comprehensive technical resource on creating fertile soil using a balanced program that does not rely on chemical fertilizers. Tables, appendixes, glossary, and index. **Price:** $39.95/paper. **Pages:** 190. **Date Publ.:** 1990. **Publisher:** agAccess. Order: (800)828-1302. **Contact(s):** Robert Parnes.

### E ◆ 50 Simple Things You Can Do to Save the Earth
Earthworks Press
Box 25, 1400 Shattuck Ave.
Berkeley, CA 94709
**Concern(s):** environment. This slim paperback furthers the eco-consciousness currently proliferating. Printed on recycled paper, it offers practical advice on protecting the environment and was such a success that a whole series of "What You Can Do's" have hit the shelf. **Publisher:** Earthworks Press.

### E ◆ Fight To Win On Hazardous Waste: A Leader's Manual
CCHW, Box 6806
Falls Church, VA 22040
**Affiliation:** Citizens Clearinghouse for Hazardous Waste. **Concern(s):** environment; health; politics; hazardous/toxic waste; grassroots organizing.

### E ◆ Fighting Toxics: A Manual For Protecting Your Family, Community, and Workplace
c/o Island Press
Box 7
Covelo, CA 95428    (800)828-1302
**Affiliation:** National Toxics Campaign. **Concern(s):** environment; health; politics; hazardous/toxic waste; grassroots organizing. Part one provides the nuts and bolts of organizing citizen campaigns. Part two offers everything you need to know on federal statutes and citizens'

legal recourse against pollution. Includes reading lists, contacts, and information about getting involved. Tables, lists, extracts, appendices, index. **Price:** $31.95 cloth; $19.95 paper. **Pages:** 346. **Date Publ.:** 1990. **Publisher:** Island Press. **Contact(s):** Gary Cohen, John O'Connor (Editors).

### J ◈ Financial Aid for Minorities in...

Garrett Park Press
Box 190F
Garrett Park, MD 20896

**Concern(s):** justice; minority rights. In 6 volumes, sources of financial aid for minorities. Volume 1 covers health occupations; volume 2 covers business and law; volume 3 covers education; volume 4 covers engineering and science; volume 5 covers journalism and mass communications; volume 6 covers financial aid for students with any major. **Frequency:** Irregular. **Price:** Set/$20; Booklets $4/ea. **Pages:** 60-70 each. **Date Publ.:** 1989-90. **Publisher:** Garrett Park Press.

### ⚕ ◈ Financial Aid for the Disabled and Their Families

Reference Service Press
1100 Industrial Rd., #9
San Carlos, CA 94070

**Concern(s):** health; disabled. Foundations, corporations, government agencies, professional associations, and other organizations that offer 900 scholarships, fellowships, grants, loans, and awards to disabled persons or their family members. Also includes list of sources of financial aid and information about financial aid for the disabled. **Frequency:** Biennial. **Price:** $35/ea. **Pages:** 225. **Date Publ.:** 2/88. **Publisher:** Reference Service Press. **Fax:** (415)594-0411. **Contact(s):** Gail Ann Schlachter, R. David Weber (Editors).

### $ ◈ Finding Co-ops

National Cooperative Business Association
1401 New York Ave. NW, #1100
Washington, DC 20005 (202)638-6222

**Affiliation:** National Cooperative Business Association. **Concern(s):** economics; labor; cooperatives. 20,000 cooperatives, cooperative associations, and resource organizations are listed geographically, alphabetically, and by sector. With this, the only directory of its kind, consumers and producers can find cooperatives and cooperatives can find one another. **Price:** $4.95/ea. **Bulk:** $4.45ea/24. **Pages:** 288. **Date Publ.:** 1990. **Publisher:** Cooperative Information Consortium. **Contact(s):** Robert Scherer (President), Leta Mach (Communications).

### E ◈ Fish and Wildlife Reference Service

5430 Grosvenor Lane, #110
Bethesda, MD 20814 (800)582-3421

**Concern(s):** environment; education; wildlife/endangered species; research; volunteers; conservation. Provides fish and wildlife management reports through a computerized information retrieval system and clearinghouse in order to encourage better management and protection of endangered species. **Other Resources:** Accepts one to five volunteer interns a year. See its newsletter under same name. **Dues:** User fees.

### H ◈ The Food Pharmacy

Bantam Books
666 Fifth Ave.
New York, NY 10103 (212)765-6500

**Concern(s):** health; nutrition; preventative medicine; hazardous/toxic; alternative consumer; consumer protection. "Dramatic New Evidence That Food Is Your Best Medicine, featuring a pharmacopoeia of more than fifty foods." Extols the therapeutic value of various foods. A landmark in preventative health. **Date Publ.:** 1988. **Publisher:** Bantam Books.

### T ◈ Food, Hunger, Agribusiness: A Directory of Resources

464 19th St.
Oakland, CA 94612-9761 (510)536-1876

**Affiliation:** Third World Resources/Data Center. **Concern(s):** Third World. For postage and handling, add $1.50 for North America and $3.00 for foreign air mail. Please, order from Third World Resources. **Price:** $12.95/ea. **Pages:** 160. **Date Publ.:** Spring 1987. **Publisher:** Orbis Books. **Other Formats:** Geonet, user **ID:** 'geo2:tfenton'. **E-Network:** Peacenet. **ID:** 'tfenton'. **Contact(s):** Thomas P. Fenton, Mary J. Heffron (Compilers/Editors).

### S ◈ Foundation Directory

The Foundation Center
79 5th Ave.
New York, NY 10003 (800)424-9836

**Affiliation:** Foundation Center. **Concern(s):** spiritual; philanthropy. 6,600+ of the largest foundations in the US, all having $1 million or more in assets or awarding $100,000 or more in grants in a recent

year. **Other Resources:** Formerly DIRECTORY OF NEW & EMERGING FOUNDATIONS. **Frequency:** Annual. **Pages:** c1,235. **E-Network:** DIALOG Information Services. **Fax:** (212)691-1828. **Contact(s):** Stan Olsen (Editor).

### S ◈ Foundation Grants Index Annual

The Foundation Center
79 5th Ave.
New York, NY 10003 (800)424-9836

**Affiliation:** Foundation Center. **Concern(s):** spiritual; philanthropy. 43,000+ grants of $5,000 or more reported in the preceding year by over 400 private, community, and company-sponsored foundations; cumulates all grant records published during the year in "Foundation Grants Index Bimonthly," plus over 30,000 grants reported separately at the end of the year. Data include Foundation name, limitations on giving; recipient name, location; grant amount, date, and description. Foundation addresses are listed separately. **Other Resources:** DIALOG Information Services as FOUNDATION GRANTS INDEX file of FOUNDATIONS database; updated bimonthly. Updated by FOUNDATION GRANTS INDEX BIMONTHLY. **Frequency:** Annual. **Price:** $65/ea. + $2/shipping. **Pages:** c1,000. **Date Publ.:** 9/90. **Fax:** (212)691-1828. **Contact(s):** Ruth Kovacs (Editor).

### S ◈ Foundation Grants to Individuals

The Foundation Center
79 5th Ave.
New York, NY 10003 (800)424-9836

**Affiliation:** Foundation Center. **Concern(s):** spiritual; philanthropy. 1,200+ foundations that make grants to individuals, classified by subject areas of grants and indexed by foundation name, subject, type of support, geographical, company-related grant, school or university-related grant. **Frequency:** Biennial. **Price:** $24/ea.+$2 shipping. **Pages:** c360. **Date Publ.:** 7/90. **Contact(s):** Stan Olsen, Margaret Feczko (Editors).

### ✏ ◈ Free and Inexpensive Materials on World Affairs

World Affairs Materials
Box 726
Kennet Square, PA 19348

**Concern(s):** education. Lists a wide range of free and inexpensive resources for use by students, educators at all levels, writers, editors, and organizations or groups. **Publisher:** World Affairs Materials. **Contact(s):** Leonard S. Kenworthy.

### A ◈ Free Range Meat Directory

Americans for Safe Food
1875 Connecticut Ave. NW, #300
Washington, DC 20009 (202)332-9110

**Affiliation:** Americans for Safe Food. **Concern(s):** agriculture; environment; health; hazardous/toxic waste; nutrition; consumer protection. Listing of meat sources. While ASF does not guarantee that these sources are sustainably and humanely raised, it provides meat eaters with a good starting point. ASF also offers and ORGANIC MAIL ORDER PRODUCE LIST. Both retail for $1.50 each.

### M ◈ Freedom of Information Clearinghouse

Public Citizen
2000 P St. NW, #605
Washington, DC 20036-0757 (202)833-3000

**Affiliation:** Public Citizen. **Concern(s):** media; politics; justice; government accountability; constitutional rights. "A project of Ralph Nader's Center, we provide technical and legal assistance to individuals, public interest groups, and the media who seek access to information held by government agencies. We are available to consult by phone or mail. The Clearinghouse also litigates a number of cases each year to protect the public's right to access government information." Nonprofit. **Contact(s):** Rima V. Silenas (Assistant Director). (202)785-3704.

### ✏ ◈ Friendly Classroom for a Small Planet

Fellowship of Reconciliation
Box 271
Nyack, NY 10960

**Affiliation:** Fellowship of Reconciliation. **Concern(s):** education; peace; conflict resolution; childhood; students. This handbook offers many techniques for developing a positive atmosphere in which children can grow and discover creative alternatives for solving problems and dealing with conflicts. It is primarily designed for grades K-6, but the activities can be adapted for older or younger children. **Price:** $12.95/ea. **Bulk:** 40% off/24. **Pages:** 130. **Publisher:** New Society Publishers. **Contact(s):** Paula Cuth Conner.

### S ◈ Fringes of Reason

27 Gate 5 Rd.
Sausalito, CA 94965

**Affiliation:** Whole Earth Institute. **Concern(s):** spiritual; future; transformation; analysis; research; ideation. Scientific knowledge has

succeeded in contradicting traditional religion, but has failed to provide meaning and hope. Into the void new mythologies emerge, strange beliefs multiply, space-age folklore spawns. The Fringes of Reason: A Field Guide to New Age Frontiers, Unusual Beliefs and Eccentric Sciences explores this world of modern mythology, its possibilities, and curiosities. **E-Network:** The WELL. **ID:** Kerwit@Well. **Contact(s):** Kelly Teevan (Executive Director).

### ✿ ◈ From Star Wars to the Alternative

3930 Franklin Ave.
Los Angeles, CA 90027 (213)661-1535

**Affiliation:** Federation of Scientists. **Concern(s):** peace; economics; politics; disarmament; economic conversion; peace dividend. A critique on the Strategic Defense Initiative for laymen. **Price:** $1/ea. **Bulk:** 50% off/24. **Pages:** 17. **Date Publ.:** 1987. **Office:** 3318 Colbert Ave., #200 Los Angeles, CA 90066. **Contact(s):** James C. Ware (Chairman), Sheldon Plotkin (Board member). (310)390-3898.

### S ◈ Fund Raising Counselors & Organizations

American Business Directories/Information Inc.
5711 S. 86th Circle
Omaha, NE 68127

**Concern(s):** spiritual; fundraising; philanthropy. 2,310 listings arranged geographically and derived form the "Yellow Pages." **Frequency:** Annual. **Price:** $105/ea.; prepaid. **Publisher:** American Business Directories, Inc. **Other Formats:** Magnetic tape; diskette. 3x5 cards. **E-Network:** Online Information Network. **Fax:** (402)331-1505.

### $ ◈ Funding - Social Responsibility

666 Broadway, 5th Fl.
New York, NY 10012 (212)529-5300

**Concern(s):** economics; politics; fundraising.

### S ◈ Fundraiser's Guide to Human Service Funding

The Taft Group; Gale Research Inc.
12300 Twinbrook Parkway, #450
Rockville, MD 20852 (800)888-8238

**Affiliation:** Taft Group. **Concern(s):** spiritual; fundraising; philanthropy. About 900 corporations and foundations that contribute to human service projects. **Frequency:** Annual. **Price:** $110/ea. **Pages:** c560. **Publisher:** Gale Research Inc. **Fax:** (301)816-0811. **Contact(s):** Susan Elnicki.

### ✿ ◈ Future Mind

American Council for the United Nations University
4421 Garrison St. NW
Washington, DC 20016 (202)686-5179

**Affiliation:** American Council for the UN University. **Concern(s):** peace; future; conflict resolution; sustainability. Handbook to resolve prejudice between mystically-oriented and technocratically oriented. Many examples of how the two orientations are necessary at this point in history to make the future integration of consciousness and high technology work for peaceful future. "Conscious Technology" as a new vision is shown to grow from contemporary world events, philosophy, and evolution of civilization. 307 pages, illustrated, and appendix. **Other Resources:** Published in English 1989 (Acropolis). Published in Japanese 1991 (TBS - Britannica). **Bulk:** 40% off/24. **Pages:** 307. **Publisher:** Acropolis. **E-Network:** Econet. **ID:** 'jglenn'. **Fax:** (202)289-8670. 531 (EIES). **Contact(s):** Jerome C. Glenn (Executive Director, ACUNU), Evan Dvorsek (Database Management, ACUNU).

### ? ◈ Future Research Directory

World Future Society
4916 St. Elmo Ave.
Bethesda, MD 20814

**Affiliation:** World Future Society. **Concern(s):** future. About 800 futurists and/or individuals with a special interest in the future. **Frequency:** Irregular. **Price:** $29.95/ea. + $2.50 shipping. **Pages:** 245. **Date Publ.:** 7/87. **Labels:** 75. **Contact(s):** Edward Cornish (Editor).

### E ◈ Gaia, an Atlas of Planet Management

Doubleday & Company, Inc.
666 5th Ave.
New York, NY 10103

**Concern(s):** environment; spiritual; planning. **Date Publ.:** 1984. **Publisher:** Doubleday & Company, Inc. **Contact(s):** Norman Myers (Editor).

### ✈ ◈ Gale Global Access: Associations

Gale Research Inc.
835 Penobscot Building
Detroit, MI 48226-4094 (800)877-GALE

**Concern(s):** education; volunteers; travel. 75,000+ nonprofit voluntary membership associations in the US and worldwide. Includes the full text of "Encyclopedia of Associations: National Organizations of the

US," "International Organizations," and "Encyclopedia of Associations: Regional, State, and Local Organizations" (see separate entries). Costs $1,620 for multi-user version. **Frequency:** Annual. **Price:** $995/ea.; includes update; $900 without update. **Publisher:** Gale Research Inc. **Fax:** (313)961-6241. Telex: (810)221-7086.

**♿ ▸ Gallaudet University Library**
See INTERNATIONAL DIRECTORY OF PERIODICALS RELATED TO DEAFNESS and COLLEGE AND CAREER PROGRAMS FOR THE DEAF.

**G ▸ Gay and Lesbian Library Service**
McFarland & Company, Inc.
Box 611
Jefferson, NC 28640
**Concern(s):** justice; health; gay/lesbian; AIDS. Sixteen main chapters, e.g. collection development, school, academic, public, special collections, subject heads, services, exhibits, reference, periodicals, censorship, AIDS information. And 16 appendices, e.g. core collection, checklist of bibliographies, filmography, discography, gay/lesbian plays, famous gays, YA material, several kinds of directories, AIDS bibliographies/filmography, policy documents. **Price:** $36.50/ea. **Pages:** 368. **Date Publ.:** 1990. **Publisher:** McFarland & Company, Inc. **Contact(s):** Cal Gough, Ellen Greenblatt (Editors).

**☮ ▸ General Electric Shaping Nuclear Weapons Policies for Profits**
Box 3223
South Pasadena, CA 91031 (818)799-9133
**Affiliation:** INFACT. **Concern(s):** peace; economics; boycott. A report on one of the largest defense contractors actions in making components for nuclear weapons. Remember, at GE they bring good things to light except their involvement in the war machine.

**P ▸ Getting Organized: A Directory of Action Alliances, Publications and Information Services**
c/o Neal-Schuman
23 Leonard St.
New York, NY 10013 (212)925-8650
**Concern(s):** politics; justice; health; education. "...provides access to a vast range of publications and services that usually escape the net of traditional bibliographic tools. The nearly 500 organizations listed here offer information and services—much of which is innovative, original, and unavailable elsewhere—that can help people make informed choices in several areas that affect the quality of life." Areas covered are similar in scope to Macrocosm's. Includes address, phone, purpose statement with alphabetical organization index. **Price:** $24.95/ea. **Date Publ.:** 1982. **Publisher:** Neal-Schuman.

**$ ▸ Gifts from Uncle Sam**
JRS Publishing
931 Village Blvd., Dept. 907-259
West Palm Beach, FL 33409
**Concern(s):** economics. "More than 15,000 different items—books, posters, pamphlets, periodicals, videos, and more—are available for purchase, for rent, or for free from the federal government. Approximately 3,000 new items are available each year. There are 200+ free catalogs available—pertaining to a distinct subject category." This booklet helps you locate these items and includes Health Tips, Fascinating Facts, and much more. Numerous numbers (many toll-free) of various federal agencies are listed. **Price:** $3.50/ea. **Pages:** 35. **Date Publ.:** 1991.

**E ▸ The Global Ecology Handbook**
Global Tomorrow Coalition
1325 G St. NW, #915
Washington, DC 20005-3014 (202)628-4016
**Affiliation:** Global Tomorrow Coalition. **Concern(s):** environment; energy; demographics; health; sustainability; population growth; forests; hazardous/toxic waste. A guide to sustaining the Earth's future with the latest information on: Air, Water, Climate Change, Energy, Toxic Waste, Tropical Forests, Population, and much more. A practical supplement to the PBS series RACE TO SAVE THE PLANET. Updated and expanded version of the GTC book CITIZEN'S GUIDE TO SUSTAINABLE DEVELOPMENT. **Publisher:** Beacon Press. **Contact(s):** Dr. Walter H. Corson.

**✍ ▸ Global Education Resource Guide**
Global Education Associates
475 Riverside Dr., #456
New York, NY 10115 (212)870-3290
**Affiliation:** Global Education Associates. **Concern(s):** education; global understanding; press; film. Extensive, fully annotated listing of books, audiovisual materials, teaching aids and other action resources on global issues, organized by subject, with recommended grade levels. Background reading for educators, global concerns and tools for the classroom. **Contact(s):** Sandra Graff. (212)870-3291.

**E ▸ Global Releaf Citizen's Action Guide**
American Forestry Association
Box 2000, National Capitol Station
Washington, DC 20013 (202)667-3300
**Affiliation:** American Forestry Association. **Concern(s):** environment; forests; conservation; global warming. **Frequency:** 4/yr. **Contact(s):** R. Neil Sampson (Executive Director).

**E ▸ Global Survival Handbook**
Box 632
Haines, AK 99827
**Concern(s):** environment; education. Saving the Earth should be a central theme in all curricula from K through PhD. High school students in Haines, Alaska, are encouraged to think of ways to live fulfilling lives while preventing global self-destruction by working through a 23-part project. From "The Concept of Survival" through "A Code of Ethics," "List of Global Problems, " "The Haves and the Have Nots," "Reflections on Place" and into "Making a Difference" and "The Voyage Goes On." Each section suggests projects for global survival. **Contact(s):** Bruce John.

**E ▸ Global Warming**
Sierra Club Books
730 Polk St.
San Francisco, CA 94109-7897 (415)776-2211
**Affiliation:** Sierra Club. **Concern(s):** environment; global warming.

**✪ ▸ Global Warming and Energy Choices**
c/o Concern, Inc.
1794 Columbia Rd. NW
Washington, DC 20009 (202)328-8160
**Affiliation:** Concern, Inc.. **Concern(s):** energy; environment; global warming. This booklet is designed to provide an introduction to the complex issues of global warming and to raise public awareness of the implications of our energy choices and their impact on the world's climate. It encourages citizens to become involved in these choices both in their personal lives and in their communities. **Est.:** 1970. **Price:** $4/ea. **Fax:** (202)387-3378. **Contact(s):** Susan Boyd (Executive Director), Burks Lapham (Chairman).

**✍ ▸ Global/International Issues and Problems: A Resource Book for Secondary Schools**
ABC-CLIO
130 Cremona Dr. Box 1911
Santa Barbara, CA 93116-1911 (800)422-2546
**Concern(s):** education; justice; Third World; peace; youth; global understanding; hunger; childhood; students. List of international and national organizations and agencies involved in current issues, such as international concerns, human rights, hunger, and peace. **Other Resources:** List of resources (print and nonprint), charts, graphs, maps of world information, and chronologies of major events in specific world issues. **Price:** $32.95/ea. **Pages:** 220. **Date Publ.:** 1989. **Publisher:** ABC-CLIO. **Fax:** (805)685-9685. **Contact(s):** Lynn Parisi, Robert D. LaRue, Jr. (Editors).

**✈ ▸ Going Off the Beaten Path**
Route 5, Box 423
Livingston, KY 40445 (606)453-2105
**Concern(s):** environment; energy; agriculture; education; travel; bioregionalism; land use; renewables; resource management. This book serves both as a guide for travelers and a source of basic information for all concerned with establishing a sustainable society. The subject coverage is broad: from renewable energy through public lands to bioregionalism. For each topic the guide describes a sampling of places that can be visited and tells how to find additional resources. **Other Resources:** Formerly FROM WALDEN POND TO MUIR WOODS: Alternative Ways Across America. **Price:** $15.95/ea. **Bulk:** 33% off/24. **Pages:** 467. **Date Publ.:** 1990. **Publisher:** ASPI Publications. **Contact(s):** Mary Davis (Author), Al Fritsch (Director, ASPI).

**L ▸ Good Works: A Guide to Careers in Social Change**
W. W. Norton & Company, Inc.
500 5th St.
New York, NY 10110 (212)354-5500
**Concern(s):** labor; education; environment; justice; peace; jobs; volunteers; travel. **Publisher:** W.W. Norton. **Contact(s):** Joan Anzalone (Editor).

**S ▸ Grantseekers Guide: A Funding Source Book**
National Network of Grantmakers
2335 18th St. NW
Washington, DC 20009
**Affiliation:** National Network of Grantmakers. **Concern(s):** spiritual; philanthropy; fundraising. 200+ foundations and corporations that have supported social change projects such as the environment, civil liberties, women's and gay issues, AIDS, etc. Classified by groups with national and regional interests, then geographical. Also includes chapters on: fund-raising planning, gaining tax-exempt status, corporate support, proposal preparation, church resources for social justice, emerging cash flow loans, management support organizations. Bibliography of recommended publications. **Other Resources:** Formerly, DIRECTORY OF CHANGE ORIENTED FOUNDATIONS (1981); GRANTSEEKERS GUIDE: A DIRECTORY FOR SOCIAL AND ECONOMIC JUSTICE PROJECTS. **Frequency:** Irregular. **Pages:** c900. **Date Publ.:** 3/89. **Publisher:** Moyer Bell Ltd. (800)759-4100 **Fax:** (914)666-9384. **Contact(s):** Jill R. Shellow, Nancy C. Stella (Editors).

**☮ ▸ Grassroots Peace Directory**
ACCESS: A Security Information Service
1730 M St. NW, #605
Washington, DC 20036 (202)785-6630
**Affiliation:** ACCESS: A Security Information Service. **Concern(s):** peace. A computer-based information service on peace organizations and resources. Peace directories for the following: South, Lower Midwest, Western States, Southwest, Northwest and Pacific Rim, New England, New York, Mid Atlantic, Upper Midwest, and California. Separate addenda are available for $3.00 a region. Full set (10 volumes): $109.75. All orders must be prepaid and include shipping and handling. **Other Resources:** See listings for directories under the above names. **Price:** $10-15/ea. **Pages:** 125-190. **Labels:** 50. **Contact(s):** Phyllis E. Emigh (Information Manager).

**H ▸ Gray Panther Network - Listing of Local Groups Issue**
Gray Panthers
1424 16th St. NW
Washington, DC 20036 (202)387-3111
**Affiliation:** Gray Panthers. **Concern(s):** health; justice; seniors. Nationwide list of local groups. **Frequency:** Annual. **Contact(s):** Abby Lederman (Editor).

**L ▸ Great Careers: The Fourth of July Guide to Careers, Internships, and Volunteer Opportunities in the Nonprofit Sector**
Garrett Park Press
Box 190D
Garrett Park, MD 20896 (301)946-2553
**Concern(s):** labor; education; economics; jobs; volunteers; travel. Written by a team of 30+ college career planning and placement counselors and other staff who felt the need for a special resource concerning service occupations. Chapters topics cover animal rights, arts, children & youth, consumer advocacy, education, energy, ecology, fundraising, government, homelessness, hunger, international internships, labor, legal aid, media, peace & disarmament, disabilities, social action & work, sustainability, urban planning, women's issues & volunteerism. **Price:** $35 prepaid. **Contact(s):** Devon Cottrell Smith (Editor).

**☮ ▸ Great Decisions**
729 7th Ave.
New York, NY 10019 (212)764-4050
**Affiliation:** Foreign Policy Association. **Concern(s):** peace; education; politics; Third World; foreign policy; intervention. A nationwide foreign policy study/discussion program (Great Decisions program) which enables concerned members of the public to become better informed about international issues and to engage in active discussion of US foreign policy options.

**E ▸ Great Lakes Directory**
435 N. Michigan Ave., #1408
Chicago, IL 60611
**Affiliation:** Center for the Great Lakes. **Concern(s):** environment; Great Lakes.

**☮ ▸ The Great Turning: Personal Peace, Global Victory**
c/o Gary Lapid
560 Oxford, #1
Palo Alto, CA 94306
**Affiliation:** Project Victory. **Concern(s):** peace; education; future; conflict resolution. Visionary approach to Conflict Resolution and how to use mediated, dialogue to create a new era of human dignity, environmental restoration and global security. **Price:** $12/ea. **Pages:** 276. **Date Publ.:** 1989. **Publisher:** Bear & Co. **Contact(s):** Gary Lapid, Craig Schindler (Co-authors).

**U ▸ A Green City Program for the Bay Area and Beyond**
Planet Drum Books
Box 31251
San Francisco, CA 94131 (415)285-6556

**Affiliation:** Planet Drum Foundation. **Concern(s):** urban; environment; sustainability; bioregionalism; volunteers. A "how-to" manual for individuals and organizations interested in a sustainable future. Premise: that urban areas can exist harmoniously with natural systems. Includes: practical and visionary applications that are applicable to any community. Also includes a partial listing of volunteer activities with ideas on how to start working towards a "green" future, and a planet wide list of green city contacts. **Price:** $9/ea. **Pages:** 90. **Date Publ.:** 1990. **Publisher:** Planet Drum/Wingbow Press. **Contact(s):** Peter Berg, Beryl Magilavy, Seth Zuckerman (Authors).

**A ◆ Green Front Report**
Box 1064
Tonasket, WA 98855

**Affiliation:** Friends of the Trees Society. **Concern(s):** agriculture; environment; health; preservation; food production; permaculture; forests. This guide focuses on reforestation, fruit picking in Washington state, gardening sourcebooks, groups world-wide, arid-land permaculture, and herbal treatments. Nonprofit. **Est.:** 1978. **Price:** $8/ea. **E-Network:** Econet. **ID:** 'fott'. **Fax:** (509)486-4726. **Contact(s):** Michael Pilarski (Director), Carol Lanigan (Office Manager).

**E ◆ Green Index**
c/o Island Press
Box 7
Covelo, CA 95428          (202)232-7933

**Concern(s):** environment. "A State-By-State Guide to the Nation's Environmental Health". "Find out how your state compares in more than 250 environmental categories in this comprehensive reference. [It] tells which policies work and which don't. It also includes an overall environmental quality score for each state." Tables, charts, figures and index. **Publisher:** Island Press. Order: (800)828-1302. **Contact(s):** Bob Hall, Mary Lee Kerr (Authors).

**E ◆ Greenhouse Crisis, A Citizen's Guide**
Greenhouse Crisis Foundation
1130 17th St. NW, #630
Washington, DC 20036  (800)ECO-LINE

**Affiliation:** Greenhouse Crisis Foundation/Council on Economic Trends. **Concern(s):** environment; global warming.

**E ◆ The Greenhouse Effect**
Box 1112
Black Mountain, NC 28711  (704)669-6211

**Concern(s):** environment; energy; global warming. "We are under the influence of the Greenhouse Effect because we have done nothing to prevent it. The seas are rising. The Earth is heating up. We will have major changes in the next decades." This report gives details on the problem and the potential solutions. **Frequency:** Annual. **Price:** $15.00/ea. **Bulk:** $9.20ea/24. **Pages:** 50. **Publisher:** Lorien House. **Contact(s):** David A. Wilson (Owner).

**E ◆ The Greenpeace Guide to Paper**
4649 Sunnyside Ave. N
Seattle, WA 98103

**Concern(s):** environment; conservation; resource management; natural resources; recycling.

**P ◆ Greens Bibliography**
443 Market St.
Williamsport, PA 17701

**Concern(s):** politics; Green. Contains 800 bibliographic references of recent news articles on the Greens. **Pages:** 70. **Contact(s):** Jay Michael Ochs.

**E ◆ Groundwater: A Community Action Guide**
c/o Concern, Inc.
1794 Columbia Rd. NW
Washington, DC 20009  (202)328-8160

**Affiliation:** Concern, Inc.. **Concern(s):** environment; health; water; public health. This booklet explains what groundwater is, its availability and depletion as well as how it is contaminated and the consequences to public health. Pertinent laws and suggestions for individual and community action are given. **Est.:** 1970. **Price:** $4/ea. **E-Network:** Econet. **Fax:** (202)387-3378. **Contact(s):** Susan Boyd (Executive Director), Burks Lapham (Chairman).

**T ◆ Guide to Action**
936 N. 34th St., #200
Seattle, WA 98103-8869    (800)888-8750

**Affiliation:** Campaign To End Hunger/Planet Earth Foundation. **Concern(s):** Third World; demographics; education; hunger; development; global understanding. **Contact(s):** Keith Blume (Executive Director), Carla Cole (Director).

**◊ ◆ Guide to Careers and Graduate Education in Peace Studies**
The Five College Program in Peace and World Studies
Hampshire College
Amherst, MA 01002

**Affiliation:** Five College Program in Peace & World Studies. **Concern(s):** peace; jobs; students; conflict resolution. Includes internships and fellowships in conflict resolution and a list of organizations across the US.

**L ◆ Guide to Careers in World Affairs**
Foreign Policy Association
729 7th Ave.
New York, NY 10019    (212)764-4050

**Affiliation:** Foreign Policy Association. **Concern(s):** labor; education; politics; jobs; travel.

**✍ ◆ Guide to Community Education Resources**
Charles Stewart Mott Foundation
Mott Foundation Building, #1200
Flint, MI 48502-1851

**Affiliation:** Charles Stewart Mott Foundation. **Concern(s):** education; economics; community self-reliance. About 120 centers in the US and about 30 international centers that develop community education programs, lend technical assistance, training, etc., to enable community involvement in decisions concerning it. **Other Resources:** Formerly, PEOPLE HELPING PEOPLE HELP THEMSELVES. **Frequency:** Annual. **Subscription:** Free. **Pages:** 25. **Date Publ.:** 12/90. **Fax:** (313)238-8482. **Contact(s):** Dr. Pat Edwards (Editor).

**✍ ◆ A Guide to Educational Programs in Non-Collegiate Organizations**
American Council on Education, Office of Educational Credits
1 Dupont Circle NW, #800
Washington, DC 20036  (202)939-9300

**Affiliation:** American Council on Education. **Concern(s):** education; students.

**S ◆ Guide to Gifts and Bequests: A Directory of Philanthropically Supported Institutions**
The Institutions Press, Inc.
114 Morningside Dr.
New York, NY 10027    (212)532-0367

**Concern(s):** spiritual; philanthropy; fundraising. Publishes paid listings for hospitals, colleges, social service agencies, museums, and other institutions and organizations that wish to bring their activities to the notice of lawyers, accountants, trust officers and prospective donors; separate editions for Illinois, California, New York, and Florida, with 150-300 listings per edition. **Frequency:** Triennial. **Subscription:** Restricted circulation. **Pages:** c160-240. **Publisher:** Institutions Press, Inc. **Contact(s):** Linda Kaplan (Editor).

**E ◆ Guide to Hazardous Products Around the Home**
901 S. National Ave.
Box 87
Springfield, MO 65804

**Affiliation:** Household Hazardous Waste Project. **Concern(s):** environment; health; hazardous/toxic waste.

**H ◆ Guide to Health-Oriented Periodicals**
Sprouting Publications
Box 62
Ashland, OR 97520    (800)543-5888

**Concern(s):** health; media; environment; justice; spiritual; economics; press; holism; green consumer; alternative consumer. 250+ newsletters, magazines, journals, and newspapers. **Other Resources:** The editor also publishes THE SPROUTLETTER, SPROUTCHART, and SPROUTGUIDE. **Frequency:** Annual. **Pages:** 128. **Date Publ.:** 1989. **Publisher:** Sprouting Publications. **Contact(s):** Michael Linden (Editor).

**S ◆ Guide to Household Alternatives**
Clean Water Action
1320 18th St. NW, #300
Washington, DC 20036  (202)457-1286

**Affiliation:** Clean Water Action. **Concern(s):** economics; environment. A 30-page booklet of consumer-oriented environmental tips. Television productions, videotapes, and a slide presentation are all being planned. **Contact(s):** Debbie Keller.

**S ◆ A Guide to Liberation Theology for Middle-Class Congregations**
CBP Press
1316 Convention Plaza
St. Louis, MO 63103

**Concern(s):** spiritual; Third World; justice; peace; politics; interfaith; development; indigenous peoples; intervention. **Date Publ.:** 1986. **Publisher:** CBP Press. **Contact(s):** Charles H. Bayer.

**P ◆ A Guide to Living and Working for Social Change**
Bantam Books
666 5th St.
New York, NY 10103    (212)765-6500

**Concern(s):** politics; grassroots organizing. **Publisher:** Bantam Books. **Contact(s):** Charles Beitz.

**J ◆ Guide to Multicultural Resources**
Praxis Publications, Inc.
2215 Atwood Ave.
Madison, WI 53704

**Concern(s):** justice; feminism; minority rights; diversity; Native Americans. Minority and multicultural organizations and associations involved with the Asian, Black, Hispanic, and Native American communities. **Frequency:** Biennial. **Price:** $58/ea. **Pages:** 500. **Date Publ.:** 1/91. **Publisher:** Praxis Publications, Inc.. **Other Formats:** Diskette. **Labels:** 60. **Contact(s):** Charles Taylor (Publisher).

**✍ ◆ Guide to Resources in Holistic Education**
Holistic Education Review
39 Pearl St.
Brandon, VT 05733-1007    (802)247-8312

**Concern(s):** education; feminism; health; justice; holism; children; child abuse; childhood; welfare rights. "Each particular movement has its own publications, resources, and opportunities for networking. However, this Guide is the only comprehensive listing of organizations and publications from all the various movements. This is, of course, an ambitious undertaking and the Guide is by no means complete. We invite readers to send information about additional resources or revisions of the information presented here." Also covers children's rights and welfare organizations. Great little directory! **Other Resources:** "The Guide will be updated periodically, with additions appearing quarterly in HOLISTIC EDUCATION REVIEW." Some of the listings in MACROCOSM were reprinted with permission from this guide. **Price:** $2/ea., free with orders. **Pages:** 16. **Publisher:** Holistic Education Review.

**$ ◆ A Guide to Socially Responsible Investing**
Social Investment Forum
711 Atlantic Ave.
Boston, MA 02111

**Affiliation:** Social Investment Forum. **Concern(s):** economics; socially-responsible investing.

**P ◆ Guide to the American Left**
Editorial Research Service
Box 2047
Olathe, KS 66061    (913)829-0609

**Concern(s):** politics; peace; justice; feminism; environment; alternative party; anti-authoritarian; activism. A current, comprehensive directory of 3,000+ Socialist, Marxist, Revolutionary, Disarmament, Anti-Nuclear, Ethnic (Minority), Nationalist, Environmentalist, Gay, Feminist, and other "left-wing" organizations, publishers, book dealers, newsletters, and journals in the US and Canada. Listings are coded to indicate special areas of interest and serials are cross-indexed with sponsoring organizations. **Other Resources:** Updated by the WILCOX REPORT, formerly THE DIRECTORY OF THE AMERICAN LEFT (1984). **Frequency:** Annual. **Price:** $24.95/ea., postpaid, prepaid. **Bulk:** 20% off/24. **Pages:** 84. **Date Publ.:** 6/90. **Publisher:** Editorial Research Service. **Contact(s):** Laird Wilcox (Publisher/Editor).

**P ◆ Guide to the American Right: Directory and Bibliography**
Editorial Research Service
Box 2047
Olathe, KS 66061

**Concern(s):** politics; social justice; discrimination. 3,000 conservative, anti-communist, libertarian, free market, racial nationalist, tax revolt, right-to-life, and other right-wing organizations and publishers of periodicals; coverage includes Canada. Bibliography of 550 historical, political, biographical, and related publications concerning rightwing movements. Updated by THE WILCOX REPORT. **Other Resources:** Formerly, DIRECTORY OF THE AMERICAN RIGHT (1984). **Frequency:** Annual. **Price:** $24.95/ea.; postpaid, prepaid. **Pages:** 100. **Date Publ.:** 6/91. **Publisher:** Editorial Research Service. **Labels:** 98. **Contact(s):** Laird M. Wilcox (Editor).

**E ◆ Guide to the Management of Hazardous Waste**
c/o Island Press
Box 7
Covelo, CA 95428    (202)232-7933

**Concern(s):** environment; economics; hazardous/toxic waste; recycling; waste management; corporate responsibility. How to influence public policy; how waste laws effect your business; proper disposal;

waste reduction; meeting regulations and assessing risks; liabilities for clean-up of hazardous waste. Includes tables, figures, glossary, directory, bibliography, and index. **Price:** $17.95 paper; $34.95 cloth. **Pages:** 308. **Date Publ.:** 1991. **Publisher:** Fulcrum. Order: (800)828-1302. **Contact(s):** J. William Haun (Author).

### H ◆ Guide to the Nation's Hospices
National Hospice Organization
1901 N. Moore St., #901
Arlington, VA 22209
**Affiliation:** National Hospice Organization. **Concern(s):** health; death/dying. About 1,500 hospices, palliative care centers, and other programs serving terminally ill persons. **Frequency:** Annual. **Pages:** 140. **Circ.:** 4.5M. **Date Publ.:** 7/89. **Fax:** (703)525-5762. **Contact(s):** Ira J. Bates (Director of Educational Services).

### ☙ ◆ A Guide to Walking Meditation
Fellowship of Reconciliation
Box 271
Nyack, NY 10960
**Affiliation:** Fellowship of Reconciliation. **Concern(s):** peace; spiritual; transformation. "Nhat Hanh's words in this book are so authentic that the quality of life seems to change as you read them. This small volume is another classic that makes a wonderful gift." Available from FOR. **Date Publ.:** 1985. **Contact(s):** Thich Nhat Hanh.

### ☙ ◆ A Guide to War Tax Resistance
War Resisters League
339 Lafayette St.
New York, NY 10012    (212)228-0450
**Affiliation:** War Resisters League. **Concern(s):** peace; war tax revolt; nonviolence. **Date Publ.:** 1986. **Contact(s):** Ed Hedemann.

### ✎ ◆ Guide to Women's Art Organizations & Directory for the Arts
Midmarch Arts Press
300 Riverside Dr.
New York, NY 10025    (212)666-6990
**Concern(s):** arts; feminism. **Price:** $8.50/ea. **Publisher:** Midmarch Arts Press.

### ☙ ◆ Handbook for Nonviolent Action
c/o Donnelly/Colt
Box 188
Hampton, CT 06247    (203)455-9621
**Concern(s):** peace; nonviolence; civil disobedience. This 36-page handbook gives an overview of issues involved in civil disobedience/ direct action. An excellent basic resource to be used by action organizers and participants, nonviolence trainers and anyone interested in learning more about nonviolence, consensus decision-making, legal issues, affinity groups, discussion of oppression, campaign strategy and a bibliography, among others. Includes 17 inspirational photographs of nonviolent actions throughout the US Priced for mass distribution. **Bulk:** 50% off/10. **Fax:** (203)455-9597.

### ☙ ◆ Handbook for Peace and Environment
Sierra Club Books
730 Polk St.
San Francisco, CA 94109    (415)776-2211
**Affiliation:** Sierra Club. **Concern(s):** peace; environment. **Date Publ.:** 1990. **Publisher:** Sierra Club Books. **Contact(s):** Carl Anthony.

### ☙ ◆ Handbook For World Peacemakers Groups
World Peacemakers
2025 Massachusetts Ave. NW
Washington, DC 20036  (202)265-7582
**Affiliation:** World Peacemakers. **Concern(s):** peace; spiritual; interfaith. A call of faith and action guided by this publication.

### ☙ ◆ The Handbook of Nonviolence
Lawrence Hill & Co.
230 Park Pl., #6A
Brooklyn, NY 11238    (718)857-1015
**Concern(s):** peace; nonviolence. **Date Publ.:** 1986. **Publisher:** Chicago Review Press. **Contact(s):** Robert A. Seeley (Editor).

### ☙ ◆ Handbook on Military Taxes and Conscience
Friends Committee for Consultation, Section of the Americas
1501 Cherry St.
Philadelphia, PA 19102
**Affiliation:** Friends Committee for Consultation, Section of the Americas. **Concern(s):** peace; Third World; politics; war tax revolt; nonviolence; intervention.

### ♿ ◆ Handicapped Driver's Mobility Guide
American Automobile Association (AAA)
1000 AAA Rd.
Heathrow, FL 32746
**Affiliation:** American Automobile Association (AAA). **Concern(s):** health; disabled. 500+ manufacturers of driving aids, driving schools, publishers, government agencies, universities, and other organizations and companies offering services and products to the handicapped driver; about 15 VA-approved hand control manufacturers. **Frequency:** Biennial. **Price:** $3.50/ea. **Pages:** 95. **Date Publ.:** 5/90. **Contact(s):** Thomas P. Luce, Charles A. Butler (Editors).

### ♿ ◆ Handicapped Funding Directory
Research Grant Guides
Box 4970
Margate, FL 33063
**Concern(s):** health; justice; disabled; philanthropy; disabled's rights. 1,000+ foundations, associations, and government agencies that grant funds to nonprofit organizations for projects related to handicapped persons. **Frequency:** Biennial. **Price:** $39.50/ea.+$3 shipping. **Pages:** 225. **Date Publ.:** 1/90. **Publisher:** Research Grant Guides. **Contact(s):** Richard M. Eckstein (Editor).

### E ◆ Harbinger File
Harbinger Communications
250 Homestead Trail
Santa Cruz, CA 95060    (408)429-8727
**Affiliation:** Harbinger Communications. **Concern(s):** environment; politics; education; activism. A directory of over 1,000 citizen groups, government agencies, and environmental education programs concerned with California environmental issues with detailed information and descriptions. **Other Resources:** The information can be accessed under the database section of Peacenet under Harbinger File. **Frequency:** 2/yr. **Price:** $17.50/ea. **Pages:** 288. **Date Publ.:** 1/ 92. **E-Network:** Peacenet. **ID:** 'harbinger'. **Contact(s):** Bill Leland (President).

### H ◆ Healing Wise: The Second Wise Woman Herbal
Wise Woman Center
Box 64
Woodstock, NY 12498
**Affiliation:** Wise Woman Center. **Concern(s):** health; spiritual; feminism; environment; nutrition; empowerment; holism; transformation. Talking plants, frolicking fairies, wild recipes, personal weed walks, and ready-to-use herbal remedies are part of the green blessings beautifully and joyously offered. This is the book that has sparked excitement about the world's oldest healing tradition: the Wise Woman way of invisibly nourishing wholeness. Introduction by Jean Houston. **Price:** $11.95/ea. **Bulk:** 40% off/24. **Pages:** 312. **Date Publ.:** 1989. **Publisher:** Ash Tree Publishing. **Contact(s):** Susun Weed (Owner), Julia Hammid (Helper).

### E ◆ The Health Detective's Handbook: A Guide to the Investigation of Environmental Health Hazards by Nonprofessionals
The John Hopkins University Press
701 W. 40th St., #275
Baltimore, MD 21211
**Concern(s):** environment; health; hazardous/toxic waste. A thorough guide for citizens to evaluate whether adverse health effects in their community may be related to toxic substances. **Date Publ.:** 1985. **Publisher:** John Hopkins University Press, The.

### H ◆ Health Funds Grants Resources Yearbook
Health Resources Publishing
Brinley Professional Plaza, 3100 Hwy.138
Wall Township, NJ 07719-1442
**Concern(s):** health; spiritual; philanthropy. Foundations, government agencies, and corporations which award grants in areas of health care. Also includes bibliography of information sources for healthcare grant seekers. **Frequency:** Annual. **Price:** $85/ea.+$4.50 shipping. **Pages:** c160. **Date Publ.:** 4/90. **Publisher:** Health Resources Publishing; Brinley Professional Plaza. **Contact(s):** Robert K. Jenkins (Editor).

### H ◆ The Health Marketing Buyers Guide
CPS Communications
7200 W. Camino Real, #215
Boca Raton, FL 33433
**Concern(s):** health. 1,200+ journals specializing in the health care industry. **Frequency:** 2/yr. **Price:** $200/ea. **Pages:** 1200. **Circ.:** 600. **Date Publ.:** 12/90. **Publisher:** CPS Communications. **E-Network:** Online through Perq Research. **Fax:** (407)368-7870. **Contact(s):** Beverly B. Reynolds (Publisher).

### A ◆ Healthy Harvest IV: A Directory
1424 16th St. NW, #105
Washington, DC 20036   (703)243-0993
**Affiliation:** National Institute for Science, Law & Public Policy (NISLPP). **Concern(s):** agriculture; energy; health; Third World; sustainability; nutrition; organic; farmland; food distribution; development; appropriate technology. The ultimate directory for sustainable/

organic agriculture. More than 1000 farmers, food distributors, and international development groups are listed. 1400 entries contain full descriptions, and all contain name, address, phone, and contact. There are both subject and geographic indexes. Includes agriculture and horticulture organizations, research institutes, development programs, political organizations, appropriate technology institutes and design groups. One of a kind! Nonprofit. **Est.:** 1985. **Dues:** $24, $50 organization. **Frequency:** Annual. **Price:** $16.95/ea. **Bulk:** 40% off/24. **Pages:** 160. **Circ.:** 5M. **Date Publ.:** 12/91. **Publisher:** Potomac Valley Press. **Fax:** (202)265-6564. **Contact(s):** Deborah Preston (Publisher's Assistant), Steve Fustero (Marketing Director). (202)462-8800.

### H ◆ Healthy Healing
1975 C Mono Way
Sonora, CA 95370
**Concern(s):** health; preventative medicine; alternative consumer; nutrition. Lists the nutritional, herbal and homeopathic remedies to just about every dis-ease. If you can't find this helpful guide in your local health food store you should be able to order it through a bookstore. **Publisher:** Crystal Star Herbs.

### H ◆ Healthy Mothers, Healthy Babies - Directory of Educational Materials
409 12th St. SW, #309
Washington, DC 20023   (202)863-2458
**Concern(s):** health; family; education; birth; day care. Approximately 70 member organizations providing educational services and materials (primarily literature) concerning prenatal and infant care; approximately 15 additional nonmember organizations offering similar services or products. **Frequency:** Irregular. **Pages:** 170. **Date Publ.:** 1990.

### ♿ ◆ HEATH Resource Directory
HEATH Resource Center
1 Dupont Circle NW, #800
Washington, DC 20036  (800)544-3284
**Affiliation:** HEATH Resource Center. **Concern(s):** justice; health; disabled; disabled's rights. About 150 publishers of information resources for the handicapped and educators in postsecondary education. **Frequency:** Biennial. **Subscription:** Free. **Pages:** 25. **Date Publ.:** 5/91. **Other Formats:** Diskette, free; audiocassette. **Contact(s):** Anne Davie (Editor).

### H ◆ Help for Children from Infancy to Adulthood: A National Directory of Hotlines, Helplines, Organizations, Agencies & Other Resources
Rocky River Publishers
Box 1679
Shepherdstown, WV 25443  (800)343-0686
**Concern(s):** health; education; counseling; youth Nearly 400 US organizations, agencies, hotlines, helplines, and other resources that provide help for children and teenagers. **Other Resources:** Formerly, HELP FOR CHILDREN: HOTLINES, HELPLINES, AND OTHER RESOURCES. **Frequency:** Biennial. **Price:** $8.95/ea. **Pages:** 210. **Date Publ.:** 1/91. **Publisher:** Rocky River Publishers. **Contact(s):** Miriam Williams-Wilson, Eugene Lincoln Gerald Wheeleter , Editors.

### E ◆ Helping Out in the Outdoors
American Hiking Society
1015 31st St. NW
Washington, DC 20007  (703)385-3252
**Affiliation:** American Hiking Society. **Concern(s):** environment; labor; jobs; volunteers; wilderness; recreation. "Annual directory listing a wide variety of over 2,000 volunteer jobs. Some of the available volunteer positions even supply housing, offer reimbursement for food and/or travel expenses, provide on-the-job training or academic credit." **Frequency:** Annual. **Contact(s):** Louise Marshall (President).

### $ ◆ High Weirdness by Mail: A Directory of the Fringe - Mad Prophets, Crackpots, Kooks, and True Visionaries
Fireside Books; Simon and Schuster, Inc.
1230 Avenue of the Americas
New York, NY 10020    (800)223-2336
**Concern(s):** economics; media; press; trade. Publications and suppliers of records, audio- and videocassettes, and other mail order items selected by the editor for their off-the-wall or parodic qualities. **Price:** $9.95/ea. **Pages:** 330. **Date Publ.:** 5/88. **Publisher:** Fireside Books; Simon and Schuster, Inc. **Contact(s):** Ivan Stang (Author).

### J ◆ Hispanic American Voluntary Organizations
Greenwood Press, Inc.
88 Post Rd. W
Westport, CT 06881

**Concern(s):** justice; demographics; volunteers; minority rights; diversity. 200+ national and local Hispanic voluntary organizations and associations in the US, serving chiefly Mexican American, Puerto Rican, and Cuban populations. **Other Resources:** This work is second in the series ETHNIC AMERICAN VOLUNTARY ORGANIZATIONS. **Price:** $45/ea. **Pages:** c370. **Date Publ.:** 1985. **Publisher:** Greenwood Press, Inc., Congressional Information Service, Inc.. **Contact(s):** Sylvia Alicia Gonzales (Editor).

J ▸ **Hispanic Americans Information Directory**
Gale Research Inc.
835 Penobscot Building
Detroit, MI 48226-4094 (800)877-GALE
**Concern(s):** justice; diversity; minority rights. Information sources on varied aspects of Hispanic American life and culture, including national, state, and local organizations; publishers of newspaper, periodicals, newsletters, and other publications and videos; television and radio stations; bilingual programs in elementary/secondary schools; library collections; museums and other cultural institutions; grants/scholarships; Hispanic studies programs and research centers; federal and state government agencies; awards, honors, & prizes. **Price:** $69.50/ea. **Pages:** c370. **Date Publ.:** 1985. **Publisher:** Gale Research Inc. **Fax:** (313)961-6241. Telex: (810)221-7086. **Contact(s):** Darren L. Smith (Editor).

J ▸ **Hispanic Resource Directory**
The Denali Press
Box 021535
Juneau, AK 99802-1535
**Concern(s):** justice; minority rights; research; analysis. A comprehensive guide of extensive information on 951 local, regional and national Hispanic organizations, associations, research centers, academic programs, foundations, chambers of commerce, museums, government agencies and other US groups. Main section is arranged by state with data access through a series of fifteen indices and nine appendices (containing an additional 1,300 entries) which are primarily directories. Extensive social, political, and economic statistics in final appendix. **Price:** $37.50/ea. **Pages:** 347. **Date Publ.:** 1991. **Publisher:** Denali Press. **Contact(s):** Alan Edward Schorr (Editor).

H ▸ **Holistic Resources Directory**
c/o Quality Books
918 Sherwood Dr.
Lake Bluff, IL 60044
**Concern(s):** health; spiritual; environment; media; holism; transformation; press. Publishers, organizations, retailers, and practitioners of holistic products and services. 10,000+ holistic health and related listings from the US and Canada with 180 subjects index. **Pages:** 265. **Date Publ.:** 1988. **Publisher:** Quality Books. **Contact(s):** Susan James.

H ▸ **Home Health Care: A Complete Guide for Patients and Their Families**
W. W. Norton & Company, Inc.
500 5th St.
New York, NY 10110 (212)354-5500
**Concern(s):** health; seniors. List of adult day care centers with instructions on obtaining medical home health care. **Date Publ.:** 1986. **Publisher:** W. W. Norton & Company, Inc.

E ▸ **Home Safe Home & Environmental Shoppers 'Starter Kit'**
Clean Water Action Project
1320 18th St. NW, #300
Washington, DC 20036 (202)457-1286
**Affiliation:** Clean Water Action Project. **Concern(s):** environment; health; economics; hazardous/toxic waste. Includes: supplies, household alternatives chart, How to be an Environmental Shopper brochure, CITIZEN'S ENVIRONMENTAL HANKBOOK; Environmental Shoppers T-shirts.

✍ ▸ **The Home School Handbook**
Box 1083
Tonasket, WA 98855
**Concern(s):** education; homeschooling. An annually revised and updated guide to home schooling. The most comprehensive book of its kind. **Frequency:** Annual. **Price:** $6.50/ea. **Bulk:** 50% off/24. **Pages:** 40. **Date Publ.:** 4/91. **Publisher:** Home Schooling Press. **Contact(s):** Mark Hegener.

✍ ▸ **The Home School Reader**
Box 1083
Tonasket, WA 98855
**Concern(s):** education; homeschooling. A collection of articles from the first five years of HOME EDUCATION MAGAZINE. Authors include most of the top writers in the field, including John Holt, Linda Winkelreid-Dobson, Helen Hegener, Nancy Wallace, and many others. **Price:** $10.75/ea. **Bulk:** 50% off/24. **Pages:** 160. **Date Publ.:** 1/89. **Publisher:** Home Education Press. **Contact(s):** Mark Hegener.

H ▸ **Hospice Alternative: A New Context for Death and Dying**
Basic Books, Inc.
10 E. 53rd St.
New York, NY 10022 (212)207-7057
**Concern(s):** health; death/dying. Appendix of hospice referral centers with discussion of hospice care. Geographically arranged. **Price:** $8.95/ea. **Date Publ.:** 6/86. **Publisher:** Basic Books, Inc. **Fax:** (212)207-7203. **Contact(s):** Anne Munley.

✈ ▸ **Host Family Survival Kit: A Guide for American Host Families**
Intercultural Press, Inc.
Box 700
Yarmouth, ME 04096
**Concern(s):** education; travel; students. List of associations offering assistance or information to families involved in hosting foreign exchange students with association name and address. Principal content is a guide to hosting a foreign exchange student. **Frequency:** Irregular. **Price:** $9.95/ea. **Date Publ.:** 1988. **Publisher:** Intercultural Press, Inc. **Fax:** (207)846-5181. **Contact(s):** Ken Huff, Nancy King (Authors).

✈ ▸ **Hosting Soviet Visitors: A Handbook**
1601 Connecticut Ave. NW, #301
Washington, DC 20009 (202)387-3034
**Affiliation:** Institute for Soviet-American Relations. **Concern(s):** education; peace; conflict resolution; travel. A practical guide in how to initiate and conduct exchanges with the Soviet Union providing information on inviting, hosting, financing and other aspects of caring for Soviet guests. **Price:** $4.95/ea. **Pages:** 52. **Date Publ.:** 6/88. **Publisher:** Delphi Press, 1019 19th St. NW, Washington DC 20036. **Other Formats:** Prepared by Yale Richmond, retired foreign service officer with 20 years experience in US-Soviet Exchange. **Fax:** (202)667-3291. **Contact(s):** Eliza Klose (Executive Director), Harriet Crosby (President).

E ▸ **Household Hazardous Waste: A Bibliography of Useful References and List of State Experts**
Environmental Protection Agency
401 M St. SW
Washington, DC 20460 (800)424-9346
**Affiliation:** Environmental Protection Agency. **Concern(s):** environment; health; hazardous/toxic waste.

E ▸ **Household Waste: Issues and Opportunities**
c/o Concern, Inc.
1794 Columbia Rd. NW
Washington, DC 20009 (202)328-8160
**Affiliation:** Concern, Inc.. **Concern(s):** environment; health; hazardous/toxic waste; recycling. This booklet provides citizens with information about household waste and to indicate how they can contribute to its reduction. It demonstrated how each individual can reduce waste by adopting new habits, making informed choices, and becoming involved in community action. **Est.:** 1970. **Price:** $4/ea. **E-Network:** Econet. **Fax:** (202)387-3378. **Contact(s):** Susan Boyd (Executive Director), Burks Lapham (Chairman).

☮ ▸ **Housemans Diary Group**
See PEACE DIARY: WORLD PEACE DIRECTORY.

E ▸ **How to Make the World a Better Place, a Beginner's Guide**
Quill Press
105 Madison Ave.
New York, NY 10016 (212)889-3050
**Concern(s):** environment; peace; agriculture; economics; socially-responsible investing. **Date Publ.:** 1990. **Publisher:** Quill Press. **Contact(s):** Jeffrey Hollender (Author).

E ▸ **How You Can Fight Global Warming: An Action Guide**
Union of Concerned Scientists
26 Church St.
Cambridge, MA 02138
**Affiliation:** Union of Concerned Scientists. **Concern(s):** environment; global warming.

♿ ▸ **Human Factors Society - Directory**
Human Factors Society
Box 1369
Santa Monica, CA 90406
**Affiliation:** Human Factors Society. **Concern(s):** health; justice; energy; appropriate technology; disabled; seniors. 5,200 psychologists, engineers, physiologists, and other scientists in related fields who are concerned with the use of human factors in the development of systems and devices of all kinds. **Frequency:** Annual. **Price:** $30/ea. + $2.50 shipping. **Pages:** 320. **Date Publ.:** 5/91. **Labels:** 80.

T ▸ **Human Rights Directory: Asia & the Pacific**
c/o Human Rights Centre, University of Ottawa, 57 Louis Pasteur
Ottawa, ON K1N 6N5 Canada (613)564-3492
**Affiliation:** Human Rights Internet. **Concern(s):** Third World; justice; peace; Asia; Pacific/Pacific Rim. **Dues:** 50% off to members. **Date Publ.:** 1991. **Fax:** (613)564-4054.

J ▸ **Human Rights Directory: Latin America & the Caribbean**
c/o Human Rights Centre, University of Ottawa, 57 Louis Pasteur
Ottawa, ON K1N 6N5 Canada (613)564-3492
**Affiliation:** Human Rights Internet. **Concern(s):** Third World; justice; peace; Latin America; Caribbean; Central America. A bilingual directory that describes nearly 800 organizations concerned with human rights and social justice in Latin America and the Caribbean worldwide. Detailed descriptions and acronyms index and is intended as resources for networking, research and policy making. It primarily focuses on non-governmental organizations (NGOs), although relevant governmental bodies are described and is meant to highlight the work and concerns as well as serve the information needs of progressives. **Dues:** 50% off to subscribers to HRI Reporter. **Price:** $50/ea. **Date Publ.:** 1990. **Fax:** (613)564-4054.

J ▸ **Human Rights Directory: The Commonwealth**
c/o Human Rights Centre, University of Ottawa, 57 Louis Pasteur
Ottawa, ON K1N 6N5 Canada (613)564-3492
**Affiliation:** Human Rights Internet. **Concern(s):** justice; peace; economics; social justice; political prisoners; racism; discrimination. **Dues:** 50% off to members. **Date Publ.:** 1991. **Fax:** (613)564-4054.

J ▸ **Human Rights Directory: Western Europe**
c/o Human Rights Centre, University of Ottawa, 57 Louis Pasteur
Ottawa, ON K1N 6N5 Canada (613)564-3492
**Affiliation:** Human Rights Internet. **Concern(s):** justice; peace; economics; social justice; political prisoners; racism; discrimination. Describes over 800 organizations based in Western Europe working on human rights and social justice. Numerous indices facilitate information retrieval. **Dues:** 50% off to subscribers to HRI Reporter. **Price:** $30/ea. **Date Publ.:** 1982. **Fax:** (613)564-4054.

J ▸ **Human Rights Internet Directory: Eastern Europe & the USSR**
c/o Human Rights Centre, University of Ottawa, 57 Louis Pasteur
Ottawa, ON K1N 6N5 Canada (613)564-3492
**Affiliation:** Human Rights Internet. **Concern(s):** justice; peace; East-West. This volume describes 200+ East European or Soviet "unofficial:" and "approved" human rights organizations, groups, and initiatives which have emerged in the region since the early 1970's and organizations throughout the world which monitor human rights developments in this area. Detailed information and reports. **Dues:** 50% off to subscribers to HRI Reporter. **Price:** $30/ea. **Date Publ.:** 1987. **Fax:** (613)564-4054.

T ▸ **Human Rights: A Directory of Resources**
464 19th St.
Oakland, CA 94612-9761 (510)536-1876
**Affiliation:** Third World Resources/Data Center. **Concern(s):** Third World; justice; media; press; film. 120 sources for books, periodicals, pamphlets, audiovisuals, and other educational resources on human rights in the Third World. Alphabetical with institution name, address, phone, description, activities, resources, and titles, prices and frequencies. For postage and handling, add $1.50 for North America and $3.00 for foreign air mail. Please, order from Third World Resources. **Price:** $12.95/ea. **Pages:** 160. **Date Publ.:** Spring 1989. **Publisher:** Orbis Books. **Other Formats:** Geonet, user **ID:** 'geo2:tfenton'. **E-Network:** Peacenet. **ID:** 'tfenton'. **Contact(s):** Thomas P. Fenton, Mary J. Heffron (Compilers/Editors).

D ▸ **Hunger Action Handbook: What You Can Do and How To Do it By Seeds**
Reform Church of America
161 W. 12th St.
Holland, MI 49423
**Affiliation:** Reform Church of America. **Concern(s):** demographics; agriculture; hunger. **Contact(s):** Leslie Withers, Tom Peterson (Editors).

## ? ◈ The Ideas Index: Fresh Ideas for Democratic Ideals

The Democracy Project
215 Park Ave. S, #1814
New York, NY 10003    (212)260-2022

**Affiliation:** Democracy Project. **Concern(s):** future; politics; ideation; grassroots organizing. This $20 book lists 50 "new ideas" in six broad categories: economic development, foreign affairs, good government, rights and freedoms, environmental safety, education. **Contact(s):** Mark Green, David Corn.

## E ◈ In Praise of Nature

c/o Island Press
Box 7
Covelo, CA 95428    (202)232-7933

**Concern(s):** environment. This is a stimulating collection of excerpts, commentary, and reviews of more than 100 works of highly respected environmental writers including Barry Lopez, George Perkins Marsh, Aldo Leopold, John McPhee, Lewis Mumford, Marc Reisner, Paul Ehrlich, E.O. Wilson, and George Orwell. A valuable reference tool for librarians, teachers, and general readers who want guidance in choosing from the wealth of environmental writing available today. Bibliography and index. **Price:** $22.95 cloth; /$14.95 paper. **Pages:** 288. **Date Publ.:** 1990. **Publisher:** Island Press. Order: (800)828-1302. **Contact(s):** Stephanie Mills (Editor/Author).

## T ◈ In Whose Interest: A Guide to US-South Africa Relations

Institute for Policy Studies
1601 Connecticut Ave. NW
Washington, DC 20009  (202)234-9382

**Affiliation:** Institute for Policy Studies. **Concern(s):** Third World; peace; politics; South Africa; foreign policy; divestment. **Date Publ.:** 1985. **Contact(s):** Kevin Danaher.

## J ◈ Indian Reservations: A State and Federal Handbook

Confederation of American Indians
c/o McFarland & Co. Inc.; Box 611
Jefferson, NC 28640

**Affiliation:** Confederation of American Indians. **Concern(s):** justice; Native Americans. Reservations arranged alphabetically and indexed by subject with name of reservation, address, status (whether state or federal), tribal headquarters, type of land (tribal, allotted, government, etc.), description of history and culture, climate, utilities, and community facilities. **Price:** $45/ea.+$2 shipping. **Pages:** 345. **Date Publ.:** 1986.

## S ◈ Institute for Theological Encounter with Science and Technology - Membership Directory

Institute for Theological Encounter with Science and Technology
221 N. Grant Blvd.
St. Louis, MO 63101

**Affiliation:** Institute for Theological Encounter with Science and Technology. **Concern(s):** spiritual; education; science; faith. About 600 member scientists, theologians, and academicians who address scientific and technological issues as they related to Christian understanding of the human and of creation. **Frequency:** Annual. **Price:** $20/ea. **Pages:** c75. **Date Publ.:** 12/89. **Contact(s):** Reverend Robert A. Brungs, S.J., (Director).

## $ ◈ Intermediate Technology Development

6 Valley Trail
Croton-On-Hudson
New York, NY 10520    (212)953-6920

**Affiliation:** Intermediate Technology Development Group of North America. **Concern(s):** economics; community self-reliance; sustainability. **Other Resources:** Bootstrap Press.

## P ◈ International Blacklist

c/o Brian Kane
Box 410151
San Francisco, CA 94141-0151

**Concern(s):** politics; anti-authorian. An anti-authoritarian's directory of 7,000+ listings for public anarchist and other similar anti-authoritarian publications, projects, groups, and individuals. Also listed are those who, though not anarchist, provide information that is helpful to an anti-authoritarian analysis of the world and which don't follow some party's line - the most comprehensive directory of alternative thinkers and actors in the public domain from nearly every country in the world. **Frequency:** Irregular. **Pages:** 200. **Date Publ.:** 1/90. **Contact(s):** Brian Kane (Editor).

## F ◈ International Centers for Research on Women

Sara Delano Roosevelt Memorial House
47-49 East 65th St.
New York, NY 10021    (212)570-5001

**Affiliation:** National Council for Research on Women. **Concern(s):** feminism. A listing of over 150 research and documentation centers in 47 countries, including the US member centers of the NCRW. **Price:** $10/ea. **Pages:** 26. **Date Publ.:** 1990. **Fax:** (212)570-5380. **Contact(s):** Mariam Chamberlain (Compiler).

## T ◈ International Development Resource Books

Greenwood Press, Inc.
88 Post Rd. W
Westport, CT 06881

**Concern(s):** Third World; development; United Nations. In each of 20 volumes in the series, lists of international periodicals. United Nations information sources, and research institutions working on the particular aspects of economic development covered by the volume. **Price:** $45-60.95/ea. **Pages:** 365-710. **Date Publ.:** 1984. **Publisher:** Greenwood Press, Inc. **Contact(s):** Pradip K. Ghosh (Editor).

## ♿ ◈ International Directory of Adult-Oriented Assistive Device Sources

Lifeboat Press
Box 11782
Marina Del Rey, CA 90295

**Concern(s):** health; disabled. Suppliers of implements and tools enabling adults with impaired functions or disabilities to perform daily living activities. **Frequency:** Biennial. **Price:** $45.95/ea. **Pages:** 350. **Date Publ.:** 5/90. **Publisher:** Lifeboat Press. **Contact(s):** Carol J. Walsh (Project Manager).

## G ◈ International Directory of Gay and Lesbian Periodicals

Oryx Press
2214 N. Central at Encanto
Phoenix, AZ 85004

**Concern(s):** justice; gay/lesbian. Over 2,000 publishers of gay and lesbian newspapers, newsletters, journals, magazines, and other publications. **Price:** $20/ea., postpaid. **Pages:** c240. **Date Publ.:** 3/87. **Publisher:** Oryx Press. **Fax:** (602)253-2741. **Contact(s):** H. Robert Malinowsky.

## E ◈ International Directory of Human Ecologists

c/o College of the Atlantic
Bar Harbor, ME 04609

**Affiliation:** Society for Human Ecology. **Concern(s):** environment. Contains self-descriptions by 750 human ecologists of their areas of expertise, active interest, address, and phone number.

## M ◈ The International Directory of Little Magazines and Small Presses

Dustbooks
Box 100
Paradise, CA 95967

**Concern(s):** media; arts; press; journalism; research; literature. A complete list of little, literary, and college periodicals and publishers. A necessity for those with an interest in the alternative press. **Price:** $24.95/ea. **Publisher:** Dustbooks.

## ♿ ◈ International Directory of Periodicals Related to Deafness

Gallaudet University Library
800 Florida Ave.
Washington, DC 20002  (202)651-5217

**Affiliation:** Gallaudet University Library. **Concern(s):** justice; health; disabled; disabled's rights. 500+ periodical titles; related to deafness; international coverage. **Frequency:** Irregular. **Price:** $5/ea. **Pages:** 125. **Date Publ.:** 1990. **Contact(s):** Steven A. Frank (Compiler).

## A ◈ International Green Front Report

Box 1064
Tonasket, WA 98855

**Affiliation:** Friends of the Trees. **Concern(s):** agriculture; environment; sustainability; forests. The Green Front Report is one of the most comprehensive sourcebooks on sustainable agriculture and world reforestation. It is a sourcebook of solutions: noteworthy deeds, projects, events, organizations, movements, individuals, periodicals, books, and articles concerning Regreening the Earth. It reviews 500 organizations and 350 books and periodicals. **Other Resources:** ACTINIDIA ENTHUSIASTS NEWSLETTERS #1-5, 1986 FRIENDS OF THE TREES YEARBOOK. **Est.:** 1988. **Price:** $7/ea. **Pages:** 196. **Date Publ.:** 1991. **Labels:** 7. **E-Network:** Econet. **ID:** 'fott'. **Fax:** (509)486-4726. **Contact(s):** Michael Pilarski (Director), Carol Lanigan (Office Manager).

## S ◈ International Organizations

Gale Research Inc.
835 Penobscot Building
Detroit, MI 48226-4094  (800)877-GALE

**Concern(s):** spiritual; Third World; philanthropy; volunteer. Two volumes, 10,000+ international nonprofit membership organizations, including multinational, binational, and national organizations based outside the US covering all subjects and a variety of activities. **Other Resources:** Formerly, ENCYCLOPEDIA OF ASSOCIATIONS: INTERNATIONAL ORGANIZATIONS. Also see ENCYCLOPEDIA OF ASSOCIATIONS: NATIONAL ORGANIZATIONS OF THE US. **Frequency:** Annual. **Price:** $410/ea., including supplement. **Pages:** 2,435/2 vols. **Publisher:** Gale Research Inc. **Other Formats:** CD-ROM as part of 'Gale GlobalAccess: Associations' (see separate entry). **Fax:** (313)961-6241. **Telex:** (810)221-7086. **Contact(s):** Linda Irvin (Editor).

## ☃ ◈ International Peace Directory

California Institute of Public Affairs
Box 189040
Sacramento, CA 95818

**Affiliation:** California Institute of Public Affairs. **Concern(s):** peace. National and international organizations working for peace worldwide. Annotated list of directories of peace organizations, published by the University of Peace. **Price:** $19.95/ea. + $1.50 shipping. **Pages:** 125. **Date Publ.:** 1984. **Fax:** (916)442-2478. **Contact(s):** Thaddeus C. Trzyna (Editor).

## A ◈ The International Permaculture Species Yearbook (TIPSY)

7781 Lenox St.
Jacksonville, FL 32221

**Affiliation:** Solutions Network. **Concern(s):** agriculture; environment; sustainability; organic; permaculture. Addresses environmental concerns and solutions through editorials, information articles, species lists, book reviews, and related coverage. Stress is on practical information useful to bring human lives back into the ecosystem context. Basic articles on permaculture and special themes — urban permaculture, wetlands, poultry forage, bee forage, etc. — are included in each issue. **Frequency:** Usually annual. **Bulk:** 20% off/24. **Pages:** 144. **Publisher:** Yankee Permaculture. **Contact(s):** Dan Hemenway (Editor/Publisher), Cynthia Baxter (Associate Editor).

## A ◈ International Rural Sociology Association - Membership Directory

Michigan State University, Sociology Department
c/o Dr. Harry K. Schwarzweller
East Lansing, MI 48824

**Affiliation:** International Rural Sociology Association. **Concern(s):** agriculture; demographics; Third World; urban; rural communities; development 1,600 professionals and paraprofessionals working in rural communities in both developed and developing countries. **Frequency:** Annual.

## ♿ ◈ International Telephone Directory of TDD Users

Telecommunications for the Deaf, Inc.
814 Thayer Ave.
Silver Spring, MD 20910

**Affiliation:** Telecommunications for the Deaf, Inc. **Concern(s):** health; disabled. About 150,000 deaf persons who use the hearing device called TDD on their telephones. **Frequency:** Annual. **Pages:** 190. **Date Publ.:** 1/91. **Contact(s):** Alfred Sonnestrahl.

## E ◈ International Tree Project Clearinghouse

United Nations
Non-Governmental Liaison Service
New York, NY 10017  (212)963-1234

**Affiliation:** UN NGO Liaison Service. **Concern(s):** environment; Third World; forests. Information on international reforestation.

## ✈ ◈ International Workcamp Directory

Box 202
Belmont, VT 05730

**Affiliation:** Volunteers for Peace/UNESCO; CCIVS at UNESCO, Paris. **Concern(s):** education; Third World; peace; travel; volunteers. This directory contains descriptions on 800+ workcamps in 34 countries throughout Europe, the USSR, Asia and Africa. workrooms are mostly in the summer months for 2-3 weeks and cost $80-$90. The directory contains all registration materials. **Other Resources:** Please write or call for a FREE copy of our newsletter. Nonprofit. **Est.:** 1982. **Dues:** $10/yr. **Frequency:** Annual. **Bulk:** 10% off/24. **Pages:** 112. **Circ.:** 4M. **Date Publ.:** 4/91. **E-Network:** PeaceNet. **ID:** 'vfpusa'. **Fax:** (802)259-2922. **Contact(s):** Peter Coldwell (Director), Megan Brook (Co-director).

**T ▶ Inventory of Population Projects in Developing Countries Around the World**
United Nations Population Fund
220 E. 42nd St.
New York, NY 10017 (212)297-5000
**Affiliation:** United Nations Population Fund. **Concern(s):** Third World; demographics; development; population growth. 4,000+ population projects in developing countries and their sponsoring organizations. **Frequency:** Annual. **Price:** $20/ea. **Pages:** 902. **Other Formats:** Microfilm. **Fax:** (212)557-6416.

**D ▶ Inventory of Private Agency Population Research**
Interagency Comm. on Population Research, Public Health Service
Dept. of Health & Human Services; Nat'l Inst. of Child Health & Dev.
Bethesda, MD 20892
**Affiliation:** Interagency Committee on Population Research, Public Health Service. **Concern(s):** demographics; population growth; research; public health; philanthropy. 500+population research projects sponsored by the Ford Foundation, the Population Council, the Rockefeller Foundation, the A. W. Melloon Foundation and the Hewlett Foundation. **Frequency:** Irregular. **Subscription:** Free. **Pages:** 100. **Date Publ.:** 1988. **Contact(s):** Margaret R. Garner (Technical Information Specialist/Biologist).

**S ▶ Invest Yourself, The Catalog of Volunteer Opportunities**
Commission on Voluntary Service & Action (CVSA)
Box 117
New York, NY 10009 (212)974-2405
**Affiliation:** Commission on Voluntary Service & Action (CVSA). **Concern(s):** spiritual; politics; Third World; volunteers; networking; philanthropy; development. A Guide to Action, the definitive directory for 45 years, listing 200+ non-government voluntary service opportunities based in North America with 40,000 placements worldwide. More than a reference, this new issue has 150+ pages of organization listings, photographs, ad articles for those interested in realizing their social concerns and faith in action through volunteering. **Est.:** 1946. **Frequency:** Annual. **Price:** $7.95/ea. **Pages:** 150. **Circ.:** 40M. **Date Publ.:** 1991. **Other Formats:** 3 1/2' disc. **Labels:** 8. **Contact(s):** Susan Angus (Editorial coordinator), Jim Rosenberg.

**$ ▶ Investing in America's Corporate Conscience**
Council on Economic Priorities
30 Irving Place
New York, NY 10003
**Affiliation:** Council on Economic Priorities. **Concern(s):** economics; environment; peace; socially-responsible investing; green consumer.

**$ ▶ The Investment Services & Directory of Alternative Investments**
c/o Interfaith Center for Corporate Responsibility
475 Riverside Dr. # 566
New York, NY 10115 (212)870-2295
**Affiliation:** Interfaith Center for Corporate Responsibility. **Concern(s):** economics; spiritual; peace; politics; interfaith; corporate responsibility; alternative markets; divestment; socially responsible; boycott; anti-nuclear; economic conversion; peace dividend; boycott. This guide challenges the financial institutions and corporations by identifying those involved with nuclear weapons production, investment in South Africa, and Star Wars, and other issues counter-productive to peace, economic justice, and stewardship of Earth. **Other Resources:** THE CONSCIENTIOUS INVESTOR'S GUIDE TO SOCIALLY-RESPONSIBLE MUTUAL AND MONEY MARKET FUNDS. **Contact(s):** Tim Smith.

**✍ ▶ It's a Free Country! A Young Person's Guide to Politics & Elections**
Atheneum Press/Juvenile Department
866 3rd Ave.
New York, NY 10022 (212)702-2000
**Concern(s):** education; politics; students; voting. **Publisher:** Atheneum Press. **Contact(s):** Cynthia K. Samuels.

**S ▶ Jewish American Voluntary Organizations**
Greenwood Press, Inc.
88 Post Rd. W
Westport, CT 06881
**Concern(s):** spiritual; volunteers; faith. National and local Jewish-American voluntary organizations and associations. **Price:** $75/ea. **Pages:** c720. **Date Publ.:** 1986. **Publisher:** Greenwood Press; Congressional Information Service. **Contact(s):** Michael N. Dobkowski (Editor).

**🕊 ▶ Keyguide to Information Sources in Animal Rights**
McFarland & Company, Inc.
Box 611
Jefferson, NC 28640
**Concern(s):** environment; animal rights; wildlife/endangered species. Includes annotated bibliography, directory of organizations, appendices, index. "Highly recommended"—Booklist/RBB; "extensively annotated 335-item bibliography...an excellent annotated international directory of 182 animal welfare organizations"—Wilson Library Bulletin; "rich overview...and the appendices handily assemble information not readily available elsewhere. Recommended"—Choice; "superior... outstanding"—RQ. **Pages:** 281. **Date Publ.:** 1989. **Contact(s):** Charles R. Magel (Editor).

**✌ ▶ L.A. Peace Directory**
1355 Westwood Bl., #202
Los Angeles, CA 90024
**Concern(s):** peace; environment; media; activism; conservation; networking. "We publish a directory of social change organizations in the greater L.A. and Orange County area. The directory includes descriptions of 300 groups as well as articles and resource information that increase grassroots empowerment and effectiveness through networking, coalition building, economics of scale, and computer utilization." **Other Resources:** Database available. **Price:** $14/ea. **Bulk:** $9ea/24. **Pages:** 160. **Date Publ.:** 6/89; 1990. **Contact(s):** Eva Kutaja, Ph.D. (Editor).

**✌ ▶ The Language of Nuclear War: An Intelligent Citizen's Dictionary**
Harper & Row
Ice House One #401, 151 Union St.
San Francisco, CA 94111-1299
**Concern(s):** peace; anti-nuclear. **Publisher:** Harper & Row. **Contact(s):** Eric Semler, Adam Gros, James Benjamin (Editors).

**T ▶ Latin America and Caribbean: A Directory of Resources**
464 19th St.
Oakland, CA 94612-9761 (510)536-1876
**Affiliation:** Third World Resources/Data Center. **Concern(s):** Third World. For postage and handling, add $1.50 for North America and $3.00 for foreign air mail. Please, order from Third World Resources. **Price:** $12.95/ea. **Pages:** 160. **Date Publ.:** Spring 1986. **Publisher:** Orbis Books. **Other Formats:** Geonet, user **ID:** 'geo2:tfenton'. **E-Network:** Peacenet. **ID:** 'tfenton'. **Contact(s):** Thomas P. Fenton, Mary J. Heffron (Compilers/Editors).

**D ▶ Latino Librarianship: A Handbook for Professionals**
McFarland & Company, Inc.
Box 611
Jefferson, NC 28640
**Concern(s):** demographics. Latino demographics, community needs, reference tools and services, Latino databases, collection development for specific subgroups. Hispanic archives, book trade, REFORMA, an "English-Only" movement bibliography, and various appendices such as the American Library Association's guidelines on library services to Hispanics. **Other Resources:** Bibliography, appendices, and index. **Price:** $29.95/ea. **Pages:** 208. **Date Publ.:** 1990. **Publisher:** McFarland & Company, Inc. **Contact(s):** Salvador Guerena (Editor).

**M ▶ The Left Index: A Quarterly Index to Periodicals of the Left**
Reference & Research Services
511 Lincoln St.
Santa Cruz, CA 95060 (408)426-4479
**Concern(s):** media; education; politics; justice; feminism; health; peace; environment; economics; press. Indexes the professional and scholarly periodical literature written from a left perspective. Newspapers, newsletter, and journalistic literature, covered by other indexes, are not generally included. Topics covered include anthropology, art, economics, history, education, sociology, philosophy, black studies, women's studies, and political science. Each contains author list; subject, book review and journal indices; & new serial list. **Other Resources:** Also publishes CONTEMPORARY SOCIAL ISSUES: A BIBLIOGRAPHIC SERIES. **Est.:** 1982. **Frequency:** 4/yr. **Price:** $15/ea. **Bulk:** 20% off/24. **Pages:** 75. **Publisher:** Reference & Research Services. **Contact(s):** Joan Nordquist (Editor).

**$ ▶ The Lemon Book**
Center for Auto Safety
2001 S St. NW, #410
Washington, DC 20009 (202)328-7700
**Affiliation:** Center for Auto Safety. **Concern(s):** economics; health; consumer rights.

**✈ ▶ Lend a Hand: The How, Where, and Why of Volunteering**
William Morrow & Co. Inc., Hearst Corporation
105 Madison Ave.
New York, NY 10016 (800)843-9389
**Concern(s):** education; volunteers; travel. 100+ national and international nonprofit organizations that accept the assistance of young volunteers. **Price:** $11.95/ea. **Pages:** c170. **Date Publ.:** 1988. **Publisher:** William Morrow & Co. Inc., Hearst Corporation. **Fax:** (212)481-3826. **Contact(s):** Sara Gilbert.

**♿ ▶ The Library Manager's Guide to Hiring and Serving Disabled Persons**
McFarland & Company, Inc.
Box 611
Jefferson, NC 28640
**Concern(s):** health; disabled. "Library planners and managers will appreciate the wealth of detailed specifications for handicapped accessibility, the physical demands checklist for communicating job requirements, and the appendixes of disabled service organizations, computerized information sources, and vendors of materials for the disabled. Highly recommended for all libraries"-Booklist; "especially pertinent for public library administrators but recommended for academics as well"-Library Journal. **Price:** $27.50/ea. **Pages:** 171. **Date Publ.:** 1990. **Publisher:** McFarland & Company, Inc. **Contact(s):** Keith C. Wright, Judith F. Davie (Consultants).

**♿ ▶ Library Resources for the Blind and Physically Handicapped**
Library of Congress
1291 Taylor St. NW
Washington, DC 20542 (800)424-8567
**Concern(s):** health; disabled. 55+ regional and 95 subregional libraries, and 8 machine-lending agencies in the US, Puerto Rico, the US Virgin Islands, and Guam that provide a free library service of braille and recorded books and magazines to visually and physically handicapped persons; other agencies distributing braille materials and talking book machines are also indicated. **Frequency:** Annual. **Subscription:** Free. **Pages:** 75. **Publisher:** Library of Congress. **Fax:** (202)707-0712.

**T ▶ List of Declared Public Sanctuaries**
Chicago Religious Task Force on Central America
59 E. Van Buren, #1400
Chicago, IL 60605
**Affiliation:** Chicago Religious Task Force on Central America. **Concern(s):** Third World; demographics; Central America; refugees; immigration. 390+ declared sanctuaries for Central American refugees in the US. **Other Resources:** Also appears in quarterly BASTA! newsletter from the same publisher. **Frequency:** 4/yr. **Pages:** 25.

**H ▶ Local AIDS Services: The National Directory**
US Conference of Mayors
1620 I St. NW
Washington, DC 20006 (202)293-7330
**Affiliation:** US Conference of Mayors. **Concern(s):** health; AIDS. Nearly 2,500 organizations that provide AIDS-related services and information including counseling, financial and legal services, health care, local health departments, community-based organizations, housing assistance, state AIDS coordinators, social security regional AIDS coordinators, NIAID, AIDS Treatment and Evaluation Units, AIDS information hotlines. Arranged geographically. **Frequency:** Annual. **Price:** $350/ea. **Pages:** 160. **Date Publ.:** 1990. **Labels:** 350. **Fax:** (202)293-2352. **Contact(s):** Alan E. Gambrell (Editor).

**✌ ▶ Lower Midwest Grassroots Peace Directory**
ACCESS: A Security Information Service
1730 M St. NW, #605
Washington, DC 20036 (202)785-6630
**Affiliation:** ACCESS: A Security Information Service. **Concern(s):** peace; national security; activism; grassroots organizing; networking. National, regional, and local groups in Illinois, Indiana, Iowa, Kansas, Missouri, and Ohio working for peace, disarmament, and international security. Arranged geographically with organization name, address, phone, contact name, congressional district served, national affiliation, geographical area served, program focus, primary concerns, methods of operation, resources available, tax status, budget, number of members, size of staff, description of projects and activities. **Other Resources:** Mailing labels available to nonprofit organizations; $50 per thousand, one time use, $20 minimum per order, plus $15-$50 for specialized searches. **Frequency:** Biennial. **Pages:** 250. **Contact(s):** Phylis Emigh (Information Manager).

**D ▶ Major Private Organizations**
Population Crisis Committee
1120 19th St. NW, #550
Washington, DC 20036 (202)659-1833

**Affiliation:** Population Crisis Committee. **Concern(s):** demographics; population growth; poverty; hunger; philanthropy.

📚 **Make a World of Difference: Creative Activities For Global Learning**
Office on Global Education
2115 N. Charles St.
Baltimore, MD 21218

**Affiliation:** Office on Global Education. **Concern(s):** education; peace; environment; global understanding; students. This "user friendly" treasure includes a handy index to activities for all ages. A handbook of innovative and fun exercises to help develop and strengthen a global perspective. **Price:** $16.95ea. **Bulk:** 40% off/ 24. **Publisher:** Friendship Press. **Contact(s):** Rose M. Downing (Secretary), Tom Hampson (Associate Director).

E ▶ **Making Polluters Pay: A Citizens' Guide to Legal Action and Organizing**
CCHW, Box 6806
Falls Church, VA 22040

**Affiliation:** Citizens Clearinghouse for Hazardous Waste/Environmental Action. **Concern(s):** environment; politics; health; hazardous/toxic waste; grassroots organizing; lobbying. **Contact(s):** Andrew Owens Moore (Author).

P ▶ **Making Things Happen**
c/o Island Press
Box 7
Covelo, CA 95428        (202)232-7933

**Concern(s):** politics; environment; volunteers; grassroots organizing. "How To Be An Effective Volunteer". Teaches volunteers the basic skills they need to make a stronger impact. Organized in a clear, easy-to-read format, this enthusiastic book offers common sense advice and helpful tips. Checklists, bibliography, appendixes, index. **Price:** $14.95 paper; $22.95 cloth. **Pages:** 240. **Date Publ.:** 1991. **Publisher:** Island Press. Order: (800)828-1302. **Contact(s):** Joan Wolfe (Author).

P ▶ **The MAP Training Manual**
721 Shrader St.
San Francisco, CA 94117

**Affiliation:** Social Movement Empowerment Project. **Concern(s):** politics; peace; nonviolence; civil disobedience; activism. This workbook helps you put into practice the theories and strategies developed by activists to the present day. SMEP's publications are a hopeful sign as well as practical guides on the continuing struggle to bring about small changes which are adding up toward an overall paradigm shift. **Other Resources:** See also, THE PRACTICAL STRATEGIST. **Price:** $1.50/ea.

M ▶ **Mass Media and Adolescent Values**
c/o McFarland & Company, Inc.
Box 611
Jefferson, NC 28640        (919)246-4460

**Concern(s):** media; education; responsibility; youth; childhood. "The average viewer in a year is exposed to 14,000 instances of some sort of sexual activity during daytime television broadcasts alone. This book reflects current research findings and analysis of mass media (especially television) products and their impact on adolescent attitudes and behavior." Covers a multitude of social issues and its directory lists 58 organizations that provide counseling and information services to adolescents. **Pages:** 100. **Date Publ.:** 1991. **Contact(s):** A. Odasua Alali (Author).

H ▶ **Mental Health Directory**
Superintendent of Documents
US Government Printing Office
Washington, DC 20402        (202)783-3238

**Affiliation:** National Institute of Mental Health. **Concern(s):** health; demographics; psychology; homelessness; substance abuse; veterans; disabled. Hospitals, treatment centers, outpatient clinics, day/night facilities, residential treatment centers for emotionally disturbed children, residential supportive programs with halfway houses and mental health centers offering mental health assistance; does not include substance abuse programs, VA programs, nursing homes, programs for the developmentally disabled, and organizations in which fees are retained by individual members. Geographically arranged. **Frequency:** Irregular. **Pages:** 355. **Date Publ.:** Fall 1990. **Publisher:** Superintendent of Documents. **Contact(s):** Marion R. Warscak. **Other:** National Institute of Mental Health, 5600 Rishers Lane, Dept. of Health & Human Welfare, Rockville, MD 20857. (301)443-4513.

🐝 **Mid Atlantic Grassroots Peace Directory**
ACCESS: A Security Information Service
1730 M St. NW, #605
Washington, DC 20036        (202)785-6630

**Affiliation:** ACCESS: A Security Information Service. **Concern(s):**

peace; national security; activism; grassroots organizing; networking. National, regional, and local groups in Delaware, Maryland, New Jersey, Pennsylvania, Virginia, West Virginia, and Washington, D.C., working for peace, disarmament, and international security. Arranged geographically and indexed by organization.

T ▶ **Middle East Human Rights Directory**
c/o Human Rights Centre, University
of Ottawa, 57 Louis Pasteur
Ottawa, ON K1N 6N5 Canada        (613)564-3492

**Affiliation:** Human Rights Internet. **Concern(s):** Third World; justice; peace; Mid-East. **Dues:** 50% off to subscribers to HRI Reporter. **Date Publ.:** 1991. **Fax:** (613)564-4054.

T ▶ **Middle East: A Directory of Resources**
464 19th St.
Oakland, CA 94612-9761        (510)536-1876

**Affiliation:** Third World Resources/Data Center. **Concern(s):** Third World; Mid-East. For postage and handling, add $1.50 for North America and $3.00 for foreign air mail. Please, order from Third World Resources. **Price:** $12.95/ea. **Pages:** 160. **Date Publ.:** Spring 1988. **Publisher:** Orbis Books. **Other Formats:** Geonet, user **ID:** 'geo2:tfenton'. **E-Network:** Peacenet. **ID:** 'tfenton'. **Contact(s):** Thomas P. Fenton, Mary J. Heffron (Compilers/Editors).

H ▶ **Migrant Health Services Directory**
Midwest Migrant Health Information Office
6131 W. Outer Dr., 4th Fl.; National Migrant Worker Council
Detroit, MI 48235

**Affiliation:** Midwest Migrant Health Information Office. **Concern(s):** health; labor; justice; agriculture; public health; farm workers; minority rights. About 60 federally funded migrant health clinics in Michigan, Ohio, Indiana, Illinois, Iowa, Wisconsin, and Minnesota. Arranged geographically by clinic. Languages used in text: English and Spanish. **Other Resources:** Maps of each state, with location of clinics, major highways, and cities noted. **Frequency:** Annual. **Pages:** 30. **Date Publ.:** 3/91.

J ▶ **Minority Business Development Agency - Directory of Regional & District Offices and Funded Organizations**
Minority Business Development Agency
Department of Commerce
Washington, DC 20230        (202)377-2000

**Affiliation:** Minority Business Development Agency. **Concern(s):** justice; economics; minority rights; trade. About 10 regional and district offices of the Minority Business Development Agency; approximately 110 agency-funded minority business development centers which offer business services for a nominal fee to current and prospective minority business operators. Arranged by separate geographical lists for regional office, district offices, and development centers. **Pages:** c15.

J ▶ **Minority Organizations: A National Directory**
Garrett Park Press
Box 190F
Garrett Park, MD 20896        (301)946-2553

**Concern(s):** justice; minority rights; diversity. 7,700+ groups composed of or intended to serve members of minority groups, including Alaska Natives, American Indians, Blacks, Hispanics, and Asian Americans. Classified by minority group and indexed by organization. **Frequency:** Irregular. **Price:** $36 prepaid; $40/ea. **Pages:** c690. **Date Publ.:** 1987. **Publisher:** Garrett Park Press. **Other Formats:** mailing labels. **Contact(s):** Robert Calvert, Jr. (Editor).

J ▶ **Missing Children**
Box 6292
Lake Worth, FL 33466

**Affiliation:** Child Keyppers International. **Concern(s):** justice; family; children; criminal system; child abuse.

E ▶ **Mono Lake Guidebook**
Box 29
Lee Vining, CA 93541

**Affiliation:** Mono Lake Committee. **Concern(s):** environment; water; rivers; preservation; conservation A citizen's group dedicated to saving Mono Lake from excessive diversion of water from its tributary streams. "We seek a compromise that will meet the real water needs of Los Angeles and leave our children a living, healthy and beautiful lake. This is our guidebook." Nonprofit. **Price:** $8.95/ea. **Pages:** 104. **Date Publ.:** 1990. **Publisher:** Kutsavi Press. **Contact(s):** Lauren Davis (Editor).

📚 ▶ **Mudpies to Magnet**
Gryphon House, Inc.
3706 Otis St.
Mt. Rainier, MD 20712

**Concern(s):** education; science; students; childhood. A collection of clearly illustrated science or curiosity building experiments for classroom or home learning. Using simple materials hundreds of fun things to do for kids and adults make science a stimulating process of discovery. This book also contains a resource guide. Fostering curiosity in teachers and children will reduce attitudinal barriers to science learning. **Publisher:** Gryphon House, Inc.

E ▶ **Multi-Material Recycling Manual**
Keep America Beautiful
Mill River Plaza, 9 W. Broad St.
Stamford, CT 06902

**Affiliation:** Keep America Beautiful. **Concern(s):** environment; recycling; beautification; conservation; preservation. A guide to finding markets for recycled materials, relevant associations and programs.

H ▶ **NAPSAC Directory of Alternative Birth Services & Consumer Guide**
Route 1, Box 646
Marble Hill, MO 63764        (800)772-9100

**Concern(s):** health; feminism; birth; holism; alternative consumer. 2,000 birth centers, midwifery schools, midwives, doctors attending to home births, childbirth educators, and others in the field of alternative childbirth; coverage includes Canada. Geographically arranged. **Frequency:** Annual. **Price:** $16/ea. **Pages:** 150. **Circ.:** 500. **Date Publ.:** Spring 1991. **Labels:** 50. **Fax:** (202)667-5890. **Contact(s):** Lee and David Stewart. (Editors).

F ▶ **National Abortion Federation - Membership Directory**
1436 U St. NW, #103
Washington, DC 20009        (800)772-9100

**Affiliation:** National Abortion Federation. **Concern(s):** feminism; pro-choice. 310 member abortion clinics, hospitals, professional corporations (medical practices) and research organizations, geographically arranged, indexed alphabetically. **Frequency:** Annual. **Pages:** 110. **Date Publ.:** 1/91. **Labels:** 50. **Fax:** (202)667-5890. **Contact(s):** Patricia Anderson (Membership Director). (202)667-5881.

👪 ▶ **National Accreditation Council for Agencies Serving the Blind and Visually Handicapped - List of Member Organization**
232 Madison Ave., #907
New York, NY 10016

**Affiliation:** National Accreditation Council for Agencies Serving the Blind and Visually Handicapped. **Concern(s):** health; disabled. About 100 accredited agencies and schools for service to the blind, arranged geographically. **Frequency:** 2/yr. **Subscription:** Free. **Pages:** 10. **Date Publ.:** 12/90. **Other Formats:** Cassette.

H ▶ **National Association of Meal Programs - Directory**
National Association of Meal Programs
204 E. St. NE
Washington, DC 20002        (202)547-6157

**Affiliation:** National Association of Meal Programs. **Concern(s):** health; nutrition. Community organizations, agencies, and individuals providing group or home-delivered meals to older persons unable to prepare meals for themselves. Geographically arranged. **Frequency:** Annual. **Price:** $50/ea. **Pages:** 45. **Date Publ.:** 1/91. **Other Formats:** computer printout: $50. **Labels:** 100. **Contact(s):** Gail Martin (Assistant Administrative Director).

H ▶ **National Association of Substance Abuse Trainers**
National Association of Substance Abuse Trainers & Educators
1521 Hillary St.
New Orleans, LA 70118

**Affiliation:** National Association of Substance Abuse Trainers & Educators. **Concern(s):** health; substance abuse. About 70 universities offering educational programs in the treatment of substance abuse, arranged geographically. **Frequency:** Annual. **Pages:** 40. **Date Publ.:** Summer 1990. **Contact(s):** Thomas P. Lief, Ph.D.

📚 ▶ **National Center for Resources in Vocational Education**
Ohio State University
1960 Kenny Rd.
Columbus, OH 43210

**Concern(s):** education; labor; jobs; volunteers. **Publisher:** Ohio State University.

$ ▶ **National Clearinghouse for Legal Services**
407 South Dearborn St., #400
Chicago, IL 60005        (800)621-3256

**Concern(s):** economics; consumer rights. Distributes some publications of the National Consumer Law Center.

**F ◆  National Clearinghouse on Marital and Date Rape**
2325 Oak St.
Berkeley, CA 94708
**Concern(s):** feminism; health; justice; politics; rape/sexual abuse; sexism; law. A project of the former Women's Historic Resource Center, is an organization of consultants, residents, speakers, and resources for legislative and medical advocates, writers, the media, students, and campus and community people. **Contact(s):** Laura X.

**D ◆  National Coalition For the Homeless**
1621 Connecticut Ave., #400
Washington, DC 20009-1013    (202)265-2371
**Concern(s):** demographics; justice; politics; hunger; poverty; homelessness; grassroots organizing; reform; law; lobbying. A national information and resource clearinghouse on the homeless; offers technical assistance to service providers; resource and educational materials; monitors federal, state and local legislation; conducts impact litigation; and aids community organizations and empowerment efforts.

**F ◆  National Congress for Men - Directory**
National Congress for Men
3623 Douglas Ave.
Des Moines, IA 50310
**Affiliation:** National Congress for Men. **Concern(s):** feminism; family; health; men's liberation; child support; sexism; counseling. About 1,000 organizations and individuals advocating or involved in private divorce mediation, parental rights, divorce reform, child location, adoptee location,; divorce support groups for children, grandparents, second spouses, stepparents, and noncustodial mothers; publishers of relevant books in print, newsletters and magazines; worldwide coverage. **Frequency:** 12/yr. **Price:** $7/ea., postpaid. **Pages:** 100. **Contact(s):** Peter T. Cyr (Editor). **Other:** 68 Deering St., Portland, ME 04101.

**S ◆  National Data Book**
The Foundation Center
79 5th Ave.
New York, NY 10003    (800)424-9836
**Affiliation:** Foundation Center. **Concern(s):** spiritual; philanthropy; fundraising. About 30,000 currently active grantmaking foundations in the US, including community and operating foundations, based on information returns to the Internal Revenue Service. Arranged geographically by state. **Other Resources:** DIALOG Information Services as NATIONAL FOUNDATIONS file of FOUNDATIONS database; revised annually. Also includes bibliography of state and local directories of grantmaking foundations. **Frequency:** Annual. **Price:** $125/ea. + $2 shipping. **Pages:** c850. **Date Publ.:** 1/91. **Fax:** (800)424-9386. **Contact(s):** C. Edward Murphy (Editor).

**H ◆  National Directory of Alcoholism and Drug Abuse Treatment and Prevention Programs**
Program Information Associates
Box 26300
Honolulu, HI 96825
**Concern(s):** health; substance abuse. 10,000+ treatment, prevention, and information programs for alcoholism and drug abuse in the US, arranged geographically. **Frequency:** Biennial. **Price:** $45/ea. **Pages:** 350. **Date Publ.:** Winter 1990. **Publisher:** Program Information Associates. **Other Formats:** Magnetic tape, diskette (IBM PC-AT).

**✍ ◆  National Directory of Alternative Community Schools**
58 Schoolhouse Rd.
Summertown, TN 38483(615)964-3670
**Affiliation:** National Association for Legal Support of Alternative Schools (NALSAS). **Concern(s):** education. Contains over 600 entries of schools and educational resources throughout the US and in 20 foreign countries. The largest and most complete directory of its kind, it is now found in libraries throughout this country. More than 300 schools described in their own words; sections on Boarding Schools, Alternative Colleges, Foreign Schools, and a special section on Innovative Ideas and Programs. If you want to find an alternative school to work at or send your kids to, use this directory. Nonprofit. **Est.:** 1975. **Frequency:** Annual. **Price:** $12.50/ea. **Pages:** 24. **Circ.:** 1.7M. **Date Publ.:** 1991. **Publisher:** NCACS. **Contact(s):** Michael Traugot (Office Coordinator), Mary Ellen Bowen (News Editor). **Other:** National Association for Legal Support of Alternative Schools (NALSAS), Box 2823, Santa Fe, NM 87504.

**♥ ◆  National Directory of Child Abuse Prosecutors**
National Center for Prosecution of Child Abuse
1033 N. Fairfax St., #200
Alexandria, VA 22314

**Affiliation:** National Center for Prosecution of Child Abuse. **Concern(s):** family; justice; child abuse; children; criminal system. 800+ prosecutors and district attorneys specializing in child abuse cases arranged geographically and indexed by personal name and jurisdiction. Includes district attorney name, assistant district attorney names. etc. **Frequency:** Annual. **Price:** $5/ea. **Pages:** 170. **Date Publ.:** 12/89. **Contact(s):** Janet L. Dinsmore (Communications Director).

**✍ ◆  National Directory of Children & Youth Services**
Marion L. Peterson, Publisher
Box 1837
Longmont, CO 80502
**Concern(s):** education; feminism; justice; health; youth; child abuse; children; counseling; juvenile; welfare rights; criminal system. Child and youth-oriented social services, health and mental health services, and juvenile court and youth advocacy services in state and private agencies, major cities, and 3,100 counties; also covers runaway youth centers, child abuse projects, congressional committees, clearinghouses, and national organizations concerned with child health and welfare; buyer's guide to specialized services and products. Arranged geographically. **Frequency:** Biennial. **Price:** $63/ea., postpaid. **Pages:** 725. **Date Publ.:** 7/89. **Publisher:** Marion L. Peterson, Publisher. **Other Formats:** Cheshire labels, $450; pressure-sensitive labels, $495; 3x5 cards, $495. **Contact(s):** Marion Peterson (Publisher).

**✍ ◆  National Directory of Community Based Adult Literacy Programs**
1804 Vernon St. NW
Washington, DC 20009    (202)462-6333
**Affiliation:** Association for Community Based Education. **Concern(s):** education; literacy. The first nationwide listing of community based adult literacy programs. Includes: Name and address of program, phone number, contact person, number of students served each year, racial/ethnic characteristics of students, gender, reading levels, methods of instruction, other activities of sponsoring organization, plus a statistical overview of the participants, the programs, and the sponsoring organizations. 786 entries. **Price:** $10/ea. **Bulk:** 40% off/24. **Pages:** 83. **Date Publ.:** 6/89. **Contact(s):** Tracy McDonald.

**E ◆  National Directory of Conservation Land Trusts**
Land Trust Exchange
1017 Duke St.
Alexandria, VA 22314
**Affiliation:** Land Trust Exchange. **Concern(s):** environment; economics; agriculture; conservation; land; wilderness; land trusts. Lists 743 organizations in 45 states, Puerto Rico and the Virgin Islands.

**H ◆  National Directory of Drug Abuse and Alcoholism Treatment and Prevention Programs**
Superintendent of Documents
US Government Printing Office
Washington, DC 20402    (202)783-3238
**Affiliation:** National Institute on Drug Abuse. **Concern(s):** health; substance abuse. 9,000 federal, state, local, and privately funded agencies administering or providing drug abuse and alcoholism treatment and prevention services, geographically arranged with name of agency, address, phone, and whether the agency's purpose is treatment or prevention of drug, alcohol, or drug/alcohol abuse. **Frequency:** Irregular. **Price:** $19/ea. **Pages:** 400. **Date Publ.:** 1990. **Publisher:** Superintendent of Documents. **Other:** National Institute on Drug Abuse, 5600 Fisher's Lane, Dept. of Health & Welfare, Rockville, MD 20857.

**J ◆  National Directory of Nonprofit Organizations**
The Taft Group, Gale Research Inc.
12300 Twinbrook Parkway, #450
Rockville, MD 20852    (800)888-TAFT
**Affiliation:** Taft Group. **Concern(s):** justice; health; environment; nonprofit organizations. About 140,000 nonprofit organizations, arranged alphabetically and indexed by area of activity, executive officer name, board officer name, donor name, and geographical location. **Other Resources:** Formerly, TAFT DIRECTORY OF NONPROFIT ORGANIZATIONS: PROFILES OF AMERICA'S MAJOR CHARITABLE INSTITUTIONS. **Frequency:** Annual. **Price:** $225/ea. **Pages:** 2600. **Date Publ.:** Spring 1991. **Publisher:** Gale Research Inc. **Fax:** (301)816-0811. **Contact(s):** Susan Elnicki (Editor).

**J ◆  National Directory of Private Social Agencies**
Croner Publications, Inc.
211-05 Jamaica Ave.
Queens Village, NY 11428
**Concern(s):** justice; social justice; welfare rights. 15,000+ listings

arranged geographically and indexed by service and agency type. Base edition supplied upon order with monthly updates. **Frequency:** 12/yr. **Pages:** 900. **Publisher:** Croner Publications, Inc.

**J ◆  National Directory of Runaway Programs**
American Youth Work Center
1751 N. St. NW, #302
Washington, DC 20036    (202)785-0764
**Affiliation:** American Youth Work Center. **Concern(s):** justice; family; children; child abuse; juvenile. 300+ programs serving runaway youth, arranged geographically with sponsoring agency, etc. **Frequency:** Irregular. **Price:** $15/ea. **Pages:** 130. **Date Publ.:** 1/88. **Labels:** 125. **Contact(s):** Virginia Hines (Deputy Director).

**E ◆  The National Environmental Scorecard**
League of Conservation Voters
1707 L St. NW
Washington, DC 20036    (202)785-8683
**Affiliation:** League of Conservation Voters. **Concern(s):** environment; politics; law. This report is the definitive guide to the environmental voting record of our Congressmen and women. Each member is rated according to the number of pro-environment votes cast every session. **Frequency:** Annual.

**S ◆  National Foundations**
The Foundation Center
79 5th Ave.
New York, NY 10003    (800)424-9836
**Affiliation:** Foundation Center. **Concern(s):** spiritual; philanthropy; fundraising. About 25,000 nongovernmental and nonprofit foundations, including 17,000 small foundations not listed in the "Foundation Directory" (see separate entry). **Other Resources:** DIALOG Information Services. Custom computer printouts.

**S ◆  National Fund Raising Directory**
Orange Glen High School Chapter, Distributive Education Clubs of America
2200 Glen Ridge; Box 27592
Escondido, CA 92027
**Affiliation:** Distributive Education Clubs of America. **Concern(s):** spiritual; fundraising; philanthropy. 1,000+ firms offering 100+ types of products for fundraising by schools, bands, church groups, etc.; products include candy, clothing, jewelry, etc. Classified by product, data include company name, address, phone, contact name, and product. **Frequency:** Annual. **Subscription:** Schools free; $5 (current & 1991 editions). **Pages:** c80. **Circ.:** 25M. **Date Publ.:** 9/90. **Contact(s):** Robert Hughes (Advisor).

**S ◆  National Guide to Corporate Giving**
The Foundation Center
79 5th Ave.
New York, NY 10003    (800)424-9836
**Affiliation:** Foundation Center. **Concern(s):** spiritual; philanthropy; fundraising. 1,500+ corporations with company-sponsored foundations and/or direct giving programs. Indexed by donor/officer/trustee name; subject; geographical; type of support; type of business; company name, direct giving programs/company-sponsored foundation, Alphabetical listings by company, etc. Summary of purpose statement and sample grants of foundations and more... **Other Resources:** Formerly, NATIONAL DIRECTORY OF CORPORATE CHARITY. **Price:** $175/ea. **Date Publ.:** 12/89. **Contact(s):** Suzanne Haile (Editor).

**H ◆  National Guide to Funding in Aging**
The Foundation Center
79 5th Ave.
New York, NY 10003    (800)424-9836
**Affiliation:** Foundation Center. **Concern(s):** health; seniors; fundraising. Nearly 600 foundations, federal and state government agencies, and private organizations which offer public and private sources of funding for programs about aging. Classified by type of organization (federal, state, foundation, private). Indexed by organization name. **Frequency:** Irregular. **Price:** $75/ea. + $3.50 shipping. **Pages:** c280. **Date Publ.:** 1989. **Contact(s):** David Weiss, Diane Mahlmann (Editors).

**H ◆  National New Age Yellow Pages: The Complete Directory to Consciousness-Raising Services, Products & Organizations**
Highgate House, Publishers
Box 547695
Orlando, FL 32854
**Concern(s):** health; spiritual; transformation. Organizations, business, and individuals that provide information, products, and services related to New Age, metaphysical, holistic, spiritual, and mystical subjects and activities. Classified by subject and indexed by subject, geography, and trade name. Entries include organization or company name, etc. Discount coupons included. **Frequency:** Biennial. **Price:**

$14.95/ea.+$2 shipping. **Pages:** c250. **Date Publ.:** 1990. **Publisher:** Highgate House, Publishers. **Contact(s):** Marcia Gervase Ingenito (Editor).

## H ◗ National Prevention Network - Directory
National Prevention Network
444 N. Capitol St. NW #520
Washington, DC 20001

**Affiliation:** National Prevention Network. **Concern(s):** health; substance abuse; preventive. State alcohol and drug abuse prevention agencies, arranged geographically with agency name, etc. **Frequency:** 4/yr. **Subscription:** Free. **Pages:** 10. **Labels:** 5. **Contact(s):** Katherine H. Ross (Prevention Project Manager).

## ☙ ◗ National Priorities Action Packet
377 Hills South
University of Massachusetts
Amherst, MA 01002     (413)584-9556

**Affiliation:** National Priorities Project (NPP). **Concern(s):** peace; government accountability; municipal; economic conversion; community investment; activism. Compiled by NPP, this kit empowers activists to research the costs to their communities of the 1980s increase in federal military spending. Includes a guide to the past decade's cutback in federal social spending and its impact on local communities, a worksheet to calculate how much your community spends on the military buildup, and a step-by-step approach to determining your community's needs.

## H ◗ National Register
435 N. Michigan Ave.
Chicago, IL 60611

**Affiliation:** American Association of Sex Educators, Counselors & Therapists. **Concern(s):** health; counseling; psychology. About 1,400 sex educators, 1,300 sex therapists, and 200 sex counselors, who are all certified. Arranged by separate geographical sections for educators, therapists, and counselors. Categories include name, address, highest degree. Details on certification requirements and procedures. **Frequency:** Irregular. **Price:** $10/ea. **Pages:** 145. **Date Publ.:** 1990. **Labels:** 270. **Fax:** (312)644-8557.

## E ◗ National Resources for the 21st Century
American Forestry Association
Box 2000
Washington, DC 20013   (202)667-3300

**Affiliation:** American Forestry Association. **Concern(s):** environment; energy; future; natural resources; forests. **Publisher:** Island Press. **Contact(s):** Neil Sampson, Dwight Hair (Editors).

## H ◗ National Treatment Directory Alcohol and Addiction
4959 Commerce Parkway
Cleveland, OH 44128

**Concern(s):** health; substance abuse. 3,000 drug and alcohol treatment programs and facilities, addiction counselors, and physicians, arranged geographically. **Frequency:** Annual. **Price:** $20/ea. **Pages:** 150. **Fax:** (216)464-1835. **Contact(s):** Duane Frayer.

## D ◗ National Volunteer Clearinghouse for the Homeless
                          (202)393-4409

**Concern(s):** demographics; volunteers. Whatever area you are living in, they will send you information on places close by that you can volunteer to help the homeless. (800)HELP-664.

## E ◗ National Wildlife Federation's Conservation Directory
1400 16th St. NW
Washington, DC 20036-2236      (800)432-6564

**Affiliation:** National Wildlife Federation. **Concern(s):** environment; education; wildlife/endangered species; conservation; research. An annual publication of the Federation that continues to be the most complete source for up-to-date detailed information on environmental conservation, education, and natural resource management. The '91 edition lists 1,900+ government, NGO's and personnel involved in conservation work statewide and worldwide. Many listings support hunting and fishing interests. **Frequency:** Annual. **Price:** $18/ea. **Pages:** 396. **Circ.:** 14M. **Date Publ.:** 1/92. **Fax:** (703)442-7332. **Contact(s):** Rue E. Gordon (Editor).

## F ◗ National Women's Mailing List
Women's Information Exchange
Box 68
Jenner, CA 95450

**Affiliation:** Women's Information Exchange. **Concern(s):** feminism. Directories supplied as a mailing list on mailing labels in zip code order; can be selected on subject of women's organizations or by demographics and interests of individual women. Lists are created from a database of 10,000 women's organizations and 60,000 individual women. Data include name, address, contact (or organiza-

tion) name. **Frequency:** 12/yr. updates. **Contact(s):** Jill Lippitt (Editor).

## J ◗ Native American Archives: An Introduction
Society of American Archivists
600 S. Federal, #504
Chicago, IL 60605

**Affiliation:** Society of American Archivists. **Concern(s):** justice; Native Americans. List of organizations and individuals who provide assistance in establishing archives. Arranged alphabetically with organization or individual name and address. **Frequency:** Irregular. **Price:** $7/ea. + $3 shipping. **Date Publ.:** 1987. **Fax:** (312)347-1452. **Contact(s):** John A. Fleckner.

## J ◗ Native American Directory: Alaska, Canada, United States
National Native American Cooperative
Box 5000
San Carlos, AZ 85550

**Affiliation:** National Native American Cooperative. **Concern(s):** justice; arts; media; Native Americans. Native American performing arts groups, craft materials suppliers, stores and galleries, Indian-owned motels and resorts; tribal offices, museums, and cultural centers; associations, schools; newspapers, radio and television programs and stations operated owned, or specifically for Native Americans; calendar of events, including officially sanctioned powwows, conventions, arts and crafts shows, all-Indian rodeos, and Navajo rug auctions. **Frequency:** Irregular. **Price:** $18.95/ea. + $3 shipping. **Pages:** 335. **Circ.:** 40M. **Date Publ.:** 9/90. **Other Formats:** 3x5 cards, $95/1,000. **Labels:** 95. **Contact(s):** Fred Synder (Editor).

## J ◗ Native American Policy Network - Directory
Barry University
11300 NE 2nd Ave.
Miami, FL 33161

**Affiliation:** Native American Policy Network. **Concern(s):** justice; Native Americans. About 350 professors, political leaders, and others interested in Native American politics, arranged geographically. **Other Resources:** Diskette, $20. **Frequency:** 4/yr. **Pages:** c15. **Other Formats:** Diskette, $20. **Labels:** 25. **Contact(s):** Dr. Michael E. Melody (Editor).

## E ◗ Natural Choices
204 N. El Camino Real, #E-214
Encinitas, CA 92024

**Concern(s):** environment; health; hazardous/toxic waste. Distributes "The Nontoxic Baby: Reducing Harmful Chemicals From Your Baby's Life" $9.95 (+$2.00 tax and shipping). An invaluable pocket-size package of easy-to-read bound reference cards highlighting Facts, Concerns and Solutions related to toxic chemicals in babies' lives.

## E ◗ Naturalists' Directory and Almanac
Sandhill Crane Press, Inc.
2406 NW 47th Terrace
Gainesville, FL 32606

**Concern(s):** environment. 6,000 active amateur and professional naturalists, worldwide, who will correspond. Arranged alphabetically and indexed geographically and by specialty. **Other Resources:** **Price:** also includes access to a file of additional names of naturalists. **Frequency:** Irregular. **Price:** $22.95/ea.; prepaid. **Pages:** 350. **Date Publ.:** 1990. **Publisher:** Sandhill Crane Press, Inc. **Fax:** (904)371-9969. **Contact(s):** Dr. Ross H. Arnett, Jr. (Editor).

## J ◗ The Negro Almanac: A Reference Work on the African American
Gale Research Inc.
835 Penobscot Building
Detroit, MI 48226-4094  (800)877-GALE

**Concern(s):** justice; social justice; minority rights; diversity. Human rights organizations and black power advocates; African Americans in law, politics; highly capitalized black companies; support programs; predominantly black colleges and universities in the US, community and state colleges with black administrative heads; blacks in the military; outstanding black athletes, literary figures, artists, scientific pioneers, astronauts, scientists, entertainers, publishers, and journalists; leaders of slave revolts in the US, etc. **Other Resources:** Principal content of publication is an all-in-one resource to significant dates, movements, legislation, and people in African American history and culture in America. **Frequency:** Triennial. **Price:** $110/ea. **Pages:** c1,625. **Date Publ.:** 12/89. **Publisher:** Gale Research Inc. **Fax:** (313)961-6241. **Telex:** (810)221-7086. **Contact(s):** Harry A. Ploski, James Williams (Editors).

## U ◗ Neighborhood Caretakers: Stories, Strategies and Tools for Healing Urban Communities
Knowledge Systems
7777 W. Morris St.
Indianapolis, IN 46231    (800)999-8517

**Concern(s):** urban; economics. Urban neighborhoods are recreating themselves using new social technologies that combine science, spirit and leadership. A compassionately hard-headed, interdisciplinary approach to tackling social disorders of urban communities, it documents many successful experiments of "social laboratories" using methods that inject energy and self-reliance. How to provide leadership in leaderless communities, land trusts, mediation, affordable housing, family empowerment, vocational adventure, and more. **Other Resources:** Bibliography, resources, financial discussion, a network of methods experts, and index included. **Contact(s):** Burt Dyson, Betty Dyson (Authors).

## E ◗ The Network Guide of Organizations
National Coalition Against the Misuse of Pesticides
701 E St. SE
Washington, DC 20003  (202)543-5450

**Affiliation:** National Coalition Against the Misuse of Pesticides. **Concern(s):** environment; agriculture; pesticides.

## P ◗ Networking: People Connecting with People
c/o Routledge & Kegan Paul
29 W. 35th St.
New York, NY 10001     (212)244-3336

**Affiliation:** Networking Institute, Inc. **Concern(s):** politics; future; economics; environment; health; media; networking; sustainability; research; analysis; ideation; computer networking; grassroots organizing. Examines what networking is, why it works and how to use it. Includes a comprehensive directory to 1,500+ key social change networks. Covers issues of ecology, health, education, communications, personal growth, cooperatives and a sustainable future. **Other Resources:** Formerly NETWORKING: THE FIRST REPORT AND DIRECTORY. **Pages:** 192. **Date Publ.:** 1986. **Contact(s):** Jessica Lipnack, Jeffrey Stamps (Editors). (617)965-3340.

## ✍ ◗ New Careers, A Directory of Jobs and Internships in Technology & Society
Student Pugwash
1638 R St. NW, #32
Washington, DC 20009  (202)328-6555

**Affiliation:** Student Pugwash, USA. **Concern(s):** education; labor; jobs; volunteers; students; science. New info on both internships and full-time employment with organizations in 30 major cities nationwide. Listed by geography and by issues: development, energy, environment, communications, peace, security, health, and general science. Special section devoted to opportunities with state and federal government. Nonprofit. **Contact(s):** Denise Nepveux.

## H ◗ New Consciousness Source Book: Spiritual Community Guide
Arcline Publications
Box 1067
Berkeley, CA 94701

**Concern(s):** health; spiritual; transformation; holism; nutrition. 3,000 yoga, health, growth, and meditation centers, ashrams, natural food stores and restaurants, spiritual bookstores, and over 600 major New Age health, self-improvement, and spiritual groups; coverage includes Canada; limited foreign listings. Organizations are classified by subject; growth centers are alphabetical; yoga classes and similar firms (paid listings) are geographical. Indexed alphabetically and by subject. **Other Resources:** Formerly, SPIRITUAL COMMUNITY GUIDE: THE NEW CONSCIOUSNESS SOURCE BOOK. Send order to: NAM Mailing Lists, Box 1067, Berkeley, CA 94701. **Frequency:** Irregular. **Price:** $8.95/ea. + $1.50 shipping. **Pages:** c210. **Circ.:** 80M. **Date Publ.:** 11/85. **Publisher:** Arcline Publications. **Fax:** (510)486-8032. **Contact(s):** Parmatma Singh, Dharam Kaur Khalsa (Editors).

## ☙ ◗ New England Grassroots Peace Directory
ACCESS: A Security Information Service
1730 M St. NW, #605
Washington, DC 20036  (202)785-6630

**Affiliation:** ACCESS: A Security Information Service. **Concern(s):** peace; national security; activism; grassroots organizing; networking. National, regional, and local groups in Connecticut, Massachusetts, Maine, New Hampshire, Rhode Island, and Vermont working for peace, disarmament, and international security. Arranged geographically. **Other Resources:** Published in cooperation with the Topsfield Foundation, Inc. Mailing labels available to nonprofit organizations, $50 per thousand, one time use, $20 minimum per order, plus $15-$50 for specialized searches. **Frequency:** Biennial. **Pages:** c210. **Date Publ.:** Spring 1990. **Contact(s):** Phyllis Emigh (Information Manager).

**◭ ◆ The New Global Resource Book**
American Forum for Global Education
45 John St., #1200
New York, NY 10038    (212)732-8606
**Affiliation:** American Forum for Global Education. **Concern(s):** education; media; global understanding; film; press. Publishers of about 500 books, audiovisual materials, and other curriculum materials for K-12 teachers of global or international topics, classified by subject or region. **Other Resources:** Formerly, GLOBAL RESOURCE BOOK. **Frequency:** Irregular. **Pages:** 300. **Date Publ.:** 1990. **Fax:** (212)791-4132.

**P ◆ New Pages - JUST Resources Section**
New Pages Press
Box 438
Grand Blanc, MI 48439
**Concern(s):** politics; economics; Third World; media; press; film. List of publishers and distributors of books, periodicals, and audiovisual materials on political, economic, and social concerns among developing countries, arranged alphabetically with lists of publishers and distributors of books, periodicals, and audiovisual materials on political, economic, and social concerns among developing countries. **Frequency:** 3/yr. **Price:** $2/ea. **Publisher:** New Pages Press. **Contact(s):** Casey Hill (Editor).

**E ◆ New York State Environmental Conservation Directory**
50 Wolf Rod., Rm. 507
Albany, NY 12233
**Concern(s):** environment; conservation.

**E ◆ Non-toxic and Natural: How To Avoid Dangerous Everyday Products & Buy or Make Save Ones**
c/o Debra Lynn Dadd
Box 1506
Mill Valley, CA 94942
**Concern(s):** environment; economics; green consumer; alternative markets. A product-specific consumer guide to non-toxic options for our homes and lives ranging from air to yarn - with over 1,000 items in 300 categories. Wherever possible do-it-yourself formulas for alternative products are included. In other cases, safer sources, suppliers, and mail-order resources are offered. This extensive listing includes building materials and even what to look for in appliances from telephones to washing machines. **Contact(s):** Debra Lynn Dadd (Author).

**F ◆ Nongovernmental Organizations in International Population Crisis Committee**
Population Crisis Committee
1120 19th St. NW, #550
Washington, DC 20036    (202)659-1833
**Affiliation:** Population Crisis Committee. **Concern(s):** feminism; demographics; population growth; family planning. About 100 organizations concerned with population issues and family planning; international coverage. Arranged alphabetically. **Other Resources:** Formerly, MAJOR PRIVATE ORGANIZATIONS IN THE POPULATION FIELD. **Price:** $5/ea. **Pages:** 20. **Date Publ.:** 12/88. **Contact(s):** Sharon L. Camp (Director, Education/Public Policy).

**F ◆ North American Directory of Programs for Runaways, Homeless Youth and Missing Children**
American Youth Work Center
1751 N. St. NW, #302
Washington, DC 20036    (202)785-0764
**Affiliation:** American Youth Work Center. **Concern(s):** feminism; justice; demographics; child abuse; children; homelessness; juvenile. Over 500 organizations offering programs or providing resources for youth workers and other professionals concerned with either runaway or homeless teenagers or missing children. Arranged geographically and indexed alphabetically. **Frequency:** Biennial. **Price:** $15/ea. **Pages:** 200. **Date Publ.:** Summer 1990. **Fax:** (202)728-0657. **Contact(s):** Virginia K. Hines (Deputy Director).

**J ◆ North American Human Rights Directory**
c/o Human Rights Centre, University of Ottawa, 57 Louis Pasteur
Ottawa, ON K1N 6N5 Canada    (613)564-3492
**Affiliation:** Human Rights Internet. **Concern(s):** justice; indigenous peoples; Native Americans; minority rights; racism; discrimination; political prisoners; sexism. Data included organization name, address, phone, names of principle staff members, publications, whether tax-exempt or registered with United Nations, and brief description of origin, purposes, and programs. Arranged alphabetically and indexed by subject geographic focus. **Other Resources:** Former title, HUMAN RIGHTS DIRECTORY (1980). **Dues:** 50% off to subscribers to

HRI Reporter. **Price:** $30/ea. **Date Publ.:** 1984. **Fax:** (613)564-4054.

**◭ ◆ North American Students of Cooperation - Campus Co-Op Directory**
North American Students of Cooperation (NASCO)
Box 7715
Ann Arbor, MI 48107
**Affiliation:** North American Students of Cooperation (NASCO). **Concern(s):** education; labor; economics; students; cooperatives. Over 200 student-run cooperatives, including housing, food, child care, retail, bookstore, and miscellaneous service cooperatives; coverage includes Canada. Arranged geographically. **Frequency:** Biennial. **Pages:** 25. **Date Publ.:** Summer 1989. **Contact(s):** Margaret Martin (Director of Member Services).

**☸ ◆ Northwest & Pacific Rim Grassroots Peace Directory**
ACCESS: A Security Information Service
1730 M St. NW, #605
Washington, DC 20036    (202)785-6630
**Affiliation:** ACCESS: A Security Information Service. **Concern(s):** peace; national security; activism; grassroots organizing; networking. 7,700+ national, regional, and local groups in Alaska, Hawaii, Oregon, and Washington working for peace, disarmament, and international security. Arranged geographically and indexed by organization. **Other Resources:** Mailing labels available to nonprofit organizations, $50/1,000, one time use, $20 minimum per order, plus $15-$50 for specialized searches. **Frequency:** Biennial. **Pages:** 130. **Contact(s):** Phyllis Emigh (Information Manager).

**☸ ◆ Nuclear Arsenal Handbook**
2216 Race St.
Denver, CO 80205    (303)377-7998
**Affiliation:** Nuclear Arsenal Project. **Concern(s):** peace. "The handbook is an annual cataloging of US and Soviet nuclear weapons. A comparison of the two countries' arsenals and a useful bibliography are important parts."-C.C. **Est.:** 1982. **Frequency:** Annual. **Subscription:** $3.75/yr. **Price:** $3.75/ea. **Contact(s):** Barbara Donachy.

**☸ ◆ Nuclear Free America**
325 E. 25th Ave.
Baltimore, MD 21218
**Concern(s):** peace; environment; health; anti-nuclear; hazardous/toxic waste. Founded as a national clearinghouse and resource center for the grassroots Nuclear Free Zone movement. NFA has assisted thousands of individual organizations and communities in their efforts to create a Nuclear Free World. There are now 3600+ NFZs in 24 countries, making this the largest anti-nuclear movement in the world. The NFZ movement challenges communities to debate and decide their own role in the nuclear arms race, independent of Congress and the President. **Other Resources:** Newsletter: THE NEW ABOLITIONIST. Also: THE TOP 50 NUCLEAR WEAPONS CONTRACTORS and PROFILES OF THE TOP 50 NUCLEAR WEAPONS CONTRACTORS. **Est.:** 1982. **Contact(s):** Albert Donnay (Director).

**☸ ◆ Nuclear Free Zone Registry**
28222 Stonehouse Rd.
Lake Elsinore, CA 92330
**Affiliation:** Nuclear Free America. **Concern(s):** peace; education.

**E ◆ Nuclear Waste Digest & Nuclear Waste Primer**
League of Women Voters
1730 M St. NW
Washington, DC 20036    (202)429-1965
**Affiliation:** League of Women Voters. **Concern(s):** environment; peace; health; politics; hazardous/toxic waste; anti-nuclear; voting. **Date Publ.:** 1985.

**☸ ◆ Nuclear Weapons Chart**
US-USSR Bridges for Peace
Box 710
Norwich, VT 05055
**Concern(s):** peace; anti-nuclear; disarmament. This chart, prepared by US-USSR Bridges for Peace, has been widely used in the Nuclear Freeze Campaign. 6,000 dots represent the 18,000 megatons in today's arsenals; 1 dot in the center represents all the firepower of WW II: 3 megatons.

**☸ ◆ Nuclear Weapons Databook**
Ballinger
Route 3, Box 20B
Hagerstown, MD 21740
**Concern(s):** peace; anti-nuclear. Vol I- US Nuclear Forces and Capabilities; Vol II- US Nuclear Warhead Production; Vol III US Nuclear Warhead Facility Profiles. **Date Publ.:** 1987. **Publisher:** Ballinger Publishing Co. **Contact(s):** Thomas B. Cochran.

**H ◆ Nutrient Data Bank Directory**
Department of Human Nutrition & Food Systems
Univ. of Missouri, 217 Gwynn Hall
Columbia, MO 65211
**Affiliation:** Department of Human Nutrition & Food Systems. **Concern(s):** health; nutrition. Producers of 100+ software packages for the analysis of nutrient content and information, with entries including software title, producer name and address, system requirement, hardware compatibility, programming language used; specific proteins, fats, carbohydrates, vitamins, and minerals available in each program. **Price:** $15/ea. **Date Publ.:** 1988. **Contact(s):** Loretta W. Hoover, Ph.D., R.D.

**$ ◆ Off The Beaten Path**
Box 190-MAC
Philomath, OR 97370
**Concern(s):** economics; homeschooling. Describes over 50 periodicals, networks and guides on alternative tech, camping, gardening, home schooling, low-cost shelters, travel, etc. Unusual how-to publications. All addresses included. **Frequency:** Annual. **Subscription:** SASE/Free. **Pages:** 4. **Date Publ.:** 4/90. **Publisher:** Light Living Library.

**E ◆ The Official Recycled Products Guide**
American Recycling Market
Box 577
Ogdensburg, NY 13669    (800)267-0707
**Affiliation:** American Recycling Market. **Concern(s):** environment; economics; recycling; green consumer. America's most comprehensive directory/reference manual on materials recycling markets. 25,000 cross referenced Company and Agency listings. 400 recycled products classifications. Consumers, brokers, dealers, processors, collectors, equipment manufacturers and distributors. **Price:** includes free Buyers' Guide. **Est.:** 1985. **Frequency:** Annual. **Price:** $125/ea. **Pages:** 800. **Fax:** (315)471-3258. **Contact(s):** Mike Fraser.

**E ◆ The Official World Wildlife Fund Guide to Endangered Species of North America**
c/o Island Press
Box 7
Covelo, CA 95428    (202)232-7933
**Affiliation:** World Wildlife Fund. **Concern(s):** environment; wildlife/endangered species. Two volumes describe more than 500 plants and animals that are federally listed as endangered or threatened, Maps, color illustrations, information on habitat, food behavior, range and conservation efforts. Bibliographies, index, and directories. **Price:** $195/cloth. **Pages:** 1180. **Date Publ.:** 1990. **Publisher:** Beacham Publishing. Order: (800)828-1302.

**H ◆ The 100 Best Treatment Centers for Alcoholism and Drug Abuse**
Avon Books, Hearst Corporation
105 Madison Ave.
New York, NY 10016    (212)481-5600
**Concern(s):** health; family; substance abuse; counseling. 100 substance abuse treatment centers, therapists, family counseling organizations, and support groups. **Price:** $10.95/ea. **Pages:** 455. **Date Publ.:** 1988. **Publisher:** Avon Books. **Contact(s):** Linda Sunshine, John W. Wright (Editors). (800)238-0658.

**E ◆ 101 Ways To Help Save The Earth**
Greenhouse Crisis Foundation
1130 17th St. NW, #630
Washington, DC 20036    (800)ECO-LINE
**Affiliation:** Greenhouse Crisis Foundation. **Concern(s):** environment; global warming.

**E ◆ Once Is Not Enough: A Citizen's Recycling Manual**
National Toxics Campaign
37 Temple Place
Boston, MA 02111
**Affiliation:** National Toxics Campaign. **Concern(s):** environment; recycling.

**F ◆ Opportunities for Research and Study**
Sara Delano Roosevelt Memorial House
47-49 E. 65th St.
New York, NY 10021
**Affiliation:** National Council for Research on Women. **Concern(s):** feminism. A descriptive listing of the fellowships, affiliated scholar programs, grants and internships sponsored by Council member centers. A resource for graduate students, academic advisors, women's centers and research institutes, scholars, and independent researchers. **Other Resources:** Annotated bibliography of financial aid resources for women at all education levels. **Frequency:** Annual. **Price:** $10/ea. **Pages:** 26. **Circ.:** 500. **Date Publ.:** 1991-92. **Contact(s):** Paulette Tulloch (Editor).

A ▶ **Organic Network**
12100 Lima Center Rd.
Clinton, MI 49236
**Affiliation:** Eden Acres, Inc.. **Concern(s):** agriculture; health; economics; organic; nutrition; alternative consumer; green consumer. Directory of organic food suppliers.

A ▶ **Organic Wholesalers Directory**
California Action Network
Box 464
Davis, CA 95617 (916)756-8518
**Affiliation:** California Action Network. **Concern(s):** agriculture; organic. This 7th edition lists hundreds of wholesalers and retail stores in the business of organic food and farm supplies. Although California has the most entries, almost every state is represented by at least a few addresses. This handbook offer a way to see who's who in the organic food distribution business. Dozens of organic farms are listed. **Frequency:** Annual. **Date Publ.:** 1990.

✈ ▶ **Organizations Involved in Soviet-American Relations**
Institute for Soviet-American Relations
1608 New Hampshire Ave.
Washington, DC 20016 (202)387-3034
**Affiliation:** Institute for Soviet-American Relations. **Concern(s):** peace; education; economics; travel; trade; East-West. About 400 nonprofit organizations involved in trade, research, cultural exchange, human rights, religious, communications, and public educational programs with the Soviet Union arranged alphabetically by organization. It includes a number of useful lists and appendices, such as trade and travel resources, language programs, and Sister Cities. **Other Resources:** Formerly titled and often cited as HANDBOOK ON ORGANIZATIONS INVOLVED IN SOVIET-AMERICAN RELATIONS. **Frequency:** Triennial. **Price:** $25/ea. **Bulk:** 40% off/24. **Pages:** 250. **Circ.:** 3M+. **Date Publ.:** 6/86; 1990. **Contact(s):** Eliza Klose (Executive Director), Nancy Graham (Senior Associate).

S ▶ **Organizations Master Index**
Gale Research Inc.
835 Penobscot Building
Detroit, MI 48226-4094 (800)877-GALE
**Concern(s):** spiritual; Third World; politics; philanthropy; volunteer; municipal; law. About 150,000 nonprofit organizations, associations, foundation, museums, research centers, and government agencies in the US, Canada, and some foreign countries which have had statistical summaries, evaluations, or profiles published about them in some 50 well-known directories and yearbooks. Arranged alphabetically with organization. **Other Resources:** A Similar Gale publication, BUSINESS FIRMS MASTER INDEX provides access to about 110,000 for-profit firms in communications and the media. **Price:** $125/ea. **Pages:** c1,120. **Date Publ.:** 11/86. **Publisher:** Gale Research Inc. **Other Formats:** Magnetic tape. **Fax:** (313)961-6241. Telex: (810)221-7086. **Contact(s):** Denise M. Allard (Editor).

☮ ▶ **Organize!**
(800)537-9359
**Concern(s):** peace; environment; justice; fundraising; activism; volunteers; grassroots organizing. "The first comprehensive manual for grassroots organizers working for social, political, environmental, and economic change. An invaluable source of information - learn strategies from recruiting volunteers to fundraising. Use it and act!" "Do the right thing. Buy the book"-Jesse Jackson. **Price:** $19.95/ea.

☮ ▶ **Organizers' Manual**
c/o Donnelly/Colt
Box 188
Hampton, CT 06247 (203)455-9621
**Affiliation:** War Resisters League. **Concern(s):** peace; politics; grassroots organizing. This is the first comprehensive book on grassroots organizing techniques in a decade. No organizer should be without one. This information is relevant to every progressive social change organization working at the grassroots. The subjects it covers are wide-ranging and universal, and apply to your work no matter what your political affiliation. 44 chapters, 70 photos. **Price:** $10/ea. **Pages:** 220. **Fax:** (203)455-9597.

P ▶ **Organizing for Social Change**
Seven Locks Press
Box 27
Cabin John, MD 20818 (800)537-5359
**Affiliation:** New Jersey Citizen Action. **Concern(s):** politics; grassroots organizing. Authors, who work with NJCA, outline various ways that citizens can affect change through community organizing with service, self-help and public interest approaches. **Price:** $19.95 ($22.95 postpaid). **Pages:** 271. **Contact(s):** Kim Bobo, Steve Max (Authors). Jackie Kendall

✈ ▶ **Overseas List - Opportunities For Living and Working in Developing Countries**
Augsburg College
731 21 Ave. S
Minneapolis, MN 55454
**Concern(s):** education; Third World; labor; development; volunteers; jobs; travel. **Date Publ.:** 1985. **Publisher:** Beckman, Mitchell & Powers.

♥ ▶ **Parental Kidnapping: An International Resource Directory**
Rainbow Books
Box 1069
Moore Haven, FL 33471
**Concern(s):** family; justice; children; criminal system; child abuse. List of about 45 government agencies, missing child organizations, and other groups concerned with kidnapping of children by their parents. International coverage; alphabetically arranged. Description of the laws of the countries covered regarding parental kidnapping of minor children. **Frequency:** Annual. **Price:** $18.50/ea. **Publisher:** Rainbow Books. **Contact(s):** Joe Teague Caruso.

♥ ▶ **Parental Kidnapping: How to Prevent an Abduction and What to Do If Your Child is Abducted**
National Center for Missing and Exploited Children
2101 Wilson Blvd., #550
Arlington, VA 22201 (800)843-5678
**Affiliation:** National Center for Missing and Exploited Children. **Concern(s):** family; justice; health; children; victims' rights; empowerment; counseling. 100+ support groups for parents of children who are victims of parental abduction. Information on preventive action, legal remedies and assistance available, counseling, rights of noncustodial parents, state, and federal laws and regulations, and international kidnapping. Prepared in cooperation with the Office of Juvenile Justice and Delinquency Protection of the Department of Justice. **Other Resources:** Microfiche from ERIC Document Reproduction Service, Computer Microfilm Corp., 3900 Wheeler Ave., Alexandria, VA 22304. (703) 823-0500. **Frequency:** Irregular. **Price:** $.85/ea. **Date Publ.:** 8/88. **Other Formats:** Microfiche from ERIC Document Reproduction Service, Computer Microfilm Corp. **Fax:** (703)235-4067. **Contact(s):** Patricia M. Hoff, Janet Kosid Uthe (Authors).

G ▶ **Parents & Friends of Gays - International Directory**
National Federation of Parents & Friends of Gays
8020 Eastern Ave. NW
Washington, DC 20012
**Affiliation:** National Federation of Parents & Friends of Gays. **Concern(s):** health; justice; counseling; self-help; AIDS; gay/lesbian. About 160 self-help, peer counseling, and support groups; 600 counselors and religious, social, community service, and other organizations serving parents, families, and friends of homosexuals and bisexuals. Arranged geographically. **Frequency:** Annual. **Price:** $3/ea. **Pages:** c.10. **Date Publ.:** 5/91. **Contact(s):** Gene Baker (National Coordinator).

✍ ▶ **Peace and World Order Studies: A Curriculum Guide**
Westview Press
5500 Central Ave.
Boulder, CO 80301
**Concern(s):** education; peace; media; spiritual; film; press; fundraising; philanthropy. List of approximately 1,020 funding sources, films, periodicals, organizations, and books concerned with peace education, including foundations and other sources of grants. Classified by subject with organization name, address, and phone. Principal content is various academic disciplines' course syllabi and outlines, as well as printed, audiovisual, and other interdisciplinary resources useful in the field of peace education. **Frequency:** Irregular. **Price:** $16.95/ea. **Date Publ.:** 1989. **Publisher:** American Business Directories, Inc.. **Contact(s):** Barbara J. Wien (Editor).

☮ ▶ **Peace Archives**
World Without War Council
1736 Martin Luther King Way
Berkeley, CA 94709
**Concern(s):** peace. Subtitle: A Guide to Library Collections of The Papers of American Peace Organizations and of Leaders in the Public Effort for Peace. **Date Publ.:** 1986. **Contact(s):** Marguerite Green (Compiler/Editor).

✍ ▶ **Peace Archives: A Guide to Library Collections**
World Without War Council
1730 Martin Luther King, Jr. Way
Berkeley, CA 94709
**Affiliation:** World Without War Council. **Concern(s):** education; peace. Lists about 30 libraries and archives with paper and manuscript collections of organizations and individuals active in the peace movement; 75 individual collections located in other libraries or archives; 30 peace organizations and whether they maintain their own collection or deposit it elsewhere; explanation of record-keeping standards and processes or archiving; bibliography. **Price:** $7/ea. **Pages:** 80. **Date Publ.:** 1986. **Fax:** (510)845-5721. **Contact(s):** Marguerite Green (Director, Historian Project).

☮ ▶ **The Peace Catalog**
Press For Peace, Inc.
5621 Seaview Ave. NW
Seattle, WA 98107
**Concern(s):** peace; economics; socially-responsible investing. Articles and essays covering all aspects of peace by many of the world's top thinkers. Directory and detailed information on over 1,000 peace organizations. Guide to socially responsible investing. List of reference books, publications, and films. **Publisher:** Press For Peace, Inc.. **Contact(s):** Duane Sweeney (Editor).

☮ ▶ **Peace Diary: World Peace Directory**
c/o Fellowship Publications
Box 271
Nyack, NY 10960
**Affiliation:** Housemans Diary Group. **Concern(s):** peace. Published in England and distributed by the Fellowship, this periodical is laid out like a personal daily calendar and includes a directory of national organizations by country with address information, contact, and publications. Also has British local directory. **Frequency:** Annual. **Price:** $7.95 paper. **Pages:** 250+. **Date Publ.:** 1989.

☮ ▶ **Peace Education**
McFarland & Company, Inc.
Box 611
Jefferson, NC 28640
**Concern(s):** peace. List of peace organizations that offer resource materials on educational strategies to promote peace. Alphabetically arranged by company or institution. Includes information on key issues and educational approaches for peace education at different age levels. **Price:** $19.95/ea.+$2 shipping. **Date Publ.:** 1988. **Publisher:** McFarland & Company, Inc. **Contact(s):** Ian M. Harris.

☮ ▶ **Peace Organizations Past and Present: A Survey and Directory**
McFarland & Company, Inc.
Box 611
Jefferson, NC 28640
**Concern(s):** peace. Nearly 100 organizations promoting peace through example, education, and advocating federation and world citizenship. Classified by type of organization. **Price:** $24.95/ea.+shipping. **Pages:** 280. **Date Publ.:** 1988. **Publisher:** McFarland & Company, Inc. **Contact(s):** Robert S. Meyer (Author).

? ▶ **Peace Pact Guide**
300 Northern Pike
Pittsburgh, PA 15235
**Affiliation:** World Peace One, Inc.. **Concern(s):** future; peace; ideation. Describes World Peace One's systems approach to peace plus the dynamics, problems and solutions to eight key systems (environment, economy, community, politics, health, psyche, personal and non-personal relationships). It also includes a step-by-step goal-attainment process (with forms), plus an eight-page section on learning how to learn. Nonprofit. **Price:** $8/ea. **Date Publ.:** 1990. **Contact(s):** Timothy L. Cimino (Executive Director).

☮ ▶ **Peace Resource Book**
Institute for Defense and Disarmament Studies
2001 Beacon St.
Brookline, MA 02146
**Affiliation:** Institute for Defense and Disarmament Studies. **Concern(s):** peace; education; disarmament. A directory of 7,000 national and local peace groups and a guide to recent literature on armaments, military policy, alternative defense, arms control, disarmament, and nonviolent conflict resolution. **Frequency:** Biennial. **Price:** $14.95/ea. **Pages:** 304. **Date Publ.:** 1990. **Publisher:** Ballinger Publishing Co. **Contact(s):** Alaina Smith (Administrative Coordinator), Ken White (Publications Director). MA 02138.

☮ ▶ **People Power: Applying Nonviolence Theory**
New Society
Box 582
Santa Cruz, CA 95061
**Concern(s):** peace; nonviolence. Straightforward guide to understanding the dynamics of nonviolent action and using them in ongoing social change struggles. Provides a framework and checklist for understanding social power and for building nonviolent action strategies. **Contact(s):** David H. Albert (Author).

**M ▶ Periodicals of Public Interest Organizations: A Citizen's Guide**
Commission for the Advancement of Public Interest Organizations
1875 Connecticut Ave. NW
Washington, DC 20009  (202)462-0505
**Affiliation:** Commission for the Advancement of Public Interest Organizations. **Concern(s):** media; justice; politics. **Date Publ.:** 1980.

**E ▶ Permaculture: A Practical Guide for a Sustainable Future**
North American Permaculture
Box 573
Colville, WA 99114
**Affiliation:** North American Permaculture. **Concern(s):** environment; agriculture; economics; permaculture. "This book delivers the very best the world of 'functional' and 'sustainable' design has to offer. Mollison shows us with his scientific eye, a world with a sustainable future. With a heart committed to repair of the Earth, he empowers us not only to see how this future can be constructed but how it can be maintained forever, using very little energy and without exploiting our natural and cultural resources." An ecological resource book that no environmentalist should be without. **Price:** $34.95/ea.+$3 S&H. **Pages:** 576. **Contact(s):** Bill Mollison (Author).

**E ▶ A Personal Action Guide for the Earth**
Transmissions Project of UNEP
730 Arizona Ave., #329
Santa Monica, CA 90401
**Affiliation:** Transmissions Project of UNEP. **Concern(s):** environment; energy. Under headings of Energy, Food, Water, Toxins, Waste, and Life Preservation, lists are given for actions you can take as an individual. In addition, under the same headings are lists of groups you can join, support or use to care for the Earth. **Contact(s):** Kathleen Gildred.

**H ▶ The Pesticide Handbook: Profiles for Action**
Pesticide Action Network
965 Mission St., #514
San Francisco, CA 94103
**Affiliation:** International Organization of Consumers Union. **Concern(s):** health; agriculture; environment; pesticides; hazardous/toxic wastes. A description of the health effects of over 40 pesticides commonly used worldwide, and useful sources of information on international pesticide issues.

**A ▶ Pesticides: A Community Action Guide**
c/o Concern, Inc.
1794 Columbia Rd. NW
Washington, DC 20009  (202)328-8160
**Affiliation:** Concern, Inc. **Concern(s):** agriculture; health; environment; hazardous/toxic waste; pesticides. **Date Publ.:** 1987.

**🐾 ▶ The PETA Guide to Compassionate Living**
Box 42516
Washington, DC 20015-0516  (202)770-7444
**Affiliation:** People for the Ethical Treatment of Animals (PETA). **Concern(s):** health; environment; agriculture; nutrition; alternative consumer; animal rights; green consumer. **Contact(s):** Susan Rich (Director, Compassion Campaign), Harold Ullman (Compassion Campaign Coordinator).

**S ▶ Philanthropy and Volunteerism**
The Foundation Center
79 5th Ave.
New York, NY 10003  (800)424-9836
**Affiliation:** Foundation Center. **Concern(s):** spiritual; philanthropy; volunteers. List of publishers of about 1,600 articles, books, reports, and essays that give information on philanthropy; also includes a list of conferences, commissions, and organizational resources. Classified by subject. Data includes bibliographic info. **Price:** $18.50/ea.+$2 shipping. **Date Publ.:** 6/87. **Contact(s):** Daphne N. Layton (Editor).

**E ▶ Planetwork**
Box 804
Ketchum, ID 83340
**Concern(s):** environment; future; ideation. A clearinghouse for Earth-friendly ideas. **Contact(s):** Ed and Jennifer Moffet.

**♥ ▶ Planned Parenthood Affiliates, Chapter & State Public Affairs Offices Directory**
Planned Parenthood Federation of America
810 7th Ave.
New York, NY 10019  (212)541-7800
**Affiliation:** Planned Parenthood Federation of America. **Concern(s):** family; feminism; family planning. 250 listings arranged geographically with affiliate or chapter. **Other Resources:** Formerly, AFFILIATE DIRECTORY: PLANNED PARENTHOOD AFFILIATES &

CHAPTERS. **Frequency:** Annual. **Subscription:** For internal distribution only. **Date Publ.:** 9/90.

**♥ ▶ Polyfidelity Primer**
Box 6306
Capt Cook, HI 96704-6306
**Affiliation:** P.E.P. **Concern(s):** family. A practical handbook for the non-monogamous. It includes chapters on lifestyle design, courtship, decision-making, money, sex, jealousy, multiple parenting and more. Also includes resources: books, videos, organizations, and publishes LOVING MORE JOURNAL and maintains a Network. A complete how-to on successful group marriage. **Other Resources:** Quarterly journal; support for local groups (networking & materials); phoneline consultation; annual conference. For Profit. **Est.:** 1990. **Dues:** $25-$60/yr. **Contact(s):** R. Nearing (Director), B. Northrop (Operations/Graphics).

**D ▶ Population Handbook**
Population Reference Bureau
1875 Connecticut Ave. NW, #520
Washington, DC 20009  (202)483-1100
**Affiliation:** Population Reference Bureau. **Concern(s):** demographics; Third World; population growth. These clear, concise guides cover the terms and concepts of demography, explaining the fundamental statistical rates and how to calculate them. An indispensable reference for students, teachers, journalists, and anyone who needs to know about population. Available: US, Caribbean, and International editions in English, French, Spanish, and Arabic. The Bureau has been in existence since 1929. Nonprofit. **Est.:** 1978. **Dues:** $45/ea. **Date Publ.:** Soon. **Labels:** 5. **Fax:** (202)328-3937. (800)877-9881(orders).

**D ▶ Population Programmers and Projects: Guide to Sources of International Population Assistance**
United Nations Population Fund
United Nations
New York, NY 10017  (212)297-5000
**Affiliation:** United Nations Population Fund. **Concern(s):** demographics; population growth. About 180 multilateral, regional, and bilateral agencies; nongovernmental organizations; universities; research institutions; and training organizations that offer technical assistance, training, or funding for population activities and studies. Arranged by type of organization, then alphabetical. **Other Resources:** Available in English, French, and Spanish editions. **Frequency:** Triennial. **Price:** $20/ea. **Pages:** 480. **Date Publ.:** 5/88. **Other Formats:** Microfilm. **Fax:** (212)557-6416.

**H ▶ Post-Traumatic Stress Disorder, Rape Trauma, Delayed Stress and Related Conditions**
McFarland & Company, Inc.
Box 611
Jefferson, NC 28640  (919)246-4460
**Concern(s):** health; feminism; counseling; rape/sexual abuse; veterans; psychology. List of 1,895 outreach programs for war veterans seeking counseling for a variety of battle-related mental disorders: post-traumatic stress disorder (PTSD), delayed stress, war neurosis, shell-shock, combat fatigue, acute combat reaction, combat- related stress, gross stress reaction, combat exhaustion, battle-induced mental disorder, and battle shock. Arranged alphabetically by institution. **Price:** $29.95/ea. **Date Publ.:** 1986. **Publisher:** McFarland & Company, Inc. **Contact(s):** D. Cheryn Picquet, Reba Best (Editors).

**✊ ▶ Power of the People, Active Nonviolence in the United States**
c/o Donnelly/Colt
Box 188
Hampton, CT 06247  (203)455-9621
**Concern(s):** peace; politics; grassroots organizing; civil disobedience; nonviolence. A pictorial encyclopedia of the struggles of US women and men working for peace and justice through nonviolent action. Illustrated with over 300 photographs, bibliography, index. **Price:** $18.95/ea. **Pages:** 272. **Date Publ.:** 1987. **Publisher:** New Society Publishers. **Fax:** (203)455-9597. **Contact(s):** Helen Michalowski (Editor), Robert Cooney.

**☉ ▶ The Power of the States: a Fifty-State Survey of Renewable Energy**
Public Citizen
2000 P St. NW, #605
Washington, DC 20036-0757  (202)833-3000
**Affiliation:** Public Citizen. **Concern(s):** energy; renewable; appropriate technology; policy. This new study by Public Citizen indicates that 10% of the US energy supply is provided by renewable energy, with California, Maine, and Georgia among the leaders in developing renewable energy.

**☉ ▶ Practical Home Energy Savings**
Rocky Mountain Institute
1739 Snowmass Creek
Old Snowmass, CO 81654
**Affiliation:** Rocky Mountain Institute. **Concern(s):** energy; environment; efficiency; water. Compiled by the Energy Program. It will serve as a complement to Water Efficiency for Your Home.

**J ▶ Pre-trial Detainee Manual**
Center for Constitutional Rights
666 Broadway
New York, NY 10012  (212)614-6464
**Concern(s):** justice; prisons; criminal system.

**H ▶ Prescription for Nutritional Healing**
Avery Publishing Group, Inc.
120 Old Broadway
Garden City, NY 11040  (516)741-2155
**Concern(s):** health; nutrition; preventative medicine. "A complete and authoritative guide to dealing with health disorders through nutritional, herbal, and supplemental therapies. Written by a medical doctor and a certified nutritionist, the book blends the latest scientific research with traditional nonsurgical treatments. This guide provides all the information needed for the average person to design his/her own nutrition program." **Price:** $16.95/ea. **Date Publ.:** 1990. **Contact(s):** Dr. James Balch, Phyllise Balch (Co-authors).

**$ ▶ The Product Safety Book: The Ultimate Consumer Guide**
E.P. Dutton
375 Hudson St.
New York, NY 10014  (212)366-2000
**Concern(s):** economics; health; consumer protection. **Publisher:** E.P. Dutton. **Contact(s):** Stephen Brobeck, Anne C. Averyt (Editors).

**♿ ▶ Programs Demonstrating Model Practices for Integrating People with Severe Disabilities into the Community**
Center on Human Policy
Box 127, University Station
Syracuse, NY 13210  (315)443-3851
**Affiliation:** Center on Human Policy. **Concern(s):** health; justice; disabled; disabled's rights. Programs that were selected as models of how to integrate severely disabled persons into the community. Classified by type of program. **Other Resources:** Also cited as MODEL PRACTICES LIST. **Frequency:** Irregular. **Price:** $2/ea. plus postage. **Pages:** 25. **Fax:** (315)443-4338. **Contact(s):** Julie Ann Racino (Associate Director).

**♥ ▶ Programs to Strengthen Families: A Resource Guide**
Family Resource Coalition
230 N. Michigan, #1625
Chicago, IL 60601  (312)726-4750
**Affiliation:** Family Resource Coalition. **Concern(s):** family; health; justice; education; child abuse; counseling; day care; self-help. Descriptions of 72 organizations offering programs providing a variety of service models for working with families of varied economic and ethnic backgrounds in different geographic (urban, rural, etc.) settings; includes parents education, prevention of child abuse and neglect, day care, neighborhood-based self-help and information support programs, and others. **Frequency:** Irregular. **Price:** $12.50/ea. **Pages:** 140. **Date Publ.:** 5/88. **Contact(s):** Carole Levine, Irene Beck (Editors).

**✎ ▶ Progressive Periodicals Directory**
Box 120574
Nashville, TN 37212
**Affiliation:** Progressive Education. **Concern(s):** education; media; arts; peace; environment; justice; journalism; press. Reviews provide details on some 600 social concerns, magazines, newsletters, and newspapers that are national in scope. The purpose is to give subscription information and to promote networking. Categories include children/youth, civil rights, culture, environment, general, health, human rights, international, labor, media, organizing, peace, the professions, public interest and religious. **Other Resources:** Several descriptions that appear in Macrocosm were reprinted from PROGRESSIVE PERIODICALS with permission from the author. Many thanks to Mr. Canan for his generosity and good work! **Frequency:** Irregular. **Price:** $16/ea. **Date Publ.:** 1990. **Other Formats:** Also available on mailing labels. **Contact(s):** Craig Canan (Author).

**H ▶ Psychoimmunity and the Healing Process: A Holistic Approach to Immunity and AIDS**
Box 7327
Berkeley, CA 94707  (510)524-1801
**Concern(s):** health; holism; AIDS; psychology. List of about 60

holistic health practitioners, organizations and centers that provide information about the treatment of immune dysfunction and AIDS. Classified by type of service and indexed alphabetically. Principal content is articles advocating a holistic approach for the treatment of AIDS. **Frequency:** Irregular. **Price:** $12.95/ea. **Contact(s):** Jason Serinus (Editor). (800)841-2665.

E ♦ **Public Interest Group Directory**
Attn: Publication Clerk, EPA
Region 10, 1200 6th Ave., Mail Stop MD-108
Seattle, WA 98101    (206)442-1519
**Affiliation:** Environmental Protection Agency. **Concern(s):** environment; education; volunteers; polar. Regional voluntary organizations, EPA regional offices, and state, local, and provincial environmental and pollution control agencies in Alaska, Idaho, Oregon, Washington, and British Columbia. Classified by type of organization. **Frequency:** Irregular. **Subscription:** Free. **Pages:** 40. **Date Publ.:** 1989. **Other Formats:** Microfiche from National Technical Information Service, Springfield, VA 22161; $6.95 (PB87-124053). **Contact(s):** Mary M. Neilson (Constituency Coordinator).

S ♦ **Public Media Center's Index of Progressive Funders**
Public Media Center
466 Green St., #300
San Francisco, CA 94133    (415)434-1403
**Affiliation:** Safe Energy Communications Council. **Concern(s):** spiritual; fundraising; networking; philanthropy. 130+ organizations that provide funding to groups concerned with progressive issues, such as disarmament, civil rights, women's issues, community organization, citizen advocacy, the elderly, and environmental problems; church-sponsored grant programs, list of publications, such as fundraising guides and other directories to funding organizations. Arranged alphabetically with indexes by subject. **Frequency:** Irregular. **Pages:** c465. **Date Publ.:** Summer 1990. **Contact(s):** Bill Hartman (Editor).

H ♦ **A Quick Guide to Food Additives**
**Concern(s):** health; nutrition; hazardous/toxic. "Nontechnical ...information-packed...easy to use. Contains new, updated sections on agricultural and processing chemicals. Includes a handy dictionary of the most common additives. The essential facts you need to make informed food choices." **Price:** $5.95/ea. **Publisher:** Silvercat.

☢ ♦ **RAINBOOK: Resources for Appropriate Technology**
c/o Rain Magazine
Box 30097
Eugene, OR 97403-9979    (919)933-5875
**Concern(s):** energy; appropriate technology. **Publisher:** Schocken Books/Pantheon Books.

✈ ♦ **Rainforest: A Guide to Research & Tourist Facilities at Selected Tropical Sites in Central & South America**
Feline Press
Box 7219
Gainesville, FL 32605
**Concern(s):** education; Third World; environment; forests; travel; Central America; South America. **Publisher:** Feline Press. **Contact(s):** James L. Castner, Ph.D. (Author).

☸ ♦ **Raising the Curtain: A Guide to Independent Organizations and Contacts in Eastern Europe**
World Without War Council
1736 Martin Luther King Way
Berkeley, CA 94709
**Affiliation:** World Without War Council. **Concern(s):** peace; environment; world order. A fact-filled book with indispensable lists, names and ideas for action: what to read (annotated guide to the best periodicals, essays, books, and pamphlets from and about the region); Whom to meet (50+ independent grassroots groups in Eastern Europe concerned with ecology, peace, jazz, civil liberties, labor, religion and youth); how to help (over 40 organizations in the US and Western Europe in close contact with independent movements in Eastern Europe); and where to go (resource for educators. **Pages:** 36. **Contact(s):** Lucy Dougall, Holt Ruffin.

☢ ♦ **Real Goods Alternative Energy Sourcebook**
See References.

♥ ♦ **Reaching Out: A Directory of National Organizations Related to Maternal and Child Health**
38th & R Sts. NW
Washington, DC 20057    (202)625-8400
**Affiliation:** National Center for Education in Maternal and Child Health. **Concern(s):** family; health; education; day care; birth; self-

help; volunteers. 500+ national and international voluntary organizations for health professionals, educators, and the public; mutual support groups; self-help clearinghouses; and selected federal Maternal and Child Health Information Centers. Classified by cause or specialty and indexed by organization, name, and subject. **Frequency:** Biennial. **Pages:** 130.

F ♦ **Recovering from Rape**
Henry Holt & Co.
Box 30135
Salt Lake City, UT 84130    (801)972-2221
**Concern(s):** feminism; rape/sexual abuse. List of US rape crisis centers. Principal content is information and advice for victims of rape and their families. **Price:** $9.95/ea. **Publisher:** Henry Holt & Co.. **Fax:** (801)977-9712. **Contact(s):** Linda E. Ledray. (800)247-3912.

H ♦ **Recovery Resource Guide**
Health Communications
3201 SW 15th St.
Deerfield Beach, FL 33442
**Concern(s):** health; education; drug/alcohol; counseling. An indispensable resource guide for anyone who has known, or has been a substance abuser. Written by Robert Ackerman, Ph.D. and Judith A. Michaels, M.A., leaders in this field. **Date Publ.:** 1990. **Publisher:** Health Communications.

H ♦ **Recovery, Incorporated - Directory of Group Meeting Information**
Recovery, Inc.
802 N. Dearborn St.
Chicago, IL 60610    (312)337-5661
**Affiliation:** Recovery, Inc.. **Concern(s):** health; health care; self-help; psychology. About 1,000 weekly group meetings providing a professionally developed method of self-help aftercare to help prevent relapses in former mental patients and relieve chronic nervous conditions. Arranged geographically with group meeting location, time and date. **Frequency:** Annual. **Subscription:** $1, members/professionals only. **Pages:** 50. **Date Publ.:** 1/91. **Contact(s):** Marybeth Murphy (Editor).

F ♦ **Recovery: How to Survive Sexual Assault**
Doubleday & Co.
510 Franklin Ave.
Garden City, NY 11530
**Concern(s):** feminism; health; rape/sexual abuse; psychology. **Publisher:** Doubleday & Company, Inc.

E ♦ **Recycling Study Guide**
Bureau of Information & Education, Dept. of Natural Resources
Box 7921
Madison, WI 53707
**Affiliation:** Department of Natural Resources. **Concern(s):** environment; recycling; natural resources.

J ♦ **Red Pages: Businesses Across Indian America**
LaCourse Communications Corp.
6 S. 2nd St., #919
Yakima, WA 98901    (509)457-3786
**Concern(s):** justice; economics; Native Americans; trade. Native American-owned businesses arranged geographically, then classified by line of business with company name, etc. **Date Publ.:** 1985.

? ♦ **Redefining Wealth & Progress: The Caracas Report on Alternative Development Indicators**
Knowledge Systems
7777 W. Morris St.
Indianapolis, IN 46231    (800)999-8517
**Concern(s):** future; economics; environment. This report contains a discussion of alternative models on how to measure the Quality of Life. Key contributors include noted futurist, Hazel Henderson, author of THE POLITICS OF THE SOLAR AGE and CREATING ALTERNATIVE FUTURES. **Member:** Co-op America.

D ♦ **Refugee and Immigrant Resource Directory 1990-1991**
The Denali Press
Box 021535
Juneau, AK 99802-1535 (907)586-6014
**Concern(s):** demographics; justice; refugees; immigration. This is an expanded version of the Directory of Services for Refugees and Immigrants (1987) and now includes detailed information on nearly 1,000 local, regional and national organizations, associations, agencies, academic programs, research centers, museums and other US groups that offer services to or provide information/policy analysis about refugees and immigrants. The main section is arranged by state. There are six indices and forty sub-indices. **Other Resources:** RIRD

90-91 proved extremely useful to Amnesty International USA and they incorporated the appendices in their 1990 campaign on seeking asylum in the US. Their essays provides an excellent overview of US refugee and immigration policy. **Frequency:** Triennial. **Price:** $37.50/ea.+$2.50 shipping. **Pages:** 352. **Date Publ.:** 1990. **Publisher:** Denali Press. **Contact(s):** Alan Edward Schorr (Editor).

♥ ♦ **Register of Marriage and Family Therapy Providers**
American Association for Marriage and Family Therapy
1100 17th St. NW
Washington, DC 20036    (202)452-0109
**Affiliation:** American Association for Marriage and Family Therapy. **Concern(s):** family; counseling. 14,000 members throughout the US and Canada, plus national and international affiliates. **Other Resources:** Formerly, AMERICAN ASSOCIATION FOR MARRIAGE. **Frequency:** Irregular. **Pages:** c500. **Circ.:** 5M. **Date Publ.:** 1/88. **Contact(s):** Kim Tilley (Editor).

H ♦ **Rehab: A Comprehensive Guide to the Best Drug-Alcohol Treatment Centers in the US**
HarperCollins
10 E. 53rd
New York, NY 10022    (212)207-7000
**Concern(s):** health; feminism; substance abuse; empowerment; psychology. 140+ drug and alcohol treatment centers; centers exclusively for women are listed in an appendix. Arranged and indexed geographically with center name, etc. **Pages:** 320. **Date Publ.:** 12/88. **Publisher:** Harper Collins. **Fax:** (717)343-3611. **Contact(s):** Stan Hart (Editor). (800)2-HARPER.

E ♦ **Rene Dubos Center for Human Environments - Directory**
100 E. 85th St.
New York, NY 10028    (212)249-7745
**Affiliation:** Rene Dubos Center for Human Environments. **Concern(s):** environment. A listing of 500 environmentalists, including college and university professors, representatives of industrial firms, and government officials; international coverage. **Frequency:** Annual.

E ♦ **Repair Manual For Planet Earth: Steps You Can Take To Heal the Land, Water, Wildlife, and Cities of America**
Restoring the Earth
1713 C Martin Luther King Way
Berkeley, CA 94709    (510)843-2645
**Affiliation:** Restoring the Earth. **Concern(s):** environment; urban; land; water; wildlife/endangered species; development; conservation; sustainability. A "how-to" handbook.

S ♦ **Resource Directory for Volunteer Programs**
Heritage Arts
1807 Prairie Ave.
Downers Grove, IL 60515    (708)964-1194
**Concern(s):** spiritual; economics; volunteers; philanthropy; trade. Volunteer organizations and suppliers of products and services for volunteer organizations, including technical assistance, trainers, consultants, and publishers of related books, audio tapes, video tapes, and computer software. Classified by product or service, etc. **Other Resources:** Also includes statistical information on volunteerism, volunteerism issues; basic guide to volunteer program management. **Frequency:** Annual. **Pages:** c105. **Publisher:** Heritage Arts. **Fax:** (708)964-0841. **Contact(s):** Steve McCurley, Sue Vineyard (Editors).

A ♦ **Resource Guide for Creating Successful Communities**
c/o Island Press
Box 7
Covelo, CA 95428    (202)232-7933
**Concern(s):** agriculture; urban; rural communities; sustainability This is the resource guide for Creating Successful Communities ($24.95 paper; $39.95 cloth). It includes charts, graphs and illustrations. **Price:** $24.95 paper; $39.95 cloth. **Pages:** 210. **Date Publ.:** 1989. **Publisher:** Island Press. Order: (800)828-1302. **Contact(s):** Michael A. Mantell, Stephen F. Harper (Co-authors). Luther Propst, Co-author.

T ♦ **Resource Guide to Sustainable Agriculture in the Third World**
1701 University Ave. SE, #202
Minneapolis, MN 55414
**Affiliation:** International Alliance for Sustainable Agriculture. **Concern(s):** Third World; agriculture; sustainability.

**H ◆ Resource List for Informational Materials on Sexually Transmitted Diseases**
Technical Information Services
Center for Disease Control
Atlanta, GA 30333       (404)639-1819
**Concern(s):** health; AIDS; public health. List of organizations that provide information on sexually transmitted diseases. **Pages:** 30. **Date Publ.:** 3/87. **Publisher:** Technical Information Services.

**⊗ ◆ Resource Manual For a Living Revolution**
New Society
Box 582
Santa Cruz, CA 95061
**Concern(s):** peace; environment; justice. **Publisher:** New Society. **Contact(s):** Virginia Coover.

**☯ ◆ Resource-Efficient Housing Guide**
Rocky Mountain Institute
1739 Snowmass Creek
Old Snowmass, CO 81654
**Affiliation:** Rocky Mountain Institute. **Concern(s):** energy; environment; economics; alternative markets; efficiency. **Contact(s):** Robert Sardinsky, Jon Klusmire.

**F ◆ Resources for Feminist Research - International Guide to Women's Periodicals and Resources Issues**
Ontario Institute for Studies in Education
252 Bloor St. West
Toronto, ON M5S 1V6 Canada       (416)923-6641
**Concern(s):** feminism; research. List of organizations, periodicals, films, research centers, and committees concerned with feminism and its movement. International coverage. Arranged geographically; includes periodical or resource. **Frequency:** Irregular. **Price:** $6.50 Canadian dollars. **Fax:** (416)926-4725.

**A ◆ Resources for Sustainable Agriculture and Alternative Enterprises in Eastern Oklahoma and Western Arkansas**
Kerr Center for Sustainable Agriculture
Box 588
Poteau, OK 74953
**Affiliation:** Kerr Center for Sustainable Agriculture. **Concern(s):** agriculture; sustainability. 80+ organizations, businesses, and specialists listed under the categories; general information, aquaculture, horticulture, livestock, trees and forestry. **Contact(s):** Lara Ervin.

**P ◆ Resources Mailing Lists**
40 Welles Ave.
Boston, MA 02124       (617)825-8895
**Concern(s):** politics; fundraising; networking. Mailing lists for progressive individuals, organizations, publications, subscribers, donors, etc. for fundraising, publicity, new members, etc. Available on self-sticking or cheshire labels; floppy disc or magnetic tape. Selective searches on just about any progressive category you might want. **Fax:** (617)288-2999.

**A ◆ The Resources of International Permaculture (TRIP)**
7781 Lenox Ave.
Jacksonville, FL 32221
**Affiliation:** Elfin Permaculture/Yankee Permaculture. **Concern(s):** agriculture; organic. An extensive green directory of groups involved with issues of sustainability.

**⊗ ◆ Resources on Gandhi**
Greenleaf Books
Weare, NH 03281
**Concern(s):** peace; nonviolence. Offers most of Gandhi's writings and some books about him. Write for complete list of available titles. **Publisher:** Greenleaf Books.

**E ◆ Resources, Environment and Policy**
Harper & Row
Ice House One #401, 151 Union St.
San Francisco, CA 94111-1299
**Concern(s):** environment; energy; politics. **Date Publ.:** 1985. **Publisher:** Harper & Row.

**G ◆ The Rights of Gay People: An American Civil Liberties Handbook**
Bantam Books
666 5th St.
New York, NY 10103       (212)765-6500
**Concern(s):** justice; gay/lesbian; civil liberties. **Date Publ.:** 1983. **Publisher:** Bantam Books.

**D ◆ Rural Sociological Society**
Wilson Hall, #2-125
Montana State University
Bozeman, MT 59717       (406)994-5248
**Concern(s):** demographics; agriculture; rural communities; rural relocation. Educators and others employed in the field of rural sociology. Arranged alphabetically with name, office or home address, phone, highest degree held, present position, personal data, and areas of occupational specialization. **Other Resources:** Formerly, RURAL SOCIOLOGICAL SOCIETY DIRECTORY. **Frequency:** Biennial. **Subscription:** Members only. **Pages:** 200. **Contact(s):** Patrick C. Jobes (Treasurer).

**H ◆ RX Home Care - Buyers Guide Issue**
341 White Pond Dr.
Akron, OH 44320       (216)867-4401
**Concern(s):** health. Listings of more than 11,300 manufacturers and exclusive distributors of home health care products and services worldwide. Alphabetically arranged and indexed by product (with address and phone), company name (with toll-free phone and locations). Categories include company name, address, phone, telex, TWX, and names of contact or key personnel. **Frequency:** Annual. **Price:** $45/ea. **Circ.:** 18M. **Date Publ.:** 10/90. **Contact(s):** Kris Kyes (Editor).

**H ◆ Safe, Strong, and Streetwise**
Joy Street Books; Little, Brown & Company
34 Beacon St.
Boston, MA 02108       (617)227-0730
**Concern(s):** health; feminism; empowerment; rape/sexual abuse; battered women; child abuse. Lists 40 organizations concerned with crises and informative counseling and prevention of sexual assault, particularly involving teenagers. Arranged geographically with organization. Principal content is discussion of types of sexual assault and methods of prevention. **Pages:** 180. **Date Publ.:** 3/87. **Publisher:** Joy Street Books. **Contact(s):** Helen Benedict, Melanie Kroupa (Editors).

**E ◆ Save Our Planet**
Zephyr Press
3316 N. Chapel Ave., Box 13448-C, Dept.
Tucson, AZ 85732-3448 (602)322-5090
**Concern(s):** environment; education; childhood; students. "750 Everyday Ways You Can Help Clean Up the Earth". Here are hundreds of simple and effective ways you and your students can improve our planet. It doesn't just repeat the recycle-your-trash sort of suggestions. The author presents an overview of the major environmental problems of our time and links the consequences of our individual efforts to each issue. Grade 4-Adult. **Pages:** 210. **Contact(s):** Diane MacEachern (Editor).

**E ◆ Saving America's Countryside: A Guide to Rural Conservation**
The John Hopkins University Press
Baltimore, MD 21218
**Concern(s):** environment; conservation; rural communities. **Publisher:** Johns Hopkins University Press.

**E ◆ Saving The Earth: A Citizen's Guide to Environmental Action**
Alfred A. Knopf, Inc.
201 E. 50th St.
New York, NY 10022       (212)751-2600
**Concern(s):** environment; activism. **Date Publ.:** 1990. **Publisher:** Alfred A. Knopf, Inc.. **Contact(s):** Will Steger.

**E ◆ Scarcity and Growth Reconsidered**
Resources for the Future
1616 P St. NW
Washington, DC 20036  (202)328-5000
**Affiliation:** Resources for the Future. **Concern(s):** environment; demographics; natural resources; population growth; sustainability. **Contact(s):** V. Kerry Smith (Editor).

**✍ ◆ School's Out—Revised**
Ten Speed Press
Box 7123
Berkeley, CA 94707       (510)845-8414
**Concern(s):** education; feminism; childhood; day care. A completely revised and updated edition of the best-ever resource book for after school, weekends, and vacation time. Extensive resource USTS and bibliographies. **Est.:** 1970. **Publisher:** Ten Speed Press. **Fax:** (510)524-1052. (800)841-2665.

**S ◆ Science & Religion**
Greenhaven Press, Inc.
Box 289009
San Diego, CA 92128       (619)485-7424

**Concern(s):** spiritual; education; science; religious reform; faith. List of organizations providing information on the relationship between science and religion; publishers of related (limited circulation) periodicals. A collection of essays offering opposing viewpoints on the conflict between science and religious teachings. **Date Publ.:** 1988. **Publisher:** Greenhaven Press, Inc. **Contact(s):** Janelle Rohr (Editor). (800)231-5163.

**S ◆ Search for Security: The ACCESS Guide to Foundations in Peace, Security, and International Relations**
ACCESS: A Security Information Service
1730 M St. NW, #605
Washington, DC 20036  (202)785-6630
**Affiliation:** ACCESS: A Security Information Service. **Concern(s):** spiritual; peace; national security; international law; philanthropy; fundraising. 150+ foundations which have spent over $120 million in support of nearly 2,500 grants in the fields of peace, security, and international relations. Analysis of foundations by issues and activities funded, and region of concern; discussion of outlook and trends based on foundation interviews and extensive research. **Frequency:** Irregular. **Price:** $50/ea.+shipping. **Pages:** c190. **Date Publ.:** Fall 1989. **Contact(s):** Anne Allen (Editor).

**⊗ ◆ Seeds of Peace: A Catalog of Quotations**
New Society
Box 582
Santa Cruz, CA 95061
**Concern(s):** peace; media; arts; nonviolence; literature. An indexed and well-organized collection of more than 1,700 quotations on war and peace, nonviolence, and the quest for justice. It has 29 chapters, including sections on patriotism, waging war, the challenge to make peace, humor, bumper stickers, graffiti, and more. With pages tabbed for easy use, complete with index and detailed table of contents. It is an invaluable resource for speechmakers, sermon writers, and newsletter editors, as well as a terrific gift. Also fun to browse through. **Publisher:** New Society.

**H ◆ Self-Care and Self-Help Groups for the Elderly: A Directory**
Professional Management Associates
2209 Distribution Circle
Silver Spring, MD 20910(202)785-6630
**Affiliation:** National Institute on Aging Information Center. **Concern(s):** health; seniors; self-help. About 100 national self-care and self-help groups, professional organizations, government agencies, and other organizations with related programs for the elderly, their families, and health care professionals. Arranged alphabetically and indexed by subject. **Frequency:** Irregular. **Subscription:** Free, limited supply. **Pages:** c150. **Date Publ.:** Fall 1987.

**H ◆ Self-Help Organizations and Professional Practice**
National Association of Social Workers
7981 Eastern Ave.
Silver Spring, MD 20910(301)565-0333
**Affiliation:** National Association of Social Workers. **Concern(s):** health; self-help. Lists of self-help groups and organizations, support groups, and mutual aid groups, classified by size of staff, geographical territory served. Includes bibliography. **Price:** $16.95/ea.+$1.75 shipping. **Pages:** 370. **Contact(s):** Thomas J. Powell.

**H ◆ Self-Help Sourcebooks**
Self-Help Clearinghouse, Pocono Rd.
St. Clares-Riverside Medical Center
Denville, NJ 07834       (201)625-9565
**Affiliation:** Self-Help Clearinghouse. **Concern(s):** health; family; disabled; substance abuse; empowerment; psychology; self-help. 700+ national and selected self-help groups for addictions, disabilities, illnesses, parenting, and other stress-causing problems. Classified by subject with group name, etc. **Frequency:** Biennial. **Price:** $10/ea. **Pages:** 150. **Date Publ.:** Summer 1990. **Contact(s):** Edward J. Madara, Abigail Meese (Editors).

**H ◆ The Senior Citizen's Handbook: A Nuts and Bolts Approach to More Comfortable Living**
Price:/Stern/Sloan, Inc.
360 N. La Cienega Blvd.
Los Angeles, CA 90048  (310)657-6100
**Concern(s):** health; senior citizens. List of organizations that provide information on issues relevant to senior citizens. Data include organization name and address. **Price:** $9.95/ea. **Date Publ.:** 4/89. **Publisher:** Price/Stern/Sloan, Inc. **Contact(s):** Wesley J. Smith (Editor).

H ▸ **Senior Citizens Service Organizations Directory**
American Business Directories/Information Inc.
5711 S. 86th Circle
Omaha, NE 68127 (402)593-4600
**Concern(s):** health; seniors. 6,715 listings compiled from the Yellow pages nationwide, arranged geographically. **Frequency:** Annual. **Price:** $235/ea.; prepaid. **Publisher:** American Business Directories, Inc. **Fax:** (402)331-1505.

H ▸ **SER Network Directory**
SER-Jobs for Progress, Inc.
1355 River Bend Dr., #240
Dallas, TX 75247 (214)631-3999
**Affiliation:** SER-Jobs for Progress, Inc.. **Concern(s):** health; labor; justice; counseling; jobs; minority rights. Nearly 110 affiliated agencies of SER ("Service, Employment, Redevelopment") Jobs for Progress, Inc., an organization of Hispanics that provides job preparation and training, adult basic education, counseling, etc. Arranged geographically with organization name, etc. **Frequency:** Annual. **Subscription:** Free. **Pages:** c30. **Date Publ.:** 4/91. **Fax:** (214)630-0132. **Contact(s):** Allison Schwartz (Editor).

J ▸ **Sex Law: A Legal Sourcebook on Critical Sexual Issues for the Non-Lawyer**
McFarland & Company, Inc.
Box 611
Jefferson, NC 28640
**Concern(s):** justice; feminism; sexism; pro-choice; equal rights; gay/lesbian. "A welcome, lucid vade mecum to the body of US law...[The author] doesn't say that he has fashioned a real godsend for anyone interested in sex law. But, in fact, he has"—Booklist;"addresses such topics as abortion," workplace sexual harassment, "AIDS, surrogate motherhood, paternity, and the rights of lesbians and gays"—Library Journal. Leading judicial precedents on these subjects are discussed and many citations to case and statutory authority are supplied to assist the reader... **Other Resources:** Includes references and index. **Pages:** 175. **Contact(s):** Scott E. Friedman (Author).

✍ ▸ **Sexual Abuse Prevention Education: An Annotated Bibliography**
c/o Network Publications
1700 Mission St. #203
Santa Cruz, CA 95061 (408)438-4060
**Affiliation:** Illusion Theater. **Concern(s):** education; family; feminism; media; health; child abuse; childhood; rape/sexual abuse; theater; AIDS; psychology. List of almost 50 organizations and consultants of help in establishing child sexual abuse prevention programs, and publishers or distributors of films, filmstrips, and videocasettes used in teaching prevention techniques or coping strategies. Guidelines and advice for establishing child sexual abuse prevention programs, information on interpersonal violence and HIV/AIDS prevention education, and listings of workshops and bibliographies on sexual health. Classified by type of program. **Other Resources:** Also publishes an excellent booklet guide, CHILD SEXUAL ABUSE PREVENTION: HOW TO TAKE THE FIRST STEPS. **Frequency:** Irregular. **Price:** $9.95/ea. **Date Publ.:** 1990. **Contact(s):** Kay Clark (Editor). (612)339-4944. **Other:** Illusion Theater, 528 Hennepin Ave. #704, Minneapolis, MN 55403.

♥ ▸ **Sexual Assault and Child Abuse: A National Directory of Victim Services and Prevention Programs**
Oryx Press
2214 N. Central at Encanto
Phoenix, AZ 85004 (602)254-6156
**Concern(s):** family; child abuse; victims' rights; rape/sexual abuse. **Price:** $55/ea. **Pages:** c305. **Date Publ.:** 7/89. **Publisher:** Oryx Press. **Fax:** (602)253-2741. **Contact(s):** Linda Webster (Editor). (800)457-6799.

U ▸ **Shading Our Cities, A Resource Guide For Urban Community Forests Communities**
c/o Island Press
Box 7
Covelo, CA 95428 (800)828-1302
**Affiliation:** American Forestry Association. **Concern(s):** urban; environment; energy; health; forests; beautification; planning; sustainability; air pollution. The first handbook to help neighborhood groups, local officials, and planners develop urban forestry projects, not only to beautify their cities, but also to help reduce energy demand, improve air quality, protect water supplies, and contribute to healthier living conditions. **Price:** $19.95 paper; $34.95 cloth. **Date Publ.:** 1989. **Publisher:** Island Press. **Contact(s):** Gary Moll, Sarah Ebenreck (Editors).

$ ▸ **Shopping for a Better World: A Guide to Socially Responsible Supermarket Shopping**
c/o Council on Economic Priorities
30 Irving Place, 9th Fl.
New York, NY 10211 (212)420-1133
**Affiliation:** Council on Economic Priorities. **Concern(s):** economics; environment; alternative markets; green consumer. This quick and easy pocket guide rates the makers of over 1800 brand name products on such issues as: environmental record; weapons contracts; South Africa; nuclear power; animal testing; advancement of women and minorities, charitable giving, labor issues, and minority hiring. It allows you to cast your "economic vote" every time you shop. 1991 added 500 new products, expanded environmental section, workplace issues, consumer 800 numbers, and larger type with an easier format. **Other Resources:** Publishes the BETTER WORLD INVESTMENT GUIDE also. Nonprofit. **Est.:** 1989. **Dues:** $25/yr. **Frequency:** Annual. **Subscription:** Membership. **Price:** $4.95/ea. **Bulk:** 40% off/24. **Pages:** 345. **Circ.:** 1,000M+. **Date Publ.:** 1/91. **Publisher:** Ballantine. **Fax:** (212)420-0988. **Contact(s):** Jacqueline Gelman (Marketing Director), Leslie Gottlied (Communications Director).

U ▸ **Signs For Main Street: Guidelines**
c/o Coalition for Scenic Beauty
216 7th St. SE
Washington, DC 20003 (202)546-1100
**Affiliation:** National Trust for Historic Preservation. **Concern(s):** urban; environment; planning; preservation; beautification. **Date Publ.:** 1987. **Contact(s):** Norman Mintz (Author).

$ ▸ **Social Services Organization**
American Business Directories/Information, Inc.
5711 S. 86th Circle
Omaha, NE 68127 (402)593-4600
**Concern(s):** economics; urban; education; health; inner city; public health. 47,830 listings arranged geographically by name and derived from the "Yellow Pages." **Other Resources:** Regional editions available: Eastern, $865; Western, $535. **Frequency:** Annual. **Subscription:** $1,295 prepaid. **Publisher:** NY Public Library. **Other Formats:** Magnetic tape, diskette. 3x5 cards. **E-Network:** Online Information Network. **Fax:** (402)331-1505.

✍ ▸ **The Social Studies School Service Catalog**
10200 Jefferson Blvd., #171
Box 802
Culver City, CA 90232
**Concern(s):** education; justice; diversity.

$ ▸ **Socially Responsible Buyer's Guide**
Covenant Fund; c/o Donald Pelz
2406 Geddes Ave.
Ann Arbor, MI 48104
**Affiliation:** Sane/Freeze; INFACT; Covenant Fund. **Concern(s):** economics; socially-responsible investing; alternative markets. **Publisher:** Covenant to End War. **Contact(s):** Donald Pelz.

$ ▸ **Socially Responsible Financial Planning Guide**
c/o Co-op America
2100 M St. NW, #403
Washington, DC 20063 (202)872-5307
**Affiliation:** Co-op America. **Concern(s):** economics; environment; justice; politics; socially-responsible investing; green consumer. This guide shows how to get involved in making financial decisions that are "values-added" and meet financial needs and goals, and to help people understand the basics of the fast-growing socially responsible investing movement. Concerns are: Environmental, community economic development, housing projects, worker-owned businesses, fair employment practices, and no- war related industries. **Frequency:** Annual. **Price:** $5/ea. **Date Publ.:** 1991. (800)424-COOP. **Contact(s):** Cindy Mitlo (Editor).

✍ ▸ **Society for Research in Child Development**
c/o University of Chicago Press
5720 Woodlawn Ave.
Chicago, IL 60637 (312)702-7470
**Concern(s):** education; health; justice; family; childhood; children. 4,300 anthropologists, educators, nurses, pediatricians, psychiatrists, psychologists, sociologists, statisticians. Arranged alphabetically by name with affiliation, address, phone, and highest degree. **Frequency:** Irregular. **Price:** $10/ea. **Pages:** 260. **Date Publ.:** 1990. **Publisher:** University of Chicago Press. **Contact(s):** Barbara Kahn (Editor).

✈ ▸ **Soft Paths**
Stackpole Books
Cameron & Keller Sts.
Harrisburg, PA 17105
**Affiliation:** American Camping Association. **Concern(s):** education; environment; recreation; travel. **Publisher:** Stackpole Books. **Contact(s):** Bruce E. Matthews.

✪ ▸ **Solar Electricity Today**
2303 Cedres Circle
Santa Fe, NM 87505 (505)473-1067
**Concern(s):** energy; economics; solar; alternative markets. "A directory of info, dealers, mail order shops, and manufacturers of PV and DC related equipment." The 4-issue subscription includes S.E.T. plus 3 issues on general PV Business News and how-to-do-it info. **Est.:** 1980. **Frequency:** 4/yr. **Date Publ.:** Directory published every May. **Labels:** 75. **Contact(s):** Paul Wilkins (Owner).

✪ ▸ **Solar Energy Applications**
Directory of the US Photovoltaic Industry
777 N. Capitol St. NE, #805
Washington, DC 20002 (703)524-6100
**Affiliation:** Solar Energy Industries Association. **Concern(s):** energy; solar. This revision of our industry directory reflects the changes that have occurred since our '87 publication. Many of the applications and companies represented then are still included here. But many firms have been added who have acquired the necessary equipment, knowledge, and skills to meet the growing demand of communities worldwide that can benefit from using photovoltaic technology. The photovoltaic's industry's annual grows rapidly due to the creativity and quality of companies listed here. **Est.:** 1987. **Fax:** (202)408-8536. **Contact(s):** Scott Sklar (Publisher), Jeanne Little (202)408-0660.

✪ ▸ **Solar Energy Education Directory**
US Government Printing Office
Superintendent of Documents
Washington, DC 20402 (202)783-3238
**Concern(s):** energy; education; solar. **Publisher:** US Government Printing Office.

E ▸ **Solid Waste Action Guide Book**
Citizens' Clearinghouse on Hazardous Waste
Box 926
Arlington, VA 22216
**Affiliation:** Citizens' Clearinghouse on Hazardous Waste. **Concern(s):** environment; recycling.

E ▸ **Solid Waste Education Recycling Directory**
c/o Island Press
Box 7
Covelo, CA 95428 (202)232-7933
**Concern(s):** environment; recycling; waste management. Summarizes recycling education curricula for each state, covering all levels, K-12. Provides names, addresses, phone numbers, information about the availability of materials, how you can get them, and how much they cost. This book will interest environmental agencies, teachers, solid waste professionals, state boards of education, city managers and planners. Teresa Jones, Edward J. Calabrese, Charles E. Gilbert, and Alvin E. Winder (Authors). **Price:** $57/paper. **Pages:** 109. **Date Publ.:** 1990. **Publisher:** Lewis Publishers. Order: (800)828-1302.

E ▸ **The Solid Waste Handbook**
John Wiley & Sons
605 3rd Ave.
New York, NY 10158 (212)850-6000
**Concern(s):** environment; recycling. **Date Publ.:** 1986. **Publisher:** John Wiley and Sons. **Contact(s):** William D. Robinson (Editor).

♥ ▸ **Solo Parenting: Your Essential Guide**
New American Library
120 Woodbine St.
Bergenfield, NJ 07621
**Concern(s):** family. List of resources intended to aid the single parent. A discussion of single parent concerns, including concerns about money, child care, career, and social life. **Price:** $4.50/ea. **Publisher:** New American Library. **Contact(s):** Kathleen McCoy.

P ▸ **SourceBook: Guide to Clubs, Groups, Associations, and Organizations**
SourceBook Division; Bernardo Press
16496 Bernardo Center Dr., #207
San Diego, CA 92128 (619)451-3790
**Concern(s):** politics; community/grassroots organizing; volunteers; networking. Group of franchised, common-format loose-leaf directories for numerous cities covering voluntary membership groups of all kinds; includes both strictly local organizations and local chapters or branches of regional or national organizations that have regular, sit-down meetings with speakers. Editions for Los Angeles, Sacramento, and San Diego, Calif.; Denver, CO; and Phoenix, AZ are available. Classified by type of group and area of interest; indexed geographically and alphabetically. **Other Resources:** Some prices as follows—$121.17/AZ & San Diego; $89.97/L.A.; $240/Denver; $87/Sacramento. **Frequency:** 4/yr. **Pages:** c300-500. **Publisher:** Source-

Book Division; Bernardo Press. **Contact(s):** Karen Alvarado, Judith Michaels,, Beverly Zirkle, Lynn Kelly (Editors).

### Sources of Financial Aid Available to American Indian Students
Indian Resource Development (IRD)
Box 30003; Dept. 31RD
Las Cruces, NM 88003   (505)646-1347

**Affiliation:** Indian Resource Development (IRD). **Concern(s):** education; justice; students; Native Americans. About 40 government agencies, private organizations, colleges and universities and other groups offering financial aid or work experience opportunities for North American Indian college students. Classified by type of student with organization or institute name, etc. **Other Resources:** Microfiche from ERIC Document Reproduction Service, Computer Mircofilm Corp., 3900 Wheeler Ave., Alexandria, VA 22304 (703) 823-0500; 85 cents. **Frequency:** Annual. **Price:** $3/ea. **Pages:** c50. **Date Publ.:** 1/90. **Other Formats:** Microfiche from ERIC Document Reproduction Service, Computer Mircofilm Corp., 3900 Wheeler Ave., Alexandria, VA 22304 (703) 823-0500; 85 cents. **Contact(s):** Roxie June, Hubert Mirabel (Editors).

### South Grassroots Peace Directory
ACCESS: A Security Information Service
1730 M St. NW, #605
Washington, DC 20036   (202)785-6630

**Affiliation:** ACCESS: A Security Information Service. **Concern(s):** peace; national security; activism; grassroots organizing; networking. National, regional, and local groups in the southeastern states working for peace, disarmament, and international security. Arranged geographically with indexes by organization name, etc. **Other Resources:** Mailing labels available to nonprofit organizations, $50 per thousand, one time use, $20 minimum per order, plus $15-$50 for specialized searches. **Frequency:** Biennial. **Pages:** 200. **Date Publ.:** Spring 1991. **Contact(s):** Phyllis Emigh (Information Manager).

### Southwest Grassroots Peace Directory
ACCESS: A Security Information Service
1730 M St. NW, #605
Washington, DC 20036   (202)785-6630

**Affiliation:** ACCESS: A Security Information Service. **Concern(s):** peace; national security; activism; grassroots organizing; networking. National, regional, and local groups in Arizona, New Mexico, Oklahoma, and Texas working for peace, disarmament, and international security. Arranged geographically and indexed by organization name, etc. **Other Resources:** Mailing labels available to nonprofit organizations, $50 per thousand, one time use, $20 minimum per order, plus $15-$50 for specialized searches. **Frequency:** Biennial. **Pages:** c100. **Date Publ.:** Spring 1991. **Contact(s):** Phyllis Emigh (Information Manager).

### The Special Child: A Source Book for Parents of Children with Developmental Disabilities
Paul H. Brookes Publishing Co.
Box 10624
Baltimore, MD 21285   (301)337-9580

**Concern(s):** health; disabled. List of nearly 100 organizations which can offer help to parents of children who are developmentally disabled. Arranged alphabetically with organization name, address, phone, and services offered. Descriptions of disabilities and possible treatments. **Price:** $22/ea. **Date Publ.:** 1988. **Publisher:** Paul H. Brookes Publishing Co. **Fax:** (301)337-8539. **Contact(s):** Siegfried M. Pueschel, Leslie E. Weidenman, James C. Bernier (Authors). (800)638-3775.

### Special Recreation Compendium of 1,500 Resources for People with Disabilities
Special Recreation Digest
362 Koser Ave.
Iowa City, IA 52246-3038   (319)337-7578

**Concern(s):** health; disabled. 1,500+ associations, national and state government agencies, companies, colleges and universities, and other contacts for 40 recreation activities for the disabled, including amusement and theme parks, toll-free phone services, suppliers of adapted equipment, special products, rehabilitation therapies, recreation vehicles, sports organizations, travel agencies, and wildlife resource agencies; worldwide coverage. Classified by type with organization name, address, phone and key contact. **Other Resources:** Formerly, SPECIAL RECREATION COMPENDIUM OF 1,500 RESOURCES FOR DISABLED PEOPLE. **Frequency:** Biennial. **Price:** $49.95/ea., postpaid. **Pages:** 500. **Publisher:** Special Recreation Digest. **Contact(s):** John A. Nesbitt (Editor).

### Spices of Life: The Well-Being Handbook For Older Americans
Public Citizen
2000 P St. NW, #605
Washington, DC 20036-0757   (202)833-3000

**Affiliation:** Public Citizen. **Concern(s):** health; seniors. **Contact(s):** Ruth Fort.

### Spinal Network: The Total Resource for the Wheelchair Community
Spinal Associates; Box 4162
1911 11th St., No. 307
Boulder, CO 80306   (303)449-5421

**Affiliation:** Spinal Associates. **Concern(s):** health; disabled. Principal content is articles describing different activities available to the disabled, and personal accounts telling how some people have handled challenges they faced; many articles are followed by lists of pertinent resource organizations and facilities. Nearly 100 national-resource organizations alphabetically arranged, some are geographical. **Date Publ.:** 1988. **Contact(s):** Sam Maddox (Editor).

### SproutChart/SproutGuide
Box 62
Ashland, OR 97570   (503)488-2326

**Concern(s):** health; nutrition; vegetarian. Sproutchart, including Sproutguide. 30,000 charts in circulation, new 4th edition. Side 1: How to sprout 39 seeds, beans, grains; Side 2: mixing them in 25 combinations. Includes suggested uses, tips, failure, alternatives, mail order resources. Sproutguide Booklet gives details on all types of sprouting. **Est.:** 1982. **Frequency:** 2/yr. **Price:** $7.90/ea. **Bulk:** 40% off/24. **Pages:** 8. **Circ.:** 30M. **Publisher:** Sprouting Publications. **Contact(s):** Michael Linden (Owner).

### Starting Early: A Guide to Federal Resources in Maternal and Child Health
8th & R St. NW
Washington, DC 20057   (202)625-8400

**Affiliation:** National Center for Education in Maternal and Child Health. **Concern(s):** family; health; birth; child care. Federal agencies and federally supported organizations offering 500+ print and non-print resources (posters, audiovisual materials, software) on prenatal, infant, and adolescent health; state and regional maternal and child health contacts; regional services networks. Agencies are classified by subject of their focus, regional contacts are geographical. **Frequency:** Irregular. **Subscription:** Free. **Pages:** 170. **Date Publ.:** 11/88.

### The State of the Earth Atlas
Zephyr Press
3316 N. Chapel Ave., Box 13448-C, Dept.
Tuscon, AZ 85732-3448 (602)322-5090

**Concern(s):** environment; education; demographics; childhood; students; population growth. Here is a concise survey of the environment through 37 full-color international maps. This important resource reveals at a glance how civilization impacts on the environment. Grades 4-12. **Pages:** 127. **Publisher:** Simon & Schuster. **Contact(s):** Joni Seager (Editor).

### State of the States
Renew America
1400 16th St. NW, #710
Washington, DC 20036   (202)232-2252

**Affiliation:** Renew America. **Concern(s):** energy; environment; appropriate technology. Annual report, first publishes in 1987, providing an easily understood report card on current developments in environmental protection across all 50 states. It ranks the performance of each state's policies and programs in dealing with five or six environmental problems. Using data from state and federal agriculture, university and private organizations, the report traces programs in addressing the issues, highlights innovative programs, and identifies needs for improvement.

### State of the World
Worldwatch Institute
1776 Massachusetts Ave. NW
Washington, DC 20036   (202)452-1999

**Affiliation:** Worldwatch Institute. **Concern(s):** environment. A basic desktop guide documenting Earth's "vital signs," a comprehensive evaluation of the threats confronting the biosphere and a battle plan for what individuals can do. Trend tracking and documentation of our (mis)use of land, air, agriculture, water, transportation and people resources, this "annual physical" of the planet is the most complete and up-to-date guide to the world's resources and how they are being managed. It is translated into 11 languages. Contains index and footnotes. **Frequency:** Annual. **Price:** $9.95 paper; $12.95 hardback. **Publisher:** W.W. Norton & Co. **Contact(s):** Lester Brown,

Linda Stark (Editors).

### State of the World Atlas
Simon & Schuster
1230 Avenue of the Americas
New York, NY 10020

**Affiliation:** Pluto Press Project. **Concern(s):** Third World; hunger; development. **Publisher:** Simon & Schuster. **Contact(s):** Michael Kidron, Michael Segal.

### State Youth Employment Initiatives: A Resource Guide and Framework for Action
Children's Defense Fund
122 C St. NW
Washington, DC 20001   (202)628-8787

**Affiliation:** Children's Defense Fund. **Concern(s):** justice; labor; urban; economics; education; children; poverty; jobs; unemployment; youth. **Contact(s):** Gary Lacy, Clifford Johnson.

### Strangers in Their Own Country: A Curriculum Guide on South Africa
Africa World Press
Box 1892
Trenton, NJ 08607

**Concern(s):** Third World; education; South Africa. **Publisher:** Africa World Press. **Contact(s):** William Begelow.

### Strategy Workbook
Institute for International Cooperation and Development
Box 705
Amherst, MA 01004

**Affiliation:** Institute for Peace and International Security. **Concern(s):** peace; grassroots organizing; activism; national security; world order; international law. A useful tool for translating Community Security ideas into local organizing strategies. Divided into 4 modules, the workbook is ideal for use by peace and justice groups of all sizes.

### The Student Conservation Association Catalog
Box 550
Charlestown, NH 03603 (603)826-4301

**Affiliation:** Student Conservation Association, Inc.. **Concern(s):** education; environment; volunteers; travel. Volunteer jobs listings for positions across the US for stewardship of our natural lands. Approximately 1400 openings per year. Nonprofit. **Est.:** 1957. **Price:** $15+/yr. **Frequency:** 2/yr. **Subscription:** Free. **Fax:** (603)826-7755. **Contact(s):** Wallace Eaton (Public Relations Director).

### Substance Abuse Training Program
S. University
6400 Press Dr.
New Orleans, LA 70126

**Concern(s):** health; substance abuse. **Contact(s):** Tom Lief.

### Suburban Newspapers of America - Membership Directory
Suburban Newspapers of America
111 E. Wacker Dr., #600
Chicago, IL 60601   (312)644-6610

**Concern(s):** media; press. About 200 publishers of community-oriented newspapers in suburban and urban areas, and suppliers of products and services. Newspapers are arranged geographically; suppliers, alphabetically. **Frequency:** Annual. **Price:** $60/ea. **Pages:** c100. **Circ.:** 1M. **Date Publ.:** 1/91. **Publisher:** Suburban Newspapers of America. **Labels:** 100. **Fax:** (312)565-4658. **Contact(s):** Larry Fleischman (Public Relations Manager).

### Suggestions for Organizers
Center for Economic Conversion
222-C View St.
Mountain View, CA 94041

**Affiliation:** Center for Economic Conversion. **Concern(s):** peace; economics; economic conversion; peace dividend; activism.

### Sunny Von Bulow National Victim Advocacy Center
307 W. 7th St., #1001
Fort Worth, TX 76102

**Concern(s):** feminism; justice; victims' rights.

### Sustainable Energy
Renew America
1400 16th St. NW, #710
Washington, DC 20036   (202)232-2252

**Affiliation:** Renew America. **Concern(s):** environment; energy; resource management. This report outlines the current status and future potential for energy efficiency in transportation, buildings, and industry, and for development of renewable energy technologies. The report describes how sustainable energy policies can overcome institutional and market barriers and bring about a 50% reduction in global warming. **Frequency:** Annual. **Price:** $10/ea. **Bulk:** $5ea/ 24. **Pages:** 48. **Date Publ.:** 12/89. **Contact(s):** Rick Piltz (Deputy Director).

### ☙ ◆ Swords into Plowshares: Nonviolent Direct Action for Disarmament
Perennial Library, HarperCollins
10 E. 53rd St.
New York, NY 10022    (212)207-7655
**Concern(s):** peace; media; spiritual; nonviolence; anti-nuclear; disarmament; faith; activism; film. Lists of peace and disarmament groups, and audiovisual resources for the disarmament movement. Principal content is a discussion of antinuclear civil disobedience in a Christian context. **Price:** $7.95/ea. **Date Publ.:** 2/87. **Publisher:** Perennial Library, Harper Collins. **Contact(s):** Arthur J. Laffin, Anne Montgomery (Editors).

### ☼ ◆ SYNERJY - A Directory of Renewable Energy
Box 1854, Cathedral Station
New York, NY 10025    (212)865-9595
**Concern(s):** energy; renewables. Bibliographic directory that lists books, articles, patents, government publications, manufacturers, research groups and conferences in the areas of: solar, biomass, hydrogen, geothermal, water and wind energy as well as energy transfer and storage. **Frequency:** 2/yr. **Circ.:** 300. **Contact(s):** Jeff Twine (Publisher), Scottie Twine (Production Director). (212)865-9595.

### F ◆ T.A.P.P. Sources: A National Directory of Teenage Pregnancy Prevention
Women's Action Alliance
370 Lexington Ave.
New York, NY 10017    (212)532-8330
**Affiliation:** Women's Action Alliance. **Concern(s):** feminism; family planning. About 600 teenage pregnancy prevention programs arranged geographically with program name, etc. **Price:** $29.95/ea. **Pages:** 560. **Date Publ.:** 1989. **Contact(s):** Dominique Treboux (Project Director). (800)537-7107.

### S ◆ Taft Foundation Reporter
The Taft Group; Gale Research Inc.
12300 Twinbrook Parkway, #450
Rockville, MD 20852    (301)816-0210
**Affiliation:** Taft Group. **Concern(s):** spiritual; philanthropy. Over 500 private philanthropic foundations with national and regional interests arranged alphabetically and indexed geographically, type of grant, recipient type, personal name, birthplace, and alma matter. **Other Resources:** The TAFT FOUNDATION INFORMATION SYSTEM and the TAFT CORPORATE INFORMATION SYSTEM are marketed together under title "BASIC II"; $627+$25 shipping. Updated monthly in FOUNDATION GIVING WATCH. **Frequency:** Annual. **Price:** $397/ea. + $15 shipping. **Pages:** c845. **Date Publ.:** 1/91. **Publisher:** Gale Research Inc.. **Fax:** (301)816-0811. **Contact(s):** Susan E. Elnicki (Editor). (800)888-TAFT.

### F ◆ Talking It Out: A Guide to Groups For Abused Women
The Seal Press
3131 Western Ave., #410
Seattle, WA 98121-1028
**Concern(s):** feminism; battered women. **Publisher:** Seal Press. **Contact(s):** K. Merriam, S. Coffman, G. McCarthy

### ✍ ◆ Tamiment Institute Library
70 Washington Square S.
New York, NY 10012    (212)998-2639
**Concern(s):** education; analysis; research; activism. The Library preserves the history of American labor and radicalism. Extensive holdings, including hundreds of progressive periodicals, are a valuable resource for contemporary activists and scholars. Sympathetic, knowledgeable staff will assist researchers, and advise individuals and organizations on identifying, preserving their historically valuable records. **Other Resources:** LIBRARY INFORMATION BULLETIN available. See LABOR HISTORY (periodicals). **Est.:** 1906. **Contact(s):** Peter Filardo, Dorothy Swanson (Archivists). (212)998-2639.

### ✍ ◆ Teacher's Resource Guide
Nuclear Information & Resource Service
1424 16 St. NW #601
Washington, DC 20036    (202)328-0002
**Affiliation:** Nuclear Information & Resource Service. **Concern(s):** education; peace; anti-nuclear; youth; students. Annotated listing of materials - films, books, videos, etc., suitable for high school classroom use on nuclear power and weapons.

### ✍ ◆ Teacher's Resource Guide, 17 Lessons on Current US Foreign Policy Issues for Secondary Social Studies Courses
Foreign Policy Association
729 7th Ave.
New York, NY 10019    (212)764-4050
**Affiliation:** Foreign Policy Association. **Concern(s):** education; politics; youth; students. **Contact(s):** M. E. Soley, B. Miller, J. S. Johnson

### ✈ ◆ Teachers Swap
Box 4130
Rocky Point, NY 11778
**Concern(s):** education; travel. Teachers swap homes in Germany, Austria, Canada, England, Thailand and the USA. The directory is arranged to help readers locate names, addresses and telephone numbers of teachers living in areas with good vacation facilities.

### A ◆ Tech and Tools Book: A Guide to Technologies Women Are Using Worldwide
International Women's Tribune Center
777 UN Plaza
New York, NY 10017    (212)687-8633
**Affiliation:** International Women's Tribune Center. **Concern(s):** agriculture; feminism; health; energy; nutrition; science. New and alternative technologies for agricultural, communications, health and sanitation, food, energy, and income-generation purposes. Classified by function with technology name, description, summary of strengths and weaknesses, names and addresses of organizations able to provide more information, user reports, and related publications. **Frequency:** Irregular. **Price:** $10/ea. **Pages:** 190. **Date Publ.:** 1988. **Fax:** (212)661-2704. **Contact(s):** Joanne Sandler, Ruby Sandhu (Editors).

### ✍ ◆ Thinking Globally...Acting Locally: A Citizen's Guide to Community Education on Global Issues
League of Women Voters
1730 M St. NW
Washington, DC 20036    (202)429-1965
**Affiliation:** League of Women Voters. **Concern(s):** education; environment; peace; politics; global understanding; voting; grassroots organizing. **Date Publ.:** 1988.

### H ◆ Third Opinion: An International Directory to Alternative Therapy Centers for the Treatment & Prevention of Cancer
Avery Publishing Group, Inc.
120 Old Broadway
Garden City Park, NY 11040    (516)741-2155
**Concern(s):** health; alternative consumer. 300+ alternative treatment cancer centers; international coverage. Classified by subject and indexed by center name, subject, and product/service. **Frequency:** Biennial. **Price:** $12.95/ea. **Pages:** 290. **Date Publ.:** Spring 1991. **Publisher:** Avery Publishing Group, Inc.. **Fax:** (516)742-1892. **Contact(s):** John M. Fink. (800)548-5757.

### S ◆ Third Sector Directory
Canadian Centre for Philanthropy
74 Victoria St., #920
Toronto, ON M5C 2A5 **Canada**
**Concern(s):** spiritual; philanthropy. About 4,000 fundraising charitable organizations in Canada. Arranged alphabetically and indexed by geography and activity. Send order to: Canadian Centre for Philanthropy, Box 116, Concord, ON L4k 1B2, Canada. **Frequency:** Annual. **Price:** $51.95/ea.

### T ◆ Third World Resource Directory
464 19th St.
Oakland, CA 94612-9761    (510)835-4692
**Affiliation:** Third World Resources/Data Center. **Concern(s):** Third World. For postage and handling, add $1.50 for North America and $3.00 for foreign air mail. Please, order from Third World Resources. **Price:** $19.95/ea. **Pages:** 304. **Date Publ.:** Spring 1984. **Publisher:** Orbis Books. **Other Formats:** Geonet, user **ID:** 'geo2:tfenton'. **E-Network:** Peacenet. **ID:** 'tfenton'. **Contact(s):** Thomas P. Fenton, Mary J. Heffron (Compilers/Editors). (510)536-1876.

### T ◆ Third World Resources Documentation Clearinghouse
Third World Resources
464 19th St.
Oakland, CA 94612-9761    (510)835-4692
**Affiliation:** Third World Resources/Data Center. **Concern(s):** Third World; media; press; film. The nation's most comprehensive, up-to-date, and accessible library collections of print resources on the full

range of Third World regions and issues. All audiovisual, organizational and print resources are kept on a computerized database. **Other Resources:** See Third World Resources under organizations. **Other Formats:** Geonet ('Geo2:tfenton'). **E-Network:** PeaceNet. **ID:** 'tfenton'. **Contact(s):** Thomas P. Fenton, Mary J. Heffron (Compilers/ Editors). (510)536-1876.

### T ◆ Third World Struggles For Peace and Justice
464 19th St.
Oakland, CA 94612-9761    (510)835-4692
**Affiliation:** Third World Resources/Data Center. **Concern(s):** Third World; peace. For postage and handling, add $1.50 for North America and $3.00 for foreign air mail. Please, order from Third World Resources. **Price:** $12.95/ea. **Pages:** 160. **Date Publ.:** Fall 1990. **Publisher:** Orbis Books. **Other Formats:** Geonet, user **ID:** 'geo2:tfenton'. **E-Network:** Peacenet. **ID:** 'tfenton'. **Contact(s):** Thomas P. Fenton, Mary J. Heffron (Compilers/Editors). (510)536-1876.

### E ◆ Tips on How to Reduce Your Waste
Coalition for Recyclable Waste
Box 1091
Absecon, NJ 08201
**Affiliation:** Coalition for Recyclable Waste. **Concern(s):** environment; recycling. **Contact(s):** Ruth Lampi.

### $ ◆ To Celebrate: Reshaping Holidays and Rites of Passage
Alternate Celebrations Catalogue
5263 Bouldercrest Rd.
Ellenwood, GA 30049    (404)961-0102
**Concern(s):** economics; spiritual; transformation. Concerns ways of celebrating holidays more simply and less expensively by emphasizing noncommercial values. **Other Resources:** Former titles, THE ALTERNATE CATALOGUE (1978); and, ALTERNATE CELEBRATION CATALOGUE (1987). **Frequency:** Irregular. **Price:** $12.95/ea. **Pages:** 190. **Date Publ.:** 6/87. **Publisher:** Westview Press. **Contact(s):** Mike Thornberry (Director).

### ♥ ♥ ◆ Total Nutrition for Breast-Feeding Mothers
Little, Brown & Company, Inc.
34 Beacon St.
Boston, MA 02108    (617)227-0730
**Concern(s):** family; feminism; health; birth; nutrition. List of about 25 resources for nursing mothers, such as organizations, books, and magazines, classified by subject with organization name, address, and phone. Principal content is information on nutrition, vitamins, recipes, and breast feeding in general. **Price:** $9.70/ea. **Date Publ.:** 7/86. **Publisher:** Little, Brown & Company, Inc. **Contact(s):** Betty and Si Kamen.

### ☙ ◆ Towards a Nuclear Free Future: A Guide to Organizing a Local Nuclear Free Zone Campaign
Mobilization for Survival
45 John St., #811
New York, NY 10038
**Affiliation:** Mobilization for Survival. **Concern(s):** peace; energy; Third World; environment; justice; anti-nuclear.

### E ◆ The Toxic 500
National Wildlife Federation
1400 16th St. NW
Washington, DC 20036    (800)432-6564
**Affiliation:** National Wildlife Federation. **Concern(s):** environment; hazardous/toxic wastes. Lists the top 500 polluters. **Frequency:** Annual.

### J ◆ Toxic Wastes and Race in the US
UCC Commission for Racial Justice
5113 Georgia Ave. NW
Washington, DC 20011    (202)291-1593
**Affiliation:** United Church of Christ. **Concern(s):** justice; environment; racism; discrimination; hazardous/toxic waste. A National Report on the Racial and Socio-economic Characteristics of Communities with Hazardous Waste Sites.

### ✈ ◆ Transitions Abroad: Educational Travel Directory
18 Hulst Rd
Amherst, MA 01002    (413)256-0373
**Concern(s):** education; travel. The annual "Educational Travel Directory" (July, included with subscription to Transitions Abroad) provides detailed descriptions - by country and subject - of the best current information on work, study, living, educational and socially responsible travel outside the US Activists, students, workers and others wishing to experience non-tourist travel can locate a trip of interest. **Other Resources:** See TRANSITIONS ABROAD newsmagazine and vari-

ous international resource guides. **Est.:** 1977. **Price:** Included with magazine subscription. **Circ.:** 20M. **Publisher:** Transitions Publishing. **Contact(s):** Clay Hubbs, Ph.D. (Editor/Publisher), Lisa Aciukewicz (Assistant).

**T ▸ Transnational Corporations and Labor: A Directory of Resources**
464 19th St.
Oakland, CA 94612-9761 (510)835-4692
**Affiliation:** Third World Resources/Data Center. **Concern(s):** Third World; corporate responsibility. For postage and handling, add $1.50 for North America and $3.00 for foreign air mail. Please, order from Third World Resources. **Price:** $12.95/ea. **Pages:** 160. **Date Publ.:** Fall 1989. **Publisher:** Orbis Books. **Other Formats:** Geonet, user **ID:** 'geo2:tfenton'. **E-Network:** Peacenet. **ID:** 'tfenton'. **Contact(s):** Thomas P. Fenton, Mary J. Heffron (Compilers/Editors). (510)536-1876.

**H ▸ Traveler's Guide to Healing Centers and Retreats in North America**
John Muir Publications
Box 613
Santa Fe, NM 87504-0613 (505)982-4078
**Concern(s):** health; holism. About 750 holistic and nondenominational institutions in the US and Canada offering programs for stress relief and other types of "healing." Arranged geographically with name, etc. Regional sections include map with location of the centers; glossary of techniques and therapies offered. **Price:** $11.95/ea. **Pages:** c220. **Date Publ.:** 1989. **Publisher:** W.W. Norton & Co., Inc.[(212)354-5500] **Contact(s):** Martine Rudee, Jonathan Blease (Authors).

**✍ ▸ TRF Food Web Game**
F Sandford Biology Dept.
Coe College
Cedar Rapids, IA 52402 (319)399-8576
**Concern(s):** education; demographics; Third World; environment; agriculture; hunger; childhood; hunger. A guide for grades 3-6 where students play the part of a plant or animal (34 possible roles). It comes with teacher's instructions, fact sheets, sample food webs and "what if" web damaging situations.

**A ▸ TRIP (The Resources of International Permaculture)**
7781 Lenox St.
Jacksonville, FL 32221
**Affiliation:** Yankee Permaculture. **Concern(s):** agriculture; environment; permaculture; sustainability. Includes: Permaculture publications, services and centers; Bioregioanal groups; Green/Green politics; Remineralization; Alternative Economics; Sustainable Food Systems; Urban Sustainability; Forest Tree Concerns; Ecology Earth Defense; Earth Spirituality; Appropriate Technology; Genetic Resources and other related activities. Cross-referencing included for assistance in locating resources. Over 1,000 listings. **Price:** $15/ea.+P&H. **Bulk:** 20% off/24. **Pages:** 50. **Circ.:** 1M. **Date Publ.:** 6/89; 1990. **Contact(s):** Dan Hemenway (Editor/Publisher).

**A ▸ Truth in Produce**
c/o Americans for Safe Food
1875 Connecticut Ave. NW
Washington, DC 20036 (202)332-9110
**Affiliation:** Maine Organic Farmers & Gardeners Association. **Concern(s):** agriculture; health; organic; consumer protection; alternative consumer. A legislative kit used by MOFGA in its successful labeling law campaign.

**✪ ▸ Uncovering the Nuclear Industry: A Research Guide**
Mobilization for Survival
45 John St., #811
New York, NY 10038
**Affiliation:** Mobilization for Survival. **Concern(s):** energy; peace; environment; anti-nuclear.

**E ▸ Understanding Environmental Administration and Law**
c/o Island Press
Box 7
Covelo, CA 95428 (202)232-7933
**Concern(s):** environment; politics; lobbying; grassroots organizing. Designed specifically for those who need a thorough, but rapid understanding of environmental law. Makes the law more accessible for mid-level managers and can increase the effectiveness for citizens, special interest groups, and others who work with environmental law. Bibliography, case lists, legislation lists, glossary, index. **Price:** $21.95 paper; $34.95 cloth. **Pages:** 224. **Date Publ.:** 1991. **Publisher:** Island Press. Order: (800)828-1302. **Contact(s):** Susan J. Buck, Ph.D. (Author).

**✌ ▸ Understanding Nuclear Weapons and Arms Control: A Guide to the Issues**
Pergamon-Brassey
8000 Westpark Dr., #400
McLean, VA 22101
**Concern(s):** peace; anti-nuclear; disarmament. **Publisher:** Pergamon-Brassey. **Contact(s):** T. K. Mayers.

**♿ ▸ Understanding the Law**
Center on Human Policy
Box 127, University Station
Syracuse, NY 13210
**Affiliation:** Center on Human Policy. **Concern(s):** health; justice; education; disability rights; disabled. Understanding the Law is an advocate's guide to the law and developmental disabilities. This handbook includes an excellent and straightforward glossary of legal terms, a chapter of how the legal system is set up and how it works, the process of litigation, a layperson's guide to researching the law, and hints on how to build a case. **Price:** $4.25/ea. **Publisher:** Human Policy Press. **Office:** 200 Huntington Hall, University Station Syracuse, NY 13244. **Contact(s):** Stephen J. Taylor, Julie Racino (Coauthors).

**E ▸ The United Nations List of National Parks and Protected Areas**
c/o Island Press
Box 7
Covelo, CA 95428 (202)232-7933
**Affiliation:** World Conservation Monitoring Centre/IUCN Commission on National Parks and Protected Areas. **Concern(s):** environment; wildlife/endangered species; forests; wetlands; conservation; preservation. An authoritative, indispensable list of national parks and other protected areas. Includes special lists of World Heritage sites, biosphere reserves, and wetlands of international importance. Tables, graphs, maps. **Price:** $25/paper. **Pages:** 284. **Date Publ.:** 1990. **Publisher:** IUCN. Order: (800)828-1302.

**D ▸ United States Committee for Refugees - Directory**
1025 Vermont Ave. NW, #920
Washington, DC 20005 (202)347-3507
**Affiliation:** United States Committee for Refugees. **Concern(s):** demographics; refugees; immigration. List of approximately 80 national organizations and local agencies in the US concerned with refugee resettlement programs and other refugee concerns. Country-by-country review of worldwide refugee situation, statistics, US policy toward refugees, and programs to assist them in the US and overseas; bibliography. Data include organization or agency name, address, and purpose. **Frequency:** Annual. **Price:** $8/ea. **Date Publ.:** 3/91.

**P ▸ The United States Congress Handbook**
Box 566
McLean, VA 22101
**Concern(s):** politics. Pictorial directory listing members of Congress with bibliographies, committee membership, office address, and phone numbers.

**✌ ▸ The United States in Search of Enemies**
WECAN Publishers
504 W. 24th, #79
Austin, TX 78705
**Concern(s):** peace; politics; national security; government accountability; CIA. An annotated national security reading list by former CIA operative, John Stockwell, who until recently has been banned from speaking in the US. Includes an essay on national and world security issues plus succinct reviews of the best 120 books on national security and world security issues. **Other Resources:** For speaking engagements contact—K & S Speakers, 875 Main St. Cambridge, MA 02139; (617)876-8090. Videos and transcripts available. **Price:** $7/ea.. **Contact(s):** John Stockwell (Author).

**H ▸ Unity-and-Diversity World Directory**
Unity-and-Diversity World Council, Inc.
1010 S. Flower St., #500
Los Angeles, CA 90015 (310)839-0758
**Affiliation:** Unity-and-Diversity World Council, Inc.. **Concern(s):** health; peace; spiritual; transformation; holism. Several hundred organizations and individuals of primarily holistic, spiritual, scientific, or peace and justice orientation working to "foster the emergence of a new universal person and civilization based on unity-and-diversity among all peoples." Classified by subject and indexed alphabetically. Data include organization or individual name, address, phone, purpose, activities. **Other Resources:** Formerly, INTERNATIONAL CO-OPERATION COUNCIL DIRECTORY; PLANETARY GUIDE TO COOPERATING ORGANIZATIONS; DIRECTORY FOR A NEW WORLD (1986). SPECTRUM - UNITY-AND-DIVERSITY WORLD DIRECTORY ISSUE (1990). **Frequency:** Annual. **Price:** $8/ea. **Labels:** 60. **Contact(s):** Louis K. Acheson (Editor).

**♿ ▸ The Unrestrictive Environment**
Center on Human Policy
Box 127, University Station
Syracuse, NY 13210
**Affiliation:** Center on Human Policy. **Concern(s):** health; justice; education; disability rights; disabled. This book outlines some basic principles of community integration, critiques the "continuum concept," describes homes and support services for adults and children with severe disabilities, discusses integrated vocational services, looks at what makes community integration work, and outlines some of the emerging controversies in community integration. An appendix outlines some strategies and resources to aid in day-to-day problem solving in integrating severely disabled into the community. **Price:** $4.25/ea. **Publisher:** Human Policy Press. **Office:** 200 Huntington Hall, University Station Syracuse, NY 13244. **Contact(s):** Steven J. Taylor, Douglas Biklen (Co-editors).

**✌ ▸ Upper Midwest Grassroots Peace Directory**
ACCESS: A Security Information Service
1730 M St. NW, #605
Washington, DC 20036 (202)785-6630
**Affiliation:** ACCESS: A Security Information Service. **Concern(s):** peace; national security; activism; grassroots organizing; networking. National, regional, and local groups in Michigan, Minnesota, and Wisconsin working for peace, disarmament, and international security. Arranged geographically and indexed by organization name, primary issue of concern, resources, constituency served, congressional district, and ZIP code. Published in cooperation with the Topsfield Foundation, Inc. **Other Resources:** Mailing labels available to non-profit organizations, $50 per thousand, one time use, $20 minimum per order, plus $15-$50 for specialized searches. **Frequency:** Biennial. **Pages:** c165. **Date Publ.:** Spring 1990.

**J ▸ Using the Freedom of Information Act, A Step by Step Guide**
ACLU
122 Maryland Ave NE
Washington, DC 20002 (202)544-1681
**Affiliation:** American Civil Liberties Union. **Concern(s):** justice; civil liberties.

**M ▸ Utne Reader Subject Index**
Fawkes Building
1624 Harmon Pl.
Minneapolis, MN 55403
**Concern(s):** media; press. "Utne Reader has explored thousands of diverse publications, selected an eclectic mix of articles (the best of the alternative press), and packaged them neatly in each issue. Now, we've organized this wealth of information in an index covering the first six years, 36 issues. Topics range from activism, health and the environment to work, women's issues and spirituality." **Price:** $10/ea. **Publisher:** Fawkes Building.

**H ▸ Vegetarian Health Directory**
21st Century Publications
401 N. 4th St.
Fairfield, IA 52556
**Concern(s):** health; spiritual; vegetarian; nutrition. **Publisher:** 21st Century Publications.

**H ▸ Vegetarian Voice - Local Vegetarian Organizations Section**
North American Vegetarian Society
Box 72
Dolgeville, NY 13329 (518)568-7970
**Affiliation:** North American Vegetarian Society. **Concern(s):** health; vegetarian; nutrition. About 100 affiliated vegetarian societies and information centers geographically arranged with a list of about 100 affiliated vegetarian societies and information centers. Categories include organization name, et al. **Frequency:** 4/yr. **Price:** $4/ea. **Contact(s):** Jennie Collura (Managing Editor).

**P ▸ The Voluntary Agencies Directory**
Bedford Square Press
26 Bedford Square
London, WC1B3HU England
**Concern(s):** politics; justice; grassroots organizing; volunteers; activism. 2,000+ organizations described in every field.

**✈ ▸ Volunteer Vacations**
Independent Publishers Group
814 N. Franklin St.
Chicago, IL 60610 (312)337-0747
**Concern(s):** education; volunteers; travel. Detailed accounts of 190+ organizations that sponsor 2,000+ expeditions for travelers wishing to combine adventure and personal growth with service to

others. Each entry lists projects locations, types, costs, and dates; tells how to apply; notes any required skills; describes work done by volunteers; and gives commentary. Five cross-referenced indexes help readers narrow their myriad options according to budget, available time, location, season of the year, and specific interests. Stories. **Other Resources:** Author publishes a newsletter, VOLUNTEER VACATIONS UPDATE, and had written many other useful books for the traveler. **Price:** $11.95/ea. **Pages:** 376. **Date Publ.:** 1991. **Publisher:** Chicago Review Press. **Fax:** (312)337-5985. **Order:** (800)888-4741. **Contact(s):** Bill McMillon (Author).

### ✈ ♦ Volunteer! The Comprehensive Guide to Voluntary Service in the US and Abroad.
Council on International Educational Exchange
205 E. 42nd St.; Information & Student Services
New York, NY 10017    (212)661-1414

**Affiliation:** Council on International Educational Exchange. **Concern(s):** education; Third World; volunteers; travel. About 200 organizations sponsoring voluntary service programs in the US and elsewhere. Arranged alphabetically and indexed by geography, skill, and organization/publication name. Data include organization name, address, description of program, prerequisites for participation, costs, skills involved, opportunities available for the disabled. **Frequency:** Biennial. **Price:** $6.95/ea.+$1 shipping. **Pages:** c180. **Date Publ.:** 1/90. **Fax:** (212)972-3231. **Contact(s):** Adrienne Downey (Editor).

### ☪ ♦ Waging Peace: A Handbook for the Struggle to Abolish Nuclear Weapons
Harper & Row
Ice House One #401, 151 Union St.
San Francisco, CA 94111-1299

**Concern(s):** peace; anti-nuclear; nonviolence; civil disobedience. **Publisher:** Harper & Row. **Contact(s):** Jim Wallis.

### E ♦ Walking Gently on the Earth: An Earthcare Checklist
Friends Committee on Unity with Nature
7899 St. Helena Rd.
Santa Rosa, CA 95404

**Affiliation:** Friends Committee on Unity with Nature. **Concern(s):** environment; economics; green consumer; recycling; social ecology. This small booklet has a checklist on recycling, pollution reduction, shopping guides, and other practical steps a person can take for environmental "gentle walking." **Contact(s):** Jack Phillips (Author).

### ☪ ♦ War Tax Manual for Counselors and Lawyers
National War Tax Resistance Coordinating Committee
Box 85810
Seattle, WA 98145

**Affiliation:** National War Tax Resistance Coordinating Committee. **Concern(s):** peace; war tax revolt. Counseling skills and detailed legal information. Indexed.

### P ♦ Washington Information Directory
1414 22nd St. NW
Washington, DC 20037

**Concern(s):** politics. Provides information on agencies of the executive branch, Congress, and private or "nongovernmental" organizations.

### E ♦ Waste in Place
9 W. Broad St.
Stamford, CT 06902    (203)323-8987

**Affiliation:** Keep America Beautiful. **Concern(s):** environment; recycling; conservation; beautification. Curriculum for K-6 school children.

### E ♦ Waste: A Hidden Resource
9 W. Broad St.
Stamford, CT 06902    (203)323-8987

**Affiliation:** Keep America Beautiful. **Concern(s):** environment; recycling; conservation; beautification. Secondary school curriculum developed by the TVA for grades 7-12, designed to stimulate interest in waste management which should, in turn, help educate parents and community members as well.

### E ♦ Waste: Choices for Communities
c/o Concern, Inc.
1794 Columbia Rd. NW
Washington, DC 20009    (202)328-8160

**Affiliation:** Concern, Inc.. **Concern(s):** environment; recycling. Provides an introduction to the many complex issues of waste management in the US. It is designed to raise public awareness of the serious impact of current waste generation and disposal practices and to promote alternatives. Nonprofit. **Est.:** 1970. **Price:** $4/ea. **Fax:** (202)387-3378. **Contact(s):** Susan Boyd (Executive Director), Burks Lapham (Chairman).

### E ♦ We All Live Downstream - a Guide to Waste Treatment That Stops Water Pollution
Route 3, Box 716
Eureka Springs, AR 72632    (501)253-9431

**Affiliation:** Water Center. **Concern(s):** environment; water; rivers/ oceans; wetlands; waste management; recycling. This book explains the water crisis, includes poems and pictures and is also a catalogue of compost toilets and other water conserving devises. Water should not be used as a waste vehicle."The poetry and superb illustrations included in We All Live Down stream add to my belief that this is the best book available on the subject of ecological home waste management. Much more than a technical manual, it was written with the intent of instilling a philosophy of water stewardship."-New Alchemy Quarterly. **Other Resources:** Publishes news magazine called AQUA TERRA. **Price:** $9/ea., post paid. **Bulk:** 66% off/24 + S&H. **Pages:** 85. **Date Publ.:** 1990. **Publisher:** Water Works Publishing. **Contact(s):** Barbara Harmony (Coordinator).

### ☪ ♦ Western States Grassroots Peace Directory
ACCESS: A Security Information Service
1730 M St. NW, #605
Washington, DC 20036    (202)785-6630

**Affiliation:** ACCESS: A Security Information Service. **Concern(s):** peace; national security; activism; grassroots organizing; networking. Covers national, regional, and local groups in North Midwest and Rocky Mountain states working for peace, disarmament, and international security. Arranged geographically with organization name, et al. **Other Resources:** Mailing labels available to nonprofit organizations, $50 per thousand, one time use, $20 minimum per order, plus $15-$50 for specialized searches. **Frequency:** Biennial. **Pages:** c135. **Date Publ.:** Spring 1991. **Contact(s):** Phyllis Emigh (Information Manager).

### T ♦ What's Wrong, Who's Right in Central America? A Citizen's Guide
Facts on File, Inc.
460 Park Ave. S
New York, NY 10016    (212)683-2244

**Concern(s):** Third World; Central America. **Date Publ.:** 1986. **Publisher:** Facts on File. **Contact(s):** Richard A. Nuccio.

### H ♦ When Someone You Know Has AIDS: A Practical Guide
Crown Publishers, Inc.
225 Park Ave. S
New York, NY 10003    (212)254-1600

**Concern(s):** health; AIDS. List of organizations dealing with AIDS related problems arranged geographically with organization name, address, phone, and geographical area served. Primary focus is on information and suggestions for people dealing with AIDS victims. **Price:** $19.95/ea. **Date Publ.:** 5/87. **Publisher:** Crown Publishers, Inc. **Contact(s):** David Groff (Editor).

### H ♦ Where Can Mom Live? A Family Guide to Living Arrangements for Elderly Parents
D.C. Heath & Company; Lexington Books
125 Spring St.
Lexington, MA 02173    (617)860-1580

**Concern(s):** health; demographics; seniors; housing. List of state government and private agencies that deal with the elderly and housing for the elderly. Categories include agency name, address, and phone. Primary focus is a discussion of housing needs and alternatives for elderly persons. **Price:** $12.95/ea. **Date Publ.:** 10/87. **Publisher:** D.C. Heath & Company. **Fax:** (617)860-1508. **Contact(s):** Ruth Mansberg. (800)235-3565.

### S ♦ Where to Go to Find Information on Grant Funds and Fundraising
Health Resources Publishing
3100 Highway 138
Wall, NJ 07719    (201)681-1133

**Concern(s):** spiritual; fundraising; philanthropy. **Price:** $8.95/ ea.+$1.50 shipping. **Publisher:** Health Resources Publishing. **Contact(s):** Robert K. Jenkins (Publisher).

### E ♦ Who Is Who
Shelton Cove Rd., #185
Waynesville, NC 28786    (704)926-2200

**Concern(s):** environment; justice; education. A directory of people, projects, and organizations in service to the Earth. Includes 41 visions written by notable writers. **Frequency:** Annual. **Price:** $19.95+$4 S&H.. **E-Network:** PeaceNet. **ID:** 'hkeller'. **Fax:** (704)926-9041. **Contact(s):** Hans Keller.

### D ♦ Who's Involved With Hunger: An Organization Guide for Education and Advocacy
Kumerian Press
630 Oakwood Ave., #119
West Hartford, CT 06110-1529

**Affiliation:** World Hunger Education. **Concern(s):** demographics; Third World; hunger. **Publisher:** Kumarian Press. **Contact(s):** Patricia L. Kutzner, Nochola Lagoudakis (Editor). **Other:** World Hunger Education, 1317 G St. NW, Washington, DC 20005.

### H ♦ Who's Who in Addiction Treatment and Recovery
Wilson, Brown & Co.
23200 Chagrin Blvd., #160
Cleveland, OH 44122    (216)464-1820

**Concern(s):** health; counseling; substance abuse. 2,000+ professional counselors, social workers, psychiatrists, writers, editors, physicians, researchers, and other professionals involved in the treatment or study of alcoholism, drug abuse, and other addictions. Arranged alphabetically and indexed geographically with individual name, et al. **Frequency:** Irregular. **Price:** $79.95/ea. **Pages:** 270. **Date Publ.:** Summer 1990. **Publisher:** Wilson, Brown & Co. **Fax:** (216)464-2980. **Contact(s):** Duane Frayer (Editor).

### ♥ ♦ Whole Again Birth Catalog: A Sourcebook for Choices in Childbirth
c/o Crossing Press
Box 1048
Freedom, CA 95019    (408)722-0711

**Concern(s):** family; health; birth; holism. A comprehensive guide for the consumer that lists organizations, publications and products concerning alternatives in childbirth, parenting and family living. Author, title and subject indices. 1,000+ periodicals, books and pamphlets listed, reviewed and excerpted. **Price:** $15.95/paper. **Pages:** 325. **Date Publ.:** 1983. **Publisher:** Crossing Press. **Contact(s):** Janet Isaacs Newton (Editor).

### H ♦ Whole Again Resource Guide
Sourcenet
Box 6767
Santa Barbara, CA 93160    (805)494-7123

**Concern(s):** health; spiritual; environment; peace; holism; transformation. 3,200+ magazines and other periodicals, sourcebooks, bibliographies, newspapers, newsletters, and directories published by associations, centers, and other groups as well as commercial publishers which are concerned with appropriate technology, holistic health, new age culture, and similar subjects. Ordered by subject; indexed by title, publisher location, editor, and subject. **Frequency:** Irregular. **Price:** $24.95/ea.+$2/shipping. **Pages:** c360. **Date Publ.:** 11/ 86. **Publisher:** Sourcenet. **Contact(s):** Tim Ryan (Editor).

### ✐ ♦ Whole Arts Directory
Midmarch Arts Press
300 Riverside Drive
New York, NY 10025    (212)666-6990

**Concern(s):** arts; feminism; economics; health; labor; justice; fine arts; culture; occupational safety; minority rights; empowerment; networking; cooperatives. "A listing of galleries, cooperatives, agencies and organizations, many focussed on women, for networking and support in the visual arts. Includes colonies and retreats, legal assistance, information hotlines." Organizations, alternative spaces, co-op galleries; artists colonies; financial help; health hazards info; arts advocacy; special focus on minorities. **Price:** $12.95/ea. **Publisher:** Midmarch Arts Press. **Other:** c/o Upper Access Books, Box 457, Hinesburg, VT 05461. Lisa & Steve Carlson , Distributors. (800)356-9315.

### E ♦ Whole Earth Ecolog
Box 38
Sausalito, CA 94966

**Concern(s):** environment; economics; green consumer. Detailed reviews of "the best environmental tools and ideas." 1000+ sources for hardware, and information on shelters, gardening, transport, health, communities, etc. It "does not attend what's wrong in the world. Instead we celebrate those doing something about it." **Price:** $17/ ea.

### ✍ ♦ The Whole Language Catalog
c/o American School Publishers
1221 Farmers Lane, #C
Santa Rosa, CA 95405

**Concern(s):** education. Covers a tremendous range of educational topics, from historical and philosophical concerns to practical approaches for teaching language arts and other subjects; from grading and assessment to the psychology of learning; from community and parent involvement to cultural diversity and environmental education; from computers to the arts. Over 500 educators, scholars, and parents contributed to the multiple perspectives of books, periodicals, videos, organizations, and learning materials. **Price:** $34.95/ea. **Pages:** 445. **Date Publ.:** 1990. **Contact(s):** Kenneth & Yetta Goodman, Lois Bridges Bird (Co-editors).

**S ▶ Whole Nonprofit Catalog**
Box 6210
Los Angeles, CA 90014 (213)689-9222
**Affiliation:** Grantsmanship Center. **Concern(s):** spiritual; economics; philanthropy; fundraising. "No not-for-profit group should fail to read this Catalog for its valuable advice on improving the outreach and inner workings of such groups. Many resource ideas are described as well. The price is right; it's free!"-C.C. **Est.:** 1985. **Frequency:** 2-3/yr. **Price:** Free. **Contact(s):** Susan Stanton.

**U ▶ Wildlife Reserves and Corridors in the Urban Environment**
c/o Island Press
Box 7
Covelo, CA 95428 (202)232-7933
**Affiliation:** National Institute for Urban Wildlife. **Concern(s):** urban; environment; sustainability; wildlife/endangered species; transportation. "A Guide to Ecological Landscape Planning and Resource Conservation". Provides guidelines and approaches to ecological landscape planning and wildlife conservation in urban regions. **Price:** $9.95/paper. **Pages:** 91. **Date Publ.:** 1989. Order: (800)828-1302. **Contact(s):** Lowell W. Adams, Louise E. Dove (Co-authors).

**☯ ▶ Wind Energy for a Growing World**
777 N. Capitol St. NE., #805
Washington, DC 20002 (202)408-8988
**Affiliation:** American Wind Energy Association. **Concern(s):** energy; environment; wind; renewables. Information about current uses of wind energy and a listing of companies (manufacturers, developers, operators of wind farms, and consultants) in the wind industry. **Est.:** 1974. **Date Publ.:** 4/90. **Labels:** 10. **E-Network:** Econet. **ID:** 'awea'. **Fax:** (202)408-8536. MCI Mail: AWEA. **Contact(s):** Randy Swisher (Executive Director), Dianne Eppler (Director of Operations).

**S ▶ Wise Giving Guide**
National Charities Information Bureau
19 Union Square W, 6th Fl.
New York, NY 10003 (212)929-6300
**Affiliation:** National Charities Information Bureau. **Concern(s):** spiritual; fundraising; philanthropy. 400 national organizations that solicit contributions from the public, and which have supplied or been requested to supply operating and financial data to the bureau. Bureau requests audit by independent auditors, detailed annual budget, etc. Evaluations are reported by listing the organization with codes indicating degree of compliance with NCIB Standards in such areas as purpose, program, fund raising and accountability. **Frequency:** 3/yr. **Price:** Free. **Fax:** (212)463-7083. **Contact(s):** Frank Driscoll (Research Associate).

**♥ ▶ Wise Woman Herbal for the Childbearing Year**
Wise Woman Center
Box 64
Woodstock, NY 12498 (914)246-8081
**Affiliation:** Wise Woman Center. **Concern(s):** family; feminism; health; family planning; holism; birth. Safe, effective, inexpensive remedies for common distresses of pregnancy and infancy are interspersed with sound emotional guidance, sensible background information, and delightful stories and drawings. Complete with "the herbal pharmacy," "herbal source list of vitamins and minerals," and "herbal birth control guide." Introduction by Jeannine Parvati Baker. **Price:** $8.95/ea. **Bulk:** 40% off/24. **Pages:** 196. **Date Publ.:** 6/86. **Publisher:** Ash Tree Publishing. **Contact(s):** Susun Weed (Owner), Julia Hammid (Helper).

**F ▶ Woman's Yellow Book**
Federation of Organizations for Professional Women
2001 S St. NW, #540
Washington, DC 20009 (202)328-1415
**Affiliation:** Federation of Organizations for Professional Women. **Concern(s):** feminism. About 575 national organizations, government agencies, research institutes, clearinghouses, and publishers concerned with women's issues. Arranged alphabetically and indexed by keyword/geography. **Other Resources:** Formerly, WOMAN'S YELLOW PAGES (1981). **Frequency:** Irregular. **Price:** $25/ea., postpaid. **Pages:** c250. **Date Publ.:** Spring 1990.

**F ▶ Women and Technology Project**
315 S. 4th St. E
Missoula, MT 59801
**Concern(s):** feminism; education; science.

**F ▶ Women in Communications**
Box 17640
Arlington, VA 22216
**Concern(s):** feminism; media.

**T ▶ Women in the Third World: A Directory of Resources**
464 19th St.
Oakland, CA 94612-9761 (510)835-4692
**Affiliation:** Third World Resources/Data Center. **Concern(s):** Third World. For postage and handling, add $1.50 for North America and $3.00 for foreign air mail. Please, order from Third World Resources. **Price:** $12.95/ea. **Pages:** 160. **Date Publ.:** Spring 1987. **Publisher:** Orbis Books. **Other Formats:** Geonet, user **ID:** 'geo2:tfenton'. **E-Network:** Peacenet. **ID:** 'tfenton'. **Contact(s):** Thomas P. Fenton, Mary J. Heffron (Compilers/Editors). (510)536-1876.

**F ▶ Women in the World: An International Atlas**
Simon & Schuster/Touchstone
1230 Avenue of the Americas
New York, NY 10020 (212)698-7000
**Concern(s):** feminism; demographics; justice. Maps the conditions of women's lives throughout the world. PublisheD by Pan Books, London 1986. **Publisher:** Simon & Schuster/Touchstone.

**F ▶ Women's Annual**
G.K. Hall & Co.
70 Lincoln St.
Boston, MA 02111
**Concern(s):** feminism. **Publisher:** G.K. Hall & Co.

**F ▶ Women's Legal Rights in the US: Bibliography**
American Library Association
50 E. Huron St.
Chicago, IL 60611
**Affiliation:** American Library Association. **Concern(s):** feminism; justice.

**F ▶ Women's Liberation Kit**
UN NGO Liaison Service
Department of Public Information
New York, NY 10017 (212)963-1234
**Concern(s):** feminism. Lists 12 UN agencies addressing women and development since the official Decade for Women ended in 1985. **Publisher:** UN NGO Liaison Service.

**F ▶ Women's Mailing List Directory**
National Council for Research on Women
47-49 E. 65th St.
New York, NY 10021 (212)570-5001
**Affiliation:** National Council for Research on Women. **Concern(s):** feminism. Makes available for the first time indexed descriptions of lists maintained by diverse US women's groups and organizations: research centers and caucuses; feminist periodicals, publishers, and bookstores; and women's policy and activist organizations, programs, centers, and networks. The Directory includes detailed information about selling and exchanging mailing lists, available formats, methods of compiling and maintaining lists. **Frequency:** Irregular. **Price:** $20/ea. **Pages:** 164. **Date Publ.:** 1990. **Contact(s):** Debra L. Schultz (Editor).

**F ▶ Women's Organizations and Leaders**
Triangle News Service
National Press Building, #1199
Washington, DC 20045
**Concern(s):** feminism; politics. **Publisher:** Triangle News Service.

**F ▶ Women's Organizations: A National Directory**
Garrett Park Press
Box 190F
Garrett Park, MD 20896 (301)946-2553
**Concern(s):** feminism. About 2,000 national and local women's organizations including professional and trade associations, government commissions, and research centers specializing in women's issues. Arranged alphabetically and indexed geographically and by type of program with organization. Also includes list of women's directories. **Frequency:** Irregular. **Price:** $22.50/ea.; prepaid. **Pages:** c310. **Date Publ.:** 1986. **Publisher:** Garrett Park Press. **Contact(s):** Martha Merill Doss (Editor).

**F ▶ Women's Studies: A Guide to Information Sources**
McFarland & Company, Inc.
Box 611
Jefferson, NC 28640
**Concern(s):** feminism. Comprehensive, beautifully crafted...a true guide to literature...a very readable, very useful book. A must purchase for every academic library."—Choice; "a vast array of topics"—

Library Journal; "essential to women's studies and ...gender studies collections"—Wilson Library Bulletin; "invaluable to those involved in teaching and research"—Booklist/RBB. In three sections: General Material, Women in the World, and Special Subjects. Broad spectrum. Includes index. **Pages:** 288. **Date Publ.:** 1990. **Contact(s):** Sarah Carter, Maureen Ritchie (Editors).

**F ▶ Words to the Wise**
Firebrand Books
141 The Commons
Ithaca, NY 14850 (607)272-0000
**Concern(s):** feminism; media; press. 100+ publishers of feminist and lesbian books and periodicals who actively solicit manuscripts from women; publishers of directories, newsletters, and other publications and resources for women writers. Arranged by separate sections for publishers, periodicals and resources. **Frequency:** 18-24 months. **Price:** $3.95/ea.+$1.75 shipping. **Pages:** 50. **Date Publ.:** 10/90. **Publisher:** Firebrand Books. **Contact(s):** Andrea Fleck Clardy.

**⚰ ▶ Working for Peace: An Annotated Resource Guide**
**Affiliation:** Joel Brooke Memorial Committee/Fund for Peace. **Concern(s):** peace; media; press; film. 200+ organizations, publishers, religious groups, and national peace groups that offer books, pamphlets, periodicals, films, slide shows, visual aids, and speakers on various peacemaking topics. Classified by product or service. Note: Out of print. Copies might still be found in college and university libraries. **Other Resources:** Formerly FIRST STEPS TO PEACE. **Frequency:** Biennial. **Price:** $5.95/ea. **Pages:** c100. **Date Publ.:** 3/89. **Contact(s):** A. M. Postag (Editor).

**F ▶ A Working Woman's Guide to Her Job Rights**
Department of Labor
200 Constitution Ave. NW
Washington, DC 20210 (202)523-8191
**Affiliation:** Department of Labor. **Concern(s):** feminism; equal rights. List of state and federal agencies in charge of enforcing the rights of working women. Major content of publication is description of employment rights for women and ways to protect those rights. (202)523-6666.

**E ▶ World Directory of Environmental Organizations**
Box 189040
Sacramento, CA 95818 (916)442-2472
**Affiliation:** California Institute of Public Affairs/Claremont Colleges. **Concern(s):** environment; education. The only comprehensive guide to organizations in all parts of the world that are concerned with the urgent problems of the environment and natural resources. Includes: Detailed profiles of environmental activities of international organizations; listings of key national governmental and non-governmental organizations. Over 2,100 entries. **Price:** $35/ea.+$2 shipping & 6.5% for CA. **Pages:** 175. **Date Publ.:** 1989. **Fax:** (916)442-2478. **Contact(s):** Thaddeus C. Trzyna (Editor).

**G ▶ World Directory of Gay/Lesbian Groups of Alcoholics Anonymous**
Box 90
Washington, DC 20044 (202)293-4022
**Concern(s):** justice; gay/lesbian. About 450 listings arranged geographically with group name and address meeting information. Some listings include name and phone of contact. **Frequency:** Biennial. **Price:** $2.50/ea. **Pages:** 40.

**J ▶ World Directory of Minorities**
St. James Press
233 E. Ontario, #600
Chicago, IL 60611 (312)787-5800
**Concern(s):** justice; Third World; demographics; diversity; minority rights. Major minorities that are, by definition, a numerically inferior portion of a national population differing from the majority in ethno-religio-linguistic ways; worldwide coverage. Arranged geographically and indexed by subject and keyword. **Price:** $85/ea. **Pages:** c430. **Date Publ.:** 1990. **Publisher:** St. James Press.

**⚰ ▶ World Directory of Peace Research and Training Institutions**
Berg                                        Publishers
New York, NY
**Concern(s):** peace. Publishers are no longer in New York and affiliate name not available. Check your local library. **Publisher:** Berg Publishers.

**? ♦ World Future Studies Newsletter - Membership Directory Issue**
Dept. of Political Science; University of Hawaii at Manoa
2424 Maile Way
Honolulu, HI 96822      (808)948-6601
**Affiliation:** World Future Society. **Concern(s):** future; research; ideation. 700+ member individuals and 60 institutions with an interest in the study of the world's future. Arranged alphabetically by sections for institutions and for individuals with names and addresses. **Frequency:** Annual. **Price:** $5/ea. **Date Publ.:** Fall 1990. **Fax:** (808)942-5710. **Contact(s):** James A. Dator (Secretary General).

**D ♦ World Hunger, a Guide to the Economic and Political Dimensions**
ABC-CLIO, Inc.
130 Cremona Dr. Box 1911
Santa Barbara, CA 93116
**Concern(s):** demographics; economics; politics; hunger. **Date Publ.:** 1981. **Publisher:** ABC-CLIO.

**♿ ♦ A World of Options: A Guide to International Educational Exchange, Community Service and Travel for Persons with Disabilities**
Mobility International USA
Box 3551
Eugene, OR 97403      (503)343-1284
**Affiliation:** Mobility International USA. **Concern(s):** education; travel. About 200 educational programs, workcamps, transportation and travel advisory services for persons with disabilities. Arranged alphabetically and indexed by names. **Frequency:** Irregular. **Price:** $15/ea.; prepaid. **Pages:** c190. **Date Publ.:** 1990. **Contact(s):** Cindy Lewis, Susan Sygall (Editors).

**☙ ♦ World Peace and World Order Studies: A Curriculum Guide**
World Policy Institute
777 UN Plaza
New York, NY 10017      (212)490-0010
**Affiliation:** World Policy Institute. **Concern(s):** peace; Third World; justice; environment; politics; world order; natural resources; social justice; foreign policy; East-West; conflict resolution; intervention.

**D ♦ World Population Data Sheet**
Population Reference Bureau
1875 Connecticut Ave. NW, #520
Washington, DC 20009   (202)483-1100
**Affiliation:** Population Reference Bureau. **Concern(s):** demographics; population growth. Demographic data and estimates for the countries and regions of the world. **Publisher:** Population Reference Bureau.

**D ♦ World Population Fundamentals of Growth, Student Chartbook**
Population Reference Bureau
1875 Connecticut Ave. NW, #520
Washington, DC 20009   (202)483-1100
**Affiliation:** Population Reference Bureau. **Concern(s):** demographics; education; students; population growth. **Date Publ.:** 1984. **Publisher:** Population Reference Bureau.

**H ♦ Worldwide AIDS Directory**
Technology Management Group
25 Science Park
New Haven, CT 06511   (203)786-5445
**Affiliation:** Technology Management Group. **Concern(s):** health; AIDS. Nearly 800 manufacturers, 700 research institutions, and 540 other AIDS-related organizations; international coverage, arranged alphabetically. **Price:** $150/ea. **Pages:** 545. **Date Publ.:** 10/87. **Other Formats:** Diskette, $500 (includes printed directory). **Fax:** (203)786-5449. **Contact(s):** Manny Ratafia (President).

**F ♦ Worldwide Directory of Women and Environment**
Box 40885
Washington, DC 20016
**Affiliation:** Worldwide. **Concern(s):** feminism; environment; demographics.

**M ♦ The Writer's Handbook**
The Writer, Inc.
120 Boylston St.
Boston, MA 02116
**Concern(s):** media; arts; press; journalism; research; literature. 100 chapters by leading writers; 2500 markets with names of editors, addresses and specific editorial requirements. A list of representative literary agents, writer's organizations, contests, awards and grants, business information for writers. What to write, how to write, where to sell. **Price:** $28.95/ea.+$2.75 S&H, hardcover. **Pages:** 756. **Publisher:** Writer, Inc., The.

**✍ ♦ Young and Old Together**
California Department of Education
Box 271
Sacramento, CA 95802
**Affiliation:** California Department of Education. **Concern(s):** education; health; youth; seniors.

**☙ ♦ Young Peacemakers Project Book**
Fellowship of Reconciliation
Box 271
Nyack, NY 10960
**Affiliation:** Fellowship of Reconciliation. **Concern(s):** peace; education; youth; childhood; conflict resolution. A valuable collection of imaginative learning activities that introduce the pre-school through elementary age child to the fundamental concepts of peacemaking. Useful for educators and other caring individuals. **Date Publ.:** 1988. **Contact(s):** Kathleen Fry-Miller, Judith Myers- Walls.

**E ♦ Your Resource Guide to Environmental Organizations**
Smiling Dolphin Press
4 Segura
Irvine, CA 92715
**Concern(s):** environment. A directory of 150 environmental organizations. Includes purposes, accomplishments, programs, voluteer opportunities, publications, and membership benefits. Three indexes, glossary, plus biographical close-ups of 14 environmental leaders. **Price:** $18.95/ea. CA include $1.04 sales tax. **Pages:** 514. **Contact(s):** John Seredich (Editor).

## Special Thanks to:

**Gale Research Inc.**, for allowing **Macrocosm USA, Inc.** to derive many of the descriptions for this section from:

***Directories in Print***, Eighth Edition, edited by Charles B. Montney. Copyright ©1991 by **Gale Research Inc.** Reproduced by permission of the publisher.

# ⑦ **People Index**

❏ Organization • Type: _____ ❏ Periodical • Type: _____

❏ Media ❏ Publisher ❏ Business ❏ Directory/Guide

Name: _____

Address: _____

City: _____ State: _____ Zip Code: _____ Country: _____

Phone: _____

Affiliation: _____

Tax Status: ❏ Nonprofit ❏ For-Profit ❏ Other: _____ Date Established: _____

Keywords (see page 195 or suggest): _____

Description (75 words or less, precisely and concisely!): _____

_____

_____

_____

_____

Other Resources: _____

_____

_____

Frequency: _____ Price: _____ Bulk Discount: _____

Subscription/Dues: _____ Circulation: _____

# pages: _____ Publication Date (books or booklets only): _____

Contact: _____ Title: _____

Contact: _____ Title: _____

Additional Phone #: _____ Fax: _____ Other: _____

E-Network: _____ user name/E-Mail Address: _____

Publisher (for books only): _____

Mailing Labels: _____

Other Formats: _____

Office Address: _____

City: _____ State: _____ Zip: _____ Country: _____

What Coalition or Network do you belong to? _____

How might you improve **Macrocosm USA**?: _____

Will you be sending us a free subscription? ❏ Will you be sending brochures, books, guides, clippings, directories or pamphlets? ❏ Will we be able to obtain reprint permission? ❏ If offered a standard discount, can you distribute and/or advertise **Macrocosm**? ❏ Are you interested in purchasing our database? ❏ Other? ❏ Explain: